About the Author of *Decision Support and Expert Systems: Management Support Systems*

Efraim Turban is the Lumpkin Distinguished Professor of Business at Eastern Illinois University. He holds an M.B.A. and Ph.D. from the University of California at Berkeley. Professor Turban has written nine books and numerous articles in professional journals. He has been a consultant to major corporations and several governments.

Professor Turban's current research is on emerging technologies for management support.

Efraim Turban has two daughters. His hobbies include traveling, fishing, swimming, and archeology.

MACMILLAN SERIES IN INFORMATION SYSTEMS

Henry C. Lucas, Jr.
New York University
Consulting Editor

Lucas: INTRODUCTION TO COMPUTER
AND INFORMATION SYSTEMS

Laudon/Laudon: MANAGEMENT INFORMATION SYSTEMS:
A CONTEMPORARY PERSPECTIVE

Turban: DECISION SUPPORT AND EXPERT SYSTEMS:
MANAGEMENT SUPPORT SYSTEMS

Decision Support and Expert Systems:

MANAGEMENT SUPPORT SYSTEMS

SECOND EDITION

Efraim Turban

Eastern Illinois University

Macmillan Publishing Company
New York

Collier Macmillan Publishers
London

Dedicated to
my daughters Daphne and Sharon,
with love

Cover: Gemini G.E.L./Art Resource, NY:
1. Frank Stella, River of Ponds IV. 1971.

Macmillan Publishing Company
866 Third Avenue, New York, New York 10022

Collier Macmillan Canada, Inc.

Library of Congress Cataloging-in-Publication Data
Turban, Efraim.
    Decision support and expert systems: management support systems/
Efraim Turban.—2nd ed.
        p.   cm.—(Macmillan series in information systems)
    Includes Index.
    ISBN 0-02-421663-1
        1. Management—Data Processing.   2. Decision support systems
3. Expert systems (Computer science)   I. Title.   II. Series
HD30.2.T87   1990   CIP
658.4′03—dc20   89-15831

Printing: 4 5 6 7 8   Year: 1 2 3 4 5 6 7 8

Preface

Overview

Computer applications for management support are on the rise. The microcomputer revolution made computers available on many managers' desks. Managers may access thousands of databases all over the country. Many organizations, private or public, are no longer making major decisions without some computerized analysis. The cost of hardware and software is declining whereas the capabilities of information systems are continuously increasing.

Corporations are developing distributed systems that enable easy accessibility to data stored in multiple locations. Various information systems are being integrated with each other and/or with other automated systems. Managers can make better decisions because they have more accurate information at their fingertips.

However, despite all these technological developments, many managers are not using computers at all, or are using them primarily to support simple decisions. Decision Support Systems (DSS), Executive Information Systems (EIS) and Expert Systems (ES) are designed to change this situation.

The purpose of this book is to introduce the reader to these technologies which we call collectively management support systems (MSS). This book presents the fundamentals of the techniques, and the manner in which they are being constructed and used.

A unique aspect of this book is the integration of the technologies which were developed independently of each other. The integration of MSS could have a synergetic effect, owing to the complementary nature of the techniques in the support of managerial decision making. For this reason, several universities are beginning to teach DSS, EIS, and ES in one course (Management Support Systems).

DSS and ES courses and portions of courses are recommended by ACM and DPMA. This course is designed to cover the material of CIS/86-11 (Decision Support and Epert Systems) of the DPMA model curriculum for computer information systems. It actually covers more than what is recommended. A secondary objective is to provide the practicing manager with the foundations of DSS, EIS, and ES. In addition, the book can be used as a sourcebook for MSS hardware and software.

The Second Edition

Four new chapters were added to this edition: Modeling, IFPS, Knowledge Acquisition and User Interface. In addition, the topics of GDSS, EIS, knowledge representation and neural computing were greatly expanded in various chapters together with case studies. The software support was expanded to include VP EXPERT and IFPS, on top of an improved 50 rules EXSYS package. In addition a separate test bank has been added to the instructional package.

The Instructional Materials

In addition to the text the instructional package consists of several components:

Instructor's Manual.   This manual includes:

a. Answers to the questions, problems and exercises at the end of the chapters.
b. Teaching suggestions (including instructions for projects).
c. Transparency masters.
d. How to use EXSYS
e. How to use IFPS
f. How to use VP EXPERT.
g. Learning objectives for both the entire course and for each chapter.

Test Bank.   The test bank includes multiple choice questions for all the chapters with answers and many test exercises for both DSS and Expert Systems with solutions.

Demo Software.   "Show and Tell" demo software for EXSYS, IFPS and VP EXPERT is available with the complementary desk copy.

Free Development Software for the Students.   Adoptors of this book can provide their students with free software. The following arrangements are available:

a. Get 2 disks of EXSYS (50 rules) or 4 disks of EXSYS Professional (50 rules). You are permitted to copy these disks for your students without charge. The improved software interfaces with Lotus and databases (see Instructor's Manual).
b. Get 2 disks of IFPS/Personal-student version. Again, you can duplicate the disks for your students without any charge.
c. Get disks of VP EXPERT for each of your students without any charge.

Further details and order forms are included in the instructor's manual.

Acknowledgments

Many individuals provided suggestions and criticisms during the long creation process. Dozens of students participated in class testing of various chapters and problems and assisted in collecting material. It is not possible to name all of the many who participated in this project; thanks go to all of them. However, certain individuals made significant contributions and they deserve special recognition for the first edition.

First, those individuals who provided formal reviews: Robert Blanning (Vanderbilt University), Charles Butler (Colorado State), Warren Briggs (Suffolk University), Sohail S. Chaudry (University of Wisconsin, LaCrosse), Joyce Elam (University of Texas), Anand S. Kunnathur (Florida International University), Hank Lucas (NYU), Dick Mason (SMU), Benjamin Mittman (Northwestern University), Larry Moore and Loren Rees (Virginia Polytechnic and State University), Roger Alan Pick (University of Wisconsin), and John Van Gigch (California State University at Sacramento).

The second edition reviewers are: Orv Greynhold (University of Denver), Steve Ruth (George Mason University), David Russell (Western New England College), Randy Smith (University of Virginia), Jung Shim (Mississippi State) and Steve Zanakis (Florida International University).

Second, those individuals who provided informal guidance: Steve Ruth (George Mason University) who class tested the manuscript; Paul Watkins (USC) worked closely with me on several of the chapters and on related projects; and Frank DeBalogh (USC) provided detailed comments. Extensive informal reviews were provided by Gerry Bedore (a management consultant), Ata Omidi (New York Institute of Technology), Craig Wolfe (COMDEX), and Mary Lou Shippe (Ford Aerospace). The last four reviewers were students in the doctoral program at Nova University.

Third, several individuals provided material for this text. Specifically, Warren Briggs (Suffolk University), Neil Dorf (Xerox Corporation), David King (Tecknowledge, Inc.), Donna Schaeffer (Claremont Graduate School), Allan Greenwood (Northeastern University), David Friend (Pilot Executive Software), Alan Rowe (USC), and Larry Moore (Virginia Polytechnic and State University).

For the second edition: Glen Gray (California State-Northridge), Janet Francis (Eastern Illinois University), Lou Frenzel (Technovat Inc), Linda Volonino (Canisius College), Gerry Drinkard (Fisher-Price, Inc.) and K. H. Scanlon and Hal Schutt (Defense Systems Management College). A special contribution was made by Paul Gray (Claremont Graduate School) who not only wrote most of the IFPS chapter, but also contributed to chapter 19 and advised me on several other topics.

Fourth, several vendors cooperated and assisted me in this task. They are:

1. EXSYS Corp. which allowed us to use its software, and whose president, Dustin Huntington, advised me on several topics and provided the EXSYS documentation.
2. Paperback Software Inc. which provided the use of the demo and the disks of VP EXPERT.
3. Execucom Systems Corp. which provided us with the IFPS demo and IFPS software and which worked closely with me during the entire

period of the second edition. The following individuals spent long hours in reviewing various chapters and provided me with considerable advice and material:

Ed Bradshaw, Staff Consultant
Donna Carter, University Support Program Manager
Dave Clark, Director of Customer Relations
Kirk Jones, Senior Vice President of Technology
David King, Director of Advanced Product Design and Development
Steve Murchie, Product Marketing Manager
Mark Wood, Product Marketing Manager
Pat Wyman, Manager, Client Services Consultant

Fifth, several individuals granted me permission to reproduce their work (they are all acknowledged in the appropriate chapters). Also, publishers and vendors permitted me to use their products.

Sixth, many individuals helped with administrative matters, editing, and production. Special thanks go to Jack Repcheck who was closely involved in this project from its inception, Charles Stewart who guided the execution of the second edition together with Robert Freese who designed both the interior and the cover; all are with Macmillan Publishing Company. Also, Hank Lucas, the series editor, provided many valuable suggestions and deserves special recognition. Janet Fisher helped me with editing and general organization. Senior production coordinator Melissa Madsen and other staff at the book composition firm of Publication Services, Inc. (Champaign, IL), were extremely helpful. Finally, special acknowledgment goes to my friend Gerry Bedore, my research assistants Diana Lanman and Bruce Williams, my assistant Judy Lang and my daughter Sharon who helped me with the tedious job of proofing the pages of the manuscript.

E. T.

Contents

ix

Chapter 3

Modeling   73

Chapter 4

Decision Support Systems and
Group DSS: An Overview   105

Chapter 5

Constructing a Decision Support System   157

Chapter 6

The DSS Development Tools

Chapter 7

The Interactive Financial Planning System (IFPS)

Chapter 8

Case Studies 303

Chapter 9

Illustrative DSS Applications 335

Chapter 10

Executive Information and Support Systems 365

Chapter 11

Applied Artificial Intelligence 399

Chapter 12

Fundamentals of Expert Systems   423

Chapter 13

Knowledge Acquisition   453

Chapter 14

Knowledge Representation and Inferencing   485

Chapter 15

Building Expert Systems: Process, Tools, and Strategy   **537**

Chapter 16

Major Case Studies   **579**

Case 1: Coopers and Lybrand's Expert System (ExperTAX)   580

Chapter 17

Expert Systems Applications Cases   607

Chapter 18

User Interface   645

Chapter 19

Management Support Systems Integration   677

Chapter 20

Implementing Management Support Systems   725

Chapter 21
Organizational and Societal Impacts
of Management Support Systems   767

Chapter 22
The Future of Management Support Systems   797

Chapter 1

Management Support Systems–An Overview

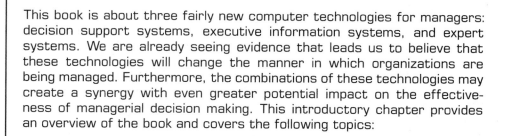

This book is about three fairly new computer technologies for managers: decision support systems, executive information systems, and expert systems. We are already seeing evidence that leads us to believe that these technologies will change the manner in which organizations are being managed. Furthermore, the combinations of these technologies may create a synergy with even greater potential impact on the effectiveness of managerial decision making. This introductory chapter provides an overview of the book and covers the following topics:

1.1   Managers and Computerized Systems

A 1984 study of top corporate executives in Fortune 500 companies revealed that one-third of these executives *personally* use computers when making critical decisions. About one quarter of these executives also used computers in their homes. A 1989 study of chief executive officers (CEOs) in the Fortune 500 indicated that 21 percent of them use computers. (See [20].) These constantly growing figures are only one of many signals indicating that we are indeed in the information age. The impact of computer technology on organizations and society is increasing as new technologies evolve and existing technologies expand. The interaction and cooperation between people and machines is rapidly growing to cover more and more aspects of organizational activities. From traditional uses in payroll and bookkeeping functions, computerized systems are now penetrating complex managerial areas ranging from the design and management of automated factories to the evaluation of proposed mergers and acquisitions.

Some clerks and technicians have been using computers for as long as two decades to support routine jobs; in contrast, most managers use computers very infrequently to support their decision-making activities. This situation began to change in 1982. The driving forces of this change are the availability of microcomputers and the introduction of relatively easy-to-use software. These innovations enable managers not only to use general-purpose programs (application programs) but also to build their own computerized systems (Martin [11]) with easy-to-use construction tools. The first construction tool for micros was the spreadsheet technology, which received lots of attention in 1979 because of VisiCalc (see Figure 1.1). The construction tools and application programs are assisting managers in building, analyzing, and utilizing models, graphs, and charts; managing time and projects; and electronically writing memos and reports. Furthermore, managers can perform these tasks by themselves instead of waiting for data processing* to do them. The executive is discovering that the computer is like a very reliable staff assistant; it works endlessly without pay, complaints, mistakes, or criticisms of other people.

Management now realizes that desktop computers are not "just another fad." Executives are recognizing that computers can provide value-added computing power to existing large-capacity computing and that computers are here to stay. These executives have started asking such questions as "What can we do with all these micros?" (9). Technological developments in hardware, software, and telecommunications are providing answers to this and similar questions by introducing products that can assist executives in their jobs. Computer applications are moving from transaction (or "backroom") processing and monitoring activities (which dominated the industry in the 1960s and 1970s) to problem analysis and solution applications in the 1980s. There is also a trend to provide managers with integrated packages that can assist them in their most important task—making decisions.

---

*The terms *data processing* (DP) and *data processing people* and *departments* are being replaced with the term *information systems* or *services* (IS). The two terms are used interchangeably in this book.

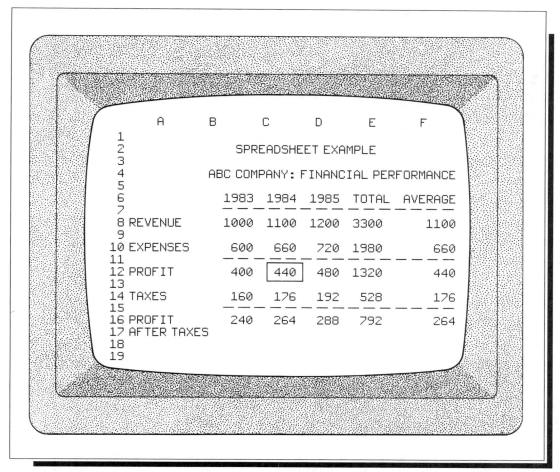

FIGURE 1.1 Simple financial statement using Visicalc.

Computer-based technologies are being developed to improve the effectiveness of managerial decision making, especially in complex tasks. Three such technologies—decision support systems (DSS),* executive information systems (EIS), and expert systems (ES)—are the subject of this book. They are collectively known as computerized management support systems. Decision support systems, about fifteen years old, have already proven themselves by providing business with substantial savings in time and money.** Expert systems, which appeared commercially in the early 1980s, may be one of the most important future breakthroughs in computerized decision making. Finally, executive information systems are now being designed to support the work of senior

---

*The abbreviations DSS, EIS, and ES are used for both the singular and plural form throughout this text.

**e.g., see *Business Computer Systems*, July 1984, and Reimann (13).

executives. These technologies appear as independent systems but they are sometimes integrated.

1.2 **Managerial Decision Making and Management Information Systems**

To better understand management support systems, let us examine two important topics: managerial decision making and management information systems (MIS).

Management is a process by which certain goals are achieved through the use of resources (people, money, energy, materials, space, time). These resources are considered to be inputs, and the attainment of the goals is viewed as the output of the process. The degree of success of a manager's job is often measured by the ratio between outputs and inputs. This ratio is an indication of the organization's *productivity*.

$$\text{Productivity} = \frac{\text{outputs (products, services)}}{\text{inputs (resources)}}$$

Productivity is a major concern for any organization because it determines the well-being of the organization and its members. Productivity is also one of the most important issues at the national level. National productivity is the sum of the productivity of all organizations and individuals, and it determines the standard of living, the employment level, and the economic well-being of a country.

The level of productivity, or the success of management, depends on the execution of certain managerial functions like planning, organizing, directing, and controlling. To carry out these functions, managers are engaged in a continuous process of making decisions.

All managerial activities revolve around decision making. The manager is first and foremost a decision maker. Organizations are filled with decision makers at various levels. Each manager is charged in fact with a certain part of an organization's decision-making activities.

For years, managers have considered decision making a pure art—a talent acquired over a long period of time through experience (learning by trial and error). Management was considered an art because a variety of individual styles could be used in approaching and successfully solving the same type of managerial problems in actual business practice. These styles are often based on creativity, judgment, intuition, and experience, rather than on systematic quantitative methods based on a scientific approach.

However, the environment in which management must operate is changing. We live in the information and the microelectronic age, where technological advancements become a major determinant of our lifestyle. Such advances in technology cannot possibly be made or sustained without concurrent advancement in management systems.

Business and its environment are more complex today than ever before, and the trend is toward increasing complexity. Figure 1.2 shows the changes

FACTOR	TREND	RESULTS
Technology	Increasing	More alternatives
Information/computers	Increasing	to choose from
Organizational size	Increasing	Larger cost of
Structural complexity	Increasing	making errors
Competition	Increasing	
International markets	Increasing	More uncertainty
Political stability	Decreasing	regarding the
Consumerism	Increasing	future
Government intervention	Increasing	

FIGURE 1.2 Factors affecting decision making. (*Source:* Adapted from Turban and Meredith [17].)

in major factors (on the left) that have had an impact on managerial decision making. The results (on the right) indicate that decision making today is more complicated than in the past. It is more difficult to make decisions for three reasons. First, the number of available alternatives is much larger today than ever before, owing to improved technology and communication systems. Second, future consequences of decisions are more difficult to predict because of increased uncertainty. Finally, the cost of making errors can be very large owing to the complexity and magnitude of operations, automation, and the chain reaction that an error may cause in many parts of the organization.

As a result of these trends and changes it is very difficult to rely on a trial-and-error approach to management, especially in decisions involving the factors shown in Figure 1.2. Managers must become more sophisticated—they must learn how to use new tools and techniques that are being developed in their field. Many of these techniques use a quantitative analysis approach; they are grouped into a discipline called *management science* (or *operations research*). (For further details, see Turban and Meredith [17].)

Management Science

The management science approach adopts the view that managers can follow a fairly systematic process for solving problems (or making decisions). Therefore, it is possible to use a scientific approach to managerial decision making. This approach involves the following steps:

1. Defining the *problem* (a decision situation which may deal with *trouble* or with an *opportunity*).
2. Classifying the problem into a standard category.
3. Constructing a mathematical model that describes the real life problem.
4. Finding potential solutions to the modeled problem and evaluating them (through experimentation or calculation).
5. Choosing and recommending a solution to the problem.

In order to follow this process it is necessary to use information regarding the problems, the relevant variables, the environment, the model, and the solution alternatives. This information is provided through a supportive management information system.

Management Information Systems

A management information system (MIS) is a formal, computer-based* system, intended to retrieve, extract, and integrate data from various sources in order to provide timely information necessary for managerial decision making. MIS has been most successful in providing information for routine, structured, and anticipated types of decisions. In addition, it has been successful in acquiring and storing large quantities of detailed data concerning transaction processing. MIS has been less successful in supporting complex decision situations. This is because of a lack of capabilities necessary for such support, and MIS traditionally has not been easy enough to be developed or even used by managers. Furthermore, as managers climb the corporate ladder, they must increasingly deal with matters outside the organization. Most MIS are built with a focus on the internal organization. Hence, the support of the traditional MIS decreases as the organizational level increases. The computerized management support systems discussed in this book are intended to complement both management science and MIS because they address those tasks that are nonroutine and require managerial judgment in addition to formal analysis.

1.3   A Framework for Decision Support

Before defining DSS, EIS, and ES, it will be useful to present a classical framework for decision support. This framework will provide us with several major concepts that are used in the definitions of DSS and ES. It will also help us in discussing several additional issues, such as the relationship among MIS, management science, and DSS, and the evolution of computerized systems. This framework was proposed by Gorry and Scott-Morton (6), who combined the work of Simon (16) and Anthony (2). The details of this framework are as follows:

According to Simon, decision-making processes fall along a continuum that ranges from highly structured (sometimes referred to as *programmed*) to highly unstructured (*nonprogrammed*) decisions. *Structured* processes refer to routine and repetitive problems for which standard solutions exist. *Unstructured* processes are "fuzzy," complex problems for which there are no cut-and-dried solutions. A detailed description of this concept, with several examples, is provided in Chapter 2.

The focus on decision making also requires an understanding of the human decision-making *process*. This process is divided by Simon into three phases:

A fully structured problem is one in which all these phases are structured. A *structured phase* is a phase whose procedures are standardized, the objectives are clear, and the input and output are clearly specified.

---

*A management information system may be in operation without a computer. However, in this book an MIS should always be thought of as computer-based.

□ Intelligence—searching for conditions that call for decisions.
□ Design—inventing, developing, and analyzing possible courses of action.
□ Choice—selecting a course of action from those available.

An *unstructured problem* is one in which none of the three phases are structured. Decisions where some, but not all, of the phases are structured are referred to as *semistructured* by Gorry and Scott-Morton.

In a structured problem, the procedures for obtaining the best (or at least a good enough) solution are known. Whether the problem involves finding an appropriate inventory level or deciding on an optimal investment strategy, the objectives are clearly defined. Frequent objectives are cost minimization or profit maximization. The manager can use the support of clerical, data processing, or management science people armed with models. In an unstructured problem, human intuition is still the basis for decision making. Typical unstructured problems include planning of new services to be offered, hiring an executive, or choosing a set of research and development projects for next year. The semistructured problems fall between the structured and the unstructured, involving a combination of both standard solution procedures and individual judgment. Keen and Scott-Morton (8) give the following examples of semistructured problems: trading bonds, setting marketing budgets for consumer products, and performing capital acquisition analysis. Here, a decision support system can improve the quality of the information on which the decision is based (and consequently the quality of the decision) by providing not only a single solution but a range of alternate solutions. These capabilities, which are described later, allow managers to better understand the nature of the problems so they can make better decisions.

The second half of this framework is based on Anthony's taxonomy (2), which defines three broad categories that encompass all managerial activities: (1) strategic planning—the long-range goals and the policies for resource allocation; (2) management control—the acquisition and efficient utilization of resources in the accomplishment of organizational goals; and (3) operational control—the efficient and effective execution of specific tasks.

Anthony and Simons' taxonomies are combined in a nine-cell decision support framework (see Figure 1.3). The right-hand column indicates the information system and other tools needed to support the various decisions. Gorry and Scott-Morton suggested that for the semistructured and unstructured decisions, the conventional MIS and management science approaches are insufficient. They proposed the use of a supportive information system, which they called *decision support system* (DSS). Expert systems (ES), which were introduced several years later, are most suitable for tasks requiring expertise. Such problems can be semistructured or unstructured but are usually in a very narrow problem area.

The more structured and operational control-oriented tasks (cells 1, 2, and 4) are being performed by low-level managers, whereas the tasks in cells 6, 8, and 9 are the responsibility of top executives. This means that DSS and ES are

Type of Decision \ Type of Control	Operational Control	Managerial Control	Strategic Planning	Support Needed
Structured	Accounts Receivable, Order Entry [1]	Budget Analysis, Short-Term Forecasting, Personnel Reports, Make or Buy Analysis [2]	Financial Management (Investment), Warehouse Location, Distribution Systems [3]	MIS, Operations Research Models, Transaction Processing
Semistructured	Production Scheduling, Inventory Control [4]	Credit Evaluation, Budget Preparation, Plant Layout, Project Scheduling, Reward Systems Design [5]	Building New Plant, Mergers and Acquisitions, New Product Planning, Compensation Planning, Quality Assurance Planning [6]	DSS
Unstructured	Selecting a Cover for a Magazine, Buying Software, Approving Loans [7]	Negotiating, Recruiting an Executive, Buying Hardware, Lobbying [8]	R & D Planning, New Technology Development, Social Responsibility Planning [9]	DSS ES

FIGURE 1.3 Decision support framework.

more often applicable for top executives and professionals tackling specialized, complex problems.

Computer Support for Structured Decisions

Structured and some semistructured decisons, especially of the operational and managerial control type, have been supported by computers since the 1960s. Decisions of this type are being made in *all functional areas,* especially in finance and production operations.

Such problems, which are encountered fairly repeatedly, have a high level of structure. It is therefore possible to abstract and analyze them and classify them into prototypes. For example, a "make-or-buy" decision belongs to this category. Other examples are capital budgeting (e.g. replacement of equipment), allocation of resources, distribution problems, planning and inventory control. For each type of problem a prescribed solution was developed through the use of some mathematical formulas. This approach was supported by two activities: modeling and computerization.

Modeling involves the transformation of the real-world problem into the prototype structure. As will be seen later, modeling is going to be used also in less structured problems (some portions of an unstructured problem may be structured). The use of computers was designed to help in finding the solution for the problem in a quick and efficient manner. While structured problems were solved with the aid of a host of mathematical models, the less structured ones can be handled by decision support systems.

1.4 Decision Support Systems

The concepts involved in DSS were first articulated in the early 1970s by Scott-Morton under the term *management decision systems*. He defined such systems as "interactive computer-based systems, which help decision makers utilize *data* and *models* to solve unstructured problems"(15). Another classical definition of DSS, provided by Keen and Scott-Morton (8), follows:

> Decision support systems couple the intellectual resources of individuals with the capabilities of the computer to improve the quality of decisions. It is a computer-based support system for management decision makers who deal with semi-structured problems.

The foregoing definitions indicate the four major characteristics of DSS:

☐ DSS incorporate both data and models.
☐ They are designed to *assist* managers in their decision processes in *semistructured* (or *unstructured*) tasks.
☐ They *support*, rather than *replace*, managerial judgment.
☐ The objective of DSS is to improve the *effectiveness* of the decisions, not the *efficiency* with which decisions are being made.

This DSS definition will be revisited and expanded in Chapter 4. It should be noted that DSS, like MIS and ES, is content-free expression (i.e., it means different things to different people). There is no universally accepted definition of DSS.

Now, let us examine a typical case of a successfully implemented DSS, as shown at the top of Page 10.

The case demonstrates some of the major characteristics of a DSS. The risk analysis performed first was based on the decision maker's initial definition of the situation using a management science approach. Then the executive vice president, using his experience, judgment, and intuition, felt that the model should be modified. The initial model, although mathematically correct, was incomplete. With a regular simulation system, a modification would have taken a long time, but the DSS provided a very quick analysis. Furthermore, the DSS was flexible and responsive enough to allow managerial intuition and judgment to be incorporated in the analysis.

How can such a thorough risk analysis be performed so quickly? How can the judgment factors be elicited, quantified, and worked into the model? How can the results be presented meaningfully and convicingly to the executive? What is meant by "what-if" questions? The answers to these questions are provided in Chapters 4 through 9.

The Houston Minerals Case

Houston Minerals Corporation was interested in a proposed joint venture with a petrochemicals company to develop a chemical plant. Houston's executive vice president responsible for the decision wanted analysis of the risks involved in the areas of supplies, demands, and prices. Bob Sampson, manager of planning and administration, and his staff built a DSS in a few days by means of a specialized planning language. The results strongly suggested the project should be accepted.

Then came the real test. Although the executive vice president accepted the validity and value of the results, he was worried about the potential downside risk of the project, the chance of a catastrophic outcome. As Sampson tells it, his words were something like this:

> I realize the amount of work you have already done, and I am 99 percent confident with it. I would like to see this in a different light. I know we are short of time and we have to get back to our partners with our yes or no decision.

Sampson replied that the executive could have the risk analysis he needed in less than an hour's time. Sampson concluded, "within 20 minutes, there in the executive boardroom, we were reviewing the results of his "what-if?" questions. Those results led to the eventual dismissal of the project, which we otherwise would probably have accepted."

For a start, let us list some of the major characteristics and benefits of DSS, some of which are evidenced in the Houston Minerals Case, others are based on Alter's observations (1).

DSS Characteristics and Benefits

The following are the major characteristics of DSS:

a. Ability to support the solution of complex problems. A DSS enables the solution of complex problems that ordinarily cannot be solved by other computerized approaches. (Or can be solved at a much slower pace.)

b. Fast response to unexpected situations that result in changed conditions. A DSS enables a thorough, quantitative analysis in a very short time. Even frequent changes in a scenario can be evaluated objectively in a timely manner.

c. Ability to try several different strategies under different configurations, quickly and objectively. As demonstrated in the preceding case, a complete "what if" analysis was carried out to examine the downside risk of the project. This analysis, which took 20 minutes, would have taken days or weeks with other computerized systems.

NOTE: A "what if" analysis, as will be shown in Chapter 2, is an important feature of DSS that enables us to find what happens to certain conclusions or results if changes are being made in the assumptions or in the input information.

d. New insights and learning. The user can be exposed to new insights through the composition of the model and an extensive sensitivity "what if" analysis. The new insights can help in training inexperienced managers and other employees as well.

e. Facilitated communication. Data collection and model construction experimentations are being executed with active users' participation, thus greatly facilitating communication among managers. The objectivity and logic of the decision process can make employees more supportive of organizational decisions. The "what if" analysis can be used to satisfy skeptics, in turn improving teamwork.

f. Improved management control and performance. DSS can increase management control over expenditures and improve performance of the organization.

g. Cost savings. Routine applications of a DSS may result in considerable cost reduction, or in reducing (eliminating) the cost of wrong decisions.

h. Objective decisions. The decisions derived from DSS are more consistent and objective than decisions made intuitively. They are also based on a thorough analysis and are executed with greater participation of the individuals affected by the decisions. Therefore, the decisions are of a high quality and have a greater chance of successful implementation.

i. Improving managerial effectiveness. All the capabilities a–h can improve managerial effectiveness (and personal efficiency) by allowing managers to perform a task in less time and/or with less effort. The DSS provides managers with more "quality" time for analysis, planning, and implementation.

j. Support for individuals and/or groups. DSS can be used to support individual managers and/or groups of managers.

Why Use a DSS?

Firestone Tire & Rubber Co. explained its reasons for implementing a DSS in *Computerworld* (September 27, 1982). The major reasons were that:

□ The company was operating in an unstable economy.
□ The company was faced with increasing foreign and domestic competition.
□ The company encountered increasing difficulty in tracking the numerous business operations.
□ The company's existing computer system did not support the objectives of increasing efficiency, profitability, and entry into profitable markets.
□ The DP Department could not begin to address the diversity of the company's needs or management's ad hoc inquiries, and business analysis functions were not inherent within the existing systems.

A survey conducted by Hogue and Watson (7) identified six main reasons why major corporations started large-scale DSS:

Factors	Cited by (percent)
Accurate information is needed.	67
DSS is viewed as an organizational winner.	44
New information is needed.	33
Management mandated the DSS.	22
Timely information is provided.	17
Cost reduction is achieved.	6

DSS at Pfizer Pharmaceutical, Inc.

As of 1973, Rachelle Laboratories, Inc. (Long Beach, CA), a competitor of Pfizer, began selling an antibiotic called Doxychel, which was the same drug as Pfizer's Vibramycin. Pfizer contended that its patent had been violated.

The disagreement came to a head in the winter of 1983 in a district court in Honolulu. Throughout the six-week trial, however, Pfizer had an edge over Rachelle. Pfizer had a DSS. Jeffrey Landau, manager of DSS at Pfizer, recalls: "We put together a team of lawyers, system-staff professionals, and others, and built a model." The model, he says, looked at one key: "what-if." If Rachelle hadn't started selling Doxychel, how much more money would Pfizer have made? The answer, of course, depended on two assumptions. One was that all Rachelle's sales were at Pfizer's expense. The other was that, without Rachelle as a competitor, Pfizer could have sold its antibiotic at a higher price.

Armed with these assumptions, the Pfizer team set up, three blocks from the courthouse, a DSS war room, complete with terminals, printers, plotters, and high-speed communication to a DEC System-10 mainframe in Connecticut. With the system in place, the opposition could not stall for time by requesting additional information. Pfizer's system accessed the requested information instantly.

When the trial got under way, however, Pfizer's decision-support system was really put to the test. "We could measure the impact of claims witnesses made about the market. Using the information provided, the lawyers would yield on points that were determined to be insignificant. If the other side made a claim that had big monetary implications, our lawyers would fight it." In effect, the Pfizer team used the model to plan its legal tactics.

The result: On June 30, 1983, Judge Martin Pence, who frequently alluded to Pfizer's model, awarded Pfizer $55.8 million. It was the largest judgment on a patent-infringement suit in U.S. history.

(*Source:* Condensed from M. Lasden, *Computer Decisions*, Nov. 1983, pp. 254–58.)

Another reason for the development of DSS is the end-user computing movement (see section 5.10)—normally, end-users who build their own systems rather than wait (frequently years) for the IS people to do it. End-users are not programmers and therefore they require easy to use construction tools and procedures. These are provided by DSS.

The overall results of using a DSS can be very impressive, as indicated by the Pfizer case.

1.5   Executive Information (or Support) Systems

The basic idea of an EIS is to provide timely information support to senior managers. The technology was developed at the Center for Information Systems

Executive Information System at Hardee's

At Hardee's (Rocky Mount) the EIS primarily provides status access, according to John Wilson, chief financial officer. Point of sale terminals at over 3000 Hardee's restaurants accumulate detailed sales information, which the corporate mainframe collects automatically each night. Financial analysts extract and analyze information from the mass of data using Express (a DSS generator discussed in Chapter 6.) This information is transformed to the EIS database.

The database also holds information on Hardee's competitors and other financial information from online information services. Five top executives, including the chairman and Wilson, tap the EIS with their own IBM PCs. The executives use a mouse to select graphs and reports from menus. Much of their work with the system involves devising and tracking marketing strategies. For example, if the figures show that sales in a region are falling off during a particular time of day, local advertising might have to be refocused.

At Hardee's, the EIS's analyst is tailoring the information to executives' needs and desires. The analyst puts together a basic package of reports and graphs. As the five users familiarize themselves with the available information and possible formats, they are requesting new reports and modifications of standing ones. Wilson expects to add more sophisticated features, like automatic exception reporting and the tracking of situations, that the executive considers critical. The system was developed with the Command Center software (see Chapter 10). "It takes no time at all to learn the system," Wilson says. "Everyone was up to speed in five minutes." (Condensed from *Computer Decisions*, Dec. 17, 1985.)

Research at MIT during the last 10 years. EIS are being developed primarily for the following objectives. They

- □ Provide extremely user friendly interface for the executive.
- □ Meet individual executives' decision styles.
- □ Provide timely and effective tracking and control.
- □ Provide quick access to detailed information behind text, numbers, or graphics (drill-down capability).
- □ Filter, compress, and track critical data and information.

Detailed description of EIS is provided in Chapter 10 and by Rochart and De Long (14). The preceding case demonstrates a successful implementation of the technology.

1.6 Expert Systems

When an organization has a complex decision to make or problem to solve, it often turns to experts for advice. These experts have specific knowledge and experience in the problem area. They are aware of the alternatives, the chances of success, and the costs the business may incur. Companies engage experts for advice on such matters as computer acquisitions, mergers and acquisitions, and advertising strategy. The more unstructured the situation, the more expensive is the advice. Expert systems are an attempt to mimic human experts.

Typically, an expert system is a decision-making and/or problem-solving package of computer hardware and software that can reach a level of performance comparable to—or even exceeding that of—a human expert in some specialized and usually narrow problem area.

Expert systems are a branch of applied artificial intelligence (AI). From applications in medical diagnosis, mineral exploration, and computer configurations, expert systems are spreading into complex business applications like managing assets and liabilities, corporate planning, tax advice, competitive bid preparations, internal control evaluations, and fault analysis. Major efforts are now underway in industry, government, and science to exploit this technology and extend it to new applications, especially in areas where human expertise is in short supply.

The basic idea behind ES is simple. Expertise, which is the vast body of task-specific knowledge, is transferred from the human to the computer. This knowledge is then stored in the computer and users call on the computer for specific advice as needed. The computer can make inferences and arrive at a specific conclusion. Then, like a human consultant, it advises the nonexperts and explains, if necessary, the logic behind the advice.

Illustrative Case

When Elf Aquitaine, the French oil company, has a drill bit stuck thousands of feet below the earth's surface, they no longer call their top troubleshooter to fix this costly problem. Instead, the drilling rig foreman calls a computer for help. The computer asks the foreman questions, just as an expert would. Once it gathers the information it needs from the foreman, the computer, by using its inferencing capabilities, makes a recommendation on how to retrieve the drill bit. The computer can also explain to the foreman why a certain action is less effective than the recommended one. The recommendation is done by drawing images on the computer screen.

To build this system, the builders interviewed Elf Aquitaine's top troubleshooter, Jacques-Marie Courte, and then programmed his answers into the computer. Thus, the computer replicates the expert's knowledge.

This case illustrates some of the distinct capabilities and characteristics of expert systems, such as their ability to:

□ Capture and preserve perishable expertise from one or several experts.
□ Apply this expertise to solve, by using inferencing capabilities, complex problems effectively and efficiently.
□ Solve problems by providing answers instead of data.
□ Provide an explanation of how solutions are derived.

How Expert Systems Can Perform Useful Tasks

Suppose you manage an engineering firm that bids on many projects. Each project is, in a sense, unique. You can calculate your expected cost, but that's not sufficient to set up your bid. You have background information on your likely competitors and their bidding strategies. Something is known about the risks—possible technical problems, political delays, material shortages, or other sources of trouble. An experienced proposal manager can put all this together and, generally, arrive at a sound judgment concerning terms and bidding price. However, you do not have that many proposal managers who have the time to concentrate on preparing and negotiating major proposals. This is where expert systems become useful. An expert system can capture the lines of thinking the experienced proposal managers can follow. It can also catalog information gained on competitors, local risks, et cetera, and can incorporate your policies and strategies concerning risk, pricing, and terms. It can help your younger managers work through to an informed bid consistent with your policy.

Suppose you are a life insurance agent and you are a very good one; however, your market has changed. You are no longer competing only with other insurance agents. You are also competing with banks, brokers, money market fund managers, and the like. Your company is now pushing a whole array of products, from universal life insurance to venture capital funds. Your clients have the same problems as ever, but they are more inquisitive, more sophisticated, and more conscious of tax avoidance and similar considerations. How can you give them advice and put together a sensible package for them when you are more confused than they are?

Financial planning systems and estate planning guides have been part of the insurance industry's marketing kit for a long time. However, sensible financial planning takes more skill than the average insurance agent has or can afford to acquire. This is one reason why the fees of professional planners are as high as they are. A number of insurance companies are currently investing heavily in artificial intelligence techniques in the hope that these techniques can be used to build sophisticated, competitive, knowledge-based financial planning support systems to assist their agents in helping their clients.

(*Source:* Publicly disclosed project description of Arthur D. Little, Inc.)

These capabilities can provide companies with improved productivity levels and increased competitive advantages owing to the following potential benefits:

1. Monetary savings. Human expertise is usually very expensive compared with a frequently used expert system.
2. Improved quality. Some ES have proved to do a better job than humans. They make fewer mistakes and are more consistent in their recommendations.
3. ES are compatible with many managers' decision styles. ES are based on judgment, which is extensively used by managers.
4. ES can be used as a training vehicle to train nonexperts and even to improve the expertise of experts.
5. ES can free experts from time-consuming, routine tasks. Many experts are too busy advising nonexperts on what to do. ES can free experts from repetitive advising and training, and/or from data search tasks, and enable them to concentrate on more creative tasks.
6. Preserving scarce expertise.
7. Enabling operation in a hazardous environment.

1.7   The Evolution of Computerized Decision Aids

Computers have been used as tools to support managerial decision making for over two decades. Table 1.1 presents a summary of the development of computerized procedures used as aids in decision making.

The computerized tools or decision aids displayed in Table 1.1 can be grouped into six categories (see Kroeber and Watson [10]):

☐ Transaction Processing Systems (TPS).
☐ Management Information Systems (MIS).
☐ Office Automation Systems (OAS).
☐ Decision Support Systems (DSS) and Group DSS (GDSS).
☐ Expert Systems.
☐ Executive Information Systems (EIS).

These systems will be called computer-based information systems (CBIS).[*]
There are several opinions about the evolution of DSS and ES and their relationship to the other systems. A common view is that the recommendations and advice provided by DSS and ES to the manager can be considered as information needed for final decisions made by humans. If we accept this approach, we can consider both DSS and ES as sophisticated, high-level types of information systems that can be used in addition to traditional transaction processing systems, office automation, and MIS.

The evolutionary view of CBIS, presented in Figure 1.4, has a strong logical basis. First, there is a clear-cut sequence through time: EDP systems appeared in the mid-1950s, MIS followed in the 1960s, OAS was developed mainly in the 1970s, and DSS is a product of the 1970s and is expanding in the 1980s. Commercial applications of expert systems are beginning to emerge and Execu-

---

[*]All these systems are supported by telecommunications and networks, a topic outside the framework of this book.

TABLE 1.1   Aids in Decision Making.

Phase	Description	Examples of Tools
Early	Compute, "crunch numbers," summarize, organize	Calculators; early computer programs; statistical models; simple operations research models
Intermediate	Find, organize, and display decision-relevant information	Database management system, MIS, filing systems
Current	Perform decision-relevant computations on decision-relevant information; organize, and display the results. Query-based and user-friendly approach. "What if" analysis	Financial models, spreadsheets, trend exploration, operations research models, CAD systems, decision support systems
	Interact with decision makers to facilitate formulation and execution of the intellectual steps in the process of decision making	Expert systems
Just beginning		2nd generation of Expert Systems, Executive Support Systems

tive Information Systems support the work of senior executives. Second, there is a common technology linking the various types of CBIS: the computer, which itself has evolved considerably over time. And third, there are systemic linkages in the manner in which each system processes data into information. Additional support for the evolutionary view is presented in Figure 1.5. This figure lists the

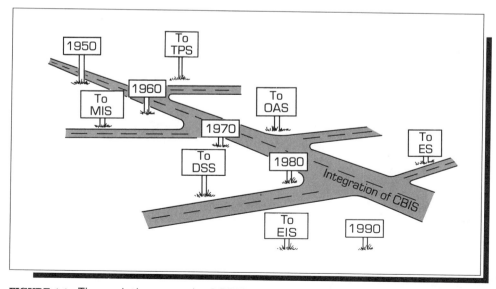

FIGURE 1.4   The evolutionary path of CBIS. (*Source:* Kroeber and Watson [10]; modified.)

Dimension	Transactions Processing Systems (TPS)	Management Information Systems (MIS)	Decision Support Systems (DSS)	Expert Systems (ES)	Executive Information Systems (EIS)
Applications	Payroll, inventory, record keeping, production and sales information	Production control, sales forecasting, monitoring	Long-range strategic planning, complex integrated problem areas	Diagnosis, strategic planning, internal control planning, maintenance strategies. Narrow domain	Support to top management decision, environmental scanning
Focus	Data Transactions	Information	Decisions, flexibility, user-friendliness	Inferencing, Transfer of expertise	Tracking, control "Drill down"
Database	Unique to each application, batch update	Interactive access by programmers	Database management systems, interactive access, factual knowledge	Procedural and factual knowledge; knowledge base (facts, rules)	External (online) and corporate
Decision Capabilities	No decision, or simple decision models	Structured routine problems using conventional operations research tools	Semistructured problems, integrated OR models, blend of judgment and structured support capabilities	The system makes complex decisions, unstructured; use of rules (heuristics)	None
Manipulation	Numerical	Numerical	Numerical	Symbolic	Numeric (mainly) some symbolic
Type of information	Summary reports, operational	Scheduled and demand reports, structured flow, exception reporting	Information to support specific decisions	Advice and Explanations	Status access, exception reporting, key indicators
Highest organizational level served	Submanagerial, low management	Middle management	Top management	Top management and specialists	Senior executives (only)
Impetus	Expediency	Efficiency	Effectiveness	Effectiveness and expediency	Timeliness

FIGURE 1.5 Attributes of computerized systems.

attributes of TPS, MIS, DSS, EIS and ES classified into several dimensions. Only the most sophisticated attributes of each level are listed. Several lesser attributes can be found (although not listed) in most of the CBIS.

The relationship among TPS, MIS, DSS, EIS and ES can be summarized as follows:

- □ All five technologies can be viewed as being unique classes of information technology.
- □ They are interrelated, and they each support some aspects of managerial decision making.
- □ The evolution and creation of the newer tools help expand the role of information technology for the betterment of management in organizations.
- □ The interrelationship and coordination between these tools is still evolving. A lot remains to be learned and theories need to be further developed.

The classification of CBIS does not imply that real world computer systems must belong to only one category. On the contrary, an MIS system may be coupled with a transaction processing system. A DSS may be combined with an MIS and integrated with an ES. The interactions among CBIS occur along two dimensions: Technology (hardware, software, processes) and applications (personnel management, scheduling, inventory control). For further discussion, see Kroeber and Watson (10) and Chapter 19.

An illustration of CBIS in a personnel department is provided in Appendix A at the end of the chapter.

1.8   Some Differences Between MIS and DSS

The DSS definitions, performance characteristics, and examples clearly indicate that there are differences between DSS and MIS. We notice that the differences are real and merit our attention. What can be expected from a DSS is less typically possible with an MIS. This does not mean that an MIS cannot have these features; rather, they are simply not common to most management information systems. The Houston Minerals Case illustrates these differences.

Specifically, a DSS can be used to address ad hoc, unexpected problems. The proposed joint venture was possibly a once-in-a-lifetime decision-making situation. Most MIS decision support is supplied by structured information flows in the form of summary and exception reports. An exception report singles out items that require special attention. Structured reports are of limited value for unique problems. Either the needed information is not provided or it is in the wrong format.

A DSS can provide a valid representation of a complex real world system. In this example, the decision maker accepted the validity of the model and the value of the results; the model builders were able to develop a model that could be trusted. The way many model builders are embedded in an MIS does not engender such trust, because they are frequently built by the management science group and left for the user as the management scientist moves on to other projects. Over time, the models become out-of-date and either are not used or are used and provide potentially misleading, outdated information.

A DSS can supply decision support within a short time frame. A model for the proposed joint venture was completed and working within days. A request for risk analysis was satisfied within one hour. In an MIS, if the model is not already available, the lead time for writing programs and getting answers is often too long to help many decision situations.

A DSS can evolve as the decision maker learns more about the problem. In many cases, managers cannot specify in advance what they want from computer programmers and model builders. In our example, the request for risk analysis occurred *after* the model was built. Many computerized applications are developed in a way that requires detailed specifications to be formalized in advance. This requirement is not reasonable in many semistructured and unstructured decision-making tasks.

A DSS is often developed by non-data processing (DP) professionals. In the Houston case, the planning and administration group created the model with no outside help. This was possible because of the software package that was available. Most MIS applications and systems are developed by data processing professionals.

These distinguishing DSS features are summarized in Table 1.2. Keen and Scott-Morton also have noted the distinctive nature of DSS. Table 1.3 summarizes the differences that they see among MIS, operations research/management science (OR/MS), and DSS.

Another way to look at the relationships between DSS and MIS is provided by McLean (12), who uses Anthony's framework. The three levels of organizational activities are shown as a triangle with an added level for transaction processing. Transaction processing is done mainly at the operational level.

In a sense, the bottom layer is not a level of decision making at all. It is an organizational activity, however, that consumes a good bit of managers' time, particularly those charged with managing the data processing function within the organization.

MIS, in theory, was to serve all levels of managerial activities. As such DSS can be considered a subset of MIS (see Figure 1.6). In practice, MIS has fallen far short of this objective. The proponents of decision support systems therefore argued that their approaches were better suited to the upper two layers of decision making.

Similar to McLean's point of view is the notion that MIS is an umbrella that supports all managerial activities. DSS is viewed as the portion that deals

---

TABLE 1.2 DSS Features

- ☐ A DSS can be used to address ad hoc, unexpected problems
- ☐ A DSS can provide valid representation of the real world system
- ☐ A DSS can provide decision support within a short time frame
- ☐ A DSS can evolve as the decision maker learns more about the problem
- ☐ DSS can be developed by non-DP professionals

TABLE 1.3 The Characteristics of MIS, OR/MS, and DSS.

Management Information Systems
- □ The main impact has been on structured tasks, where standard operating procedures, decision rules, and information flows can be reliably predefined
- □ The main payoff has been in improving efficiency by reducing costs, turnaround time, and so on, and by replacing clerical personnel
- □ The relevance for manager's decision making has mainly been indirect, for example, by providing reports and access to data

Operations Research/Management Science
- □ The impact has mostly been on structured problems (rather than tasks), where the objective, data, and constraints can be prespecified
- □ The payoff has been in generating better solutions for given types of problems
- □ The relevance for managers has been the provision of detailed recommendations and new methodologies for handling complex problems

Decision Support Systems
- □ The impact is on decisions in which there is sufficient structure for computer and analytic aids to be of value but where managers' judgment is essential
- □ The payoff is in extending the range and capability of computerized managers' decision processes to help them improve their effectiveness
- □ The relevance for managers is the creation of a supportive tool, under their own control, that does not attempt to automate the decision process, predefine objectives, or impose solutions

Source: Keen and Scott-Morton (8), p. 1.

with unstructured situations while management science deals with structured problems.

NOTE: For a discussion on the differences between DSS and EIS, see Chapter 10.

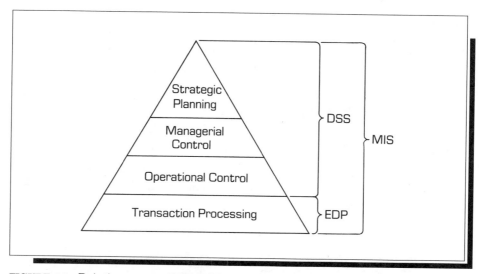

FIGURE 1.6 Relation among EDP, MIS, and DSS. (*Source:* McLean [12].)

1.9   The Decision Support-Expert Systems Connection

DSS and ES seem to be completely different and unrelated computerized systems. As can be viewed in Table 1.4, there are significant philosophical, technological, and managerial differences between the two tools. These differences are discussed in detail in Chapter 19.

The disciplines of ES and DSS grew up along parallel, but largely independent, paths. Only recently has the potential of integrating the two been recognized. As a matter of fact, because of the different capabilities of the two tools, they can complement each other, creating a powerful, integrated, computer-based system that can considerably improve managerial decision making.

1.10   Support of Decision Making

The techniques discussed in this book can be used as independent, stand alone tools, or they can be integrated. The manner in which they are applied depends on the nature of the decision, the nature of the organization and the individuals involved in the decision making. To show the potential support of the techniques discussed in this book we revisit Simon's decision making process, discussed earlier. The process is shown in Figure 1.7 (slightly modified). We also show the potential support of DSS, GDSS, EIS and ES.

TABLE 1.4   Differences Between DSS and ES.

	DSS	**ES**
Objective	Assist human decision maker	Replicate (mimic) human advisers and replace them
Who makes the recommendations (decisions)?	The human and/or the system	The system
Major orientation	Decision making	Transfer of expertise (human-machine-human) and rendering of advice
Major query direction	Human queries the machine	Machine queries the human
Nature of support	Personal, groups, and institutional	Personal (mainly), and groups
Manipulation method	Numerical	Symbolic
Characteristics of problem area	Complex, integrated, wide	Narrow domain
Type of problems	Ad hoc, unique	Repetitive
Content of database	Factual knowledge	Procedural and factual knowledge
Reasoning capability	No	Yes, limited
Explanation capability	Limited	Yes

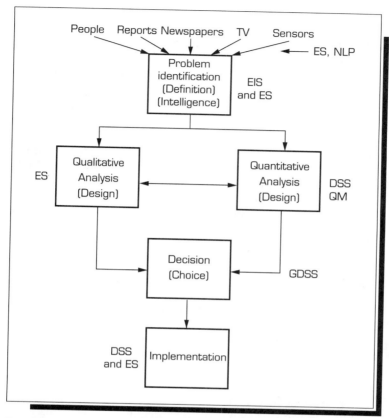

FIGURE 1.7 Computerized Support to the Decision-Making Process.

The steps of the process are:

Step a. Problem (opportunity) finding. This step involves the collection of information from various sources in order to identify problems and opportunities. This step is primarily supported by EIS. The system monitors the environment, prepares reports, concentrates on key indicators, permits "drill-down" investigations, etc.

An ES can help in the design of the flow of information to the executive (e.g., what to monitor, when), and in the interpretation of the collected information. Because some of the information is fuzzy, a combination of ES and neural computing (Chapter 22) can be very helpful. The entire area of scanning, monitoring, forecasting (e.g., trends) and assessment (or interpretation) can be greatly helped by automation in general (e.g., E-mail, etc.) and by ES in particular. Also, Natural Language processors (NLP, see Chapter 18) can be useful in summarizing information.

Step b. Analysis. Once the problem (opportunity) has been identified, a question is posed: what to do about it? At this step an analysis is called for. The analysis can be qualitative or quantitative (or combined). The quantitative analysis can be supported by a DSS and by structured quantitative analysis tools. The qualitative analysis can be supported by an ES.

Step c. Choice. In this step, a decision is made regarding the problem (or opportunity) based on the results of the analysis. The step can be supported by a DSS (if the decision maker is an individual) or by a GDSS (if the decision is made by a group).

Step d. Implementation. In the event that the decision is to implement a proposed solution a DSS and/or ES can provide the support.

Group Decision Support Systems

Many decisions, especially of managerial and strategic nature are being made by groups (committees, task forces) rather than by individuals. DSS, EIS and ES support decisions made by groups by providing *information* and *advice* to the group. However, they do not support the *process* of group decision making. Such a support is provided by a technology called Group Decision Support Systems (GDSS) which is described in Chapter 4.

1.11   Plan of the Book

This book is composed of 22 chapters, divided into 4 parts. Part I (Chapters 1, 2, and 3) contains an introduction (Chapter 1), the conceptual foundations of decision making necessary for understanding MSS (Chapter 2), and modeling (Chapter 3).

Part II contains 7 chapters about DSS. Chapter 4 includes the definitions, structure, functions, capabilities, and limitations of DSS. The process of building a DSS is presented in Chapter 5 with the different construction strategies. Chapter 6 presents the DSS construction tools. Chapter 7 is dedicated to IFPS including a detailed IFPS project. Chapter 8 presents two detailed cases that demonstrate the construction process. Chapter 9 presents case studies of applications in various business functional areas. Chapter 10 deals with executive information systems (EIS).

Part III is similar in structure to Part II (see Figure 1.8). In this part, however, the subject is expert systems. Specifically, Chapter 11 presents an overview of applied artificial intelligence tools of which expert systems is a prominent category. Chapter 12 presents the definitions, structure, capabilities, and limitations of ES. Chapter 13 deals with knowledge acquisition issues, including validation and verification. Chapter 14 deals with knowledge representation and inferencing. Chapter 15 deals with construction tools and available development strategies. Chapter 16 gives two detailed cases to demonstrate the development process. Part III ends with a brief description of more than a dozen cases (Chapter 17), which illustrates applications in several functional areas.

Part IV deals with topics common to both DSS, EIS, and ES. First, Chapter 18 deals with user interface and Natural Language Processors. Second, Chapter 19 covers the interaction and integration of the three technologies. The implementation of MSS is presented in Chapter 20. The determinants of successful implementation are presented together with some suggestions that could increase the chances of a successful implementation. Chapter 21 deals with potential consequences of introducing MSS into organizations. These consequences range from management power struggles and the difficulties with the

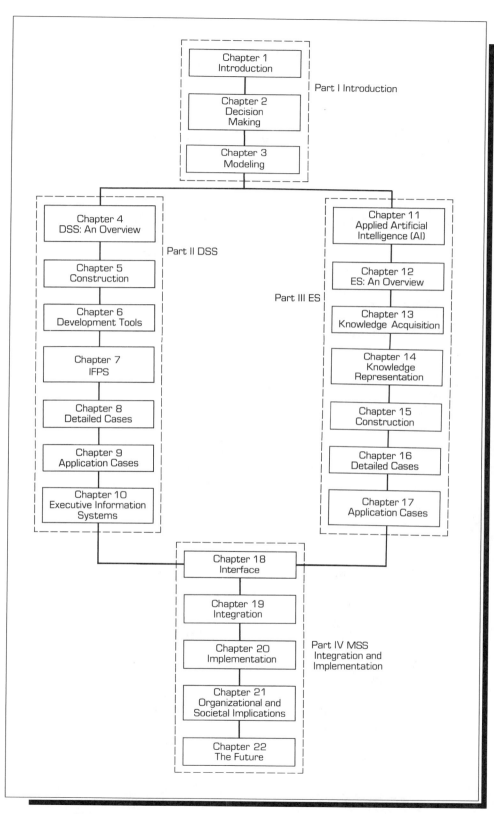

FIGURE 1.8 Plan of the book.

human-machine interfaces to the possible increase in unemployment. The book ends with an exposition of future developments (Chapter 22), ranging from neural computing to the automated, intelligent factory.

1.12 Summary

To summarize and reinforce some of the ideas expressed in this chapter, we present representative quotations from several practitioners:

> Our bank, the nation's fourth largest, would hardly make a major decision without marshalling the facts and figures in computer-generated presentations.

> The PC has become an essential part of the CEO's business life, as essential as the company telephone.

> Managers now have a more broadly perceived need for decision support, and in many cases, a belief that computer systems can be a valuable source of help.

> The basic function of innovational technology is replacement and amplification of mental labor.

> We've got information coming out of our ears and what we need now is some way to make sense of it.

> About $30 billion of DP funds in the USA goes to support $450 billion of managerial/professional activities, while $50 billion of DP dollars go to support $150 billion of clerical activities. It is time for a change.

> A study of DP departments by IBM indicates that in major companies there is an average 2.5 year backlog for major system applications, with 15% experiencing more than 4 years of backlog.

> Information consumers might want to help themselves to information instead of being spoon-fed by professionals.

> Expert systems provide direct answers to questions, not merely information. Furthermore, they are capable of using incomplete or even inconsistent input data to infer a conclusion.

Why is there current interest in management support systems?

- Growing awareness of the potential benefits.
  - —by users
  - —by the MIS departments
  - —by top management
- Dramatic reduction in the cost of hardware.
- Widespread availability of hardware.
- Widespread availability of software at decreasing costs.
- Growing sophistication on the part of users.
- User-friendly languages to simplify development of systems.
- Easier access to data through database management systems and intelligent interfaces.
- Compatibility of DSS with related developments in office automation, professional work stations, distributed computing, interactive computering, graphics, and advanced integrated systems.

☐ Growing end-user computing activities.
☐ Increasing pressures to increase productivity.

Key Words

artificial intelligence
decision support systems
   (DSS)
electronic data processing
   (EDP)
Executive Information
   Systems (EIS)
expertise
expert systems (ES)
hardware
integrated computer systems

management information
   systems (MIS)
management science (MS)
Management Support
   Systems
mathematical models
microcomputers
microelectronics
nonprogrammed decision
operations research

productivity
programmed decisions
semistructured decisions
software
spreadsheets
structured decisions
telecommunications
unstructured decisions
user-friendly
"what if" analysis

Questions for Review

1. What caused the latest revolution in management use of computers? List at least two causes.
2. What is a computer-based information system (CBIS)?
3. List the three phases of the decision-making process (according to H.A. Simon).
4. Define DSS.
5. Discuss the major characteristics of DSS.
6. List five major benefits of DSS.
7. Management is often equated with decision making. Why?
8. Discuss the major trends that impact managerial decision making.
9. Define management science.
10. Define MIS and relate it to the decision-making process.
11. Relate MIS and DSS to the degree of structuredness of managerial decisions.
12. Define structured, semistructured, and unstructured decisions.
13. Categorize managerial activities (according to Anthony).
14. Define expert systems.
15. Define expertise.
16. List the major benefits of ES.
17. Trace the evolution of MIS through DSS to ES.
18. Discuss the major differences between MIS and DSS.
19. Discuss the major differences between DSS and ES.
20. Describe the objectives and characteristics of EIS.

Problems and Discussion Questions

1. Give additional examples for each of the cells in Figure 1.3.
2. Read *MIS Week* of September 8, 1982, p. 23, for an article by Hiller titled "Personal Computer Revolution: How to Manage It." Answer the following questions:
   a. How are information centers, office automation, personal computers, and DSS interrelated?
   b. How can the personal computer revolution impact a DSS?
3. Design a computerized system for a brokerage house that trades in securities, conducts research on companies, and provides information and advice to customers (e.g.,

"buy," "sell," "hold"). In your design, clearly distinguish five parts: transaction processing, MIS, office automation, DSS, and ES. Be sure to deal with input and output information.

For extra credit: List the hardware and the software that you recommend. List all your assumptions.

Note: Assume that the brokerage company is a small one with only 20 branches in four different cities. (Submit this special assignment at the end of the semester.)

4. Survey the literature of the last six months to find one application each of DSS, EIS, and ES. Summarize the applications on one page and submit it with a photocopy of the article.

5. Observe an organization that you are familiar with. List five decisions it makes in each of the following categories: strategic planning, management control (tactical planning), and operational planning and control.

MINICASE: The Ohio Association of Realtors (OAR)

The OAR headquarters, an organization with 27 employees, serves 33,000 members in Ohio. The association has been using computers since 1970. In 1985 the system was upgraded to a network of mini- and microcomputers that provide the following services and capabilities: (1) Electronic mail is now available in the office. (2) A list (tracking) of all members is updated monthly. (3) Word processing is done. (4) Several periodical reports are generated. (5) Bookkeeping is done. (6) Information about educational activities is mailed to members. (7) Standard mortgage evaluation models are accessed. (8) Executive calendars and calendars of activities are produced. (9) A statistical analysis of home sales is compiled monthly. (10) Standard management science models (like PERT/CPM) are available on the system. A telecommunications package is available for receiving information from commercial databases.

The system is centered around IBM Systems /34 and /36 and it includes IBM PCs, Compaqs, and a MacIntosh. (The MacIntosh is used to create flyers, charts, and graphs.) The association plans to buy spreadsheet software (Supercalc II) and train employees to use it.

QUESTIONS

1. What kind(s) of CBIS exist at OAR? (Refer to Figure 1.4.)
2. What attributes of DSS or ES can be found in this system? (Be specific!)
3. Can EIS be useful to this organization: Why or why not?

References and Bibliography

1. Alter, S. L. *Decision Support System, Current Practice and Continuing Challenges.* Reading, Mass: Addison-Wesley, 1980.
2. Anthony, R. N. *Planning and Control Systems: A Framework for Analysis.* Cambridge, MA: Harvard University Graduate School of Business, 1965.
3. Bullerx, W. I., and Reid, R. A. "Management Systems: Four options, one solution." *Journal of Information Systems Management,* Spring 1987.
4. Chung, C. "A network of management support systems." *Omega,* Vol. 13, No. 4, 1988.

5. Fersko-Weiss, H. "Personal Computing at the Top."*Personal Computing,* March 1985.
6. Gorry, G. M., and M. S. Scott-Morton. "A Framework for Management Information Systems." *Sloan Management Review,* Fall 1971.
7. Hogue, J. T., and H. J. Watson. "Management's Role in the Approval and Administration of Decision Support Systems."*MIS Quarterly,* June 1983.
8. Keen, P. G. W., and M. S. Scott-Morton. *Decision Support Systems, An Organizational Perspective.* Reading, MA: Addison-Wesley,1978
9. Keen, P. G. W., and L. A. Woodman. "What to Do With All Those Micros?"*Harvard Business Review,* 1984.
10. Kroeber, D. W., and H. J. Watson. *Computer-based Information Systems: A Management Approach.* 2nd ed. New York: Macmillan, 1988.
11. Martin, J. *Applications Development Without Programmers.* Englewood Cliffs, NJ: Prentice-Hall, 1982.
12. McLean, E. R. *Decision Support Systems and Managerial Decision Making.* Working paper 1-83, Graduate School of Management, UCLA, Los Angeles, CA, 1982.
13. Reimann, B. C. "Decision Support Systems: Strategic Management Tools for the Eighties" *Business Horizons,* 1985.
14. Rockart J. F., and D. W. DeLong, *Executive Support Systems,* Homewood, IL: Dow-Jones, Irwin: 1988.
15. Scott-Morton, M. S. *Management Decision Systems: Computer-Based Support for Decision Making.* Cambridge, MA: Division of Research, Harvard University, 1971.
16. Simon, H. *The New Science of Management Decision.* New York: Harper & Row, 1960.
17. Turban E., and J. Meredith. *Fundamentals of Management Science.* 5th ed. Homewood Il, Irwin, 1991.
18. Waterman, D. *A Guide to Expert Systems.* Reading, MA: Addison-Wesley, 1986.
19. Yoneji, M. *Information Society.* Tokyo: Institute for Information Society, 1980.
20. *Personal Computing,* April 1989.

APPENDIX A: Computer Based Information Systems in a Personnel Department

The purpose for this appendix is to illustrate the content of typical CBIS in a personnel department. The classification is somewhat arbitrary since we do not have information on the content of each task. In reality these tasks can be placed in different categories or one task can be classified in two categories, since the boundaries of the categories are not precise and several real-life systems combine several of the categories.

Category	Tasks
Transaction processing	Keep inventory of personnel. Payroll preparation; compute salaries and incentive plans.
Management Information System	Summary reports (e.g., average salaries in town). Performance tracking of employees, labor budget. Preparation, monitoring, and analysis. Short-term scheduling. Match positions and candidates. Positions control systems. Fringe benefits monitoring and control.

Decision Support Systems	Special reports (e.g.,) safety records, equal opportunity achievements). Long-range planning for human resources. Design of a compensation plan. Quantitative support of labor-management negotiation.
Expert Systems	Advice on legal and tax implications during management-labor negotiations. Develop a social responsibility plan. Select training media. Design comprehensive training programs.
Office Automation	Online job interviews and recruiting, schedule meetings, mailing lists, schedule training, electronic mail, labor news and statistics received online, preparation of training materials.
Executive Information System	Exists at the corporate level only. Will measure key performance indicators of the department (such as dollar per employee).

Chapter 2

Decision Making, Systems, Modeling, and Support

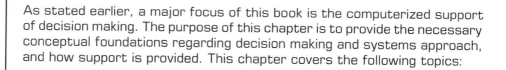

As stated earlier, a major focus of this book is the computerized support of decision making. The purpose of this chapter is to provide the necessary conceptual foundations regarding decision making and systems approach, and how support is provided. This chapter covers the following topics:

31

2.1   Definitions[*]

Decision making is a process of choosing among alternative courses of action for the purpose of attaining a goal or goals. According to Herbert A. Simon (21), managerial decision making is synonymous with the whole process of management. To illustrate the idea, let us examine the important managerial function of planning. Planning involves a series of decisions, for example, What should be done? When? How? Where? By whom? Hence, planning implies decision making. Other functions in the management process like organizing and controlling can also be viewed as decision making.

Decision Making and Problem Solving

Much confusion exists between the terms *decision making* and *problem solving*. One way to distinguish between them is to examine the phases of the decision process. These phases are (1) intelligence, (2) design, (3) choice, and (4) implementation. One school of thought considers the entire process (steps 1–4) as problem solving; the choice step is considered decision making. Another viewpoint is that steps 1–3 constitute decision making that ends with a recommendation—whereas problem solving additionally includes implementation of the recommendation (step 4). The terms decision making and problem solving are used here interchangeably.

2.2   Systems

DSS, EIS, and ES (to be called, collectively, Management Support System—MSS) include the term *systems*. A system is a collection of people, resources, concepts, and procedures intended to perform an identifiable function or to serve a goal. A clear definition of that function is most important for the design of MSS. For instance, the purpose of an air defense system is to protect ground targets, not just to destroy attacking aircraft or missiles.

The notion of levels (or a hierarchy) of systems reflects that all systems are actually subsystems, since all are contained within some larger system. For example, a bank includes such subsystems as (1) the commercial loan department, (2) the consumer loan department, (3) the savings department, and (4) the operations department. The bank itself may also be a subsidiary of a holding corporation, such as Bank of America, which is a subsystem of the California banking system, which is a part of the national banking system, which is a part of the national economy, and so on. The interconnections and interactions among the subsystems are terms *interfaces*.

---

[*]A large portion of the material in this chapter was adapted, with permission, from Turban and Meredith (24).

The Structure of a System

Systems are divided into three distinct parts: inputs, processes, and outputs. They are surrounded by an environment (Figure 2.1) and frequently include a feedback mechanism.

Inputs.   Inputs include those elements that enter the system. Examples of inputs are raw materials entering a chemical plant, patients admitted to a hospital, or data input into a computer.

Processes.   All the elements necessary to convert or transform the inputs into outputs are included in the processes. For example, in a chemical plant a process may include heating the materials, using operating procedures, employing the materials handling subsystem, and using employees and machines. In a hospital the process includes conducting tests and performing surgery. In a computer a process may include activating commands, executing computations, and storing information.

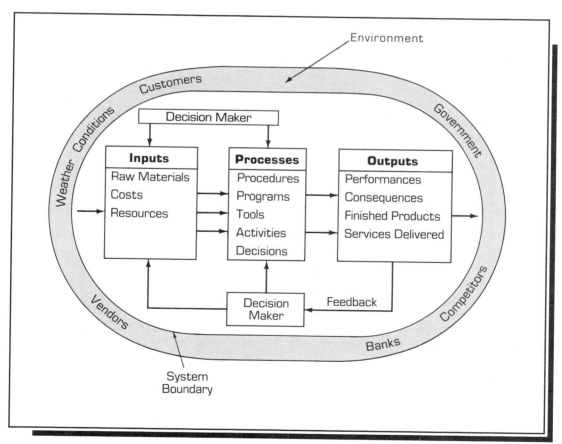

FIGURE 2.1   The system and its environment.

Outputs.   Outputs describe the finished products or the consequences of being in the system. For example, fertilizers are one output of a chemical plant, cured people are an output of a hospital, and reports may be the output of a computerized system.

Feedback.   There is a flow of information from the output component to the decision maker concerning the system's output or performance. Based on this information the decision maker, who acts as a control, may decide to modify the inputs or the processes, or both. This flow, which appears as a closed loop (Figure 2.1), is termed *feedback*.

Productivity.   Productivity is sometimes defined as the ratio of outputs (results) to inputs (resources). A more accurate definition is that productivity is the ratio of output to the combined efforts of inputs and processes:

$$\text{Productivity} = \frac{\text{outputs}}{\text{inputs} + \text{processes}}$$

For a detailed discussion of these two and other definitions of productivity, see Sumanth (23).

The Environment.   The environment of the system is composed of several elements that lie outside it in the sense that they are not inputs, outputs, or processes. However, they have an impact on the system's performance and consequently on the attainment of its goals. One way to identify the elements of the environment is by answering two questions as suggested by Churchman (3):

1. Is the element matter relative to the system's goals?
2. Is it possible for the decision maker to significantly manipulate this element?

If and only if the answer to the first question is *yes*, but the answer to the second is *no*, the element should be considered part of the environment. Environmental elements can be social, political, legal, physical, and economical. For example, in the case of a chemical plant the suppliers, competitors, and customers are elements of the environment. In a decision support system that deals with capital budgeting, the Dow-Jones database, the production system of the company, a telecommunications network, and the personnel department may represent some elements of the environment.

The Boundary.   A system is separated from its environment by a boundary. The system is inside the boundary whereas the environment lies outside. Boundaries may be physical (e.g., the system is a department in Building C), or the boundary may be some nonphysical factor. For example, a system can be bounded by time. In such a case we may analyze an organization for a period of only one year.

When systems are studied or worked with it is often necessary to arbitrarily define the boundaries in order to simplify the analysis. Such boundaries are related to the concepts of closed and open systems.

Closed and Open Systems. Because every system can be considered a subsystem of another, the application of system analysis may never end. Therefore it is necessary, as a matter of practicality, to confine the analysis to defined boundaries. Such confinement is termed *closing* the system.

A *closed system* represents one extreme along a continuum (the *open system* is at the other extreme), which reflects the degree of independence of systems. A closed system is totally independent, whereas an open system is very dependent on its environment (and/or other systems). The open system accepts inputs from the environment and may deliver outputs into the environment, but there are no interactions during the transformation process.

When determining the impact of decisions on an open system, we must check the environment and vice versa. In a closed system, however, it is not necessary to conduct such checks because it is assumed that the system is isolated. Traditional computer systems like transaction processing systems (TPS) are considered to be closed systems. Many management science models are also confined to closed systems or include very limited environmental elements.

Open systems exchange information, material, or energy with the environment. Living systems are the best examples of open systems. Most organizations are open systems and readily adapt to changes in their environment.

A special type of closed system is called the *black box*. In such a system inputs and outputs are well defined but the process itself is not specified. Many managers like to treat computer systems as a black box; in other words, they do not care how the computer works. They consider it as they would consider a telephone or an elevator. They use these devices but do not care how they operate.

Decision support systems attempt to deal with systems that are fairly open. Such systems are complex, and during their analysis it is necessary to check the impacts on and from the environment. To illustrate the difference between a DSS and a management science approach, let us look at an inventory system (Table 2.1), which compares a well-known inventory model, the economic order quantity (EOQ) model, with a hypothetical DSS for an inventory system.

TABLE 2.1 A Closed vs. an Open Inventory System.

Management Science, EOQ (Closed System)	DSS (Open System)
Constant demand, constant per unit cost, constant lead time.	Variable demand influenced by many factors; cost can be changed any day; lead time varies and is difficult to predict.
Vendors and users are excluded from the analysis	Vendors and users are being considered.
Weather and other environmental factors are ignored.	Weather conditions could determine both demand and lead time.

System Effectiveness and Efficiency

Systems are evaluated and analyzed with two major classes of performance measurement: effectiveness and efficiency.

Effectiveness is the degree to which goals are achieved. It is therefore concerned with the results or the outputs of a system. These outputs may be total sales of a company or of a salesperson, for example.

Efficiency is a measure of the use of inputs (or resources) to achieve results; for example, how much money is used to generate a certain level of sales.

Effectiveness is frequently confused with efficiency. Effectiveness measures the degree of a goal's attainment; efficiency measures how well resources are utilized. Effectiveness does not necessarily imply efficiency. A system may be effective but very inefficient if it attains its goals at a tremendous expense. On the other hand, a system may be efficient (making best use of its resources) but ineffective (not achieving its objectives).

An interesting way to distinguish between the two was proposed by Peter Drucker, who makes the following distinction:

> Effectiveness = doing the "right" thing
>
> Efficiency = doing the "thing" right

An important characteristic of DSS and ES is their emphasis on the effectiveness, or "goodness," of the decision produced, rather than on the computational efficiency, which is usually a major concern of a transaction processing system.

In many managerial systems, and especially those involving the delivery of human services (such as education, health, or recreation) the measurement of the system's effectiveness and efficiency constitutes a major problem. The reason for the difficulty is due to the existence of several, often nonquantifiable, conflicting goals. In addition, indirect costs and benefits may be involved. For further discussion and references, see Van Gigch (25).

The systems concept is important not only because it is a part of MSS but also because it is actually used in the decision-making process.

2.3 Models

A major characteristic of decision support systems is the inclusion of a modeling capability. The basic idea is to execute the DSS analysis on a model of reality rather than on reality itself.

A *model* is a simplified representation or abstraction of reality. It is usually simplified because reality is too complex to copy exactly and because much of the complexity is actually irrelevant to the specific problem. The characteristics of simplification and representation are difficult to achieve simultaneously in practice (they *contradict* each other). For example, a model can be simple but inadequately representative of a given phenomenon.

The representation of systems or problems through models can be done at various degrees of abstraction; therefore models are classified, according to their degree of abstraction, into three groups.

Iconic (Scale). An iconic model—the least abstract model—is a physical replica of a system, usually based on a different scale from the original. Iconic models may appear to scale in three dimensions such as an airplane, car, bridge, or production line. Photographs are another type of iconic scale model but in only two dimensions.

Analog. An analog model does not look like the real system but behaves like it. It is more abstract than an iconic model and is considered a symbolic representation of reality. These are usually two-dimensional charts or diagrams: that is, they could be physical models, but the shape of the model differs from that of the actual system. Some examples are

- Organization charts that depict structure, authority, and responsibility relationships.
- A map where different colors represent water or mountains.
- Stock market charts.
- Blueprints of a machine or a house.
- A speedometer.
- A thermometer.

A special class of symbolic model is where symbolic logic is used. This topic is revisited in Chapter 11.

Mathematical (Quantitative). The complexity of relationships in some systems cannot be represented physically, or the physical representation may be cumbersome and time-consuming. Therefore a more abstract model is used with the aid of mathematics. Most DSS analysis is executed numerically with the aid of mathematical models.

The Benefits of Models

The following are the major reasons why an MSS employs models:

1. The cost of the modeling analysis is much lower than the cost of a similar experimentation conducted with a real system.
2. Models enable the compression of time. Years of operations can be simulated in minutes of computer time.
3. Manipulation of the model (changing variables) is much easier than manipulating a real system. Experimentation is therefore easier to conduct and it does not interfere with the daily operation of the organization.
4. The cost of making mistakes during a trial-and-error experiment is much less when models are used rather than real systems.
5. Today's environment involves considerable uncertainty. The use of modeling allows a manager to calculate the risks involved in specific actions.
6. The use of mathematical models enables the analysis of a very large, sometimes infinite number of possible solutions. With today's advanced

technology and communications, managers frequently have a large number of alternatives to choose from.

7. Models enhance and reinforce learning.

Note: With recent advances in computer graphics, there is an increased tendency to use iconic and analog models to complement mathematical modeling in MSS. For example, visual simulation (see Chapter 18) combines the three types of models.

2.4   The Modeling Process—A Preview

Ma-Pa Groceries is a small neighborhood food store on the West Side of New York City. Bob and Nancy, the owners, are very sensitive to their clients' wishes. They also are concerned with the financial viability of the store. A major product they sell is bread. Bread causes them headaches. Some days there is not enough bread, other days bread is overstocked. Their problem is simple: How much bread to stock each day?

Bob and Nancy can apply several solution approaches to the problem. Three such approaches are discussed here: trial-and-error, simulation, and optimization.

Trial and Error.   In this approach the owners try to learn from experience. They conduct experiments with the real system. Namely, they change the quantities of bread stocked and observe what happens. If they find they are short on bread, they will increase the quantities ordered. If they find that too much bread is left, they will decrease the quantities ordered. Sooner or later they will find out how much bread to order.

Although this approach may be very successful for Bob and Nancy, it may fail in many other cases. Trial-and-error may not work if one or more of the following conditions exists:

1. There are too many alternatives ("trials") to experiment with.
2. The cost of making errors (which is part of the trial-and-error approach) is very high.
3. The environment itself keeps changing. Therefore learning from experience is difficult or even impossible. By the time you have experimented with all the alternatives, the environmental conditions have changed— you have a new "ball game" to deal with.

In such cases Nancy and Bob can try modeling approaches; instead of dealing with the real system, they will deal with a model of it. The two types of modeling approaches they can use are typical of DSS: simulation and optimization (or a combination of the two).

Simulation.   In this case Nancy and Bob play a "make believe" game. They ask themselves a question: *If* we order 300 loaves of bread, *what* will the results be? The results of course will depend on the demand, which may be constant or may vary. This simulation can deal with both situations. The model that represents Ma-Pa Groceries is used to calculate results like total profit (or loss), percentage of unsatisfied customers, and amount of leftovers. A big advantage of modeling is that months of operations can be simulated in seconds (if a computer is used). Next, Nancy and Bob change the order quantity to 350, 400, 450, 250, and so on. They "run the store" with each order quantity for several months and calculate the results. Finally, they compare the results of each order quantity and decide how much to order.

The problem with the simulation approach is that once the experiment is completed, there is no guarantee that the selected order level is the best one. It will be the best of all levels experimented with, but it is possible that the true best level (the optimal one) is 675, a level not checked in the experiment. Another problem with the simulation is that Nancy and Bob will need professional help to design the simulation study and program it on a computer, and to statistically interpret the results. The cost may not be justified.

Optimization. The fastest, most direct approach to the problem is to use an optimization model. Ideally such a model will generate in seconds an optimal (best) order level, say, 675. Usually there is a very user-friendly software to conduct such an analysis. The problem with this approach is that it will work only if the problem is very structured. Specifically, such a model will specify the required input data and the mathematical relationship in a precise manner. Obviously if reality differs significantly from this structure, optimization cannot be used.

As stated earlier, DSS deals with unstructured problems. Does this preclude optimization? Not necessarily. Many times it is possible to break a problem into subproblems, some of which are structured enough to justify optimization. As a matter of fact, optimization can be combined with simulation.

The Decision-Making Process. To better understand the modeling process, it is advisable to follow the decision-making process. To do so let us return to the work of H. Simon (21). The decision-making process, according to Simon, involves three major phases: intelligence, design, and choice. A fourth phase, implementation, was added later. A conceptual picture of the modeling process is shown in Figure 2.2. There is a flow of activities from intelligence to design to choice, but at any phase there may be a return to a previous phase. The figure includes the additional phase of implementation.

The modeling process starts with the intelligence phase. At this time reality is examined and the problem is identified and defined. In the design phase a model that represents the system is constructed. This is done by making assumptions that simplify reality and by writing the relationships among all variables. The model then is validated and criteria are set for the evaluation of the alternative courses of action that are also being identified. The choice phase includes a solution of the model (not of the problem that it represents). This solution is being tested "on paper," (that is, in the modeling framework). Once the proposed solution seems to be reasonable, it is ready for the last phase—implementation. Successful implementation results in solving the original problem. Failure leads to a return to the modeling process. Detailed discussion of the process is given in the following sections.

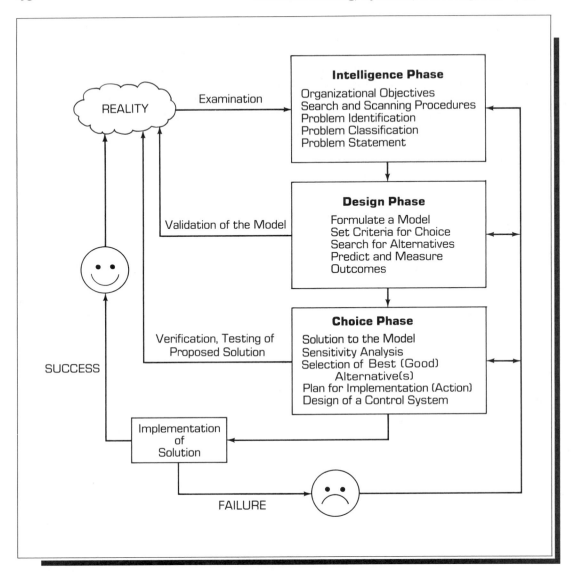

FIGURE 2.2 The decision making/modeling process.

2.5 **The Intelligence Phase**

Intelligence entails scanning the environment, either intermittently or continuously. It includes several activities aimed at identifying problem situations or opportunities.*

---

*The discussion in this chapter is geared toward problem solving. However, decision making should also be viewed as dealing with opportunities in addition to problems.

Finding the Problem. The intelligence phase begins with the identification of organizational goals and objectives. Problems arise out of dissatisfaction with the way things are going. Such dissatisfaction is the result of a difference between what we desire and what is (or is not) happening. In this phase, one attempts to find out if a problem exists, find the symptoms of the problem, find its magnitude, and define the problem. Often what is described as a problem (e.g., excessive costs) may be only a symptom of a problem (e.g., improper inventory levels). Because so-called real world problems are usually complicated by many interrelated factors, it is sometimes difficult to distinguish between the symptoms and the real problem.

The existence of a problem in an organization can best be appraised by monitoring the organization's productivity level (assuming that the goals are specified and correct). In order to do so it is necessary to study the organization's inputs, processes, and outputs. The measurement of productivity, as well as the construction of the model, are based on data. The collection of existing data and the estimation of future data is one of the most difficult steps in the analysis. Following are some of the issues that arise during data collection and estimation:

1. Outcome variables may occur over an extended period of time. As a result, revenues (or profits) and expenses will be recorded at different points in time. To overcome this difficulty a present-value approach should be used.
2. It is often necessary to use a subjective approach to data estimation.
3. It is assumed that the data used for assessment and modeling are the same as those expected to prevail when the solution is later implemented. If not, it is necessary to predict the nature of the change and include it in the analysis as well.

Once the preliminary analysis is completed it is possible to determine whether a problem really exists, where it is located, and how significant it is (i.e., what is the priority of solving the problem). In addition, the intelligence phase involves other activities such as problem classification, problem decomposition, and determination of problem ownership.

The Classification. This activity is the conceptualization of a problem in an attempt to classify it into a definable category. An important classification is according to the degree of structuredness evident in the problem.

Programmed Versus Nonprogrammed Problems. Herbert A. Simon (21) has distinguished two extreme situations regarding structuredness of decision problems. At one end of the spectrum are the well-structured problems that are repetitive and routine, and for which standard models have been worked out. Simon termed these *programmed problems*. Examples of such problems are weekly scheduling of employees and monthly determination of cash flow and selection of an inventory level for a specific item. At the other end of the spectrum are the poorly structured (called *nonprogrammed* by Simon) *problems*, which are novel and nonrecurrent. For example, acquisition and merger decisions, undertaking a complex research and development project, reorganizing a corporation, and opening a university are all nonstructured problems. As mentioned earlier, DSS is a tool for handling unstructured (and semistructured) problems.

Problem Decomposition.   Every complex problem can be broken apart into subproblems for separate analyses. Such an approach is useful in starting some MSS. It also facilitates communication between the people involved in the solution process.

To Whom a Problem Belongs.   In the intelligence phase, it is important to establish the "ownership" of the problem. A problem exists in an organization only if the organization has options to solve it. For example, many companies feel that they have a problem because interest rates are too high. Since interest rate levels are determined at the national level and most companies can do nothing about them, high interest rates are the problem of the federal government and not of a specific company. The problem that companies face is how to operate in an environment in which the interest rate is high. For the individual company the interest rate level is an uncontrollable factor.

The intelligence phase ends with a problem statement. At that time the design phase can be started.

2.6   The Design Phase

The design phase involves inventing, developing, and analyzing possible courses of action. This includes activities such as understanding the problem, generating solutions, and testing solutions for feasibility. Also in this phase, a model of the problem situation is constructed, tested, and validated.

Modeling involves the conceptualization of the problem and its abstraction to a mathematical-numerical model and/or a symbolic form. In case of a mathematical model, the dependent and independent variables are identified and the equations describing their relationships are established. Simplifications are made, whenever necessary, through a set of assumptions. For example, a relationship between two variables may be assumed to be linear. It is necessary to find a proper balance between the level of simplification of the model and the representation of reality. A simpler model leads to easier manipulations and solutions, but is also less representative of the real problem.

The task of modeling involves a combination of art and science. The following topics of modeling are presented here:

- ☐ The components of the model.
- ☐ The structure of the model.
- ☐ Selection of a principle of choice (criteria for evaluation).
- ☐ Developing (generating) alternatives.
- ☐ Predicting outcomes.
- ☐ Measuring outcomes.
- ☐ Scenarios.

The Components of Mathematical Models

All mathematical models are comprised of three basic components: decision variables, uncontrollable variables and parameters, and result (outcome) variables. These components are connected by mathematical (logical) relationships, as shown in Figure 2.3.

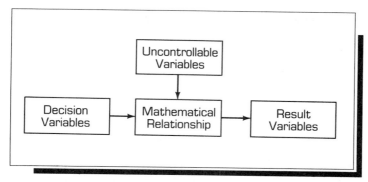

FIGURE 2.3 The general structure of a model.

As can be seen in Figure 2.3, the results (or outcome) of decisions are determined by (1) the decision being made; and (2) other factors that are uncontrollable by the decision maker.

Result Variables. These variables reflect the level of effectiveness of the system; that is, they indicate how well the system performs or attains its goals. Examples of result variables are shown in Table 2.2. The result variables are considered to be dependent variables.[*]

Decision Variables. Decision variables describe the alternative courses of action. For example, in an investment problem, the amount of money to be invested in each alternative is a decision variable. In a scheduling problem, the decision variables are people and hours. These variables can be manipulated by the decision maker. Other examples include the quantities of products to produce, the number of units to be ordered, and the number of tellers to use in a bank (more are listed in Table 2.2). Decision variables are classified mathematically as independent variables (or unknown variables). An aim of DSS is to find good enough, or possibly the best, values for these decision variables.

Uncontrollable Variables and Parameters. In any decision situation there are factors that affect the result variables but are not under the control of the decision maker. Examples are the prime interest rate, a city's building code, tax regulations, and prices of supplies (others are shown in Table 2.2). Most of these factors are uncontrollable because they emanate from the environment surrounding the decision maker. These variables are also classified as independent variables since they affect the dependent (result) variables. These variables and parameters might place limits on the decision maker, and, therefore, are called the *constraints* of the problem.

Intermediate Variables Intermediate variables are any variables necessary to link the decision variables to the results. These variables are usually uncontrollable. Sometimes they reflect intermediate outcomes. For example, in determining machine's scheduling, spoilage, is an intermediate variable while total profit is the result variable.

---

[*]A dependent variable means that for the event described by this variable to occur, another event must occur first. In this case the result variables depend on the occurrence of the decision and the uncontrollable variables.

TABLE 2.2   Examples of the Components of Models.

Area	Decision Variables	Result Variables	Uncontrollable Variables and Parameters
Financial investment	Investment amounts Period of investment Timing of investment	Total profit Rate of return Earnings/share Liquidity	Inflation rate Prime rate Competition
Marketing	Advertising budget Product lines Zonal sales reps	Market share Customer satisfaction	Customers' income Competitors' actions
Manufacturing	Production amounts Inventory levels Compensation program	Total cost Quality level Spoilage (%)	Machine capacity Technology Materials prices
Accounting	Audit schedule Use of computers Depreciation schedule	Data processing cost Error rate	Legal requirements Tax rates Computer technology
Transportation	Shipments schedule	Total transport cost	Delivery distance Regulations
Services	Staffing levels	Customer satisfaction	Demand for services

Another example is employee bonus, which is a decision variable, the bonus determines employees' satisfaction (intermediate outcome) which determines productivity level (result).

The Structure of Mathematical Models

The components of a mathematical model are tied together by sets of mathematical expressions such as equations or inequalities.

A simple financial-type model may look like this: $P = R - C$, where P stands for profit, R stands for revenue, and C stands for cost. Another well-known financial-type model is a present-value model, which may look like this:

$$P = \frac{F}{(1 + i)^n}$$

where

P is the present value

F is a future single payment in dollars

i is interest rate

n is number of years

Using this model, one can find, for example, the present value of a payment of $100,000, to be made five years from today, considering 10 percent interest rate, to be

$$P = \frac{100,000}{(1.1)^5} = \$62,110$$

A more complex product-mix model is presented next. This model is a management science optimization model that helps determine the best production plan.

Example: The Product-mix Model

MBI Corporation makes special computers. A decision must be made: How many computers should be produced next month in the Boston plant? Two types of computers are considered: PC-7, which requires 300 days of labor and $10,000 in materials; and PC-8, which requires 500 days of labor and $15,000 in materials. The profit contribution of PC-7 is $8000, whereas that of PC-8 is $12,000. Currently, the plant has a capacity of 200,000 days per month while the material budget is $8,000,000 per month. Marketing requires that at least 100 units of PC-8 be produced while the market will absorb any quantity produced. The problem is how many units of PC-7 and how many units of PC-8 to produce each month to maximize the company's profits.

Modeling

The mathematical model has three components (per Figure 2.3):

Decision variables: X_1 = units of PC-7 to be produced; X_2 = units of PC-8.
Result variable: The total profit.
    The objective is to maximize total profit.
    Total profit is: $8000\ X_1 + 12{,}000\ X_2$.
Uncontrollable constraints:
    Labor constraint: $300\ X_1 + 500\ X_2 \leq 200{,}000$ (in days)
    Budget constraint: $10{,}000\ X_1 + 15{,}000\ X_2 \leq 8{,}000{,}000$ (in dollars)
    Marketing requirement: $X_1 \geq 100$ (in units)
    This information is summarized in Figure 2.4.

Linear Programming

Linear programming is perhaps the best-known optimization model. It deals with optimal allocation of resources among competing activities. The allocation problem is presented in the model as follows:

The problem is to find the value of the decision variables X_1, X_2, and so on (Figure 2.4) such that the value of the result variable Z is maximized, subject to a set of linear constraints that express the technology, market conditions, and other uncontrollable variables. The mathematical relationships are all linear equations and inequalities. Theoretically, there are an infinite number of possible solutions to any allocation problem of this type. Using special mathematical procedures, the linear programming approach applies a unique search procedure that finds the best solution(s) in a matter of seconds. Furthermore, the solution approach provides automatic sensitivity analysis (see Section 2.8).

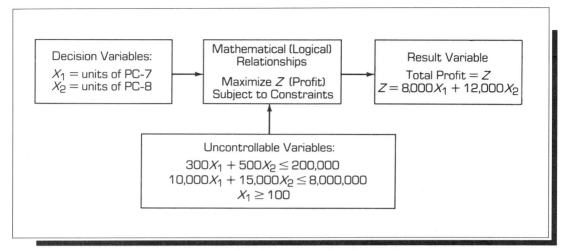

FIGURE 2.4 Mathematical model of a product mix.

Solution. The solution to this problem (derived by a computer) is $X_1 = 666.667$, $X_2 = 0$, Profit $= \$5,333,333$.

The model of the product mix just presented has an infinite number of possible solutions. Assuming that a production plan is not restricted to whole numbers—which is a reasonable assumption in a monthly production plan—finding the one that maximizes total profit requires a technique called *linear programming.* Determining which technique to use relates to the discussion of our next topic, the principle of choice.

The Principle of Choice

The evaluation of alternatives and the final choice depend on the type of criteria we want to use. Are we trying to get the best solution? Or will the "good enough" result be sufficient? This issue is discussed next.

Selection of a Principle of Choice.   A principle of choice refers to a decision regarding the acceptability of a solution approach. Is the best possible alternative sought, or will a "good enough" solution do? Are we willing to assume risk or do we prefer a conservative approach? Of the various principles of choice, two are of prime interest: normative (optimization) and descriptive.

Normative Models.   The optimal alternative is demonstrably the best of all possible alternatives. To find it, one should examine all alternatives and *prove* that the one selected is indeed the best.

In operational terms, optimization can be achieved in one of three ways:

□ Get the highest level (maximum) of goal attainment from a given set of resources. In this case the cost (budget) is fixed and the effectiveness may vary to a maximum.

□ Find the alternative with the lowest cost (minimization of resources) that will fulfill a required level of goal(s); that is, given fixed effectiveness, use the least cost.

□ Find the alternative with the highest ratio of goal attainment to cost (e.g., profit per dollar invested), or in other words, maximize productivity. In this case, both the cost and the effectiveness may vary.

Optimization models are also referred to as normative models. Normative decision theory is based on the following assumptions:

□ Humans are economic beings whose objective is to maximize the attainment of goals; that is, the decision maker is rational.

□ In a given decision situation, all viable alternative courses of action and their consequences, or at least the probability and the values of the consequences, are known.

□ Decision makers have an order or preference that enables them to rank the desirability of all consequences of the analysis.

Suboptimization. By definition, optimization requires the decision maker to consider the impact of each alternative course of action on the entire organization. The reason for this is that a decision made in one area may have significant effects in other areas. Take as an example a production department that plans its own schedule. For that department it would be beneficial to produce only a few products but in large quantities to reduce manufacturing costs. However, such a plan may result in large, costly inventories and marketing difficulties owing to the lack of a variety of products.

Using a systems point of view affords consideration of the impact on the entire system. Thus the production department should make its plans in conjunction with other departments. Such an approach, however, may require a complicated, expensive, and time-consuming analysis. As a matter of practice the MSS builder may "close" the system within narrow boundaries, considering

Optimization Models

□ Assignment
□ Dynamic programming
□ Goal programming
□ Investment (maximize rate of return)
□ Linear programming
□ Maintenance (minimize cost of maintenance)
□ Network models
□ Nonlinear programming
□ Replacement (capital budgeting)
□ Simple inventory models (e.g., economic order quantity)
□ Transportation
□ Waiting line management (simple)

only part of the organization under study (the production department in this case.) Such an approach is called *suboptimization*.

If a suboptimization decision is made in one part of the organization without consideration of the rest of the organization, then a solution that is optimal from the point of view of that part may be suboptimal from the point of view of the whole. This may produce inferior or even damaging results.

Suboptimization, however, may still be a very practical approach, and many problems are first approached from this perspective. The primary reason for this is that analyzing only a portion of a system allows some tentative conclusions to be made without bogging down the organization in a deluge of details. Once a solution is proposed, its potential effects on the remaining departments of the organization can be checked. If no significant negative effects are found, the solution may then be adopted. This approach fits nicely with the iterative (step-by-step) development approach to DSS.

Descriptive Models.   Descriptive models describe things as they are. Such models are extremely useful in DSS for investigating the consequences of various alternative courses of action under different configurations of inputs and processes. However, because a descriptive analysis checks the effectiveness of the system for a given set of alternatives (rather than for *all* alternatives), there is no guarantee that an alternative selected with the aid of a descriptive analysis is optimal. In many cases it is only satisfactory or "good enough."

Good Enough or "Satisficing."   Most human decision making, according to Simon (21), whether organizational or individual, involves a willingness to settle for a satisfactory solution, "something less than the best." In a "satisficing" mode the decision maker sets up an aspiration, goal, or desired level of performance and then searches the alternatives until one is found that achieves this level. The usual reasons for satisficing are lack of time or ability to achieve optimization as well as unwillingness to pay the price for the required information.

A related concept is that of *bounded rationality*. Humans have a limited capacity for rational thinking; they generally construct a simplified model of the real situation in order to deal with it. Their behavior with respect to the simplified model may be rational. However, it does not follow that the ratio-

Descriptive Models

- □ Information flow
- □ Scenario analysis
- □ Financial planning
- □ Inventory management (complex)
- □ Markov analysis (predictions)
- □ Environmental impact analysis
- □ Simulation (different types)
- □ Technological forecasting
- □ Waiting line management (complex)

nal solution for the simplified model is rational in the real world situation. Rationality is restricted or bounded not only by limitations on human processing capacities but also by individual differences such as age, education, and attitudes. For this reason, many models are descriptive rather than normative.

Developing (Generating) Alternatives

A significant part of the process of model building is generating (or searching for) alternatives. In optimization models (such as linear programming) the alternatives may be built into the model. In most DSS situations, however, it is necessary to generate alternatives. This can be a lengthy process that involves search and creativity, and it takes time and costs money. Issues such as when to stop generating alternatives can be very important. Generating alternatives is heavily dependent on the availability and cost of information and requires expertise in the problem area. This is the least formal portion of problem solving. Creativity can be enhanced by aids like brainstorming, group dynamics sessions, checklists, and special training. In some cases, the search may continue while an evaluation is proceeding. Consider, for example, the selection of a person to fill a position. Typically, candidates are evaluated and compared while the search for additional candidates is still going on.

Notice that the search for alternatives comes *after* the criteria for evaluating the alternatives are determined. This sequence can reduce the search for alternatives and the efforts involved in the evaluation of the alternatives.

Generating alternatives is done manually in most DSS; however, as will be shown later, this activity can be automated if an expert system is used.

Predicting the Outcome of Each Alternative

To evaluate and compare alternatives it is necessary to predict the outcome of each proposed alternative. Predicting the outcome of alternatives means forecasting, because the specific outcomes will occur in the future. Decision situations are frequently classified on the basis of what the decision maker knows (or believes) about the forecasted results. It is customary to classify this knowledge into three categories (see Figure 2.5), ranging from complete

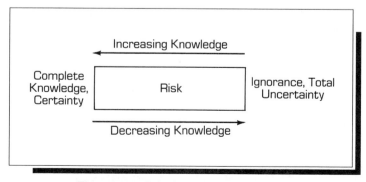

FIGURE 2.5 The zones of decision making.

knowledge, on the left, to ignorance, on the right. Specifically, these categories are

- □ Certainty (complete information).
- □ Risk (less than complete information).
- □ Uncertainty (least information).

Decision Making Under Certainty.   In decision making under certainty, it is *assumed* that complete information is available so that the decision maker knows exactly what the outcome of each course of action will be. The decision maker is being viewed as a perfect predictor of the future, because it is assumed that there is only one outcome for each alternative. For example, the alternative of investing in U.S. Treasury bills is one for which it is reasonable to assume complete availability of information about the future return on the investment. Such a situation is also termed *deterministic*. It occurs most often with short time horizons (up to one year). Decision making under certainty is most suitable for a management science approach. However, some problems under certainty are not structured enough to be approached by management science; they thus require a DSS approach.

Decision Making Under Risk (Risk Analysis).   A decision made under risk (also known as a probabilistic or stochastic decision situation) is one in which the decision maker must consider several possible states of nature, each with a given probability of occurrence. Thus multiple possible outcomes of each alternative are identified. In addition, it is assumed that the long-run probabilities of the occurrences of the given states of nature (and their conditional outcomes) are known or can be estimated. The decision maker can assess the degree of risk assumed (termed *calculated* risk).

Risk analysis is usually executed by computing the expected value of each alternative and selecting the alternative with the best expected value.

Decision Making Under Uncertainty.   In decision making under uncertainty,[*] the decision maker considers situations in which several outcomes are possible for each course of action. In contrast to the risk situation, the decision maker does not know, or cannot estimate, the probability of occurrence of the possible states of nature (with their conditional outcomes).

Decision making under uncertainty is more difficult to evaluate because of insufficient information. Modeling of such situations involves the assessment of the decision maker and/or the organizational attitude toward risk (e.g., being a conservative or a risk taker).

Measuring Outcomes (Goal's Attainment Level)

The value of an alternative is judged in terms of the goal's attainment. Sometimes an outcome is expressed directly in terms of a goal. For exam-

---

[*]The definitions of the terms *risk* and *uncertainty*, as presented here, were suggested by Professor F. H. Knight of the University of Chicago in 1933. Several other definitions are being used by different organizations and authors.

ple, profit is an outcome, whereas profit maximization is a goal, and both are expressed in dollar terms. In other cases an outcome may be expressed in other terms than that of the goal. For example, the outcome may be in terms of the number of new customers, whereas the goal is expressed in terms of dollars. In such cases it is necessary to transform the outcome so that it is expressed in terms of the goal.

Scenarios

A *scenario* is a statement of assumptions about the operating environment of a particular system at a given time. In other words, a scenario is a narrative description of the setting in which the decision situation is to be examined. A scenario describes the decision and uncontrollable variables and parameters for a specific modeling situation. It also may provide the procedures and constraints for the modeling itself.

Scenarios were originated in the field of drama. The term was then borrowed for war gaming and large-scale simulations. More recently scenarios have entered the realm of MSS. For example, a scenario may describe the set of assumptions about the behaviors, intentions, and effects of the various processes represented in a merger proposal to be evaluated by a DSS.

A scenario is especially helpful in simulation and in "what if" analysis. In both cases we keep changing scenarios. For example, one can change the anticipated demand for hospitalization (which is an input variable for planning), thus creating a new scenario. Then one can measure the anticipated cash flow of the hospital for each scenario.

Scenarios play an important role in MSS because they

□ Help identify potential opportunities and/or problem areas.
□ Provide flexibility in planning.
□ Identify the leading edges of changes that management should monitor.
□ Help *validate* major assumptions used in modeling.

Possible Scenarios Thousands of possible scenarios may exist for every decision situation. However, the following are of a special value:

□ The "worst possible" scenario.
□ The "best possible" scenario.
□ The "most likely" scenario.

The scenario sets the context of the analysis (or the evaluation) to be performed, defines many of the inputs, and to a large degree establishes the evaluation criteria.

2.7 The Choice—Search Phase

The boundary between the design and the choice phases is not clear because certain activities may be performed both during the design and the choice phases. The choice phase includes search, evaluation, and finding an appropriate solution to the model.

A *solution* to a model is a specific set of values for the decision variables. The solution of the model identifies the alternative selected. Finding an appropriate solution basically implies search and evaluation.

Note: Solving the model is not the same as solving the problem that the model represents. The solution to the model yields a recommended solution to the problem. Only if this recommended solution is successfully implemented is the problem considered to be solved.

Search Approaches

The choice phase involves the search for the appropriate course of action (among those identified during the design phase) that will solve the real problem. Several major search approaches exist, depending on the criteria of choice. For normative models either an analytical approach is used or a complete, exhaustive enumeration (comparing all alternatives to one another) is applied. For descriptive models a comparison of a limited number of alternatives is used, either blindly or by using heuristics. These search approaches are shown in Figure 2.6.

Analytical Techniques.   Analytical techniques use mathematical formulas to directly either derive an optimal solution or predict a certain result. Analytical techniques are used mainly for solving structured problems, usually of a tactical or operational nature, in areas like allocation of resources or inventory management. For more complex problems that are addressed by MSS the blind or heuristic search approaches are generally used.

Algorithms.   Analytical techniques may use algorithms to increase the efficiency of the search. An *algorithm* is a step-by-step search process (see Figure 2.7) for arriving at an optimal solution. Solutions are generated and tested for possible improvements. An improvement is then made and the new solution is subjected to the improvement test. The process ends when no further improvement is possible.

Blind and Heuristic Search Approaches

In conducting a search, a description of a desired solution is given. This is called a *goal*. A set of possible steps leading from initial conditions to the goal is viewed as the *search steps*. Problem solving is carried out by searching through the space of possible solutions. Two search methods are considered: the blind search and the heuristic search.

Blind Search.   Blind search techniques explore the alternatives and events of a decision situation, one at a time. Two types of blind search exist: *complete enumeration*, in which case all the alternatives are considered, and therefore an optimal solution is discovered; and *incomplete enumeration* (partial search), which continues until a "good enough" solution is found.

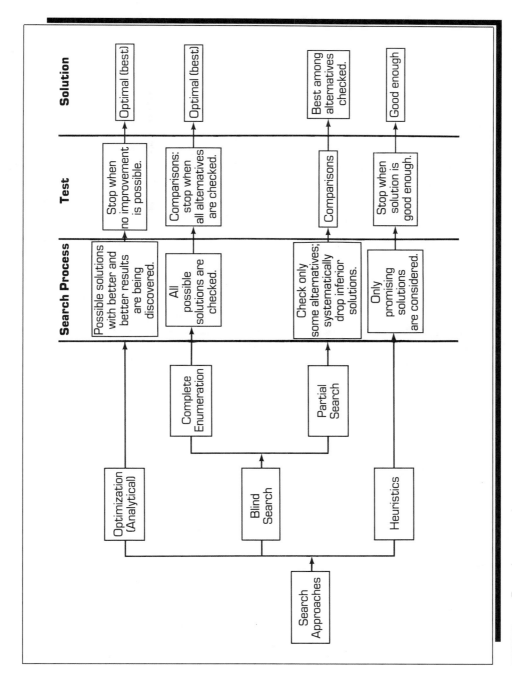

FIGURE 2.6 Search approaches.

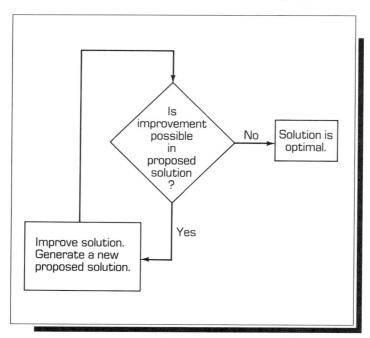

FIGURE 2.7 The process of using an algorithm.

There are practical limits on the amount of time and computer storage available for blind searches. Although in principle blind search methods can eventually find a solution to most search situations, the method is not practical for large problems because too many nodes must be visited before a solution is found.

Heuristic Search. For many applications, it is possible to find specific information to guide the search process and reduce the amount of necessary computations. This is called heuristic information, and the search procedures that use it are called heuristic search methods.

Heuristics (derived from the Greek word for "discovery") are decision rules regarding how a problem should be solved. Heuristics are developed on a basis of solid, rigorous analysis of the problem, sometimes involving designed experimentation. In contrast, "rules of thumb" are usually developed as a result of a trial-and-error experience. Some heuristics were derived from rules of thumb (as a starting point). *Heuristic searches* (or *programming*) are step-by-step procedures that are repeated until a satisfactory solution is found. In practice, such a search is much faster and cheaper than a blind search, while the solutions can be very close to the ones generated by a blind search. For details see Pearl (17) and Zanakis and Evans (27). Examples of heuristics are given in Table 2.3.

The Direction of a Search

A search can be goal-directed, data-directed, or a combination of both. These two approaches are discussed further when expert systems methodology is presented.

TABLE 2.3 Examples of Heuristics.

Sequence jobs through a machine	Do the jobs that require the least time first.
Purchase stocks	Do not buy stocks whose price-to-earnings ratio is larger than 10.
Travel	Do not go on the freeway between 8 and 9 A.M.
Capital investment in high-tech projects	Consider only projects whose estimated payback period is less than two years.
Purchase of a house	Buy only in a good neighborhood, but buy there only at the lower price range.

Data-directed Search. This type of search starts from available information (or facts) and tries to draw conclusions regarding the situation or the goal attainment. For example, if a company is losing sales volume, the search attempts to find out why (e.g., because of insufficient advertisement).

Goal-directed Search. This search starts from expectations of what the goal is or what is to happen; then it seeks evidence that supports (or contradicts) those expectations (or hypotheses). For example, we expect that sales declined because we feel that our advertising budget is insufficient. The goal-directed search will confirm or deny our expectations.

2.8   Evaluation: Multiple Goals, Sensitivity Analysis, and Goal Seeking

The search process described earlier is coupled with evaluation. The evaluation is the final step that leads to the recommended solution. Several topics are important in the evaluation of MSS solutions: multiple goals, sensitivity analysis, "what if" analysis, and goal seeking. They are discussed next.

Multiple Goals

The analysis of management decisions aims at evaluating, to the greatest possible extent, how far each alternative advances management toward its goals. Unfortunately, managerial problems are seldom evaluated in terms of a single goal such as profit maximization. Today's management systems are becoming more and more complex, and a single goal is rare. Instead, managers want to attain simultaneous goals, some of which conflict with each other. Therefore it is often necessary to analyze each alternative in light of its potential impact on several goals.

For example, consider a profit-making firm. In addition to making money, the company wants to grow, to develop its products and its employees, to provide job security to its workers, and to serve the community. Managers want to satisfy the shareholders and at the same time enjoy high salaries and expense accounts, while employees wish to increase their take-home pay and fringe benefits. Needless to say, some of these goals complement each other while others are in direct conflict. Add to this social, and ethical considerations and the system of goals begins to look quite complex.

Most quantitative approaches to decision theory are based on comparing a single measure of effectiveness. Therefore, it is necessary to transform, mathematically, the multiple-goal problem into a single-goal problem prior to the final comparison, or to develop another method of comparison.

Several methods of handling multiple goals can be used when working with MSS. The most common ones are:

    □ Use of utility theory.
    □ Goal programming.
    □ Expression of goals as constraints, using linear programming.
    □ Using a point system.

For further details, see Keeney and Raiffa (9) or Turban and Meredith (24). The analysis of multiple goals involves the following difficulties:

1. It is usually difficult to obtain an explicit statement of the organization's goals.
2. Various participants assess the importance (priorities) of the various goals differently.
3. The decision maker may change the importance assigned to specific goals with the passage of time or in different decision situations.
4. Goals and subgoals are viewed differently at various levels of the organization and in various departments.
5. The goals themselves are dynamic in response to changes in the organization and its environment.
6. The relationship between alternatives and their impact on goals may be difficult to quantify.

Sensitivity Analysis

Sensitivity analysis attempts to help managers when they are not certain about the accuracy or relative importance of information, or when they want to know the impact of changes in input information of a model on some results or measures of performance.

The topic of sensitivity analysis is extremely important in MSS because it enables flexibility and adaptation to changing conditions and to the requirements of different decision-making situations.

Sensitivity analysis is conducted in order to gain a better understanding of the model and the world it purports to describe. It checks relationships such as:

    □ Effect of uncertainty in estimating external variables.
    □ Effects of interactions among variables.
    □ Robustness of decisions.

Specific kinds of sensitivity analyses are:

- The impact of changes in external (uncontrollable) variables and parameters on the outcome variable(s).
- The impact of changes in the decision variables on the outcome variable(s).

Sensitivity analyses are used to:

- Revise models to eliminate too large sensitivities.
- Add details about sensitive variables or scenarios.
- Obtain better estimates of sensitive external variables.
- Alter the real-world system to reduce actual sensitivities.
- Live with a sensitive (and hence vulnerable) real world, monitoring actual results closely.

Two types of sensitivity analysis exist: automatic and trial and error.

Automatic Sensitivity Analysis. This kind of analysis is provided with some standard quantitative models such as linear programming. It tells the manager, for example, the range within which a certain input variable (e.g., unit cost) can vary without any significant impact on the value of the proposed solution. Automatic sensitivity analysis is usually limited to one change at a time, and only for certain variables. It is, however, very powerful because of its ability to establish ranges and limits very fast (and with little or no additional computational cost).

Trial and Error. The trial-and-error sensitivity approach is generally used with MSS. The impact of changes in any variable, or in several variables, can be determined through a trial-and-error approach. Such flexibility makes this sensitivity analysis an integral part of using almost any MSS. It appears in two forms: "what if" and goal seeking.

"What If" Analysis. A model builder makes predictions and assumptions regarding the input data, many of which deal with the assessment of uncertain futures. When the model is solved, the results depend, of course, on these data. Sensitivity analysis attempts to check the impact of a change in the input data on the proposed solution (the result variable). This type of sensitivity analysis is called "what if" analysis, because it is structured as "*What* will happen to the solution *if* an input variable, an assumption, or a parameter value is changed?"
Examples include the following:

- *What* will happen to the total inventory cost *if* the cost of carrying inventories increases by 10 percent?
- *What* will be the market share *if* the advertising budget increases by 5 percent?

Assuming the appropriate user interface, managers can ask these types of questions of the computer. Furthermore, they can repeat the question and change the percentage of any other data in the question, as desired. Note that "what if" is concerned with what will happen to the *output* of the system if a change is being made in the *inputs*.

Figure 2.8 shows a "what if" query in the case of five years financial planning. The user asks "what if" material cost equals $22.00 (this figure is different from the original material cost). Then the user commands the computer to calculate all the affected data. Once the computer informs the user that the computation is completed, the user commands the computer to print any desired data (in this case, projected gross income for the next five years). What if analysis can be executed with expert systems as well. Users are given the opportunity to change their answers to some of the computer's questions, then a revised recommendation is shown and compared to the previous one. For details see Chapter 16, case #2.

Goal Seeking.   Goal seeking is a type of sensitivity analysis that works in a somewhat different fashion than "what if." It represents a "backward" solution approach. For example, let us say that our initial analysis yielded a profit of $2 million. Management might then want to know what sales volume would be necessary to generate a profit of $2.2 million.

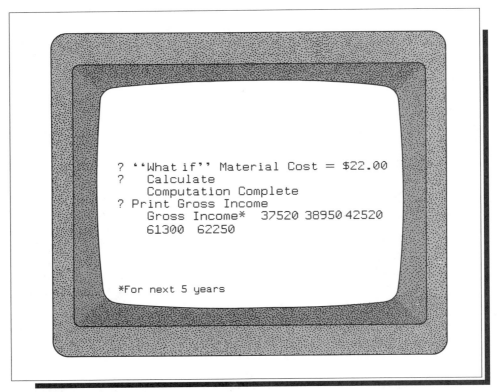

FIGURE 2.8   "What if?" analysis (? is the user's input).

Other examples are as follows:

☐ What is the annual R&D budget needed for an annual growth rate of 15 percent by 1990?
☐ How many nurses are needed to reduce the average waiting time of a patient in the emergency room to less than 10 minutes?
☐ How many auditors are needed to complete the audit by November 15?

Goal seeking analysis is concerned with the inputs necessary to achieve given output(s).

A computer printout of goal-seeking dialogs is shown in Figure 2.9, which shows a goal-seeking process. The user wants to determine the per unit price necessary to achieve a profit of $100,000 the first year and $5000 more in each of the following years. The computer calculates the necessary price (per unit) for each of the five years in the planning document.

Computing a Break-even Point Using Goal Seeking. An interesting application of goal seeking for computing break-even points is available in some computer packages (e.g., in IFPS, see Chapter 7). This can be done, for example, by finding what quantity is needed to be produced in order to generate zero profit.

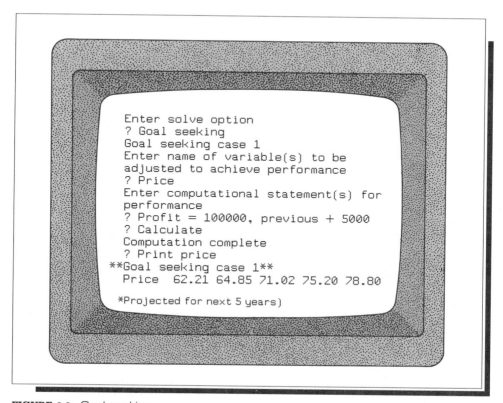

```
Enter solve option
? Goal seeking
Goal seeking case 1
Enter name of variable(s) to be
adjusted to achieve performance
? Price
Enter computational statement(s) for
performance
? Profit = 100000, previous + 5000
? Calculate
Computation complete
? Print price
**Goal seeking case 1**
   Price   62.21 64.85 71.02 75.20 78.80

   *Projected for next 5 years)
```

FIGURE 2.9 Goal seeking.

Sensitivity analysis is important because it can be used to improve confidence in the model and thus increase the rate of application and implementation of quantitative analysis. In many regular computer-based decision systems, it is difficult to conduct such an analysis because the prewritten routines usually present only a limited opportunity for "what if" questions. In a DSS the "what if" and the goal seeking options are easy to execute and provide ample opportunity for flexibility and adaptability.

"What if" and goal seeking are important properties of DSS. Both topics are revisited in Chapter 7-9.

2.9   Critical Success Factors

The final issue that relates to "choice" is the technique of critical success factors. Critical success factors (CSF) is a diagnostic technique (see Rockart [18]) for identifying the factors that are the most critical to the achievement of organizational objectives. The process involves conducting interviews with individual executives, followed by a structured group discussion for the purpose of identifying success factors and agreeing on their importance. The identification of such factors is essential both for determining the information needs required by management to achieve their objectives and for prioritizing the criteria used in evaluating alternative courses of action. The CSF technique (or a similar process) is one of the first steps in developing a MSS.

Once the critical factors are determined, it is possible to identify information gaps, that is, to find out which critical factors are not being adequately supported by the current information system. The lack of such information prevents management from measuring the effectiveness of areas that are critical to the organization. Therefore it is necessary to identify the critical factors and structure the appropriate information system before developing the MSS. In addition to its use in determining information requirements, CSF has been used in feasibility studies of DSS, EIS, and ES and in other phases of the development process of these techniques as well as information systems in general. For example, it was used in DSS software selection (Shank et al. [20]). The CSF approach can be applied to many other decision-making situations.

Once the choice phase has been completed, the recommended solution must be implemented. This issue is discussed next.

2.10   Implementation

What is implementation? Machiavelli astutely noted over 400 years ago that there was "nothing more difficult to carry out, nor more doubtful of success, nor more dangerous to handle, than to initiate a new order of things." The implementation of a proposed solution to a problem is, in effect, the initiation of a new order of things, or in modern language—the introduction of a change.

The definition of implementation is somewhat complicated because implementation is a long and involved process whose boundaries are vague. In a simplistic manner, it may be defined as putting a recommended solution to work.

The concept of implementation defined above is applicable to recommendations made by DSS and ES. Furthermore, many of the generic issues of implementation, such as resistance to change, degree of support of top management, and user's training, are important in dealing with MSS. Such topics and others that are unique to DSS and ES are presented in Chapter 20.

The decision-making process described in Sections 2.5 through 2.10 is conducted by people, but it can be improved if supported by computers. The manner in which such support can be provided is the subject of the next section.

2.11 How Decisions Are Being Supported

The discussion in this chapter has centered so far on decisions and systems; equally important is the notion of *support* in MSS. Chapter 1 illustrated, in general terms, how computers have supported management decisions since the early 1950s (Table 1.1). Now that we are familiar with the decision process, we will discuss the support from this point of view. Simon's phases of intelligence, design, and choice will be used as a framework, with the addition of the implementation phase.

As noted by Sprague and Carlson (22), a DSS could support all phases of the decision-making process (see Figure 2.10). In contrast, MIS supports mainly the intelligence phase, whereas management science supports mainly the choice phase. EIS would support the intelligence phase while ES can support any of the phases.

Support for the Intelligence Phase

The primary requirement of decision support for the intelligence phase is the ability to scan external and internal databases for opportunities and problems. Computerized systems store large volumes of information. An EIS, as will be described later, helps in accessing databases rapidly and efficiently. Furthermore, a DSS through its modeling capabilities can analyze data very fast. That is, the scanning done during the intelligence phase can be executed much faster with the aid of a DSS and EIS.

Another area of support is that of reporting. Both routine and ad hoc reports can aid in the intelligence phase. For example, regular reports can be designed to assist in the problem-finding activity by comparing expectations with current and projected performance. Table 2.4 lists report elements that can assist in problem finding.

The major purpose of an EIS is to support the intelligence phase. This is done by continuously monitoring both internal and external information, looking for early signs of problems and/or opportunities. For example, EIS will detect below normal performance and through a detailed investigation will attempt to pinpoint its sources.

Finally, ES can render advice regarding the nature of the problem, its classification, its seriousness, and the like. ES can advise on the suitability of a solution approach and on the likelihood of successfully solving the problem. One of the primary areas of ES success, as will be shown later, is in *interpretation*

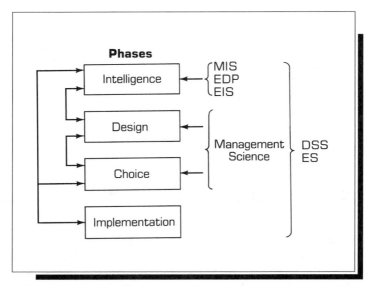

FIGURE 2.10 DSS support. (*Source:* Sprague R.H., Jr., "A Framework for the Development of DSS." MIS Quarterly [Dex. 1980], Fig. 5, p. 13. Reprinted by special permission of the MIS Quarterly. ©1980 by the Society for Information Management and the Management Information Systems Research Center at the University of Minnesota.)

of information and in *diagnosing* problems. This capability can be utilized during the intelligence phase.

The phase of intelligence, according to a study conducted by Lucas (11), is a primary target for DSS and other computer-based information systems that deal with nonstructured problems.

TABLE 2.4 Report Elements. (Condensed from Brooks [2].)

Report Element	Problem Finding Use
Summarization	Current performance is summarized by expectations provided by the user of the report
Comparison	The report has explicit comparisons with current performance expectations: Comparison with plans, budgets, or standards. Variance (from standards) reports. Comparison with competitors, industry averages, and other extraorganizational standards and measures. Exceptions reports.
Prediction	Forecasts of future performance: Prediction based on budget or planning model or historical ratios Prediction based on seasonally adjusted (or other method) data Forecast of current performance to the end of the planning period
Confirmation	Data items that allow the user to validate or audit the report to provide assurance that it corresponds to underlying detail or other data available to the user. Confirmation may use historical data, planning data, or data from elsewhere in the organization.

Support for the Design Phase

The design phase involves generation of alternative courses of action, decisions about the criteria for choice and their relative importance, and forecasting the future consequences of using various alternatives. Several of these activities could use standard models provided by the DSS (e.g., forecasting). Generation of alternatives for structured problems could be provided by a DSS through the use of either standard or special models. However, generation of alternatives for complex problems requires expertise that could be provided by a human or an expert system. Information about technology, availability of resources, market conditions, and the like could be provided to the decision maker by the computer's database. This information is essential for the development of alternative solutions to the problems and for the prediction of decision consequences. Finally, most DSS have forecasting capabilities while an added on ES can assist with qualitative methods of forecasting as well as with expertise required in applying quantitative forecasting models.

Support for the Choice Phase

A decision support system, by definition, does not make a choice. However, optimization and other mathematical models identify potential solutions and can rank the alternatives according to any desired criteria. That is, a choice is recommended.

In addition to the use of models that rapidly identify the best or "good enough" alternative, a DSS can support the choice phase through the "what if" and goal seeking sensitivity analysis. Different scenarios can be tested for the selected option to reinforce the final decision. An ES can be used to assess the desirability of certain solutions as well as to recommend an appropriate solution.

Support for the Decision Implementation

Interviews conducted by Mittman and Moore (15) suggest that the DSS benefits provided during implementation are frequently as important or more important than those mentioned in the previously discussed phases.

These interviews showed many instances of computer support of activities that can be interpreted both as decision making and decision implementation. It is difficult to maintain that the support is solely intended for one or the other role in such instances. However, activities that clearly belong to only one of the two categories were also seen; particularly, respondents reported numerous uses of DSS in implementation activities like decision communication, explanation, and justification. (Note: the last two activities are strongly supported by ES.) For example, a copy containing DSS results was frequently sent to parties who were both internal and external to companies. The recipients included senior managers' peers and subordinates, the board of directors, bankers and financial analysts, customers and clients, suppliers, and others from whom cooperation and coordination are needed.

Benefits of DSS in the implementation phase are due in part to the vividness and detail of the analysis and resulting output. For example, one CEO gives subordinates and external parties not only the aggregate financial goals and cash needs for the near term, but includes the calculations, intermediate results, and statistics used in determining the aggregate figures. In addition to communicating the financial goals unambiguously, the CEO signals other messages. Subordinates know that the CEO has thought through the assumptions behind the financial goals and is serious about their importance and attainability. Bankers and directors are shown that the CEO was personally involved in analyzing cash needs, and is aware of and responsible for the implications of the financing requests prepared by the finance department. Each of these messages improves decision implementation in some way. Decisions requiring authorization by directors and/or external parties were also seen to be important candidates for computer support of implementation. Expansion, acquisition, and other major capital expenditure requests were among the examples of decision support cited in the study.

The evidence just discussed indicates that senior managers are using computers primarily in support of the implementation aspects of the decision process—explaining, justifying, and communicating decisions. Numerous indications of the DSS role in decision implementation appear in other studies (e.g., see Alter [1] and Keen and Scott-Morton [8]).

All phases of the decision-making process can be supported by improved communication in cases of group decision making. Computerized systems can facilitate communication by allowing people to explain and justify their suggestions and opinions, usually with graphic support. Quantitative support can also be quickly provided for various possible scenarios while a meeting is in session.

Decision implementation can be supported by ES. Some ES include, like a DSS, a "what if" mechanism that intends to increase the *confidence* in the system. Furthermore, an ES can be used as an advisory system regarding implementation problems (e.g., resistance to change). Finally, an ES can provide training that may smooth the course of implementation.

Other Views of Support

Another view of support is to divide it into technical, decision process, and behavioral aspects.

Technical Aspects. These include computational efficiency, accuracy, optimization capability, and communication capabilities.

Decision Process. This includes quality issues such as efficient methodology, support to individual creativity, insight, and learning (e.g., through feedback).

Behavioral Process. This includes the fostering of group decision making (group and organizational dynamics and team building.)

Support of Other Related Activities

The decision process as described in this chapter ended with implementation. However, an extended view of the decision process includes additional activities like evaluation and control. Evaluation may occur 6 to 12 months after implementation and is intended to check whether the implemented solution indeed solved the problem. Control may involve adjustments in the solution. MSS can support these types of activities by providing a monitoring and reporting system and by signaling exceptions.

Support was viewed in this section as related to the phases of the decision-making process. However, support depends not only on the decision-making phases but also on the individuals (or groups) it supports. Specifically, different people may require different support owing to their personalities and other personal characteristics. This topic is briefly described next.

2.12   Human Cognition and Decision Styles

Cognition Theory.   Cognition refers to the activities by which an individual resolves differences between an internalized view of the environment and what actually exists in that same environment. In other words, it is the ability to perceive and understand information. Cognitive models are attempts to explain or understand various human cognitive processes. For instance, they explain how individuals revise previous opinions to conform with a particular choice after they have made that choice.

Cognitive Style.   Cognitive style refers to the subjective process through which individuals perceive, organize, and change information during the decision-making process. One model classifies individual styles along two continua (Figure 2.11). The information-gathering dimension relates to the perceptual processes by which the mind organizes verbal and visual stimuli. At one extreme of this dimension, perceptive individuals focus on relationships among data items and attempt to generalize from them about the environment. At

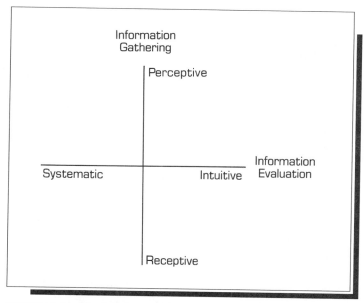

FIGURE 2.11 Model of cognitive style. (*Source*: McKenney and Keen [12], p. 81.)

the other extreme, receptive individuals focus on details and attempt to derive specific knowledge about the environment from the available data.

Information evaluation refers to the sequence by which the individual analyzes data. At one extreme, systematic individuals (also referred to as analytic) pursue a structured, deductive approach that, if followed through, leads to a likely solution. Intuitive (or heuristic) individuals use trial-and-error strategies, act spontaneously on the basis of new information, and respond to and incorporate, nonverbal cues.

Another cognitive model is the "cognitive contingency" model, which considers the manager's cognitive style and the environment's complexity (e.g., concern for technical vs. sociotechnical systems) as a basis for understanding preferences that managers exhibit in making decisions. For details see Rowe (19).

Cognitive style may be important because in many cases it determines peoples' preference for human-machine interface. For example, should data be raw or aggregate, should they be detailed or summarized, should they be tabulated or presented as graphs. Furthermore, cognitive styles impact on preferences for qualitative versus quantitative analysis as well as on the preferences for decision-making aids.

The research on cognitive styles is directly relevant to the design of management information systems. MIS and transaction processing systems tend to be designed by individuals who perceive the decision-making process to be systematic. Systematic managers are generally willing to use such systems; they are typically looking for a standard technique and view the system designer as an expert with a catalog of methods. However, such systems do not conform to the natural style of a heuristic decision maker. For this individual, a system should allow for exploration of a wide range of alternatives, permit changes in priorities or in processing, allow the user to shift easily between levels of detail and generality, and permit some user control over the output form (e.g., visual, verbal, graphic, and so on). And this is precisely what DSS is attempting to do. Other interesting implications of cognitive style will be presented when DSS and ES implementation is discussed.

Although cognitive style is a useful concept, it may be overemphasized in the MIS literature. There are difficulties in applying it to information systems and decision making (see Huber [7]). For one thing, cognitive style is a continuous variable. Many people are not completely heuristic nor analytic, but are somewhere in between. Related to the cognitive styles is the concept of decision styles.

Decision Styles. The manner in which decision makers think and react to problems, the way they perceive, their cognitive response, their values and beliefs, vary from individual to individual and from situation to situation. As a result people make decisions differently. Although there is a general process of decision making, it is far from being linear. People do not follow the same steps of the process in the same sequence, nor do they use all of the steps. Furthermore, the emphasis, time allotment, and priorities given to each step vary significantly—not only from one person to another, but also from one situation to the next. The manner in which managers make decisions (and the way they interact with other people) describes their decision style. Because decision styles depend on the several factors described earlier, there are many decision styles. For example, Gordon et al. (6) identified 40 processes in looking at nine types of decisions, and Mintzberg (14) identified seven basic styles with many variations.

In addition to the heuristic and analytic styles discussed earlier, one can distinguish autocratic versus democratic styles; another style is consultative (with individuals or groups). Of course, there are many combinations and variations of styles. For example, one can be analytic and autocratic, or consultative (with individuals) and heuristic. For further details on how decision styles relate to DSS and the provided support, see Wedley and Field (26).

For a computerized system to successfully support a manager, it should fit the decision situation as well as the decision style. Therefore the system should be flexible and adaptable to different users. The capability of asking "what if" and goal seeking questions provides flexibility in this direction. Availability of graphics is also desirable in supporting certain decision styles. If an MSS is to support varying styles, skills, and knowledge, it should not attempt to enforce a specific process. Rather, the MSS should help decision makers use and develop their own styles, skills, and knowledge.

Different decision styles require different types of support. A major factor that determines the type of required support is whether the decision maker is an individual or a group.

2.13 Group Decision Making

Many complex decisions in organizations are being made by groups of people. With the increased complexity of organizational decision making (see Chapter 1, Section 1.2), there is an increased need for meetings and working in groups. This demand is resisted by many who feel that meetings are frequently a waste of time. Groups often produce inadequate solutions to problems. "A camel is a horse designed by a committee" is a well-known quotation that describes the ineffectiveness of many committees.

One approach to the group problem-solving process has been a normative one, where an attempt is made to improve the effectiveness of the group. Most such theories try to overcome difficulties encountered during meetings. Typical examples are brainstorming, nominal group technique, and the DELPHI method (10).

The complexity of the tasks that are subject to DSS analysis suggests that a group DSS may be appropriate. However, supporting a group is much more complicated than supporting an individual. And indeed there is an increasing interest in this topic lately (for an overview and research directories see DeSantis and Gallupe [4]).

The topic of group decision making will be revisited when the concept of group DSS is introduced in Chapter 4.

2.14 Summary

Decision making is viewed as a four-phase process: intelligence, design, choice, and implementation. To understand this process the concept of a system was first presented. The major components of a system are the inputs, processes, and outputs, which are surrounded by an environment. Using the feedback concept, organizations can monitor their performance to recognize problems and improve productivity.

To apply a DSS to help solve these problems the methodology of modeling is used. The essentials of a problem under investigation are presented as a mathematical model. Alternative courses of action are tested to evaluate their potential success in solving the problem. Dealing with a model rather than with reality can save a significant amount of money and time. Using modeling in decision making is a complex task because it involves a host of issues like uncertainty and risk, information availability and accuracy, and search strategies. Despite these difficulties the approach of modeling as a support to decision making is gaining popularity and is a major building block in using decision support systems.

Key Words

algorithm	enumeration	problem solving
analog model	goal seeking	productivity
analytical approach	heuristics	programmed decisions
cognitive style	iconic model	risk analysis
controllable variables	implementation	satisfice
critical success factors	independent variables	scenario
decision styles	inputs	sensitivity analysis
DELPHI	linear programming	simulation
dependent variables	mathematical model	suboptimal
descriptive models	normative	system
deterministic models	optimization	uncertainty
effectiveness	outputs	uncontrollable variables
efficiency	principle of choice	"what if"

Questions for Review

1. What is the difference between making decisions and solving problems?
2. Define a system.
3. List the major components of a system.
4. Define productivity.
5. Define an environment of a system.
6. Define open and closed systems. Give an example of each.
7. What is meant by a "black box"?
8. Define efficiency and contrast it with effectiveness.
9. Define the phases of intelligence, design, and choice.
10. Define a problem and distinguish it from the symptoms of the problem.
11. Define programmed versus unprogrammed problems; give one example of each in each of the following areas: accounting, marketing, personnel administration.
12. List the major components of a mathematical model.
13. Define optimization and contrast it with suboptimization.
14. Compare and contrast normative versus descriptive approaches to decision making.
15. Why do people have a bounded rationality?
16. Distinguish between decision making under risk and under uncertainty.

17. What is the major advantage of optimization?
18. What is the major disadvantage of complete enumeration?
19. Define heuristics.
20. Why is a heuristic search superior to a blind one?
21. Define data-directed search and give an example.
22. Define goal-directed search and give an example.
23. Define "what if" analysis and provide an example.
24. Define goal seeking analysis and provide an example.
25. Define critical success factors (CSF) and describe the steps in this process.
26. Define implementation.
27. Define a scenario. How is it used in decision making?
28. Define cognition and cognitive style.
29. Compare simulation and optimization.
30. Define sensitivity analysis.
31. Compare decision style to cognitive style.
32. Discuss the various types of computerized support.

Problems and Discussion Questions

1. Specify in a table the inputs, process, and output of the following systems:
   a. post office
   b. elementary school
   c. social service agency
   d. paper mill
2. List a possible mode of feedback for the systems in the previous question.
3. A hospital includes a dietary, radiology, housekeeping, and nursing (patient care rooms) department, and an emergency room. List four system interfaces between pairs of these departments.
4. How would you measure the productivity of:
   a. a letter carrier
   b. a salesperson
   c. a professor
   d. a social worker
5. Give an example of five elements in the environment of a university.
6. Analyze a managerial system of your choice and identify the following:
   a. the components, inputs, and outputs
   b. the environment
   c. the process
   d. the system's goals
   e. the feedback
7. What are some of the "measures of effectiveness" in a manufacturing plant, a restaurant, an educational institution, and the U.S. Congress?
8. What are some of the controllable and uncontrollable variables in the following systems: automotive manufacturing, hospital, courthouse, airline, restaurant, hotel, bank, oil refinery, atomic power plant? Specify a typical decision in each of the above.
9. Assume a marketing department is an open system. How would you "close" this system?
10. What could be the major advantages of a mathematical model that would be used to support a major investment decision?
11. Your company is considering opening a branch in China. List typical activities in each phase (intelligence, design, choice, implementation).

12. Most farm equipment manufacturers have had major losses in recent years because farmers have had no money to purchase farm equipment. What is the problem that the manufacturing companies are faced with?

13. You are about to sell your car. What criteria (or principles of choice) are you most likely to employ in deciding about accepting or rejecting offers? Why?

14. You are about to decide on driving to work via the freeway or via the parallel road. There is no immediate traffic information. Is your decision under certainty? risk? uncertainty? Why?

15. There are $n!$ (n factorial) ways to schedule n jobs through one machine. You have 50 jobs to schedule. You must decide which job to run first, second, etc. There is no analytical solution to the problem. What type of search would you use in your analysis and why?

16. List five heuristics (or rules of thumb) that are being used in your company, a university, a bank, or a fast-food restaurant.

17. A hospital desires to know what level of demand for its services will guarantee an 85 percent bed occupancy. What type of sensitivity analysis should the hospital use and why?

18. Apply the method of critical success factors to determine which computer to buy for your home. Assume that at least three people will use the computer and you can afford only one PC.

19. The use of scenarios is becoming popular in computerized decision making. Why? For what type of decisions is this technique most appropriate?

20. Explain how cognitive style relates to decision style. How might these concepts impact the development of information systems?

21. Discuss the major issues related to group decision making.

22. Explain, through an example, the support given to decision makers by computers in each phase of the decision process.

23. Some experts believe that the major contribution of DSS is to the implementation of the decision and not to the intelligence, design, or choice. Why is this so?

24. Table 2.5 shows the differences between heuristic and analytic cognitive styles.
    a. Would you consider yourself heuristic or analytic? Why?
    b. Read Huber's article (*Management Science*, May 1983). Do you agree with Huber's position? Why or why not?
    c. Assume you are making a presentation to two managers—one heuristic, the other analytic—regarding a decision about adding a service by the bank you work for. How would you appeal to their cognitive styles? (Be specific.)

25. How is the term *model* used in this text? What are the strengths and weaknesses of modeling?

26. Most managers are capable of utilizing the telephone without understanding or even considering the electrical and magnetic theories involved. Why then is it necessary for managers to understand analytic tools to use them wisely?

27. Decision-making styles vary from analytical to heuristic-intuitive. Does a decision maker consistently use the same style? Give examples from your own experience.

References and Bibliography

1. Alter, S. L. *Decision Support Systems: Current Practice and Continuing Challenge*. Reading, MA: Addison-Wesley, 1980.
2. Brookes, C. H. P. "A Framework for DSS Development." Information Systems Forum Research Report, Department of Information Systems, University of New South Wales, Sydney, Australia, 1984.
3. Churchman, C. West. *The Systems Approach*. Rev. ed. New York: Delacorte, 1975.

TABLE 2.5 Cognitive-style Decision Approaches.

Problem-solving Dimension	Heuristic	Analytic
Approach to learning	Learns more by acting than by analyzing the situation and places more emphasis on feedback.	Employs a planned sequential approach to problem solving; learns more by analyzing the situation than by acting and places less emphasis on feedback.
Search	Uses trial and error and spontaneous action.	Uses formal rational analysis.
Approach to analysis	Uses common sense, intuition, and feelings.	Develops explicit, often quantitative models of the situation.
Scope of analysis	Views the totality of the situation as an organic whole rather than as a structure constructed from specific parts.	Reduces the problem situation to a set of underlying causal functions.
Basis for inferences	Looks for highly visible situational differences that vary with time.	Locates similarities or commonalities by comparing objects.

Source: G. B. Davis; *Management Information Systems: Conceptual Foundations, Structure, and Development* New York: McGraw-Hill, 1974, p. 150.

4. DeSantis, G., and B. Gallupe. "Group Decision Support Systems: A New Frontier." *Data Base*, Winter 1985.
5. Emory, C. W. *Business Research Methods.* Homewood, IL: Irwin, 1980.
6. Gordon, L. A., et al. *Normative Models in Managerial Decision Making.* New York: National Association of Accounting, 1975.
7. Huber, G. P. "Cognitive Style as a Basis for MIS and DSS Designs: Much Ado About Nothing?" *Management Science*, Vol. 29, No. 5, May 1983.
8. Keen, P. G. W., and M. S. Scott-Morton. *Decision Support Systems: An Organizational Perspective.* Reading, MA: Addison-Wesley, 1978.
9. Keeney, R., and H. Raiffa. *Decisions with Multiple Objectives, Preferences, and Value Tradeoffs.* New York: Wiley, 1976.
10. Linstone, H. A., and M. Turoff. *The Delphi Method: Techniques and Applications.* Reading, MA: Addison-Wesley, 1975.
11. Lucas, H. C. "Top Management Problem Solving and Information Systems," Working Papers CRIS #11, Center for Research on Information Systems; New York University, 1980.
12. McKenney, J. L., and P. G. W. Keen. "How Managers' Minds Work." *Harvard Business Review*, May–June 1974.
13. Mayer, R. E. *Thinking, Problem Solving, Cognition.* New York: Freeman, 1983.
14. Mintzberg, H. *The Nature of the Managerial Work.* New York: Harper & Row, 1973.
15. Mittman, B. S., and J. H. Moore. *Senior Management Computer Use: Implications for DSS Design and Goals.* Paper presented at the DSS-84 meetings, Dallas, Texas, April 1984.
16. Newell, A, and H. A. Simon. *Human Problem Solving.* Englewood Cliffs, NJ: Prentice-Hall, 1972.

17. Pearl, J. *Heuristics: Intelligent Search Strategies for Computer Problem Solving.* Reading, MA: Addison-Wesley, 1984.
18. Rockart, J. F. "Chief Executives Define Their Own Data Needs." *Harvard Business Review,* July–August 1981.
19. Rowe, A. J. "Decision Making in the 80s." *Los Angeles Journal of Business and Economics,* Winter 1981.
20. Shank, M. E., et al. "Critical Success Factor Analysis as a Methodology for MIS Planning." *MIS Quarterly,* June 1985.
21. Simon, H. *The New Science of Management Decisions.* Rev. ed. Englewood Cliffs, NJ: Prentice-Hall, 1977.
22. Sprague, R. H., and E. D. Carlson. *Building Effective Decision Support Systems.* Englewood Cliffs, NJ: Prentice-Hall, 1982.
23. Sumanth, D. *Productivity Management.* New York: McGraw-Hill, 1984.
24. Turban, E., and J. Meredith. *Fundamentals of Management Science.* 5th ed. Homewood, Il: Richard D. Irwin, 1991.
25. Van Gigch, J. P. *Applied General Systems Theory.* 2nd ed. New York: Harper & Row, 1978.
26. Wedley, W. K., and R. H. C. Field. "A Predecision Support System." *Academy of Management Review,* October 1984.
27. Zanakis, S. H., and J. R. Evans. "Heuristic Optimization: Why, When and How to Use It." *Interfaces,* October 1981.

Chapter 3

Modeling

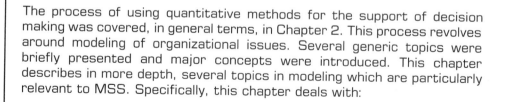

The process of using quantitative methods for the support of decision making was covered, in general terms, in Chapter 2. This process revolves around modeling of organizational issues. Several generic topics were briefly presented and major concepts were introduced. This chapter describes in more depth, several topics in modeling which are particularly relevant to MSS. Specifically, this chapter deals with:

3.1 Modeling in MSS

Modeling in MSS can be executed in many ways.* In order to understand how modeling works in MSS, the case of the Frazee Company in Chapter 7 gives an illustrative example. This DSS includes three types of models:

1. A statistical model, which is being used for validating the relationship in the DSS. This model is preprogrammed in the DSS development software tool.
2. A financial model for developing income statements and projecting financial data for several years. This model is semistructured and is written with a special DSS language called IFPS.
3. An optimization model is performed using a linear programming approach in order to determine media selection.

The Frazee case demonstrates that a DSS can be composed of *several models*, some standard and some custom made, which are used collectively to support the advertisement decisions in the company.

Other aspects of modeling must also be considered, such as the following:

Identification of the Problem (Task). This issue was discussed in Chapter 2. One aspect that was not discussed is the topic of *environmental scanning*, which refers to the monitoring, scanning, and interpretation of the collected information. The issue of information and knowledge acquisition is discussed in Chapter 13 as it is related to expert systems. In the Frazee Corp. case we illustrated some of these issues. The problem in this case is actually composed of several subproblems (How much to allocate for advertisement, how much to allocate to each product, and how much to spend in each media). For a complete description of problem identification see Weber and Konsynski (24).

Environmental Analysis. It is frequently advisable to analyze the scope, the abstraction of the domain, and the forces and dynamics of the environment. It is necessary to identify the organizational culture and the corporate decision-making process (who makes decisions, degree of centralization, etc.). This information is particularly important to the success of implementation (Chapter 20). For further discussion see Ariav and Ginzberg (1).

Identification of the Variables. The identification of the various variables is of utmost importance and so are their relationships. Influence diagrams, which are described in Section 3.7, can be very helpful in this process.

Data Collection and Forecasting. Models require data, some of which is historical and some of which is forecasted. Data collection and interpretation is important for the identification of the problem and the environmental analysis. Forecasting is essential for the creation and manipulation of the models. Fore-

---

*Sections 3.4, 3.5, 3.6, and 3.8 are adapted from Turban and Meredith (23).

casting is described in Section 3.8. Data collection and validation is discussed in Chapter 2.

Model Selection. Model selection depends on appropriate diagnosis of the problem area. For use of an expert system for such a diagnosis see Courtney et al. (4). The issue of model selection is part of model management, which is discussed in Chapters 4 and 6.

Decision Support Systems may include several models, as shown in our opening case. Some of these models are fairly standard and they are built into the DSS development software. Others are standard but are not available as built-in functions. Instead they are available as a free-standing software that can interface with the DSS. The nonstandard models need to be constructed from scratch.

The DSS builder is often faced with the dilemma of which models to use. Then the decision must be made as to whether to build them, to use the ready-made ones, or to modify existing models. The classification of models into categories will assist the DSS builder in making a decision.

Table 3.1 summarizes the categorization of models used in DSS into seven groups. It also lists several representative techniques in each category, and indicates the section number in which each category is discussed in this chapter.

Each of the techniques may appear in a form of either a static or a dynamic model (Section 3.2), and it may be constructed under assumed certainty, uncertainty or risk (Section 3.3).

TABLE 3.1 Types of Models.

Category	Process and Objective	Representative Techniques
Complete enumeration Section 3.3	Find the best solution from a relatively small number of alternatives	Decision tables, decision tree, decision analysis
Optimization via algorithm Section 3.4	Find the best solution from a large or an infinite number of alternatives, using a step-by-step improvement process	Linear and other mathematical programming models, network models
Optimization via analytical formula	Find the best solution, in one step, using a formula	Some inventory models
Simulation Section 3.5	Finding "good enough" solution, or the best among those alternatives checked using experimentation	Several types of simulation
Heuristics Section 3.6	Finding "good enough" solution using rules	Heuristic programming, expert systems
Other descriptive models	Finding "what if" using a formula	Financial modeling, waiting lines
Predictive models Section 3.8	Predict future for a given scenario	Markov analysis, forecasting models

Finally, most of these techniques can be supported by built-in functions in DSS software, or by standard software. For a list see Chapter 6.

3.2 Static and Dynamic Models

DSS can be static or dynamic:

Static Analysis. Static models take a single snapshot of a situation. During this snapshot everything occurs in a single interval, which can be short or long in duration.

For example, a decision on whether to make or buy a product is static in nature. A quarterly or annual income statement (such as performed by IFPS in Chapter 7) is static and so is the investment decision shown in Section 3.3.

During a static analysis it is assumed that there is stability. There are no changes in the data.

Dynamic Analysis. Dynamic models are used to evaluate scenarios that change over time. A simple example would be a five-year profit projection, where the input data, such as costs, prices, and quantities are changed from year to year. An example of such an analysis is given in Chapter 7.

Dynamic models are time dependent. For example, in determining how many employees to have in the checkout points in a supermarket, it is necessary to consider the time of the day. This is because there are changes in the number of people that arrive at the supermarket at different hours.

Dynamic models are important because they show *trends* and patterns over time. They also show averages per period, moving averages, and comparative analysis (e.g., profit this quarter against the same quarter last year).

3.3 Treating Certainty, Uncertainty, and Risk

Introduction

The concepts of certainty, uncertainty, and risk were introduced in Chapter 2. When we build models any of these conditions may occur. The following are some of the issues involved in each condition:

Certainty Models. Everyone loves them because they are easy to work with and can yield optimal solutions. Of a special interest are problems that have an infinite (or a very large) number of feasible solutions. They are discussed in Sections 3.4 and 3.6. Many financial models (Chapter 7) are being conducted under assumed certainty. Unfortunately, very little is certain in this world.

Uncertainty. Managers attempt to avoid uncertainty as much as possible. Instead they attempt to acquire more information so that the problem can be treated under risk. If you can not acquire more information, you can use one of the approaches described in Turban and Meredith (23).

Risk. Most major business decisions are being made under assumed risk. Several techniques can be used to deal with risk analysis. They are discussed in Sections 3.3, 3.5 and in Chapter 7.

Decision Analysis

Decision situations that involve a finite and usually not too large a number of alternatives are modeled by an approach called decision analysis. In this approach the alternatives are listed and their forecasted contributions to the goal(s) are assessed. Then, an evaluation takes place in order to select the best alternative.

Two cases are distinguished: single goal and multiple goals. Single goal situations are approached by the use of decision tables or decision trees. Multiple goals can be approached by several techniques (to be described later).

Decision Tables—Single Goal

Decision tables are a convenient way to organize information in a systematic manner.

Example: An investment company is considering investing in one of three alternatives: Bonds, stocks, or certificates of deposit (CDs).

The company is interested in one goal—maximizing the yield on the investment after one year. If it were interested in other goals such as safety or liquidity, then the problem would be classified as *multiple criteria decision analysis*.

The yield depends on the status of the economy, which can be either in solid growth, stagnation, or inflation. The following estimates of yield were solicited from the experts:

1. If there is solid growth in the economy, bonds will yield 12 percent; stocks, 15 percent; and time deposits, 6.5 percent.
2. If stagnation prevails, bonds will yield 6 percent; stocks, 3 percent; and time deposits, 6.5 percent.
3. If inflation prevails, bonds will yield 3 percent; the value of stocks will drop 2 percent; and time deposits will yield 6.5 percent.

The problem is to select the best investment alternative. Note: investing 50 percent in bonds and 50 percent in stocks is another alternative, and it can be added as a fourth alternative. Obviously, in reality the company may be faced with many other alternatives.

The investment problem can be organized in a table (see Table 3.2).

TABLE 3.2 Investment Problem

Alternative	Solid Growth	Stagnation	Inflation
Bonds	12.0%	6.0%	3.0%
Stocks	15.0%	3.0%	−2.0%
CDs	6.5%	6.5%	6.5%

This is a mathematical model. According to our definition in Chapter 2, it includes: *Decision variables* (the alternatives), *uncontrollable variables* (the states of the economy), and *result variables* (the projected yield; the numbers inside the table).

Two cases can be distinguished: uncertainty and risk. In the case of uncertainty we do not know the probabilities of each state of nature. In the case of risk we assume we know the probabilities with which each state of nature will occur.

Treating Uncertainty. The intuitive reaction of any manager is not to make a decision under uncertainty until the chances of the economy can be assessed. In such a case the problem will be one of a risk. However, if there is no information that will support the risk assessment (or if there is no time to collect such information), one can use one of several approaches to handle the uncertainty. For example, the *optimistic approach* involves considering the *best* possible outcome of each alternative and selecting the best of the bests (stocks). The *pessimistic (conservative) approach* involves considering the *worst* possible outcome for each alternative and selecting the *best* one (CDs).

For details on these and other approaches, see Turban and Meredith (23). All the approaches of handling uncertainty have serious deficiencies. Therefore, any modeler should attempt to collect sufficient information so that the problem can be treated under assumed risk.

Treating risk. Let us assume that the chance of solid growth is 50 percent, that of stagnation 30 percent and that of inflation 20 percent. In such a case the decision table is rewritten with the added information (see Table 3.3). The most common method for solving this problem is to select the alternative with the largest expected value. An expected value is computed by multiplying the results (outcomes) by their respective probabilities and adding them. For example, for bonds we get: $12(0.5) + 6(0.3) + 3(0.2) = 8.4$ (invest in bonds, for an average return of 8.4 percent).

Decision Trees. An alternative presentation of the decision table is a decision tree. A decision tree has two advantages: First, it shows graphically the relationships of the problem and second, it can deal with more complex situations in a compact form (e.g., multiperiod investment problem).

Other Methods of Treating Risk. Several other methods of treating risk are discussed in this book. Specifically: simulation (Section 3.5 and Chapter 7), certainty factors, and fuzzy logic (Chapter 14).

TABLE 3.3 Decision Under Risk and Its Solution.

Alternative	Solid Growth 0.50	Stagnation 0.30	Inflation 0.20	Expected Value
Bonds	12.0%	6.0%	3.0%	8.4%
Stocks	15.0%	3.0%	−2.0%	8.0%
CDs	6.5%	6.5%	6.5%	6.5%

TABLE 3.4 Multiple Goals.

Alternatives	Yield	Safety	Liquidity
Bonds	8.4%	High	High
Stocks	8.0%	Low	High
CDs	6.5%	Very High	High

Multiple Goals

A simplified case of multiple goals is shown in Table 3.4. Three goals (or attributes) are considered: yield, safety, and liquidity.

Notice that this situation is under assumed certainty, i.e., only one possible consequence is projected for each alternative. (Obviously, in the more complicated cases, a risk or uncertainty can be considered.) Notice also that some of the results are *not numerical* but symbolic (e.g., Low, High). For methods of dealing with multiple goals see Hwang and Yoon (14).

Extensive software is available for dealing with multiple criteria decision making (see Chapter 6, Decision aid software.)

3.4 Optimization via Mathematical Programming

The concept of optimization was introduced in Chapter 2 where an example of linear programming was developed. Linear programming is the most known technique in a family of tools called mathematical programming. Optimization is achieved by the use of an *algorithm* (see Chapter 2).

Mathematical Programming

Mathematical programming is the name for a family of tools designed to help solve managerial problems in which the decision maker must allocate scarce (or limited) resources among various activities to optimize a measurable goal. For example, distribution of machine time (the resource) among various products (the activities) is a typical allocation problem. Allocation problems usually display the following characteristics and necessitate making certain assumptions.

Characteristics.

1. A limited quantity of economic resources (such as labor, capital, machines, or water) is available for allocation.
2. The resources are used in the production of products or services.
3. There are two or more ways in which the resources can be used. Each is called a solution or a program. (Usually the number of ways is very large, or even infinite.)
4. Each activity (product or service) in which the resources are used yields a return (or reward) in terms of the stated goal.

5. The allocation is usually restricted by several limitations and requirements called constraints.

Assumptions.

1. Returns from different allocations can be compared; that is, they can be measured by a common unit (such as dollars or utility).
2. The return from any allocation is independent of other allocations.
3. The total return is the sum of the returns yielded by the different activities.
4. All data are known with certainty.
5. The resources are to be used in the most economical manner.

The allocation problem can generally be stated as: Find the way of allocating the limited resources to various activities so the total reward will be maximized. Allocation problems, typically, have a large number of possible alternative solutions. Depending on the underlying assumptions, the number of solutions can be either infinite or finite. Usually, different solutions yield different rewards. Of the available solutions, one (sometimes more than one) is the *best*, in the sense that the degree of goal attainment associated with it is the highest (i.e., total reward is maximized). This is referred to as the optimal solution.

A survey would find that many, or even most, problems in organizations are related to the allocation of resources (money, people, time, power, space, equipment). The reasons for this are that the resources are limited, there are many ways of allocation, it is difficult to measure the contribution of the allocation to the goals, and there is disagreement concerning the importance of the results. Mathematical programming provides a relatively unbiased approach to the allocation problem.

The field of mathematical programming is composed of several techniques:

Linear Programming (LP).   Linear programming deals with allocation problems in which the goal (or objective) and all the requirements imposed on the problem are expressed by linear functions.

Integer Linear Programming.   When the requirement that some or all of the decision variables must be integers (whole numbers) is added to a linear programming problem, it becomes one of integer (linear) programming.

Nonlinear Programming.   Mathematical programming problems, where the goal and/or one or more of the requirements imposed on the problem are expressed by nonlinear functions are referred to as nonlinear programming problems.

Goal Programming.   This is a variant of linear programming that is used when multiple goals exist.

Distribution Problems.   The *transportation* of a commodity from sources of supply to destinations, at minimum cost (or maximum profit), and the *assign-*

ment of workers (or equipment) to jobs are examples of what are termed *distribution problems*.

The uses of mathematical programming, especially of linear programming, are so common that "canned" computer programs can be found today in just about any organization that has a computer.

DSS development tools, such as IFPS, can be used to model and solve linear programming situations, or have the capability to interface with a "canned" LP program. (For a software list see Chapter 6.)

Linear Programming

In Chapter 2 we presented a simple product-mix problem and formulated it as linear programming. Here we will introduce another typical LP problem called the blending problem.

Example: The Blending Problem (Minimization).   In preparing Sungold paint, it is required that the paint have a brilliance rating of at least 300 degrees and a hue level of at least 250 degrees. Brilliance and hue levels are determined by two ingredients, Alpha and Beta. Both Alpha and Beta contribute equally to the brilliance rating, one ounce (dry weight) of either producing one degree of brilliance in one case of paint. However, the hue is controlled entirely by the amount of Alpha, one ounce of it producing three degrees of hue in one case of paint. The cost of Alpha is 45 cents per ounce, and the cost of Beta is 12 cents per ounce. Assuming that the objective is to minimize the cost of the resources, then the problem is to find the quantity of Alpha and Beta to be included in the preparation of each case of paint.

Formulation of the Blending Problem.   The *decision variables* are

x_1 = Quantity of Alpha to be included, in ounces, in each case of paint

x_2 = Quantity of Beta to be included, in ounces, in each case of paint

The objective is to minimize the total cost of the ingredients required for one case of paint. Since the cost of Alpha is 45 cents per ounce, and since x_1 ounces are going to be used in each case, then the cost per case is $45x_1$. Similarly, for Beta the cost is $12 x_2$. The total cost is, therefore, $45 x_1 + 12x_2$, and as our objective function, it is to be *minimized* subject to the constraints of the following specifications:

1. To provide a brilliance rating of at least 300 degrees in each case. Since each ounce of Alpha or Beta increases the brightness by one degree, the following relationship exists:

Supplied by Alpha		Supplied by Beta		Demand
$3x_1$	$+$	$0x_2$	$\geq$	250

2. To provide a hue level of at least 250 degrees, the effect of Alpha (alone) on hue can similarly be written as:

Supplied by Alpha		Supplied by Beta	Demand
$3x_1$	+	$0x_2$	$\geq$ 250

In summary, the blending problem is formulated as follows: Find x_1 and x_2 that

> minimize $z = 45x_1 + 12x_2$
> subject to
> $1x_1 + 1x_2 \geq 300$ (brightness specification)
> $3x_1 + 0x_2 \geq 250$ (hue specification)

Solution. (derived by IFPS)

$$x_1 = 83.333$$
$$x_2 = 216.667$$
$$\text{Total cost} = \$6350$$

General Formulation and Terminology

In the previous section, two classical managerial problems were formulated. Let us now generalize the formulation.

Every LP problem is composed of:

Decision Variables. The variables whose values are unknown and are searched for. Usually they are designated by x_1, x_2, and so on.

Objective Function. This is a mathematical expression, given as a linear function, that shows the relationship between the decision variables and a *single goal* (or objective) under consideration. The objective function is a measure of goal attainment. Examples of such goals are total profit, total cost, share of the market, and the like.

If the managerial problem involves multiple goals, one can use the following two-step approach:

1. Select a primary goal whose level is to be maximized or minimized.
2. Transform the other goals into constraints, which must only be satisfied.

For example, one may attempt to maximize profit (the primary goal) subject to a growth rate of at least 12 percent per year (a secondary goal).

Optimization. Linear programming attempts to either maximize or minimize the values of the objective function.

Profit or Cost Coefficients. The coefficients of the variables in the objective function (e.g., 45 and 12 in the blending problem) are called the profit (or cost) coefficients. They express the *rate* at which the value of the objective function increases or decreases by including in the solution one unit of each of the decision variables.

Constraints. The maximization (or minimization) is performed subject to a set of constraints. Therefore, linear programming can be defined as a *constrained optimization problem*. These constraints are expressed in the form of linear inequalities (or, sometimes, equalities). They reflect the fact that resources are limited or they specify the product requirements.

Input-Output (Technology) Coefficients. The coefficients of the constraints' variables are called the *input-output* coefficients. They indicate the rate at which a given resource is depleted or utilized. They appear on the left-hand side of the constraints.

Capacities. The capacities (or availability) of the various resources, usually expressed as some upper or lower limit, are given on the *right-hand side* of the constraints. The right-hand side also expresses minimum requirements.

Example. These major components of a linear programming model are illustrated for the blending problem:

Find x_1 and x_2 (decision variables) that will minimize the value of the linear objective function

$$\text{cost coefficients}$$

$$z = 45x_1 + 12x_2$$

$$\text{decision variables}$$

subject to the linear constraints

$$1x_1 + 1x_2 \geq 300$$
$$3x_1 + 0x_2 \geq 250$$

input-output   capacities or
coefficients   requirements

3.5   **Simulation**

Simulation has many meanings, depending on the area where it is being used. To *simulate*, according to the dictionary, means to assume the appearance of characteristics of reality. In MSS it generally refers to *a technique for conducting experiments (such as "what if") with a digital computer on a model of a management system*.

Major Characteristics

To begin, simulation is not strictly a type of model; models in general *represent* reality, while simulation *imitates* it. In practical terms, this means that there are fewer simplifications of reality in simulation models than in other models.

Second, simulation is a technique for *conducting experiments*. Therefore, simulation involves the testing of specific values of the decision or uncontrollable variables in the model and observing the impact on the output variables.

Simulation is a *descriptive* rather than a normative tool; that is, there is no automatic search for an optimal solution. Instead, a simulation describes and/or predicts the characteristics of a given system under different circumstances. Once these characteristics are known, the best among several alternatives can be selected. The simulation process often consists of the repetition of an experiment many, many times to obtain an estimate of the overall effect of certain actions. It can be executed manually in some cases, but a computer is usually needed.

Finally, simulation is usually called for only when the problem under investigation is too complex to be treated by numerical optimization techniques (such as linear programming). Complexity here means that the problem either cannot be formulated for optimization (e.g., because the assumptions do not hold or the formulation is too involved for a practical or economic solution).

Advantages and Disadvantages of Simulation

The increased acceptance of simulation is probably due to a number of factors:

1. Simulation theory is relatively straightforward.
2. The simulation model is simply the aggregate of many elementary relationships and interdependencies, much of which is introduced slowly by request of the manager and in a patchwork manner.
3. Simulation is descriptive rather than normative. This allows the manager to ask "what if" type questions. Thus, managers who employ a trial-and-error approach to problem solving can do it faster and cheaper with less risk, using the aid of simulation and computers.
4. An accurate simulation model requires an *intimate* knowledge of the problem, thus forcing the MSS builder to constantly interface with the manager.
5. The model is built from the manager's perspective and in his or her decision structure.
6. The simulation model is built for one particular problem and, typically, will not solve any other problem. Thus, no generalized understanding is required of the manager; every component in the model corresponds one to one with a part of the real-life model.
7. Simulation can handle an extremely wide variation in problem types such as inventory and staffing, as well as higher managerial level functions like long-range planning. Thus, it is "always there" when the manager needs it.

8. The manager can experiment with different variables to determine which are important, and with different alternatives to determine which is the best.
9. Simulation, in general, allows for inclusion of the real-life complexities of problems; simplifications are not necessary. For example: simulation utilizes the real-life probability distributions rather than approximate theoretical distributions.
10. Due to the nature of simulation, a great amount of *time compression* can be attained, giving the manager some feel as to the long-term (1 to 10 years) effects of various policies, in a matter of minutes.

The primary disadvantages of simulation are:

1. An optimal solution cannot be guaranteed.
2. Constructing a simulation model is frequently a slow and costly process.
3. Solutions and inferences from a simulation study are usually not transferable to other problems. This is due to the incorporation in the model of the unique factors of the problem.
4. Simulation is sometimes so easy to sell to managers that analytical solutions that can yield optimal results are often overlooked.

The Methodology of Simulation

Simulation involves setting up a model of a real system and conducting repetitive experiments on it. The methodology consists of a number of steps (Figure 3.1). The following is a brief discussion of the process.

Problem Definition.   The real-world problem is examined and classified. Here we should specify why simulation is necessary. The system's boundaries and other such aspects of problem clarification (see Chapter 2) are attended to here.

Construction Of The Simulation Model.   This step involves gathering the necessary data. In many cases, a flowchart is used to describe the process. Then a computer program is to be written.

Testing And Validating The Model.   The simulation model must properly imitate the system under study. This involves the process of validation, discussed later.

Design Of The Experiments.   Once the model has been proven valid, the experiment is designed. Included in this step is determining how long to run the simulation and which data to include. This step deals with two important and contradictory objectives: accuracy and cost.

Conducting The Experiments.   Conducting the experiment may involve issues such as random number generation, stopping rules, and derivation of the results.

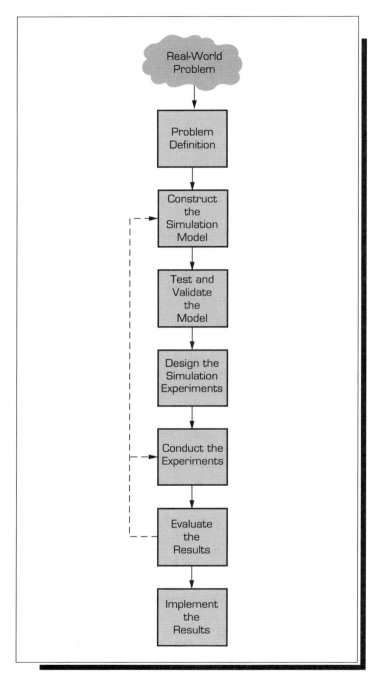

FIGURE 3.1 The process of simulation.

Evaluating the Results.   The final step is the evaluation of the results. Here, we deal with issues such as "What do the results mean?"   In addition to statistical tools, we may use a sensitivity analysis (in the form of "what if" questions).

Implementation. The implementation of simulation results involves the same issues as any other implementation. However, the chances of implementation are better since the manager is usually more involved in the simulation process than with analytical models.

Types of Simulation

There are several types of simulation. The major ones described in this book are:

Probabilistic Simulation. In this type of simulation one or more of the independent variables (e.g., the demand in an inventory problem) is probabilistic. That is, it follows a certain probability distribution. Two subcategories are recognized: discrete distributions and continuous distributions.

Discrete distributions involve a situation with a limited number of events (or variables) that can only take on a finite number of values. This situation is illustrated in the inventory example in this section.

Continuous distributions refer to a situation with an unlimited number of possible events that follow density functions such as the normal distribution. (See the IFPS example in Chapter 7.)

The two types of distributions are shown in Table 3.5.

Probabilistic simulation is conducted with the aid of a technique called Monte Carlo.

Time Dependent and Time Independent Simulation. *Time independent* refers to a situation where it is not important to know exactly when the event occurred. For example, we may know that the demand for a certain product is three units per day, but we do not care *when* during the day the item was demanded. Or in some situations, such as financial or organizational simulation, time may not be a factor in the simulation at all.

On the other hand, in waiting line problems, it is important to know the precise time of arrival (to know if the customer will have to wait or not). In this case, we are dealing with a *time dependent* situation.

Visual Simulation. This graphic display of computerized results is one of the more successful new developments in computer-human problem solving. It is described in Chapter 18.

TABLE 3.5 Discrete and continuous distributions.

Discrete		Continuous
Daily demand	**Probability**	
5	0.10	Daily demand is normally
6	0.15	distributed with a mean of 7 and
7	0.30	a standard deviation of 1.2
8	0.25	
9	0.20	

Simulation Experimentation (Probabilistic)

The process of simulation experimentation involves eight steps:

1. Describe the system and obtain the probability distributions of the relevant probabilistic elements of the system.
2. Define the appropriate measure(s) of system performance. If necessary, write in the form of an equation(s).
3. Construct cumulative probability distributions for each of the stochastic elements.
4. Assign representative numbers in correspondence with the cumulative probability distribution.
5. For each probabilistic element, take a random sample (generate a number at random or pick one from a table of random numbers).
6. Derive the measures of performance and their variances.
7. If stable results are desired, repeat steps 5 and 6 until the measures of system performance "stabilize."
8. Repeat steps 5–7 for various alternatives. Given the values of the performance measures and their confidence intervals, decide on the appropriate alternative.

The *Monte Carlo* procedure is not a simulation model per se, although it has become almost synonymous with probabilistic simulation. It basically includes steps 3 through 6 in the process. Namely, the procedure generates random observations of the variable(s) of interest.

The following example (which is a time-independent, discrete simulation) will illustrate the simulation experimentation of an inventory control situation.

The example is being worked manually. In real DSS computers are being used.

Example. Marin's Service Station sells gasoline to boat owners. The demand for gasoline depends on weather conditions and fluctuates according to the following distribution.

Weekly demand (gal)	Probability
2000	0.12
3000	0.23
4000	0.48
5000	0.17

Shipments arrive once a week. Since Marin's Service Station is located in a remote place, it must order and accept a fixed quantity of gasoline every week. Joe, the owner, faces the following problem: If he orders too small a quantity, he will lose, in terms of lost business and goodwill, 12 cents per gallon demanded and not provided. If he orders too large a quantity, he will have to pay 5 cents per gallon shipped back due to lack of storage. For each gallon sold he makes 10 cents profit. At the present time, Joe receives 3500 gallons at the beginning of each week before he opens for business. He feels that he should receive more, maybe 4000 or even 4500 gallons. The tank's capacity is 5500 gallons. The problem is to find the best order quantity.

This problem can be solved by trial and error. That is, the service station can actually order each quantity for, say, 10 weeks, then compare the results. However, simulation can give an answer in a few minutes and a simulated loss is only a loss on the paper.

Solution by Simulation.   To find the best ordering quantity, it is necessary to compute the profit (loss) for the existing order quantity (3500 gallons) and for other possible order quantities. For example, 4000 and 4500 (as suggested by Joe) or any other desired figure (e.g., 3600, 3750, 3800, and so on) may be tried. Each quantity is a proposed solution, and steps six and seven must be executed for each; the eighth step then concludes the analysis. Assume that today is the first day of the week, a shipment has just arrived, and there is now an inventory of 3800 gallons.

Before constructing a simulation, particularly if computerized, it is wise to construct a flowchart of flow diagram of the tasks. A flowchart is a schematic presentation of all computational activities used in the simulation. Its major objective is to help the computer programmer in writing the computer program. Figure 3.2 shows a flowchart for the inventory problem. We will discuss the equations a bit later, but the logic flow for the simulation process is clear. Therefore, let us begin the eight steps for the simulation and then follow the steps in the flowchart.

Step 1: Describe the system and determine the probability distributions. There is only one probability distribution in this case. It describes the demand. In more complicated Monte Carlo simulations there are several distributions involved.

Step 2: Decide on the measures of performance.   The primary measure of performance is the *average daily profit*, which is computed as (all quantities are in gallons)

$$\text{Average daily profit} = 10\text{¢} \times (\text{sales}) - 12\text{¢} \times (\text{Unsatisfied demand})$$

$$-5\text{¢} \times (\text{Quantity shipped back})$$

Several less important measures such as the average shortage are discussed at the end of this example.

Step 3: Compute cumulative probabilities.   The cumulative probabilities are computed in Table 3.6.

TABLE 3.6 Assignment of representative numbers.

(A) Weekly demand (gal)	(B) Probability	(C) Cumulative probability	(D) Representative numbers (range)
2000	0.12	0.12	01–12
3000	0.23	0.35	13–35
4000	0.48	0.83	36–83
5000	0.17	1.00	84–00

The cumulative probability column indicates the chance for a certain demand or less to occur. For example, there is a 0.35 chance for a demand of 3000 or less.

   Step 4: Assign representative ranges of numbers. For each possible demand, a range of representative numbers is assigned in proportion to the probability

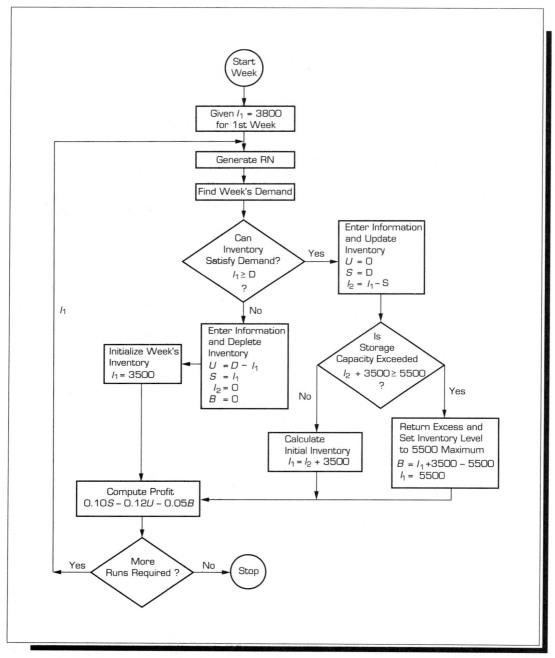

FIGURE 3.2 Flow diagram for the inventory example (I beginning = I_1, I end = I_2)

distribution. For example, there is a chance of 0.12 for a demand of 2000 to occur. Therefore, out of 100 numbers (all two-digit numbers), 12 will be assigned to represent a demand of 2000*. An easy way of doing this is to assign the numbers 01, 02, 03, . . . , 12. (This information is entered in Table 3.6. Next, the demand of 3000 is represented by 23 numbers, since it has a 0.23 chance of occurring. Since the numbers 01–12 have already been used, it is logical to use the next 23 two-digit numbers, 13–35.

Step 5: Generate random numbers and compute the system's performance. The first inventory system that will be considered is the current order policy of 3500 gallons per week. For purposes of demonstration, step 5 is repeated here only 10 times to simulate 10 weeks. In reality, it should continue until the measure of performance (average weekly profit) achieves *stability*, as will be explained later in step 7. The detailed computations are shown in Table 3.7 and are executed as follows:

Column 1 designates the simulated week. In this example, only 10 weeks are simulated.

Column 2 is a list of random numbers (RNs), taken from a table of random numbers. Here, we are interested in two-digit numbers, so the first and second of a four-digit random number are used, starting with 32, then the next two digits, 08, and so on.

Column 3 represents inventory at the beginning of each week (I_b). The column is computed by adding the 3500-gallon shipment to the inventory at the end of the previous week (I_e). The *maximum inventory* is 5500 gallons, due to limited storage capacity. Thus, $I_b = I_e + 3500$ (up to 5500 as an upper limit).

Column 4 represents the forecasted demand, D, based on the RN in column 2 and the range of RNs in Table 3.6. For example, the first RN, 32, falls in the representative range of 13–35, which is equivalent to a weekly demand of 3000. Once the second column (RN) is generated, the entire fourth column can be computed quickly.

Column 5 represents the amount sold. Two cases may occur.

1. The demand, D, is equal to or smaller than the inventory of hand, I_b. In this case, sales equal demand (i.e., $S = D$ as in weeks 1, 2, 3, and 4).
2. Demand is *larger* than the inventory on hand. In this case, sales are limited to the inventory on hand, I_b (i.e., $S = I_b$). The difference between the demand and the inventory on hand, $D - I_b$, is thus the unsatisfied demand, U (column 7). For example, in week 5 there is a demand of 4000, but an inventory of 3500. Therefore, the sales are 3500 and there is an unsatisfied demand of 500.

In Column 6 the inventory at the end of each week, I_e, is listed. It is computed by subtracting the amount sold (column 5) from the beginning inventory (column 3), $I_e = I_b - S$.

Column 7 designates the unsatisfied demand, U. This column shows the difference between the demand and the beginning inventory whenever demand is larger (e.g., in week 5). Thus, $U = D - I_b$.

---

*In this case, a two-digit random number is used. If the probability of demand were given by three-digit figures, for example, 0.115 then three-digit random numbers would have to be used.

TABLE 3.7 The simulation for 10 weeks.

(1) Week number	(2) RN	(3) Inventory at beginning of week $I_b = I_e + 3500$	(4) Simulated demand D	(5) Sold S	(6) Inventory at end of week $I_e = I_b - S$	(7) Unsatisfied demand $U = D - I_b$	(8) Shipped back B	(9) Weekly profit	(10) Average weekly profit
1	32	3800	3000	3000	800			$ 300.00	$300.00
2	08	4300	2000	2000	2300			200.00	250.00
3	46	5500	4000	4000	1500		300	385.00	295.00
4	92	5000	5000	5000	0			500.00	346.25
5	69	3500	4000	3500	0	500		290.00	335.00
6	71	3500	4000	3500	0	500		290.00	327.50
7	29	3500	3000	3000	500			300.00	323.57
8	46	4000	4000	4000	0			400.00	333.12
9	80	3500	4000	3500	0	500		290.00	328.33
10	14	3500	3000	3000	500			300.00	325.50
Total	—	40,100	36,000	34,500	5600	1500	300	$3255.00	—
Average per week	—	4010	3600	3450	560	150	30	325.50	325.50

Column 8 designates the amount shipped back, *B*. Such a situation occurs when the "end-of-the-week inventory" plus the shipment (3500 gallons in the system under study) exceed the 5500-gallon tank capacity. In this case, the excess supply is shipped back and the beginning inventory is 5500. For example, in week 3, the shipment of 3500, added to the weekend inventory of week 2 of 2300, gives a total of 5800 gallons. Therefore, 5800 − 5500 = 300 gallons are shipped back.

Column 9: The measure of performance in this problem is profit. The profit is calculated, every week, according to the formula

$$\text{profit} = 0.10S - 0.12U - 0.05B$$

For example, in week 1: *S* = 3000, *U* = 0, Profit = 0.1(3000) = \$300. In week 3: *S* = 4000, *U* = 0, *B* = 300. Profit = 0.1(4000) − 0.05(300) = \$385.

Column 10: The *average* weekly profit at any week is computed by totaling the weekly profits up to that week (cumulative profit) and dividing it by the number of weeks. For example, in week 3: Cumulative profit = \$300 + \$200 + \$385 = \$885. The weekly average: \$885/3 = \$295.

Step 6: Computing the measures of performance. Each simulation run is composed of multiple *trials*. The question of how many trials to have in one run (or finding the *length* of the run) involves statistical analysis. The longer the run, the more accurate are the results, but the higher the cost. This issue concerns what is labeled as *stopping rules*. The stopping rules are usually built into the simulation program. For example, the run could be terminated when a desired standard error in the measures of performance is attained. These measures are computed continuously during the simulation, since they determine stability and the stopping time.

The simulation performed thus far indicated an average weekly profit of \$325.50. In addition to total profit, the following measures of performance can be computed:

1. *The probability of running short and the average shortage.* In 3 out of the 10 weeks there was an unsatisfied demand. Therefore, there is a 3/10 = 30 percent chance of running out of stock. The average shortage, per week, is 1500/10 = 150 gallons.
2. *The probability of shipping back and the average quantity shipped back.* In 1 out of the 10 weeks some gasoline was shipped back. On the average there is 1/10 = 10 percent chance of shipping back; the average amount is 300/10 = 30 gallons per week.
3. *The average demand.* The average weekly demand is computed as 3600, which is close to the expected value of the demand (from Table 3.6, of 3700. (In a stabilized process, these two numbers will be very close.)
4. *The average beginning inventory* is computed as 4010 gallons.
5. *The average weekly sales* are computed as 3450 gallons.
6. *The average ending inventory* is computed as 560 gallons.

Step 7: Stabilization of the simulation process. Simulation begins to represent reality only after stabilization has been achieved. Examination of column 10 in Table 3.7 indicates that the process, although close to stabilizing, has not yet stabilized; that is, the *average* weekly profit is still fluctuating. Notice, however, that after six weeks, the differences are becoming very small.

Step 8: Find the best ordering policy. Steps 5, 6, and 7 are now repeated for other ordering policies in order to find the best. In the example just presented, the ordered quantity was 3500; other values (e.g., 3300, 3700, 4000) should next be considered. Each quantity constitutes an independent system for which the various measures of effectiveness such as average profit, average sales, and unsatisfied demand are computed. Each such experiment is called a *simulation run*. The best results seem to occur at about 4100 gallons.

3.6 Heuristic Programming

The determination of optimal solutions to some complex decision problems could involve a prohibitive amount of time and cost, or it may even be an impossible task. In such situations, it is sometimes possible to arrive at *satisfactory* solutions more quickly and less expensively by using *heuristics*.

While heuristics are used primarily for solving ill-structured problems, they can also be used to provide satisfactory solutions to certain complex, well-structured problems much more quickly and cheaply than algorithms. The main difficulty in using heuristics is that they are not as general as algorithms. Therefore, they can normally be used only for the specific situation for which they were intended. Another problem with heuristics is that they may result in a poor specific solution.

Heuristic programming is the approach of employing heuristics to arrive at feasible and "good enough" solutions to such complex problems. "Good enough" is usually in the range of 90–99.9 percent of the true optimal solution.

In studying examples of applied heuristic programming, one can observe the attempt to reduce the amount of search for a satisfactory solution. In such a search, the computer is "taught" how to explore only relatively fertile paths and ignore relatively sterile ones. The computer choices are made by using heuristics that can be improved in the course of the search.

Methodology*

Heuristic thinking does not necessarily proceed in a direct manner. It involves searching, learning, evaluating, judging and then again searching, relearning, and reappraisal as exploring and probing take place. The knowledge gained from success or failure at some point is fed back and modifies the search process. More often than not, it is necessary either to redefine the objectives or the problem, or to solve related or simplified problems before the primary one can be solved.

Heuristic methods have been described by Pearl (19) based on intelligent search strategies for computer problem solving using split and prune methods, repetitive splitting, branch and bound algorithms, state space graphs, logical reasoning, and sampling.

---

*Based on Rowe (21).

The heuristic procedure has been described as finding rules that help to solve intermediate problems; to discover how to set up these problems for final solution by finding the most promising paths in the search for solutions; finding ways to retrieve and interpret information on each experience; and then finding the methods that lead to a computational algorithm or general solution. The term heuristic has been used to include any and all of these steps.

Thus, heuristic reasoning is not regarded as final and strict but as provisional and plausible only, whose purpose is to discover an approach that will lead to a general solution. Intermediate solutions that make use of information previously learned and that are plausible are indicators of progress; while the absence of these indicators warn of blind alleys and their presence focuses on the high payoff areas. However, to interpret these indicators correctly, it takes both experience and judgment.

A logical approach to heuristic rules incorporates:

1. A classification scheme that introduces structure into a problem.
2. Analysis of the characteristics of the problem elements.
3. Rules for selecting elements from each category to achieve efficient search strategies.
4. Rules for successive selections, where required.
5. An objective function that is used to test the adequacy of the solution at each stage of selection or search.

Problems in Using Heuristics

Geoffrion[*] identifies the following shortcomings of heuristics:

1. Enumeration heuristics that consider all possible combinations, in practical problems can seldom be achieved.
2. Sequential decision choices can fail to anticipate future consequences of each choice.
3. "Local improvement" can short circuit the best solution because heuristics lacks a global perspective.
4. Interdependencies of one part of a system can sometimes have a profound influence on the whole system.

Goeffrion maintains that "common sense approaches and heuristics can fail because they are *arbitrary*. They are arbitrary in the choice of a starting point, in the sequence in which assignments or other decision choices are made, in the resolution of ties, in the choice of criteria for specifying the procedure, in the level of effort expended to demonstrate that the final solution is in fact best or very nearly so. The result is erratic and unpredictable behavior—good performance in some specific applications and bad in others."

He also expressed concern about a more profound weakness of heuristics in the planning process. It is precisely this kind of problem that requires more

[*]Geoffrion, A. M., and Van Roy, T. J. "Caution: Common Sense Planning Methods Can Be Hazardous to Your Corporate Health." *Sloan Management Review*, 1979.

robust heuristics that utilize both the analytic and the intuitive capability of decision makers. He sees a critical need to *solve* planning problems under several alternative sets of assumptions. Consequently, the ability to ask "what if" questions is more important than finding a so-called optimum plan. The reasons can be summarized as follows:

1. The planning team has to come up with good recommendations, and also convincing justification to gain acceptance of the plan.
2. It is important to work simultaneously with more than one set of assumptions.
3. It is important to compare solutions under different sets of assumptions.

When to Use Heuristics (per Zanakis And Evans [25])

The following are some scenarios where the use of heuristics (instead of optimization) is appropriate:

1. The input data are inexact or limited.
2. Reality is so complex that the optimization model is oversimplified.
3. A reliable, exact method is not available.
4. The computation time of optimization is too excessive.
5. It is possible to improve the efficiency of the optimization process (e.g., by producing good starting solutions using heuristics).
6. Problems that are being solved frequently (and repeatedly) and consume computer time.
7. Complex problems that are not economical for optimization or take too long a time and the heuristic can improve the noncomputerized solution.
8. When symbolic rather than numerical processing is involved.

Advantages of Heuristics

The major advantages of heuristics are that they:

1. Are simple to understand and therefore are easier to implement.
2. Help in training people to be creative and come up with heuristics for other problems.
3. Save formulation time.
4. Save programming and storage requirements on the computers.
5. Save computer running time (speed!).
6. Produce multiple solutions.

For further discussion see Zanakis and Evans (25). For a categorized survey with several hundred references see Zanakis et al. (26).

With the reduction in cost of using computers, there is an increased tendency to use heuristics as an alternative to optimization methods. Heuristics can be fun to develop and use. What is required is an understanding of the nature of the problem and some ingenuity, as illustrated in the following example:

The Traveling Salesperson Problem (TSP)

The Problem. A traveling salesperson must visit N cities in a territory. The salesperson starts from a base and visits each city once, returning to his or her home city at the end. The TSP attempts to find out the best route (in terms of least cost, or least distance).

The Difficulty. The number of routes (counting only one direction route) is
$$R = 0.5(N - 1)!$$
For 10 cities there are 181,440 routes, for 11 cities there are about 2 million different routes, and for 20 cities there are approximately 6.1×10^{16} routes. This is a typical combinatorial problem. With the addition of just a few more cities, the problem grows to an astronomical number of alternatives.

The Solutions. Complete enumeration and algorithms are inefficient or ineffective. Heuristic solutions provide good enough solutions, sometimes very quickly, as will be shown in the following examples. *Note*: Neural computing (Chapter 22) may be the best approach in the future.

Heuristic Solutions. "Start at any city and move to the closest city. Continue until the last city is visited, then return to the original city."

Another heuristic is shown in Figure 3.3. This time the solution has been derived in a single iteration. The heuristic is: "Start from any point, build up an *exterior* path, with no crossovers or backtracking, and return to the original city."

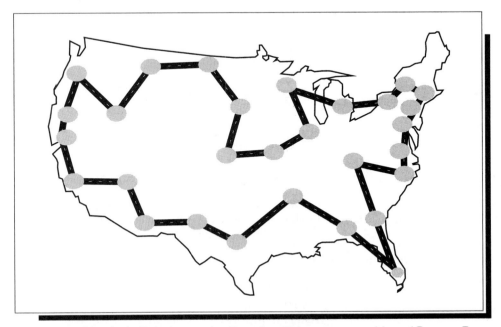

FIGURE 3.3 Heuristic Solution to the Traveling Salesperson problem. (*Source:* Rowe [21])

3.7   **Influence Diagrams**

An influence diagram provides a graphical presentation of a quantitative model. It provides a visual communication to the model builder. It also serves as a framework for expressing the exact nature of the relationship within the MSS model. The term *influence* refers to the dependency of a variable on the level of another variable. An influence diagram maps all the variables in a decision problem.

Influence diagrams appear in several shapes. We will use the following convention, suggested by Bodily (3):

Rectangle = a decision variable

Circle = uncontrollable or intermediate variable

Oval = result (outcome) variable; intermediate or final

The variables are connected with arrows, which indicate the direction of the influence. The shape of the arrow also indicates the type of relationship. The following are typical relationships:

1. Certainty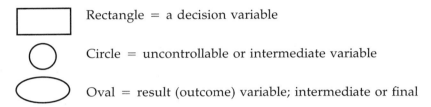

2. Uncertainty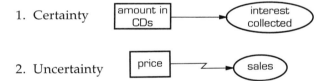

3. Random variable: place ~ above the variable's name.

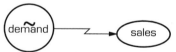

4.   Preference (usually between outcome variables). This is shown as a double-line arrow.

Arrows can be one way or two-way (bidirectional).

Influence diagrams can be constructed at any degree of detail and sophistication. It enables the model builder to remember *all* the relationships in the model, as well as the direction of the influence.

Example.   Given a model:

Income = units sold × unit price
Units sold = 0.5 × amount used in advertisement
Expense = unit cost × units sold + fixed cost
Profit = income − expense

An influence diagram of this simple model is shown in Figure 3.4.

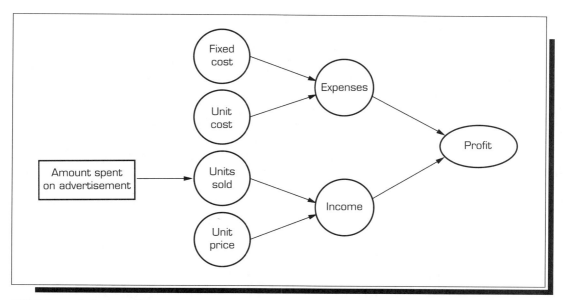

FIGURE 3.4 Influence Diagram

Software.   An influence diagram software product named David, is available from the Center for Academic Computing of Duke University. It is supported by a user's manual (written by Shachter). It helps the user to build, modify, and analyze models in an interactive graphical environment. Also, several computer graphic software and CASE packages can be used.

3.8 Forecasting

As the reader may recall, decision making involves choosing an alternative course of action by evaluating the possible consequences of the alternatives. Although the choice is made today, the possible consequences will occur some-time in the future. Therefore, the quality of the decision largely depends on the quality of the forecast.

Forecasting models are an integral part of many DSS. One can build a fore-cast model or one may use preprogrammed software packages. (See Chapter 6.) Many DSS development tools have some built-in forecasting capabilities.

The Uses of Forecasts

The major use of forecasting, as it relates to modeling, is to predict the value of the model input data, as well as the logical relationship of the model, at some time in the future. The future time of interest depends on "when" we want to evaluate the results. For example, in a regular investment decision we may be interested in prices a year from today, while in a capital investment decision we may be interested in projected prices during the next five years. Generally speaking, we distinguish between two types of forecasts: (a) short run (up to one year), where the forecast is used mainly in deterministic models and (b) long run (beyond one year), where the forecast is used in both deterministic and probabilistic models.

Forecasting Models and Methods

There exist many types of forecasting models because forecasting is an extremely difficult task. What is going to happen in the future depends, in many cases, on a multiplicity of factors, most of which are uncontrollable. Furthermore, data availability, accuracy, cost, and the time required to make the forecast also play an important role.

Forecasting methods can be grouped in several ways. One classification scheme distinguishes between formally recognized forecasting techniques (formal) and informal approaches such as intuition, spur-of-the-moment guesses, and seat-of-the-pants predictions. Our attention in this section is directed to the formal methods.

Formal methods can be divided into four categories: judgment methods, counting methods, time-series methods, and association or causal methods.

Each category is briefly discussed below. For a more detailed discussion see Georgoff and Murdick (9) and Makridakis and Wheelwright (18).

Judgment Methods. Judgment methods are those based on subjective estimates and expert opinion, rather than on hard data. They are often used for long-range forecasts, especially where external factors (e.g., technological or political developments) may play a significant role. They also are used where historical data are very limited or nonexistent, such as in new product/service introductions.

Counting Methods. Counting methods involve some kind of experimentations or surveys of a sample with an attempt to generalize about the entire market. These methods are primarily used for forecasting demand for products/services, a part of marketing research.

The next two types of forecasting methods are quantitative in nature. They are based on hard data and are thus generally considered more objective than the previous types. They typically use historical data and are commonly divided between time-series and causal methods.

Time-series Analysis. A time series is a set of values of some business or economic variable, measured at successive (usually equal) intervals of time. For example, quarterly sales of a firm make up a time series, as does the yearly growth of people in a city, the weekly demand for hospital beds, and so on. We undertake time-series analysis in decision making because we believe that knowledge of past behavior of the time series might help our understanding of (and therefore our ability to predict) the behavior of the series in the future. In some instances, such as the stock market, this assumption may be unjustified, but in managerial planning we assume that (to some extent, at least) history will repeat itself and that past tendencies will continue. Time-series analysis efforts conclude with the development of a *time-series forecasting model* that can then be used to predict future events.

Association or Causal Methods. Association or causal methods include data analysis for finding data associations and, if possible, cause-effect relationships. They are more powerful than the time-series methods, but they are also more complex. Their complexity comes from two sources. First, they include more variables, some of which are external to the situation. Second, they enjoy sophisticated statistical techniques for segregating the various types of variables. Causal approaches are most appropriate for midterm (between short and long-term) forecasting.

Generally speaking, judgment and counting methods, which are subjective in nature, are used in those cases where quantitative methods are inappropriate or cannot be used. Time pressure, lack of data, or lack of money may prevent the use of quantitative models. Complexity of historical data (due to interactions or fluctuations, for example) may also inhibit the use of hard data.

3.9 Conclusion

The description of modeling that was initiated in Chapter 2 has been expanded in this chapter focusing on four major types of models: Decision analysis, mathematical programming, simulation, and heuristic programming. In addition the technique of influence diagrams was described. This technique helps in visualizing the relationships among the various components of models. Finally, a brief overview of forecasting techniques was presented.

Key Words

blending problem	forecasting	optimization
decision trees	heuristic programming	random numbers
decision analysis	heuristics	simulation
dynamic models	influence diagrams	static models
enumeration	Monte Carlo	time-series analysis
environmental analysis		

Questions for Review and Discussion

1. Distinguish between built-in models and models that need to be built.
2. What is environmental analysis of MSS?
3. What is the difference between environmental analysis and environmental scanning?
4. What are the major issues in model selection?
5. What is the difference between built-in models and ready-made models that are not built-in?
6. What is complete enumeration?
7. Distinguish between a static and a dynamic model.
8. What is the difference between a decision analysis with a single goal and decision analysis with multiple goals (criteria)?
9. What is the difference between an optimistic approach and a pessimistic approach to decision making in uncertainty?
10. What is an expected value?
11. What is a decision tree?
12. What is an allocation problem?
13. Why is an allocation problem so difficult to solve?
14. List and briefly discuss the three major components of linear programming.

15. Describe the general process of simulation.
16. Describe the role of Monte Carlo in simulation.
17. List some of the major advantages of simulation over optimization.
18. List some advantages of optimization over simulation.
19. Give examples of three heuristics that you are familiar with.
20. What is heuristic programming?
21. What is an influence diagram? What is it used for?
22. Describe judgmental forecasting methods.
23. What is a time-series analysis?
24. What are causal forecasting models?

EXERCISES

1. Many managers know that a small percent of the customers contribute to most of the sales. Similarly most of the wealth in the world is concentrated in the hands of a few. This phenomenon is called the 20-80, the A-B-C, and the value-volume and it is attributed to the famous economist, Pareto. How can this phenomenon be used in the modeling? What kind of approach is this: optimization, simulation, or heuristic?

2. Assume that you know that there is one irregular coin (either lighter or heavier) among 12. Using a two-pen scale you must find that coin (Is it lighter or heavier?) in no more than three tests.

a. Solve this problem and explain the weighing strategy that you use.

b. What approach to problem solving is used in this case?

3. Simulate the inventory problem of Section 3.5 for a demand of 3800.

References and Bibliography

1. Ariav, A., and Ginzberg, M. J. "DSS Design: A Systematic View of Decision Support." *Communications of the ACM*, October 1985.

2. Banks, J., and J. S. Carson. *Discrete Event System Simulation.* Englewood Cliffs, NJ: Prentice-Hall, 1984.

3. Bodily, S. E. *Modern Decision Making.* New York, McGraw-Hill, 1985.

4. Courtney, J. E. Jr. et al. "A Knowledge-based DSS for Managerial Problem Diagnosis." *Decision Sciences*, Vol. 18, No. 3, 1987.

5. Davis, M. W. *Applied Decision Support.* Englewood Cliffs, NJ: Prentice-Hall, 1988.

6. De, Suranjan. "Providing Effective Decision Support Modeling." *Decision Support System*, December 1986.

7. Farnum, N. R., and Stanton, L. W. *Quantitative Forecasting Methods.* PWS-Kent, 1989.

8. Gavett, J. W. "Three Heuristic Rules for Sequencing Jobs to a Single Production Facility." *Management Science*, Vol. 11, 1965.

9. Georgoff, D. M., and R. G. Murdick. "Manager's Guide to Forecasting." *Harvard Business Review*, January–February 1986.

10. Gutierrez, O., and Tseng, V. P. "Problem Definition for Supporting Decision Making." *DSS 88-Transactions*, S. E., Weber ed., 1988.

11. Harrald, J. R., et al. "The Use of Influence Diagrams as a Design Tool For a Disaster Management Decision Support System." *DSS 88-Transactions*, S. E. Weber, ed., 1988.

12. Hertz, D. *Practical Risk Analysis.* New York: Wiley, 1983.

13. Houston, T. R. "Why Models Go Wrong." *Byte*, October 1985.

14. Hwang, C. L., and K. Yoon. *Multiple Attribute Decision Making: Methods and Applications: A State of the Art Survey.* New York: Springer-Verlag, 1981.

15. Jacoby, S. L. S., and J. S. Kowalik. *Mathematical Models with Computers.* Englewood Cliffs, NJ: Prentice-Hall, 1980.

16. Jeter, M. W. *Mathematical Programming—An Introduction to Optimization*. New York, Dekker, 1986.
17. Law, A. M., and W. D. Kelton, *Simulation Modeling and Analysis*. New York: McGraw-Hill, 1982.
18. Makridakis, S., and S. C. Wheelwright. *The Handbook of Forecasting: A Manager's Guide*. New York: Wiley, 1982.
19. Pearl, J. *Heuristics*. Reading, MA: Addison-Wesley, 1984.
20. Raiffa, H. *Decision Analysis*. Reading, MA: Addison-Wesley, 1970.
21. Rowe, A. J. "The Meta Logic of Cognitively Based Heuristics." Special Report, University of Southern California, April 1988.
22. Taylor, J., and W. Taylor "Searching for Solutions." *PC Magazine*, September 15, 1987.
23. Turban, E., and J. Meredith. *Fundamentals of Management Science*. Homewood, IL: Irwin, 5th ed. 1991.
24. Weber, E. Sue, and B. R. Konsynski. "Problem Management: Neglected Elements in Decision Support System." *JMIS*, Vol. 4, No. 64–81, Winter 1987–1988.
25. Zanakis, S. H., and J. R. Evans. "Heuristic Optimization: Why, When and How to Use It." *Interfaces*, October 1981.
26. Zanakis, S. H., et al. "Heuristic Methods and Applications: A Categorized Survey." *European Journal of Oper. Resc.*, June 1989.

Chapter 4

Decision Support Systems and Group DSS: An Overview

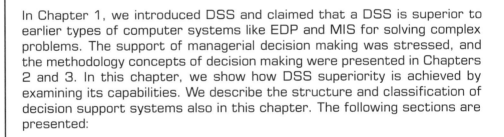

In Chapter 1, we introduced DSS and claimed that a DSS is superior to earlier types of computer systems like EDP and MIS for solving complex problems. The support of managerial decision making was stressed, and the methodology concepts of decision making were presented in Chapters 2 and 3. In this chapter, we show how DSS superiority is achieved by examining its capabilities. We describe the structure and classification of decision support systems also in this chapter. The following sections are presented:

4.1   The Case: Gotaas-Larsen
Shipping Corp. (GLSC)[*]

Strategic planning is one of the most difficult tasks of modern management. It involves all functional areas in an organization and several relevant outside factors, a fact that complicates the planning process, especially when one deals with the uncertainties of the long run. As such, strategic planning is clearly not a structured decision situation; therefore it is a potential candidate for DSS applications.

GLSC, a subsidiary of International Utilities (IU), operates cargo ships all over the world. The company developed a comprehensive decision support system for executing both short- and long-term planning in the mid-1970s. The system, like any other DSS, is composed of two major parts: data and models.

The data include both external data (port or canal characteristics, competitors' activities, and fares) and internal data (existing plans, availability of resources, and individual ships' characteristics). In addition, users can utilize their own data or express their attitudes (e.g., add their own risk preferences).

The models include routine standard accounting and financial analysis models (like cash flow computations and pro forma income and expenses) organized on a per ship, per voyage, per division, and per entire company basis. These models permit elaborate financial analyses. A simulation model is used to analyze short- and long-term plans and to evaluate the desirability of projects. In addition, the system interfaces with a commercially available time-sharing application program for analyzing individual voyages (time-charter analysis).

A highly decentralized, 15-month operational planning and control document is prepared within the framework of the long-term strategic plan. This 15-month document is used as the basis for detailed goal formation for the various ships and the individual voyages. A detailed monitoring and control mechanism is also provided, including a regular variance report and diagnostic analysis. In addition, a detailed performance tracking report is executed (by voyage, ship, division, and entire corporation).

Once the assessment of the opportunity of individual projects (such as buying a ship or contracting a voyage) is examined by a charter analysis, an aggregation is performed. The objective is to determine whether a series of individually profitable projects adds up to a feasible and effective long-range plan. The DSS utilizes a simulation model that examines various configurations of projects in an attempt to conduct a "fine tuning" of the aggregate plan. Specifically, when several projects are executed, the resources (like labor and finance) might be insufficient. Therefore modifications in scheduling and financial arrangements might be necessary. This fine tuning provides a trial-and-error approach to feasibility testing and sensitivity analyses. The "what if" capabilities of the DSS are especially important in this case. The strategic plan of GLSC is very detailed and accurate because of the contractual nature of both the sales

---

[*]For a complete description, see Alter (1).

and some of the expenses. The model is geared to a traditional business policy structure, which helps in assessing the threats and risks in the general operating environment and makes possible an examination of the impacts of new opportunities on existing plans.

The GLSC case is an example of a large-scale DSS. We will refer to this case in the forthcoming sections.

4.2 Introduction

The early definitions of a DSS identify it as a system intended to support managerial decision makers in semistructured decision situations. DSS were meant to be an adjunct to decision makers, to extend their capabilities but not to replace their judgment. They were aimed at decisions where judgment was required, decisions that could not be completely specified as an algorithm and turned over to a computer. Not specifically stated, but implied in the early definitions, was the notion that the system would be computer-based, would operate on-line, and preferably would have graphic-output capabilities.

The early definitions were open to several interpretations. Soon several other definitions appeared that occasioned considerable disagreement as to what a DSS is. Some skeptics even suggested that DSS was just another buzz word. The purpose of this chapter is to show that this is not the case, and that there is a significant amount of content behind the label DSS. To do so we present the essential characteristics that could help in determining whether a system is a DSS or not. Also, the structure of DSS will be presented as well as the various types of systems. Let us begin by reviewing some definitions (based on Ginzberg and Stohr [7]) and then delve into the DSS content and structure.

4.3 What Is a DSS?

A refinement of Gorry and Scott-Morton's DSS definition was provided by Little (16), who defines DSS as a "model-based set of procedures for processing data and judgments to assist a manager in his decision making." He argues that in order to be successful, such a system must be (1) simple, (2) robust, (3) easy to control, (4) adaptive, (5) complete on important issues, and (6) easy to communicate with. Implicit in this definition, too, is the assumption that the system is computer-based and serves as an extension of the user's problem-solving capabilities.

Throughout most of the 1970s, definitions of DSS, like those just presented, were accepted by practitioners and researchers. By the end of the decade, however, new definitions began to emerge. Alter (1) defines DSS by contrasting them with traditional EDP systems on five dimensions, as shown in Table 4.1.

Three other definitions of DSS are offered by Moore and Chang (19), Bonczek, Holsapple, and Whinston (3), and Keen (13). Moore and Chang argue

TABLE 4.1 DSS vs. EDP.

Dimension	DSS	EDP
Use	Active	Passive
User	Line and staff management	Clerical
Goal	Effectiveness	Mechanical efficiency
Time Horizon	Present and future	Past
Objective	Flexibility	Consistency

that the "structuredness" concept, so much a part of early DSS definitions (i.e., that DSS can handle semistructured and unstructured situations), is not meaningful in general; a problem can be described as structured or unstructured only with respect to a particular decision maker (i.e., structured decisions are structured because we choose to treat them as such). Thus, they define DSS as (1) extendable systems, (2) capable of supporting ad hoc data analysis and decision modeling, (3) oriented toward future planning, and (4) used at irregular, unplanned intervals.

Note: Computerized systems for decision support are being developed today by end-users on microcomputers for dealing with fairly structured problems. The advantage here is that the user can build systems with little or no help from information systems people.

Bonczek et al. (3) define a DSS as a computer-based system consisting of three interacting components: (1) a language system—a mechanism to provide communication between the user and other components of the DSS, (2) a knowledge system—the repository of problem domain knowledge embodied in DSS, either as data or procedures, and (3) a problem-processing system—the link between the other two components, containing one or more of the general problem-manipulatory capabilities required for decision making.

Note: The concepts provided by this definition are important for understanding the structures of DSS and ES and the interrelationship between the two technologies.

Finally, Keen (13) applies the term DSS "to situations where a 'final' system can be developed only through an *adaptive process* of learning and *evolution.*" Thus, he defines DSS as the product of a developmental process in which the DSS user, the DSS builder, and the DSS itself are all capable of influencing one another, resulting in an evolution of the system and the pattern of its use.

These definitions are compared and contrasted by examining the types of concepts each employs to define DSS (see Table 4.2). It seems that the basis for defining DSS has been developed from the perceptions of what a DSS does (e.g., support decision making in unstructured problems) and from ideas about how the DSS's objective can be accomplished (e.g., components required, appropriate usage pattern, and the necessary development processes).

One result of these definitions is a narrowing of the population of systems that each author would identify as DSS. For example, Keen would exclude systems built without following an evolutionary strategy, and Moore and Chang would exclude systems used at regular, planned intervals to support decisions

TABLE 4.2 Concepts Underlying DSS Definitions.

Source	DSS Defines in Terms of
Gorry and Scott-Morton (8)	Problem type, system function (support)
Little (16)	System function, interface characteristics
Alter (1)	Usage pattern, system objectives
Moore and Chang (19)	Usage pattern, system capabilities
Bonczek et al. (3)	System components
Keen (14)	Development process

about current operations. The narrowing of a population is indeed a proper function of a definition. By dealing with a smaller population of objects, we can identify those characteristics that the population members have in common, as well as characteristics that differentiate one population from another.

Unfortunately, the definitions above of DSS do not provide a consistent focus, because each tries to narrow the population in a different way. Furthermore, they collectively ignore the central issue in DSS; that is, support and improvement of decision making. There seems to have been a retreat from the consideration of outputs, and a focus on the inputs instead. A very likely reason for this change in emphasis is the difficulty of measuring the outputs of a DSS (e.g., decision quality). Although such measurement difficulties no doubt exist, they must not be used as an excuse for ignoring what should be our central concern.

Working Definition

A DSS is an interactive, flexible, and adaptable CBIS that utilizes decision rules, models, and model base coupled with a comprehensive database and the decision maker's own insights, leading to specific, implementable decisions in solving problems that would *not* be amenable to management science optimization models per se. Thus, a DSS supports complex decision making and increases its effectiveness.

This working definition is used as a guideline throughout this book for analyzing and discussing issues like the next topic: the characteristics common to an ideal DSS.

4.4 Characteristics and Capabilities of DSS

Note: Because there is no consensus on what a DSS is, there is obviously no agreement on the characteristics and capabilities of DSS. Therefore we label the forthcoming list as an ideal set. Most DSS have only some of the items on the list.

1. DSS provides support for decision makers mainly in semistructured and unstructured situations by bringing together human judgment and computerized information. Such problems cannot be solved (or cannot be solved conveniently) by other computerized systems, such as EDP or MIS, nor by management science.
2. Support is provided for various managerial levels, ranging from top executives to line managers.
3. Support is provided to individuals as well as to groups. Many organizational problems involve group decision making. The less structured problems frequently require the involvement of several individuals from different departments and organizational levels. DSS assist integration among individuals whenever appropriate.
4. DSS provides support to several interdependent and/or sequential decisions. (See Section 4.11 for definitions.)
5. DSS supports all phases of the decision-making process: intelligence, design, choice, and implementation.
6. DSS supports a variety of decision-making processes and styles; there is a fit between the DSS and the attributes of the individual decision makers (e.g., the vocabulary and decision style).
7. DSS must be adaptive over time. The decision maker should be reactive, being able to confront changing conditions and adapt DSS to meet these changes. DSS must be flexible so users can add, delete, combine, change, or rearrange basic elements (providing fast response to unexpected situations). This capability makes possible timely, quick, ad hoc analyses.
8. DSS should be easy to use. Users must feel "at home" with the system. User-friendliness, flexibility, strong graphic capabilities, and an English-like dialog language can greatly increase the effectiveness of DSS. This ease of use implies an interactive mode.
9. DSS attempts to improve the effectiveness of decision making (accuracy, timeliness, quality), rather than its efficiency (cost of making the decision, including the charges for computer time).
10. The decision maker has complete control over all steps of the decision-making process in solving a problem. A DSS specifically aims to support and not to replace the decision maker. The decision maker can override the computer's recommendation at any time of the process.
11. DSS leads to learning, which leads to new demands and the refinement of the system, which leads to additional learning, and so forth, in a continuous process of developing and improving the DSS.
12. DSS should be easy to construct. End-users should be able to construct simple systems by themselves. Larger systems could be built in users' organizations with only minor assistance from information systems (IS) or information center specialists.

These capabilities and characteristics, summarized in Figure 4.1, are provided by three major components of DSS, which are presented next.

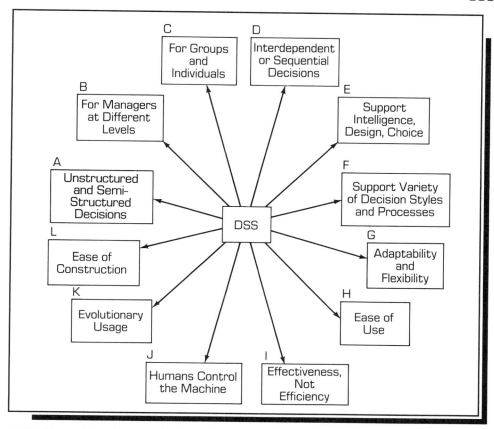

FIGURE 4.1 The characteristics and capabilities of DSS.

4.5   Components of DSS

A DSS is composed of the following:

1. Data Management. The data management includes the database(s), which contains relevant data for the situation and is managed by software called database management systems (DBMS).
2. Model Management. A software package that includes financial, statistical, management science, or other quantitative models that provide the system's analytical capabilities, and an appropriate software management.
3. Communication (dialog) subsystem. The subsystem through which the user can communicate with and command the DSS.

These components constitute the software portion of the DSS. They are housed in a computer and could be facilitated by additional hardware pieces (peripherals). Finally, the manager or user is considered to be a part of the system. Researchers assert that some of the unique contributions of DSS are derived from the interaction between the computer and the decision maker.

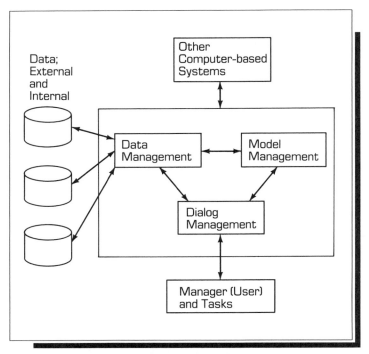

FIGURE 4.2 Conceptual model of DSS.

A conceptual model of the DSS is given in Figure 4.2. It provides a basic understanding of the general structure and components of a DSS. A more detailed look at each of the components is given in the forthcoming sections.

4.6   The Data Management Subsystem

The data management subsystem is composed of the following elements:

□ DSS database.
□ Database management system.
□ Data directory.
□ Query facility.

These elements are shown schematically in Figure 4.3 (inside the broken lines). The figure also shows the interaction of the data management subsystem with the other parts of the DSS, as well as the interaction with several data sources. A brief discussion of these elements and their function follows.

The Database

A *database* is a collection of interrelated data organized in such a way that it corresponds to the needs and structure of an organization and can be used by

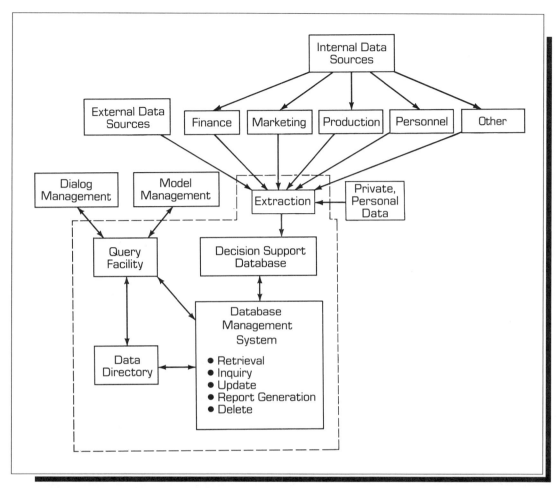

FIGURE 4.3 The data management subsystem.

more than one person for more than one application. In order to understand better what a database is, let us consider information kept in separate files.

A file traditionally contains information regarding one application. For example, a company may have a personnel file listing all employees, a customer file listing all customers, and so on. Such files may contain extensive information such as addresses, telephone numbers, and volume of purchases for each customer. In a computerized system, a file can be on an auxiliary storage device, such as a tape or disk.

Example. Let us assume that a company has four files: a parts inventory file, a product file, a parts usage file (quantity used), and a customer file. Although each file has a different purpose, the data within the files are interrelated. For example, the parts usage file is required in preparing the monthly inventory report. And the purchasing data of products recorded in the customer files are used to compute the products' projected monthly demand.

In addition to routine reports, management may require special reports from time to time (called *ad hoc reports*) based on information available in two or more files. In some companies, as much as 80 percent of all reporting is ad hoc and special analysis. In the past, programmers and system analysts had to sort files, create new programs, and manipulate data to meet management's needs, usually at tremendous cost. These needs are now being met quickly and inexpensively by the database and its management. Many times, users can create the reports by themselves.

The data in the database are stored together with a minimum of redundancy to serve multiple applications, so the database is independent of the computer program that uses it and the type of hardware where it is stored. The database is organized so that the firm's files still exist, but they are linked in certain ways so that they form an integrated unit. This arrangement is very important when information is updated. In addition, there could be a considerable savings of storage space.

The data in the DSS database, as shown in Figure 4.3, may include internal transactions, other internal data sources, external data, and private (personal) data belonging to one or more users.

Internal data come from the organization's transaction processing (or data processing) system. Depending on the needs of the DSS, data from functional areas like accounting, finance, marketing, production, and personnel might be included. Transaction data are the major source of information regarding internal company operations. A typical example of such data is the monthly payroll.

Other internal data might also be important to the DSS. Examples include planned dividend rates, machine maintenance scheduling, forecasts of future sales, cost of out-of-stock items, and future hiring plans.

External data may include industry data, marketing research data, census data, regional employment data, government regulations, tax rate schedules, or national economic data. These data might come from the U.S. government, trade associations, marketing research firms, econometric forecasting firms, and the organization's own efforts in collecting external data. Like internal data, the external data may be permanently maintained in the DSS database or may be entered when the DSS is used. External data are provided, in many cases, by computerized online services, a topic that will be discussed later.

Private data may include rules of thumb used by specific decision makers and assessments of specific data and/or situations.

An example of a DSS database for a bank is shown in Figure 4.4.

Organization. The data in the database can be organized in different configurations. For details see Appendix A.

Should a DSS have an independent database? Most large DSS have their own fully integrated, multiple-source DSS database. The major advantages and disadvantages of a separate database are summarized as follows.

Advantages:

1. A greater control exists over the data.
2. A better fit exists with the software that manages the database.
3. Most organizational databases are oriented toward transaction processing; therefore a separate database may be more efficient for a DSS.

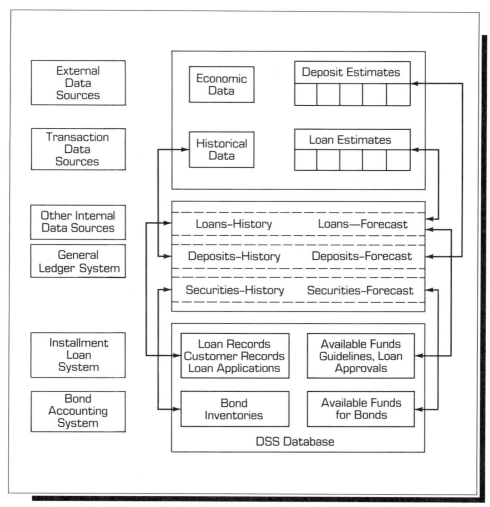

FIGURE 4.4 A DSS database for a bank. (*Source*: Sprague and Watson [24], Fig. 5, p. 665.)

4. Changes and updates are faster, easier, and cheaper.
5. Easier access and data manipulation are provided.
6. Can adopt a database structure that is optimal for DSS use (like relational).

Disadvantages:

1. A second database is more expensive to build, secure, and maintain than one database.
2. Separate databases can be individually modified by each user. If redundant data are stored in different places, and if the data are modified differently, we may have inconsistent data in the organization. A separate DSS database does not have to be physically separated from the corporate database. It can be located at the same place as the corpo-

rate database for economic reasons. It also can be merged with other databases (see Figure 4.5).

Extraction. In order to create a DSS database it is often necessary to capture data from several sources. This operation is called *extraction*. It is basically importing of files, summarization, filtration, and condensation of data. Extraction also occurs when the user produces reports from the data in the DSS database. The extraction process is managed by the database management system (DBMS).

Database Management System

The database is created, accessed, and updated by a set of software programs called DBMS, ranging in price from $99 for a microcomputer version to $100,000 for complex mainframe software. DBMS have varied capabilities and are fairly complex so that only a few users can program and develop their own DBMS software. Instead, usually a standard software package is purchased. Examples of micro DBMS are dBASE IV, R base 5000, and ORACLE. These and other commercial packages are presented in Chapter 6. The data management capabilities are provided by a set of software programs and are sometimes supported by special hardware and/or communication components.

A DBMS performs three basic functions. It enables storage of data in the database, retrieval of data from the database, and control of the database.

Storage. DBMS vary in the configuration of the stored data. Mainframe systems store many large files, each file containing many records, each record containing many data items, and the data items containing many characters. The systems for microcomputers offer more constrained capacities because of limited primary and secondary storage space. (This limitation is becoming less and less of a factor).

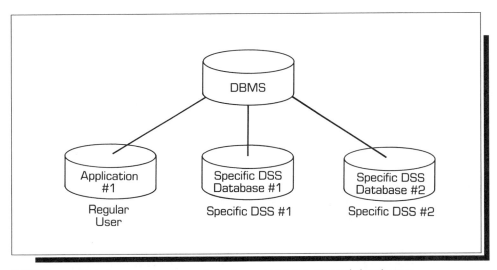

FIGURE 4.5 Database management system manages several databases.

The Capabilities of DBMS in a DSS

- □ Captures/extracts data for inclusion in a DSS database.
- □ Quickly updates (adds, deletes, edits, changes) data records and files.
- □ Interrelates data from different sources.
- □ Quickly retrieves data from a database for queries and reports.
- □ Provides comprehensive data security (protection from unauthorized access, recovery capabilities, etc.).
- □ Handles personal and unofficial data so that users can experiment with alternatives based on their own judgment.
- □ Performs complex retrieval and data manipulation tasks based on queries.
- □ Tracks usage of data.

Retrieval. The feature of the DBMS most visible to the user is data retrieval. Current DBMSs offer great flexibility in terms of how the information is retrieved and displayed. With a sophisticated DBMS, the user can specify certain processing of data and customize the output (e.g., reports or graphs) in terms of heading and spacing.

Control. Much of the control activity of the DBMS is invisible to users. They ask for some information and receive it without knowing the processes that the DBMS has performed. The DBMS can be designed to screen each request for information and determine that (1) the person making the request is indeed an authorized user, (2) the person has access to the requested file, and (3) the person has access to the requested data items in the file. A mainframe DBMS might perform all the control functions very well. The micro DBMS may perform some. This is an area of great variety among the various DBMS products on the market.

The manager can obtain information from the DSS in the form of periodic reports, special reports, and output of mathematical models. In all three of these instances, the DBMS serves as a gatekeeper and makes the data available (see Figure 4.6). The periodic reports are frequently prepared by application programs. These programs make requests of the DBMS for data needed from the database. The DBMS might offer a query language that can be manipulated by the user to create special reports. The user enters a few instructions, and this is all that is needed to trigger the preparation of a report. Mathematical models may also obtain their data from the database, and the data are provided by the DBMS.

Each application program, query request, and mathematical model is used to support the manager in some way as decisions are made and problems are solved. The DBMS provides the all-important link between the DSS and the database.

An effective database and its management can provide support for many managerial activities; general navigation among records, support for a diverse set of data relationships, and report generation are typical examples. However, the real power of the DSS is provided when the database is integrated with models.

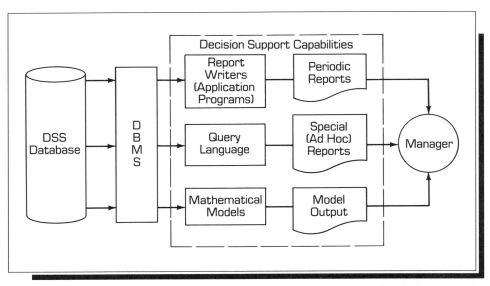

FIGURE 4.6 The role of DBMS. (*Source:* Adapted from McLeod [17]. Reprinted by permission. Copyright ©1985 by Science Research Associates, Inc.)

The Query Facility

This element provides the basis for access to data. It accepts requests for data (from other DSS components; see Figure 4.3), determines how these requests can be filled (consulting, if necessary, the data directory), formulates the detailed requests, and returns the results to the issuer of the request. The query facility includes a special query language. Important functions of a DSS query system are the "selection" and "manipulation" operations. For example, the ability to follow an instruction such as "search for all sales in zone *B* during January 1988 and summarize sales by salesperson."

The Directory (Dictionary)

The data directory is a catalog of all the data in the database. It contains the data definitions, and its main function is to answer questions about the availability of data items, their source, or their exact meaning. The directory is especially appropriate for supporting the intelligence phase of the decision-making process by helping to scan data and identify problem areas or opportunities. The directory, as does any other catalog, supports the addition of new entries, deletion of entries, and retrieval of information on entries.

4.7   The Model Management Subsystem

The model management subsystem of the DSS is composed of the following elements:

□ Model base.
□ Model base management system.

□ Model directory.
□ Model execution, integration, and command.

These elements and their interface with the other DSS components are shown in Figure 4.7.

The definition and function of each of these elements will now be described.

Model Base

A model base contains routine and special statistical, financial, management science, and other quantitative models that provide the analysis capabilities in a DSS. The ability to invoke, run, change, combine, and inspect models is a key capability in DSS that differentiates it from the traditional CBIS. The models in the model base can be divided into four major categories: strategic, tactical, operational, and model building blocks and subroutines.*

Strategic models are used to support top management's strategic planning responsibilities. Potential applications include developing corporate objectives, planning for mergers and acquisitions, plant location selection, environmental impact analysis, and nonroutine capital budgeting. Strategic models tend to

*The details of these are based on Kroeber and Watson (15).

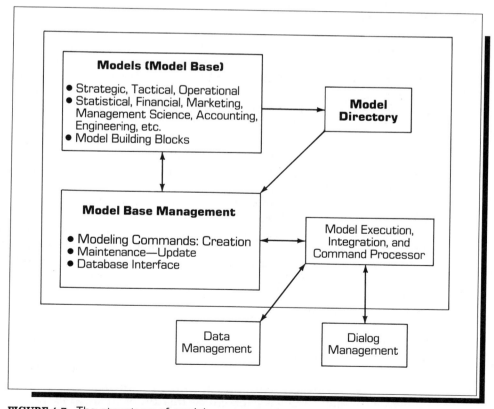

FIGURE 4.7 The structure of model management.

be broad in scope with many variables expressed in a compressed form. The time horizons for these models are expressed in years. The models tend to be of a descriptive (simulation) type rather than of an optimization nature. The GLSC case includes a long-range planning model. For details regarding planning models, see Naylor (20).

Tactical models are employed mainly by middle management to assist in allocating and controlling the organization's resources. Examples of tactical models include labor requirement planning, sales promotion planning, plant layout determination, and routine capital budgeting. Tactical models are usually applicable only to an organizational subsystem like the accounting department. Their time horizon varies from one month to less than two years. Some external data are needed, but the greatest requirements are for internal data. Some tactical models include optimization capabilities while others are descriptive in nature. The GLSC case includes mainly tactical models for their 15-month plan.

Operational models are used to support the day-to-day working activities of the organization. Approving personal loans by a bank, production scheduling, inventory control, maintenance planning and scheduling, and quality control are all examples of operational areas with potential DSS application. Operational models support mainly first-line managers' decision making with a daily to monthly time horizon. The models normally use internal data and sometimes include optimization features.

In addition to strategic, tactical, and operational models, the model base could contain model building blocks and subroutines. Examples include a "random number generator mechanism," "curveline fitting routine," "present-value computational routine," or "regression analysis." Such building blocks can be used in several ways. They can be used on their own for applications like data analysis. They can also be employed as components of larger models. For example, a present-value component can be part of a "make or buy" model. Some of these building blocks are used to determine the values of variables and parameters in a model, as in the use of regression analysis to create trend lines in a forecasting model.

The models in the model base can also be classified by functional areas (e.g., financial models, production control models) or by discipline (e.g., statistical models, management science allocation models). A list of representative models is given in Appendix B. The number of models in a DSS can vary from a few to several hundred. For example, a DSS for a large transportation company includes over 175 models (see Oliff [22]).

DSS holds the potential for reducing or eliminating several typical problems associated with the use of conventional quantitative models in decision making. One such problem is the difficulty of keeping models up-to-date. An all too common situation has been one in which model builders create a model, turn it over to users, and then move on to other projects. Because no easy way exists in a traditional system for updating and changing models, the models eventually become obsolete. Then one of two unfortunate conditions occur. Either the user stops using the model or the user continues to use the model, while the model's output is no longer valid. With a well-thought-out DSS, users have the capability of updating and changing the models by themselves.

Another major problem with quantitative models has been the lack of integration among models. To reduce this problem, models need to be able to "talk" to one another. With a DSS approach to modeling, this integration is accomplished with the help of a software system called model base management system (MBMS), which is presented in the next section. The models feed their output to the database, which makes the output from each model available to all other models. The MBMS also facilitates entering and extracting model output in and out of the database. Other problems that are typical of quantitative models and that could be eliminated by using DSS are inadequate tools to support model development, output in a form that is difficult to use, inflexible inputs and outputs, and lack of support for user understanding of large (complex) models.

The Model Base Management System (MBMS)

The model base management system is a software system with the following functions: model creation, using subroutines and other building blocks; generation of new routines and reports; model updating and changing; and data manipulation. The MBMS is capable of interrelating models with the appropriate linkages through a database.

The Model Directory

The role of the model directory is similar to that of a database directory. It is a catalog of all the models in the model base. It contains the model definitions, and its main function is to answer questions about the availability and capability of the models.

An interesting issue in a DSS might be "Which model should be used for what occasion?" Model selection cannot be done by the MBMS because it requires expertise; it is a potential area for an expert system "assisting" in the DSS. This issue is discussed in Chapter 19.

The Major Functions (or Capabilities) of the MBMS

- Ability to create models easily and quickly, either from scratch or from existing models or from the building blocks.
- Ability to allow users to manipulate the models so that they can conduct experiments and sensitivity analyses ranging from "what if" to "goal seeking."
- Capability of storing and managing a wide variety of different types of models in a logical and integrated manner.
- Ability to access and integrate the model building blocks.
- Ability to catalog and display the directory of models for use by several individuals in the organization.
- Tracking of models, data, and application usage.
- Interrelate models with appropriate linkages through the database.
- Manage and maintain the model base with management functions analogous to database management: store, access, run, update, link, catalog, and query.

Model Execution, Integration, and Command

The following activities are usually controlled by model management:

- ☐ Model execution—controlling the actual running of the model.
- ☐ Model integration—combining the operations of several models when needed (e.g., directing the output of one model to be processed by another one). Especially important is the use of semantics in model integration. This topic is further discussed in Chapter 19.

A modeling command processor is used to accept and interpret modeling instructions as they flow out of the dialog component, and to route them to the MBMS, the model execution, or to the integration functions.

The execution of computations with the models requires retrieval of data items from the database. This activity is performed through a database interface. The model management is accessed via the dialog subsystem.

4.8   The User Interface (Dialog) Subsystem

The dialog component of a DSS is the software and hardware that provides the user interface for DSS. The term *user interface* covers all aspects of the communications between a user and the DSS. It includes not only the hardware and software, but also factors that deal with ease of use, accessibility, and human-machine interactions. Some DSS experts feel that user interface is the most important component because much of the power, flexibility, and ease-of-use characteristics of DSS are derived from this component (e.g., Sprague and Carlson [23, p. 29]). An inconvenient user interface is one of the major reasons why managers have not used computers and quantitative analyses to the extent that these technologies have been available.

A definition of the content of a dialog system is provided by Bennett (2), who divided the system into three components: terminal, software, and user. In addition he divided the dialog process itself into the following three parts: action language, display, and knowledge base.

1. The action language is what the user can do to communicate with the system. It includes such data input options as the use of a regular keyboard, function keys, touch panels, mouse, joystick, voice activation, and an optical reader for typed or written material.
2. The display or presentation language is what the user sees or hears. The display language includes options such as a character or line printer, a display screen, graphics, plotters, and audio output. A variety of studies have shown that the type of output provided has an impact on the quality of the decisions made and on the user's perception of the system (see Dickson et al. [5]). It is important to provide output that is appropriate for the users of the systems and for the decisions being supported.
3. The knowledge base includes the information that the user must know. The knowledge base consists of what the user needs to bring to the session with the system in order to use it effectively. The knowledge

may be in the user's head, on a reference card or instruction sheet, in a user manual, or in a series of "help" outputs available on request.

Note: This definition of a knowledge base differs considerably from the term used to describe the storage of knowledge in an expert system (Chapter 12).

Dialog Styles. The effectiveness of the interface depends on the strength and variety of capabilities in each of the dialog elements just presented. Combinations of these elements comprise what might be called a *dialog style*. Dialog styles determine how the DSS is directed and what the DSS requires as an input and provides as output. Dialog styles are described in detail in Chapter 18.

Management of the Dialog Subsystem

The dialog subsystem is managed by software called dialog generation and management software (DGMS). The DGMS is composed of several programs that provide the following capabilities:

□ Interacts in several different dialog styles.
□ Captures, stores, and analyzes dialog usage (tracking), which can be used for improving the dialog system.
□ Accommodates the user with a variety of input devices.
□ Presents data with a variety of formats and output devices.
□ Users are given "help" capabilities, prompting, diagnostic and suggestion routines, or any other flexible support.
□ User interface exists with database and model base.
□ Creates data structures to describe outputs (output formatter).
□ Stores input and output data.
□ Provides color graphics, three-dimensional graphics, and data plotting.
□ Has windows to allow multiple functions to be displayed concurrently.
□ Has the ability to support communication among and between users and builders of DSS.
□ Provides training by examples (guiding users through the input and modeling process).
□ Provides flexibility and adaptiveness so the DSS will be able to accommodate different problems and technologies.

The Dialog Process

The dialog process is shown schematically in Figure 4.8. The user interacts with the computer via an action language processed via the DGMS. In advanced systems the dialog component includes a natural language processor. This device enables users to communicate with the computer in a natural language (such as English or Japanese) even during the construction of the DSS. This makes the construction of the DSS and its modifications fairly easy for nonprogrammers.

The DGMS provides the capabilities listed in the box, and enables the user to interact with the model management and the data management subsystems.

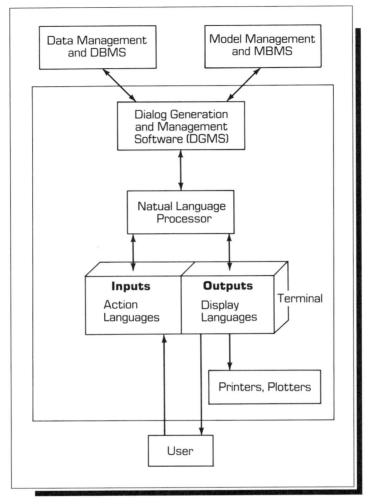

FIGURE 4.8 Schematic view of dialog management.

The dialog management subsystem offers a user interface system, which includes the input-output devices and provides the physical means of communication with the DSS; a function that controls the flow of information through the dialog subsystem as data are being inputted and outputted; and a function that transforms the input from the user into languages that can be read by the DBMS and the MBMS and that can translate output from the DBMS and MBMS into a form that can be understood by the user. For further discussion see Stohr and White (25).

4.9 The User

The person faced with the problem or decision that the DSS is designed to support has been referred to as the *user*, the *manager*, or the *decision maker*.*

---

*The material in sections 4.9 and 4.10 was adapted from Kroeber and Watson (15).

Usage Patterns

The ultimate "user" of a decision support system is the decision maker. However, he or she may not actually run the system. Based on his research on 56 decision support systems, Alter ([1], p. 115) identified four distinct usage patterns:

1. *Subscription mode.* The decision maker receives reports generated on a regular basis. Although some data analysis systems or accounting models might be used in this way, it is not typical for decision support systems.
2. *Terminal mode.* The decision maker is the direct user of the system through online access.
3. *Clerk mode.* The decision maker uses the system directly but off line, preparing input on coding forms. The primary difference between this mode and the terminal mode is in the technology employed (batch versus online).
4. *Intermediary mode.* The decision maker uses the system through intermediaries, who perform the analysis and interpret and report the results. The decision maker does not need to know how the intermediary used the system to arrive at the requested information.

The role of an intermediary is common in the use of decision support systems and merits separate attention. The use of an intermediary allows the manager to benefit from the decision support system without actually having to use the keyboard. Some managers resist using the keyboard, and until speech recognition devices become available, there will continue to be some resistance to self-input of data via the terminal keyboard.

There are three types of intermediaries that reflect different types of support for the manager:

1. *Staff assistant.* This person has specialized knowledge about management problems and some experience with the decision support technology.
2. *Expert tool user.* This person is skilled in the application of one or more types of specialized problem-solving tools. The expert tool user performs tasks that the problem solver does not have the skills or training to perform.
3. *Business (system) analyst.* This person has a general knowledge of the application area, formal business administration education (not computer science), and considerable skill in DSS (and/or expert systems) construction tools.

These terms fail to reflect, however, the heterogeneity that exists among users of DSS. There are differences in the positions that the users hold, the way in which a final decision is reached, the users' cognitive preferences and abilities, and ways of arriving at a decision (decision styles).

A DSS has two broad classes of users: managers and staff specialists. Staff specialists, like planning analysts, production planners, and marketing researchers, outnumber managers by about three to two and are using computers by a much larger ratio. Knowing who will actually have hands-on use of the DSS is important when one is designing it. In general, managers expect systems to be more user-friendly than do staff specialists. Staff specialists tend to be more detail-oriented, are more willing to use complex systems in their day-to-day work, and are interested in the computational efficiency of the DSS. In many cases the staff analysts are the intermediaries between management and the DSS.

Even within the categories of managers and staff specialists, there are important subcategories that influence DSS design. For example, managers differ by organizational level, functional area, education background, and need for analytic support. Staff specialists differ in areas such as education, the functional area that they operate, and relationship to management.

4.10   DSS Hardware and Software

Decision support systems have evolved simultaneously with advances in computer hardware and software technologies. Hardware affects the functionality and the usability of the DSS. Although the choice of hardware may be made before, during, or after the design of the DSS software, in many cases the hardware choice is predetermined by what is already available within the organization. A DSS runs on standard hardware, in contrast to expert systems that may require specially designed hardware. The major hardware options are a time-sharing network, the organization's mainframe computer, a minicomputer, a personal computer, or a combination of the above. Each option offers advantages and disadvantages. These are briefly discussed next.

Time-sharing Network

Companies like Boeing Computer Services, Tymshare, and CompuServe offer national time-sharing networks on which DSS software can be placed. In addition, several DSS vendors offer tools for building DSS via time-sharing. Time sharing is an ideal option if you do not have a mainframe computer. But it is also used by companies that already have a mainframe because in some instances better response times can be obtained from a time- sharing network than from an in-house computer system. It is not unusual for companies to experience poor response times when computer production runs with high priority (e.g., accounts receivable and payroll) are being processed. If the timing of these runs conflicts with the use of the DSS, a time-sharing network may be an attractive alternative. Another benefit is the quickness with which a DSS can be constructed when the vendor is the DSS builder. Because the vendor has experience in using the software and building similar DSS, a great deal of time can be saved. Time sharing also offers an alternative to transient capacity problem, which may occur seasonally, for example.

Time-sharing networks offer a variety of capabilities that are not available on an in-house system but may be important to the DSS. Most time-sharing networks have an extensive set of software packages, including a variety of

DSS building tools. This is an extremely important point in building a DSS. As is discussed later, there are dozens of construction tools that can be used to build a DSS. The more of these that are available, the better the potential fit between the tools and the problem attacked by the DSS. Most organizations can afford to buy only a few of the tools; however, with time sharing one can "rent" the best tool for each specific purpose. Because computing is usually their only business, time-sharing networks tend to keep up with, and use, the latest in both hardware and software.

A time-sharing network also typically offers a variety of support services. These services include training sessions for users, hotlines to answer questions, and management consulting. These services are sometimes easier to obtain from a time-sharing network than to arrange in-house. Some in-house systems do not have network support for strategic businesses in outlying geographic areas (e.g., out of state). A time-sharing vendor helps avoid added telecommunications investment.

Another potential advantage of a time-sharing network is that at a reasonable cost (sometimes at no cost) the user can try the DSS approach on a problem or a set of problems and see whether the approach looks promising. If the results are disappointing, relatively little is lost, because the start-up costs have been relatively small. If successful, often the vendor will offer the DSS tool for sale on the user's in-house computer. The ability to try out the DSS lowers the risk of a bad investment.

The major disadvantage of a time-sharing network is cost control. If a DSS is frequently used, time-sharing costs can become quite high. What frequently happens in this case is that the DSS is then brought in house.

Mainframe, Workstation, Mini-, or Personal Computer

If the DSS is located in-house, a mainframe, workstation, mini-, or personal computer might be used (or a combination of these). A variety of factors influence the type of computer used, including what kind of computers are available in-house, the type of decision support to be provided, the data needs of the DSS, the computational power that is needed, the existing network (communication) system, and the software demands of the DSS.

A major reason for placing a DSS in house is that the required hardware and software may already be available there. However, this situation need not be the limiting consideration. It is not unusual for software and sometimes hardware to be purchased specifically for DSS.

The range of DSS users also influences what hardware is to be used and where it is placed. If the system is to support users throughout an organization, a large mainframe system like an IBM 3090 or CYBER 170 might be required. On the other hand, if the DSS is to provide decision support for one person, a personal computer might be used (e.g., see Hackathorn and Keen [11]).

The latest developments in the area of super micros and micro-to-mainframe communication and networks of computers could have a major impact on hardware selection.

The data needs of the DSS may also play a role in determining the hardware selection. Some DSS require considerable data from the organization's (corporate) database. Then it may be advantageous to place the DSS on the same system where the database is maintained. However, this may not be as important a consideration as it might first seem. Experience has shown that the data needs of many decision support systems differ considerably from what is maintained in existing databases. Therefore, as mentioned earlier, it may be more practical to download and extract data from the corporate database to the DSS database or even directly to a microcomputer's memory.

Some decision support systems require significant computational power, which necessitates the use of large, fast machines. Some simulation models especially require a large number of calculations. Multidimensional reports constructed from a large number of files also require a significant memory.

In addition to the selection of the computer itself, there is the problem of selecting several additional pieces of hardware that are used to support activities ranging from graphics to auxiliary storage. The selection of specific hardware and peripherals, which requires expertise, is beyond the scope of this book.

The DSS software, as outlined earlier, is composed of the DBMS, MBMS, and dialog management. There may also be additional software for added capabilities (e.g., word processing). The software selection issue is also very important and will be discussed with other software topics in Chapter 6.

4.11   Classifications of DSS and Their Support

There are several classifications of DSS, some of which overlap. The design process, as well as the operation and implementation of DSS, depends in many cases on the type of DSS involved. Six classification schemes are presented next.

Support Provided by DSS

DSS may provide several types of support. The following structure is based on Alter [1]. Each level of support contains and adds on the previous level (but may also contribute to the previous level).

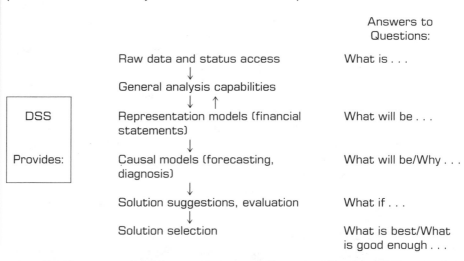

Type of Support (Alter [1])

This classification is based on the "degree of action implication of system outputs"; that is, the extent to which system outputs can directly support (or determine) the decision. According to this classification, there are seven categories of DSS software (see Table 4.3). The first three types are data-oriented, performing data retrieval and/or analysis. The remaining four are model-oriented, providing either simulation capabilities, optimization, or computations that "suggest an answer." Not every DSS fits neatly into this classification system; some have equally strong data and modeling orientation (e.g., the GLSC case).

TABLE 4.3 Characteristics of Different Classes of Decision Support Systems.

Category	Type of Operation	Type of Task	User	Usage Pattern	Time Frame
File drawer systems	Access data items	Operational	Nonmanagerial line personnel	Simple inquiries	Irregular
Data analysis systems	Ad hoc analysis of files of data	Operational or analysis	Staff analyst or managerial line personnel	Manipulation and display of data	Irregular or periodic
Analysis information systems	Ad hoc analysis involving multiple databases and small models	Analysis, planning	Staff analyst	Programming special reports, developing small models	Irregular, on request
Accounting models	Standard calculations that estimate future results on the basis of accounting definitions	Planning, budgeting	Analyst or manager	Input estimates of activity; receive estimated monetary results as output	Periodic (e.g., weekly, monthly, yearly)
Representational models	Estimating consequences of particular actions	Planning, budgeting	Staff analyst	Input possible decisions; receive estimated results as output	Periodic or irregular (ad hoc analysis)
Optimization models	Calculating an optimal solution to a combinatorial problem	Planning, resource allocation	Staff analyst	Input constraints and objectives; receive answer	Periodic or irregular (ad hoc analysis)
Suggestion models	Performing calculations that generate a suggested decision	Operational	Nonmanagerial line personnel	Input a structured description of the decision situation; receive a suggested decision as output	Daily or periodic

Source: Adapted from Alter (1), p. 90-99.

Institutional vs. Ad Hoc DSS
(Donovan and Madnick [6])

This classification is based on the nature of the decision situation that the DSS are designed to support. There are two categories.

Institutional DSS. This type of DSS deals with decisions of a *recurring* nature. A typical example is a portfolio management system (PMS), which has been used by several large banks (see Alter [1]). Another example is the GLSC case presented earlier. An institutional DSS may be developed and refined over a number of years because the DSS will be used over and over (with appropriate updating of the database and models) to solve identical or similar problems. Institutional DSS deal mainly with operational and management control problems.

Ad Hoc DSS. This type of DSS deals with specific problems that are usually neither anticipated nor recurring. For example, the Houston Minerals DSS was created specifically to evaluate the feasibility of a joint venture. Economic support for this type of situation requires general-purpose software for information retrieval, data analysis, modeling, and the like that can be quickly customized to a specific application. The concept of DSS generators, which will be introduced later, was developed to provide a means for satisfying ad hoc needs for decision-making support. Ad hoc decisions frequently involve strategic planning issues and sometimes management control problems.

Many of the DSS developed up to 1983 were institutional in nature (see Alter [1] and Meador et al. [18]), mainly owing to the high cost of developing a DSS for nonrecurring use. However, with the increased availability of DSS tools, with their steadily decreasing costs and increasing capabilities, and with the appearance of DSS software for microcomputers, it is probable that relatively more ad hoc DSS will be constructed in the future.

Degree of Nonprocedurality (Bonczek et al. [3])

This classification is based on the degree of nonprocedurality of the data retrieval and modeling languages provided by the DSS. Procedural languages, such as BASIC and COBOL, require step-by-step specifications of how data are to be retrieved and how computations are to be performed. In nonprocedural languages the system itself is programmed so that programmers are required to specify only what action is needed. There is no need to specify the sequence of execution. At an intermediate level of procedurality are systems that utilize a command language allowing users to call up a desired prespecified report, model, or function. Most DSS users find nonprocedural languages more convenient for both data retrieval and modeling activities. Nonprocedural languages (also called fourth-generation languages) are discussed in Chapter 6.

Personal, Group, and Organizational
Support (Hackathorn and Keen [11])

The support given by DSS can be separated into three distinct but interrelated categories:

Personal Support. Here the focus is on an individual user (or a group of users) performing the same activity in a discrete task or decision (e.g., selecting stocks). The task is relatively independent of other tasks.

Group Support. The focus here is on a group of people, each of whom is engaged in separate but highly interrelated tasks. An example is a typical finance department where one DSS may serve most of the employees.

Organizational Support. Here the focus is on organizational tasks or activities involving a *sequence* of operations, different functional areas, and required resources. For example, the GLSC case illustrates a sequence of decisions composed of long-term planning, short-term planning, resource allocation, and job assignment decisions.

Degree of Dependency

Sequential interdependent decisions may require a decision maker to make part of a decision and then to pass it on to other decision makers, who make their own contributions to the decision. The GLSC case is an example of such a situation. Decision support systems that support sequential interdependent decision making provide organizational support. Capabilities such as access by multiple users throughout the organization (e.g., using networks) and the ability to store and retrieve data, models, and other users' contributions to the decision are important in providing organizational support. *Pooled interdependent* decisions are made by a group after interaction and negotiation by group members. A DSS for this type of decision making is described as Group DSS (GDSS).

Group DSS

The term *group support* introduced earlier should not be confused with the concept of group DSS. In group support the decisions are made by individuals whose tasks are interrelated. Therefore they should check the impact of their decisions on others, but not necessarily make decisions as a group. In a group DSS each decision (sometimes only one decision) is made by a group.

4.12   Group DSS

Many DSS researchers and practitioners (e.g., Keen [14]) pointed out that the fundamental model of DSS—the lonely decision maker striding down the hall at high noon to make a decision—is true only for minor decisions.[*] In most organizations, be they public or private, Japanese, European, or American, most *major* decisions are made collectively.

In this section we consider group decision support systems, usually referred to as GDSS. This is an emerging subfield within DSS in which there

[*]This section was prepared by Janet Francis, Eastern Illinois University. It is based, in part, on Gray (9) and (10).

has been a marked increase in activity since the mid-1980s (e.g., see DeSanctis and Gallupe [4]).

Here are some typical definitions of GDSS: "A GDSS consists of a set of software, hardware, and language components and procedures that support a group of people engaged in a decision-related meeting" (Huber [12]).

"A GDSS is an interactive, computer-based system that facilitates the solution of unstructured problems by a set of decision makers working together as a group" (DeSanctis and Gallupe [4]).

A GDSS supports the *process* of decision making rather than the solution of a specific problem.

The Nature of Group Decision Meetings

Although most business organizations are hierarchical, decision making is usually a shared process. Face-to-face meetings among groups of managers are an essential element of reaching a consensus. The group may be involved in a decision or in a decision-related task like creating a short list of acceptable alternatives or deciding on criteria for accepting an alternative. These group meetings are characterized by the following activities and processes:

- ☐ Meetings are a joint activity, engaged in by a group of people usually of equal or near equal status, typically involving 5 to 20 individuals.
- ☐ The outcome of the meeting depends in an essential way on the knowledge, opinions, and judgments of its participants.
- ☐ The outcome of the meeting also depends on the composition of the groups and on the decision-making process used by the groups.
- ☐ Differences in opinion are settled either by the ranking person present or, more often, by negotiation or arbitration.

Components of GDSS

A typical GDSS configuration, and a rather basic one, includes a group of decision makers which has access to a database, a model base, and GDSS application software during the course of a decision-related meeting. There is at least one computer processor, one input/output device, and one viewing screen for the group and preferably for each participant. A group facilitator coordinates the group's use of the technology, and there is a flexible, friendly, user-interface language available for use by the facilitator and each group member.

DeSanctis and Gallupe (4) define the components of GDSS as being *Hardware, Software, People*, and *Procedures*. (See Figure 4.9)

Hardware.   Regardless of the specific situation, the group as a whole or each member of the group must be able to access a minicomputer processor and a display of information. The minimal hardware requirements of the system include: an input/output device and the processor, and either a common viewing screen or individual monitors for use in displaying information to the group. However, a design that allows each participant to work independently of the others—through its own I/O terminal or desktop computer—to publicly demon-

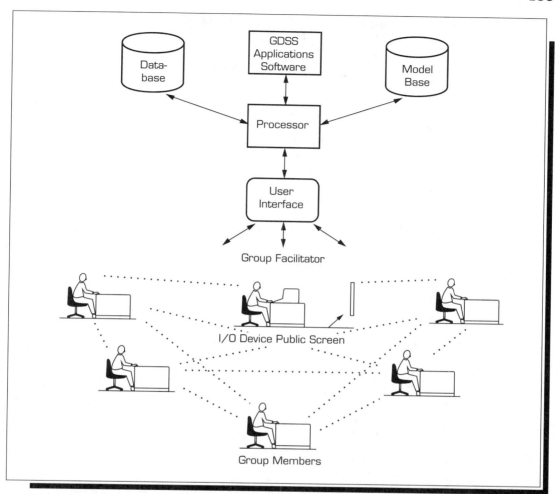

FIGURE 4.9 A model of GDSS. (*Source:* DeSanctis and Gallupe [4].)

strate personal work, and to see the work of other individuals and the group as a whole, is preferred, as it enhances the efficiency of the participation.

Software. The software component of the GDSS includes a database, a model base, specialized application program(s) to be used by the group, and an easy-to-use, flexible, user interface. GDSS software includes packages to support the individual and the group, the process, and specific tasks. It allows each individual to do private work; the usual collection of text and file creation, graphics, spreadsheet, database, and help routines are provided at the individual workstations. Typical group features include:

1. Numerical and graphical summarization of group members, ideas, and votes.
2. Programs for calculation of weights for decision alternatives; anonymous recording of ideas; formal selection of a group leader; progressive

rounds of voting toward consensus building; or elimination of redundant input during brainstorming.

3. Text and data transmission among the group members, between the group members and the facilitator, and between the members and a central computer processor.

People. The people component of the GDSS includes the group members and a facilitator who is responsible for the smooth operation of the GDSS technology. The facilitator is usually present at all group meetings and serves as the group's "chauffeur," operating the GDSS hardware and software and displaying requested information to the group as needed.

Procedures. The final component of the GDSS consists of procedures that enable ease of operation and effective use of the technology by group members. These procedures may apply only to the operation of the hardware and software, or they may extend to include rules regarding verbal discussion among members and the flow of events during a group meeting.

GDSS Typology

Since the early 1980s group decision support system technology has made enormous theoretical advances. This technology has been studied from both conceptual and design perspectives. DeSanctis and Gallupe (4) have developed a framework for group decision support systems (see material in box). The precise configuration of a GDSS varies considerably depending on the type of problem to be solved and the organizational context in which the problem is addressed. This framework emphasizes that the purpose and configuration of a GDSS varies according to the duration of the decision-making session and the degree of physical proximity of group members. Based on these two dimensions, at least four scenarios are possible:

1. *Decision Room.* This scenario may be thought of as the electronic equivalent to a traditional meeting. This GDSS incorporates a conference room with terminal/nodes for each participant, and any decision making that takes place in this environment is conducted within a certain period of time. This type of GDSS is often referred to as a war room, decision laboratory, or face-to-face conference.

2. *Local Decision Network.* This type enables participants to communicate through their terminals, thus allowing people to make decisions even if they are not in the same room or the same city. A central processor stores common GDSS software and databases, and a local area network provides member-to-member and member-to-central-processor communication. This approach removes the one-place/one-time constraint of the first scenario. There is the disadvantage of removing face-to-face communication, but face-to-face meetings could be held when necessary.

3. *Teleconferencing.* This type of GDSS is used in groups whose members are geographically distant from one another but who nevertheless must come together for the purpose of making a decision. In this case two or

A Group Decision Support System

A group decision support system (GDSS) is an interactive computer-based system that facilitates the solution of unstructured problems by a set of decision makers working together as a group. Components of a GDSS include hardware, software, people, and procedures. These components are arranged to support a group of people, usually in the context of a decision-related meeting. Important characteristics of a GDSS can be summarized as follows:

1. The GDSS is a specially designed system, not merely a configuration of already existing system components.
2. A GDSS is designed with the goal of supporting groups of decision makers in their work. As such, the GDSS should improve the decision-making process and/or the decision outcomes of groups over outcomes which would occur if the GDSS were not present.
3. A GDSS is easy to learn and easy to use. It accommodates users with varying levels of knowledge regarding computing and decision support.
4. The GDSS may be specific (designed for one type of problem) or general (designed for a variety of group-level organizational decisions).
5. The GDSS contains built-in mechanisms that discourage development of negative group behaviors, such as destructive conflict, miscommunication, or "group think."

The definition of GDSS is quite broad and, therefore, can apply to a variety of group decision situations, including committees, review panels, task forces, executive board meetings, remote workers, and so forth. Appropriate settings for a GDSS range from an executive group meeting that occurs in a single location for the purpose of considering a specific problem (such as a merger/acquisition decision) to a sales managers' meeting held via telecommunications channels for the purpose of considering a variety of problems (such as hiring of sales representatives, product offerings, and sales call schedules). Because the contexts of group decision making vary so greatly, it is useful to think of a GDSS in terms of the common "group" activities that, therefore, are in need of computer-based support. They are information retrieval, which includes selection of data values from an existing database as well as simple retrieval of information (including attitudes, opinions, and informal observations) from other group members; information sharing, which refers to the display of data to the total group on a viewing screen or sending of data to selected group members' terminal sites for viewing; and information use, which involves the application of software technology (such as modeling packages or specific application programs), procedures, and group problem-solving techniques for reaching a group decision.

(*Source:* DeSanctis and Gallupe (4).)

more decision rooms are connected together by visual and/or communication facilities. The approach is essentially the same as in scenario 1 except that teleconferencing is used to supplement the communication component of the GDSS; thus, flexibility in terms of time and duration of holding a meeting, is advantageous.

4. *Remote Decision Making.* This scenario is not yet common but it offers possibilities for the near future. Here there is uninterrupted communication between remote decision stations in a geographically dispersed organization, which has a fixed group of people who must regularly make joint decisions. This scenario removes the constraint of a single central meeting location and addresses the needs of decision makers who must work together on a regular basis but cannot meet face to face.

In a recent study, Straub and Beauclair (26) analyzed the overall intentions of 135 randomly selected Data Processing Management Association members concerning the implementation of GDSS technology at some future date. The study indicates that government organizations plan to introduce all four systems discussed. Financial institutions and computer service bureaus intend to introduce decision room GDSS while utilities and financial institutions plan teleconferencing and remote decision-making GDSS.

Because of cost and complexity considerations, teleconferencing GDSS seems least likely to experience much growth in the near future. However, the data suggests that interest in decision rooms will continue to run high while interest will remain steady for local decision network systems.

The GDSS Facilities and Software

The University of Arizona Planning and Decision Laboratory provides two GDSS facilities (one small and one large) for the study of the impact of automated support on planning and decision processes. Executives, managers, and professional staff from organizations use the facilities for organizational planning and to address complex, unstructured decision problems. The facilities are based on the decision room approach. The facilities are available for rent for corporations who want to use them for GDSS.

The small facility is shown in Figure 4.10. It consists of a large U-shaped table equipped with 16 networked microcomputers that are recessed into a table to facilitate interaction among participants. A microcomputer attached to a large-screen projection system is connected to the network and permits the display of work done at individual workstations of aggregated information from the total group. Breakout rooms are equipped with microcomputers that are networked to the microcomputers at the main conference table. The output from these small group sessions can also be displayed on the large "public" screen projector for group presentations and can be updated and integrated with planning session results.

Participants interact with a variety of automated software products for planning and problem-solving models suitable for use by executives. Some of the currently available tools used in this GDSS as described by Nunamaker, et al. (21) follow:

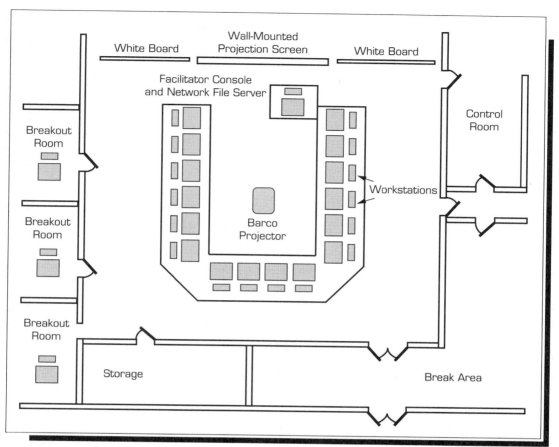

FIGURE 4.10 University of Arizona Small GDSS Facility.

The *Electronic Brainstorming* (EBS) tool allows participants, using the networked microcomputers, to anonymously share comments on a specific question with other participants. For example, members enter a comment to a question on their individual computer screen and send it out onto the network to be received by other participants who review previous comments, append an additional comment, and return the response to the network (see Figure 4.11 for an example). Comments from all participant screens are consolidated after the session and systematic analysis support is used to identify common issues or concerns, associated attributes, and relationships between categories. This interchange of ideas was found to increase creativity and generate alternative possible courses of action.

The *Stakeholder Identification and Analysis* (SIAS) tool is used to identify stakeholders pertinent to a proposed plan, record assumptions or expectations of those stakeholders, and rate the stakeholder assumptions in terms of importance to the stakeholder as well as importance to the proposed plan. Assumption ratings are captured, consolidated, and displayed graphically for review and consideration by the group.

```
┌──────────────────────────────────────────────────────────────┐
│     ┌────────────────── ELECTRONIC BRAINSTORMING ──────────────┐ ▐
│     │ PRIOR COMMENTS:  To Scroll PRIOR COMMENTS, Use PgUp, PgDn, Home, End │ ▐
│     │                                                          │ ▐
│     │ What new products would have high impact in our existing market │ ▐
│     │ distribution chain?                                      │ ▐
│     │                                                          │ ▐
│     │ An add-in program that allows users to create 3-dimensional spreadsheets │ ▐
│     │ would make our product competitive with the new generation coming out. │ ▐
│     │                                                          │ ▐
│     │ Improve our graphics so that users can change graph height as in │ ▐
│     │ Javelin.  It ought to be mouse driven rather than cursor driven. │ ▐
│     │                                                          │ ▐
│     │ The 3-dimensional spreadsheet is a gimmick.  Real analysts don't use │ ▐
│     │ them.  People have great difficulty in thinking in 3 dimensions. │ ▐
│     ├──────────────────────────────────────────────────────────┤ ▐
│     │   YOUR COMMENTS (limit of 5 lines):                      │ ▐
│     │ You are right on with the interactive graphics input.  Managers can │ ▐
│     │ relate to that.  Would we have to buy rights to that or is the idea a │ ▐
│     │ public domain?                                           │ ▐
│     └──────────────────────────────────────────────────────────┘ ▐
│                                                                  │
│     PRESS F10 TO SUBMIT COMMENTS & CONTINUE            F1 = HELP │
└──────────────────────────────────────────────────────────────┘
```

FIGURE 4.11 Electronic brainstorming screen as seen by participant after several rounds; Arizona GDSS interface. (*Source:* Gray [10].)

The *Voting* tool can be used to consolidate group sentiments at any stage of the planning process, using several different formats including agree/disagree, multiple choice, 10-point scale ranking, or ranking in order.

The *Policy Formulation* (PF) tool enables group members to develop policy statements, based on the issues identified. The facilitator enters the initial wording of a proposed policy on the groups' verbal direction. This policy is then sent to individual participants who edit it and send it back for group comments until a group consensus is reached.

The *Enterprise Analyzer* (EA) is the means through which an organization can be represented in the knowledge base. It is conceptually similar to IBM's Business Systems Planning (BSP) methodology, but it is a computerized version updated to reflect a user friendly approach to the definition of organization structure and resources.

Additional tools and models provide support for session initialization, agenda generation, issue prioritizing, statistical analysis, interface and display. The output from the models serves as input to a knowledge base that provides a mechanism for representation and storing the planning knowledge using a variety of knowledge representation techniques including semantic inheritance networks, frames, and production rules (see Chapter 14).

Determinants of GDSS Success

The experience gained from almost two years of experimentations at the University of Arizona Planning and Decision Laboratory has been analyzed. Of special interest are the detected determinants of GDSS success. This analysis focuses on the effectiveness and efficiency of GDSS in facilitating the decision-making process, and the degree of satisfaction of the group members (Vogel, et al. [27]). These experiments suggest the following attributes of successful GDSS:

- The setting should be multipurpose and flexible to better meet the needs of different group sizes and task environments. Aesthetics should provide a measure of executive appeal in terms of comfort and familiarity to allow decision makers to better focus on issues at hand.
- The provision of an electronic interface for each group member encourages all group members to participate and enhances the efficiency of that participation. Each workstation should have a high degree of local intelligence and in-residence software options. As such, each participant can maintain some independence while contributing to the group as a whole through an interface that is flexible and individually supportive.
- The software should not be merely user-friendly but *user seductive*, to present a professional image and encourage end-user involvement in group decision-making sessions. The software should not impose on or frustrate users, but encourage user interaction through effective use of color, overlays, windowing, and other features.
- Anonymity is important to groups especially when sensitive issues are being discussed. For groups of differing organizational levels, anonymity provides a sense of equality and encouragement for participation by all members in the group independent of perceived status. Problems of group-think, pressures for conformity, and dominance of the group by strong personalities of particularly forceful speakers are minimized. Members can contribute without the personal attention and anxiety associated with singularly gaining the floor and being the focus of attention.
- Tasks that involve generating ideas or plans, solving problems with or without optimal solutions, and resolving conflicts of different viewpoints or interests are particularly good candidates for effective GDSS utilization. Those that involve resolving conflicts of power or group leadership, and those that are more related to actual detail execution, that more often resides with individuals, are less effectively addressed by a GDSS.
- The use of a GDSS, however, tends to heighten conflict within a group as members tend to become more blunt and assertive in their comments. Members tend to express themselves more forcefully and are often not as polite when interfacing through the system rather than in person.
- Efficiency considerations (measured by the time it takes to reach a decision) of group decision support systems become increasingly apparent as group size increases. It is difficult to demonstrate that GDSS promotes group efficiency for small groups (e.g., of size 3 to 5). For larger groups (e.g., of size 8 and up), the GDSS enhances group efficiency by facilitating input from all group members in a relative simultaneous fashion.
- Group effectiveness (measured by the quality of the decisions) when using GDSS is also enhanced as group size increases. For groups of size 6 to 8 or more, the effectiveness of GDSS becomes particularly apparent in the facilitation and coordination of large numbers of issues associated with a complex question. Small groups, by contrast, often find that while

the GDSS is interesting, it is difficult to suggest that any striking measure of increased effectiveness has been attained.

☐ Member satisfaction with the group process is also better when groups are larger. Larger groups appreciate the structuring inherent with the GDSS to keep the group from becoming bogged down or subject to domination by member personalities. Small groups are more frustrated by GDSS constraints, and are less likely to conclude that the GDSS is more effective or efficient than an unstructured face-to-face meeting for the relatively less complex questions typically addressed by small groups.

Conclusions. The University of Arizona's experience confirms that the key to success rests in an appreciation of the need for:

1. Facilities that provide a professional setting in which sophisticated software and hardware are well organized and effectively supported.
2. Ability to accommodate groups of sufficient size that may vary considerably in composition and experience and which address tasks that are real and complex by nature.
3. Facilitation that demonstrates technical competence in combination with an appreciation for group dynamics with a research orientation that encompasses a multidisciplinary approach.

GDSS Research

GDSS is a state-of-the-art technology. Unlike other technologies in MIS research, such as end-user computing or system development techniques, it cannot yet be widely investigated for its use in the hands of practitioners. Few organizations use GDSS technology as researchers know it today. Findings from GDSS lab experimentations have been distinctly different from those of GDSS field studies, due in part to the fact that the use of GDSS by organizations has been distinctly different than the use of GDSS in previous laboratory experiments. The first step toward the closing of the gap between the laboratory experiments and field studies is to embark on multimethodological research programs that provide individual researchers with first-hand understanding of the key GDSS issues from both the experimental and field research perspectives. The absence of either experiments or field studies in a research program reduces the strength within which conclusions can be drawn, and the applicability of those conclusions to actual organizations. A second challenge would be to understand the effects that these differences have on the process and outcome of group meetings, and to use this understanding in interpreting and applying the conclusions of experiments to the use of GDSS by business organizations. From this understanding, we can develop new research designs: field studies with greater rigor (internal validity) and experiments with greater relevancy to the organizational use of GDSS (external validity).

For a summary of GDSS experiments, see George, J. F. "A Comparison of Four Recent GDSS Experiments," Proc Hawaii Int Conf Syst Sci 22, January 1989.

Relation of GDSS to DSS

GDSS contains a conventional DSS within it. That is, the concepts of model base, database, and human interface all apply. Thus as group size shrinks to one, a GDSS reduces to a DSS. Conversely, in moving from a DSS to a GDSS, some new requirements are introduced:

1. Addition of a communications base.
2. Enhancement of the model base to provide voting, ranking, rating, and so on for developing consensus.
3. Greater uptime is desired.
4. Increased setup before use of the system.
5. Expanded physical facilities.

The first two requirements have already been discussed. Uptime has to be much greater for a GDSS than for a DSS. If a GDSS goes down, many people are affected, not just one. Because these people are important and well paid, there is a much greater loss in terms of both financial cost and trust in the system. A GDSS requires much more setup before the system can be used because both the people and the facility must be scheduled, an agenda must be prepared, participants must have the ability to prepare for the meeting by seeing its data files and models, and so on.

A GDSS requires capital investment in physical facilities. If the GDSS is located in a decision room, the room has to be elegantly furnished and have the feel of the executive conference room. A GDSS also requires much more display and communications hardware.

Commercial Experience with GDSS

The number of group decision support systems built and/or offered for sale is quite small. Facilities that are single purpose and have been offered for rent by vendors seem, thus far, to have survived longer than permanent single-site installations at user locations. The reason appears to be that single-site installations have typically not offered a broad enough range of services to make them economically viable. A system that has low frequency of use does not survive.

4.13 Summary and Conclusions

This chapter attempts to explain what a DSS is and describe its major capabilities and components, as well as the computing environment required for its operation. The DSS is composed of three basic components: the database and its management, the model base and its management, and the dialog subsystem. Figure 4.12 presents the various DSS components as reflected in the GLSC case. Each of these parts possesses certain capabilities. These capabilities contribute to general capabilities and overall objectives of the DSS. Figure 4.13 summarizes the major capabilities at all levels.

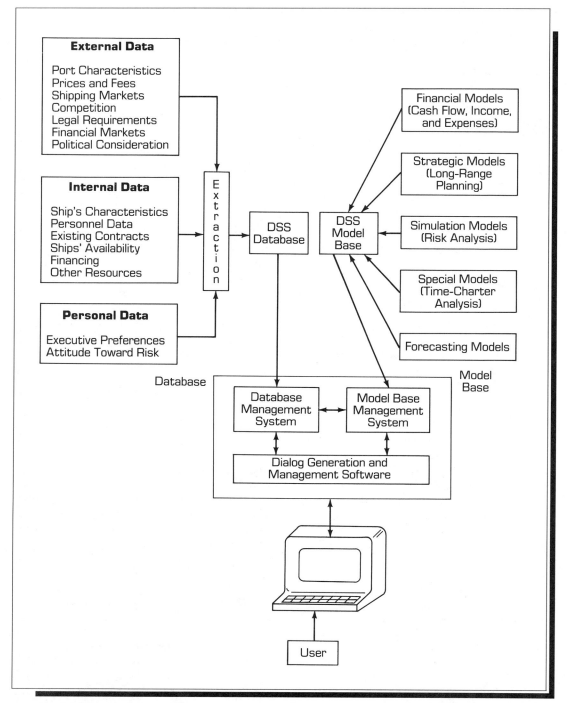

FIGURE 4.12 The GLSC DSS—an overview.

Group DSS is a special case of DSS in which decisions are being made by a group. The technology here aims at facilitating communications, private workspaces, ranking capabilities, and information retrieval and displays.

One important topic not discussed in this chapter is the construction of a DSS. This topic is treated in Chapter 5.

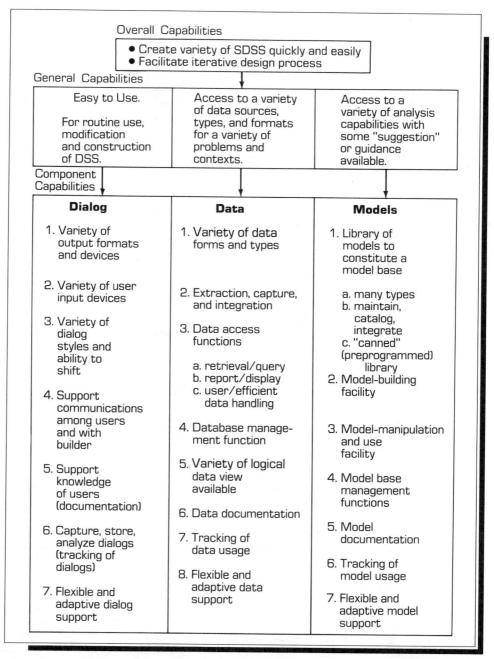

FIGURE 4.13 Summary of DSS capabilities. (*Source:* Sprague and Carlson [23], p. 313.)

Key Words

adaptive process	dialog system	natural language
ad hoc data analysis	directory	processor
(reports)	English-like language	nonprocedural languages
applications programs	extraction	operational models
database	group DSS	peripherals
database management	institutional DSS	procedural languages
system (DBMS)	interdependent decisions	query system
decision room	interface	sequential decisions
dialog generation and	model base	strategic models
management system	model base management	tactical models
(DGMS)	system (MBMS)	user-friendly
dialog style	model building blocks	user interface

Questions for Review

1. Give two definitions of DSS.
2. Why do people attempt to narrow the definition of DSS?
3. Give your own definition of DSS.
4. List the major components of DSS and define each of them briefly.
5. How does a database differ from a collection of files?
6. What are the major functions (capabilities) of DBMS?
7. What is meant by "extraction"?
8. What is the function of a query facility?
9. What is the function of a directory?
10. Models are classified as strategic, tactical, or operational. What is the purpose of such classifications? Give an example of each.
11. List some of the major functions of MBMS.
12. What is the major purpose of the user interface system?
13. List some input (or action language) devices.
14. List some display (or presentation language) devices.
15. What is meant by "dialog style"?
16. What are the major functions of a dialog management system?
17. List the major classes of DSS users.
18. What types of support are provided by DSS?
19. What are the major advantages of time sharing?
20. What are the major disadvantages of time sharing?
21. What are the major software components included in a DSS?
22. Define a procedural computer language and contrast it with a nonprocedural one.
23. List the major characteristics of group DSS.
24. List three benefits of GDSS.
25. Describe a "decision room" and contrast it with other GDSS scenarios.

Problems and Discussion Questions

1. Review the major characteristics and capabilities of DSS. Relate each of them to the three major components of DSS.
2. List some internal data and external data that could be found in a DSS for selection of a portfolio of stocks for an investor.

3. List some internal and external data in a DSS that will be constructed for a decision regarding the expansion of a hospital.
4. Provide a list of possible strategic, tactical, and operational models in a university, in a restaurant, in a chemical plant.
5. Show the similarity between DBMS and MBMS. What is common to both?
6. Compare a Group DSS to noncomputerized group decision making.
7. It is said that GDSS supports the *process* while DSS supports the *task.* Comment.
8. How can GDSS support creativity?
9. Explain why most DSS use a relational database.

CASE 1: Financial Planning at the Louisiana National Bank*

The Louisiana National Bank (LNB) is located in Baton Rouge, the state capital of Louisiana. In 1958, Charles McCoy became the bank's chief executive officer. Under his leadership, the LNB has developed a reputation for innovation. By 1978 the LNB became the largest bank in Baton Rouge with assets in excess of $600 million.

In the fall of 1973, the LBN was facing serious problems. Profits had been declining for over a year. Traditional policies for managing the bank were failing. There was a lack of coordination among decision makers. The bank was slow to react to market and regulation changes.

In response to this deteriorating situation, McCoy designated Gil Urban as corporate planner and charged him with the responsibility of developing a system to help analyze the bank's performance and to support top management decision making. Urban was an excellent choice for this position because he had extensive banking experience and a personal interest in planning and analysis activities.

The Development of FPS

After an intensive six-week study, Urban began developing the financial planning system (FPS). The initial system was designed to produce reports of the type and format that top management had been receiving in the past. Over time, management understanding of FPS grew, and the capabilities of the system were refined and expanded.

System Components

FPS has three components: data, reports and analyses, and forecasts. Each component plays an important role in the functioning of FPS.

Data

On a monthly basis, summary data from the bank's general ledger accounting system are extracted and entered into the FPS. The data are added to a matrix of historical data in which the rows are items in the summary chart of accounts and the columns are time periods. The database maintains up to three years of monthly figures and up

*Condensed from Ralph H. Sprague, Jr., and Ronald L. Olson. "The Financial Planning Systems at Louisiana National Bank." *MIS Quarterly*, September 1979, pp. 35–46.

to 7.5 years of quarterly figures. The database also stores 12 periods of forecast data, based on the system's forecasting and simulation capabilities.

Reports and Analyses

Each month, FPS produces a complete set of summary financial statements, including the balance sheet, the income statement, and standard operating reports. Data from the current month are compared with the forecast, the budget, and the actual data for the previous year. A number of special reports are also generated. Of particular importance to the LNB management are the interest rate-volume-mix analysis and the line-of-business-analysis reports. The latter show the sources and uses of funds for three major segments of the bank: the retail or customer sector, the public sector, and the commercial sector.

Forecasts

The system produced a forecast of the information included in the reports for a period of 12 months into the future. A forecasting model was developed and values for the independent variables were entered by management or statistically estimated by FPS with a management override capability. The system contains a built-in linear programming submodel that can be used to optimize projected earnings with respect to yields, subject to constraints or guidelines defined by management. The system can also be used to forecast as far into the future as desired on a monthly or quarterly basis.

Use of the System

FPS is employed in several ways. On the first Tuesday of each month, FPS is used to supply the planning committee with reports and graphs that show the previous month's activities. The planning committee is also given the newly prepared 12-month forecast.

During the meeting of the planning committee, anticipated changes and pending issues are discussed. Frequently, there are questions and possibilities that need to be explored further at the next meeting after additional runs of FPS.

Urban also uses FPS to prepare forecasts for other bank officers who wish to investigate the consequences of possible strategies.

Urban also uses FPS on his own initiative. He investigates areas such as the impact of pending changes in money market rates, banking regulations, market trends, and internal policy changes. Urban considers it part of his job to watch systematically for opportunities that will require management action.

FPS also plays an important role in the bank's budgeting process. Each fall a "grass roots" budget, as it is called, is prepared. It is composed of about 9,000 data items: one for each budget line item, for each of the cost centers, for each of the 12 months of the coming year. Once the tentative budget is prepared, summaries are then extracted and entered into the FPS the same way that actual data are transferred after the end of each month. FPS is then used to assess the combined impact of the budget estimates, to examine the reasonableness of the estimates compared with top management's judgment, and to search for any inconsistencies in interrelated areas. Any adjustments of the tentative budget are made through a process of negotiation between top management and the cost center managers. The detailed final budget is approved by mid-December and is then carried in the automated accounting system, which produces monthly budget variance reports for each cost center during the coming year.

Benefits

The LNB has benefited considerably from the use of FPS. Most important, it has made the bank profitable. After-tax profit grew from 2 to 6 million dollars between 1974 and 1978.

The use of FPS has led to new policies for asset-liability management. An example of this occurred in 1975 when the government authorized consumer certificates of deposit (CDs) in small denominations for four- and six-year maturities. Many banks hesitated to offer these CDs because of the fear that savers would shift their regular savings to higher-paying CDs. By using FPS, the management at the LNB became convinced that the CDs were an excellent way to obtain long-term funds on which to build their consumer loan portfolio. Consequently, they gave heavy promotion to the CDs, which resulted in increased funds, increased loans, and increased profitability in the retail segment of the LNB's business.

FPS has also provided a framework, a structure, and a discipline for unified decision making. Recently, the LNB experienced a growth in credit card loans and decided to sell a large portion of the loans to a New York bank. Without the convincing analysis provided by FPS, this move would have been strongly opposed by several of the bank's managers because of the bank's history as the leading regional credit card lender.

Reporting and negotiating with bank regulators has been facilitated by FPS. In 1978, management noted that FPS forecasted a need for additional capital because of a growing demand for loans. Using FPS, management developed a "balanced growth" plan.

The use of FPS has made it possible to respond to changes faster. In March 1978, after several years of liquidity shortages, the LNB was experiencing an average excess liquidity of 30 million dollars a day. FPS forecasted, however, that loan growth and deposit shrinkage would create liquidity problems by early fall. Based on this forecast, the planning committee set maximum growth goals for all departments and took some other preemptive actions. By October, it was clear that the LNB had averted a major liquidity crisis because of the early warning provided by FPS.

FPS produces the normal monthly reports less expensively than when they were prepared manually. However, the cost of additional runs to explore alternative plans and assumptions more than consumes this saving.

This additional cost does not bother management. As McCoy has said, "FPS clearly paid for itself in helping us generate that first set of strategic plans. Now we don't even think about what it costs, because we couldn't run the bank without it."

QUESTIONS

1. Discuss the data, models, software interface, and user components in this case.
2. Is the financial planning system at the Louisiana National Bank best categorized as an MIS or a DSS? Why? Is the distinction clear? Why?
3. Decision support systems have the potential for supporting top-, middle-, and lower-management decision making. To what extent is decision making at these levels supported by the decision support systems described in this case?
4. Decision support systems can be used for ad hoc and for repetitive decision making. How would you classify the decision support systems described in this case?
5. Decision support systems have the potential for supporting the intelligence, design, and choice phases of decision making. To what extent are these decision-making phases supported by the decision support systems described in this case?

6. Decision support systems can support independent and sequential interdependent decision making. What kind of decision support is provided by the decision support systems described in this case?

7. Explain the following statement: "Values for the independent variables were entered by management or statistically estimated by FPS with a management override capability." What is the significance of this statement?

8. An evolutionary developmental approach is best for most decision support systems. To what extent was an evolutionary approach used with the decision support systems described in this case? Do you agree with the approaches that were used? Why?

9. The objective of a DSS is to create organizational benefits. Describe the benefits generated by the decision support systems described in this case.

CASE 2: GDSS in City Government*

Problem.

In Louisville, Kentucky, one volunteer group called Third Century is working to define a future for the inner city. Nearly 500 community members from all neighborhoods, public and private sector business organizations, and education meet regularly to identify the major issues confronting the city. Their activities include open forums to discuss critical issues, gathering data to understand the opportunities and problems facing the city, and sponsoring meetings and festivals to help revitalize the downtown as a viable place to live, work, and shop. Third Century's major goal is to develop a set of policy priorities for the future of the community.

The University of Louisville developed a limited GDSS to help the large, dispersed, heterogeneous group to arrive at consensus goals.

Most GDSS operate in laboratory conditions. Very few GDSS involve actual decision makers, usually in the private sector where there is less conflicting environment.

The problem, common to every community, is to provide an arena in which each agenda can be dealt with openly while sharing realistic expectations regarding what is possible, given existing resources and competing agendas.

Third Century first identified a list of critical community concerns, which included a wide variety of issues. From their data gathering they found education was at the top of the list in terms of community interest. Third Century planners then refined a list of ten specific education-related items most often cited in the community survey. They identified executives, neighborhood and community leaders, and key government people who were the opinion leaders and invited them to participate in a consensus-building exercise.

Design and Implementation.

The first step was to design the GDSS to assure that all of the leaders had an opportunity to make a case for the educational priorities they felt appropriate.

A flow chart was developed to clarify the GDSS process to technical and non-technical users (see Figure 4.14). A programmer then translated the chart into usable

*Taylor, R. L., and Beauclair, R. A., "GDSS as a Tool in Public Policy: The Louisville Experience," *DSS 89 Transactions*, with permission of the authors and the Institute of Management Sciences.

code. Because of excessive costs and the unavailability of existing packaged software, university faculty developed the GDSS application to support the process.

Representatives from Third Century visited each group leader (representatives from the local school board, teachers, parents, parochial and private school heads, business people, political leaders, and individuals from higher education). From these

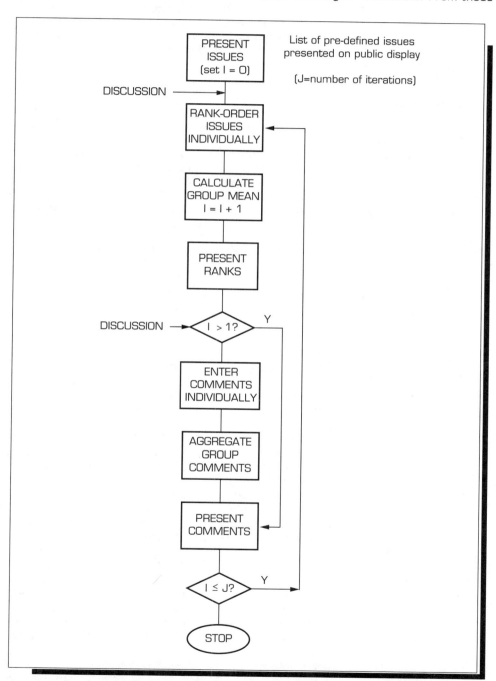

FIGURE 4.14 System Flowchart.

interviews, a list of the ten most frequently cited educational concerns was identified and each was rephrased as an action item. The action items were short statements clarifying each main concern. The cost to implement the ten action items far exceeded the available resources of the community; furthermore, some actions had to be taken before others could be accomplished. Priorities had to be established.

The Third Century representatives were invited to discuss the list in the GDSS research room which included seven networked microcomputers in a comfortable discussion setting. They participated in a pilot exercise to determine whether consensus could be achieved and whether the GDSS configuration was "user friendly." From the testing, the action items and software were revised.

Group Process.

Fifty individuals were identified by Third Century to participate. They included the U.S. senator from Louisville, school superintendents from public and private schools, university administrators, outstanding teachers, principals, community leaders, neighborhood advocates, minority leaders, and citizen activists. They were invited to participate in one of four GDSS sessions. Because of scheduling constraints, the number of participants was reduced to 28.

Four sessions of seven participants each were conducted. After a brief orientation to the GDSS process, each of the ten issues was discussed. Participants often advocated their position during this discussion but, more importantly, everyone seemed to achieve a common understanding about the nature and scope of the issues. The ten specific issues were:

1. Corporate and Community Involvement.
2. Curriculum.
3. Early Childhood Education.
4. Funding.
5. Higher Education.
6. Holding Power (reducing dropout rate).
7. Literacy.
8. Research and Technology.
9. Responsiveness to Student Needs.
10. Teaching Profession.

Each session was scheduled for three hours. The orientation and discussion took about an hour, and then the first iteration of the GDSS process began.

The university provided facilitators and technical assistants so that the process would go smoothly and the participants could overcome any fears they might have about using a computer or an unfamiliar program. Deliberations were tape recorded to provide a record of the session and for researchers to analyze the process. An electronic log of each session was compiled by the system.

In the first iteration, participants were asked to rank order the issues, assigning a value of 10 to the most important and 1 to the least important. The system collected this information and calculated mean ranks for the group. A consensus list was displayed to the group in order of ranking. Group members were then asked to enter comments about their rankings relative to the group ranking for each of the ten issues. The system collected these comments and then presented them *by issue* back to the group. Lively discussion followed. In general, the first iteration took approximately one hour.

Substantive arguments were made for each of the issues. It was found that the participants spent more time listening than they did advocating their own points of view. There seemed to be a greater degree of understanding about others' points of view and a willingness to rethink initial positions. While the artificiality of the process seemed to encourage participants to be on their best behavior, it is unlikely that this accounts for all of the activity expressed by group members; the GDSS also appeared to have a positive effect. Much of the discussion in this first iteration centered on what could realistically be done given limited resources.

A second iteration was then initiated, and participants reprioritized the issues on the basis of prior discussion. There was a greater degree of consensus the second time around. A brief discussion was then held, but comments were not collected electronically. This second iteration took no more than thirty minutes.

A final iteration allowed participants to prioritize the issues once more. In each case, there was a surprising degree of consensus, and participants felt they had accomplished something significant. A wrap-up discussion was then held to talk about the list and highlight the importance of advocating this priority list to implement change.

QUESTIONS

1. Why is this a "limited GDSS"?
2. The decision room accommodates the participants in shifts, due to the small size of the facility. What could be the impact of such a restriction?
3. Compare this case to a Delphi process.
4. What are some of the major advantages of this GDSS?
5. How would a GDSS for public policy compare with one in a for-profit organization?

References and Bibliography

1. Alter, S. L. *Decision Support Systems: Current Practices and Continuing Challenges.* Reading, MA: Addison-Wesley, 1980.
2. Bennett, J. "User Orientated Graphics, Systems for Decision Support in Unstructured Tasks." In *User-Orientated Design of Interactive Graphic Systems*, S. Treu, ed. New York: ACM, 1977.
3. Bonczek, R. H., C. W. Holsapple, and A. B. Whinston. "The Evolving Roles of Models in Decision Support Systems." *Decision Sciences*, Vol. 11, No. 2, 1980.
4. DeSanctis, G., and B. Gallupe. "Group Decision Support Systems: A New Frontier." *Data Base*, Winter 1985. Also see *Management Science*, May 1987.
5. Dickson, G. W., et al. "Research in Information Systems: The Minnesota Experiments." *Management Science*, May 1977.
6. Donovan, J. J., and S. E. Madnick. "Institutional and Ad Hoc Decision Support Systems and Their Effective Use." *Data Base*, Vol. 8, No. 3, Winter 1977.
7. Ginzberg, M. J., and E. Stohr. "Decision Support Systems: Issues and Perspectives." In *Decision Support Systems*, M. J. Ginzberg et al., ed. Proceedings, NYU Symposium on DSS; New York, 1981. Amsterdam: North-Holland, 1982.
8. Gorry, G. A., and M. S. Scott-Morton. "A Framework for Management Information Systems." *Sloan Management Review*, Vol. 13, No. 1, Fall 1971.
9. Gray, P. "Group Decision Support Systems." *Transactions DSS 86*, Washington, D.C., April 21–23, 1986.
10. Gray, P. "The User Interface in GDSS." *Transactions DSS 88*, Boston, 1988.
11. Hackathorn, R. D., and P. G. W. Keen. "Organizational Strategies for Personal Computing in Decision Support Systems." *MIS Quarterly*, September 1981.

12. Huber, G. P. "Issues in the Design of Group Decision Support Systems." *MIS Quarterly*, September 1984.

13. Keen, P. G. W. "Adaptive Design For Decision Support Systems. *Data Base*, Vol. 12, Nos. 1 and 2, Fall 1980.

14. Keen, P. G. W. "Value Analysis: Justifying Decision Support Systems." *MIS Quarterly*, March 1981.

15. Kroeber, D. W., and H. J. Watson. *Computer-Based Information Systems*. 2nd ed. New York: Macmillan, 1986.

16. Little, J. D. C. "Models and Managers: The Concept of a Decision Calculus." *Management Science*, Vol. 16, No. 8, April 1970.

17. McLeod, R., Jr. *Decision Support Software for IBM Personal Computer*. Chicago: SRA, 1985.

18. Meador, C. L., et al. "Setting Priorities for DSS Development." *MIS Quarterly*, June 1984.

19. Moore, J. H., and M. G. Chang. "Design of Decision Support Systems." *Data Base*, Vol. 12, Nos. 1 and 2, Fall 1980.

20. Naylor, T. H. "Strategic Planning Models." *Managerial Planning*, Vol. 30, No. 1, 1983.

21. Nunamaker, J. F., et al. "Computer-aided Deliberation: Model Management and Group Decision Support." *Operations Research*, Vol. 36, No. 6, November–December 1988.

22. Oliff, M. D. "FAST Decision Support." *Proceeding Amer. Inst. of Dec. Sciences*, National Meeting, Toronto, Canada, November 1984.

23. Sprague, R. H., Jr., and E. D. Carlson. *Building Effective Decision Support Systems*. Englewood Cliffs, NJ: Prentice-Hall, 1982.

24. Sprague, R. H., Jr., and J. J. Watson. "A Decision Support System for Banks." *Omega*, Vol. 4, No. 6, 1976.

25. Stohr, E. A., and N. H. White. "User Interfaces for Decision Support Systems: An Overview." *Inter. Jour. of Policy Analysis and Infor. Systems*, Vol. 6, No. 4, 1982.

26. Straub, D. W., Jr., and Renée A. Beauclair. "Current and Future Uses of Group Decision Support System Technology: Report on a Recent Empirical Study." *Journal of Management Information System*, Vol. 5, No. 1, Summer 1988.

27. Vogel, Doug, et al. "Group Decision Support Systems: Determinants of Success." *Transactions DSS 87*. San Franscisco, June 1987.

APPENDIX A: Database Structures

The relationships between the many individual records stored in a database can be expressed by several logical structures. DBMS are designed to use these structures to execute their functions. The three fundamental structures are relational, hierarchical, and network. They are shown in Figure 4.15.

Relational Database

This prominent form of database organization—described as tabular or flat—allows the user to think in the form of two-dimensional tables, which is the way many people see data reports. It takes its name from the mathematical theory of relations. This structure is most popular for DSS databases.

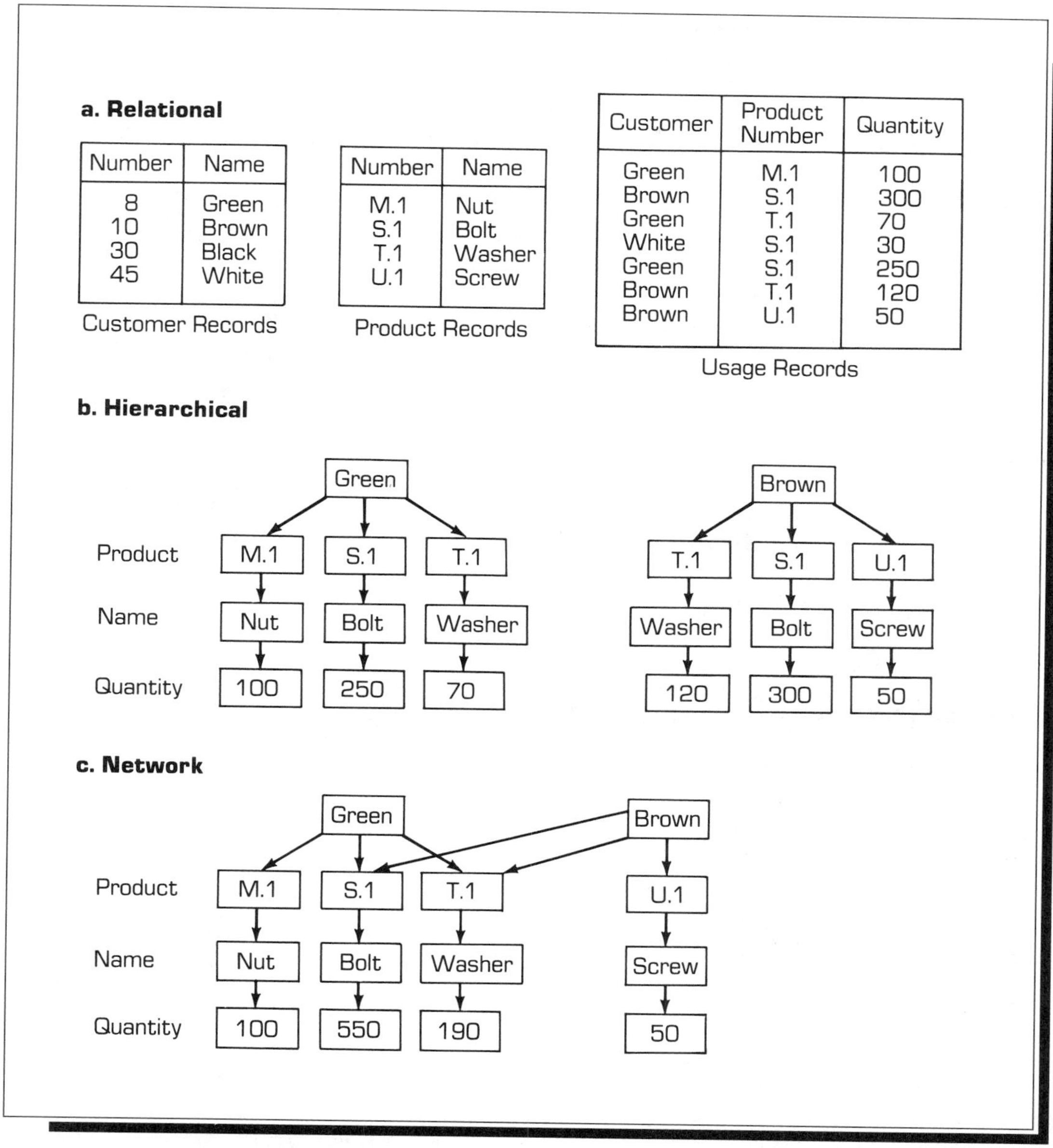
a. Relational
Number Name
8 Green
10 Brown
30 Black
45 White
Customer Records
Number Name
M.1 Nut
S.1 Bolt
T.1 Washer
U.1 Screw
Product Records
Customer Product Number Quantity
Green M.1 100
Brown S.1 300
Green T.1 70
White S.1 30
Green S.1 250
Brown T.1 120
Brown U.1 50
Usage Records
b. Hierarchical
Green
Product M.1 S.1 T.1
Name Nut Bolt Washer
Quantity 100 250 70
Brown
T.1 S.1 U.1
Washer Bolt Screw
120 300 50
c. Network
Green
Brown
Product M.1 S.1 T.1
U.1
Name Nut Bolt Washer
Screw
Quantity 100 550 190
50

FIGURE 4.15 Database structures.

Thus, a data file consists of a number of columns proceeding down a page. These columns are considered individual fields. The rows on a page represent individual records made up of several fields. This is the very same design employed by spreadsheets. Several such data files may be "related" by means of a common data field found in the two (or more) data files. These common fields must be spelled exactly alike and must be the same size (number of bytes) and type (e.g., alphanumeric, dollar, etc.). For example, in Figure 4.15 the data field called customer name is found in both the customer and the product files, and they are thus related. The data field called product number is found in the product file and the usage file. It is through these common linkages that all three files are related and in combination form a relational database.

The advantage of this form of database is that it is simple for the user to learn, can be easily expanded or altered, and may be accessed in a number of formats not anticipated at the time of the initial design and development of the database.

Hierarchical

The hierarchical model orders the data items in a top-down fashion, creating logical links between related data items. It looks like a tree, or an organizational chart.

Network

This structure permits more complex links, including lateral connections between related items. This structure is also called the CODASYL model. It can save storage space owing to sharing of some items (e.g., Green and Brown are sharing S.1 and T.1).

APPENDIX B: Representative Models

The following list includes representative quantitative models categorized by major business functions. It also includes a list of management science and statistical models.

Area	*Models*
Accounting	Cost analysis, discriminant analysis, break-even analysis, auditing (e.g., sampling), tax computation and analysis, depreciation methods, budgets.
Corporate level	Corporate planning, venture analysis, mergers and acquisitions.
Finance	Cash flow, return on investment, buy or lease, budgeting for optimal capital expenditure, bond refinancing, selecting optimal stock portfolio, Treasury bill values, compound interest, after-tax yield, foreign exchange values.
Marketing	Product demand forecast, advertising strategy analysis, pricing strategies, market share analysis, sales growth evaluation, sales performance.

Personnel	Labor negotiations, labor market analysis, personnel skill, training, employee business expense, fringe benefits computations, payroll and deductions.
Production	Product design, production schedule, transportation, product-mix inventory level (EOQ, ELS), quality control, learning curve, plant location, material allocation, maintenance analysis, machine replacement, job assignment, and MRP.
Management science	Linear programming, decision trees, Markov analysis, simulation, PERT, CPM, queuing models, dynamic programming, network models.
Statistics	Regression and correlation analysis, exponential smoothing, sampling, time-series analysis, hypothesis-testing models, Bayesian statistics.
Other	Econometric models.

Chapter 5

Constructing a
Decision Support System

The previous chapter presented an overview of DSS. The capabilities of DSS were stressed and a sample case was given. The first question that may enter a manager's mind is what must be done to acquire a DSS? Unfortunately DSS are designed to deal with complex situations and therefore they cannot simply be acquired. Rather they must be custom tailored to the specific use. This chapter deals with the DSS construction process, and includes the following sections:

5.1   Introduction

The construction of a DSS is a complicated process. It involves issues ranging from the technical, such as hardware selection, to the behavioral, such as person-machine interfaces and the potential impact of DSS on individuals and groups. This chapter concentrates mainly on construction issues involving DSS software.

Because there are several types and categories of DSS, there is no single best approach to the construction of a DSS. There are also variations because of the differences in organizations, individual decision makers, and the DSS problem area. For example, the Houston Minerals DSS was constructed to support a one-time decision, whereas the GLSC DSS was developed for repetitive use. The Houston case was constructed in only a few days with the help of a specialized planning language. In contrast, the GLSC DSS was developed over a four-year period. Why was one DSS developed so quickly, yet the other took so long? What is a "specialized planning language"? What are some of the managerial aspects of DSS construction? These questions and several others are addressed in this and the forthcoming chapters.

5.2   The System Development Life Cycle (SDLC)

The development (or modification) of a computerized information system can be an event of major consequence to an organization. It usually follows a lengthy process termed the *life cycle* of the computerized system. Although there are many versions of this process, it can be generalized into six basic phases. (For details, see Dickson and Wetherbe [7], Lucas [14], and Zmud [26].)

The process, described in Figure 5.1, is appropriate for most transaction processing systems, traditional MIS, and for some DSS. However, building most DSS is quite a different proposition. Specifically, the design, implementation, and evaluation of DSS tend to proceed concurrently. These processes are evolutionary in that the DSS is likely to be incomplete when put to work for the first time. Because of the semistructured or unstructured nature of problems addressed by decision support systems, managers' perceived needs for information will change and so the DSS must also change. Therefore most DSS are developed by a process that is different from the classical SDLC.

5.3   The DSS Development Process

The development process described in this section includes all the activities that could go into a complex DSS development. However, not all the activities are performed for every DSS. For example, a simple ad hoc DSS goes through a shorter process, and a user-developed DSS may involve both a shorter process and a different development orientation. The illustrated process is based on an integration of the work of Keen and Scott-Morton (12) and Meador et al. (17). The process is summarized in Figure 5.2. The various phases are described below.

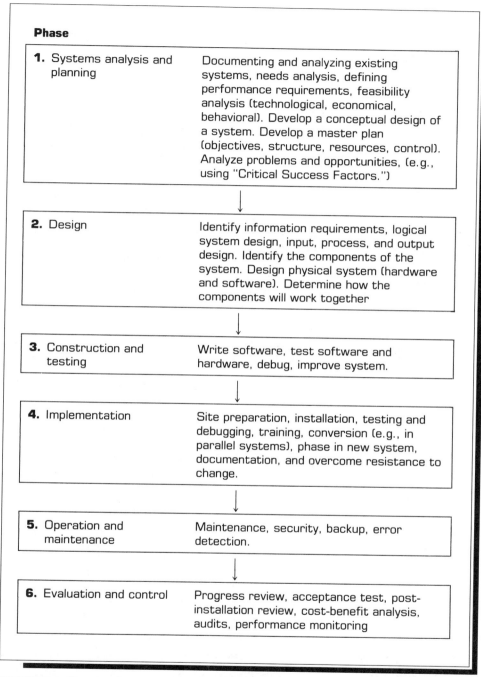

FIGURE 5.1 The development phases of a computerized information system.

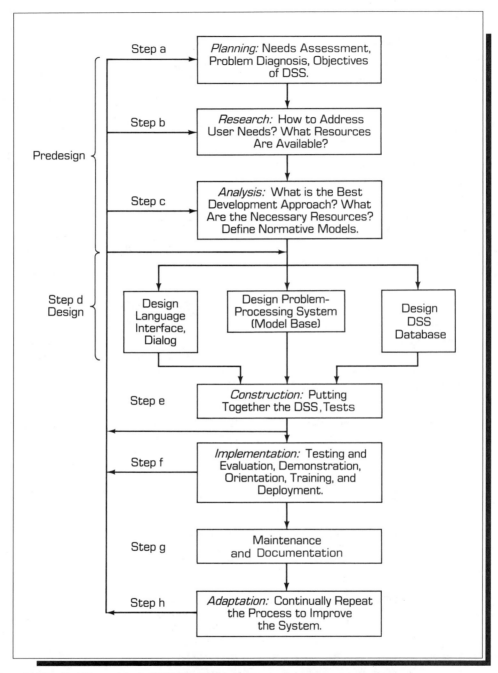

FIGURE 5.2 Phases in building a decision support system.

Planning

Planning deals mainly with need assessment and problem diagnosis. Here the objectives and goals of the decision support effort are defined. A crucial step in the planning effort is determining the key decisions of the DSS. For example, in a portfolio management system, a key decision might be selecting the correct stocks for a particular customer's needs. It could be difficult to provide information that would advise a portfolio manager which stocks to select because of the many factors involved. Some customers might be very conservative and desire low-risk stocks only. Others might prefer higher-risk situations because of the greater potential returns. Two points should be emphasized relative to the key decisions. First, the DSS is only a tool providing information to the manager. The portfolio manager, not the DSS, makes the final decision on which stocks to select. Second, though we may find it difficult to provide relevant information for a decision, it is still crucial to identify the key decisions. The method of critical success factors (CSF) is recommended for this stage (see Shank et al. [22]) to help with this identification.

Research

This phase involves the identification of a relevant approach for addressing user needs and available resources (hardware, software, vendors, systems, studies or related experiences in other organizations, and review of relevant research).

Analysis

This phase includes the determination of the best approach and specific resources required to implement it, including technical, staff, financial, and organizational resources. It is basically a *conceptual* design followed by a feasibility study.

A normative approach is suggested here (by Keen and Scott-Morton [12]) to define the ideal models that can provide information for key decisions. Such models are likely to be theoretical. In the actual implementation of the DSS it is unlikely that we will attain the level of the normative model. But it represents a goal we should try to attain in a real-world situation. Even though it may not be practical or advisable to implement the normative model, we should keep it in mind when designing the actual DSS. Such normative models are a major part of our design objectives, because the models tell us the ideal level of performance.

Design

The detailed specifications of the system components, structure, and features are determined here. The design can be divided into three parts corresponding to the three major components of a DSS: database and its management, model base and its management (the problem-solving part of the DSS), and the dialog subsystems. Here one selects appropriate software tools and generators (such as database manager and a spreadsheet) or writes them. A major issue in the design effort is deciding what commercially available software to use. This issue is discussed in detail in Chapter 6.

Construction

A DSS can be constructed in different ways depending on the design philosophy and the tools being used. The construction is the technical implementation (programming) of the design. The system is being tested continuously and improvements are being made.

Implementation

At the end of the construction phase, the system is ready to be implemented in the real world. The implementation phase consists of the following tasks: testing, evaluation, demonstration, orientation, training, and deployment. Several of these tasks happen simultaneously.

Testing. In this phase, data on the system's performance are collected and compared against the design specifications.

Evaluation. During this phase, the implemented system is evaluated to see how well it meets users' needs. Technical and organizational loose ends are also identified. Evaluation is particularly difficult with a DSS because the system is continuously being modified or expanded, and therefore does not have neatly defined completion dates or standards for comparison. The testing and evaluation usually result in changes in the design and the construction. The process is cyclical and repeats itself several times.

Demonstration. Demonstration of the fully operational system capabilities to the user community is an important phase. Viewers can become believers. As a result they accept the system with less or no resistance.

Orientation. This involves instruction of managerial users in the basic capabilities of the system.

Training. Operational users are trained in system structure and functions.

Deployment. The full system is operationally deployed for all members of the user community.

The development effort ends with two additional phases: maintenance and adaptation.

Maintenance and Documentation

Maintenance involves planning for ongoing support of the system and its user community. Proper documentation for using and maintaining the system is also developed.

Adaptation

Adaptation requires recycling through the steps above on a regular basis to respond to changing user needs. As mentioned earlier, these steps are not linear (i.e., there are loops and cycles, see Figure 5.2).

Summary. The preceding process has many variations (owing to the many variations of DSS), two of which are presented in Sections 5.9 and 5.10.

To enhance the understanding of specific design processes, we explore the following conceptual foundations, which are unique to DSS:

□ Technology level classification
□ Participants in the process
□ Approaches to DSS construction
□ Iterative nature of the process
□ Team-developed versus user-developed DSS

5.4 Technology Levels

A useful framework for understanding DSS construction issues was devised by Sprague (23), who identified three levels of DSS technology: specific DSS, DSS generators, and DSS tools.

Specific DSS

The "final product," or finished DSS that actually accomplishes the work, is called a *specific DSS* (SDSS). It is used to support a specific application. For example, the Houston Minerals case presented earlier is a specific DSS for analyzing a joint venture.

A well-known example of a specific DSS is the police-beat allocation system, which was implemented by IBM in San Jose, California. This system allows a police officer to display a map outline on a video display terminal and call up data by geographical zones showing police calls for service, response times, and activity level. An officer can manipulate the map, zones, and data, and experiment with a variety of police patrol alternatives. Incidentally, this DSS yielded superior results (in terms of acceptance by users and consistency with the problem requirements) over a solution derived by linear programming.

DSS Generators

A generator is a package of software that provides a set of capabilities to build a specific DSS quickly, inexpensively, and easily. A popular microcomputer-based generator is Lotus 1-2-3. A generator possesses diverse capabilities ranging from modeling, report generation and graphical display to performing risk analysis. These capabilities, which have been available separately for some time, are integrated into an easy-to-use package.

> The term *DSS generator* emerged from the concept of *program* (or application) *generator*. Application generators are tools used by programmers and system analysts to expedite programming and systems development. For example, a program generator can be used to build an inventory control system.
>
> Program generators add convenience and reduce costs for the creation of programs. The programs produced are not as efficient, in terms of processing throughout, as those coded from scratch by experienced programmers. Therefore generators are more suitable for applications that run infrequently or that do not involve large-volume data processing.

One of the first DSS generators, Geodata Analysis and Display (GADS), was developed by IBM and used to build the police-beat specific DSS described earlier. This generator contains maps, data, a data dictionary, and statements for special procedures that can be changed from one application to another. Originally developed from a specific DSS, GADS was also used to build (in less than a month) a specific DSS to support the planning of territories for IBM customer service engineers. In other applications, GADS was used to set school attendance boundaries, to establish sales territories, to route copier repairmen, and to plan equipment placement for fire stations.

There has been an evolutionary growth from two directions toward what might be described as an "ideal" DSS generator. One direction is *special-purpose languages* initially developed for the mainframes. In fact, many commercial DSS generators evolved from planning (or modeling) languages, usually with added report generation and graphic display capabilities. Examples of such languages are the Interactive Financial Planning System (IFPS) and Evaluation Planning Systems (EPS). Other types of specialized languages are those initially developed around strong DBMS capabilities. Examples of such languages are Nomad 2, Ramis II, and Focus. The second direction is microbased *integrated software* systems like Lotus 1-2-3, Symphony, and Framework, which are constructed around spreadsheet technology. Both types of generators are discussed in Chapter 6.

DSS Tools

At the lowest level of DSS technology are the software utilities or tools. These elements facilitate the development of either a DSS generator or a specific DSS. Examples of tools are graphics (hardware and software), query systems, random number generators, spreadsheets, and programming languages.

Relationships Among the Three Levels

The relationships among the three levels are presented in Figure 5.3. The tools are used to construct generators, which in turn are used to construct specific DSS. However, tools can also be used directly to construct specific DSS. In

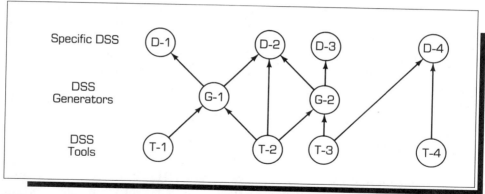

FIGURE 5.3 Technology levels.

addition (not shown in the figure), there may be simpler tools for constructing more complicated tools.

The use of DSS generators is extremely helpful in constructing specific DSS and enabling them to quickly adapt to changes. Using generators can save a significant amount of time and money, thus making a DSS financially feasible. Constructing DSS only with tools, without generators, can be a very lengthy and expensive proposition, especially if the tools themselves need to be developed. Although most of the early DSS were developed without generators, this is no longer the usual case.

Significance. The classification of technology levels is not only important for understanding the construction of DSS (and also ES) but also for developing a framework for their use. A field study (Mittman and Moore [18]) revealed that DSS generators and tools are extremely useful even for senior managers. There is a wide range of decision situations faced by senior management that require ad hoc DSS. Ad hoc DSS can be developed economically, and in a timely manner, only with the aid of generators.

5.5   The Participants

Several types of participants play major roles in the construction and operation of DSS. The number of participants involved in developing a DSS vary. In some cases, the user is the sole participant; in other cases, several parties participate, each with a different degree of involvement.

The User.   The user is the manager, the analyst, or a committee—the individual(s) responsible for making the decision, conducting some analysis, or solving a problem. The user may be an individual or a group.

The Intermediary.   Sometimes called the *chauffeur*, this individual, who is usually a staff analyst, helps the manager to use the DSS. Because most early DSS were not very "user-friendly," they generally required an intermediary.

The DSS Builder (or Facilitator). This individual is responsible for technical decisions like what tools and/or generators to use, and whether to use a micro-, a mini-, or a mainframe computer (i.e., what software and hardware are necessary to provide the required capabilities). The builder must possess an understanding of both the problem area and DSS technology. During the 1970s (and today for large DSS), this role was carried on by a special DSS group. Currently, especially for smaller DSS, the functions of a DSS builder are most likely to be provided by a member of the *information center*.

The Technical Support Person. This participant develops additional information system capabilities or components as needed and may also provide technical assistance to the DSS builder. This individual is a computer scientist and/or programmer who participates mainly in large-scale DSS development. He or she does the necessary programming to "glue" together the DSS and to connect it with other CBIS if needed.

The Toolsmith. Although the trend is to use existing tools, it is possible that some large-scale DSS will be enriched by new hardware, software, or even programming languages. The toolsmith's responsibility is to research and develop tools that improve the efficiency and/or effectiveness of the DSS package.

Note: One individual may assume several of the above roles or several individuals may fill one role.

The typical participation in many personal DSS consists of a manager (user) with some help from the Information Center. There is less involvement of the technical people from the information systems (IS) department in building DSS, especially in micro-DSS. The technical support and toolsmithing in such cases

The Information Center (IC)

The information center concept was conceived in an attempt to reduce the growing number of requests for computer applications and to alleviate the "backlog" problem. It is a user-oriented organizational unit that provides service to end-users. The concept means different things to different people, and it appears under different structures and names.

The information center provides the end-user with appropriate education, technical support, usable tools, consulting (e.g., selection of DSS software), accessibility to databases, and convenient access to other computer systems. It is designed to improve turnaround time to users' requests for information, and to facilitate data analysis, special reports, and other one-shot, brief information needs. It is staffed mainly by user-oriented people experienced in the functional business areas who are specifically trained in the use of DBMS (particularly query language and report writing) and in modeling languages. It is designed mainly for PC users but can serve other end-users. It also protects the IS staff from being "bogged down" by users' requests for assistance. See Chapter 21 for details.

can be provided by vendors. Thus the role that the information center plays in DSS (and in ES) construction is expanding rapidly. Some organizational implications of this situation are discussed in Chapter 21. The technology level concept and the specification of the participants provide the necessary background for understanding the development process, which is reviewed next.

5.6   Approaches to DSS Construction

There are several approaches to DSS construction. These are classified into three categories: quick-hit, staged development, and development of a complete DSS (Sprague and Carlson [24]).

Quick-hit.   According to this approach, a specific DSS is constructed when there is a recognized need and a high potential payoff, or a difficult problem exists. The Houston Minerals DSS was constructed in this manner. Many micro-DSS are being constructed this way, using an available generator. In the quick-hit approach, costs and risks are low, the latest technology can be utilized, and the DSS can be constructed relatively quickly. A major advantage is that it uses commercially available generators. Thus much of the software updating and maintenance is done by software vendors rather than by the user's organization. The disadvantages are that quick-hit DSS are usually constructed for one person or for one purpose, they do not relate to other DSS, and there is usually limited carryover of experience to the next DSS. They are also inefficient in computing time as compared with the complete DSS.

When Is a Quick-Hit Appropriate?

□ *Clear-cut goals*—The goals of the project should be both settable and set at the outset; no research should be needed to define them.
□ *Clear-cut procedure*—The DSS should be based on existing types of well-understood procedures and calculations; again, no research should be needed to define them.
□ *Available data*—The needed data should be readily available.
□ *Fewer users*—The DSS should be for the benefit of one or a few highly motivated users with common goals and concerns. The DSS should not cross organizational boundaries, nor should major selling or educational efforts be required.
□ *Independent system*—Although the DSS may use input data prepared by other systems, it should operate independently of all other systems once those data have been received.

Source: S. Alter, in D. Young and P. G. W. Keen, eds., *DSS-81 Transactions*, Austin, TX: Execucom System Corp., 1981.

Staged Development. According to this approach, a specific DSS is constructed with some advanced planning, so that part of the effort in developing the first system can be reused in future DSS. Such an approach can lead to the development of an in-house DSS generator. The staged development approach takes more time than the quick-hit, yet it can yield similar success and visibility.

Complete DSS. This approach requires the development of a full-service, large-scale, DSS generator; large-scale, specific DSS; and an organizational unit to manage such a project. An example of such an approach is the development of the GADS system by IBM, which included a generator and several specific DSS. It is lengthy process that is likely to result in an efficient generator with excellent integration of basic tools. It may take several years to develop such a system; therefore, success and visibility are delayed. Furthermore, there is a high risk of technological obsolescence.

The approach to be selected will depend on the specific situation (i.e., the organization, purpose of the DSS, users, tasks, available tools, and builder). In some companies a combination approach is used—namely, there is a large-scale, companywide DSS and several unrelated quick-hit DSS. With the development of more commercial DSS generators and increased capabilities of microcomputers, the quick-hit will probably become the most frequently used approach.

5.7 The Development Process: Iterative and Adaptive

DSS construction can be executed in several different ways. We will differentiate between what we call the *traditional (life cycle) technique* and the *iterative process*.

The Traditional System Design Technique

This design strategy, which was presented in Section 5.2, involves the fundamental assumption that the information requirements of a system can be predetermined. Therefore there has been a keen interest in the last decade in information requirements definition (IRD) as a formalized approach to systems analysis. Traditionally, IRDs are determined by combining logical analysis with investigation of user information processing behavior. For example, the requirements of an accounts receivable information system can be determined by examining accounting procedures and by speaking with experienced accountants. The concept of CSF can also be used to determine IRD.

But where does the traditional approach leave us with decision support systems? DSS are designed to enhance the decision processes of managers faced with poorly structured problems. By definition, we do not, perhaps cannot, completely understand the user's needs. As a result, we must explicitly acknowledge the role of learning in our design strategy. That is, it is expected that as part of the design and implementation effort, users will "learn" more about their problem or environment and therefore will identify new and unanticipated information needs.

Generally, DSS designers have recognized a need for a departure from the traditional design strategy. The strategy suggested as most appropriate is called *evolutionary* (Keen [11]), *iterative* (Sprague and Carlson [24]), or *prototyping* (Henderson and Ingraham [9]). Other names are middle-out process, adaptive design, and incremental design.

The Iterative Approach

The iterative approach aims at building a DSS in a series of short steps with immediate feedback from users to ensure that development is proceeding correctly. DSS tools and generators must, therefore, permit changes to be made quickly and easily.

The iterative design process combines four major phases of the traditional SDLC (analysis, design, construction, and implementation) into a single step that is repeated. The iterative process includes the following four activities (per Courbon et al. [6]):

1. Select an important subproblem (or a segment of a problem). The user and the builder jointly identify a subproblem for which the initial DSS is constructed. This early joint effort sets up initial working relationships between the participants and opens the lines of communication. The subproblem should be small enough so that the nature of the problem, the need for computer-based support, and the nature of that support are clear. It should have high interest value to the decision maker even if that interest may be short-lived.

2. Develop a small but usable system to assist the decision maker. No major systems analysis or feasibility analysis is involved. In fact, the builder and the user go through all the steps of the system development process quickly, though on a small scale. The system should, out of necessity, be simple.

3. Evaluate the system constantly. At the end of each cycle the system is evaluated by the user and the builder. Evaluation is an integral part of the development process, and it is the control mechanism for the entire iterative design process. The evaluation mechanism is what keeps the cost and effort of developing a DSS consistent with its value.

4. Refine, expand, and modify the system in cycles. Subsequent cycles expand and improve the original version of the DSS. All the analysis-design-construction-implementation-evaluation steps are repeated in each successive refinement.

This process is repeated several times until a relatively stable system evolves. The interaction between the user, the builder, and the technology are extremely important in this process (Keen [11]). Note that user involvement is very high. There is a balance of effort and cooperation between the user and the builder: the user takes the lead in the utilization and evaluation activities, while the builder is stronger in the design and implementation phases. The user plays a joint and active role in contrast to conventional systems development, where the user frequently operates in a reactive or passive role.

The iterative design approach produces a specific DSS. The process is fairly straightforward for a DSS designed for personal support. The process becomes more complicated, although not invalidated, for a DSS that provides group support or organizational support. Specifically, there is a greater need for mechanisms to support communication among users and builders. There is also a need for mechanisms to accommodate personal variations while maintaining a common core system that is standard for all users. This is not a completely new concept; mechanisms that provide personal, group, and public data files have been a standard part of time-sharing systems for years.

As the number of users for a given system increases, the communication links required to operate the iterative design process must become more formal and structured. It may be necessary to establish checkpoints to define the beginning of each usage-evaluation cycle. When a DSS has many users and is designed for organizational support, it must be integrated into the organization by formalizing some of the stages in the systems development process.

The iterative process can be summarized as follows. It begins with a model of a part of the problem or with a simplified version of the entire problem. This gives end-users something concrete to react to. End-users then offer suggestions that may be incorporated into the DSS and they are then given a new version of the DSS. The process continues until the end-user is satisfied (at least temporarily) with the model. This process is necessary because in complex decisions the users often do not know what they want and the DSS builder does not understand what end-users need or will accept. The iterative process permits mutual learning to occur.

The iterative process is often referred to as *prototyping*. However, there is a difference between conventional prototyping and the iterative process. It is only lately that prototyping has been modified and is now similar to the iterative process. This issue is presented in Appendix A.

DSS and the Iterative Approach—Summary

DSS are constructed in several different ways. Some are constructed by following the system development life cycle approach; the majority, however, are built by using the evolutionary prototyping approach.

The iterative process has three main advantages:

- Short development time.
- Short user reaction time (feedback from user).
- Improved users' understanding of the system, its information needs, and its capabilities.

There is also a disadvantage to the iterative process. When such an approach is used, the gains obtained from cautiously stepping through each of the system's life-cycle stages might be lost. These gains include a thorough understanding of the information system's benefits and costs, a detailed description of the business's information needs, an information system design that is easy to maintain, a well-tested information system, and a well-prepared group of users.

The construction method that the DSS builder will use depends, in many cases, on whether the DSS is built by the end-user or by a DSS team.

5.8 Team-developed vs. User-developed DSS

Many of the DSS developed in the 1970s and early 1980s were large-scale, complex systems designed primarily to provide organizational support. Such systems are still being developed for complex problems and for companywide applications. These systems are constructed by a team composed of users, intermediaries, DSS builders, technical support experts, and toolsmiths. Because there can be several individuals in each category, these teams are often large and their composition may change over time. Constructing a DSS with a team is a complex, lengthy, and costly process.

Another approach to the construction of a DSS is a user-developed system. This approach gained momentum in the 1980s owing to the development of microcomputers, computer communication networks, and micro-mainframe communication. In addition, the spread of user-developed DSS was fueled by the increasing amount of friendly development software for microcomputers, the reduced cost of both software and hardware, and the increased capabilities of microcomputers. Finally, the establishment of Information Centers contributed to an even greater proliferation of DSS constructed by users.

Often a mixture between these two extremes is developed. For example, a team can develop the basic DSS and a specific user can then develop additional applications. In addition, one can find other approaches to development such as that of Security Pacific Bank (Los Angeles), which has a DSS unit within its financial services division. This unit is completely separated from the IS department, and it is the major contributor to DSS construction in the bank. In the forthcoming sections we outline the process involved in each of the two extreme approaches.

5.9 Team-developed DSS

A team-developed DSS requires a substantial effort. Therefore it needs extensive planning and organization. The planning and organization depends on the specific DSS, the organization where it will be used, and so on. However, certain activities are generic and can be executed by any team. The planning and organizing activities discussed here include the following:*

- □ Forming the DSS group.
- □ An action plan.
- □ Planning for a DSS generator and the specific DSS.
- □ Representations, operations, memory aids, and control mechanisms, (ROMC).
- □ Flexibility in DSS.

---

*The material in this section has been condensed, with permission, from Chapters 3–5 of Sprague and Carlson (24). Other team-developed DSS approaches are used by many organizations, but they are not documented in the literature.

Forming the DSS Group

A complex DSS requires a group of people to build and to manage it. The number of people in the group will depend on the size of the effort and the tactical development option used (e.g., prototyping vs. SDLC). Some companies have initiated a DSS effort with as few as 2 or 3 people; others have used as many as 12 to 15 people.

In general, the responsibilities of the DSS group include the following:

1. To develop a good understanding of the DSS philosophy and formulate a group mission based on that philosophy.
2. To become familiar with the procedures for implementing DSS.
3. To manage the DSS generator(s) and the collection of tools used to provide DSS building services to users.
4. To play the role of a facilitator helping users bring the technology to bear on their problems.

The builder's role is needed to bridge the gap between the technology and the user. This is the same role that applications-oriented systems analysts have occupied in building traditional systems. Sometimes the builder must act as the intermediary and counsel the user, while at other times the builder must play the role of technical support when working with the toolsmith.

In some cases, the builder's role develops a dual focus: One role is technology-oriented, developing and managing the DSS generator; the other is sales-oriented, promoting the use of DSS by working directly with the users or intermediaries.

The DSS group can be formed by redefining and extending the charter of an existing group, or it can be newly initiated. In either case, the group or individuals can come from several sources.

1. A special-purpose team of applications systems analysts.
2. A reoriented software tools group.
3. A management science or industrial engineering group.
4. The planning department.
5. A staff analysis group from one of the functional areas such as a market research group, or a budget analysis group from accounting/finance.

The organizational placement of the DSS group varies. Here are some typical locations:

1. Within the information services (IS) department (or the data processing department).
2. As a highly placed executive staff group.
3. Within the finance or other functional area.
4. Within the industrial engineering department.
5. Within the management science group.
6. Within the Information Center group.

Regardless of the organizational location, the DSS group will have to confront the issue of centralization versus decentralization. In a centralized organization, the DSS group is more likely to have the full responsibility for the DSS generators and tools, and for handling all users. In a decentralized organization, the group may provide the technical expertise to manage the generators and tools while supporting work done by or with users in each division or geographic region. In the past there was reluctance by the IS staff to participate in the DSS team whenever it was constructed with a non-SDLS approach. This situation is changing and there is more willingness by the IS staff to participate in the DSS team. Once the group is formed, an action plan is developed.

Action Plan

The action plan comprises four phases.

Phase 1. Preliminary study and feasibility assessment. This phase includes needs assessment (present and future) and review of all requests for DSS. Conduct a few pilot projects. Prepare for phase 2.

Phase 2. Developing the DSS environment. Activate the DSS group, acquire the tools, and find the necessary data. Plan the development process (e.g., what to make and what to buy), and prepare for phase 3.

Phase 3. Developing the initial DSS. Use the iterative process. Improve and redesign until the DSS is in full working condition. Plan phase 4.

Phase 4. Developing a subsequent DSS. Search for a second DSS that can "fit into" the first. For example, if the first DSS deals with budget planning, the second can be expense analysis (to be compared with the budget). However, in many cases one may not find a fit, or the second related DSS is of a low priority. In such a case, the best way is to look at successive applications needs.

The DSS group may be formed as the first step in a DSS effort based on upper management's conviction that such an effort is necessary. More often, the decision to form a group is a step in a broader plan to evaluate potential benefits and the feasibility of a DSS effort. Because the fundamental rules in DSS are determined by user needs, a DSS effort should not be undertaken unless the need is apparent. Assessing the extent of need, however, requires some understanding and commitment to the DSS in advance (another chicken-and-egg issue).

Planning for a DSS Generator

The staged development approach discussed earlier leads to the development (or purchase) of a DSS generator(s). What would an ideal DSS generator look like, and what should it do? Identifying the necessary and desirable characteristics of a DSS generator is a crucial step in phase 2 of the plan (development of the DSS environment). A typical but inappropriate approach to this task would be to list all possible features a DSS generator should have, then prepare a checklist to see which existing software system provides the most features. Such an approach is inappropriate for two reasons. First, because there is little rationale for choosing items on the initial list, it could be difficult to assess the importance of their presence or absence in a given DSS generator. Second, there is no ideal "full-service" generator currently available, either in the software market or in a user organization, against which existing software may be compared.

The construction approach suggested by Sprague and Carlson is in a form of "top-down" analysis at four levels (see Figure 5.4):

1. Identify the *overall objectives* for a DSS generator.
2. Infer from level 1 the *general capabilities* that a DSS generator must have to respond to the objectives. Segregate the general objectives into those related to the data, models, and dialog components of the DSS.
3. Infer from level 2 a set of *specific capabilities* that are required to accomplish the general capabilities.
4. Infer from levels 2 and 3 *specific devices, strategies,* and *hardware/software* features necessary to implement the specific capabilities.

The general objectives, capabilities, and features of DSS generators are described as follows:

Level 1 Overall Objectives.   There are two basic objectives of a DSS generator:

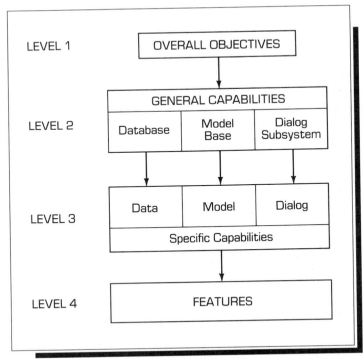

FIGURE 5.4   A top-down criterion for a DSS generator. (*Source:* Adapted from Sprague and Carlson [23], pp. 70–72.) Details are shown in Fig. 4.13

1. To permit quick and easy development of a wide variety of specific DSS.
2. To be flexible and adaptive enough to facilitate the iterative design process. This allows specific DSS to respond quickly to changes in the organizational or physical environment, in the style of the user, or in the nature of the task. The generator must also facilitate communication and interaction between the user and the builder.

Level 2 General Capabilities.

1. The generator should be easy to use. Specifically,
   a. The generator should be able to create a specific DSS that is easy and convenient for nontechnical people to use.
   b. The generator should be easy and convenient for a builder to use for developing and modifying a specific DSS. This capability is related to the dialog subsystem.
2. A DSS generator should provide access to a wide variety of data sources. This capability is related to the DBMS.
3. A DSS generator should provide access to analytical capabilities. This capability is related to the model base. The overall objectives and general capabilities for an "ideal" DSS generator define the characteristics of the long-range target.

Levels 3 and 4 Capabilities and Features.
The specific capabilities and features in the dialog, data management, and model management subsystems were presented in Chapter 4.

The Representations, Operations, Memory Aids, and Control Mechanisms Approach (ROMC Approach)

The ROMC approach is a framework for DSS systems analysis and design that was developed by Sprague and Carlson (24). The major objective of this approach is to identify the characteristics and capabilities that a specific DSS needs to have.

The major difficulty in building a DSS is that the information requirements, which are the starting point for systems design, are usually poorly specified (owing to the unstructured nature of the problems solved by a DSS). The ROMC approach helps overcome this difficulty. It is composed of a set of four user-oriented entities:

- □ Representations. The ability to provide representations, if possible visual, to help conceptualize and communicate the problem. This is the context in which users interpret output and invoke operations.
- □ Operations. The ability to provide operations to analyze and manipulate those representations (the ways in which users manipulate objects in the given context).
- □ Memory Aids. To assist the user in linking representations and operations, a set of memory aids is used. These are fundamental learning aids in making decisions.

□ Control Mechanisms. Those mechanisms used to control and operate the entire system—the framework for integrating the three entities into a useful decision-making system.

Note: For a detailed list of items included in ROMC, see Appendix B.

The ROMC approach, which is process-independent, is based on five observed characteristics regarding decision making:

1. Decision makers have difficulties describing situations. They prefer to use graphical conceptualizations whenever possible.

2. The decision-making phases of intelligence, design, and choice can be applied to DSS analysis.

3. Memory aids (such as reports, "split screen" displays, data files, indexes, mental rules, and analogies) are extremely useful in decision making and should be provided by a DSS.

4. Decision makers differ in style, skills, and knowledge. Therefore the DSS should help decision makers use and develop their own styles, skills, and knowledge.

5. The decision maker expects to exercise direct, personal control over the support system. This observation does not suggest that users must work without an intermediary; it does suggest, however, that they must understand the DSS capabilities and be able to analyze the inputs and interpret the outputs of the DSS.

Examples based on these five observations are summarized in Table 5.1 (left column) and are compared with the corresponding ROMC components (right column). The closer the match between the left and right columns (and this is precisely what the ROMC approach aims to do), the better the DSS will be.

The ROMC components are identified and integrated during the actual system analysis (i.e., the DSS is designed as a set of representations with associated operations).

Flexibility in DSS

DSS must be flexible to react to the frequent changes in the environment, tasks, and users of the DSS. Flexibility is a significant consideration in all aspects of building and using DSS, but it requires special attention during the process of design. The ROMC approach provides a framework for design, and the process of design results in the particular configuration of elements that becomes a specific DSS. It is the configuration that must be flexible and easily changed to serve the decision-making needs of users over time.

The Case for Flexibility. Some observations on the characteristics of DSS users, tasks, and environment that illustrate the need for flexibility include the following, according to Keen (11):

□ Neither the user nor the builder is able to specify functional requirements in advance.

□ Users do not know, or cannot articulate, what they want and need. Therefore they need an initial system to react to and improve on.

☐ The users' concept of the task, and perception of the nature of the problem, change as the system is used.

☐ Actual uses of DSS are almost always different from those originally intended.

☐ Solutions derived through a DSS are subjective.

☐ There are wide variations among individuals in how they use DSS.

In summary, there are two basic reasons for the importance of flexibility in DSS:

1. A DSS must evolve or grow to reach an operational design because no one can completely predict or anticipate in advance what is required.

2. The system can seldom be final; it must change frequently to adjust to changes in the problem, user, and environment because these factors are inherently volatile.

Let us now consider the nature of this flexibility. Sprague and Carlson (24) distinguish four levels of flexibility:

TABLE 5.1 Decision Requirements vs. DSS Capabilities

Decision-Makers Use	DSS Provides
1. Conceptualizations: 　A city map 　Relationship between assets and 　　liabilities	1. Representations: 　A map outline 　A scatterplot of assets vs. liabilities
2. Different decision-making processes 　and decision types, all involving 　activities, for intelligence, design, 　and choice 　Gather data on customers 　Create alternative customer 　　assignments for salespeople 　Compare alternatives	2. Operations for intelligence, design, 　and choice: 　Query the data base 　Update lists to show assignments 　Print summary statistics on each 　　alternative
3. A variety of memory aids: 　List of customers 　Summary sheets on customers 　Table showing salespeople and their 　　customer assignments 　File drawers with old tables 　Scratch paper 　Staff reminders 　Rolodex	3. Automated Memory Aids: 　Extracted data on customers 　Views of customer data 　Workspace for developing assignment 　　tables 　Library for saving tables 　Temporary storage 　DSS messages 　Computerized addresses
4. A variety of styles, skills, and 　knowledge, applied via direct, 　personal control: 　Accepted conventions for 　　interpersonal communication 　Orders to staff 　Standard operating procedures 　Revise orders or procedures	4. Aid to direct personal control 　conventions for user-computer 　communication: 　Training and explanation in how to 　　give orders to the DSS 　Procedures formed from DSS 　　operations 　Ability to override DSS defaults or 　　procedures

Source: Carlson (5).

1. The flexibility to *solve*. The first level of flexibility gives the user of a specific DSS the ability to confront a problem in a flexible, personal way. It is the flexibility to perform intelligence, design, and choice activities and to explore alternative ways of viewing or solving a problem. Such flexibility is provided, for example, by the "what if" capability.

2. The flexibility to *modify*. The second level of flexibility is the ability to modify the configuration of a specific DSS so that it can handle somewhat different problems, or an expanded set of problems. This flexibility is exercised by the user and/or the builder.

3. The flexibility to *adapt*. The third level of flexibility is the ability to adapt to changes that are extensive enough to require a completely different specific DSS. This adaptability may require changes in the DSS generator (e.g., new capabilities). This flexibility is exercised by the DSS builder.

4. The flexibility to *evolve*. The fourth level of flexibility is the ability of the DSS and the DSS generator to evolve in response to changes in the basic nature of the technology on which DSS are based. This level requires a change in the tools and the generator for better efficiency.

Note: The DSS flexibility also implies that the DSS builders must be flexible. This characteristic is at odds with many traditional IS staff and may create a problem in developing and implementing DSS.

5.10   End-user Computing and User-developed DSS

End-user Computing

A user-developed DSS is directly related to a trend in information systems called end-user computing. Broadly defined, *end-user computing* is the development and use of computer-based information systems by people outside the formal data processing or information systems areas. This definition includes managers and professionals using personal computers, word processing done by secretaries, electronic mail used by the CEO, and time-sharing systems used by scientists and researchers. Relevant to DSS is a more narrow definition, which includes decision makers and professionals (such as financial or tax analysts and engineers) *building* and *using* computers to solve problems or enhance their productivity mainly through personal computers, although they may also use terminals connected to a large computer or a time-sharing network.

The end-user can be on any level of the organization, or in any functional area. Their levels of computer skill can also vary substantially. End-user computing can be classified according to the extent and method of use, type of application, training requirements, and required support. The number of end-users is growing at a rate of 50 to 100 percent annually (Rockart and Flannery [20]).

It is only natural that many end-users will attempt to construct their own DSS. Although we do not have much empirical evidence, it seems from discussions with users in small and large organizations that many DSS are being constructed today by information centers with the active participation of end-users, or by end-users themselves. Furthermore, a study conducted by Mittman

An End-User's Story

The vice president for management services at Florida Power and Light, D. L. Dady, is one of the major users of an end-user facility that includes color graphics. He cites an experience to demonstrate the value of the system to him.

"I had a telephone call about a quarter of five on a Tuesday afternoon relative to some information I was going to need at a meeting the next morning. The staff had just left for the evening. I was able to go to the terminal and compare some payroll information from Florida Power and Light with several other companies. From the COMPUSTAT database I had access to 20 years of payroll data from all utilities. I was able to put in parameters on what I wanted to look at—companies with nuclear plants (as we have) and companies that are over a certain size by number of customers and kilowatt hours produced annually. In a few seconds I had a list of 23 utility companies that met the criteria. There was one other company I also wanted to include, so I keyed that company in."

"I asked the terminal to do a calculation: I wanted to know what the average payroll was per employee among those utility companies. It takes longer to tell about it than it took to do it. I got back the average figures for as many years as COMPUSTAT had data from the companies. I had the information in my hands in 20 minutes and was able to go home and look it over quietly that evening. There I added the numbers together and produced some averages, which took me another 30 minutes."

"The next morning it took me 25 minutes with the manual and inter-active facility to produce a new graph of the data. I decided then to plot the data for only five years. On one graph I was able to show Florida Power and Light compared with the average of 24 selected companies, with the average of 8 selected companies, as well as with the high and low companies."

"Developing this kind of information would have taken weeks without the system. Moreover, it allowed me to refine my own thinking as I proceeded, depending on the significance of the numbers I generated."

Source: "Graphic Systems Aid Executive Fact Finding." *IBM Information Processing*, Vol. 1, No. 3, June–July 1982, pp. 5–6.

and Moore (18) indicated that even some top executives like to build their own DSS (using Lotus 1-2-3, for example).

User-developed DSS: Advantages and Risks

There are several advantages for users building their own DSS:

1. **Short delivery time.** You do not have to wait in line for the information services (IS) people to come. A backlog of two to three years is rather common in IS (e.g., see Rockard and Flannery [20]).

2. The prerequisites of extensive and formal user requirements specifications, which are part of system analysis in a conventional system development life cycle, are eliminated. These specifications (Zmud [26]) are often incomplete or incorrect owing to such issues as the users' inability to specify the requirement, or the communication difficulties between analyst and user. They also take a long time to develop.

3. Some DSS implementation problems could be greatly reduced by transferring the implementation process to the users.

The risks of user-developed DSS are listed as follows:

1. User-developed DSS could be of poor quality (e.g., see Alavi [1]). Lack of practical DSS design experience and the tendency of end-users to ignore conventional controls, testing procedures, and documentation standards can lead to low-quality systems. (See boxed material.)

Using a spreadsheet package, a California executive predicted in 1984, $55 million in sales over the first two years for a computer his company planned to introduce. Based on this projection, other managers began making plans for hiring additional staff and expanding inventories. Unfortunately the sales projections were wrong because the executive had forgotten to include a price discount planned for a key component. On closer examination of the model, he discovered the sales estimates were inflated by $8 million because of an error in the pricing formula. Had the executive's mistake not been detected, the actual profit margins would have been considerably lower than the projection.

---

2. Potential quality risks may be classified in three categories: (a) substandard tools and facilities used in DSS development, (b) risks associated with the development process (e.g., inability to develop workable systems, or developing of systems that generate erroneous results), and (c) data management risks (e.g., loss of data).

To reduce these risks and enhance the quality of the DSS, Alavi suggested four general approaches and eight specific tactics (see Appendix C). In addition, cooperation with an Information Center (which uses some of the specific methods suggested by Alavi) may be sufficient to assure quality DSS.

The Construction Process

The construction of user-developed DSS varies from situation to situation. It depends on the user's skill level, the availability of organizational resources (see Zmud [26]), the nature of the DSS, and the type of software used, to mention a few. Furthermore, the extent of end-user computing depends on the availability of formal mechanisms for linking end-users with the information services function (one of which is the Information Center). A typical process may be composed of the following phases (see Figure 5.5):

1. *Deciding on the project (or problem to be solved).* Execution of this phase may involve a formal cost-benefit analysis. Such analysis is not usually needed because the cost of a user-developed DSS, especially when the software and hardware are already available, is fairly small. Selection of the project by the user will contribute to an increased likelihood of successful implementation. (This situation is somewhat analogous to quality circles, a method developed in Japan to enhance participation in decision making. The members of a quality circle decide what

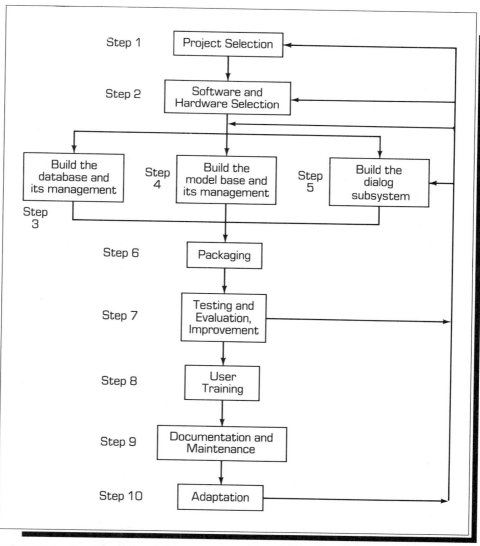

FIGURE 5.5 The development process of a DSS constructed by end-users.

project they are going to tackle.) Sometimes (as illustrated in the Chesebrough-Pond's case, see Chapter 20) the Information Center staff will look for DSS opportunities.

2. *Selecting software and hardware.* An end-user DSS is usually constructed using a commercial software package and existing hardware. The selection of hardware and software are interrelated issues. Some companies already have a variety of software (e.g., a package that is most suitable for financial planning, or another one which is better for reporting). Some software is available for micros while other is available only for a mainframe (or it is available via time sharing). The less sophisticated end user will need help in the selection. Such help can be provided by the Information Center.

3. *Model subsystem acquisition and management.* Users can write their own models and reports, but they may use standard models at times (e.g., for forecasting or for present-value calculations). Standard models may be part of the DSS generator, or they could be acquired separately to supplement the DSS generators. For example, a forecasting template can be used in conjunction with Lotus 1-2-3, and an SAS statistical package can supplement a DSS generator such as Encore. (See Chapter 6)

4. *Data acquisition and management.* The DSS may require data that are available in external and/or internal databases. Several questions will have to be answered: what data to use, how to ensure the quality of the data, where the data are available, how to transfer the data to the user (e.g., how to download the data from the mainframe to the micro), how these data can be kept secure, and how the data are incorporated into the DSS. Again, the Information Center can be of great help because the nontechnical DSS users may have difficulties in building their own databases. A DBMS that can be a part of the DSS generator or a package of its own is also needed.

5. *Dialog subsystem and its management.* Several hardware and software components make up the dialog subsystem. They range from a natural language processor to a graphics software package. Further discussion is presented in Chapter 6.

6. *Packaging.* Once the components have been acquired and the data identified, the DSS can be put together. Sometimes it is possible to modify an existing DSS software to save time. The packaging can be executed by end-users if they have experience and basic computer skills. Otherwise, help will be required from the Information Center or the information services department. The programming is usually done in procedural languages (such as Pascal or PL-1) to bond together the various software components of the DSS. Lately, there is an increased tendency to use integrated packages (such as Framework and Lotus' Symphony). When such integrated packages are used, the packaging job is minimal.

7. *Testing, evaluation, and improvement.* The user should test the DSS on sample problems, improve it if necessary, and analyze the results provided by the DSS to make sure they are reliable and valid.

8. *Training.* End-user training is very important. It can be provided by various sources ranging from the Information Center to the vendor who provides the DSS generator. (For a discussion, see *EDP Analyzer [8].*)

9. *Documentation and maintenance.* Most end-users do not like to write documentation for their personal DSS nor to develop formal maintenance plans. However, both activities should be carried out by the user. A formal documentation approach can eliminate potential problems that arise, for example, when the DSS builder-user leaves the organization.

10. *Adaptation.* This should be the easiest part of the process, because the developer is also the user. If the DSS is effective and easy to use, it will be used whenever relevant problems occur.

As indicated earlier, this development process is a typical one; however, variations can be found. For example, some end-users could use extensive planning, which is usually associated with the team-developed approach.

5.11 Some Constructive Comments

Abbreviated Process. Not all DSS are created with the entire iterative approach. Simple or user-developed systems use an abbreviated cycle that may not even be iterative (especially if an ad hoc DSS is constructed).

Use of System Development Life Cycle. Sometimes the traditional system development life cycle (SDLC), or some variation of it, is used to build a DSS. This may happen when a complex companywide DSS is being developed from scratch (without generators, using only tools). If IS people control the development of the DSS, they tend to use the SDLC. Obviously, if the information requirements are clear (a rare but possible situation), there may be less need for the iterative approach. The SDLC approach was found to be useful for building DSS that support operational control decisions while the iterative approach was more often used in support of stragetic planning systems (see Hogue and Watson [10]).

Organizational Decision-making Style. For a DSS to be effective, its design should take into consideration the organization's attitudes and approaches toward decision-making; for example, the degree of participative management, the amount of reliance on quantitative methods, and the decision making process used. For further details, see Taylor (25).

Make-or-Buy Considerations. Most companies will buy some software for the DSS rather that write it. But even the best packages may require supplemental programming and tool integration, especially for large DSS. Several questions may be considered when the make versus buy issue surfaces:

1. Which alternative is more economical?
2. Which alternative is faster?
3. Should time-sharing be considered?
4. Should a mainframe and/or micro version be acquired?
5. Should a consultant be hired to build the DSS?
6. What networking is needed?

To make the final decision a checklist may be developed. Using a multiple-criteria method (see Chapter 2), one can compare the "buy" option against the "make" for a final decision.

Building a New DSS from an Old One.   Some companies are facing decision situations that are similar in nature yet differ on specific details. For example, a commercial loan requested by a certain company in a particular industry may be similar to a loan request of another company in the same or a related industry. In such cases management faces a series of ad hoc decisions. There is no need, however, to develop a DSS from scratch for each loan request. Morgan Guaranty Trust (of New York City) uses the following approach:

The company is using a mainframe DSS generator (called IFPS, See Chapter 7) to build a specific DSS for each loan requested. A team composed of the experts on the industry, the finance people, and an analyst are assigned to each loan. The DSS is constructed by the company analyst, who was, in 1986, the only one interacting directly with the computer for loan analysis.

Once a DSS is completed, it is used to help decide whether to approve or reject the loan request. The computer program is then stored. For example, Loan L-13 was granted to a company in the chemical industry; a few weeks or months later, when a similar request for a loan arises, the DSS for L-13 can be modified to a new ad hoc DSS in only a few days.

Construction of the DSS in a day or a few days illustrates another important point. As in many quantitative analyses, a major difficulty may not be the model construction or computing the solution but getting the required data. It usually takes Morgan Guaranty Trust several weeks to acquire the data for a DSS, which is constructed in days and may be used for only a few minutes.

Project Selection and Approval.   In small-scale DSS the problem area, or the project, is selected by the user. In most cases, the existing hardware and software provide an environment that enables building the DSS at a very low cost. Therefore there is no need for a formal process for project selection and approval. However, large systems may be fairly expensive, and in addition may involve people from several departments. In the latter case, a formal approach would probably be necessary.

According to Meador et al. (17), the construction of a DSS is usually quite well done. However, this effort could be merely a waste if the DSS does not appropriately address the *right* problem. Several factors must be considered when deciding whether a project should be approved. They are listed in order of importance in Table 5.2.

Reasons for Developing DSS.   In addition to its declared objective of improving (or supporting) decision making, DSS are being developed, according to Sprague and Carlson (24), for the following reasons:

1. To establish a power base and control (or other hidden agendas).
2. To get attention.
3. To change the decision-making process.
4. To change the organizational goals.
5. To challenge the "old line" (status quo).

TABLE 5.2   Average Rated Importance of Factors in DSS Project Approval Process.

Factor	Average Rated Importance
Top management emphasis	5.91
Return on investment (cost/benefit)	5.04
Technically do-able	4.87
DSS development costs	4.76
Impact on data processing resources	4.70
Degree of user commitment	4.70
Increase in user effectiveness	4.67
DSS operating costs	4.64
Increase in user efficiency	4.61
Adaptability of organization to change	4.52
Urgency of user needs	4.49
Uncertainty of objectives for DSS design	4.27
Qualitative or "soft" benefits	4.11
Company politics	4.09

Scale: 1, Low; 7, High.

Source: Meador et al. (17), reprinted by special permission of the *MIS Quarterly*, © 1984.

It is important to identify the purpose of the DSS prior to its design, and obviously the purpose should be considered throughout the construction process.

DSS Architecture.   The integration (or "gluing") of the basic components of DSS into one system can be done in different ways. Four different arrangements or architectures have been proposed by Sprague and Carlson (23): DSS *network*, DSS *bridge*, DSS *sandwich*, and DSS *tower*. The details of the four configurations are beyond the scope of this book. However, the importance of the topic should be recognized by management.

Incorrect integration of the DSS components will result in an incorrect DSS, even when all the components are properly designed. Incorrect integration can affect many of the DSS capabilities, thus causing the DSS to fail.

5.12   Summary and Conclusions

To be successful, a DSS must offer certain capabilities: it must be responsive to changes and be easy to use. To achieve these capabilities one needs to design and construct the DSS very carefully. The development process of a DSS differs from the development process of conventional information systems, mainly because of the use of the iterative design and development strategy. This strategy calls for a small-scale, working prototype that is incrementally enlarged and/or improved. The system should be built quickly, using the latest technology, and the responsibility for the development should be in the hands of the user if at all possible.

This chapter described the traditional system development life cycle and extended it to the DSS development process. Several DSS development approaches exist. Two important approaches are team-developed DSS and user-developed DSS. In practice one can find many variations of the two.

A methodology for a team-developed process, as proposed by Sprague and Carlson, was presented here.

Most DSS are constructed with the aid of generators and tools. The details regarding the availability and use of these are the subject of Chapter 6.

Key Words

action plan	flexibility in DSS	ROMC (representation,
complete DSS	generators	operations, memory
critical success factors	information center	aids, mechanism
(CSF)	information requirements	control)
DSS builder	intermediary	specific DSS
DSS generators	iterative process	staged development
DSS tools	make-or-buy	systems analysis
end-user computing	planning language	system design
evolutionary process	prototyping	system development life
feasibility study	quick-hit	cycle (SDLC)

Questions for Review

1. List the six phases of the traditional life cycle development process.
2. List some activities that are included in systems analysis.
3. List some activities that are included in the design phase of SDLC.
4. List all the phases of the DSS development process.
5. List and discuss the various technology levels.
6. Define "DSS generators" and discuss their objectives.
7. List the participants in the DSS construction.
8. What is an Information Center?
9. What does a quick-hit, a staged development, and a complete DSS strategy imply?
10. What is the major difference between the iterative design process and the SDLC?
11. List the major steps of the iterative process (per Courbon et al. [6]).
12. List the five features of prototyping. (See Appendix A.)
13. Summarize the process of forming a DSS group.
14. To whom may a DSS team report?
15. List the four phases of a DSS action plan.
16. Describe the "top-down" criteria-setting and steps for a DSS generator.
17. List the potential quality risk areas in user-developed DSS.
18. List the four types of flexibility in DSS.
19. Define "end-user" and "end-user computing."
20. List the major advantages of user-developed DSS.
21. List the steps in the construction process of a user-developed DSS.

Problems and Discussion Questions

1. Why is the classical SDLC not appropriate for most DSS?
2. Explain how the critical success factor methodology can help the DSS development process. (See Shank [22].)
3. Explain how the classification to technology levels can improve the understanding of the DSS development process.
4. Why do managers use intermediaries? Will they continue to use them in the future? Why or why not?

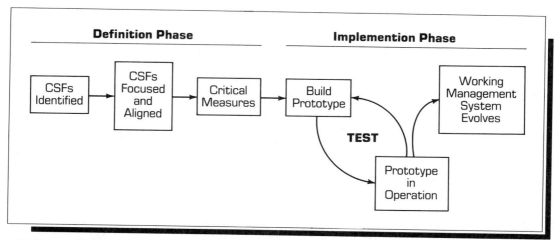

FIGURE 5.6 Combining CSF and prototyping. (*Source:* A.D. Crescenzi and R.H. Reck, "CSF helping as managers pinpoint information needs." Reprinted from *Infosystems,* July 1985. © Hitchcock Publishing Company.)

5. Discuss under what conditions people will tend to select each of the following strategies: quick-hit, staged development, and a complete DSS.
6. Explain the relationship between prototyping and CSF (see Figure 5.6).
7. Explain how the iterative approach bypasses the life cycle step of information requirements definition.
8. Explain how the establishment of Information Centers contributed to user-developed DSS.
9. How would you choose the participants in a DSS group?
10. Can a DSS group that completed its job be assigned to another DSS? Why or why not?
11. Why is the "top-down" approach for setting up the DSS objectives, capabilities, and features better than a "bottom-up" approach?
12. Discuss the five observations used to support the idea of ROMC. Do you agree with these observations?
13. Explain why flexibility is essential to DSS.
14. Discuss the reasons why user-developed DSS can be of poor quality. What can be done to improve the situation (per Alavi, Appendix C)? Do you agree with her suggestions?
15. Why is building a DSS from an old one desirable? Under what conditions will it work?
16. Compare Figures 5.2 and 5.5 and comment on their major differences.
17. How does the iterative process secure more user input than the conventional approaches?
18. What are the disadvantages of *not* having complete specifications for a CBIS, but instead letting it grow from a small prototype?
19. How does prototyping relate to nonprocedural languages? (See Appendix A.)
20. Given the relative ease of using nonprocedural languages, why do users need support from the Information Center?
21. Explain why the user is considered a component of the DSS.
22. Give two examples each, not mentioned in this text, of specific DSS, DSS generators, and DSS tools.
23. Why are most micro-based DSS being developed with the quick-hit approach?
24. Compare the process described in Figure 5.2 with that proposed in Section 5.9. Comment on the differences.

Exercise

  a. Think of a decision problem that is relevant to you that you believe could be aided by the development of a "mini" decision support system. A problem that is currently real to you is best, although hypothetical problems, either in the past or anticipated for the future, are acceptable. The problem can be either a "one-shot" decision or recurring. Describe this decision problem.

  b. How would you normally make this decision(s), without the aid of DSS? Specifically, what information would you need to gather? With whom would you need to consult? Would you need to make any "back of the envelope" calculations? If so, what would they be?

  c. Use the ROMC approach to sketch a mini-DSS for aiding your decision problem. Without making reference to specific software, discuss possible representations, operations, memory aids, and control mechanisms for such a mini-DSS. Be creative, but realistic.

CASE: Developing a DSS for Affirmative Action at Xerox Corporation*

Background

Affirmative Action (A.A.) programs at Xerox require management participation at various levels in the company. The corporate hierarchy of activities as it pertains to A.A. is as follows:

  1. The Corporate Affirmative Action Office performs the following activities:

  - Collects external data from several sources (e.g., from U.S. Census Bureau).
  - Aggregates Xerox's manpower statistics by geographical location, seniority (grade level), and job skill.
  - Extrapolates the availability of various labor pools by EEO categories (e.g., race and sex) for each grade level and skill in each geographical area.
  - Represents the corporation at meetings with federal, state, and local agencies.

  2. The Group Level Affirmative Action Manager performs the following activities:

  - Works with group-level top management to establish A.A. objectives for the group and for each operating unit within the group. (There are several operating units within each group.)
  - Works with each operating unit to monitor progress toward annual and long-range A.A. objectives on both a monthly and quarterly basis.
  - Reports to group-level top management on overall A.A. progress and trends at the group level and company wide.

  3. The Operating Unit Affirmative Action Manager performs the following activities:

---

*This case was developed by Neil Dorf, information systems consultant and DSS builder, at Xerox Corp., Los Angeles, Calif.

- Works with line management to report on progress and stresses hiring objectives consistent with A.A. objectives and the overall business plan.
- Reports to operating unit top management on A.A. progress and potential problems or legal exposure.

Need for the DSS

The DSS described in this case was developed exclusively for one of three groups in the corporation, the Xerox Systems Group (XSG). No formal cost-benefit analysis preceded the initiation of the DSS. However, it was known that the preparation of a large number of periodic and ad hoc reports consumed a great deal of management time. In addition, many ad hoc reports are needed on short notice to support various planning operations.

The major decisions supported by this DSS are as follows:

- Recruiting and hiring new employees.
- Transfer of employees.
- Promotion of employees.
- Long-range human resources planning.
- Succession planning and grooming of potential candidates for managerial positions.

These major decisions and some minor ones are performed with the objective of assuring both overall sex and minority representation.

Although some of the decisions are fairly straightforward, others are complex and involve judgment. Some of the ad hoc reports are also fairly complicated, involving several dozen variables.

Objectives and the DSS Builder

Top management recruited a DSS builder for the purpose of building the DSS. The entire project took one year, involving eight person-months.

The requirements of the DSS are flexibility, expandability, and simplicity. Ease of use was stressed as well as the ability to quickly generate reports.

The DSS is designed to support the A.A. manager at the group level, and six A.A. managers at the operating units' level.

Software and Hardware Selection

To save time and money, NOMAD 2, a DSS generator (see Chapter 6) was used to build the system. There are several reasons why this product was selected. First of all, it is a mainframe DSS generator. The large amounts of data that have to be extracted and analyzed, and the many reports that must be generated require the capabilities of a mainframe. Furthermore, NOMAD 2 was already in use at Xerox Corp. for other applications. Other reasons why NOMAD 2 was selected include its strong DBMS capabilities and its modeling features. (Lately, a comprehensive statistical analysis capability was added.) To enhance the modeling capabilities, a spreadsheet program (Multiplan) (see Chapter 6) was added. NOMAD 2 at the XSG group resides on IBM 4341 running VM/CMS, located in Columbus, Ohio. The corporate databases and a model base that feed the group DSS reside on an IBM mainframe running MVS/TSO.

The DSS Team

The DSS builder happened to be located just down the hall from the group A.A. manager in the Los Angeles XSG headquarters. This proximity enabled the builder and one user to engage in direct and spontaneous dialog during the development process.

On the team, the A.A. group manager represented all unit A.A. managers. The unit managers did not participate during the initial development stages but were involved in the process later on, when the system was tested and evaluated.

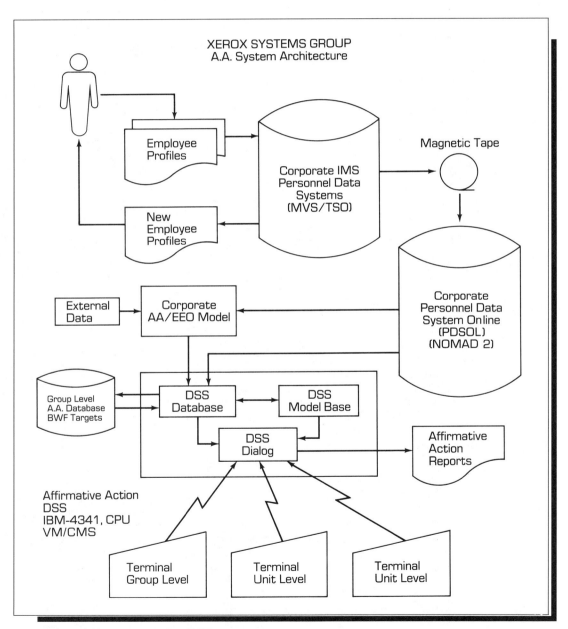

FIGURE 5.7 Affirmative action DSS.

The Data and the Database

Large amounts of data are being used in this DSS. The data come from three sources: external, corporate, and internal (group). Figure 5.7 shows schematically the various databases and their relationship to the DSS. The details are listed here:

1. Corporate level

The personnel data system (IMS) that contains permanent records (e.g., for payroll purposes) is being updated three to four times a week. Data are downloaded (via magnetic tape) to the online personnel data system twice monthly. The online database is managed by NOMAD 2 and it feeds the DSS database on request.

An Equal Employment Opportunity (EEO) model is used to conduct heavy computations and analysis for each group. The model uses data from external sources and from the on-line corporate data system to generate EEO targets and time tables known as the corporate Balanced Workforce (BWF). This BWF is then used to generate targets for the groups. For each group and operating unit, a BWF target is generated, divided into grade levels (from 1 to 18), into job categories (skills) such as engineers, marketing, or manufacturing; into sex (female, male), and into the different minority and ethnic classification.* Current company A.A. representations are compared against population (e.g., in national, states, and regions and in specific industries).**

The corporate office periodically generates management reports that show the overall achievement of BWF as compared with the targets.

2. Group Level

A special A.A. database is maintained at the group level. It shows the BWF targets and actual achievement.

The DSS DBMS is the most active part of the DSS. It generates both regular and ad hoc reports. There is a very large demand for ad hoc reports. Therefore the DSS team developed a special form for users to request reports. A routine report produced by the DSS is shown in Figure 5.8.

The Model Base

The model base includes models that compute A.A. ratios and generate recruitment feasibility plans. A new addition are medium and long-range planning models developed with Multiplan. The model base includes several forecasting models, (e.g., trend analysis using multiple regresssion), as well as inferential statistics capabilities.

The Dialog Subsystem

Users at the group level and in the operational units can access the DSS through their terminals. At the moment there are no graphics on the DSS. However, users can download information from the DSS to their PCs and then create graphics or perform further analysis.

The Development Process

The primary goal of the DSS is to act as a high-payoff, low-investment system allowing A.A. managers to compare their group or division with the federal A.A.

---

*Minority Female = Female—Black, Asian, Hispanic, American Indian
Majority Female = Female—White
Minority Male = Male—Black, Asian, Hispanic, American Indian
Majority Male = Male—White

**Xerox actually exceeds regulatory compliance monitoring requirements, in that only "minorities" and "females" (two categories) need be monitored, whereas Xerox dissects these further.

```
                    XEROX Systems Group
                       PMIS Overview

                    Effective May 14, 1986

                              Transfers
                               in from                  Transfers    May 14, 1986
      EEO      010186                    Non-XSG    Terminations   out of XSG    Population
   Category   Population  New Hires   ---------   ------------   -----------   ----------
   --------   ----------  ---------

Female  Black
        Asian
        J & A
        Hispanic
        Majority

Males   Black
        Asian
        J & A
        Hispanic
        Majority
           ==========  ==========  ==========  ============  ===========  ==========

*****Produced by XSG Personnel Systems on 05/27/86 ******
*****Report QTRAA    Run on ACCT XSGSTF6 *****
```

FIGURE 5.8 A sample report.

requirements and corporate A.A. goals. The managers can retrieve and review data and make recruitment decisions on a monthly basis. In the first iteration, the DSS builder put together a menu-driven retrieval system, including dummy figures, rough menu formats, sample reports, and the like. He then met with the A.A. group manager on a weekly basis to review, refine, and expand the initial DSS. Enhancement ideas and requirements began to evolve during this DSS design stage.

What the firm was experiencing was a typical prototyping; the frequency of the iterations was about once a week. The representative end-user participated on a continual basis by defining his and the other managers' needs, while learning the limitations of the support system. In a sense, the builder clarified user/analyst needs by actively involving the A.A. manager in the development/design process.

Testing, Evaluation, and Improvement

The initial system was tested at the Xerox System Group and refined several times. Then the system was deployed to all units of the group. As with most other DSS, the DSS builder is continually modifying and expanding the DSS as users become more dependent on its information. Although the pace is not quite as furious as at the beginning stages, the design stage is still repeated as the needs of the users change. The design phase continues as long as the needs of the user continue to change. At the present time the system is a stable one. Until the needs of the users change, the DSS will remain unchanged.

User Training

A one-on-one training was first conducted with the XSG Group A.A. manager in the comfortable surroundings of his office. Having previously used his desktop computer for simple spreadsheets and word processing, he was comfortable with the use of a computer keyboard and needed only to be trained in the use of a specific terminal program and a modem.

Once the XSG A.A. manager was trained, Operating Unit A.A. managers were trained one-on-one in succession, until gradually the XSG system supported all six unit A.A. managers.

Maintenance

Maintenance of the database is performed by the network of personnel systems analysts and consultants located in the group and corporate personnel functions. Most of the enhancement work is being done at the group level, where the need for reporting the same data in different formats is ongoing. Maintenance of the Balanced Workforce goals is accomplished by the group A.A. managers, while computation of Balanced Workforce availability is an ongoing corporate function. Maintenance of the DSS itself is done by the DSS builder who now plays the role of a consultant.

Security and Documentation

The desktop computer and modem is the users' connection to the A.A. system, which is protected by a series of log-in prompts and various password levels. Once logged in, the various reports and analyses are displayed on the screen as a menu, making the use and the learning of the system very easy. A 30+ page User Guide can also be used as a training aid as it includes samples of different types of reports and instructions on how to generate them.

Dissemination

The acceptance of the XSG A.A. report formats has been so overwhelming that these have been sought out by other groups in the organization. These other groups could not be simply added onto the XSG A.A. system, however, because of security restrictions preventing one group entity from access to the private data of another. As a result, each group will have its own A.A. DSS. However, the construction of these specific DSSs will be much faster because the experience and programs developed at XSG will be used.

Use of the DSS

The DSS was initially used through an intermediary, who is the DSS builder-consultant. He received the requests for ad hoc reports from the A.A. managers and other managers and generated the reports. Within two years all managers became proficient in the use of the system.

Questions

1. What was the major reason for the creation of this DSS?
2. Why was it not appropriate to conduct a monetary cost-benefit analysis in this case?
3. Compare the development process described here to that suggested in Section 5.10. Discuss your comparison.
4. List the various development tools used in the construction of this DSS.
5. Why was it necessary to run this DSS on a mainframe?

References and Bibliography

1. Alavi, M. "End-User a Devloped DSS: Steps Towards Quality Control." *Proceedings: Managers, Micros and Mainframe*, NYU Symposium, New York, May 1985.
2. Ariav, G., and M. J. Ginzberg. "DSS Design: A Systematic View of Decision Support." *Communications of the ACM*, October 1985.
3. Bernstein A. "Shortcut to System Design (Fourth- Generation Prototyping)." *Business Computer System*, June 1985.
4. Bonczek, R. H., et al. "The DSS Development System." AFIPS Conference Proceedings, AFIPS Press, Arlington, VA 1983.
5. Carlson, E. D. "An Approach for Designing Decision Support Systems." *Data Base*, Winter 1979.
6. Courbon, J. C. , J. Grajew, and J. Tolovi, Jr. "Design and Implementation of Decision Support Systems by an Evolution Approach." Unpublished working paper, 1980.
7. Dickson, G. W., and J. C. Wetherbe. *The Management of Information Systems.* New York: McGraw-Hill, 1985.
8. *EDP Analyser*, "Computer-Based Training For End-Users," Vol. 12, No. 12, 1983."
9. Henderson, J. C., and R. S. Ingraham. "Prototyping for DSS: A Critical Appraisal." In *Decision Support Systems*, M. J. Ginzberg et al., eds. New York: North-Holland, 1982.
10. Hogue, J. T., and H. J. Watson. "Current Practices in the Development of Decision Support Systems." *Proceedings, 5th International Conference of Information Systems*, Tucson, AZ, November 1984.
11. Keen P. G. W. "Adaptive Design for Decision Support Systems." *Data Base*, Vol. 12, Nos. 1 and 2, Fall 1980.
12. Keen P. G. W., and M. S. Scott-Morton. *Decision Support Systems: An Organizational Perspective.* Reading, MA: Addison-Wesley, 1978.

13. Keen P. G. W., and R. D. Hackathorn. "Decision Support Systems and Personal Computing." *MIS Quarterly*, Vol. 5, No. 1, March 1981.

14. Lucas, H. C., Jr. *The Analysis, Design and Implementation of Information Systems*. 3rd ed. New York: McGraw-Hill, 1985.

15. McKeen, J. D. "Successful Development Strategies for Business Applications Systems." *MIS Quarterly*, Vol. 7, No. 3, September 1983.

16. Martin, J. *Application Development Without Programmers*. Englewood Cliffs, NJ: Prentice-Hall, 1982.

17. Meador, C. L., et al. "Setting Priorities for DSS Development." *MIS Quarterly*, June 1984.

18. Mittman, B. S., and J. H. Moore. "Senior Management Computer Use: Implications for DSS Design and Goals." Paper presented at DSS-84, Dallas, TX, April 1984.

19. Nordbotten, J. C. *The Analysis and Design of Computer-Based Information Systems*. Boston: Houghton-Mifflin, 1985.

20. Rockart, J. F., and L. S. Flannery. "The Management of End-User Computing." *Communications of the ACM 26*, Vol. 10, 1983.

21. Sauter, V. L., and Schofer, J. L., "Evolutionary Development of DSS." *JMIS*, Spring 1988.

22. Shank, M. E., et al. "Critical Success Factor Analysis as a Methodology for MIS Planning." *MIS Quarterly*, June 1985.

23. Sprague, R. H., Jr. "A Framework for the Development of Decision Support Systems." *MIS Quarterly*, December 1980.

24. Sprague, R. H., Jr., and E. D. Carlson. *Building Effective Decision Support Systems*. Englewood Cliffs, NJ: Prentice-Hall, 1982.

25. Taylor, S. P. "Organizational Decision Making and DSS Design." *Systems Development Management*. Pennsauken, NJ: Auerbach Publishers, 1984.

26. Zmud, R. W. *Information Systems in Organizations*. Glenview, IL: Scott, Foresman, 1983.

27. Zmud, R. W. "Management of Large Software Development Efforts," *MIS Quarterly*, June 1980.

APPENDIX A: Prototyping

Prototyping refers to a process of building a "quick and dirty" version of information systems. Two kinds of prototyping are recognized: the throwaway and the evolutionary.

The *throwaway* concept is based on traditional prototyping centered around a pilot test program, which was developed to achieve a better understanding of the system performance and user's requirements. Once the pilot test is done, the prototype is discarded and a preliminary design takes place. After that, the final system is completed (see Figure 5.9).

The *evolutionary* approach, on the other hand, starts with a minisystem that is refined iteratively, over a long trial period. The process, which is shown in Figure 5.9, includes the following steps (per Dickson and Wetherbe [7]):

1. Identify user's information and operating requirements in a "quick and dirty" manner.
2. Develop a working prototype that performs only the most important function (e.g., using a sample database).

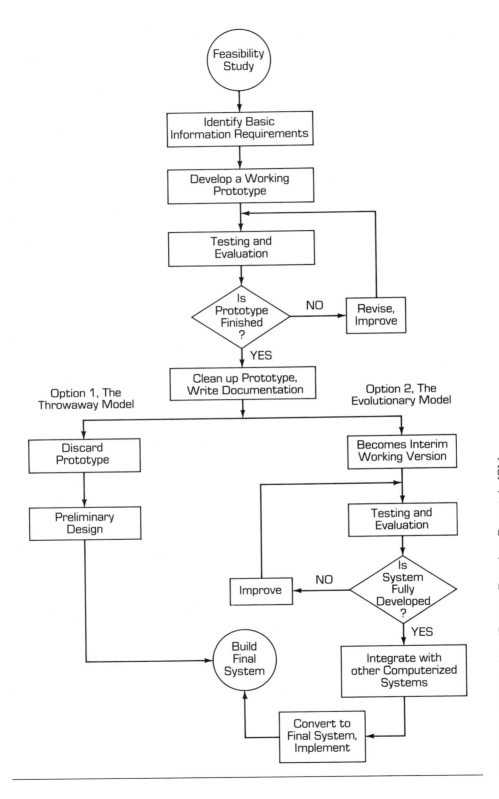

FIGURE 5.9 Prototyping. (*Source:* Based on Bernstein [3].)

3. Test and evaluate (done by user and builder).
4. Redefine information needs and improve the system.

The last two steps are repeated several times. This new concept of proto-typing is gaining popularity as an approach to developing computerized systems in general. Actually, "new prototyping" and the iterative DSS development process are very similar to each other. For further details, see Henderson and Ingraham (9).

The Primary Features of Prototyping

There are five distinct features of prototyping.

First, learning is explicitly integrated into the design process. This is normally accomplished by designing systems in an iterative fashion. A prototyped system is built and placed in the hands of the user. The user evaluates the system, determines necessary enhancements, and returns it to the analyst. The analyst updates the prototype and returns it to the users for more "commercial" testing. In other words, the designer expects to err but attempts to learn as much as possible from such errors. This learning aspect of prototyping can be contrasted with the traditional design approach, which is based on a single, sequential iteration of the design life cycle. Recycling or looping back to early stages implies that the initial analysis was incomplete. The key to success in the traditional approach is to do it right the first time. Obviously this greatly reduces the opportunity to apply lessons learned during later stages.

Second, a key criterion associated with prototyping is the short intervals between iterations. The feedback must be relatively fast. This criterion results from the required learning process; good and timely feedback is a prerequisite to effective learning.

Third, involvement of users is a very important feature. Prototyping assumes that the user may actively participate in and direct the design. This requirement stems from a need for user expertise in the design effort, and also recognizes that successful implementation will be more easily achieved with active involvement.

Fourth, the initial protoytpe must be "low cost." It must fall below the minimum threshold of capital outlays requiring special justification. The development of a prototype may be a risky decision, particularly for a DSS. However, because the benefits of a DSS are often intangible, relating to such issues as "improved decision making" or "better understanding," a high initial investment may result in a decision *not* to proceed.

Fifth, prototyping essentially bypasses the life-cycle stage of information requirements definition. Rather, it allows requirements to evolve as experience is gained. This strategy assumes that the requirements can be known only partially at the beginning of the system development, and it attempts to clarify users' needs by actively involving them in a low-cost, fast-feedback development process.

The association between prototyping and DSS is significant. First, many DSS go through the iterative process, which is basically prototyping. Second, prototyping of non-DSS is executed with the same software packages that the

How Can Prototyping Help?

Users often find it hard to state their information needs. A major cause of this difficulty lies in users' inability to "see" how they might use an information system. By providing a user with sample CRT screens or management reports, the user is able to "experience" the information system. If good software tools are available, user suggestions for improving a CRT screen or management report can quickly be tried out.

DSS is constructed with, including DSS generators and DSS tools like report generators, CRT screen generators, and electronic spreadsheets. As a matter of fact, the "application generator" mentioned earlier is a collection of prototyping tools that enables a full range of systems development activities, and as such it is very similar to a DSS generator.

DSS may take on some of the characteristics of prototyping. As a matter of fact, not all DSS are constructed using the evolutionary approach. Several companies are using the concept of throwaway DSS, that is, the building of a "quick and dirty" DSS in a process similar to that of throwaway prototyping. Instead of refining the DSS after some use, they discard it and build a completely new one. This approach is made economically feasible by the availability of DSS generators.

APPENDIX B: Items in the ROMC Approach

Representations.   Lists, graphs, cross-tabulation, economic curves, scatterplot, icons, pie charts, reports, windows, maps, spreadsheets, and organizational charts.

Operations.   Examples of general decision-making operations classified as intelligence, design and choice:

Intelligence	*Design*
☐ Gather data.	☐ Gather data.
☐ Identify objectives.	☐ Manipulate data.
☐ Diagnose problem.	☐ Quantify objectives.
☐ Validate data.	☐ Generate reports.
☐ Structure problem.	☐ Generate alternatives.
☐ Plot data, analyze.	☐ Assign risks or values to alternatives.
☐ Windowing.	☐ Superimpose partitions.

Choice
☐ Generate statistics on alternatives.
☐ Simulate results of alternatives.
☐ Explain alternatives.

- □ Choose among alternatives.
- □ Explain choice.
- □ Rank.
- □ Generate and weigh criteria.

Memory Aids. Several types of memory aids can be provided in a DSS to support the use of representations and operations. The following are examples:

- □ A database from sources internal and external to the organization.
- □ Views (aggregations and subsets) of the database.
- □ Workspaces for displaying the representations and for preserving intermediate results as they are produced by the operations.
- □ Libraries for saving work space contents for later use.
- □ Links for remembering data from one work space or library that is needed as a reference when operating on the contents of another work space.
- □ Triggers to remind a decision maker that certain operations may need to be performed.
- □ Profiles to store default and status data.
- □ Directory for quick reference.
- □ Rolodex card file.
- □ Note pad.

Control Mechanisms. Menus, function keys for operation selections, repeated procedures, windows, error messages, help comments, exception reporting, tutoring, editing, devices for correcting errors and making changes.

Source: Carlson (5).

APPENDIX C: Specific Tactics Within Different Quality-control Approaches Aimed at Controlling the Risks of User-developed DSS

Quality-control Approaches	Specific Tactics	User-developed DSS Risks
☐ Analyst reviews and audits	☐ Formation of quality assurance teams	☐ Incorrect problem specifications ☐ Piecemeal and incremental development approach ☐ Modeling errors
☐ Organizational and management policies	☐ Data management policies ☐ Hardware/software standards ☐ Formal justification policies	☐ Threats to data security and integrity ☐ Device/software incompatibility ☐ Misconceived investment of organizational resources
☐ Support and training	☐ Organizational consultants	☐ Incorrect problem specifications ☐ Insufficient search for solution ☐ Modeling errors ☐ Piecemeal development approach ☐ Threats to data integrity and security
	☐ Training in end-user computing and DP concepts	☐ Incorrect problem specifications ☐ Modeling errors ☐ Piecemeal development approach ☐ Threats to data integrity and security
☐ Hardware/software techniques	☐ Software for spreadsheet audits ☐ Software/hardware for access and monitoring	☐ Poor data integrity ☐ Calculation errors ☐ Poor data security

Source: Alavi (1).

Chapter 6

The DSS Development Tools

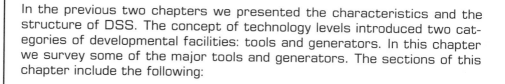

In the previous two chapters we presented the characteristics and the structure of DSS. The concept of technology levels introduced two categories of developmental facilities: tools and generators. In this chapter we survey some of the major tools and generators. The sections of this chapter include the following:

6.1   Introduction

Most users would like their DSS to be constructed as fast and as inexpensively as possible. To achieve these goals DSS builders use tools and generators. Building a DSS from scratch (using system analysts, procedural languages, and programmers to do the entire job) is a rarity. It is just too slow and/or expensive in most cases. However, the use of tools may result in a problem. There are hundreds of software packages on the market that can be used as DSS tools, and there is an extremely large number of possible combinations of putting together a DSS out of these packages.

The purpose of this chapter is to briefly survey the DSS tools that are available, explain their capabilities, discuss the selection problem and process, and explain how DSS builders are using the tools and generators to put together specific DSS.

6.2   Software Classification

A DSS comprises three basic components: database, model base, and dialog subsystem. Therefore it makes sense for DSS construction tools to be geared toward these three components. The problem is that because of the trend toward software integration, there is not a clear one-to-one relationship between the DSS components and the software. Nevertheless, it is possible to classify most DSS development tools according to this framework.

These three basic components are needed to be glued together. The more integrated the construction tools, the less cementing is needed.

Table 6.1 presents the framework we use for DSS software classification. This classification provides the sequence in which the sections of this chapter are organized.

TABLE 6.1   A Framework for Classifying DSS Software.

Component	DSS Software	Section
All	Programming languages	6.3
Dialog subsystem	Graphics	6.4
Database	Database management systems	6.5
	Fourth-generation systems	6.6
Model base	Electronic spreadsheets	6.7
	Templates and macros	6.8
	Financial modeling	6.9
	Statistical and other quantitative methods	6.10
	Model base management	6.11
Putting the components together	Integrated micro systems	6.12
	Distributed DSS and data communication	6.13
	Selecting and evaluating software	6.14
	Putting the system together and the ideal DSS generator	6.15
	Ready-made DSS	6.16

6.3 Programming Languages

Programming languages are used for developing a DSS and for communicating with it. The major categories of languages are listed here.

Machine Language

Machine language (referred to as first-generation) was the first programming language developed for computers. It is based on a binary code, which uses the two binary digits, 0 and 1, to describe all other numbers and characters. The machine language is what the computer "understands" *directly*, because 0 and 1 represent two electronic conditions (e.g., "on" and "off," or two levels of voltage). Such a language is machine-dependent; that is, a program written for one type of computer is usually not transferable to another. At the present time, computers "understand" only this language. Other languages must be "translated" one way or another to machine language for the computer to "understand" them.

Assembly Languages

Developed in the 1950s, assembly languages (referred to as second-generation) include assemblers that convert alphabetical letters and other symbols to binary code. These languages are easier to write than machine languages. The alphabetic operation codes are also easier to remember than numeric codes composed of 0 and 1. For example, storage location ("address"), which is expressed by a number in a machine language, is written here by the variable name (e.g., units produced is abbreviated to "UPR").

Procedural Languages

The DSS builders do not use the previous language categories. They do, however, use procedural (also called high-level or third-generation) and non-procedural programming languages.

Procedural languages, which include such well-known names as BASIC, COBOL, FORTRAN, and Pascal, use symbols extensively. They have been developed as of the late 1950s. As the name implies, with these languages the programmer defines the detailed procedures that the computer is to follow. The main advantage of using procedure-oriented languages is that they are widely known and are available on most computer systems. Their major limitation is that they do not contain features that facilitate the creation and use of DSS.

Certain procedural languages are better suited to DSS than others. Such languages may still require programmers to describe a procedure for the computer to follow, but features have been included in the languages that make them especially attractive for certain applications. Three languages that are used in some large-scale decision support systems are APL, PL/1, and Pascal. APL is especially appropriate for mathematical modeling applications that involve cumbersome mathematical operations like inverting a matrix. Pascal has useful data-handling features.

Some DSS are written completely with procedural languages. However, these languages are used mainly for "gluing together" DSS components. This is especially true in complex DSS where much programming is needed.

The first three generations of computer languages are derivatives of the work of the late mathematician John von Neumann, whose concept of the stored program computer is still embodied in systems that use a program counter. This counter controls program flow by indicating the next instruction to be processed.

Nonprocedural Fourth-generation Languages (4GLs)

In contrast to procedural languages, programmers who use a nonprocedural language have to specify only the major steps of the program; there is no need to specify low-level details such as the sequencing of computations or the exact data representation. Nonprocedural languages are the backbone of most DSS generators and tools.

The fundamental concept behind a nonprocedural language is to transfer the entire concern about program flow from the programmer to the computer software. With nonprocedural languages the programmer instructs the computer by specifying the desired result, rather than specifying actions needed to achieve that result. To do this it is necessary to use a memory-hungry software to translate the 4GL code into machine language.

For example, assume that a report is desired showing the total units sold for each product, in each month and year, with a subtotal for each customer. In addition, each new customer must start on a new page. A 4GL request would look something like this:

```
TABLE FILE SALES SUM UNITS BY
YEAR BY MONTH BY CUSTOMER BY
PRODUCT ON CUSTOMER SUBTOTAL PAGE BREAK
END
```

The logic flow of the same request, using a procedural language like COBOL, would be represented (for a complex situation) by a flowchart with over 50 active procedural blocks and could require hundreds of lines of coding. By eliminating most of the programming, nonprocedural languages tend also to improve application reliability by an even larger margin than their program size reduction would suggest.

In Appendix A we show an example of a program done with FOCUS vs. the same programming done in COBOL. The FOCUS programming required 4 lines vs. 115 lines in COBOL.

4GLs are beneficial because:

□ They are result-oriented.
□ They improve programmers' productivity by at least 5 to 1, and by as much as 300 to 1 for some activities (e.g., see Cobb [4]).
□ A large percentage of end users can build systems with 4GLs without going through intermediaries, because fourth-generation languages are designed for both computer specialists and end-users.

Fourth-generation languages are used to build information systems quickly and inexpensively. Therefore they can be considered effective development tools. In the non-DSS environment they are considered to be efficient applications generators for improving programmers' productivity. In the DSS environment they can be used as follows:

- ☐ As one of the tools used when a DSS or a DSS generator is built from scratch.
- ☐ As a basis for building other tools or components of a DSS; for example, a DSS DBMS is usually written in 4GL.
- ☐ As a DSS generator for building specific DSS.
- ☐ They are the ideal tool for the Information Centers being established by corporations today.

Fifth-generation Languages

Fifth-generation languages are symbolic languages used in artificial intelligence. They are discussed in Chapter 15.

Problem-oriented Languages

These languages allow the programmer to describe the characteristics of a problem to be solved rather than a procedure to be followed. A variety of problem-oriented languages has been developed for different types of problems or functions. For example, GPSS is used to expedite the construction of simulation models and can be used in the construction of a large DSS.

Report Generators and Query Languages

The procedures for preparing a report—performing subtotals and breaks for each group of items, page breaks, page headings on first and subsequent pages, page numbering, grand totals, and the like—can be quite complex. Yet they follow fairly regular rules. The regularity of the procedures and rules for report layout are the basis for report generators.

Using a report generator, the programmer describes the format of the report and characteristics of the data. The detailed procedures are generated by the software. An older but rather widely used report generator is RPG (Report Program Generator, currently at RPG III version). Report generators are now generally incorporated in very high-level languages and database query languages.

Query languages are designed to enable the user to easily communicate with the computer mainly for retrieval of data from the database. Representative query languages are ADAM, CUPID, IQF, 24, QUEL, SEQUEL II, SQL, SQUARE, and System 2000. A special class of query languages is the natural language processor, which utilizes artificial intelligence (e.g., CLOUT, Q&A, and INTELLECT). This class is discussed in Chapter 18.

6.4   The Dialog Subsystem-Graphics

The dialog subsystem provides the interface between the user and the computer. Many researchers and practitioners believe that the key to the success of MSS is a user friendly interface. For this reason we decided to dedicate a special chapter (18) to this topic, which is related to all MSS techniques, and it includes a section on natural language processors, which is an applied artificial intelligence technology.

In this chapter, however, we will deal with one topic of user interface, the graphics.

Introduction

Many factors can affect a manager's decision-making capabilities. One of the most important factors is the way in which data are presented. If there are large volumes of data, the manager must reduce the volume to a manageable size and focus on those data points that are crucial. One approach in this case is to use *exception reporting*, where those data that do not meet certain standards are highlighted. Another way to handle large volumes of data is to summarize them by using statistics, tables, and graphs. Summarization provides, in a few chunks, the same information as a large number of data items would.

Graphics enable the presentation of information in a way that more clearly conveys to many managers the meaning of data and that permits managers to visualize relationships. The value of charts and graphs in the communication of numeric data has long been recognized (see the Wharton Experiment in Appendix B).

Graphics can be produced by two methods, the traditional and the computerized. The traditional method employs graphic artists to produce visuals for meetings and formal presentations. The major deficiencies of this method are the long lead times and the significant cost. The second method, which is usually referred to as *computer graphics*, is gaining popularity (e.g., see Van Dam [34]). It makes it possible to generate graphics automatically from a computer-based information system. Computer graphics permit the user to quickly and inexpensively generate graphic information from a DSS without the aid of a graphic artist. Furthermore, this information can be presented in a dynamic mode.

Graphics Software

The primary purpose of graphics software is to present visual images of information on a computer monitor, a printer/plotter, or both. The information presented may be constructed from numeric data and shown as graphs or charts, or it may be generated from text and symbols and expressed as drawings or pictures. The boundaries between drawing-oriented applications and chart applications using numeric data are often hazy, and many software products support both.

The role of graphics in DSS is presented in Figure 6.1. As shown, the graphics present the output of various software components. The graphics

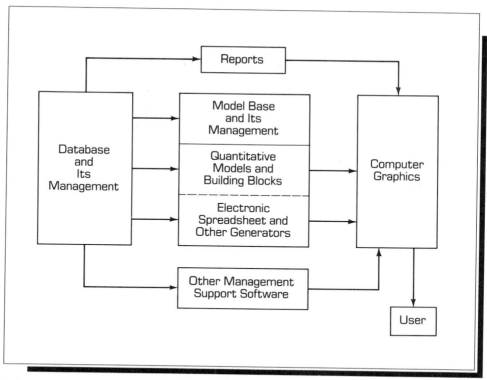

FIGURE 6.1 Computer graphics in DDS.

software can be a stand-alone package, or it can be integrated with other software routines (e.g., with a database management system).

Integrated software packages allow managers to create graphic output directly from databases or spreadsheets in a nontechnical and user-friendly way (e.g., Lotus 1-2-3). Therefore the user does not have to worry about the capability of transferring data from the spreadsheet or the database to the graphics modules. This transfer may be a problem in stand-alone graphics, plus it may be a time-consuming process.

Stand-alone graphics (like most other stand-alone packages) are usually more powerful than the integrated ones. They permit more graph styles. They often handle more data than the integrated graphics products can. Another capability of some stand-alone packages is that several graphs can be combined on one screen, compared with the one-graph-at-a-time capability of many of the integrated packages. Of course, with the integrated package, one does not have to buy the extra software. A list of representative software is given in Table 6.2.

Research on Graphics

The issue of how to present data to decision makers occupied the mind of researchers for a long time. Recognizing that the presentation is important, researchers designed experiments attempting to find the most appropriate ways of presentation. For example, Remus (29) compared the impact of graphical and tabular presentations on decision making and found no significant difference between the two. (For other studies, see DeSanctis [5].) The Wharton Experiment (Appendix B) shows the power of ordinary overhead projectors. Its conclusions, however, can be generalized to computer graphics as well, because computer graphics can be projected on a screen much like the ordinary overhead transparencies.

Hardware for Graphics

To get a hard copy, transparencies, or slides of what is presented on the screen, one can choose from a variety of plotters, ink-jet printers, or dot-matrix printers. Slide-making hardware, using Polaroid's fast-developing film, is an example of DSS optional equipment. Finally, it is possible to buy a projector that transfers the graphs (and text) onto a giant screen directly from the computer CRT. Other hardware includes boards, monitors, and printers. For a complete survey for micros, see *PC Week*, November 27, 1984.

The Role of Computer Graphics in DSS

For almost two decades, supporters of computer graphics systems have been urging their use for business management purposes. The military has pioneered in the use of computer graphics for command and control. Graphics may be especially important for business problem solving and decision making because they help managers "visualize" data, relationships, and summaries.

TABLE 6.2 Representative Graphic Software.

Product	Vendor
Artpak	PalSoftware, Inc., Stevens Point, WI
Benchmark Graphics	Metasoft Corp., Chandler, AZ
Chart Start	Micropro Inter., San Rafael, CA
DISSPLA	Integ. Soft Syst. Corp. (ISSCO), San Diego, CA
Dr. Halo	Media Cybernetics, Inc., Takoma Park, MD
Harvard Graphics	Software Publishing Co., Mountain View, CA
GEM	Digital Research, Pacific Grove, CA
GDSS	Data Business Vision, Inc., San Diego, CA
Giraph	IMRS Inc., Stamford, CT
Graftalk	Redding Group, Ridgefield, CT
Graphic Assistant	IBM, Boca Raton, FL
Graphic Environment Manager	Microsoft, Bellevue, WA
Graph in the Box	New England Software, Greenwich, CT
Mirage	Zenographics, Inc., Irvine, CA
SAS/Graph	SAS Institute, Inc., Cray, NC
Tell-A-Graf	ISSCO, San Diego, CA
Windows	Microsoft, Bellevue, WA

Types of Graphics. A wide variety of graphics forms are in use today.* All can be generated by computer, many by microcomputers.

☐ *Text* plays a critical role in graphics—listing points that the speaker is discussing, showing subject titles, identifying components and values of a chart, and so on.

☐ *Time-series charts* show the value of one or more variables over time.

☐ *Bar and pie charts* can be used to show total values (by the size of the bar or pie), as well as component values, such as breakdowns of, say, "source of money received."

☐ *Scatter diagrams* show the relationship between two variables, such as the number of air travelers who fly on Mondays, on Tuesdays, and so on.

☐ *Maps* can be two- or three-dimensional. Two-dimensional maps are useful for showing spatial relationships, for example, the locations of customers and the locations of a company's customer service facilities. Three-dimensional maps show surface contours with a three-dimensional effect.

☐ *Layouts* of rooms, buildings, or shopping centers convey much information in relatively simple diagrams.

☐ *Hierarchy charts,* such as organizational, are widely used.

☐ *Sequence charts,* such as flowcharts, show the necessary sequence of events, and which activities can be done in parallel.

☐ *Motion graphics,* such as motion pictures and television, clearly will continue to perform vital functions.

☐ *Desktop publishing.* In-house computerized publishing systems are fairly new on the market (started in 1986). These systems that have extensive graphic capabilities (e.g., transferring a picture into the computer, laying it in a desirable position and then printing it), are gaining in popularity.

Use of Graphics in Decision Making

Here are some of the ways that people in business use these various types of graphics in decision making:*

Reports. Graphics are widely used in reports, such as those prepared for management. Perhaps the most common graphs are bar charts and time-series charts.

Presentations. Graphics are used in 35 mm slides and overhead transparencies for presentation of information at briefings, meetings, and conferences.

Management Tracking of Performance. "Management chart rooms" are common in business and industry, where the charts give reasonably up-to-date information on actual versus planned performance.

*Based on Sprague and McNurlin (33). Reprinted by permission of Prentice-Hall, Inc.

Analysis, Planning, and Scheduling. Certain types of graphics have proved to be very helpful for supporting management decisions. Maps, discussed above, are one type applicable to analysis, planning, and scheduling. Critical path charts (such as PERT and CPM) have been effective in vividly showing the critical activity path of (small) projects.

Communication, Command and Control. Although not often found in business and industry, communication, command and control centers are widely used in the military. Some local governments also use them for controlling the operation of police, fire, and other vital public services. Maps and other graphics techniques play a key role in these centers.

Manufacturing Control Centers. Incorporating graphics with DSS and real time systems for production equipment experimentation and control is becoming very popular. This combination permits dynamic modeling and "what if" analysis. The graphic outputs help visualize both the problem and the potential solutions.

Other Uses. One of the main uses of graphics is for providing design, engineering, and production drawings for the manufacture of products. Computer-aided design (CAD) and computer-aided manufacturing (CAM) systems are receiving a lot of attention these days. And graphics are being used in teleconferencing and videotex systems.

Graphics in Motion. Graphics can also be used in dynamic modeling. Of special interest are animation and visual interactive modeling which are presented in Chapter 18.

Graphics in Action. The fact that some theoretical studies and limited experimentations indicate that tabular display is as good (or even better) than graphical aids* (e.g., see Remus [29]) does not seem to impress the buyers of graphics software. Sales of graphic products are increasing at a rate of 30 percent a year. In some cases computer graphics have become strategic tools. Companies that have realized high payoff applications are not broadcasting their successes for competitive reasons. For example, the August 13, 1985, issue of *Business Week* reports that General Motors considers its graphically supported financial DSS so competitive that it will not even discuss it. Table 6.3 includes some examples of successful graphical support for DSS. The list was extracted from Paller (27). One of the major features of EIS is strong and flexible graphical capabilities (see Chapter 10).

Three-dimensional Graphics

An example of 3-D graphics is shown in Figure 6.2. Not shown in this figure are the original different colors of the various geometrical shapes. The figure shows operating capacity of electrical companies organized by state and by fuel type in the Northeast.

*Note that these experiments were conducted several years ago with inferior graphics.

TABLE 6.3 Graphics Applications.

Company	Hardware	Software	Graphical Application/Benefits
McDonald's	Xerox 9700 laser printer	DISSPLA, Tell-A-Graf	Proven monetary benefits. Charts of financial reports. Help store managers to monitor performance.
First National Bank of Chicago	Nicolet Zeta Plotters	Tell-AGraf	Chartbook of 80 productivity measures. Used in marketing (best sales tool).
Electronic Data Systems	IBM 3287 and ISSCO slides service	DISSPLA, Tell-A-Graf	Monitor performance, revenue, and costs. Early warning system for clients. Data summaries.
"Chemco"	Plotters	DISSPLA, Tell-A-Graf	Support instant decision on buying raw materials. Convert results of mathematical programming to graphs
Ford Motor Company	Dicomed film recorder	DISSPLA, Tell-A-Graf	Graph planning data. Large savings in transportation cost. Confidence in results.
"Epco"	Calcomp plotter	Tell-A-Graf	Proposal for rate increase, used during public hearings on rates.
"Foodco"	Xerox color laser printer	Tell-A-Graf	Sales data, including competition. Quick responses to competition. Visual analysis of alternatives
Kodak	HP plotter, Nicolet Zeta plotters and Dicomed film recorders	DISSPLA, Tell-A-Graf	Feedback of data from service to manufacturing. Checking corrective alternatives. Improved quality.
Martin Marietta Energy Systems	III FR-80 and plotters	DISSPLA, Mapper, Tell-A-Graf,Tell-A-Plan	Save time on visual presentations. $2 million annual savings.
Monsanto	Matrix QCR film recorder	DISSPLA, Beauchart, Tell-A-Graf, SAS/Graph, FloChart	40,000 slides made directly from computer output. $1 million savings.
"Aerocorp"	Plotters, printers, laser printers, and film recorders	DISSPLA, Tell-A-Graf, Tell-A-Plan	Graphics for project management, for bidding, planning, monitoring, and control. Reports to clients.
New England Telephone	Xerox 6500 color laser printer and matrix QCR film recorder	Tell-A-Graf	Color printing. Investment recovered in three months.

Graphics on Micros and on Mainframes

Computer graphics are available for both micros and larger computers. Although for a short period micro software was considered superior, this is no longer the case. In addition to better resolution and the ability to work with larger amounts of data, workstations and larger computers provide a better opportunity for visual simulation, a topic discussed in Chapter 18.

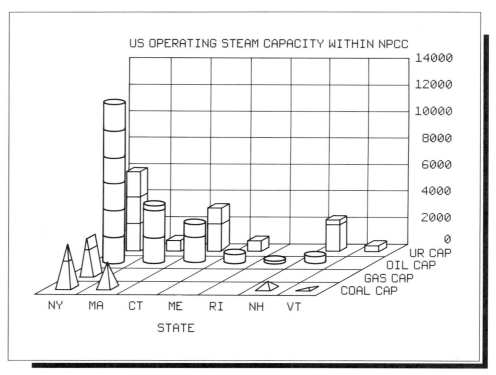

FIGURE 6.2 Three-dimensional graphics.

Some Facts About Graphics

A national study conducted at the University of Minnesota in 1984 regarding computer (business) graphics indicated (see Lehman et al. [16]):

□ SAS/GRAPH—the most widely available mainframe package.
□ TEL-A-GRAF—a close second
□ Lotus 1-2-3 (contains a graphics component)—the most widely available micro package.
□ User demand is the major factor influencing the decision to buy computer graphics.
□ The heaviest users of graphics are finance, information systems, and marketing departments.
□ About 34% of all professionals, 23% of managers, and 21% of all managerial assistants are the major interactors with software graphics to create graphs and charts. Only 9% of all executives work with these systems.
□ Most useful applications of computer graphics are the support of written reports and oral presentations. Less frequent is the use for decision support and data analysis.

- ☐ Responsibility for computer graphics usually resides at the information systems department (or the Information Center).
- ☐ The major impediments to use are poor integration of graphics software with the database (and other DSS components) and insufficient user knowledge of graphics.
- ☐ The use of graphics will increase in the future.

6.5 Databases and Database Management Systems—An Introduction

The construction of a DSS may involve the creation of a separate DSS database. In such a case the DSS builder will need help to design the database, to prepare the data, and so on. Later, it will be necessary to administer the database.

The complexity of most corporate databases and/or large-scale independent DSS databases makes the standard computer operating systems inadequate for an effective and/or efficient interface between the user and the database. A database management system (DBMS) is designed to supplement the standard operating systems by allowing for greater integration of data, complex file structure, quick retrieval and changes, and better data security, to mention a few of the advantages. Specifically, a DBMS is a software program for entering (or adding) information into a database, updating, deleting, manipulating, storing and retrieving the information. A DBMS combined with a *modeling language* is a typical system development pair, which is used in constructing DSS as well as other systems.

DBMS are designed to handle large amounts of information. Often, data from the database are extracted and put in a statistical, mathematical, or financial model for further manipulation or analysis. This is basically what is happening in a DSS.

Database Hardware

Database operations may place heavy demands on computing resources. Sorts and searches, the most common database activities, require considerable CPU time and overload the input/output ports between the processor and the disk storage. A *database machine* is a special-purpose, add-on unit dedicated to performing database operations. Using such a machine may eliminate the need for a larger computer. Representative machines are DBC/1012 (Teradata, Inc.) and Britton Lee's database machine. For further information see a special report from Britton Lee Inc.

Database Software

The most powerful DSS generators include both 4GL and procedural languages as well as relational and hierarchical data structures. This composition gives them more flexibility and capabilities; obviously they also sell at a higher price.

There are several hundred DBMS on the market with varying degrees of sophistication (for details, see Pallatto [26]). Frequently the DBMS is combined with other software packages.

SQL

SQL is a data language that is becoming a standard for data manipulation in relational database management systems. It is an English-like language consisting of several "layers" of increasing complexity and capability.

SQL is used for on-line access to databases, for DBMS operations from programs, and for database administration functions. It is also used for data access and manipulation functions of some leading DBMS software products (such as ORACLE, DB2, Ingres, and Supra).

SQL is nonprocedural and very user friendly, so people can use it for their own queries and database operations. SQL can be used from programs written in all standard programming languages; thus it facilitates software integration.

SQL statements are free format. For example, "Alter Table Employees, ADD Bonus Number" is a command to change an existing table (called "employees") by adding a column called bonus.

A simple query to identify the employees whose monthly salary is greater than $2000 is written as:

```
SELECT     Name, Salary
FROM       Employees
WHERE      Salary > 2000
```

6.6 Fourth-generation Systems

A DBMS, when used as a development tool for DSS, is usually written in a 4GL and is integrated with several other elements.[*] Such an arrangement is an especially popular combination for mainframe computers and is called a complete *fourth-generation system.*

A complete fourth-generation system typically includes several features that make it easy for the user to communicate with the computer and for the builder to build a DSS (see Figure 6.3). The most common features are:

- □ Fourth-generation DBMS.
- □ Nonprocedural report writer (or report generator).
- □ Nonprocedural language for data maintenance.
- □ Screen definition and management facility.
- □ Business graphics.
- □ Query language.
- □ Relational language.
- □ Applications manager.

[*]Based on Cobb (4).

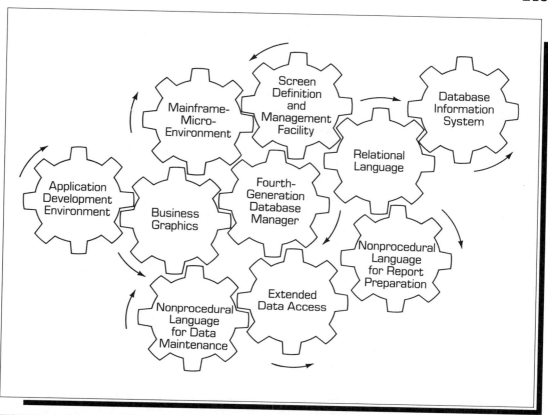

FIGURE 6.3 Integrated fourth-generation system. (*Source:* Cobb [4].)

- □ Extended data access.
- □ Database information system.
- □ Environment for applications development.
- □ Environment for information consumers.
- □ Micro-to-mainframe environment.

A complete fourth-generation system is approaching a full-fledged DSS generator. This occurs when modeling capabilities are added (e.g., a spreadsheet in a microcomputer.)

Another way to look at the classification of fourth-generation systems is to distinguish between those that are used as DSS generators by end-users (or by Information Center people) and those that are used as application generators (usually for non-DSS applications) by DP professionals. Examples of the first category are FOCUS, NOMAD 2, RAMIS II, and SAS. Examples of the second category are IDEAL, MANTIS, NATURAL, and ADS/on-line.

There are two ways to acquire a complete fourth-generation system. One is to obtain each component separately and build bridges between the components. Although a feasible solution, it is difficult to implement because the separate components available are not designed to fit together.

TABLE 6.4 Representative Mainframe Fourth-generation Complete Systems.

Product	Vendor	Used in
ADF	IBM (White Plains, NY)	
ADS/ON-LINE	Cullinet (Westwood, Mass.)	IDMB/R
DB2	IBM (White Plains, NY)	
FOCUS	Information Builders, Inc. (New York, NY)	
IDEAL	ADR (East Syracuse, NY)	DATACOM
INGRES	Relational Technology Inc. (Alameda, CA)	
MANTIS	CINCOM (Cincinnati, OH)	TOTAL, TIS
NATURAL	Software A & G (Reston, VA)	ADABAS
NOMAD 2	D & B Computer Services (Wilton, CT)	
RAMIS II	Martin Marietta Data (Princeton, NJ)	
Rdb	Digital Equipment Corp. (Nashua, NH)	

The second solution is to acquire all the functions from one vendor in a single integrated system containing components designed and implemented specifically to work together.

Currently, several vendors are working toward offering such complete systems. Representative mainframe vendors and their fourth-generation products are listed in Table 6.4.

Representative fourth-generation systems for microcomputers with strong database capabilities are listed in Table 6.5.

Not all DSS are constructed with 4GL. Some are being constructed with third-generation languages and many are being constructed with *both* third and fourth generations. One reason is that 4GLs are relatively new and many programmers are unfamiliar with the tools. In general, programs written in 4GL are considered less efficient than those written with 3GL (the computer run time is longer). This gap is being closed rapidly, however. Furthermore,

TABLE 6.5 Representative Micro-based DBMS for DSS.

Product	Vendor
Condor 3	Condor Computer Corp. (Ann Arbor, ,MI)
dBase III +, dBase IV	Ashton-Tate (Culver City, CA)
Infoscope	Microstuf, Inc. (Roswell, GA)
InfoStar +	MicroPro Int. Corp. (San Rafael, CA)
Knowledge Man/2	Micro Data Base Systems (Lafayette, IN)
Oracle	Oracle, Inc. (Belmont, CA)
PC/Focus	Information Builders, Inc. (New York, NY)
Power-base	PowerBase Systems, Inc. (New York, NY)
Present	Data General Corp. (Westboro, MA)
R:Base 5,000	Microrim, Inc. (Bellevue, WA)
Reflex	Borland International (Scotts Valley, CA)
Revelation	Cosmos, Inc. (Seattle, WA)

4GLs are starting to be integrated with artificial intelligence products, a fact that could make them *the* dominating tool in DSS construction. Of special interest is the combination of natural language processors and databases. A brief review of three products—CLOUT, PARADOX, and Q & A—is given in Chapter 18.

Three typical DSS capabilities provided by the NOMAD 2 generator are shown in Figure 6.4 ("what if"), Figure 6.5 (goal seeking), and Figure 6.6 (graphics).

Fourth-generation languages are popular not only for DSS databases; they are also used in several of the most powerful modeling tools, a topic presented next.

```
>what if revenue increases by 3 pct sales exp increases by 5 pct -

>list by region by repname sum(revenue) -
>sum(sales exp) as $99,999 sum(bonus) subtotal all total all -
>title 'effects on company bonus program' fold -
>'if sales increase 3% and direct expenses increase 5%'

PAGE    1

              EFFECTS ON COMPANY BONUS PROGRAM
       IF SALES INCREASE 3% AND DIRECT EXPENSES INCREASE 5%
```

REGION	SALESREP	SUM REVENUE	SUM EXPENSES	SUM BONUS
NORTHEAST	MARY BRENNER	$40,756	$3,432	$0
	SAM CONNERS	$117,656	$4,346	$13,084
*		$158,412	$7,778	$13,084
NORTHWEST	STAN ROBERTS	$202,995	$5,973	$31,826
	TOM FILBRITE	$83,072	$6,205	$0
*		$286,067	$12,178	$31,826
SOUTHEAST	BOB STEVENS	$83,711	$6,695	$0
	ROGER ARNESS	$37,212	$3,528	$0
*		$120,923	$10,223	$0
SOUTHWEST	CHRIS STERNMAN	$146,395	$6,953	$6,428
	JACK MILNER	$81,544	$4,129	$1,697
	PETER HANLEN	$85,665	$6,001	$0
*		$313,604	$17,083	$8,125
		$879,006	$47,263	$53,035

FIGURE 6.4 Example of "what if" analysis done by NOMAD 2. The upper part of the figure shows the commands as programmed with NOMAD 2; the lower part shows the projections and their impacts. (*Source:* Courtesy of D & B Computer Services.)

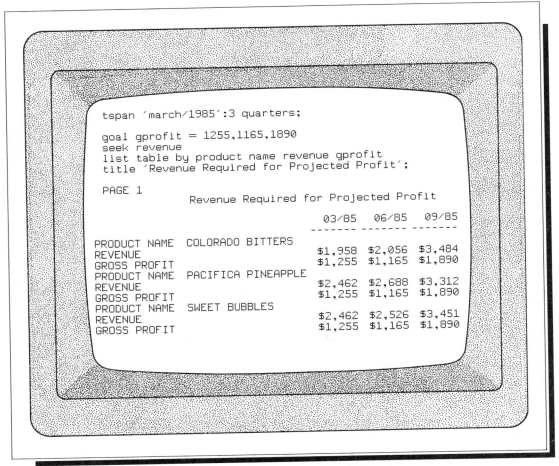

```
tspan 'march/1985':3 quarters;

goal gprofit = 1255,1165,1890
seek revenue
list table by product name revenue gprofit
title 'Revenue Required for Projected Profit';

PAGE 1
                    Revenue Required for Projected Profit

                         03/85   06/85   09/85
                        ------- ------- -------

PRODUCT NAME  COLORADO BITTERS
REVENUE                 $1,958  $2,056  $3,484
GROSS PROFIT            $1,255  $1,165  $1,890
PRODUCT NAME  PACIFICA PINEAPPLE
REVENUE                 $2,462  $2,688  $3,312
GROSS PROFIT            $1,255  $1,165  $1,890
PRODUCT NAME  SWEET BUBBLES
REVENUE                 $2,462  $2,526  $3,451
GROSS PROFIT            $1,255  $1,165  $1,890
```

FIGURE 6.5 NOMAD 2: Goal seek analysis—time span. (*Source:* Courtesy of D & B Computer Services.)

The Model Base—Preview: Sections 6.7–6.12 present topics related to the model base and its management. In Sections 6.7 and 6.8, there is a brief presentation of spreadsheets and their templates, which are essentially modeling devices. Financial planning building tools are presented in Section 6.9; statistical and other models are described in Section 6.10. Finally, the model management issue is briefly presented in Section 6.11.

6.7 Electronic Spreadsheets

A very popular DSS modeling tool for microcomputers is the electronic spreadsheet. This tool is the equivalent of an accounting spreadsheet, which is basically a column-and-row pad. The spreadsheet is represented electronically in the computer's memory. The intersections of the columns and rows are called

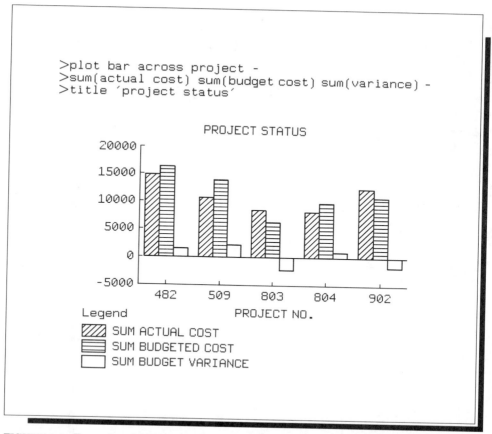

```
>plot bar across project -
>sum(actual cost) sum(budget cost) sum(variance) -
>title 'project status'
```

FIGURE 6.6 Example of NOMAD 2 graphics. The nonprocedural language allows you to use one simple command. "Title" personalizes the graph. (*Source:* Courtesy of D & B Computer Services.)

cells (see Figure 6.7). The user places numeric data or text in these cells. Then, the programmer can manipulate the data (e.g., "Multiply the content of cell C-5 by that of D-7"). Spreadsheets have many advantages over an accounting worksheet. Most notable is the modeling capability; users can write their own models and also conduct "what if" analysis. In addition, departmental reports can be consolidated, and data can be organized in alphabetical or numerical order. Other capabilities include setting up windows for viewing several parts of the spreadsheet simultaneously and executing mathematical manipulations. These enable the spreadsheet to become an important tool for analysis, planning, and modeling. In short, it is a limited DSS generator.

The first spreadsheet, VisiCalc, was introduced in 1979. Within five years close to 100 such packages appeared on the market. The electronic spreadsheet is a user-friendly modeling tool. The user uses commands rather than a programming language. During the period 1981–1989, close to eight million copies of spreadsheets were sold in the United States. The current trend is to integrate the spreadsheet with development and utility software, such as database man-

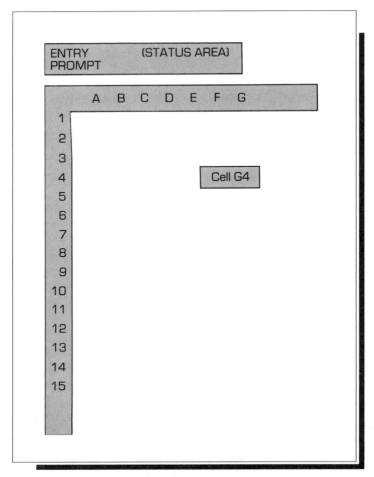

FIGURE 6.7 Typical spreadsheet screen.

agement, communication, and graphics. Integrated micropackages like Lotus 1-2-3, Excel, and Quattro are currently more popular than the stand-alone spreadsheets. Integrated packages are presented in Section 6.12.

A major capability of spreadsheet programs is that formulas can be embedded using numbers in the spreadsheet; these numbers can be changed and the implications of these changes can immediately be observed and analyzed.

A spreadsheet can be used to build static or dynamic models. A static model does not include time as a variable. For example, spreadsheets are used to build balance sheets. A balance sheet presents the condition of a company in terms of its assets and liabilities on a certain date (e.g., the end of the year). A dynamic model, on the other hand, represents behavior over time (i.e., it *does* include a time element). For example, the balance sheet for a given year can be shown together with those of the five previous years. An income statement is another example of a dynamic financial report usually produced by a spreadsheet; it normally covers a period of one year broken into quarters.

Spreadsheets are used in almost every kind of organization in all functional areas. For example, the October 1983 issue of *Personal Computing* presents typical applications of the following business models constructed with VisiCalc and Lotus 1-2-3 (pp. 82–195):

- ☐ Sales forecasts (units sold at various price levels based on regression analysis).
- ☐ Inventory models.
- ☐ Cash flow.
- ☐ Profit-and-loss statement and a balance sheet.
- ☐ Sales forecast (based on price and distributor rating).
- ☐ Graphical presentations of the above.

An example of solving an inventory management problem with a spreadsheet (using Lotus 1-2-3) is given in Appendix C.

The models constructed with spreadsheets can be linked to each other (e.g., the output of the sales forecast can be used as an input to the inventory and cash flow models). Some of these applications are not strictly DSS; they are more in the nature of the traditional MIS, or even transaction processing. The point is that with a spreadsheet, users do not have to wait a long time anymore for the IS department to build a CBIS. They can build CBIS on their own (or with minimal help from the Information Center or the IS department) very quickly and inexpensively.

Spreadsheets were developed for micros, but they are also available for larger computers with increased capabilities. Spreadsheets are very popular modeling tools, but they have limitations. For example, several spreadsheets execute only modeling under certainty: they cannot handle risk (e.g., via Monte Carlo simulation). Other areas of deficiency are the lack of optimization capability and the two-dimensional constraints. (Some of the limitations may be removed with easy interfaces, or with improved technology.) Therefore, we need more powerful modeling tools. Such tools are described in Section 6.9.

A representative list of spreadsheet software is given in Table 6.6.

TABLE 6.6 Representative Spreadsheet and Spreadsheet-based Integrated Products for Micros.

Product	Vendor
Calcstar	Micro Pro Inter. (Comming, GA)
Excel	Microsoft (Redmond, WA)
Goldengate	Cullinet Software (Bellview, MA)
LogiCalc	Corvus Systems (San Jose, CA)
Lotus 1-2-3	Lotus Development Co. (Cambridge, MA)
Master Plan	Phase One Systems Inc. (Oakland, CA)
Multiplan	Microsoft Corp. (Bellview, WA)
Peachcalc	Peachware Co. (Atlanta, GA)
Quattro	Borland International
Supercalc-4	Sorcim (San Jose, CA)
The Smart Spreadsheet	Innovative Software (Overland Park, KS)
Visi On Calc and VisiCalc	Visi Corp (San Jose, CA)
VP planner +	Paperback Software (Berkeley, CA)
20/20	Access Technology (South Natick, MA)

6.8 **Templates and Macros**

The programming productivity of building DSS can be increased further with the use of templates and macros. *Templates* are preprogrammed, reusable spreadsheet models with built-in titles and formulas, developed for specific applications. They are dataless files that contain formulas; the only task left to the user is to input the data. (See Exercise 5 at the end of this chapter.) For example, there are income tax preparation templates, real estate analysis templates, general financial planning templates, and budgeting templates. Users can build their own templates or buy prebuilt ones. Templates are available on diskettes and are used in conjunction with the spreadsheet programs (see Appendix D).

For example, in preparing a budgeting template, the user can develop an overlay customized to a specific budgeting requirement using a spreadsheet program such as Multiplan (or an integrated package like Lotus 1-2-3). This "budgeting overlay" would be used as a shell to meet the budgeting application requirements and to keep the general budgeting categories and formats the same from year to year. Templates that are available on the market are quite general in nature, but they usually can be adapted fairly easily to specific requirements.

Templates provide a fast and flexible means for conducting calculations. Because the formulas are preprogrammed, the possibility of calculation errors is reduced. Finally, templates permit automatic transfer of entries among various tables or forms as required. The power of Lotus 1-2-3 (or a similar package), when used with templates, enables the user to review the result, ask "what if" questions, and make quick changes and recalculations.

Templates can be fairly simple, containing financial, statistical, or mathematical models. Others are more advanced, allowing the manipulation of specified data items to show the impact of changes in one or more values on the dependent variables throughout the entire spreadsheet. Templates for micros are selling for about $100. Examples of popular templates are Multi-Tool Financial Statement, Multi-Tool Financial Budget, Investment Tax Analyst, Financial Projections, Business Forecasting Model, TK! Solver, and Loan Analyzer.

Macros.   Suppose a marketing DSS includes a spreadsheet with information about the sales of various products in five regions, supported by bar charts. The marketing manager often tries out "what if" scenarios by changing the variables that determine sales. The manager, using a spreadsheet, would have to make the changes in the spreadsheet and view each graph by typing in the many necessary commands to call up each graph. The commands would have to be repeated for all five graphs.

An alternative to this process is to use macros. Macros are collections of keystrokes representing commands, which are stored in the spreadsheet. To execute the commands, the user now has only to press the "alternate key" while typing the letter code for the macro.

The left side of the boxed material shows the commands that the marketing manager would have to type to create and view the five bar charts. The right side of the box shows what the manager would have to type to invoke a slide show of the graphs if a macro, named g (for graphs), had been created.

Lotus 1-2-3 would automatically display each of the graphs, one at a time, on the screen and return to the ready mode so the manager could try out some

```
Lotus 1-2-3 spreadsheet for marketing example:
A                  B          C          D          E          F
1            Region A Region B Region C Region D Region E
2 Sales:
3 Prod 1          100        400        900       1000       1500
4 Prod 2          200        500        800       1100       1400
5 Prod 3          300        600        700       1200       1300
  Lotus Commands:                      Macro:
  G (for graph)                        ``Alternate key''
  T (for type)                         and g
  B (for Bar chart)
  A (for data range)
  B3. . .B5
  X (for labeling)
  A3. . .A5
  O (for options)
  T (for title)
  F (for first line)
Sales Report for
  T (for title)
  S (for second line)
Region A
  T (for title)
  X (for X-axis)
Products


  T (for title)
  Y (for Y-axis)
Sales
  Q (for quitting options)
  N (for name)
  C (for create)
Region A
  V (for view)
Repeat for each region,
substituting the appropriate
information
```

new assumptions on the spreadsheet (performing "what if" analysis). To view the effects of these changes, the manager would simply invoke the macro again.

Macros make spreadsheets easier and faster to use and they greatly enhance the "what if" analysis.

Although templates and macros increase the modeling power of spreadsheets, the capabilities of the latter are fairly limited when compared with mainframe DSS generators that are based on financial planning software.

Note: For further discussion on the limitations of spreadsheet as compared with financial modeling see: C. Spencer, "Financial Modeling—Going Beyond the Spreadsheets," *Personal Computing*, April 1987.

6.9   Financial Modeling-oriented Generators

Many DSS generators are being developed around financial and planning modeling software.[*] Since the 1960s, planning models have advanced from an obscure concept for large corporations to an appropriate tool for planning in almost any size company. The proliferation of planning models has been due largely to the increasing availability of affordable computers over the last 20 years, which quickly enhanced the applications and practicality of modeling for all types of businesses. This trend has been accelerated in the 1980s due to the availability of microcomputers and inexpensive software.

A major property of financial modeling is that their models are *algebraically* oriented. That is, the formulas are written in the manner that one would write equations. Spreadsheets, on the other hand, write their models with a computation or *calculation* orientation.

Definition and Background of Planning Modeling

The definition of a planning model varies somewhat with the scope of its application. For instance, financial planning models may have a very short planning horizon and entail no more than a collection of accounting formulas for producing pro forma statements (i.e., a static model). On the other hand, corporate planning models often include complex quantitative and logical interrelationships among a corporation's financial, marketing, and production activities. In this sense, the model has great utility because any of the coordinated subroutines composing the comprehensive model may be isolated for narrower applications. Further on, most financial models are dynamic, multiyear models.

History of Planning Models

The rudiments of corporate modeling can be traced to the early 1960s with the large, expensive, cumbersome simulation models developed by major corporations (e.g., AT&T, Wells Fargo Bank, Dow Chemical, IBM, and Sun Oil). Most of the models were written in one of the third-generation general programming languages like FORTRAN, and were used for generating pro forma financial statements. Financial models were considered an untested concept suitable only for those corporations large enough to absorb the costs and risks of development.

Important advancements in computer technology in the early 1970s provided the means for greater diversity and affordability in corporate modeling. Interactive computing facilities all allowed for faster and more meaningful input/output sequences for modelers; trial-and-error adjustments of inputs and analyses were possible while online to the central computer or to an outside time-sharing service. By 1979, nearly every Fortune 1000 company was using a corporate simulation model.

[*]Much of the discussion in the first half of this section is based on Shim and McGlade (31).

According to several surveys, financial models were found to provide real support for upper management. The nature of the decisions made was clearly semistructured or unstructured. However, most of the models dealt only with deterministic situations. For a conceptual structure of a typical financial planning model, see Appendix E.

Planning and modeling languages (PML) have been a major incentive in involving higher management in modeling. General (third generation) programming languages are seldom used in current models; even COBOL, the "business language," has never been used extensively in modeling. The PML are steadily edging out general programming languages. Models are built more easily and with shorter development time, are more easily understood by upper management, and are periodically updated with enhancements from the PML vendor. Most of the powerful PML are written in fourth-generation, nonprocedural languages.

A further convenience offered to companies looking into modeling is premade planning packages sold by software vendors. Included in this category are templates for spreadsheets discussed earlier. These packages have often been criticized for their inflexibility, but the newer models allow for more user specificity. For example, analytical portfolio models tell an organization how to distribute resources across a portfolio of profit centers. Boston Consulting Group, Arthur D. Little, and McKinsey have developed models that categorize investments into a matrix of profit potentials and recommended strategies. A model for profit impact of market strategy (PIMS) is offered by the Strategic Planning Institute. The package uses a large, multiple regression-based model to identify the optimal strategy in a given business environment. In addition to generic DSS-based planning models, there are several industry-specific ones, notably for hospitals, banks, and universities. For example, Educom's Financial Planning Model (EFPM) is used by about 200 universities as a DSS generator for financial, long-range planning, and other university administration decisions. Similar packages are likely to proliferate in the future as more companies are forced to use DSS to remain competitive.

Today, there are about 100 PML on the market. They are available on time-sharing networks as well as packages for mainframe, mini- and microcomputers.

Typical Applications of Planning Models

Financial forecasting
Pro forma financial statements
Capital budgeting
Market decision making
Mergers and acquisitions analysis
Lease vs. purchase decisions
Production scheduling
New venture evaluation
Manpower planning

Profit planning
Sales forecasting
Investment analysis
Construction scheduling
Tax planning
Energy requirements
Labor contract negotiation fees
Foreign currency analysis

EDUCOM's Financial Planning Model (EFPM)

EFPM is the best-known modeling system used in higher education. It has been used in about 200 universities and colleges. In contrast to a regular model that has predefined data definition and equations, this DSS generator is content free. Each institution can create models unique to its mission, structure, and decision-making styles. Thus, EFPM enables a wide range of administrative applications, a sample of which is shown as follows:

Area	*University*
Athletics	Stanford University
Buildings and Grounds	Harvard University
Business School	University of Pennsylvania
Cash Flow	Pepperdine University
Central Services Allocation	Claremont University Center
Computer Center Cost Recovery	Purdue University
Conference Center	Oregon State University
Continuing Education	University of Minnesota
Dental School	Tufts University
Dining	Harvard University
Endowment Portfolio	Lexington Theological Seminary
Equipment Replacement	Purdue University
Faculty Tenure	Michigan State
Formula Funding	San Jose State University
Graduate Student Apartments	Brite Divinity School
Fringe Benefits	Cornell University
Indirect Cost Allocations	Purdue University
Legislative Budget Requests	Purdue University
Medical School	University of Southern California
Music School	University of Rochester
Oil and Gas Capitalization	Texas Christian University
Off-Campus Operations	College of New Rochelle
Parking Facilities	Purdue University
Residence Hall Financing	Harvey Mudd College
Residence Hall Operations	University of Wisconsin
Wage and Salary Administration	Pepperdine University

Several of these packages include additional capabilities starting with "what if" and goal seeking and ending with report preparation. With these added capabilities, several of the packages (for a list, see Table 6.7) are getting close to full-fledged DSS generators. Chapter 7 represents the IFPS package.

The major differences between financial modeling-based generators and DBMS-based generators are shown in Table 6.8.

TABLE 6.7 Representative DSS Generators with a Financial Modeling Base.

Product	Vendor
CONTROL STRATEGIST	Xerox Corp. Comp. Services, (Los Angeles, CA)
CUFFS	Cuffs Planning (New York, NY)
EIS	Boeing Computer Services (Vienna, VA)
EMPIRE	Applied Data Research (Princeton, NJ)
ENCORE	Ferox Microsystems (Arlington, VA)
EXPRESS, PC EXPRESS	Information Resources (Waltham, MA)
FAME	Fame Software, Citicorp (New York, NY)
FCS/EPS	THORN EMI Comp. Software (Chelmsford, MA)
FORESIGHT	Information Systems of America (Norcross, GA)
FINANCIAL PLANNER	Computer Associates (San Jose, CA)
IFPS, IFPS/Personal	Execucom Systems (Austin, TX)
INGOT	Pansophic Systems, Inc. (Oak Brook, IL)
Mapper	Unisys, (Blue Bell, PA)
MODEL	Lloyd Bush & Assoc. (New York, NY)
PLANS+	IBM (Menlo Park, CA)
SIMPLAN	Simplan Systems (Chapel Hill, NC)
STRATAGEM	Integrated Planning (Boston, MA)
SYS/PLANER	System Research Services (McLean, VA)
System W	Comshare (Ann Arbor, MI)
XSIM	Interactive Data Corp. (Lexington, MA)

TABLE 6.8 Comparison of Financial Modeling Generators with Those Based Around DBMS.

	Major Advantages (Strong Points)	Major Disadvantages (Weak Points)
Financial Modeling-based Generators	Financial reporting (and consolidations with some systems) Forecasting Sensitivity analysis Usually easier to learn for financial people Many built-in financial and statistical routines	Limited sorting with older two-dimensional packages Limited data entry Limited handling of text with data Some systems are two-dimensional and require DBMS for consolidations
DMBS-based Generators	Data (record)-oriented Best text handling Best sort/merge Data integrity Strong in ad hoc, unstructured queries and analysis	Cumbersome with time-series problems Cumbersome with multidimensional applications (multiple "passes" of the data required) Cumbersome in sensitivity analysis applications

Source: Developed by Neil Dorf, Xerox Corporation, Los Angeles, CA.

6.10 Quantitative Models

Decision support systems offer several quantitative models in areas like statistics, financial analysis, accounting, and management science. These models can be called in the DSS generator by one command. For example, in IFPS (Chapter 7) there is a list of several such models. Examples of commands are:

Monte Carlo 100	meaning: execute 100 runs of Monte Carlo simulation.
NPV	meaning: execute a net present value.

In addition, many DSS generators can easily interface with powerful quantitative methods stand-alone packages. Such packages are usually much more powerful than the build-in routines. Another organization of preprogrammed quantitive models is via templates.

Preprogrammed models can be used to expedite the programming time of the DSS builder, especially when they are built-in or when an interface exists.

Some of these models are building blocks of other quantitative models. For example, a regression model can be a part of a forecasting model that supports a financial planning model. Another example is the *functions* in Lotus 1-2-3 such as:

SQRT: This function calculates the square root of a number that may be a part of an inventory model.

NPV: This function calculates the net present value of a collection of future cash flows for a given interest rate. It also may be a part of a make versus buy model.

Statistical Packages

Statistical functions are built into many DSS generators; for example:

□ DSS/A (from Addison-Wesley) includes analysis of variance, chi-square cross tabulation, multiple linear regression, correlations and frequency distributions; all supported by graphics.
□ NOMAD 2: mean, median, variance, standard deviation, kurtosis, *t* test, chi-square, regression (linear, polynomial, and stepwise).

An example of a regression analysis executed in NOMAD 2 is shown in Figure 6.8. Notice the following three features:

1. One-word command triggered the analysis ("multireg").
2. The equation for best-fit for the model is clearly identified.
3. The report is automatically formatted.

More power can be obtained from stand-alone statistical packages, a list of which is given in Table 6.9.

```
        1
        │
        ▼
      >multireg promotion accounts

      * NOMAD2 * Multiple Linear Regression

      Dependent variable (Y):    PROMOTION
      Independent variable (X):  ACCOUNTS

  2 ──▶ The best fit for the model:  Y = a + b1*(X1) + ... +  bk*(Xk) + e

      is:       PROMOTION      =      568.860 +    5.932 * (ACCOUNTS)
                                                                              3
      Number of observations used:    12                                     ┐
          No.      Variable name        Mean
        --------  ----------------    ----------
          1 (i)   ACCOUNTS             44.583
          2 (d)   PROMOTION           833.333

                                     Regression   Standard    Partial    F-Proba-
          No.      Variable name     coefficient    error     F-Value     bility
        --------  ----------------   -----------  ----------  ----------  --------
          1       ACCOUNTS              5.932       1.500      15.634      0.003
        --------
      Intercept                        568.860      68.173

      Percent of variation explained by the model:    60.989
      Standard deviation of residuals:                45.628

      Analysis of variance for the regression
      ----------------------------------------

      Variation   Degr of     Sum        Mean                   F-Pro-
        due to    freedom  of squares    square     F-Value    bability
      ---------   -------  ----------  ----------   ---------   --------
      Regression      1    32547.930   32547.930     15.634      0.003
      Residuals      10    20819.309    2081.931
                   -------  ----------
      Total          11    53367.238                                        ┘
```

FIGURE 6.8 Regression analysis performed by NOMAD 2. (*Source:* Courtesy of D & B Computer Services.)

TABLE 6.9 Representative Statistical Packages.

Product	Vendor
APL forecasting and time-series analysis	IBM (White Plains, NY)
BMDP	BMDP Statistical State, Inc.
Crosstab	Cambridge Comp. Assoc. (Cambridge, MA)
Forecast IV	Resource Software Intl. (Fords, NY)
Microstat	ECOSOFT, Inc. (Indianapolis, IN)
SAM	Decision Sciences Inc. (Sugar Land, TX)
SAS	SAS Institute, Inc. (Cary, NY)
SPSS and SPSS/PC+	SPSS, Inc. (Chicago, IL)
Systat	Systat, Inc. (Evanston, IL)

Forecasting Model

The following is a list of representative forecasting packages.

Autobox, BOXX	Automatic Forecasting Systems, Inc. (Hatboro, PA)
EXEC*U*STAT	EXEC*U*STAT Inc. (Princeton, NJ)
Forecast Master	Scientific Systems, Inc. (Cambridge, MA)
Forecast Plus	Walonick Associates (Minneapolis, MN)
Futurcast	Futurion Assoc, Inc. (Pittsburg, CA)
Micro TSP	McGraw-Hill (New York, NY)
Soritec Econometrics	The Soritec Group (Springfield, VA)
SPSS/PC +	SPSS, Inc. (Chicago, IL)
Systat	Systat Inc. (Evanston, IL)
The Forecasting Edge	Human Edge Software (Palo Alto, CA)
1,2,3 Forecast	1,2,3 Forecast (Salem, OR)

Management Science Packages

There are several hundred management science packages on the market for management science models ranging from inventory control to project management. Some of the packages interface with Lotus 1-2-3 or other generators. Several DSS generators include optimization and simulation capabilities. For example, see Figure 6.9 and the description of IFPS in Chapter 7.

Given are representative packages of management science packages:

Topic	Product	Vendor
Simulation	GPSS/PC	Mainstream Software (Stow, MA)
	P C Simscript	CACI (La Jolla, CA)
	SLAM II/PC	Pritsker Assoc, Inc. (Lafayette, IN)
	PRISM Simulation	Tempus Development (Arlington, VA)
Decision Trees	Decision 1-2-Tree	Fast Decision Systems (Cambridge, MA)
	SUPERTREE	SDG Decision Systems (Menlo Park, CA)
Mathematical Programming	MP1-MP8	Eight programs for different mathematical programming models. SCI Computing (Wilmette, IL)
	LINDO, GINO, VINO	Lindo System Inc. (Chicago, IL)
	MPS III	Ketron, Inc. (Arlington, VA)
	MPSX	IBM (Armonk, NY)
	GAMS/MINOS	Stanford University (Stanford, CA)
	LP 83	Sunset Software (San Marino, CA)

Financial Modeling

Financial functions (such as Net Present Value and Internal Rate of Return) are built into many DSS generators. However, there is a large number of free standing packages on the market. Some representative packages are:

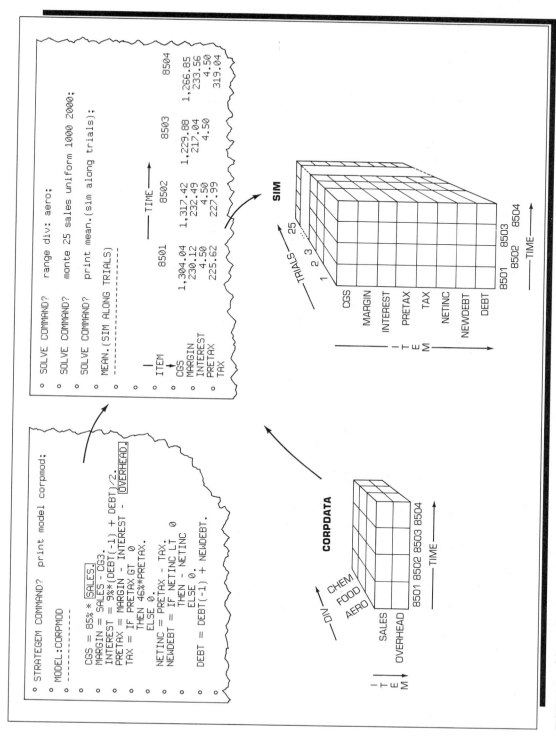

FIGURE 6.9 Monte Carlo analysis performed with Stratagem. (*Source:* Courtesy of Integrated Planning, Inc.)

231

Product	*Vendor*
FINAR	Finar Research Corp. (Denver, CO)
Micro-DSS/Finance	Addison-Wesley Pub. Co. (Reading, MA)
Peach Plan	Peachtree Software (Atlanta, GA)
PlanStar	MicroPro International (San Rafael, CA)
Target Financial	Comshare, Inc. (Ann Arbor, MI)

Special Decision Aid Tools

Several software packages may be considered interesting decision aids. They can be incorporated into the DSS model base, or be used to supplement it either by providing input data (e.g., subjective judgments) or by "massaging" the output data of the DSS. Representative examples are listed as follows:

Expert Choice. Expert Choice (from Decision Support Software, McLean, VA) is a structured decision aid that allows users to graphically portray a complex decision analysis problem with multiple criteria for evaluation.

An example of Expert Choice's site selection model is shown in Figure 6.10. Six attributes are considered, each of which is assigned a subjective weight ("How important the attribute is"). Alternatives are then outlined as they relate to each attribute. As with several other microcomputer programs, here too there are limitations on the number of attributes and alternatives.

Decision Master. Decision Master (from Generic Software, Inc., Bellevue, WA) helps the user to make decisions involving multiple choices and multiple

Use of Expert Choice in International Banking

EXPERT CHOICE is now being used by a leading bank to evaluate lending risks and opportunities in foreign countries. This bank had previously used studies to weigh economic, financial, and political considerations. While the bank was satisfied with the quality of the reports, both the bank and the consultant preparing the reports felt the information was not being put to best use. The complex data and decision-making process often resulted in "too much" or "too little" weight being placed on various aspects of the decision process. The bank's credit committee also had difficulty integrating the "expert information" into the deliberation process. Consequently, the bank's consultant prepared an EXPERT CHOICE model, enabling the credit committee to use the most recent information in making comparisons among factors. Without any prior exposure to microcomputers or EXPERT CHOICE, the bankers began using the software and evaluating the subject country within a matter of minutes.

Source: Courtesy, Decision Support Software.

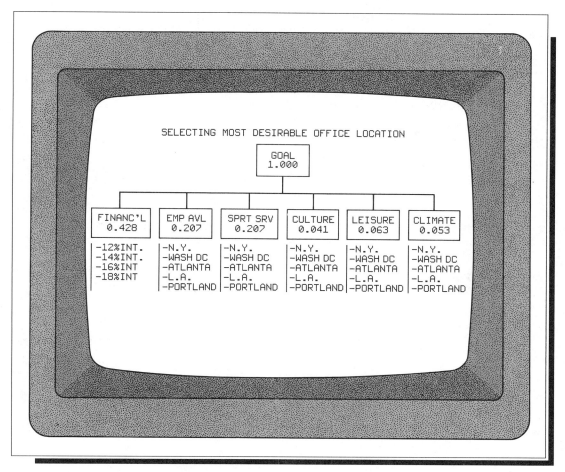

FIGURE 6.10 Expert choice, site selection model.

criteria for each choice. It also allows each criterion to be separately weighted and each choice/criterion to be individually rated.

Decision Aid. Managerial problem-solving Decision Aid (from Computer Software Consultants, Inc., New York, NY) consists of several components: personnel selection, decision simulation, time-series analysis and projections, multiple regression, statistical hypothesis testing, financial planning, and project management.

Orion. This package (from Comshare, Inc., Ann Arbor, MI) provides a data analysis system for marketing and financial managers. It offers sales forecasting, market share analysis, cash flow projections, quality control charting, and production scheduling.

Arborist. Arborist (from Texas Instruments, Dallas, TX) is a tool for solving decision situations under risk that are presented as decision trees. Using extensive graphics, the program allows one to view, over several windows, the entire decision tree, and/or portions of it. The probabilities of the states of nature are entered numerically (or the "probability wheel" can be used to graphically assist in estimating probabilities). With direct interface to Lotus 1-2-3, Arborist can be used for financial planning and for investment analysis.

Lightyear. Lightyear (from Lightyear, Santa Clara, CA) enables the user to weigh different factors in a decision-making process. The weighing is done numerically, or by using subjective ratings (such as "good" or "excellent"). The program, which uses graphics extensively, enables easy "what if" sensitivity analysis.

Decision PAD. This package deals with multiple objective decision making (From Apian Software, Menlo Park, CA).

Decision AIDE II. Use of the vendor's methodology for mulitcriteria decision making (From Kepner-Trego, Inc., Princeton, NJ).

Other DSS Products

Listed below are other DSS products.

Product	Description	Vendor
Business-modular	Business modeling, forecasting, financial system	Business Model Systems (Westmont, IL)
Activator	Organizes, computes critical information	Control Data Corp. (Greenwich, CT)
Marksman	Supports sales and marketing decisions	Control Data Corp. (Greenwich, CT)
ICMS	Accesses summary level information from databases, links to network PCs	Cullinet (Westwood, MA)
BPCS DSS	Business modeling information retrieval, E-mail, interfaces.	System Software Assoc. (Chicago, IL)
Direct Test	Evaluates direct marketing test activities	SPSS Inc. (Chicago, IL)
Simplan and Micro Simplan	Forecasting, risk analysis, modeling, simulation	Simplan Systems, Inc. (Chapel Hill, NC)
Planning Tool	Planning	ATR Inc. (Redondo Beach, CA)
MaxThink	60 different thought processing modules, helps creativity.	MaxThink Inc.

6.11   Model Base Management System Software

The concept of model base management, as developed by Sprague (32), calls for a software package with capabilities similar to that of the DBMS in the database. Unfortunately, while there are dozens of commercial DBMS packages, there are no comprehensive model base management packages currently on the market. Limited capabilities, which a model management package should exhibit, are provided by some spreadsheet programs and financial planning-based DSS generators (such as IFPS). One reason for this situation is that each company uses the models differently. Another reason is that some of the MBMS capabilities (e.g., selecting which model to use, deciding what values to insert, etc.) require expertise and reasoning capabilities. Thus, MBMS could be an interesting area for future application of expert systems. In the meantime most of the capabilities of the MBMS must be developed from scratch by systems analysts and programmers.

6.12 Integrated Packages for Micros

Integrated packages combine the ability to do several general-purpose applications in one program. It is an alternative to the use of several separate, single-function (stand-alone) packages (see Figure 6.11). In the latter case, it is

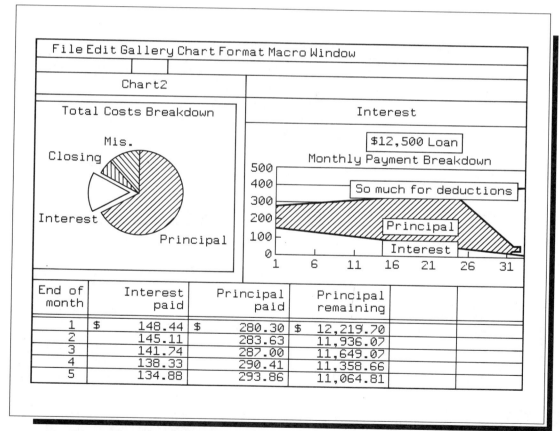

FIGURE 6.11 An integrated package provides graphics, modeling, and other capabilities. This example is provided by an integrated package based on an expanded spreadsheet, Excel (from Microsoft Corp.). The program enables the user to change or edit individual chart components (e.g., text or arrow, or resize the legend). These strong graphics capabilities are performed on Apple's Macintosh.

necessary to load each package and the same data files into the computer each time a package is used. Sometimes stand-alone packages "refuse" to work with data files created by other programs. Integrated packages have solved these problems by allowing the user to work with a variety of tools that use standardized commands and allow shifting among various applications (in a manner similar to a "call waiting" in a telephone). Thus, for example, data can pass from one function to another rather easily. The integration of several programs into one allows a user to follow a natural thought process.

The following programs are typical "raw materials" for integrated packages:

  □ Spreadsheet.
  □ Data management.
  □ Word processing.
  □ Communication.
  □ Business graphics.
  □ Calendar (time management).
  □ Desk management.
  □ Project management.

The most popular integrated package, Lotus 1-2-3, includes three components: spreadsheet, graphics, and database management. More recent packages (e.g., Lotus's Symphony and Framework from Ashton-Tate) include five or more components. The integrated micropackages (see Table 6.10) exhibit many of the ideal DSS generator capabilities described earlier.

Integrated products are continuously improving, but most of them, especially the micro based, are still no match for a group of stand-alone packages. An integrated package may have an excellent word processor but only a good spreadsheet and mediocre graphics. None of the database managers in integrated programs is powerful enough for heavy data handling. The more

TABLE 6.10   Representative Micro-integrated Packages.

Product	Vendor
AURA	BTI Systems (Austin, TX)
Corporate MBA	Context Management Systems (Torrence, CA)
ENABLE	The Software Group (Ballston Lake, NY)
First Choice	Software Pub. Co. (Mountain View, CA)
FRAMEWORK	Ashton-Tate, Inc. (Culver City, CA)
Integrated 7	Mosaic Software, Inc. (Cambridge, MA)
Lotus 1-2-3	Lotus Development Co. (Cambridge, MA)
Open Access	Software Product Intl., Inc. (San Diego, CA)
Quattro	Borland International
SMART	Innovative Software, Inc. (Overland Pk., KS)
SYMPHONY	Lotus Development Co. (Cambridge, MA)
VP Planner +	Paperback Software (Berkeley, CA)
WORKS	Microsoft, Bellevue, WA

application programs integrated into one package, the more difficult the learning and operation of the package becomes. For example, Lotus 1-2-3 has several customized features that make it easy to use by a novice. Lotus's Symphony, which includes more programs, does not have some of these features. Furthermore, Symphony requires more diskettes arranged in a manner that may baffle many novices. Another possible deficiency of integrated packages is that they require vast amounts of memory. This can slow many PCs to a frustrating crawl (or it may require additional memory purchases).

Recognizing these deficiencies, some software vendors offer both integrated packages and individual tools. For example, the IFPS family includes DATASPAN, GRAPHICS, OPTIMUM, and SENTRY, as well as the IFPS integrated package.

Modularly Integrated Systems

A relatively new approach to software integration is the "modularly integrated" systems of stand-alone products that function as one by using the same commands. For example, a spreadsheet user can pass the data disk *directly* to the word processing user. Two representative examples of this approach are ENABLE (from the Software Group, Ballston Lake, NY) and SMART (from Innovative Software, Overland Park, KS). SMART includes several stand-alone systems: spreadsheet, word processing, graphics, communications, time manager, and data manager. All systems use the same commands for easy data interchange. The modularly integrated systems are much more powerful than the fully integrated systems (such as Lotus 1-2-3), because stand-alone packages are usually more powerful than components in an integrated system; however, they cost more money.

Modular integration can also be achieved by software packages called *task managers* (such as DESQVIEW and TOPVIEW).

6.13 Distributed DSS and Data Communication

The various components of the DSS and/or its users do not have to be in one location. They can be dispersed both geographically and organizationally throughout an organization and its environment. For example, the GLSC case illustrates a system of this kind where the DSS is used in many locations; data are purchased from online services (external databases) and one of the models is located outside the company. In such cases there is a need to communicate. This need is fulfilled by data communication systems.

Data communication systems (DCSs) provide for the transmission of data over communication links between one or more computer systems and a variety of input and/or output terminals. DCSs are part of the general area of telecommunications.

The DCSs are not generally considered to be a component of a DSS. However, almost any large DSS uses a DCS extensively. In addition, a DCS can greatly increase the power of micro-based DSS. Furthermore, DSS software contains the monitors and controls for accessing the DCS. (For more information, see Champine et al. [3], Fitzgerald and Eason [6], and Martin [19].)

The following related topics will briefly be discussed:

- □ Micro-DSS.
- □ Distributed DSS.
- □ Local area networks (LANs).
- □ Commercial databases (or data banks).

Micro-DSS

During the last few years we have witnessed an increased number of DSS being constructed and operated on microcomputers. Many vendors have already created micro-versions of their mainframe DSS generators and tools. The rapid influx of microcomputers into the corporate environment is giving rise to a new concept, which is called the executive workstation. These stations support not only decision making but also communications (via electronic mail) and calendaring, to mention a few.

The success of the micro-DSS depends on its ability to integrate with the mainframe, to access data on a host (mainframe) computer, and on the capabilities provided by distributed systems and networks.

Distributed DSS

Distributed processing, also referred to as distributed data processing (DDP), is a form of information processing made possible by a network of computers "dispersed" throughout a single organization or over several organizations. Processing of user applications is accomplished by several computers (or workstations) interconnected by a network. For example, a distributed system may exist in a school or in a manufacturing plant.

Distributed processing permits users to work with their own microcomputers independently, yet communicate with other computers, and usually share a database. Therefore DDP is a movement *away* from a centralized processing approach, yet it is not a completely independent decentralized system either. It possesses five important characteristics:

- □ Computers are dispersed throughout an organization.
- □ Computers are connected by a DCS.
- □ A common database is shared by all (additional databases may exist).
- □ All computers are *centrally* coordinated with an information resource management plan.
- □ Input and output operations are done within user departments.

DDP permits centralized control over policies and processing while the system retains the flexibility of decentralization. The facilities at the sites are tailored to local needs and controlled by local management, avoiding the rigidity of centralized hardware and personnel, while integrating the sites and minimizing duplication of efforts. A typical distributed system is shown in Figure 6.12.

The DDP arrangement seems to offer the best of two worlds: the advantages of centralization and decentralization without the disadvantages of either. Distributed systems also enable the PC to be integrated with other computers and peripherals. One concept that helps in such integration is emulation.

DSS and Emulation. *Emulation* is the ability to imitate other machines. Usually, a microcomputer will emulate a (mainframe) terminal so that the user can communicate with the company's central computer. Accessing the corporate database from a microcomputer is a tremendous benefit. Data files can be transferred from the mainframe and then used in the DSS. In effect, the microcomputer replaces a dumb terminal and is still used for generating spreadsheets, providing word processing support, and generating reports.

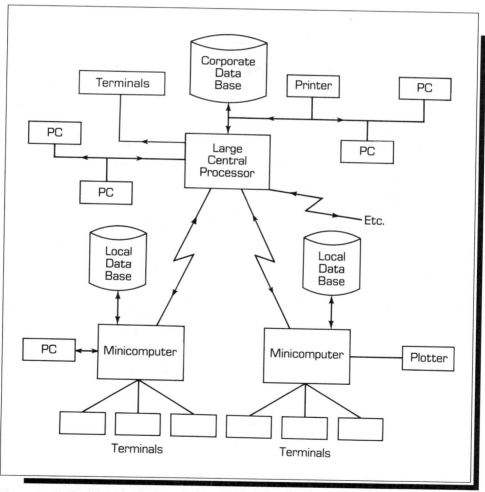

FIGURE 6.12 Distributed computer system.

Local Area Networks (LANs)

A special case of distributed processing is the local area network. Computer networks consist of interconnected hardware, software, and communication channels that support several types of data communications activity for many users. Local area networks are *privately owned* networks that connect information processing devices within a *limited* physical area, such as an office building or a manufacturing plant or a university. The LANs are usually connected to larger external networks (private or public) by special communications interface devices. This connection enables, for example, communication between a PC and a mainframe computer (e.g., for downloading of data). It also allows a DBMS to extract data from an online service, and it permits electronic mail.

A possible problem in networks is ensuring compatibility of equipment served by the network. Several vendors offer complete systems including hardware, software, procedures, and protocols. Representative examples are:

- □ Decnet, from Digital Equipment Corp.
- □ Wang-Net, from Wang Labs.
- □ Ethernet, from Xerox or from 3-Com (Ethernet is an open architecture).
- □ STARLAN, from AT&T.

Local area networks can be very useful for DSS because they can connect the internal parts of the DSS as well as the DSS with related computer-based systems. For example, a production DSS can be connected with numerically controlled machines, and a stock selection DSS may be connected with a brokerage house information and stock purchasing ordering system.

Because the LAN is owned by the using company, there is no need to pay for the use of the communication lines; in contrast, a DDP that does not use an LAN must pay for the communication (e.g., to a telephone company).

An LAN could provide the necessary access to external databases, primarily to commercial database (or data bank) services.

DSS and Commercial Database Services

A commercial database service (online service) sells access to large (usually nationwide) databases. Such a service can add external data to the DSS in a timely manner and at reasonable cost. All that is necessary to retrieve data from such a service is a computer terminal, modem, telephone, password, and some service fees. Sometimes described as a computerized data bank, this form of information supply is becoming extremely popular. Several thousand services[*] are currently available. For an overview of this business, see Seligman (30). Table 6.11 lists several representative services.

Some of these services also offer time-sharing capabilities for the use of DSS generators like IFPS, EXPRESS, and EPS. Several services use other databanks as a source of information.

---

[*]*Directory of Online Databases* is a quarterly publication by Cuadra Assoc., Inc., Santa Monica, CA (with Elsevier Publishing Co., New York) that provides current information on commercial databases. This directory is also available online.

TABLE 6.11 Representative Commercial Database (Data Bank) Services.

CompuServe and The Source. Personal computer networks providing statistical data banks (business and financial market statistics) as well as bibliographic data banks (news, reference, library, and electronic encyclopedias). CompuServe is the largest supplier of such services to personal computer users.

Data Resources, Inc. Offers statistical data banks in agriculture, banking, commodities, demographics, economics, energy, finance, insurance, international business, and the steel and transportation industries. DRI economists maintain a number of these data banks. Standard & Poor's is also a source. It offers services under *U.S. Central Data Bank.*

Dow Jones Information Service. Provides statistical data banks on stock market and other financial markets and activities, and in-depth financial statistics on all corporations listed on the New York and American stock exchanges, plus 800 selected other companies. Its Dow-Jones News/Retrieval system provides bibliographic data banks on business, financial, and general news from the *Wall Street Journal, Barron's,* the Dow Jones News Service, *Wall Street Week,* and the 21-volume *American Academic Encyclopedia.*

Interactive Data Corporation. A statistical data bank distributor covering agriculture, autos, banking, commodities, demographics, economics, energy, finance, international business, and insurance. Its main suppliers are Chase Econometric Associates, Standard & Poor's, and Value Line.

Lockheed Information Systems. The largest bibliographic distributor. Its DIALOG system offers excess and summaries of over 150 different data banks in agriculture, business, economics, education, energy, engineering, environment, foundations, general news publications, government, international business, patents, pharmaceuticals, science, and social sciences. It relies on many economic research firms, trade associations, and governmental groups for data.

Mead Data Central. This data bank service offers two major bibliographic data banks. *Lexis* provides legal research information and legal articles. *Nexis* provides a full-text (not abstract) bibliographic database of over 100 newspapers, magazines, newsletters, news services, government documents, and so on. It includes full text and abstracts from the *New York Times* and the complete 29-volume *Encyclopedia Britannica.* Also provided is the Advertising & Marketing Intelligence (AMI) data bank, and the National Automated Accounting Research System.

Source: Standard & Poor's Compustat Services, Inc., statistics on 6000 companies, financial reports.

6.14 Selection of a DSS Generator and Other Software Tools

A large number of DSS generators and other tools are commercially available at price tags that vary from hundreds to hundreds of thousands of dollars. Some of the software has been created for personal computers, whereas other software programs are available only for minicomputers or mainframes.

Two interrelated questions must be answered by an organization that would like to use a DSS generator. (1) Which generator(s) should be used, and (2) which hardware should it run on—mainframe, mini, micro, or time sharing?

Mainframe DSS Software

Mainframe DSS software costs between $30,000 and $300,000 and has several powerful capabilities. Table 6.12 lists about 60 such DSS generators. Several of these were listed previously in Tables 6.4 and 6.7.

TABLE 6.12 DSS Generators for Mainframe.

Product	Author/Vendor	Product	Author/Vendor
ABC FPRS	ABC Management Systems, Inc.	G/L PLUS	McCormack & Dodge Corporation
Analect	Dialog, Inc.	GE F/M&RS	GE Software International
Accent R	National Information Systems, Inc.	Genesys	Analysis Research & Computation, Inc.
Autotab, 300, 3000	Capex Corporation	GO	Mellonics Information Center
BBL II	Core & Code, Inc.		
Business Modeler	Business Model Systems, Inc.	IFPS	Execucom Systems Corporation
Callplan	Calldata Systems, Inc.		
CDIS-Financial	Computer Data Corporation	IMPACT	MDCR, Inc.
Context/MBA	Context Management Systems, Inc.	Infotab II	National CSS, Inc.
		Insight	Insight Software
Control & Control Strategist	Xerox Computer Services, Inc.	Insight FP	Interactive Program Products, Inc.
CSS/Final*	D&B Computing Services	ITS/73	GMI
Cuffs 88	Cuffs Planning & Models, Ltd.	Long Range Planning	STSC, Inc.
Dollarflow	Quasar Systems, Ltd.	Maps/Model	Ross Systems, Inc.
Decision Support System	MDCR, Inc.	Model	Lloyd Bush & Associates
		Mosaic	Informetrics, Ltd.
EIS	Boeing Computer Services, Inc.	MSA/F&M	Management Science America
Empire	Applied Data Research, Inc.	NYPLAN	National Information Systems, Inc.
EMS	Economic Sciences Corporation		
		Performa	Data-TEK
Enterprise	Citishare, Inc.	Perspective	PBL Associates
EPS	Data Resources, Inc.	Plancode	IBM
Express	Management Decisions, Inc.	Plato	OR/MS Dialogue, Inc.
Fame	Gemnet Software Corporation	Profile	Strategic Planning Associates
		Proforma	Decision Development, Inc.
FASS	Decision Sciences Corporation	Prophit II	VIA Computer, Inc.
		Reveal	Decision Products, Inc.
FCS-EPS	EPS, Inc.	SAM	Decision Sciences Corporation
Feast	Economic Analysis Software, Inc.		
		Simplan	Simplan Systems, Inc.
Ferox Modeler	Ferox Microsystems, Inc.	Spread	Lupfer & Long, Inc.
Fiscal Plus	Applied Advanced Management Research, Inc.	Stratagem	Integrated Planning, Inc.
		System W	Comshare, Inc.
FML	ADP Network Services	Tabol	GE Software International
Foresight	Information Systems of America	TSAM	ADP Network Services
FPI/3	Fusion Products International	XSIM	Chase Decision Systems

Note: Many of these products have a microcomputer version. Some of the vendors have been changed since the list was compiled.

*CSS/Final is now available as the Decision Support System of NOMAD 2, a fourth-generation–language database management system.

Source: Reimann and Waren (28). Copyright 1985, Association for Computing Machinery, Inc. Reprinted by permission.

Micro DSS Software

Several vendors offer a microversion of their mainframe product at a considerably lower price. With the increased capabilities of micros and the improvement of the micro to mainframe connection, it is likely that more micro-DSS will be used in the future. Table 6.13 lists several representative micro-DSS generators.

Software Selection. The basic software tools to be considered are:

☐ Relational database facilities with powerful report generation and ad hoc inquiry facilities.
☐ Graphics generation languages.
☐ Modeling languages.
☐ General-purpose statistical data analysis languages.
☐ Other special languages (e.g., for building a simulation).
☐ Programming languages (third generation).

In building a DSS, the builder must select these tools and/or a comprehensive DSS generator that is a set of all (or some) of the above.

Selecting the tools and/or generator is a complex process for the following reasons:

TABLE 6.13 Representative Micro-DSS Generators.

Product	Company
Econometric Software	Alpha Software Co. (Burlington, MA)
Encore	Ferox Microsystems (Arlington, VA)
Focus/PC	Information Builders, Inc. (New York, NY)
GSA/GSM	Prediction Systems, Inc. (Manasquan, NJ)
Horizon 370	Chase Decision Systems (Waltham, VA)
IFPS/Personal	Execucom Systems, Inc. (Austin, TX)
Informix	Relational Database Systems, Inc. (Manlo Park, CA)
Ingres/ABF	Relational Technology, Inc. (Almeda, CA)
MAPS/PRO	Ross Systems, Inc. (Palo Alto, CA)
Micro-FCS	Thorn EMI Computer Software (Chelmsford, MA)
MicroPROphit	Via Computer, Inc. (San Diego, CA)
Micro SIM	Simplan Systems (Chapel Hill, NC)
Micro W	Comshare, Inc. (Ann Arbor, MI)
Nomad 2 PC	D&B Computing Services (Wilton, CT)
PC Analect	Dialogue, Inc. (New York, NY)
PC Express	Information Resource, Inc. (Manhasset, NY)
SPSS/PC	SPSS, Inc. (Chicago, IL)
TM/1	Sinper Corp. (North Bergen, NJ)
20/20	Access Technology (South Natick, MA)
Plans +	IBM (Menlo Park, CA)

Source: Horwitt (10).

1. At the time of the selection the DSS information requirement and outputs are not completely known.
2. There are hundreds of software packages on the market.
3. The software packages are being changed (usually improved) very rapidly (especially for micros).
4. Price changes are frequent.
5. Several people may be involved in the evaluating team.
6. One language may be used in the construction of several DSS. Thus the required capabilities of the tools may change from one application to another.
7. The selection decision involves dozens of criteria against which competing packages are compared.
8. Technical, functional, end-user, and managerial issues are all considered.
9. Commercially available evaluations by companies such as Data Decisions, Data Pro, and Software Digest, Inc., and the buyer's guides of journals, such as *PC Week* and *Infosystems*, are frequently superficial. They can be used as one source of information.

The Selection Process of a DSS Generator

When an organization has a DSS generator or has access to one on a time-sharing network, it is likely that this generator will be the one used for DSS applications. However, firms do not necessarily use only one generator. Some DSS generators are better for certain types of applications than others. Thus, organizations may need to purchase a new DSS generator at times.

A Proposed Methodology for DSS Generator Selection

The following procedures are proposed by Warren and Reimann (35) for selecting DSS software. The procedure is participative (i.e., it involves users). A similar process has been proposed by Meador and Mezger (21) and by Briggs (2).

Warren and Reimann's approach goes beyond the traditional software selection approach in three basic ways. First, end-users are extensively involved in the evaluation from beginning to end. Second, the technical features to be evaluated are listed in detail and given in terms that end-users can understand. Third, the traditional role of the data processing department as the leader in software selection is abandoned in favor of end-user control.

The proposed selection process consists of a number of steps, as illustrated in Figure 6.13. First comes the initial organization of the selection team, or task force. The next step is the development of a set of user-oriented evaluation criteria, based on a survey of user needs and a survey of vendor product capabilities. Then comes a series of increasingly demanding and thorough screenings of the candidate products. The first three screens should eliminate all but one or two "finalists." These would then be brought in house (one at a time, or in parallel) for the development of a "prototype" application. This approach should enable

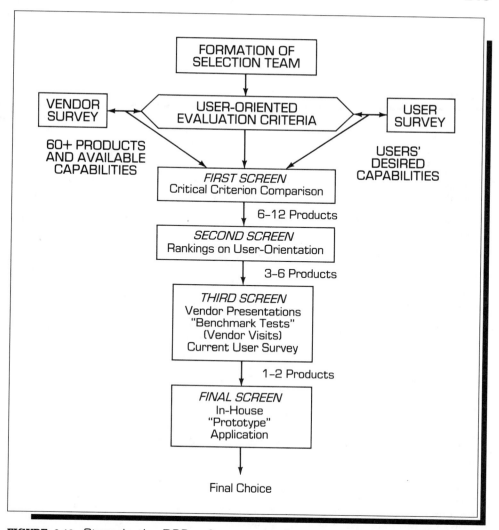

FIGURE 6.13 Steps in the DSS software selection process. (*Source:* Warren and Reimann [35].)

the selection team to choose a generator that will satisfy most of the intended users' needs.

The proposed process, which is applicable mainly to mainframe and minicomputer DSS generators, can be used (with modifications) for selecting microsoftware or any DSS tool.

Table 6.14 contains some of the items that would be on a typical checklist for mainframe software, except that an actual checklist would tend to be more detailed. For example, in regard to "forecasting capabilities," the checklist should include the specific forecasting methods that will be needed. Unnecessary features should be excluded from the checklist. There are also factors not shown in Table 6.14 that are likely to be important. These include the reputation of the vendor, training programs and their cost and location, and customer services. Several promising DSS generator candidates should emerge from the checklist.

Testing the most promising DSS generators on typical organizational applications is very important. A common mistake is to test the DSS generators on

TABLE 6.14   Evaluation Criteria for DSS.

Technical Considerations	Functional Capabilities	Functional Capabilities (continued)
Hardware and Operating System	Modeling	Reporting
Time-sharing option	Multidimensionality	Customized report formats
Mainframe compatability	Nonprocedurality	Standard (default) report format(s)
Operating system compatability	Procedural logic (within definitions)	Editing and testing of report formats
Microcomputers supported	Simultaneous equation detection and solution	Standard symbols and conventions
Support of peripherals	Complex consolidations and allocations	Report variables and computations
Hardware vendor recommendation	Common functions (math, financial, etc.)	**End-user Orientation**
Data Management	User-defined functions (customized)	User-friendliness
Common database manager	Time and currency conversions	Consistent, natural language commands
Data security	Size restrictions	Integration across modules
Simultaneous access	Model analysis and interrogation	Command abbreviations
Data selection capability	Sensitivity and "what if?"	Command recall, repeat, and edit
Data dictionary	Impact	Help facility
Automatic audit trails	Goal seeking	Clear, meaningful error messages
Communication Linkages	Monte Carlo (risk analysis)	Error recovery (e.g., "undo" command)
"Foreign" databases	Optimization (linear and nonlinear)	Optional menus or prompts
Other computer languages	Forecasting and statistics	Novice and expert modes
Special-purpose software	Time as a special dimension	Meaningful identifiers
Other computers	Time-series analysis	Helpful documentation
Costs and resource usage	Seasonal adjustment options	Data entry and editing (full-screen)
Command Language	Curve-fitting options	Spreadsheet display of data and results
User-defined commands	Basic statistical functions	Vendor Support
Customized menus and prompts	Analysis of Variance	Technical support
Input/output	Multiple regression	Applications consulting
Warnings and error messages	Multivariate statistics	Problem support (e.g., "hotline")
Costs and Resource Usage	Graphics	User training
Initial license fee	Basic plots and charts	Product improvement and updating
Pricing (e.g., bundled or unbundled)	Complex charts	Local branch office support
Annual maintenance fee	Multicolor support	Time-sharing access
Support costs (manuals, training, etc.)	Format and layout control	Size of installed customer base
Resource use (CPU, memory, storage)	Multiple graphs per page	User group
Installation/conversion costs	Compatibility with graphics devices	University support group
	Previewing of output	Financial stability

Source: Warren and Reimann (35).

problems that are too simple. Sometimes the differences among DSS generators become apparent only with more difficult applications.

6.15 Putting the System Together and the Ideal DSS Generator

Development tools increase the productivity of builders and help them produce, at a moderate cost, a DSS responsive to the true needs of users. The philosophy of the development tools and generators is based on two simple, yet very important, concepts: (1) the use of highly automated tools and/or a generator throughout the development process, and (2) the use of prefabricated pieces in the manufacturing of a whole system, whenever possible. The first concept increases the productivity of the builder in the same way an electric saw improves the productivity of a carpenter formerly using a hand saw. The second concept increases productivity analogous to the way a prefabricated wall increases the productivity of the carpenter building a house.

A DSS development system can be thought of as a workshop with several tools and components. Such a system includes the major components discussed earlier:

- □ Request (query) handler (obtains information from database).
- □ System analysis and design facility (editing, interpreting, etc.).
- □ Dialog management system (user interface).
- □ Report generator (formats output reports).
- □ Graphics generator.
- □ Source code manager (stores and accesses built-in and user-developed models).
- □ Model base management system.

Some of these components may be integrated into a DSS generator. Other components may be added as needed. These components and tools can be used to build a new DSS, or upgrade or repair an existing one. The core of the system includes a development language or a DSS generator. The construction is done by combining programming modules. (A *programming module* is a set of executable lines of code that has a name and is written to do a certain job.)

Modules can be written in command languages, which are available in all DSS generators, or in other programming languages (e.g., COBOL or PASCAL). A module can be used independently, or it can be used in conjunction with other modules to build a more complex module. A module can perform computations, read and write operations, transform data, or perform any other computer operation to achieve a certain objective. A DSS generator may include several preprogrammed modules.

The Ideal DSS Generator

The concept of an ideal DSS generator developed by Sprague in the 1970s followed the framework of GADS (see Chapter 5). According to this concept, the generator has to be developed over a long period of time in a fairly narrow area. Once developed, the generator could be used to build specific DSS. And indeed, GADS was used to construct dozens of DSS in different applications involving the allocation of people and/or equipment to geographical zones. Several companies developed DSS generators similar to GADS and used them to construct specific DSS. However, today the vast majority of DSS is being developed with general-purpose DSS generators like FOCUS, EXPRESS, and Lotus 1-2-3. Although none of these general-purpose generators is as powerful as the ideal DSS generator, several of these tools are fairly close to it. Therefore, it is not surprising that many of the fourth-generation systems and some of the modeling languages are being marketed as DSS generators. Such generators differ from the ideal DSS generator in several ways. First, they are general-purpose in nature. They are therefore developed by software companies rather than by the user companies. Second, many of them are available for microcomputers as well. Third, two or more general-purpose generators can be combined to construct a specific DSS. Fourth, they are widely available on time-sharing networks. Finally, they include dozens, sometimes hundreds, of support functions (e.g., NOMAD 2 PC has about 150 support functions).

All these make today's generators much more accessible than during the 1970s. The fact that there is no need to develop and maintain such generators makes the DSS construction process much faster and cheaper.

6.16   Ready-made (Application) DSS

The initial idea of DSS envisioned a complex system designed to support specific decision makers in semistructured (or even unstructured) situations. As such, a DSS was viewed as a custom-made product that could not be used in different settings.

As companies began to develop their DSS, they realized that their specific DSS might be transferable with only minor modifications to other settings. For example, a DSS developed for planning in one airline can be used by other airlines. The "what if" capabilities, the ease with which models can be altered, and the flexibility at various levels and dimensions make the idea of transferability of DSS very attractive.

An interesting analogy can be found in the world of clothing. A regular DSS is the counterpart of a tailored suit, which is made for a specific customer at a perfect fit. However, you can also buy a suit and alter it in several minor ways. The modified suit will not fit as well as the custom-made one. But it will be a lot cheaper and you can use it much sooner. This is basically what a ready-made DSS is.

A ready-made DSS is usually *not* as general-purpose as the DSS generators. Rather, it is a specific DSS, designed for a narrow functional area (such as quality control in manufacturing or capital budgeting). It differs from traditional MIS application software by its flexibility (e.g., the "what if" questions) and by the user's ability to introduce changes rapidly. For examples of ready-made DSS, see Cases 13-16 in Chapter 9.

6.17 Summary

The construction process of a DSS could be very lengthy and expensive. To increase the productivity of the builders, special tools have been developed. Furthermore, a variety of tools have been combined into DSS generators, which can be used to expedite considerably the construction job. The availability of such generators helps users build specific DSS with little assistance from the IS people, who are usually backlogged on large IS projects.

A special class of DSS generators are the micro-integrated software packages that include electronic spreadsheet technology. The integrated packages may provide other capabilities that are useful to managers (such as electronic mail and calendar).

DSS tools and generators can be classified into three major categories: those used in the dialog system, those built around the database, and those based around the model base.

Altogether, there are hundreds of tools on the market. Selecting the best tools for your purposes is a major problem because it involves many evaluating criteria.

Once tools and generators are selected, building the specific DSS can begin. In Chapters 8 and 9 we present a sample of about a dozen specific DSS. Some of these examples show the use of the tools described in this chapter.

Key Words

application generators
assembly language
binary code
computer graphics
CPU
database
database management
   system (DBMS)

fourth-generation
   languages (4GLs)
fourth-generation systems
macros
modeling tools
nonprocedural languages
problem-oriented
   languages
procedural languages

programming languages
query language
relational database
report generation
simulation
spreadsheet (electronic)
system software
templates
"what if" capability

Questions for Review

1. What is a programming language?
2. What is the difference between a machine language and other programming languages?
3. Define a procedural language and contrast it with a nonprocedural language.
4. Define a problem-oriented language.
5. Define RPG and explain its uses.
6. List some of the major advantages of computer graphics for management.
7. What is SQL?
8. Describe a database machine.
9. Describe a complete fourth-generation system.
10. What is an application generator? How does it relate to a DSS generator?

11. Define electronic spreadsheet.
12. List the three components of Lotus 1-2-3.
13. Define templates and explain their use.
14. Define a planning model and compare it with a financial planning model.
15. What is an integrated package? How does it differ from a "modularly integrated package"?
16. List three advantages and three disadvantages of integrated packages (as compared with stand-alone packages).
17. What is an executive workstation?
18. List some of the characteristics of distributed DSS.
19. Define and describe a commercial database (on-line) service. Name one or two that you are familiar with.
20. List five major criteria to consider in selecting a DSS generator.
21. Define a ready-made DSS.

Problems and Discussion Questions

1. Discuss some methods and tools that can improve the productivity of DSS programmers.
2. Why are nonprocedural languages more suited to DSS? Be specific. Give an example if possible.
3. The most powerful DSS generators include both procedural and nonprocedural languages. What advantages may be derived from such a pairing?
4. What type of language is Lotus 1-2-3?
5. 4GLs can clearly improve programmers' productivity, but they are not used much in transaction processing systems. Why?
6. Query languages and RPGs are extremely important in DSS construction. Explain why this is so. Use a managerial point of view.
7. Results of research indicated that graphical presentation is not more effective than tabular presentation. Practitioners disagree. They claim that graphics are superior. Explain why such differences may occur. For extra credit, read Remus's paper (*Management Science*, May 1984) and discuss it.
8. What are the major advantages of a template?
9. What is the major benefit of a macro?
10. Spreadsheet software is appearing now in three dimensions. Explain how this is possible.
11. Explain the relationship between SQL and a DBMS.
12. What is a database machine? Conduct some research to find the latest progress in this area and explain the potential impact on DSS.
13. Which of the following statements is correct and why?
    a. Any DSS generator is an application generator.
    b. Any application generator is a DSS generator.
14. Lotus 1-2-3 is probably the most popular PC software. Why is this so? What can you do with this package that makes it so attractive?
15. Visit a computer store and review the latest capabilities of Lotus 1-2-3. Compare them with the capabilities of an ideal DSS generator as discussed in Chapters 4 and 5. How wide is the gap? Be specific.
16. Explain how templates are related to Lotus 1-2-3 (or to a similar package). Explain the advantages of using templates in DSS construction.
17. Templates can be purchased in a computer store or can be developed "in house." Explain the difference between the two types.

18. What is the role of a "planning and modeling language"? How does it differ from a general programming language? How does it relate to DSS?

19. The PIMS model discussed in the text uses "a large multiple regression model." Explain the connection between regression analysis and the role of PIMS.

20. There are over 100 DBMS packages on the market for micros and several dozen for mainframes. Why don't we have such packages for model base management systems (MBMS)?

21. NOMAD 2, RAMIS II, and FOCUS share certain common characteristics. What are they? How do these packages relate to an ideal DSS generator?

22. IFPS has an interface to FOCUS. In some cases they are packaged together. FCS and RAMIS is another such pairing. What are the benefits of such a packaging?

23. A university is installing a distributed DSS for budget preparation, expense monitoring and financial planning. There are four schools at the university and 18 departments. In addition there are two research institutions and many administrative services. Prepare a diagram that shows the distributed DSS. Suggest what decisions could be supported at each managerial level.

24. Why is selecting a DSS generator such an important issue? What are some of the difficulties in the selection process?

25. Compare a custom-made DSS vs. a ready-made one. List some advantages and disadvantages of each.

26. Helix (from Odesta, Inc., Northbrook, IL) is billed as "database information management and DSS for the Apple Macintosh." It makes heavy use of graphics and icons (instead of command strings and different "modes" of operation). Helix uses Mac icons to create unique database applications. Helix's icons store instructions for processing and retrieving information. Instructions can be created and used entirely through the Mac's mouse controller without even touching a keyboard. Answer the following questions:

    a. It is said that Helix "gives the novice or the modest user of computers more flexible access to data." Explain why.

    b. It is said that Helix's graphic features "are functionally more intuitive than most command-oriented programs." Explain why.

    c. What is Helix: DSS, model base, database, dialog subsystem, or what? Explain your answer.

Exercises*

1. It has been suggested that DSS generators are English-like and have a variety of analysis capabilities. Even though you have no formal training in IFPS, see if you can identify the purpose and the analysis capabilities of the following IFPS program:

```
MODEL RISK VERSION OF 05/08/89 13:11
1 COLUMNS 1-5
2 *
```

*These exercises require a knowledge of spreadsheet or IFPS and can be assigned after finishing Chapter 7. Additional exercises are provided at the end of Chapter 7.

3 *   INCOME STATEMENT

4 *

5 VOLUME = VOLUME ESTIMATE, PREVIOUS VOLUME*VOLUME GROWTH RATE

6 SELLING PRICE = PRICE ESTIMATE, PREVIOUS SELLING PRICE*1.06

7 SALES = VOLUME*SELLING PRICE

8 UNIT COST = UNIRAND(.80,.95)

9 VARIABLE COST = VOLUME*UNIT COST

10 DIVISION OVERHEAD = 15%*VARIABLE COST

11 STLINE DEPR (INVESTMENT, SALVAGE, LIFE, DEPRECIATION)

12 COST OF GOODS SOLD = VARIABLE COST + DIVISION OVERHEAD
 + DEPRECIATION

13 GROSS MARGIN = SALES − COST OF GOODS SOLD

14 OPERATING EXPENSE = .02*SALES

15 INTEREST EXPENSE = 15742, 21522, 21147, 24905, 21311

16 *

17 NET BEFORE TAX = GROSS MARGIN − OPERATING EXPENSE − INTEREST
 EXPENSE 18 TAXES = TAX RATE*NET BEFORE TAX

19 NET AFTER TAX = NET BEFORE TAX − TAXES

20 *

21 INVESTMENT = 100000, 125000, 0, 100000, 0

22 *

23 RATE OF RETURN = IRR(NET AFTER TAX + DEPRECIATION, INVESTMENT)

24 *

25 * DATA ESTIMATES

26 TAX RATE = .46

MONTE CARLO 200

SEED .4

COLUMNS 5

HIST RATE OF RETURN, NONE

Note: This question was borrowed from Kroeber and Watson(13). The computer program was adapted from *IFPS Tutorial* (Austin, TX: Execucom Systems Corporation, 1979).

2. Prepare to hand in a printout of a spreadsheet program to analyze the following proposed new product investment. This exercise can use any popular microcomputer spreadsheet software, such as Lotus 1-2-3, Multiplan, Excel, or QUATTRO. It also could use the IFPS financial modeling software. Your hand-in should include a printout of the numerical analysis for each part of the exercise, along with a printout of the formulas used in the calculations (i.e., use PRINT Formulas in Lotus or Multiplan, or LIST in IFPS). Each printout must include a title heading that includes your name, your instructor's name, your course and section number, and the date prepared.

Your client is considering an investment of $1000 in a new product venture that will cause an immediate increase of $400 in the client's annual gross sales. It is assumed the usefulness of this new product will end after five years, that its sales will increase by 15 percent per year for years 2 thru 4, and that sales in the final or fifth year will be half those of the fourth year. Although this illustrative exercise involves only a few trivial calculations, please use formulas throughout your model that could easily be extended over more time, with more complex relationships; thus showing the power of spreadsheets.

The incremental variable costs for this new product are estimated at 40 percent of sales. The estimated incremental annual fixed costs begin at $30 for year 1, increase by $5 during each of the remaining 4 years of the new product's useful life, and then end. The initial investment, all during year 1, includes $400 of expenses that are immediately deductible from the firm's taxable profits. The remaining $600 of the investment is capitalized, and charged out as depreciation expense over several years, starting during year 1. The income tax rate applicable to the incremental net profit contribution of this new product is 28 percent for all years and all amounts. Because a reported accounting loss on this new product reduces other taxable profits, a cash savings of taxes payable of this same percentage will occur for years that show an accounting loss.

Part 1 Develop a spreadsheet model for this proposed new product investment that shows each item of incremental investment, revenue, expenses, taxes, and net profit for each of the five years. Assume the $600 capitalized part of the investment is depreciated in equal amounts ($150 per year) over years 1 through 4.

Part 2 Now extend the spreadsheet model of Part 1 to include the incremental cash flow for each of the five years, and the cumulative cash flow for each year. Cash flow includes all investments, expenses, and taxes as outflows, and revenues as inflows.

Part 3 Extend Part 2 to show the net present value, at a 20 percent annual discount factor, of the incremental cash flow for this proposed five-year investment venture. If possible, also show the internal rate of return, or yield, of this investment.

Part 4 The time period and calculation method for charging the depreciation expense of an investment against incremental taxable income can influence the cash flow pattern, and hence the attractiveness, of an investment. Please extend the spreadsheet of Part 3 to examine the impact on periodic net cash flow, and the total net present value and the internal rate of return, of the following different depreciation options:

a. Current option of equal allocation of the $600 total over four years—that is, a straight-line depreciation schedule over four years.
b. Then show straight-line over five years.
c. And, straight-line over three years.
d. Finally, use sum-of-years-digits method over four years. Notice that the digits 1, 2, 3, and 4 sum to 10; hence first-year depreciation is 4/10 of the total capitalized investment, and the following years are 3/10, 2/10, and 1/10, respectively.[*]

3.   Finding a Seasonal Index. A seasonal index is an extremely important concept for both forecasting and analysis. Most government statistics are reported as "seasonally adjusted," meaning that the actual data were adjusted to reflect seasonal impacts. One method of finding a quarterly seasonal index is described as follows:

Step 1. List all historical data by quarter.
Step 2. Use a four-quarter moving average to smooth the data (take the sum of the first four quarters and divide it by four, then sum quarters two through five and divide by four, and so on).
Center the first average against quarter 3.
Step 3. Total the moving averages and find the simple average of the numbers. Call this SQA (smoothed quarterly average).

[*]This exercise was prepared by Dr. Warren Briggs of Suffolk University.

Step 4. Find the entry for every first quarter of the SQA and delete the highest and lowest numbers. Repeat this process for the second, third, and fourth quarters.

Step 5. Find the simple average for each quarter from the results of step 4. Call it AQ1, AQ2, AQ3, and AQ4 respectively.

Step 6. Add the quarters' simple averages and divide by 4. Call this AQ.

Step 7. Compare the results of Step 6 to SQA. There should be a small discrepancy. Divide SQA by QA. You should get a result that is close to 1 (e.g., 1.05).

Step 8. Multiply AQ1 by the result of Step 7. Repeat this step for AQ2, AQ3, and AQ4. This is the adjusted quarterly average.

Step 9. Add the result of Step 8. It should equal, or be very close to, SQA.

Step 10. Multiply each of the adjusted quarterly averages by 400 and divide the result by SQA. The final result is a seasonal index based on 100 = average season.

Note: This procedure assumes no trend. For simplicity, the moving average in step 2 is placed against quarter 3 instead of between quarters 2 and 3, which would have required additional computation.

Use a spreadsheet or IFPS to build a DSS for this situation. In addition,

□ Perform sensitivity analysis.
□ Show the smoothed data over the original data on a graph.
□ Show the four seasonal indices (found in step 10) as bar and pie charts.

The input data are

	Quarter			
Year	1	2	3	4
1980	108	104	93	134
1981	110	100	90	125
1982	112	96	88	130
1983	106	93	85	142
1984	111	108	100	138
1985	98	112	94	155
1986	115	98	96	144
1987	104	102	91	150

4. Given a list of employees in a manufacturing company, use the DBMS functions and/or modeling to perform the following:

a. Sort the employees by department
b. Sort by salary in ascending order
c. Sort by department and each department by ascending order of age
d. Calculate average salary
e. Calculate average salary of female employees
f. Calculate the average age in department "A."
g. Find the females who were hired after December 31, 1985.
h. Show graphically the age distribution (use a five-year grouping) as a pie.
i. Compute the age to salary linear regression of all employees.

Name	Sex	Age	Hired at	Dep	Salary
Martin Dean	M	28	06-Jan-78	A	$22,000
Jane Hanson	F	35	15-Mar-86	D	$33,200
Daniel Smith	M	19	06-Dec-80	C	$18,500
Emily Brosmer	F	26	10-Jan-78	B	$27,000
Jessica Stone	F	45	26-May-73	A	$38,900
Tom Obudzinski	M	38	01-Dec-88	B	$29,800
Kathleen Braun	F	32	18-Apr-82	B	$35,600
Lisa Gregory	F	48	03-Sep-81	C	$32,400
Timothy Parker	M	29	03-Aug-83	A	$21,200
Jessica Hibscher	F	53	30-Jul-84	D	$38,900
Adam Handel	M	62	29-Nov-85	A	$40,250
Melissa Black	F	42	01-Dec-87	B	$26,400
Ray Ernster	M	29	02-Jul-79	C	$23,200
Daniel Baim	M	38	26-Feb-77	C	$31,000
Amy Melnikov	F	45	30-Apr-76	A	$36,400
Adrienne Cammizzo	F	30	15-Jun-76	A	$25,400
Steven Knowless	M	48	22-Oct-75	D	$33,200
Patricia Salisbury	F	56	26-Feb-74	B	$42,600
Matthew Broekhuizen	M	44	01-Jan-78	C	$45,400
Sarah Parent	F	64	03-Jan-89	A	$38,200

5. Given a Lotus template on the top and the formulas on the bottom, use Lotus to compute the values in rows 12–19. (Source: *Lotus*, February 1986)

	A	B
1	Selling Price of Order	$1200.00
2	Total Cost of Order	$1000.00
3	Discount for PV (1)	13.50%
4	Days to Payment	30
5	Probability of Payment	80.00%
6	Customer Will Reorder	
7	Yes (=1) or No (=0)	1
8	Days to Reordering Date	30
9	Discount for PV (2)	13.75%
10	Probability of Payment (2)	95.00%
11		
12	Present Value of Order	
13	Present Value of Cost	
14	Expected Value of Order	
15		
16	Present Value of Reorder	
17	Present Value of Cost (2)	
18	Expected PV of Reorder	
19	Discounted EV of 2 Orders	

Formula Table

B12:	$+B1*(1+B3/365)\wedge-B4$
B13:	$+B2$
B14:	$+B5*(B12-B13)-(1-B5)*B13$
B16:	$+B1*(1+(@MAX(B3,B9)/365))\wedge-(B8+B4)*B7$
B17:	$+B2*(1+(@MAX(B3,B9)/365))\wedge-B8*B7$
B18:	$+B10*(B16-B17)-(1-B10)*B17$
B19:	$+B14+B5*B18/(1+@MAX(B3,B9))$

References and Bibliography

1. Bernknopf, J. "4GLs Without Philosophy." *Information Center,* June 1986.
2. Briggs, W. G. "An Evaluation of DSS Packages." *Computerworld,* March 1, 1982.
3. Champine, G. A., et al. *Distributed Computer Systems: Impact on Management Design and Analysis.* New York: Elsevier, 1980.
4. Cobb, R. H. "In Praise of 4GLS." *Datamation,* July 15, 1985. See also *Computerworld,* October 14, 1985.
5. DeSanctis, G. "Computer Graphics as Decision Aids: Direction for Research." *Decision Sciences,* Vol. 15, 1984.
6. Fitzgerald, J. and T. S. Eason. *Fundamentals of Data Communications.* 2nd ed. New York: Wiley, 1984.
7. Furge, S. , and D. H. Mau. "Fourth-generation application Development." *Information Center,* June 1986.
8. Hackathathorn, R. D., and P. G. W. Keen. "Organizational Strategies for Personal Computing in Decision Support Systems." *MIS Quarterly,* September 1981.
9. Hollocks, B. "Personal Computers and Operations Research—Experience in British Steel." *Journal of Operational Research Society,* April 1982.
10. Horwitt, E. "Up from Spreadsheets." *Business Computer Systems,* June 1985.
11. Horwitt, E., et al. "A Survey of Application Generators." *IEEE Software,* January 1985.
12. Klein, R. "Computer-based Financial Modeling." *Journal of Systems Management,* May 1982.
13. Kroeber, D. W., and H. J. Watson. *Computer-Based Information Systems.* 2nd ed. New York: Macmillan, 1987.
14. Kroenke, D. M., and K. A. Dolan. *Database Processing.* 3rd ed. Chicago: SRA, 1988.
15. Lee, D. T. "Decision Support in a Distributed Environment." *National Computer Conference,* 1984.
16. Lehman, J. A., et al. "Business Computer Graphics." *Datamation,* November 15, 1984.
17. Mamis, R. "A Manager's Guide to Integrated Software." *INC,* February 1985.
18. Martin, J. *Application Development Without Programmers.* Englewood Cliffs, NJ: Prentice-Hall, 1982.
19. Martin, J. *Telecommunication and the Computer.* 3rd ed. Englewood Cliffs, NJ: Prentice-Hall, 1983.
20. Martin, J. *Fourth-Generation Languages.* 3 vols. Englewood Cliffs, NJ: Prentice-Hall, 1985.
21. Meador, C. L., and R. A. Mezger. "Selecting an End-user Programming Language for DSS Development." *M.I.S. Quarterly,* December 1984.
22. Miller, H. "Introduction to Spreadsheets." *PC World,* August 1984.
23. Neal, S., and K.L. Traunik. *Database Management System in Business.* Englewood Cliffs, NJ: Prentice-Hall, 1986.
24. O'Brien, J. A. *Computers in Business Management.* 4th ed. Homewood, IL: Irwin, 1985.
25. O'Malley, C. "Your Own Spreadsheet Templates." *Personal Computing,* September 1985.
26. Pallatto, J. "Database Management Systems: Sorting Through the Madness." *PC Week,* August 14, 1984.
27. Paller, A. "Million-dollar Applications." *Information Center,* February 1986.
28. Reimann, B. C., and A. D. Warren. "User-oriented Criteria for the Selection of DSS Software." *Communication of ACM,* February 1985.
29. Remus, W. "An Empirical Investigation of the Impact of Graphical and Tabular Data Presentations on Decision Making." *Management Science,* May 1984.
30. Seligman, D. "Life Will Be Different When We're All On-line." *Fortune,* February 4, 1985.

31. Shim, J. K., and R. McGlade. "Current Trends in the Use of Corporate Planning Models." *Journal of Systems Management*, September 1984.

32. Sprague, R. H., Jr., and E. D. Carlson. *Building Effective Decision Support Systems*. Englewood Cliffs, NJ: Prentice-Hall, 1982.

33. Sprague, R. H., Jr., and B. McNurlin. *Information Systems Management in Practice*. Englewood Cliffs, NJ: Prentice-Hall, 1986.

34. Van Dam, A. "Computer Graphics Comes of Age." *Communication of the ACM*, July 1984.

35. Warren, A. D. , and B. Reimann. "Selecting DSS Generator Software: A Participative Process." *International Journal on Policy and Information*, December 1985.

36. Wilson, R. "The 4GL Evaluation Team." *Information Center*, February 1986.

APPENDIX A: COBOL vs. FOCUS

Without Focus (a)

```
IDENTIFICATION DIVISION.
PROGRAM-ID. SAMP1.
AUTHOR. K. MCKENNA.
DATE-WRITTEN. AUG 17 1979.
DATE-COMPILED. AUG 17 1979.
SECURITY, NON-CLASSIFIED.
REMARKS. SAMPLE REPORT.
ENVIRONMENT DIVISION.
CONFIGURATION SECTION.
SPECIAL-NAMES.
    C01 IS TOP-OF-PAGE.
INPUT-OUTPUT SECTION.
FILE-CONTROL.
    SELECT INPT-FILE ASSIGN UT-S-INPT.
    SELECT SORT-FILE ASSIGN UT-S-SRT1.
    SELECT REPORT-FILE ASSIGN UT-S OUTPT.
DATA DIVISION.
FILE SECTION.
FD INPT-FILE
    LABEL RECORDS OMITTED
    RECORD CONTAINS 60 CHARACTERS.
01 INPT-HEC          PIC X (80).
SD SORT-FILE
    RECORD CONTAINS 80 CHARACTERS.
01 SORT-REC.
    05 ACCOUNT-NUMBER    PIC X(5).
    05 ACCOUNT-DOLLARS   PIC S9(5)V99.
    05 FILLER            PIC X(68).
FD REPORT-FILE
    LABEL RECORDS ARE OMITTED.
01 REPORT-RECORD     PIC X (133).
WORKING-STORAGE SECTION.
01 FLAGS.
    05 FLAG-INPT         PIC XX VALUE ZEROS.
        88 MORE-DATA     VLLUE 'YES'.
        88 NO-MORE       VALEE 'NO'.
        88 FIRST-TIME    VALEE ZEROS.
01 COUNTS.
    05 LINE-NUMBER       PIC S99 VALUE +1.
    05 PAGE-NUMBER       PIC S999 VALUE +1.
01 PREVIOUS-ACCOUNT  PIC S(5) VALUE
SPACES.
01 TOTALS.
    05 ACCOUNT-TOTAL     PIC S9(6)V99 VALUE
ZERO.
    05 FINAL-TOTAL       PIC S9(6)V99 VALUE
ZERO.

    SORT SORT-FILE
        ASCENDING KEY ACCOUNT-NUMBER
    USING INPT-FILE
        OUTPUT PROCEDURE SALES-RPT THRU SALES-
END.
    CLOSE REPORT-FILE.
    STOP RUN.
SALES-RPT SECTION.
    OPEN OUTPUT REPORT-FILE.
    PERFORM HEAD-RTN THRU READ-EXIT.
    PERFORM PROCESS-INPUT THRU PR-EXIT UNTIL
NO-MORE.
    PERFORM FINAL-PROCESSING THRU FINAL-EXIT.
SALES-END. EXIT.
PROCESS-INPUT.
    IF ACCOUNT-NUMBER IS NOT EQUAL TO
PREVIOUS-ACCOUNT
        PERFORM ACCOUNT-TOTAL-PROCESSING THRU
ACCOUNT-EXIT.
    ADD ACCOUNT-DOLLARS TO ACCOUNT-TOTAL
FINAL-TOTAL.
    PERFORM READ-RTN THRU READ-EXIT.
PR-EXIT. EXIT.
READ-RTN.
    RETURN SORT-FILE AT END
        MOVE 'NO' TO FLAG-INPT.
READ-EXIT. EXIT.
FINAL-PROCESSING.
    PERFORM ACCOUNT-TOTAL-PROCESSING THRU
ACCOUNT-EXIT.
    MOVE SPACES TO DETAIL-LINE.
    MOVE FINAL-TOTAL TO ACCOUNT-TOT-OUT.
    MOVE 'TOTAL' TO ACCOUNT-TIT.
    PERFORM LINE-OUT THRU LINE-EXIT.
FINAL-EXIT. EXIT.
ACCOUNT-TOTAL-PROCESSING.
    IF FIRST-TIME
        MOVE 'YES' TO FLAG-INPT
        MOVE ACCOUNT-NUMBER TO PREVIOUS
ACCOUNT
    ELSE
        MOVE SPACES TO DETAIL-LINE
    MOVE PREVIOUS-ACCOUNT TO ACCOUNT-NO-OUT
    MOVE ACCOUNT TOTAL TO ACCOUNT-TOT-OUT.
    PERFORM LINE-OUT THRU LINE-EXIT
    MOVE ACCOUNT-NUMBER TO PREVIOUS-ACCOUNT
    MOVE ZERO TO ACCOUNT-TOTAL.
```

```
01 DETAIL-LINE.                                ACCOUNT-EXIT. EXIT.
   05 CARRIAGE-CONTROL   PIC X.                LINE-OUT.
   05 ACCOUNT-NO-OUT     PIC ZZZZ9.               IF LINE-NUMBER = 1
   05 ACCOUNT-TIT-REDEFINES ACCOUNT-NO-OUT           MOVE PAGE-NUMBER TO PAG-NUMBER-OUT.
PIC X (5).                                            WRITE REPORT-RECORD FROM HEADING-LINE
   05 FILLER             PIC XXX.                         AFTER ADVANCING TOP-OF-PAGE
   05ACCOUNT-TOT-OUT     PIC $$$$, $$9.99.            MOVE SPACES TO REPORT-RECORD
   05 FILLER             PIC X(100).                  WRITE REPORT-RECORD AFTER ADVANCING 2
01 HEADING-LINE.                               LINES
   05 CARRIAGE CONTROL   PIC X.                    MOVE 4 TO LINE-NUMBER
   05 FILLER             PIC X (41).                ADD 1 TO PAGE-NUMBER.
       VALUE 'ACCOUNT      TOTAL      PAGE'.    WRITE REPORT-RECORD FROM DETAIL-LINE
   05 PAGE-NUMBER-OUT    PIC 29.                    AFTER ADVANCING 1 LINES.
PROCEDURE DIVISION.                                IF LINE-NUMBER = 55
PREPARE SALES REPORT.                                  MOVE 1 TO LINE-NUMBER
                                                   ELSE
                                                       ADD 1 TO LINE-NUMBER.
                                               LINE-EXIT. EXIT.
```

With
Focus
(b)

```
TABLE
>  SUM SALES AND COLUMN-TOTAL
>  BY ACCOUNT
>  END
```

```
ACCOUNT              SALES

 45452            $120.12
 45453            $869.04
 45632            $589.12

 TOTAL          $1,578.28
```

Result

APPENDIX B: The Wharton Experiment

In a study of the effectiveness of business meetings, conducted by the Wharton School, University of Pennsylvania, overhead projection was shown to significantly influence the actual decisions reached, how the presenter of information was perceived by meeting participants, and whether or not the meeting leader could quickly reach a consensus.

The six-month study was conducted with masters in business administration candidates assuming the roles of corporate decision makers grappling with a major marketing decision.

The Wharton MBA students were divided into 36 groups of three or four and given the task of making a group marketing decision on whether or not to introduce a new product, "Crystal, a light beer." The group was urged to reach a consensus decision on whether or not to market the beer—"go" or "no go."

The student presenters, playing the role of marketing experts, then gave opposing viewpoints for and against the product: one used overhead transparencies and the other used a white board to emphasize certain points. In one-third of the meetings the presenters in favor of a marketing decision used transparencies, in one-third those against used transparencies, and in one-third no transparencies were used.

Results: Regardless of which side they were favoring, the presenters were able to convince more people when they used the visual than when they did not. Sixty-seven percent agreed with the presenter promoting a "go" decision using visuals, and the same percent agreed when the presenter using visuals argued for a "no go" decision. When no overhead projector was used, deadlock at 50-50 occurred. In addition, the meeting groups rated presenters using overhead transparencies as "significantly better prepared, more professional, more persuasive, more credible, and more interesting."

Finally, the study indicated that the leader of the group that was supported with graphics achieved consensus in a 28 percent shorter meeting time. *Note:* A 28 percent reduction in meeting length could produce savings for American business equal to several billion dollars a year, or a time savings of up to 42 extra working days per year for average executives who spend half their time in business meetings.

Source: L. Oppenheim, C. Kydd, V. P. Carroll, and G. Carroll, "A study of the effects of the use of overhead transparencies on business meeting," Report of the Applied Research Center of the Wharton School, University of Pennsylvania, October 1981.

APPENDIX C: Spreadsheet Analysis for Quantity Discounts Using Lotus 1-2-3 *

The Problem.   Many vendors offer discount prices for products if purchased in large quantities. The buyers can save on the product price, but they have to pay for carrying large inventories. The formulas for determining whether to accept or reject a discount offer are not too complicated. However, they may not be found in many commercial application software packages. Writing these formulas with Lotus 1-2-3 takes only a few minutes. Furthermore, a "what if" analysis can easily be performed. The decision is determined by the following variables:

- □ Annual usage (units per year).
- □ Unit price.
- □ Cost per order (fixed).
- □ Holding cost (for each dollar value of inventory, in dollars per year).
- □ The minimum quantity that must be purchased in order to receive a discount.
- □ The discounted price.

Example.   In this example we will show only one possibility of a discount (price break). However, our analysis can easily be extended to include several price breaks. The data for our case are:

Annual usage = 1000 units
Unit price = $50.00
Ordering cost = $25.00 per order
Holding cost = $0.35 per dollar value in inventory, per year (or $17.50 per unit)

---

*Condensed from: Gardner, E. S. Jr. "Should You Take That Quantity Discount?" *Lotus,* June 1986.

The discount offer is $48.00 (a 4 percent discount per unit if a minimum of 500 units is purchased). The problem is whether to accept the offer or not.

Solution. The solution is based on the well-known economic order quantity (EOQ) formula, which states:

$$EOQ = \sqrt{\frac{2 \times \text{annual usage} \times \text{ordering costs}}{\text{unit price} \times \text{holding cost}}}$$

The Lotus Model. (A minimum competence in Lotus 1-2-3 is assumed.) The Lotus 1-2-3 program enables the organization of the input and output information in a table (Table 6.15).

Developing this analysis involved the following steps:

Cell		Formula	Explanation
E12	EOQ	@SQRT((2*E5*E7/ (E6*E8))	This calculates the value of the EOQ according to the formula
E13	Actual order quantity	@Round(E12,0)	This command rounds the result of the EOQ formula to the nearest integer
E14	Number of orders	+ E5/E13	The number of orders placed annually is computed by dividing the annual usage by EOQ
E15	Average inventory	+ E13/2	The average inventory is computed to be equal to half of the EOQ
E17	Order costs	+ E7*E14	Multiplies the cost per order by the number of orders per year
E18	Holding costs	+ E15*E6*E8	Multiplies the average inventory times the unit cost times holding cost per unit
E19	Purchase costs	+ E6*E5	Multiplies the unit cost by the annual usage
E20	Total costs	@SUM(E17..E19)	Totals the data in cells E17 through E19

Now, column G is to be completed for the discounted price. Some of the information and formulas can be copied from column E. Other information, such as the unit price in cell G6 must be entered directly or with a formula (+ E6*.96). The minimum amount required to be purchased in order to receive a discount (500) is also entered in cell G9.

The following formula should be entered into cell G13 to assure that the minimum quantity necessary for the discount is entered:

$$@IF(G12 > = G9, @ROUND(G12,0),G9)$$

This formula compares the new EOQ against the minimum order requirement and selects the appropriate one.

TABLE 6.15 The Lotus 1-2-3 Screen.

	A	B	C	D	E	F	G
1					Quantity Discount Calculator		
2							
3					Standard Price		Discount Price
4	INPUT						
5	Annual usage (units)				1000		1000
6	Unit price				$50.00		$48.00
7	Cost per order				$25.00		$25.00
8	Holding cost per $				$0.35		$0.35
9	Minimum order quantity				0		500
10							
11	OUTPUT						
12	EOQ				53.45		54.55
13	Actual order quantity				53		500
14	Number of orders				18.87		2.00
15	Average inventory				26.50		250.00
16	Annual costs:						
17	Ordering				$471.70		$50.00
18	Holding				$463.75		$4,200.00
19	Purchasing				$50,000.00		$48,000.00
20	Total				$50,935.45		$52,250.00

"What If" Analysis. "What if" analysis is easy to conduct with Lotus 1-2-3. Any of the input data can be changed and the entire output portion is recalculated instantly.

Extended Analysis. The same approach can be used to examine other discount offers; for example, the vendor may offer larger discounts (e.g., $47.00 and $46.00) for larger quantities (e.g., a minimum of 750 and 1000 units). These offers can be entered in columns H and I in a similar manner as the information in column G was entered. Such an extended analysis can aid in negotiating discounts with vendors.

Goal Seeking. Adding additional formulas can allow the user to conduct goal seeking. For example, the user may want to know the discounted unit price that will make the total cost $48,000. The execution of this formula is left to the reader as a homework exercise. Other goal-seeking information requires additional formulas.

Graphic Support. The input and/or output data can easily be converted to bar charts, histograms, or any other presentation available in Lotus 1-2-3. For example, the costs in cells E19 and G19 can be shown as a bar graph. It is also possible to show how total cost relates to EOQ (both the theoretical and the actual).

Conclusion. The solution shown in Table 6.15 indicates that the discount offer should be rejected. Through trial-and-error or via goal seeking, one can find that the break-even discount unit price is $46.79 (for a 500 unit order size). This can be used as starting point for price negotiations.

APPENDIX D: Templates Support to Lotus 1-2-3

Financial Statistics
  1. Financial Performance
  2. Financial History
  3. Balance Sheet Performance
  4. Balance Sheet History
  5. Income Statement Performance
  6. Income Statement History
  7. Balance Sheet Projection
  8. Income Statement Projection

Sales and Marketing
  9. Sales and Marketing
     Performance
  10. Sales and Marketing Projections
  11. Regional Sales Performance
  12. Regional Sales History
  13. Sales Performance Reports and
      Quotas
  14. Sales Districts Historical Sales and
      Quotas
  15. Competitive Sales Performances
  16. Competitive Sales Histories
  17. Projected Sales by Region,
      Quarterly and 5 Year
  18. Price List by Product/Region
  19. Competitive Sales Projections
  20. Product Market Share
      Projections

Organization and Budget
  21. Department Budgets
  22. Department Budgets' History
  23. Breakdown of SG&A Expenses
  24. History of SG&A Expenses
  25. Consolidated Manpower &
      Expenses
  26. Consolidated Manpower &
      Expense History
  27. Projected SG&A Expenses
  28. Department Budget Projections

Personnel
  29. Employee Business Expenses
  30. Employee Time Analysis

  31. Employee Directory
  32. Employee Time Reporting

Sales Tools
  33. Sales Follow-up Reports
  34. Sales Call Reports
  35. Customer Mailing List

Asset Management
  36. Asset Management
      Performance
  37. Asset Management History
  38. Inventory Performance
  39. Accounts Receivable
      Performance
  40. Fixed Asset Performance
  41. Fixed Asset History

Cash Management
  42. Cash Flow Projections
  43. Capital Expenditures Analysis
  44. Petty Cash Manager

Personal Organization
  45. Bank Account Reconciliations
  46. Credit Card Report
  47. Monthly Calendar
  48. Reservations and
      Appointments

Private and Financial
  49. Investment Management
  50. Personal Budgeting
  51. Activity Reports
  52. Graph Maker
  53. Personal Mailing List
  54. Phone Messages
  55. Personal Income Tax (Form
      1040)
  56. Asset Records for Insurance

Vendor: Optionware Corp.

APPENDIX E: Financial Decision Support Model*

This model monitors profit and return in asset performance by tracking sales, price, production, costs, payroll levels, and investment expenditures. Corporate financial objectives are then tracked in terms of both productivity (billings-per-person and asset turnover) and operating performance (units, sales, profits, return on assets, etc.).

These decision-support models incorporate hierarchical databases that allow reports to be consolidated at each successive management level. The system must also incorporate historical and current results with the short- and long-range plans.

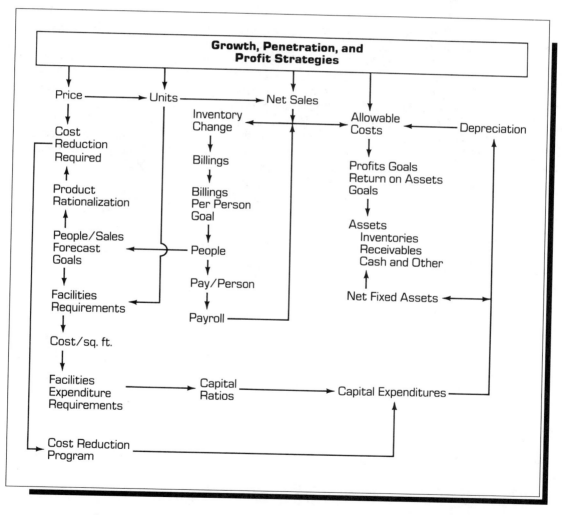

*Adopted from a paper delivered by Beudton and Davis at the 1983 National Meeting of the Institute of Decision Sciences, Las Vegas, Nevada.

APPENDIX F: Some Interesting DSS Tools

Several DSS tools can be added to a DSS generator to enhance its capability. Many of these tools are designed to support Lotus 1-2-3. However, many are designed to support other generators. Representative examples are given as follows:

1. *Spreadsheet optimization using What's Best.* What's Best (from General Optimization Inc., Chicago, IL) is a linear programming package specifically designed for compatible interface with Lotus 1-2-3 and Symphony, for model formulation and interpretation. A complete description of the product is given in *Lotus*, April 1987 (by Scharf). The use of the products enable the user to solve linear and integer programming problems as well as to conduct "what if" and goal-seeking analysis. What's Best is an external program allowing extensive sensitivity analysis, including adding constraints, changing coefficients, or adding variables.

2. *Goal Seeking.* Goal Seeker (from Brown Bag Software) provides goal-seeking capabilities (including multiple goal option, which is not provided by most generators). It supports the most popular spreadsheet packages.

3. *ORACLE for 1-2-3 Add On.* Typical shortcomings in many DSS generators is that micro-based spreadsheets are usually designed to work efficiently, and be user friendly, only when the data are stored in the program itself. When it is necessary to access the databases, performance and user friendliness degrade.

ORACLE ADD ON overcomes this problem. It serves as an extension to Lotus's spreadsheet format. At the same time it allows a direct and simple access to ORACLE's relational database and its commands. This product looks and feels like Lotus, and therefore even a novice user can easily execute SQL-based operations. Lotus itself can also be invoked from the ADD ON.

Chapter 7

The Interactive Financial Planning System (IFPS)

Prepared by Paul Gray[*]

IFPS is a powerful financial planning-based DSS generator. It is available for both mainframe and PCs as well as in a special student version (see Ref. 2).

The following topics are discussed here:

In addition, 19 exercises and an illustrative student term project written in IFPS are provided at the end of this chapter.

[*]Reproduced with the permission of the author.

265

7.1 Why IFPS?

The Interactive Financial Planning System (IFPS) is a nonprocedural fourth-generation computer language developed by Execucom Systems Corporation of Austin, Texas as a DSS generator.[*] The language was developed as a mainframe tool in the early 1970s, long before current spreadsheets such as Excel or Lotus 1-2-3. Like those languages, its principal output is a spreadsheet of numbers. Unlike those languages, which are cell oriented, IFPS is a modeling language oriented to communicating with managers. It allows you to represent your ideas in a near natural language form. Because it is a modeling language, the users can see what is in the model and can understand the assumptions that were made in creating it. As pointed out in Chapter 2, the quality of decisions depends on the quality of the underlying assumptions of the model used.

The importance of a computer language that allows easy communications cannot be overstressed. IFPS provides a number of other features that help in the communications process:

- Instructions are written in natural language form, with no restrictions on the lengths of names. Thus, for example, you can write

  PROFIT BEFORE TAX = SALES − COST OF GOODS SOLD

  which is much more understandable than, say, PBT = S − C.
- There are no order restrictions. Ideas can be written in the order in which you and your managers feel comfortable in thinking about them, as long as each variable is defined at some point in your model. The computer takes care of computing things in the right order.
- The interface allows you to create either spreadsheet output or graphic output or to create custom reports that are in the format people in your organization use.
- The user can easily write models in such a way that the assumptions made are pointed out explicitly.
- Command files allow creation of large models that can be operated simply and with little knowledge of IFPS by managers and others in the organization.
- An optional module can be added to perform linear and nonlinear programming optimizations.
- The mainframe version of IFPS includes an expert's system component, called the *explanation facility*, that helps to explain how and why specific results are obtained.

In Chapter 19, you will see how IFPS extends its "ease-of-use" capability to AI-based (rule-based) explanation commands.

Questions such as "Why did net profit increase so much in 1992" are representative WHY inquiries you might ask IFPS (in everyday plain English

---

[*]IFPS, IFPS/Plus, IFPS/Personal, and Mindsight are all registered trademarks belonging to Execucom Systems Corporation.

sentences) after reviewing the solution of a model. IFPS responds in equally plain English sentences with those factors that were most important in causing the change to net profit.

Communication is improved further by the ability to ask "what if" questions. These questions can be in the form of altering assumed values, asking for sensitivity to specific ranges of variables, and performing goal seeking.

The mainframe version of IFPS also allows you to undertake risk analysis because it allows you to perform Monte Carlo simulations.

Finally, IFPS is a full-featured language. It contains a variety of built-in functions. It allows use of databases, consolidation of spreadsheets, full-page editing, and much more.

In this chapter, we introduce you to some of the key ideas in the language. The discussion is in terms of the mainframe version of IFPS, now called IFPS /Plus since it contains integrated database management capabilities. The PC version of IFPS[*] is called IFPS/Personal and the Macintosh version is Mindsight. The differences between the mainframe version and the PC version are relatively minor but not all features are available on both systems. These differences are discussed briefly at the end of this chapter.

7.2 The Structure of IFPS

IFPS consists of five subsystems: the executive subsystem, the modeling language subsystem, the report generator subsystem, the data file subsystem, and the command file subsystem.

The *executive subsystem* is the highest level of IFPS operation. It is used to accomplish the following activities:

- □ Specify permanent files.
- □ List models and reports.
- □ Delete models and reports.
- □ Combine models.
- □ Consolidate models and data files.
- □ Copy models and reports.
- □ Call other subsystems.

The *modeling language subsystem* is called by issuing a MODEL command. The modeling language subsystem is the primary vehicle for analyzing the situation of interest to the IFPS user. The following activities are performed in the modeling language subsystem:

- □ Create new models.
- □ Edit models.
- □ Produce solutions to the model.
- □ Plot model results.

[*]For instruction on using the PC version see Gray [2]. Abbreviated instructions are given in the instructor's manual to this text. IFPS/Personal is menu driven and is very user friendly.

□ Print complete reports.
□ Ask "what if" questions.
□ Perform goal seeking.
□ Perform risk analysis.

The *database subsystem* is a relational data manager for IFPS applications. It supports multidimensional modeling, reporting and querying using the structured query language, SQL.

The *report generator subsystem* is called by issuing a REPORT command. This subsystem is used for the following purposes:

□ Creation of special report definitions.
□ Editing of special report definitions.

The *data file subsystem* is entered by issuing a DATAFILE command. The data file subsystem is used for

□ Creation of IFPS data files.
□ Editing and maintenance of IFPS data files.

The *command file subsystem* is entered by issuing a CMDFILE command. This subsystem allows the user to create stacks of commands that may be executed with a single command.

Figure 7.1 is a schematic of IFPS flow and a partial list of commands.

7.3   A Simple IFPS Model

The easiest way to learn IFPS is to study a simple model and its output. Figure 7.2 shows a model that computes the dividends expected to be paid out by a firm from 1991 through 1995 under a set of highly simplifying assumptions about income and costs:

□ Half of the net profit after tax each year is declared as dividend.
□ Selling price will be $5.00 in 1991 and will increase by 5% per year, compounded annually.
□ Cost of goods sold (COGS) includes all expenses and will be 80 percent of sales.
□ Tax rate will be 28 percent and taxes will be paid on the excess of sales over cost of goods sold.
□ Quantity sold in 1991 and 1992 will be 1000. It is expected to increase to 1250 for 1993 and 1994 and to increase again in 1995 to 1450.

If you examine Figure 7.2, you will see that each of these assumptions is built into the model. Before showing the output of the model, we will explain each line. To help you follow the explanations, we show the individual lines of Figure 7.2 before discussing them.

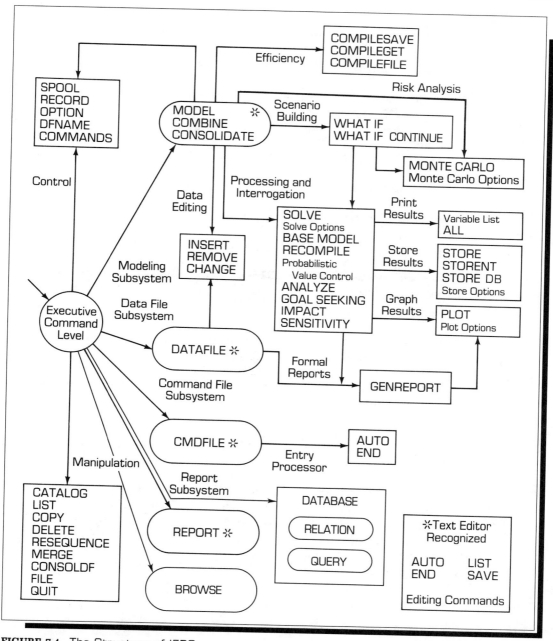

FIGURE 7.1 The Structure of IFPS.

IFPS models are like spreadsheets, containing rows and columns. The first line has to tell IFPS how many columns you want and what to name them. The first number represents the starting year (1991) and the second number the ending year (1995). The two dots tell IFPS to include all years in between. Alternatively, writing COLUMNS 1..6 would have specified that the columns should be called 1 through 6. If the column titles are to have names rather than numbers (e.g., YEAR1 or TOTAL), they have to be spelled out individually.

```
 10 COLUMNS 1991..1995
 20 \
 30 \          IFPS MODEL FOR COMPUTING DIVIDEND FORECAST
 40 \
 50 DIVIDENDS = .50*NET PROFIT AFTER TAX
 60 NET PROFIT AFTER TAX = SALES - COGS - TAXES
 70 SALES = SELLING PRICE*QUANTITY SOLD
 80 COGS = 0.8*SALES
 90 TAXES = TAX RATE*(SALES-COGS)
100 \
110 \ ASSUMPTIONS
120 \
130 SELLING PRICE = 5, PREVIOUS*1.05
140 TAX RATE = 28%
150 QUANTITY SOLD = 1000 FOR 2. 1250 FOR 2. 1450
```

FIGURE 7.2 Simple IFPS model.

Each line begins with a line number. You do not need to type these numbers in when you create a model. IFPS can assign line numbers automatically for you. However, we recommend that you do assign them yourself because this gives you much more control over your model. Line numbers are used in mainframe IFPS but not in IFPS/Personal.

```
 20 \
 30 \          IFPS MODEL FOR COMPUTING DIVIDEND FORECAST
 40 \
```

The \ symbol tells IFPS that this line is a comment. Thus, lines 20 through 40 in Figure 7.2 are comments. Comments are printed verbatim. That is, the output specified by these three lines consists of a blank line followed by a line that prints the heading IFPS MODEL FOR COMPUTING DIVIDEND FORE-CAST and another blank line. The backslash is not printed. These comment lines allow a primitive form of labeling and formatting.

```
 50 DIVIDENDS = .50*NET PROFIT AFTER TAX
```

Dividends are defined as being 50 percent of net profit after tax. In IFPS, a single variable name appears to the left of the equal sign and an expression appears on the right. Multiplication is specified by the *. Addition, subtraction, and division are specified by +, -, and /.

Unlike conventional, procedural programming languages, it is possible to use a variable in IFPS before it is defined. Variable names are not restricted in length and can include multiple words.

```
 60 NET PROFIT AFTER TAX = SALES - COGS - TAXES
```

This line is an accounting relation. It defines NET PROFIT AFTER TAX as being income (SALES) less cost of goods sold (COGS) and taxes.

```
70 SALES = SELLING PRICE * QUANTITY SOLD
```

Sales is the dollar income resulting from multiplying the selling price for each unit by the quantity sold. Both selling price (line 130) and quantity sold (line 150) are *assumptions* of the model.

```
80 COGS = 0.8*SALES
```

This arithmetic statement contains the assumption that cost of goods sold will be 80 percent of sales.

```
90 TAXES = TAX RATE*(SALES−COGS)
```

Taxes are paid at an average tax rate on the excess of sales revenue over cost. Note that this statement could contain a modeling error if, in any year, costs exceed sales and a loss is incurred. You could guard against such a mistake by writing line 90 as

```
90 TAXES = IF (SALES − COGS) .GT. 0 THEN'
95 TAX RATE * (SALES − COGS) ELSE 0
```

In this form, IFPS first tests to see if (SALES-COGS) is greater than 0. If it is, the previous definition of TAXES is used; if it is not then taxes are 0. Note that the apostrophe on line 90 allows "continuation" of the model statement onto the next line.

```
100 \
110 \ ASSUMPTIONS
120 \
```

Lines 100 through 120 are comment lines to indicate that what follows are assumptions of the model.

```
130 SELLING PRICE = 5, PREVIOUS * 1.05
140 TAX RATE = 28%
150 QUANTITY SOLD = 1000 FOR 2, 1250 FOR 2, 1450
```

The last three lines specify the assumptions of the model.

Selling price is forecasted to have an initial value in 1991 and then to increase by 5 percent each year. The way this is done is to put a comma between the value in the first column (selling price) and what follows. In general, a comma separates column values in a model. The next statement introduces the important concept of PREVIOUS. PREVIOUS is a reserved word that refers to the value in the previous column of the model. Thus, in 1992, the value of the selling price in 1991 is used; in 1993, the sales in 1992; and so on. IFPS also has the reserved word FUTURE which allows you to refer to values in the succeeding column. If you want to refer to something three periods ago, you use PREVIOUS 3; if you want to refer to something two periods from now, use FUTURE 2. Multiplying the previous value by 1.05 increases it by 5 percent. This is a convenient way of computing an annual growth rate. For line 130, selling price, only one comma separates column 1 from column 2. IFPS therefore assumes that the expression in column 2 is to be extended through to the last column, 1995. There is no need to repeatedly type this expression for every column in this model.

A continuation of a 28 percent effective tax rate for the company is assumed throughout the time interval, and the specified quantity sold. Note that in a case such as that of "quantity sold" we can repeat values over more than one column by using the IFPS reserved word FOR. Thus, writing 1000 FOR 2 is the same as writing 1000, 1000.

7.4 Output from the Simple IFPS Model

The output from the Simple IFPS Model is shown in Figure 7.3. The output is obtained by asking IFPS to SOLVE the model. We have actually done more than that as can be seen from the dialog shown as follows:

```
?solve
MODEL SIMPLE VERSION OF 7/21/89 13:00-5 COLUMNS 8 VARIABLES
ENTER SOLVE OPTIONS
?width 78 20 8 2
?all
```

Note: As a convention, model definitions and output from the computer are shown in capital letters but what you type is shown in small letters. Thus, in this example, you type **solve** and the computer responds with **MODEL SIMPLE** etc.

In response to a question mark from the computer, we first told IFPS to **solve** the model. It came back and asked for solve options. These options allow you some additional simple formatting capabilities. In our case, we wrote **width 78 20 8 2** to tell IFPS that we wanted output that was 78 spaces wide, that used 20 of those spaces for the names of variables, 8 spaces for each column, and gave all numbers two decimal points.

We next specified ALL to indicate that we wanted output for all columns and all variables. IFPS responded by printing out all five columns and all variables and comment lines. If we had specified COLUMNS 1,3,5, for example, only 1991, 1993, and 1995 would have been printed. If we had specified DIVIDENDS, SALES THROUGH TAXES only the DIVIDENDS, SALES, COGS, and TAXES lines would have printed.

Study the output. It shows that, as specified by the IFPS model, selling price is $5.00 initially and grows by 5% each year thereafter. In each case,

```
MODEL SIMPLE VERSION OF 07/21/89 13:00 — 5 COLUMNS 8 VARIABLES

ENTER SOLVE OPTIONS
?WIDTH 78 20 8 2
? ALL


                         1991      1992      1993      1994      1995

            IFPS MODEL FOR COMPUTING DIVIDEND FORECAST

DIVIDENDS                360.00    378.00    496.13    520.93    634.49
NET PROFIT AFTER TAX     720.00    756.00    992.25   1041.86   1268.99
SALES                   5000.00   5250.00   6890.63   7235.16   8812.42
COGS                    4000.00   4200.00   5512.50   5788.13   7049.94
TAXES                    280.00    294.00    385.88    405.17    493.50

  ASSUMPTIONS

SELLING PRICE              5.00      5.25      5.51      5.79      6.08
TAX RATE                   0.28      0.28      0.28      0.28      0.28
QUANTITY SOLD           1000.00   1000.00   1250.00   1250.00   1450.00
```

FIGURE 7.3 Output of a simple IFPS model.

COGS is 80 percent of the SALES value and TAXES are 28 percent of the excess of SALES over COGS. In looking at this forecast as a stockholder you would be pleased that your dividends are going to increase.

7.5 Exploring IFPS Output— "What If" and Goal Seeking

As a stockholder, you may want to explore the assumptions made by your company about its future dividend payments. Although the model lists only three assumptions, we know there are others. Figure 7.4 shows a revision of the model that makes all the assumptions explicit.

Here, all numeric values have been deleted from the model itself (lines 50, 80, 130) and replaced with variable names. Specifically, the assumptions of a 50 percent dividend payout rate, a 5 percent annual selling price growth rate, and an 80 percent sales cost rate are made explicit by replacing these numbers with their variable names in the model and recording the variable names and their values in the assumptions section of the model (lines 140 through 200). Using variable names rather than numbers in your model is good practice and should be followed as a basic principle.

```
MODEL SIMPLE1 VERSION OF 07/21/89 12:46
10 COLUMNS 1991..1995
20 \
30 \          IFPS MODEL FOR COMPUTING DIVIDEND FORECAST
40 \
50 DIVIDENDS = DIVIDEND PAYOUT RATE*NET PROFIT AFTER TAX
60 NET PROFIT AFTER TAX = SALES - COGS - TAXES
70 SALES = SELLING PRICE*QUANTITY SOLD
80 COGS = SALES COST RATE*SALES
90 TAXES= TAX RATE*(SALES-COGS)
100 \
110 \ ASSUMPTIONS
120 \
140 TAX RATE = 28%
150 DIVIDEND PAYOUT RATE =   0.50
170 SALES COST RATE = 0.80
180 QUANTITY SOLD = 1000 FOR 2, 1250 FOR 2, 1450
190 SELLING PRICE = 5, PREVIOUS * SELLING PRICE GROWTH RATE
200 SELLING PRICE GROWTH RATE = 1.05
END OF MODEL
```

FIGURE 7.4 Simple IFPS model; all assumptions stated explicitly.

"What If."   The model in the form shown in Figure 7.4 is better suited for asking questions. Let us begin by challenging the selling price assumptions. Suppose you are pessimistic about the selling price and believe selling price will only reach $4.50 per unit and increase only 3 percent per year. You do not need to redo the model to see the effect these changes could have. Rather, you would have the following dialog with the computer:

```
ENTER SOLVE OPTIONS
? what if
ENTER STATEMENTS
? selling price = 4.50, previous * selling price growth rate
? selling price growth rate = 1.03
? solve
ENTER SOLVE OPTIONS
? all
```

What you do is create a "what if" case. To do so, you type WHAT IF in response to a question mark. IFPS responds with ENTER STATEMENTS. You then write the new assumptions. To do so, you write the complete IFPS line as you want it to read. In a "what if" case, IFPS temporarily replaces each variable by its new definition. You enter one change at a time. When you have finished, you ask IFPS to SOLVE and then give it the solve options desired. The result of this "what if" dialog is shown in Figure 7.5. In examining Figure 7.5 you see that the selling price and the selling price growth rate have been replaced according to our instructions and the calculations reflect the changes in the assumption.

```
***** WHAT IF CASE 1 *****
2 WHAT IF STATEMENTS PROCESSED

                              1991      1992      1993      1994      1995

        IFPS MODEL FOR COMPUTING DIVIDEND FORECAST

DIVIDENDS                   324.00    333.72    429.66    442.55    528.76
NET PROFIT AFTER TAX        648.00    667.44    859.33    885.11   1057.53
SALES                      4500.00   4635.00   5967.56   6146.59   7343.94
COGS                       3600.00   3708.00   4774.56   4917.27   5875.16
TAXES                       252.00    259.56    334.18    344.21    411.26

   ASSUMPTIONS

TAX RATE                      0.28      0.28      0.28      0.28      0.28
DIVIDEND PAYOUT RATE          0.50      0.50      0.50      0.50      0.50
SALES COST RATE               0.80      0.80      0.80      0.80      0.80
QUANTITY SOLD              1000.00   1000.00   1250.00   1250.00   1450.00
SELLING PRICE                 4.50      4.63      4.77      4.92      5.07
SELLING PRICE GROWTH RATE     1.03      1.03      1.03      1.03      1.03

ENTER SOLVE OPTIONS
?
```

FIGURE 7.5 Results of first WHAT IF case.

As a second "what if" test, assume that not only will sales performance be poorer but that the SALES COST RATE, which had been assumed constant for five years at 80 percent, will go up starting in 1993 to 90 percent because increased advertising will be needed to sustain sales growth. The dialog required follows:

```
ENTER SOLVE OPTIONS
? what if continue
? what if case 2
ENTER STATEMENTS
? sales cost rate = 0.80 for 2, 0.90
? solve
ENTER SOLVE OPTIONS
? all
```

By writing **what if continue** you are telling IFPS that you want to keep the immediately preceding WHAT IF conditions and add new ones. The results of this **what if continue** case are shown in Figure 7.6. IFPS reassures you that three "what if" statements were processed, your original two plus the **what if continue**. Here you find that if the sales cost rate increases to 90 percent in year 3, dividends start going down rather than increasing.

```
***** WHAT IF CASE 2 *****
3 WHAT IF STATEMENTS PROCESSED

                              1991    1992    1993    1994    1995

          IFPS MODEL FOR COMPUTING DIVIDEND FORECAST

DIVIDENDS                   324.00  333.72  214.83  221.28  264.38
NET PROFIT AFTER TAX        648.00  667.44  429.66  442.55  528.76
SALES                      4500.00 4635.00 5967.56 6146.59 7343.94
COGS                       3600.00 3708.00 5370.81 5531.93 6609.55
TAXES                       252.00  259.56  167.09  172.10  205.63

  ASSUMPTIONS

TAX RATE                      0.28    0.28    0.28    0.28    0.28
DIVIDEND PAYOUT RATE          0.50    0.50    0.50    0.50    0.50
SALES COST RATE               0.80    0.80    0.20    0.90    0.90
QUANTITY SOLD              1000.00 1000.00 1250.00 1250.00 1450.00
SELLING PRICE                 4.50    4.63    4.77    4.92    5.07
SELLING PRICE GROWTH RATE     1.03    1.03    1.03    1.03    1.03

ENTER SOLVE OPTIONS
?
```

FIGURE 7.6 WHAT IF CONTINUE case

Goal Seeking.   A different way to ask "what if" questions is to use *goal seeking*. Goal seeking involves specifying the outcome and IFPS tells you what needs to occur to achieve this outcome. For example, under the original assumptions of Figure 7.3 the dividend is 360 in the first year, but it grows slowly thereafter.

   To cope with anticipated inflation, a more appropriate goal might be an annual dividend increase of 20 percent from the previous year. What quantity sold is necessary to achieve this goal? You would have the following dialog with IFPS:

```
ENTER SOLVE OPTIONS
? base case
? goal seek
GOAL SEEKING CASE 1
ENTER NAME OF VARIABLE(S) TO BE ADJUSTED TO ACHIEVE PERFORMANCE
? quantity sold
ENTER 1 COMPUTATIONAL STATEMENT(S) FOR PERFORMANCE
? dividends = 360, previous * 1.20
```

   The first instruction, base case, is designed to reinstate the original assumptions. (If you do not include it, IFPS will perform goal seeking on the current "what if" case). When you ask for **goal seek**, IFPS asks you first which variable you want changed to achieve the desired goal and then to specify the goal as an IFPS statement. The results of the dialog are shown in Figure 7.7.

```
***** GOAL SEEKING CASE 1 *****

                           1991       1992       1993       1994       1995

        QUANTITY SOLD    1000.00   1142.86   1306.12   1492.71   1705.96
```

FIGURE 7.7 Goal seeking.

```
ENTER SOLVE OPTIONS
?DIVIDENDS, NET PROFIT AFTER TAX

                           1991       1992       1993       1994       1995

DIVIDENDS                360.00    432.00    518.40    622.08    746.50
NET PROFIT AFTER TAX     720.00    864.00   1036.80   1244.16   1493.00
```

FIGURE 7.8 Obtaining additional output from goal seeking.

Goal seeking only provides output on the variable adjusted (sales in Figure 7.7). However, IFPS does follow that up immediately with the ever-present **ENTER SOLVE OPTIONS**. You can gain additional information by typing ALL in response to the question mark or, as is done in Figure 7.8, listing specific variables for which output is wanted. (Dividends and net profit after tax in Figure 7.8.)

The foregoing discussion has centered on a relatively simple situation. IFPS can be used to model much more complex situations. A variety of models from finance, statistics, operations management, and decision making are illustrated in Gray (1) and in Plane (3).

7.6 IFPS Built-In Functions and Subroutines

IFPS contains a large number of preprogrammed functions and subroutines to make your work easier. The functions include financial functions (for computing net present value, internal rate of return, etc.), mathematical functions, and trend extrapolation functions. The subroutines provide amortization and depreciation capabilities. For example, suppose you wanted to find out the net present worth and the growth rate associated with the stream of dividends in our simple model. You would add the following statements to Figure 7.4:

```
92 NET PRESENT WORTH OF DIVIDENDS = NPVC (DIVIDENDS,.12,0)
94 DIVIDEND GROWTH PERCENTAGE = GROWTHRATE (DIVIDENDS)
```

The NPVC function asks you to specify the cash inflow, the discount rate, and the cash outflow. In our case, the inflows are the dividends. The discount rate is 12 percent, and there are no (zero) outflows. The output of

TABLE 7.1 IFPS Subroutines.

Name	Description
ACRS DEPR	Accelerated cost recovery depreciation
AMORT	Amortization
DECBAL	Declining balance depreciation
GENDECBAL DEPR	General declining balance
STLINEDEPR	Straight line depreciation
SUM DEPR	Sum of the years digits depreciation

the NPVC function is the cumulative net present value of the dividends. The GROWTHRATE function measures the annual percentage growth in the variable; in our case, in dividends.

NPVC and GROWTHRATE are just two of the functions and subroutines available in IFPS. Table 7.1 lists the subroutines and Table 7.2 lists the built-in functions.

TABLE 7.2 Built-in Functions in IFPS.

Name	Description	Name	Description
Financial			
BCRATIO	Benefit/Cost ratio for given discount rate	NPV	Net present value of future earnings from one investment
CIRR	Internal rate of return from continuous cash flows and compounding	NPVC	Present value from future earnings and investments
IRR	Internal rate of return	NTV	Terminal value of future earnings and investments
MDIRR	Internal rate of return assuming mid-period cash flows		
Mathematical			
ABS	Absolute value	NATLOG	Natural logarithm
DEFINITION	Defines probability distribution	ROUND	Rounds decimals to nearest integer
GROWTHRATE	Compound growth rate of variable	ROUNDUP	Rounds decimal to next highest integer
LOG10	Logarithm to base 10	STDDEV	Standard deviation of variable
MATRIX	Selects row and column element	STEP	Step function
MAXIMUM	Maximum of a list	SUM	Adds values in row or column
MINIMUM	Minimum of a list		
MEAN	Average of a variable	TRUNCATE	Deletes decimal part of number
MEDIAN	Median of a variable	VMATRIX	Selects row and column where column number is computed
NATEXP	e to the power x	XPOWERY	Raises x to the power y
Extrapolation			
MOVAVG	Moving average	TREND	Fits a trend line
POLYFIT	Fits a polynomial curve		

7.7   **Uncertainty and Risk Analysis**

Although spreadsheets have fixed numbers in them, many of those numbers have uncertainty associated with them. These uncertainties represent risk. We have seen one way of coping with uncertainty through the use of "what if" analysis. A second important way of dealing with uncertainty and risk in IFPS is through the use of probability distributions and simulation.

Probability Distributions.   In most situations, something is known about the uncertainties being faced. For example, in our dividend example, the manager may not be sure about the selling price but can estimate, say, based on market surveys, that the initial selling price is not likely to be less than 2.50 nor more than 7.50. Furthermore, the manager may estimate the selling price growth rate to be between 3 and 7 percent per year. These estimates can be expressed as probability distributions. IFPS provides three standard built-in probability distributions (uniform, triangular, and normal) and two ways to create custom distributions. The built-in distributions are shown in Figure 7.9. Here we show

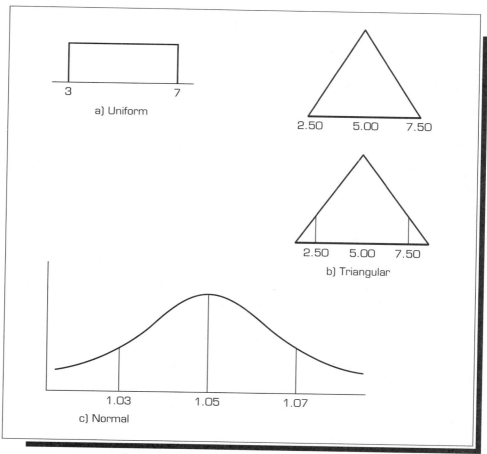

FIGURE 7.9   Built-in Probability Distributions.

□ A uniform distribution between 3 and 7 and a normal distribution with mean 1.05 and standard deviation of 0.02. One of these distributions might represent the manager's view of the uncertainty about the selling price growth rate.

□ A triangular distribution between 2.50 and 7.50 with most likely value (peak) at 5.00. The triangular distribution, which might represent the manager's view of the uncertainty about initial selling price, can be asymmetric. This has the advantage of allowing different views of upside and downside risks. Triangular distributions can be specified in terms of their peak and either the end points (top triangle in Figure 7.9) or their 10th and 90th percentile points (bottom triangle in Figure 7.9).

To use probability distributions in a model, the following built-in probability distribution functions: NORRAND, TRIRAND, T1090RAND, or UNIRAND are available. Suppose we choose NORRAND to represent the initial selling price growth rate and T1090RAND to represent selling price. Then the quantities used in line 70 in Figure 7.4:

```
70 SALES = SELLING PRICE * QUANTITY SOLD
```

would be written as:

```
190 SELLING PRICE = T1090RAND(2.50,5.00,7.50)'
195 PREVIOUS * SELLING PRICE GROWTH RATE
200 SELLING PRICE GROWTH RATE = NORRANDR (1.05, 0.02)
```

To use T1090RAND, three numbers must be specified: the 10 percent point (2.50), the maximum of the triangle (5.00), and the 90 percent point (7.50). In the case of NORRANDR we specified the mean (1.05) and the standard deviation (0.02). Note: NORRANDR was used rather than NORRAND because, by adding R, IFPS selects a different value each period from the distribution. If we had specified NORRAND, IFPS would have chosen a value in period 1 and kept the same value for every period thereafter. (Do you see the difference?)

Probability distributions can be specified directly in the model or they can be introduced in "what if" statements. For example, in the simple model shown in Figure 7.4, the built-in probability distributions can be part of a "what if" case. The advantage of the "what if" approach is that it is easier to write the deterministic model first and test it out. Once you are satisfied with it, you can then examine the effects of risk.

Simulation. A simulation procedure is used with a model that includes probability distributions. The basic idea in simulation is that the model is run many times, with each replication using a different combination of values drawn randomly from the probability distributions. The objective is to obtain not only the average (i.e., the mean) outcome, but also information on the distribution of the possible results to be anticipated.

If you tell IFPS to SOLVE, as was done in the previous sections, IFPS finds and uses the mean of each distribution to obtain an answer. If, however, you ask for MONTE CARLO, IFPS runs a simulation. MONTE CARLO requires specifying how many replications are to be run and which variables are to be printed out. The following "what if" dialog adds two probability distributions to the model of Figure 7.4, runs 100 replications, and prints out selected data.

```
? what if
MODEL SIMPLE VERSION 01/01/89 19:16—5 COLUMNS 10 VARIABLES
WHAT IF CASE 1
ENTER STATEMENTS
? selling price = t1090rand(2.50,5.00,7.50),
previous * selling price growth rate
? selling price growth rate = norrandr(1.05,.02)
? monte carlo 100
ENTER MONTE CARLO OPTIONS OR NONE
? columns 1991, 1995
ENTER MONTE CARLO OPTIONS OR NONE
? hist dividends, freq sales
ENTER MONTE CARLO OPTIONS OR NONE
? none
```

After entering the "what if" statements, you specify MONTE CARLO 100 to tell IFPS to run 100 replications (i.e., a sample size of 100). Note that the cost to run a simulation is proportional to how many replications you run since each replication takes the same amount of time. A sample of 100 is usually sufficient; however, statistical analysis may be needed to determine the appropriate sample size.

IFPS asks you to specify the Monte Carlo Options. These options involve the columns and variables to be recorded and printed. Because IFPS has to store data for each option you want, you should use them sparingly. If you do not specify columns, IFPS uses the last column as the default value. In the example, we asked for both 1991 and 1995 to show you the effects of the two probability distributions. The results obtained are shown in Figure 7.10 (the histogram for 1995 has been omitted).

The output shown in Figure 7.10 provides a lot of information. The frequency table and the sample statistics are the result of asking for FREQ; the histogram is the result of the HIST command. Each row of the frequency table shows you the 90th, 80th, . . . 10th percentile point of the observed data. Thus, for example, 80 percent of the observed sales values in 1991 equaled or exceeded 3313 while 20 percent exceeded 6355. The statistical tables tell you the mean, the standard deviation, skewness, kurtosis, and the 80 percent confidence interval about the mean. In this example, the average dividend was 501.3 in 1995 which is 65 less than the 634.5 shown in the deterministic case in Figure 7.3. However, as shown in the frequency table, it could range from 294 to 802. The decision you have to make in this case is whether you would invest under these risk conditions.

By performing risk analysis in IFPS, you develop a better understanding of the range of outcomes that can occur. By using simulation, you can start discussing the real risks associated with a venture.

```
***** WHAT IF CASE 1 *****

                         FREQUENCY TABLE

             PROBABILITY OF VALUE BEING GREATER THAN INDICATED

          90      80      70      60      50      40      30      20      10

DIVIDENDS
1991     203     239     270     301     330     360     388     458     553
1995     294     346     392     436     478     522     562     663     802

SALES
1991    2819    3313    3751    4174    4582    5000    5384    6355    7685
1995    4087    4804    5439    6053    6643    7250    7806    9215   11144

      SAMPLE STATISTICS

          MEAN  STD DEV  SKEWNESS  KURTOSIS  10PC CONF MEAN    90PC

DIVIDENDS
1991     345.8   134.1      .4       2.7         328.6        362.9
1995     501.3   194.4      .4       2.7         476.5        526.2

SALES
1991     4802    1862       .4       2.7         4564         5040
1995     6963    2700       .4       2.7         6617         7309

       HISTOGRAM FOR COLUMN 1991 OF DIVIDENDS
       19- 20              *
       17- 18            * *
       15- 16            * * *
       13- 14          * * * *
       11- 12          * * * *
        9- 10          * * * *
        7-  8          * * * * *
        5-  6      *   * * * * * * * *
        3-  4      * * * * * * * * * *
        1-  2      * * * * * * * * * *
                  _____

                      2       4       6
                9     7       4       2
                9     3       7       1
    START      70.0  STOP      650.0 SIZE OF INTERVAL      58.00
```

FIGURE 7.10 Results of Monte Carlo simulation.

7.8 **Optimization**

The IFPS "what if" and goal seeking capabilities show what can be achieved under specific assumptions. However, they cannot be used to find out what the optimum policy should be unless a large number of trial and error cases are run. For example, in the simple IFPS model shown in Figures 7.2 and 7.4, the dividend payout rate was assumed to be 50 percent every quarter. Is this payout rate optimal? The answer depends on what the objective is. For simplicity of illustration, assume that

- The firm's objective is to maximize the net present worth of the total dividend payout over the time horizon.
- Sales growth depends on advertising. Each dollar diverted from dividends to advertising is estimated to result in $10 of additional sales. Since each dollar of sales results in 14.4 cents of net profit after tax, a dollar invested in advertising results in $1.44 of additional net profit.

To deal with the possibility of advertising, the model has to be revised to take the facts just stated into account. (See Problem 3 at the end of this Chapter). The problem now involves a tradeoff. Paying out more dividends reduces sales in the future because less money is available for advertising, and hence profit and dividends are reduced in the future. Paying out less dividends now increases sales now, and profit and potentially dividends in the future. What is the optimal policy?

What we have formulated is a classic problem in optimization faced by managers. A separate module of IFPS/Plus for the mainframe, IFPS/Optimum, is available for solving optimization problems using mathematical programming.

To use IFPS/Optimum, begin with a standard IFPS model. Then write a separate routine, called a *Directive*, which specifies the conditions of the optimization. A directive includes

1. A statement of the objective function (e.g., maximize the net present worth of the dividends).
2. A statement of the decision variables (e.g., Dividends and Advertising).
3. Statements specifying the constraints on the problem (e.g., maximum amount that can be spent on advertising).

The output provided not only shows the manager the *best* policy in terms of the values of the decision variables and the resultant value of the objective function, but also provides sensitivity analysis information about the solution. Sensitivity analysis in the case of linear programming includes answers to such questions as

- How much the value of the objective function will change as a result of a change in the constraints.
- How much the value of the objective function will change as a result of a change in the values of the payoff coefficients in the objective.
- What the range is within which input variables can be changed without changing the values of the decision variables in the optimal solution.

From the point of decision support systems, IFPS/Optimum takes a managerial view. It begins with the assumption that managers faced with a decision want to find out what the best thing to do is. It recognizes that in many cases, a spreadsheet output is a natural way to formulate a problem and that optimization should be performable on the spreadsheet formulation. Selecting the right optimization technique is done by the computer rather than requiring specialized knowledge on the part of the manager. Finally, the manager is able to explore the implications of the optimization result in terms of the effect of changes in the assumptions, in the constraints, and in the objective. The result is a much more powerful approach to decision making.

7.9 Command Files

Command files provide a user-friendly way of using IFPS models without knowing much about IFPS. They automate the command sequences that otherwise have to be performed manually in IFPS. The simplest way of thinking about command files is that they contain a list of the commands that you would enter in an interactive session. For example, Figure 7.11 shows a command file that retrieves the simple IFPS model and solves it. To execute this command file, type

```
? commands command1
```

That is, type the keyword COMMANDS followed by the name of the command file.

A command file consists of *instructions* and *directives*. Instructions are the commands given to IFPS during an interactive session such as LIST or SOLVE. Directives are specific to command files. They consist of an exclamation point followed by a keyword. The following are typical directives:

!COMMENT	Treats the rest of the line as a comment
!MESSAGE	Displays the line on the screen for the user
!INPUT	Requires one line of input from the user

```
FILE COMMAND1
1 !COMMENT  This command File gets, lists, and solves
2 !COMMENT  the Simple IFPS model
3 MODEL SIMPLE
4 LIST
5 SOLVE
6 WIDTH 78 20 9 2
7 ALL
END OF COMMAND1
```

FIGURE 7.11 Command file for listing and solving the simple IFPS model.

!INPUTC	Allows multiple lines of input from the user
!END	Last line typed by user in response to !INPUTC
!MENU	Displays the choices on a menu screen
!PAUSE	Causes the program to wait for a carriage return (user's action)
!GO TO n	Makes line n the next one to be executed
!EXIT	Ends execution of command file

To see how these directives can be used, Figure 7.12 shows a command file to prompt the user on WHAT IF and GOAL SEEK in the simple IFPS model.

In Figure 7.12, the messages on lines 4 through 11 display a menu on the screen. Line 12, **MENU 20, 30, 40** transfers you to line 20, 30, or 40 depending on whether you type 1, 2, or 3. In general, the MENU command looks at the number you input and transfers you to the line number in the corresponding position. Lines 20 through 26 prompt you through the WHAT IF sequence and

```
 1 !COMMENT  Example of What If and Goal Seek for
 2 !COMMENT  Simple IFPS Model
 3 MODEL SIMPLE
 4 !MESSAGE
 5 !MESSAGE ENTER 1,2, OR 3 DEPENDING ON WHAT YOU WANT TO DO
 6 !MESSAGE
 7 !MESSAGE     1 = WHAT IF
 8 !MESSAGE
 9 !MESSAGE     2 = GOAL SEEK
10 !MESSAGE
11 !MESSAGE     3 = END THE RUN
12 !MENU 20,30,40
20 !COMMENT WHAT IF
21 WHAT IF
22 !MESSAGE INPUT CHANGES YOU WANT.LAST LINE MUST BE !END
23 !INPUTC
24 SOLVE
25 WIDTH 78 20 9 2
26 ALL
27 !GOTO 4
30 !COMMENT GOAL SEEK
31 !GOAL SEEK
32 !INPUT
33 !INPUT
34 WIDTH 78 20 9 2
35 ALL
36 GOTO 4
40 !COMMENT END THE RUN
41 !EXIT
```

FIGURE 7.12 Command file for assisting WHAT IF and GOAL SEEK.

automatically displays the results of the "what if." Line 27 causes the menu to reappear. Similarly, lines 30 through 36 help you through GOAL SEEK. Note that there are two !INPUT lines since GOAL SEEK requires two separate inputs. Line 41 uses the !EXIT directive to complete execution of the command file.

Command files are powerful. They not only allow unsophisticated users to interact with IFPS through menus and through prompts as in Figure 7.12, but they also make it easier to perform production tasks (such as running the same model with different data each month) and to create complex applications that combine several models or several reports.

7.10 Differences Between IFPS/Plus and IFPS/Personal

Because IFPS/Personal is restricted to the 640 kilobyte memory limitations of the IBM Personal Computer (PC), several features available on the mainframe version are not available in the PC version. Most important of these is the Monte Carlo simulation capability. Other features not available involve advanced capabilities such as optimization, complex consolidation of models, and the built-in IFPS relational data base.

IFPS/Personal and IFPS/Plus differ in a number of conventions that are used in writing models. The most important of these is the use of line numbers. In the mainframe version, each line has a line number either assigned by you or automatically assigned by IFPS, whereas in IFPS/Personal line numbers are not needed. To help you communicate between the mainframe and PC version, the PC version contains communications capabilities for uploading and downloading models and files as well as translation facilities that take care of making the changes needed to convert models from one form to the other.

Another important difference is in the quality of the graphs. Because IFPS/Personal uses the graphics capabilities of PCs, high-quality graphics can be obtained. In IFPS/Plus, the graphics are created with the mainframe's line printer and are relatively simple.

IFPS/Personal for the PC is available in both a full-size version that allows very large models to be written and solved, and a student version. The student version is bound into *Guide to IFPS/Personal* by Gray (2). The student version is functionally the same as the full-size version except that it is restricted in the size of matrix it will handle (60 rows, 40 columns), does not allow communication with the mainframe, and provides help information in the text rather than online.

Exercises

1. Modify line 50 in the program shown in Figure 7.2 so that it checks to see if NET PROFIT AFTER TAX is positive. If it is not, arrange to pay zero dividends.
2. How would the output of the program in Figure 7.2 be affected if line 130 were written as SELLING PRICE = 5?
3. Suppose you can reinvest some or all of the dividend money to advertise. That is, modify the model in Figure 7.4 as follows:

```
ADVERTISING = ADVERTISING RATE * PREVIOUS NET PROFIT
                AFTER TAX
NET PROFIT AFTER TAX = SALES - COGS - TAXES - ADVERTISING
SALES = (SELLING PRICE * QUANTITY SOLD) '
        + ADVERTISING LEVERAGE * ADVERTISING
```

Here, ADVERTISING RATE indicates the fraction of the previous year's net profit invested into advertising and advertising leverage is the number of dollars of sales achieved from each dollar invested in advertising. Add the following assumptions:

```
ADVERTISING RATE = 0.2
ADVERTISING LEVERAGE = 5
```

To determine effectiveness of the advertising policy, compute the net present worth of the dividends from the statement:

```
NET PRESENT WORTH OF DIVIDENDS = NPVC(DIVIDENDS,.12,0)
```

SOLVE the model. Then run a series of WHAT IF cases.

1. Vary ADVERTISING RATE between 0 and 0.5 in steps of 0.1.
2. Vary ADVERTISING RATE between 0.6 and 0.9 in steps of 0.1 and, in addition, set

```
DIVIDEND PAYOUT RATE=(1 - FUTURE ADVERTISING RATE) '
FOR 4, 0.5.
```

(Note: Changing the DIVIDEND PAYOUT RATE is required to make funds available for advertising).
Use the data you obtain to draw a graph showing the Net Present Value of Dividends as a function of the Advertising Rate. What is the optimal advertising rate?

4. *Income Statement Exercise.*
   Given: A company is producing and selling several products for a gross sales (income) of 2.15 million dollars (in 1989). Returns and allowances are 3 percent of gross sales, reducing the income to net sales. Marketing expenses, management, and general (MM&G) are figured to be 20 percent of net sales. Cost of goods sold is the sum of labor ($325,000), materials ($600,000), and overhead. Overhead is figured to be 30 percent of the combined cost of labor and materials plus $70,000.
   Gross profit is the difference between the net sales and the cost of goods sold. To figure the profit before tax, the MM&G expenses need to be subtracted from the gross profit. Finally, there is a 28 percent federal tax and 7 percent state tax that needs to be considered.
   a. Prepare an income statement and compute the taxes and profit after tax, for 1989. (Figures in thousands of dollars).
   b. Find the profit after tax if gross sales decline to $1.9 million.
   c. Find the federal tax paid if the tax rate is 32 percent. (Use original data.)
   d. Find the gross sales needed to generate a profit after tax of $1,000,000 (net profit).
5. *Five-Year Projection Exercise.* Use the original data of Exercise 4 to prepare a five-year projection (1989–1993) using the following growth assumptions:

   ☐ Gross sales increases 6 percent per year.
   ☐ Labor increases 5 percent per year.

☐ Material increases 7 percent per year.
☐ The fixed overhead increases $10,000 per year.

a. Prepare a five-year projection.
b. Show the net profit if labor increases 10 percent.
c. Show *graphically* the net profit under "a" and "b." Use bars if IFPS/Personal is used.

6. *Personnel Hiring Policy Exercise.* The current 1989 employment mix in the City of Hope is: Asians 15 percent, Blacks 8 percent, Latinos 7 percent, and Caucasians 70 percent. There is a total of 500 employees. Each year 10 percent of the employees, in each category, leave the city. Replacement is done according to a hiring policy. The city is considering two hiring policies (in percent):

	Asians	Blacks	Latinos	Caucasians
Policy A	20	20	30	30
Policy B	30	15	25	30

Prepare a five-year (1990–1994) hiring plan for vacant positions using the two policies. Show the number of people to be hired and the total number of employees.

Note:
1. The city expects a growth rate of 7 percent per year in its total employment.
2. Work with two decimals accuracy level.

7. A company's marketing research group prepared the following report on a proposed new product:

It is difficult to assess with certainty how any new product will do. The best we can do is quantify the risk. We believe that the proposed new product has an economically useful lifetime of five years. The total market at the time of introduction should be 500,000 units per year, and this market should grow at a rate of 10 percent per year. At a price of $9/unit we believe that the product can capture a significant share of the market, most likely 5 percent. We expect that we can produce the product for $6.75 per unit and that annual overhead cost will be $12,000. Engineering advises that an initial investment of $95,000 will be required to create the product. As you know, we use a discount rate of 15 percent for analyzing all new product proposals.

Based on our analysis, we recommend going ahead with this product since, based on the foregoing assumptions, the net present value for this product is over $88,000.

Your task is to check whether the marketing research group's claim that the anticipated net present value is over $88,000 is correct.

8. The vice president of marketing who received the report described in the previous exercise was quite risk averse. He felt that the uncertainties referred to by the marketing group were real and that they should introduce these uncertainties into their model. He called the head of the marketing research group into his office and they agreed that the following uncertainties existed:

□ Market share is normally distributed with a mean of 5 percent and a standard deviation of 1 percent.
□ Overhead may be as low as $10,000/year and as high as $15,000/year, but is most likely to be $12,000/year. A triangular distribution should describe this uncertainty.
□ Unit costs can also be described by a triangular distribution. The range is from $6.50 to $7.25, with $6.75 as the most likely unit cost.
□ Initial investment requirements are uniformly distributed between $90,000 and $100,000.

It is your job, using Monte Carlo analysis in IFPS, to determine whether the company should proceed under these uncertainties. The vice president of marketing is unwilling to proceed if there is even a 10 percent chance that the net present value will be negative. Based on your results, what decision will he reach?

9. When the proposal reached the CEO, she became concerned about the assumptions because the company had experienced recent overruns in production cost. She felt that a "what if" analysis should be done using a triangular distribution with a range from $7 to $8 per unit and a most likely value of $7.50. She was, however, less risk averse than the vice president of marketing and was willing to go ahead with the product if there was at least a 70 percent chance that the net present value would be positive.

Your assignment is to make the "what if" analysis requested. Based on your data, would she give a go ahead decision?

10. Refer to the EOQ example of chapter 6, (Appendix C) solved with Lotus 1-2-3.
    a. Write an IFPS program for the same problem.
    b. Solve the model.
    c. Find the new EOQ if the annual usage changes to 1100.
    d. Find the required discount (in %) which will make the total cost of the discount option equal to that of the EOQ.
    e. Compare the Lotus vs. the IFPS Solutions and procedures.

11. Find the present value of
    a. Investment today is $3500. Discount rate is 12 percent, and return for year 1 to year 5 is $1000, $1500, $2000, $1200, and $1000.
    b. Adjust initial investment (using goal seeking) in order to get NPV = $2500 at year 5.
    c. What if investment is $4000?

12. Find the growth of return value of (use Growthrate built-in function)
    a. Investment today is $3500. The cumulative returns for year 1 to year 5 are $1000, $2500, $4500, $5700, and $6700. Discount rate is 10 percent.
    b. What if returns for the first three years are $1000, $1555, and $1800?
    c. Adjust returns in order to get growth of return equals to 125%(every year).

13. Find internal rate of return of
    a. Investment is $3500. Return for year 1 to year 5 is $1000, $1500, $2000, $1200, and $1000.
    b. What if investment is $1000?

14. Find the value of benefit cost ratio of
    a. Investment is $3500. Return for year 1 to year 5 is $1000, $1500, $2000, $1200, and $1000. Discount rate is 10 percent.
    b. What if investment is $2500?
    c. How high does the initial investment have to be if the benefit-to-cost ratio equals 1.03 at year 5?

15. Find the cumulative straight line depreciation of:
    a. Investment is $3500, salvage value is 0.04. The life is 5 years.
    b. Adjust investment in order to get a period depreciation of 900.

16. Find the cumulative straight line depreciation of:
   a. Investment is $3500. Category is 5. Purchase year is 1982.
   b. What if investment equals $2000?

17. Find the cumulative depreciation using declining balance method of:
   a. Investment is $3500. Salvage is 0.04. The life is 5 years. Acceleration constant is 1.4.
   b. What if investment is $2800, and salvage is 0.05.

18. Given demand, in thousands of units for the last seven years, per quarter.

Year	Quarter 1	Q2	Q3	Q4
1	12	20	16	15
2	11	15	19	18
3	15	12	16	20
4	18	18	14	26
5	13	16	17	17
6	10	13	22	20
7	14	13	15	23

Use IFPS to write a program that will compute:
   a. The mean, median, and standard deviation of the demand
   b. Moving average (basis = 4 quarters)
   c. Centered moving average (basis = 3 quarters)
   d. Linear regression; Find the equation and the projected demand in the 20th and the 40th quarters
   e. The seasonal index
   f. The cyclical elements for each period
   g. Random variations (trendline, mean, median)
   h. Show the graphics, for the above, for the first six periods.

19. *To hedge or not to hedge.* Farmers in Eastern Illinois grow corn that they can sell either at prevailing market prices or at a predetermined contract price. Mike Orange owns a small farm (net worth $500,000) that produces 150,000 bushels of corn in a normal year, 200,000 bushels in a good year, and 80,000 bushels in a poor year. Prices in the open market vary from $3.50 to $5.60 per bushel. The most likely price is $4.10. The statistical distribution of the above data approximates a *triangular* shape.
The cost of producing corn is $0.70/bushel in addition to a fixed cost of $300,000/year for the upkeep of the farm.

   The tax schedule on farms is such that no tax is paid on an annual profit of $42,000 (depreciation is to be disregarded); 42,001– 65,000 profit results in an 18 percent tax on this amount. Any profit above 65,000 is subject to 28 percent tax.

   As stated earlier, the farmer can sell at the market price or at the contract price. Currently the contract price is $4.10/bushel for either a quantity of 60,000 bushels or 120,000 bushels. In such a case the farmer must deliver the entire quantity. If the crop is lower than that amount he must buy the difference, in the open market, at the prevailing price.
   a. Build an IFPS model to describe the farmer's problem.
   b. Prepare an influence diagram.
   c. Find which alternative is superior.
   (You need the IFPS mainframe version, use the TRIRAND and INTERPOLATION function).

CASE: The Frazee Advertising Campaign*

Introduction

This paper describes the development of a DSS to aid management evaluation of alternative levels of advertising expenditures required to meet sales growth objectives.

At its first iteration, the DSS develops a model of the relationship between total advertising expenditures and San Diego county's population growth (independent variables), and company sales (dependent variable). In a further refinement of the model the advertising-to-sales relationships for the company's two major departments is developed. This improved model allowed management to evaluate alternative investments in advertising for each of the company's departments and obtain quantitative projections of relative departmental growth. A third iteration deals with the allocation of the advertisement budget among three possible media. (Due to time limitation only three iterations are reported in this case.)

The DSS has been developed on an IBM-compatible PC to allow inexpensive implementation. IFPS/Personal and Lotus 1-2-3 have been used in the development.

The Decision Problem and Setting the Business

The Frazee Company, a San Diego retailer of paint and wallpaper supplies, has just been purchased by an aggressive parent organization, Worldwide Decorating Inc. This parent company has set for itself a goal of doubling the annual sales of the newly acquired Frazee Company within the next five years.

To a large degree Frazee purchases products in bulk at wholesale and provides retail store conveniences such as trained personnel, color samples, and wallpaper catalogs to its clientele. Only a small portion of its business is involved in the actual manufacturing of paints.

The Analysis

The three major product areas of interior paints, exterior paints, and wall coverings are analyzed to determine significant relationships between past sales, advertising expenditures, population growth, and general economic trends. In addition, seasonal variations in the product area sales are determined.

The Decision Support System Design

Using historical data, three linear regression analyses are run, linking sales in each of the product areas (independent variable) to various factors such as level of advertising, population growth, etc. (independent variables). The three regression models are then combined to provide a company composite relationship between the various independent variables and total sales (dependent variable). Seasonal adjustments, if found to be significant, will be used.

A five-year business plan, including required advertising expenditures, is then generated. Data are presented in both tabular and graphic formats.

---

*This case is based on a paper written in 1987 by Ken Campbell and Fred Orton, doctoral candidates at United States International University, San Diego, California. It is an illustrative students' project.

Feasibility Study and Assessment

The first requirement was that Frazee management have available to them a terminal with DSS information showing key data items displayed in usable form. The second requirement was that this display, and information available on it, be up-to-date and accurate enough to enable management to project the amount of advertising money to be spent in specific areas during specific seasons. In other words, the DSS must be capable of enabling management to make timely and effective decisions that would positively impact the next quarter's sales volume.

Based on an interview with Worldwide Decorating, Inc., it was determined that neither computer equipment nor computer literacy was available at Frazee; therefore, the DSS clearly had to be constructed off-site and one member of the Frazee management had to be trained to operate the terminal that was to be placed in Frazee headquarters. That individual also had to be responsible for inputting data that Frazee generates in order to keep the projections current.

The Worldwide Decorating, Inc. management provided insight on important information concerning the critical success factors, operation, and structure of Frazee management. Meetings with Frazee management's key personnel were used to identify those critical factors that must be considered in order to achieve and maintain high sales volumes. Once those items were identified, the feasibility of collecting those key data items was addressed. It was discovered that sufficient data were available for developing the DSS model through use of internal data, and significant public data was available to complete the data requirements for the model.

The purpose of the DSS was discussed with the staff of Frazee, and they concurred with the development of a prototype DSS that would assist them in meeting their ambitious goals.

Model Updating

The Frazee Advertising Campaign DSS models the effect of advertising on company sales. After the model is constructed and validated, it provides the user with projected sales figures based on given levels of advertising expenditures. After an advertising expenditure decision is made for the upcoming period, the results of sales in that period are used to verify the continued validity of the model. In addition, this information will be used to update the model. At update time the DSS designer is faced with the option of simply adding the recent sales data to the database and recomputing the regression analysis, or adding the recent sales data and additionally deleting five-year-old sales and advertising data before recomputing the regression analysis. The latter case would result in a "moving regression" analysis. The benefit of the former alternative is that it provides a larger sample of the relationships, while the latter option should be selected if the DSS designer feels there have been fundamental changes in the effectiveness of advertising. An example of the fundamental changes would be those brought about by advances in technology (e.g., at-home cable network shopping).

Description of the Database

The data used for the first iteration DSS were provided by Frazee Company records. This data included quarterly sales revenue and quarterly expenses broken down by department (Paint or Wall Covering) and by quarter.

The second iteration DSS added the use of annual San Diego County population data obtained at the city library. This data included annual population historical data as well as an eight-year forecast for population growth in the county. The company's projected advertising expenses were used as initial data in the sales forecast model, also.

Description of the Model Base and Models' Validation

Several models are used in this DSS. For executing the regression analysis, a Lotus 1-2-3 was used since the student version of IFPS does not provide for a built-in multiple regression analysis routine. Second, IFPS was used to build several financial planning and statement models and to run the "what if" and the "goal seeking" analyses.

The model was validated by performing a multiple linear regression analysis of Frazee sales against advertising expenditures and county population for the past five years. Having achieved a satisfactory level of predictive ability ($R^2 = 0.93$), the model was used to forecast sales based on projected population growth and the level of advertising selected by Frazee management.

The second iteration model was refined by separately analyzing the relationships between paint advertising and paint sales, and wallcovering advertising and wallcovering sales. This refined model showed that there was a stronger correlation between advertising and sales for wall covering than for paints. Finally, an optimization model was used to determine the optimal allocation of the advertisement budget.

Hardware and User Interface

User interface is accomplished through a PC placed in Frazee's office and the management person trained to use that PC. The computer hardware is an IBM compatible with a dual disk drive, a high resolution color monitor, and a letter quality dot matrix printer.

Since only one member of Frazee's management staff is trained in the operation of their on-site PC, plans are being discussed to have that manager train peers in PC operation procedures. The procedures and management information available within this DSS could easily be made available to the entire management staff once they become computer literate. It is assumed that, given the usefulness of this DSS, all the management staff will become capable of using it within one year. Until the management staff become experienced in the use of the DSS, the user interface will be conducted primarily through the one trained member of the management staff.

Prototyping

The First Iteration

The first step in the modeling process was to define a relationship between sales and those factors that influence sales. Likely independent variables that would be good candidates for investigation include advertising expenditures, area housing starts, and local population growth. As a first cut, a linear regression analysis was performed with total Frazee advertising expenditures as the independent variable and total sales the dependent variable. Five-year history data were used.

The results of the analysis showed that, although advertising expenditures did account for a significant portion of total sales ($R^2 = 0.45$), other variables also needed to be taken into account. Figure 7.13 provides a scatter diagram of "explained" sales versus actual sales. Table 7.3 contains the regression analysis printout.

San Diego County population, which reflected Frazee's reachable market, was added as a second independent variable. As may be noted in the regression printout in Table 7.4, the addition of the population variable increased the ability of the model to explain sales to a fully acceptable level ($R^2 = 0.93$).

Based on the relationships established by this regression model, an income projection model was constructed. The yearly planned expenditure data for the model were obtained from planning data maintained by the Frazee Company.

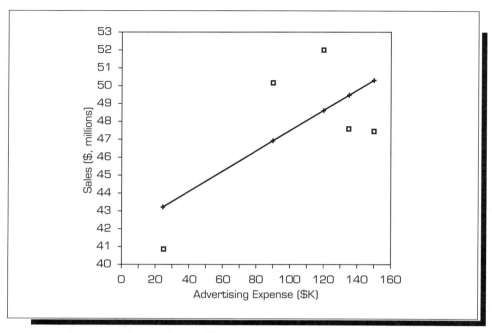

FIGURE 7.13 Regression analysis, $K = thousands of dollars.

Given a reasonably accurate forecast of sales, cost of goods can be estimated. Since the Frazee Company does very little actual manufacturing of its products and purchases them wholesale in nearly final form, it is expected that significant increases in the level of sales may take place with minimum requirements for increased capital asset acquisition (e.g., land, buildings, etc.).

Influence Diagram

Before the model was constructed, an influence diagram was built (see Figure 7.14). The model itself, as written in IFPS, is shown in Table 7.5 with the results.

TABLE 7.3

Year	Advertising ($K)	Sales ($K)
1982	25	40898
1983	150	47472
1984	135	47722
1985	120	52043
1986	90	50186

Regression Output:

Constant		41679.34
Std Err of Y Est		3605.529
R Squared		0.453433
No. of Observations		5
Degrees of Freedom		2
X Coefficient(s)	57.54631	
Std Err of Coef.	36.47721	

TABLE 7.4

Year	Population (000)	Advertising ($K)	Sales ($K)
1982	800	25	40898
1983	840	150	47472
1984	880	135	47722
1985	920	120	52043
1986	960	90	50186

Regression Output

Constant		1117.245
Std Err of Y Est		1628.419
R Squared		0.925673
No. of Observations		5
Degrees of Freedom		2
X Coefficient(s)	48.43695	37.71541
Std Er of Coef.	13.58794	17.38867

Annual sales had been expected to increase from $45,942,000 to $55,861,000 over the succeeding five years.

Sensitivity Analysis

As stated earlier, it is Worldwide Decorating's goal to double sales within a five-year period. To determine what level of advertising would be required to stimulate such an increase in sales, IFPS/Personal's What If and Goal Seeking capabilities were

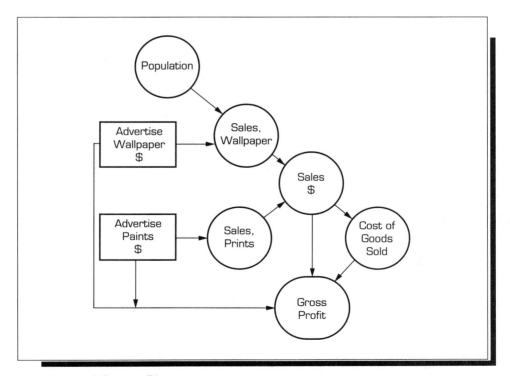

FIGURE 7.14 Influence Diagram.

TABLE 7.5   Five Years Plan

	1988	**1989**	**1990**	**1991**	**1992**
Independent Variables					
Population	800	840	880	920	960
Advertising	150	165	182	200	220
Sales	45492	47994	50552	53172	55861
Cost of Goods Sold	34619	36495	38414	40379	42396
Gross Profit	10723	11333	11956	12593	13246
Taxes	3324	3513	3706	3904	4106
Net Income	7399	7820	8250	8689	9139

The Model:
Population = 800, previous +40
Advertising = 150, previous*1.10
Sales = 48.4*population + 37.7*advertising + 1117.2
Cost of Goods Sold = 500 + .75*sales
Gross Profit = sales − cost of goods sold − advertising
TAXES = .3*gross profit
Net income = gross profit − taxes

called into action. Setting sales as the goal and advertising as the variable to adjust, IFPS/Personal determined the level of expenditure required to double the sales. As shown in Table 7.6 a level slightly over $576,000 in 1989, and a compound growth of 25 percent, will be required to achieve the stated sales growth objective. The graphical expression of these data is shown in Figure 7.15.

The Second Iteration

The Management of Worldwide Decorating noted that the model forecasts the combined total paint and wallcovering sales as a function of total advertising expenditures. They wondered what the individual relationships were for each of the departments. If, for example, it was found that there were a stronger relationship between paint advertising and paint sales, then it would imply that more profit would result from a paint advertising expenditure than from an equal wallcovering advertisement. On the other hand, management was also aware that there is a significant amount of synergistic sales that result from one-stop-shopping for both paint and wallcoverings; therefore, management desired to keep the sales levels of these two departments relatively equal.

TABLE 7.6

	1988	**1989**	**1990**	**1991**	**1992**
Population	800.00	840.00	880.00	920.00	960.00
Advertising	150.00	576.09	720.11	900.13	1125.17
Sales	45492.20	63491.63	70857.23	79580.24	90000.00
Cost of Goods Sold	34619.15	48118.72	53642.92	60185.18	68000.00
Gross Profit	10723.05	14796.82	16494.20	18494.93	20874.83
Taxes	3324.15	4587.01	5113.20	5733.43	6471.20
Net Income	7398.90	10209.81	11381.00	12761.50	14403.63

Goal Seek Solution
Goal: sales[1992] = 90000
Adjust: advertising[1989]

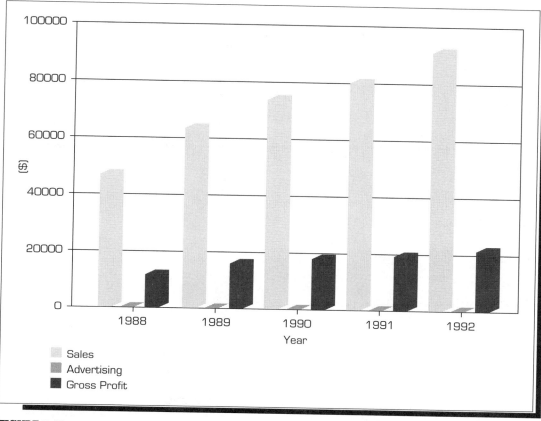

FIGURE 7.15

In order to answer management's question regarding the individual relationships of each department, additional regression analysis was performed by using data from each of the departments. As can be noted in the printouts shown in Tables 7.7 and 7.8, wallcovering sales showed a slightly stronger relationship to the level of advertis-

TABLE 7.7

Year	Pop. (000)	Paint Advert ($K)	Wallcov Advert ($K)	Total Advert ($K)	Paint Sales ($K)	Wallcov Sales ($K)	Total Sales ($K)
1982	800	10	15	25	20465	20433	40898
1983	840	50	100	150	21468	26004	47472
1984	880	50	85	135	24321	23401	47722
1985	920	50	70	120	24798	27245	52043
1986	960	35	55	90	25432	24754	50186

Regression Output:

Constant		−4791.6
Std Err of Y Est		837.341
R Squared		0.92706
No. of Observations		5
Degrees of Freedom		2
X Coefficient(s)	31.2368	15.3855
Std Err of Coef.	7.42398	26.8854

TABLE 7.8

Year	Pop. (000)	Wallcov Advert ($K)	Paint Advert ($K)	Total Advert ($K)	Paint Sales ($K)	Wallcov Sales ($K)	Total Sales ($K)
1982	800	15	10	25	20465	20433	40898
1983	840	100	50	150	21468	26004	47472
1984	880	85	50	135	24321	23401	47722
1985	920	70	50	120	24798	27245	52043
1986	960	55	35	90	25432	24754	50186

Regression Output:

Constant		4828.75
Std Err of Y Est		2021.65
R Squared		0.70299
No. of Observations		5
Degrees of Freedom		2
X Coefficient(s)	18.5877	48.9443
Std Err of Coef.	16.4744	31.9651

ing expenditures than did paint sales. Management thought that this was reasonable since a large percentage of wallcovering purchasers were individual homeowners who would be more influenced by advertising than construction contractors who purchased most of the paint.

At the second iteration, the advertising budgets for the paint and wallcovering departments were placed within the department income statement, and sales for each department were forecasted based on the advertising-to-sales relationships determined by the regression models. The report from this base model is shown in Table 7.9.

It was noted by management that due to the stronger influence of advertising on wallcovering sales, the department was gaining an increasingly larger share of the

TABLE 7.9

	1988	1989	1990	1991	1992
Independent Variables					
Population	800	840	880	920	960
paint adv	75	288	360	450	563
wallcov adv	75	288	360	450	563
Paint Department					
psales	21324	25852	28209	30843	33824
cost of pgoods sold	16293	19689	21457	23432	25668
gross pprofit	4956	5875	6392	6961	7593
Wallcovering Department					
wsales	23377	34536	38801	43946	50191
cost of wgoods sold	17732	26102	29301	33160	37843
gross wprofit	5569	8146	9140	10337	11785
FRAZEE totals					
Sales	44701	60388	67010	74789	84015
Gross Profit	10525	14021	15533	17297	19379
Taxes	3263	4347	4815	5362	6007
net income	7262	9675	10717	11935	13371

company business. However, they also realized that any shift in advertising expenditures from wallcoverings to paints could have a detrimental effect on net income.

To further explore the potential impact of such a move, management used the "what if" capability to investigate the impact of a $20,000 shift each way in advertising from the original model. The results (not shown here) supported management's intuitive impact estimates.

The Third Iteration

A third iteration was added a few months later. It is described in the last section of this chapter.

Implementation

Because Frazee does not presently have personnel who are computer and IFPS literate, full implementation of this DSS may be somewhat of a problem. As addressed in the Maintenance section of this report, it will undoubtedly be necessary for the DSS development team to stay in close contact with the Frazee individual to whom the responsibility for adding more iterations and monitoring the system was given.

Maintenance and Future Iterations

Maintenance

The maintenance of the database will be performed by one trained individual in the Frazee management staff. Quarterly updates of sales volume data and advertising budget data will be entered into the database on a remote terminal located in the Frazee management office. The terminal is networked to the parent company's computer where IFPS resides. This data update will allow management to query the computer periodically to determine if the company is "on target" throughout the year.

Annual maintenance and verification of the database and system will be performed by a consultant (one of the DSS builders). New data will be analyzed, goals will be reviewed, and the program will be modified as needed to adjust for any anomalies observed in the input data or model performance.

The DSS is very flexible and can easily incorporate new information through additions of databases and/or model bases.

Future Iterations

This DSS can be expanded in several directions to make it more usable. Initially, sales can be broken down into four seasons and sales can also be broken down into specific products for each season. The amount of budget allocated for a specific product in a certain season could have a significant impact on quarterly sales.

A second area worthy of consideration is the number of housing starts. Since new houses require paint, both interior and exterior paint sales could potentially increase when housing starts increase, especially if the advertising budget for the commercial users is enhanced to attract more developers and subcontractors as customers.

Another area for investigation is the employment level of union painters. If the employment level is high and the commercial advertising budget is sufficient, sales of both interior and exterior paint should increase since painting is primarily done by professional painters. Another impact may be the fact that since wallpapering is done by both contractors (new homes) and individuals (private homes), then when construction is increasing and a large percentage of the population is on vacation, the sale of wall coverings could increase if the advertising budget is sufficient ("do it yourself during your vacation").

Allocation of the Money Among Various Media Options (Third Iteration)

Once the total amount of advertisement dollars is determined, as well as its distribution between paint and wallpaper, it is necessary to decide on the appropriate media. That is, determine how much to spend on advertising in TV, direct mail, newspapers, et cetera. Historical data are available on the exposure of potential customers to the various media and on the success of such exposure. In such an event we can use an optimization approach utilizing linear programming. A hypothetical example for the advertisement of paints follows:

The Frazee Company plans to allocate some or all of its advertising budget of $82,000 in the San Diego Metropolitan area. It can purchase local radio spots at $120 per spot, local TV spots at $600 per spot, and local newspaper advertising at $220 per insertion.

The company's policy requirements specify that the company must spend at least $40,000 on TV and allow newspaper expenditures up to either $60,000 or 50 percent of the TV expenditures, whichever is more profitable, overall, for the company.

The payoff from each advertising medium is a function of the size of its audience. The general experience of the firm is that the values of insertions and spots in terms of "audience points" (an arbitrary unit), are as follows:

Radio	40 audience points per spot
TV	180 audience points per spot
Newspapers	320 audience points per insertion

It is necessary to find the optimal allocation of advertising expenditures among the three media. A linear programming model is used in this case:

Formulation

1. The decision variables

$$x_1 = \text{No. of spots allocated to radio}$$
$$x_2 = \text{No. of spots allocated to TV}$$
$$x_3 = \text{No. of insertions allocated to newspapers}$$

2. The objective function

$$\text{maximize } z = 40x_1 + 180x_2 + 320x_3$$

3. The constraints

$$120x_1 + 600x_2 + 220x_3 \leq 82,000 \tag{1}$$
$$600x_2 \geq 40,000 \tag{2}$$

and either

$$220x_3 \leq 60,000 \tag{3a}$$

or

$$220x_3 \leq 300x_2 \tag{3b}$$

where x_1, x_2, x_3 are integers.

The Solution

The problem must be solved twice, once for each set of "either/or" constraints, and the better solution selected. Either

$$x_2 = 66 2/3, \quad x_3 = 190.9, \quad z = 73,090.9 \quad \text{for (3a)}$$

or

$$x_2 = 91.1, \quad x_3 = 124.24, \quad z = 56,177.6 \quad \text{for (3b)}$$

The first solution is better. Rounding to integers:

$$x_2 = 66 \text{ (spots on radio)}$$
$$x_3 = 191 \text{ (spots on newspaper)}$$
$$z = 73,000 \text{ (audience)}$$

Note: the solution was derived by an LP package since the student version of IFPS does not have optimization capabilities.

References and Bibliography

1. Gray, P. *Guide to IFPS, Second Edition.* New York: McGraw-Hill, 1987.
2. Gray, P. *Guide to IFPS/Personal.* New York: McGraw-Hill, 1988.
3. Plane, D.R. *Quantitive Tools for Decision Making Using IFPS.* Reading, MA: Addison-Wesley, 1986.

Chapter 8

Case Studies

In the previous chapters we presented the development process of DSS and the software used in this process. Chapters 8 and 9 describe several cases that attempt to reinforce the material covered in the previous chapters, illustrate some important issues, and show readers the diversity of DSS applications. Chapter 8 presents two major case studies in detail. The first case, the University Tuition and Fee Policy Analysis, is an example of a team-constructed mainframe project using several DSS generators and other tools. The second case, the Wheels Project, is an example of a DSS developed by users with the aid of Lotus 1-2-3, on a microcomputer.

Case 1: A Computer-based Decision Support System for University Tuition and Fee Policy Analysis

8.1   Introduction

The purpose of this case is to describe the design, construction, and implementation of a comprehensive computer-based decision support system that serves as an online interactive decision-making environment for tuition and fee analysis at a major state university, Virginia Polytechnic Institute and State University (VPI & SU).*

The DSS example presented here was developed to analyze tuition-and-fee policy alternatives. The system was designed to enhance the administration's ability to deal effectively with tuition-and-fee policy issues at a detailed and sophisticated level without directly handling large amounts of data. The DSS is intended to support the planning, decision-making, and policy-setting processes by providing a way to readily analyze the effect of changes in the variables and parameters that impact tuition charges and by providing a means to test present and alternative policies under different scenarios. The targeted users for this system are middle- and upper-level administrators directly involved in the decision-making activities of the institution.

Tuition and fees are a major source of income for colleges and universities and are a major portion of the cost of a student's education. University administrations' task of making tuition-and-fee policy decisions is becoming more critical and more difficult. This is a result of the increased reliance on student-generated tuition-and-fee income, the declining college-age student population, reductions in state and federal funds, escalating costs of operation, and movement in the state legislature to shift more of the payment burden of the cost of the university to the students.

A major concern in establishing tuition charges is how the institution's revenue requirements should be allocated to various student categories (e.g., resident versus nonresident, undergraduate versus graduate, on-campus versus off-campus, and full-time versus part-time). Overall, tuition is a source of revenue primarily used to balance the institution's budget (i.e., offset the difference between all the other sources of revenue and the costs of operating the institution). That overall need must subsequently be distributed to charges for individual student categories, thereby establishing the tuition charge structure. In deciding on the allocation policy, the university administration attempts to balance stark financial considerations. For example, a university's policy on

---

*This case is based on the work of Allen G. Greenwood (Northeastern University) and Laurence J. Moore (Virginia Polytechnic Institute and State University).

how much more to charge an out-of-state student, as compared with a state resident, depends on charges at peer academic institutions, future enrollment levels, anticipated operating costs, and policy decisions established at the state level.

The development of the tuition charge structure is further complicated by policies and decisions made in an uncertain environment confounded by changing demographic, political, and economic conditions. Because of the dynamic environment, flexible planning is essential—policies that suffice today may not be satisfactory in a few years. The tuition-and-fee allocation process also requires the assimilation of large amounts of information, the application of numerous models, and the consideration of a large number of interrelated variables.

To address these problems and thereby enhance the planning decision making—the policy-setting processes associated with establishing tuition-and-fee charges—a decision support system with an imbedded goal programming model[*] was developed.

8.2   How This DSS Started

No formal need assessment or cost-benefit analysis was conducted prior to the initiation of the DSS. Rather, the DSS was created as a part of a natural process described in what follows.

The university recognized that the joint economic, political, and demographic pressures that it had been experiencing were not likely to subside in the foreseeable future. As an illustration of the combined effect of these pressures, between 1978 and 1984 at the institution where this system was developed, operating expenses doubled whereas the tuition revenue requirement nearly tripled. By comparison, the Consumer Price Index increased only 59 percent over the same period.

The concept for the development of the DSS evolved from several tuition studies performed at VPI & SU by the Office of Financial Planning and Analysis (OFPA) and the Office of Institutional Research between June 1982 and June 1983. It became apparent from these studies that the process of establishing tuition charges was becoming both increasingly more critical and more complex.

The first step taken by the OFPA in examining the tuition-and-fee policy issues and problems was to develop financial planning models using the spreadsheet-oriented language IFPS (Interactive Financial Planning System). One model allowed the administration to easily and quickly generate a series of reports to compare various operating environments and policy alternatives (e.g., to perform "what if" analysis). Another model, developed also using IFPS, helped the administration assess the state legislature's newly adopted "recovery rate" formula. The formula is used to determine what percentage of each state college or university's operating budget is to be derived from tuition revenue.

As these models were being developed and automated, it became apparent that the process of establishing tuition-and-fee charges is a multicriteria resource allocation problem. Universities attempt to set tuition charges that reflect the particular institution's philosophy on the level of tuition that each student

[*]For a brief description of goal programming, see the Appendix to this chapter.

category should be assessed; but this is not done without considering the economic climate, political climate, and market conditions.

The system up to this point could have been labeled a DSS, although it was not called so. It generated periodical and ad hoc reports, it had a "what if" capability, and it was structured around IFPS. However, it was only at this stage that the formalization of DSS took place.

A goal programming (GP) model was subsequently developed that described the university's tuition philosophies and policies in mathematical form. One task in the research effort was to develop a comprehensive list of all the goals the university *might* consider in establishing tuition charges. In addition to several reviews with the DSS team (which are described later), the goals included in the DSS were reviewed (in conjunction with a seminar) by a group of statewide higher education administrators.

As the model was being formulated, it became apparent that it would not be utilized if the administration had to formulate and solve the GP model every time a question arose. The administration did not have the resources or the time available to do this unless the process was highly automated.

In addition to formulating and solving the GP model, the parameter values had to be calculated; this requires a significant number of computations, a considerable amount of data, and integration of all the necessary data and models.

The DSS described in this case did not begin with a set of preconceived, detailed plans for its development—it began with the automation of several existing models that were used in the tuition-and-fee decision-making process and *evolved* into a large, comprehensive, complex, yet user-friendly DSS.

8.3 DSS Development Team

At the beginning of the effort, four university administrators were identified as being the primary contacts and supporters of the system. They were considered the "support group" for the designer/builder of the system. They were selected because of their direct involvement in the tuition-and-fee decision-making process and because they were the most likely users of the system.

The system is primarily used within the finance organization; therefore the support group included the vice president for finance and two of his staff: the director of the Office of Financial Planning and Analysis (OFPA), and the university budget director. The Office of Institutional Research is directly involved in a lot of tuition-related work; in fact, it was a strong proponent of an integrated system for tuition analysis. Therefore the assistant director was an important member of the support group. The fifth member of the team, the DSS designer/builder, was a member of the OFPA and a doctoral student in the College of Business.

Much of the users' involvement was informal, on a daily basis answering specific questions on how the decision process worked, reviewing display screens and data file layouts, clarifying calculations that would be performed by a computer model, identifying sources of data, and so on. The primary interaction was between the designer/builder and the director of the OFPA. The support group was a resource for the designer/builder to use as necessary—any problem could usually be resolved by working directly with the most appropriate individual in the support group. The primary interactions were between the designer/builder and each member of the support group individually—there was never a need for the entire group to meet.

8.4 The Modeling Process

The tuition-and-fee allocation process is represented as a multi-year goal programming model.

Tuition charges are established, as shown in Figure 8.1, by allocating the institution's annual revenue requirement to tuition charges for each individual student category based on a set of university goals, constraints, and priorities. Each student category is assessed a different tuition charge; the distinction between student categories is based on academic level, residency status, campus location, and so forth. The initial step in the process is the determination of the institution's expected operating expenses over the duration of a planning horizon. Subsequently, the revenue required to cover the expenses is established by source (state funds, tuition, fees, private, etc.).

The third step, the heart of the DSS, generates the tuition-and-fee charge structure—a set of tuition charges for all student categories based on specific assumptions, expectations, and conditions. It represents a compromise between the institution's financial considerations and its philosophical concerns.

The goals that the GP model comprises are descriptions of the university's tuition philosophy and policy expressed in mathematical form. The three types of goals shown at the top of Figure 8.1 are used by the DSS to allocate the university's annual revenue requirements to student charges. The lower portion of the figure shows the factors that must be considered when formulating the GP model and subsequently in setting tuition-and-fee policy (e.g., enrollment projections, state and university policy, other student charges, costs, and economic factors).

The first group of goals included in the DSS (shown at the top of Figure 8.1) are *aggregate goals*, which include all the student categories in the goal formulation. The second set of goals, *individual goals*, considers each student category by itself, or apart from the others. Third, *comparison goals* directly specify absolute or relative relationships among the student categories. For example, an absolute goal is used to establish a different charge for on-campus and off-campus programs; a relative goal is used to reflect a policy that nonresident students pay at least twice the in-state rate.

8.5 Translating the Model into a Usable Decision-making Aid

The core of the DSS is the GP model, as shown in Figure 8.2. However, the emphasis of the DSS is on translating the GP model into a usable and effective technique for the university administration. The DSS handles the arduous tasks

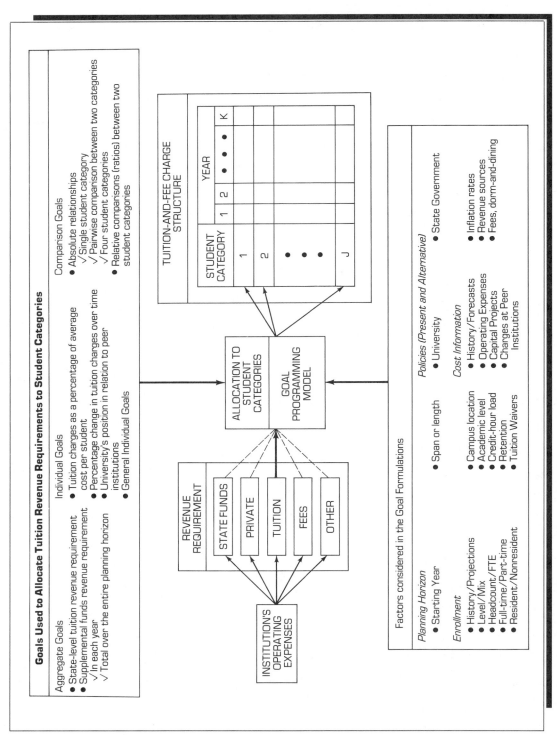

FIGURE 8.1 Tuition charges established by allocating the institution's annual revenue requirements to tuition charges for individual student categories based on a set of constraints, goals, and priorities.

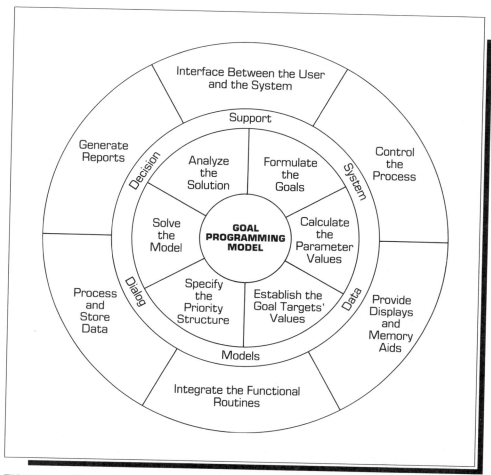

FIGURE 8.2 The tasks performed by the DSS to translate the GP model into a usable and effective technique.

associated with the GP model. As shown in Figure 8.2, these include formulating goals, calculating parameter values, establishing goal targets, specifying the priority structure, solving the model, and analyzing the solution. Figure 8.2 also shows that the DSS performs certain supporting tasks: processing and storing data, interfacing between user and system, providing displays and memory aids, generating reports, integrating functional routines, and controlling the overall process.

Figure 8.3 illustrates conceptually how the user interacts with the system in a typical application. Because the data and the user are influenced by exogenous factors—economic, political, and demographic conditions—the specific actions taken will vary from application to application, but the overall process should be similar to that shown in Figure 8.3.

There are two basic inputs to the GP model—parameter estimates and goals—both of which are controlled by the user, as illustrated in Figure 8.3. From a predefined set, the user decides which goals to include in the GP model and ranks them in the order of importance to the university, thereby

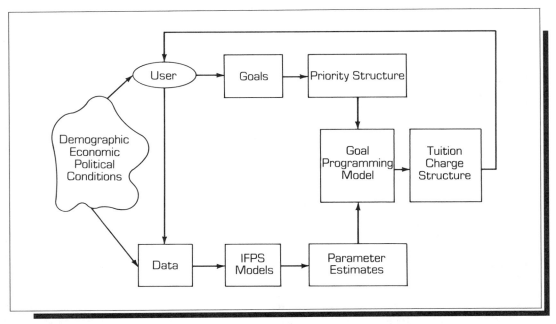

FIGURE 8.3 Interaction between the user and the decision support system in a typical application.

constructing a priority structure. The parameter estimates either are obtained directly from the user or are calculated by supporting models. The user controls the data (enrollment levels, cost information, inflation rates, fee charges, etc.) that drive the support models. The DSS automatically formulates the goals, translates them into the form required by the optimization routine, estimates the appropriate parameter values, solves the problem interactively, and generates a set of reports. Once this has been completed and the charges have been established, control is returned to the user, as illustrated by the feedback loop at the top of Figure 8.3, for the purpose of exploring and testing alternatives and performing sensitivity analyses.

8.6   An Example of Goal Processing

The example described below (refer to Figures 8.4 and 8.5) illustrates the interaction between the user and system to establish the relative comparison goals. Only two of the three steps involved are illustrated (goal selection and establishing the goal target values), because these directly concern the user. The third step (to be defined later) is to convert the specified goal into MPS format[*] for use in the optimization routine.

1. *Goal selection.* The DSS generates a list of all possible pairwise combinations of student categories. The user selects the appropriate goals by changing, directly on the screen, the N to a Y in the first column of

---

[*]MPS format is a widely accepted format for describing and storing LP models on a computer. Most commercial LP software packages recognize this format.

```
┌─────────────────────────────────────────────────────────────────┐
│             Dialog to Access the List of Goals                   │
├─────────────────────────────────────────────────────────────────┤
│                            •                                     │
│                            •                                     │
│                            •                                     │
│        ***********************************************           │
│        *                                             *           │
│ *********** RELATIVE AND ABSOLUTE COMPARISON GOALS ***********    │
│        *                                             *           │
│        ***********************************************           │
│ NOTES:                                                           │
│   1) IF YOU WISH TO ADD OR DELETE ANY RELATIVE OR ABSOLUTE GOAL, │
│      YOU MUST USE THE CHANGE COMMAND.                            │
│       MAKING CHANGES UNDER THE DISPLAY OPTION WILL NOT BE RECOGNIZED
│      BY THE SYSTEM.                                              │
│   2) IF YOU USE THE CHANGE OPTION, YOU MUST:                     │
│      A) RE-ENTER ALL OF THE RELATIVE AND ABSOLUTE GOAL TARGET VALUES.
│      B) RE-ENTER THE ENTIRE PRIORITY STRUCTURE.                  │
│    (YOU WILL BE PROMPTED FOR THESE AT A LATER TIME IN THE SESSION)
│                                                                 │
│        .. IF YOU WANT TO VIEW THE GOALS IN EFFECT,              │
│           >>> ENTER: DISPLAY                                     │
│        .. IF YOU WANT TO CHANGE THE BASIC GOALS,               │
│           >>> ENTER: CHANGE                                      │
│        .. IF NEITHER OF THE ABOVE,                             │
│           >>> ENTER: NO                                          │
│                            •                                     │
│                            •                                     │
│                            •                                     │
└─────────────────────────────────────────────────────────────────┘
                                │
                                ▼
┌─────────────────────────────────────────────────────────────────┐
│                      Goal-List File                              │
├─────────────────────────────────────────────────────────────────┤
│          VIRGINIA POLYTECHNIC INSTITUTE AND STATE UNIVERSITY     │
│         DECISION SUPPORT SYSTEM FOR TUITION AND FEE POLICY ANALYSIS
│              ALL OF THE POSSIBLE COMPARISON GOALS               │
│                                                                 │
│ RELATIVE-COMPARISON GOALS                                        │
│ Y    2  1      NRES_UG       / RES_UG      = VALUE              │
│ Y    3  1      RES_GR        / RES_UG      = VALUE              │
│ N    4  1      NRES_GR       / RES_UG      = VALUE              │
│ N    5  1      RES_GR_OFC    / RES_UG      = VALUE              │
│ N    6  1      NRES_GR_OFC   / RES_UG      = VALUE              │
│ N    3  2      RES_GR        / NRES_UG     = VALUE              │
│ N    4  2      NRES_GR       / NRES_UG     = VALUE              │
│ N    5  2      RES_GR_OFC    / NRES_UG     = VALUE              │
│ N    6  2      NRES_GR_OFC   / NRES_UG     = VALUE              │
│ N    4  3      NRES_GR_OFC   / RES_GR      = VALUE              │
│ N    5  3      RES_GR_OFC    / RES_GR      = VALUE              │
│ N    6  3      NRES_GR_OFC   / RES_GR      = VALUE              │
│ N    5  4      RES_GR_OFC    / NRES_GR     = VALUE              │
│ N    6  4      NRES_GR_OFC   / NRES_GR     = VALUE              │
│ N    6  5      NRES_GR_OFC   / RES_GR_OFC  = VALUE              │
│                            •                                     │
│                            •                                     │
│                            •                                     │
├─────────────────────────────────────────────────────────────────┤
│ Key: RES, residents; NRES, nonresidents; GR, graduate; UG, undergraduate;
│      OFC, off campus.                                            │
└─────────────────────────────────────────────────────────────────┘
```

FIGURE 8.4 Display illustrating the process of goal selection.

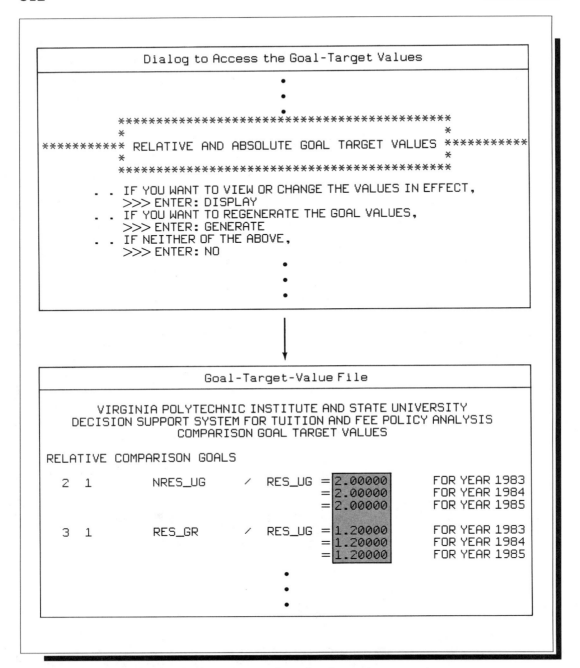

FIGURE 8.5 Display illustrating the process of setting the goal-target values.

the goal list file (highlighted in Figure 8.4). In this case the user has selected two relative-comparison goals: the ratio of tuition charges for nonresident undergraduate to resident undergraduate and the ratio of resident graduate to resident undergraduate.

2. *Goal target values.* The DSS automatically creates another file (Figure 8.5) that contains a description of each goal to be included in the model.

(*Note*: the DSS screens the goals selected [i.e., it does not include all possible goals as in Figure 8.4]). The user then specifies, directly on the screen (as highlighted in Figure 8.5), the goal target value for each year in the planning horizon. In this example, the administration wants to maintain a two-to-one ratio between the nonresident and resident undergraduate charges in each year of the planning horizon.

3. *Entering the priority structure.* Once all of the goals have been established, they must be ranked in order of importance, thereby creating a priority structure. The DSS creates the priority-structure file shown in Figure 8.6, depending on the goals selected by the user. The priority levels are entered directly on the screen in the appropriate column (highlighted area in Figure 8.6). Entering a value in the left column implies that the goal target is the minimum acceptable value; entering a value in the right column implies that the goal target is the maximum acceptable value; entering a value in both columns implies that the goal target is to be met exactly; a zero in both columns means the goal is not to be considered in the GP solution. The user also specifies the subgoals' weights (the default and most commonly used value is 1.0). The DSS, transparent to the user, then translates the information in this file to another format that is more conducive to the optimization routine. It also checks to see that the priority levels have been entered sequentially.

8.7 Application of the DSS

The specific steps involved in a typical application of the DSS are shown in Figure 8.7. The diagram at the left of the figure indicates that the user has the choice of starting the session at various points or being guided through each step of the process. The figure also indicates that the user can "loop" through the process and easily explore alternatives and perform sensitivity analyses.

As shown in Figure 8.7, the process of establishing tuition charges using the DSS involves dual and shared responsibilities between the DSS and the decision maker. Although the DSS calculates most of the model's parameter values, some must be directly entered by the user. Likewise, whereas the decision maker supplies most of the goal-target values, some are automatically calculated by the DSS. The final step in the process, analyzing the solution, is also a joint effort; the DSS supplies the reports and information to the decision maker, who ultimately selects the "best" solution.

8.8 The System Architecture

The architecture of the DSS is defined in terms of three highly integrated subsystems: dialog, data, and models. These three subsystems and their functions are summarized in Figure 8.8. The dialog subsystem controls most of the operations and provides the interface between the user and the system. The memory and information handling functions are provided by the data subsystem. The analytic function for calculating the parameter values and solving the GP model is provided by the model base subsystem.

```
Priority Structure File

                    VIRGINIA POLYTECHNIC INSTITUTE AND STATE UNIVERSITY
                   DECISION SUPPORT SYSTEM FOR TUITION AND FEE POLICY ANALYSIS
                                  GOAL PRIORITY STRUCTURE

            IF THE GOAL TARGET IS THE MINIMUM ACCEPTABLE VALUE,
                ENTER THE PRIORITY LEVEL IN THE 1ST COLUMN
            IF THE GOAL TARGET IS THE MAXIMUM ACCEPTABLE VALUE,
                ENTER THE PRIORITY LEVEL IN THE 2ND COLUMN

                                      PRIORITY LEVEL      SUBGOAL
                                        >=      <=        WEIGHTS
```

	>=	<=	SUBGOAL WEIGHTS	
STATE REVENUE REQUIREMENT	01	00	01.000	01.000
SUPPLEMENTAL REVENUE RQMT. - YEARLY	09	00	01.000	01.000
PERCENTAGE OF AVERAGE TOTAL COST GOALS				
RESIDENT_ UNDERGRADUATE	00	04	01.000	04.000
NON-RESIDENT_UNDERGRADUATE	00	06	01.000	01.000
RESIDENT_GRADUATE	00	04	01.000	02.000
NON-RESIDENT_GRADUATE	00	04	01.000	01.000
RESIDENT_GRADUATE_OFF-CAMPUS	00	06	01.000	01.000
NON-RESIDENT_GRADUATE_OFF-CAMPU	00	06	01.000	01.000
CHANGE OVER TIME GOALS				
RESIDENT_UNDERGRADUATE	00	03	01.000	01.000
NON-RESIDENT_UNDERGRADUATE	00	03	01.000	01.000
RESIDENT_GRADUATE	00	03	01.000	01.000
NON-RESIDENT_GRADUATE	00	03	01.000	01.000
RESIDENT_GRADUATE_OFF-CAMPUS	00	03	01.000	01.000
NON-RESIDENT_GRADUATE_OFF-CAMPU	00	03	01.000	01.000
PEER INSTITUTIONS GOALS				
RESIDENT_UNDERGRADUATE	00	05	01.000	01.000
NON-RESIDENT_UNDERGRADUATE	00	05	01.000	01.000
RESIDENT_GRADUATE	00	07	01.000	01.000
NON-RESIDENT_GRADUATE	00	05	01.000	02.000
RESIDENT_GRADUATE_OFF-CAMPUS	00	07	01.000	01.000
NON-RESIDENT_GRADUATE_OFF_CAMPU	00	07	01.000	01.000
GENERAL INDIVIDUAL GOALS				
RESIDENT_UNDERGRADUATE	00	00	01.000	01.000
NON-RESIDENT_UNDERGRADUATE	00	00	01.000	01.000
RESIDENT_GRADUATE	00	00	01.000	01.000
NON-RESIDENT_GRADUATE	00	00	01.000	01.000
RESIDENT_GRADUATE_OFF-CAMPUS	00	00	01.000	01.000
NON-RESIDENT_GRADUATE_OFF_CAMPU	00	00	01.000	01.000
RELATIVE GOALS				
NRES_UG VS. RES_UG	08	00	01.000	01.000
RES_GR VS. RES_UG	08	00	01.000	01.000
SINGLE-CATEGORY ABSOLUTE GOALS				
PAIRWISE ABSOLUTE GOALS				
NRES_GR VS. RES_GR	02	00	01.000	01.000
NRES_GR VS. RES_GR	00	02	01.000	01.000
RES_GR_OFC VS. RES_GR	00	02	01.000	01.000
FOUR-CATEGORY ABSOLUTE GOALS				
NRES_GR — RES_GR — NRES_GR_OFC + RES_GR_OFC	02	02	01.000	01.000
SUPPLEMENTAL REVENUE RQMT. - OVERALL	09	00	01.000	01.000

FIGURE 8.6 Display illustrating the establishment of the priority structure.

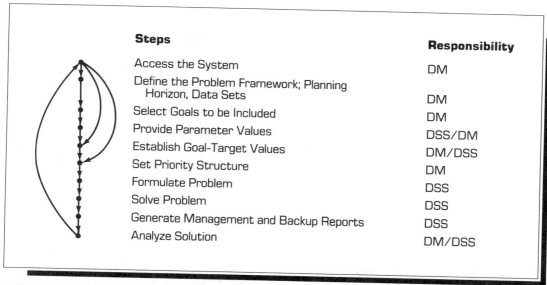

Steps	Responsibility
Access the System	DM
Define the Problem Framework; Planning Horizon, Data Sets	DM
Select Goals to be Included	DM
Provide Parameter Values	DSS/DM
Establish Goal-Target Values	DM/DSS
Set Priority Structure	DM
Formulate Problem	DSS
Solve Problem	DSS
Generate Management and Backup Reports	DSS
Analyze Solution	DM/DSS

FIGURE 8.7 The process of establishing tuition charges, involving dual and shared responsibilities between the decision support system (DSS) and the decision maker (DM).

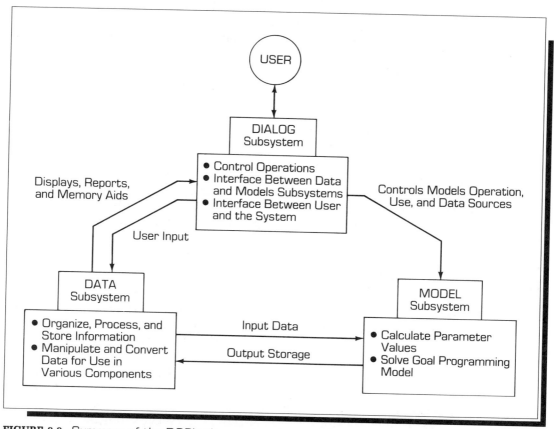

FIGURE 8.8 Summary of the DSS's three subsystems and their functions.

315

The dialog subsystem is most important because it provides the interface between the user and the system. It is linked to the models subsystem to control the models' operation and data sources; it is linked to the data subsystem to provide the user with displays, reports, and memory aids and to store the user's input values in data files.

The dialog subsystem comprises two types of programs: an executive control program (ECP) and 15 component control programs (CCP). The ECP serves several functions: (1) it is the primary link between the user and the system; (2) it controls and manages the user's session through menus, displays, and control mechanisms that initiate operations when certain conditions exist; and (3) it assigns tasks and operations to the appropriate programs. The CCP perform five basic functions: data control, goal formulation, priority structure definition, problem solution, and report generation. Most of the interface between the models and the data is provided by the CCP.

The data subsystem, through its memory function, integrates the dialog and model subsystems, as shown in Figure 8.8. It organizes, processes, and stores information as well as manipulates and converts data for use in the different components of the DSS. The data subsystem supplies input data to models, provides work space for intermediate calculations, stores output reports, and maintains displays and memory aids for the user. A few examples of the type of information supported by the data subsystem are historical tuition and fee data (both at the subject university and at its peer institutions), enrollment history and projections, relevant data on capital projects, and cost and financial information.

The models subsystem, which provides the analytical portion of the DSS, has two primary functions. The first is the calculation of the GP model's parameter values—the decision variable coefficients and the goal target values. Its second function is solving the GP model.

The models subsystem is an integrated collection of IFPS models, each dealing with a distinct problem. For example, one model determines the percentage of the institution's operating expenses that must be offset by tuition charges; another amortizes debt service charges on new capital projects to the appropriate student fee category; another provides a means to use regression analysis to predict tuition charges at peer institutions; and there is a set of models to determine student fee charges (e.g., health service, student center).

8.9 Tools and Generators

In this complex system the builder used several tools and generators. It was found that even IFPS cannot provide, by itself, all the features needed to develop a comprehensive DSS. The tools and generators used are:

1. *IFPS*. IFPS was used as a modeling language to define relationships between variables and time periods and to perform the financial/quantitative computations and projections necessary to calculate the GP model's parameter values. It was also used to generate quality reports and organize, change, manipulate, and update data files. The user in no way

needs to be familiar with IFPS, because it is imbedded in the system (i.e., all interfaces with IFPS are automatically handled by the DSS).

2. *LINDO (Linear INteractive and Discrete Optimizer)*. LINDO is a comprehensive management science modeling software package used to solve the GP model. LINDO is a very powerful yet easy-to-use interactive command-oriented program designed to solve complex linear programming problems.

   LINDO is designed to solve single-objective linear programming models, not multiobjective (goal programming) models as required by this DSS. But LINDO has a FORTRAN user-interface capability; through this feature the GP model is solved as a sequence of linear programs in one execution. The GP algorithm that controls the solution process is written in FORTRAN and is interfaced with LINDO so that it can utilize the simplex algorithm subroutines contained in LINDO.

3. *FORTRAN*. This classical language was found to be very effective in formulating the goals of the GP model in MPS format so that the model could be solved by an optimizer.

   FORTRAN was also used to generate a set of reports for the decision maker to assess and analyze the GP model's solution. One report, the goal achievement report, compares for each goal, in each year of the planning horizon, the goal's target value and the actual value derived by the solution.

   In addition, FORTRAN was used to create and modify display and data files to support IFPS. IFPS is used to calculate the quarterly charges per student for each new facility. However, the input format required by IFPS was found to be very cumbersome by the users; as a result, a FORTRAN program was developed that creates a user-oriented file (easy to read and easy to edit) that contains the basic capital projects data (cost, interest rate, economic life, etc.). After the user-oriented file is accessed, the DSS automatically executes another FORTRAN program that translates it into an IFPS-readable file.

4. *EXEC-2*. EXEC-2 is an IBM command programming language (a DSS tool) used to write the DSS control program. The control program integrates all the other programs, and controls the flow of information not only between itself and the support programs but also between the system and the user.

   EXEC-2 was also used to create and manipulate files, communicate with the operating system, access IFPS and LINDO, execute FORTRAN programs, store and manipulate variables, and perform logical operations.

   Note: Although IFPS includes command, control, and logic statements, they are not as powerful or as flexible as those included in EXEC-2.

5. *XEDIT*. This IBM full-screen mainframe editor facilitates the user's entry of data into files by allowing the user to move the cursor around the screen, entering or changing information when necessary. Whenever the user views or changes a data file, the DSS automatically accesses XEDIT so that the user can "page" through the information, change data, copy files, and save updated files. PF (program function)

TABLE 8.1 Summary of How Tools and Generators Perform DSS Functions.

DSS Function	Tools and Generators				
	EXEC-2	**FORTRAN**	**IFPS**	**LINDO**	**XEDIT**
COMMUNICATION/INTEGRATION					
☐ User Dialog (Messages, Prompts, Menus)	X				
☐ Operating System Interface	X				
☐ Intrasystem Links (Access/Execute Ancillary Programs/Packages)	X				
PROCESS MANAGEMENT					
☐ Procedure Controls and Links	X	X			
☐ Memory Aids	X				
☐ Error Checks and Diagnostics	X	X			
INFORMATION HANDLING					
☐ Data Input/Output (Historical/Protected Values, Problem Framework, etc.)	X	X	X		
☐ Variable Manipulation	X	X	X		
☐ File Creation and Manipulation (Displays, Data Entry Templates, Special Format for Imbedded Commercial Packages—IFPS, LINDO)	X	X	X		
☐ Report Generation (Management Summary and Analysis, Supporting Documentation)		X	X		
☐ Editing					X
MODELING					
☐ Goal Selection	X	X			X
☐ Parameter Value Determination	X	X	X		X
☐ Accounting, Financial, Statistical Computations			X		X
☐ Priority Structure	X	X			X
☐ Model Formulation	X	X			
☐ GP Solution Procedure		X		X	
☐ Analysis Reports		X	X		

keys are used to execute many of the edit commands by pressing a single key.

Table 8.1 provides a summary of how the tools and generators are utilized in the DSS. The table shows that a comprehensive system, such as this DSS, cannot be developed using a single language or generator. The best features of each are utilized in the software's design and development. Table 8.1 shows that most of the tools and generators serve multiple functions in the DSS; also many of the functions utilize more than one tool or generator.

8.10 Hardware

The system is situated on an IBM 3084 Processor Complex running IBM/SP HPO Release 3 with CMS (Conversational Monitoring System) Release 3. Sessions are conducted on interactive computer terminals.

8.11 Development Time

Most of the DSS was designed, programmed, tested, implemented, and documented within a one-year time span. Although no records were kept on the time spent on this process, the best estimate is approximately 2500 worker-hours. Some of the IFPS models had been previously developed; hence they only had to be modified and integrated into the DSS. Also, at the start of the project, the DSS builder was quite familiar with the budgeting process and tuition-and-fee issues, had a good working knowledge of the institution's computer system, and was proficient in all the languages used in the DSS.

Despite the builder's proficiency and the use of IFPS and LINDO, the task of integrating all the components and getting all the subsystems and packages "talking" to one another accounted for a large portion of the development time (extensive programming was required). The interfaces and integration added greatly to the complexity of the system.

8.12 Interactive/Prototyping Activities

The interfaces and models within the system were tested as the system was developed. The DSS modular structure greatly facilitated the development process, because small, manageable portions of the system could be developed and debugged before being integrated into the overall system. The system's modularity also makes it conducive to modification, extension, and updating at a later time.

The philosophy used in the development process was to have the large complex system evolve from a series of small operable and proven components. The system's development was iterative in that quite often the components had to be modified after they were integrated into the system. Modification was necessary because all the requirements of the system could not be foreseen initially and improvements were identified as the development process progressed. The modular structure facilitated this process because the components that had to be modified could often be changed and tested apart from the overall system.

Each of the models developed to calculate the GP model's input parameter values was tested separately before being integrated into the system. Likewise, the programs that organize the goals in MPS format, translate the user's priority structure into an achievement function and generate the displays and reports, were developed and tested outside the DSS. Users were also provided with alternative input file formats, output report layouts, screen arrangements, and menu/prompt/instruction dialog, so that they could select the "best" for their needs. All the model, data, and dialog routines were then integrated into the overall system, once they were found to be operating correctly and were satisfactory with the user. Even the component control programs (CCP) were developed and tested independently of the executive control program (ECP). The links between the various programs and the interactive interface between the system and the user underwent an evolutionary development as well.

8.13 Testing and Evaluation

Formal review sessions were held as the system became operational. The system was presented individually to each of the support group members. Each presentation lasted between two and three hours and involved a "live" demonstration of the system using a hypothetical yet representative set of data, goals, and priorities. A hypothetical example was used in the demonstrations so that as many of the system's features could be examined as possible. The session was an online "walk through" of typical applications of the system. Each person was also provided with a printed version of the session. This made it easier to follow what was happening on the screen and to see the details of the displays; it also provided the administrator with a means to review and study the output after the session was over.

Many of the comments and suggestions that resulted from the demonstrations were incorporated into the DSS; most were suggestions for clarifying displays, instructions, and reports. There were several additions to the system—new models and new reports—as a direct result of the demonstrations. The sessions also illustrated how powerful the DSS would be in the decision-making process, especially for generating alternative solutions and assessing the sensitivity of certain policies to changes in certain variables.

8.14 Implementation Issues and Problems

Documentation

Extensive documentation was developed for this DSS. The only criticism of the documentation was that it was too voluminous. Although very complete—both in terms of the system description and the tuition-and-fee allocation process—users felt that a short, condensed supplemental guide or reference manual would be of great value.

Maintenance

The system is in its third year of operation and is working well, even though the DSS designer/builder is no longer at the university. The finance staff can easily use the system and change the GP model formulation (update and alter the goals, priorities, planning horizon, basic data, etc.). But if any of the imbedded models change significantly, it is anticipated that the university will have to hire the DSS builder as a consultant to make the changes. The system, although simple to use and update, is extremely complex. As with many systems of this magnitude, the simpler it is on the surface (for the user), the more complex it is behind the scenes.

Installation

During the first "real" application of the DSS to establish tuition charges for the university, the DSS was used in parallel with the existing manual approach.

This helped check and validate the computer models, as well as give the administration a point of reference from which to compare the alternatives generated by the DSS.

User's Involvement

By the time the DSS was operational, there were some organizational and personnel changes. The OFPA had been reorganized and there was a new manager—the primary end-user.

The new manager and an assistant were given a demonstration of the system by the DSS builder (similar to that given to each member of the development support group). Subsequently, they reviewed the documentation and another meeting was held where the users operated the system and asked specific questions. Because the new users had not been directly involved in the tuition allocation process before, many of the questions had to do with the process and not with the DSS.

They basically used the DSS on their own to generate a set of alternative tuition charge structures for review by the president's staff. The OFPA primarily worked with the budget director and the vice president for finance; there was very little interaction with the DSS builder. The administration used the system directly with no need for an intermediary.

System Problems

As the system was implemented and demonstrated to the members of the support group, several minor problems arose and several suggestions were incorporated into the system.

There were very few requested changes because the users were an integral part of the design process—questions were resolved quickly as the system was being tested. The support group was also kept up to date on the dialog, data, and model development. Some minor changes were made in the displays, instructions, and reports once the support group saw the entire system in operation.

During one session, the system ran out of computer storage; as a result, a feature was added to test, whenever the system is activated, to see that there is enough storage to run all the routines. If there is not, a message is displayed, warning the user of this condition.

Several problems became apparent when the system was used for the first time to set tuition charges. The DSS had to be able to use two different sets of enrollment data, because often there is a difference in the expected enrollment level or mix between the time the state's recovery rate is determined and the time the tuition charges are established.

After all the necessary "real" data had been gathered and entered, a meeting was held with several administrators so that they could "experiment" with the DSS (e.g., try different goals and priority structures). The first time the model was to be solved, a "bug" reared its ugly head—a system error prevented the model from being solved. Much to the embarrassment of the DSS builder, the meeting was adjourned; it was rescheduled and the experimentation was successfully completed after the problem had been identified and fixed.

8.15 "What If" and Goal Seek Capabilities

The "what if" and goal seek capabilities are inherent in the DSS. The implementation of these capabilities in the DSS is somewhat different from how they are used in some commercial packages (e.g., IFPS). Planning languages like IFPS have explicit model interrogation commands for sensitivity analysis that temporarily change the model or data. A "what if" command resolves the current model based on temporary changes in the model's data or logic. A "goal seek" command allows the user to specify desired levels of goals' attainment and the variables that affect those goals and then solve the model to find out the value of the variables necessary to meet the goals.

This DSS does not include explicit interrogation commands, as in IFPS; but these capabilities have been implicitly incorporated in the system's design. After a solution has been generated, the system returns to the beginning of the analysis process and lets the user easily consider alternatives. Once a solution has been generated, the user may either end the current session or proceed to another analysis following one of three paths, as shown in Figure 8.9. The first path is to change only the priority structure—reorder the goals and resolve the GP. The second option lets the user modify only the goal target values and then resolve the GP. The final option permits the user to "step" through the entire process and change information in any of the data sets that affect the model or alter the goals that are included in the formulation and then resolve the GP. The user can easily access any data set—financial, enrollment, and so on—from within the DSS.

Because the core of the DSS is a GP model, the decision maker is always working in a goal seek environment. The model that the DSS constructs and

```
$$$$$$$$$$$$$$$$$$$$$$$$$$$$$$$$$$$$$$$$$$$$$$$$$$$$$$$$$$$$$$$$$$$$$$$
$                                                                   $
$        VIRGINIA POLYTECHNIC INSTITUTE AND STATE UNIVERSITY        $
$    DECISION SUPPORT SYSTEM FOR TUITION AND FEE POLICY ANALYSIS     $
$                                                                   $
$$$$$$$$$$$$$$$$$$$$$$$$$$$$$$$$$$$$$$$$$$$$$$$$$$$$$$$$$$$$$$$$$$$$$$$

 . .  IF YOU WANT TO GO DIRECTLY TO THE PRIORITY STRUCTURE AND NOT CHANGE
      ANY OF THE MODEL'S GOAL TARGETS OR BASIC DATA, >>> ENTER PRIORITY

 . .  IF YOU WANT TO GO DIRECTLY TO THE GOAL TARGET VALUES AND NOT CHANGE
      ANY OF THE MODEL'S BASIC DATA, >>> ENTER TARGET

 . .  IF YOU WANT TO STEP THROUGH THE PROCESS AND HAVE THE OPPORTUNITY TO
      VIEW OR CHANGE THE MODEL'S BASIC DATA, >>> ENTER STEP
```

FIGURE 8.9 Dialog demonstrating the three possible paths that can be followed in the DSS.

solves is composed of a set of user-specified and user-ranked goals that math-ematically express the university's philosophy on how tuition revenue require-ments should be allocated to various student categories.

8.16   Benefits

The DSS provides the administration with a rational and traceable, yet flexible, means to analyze and establish tuition charges. It serves as a central storage for a large amount of data and a variety of models that previously were not integrated. In addition to allowing the user to control the data, the DSS allows the user to set tuition charges based on a wide variety of prioritized goals over a multiyear planning horizon.

The DSS makes a very powerful decision-making tool directly and readily accessible to the administration (i.e., tuition-and-fee problems can be addressed at a detailed and sophisticated level without directly handling large amounts of data, structuring the problem, formulating and solving complex analytical models, and composing a series of reports to document the results). The DSS places the process directly into the hands of the decision maker without having to rely on intermediaries.

The system is not used just at an operational level to set tuition charges, but also at a strategic level. It is used to forecast or project future values, "design" tuition charge structures rather than just extrapolate from the past year, generate and evaluate alternative courses of action, decide how to phase in new policies or changes in the tuition charge structure, assess the impact of policy changes and analyze the effect of changes in factors that influence tuition charges, and perform sensitivity analyses.

8.17   Users of the System

The primary users of the system in the administration are the director of financial planning and analysis and the budget director. The uses are often in response to the needs of the vice president for finance. The DSS is directly used by the administrators, with no help from intermediaries, except for some clerical support to update the data.

8.18   Management Reports: An Example

One of the many reports that the DSS can generate is a summary of total charges, an example of which is provided in Figure 8.10. The IFPS-generated report summarizes for each student category the annual charges for a full-time student for each year in the planning horizon and the base year. It also provides the absolute and percentage change between years and relative to the base year.

```
                          Management Report

              VIRGINIA POLYTECHNIC INSTITUTE AND STATE UNIVERSITY
              DECISION SUPPORT SYSTEM FOR TUITION AND FEE POLICY ANALYSIS
                SUMMARY OF POTENTIAL ANNUAL TUITION AND FEE CHARGES
            FULL-TIME ON-CAMPUS NON-RESIDENT UNDERGRADUATE    04/12/84

                                  1982       1983       1984       1985
                                -------    -------    -------    -------

TUITION AND FEES:
-----------------
TUITION                          $2,322     $2,781     $3,477     $3,576
PERCENT INCREASE OVER PRIOR YEAR      -       19.8%      25.0%       2.8%
PERCENT OF AVERAGE COST           51.4%      57.0%      62.6%      60.2%


FEES:
    ATHLETIC ASSOCIATION FEE         66         72         78         84
    BUS SYSTEM FEE                   12         12         15         15
    STUDENT CENTER FEE               60         63        132        138
    HEALTH SERVICE FEE               66         69         72         84
                                -------    -------    -------    -------
A.  TOTAL TUITION AND FEES       $2,526     $2,997     $3,774     $3,897

DORM & DINING:
--------------
BASE ROOM                          $444       $474       $507       $534
BASE BOARD                       $1,023     $1,035     $1,107     $1,164
    NEW FACILITIES                    -         29         88         88
                                -------    -------    -------    -------
B.  TOTAL ROOM AND BOARD         $1,467     $1,538     $1,702     $1,786



NON-RESIDENT UNDERGRADUATE LIVING OFF-CAMPUS
--------------------------------------------
    TOTAL CHARGES (A)            $2,526     $2,997     $3,774     $3,897
    DOLLAR INCREASE OVER PRIOR YEAR   -       $471       $777       $123
    PERCENT INCREASE OVER PRIOR YEAR  -       18.6%      25.9%       3.3%
    PERCENT INCREASE OVER BASE YEAR   -       18.6%      49.4%      54.3%

NON-RESIDENT UNDERGRADUATE LIVING ON-CAMPUS
-------------------------------------------
    TOTAL CHARGES (A + B)        $3,993     $4,535     $5,476     $5,683
    DOLLAR INCREASE OVER PRIOR YEAR   -       $542       $941       $207
    PERCENT INCREASE OVER PRIOR YEAR  -       13.6%      20.8%       3.8%
    PERCENT INCREASE OVER BASE YEAR   -       13.6%      37.1%      42.3%
```

FIGURE 8.10 Example of a management report that summarizes the annual tuition and fee charges for one student category.

8.19 Conclusions

Through the system's successful implementation, the DSS demonstrates how computer hardware and software technology can be combined with management science modeling and analysis to provide an extremely powerful and effective DSS to assist university administration in making sound and effective tuition-and-fee policy decisions. The system integrates a series of analytic models and a significant amount of data into a package that provides the decision maker with an interactive and direct role in the solution of a complex, dynamic, multidimensional problem.

The DSS was used to assist in the decision-making process for establishing the tuition-and-fee charges for the 1984–1985 academic year and to aid in setting the 1985–1986 charge structure. In its first year all the DSS's features were not fully utilized, partly because of a tight schedule and partly because the administration wanted to closely parallel the previous decision-making process. In the next application of the system, most of the DSS's features were utilized, and the system was also used as a strategic planning tool.

Although the system was developed, tested, and implemented at a major comprehensive state university, the concepts developed in this case are general enough to be applied to any public institution of higher education. Also, the system could be used by state-level agencies to support aggregate planning and decision-making activities.

As a result of this work the administration has a rational and trackable, yet flexible, means to (1) "design" tuition charge structures, (2) quickly generate and evaluate alternative plans and courses of action, (3) perform sensitivity analyses and address "what if" questions, and (4) assess the impact of policy changes and analyze the effect of changes in factors that influence tuition charges.

References for Case 1

1. EXECUCOM, *IFPS User's Manual* (Release 9.0). Austin, TX: EXECUCOM Systems Corporation, 1983.
2. Greenwood, A. G., and L. J. Moore. "A Computer-Based Decision Support System for University Tuition and Fee Policy." Joint National Meeting of TIMS/ORSA, Boston, MA, April 1985.
3. Greenwood, A. G. *A Decision Support System for Tuition and Fee Policy Analysis.* Ph.D. Dissertation, College of Business, Virginia Polytechnic Institute and State University, 1984.
4. Ignizio, J. P. *Goal Programming and Extensions.* Lexington, MA: D. C. Heath, 1976.
5. Ignizio, J. P. "A Review of Goal Programming: A Tool for Multiobjective Analysis." *Journal of the Operational Research Society*, Vol. 29, 1978, pp. 1109–1119.
6. Ignizio, J. P. "Sequential Linear Goal Programming: Implementation Via MPSX." *Computers and Operations Research*, Vol. 6, 1979, pp. 141–145.
7. Keen, P. G. W. "Decision Support Systems Translating Analytic Techniques into Useful Tools." *Sloan Management Review*, Vol. 21, Spring 1980, pp. 33–44.
8. Lee, S. M. *Goal Programming for Decision Analysis.* Philadelphia: Auerbach, 1972.
9. Moore, L. J., and A. G. Greenwood. "Decision Support Systems for Academic Administration." *The AIR Professional File*, Vol. 18, Summer 1984.
10. Schrage, L. *User's Manual for LINDO.* Palo Alto, CA: Scientific Press, 1982.
12. Turban, E., and J. Meredith. *Fundamentals of Management Science.* 5th ed. Homewood, IL, Irwin: 1991.

APPENDIX: Goal Programming

Goal programming (GP) is an extension of linear programming (LP); it offers a different approach to the solution of optimization problems involving multiple, conflicting goals.

Linear programming as described earlier is a technique for finding optimal solutions to various types of allocation problems. Its structure, however, is relatively inflexible with several restrictive assumptions. First, there is one primary goal whose level of attainment is to be maximized (or minimized). If there are additional goals, they must be satisfied. The maximization is done subject to a number of constraints, none of which can be even slightly violated. Finally, the secondary goals that must be satisfied are all equal in importance.

Goal programming attempts to alleviate this inflexibility. First, the goals are ranked by order of importance; second, deviations from goals and/or restrictions are permitted. However, the more important a goal, the less the permissible deviation. Finally, there is no primary goal to be optimized. Instead an attempt is made to minimize the sum of the undesirable deviations, weighted by their importance. This enables higher-priority goals to be attained at the expense of lower-priority goals.

Goal programming is used to perform three types of analysis:

1. Determining the required resources to achieve a set of desired objectives.
2. Determining the degree of goal attainment given the available resources.
3. Providing the best solution under a varying amount of resources and the priorities of the goals.

Goal programming is especially useful in complex allocation decisions that involve multiple conflicting objectives. Such situations occur quite frequently in service organizations, especially public ones (e.g., hospitals, universities, social agencies).

Goal programming is usually conducted in a "what if" manner. Once a solution is established, one can see the deviations for each goal. By changing the priorities of the goals, one gets different solutions with different deviations. In addition to changing the ranking of the goals, it is possible to change the *relative importance* of the goals within the "what if" model.

Case 2: Wheels Project (or Which Car to Purchase in Europe)

8.20   The Problem

U.S. diplomats, Department of Defense employees, and other U.S. government employees who work in Europe are authorized to purchase, tax-free, European cars that they use while in Europe. Then they are permitted to bring the cars, tax-free, to the United States. The problem is that there are dozens of car manufacturers, each with several models. The car-buying decision is a typical multiattribute decision process. Car attributes like design, top speed, price, and color are evaluated subjectively by buyers. The forthcoming DSS, which is titled "Wheels Project," was developed to enable potential buyers to make a better purchase decision. The case presented here summarizes the first three development iterations of the DSS. The final product would include a much larger database and more decision attributes.

The DSS* attempts to guide buyers to select the vehicle best suited for their needs and financial resources.

8.21 Initiation of the Project

Like many other user-built DSS, this project was initiated by users because they faced a difficult problem and at the same time were exposed to DSS technology. European car buying is a major subject for discussion among military and other eligible personnel in Europe. The developers felt that they could help themselves and their friends by developing the DSS and at the same time acquaint themselves with DSS methodology and Lotus 1-2-3. There was no formal planning or managerial authorization, because the out-of-pocket expenses were negligible and the developers worked on the project on their free time. Published data were readily available, and because the project was carried out in the framework of a university course, the developers consulted the professor, who played the role of a person from the Information Center.

8.22 Benefits and Costs

The DSS, once completed, could be used by thousands of military personnel in Europe. Although it is difficult to put a dollar value on the benefits of such a DSS, it certainly helped people make decisions. The phases presented here took 150 hours to develop. The builders/users were unfamiliar with Lotus 1-2-3 and knew very little about computers or programming. The software and hardware costs in this case were negligible, as is true with most user-developed DSS constructed with *existing* software and hardware.

8.23 Software and Hardware

The project was developed with the aid of Lotus 1-2-3, which is a limited DSS generator with good modeling capabilities, satisfactory database management, and reasonable graphic support. The microcomputer used was a DEC Rainbow 100. In this case, there was no software and hardware selection issue because both were dictated by the framework of the course. As will be seen later, for an expanded DSS of this nature, different software and/or hardware could have been more beneficial.

8.24 The Construction Process

Because the project was done in the framework of a formal course, the builders were asked to follow the ROMC process (see Chapter 5). The builders used

*This case is based on the work of J. Citizen, J. Peranteaux, and B. Zimmerlin, who developed the DSS as a team project in their DSS graduate-level course at the Institute of Safety and Systems Management, University of Southern California, Los Angeles.

the iterative approach, and most of the material presented here was completed during the first three iterations.

8.25   The Structure of the DSS

Like any other DSS this one too is composed of a database, a model base, and a dialog subsystem. A brief description of these follows.

The Data Base

The data base includes two parts.

a. *List of available cars.* At this stage only 48 *popular* cars were included (e.g., BMW, VW, Volvo, Jaguar, Mercedes). A sample of this information, including the U.S. and the European prices, is shown as follows:

Make/Model	U.S. List Price	European Price
BMW 535i	$30,760	$25,593
VW Vanagon	$17,460	$16,171

b. *List of attributes for each car.* In the current version of the DSS there are five attributes:

- ☐ Acceleration (time it takes from 0–60 mph).
- ☐ Top speed (maximum average).
- ☐ Braking (stopping distance from 70 mph without sliding).
- ☐ Fuel economy (estimated by EPA, in miles per gallon).
- ☐ Interior sound level at 70 mph (in decibels, measured with a sound-level meter).

The definition for each attribute is available by requesting "DEFINITIONS." The data for each attribute were extracted from the April, May, and June 1985 issues of *Car and Driver* and the May 1985 issue of *Stars and Stripes*. Here are examples of such attributes.

Make/Model	Acceleration (seconds)	Top Speed (mph)	Braking (feet)	Fuel Econ. (mpg)	Sound Level (decibels)
BMW 535i	7.7	135	185	17	73
VW Vanagon	16.0	105	220	23	78

These data can be updated by the user when new data become available. The user can also add/delete potential cars, or add attributes. (Changes can be made with Lotus 1-2-3.) The database is organized as a relational database.

The Model Base

The model used for the decision is based on a multiple attribute approach. Six attributes were considered: the five attributes listed in the database and the savings. The savings are the difference between the U.S. price and the European price.

The selection model is based on weights that were assigned to each of the six attributes according to the following procedure. For each attribute the cars with the *best* and the *worst* performance were selected as bench marks. For example, in the "top speed," the Porsche 928 was ranked fastest at 154 mph, and the VW Jetta ranked slowest at 100 mph. Therefore a weight of 0 was assigned to the VW and 1.0 to the Porsche (then .01 was added to eliminate the zero in the formula). A sample of the appropriate weights for the four cars is shown in the accompanying table.

	BMW 535i	BMW 635CSi	BMW 528e	BMW 735i
1st Wt.	0.60	0.40	0.71	0.48
Approx. Savings	$5,167	$6,815	$4,200	$6,161
2nd Wt.	0.76	1.01	0.62	0.91
Acceleration (0 to 60 mph), seconds	7.7	8.2	10.0	9.5
3rd Wt.	0.82	0.77	0.59	0.64
Top Speed (mph)	135	132	128	130
4th Wt.	0.66	0.60	0.53	0.57
Braking 70–0 mph, ft.	185	189	189	195
5th Wt.	0.81	0.74	0.74	0.62
EPA Est. Fuel Econ. mpg	17	16	20	17
6th Wt.	0.24	0.17	0.43	0.24
Interior Sound Level @ 70 mph	73	72	70	68

A second formula was then developed to find the overall rating of each car (make/model). This was done by using a complicated weighted average approach. At the end, each car was given a "normalized overall rating" over 100 units, as shown in the accompanying table.

Make/Model	Normalized Rating
BMW 535i	38.55
BMW 635CSi	16.36
BMW 528e	60.50
BMW 735i	25.82
::::::::	:::::
Total	1000.00

This point system tells the potential buyer that the BMW 528e is about 2.4 times more "worthy" than the BMW 735i. Such a calculation is a typical management science approach. The advantage of the DSS so far is mainly the ease of writing the program with the aid of Lotus 1-2-3, and introducing changes without the need of a programmer. The primary contribution of the DSS is that it permits the inclusion of the user's preferences.

User Preference

User preference in this version of the DSS is centered around three variables:

1. *Price*, which is a reflection of a combination of the purchasing price and the potential savings.
2. *Performance*, which is the combined effect of top speed, acceleration, and braking.
3. *Fuel Economy*, which is a function of the estimated mpg.

Each user is asked to rank these three variables as most important (value = 1), second most important (value = 2), and least important (value = 3).

The model then adjusts the six weights as follows: a value of 1 will double the weight, a value of 2 will keep it unchanged, and a value of 3 will reduce it to zero. This adjustment can be challenged by the user, who can override the program and treat the 1-2-3 ranking differently.

In addition to the preceding variables, the user is asked to set a constraint on the price (price range) and to indicate a "make" preference, called "make range" (i.e., to indicate the three makes of cars that the user is most interested in purchasing). An automatic data sort and extract are used to display those cars fitting the user's last two criteria. The cars will be ranked by the overall weight adjusted by the user's preference of price, performance, and fuel economy.

The Dialog Subsystem

The discussion in the last paragraph illustrates some of the display capabilities. The dialog, as will be shown, is done in English. "Help" support is available in several places and graphical support of the data is also available.

8.26   Consultation with the DSS

The user's interaction with the system is shown in Figure 8.11. The input data include the user's answers to three questions: price range, desired three makes of cars, and preferences.

The recommendation given by the DSS is a list of cars ranked by their total utility to the user (see Figure 8.12).

```
42  CARS: ALFA ROMEO AUDI BMW JAGUAR MERCEDES PEUGEOT SAAB VW VOLVO
43        [NOTE] AN ''*'' IS REQUIRED AFTER NAME OF CAR.
44
45     1. SELECT A PRICE RANGE ACCEPTABLE TO YOU  (LOWEST):     $14,000
46                      TO                      (HIGHEST):     $21,000
47     2. LIST THREE MAKES OF CARS THAT INTEREST YOU THE MOST    MODEL
48        (  IN ORDER OF PRIORITY  ):                    A:   SAAB*
49                                                       B:   VOLVO*
50                                                       C:   VW*
51     3. RATE THE FOLLOWING CATEGORIES ON A SCALE OF 1 - 3.
52        (ONE IS THE HIGHEST RATING POSSIBLE).
53                                              PRICE:          1
54                                        PERFORMANCE:          2
55                                       FUEL ECONOMY:          3
56                                     (STOP   INPUTS)
57  <<<<<<<<<<<<<   REMEMBER PRESS [ALT Z]   TO ENTER DATA  >>>>>>>>>>>>>
```

FIGURE 8.11 Sample consultation.

MAKE/MODEL	U.S. PRICE.1	EUROPEAN PRICE.2	SAVINGS	POINTS VALUE
VOLVO 740 TURBO	$20,565	$18,725	$1,840	0.09
SAAB 900 TURBO	$19,020	$16,495	$2,525	0.04

FIGURE 8.12 The DSS recommendation.

8.27 Use of the ROMC Approach

The representation, operations, memory aids, and control mechanisms (ROMC) approach was suggested in Chapter 5 as a systematic development approach for aiding the construction of DSS. By applying the ROMC approach to this case, the car buyer is permitted to conceptualize the process of selecting a European car. Furthermore, the approach allows the decision maker the opportunity to exercise direct, personal control over what the DSS does.

The four components of the ROMC are listed as follows:

1. *Representation.* The "representation" feature allows the display of information in the database. In the existing version the database included 48 makes/models. The user can easily update or change the database. Additionally, the representation feature built into the program provides

a recommended list of vehicles as well as the capability of displaying a
bar graph illustrating the automobile that best meets the user's criteria.

2. *Operations*. The "user's worksheet" section permits the decision maker
much flexibility in manipulating the "operations" of this DSS to meet the
user's needs. Through making simple input changes in the price range,
make of car, and/or the ratings of price, performance, or fuel economy
criteria, users can generate a variety of comparisons to best facilitate
their decision. The operations feature also provides the decision maker
with the capability of differently weighing various options in order to
determine the most cost-effective alternative.

3. *Memory aids*. The Wheel Project's memory aids link the representation
and operation aspects of the program. Lotus 1-2-3's capabilities were
used to provide the buyer an easily accessible list of definitions of the
attributes and other technical terminology required to evaluate each
automobile (e.g., braking, acceleration). A Help screen was also created
to assist the user while running the program.

4. *Control mechanisms*. The "control" aspect of the ROMC approach is exercised by the user through the combination of the user's worksheet and
the database. For example, users may be able to change the car's price
in the database if they can negotiate a cheaper price with their dealer.
To update the database to reflect this factor, users would simply access
the database and enter the new information under the appropriate field.
Then "what if" analysis could be performed using this new information.
The same applies to the other updatable fields contained in the database.
The control feature of this DSS allows users to integrate their individual
preferences and add new information as it is obtained.

8.28 Expanding the DSS

This DSS can be expanded by including more attributes and factors. For example, data on insurance cost, maintenance cost, and resale value could have been
added as monetary considerations. Similarly, one may add attributes like comfort, prestige, or ease of ride. Such data are more difficult to obtain than data
on fuel economy or acceleration. The model can also be expanded to include
used cars (e.g., for the last five model years).

The existing version of the DSS does not have "what if" or goal seeking
functions. To execute a "what if" the user must reenter all data, then rerun the
program. However, such functions can be added. Lack of experience with Lotus
1-2-3 prevented the builders from adding these functions, which can improve
later versions.

8.29 Summary

The limited experience of the builders, the fact that this was a class exercise,
and the brief time of the project (six weeks) limited the sophistication of this
DSS. One problem observed in this case was the slow processing time. The

combination of the inexperienced programmers and the limitations of Lotus 1-2-3 forced the builders to contain the dimensions of the DSS. For example, the attribute "prestige" was attempted and then dropped because it significantly increased the processing time. Future expansion may require heavier tools and/or hardware. This is a very important point in DSS construction (i.e., whenever tools and generators are used one may be forced to tailor the problem, or the model, to fit the available DSS tools and generators).

Wheels is a working decision support system. Despite its limitations, which were imposed by both hardware, software, and the inexperience of the builders, it provides the user with a simple means of getting around complicated selection problems. It allows the examination of a wide range of choices, provides graphic representation of the results, and allows users to change preferences and receive an entirely new range of alternatives tailored to those preferences. In short, even though it was constructed in only six weeks "after hours," the DSS can help in making decisions about which is the best car to buy in the European market.

8.30 Conclusions

The two cases in this chapter illustrate some of the major steps in DSS construction and point to several issues in design, implementation and operation of DSS. These cases are very different from each other (see Question 21 in the discussion questions). The first is a team-developed, complex DSS designed for organizational support. The second is typical for personal support, using a PC. An attempt was made to show the structure, process, and use of DSS in some detail. It is evident that the two systems are very different, and this is one of the virtues of DSS. The differences permit the flexibility and adaptability so important in DSS. However, the presentation of two cases is too limited to call attention to all issues related to DSS or to show the extent of its use. Therefore we elected to present about a dozen minicases in the next chapter to illustrate several additional issues and reinforce several DSS fundamental concepts and ideas.

Questions for Discussion

1. Why are the tuition-and-fee decisions unstructured (Case 1)?
2. What type(s) of flexibility (see Chapter 5) are provided by the university planning case?
3. Examine Figure 8.7. Explain why it indicates that DSS *supports* rather than replaces decision makers. Also explain the *improvement* in the decision-making process.
4. The two DSS cases were started without any formal need assessment or cost-benefit analysis. What are the reasons for this situation? Can you generalize for DSS initiation?
5. Trace the builder-users' relationships in Case 1. What can you conclude from these relationships?
6. Data processing people were not involved in Case 1, even though the system is running on the mainframe. How do you feel about this?

7. Review the testing and evaluation activities in Case 1 and discuss their effectiveness.
8. The lack of experience of the builders of the Wheels project caused several problems and limited the capabilities of the DSS. Trace the problems and suggest how they could be eliminated.
9. Discuss the advantages of introducing a new system in parallel with the old one (Case 1).
10. What type(s) of flexibility are provided by the Wheels Project DSS?
11. Discuss evidence of the use of the iterative approach in both cases.
12. Management science approaches were used in both cases. Identify the uses and explain the difference between the two cases.
13. Decision makers' judgment is considered an important characteristic of DSS. Explain how judgment is integrated in the two cases.
14. The dialog subsystem is considered very important in DSS. Review the dialog components in both cases and discuss their contribution to the decision makers.
15. Develop an ROMC table for Case 1.
16. Discuss some of the difficulties in expanding the Wheels Project with existing DSS technology. From your experience and the material in Chapter 6, suggest how to overcome these difficulties.
17. Why is the Wheels Project considered a semistructured situation?
18. What are the major differences between the model base in the two cases?
19. What lessons for implementation can be derived from Case 1? (Relate your answer to material in Chapter 20.)
20. Why was it necessary to use several tools/generators in Case 1?
21. Summarize the major differences between the two cases in the following table (you may expand it).

Area	Case 1	Case 2
Objective of support		
Tools/Generators		
Builders		
Hardware		
Time to build		
Implementation		
Database		
Modelbase		
Dialog Subsystem		
User(s)		
Other Areas		

Comment on the differences.

Chapter 9

Illustrative
DSS Applications

9.1 Introduction

The scope of application of DSS depends on what one considers a DSS to be. If we include the many systems developed by end-users on microcomputers with the assistance of spreadsheets, it would probably be possible to count millions of operating DSS. Even if only large-system DSS are counted (those that exhibit most of the characteristics and capabilities listed in Chapters 1 and 4), it would probably be possible to find hundreds of such systems in almost all industries, services, and functional areas. A DSS can be found in a single functional area (e.g., marketing) or one DSS can cover several functional areas (manufacturing, finance, and marketing). For an overview of applications, see Table 9.1. Systems exist in large as well as small organizations. DSS can be located in both the public and private sectors. Some organizations employ one DSS, whereas others use dozens. Systems support individuals and groups, top managers, and secretaries. The use of DSS is spreading as fast as the use of microcomputers and spreadsheet packages.

The purpose of this chapter is to illustrate, through more than a dozen actual examples, the various dimensions of DSS applications. The cases covered are listed in Table 9.2 with some preliminary details. In each case a different aspect may be highlighted. For example, in Case 1, DSS implementation is emphasized. The review questions at the end of this chapter reinforce the theoretical material presented in Chapters 4–6.

9.2 CASE 1: Connoisseur Foods

The Company

Connoisseur Foods is a diversified foods company.* Their main divisions are farm products, beverages, frozen foods, toiletries, and other subsidiaries. Each division is autonomous and has a different background and history. In the farm products division, for example, top managers have been with the company for many years and have worked their way up the organization. Often they rely on their experience and judgment to make major decisions. In other divisions, management is younger and more quantitatively oriented.

TABLE 9.1 Functional Applications of DSS.

Accounting: Budgeting, cost-control, auditing, estate planning.

Finance: Cash flow and pro formas, make or buy, debt structure, investment.

Marketing: Sales forecast, advertisement and promotion, market penetration, pricing, and product profitability.

Engineering: Alternative material cost evaluation, bidding, design, simulation.

Manufacturing: Capacity planning, scheduling, blending and mixing, manpower leveling, quality control, production flow, flexible manufacturing.

Purchasing and Inventory: Make-or-buy, physical distribution, MRP coordination.

---

*Adapted from Alter (1).

TABLE 9.2 Cases Covered.

Case Company	Sector	Functional Area
1. Connoisseur Foods	Food	Marketing (promotions)
2. Great Eastern Bank	Banking	Finance, marketing, portfolio selection
3. American Airlines (AAIMS)	Transportation	Finance, marketing, operations
4. RCA (IRIS)	Manufacturing	Human resources, industrial relations
5. Wesleyan University	Education	Financial aid, budgeting
6. National Audubon (EPLAN)	Energy	Energy planning, environmental impacts
7. Manufacturing DSS	Manufacturing	Production scheduling
8. Conrail	Transportation	Marketing, operations
9. FAST	Textile	Real-time: transportation, manufacturing
10. Lox, Stock, & Bagel	Restaurants	Small company, operations, budgeting
11. Abbott Labs	Health, hospitals	Marketing, strategy, budgeting
12. San Diego Utility	Electric utility	Strategic planning
13. Hewlett Packard	Electronics	Ready-made: quality control, engineering
14. Equitable Life	Real estate	Ready-made and time sharing: finance, management, accounting
15. RealPlan	Real estate	Ready-made, investment analysis, forecasting

Situation Analysis

Albert Leland, manager of applications in the corporate MIS group, invited an external consultant to conduct several seminars that led to more consulting and later to the introduction of a DSS. Leland's goal was to apply sophisticated computer-based analysis to marketing issues. To achieve this goal a marketing model was first developed. The model captured historical and intuitively practical responses to competitors' marketing strategies such as promotions and advertising.

The DSS

The Connoisseur Foods' forecasting models were designed to help managers establish levels of marketing variables like advertising, pricing, and promotion, among others, and to track results for various configurations of the decision variables. To implement the models, market conditions were expressed as response functions. Response functions are S-shaped curves that have a projected sales multiplier on the y axis and a decision variable (e.g., advertising) on the x axis. Historical data, if available, are used to construct the curves. Otherwise marketing experts provide subjective data for constructing them. The model requires that a response multiplier curve be built for each decision variable and includes the impact of uncontrollable variables such as seasonality and trend. The model includes similar curves for competing products.

The databases for the farm products division contain dollar and unit sales for 400 items sold in 300 branches since 1960. It included, at the time that the DSS was constructed (1974), about 20 million data items. Because at that time it was not possible to store all this information on a disk, most of the data were on tapes.

Implementation Lessons

Several implementation problems were observed during the development of the first models, and to a lesser degree in subsequent DSS models. For example, the models required many subjective estimates, which sometimes conflicted with each other. The modeling process lacked support from middle management, but was backed by top management. There was a strong resistance to change from middle managers. Many managers were too busy "putting out fires" to have time for the model. Top management also had not been kept up-to-date about progress made on the project. Mr. Leland stressed that advocates at very high managerial levels are important because they make decisions on resource allocation. They themselves do not need to be end-users of the DSS.

Advocacy from top management is not sufficient for the success of a DSS. For a DSS to continue over the long run, it must be evaluated for its costs and benefits. To increase the benefits of any DSS, it must be adopted by more managers and more divisions. Only then will it be supported by middle management. Top management should be kept up-to-date with respect to the progress of the implementation, and also on how it can benefit from the new system. Top management should be able to understand the methods developed and used by subordinates to facilitate communications and value the information and decisions made by DSS users.

There is resistance to change in any organization and it must be dealt with. To do this it is necessary to consider the corporate culture and the style and needs of individuals involved. Moreover, the individual trying to bring about changes has to be in the right position within the organization. Leland stated that the real goal of his effort was not the implementation of isolated systems or models. Rather, it was the institutionalization of new approaches in corporate decision making.

9.3   CASE 2: Great Eastern Bank— A Portfolio Management System

The Company

The trust division of Great Eastern Bank employed (in 1975) 50 portfolio managers in several departments.[*] Four of these departments (investment research, trust and estate, pension, and capital management) were involved in the institution and use of an online DSS portfolio management system (called OPM).

[*]Adapted from Alter (1).

Situation Analysis

The investment research department provides information to the other three departments. Investment research analysts prepare a list of stocks from which portfolio managers can buy. They also prepare information and analysis on particular industries. The other departments manage a large number of relatively small accounts, each with specific objectives. The pension department handles large pension funds, emphasizing performance. Capital management deals with wealthy individuals who are willing to take risks and expect high returns.

OPM was designed to help the portfolio managers make their decisions. It is basically a data retrieval system that can display portfolios as well as specific information on securities. OPM is a modular system designed to grow with time. The system was not completely predefined when it was conceived. In the beginning it had a limited number of terminals and was available to users only during a few hours a day. Several bugs in the software caused much frustration among users. Every morning managers obtained a hard copy of reports that they were interested in and examined them at their desks. One reason for using OPM that way was that managers kept their own manual records of the portfolios. There was a delay of five days between the commitment for a transaction and the actual booking, which was normal in trading but was not reflected in OPM. Finally, management forced the use of OPM in account reviews, and provided training sessions for managers.

Database and Model Base Elements

The database of OPM contains information about particular securities, listings of holdings within each account, and a cross-reference from each portfolio manager to the respective accounts. The system allows the user to generate reports with the following functions: Directory by account (by aggregate figures), Scan (table by account, holdings of one security), Groups (graphics, showing the breakdown by industry and security for an account), Table (listing of all securities within an account), Histogram (distribution of one data item over all securities within an account), Scatter (relationship between two data items), Summary (of an account), and Issue (data about a security). Newer extensions of the system include models to evaluate hypothetical portfolios using investment portfolio theory (e.g., the Markowitz model). A feature to monitor the performance of current portfolios and warn the portfolio manager of deviations from guidelines was added two years later. Tax implications were added to the DSS three years later.

Cost-Benefit Analysis

The project was proposed initially as an experiment, without rigid specifications. No cost-benefit analysis or feasibility study was conducted. Top management backed the project from the beginning despite the uncertainties surrounding it. At a later stage, when the system was operational, it was still hard to make a cost-benefit evaluation, because it was difficult to measure the improvement in the quality of the decisions made by the portfolio managers. There were many benefits such as better information, better formats, less clerical work, better communications, and an improved image. Many managers mentioned that it was an excellent marketing tool, and that the hard copy reports they could give to their customers enhanced the image of the bank.

Implementation Issues

Problems in implementation included system unavailability, insufficient number of terminals, and lack of qualified personnel necessary to carry forward such a project. As with any new system, some people adopted it early and became opinion leaders while others, who jumped in only after they saw results, were followers. Some people resisted change and preferred the old ways. Management demonstrated that it was serious about changing the procedures, and that all portfolio managers had to use the system. The initial period of usage for the system caused some frustration until all the bugs were ironed out.

9.4 CASE 3: AAIMS (An Analytic Information Management System)

A typical DSS developed in the early 1970s is AAIMS.[*] It is used by several airlines for a cross section of operations, planning, marketing, and financial decisions. For example, AAIMS has proven to be an invaluable management tool in areas such as productivity measurement, seating configuration, utilization, and load factor and operating statistics. It is basically a data retrieval and forecasting system designed initially to reduce clerical work.

The database includes collections of data on virtually all U.S. scheduled airlines and on over 300 major airports in the world. Data on traffic, fuel consumption, maintenance schedules, flight time, and operating expenses, for example, are available for all major types of aircraft. In addition, the database includes financial data for participating airlines. The primary sources for the data are the reports submitted periodically to the Civil Aeronautics Board[**] (called Form 41). The availability of large amounts of data made this project feasible. Had it been necessary to acquire the data, the cost would have been too high to justify the project.

In addition, the database includes individual users' private files. Thus users may enter their own data and perform manipulations on these data independent of, or in conjunction with, industry files. The 1983 database contained more than 200,000 items and was updated monthly.

The model base includes several forecasting models (like regular and multiple regression, econometric models, moving averages, time series, trend analysis, and period over period ratios).

The AAIMS is written in APL, a flexible programming language that allows easy additions to the DSS program. Furthermore, APL allows the formation of higher-level languages or special-purpose "dialects" that can be used to

---

[*]For a detailed description, see Klass, in Carlson (3), or Alter (1). AAIMS was developed by American Airlines and is marketed through APL Services, Inc. (a time-sharing vendor).
[**]The Federal Aviation Administration has replaced the Civil Aeronautics Board.

write new DSS or expand existing ones. As with most other DSS, a graphic display is an integral part of the system. In addition to standard reports and graphs (like "operating expenses as a percent of revenue"), it is possible to construct ad hoc reports and to get an answer to questions. For example, "What has been American Airlines' domestic yield, as defined by passenger revenue divided by revenue passenger-miles, from January 1982 to date?" An interesting application of AAIMS is the collection of corporate performance and productivity indicators that include over 100 graphs, tables, and trends. The system also monitors fuel usage; for example, trends in fuel use characteristics are monitored and compared against standards. This DSS is also used to monitor total factor productivity. The productivity model includes inputs like labor, maintenance, interest expense, and purchased goods and services. It also enables management to evaluate specific proposals for productivity improvement as well as proposals for price and schedule changes. A special analysis was performed in 1976–1977 in anticipation of airline deregulation. Another special analysis was the evaluation of a proposed merger.

The use of AAIMS was (and still is) voluntary, backed with a "soft sell" approach, emphasizing training programs. Although it achieved widespread use, many individuals that had been with the company for 15 to 20 years would rather do things manually. During the first five years of its operation, the system was used on occasion by top-level executives and lower-level employees; however, the majority of users were professionals (e.g., planners).

Among the advantages of AAIMS are the following:

1. Easy to learn.
2. Can be used by people with different levels of computer sophistication.
3. Interactive.
4. Permits effective use of the database.
5. Ad hoc and standard reports.
6. Can intermix APL and AAIMS commands.
7. Time-series analysis orientation (in forecasting).
8. Reduced amount of clerical effort.

The case mentions some disadvantages of AAIMS:

1. Limited set of APL functions.
2. Time-series orientation (only).
3. Not suited for modeling and "what if" analysis.
4. Limited report formatting.
5. Database management system suited for large amounts of data only.
6. Expensive for cross-sectional reports.
7. Functions occupy large amount of core memory.
8. Can be used only with AAIMS database.
9. Difficulties in handling missing values in Form 41 reports.

Many of these disadvantages and problems have been eliminated in the 1980s owing to improved technology. The usefulness of AAIMS depends on the environment where it is applied. If large amounts of time-series data are easily available for manipulation, it is well suited.

9.5   CASE 4: RCA—A DSS
for Human Resource Management

RCA, like many other large organizations, had several computer systems dealing with the management of its personnel. Among them were systems for payroll, pension plan administration, insurance, labor relations, affirmative action
programs, and general personnel management. Each subsystem existed on a
stand-alone basis. The conclusion was that these nonintegrated stand-alone
systems had little chance of supporting complex management decision making.
Therefore a decision was made in 1975 to develop a DSS for human resources
management that would provide for clerical processing and allow the integration and ease of interaction to support decision making. The system was called
"industrial relations information system" (IRIS). It is in regular daily use in
the highly diverse industrial enterprise as a transaction-driven data system.
However, it is designed for the noncomputer-oriented manager in a problem-
solving situation.

The system was designed to deal with questions that (1) are largely unanticipated, (2) will never again occur in exactly the same form, and (3) must be
answered within one hour of their occurrence. Such situations may develop
during labor-management negotiations, during court hearings (see the Pfizer
case in Chapter 1), or during labor planning and budgeting sessions. IRIS was
built on an interactive computer system using a commercial database management system coupled with a query capability. An extensive command language
was designed and implemented to stand between the end-user and the data
management system.

The system is used on four levels. One is ad hoc analysis of existing data.
A second is to receive prespecified reports. The third use is to evaluate the
consequences of proposed decisions. The fourth use is the most infrequent:
the retrieval of isolated individual data items, say, a salary rate for a particular
employee.

Over its years of operation, IRIS was subjected to extensive cost-benefit
analysis, which was facilitated by the fact that some of RCA's divisions were
using IRIS and others were not. These analyses showed that the IRIS system
had a 60 percent annual rate of return on the investment made to develop the
system (see Edelman [9]).

9.6   CASE 5: Wesleyan University—
A DSS for Student Financial Aid

The annual rate of increase in financial aid provided by Wesleyan University
was in the 20 to 30 percent range in the late 1970s.* This rate was much faster
than the university's income increase, and the situation was greatly exacerbated
by the reduction in federal grants and student loan programs, as well as by
declining enrollment.

The increased competition among universities for the very best students,

---

*Condensed from Hopkins et al. (8), with permission.

coupled with the budgetary strains mentioned previously, forced many universities to rethink their policies and procedures regarding financial aid.

Wesleyan University used an aid-blind admission policy during the 1970s. Under this policy, students were admitted without regard to financial need. Financial aid was provided later to all those admitted who requested it. Thus over 40 percent of the students received scholarships, whereas over 50 percent received loans, job assistance, or grants.

A five-year budget forecast predicted a potential financial crisis if this policy were to have continued. As a result, a detailed financial aid model was developed using a DSS to assess alternative strategies that could prevent the crisis. The DSS was constructed in 1979 to solve the problem. A DSS generator specifically designed for use in universities, called EFPM, was used.

The financial aid model is shown schematically in Figure 9.1.

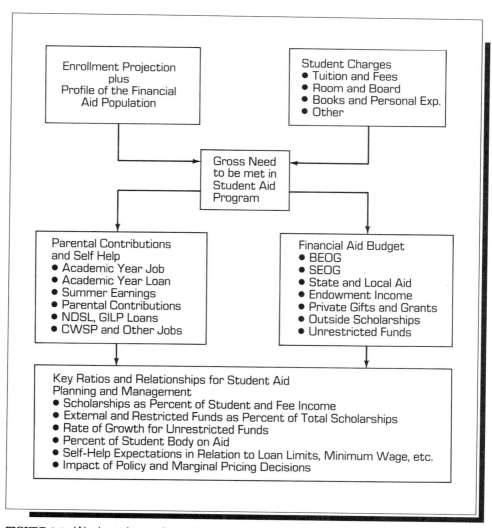

FIGURE 9.1 Wesleyan's student aid planning model.

The model brings together the multitude of policy and planning variables that affect financial aid. The model is particularly useful in computing "what if" questions relating to the input variables. For example, what if inflation remains high and there is a reduction in federal support? What if self-help expectations bump up against legislated limits in student loans? What is the budgetary impact of admitting more students? What policy changes are required to contain the program within certain limits? The model reaffirmed the projected financial crisis, and Wesleyan's president appointed a faculty/student/administration advisory committee to deal with the situation. The committee used another EFPM-based model—the budgetary model (the two are linked) to examine alternative policies. As a result, budget limits were set on financial aid. The board of trustees adopted the recommendations and the crisis was averted. The model is being continuously used to monitor the financial aid situation.

9.7 CASE 6: An Iterative Decision Support System for Energy Policy Analysis (EPLAN)

Background

The National Audubon Society is involved in an ongoing project to develop an interactive computer system that models the impacts of various public policies on U.S. energy demand. The system (EPLAN, or Energy Plan) uses a decision support system framework that assists the user by managing a large amount of engineering and economic data, performing calculations, permitting the evaluation of different energy-use scenarios, and keeping track of various constraints.

In 1981 the National Audubon Society published its first energy plan based on an energy-demand model that projected the amount of energy needed in various U.S. energy-demand sectors. At that time the process was manual and limited in scope by the volume and complexity of the information involved. The consequence was that only one scenario could have been examined and a number of approximations had to be made; it was clear that computer assistance was needed.

Database

EPLAN has a number of stored data sets for use in displays and calculations. The user can choose from among the sets of stored values and, in some cases, modify the data. The model base contains formulas that calculate yearly values of energy demand for each fuel type in each energy sector. The initial values used in the computations are the actual data for 1980, and those quantities are subsequently updated.

Auxiliary data are stored for use in the calculations as well. For example, projected oil prices are stored for each future year through 2010. Another structure in the database contains data on industrial energy use each year, starting in 1979, recorded by industry type and fuel type. The auxiliary data in the database can be modified during the session so that the user can test different scenarios ("what if" and goal seeking analyses).

The Audubon model for U.S. energy demand focuses on how and why people use energy and how energy demand can be reduced. The underlying assumption of the model is that reduced energy production and use, especially for nonrenewable resources, is beneficial to wildlife and the environment.

This energy model is used to evaluate present and planned governmental actions that could affect energy consumption. The impacts of development of alternative energy technologies are examined also. The model incorporates target levels of energy efficiencies for a variety of technologies that are consistent with realistic engineering and economic considerations. Policy options are examined in terms of their efficiency in relation to the target levels in various sectors of the economy, and energy use is broken down by the particular fuel types in each sector. At the end, policy recommendations are made by the society.

One of the goals of the computerization effort has been to stimulate the analysis carried out by energy experts who devised the original model and, at the same time, to advance the model's policy analysis capabilities.

Software and Hardware

A Wang VS minicomputer was used, with the Wang VS Basic high-level scientific language. The Wang text editor was found especially useful in developing the EPLAN software.

Issues in Implementation

In implementing the system, first the skeleton of the whole system was set up with a module for the initialization phase for each of the five energy-demand sectors. After testing to verify structural accuracy, subroutines were added to each sector to represent calculations of energy consumption for each of the fuel types. The systematic, top-down testing assured that each phase of the implementation was error-free before the next layer of complexity was added. The rest of the project involved adding the details for each sector-fuel calculation, providing constraints and dependencies among competing fuel uses, and creating the many displays.

Implementation enabled programmers to work on modules in parallel, and periodic testing of their enhancements and checks on performance of the whole system allowed manageable growth in complexity without introducing untraceable bugs.

Hints for Successful Implementation

The following DSS features and capabilities were highlighted as being important for creating a successful system like EPLAN:

1. *Adaptive filtering.* The system should enable users to filter information so that only relevant data will be highlighted for a given issue and information overload can be avoided.
2. *System memory.* Information processed at one stage should be available at another stage without having to be reanalyzed.
3. *Processing facilities.* Users should have access to a variety of capabilities including the ability to combine, weigh, alter, and otherwise put information into usable, convenient forms.

4. *Communication.* The DSS should provide a vehicle for sharing ideas among group members in ways that sharpen the decision points.
5. *Inquiry/Response.* As they go through learning stages, users should be able to incorporate feedback into the decision process.

Note: For more information about this case, please see: Medsker, L. R. "An Interactive DSS for Energy Policy Analysis." *Communication of the ACM*, November 1984.

9.8 CASE 7: Manufacturing Decision Support System (MDSS)

MDSS is a system developed at Purdue University for improving human supervision of a complicated automated manufacturing facility.[*] The system provides the decision maker with an opportunity to quickly evaluate (via simulation) the impact of various control decisions on production performance. Because MDSS provides updated information about the dynamic status of the various components of the manufacturing system, it is possible to make timely decisions in light of current management objectives. As such, MDSS can extend the control capabilities of the operations manager and eventually increase the productivity of the manufacturing system (even in a real-time environment).

The manufacturing system is a numerically controlled process system coupled with programmable materials-handling devices. The system is composed of three pairs of machining centers interconnected by conveyor loops. Parts are fixed manually on pallets, then transported to the machine centers. Routing of parts, selection of machining operations, part entry, and the machining itself are all controlled by a digital computer system.

The database includes the production specifications and the system capabilities. An error-checking routine ensures the quality of the database. The user can update and interrogate the database, plus retrieve, analyze, or aggregate data items.

The model base includes a discrete simulation model that enables the user to test various operating rules under various control parameters. In addition, the simulator allows statistical comparisons of performance measures and the construction of operation summary reports.

MDSS attempts to support decision making by following a five-step decision analysis process: (1) evaluating the problem, (2) establishing feasible alternative actions, (3) evaluating the alternatives, (4) selecting an alternative, and (5) implementing the chosen alternative. The system also includes "what if" capability. Once the user decides on the desired action, the MDSS also directs the implementation.

MDSS has a significant potential for numerically controlled manufacturing and Computer Aided Manufacturing/Computer Aided Design facilities. To assure its efficiency, however, further developments are needed in the area of versatile queries and the incorporation of computer intelligence in the MDSS.

---

[*]Adapted from Nof and Gurecki (11).

9.9 CASE 8: A Marketing Decision Support System at Conrail

Introduction

Conrail is a nonprofit corporation created in 1976 by the U.S. Congress to revitalize the freight service of six bankrupt railroads.[*] The company operates in a very competitive environment (mainly against the trucking industry); therefore marketing strategies are extremely important.

The Problem

The success of Conrail depends on marketing strategy. Appropriate pricing is crucial, as are cost-reduction opportunities like that provided by the "piggybacking" business. Requests for ad hoc information by the many decision makers at remote locations must be answered quickly.

The Database

A huge database of historical data (about 5 million records per year, each containing about 100 fields of data) is used for information retrieval.

To reply to users' requests means a search for data, sorting, summarization, consolidation (data combination), computation, data presentation, and data transfer. Most users do not have computer experience and therefore it is necessary to have a very friendly DBMS.

In addition to internal data, the database includes industry and other environmental information provided by external data banks, as well as information about clients and competitors.

The Model Base

The model base includes statistical models available in the standard SAS package.

Structure

The DSS, constructed in 1980–1981 and running on an IBM mainframe, with software that was existing at that time, is shown in Figure 9.2. Owing to the nature of the DSS, the emphasis is on DBMS. The necessary capabilities were provided by RAMIS II (a 4GL) and ADABAS (an inverted list database manager).

The DSS construction, which followed the prototyping approach, used existing interfaces between software packages whenever possible (e.g., RAMIS II and SAS, RAMIS II and ADABAS). Additional interfaces were developed using procedural languages like PL1 and COBOL. The DSS was constructed in five months.

---

[*]Adapted from Hoover (7).

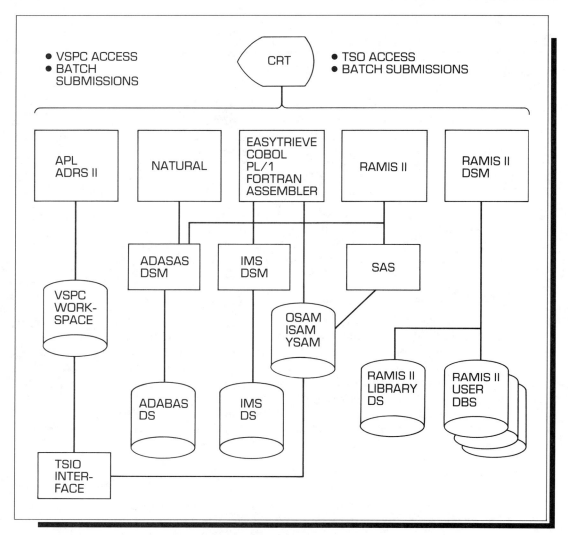

FIGURE 9.2 Conrail's interactive computing software.

Implementation

1. The system was expanded from marketing to include production (operations), creating a slow computer response time at the beginning. A special DSS database was created then for the new application.
2. Users' requests caused terminals and printers to be tied up for hours. Improvements made by software vendors solved these problems. (*Note*: Vendors of large software products are usually very cooperative in their attempt to solve problems involving their products.)
3. A committee was established to determine the content of the database (e.g., to answer questions like "How far back should one go into history?").

4. A training program was developed for users. Initially, lack of training was a major implementation constraint.
5. Several devices were developed to decrease input and output loads.
6. New and more friendly DSS features were added in the mid-1980s to alleviate both the training requirement and the heavy load on the CPU.
7. Personal computers were added to the DSS to make it a distributed DSS during 1984 and 1985. These micros are used to exchange data with mainframes (host computers). Response time has been considerably reduced and the great reservoirs of shared data in the corporate database become available to many users. Most micro-users work with integrated spreadsheet packages (primarily Lotus 1-2-3).
8. A natural language processor (see Chapter 18) is being developed to allow easier communication with the database.
9. Voice and speech recognition (see Chapter 18) are being developed to allow even easier person-machine dialog.
10. The initial investment of $4 million paid for itself in just a few months. Savings, resulting from more sensible bidding and pricing, increased market share and profit margins.

9.10   CASE 9: Freight Automatic Scheduling and Transportation—FAST

This relatively complex DSS was constructed by a large textile manufacturer (who requested to remain anonymous).[*] This manufacturer has changed from a manual trucks scheduling and dispatching system to a complex corporate DSS.

The objectives of this DSS are to provide cost reduction incentives and a fast freight rate revision system, develop an integrated planning system that associates physical transport with real-time transit information, enable computer-aided scheduling and decision support, provide real-time visibility of in-transit materials and requirements, improve communication, and provide flexibility for linkage to other CBIS.

The DSS, FAST, includes the integration of information flow throughout a vertical manufacturing process that stretches from raw material vendors through dyeing and finishing, and up to finished goods warehouses or finished goods customers. The major decisions are routing and scheduling. Routes are composed of ordered sequences of pickup/delivery points originating and ending at a depot. Scheduling consists of sequences of pickup/delivery points with prescribed arrival and departure times. Decisions in these areas are complex, because they are influenced by many variables and constraints.

The System's Structure

The system is based on three components: *real-time* information retrieval, on-line information visibility, and integrated information processing. Each plant or other physical location is equipped with a microcomputer that operates as a real-

[*]Adapted from Oliff (12).

time terminal connected to the mainframe in the network. In addition there is a corporate database. The real-time capabilities are supported by an "automatic vehicle location system" (from Motorola). Thus the exact location of each vehicle is always known. All plants and warehouses are connected through a network of dedicated data lines to the mainframe computer.

Construction

The system was constructed over a period of one year using more than 175 commercial software application (including many models) and development programs (the cost of the software alone exceeded $1 million). The system includes extensive DBMS capabilities and an optimization routine for automatic vehicle routing and scheduling.

Main Features of the System

1. FAST is a real-time DSS developed at a cost of about $2 million, with anticipated annual benefits of over $1.2 million.
2. The major objective of the system is to conduct day-to-day routing and scheduling. However, the system also supplies strategic support to capacity planning decisions.
3. The system is flexible. For example, it allows the transportation scheduler either to initiate and complete the routing manually or to rely totally on the automated system. Furthermore, the user can add constraints to the optimal scheduling model and change assumptions and/or other input data.
4. The system makes actual dispatch assignments of drivers to routes, eliminating the biases of manual dispatching. The system considers drivers' preferences and equitable rotations of less desirable routes.
5. The schedule, which is made 12 hours in advance, is constantly updated by real-time information (e.g., breakdown of vehicles, no show of drivers, etc.).
6. Attempts are made to minimize both drivers' wait time and mileage driven.

9.11 CASE 10: DSS at LS&B— An Application in a Small Business

Introduction

Lox, Stock & Bagel (LS&B) is a small independent food service company in Champaign, Illinois.* The company operates a restaurant and a bakery. The DSS was developed to support short-term (daily, weekly) planning and control decisions essential to small business operations. This DSS is typical of small

---

*Adapted from Chandler et al. (4).

businesses, but similar DSS are used for personal support in large organizations. A DSS of this type is constructed today with an integrated micropackage (such as Lotus 1-2-3, or with an expanded DBMS, such as dBASE IV), and it runs on a microcomputer. However, at the time this system was constructed (1980), such tools were not available; therefore this DSS was developed from scratch and completely programmed in DIBOL (a procedural language similar to COBOL). It runs on a DEC minicomputer on a time-sharing basis.

The Decision Supported

The planning and control model is shown schematically in Figure 9.3. The decisions are structured and semistructured and of the operation control nature. The major objective of the system is to monitor actual performance of labor and material, compare it with the budget, generate variance reports, and perform a standard variance analysis. Management then can reschedule, rebudget, and so forth.

Components of the DSS

There is no database per se in this small DSS. The necessary data are input whenever needed. When actual quantities are entered, the computer figures theoretical labor needed and compares it with the actual. Built into the formulas are reasonable variances (broken down into periods and/or food types). This arrangement allows the computer to flag exceptions. Daily data are saved in interim storage for weekly summaries. These weekly summaries can be organized in a database if further analysis is desired. The model base includes all necessary formulas.

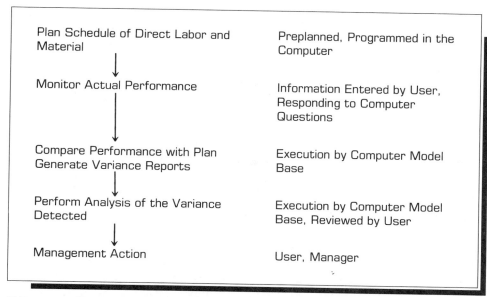

FIGURE 9.3 Planning and control model at LS&B.

TABLE 9.3 Direct Labor Variance Analysis (Sample Daily Results Page).

Prod 1	Prod 2	Serv 1	Serv 2	Serv 3	Serv 4	Serv 5
Friday						
Budgeted hours						
18.0	10.0	8.0	55.0	14.0	54.0	14.0
Actual hours						
18.0	10.0	10.0	58.0	20.0	57.0	16.0
Man-hour variance						
0.0	0.0	2.0	3.0	6.0	3.0	2.0
Expected variance						
1.1	0.6	0.5	3.5	0.9	3.4	0.9

	Budgeted	Variance	Actual	Expected variance
Man-hours	173.0	16.0	189.0	11.0
Dollar pool	656.25	62.95	718.20	41.62
Sales	4375.00	277.50	4652.50	200.00

The dialog is conducted in English. It permits changes to be made in the formulas' parameters (see Figure 9.4). An example of a report is given in Table 9.3.

Characteristics of the DSS

1. This DSS is limited to simple periodic reports. However, today with the capabilities of a spreadsheet or a DBMS, the user can quickly generate ad hoc reports as well.
2. This DSS has detection mechanisms on the reasonableness and accuracy of the data entered, which are provided by built-in limits and tests.
3. Help and explanatory material are provided on request (e.g., presentation of the formula used).
4. The system reduced weekly labor variances from about 22 percent to about 6 percent, because managers were able to change schedules quickly and achieve fairly accurate results. In addition, managers improved their forecasting and planning capabilities. Being more accurate on required labor resulted in an improved schedule, which is translated into a savings of over $10,000 a year. This savings easily recouped the initial investment the company made in the DSS.

9.12   CASE 11: Abbott Labs— Hospital Product Division

Introduction

Abbott Labs sells over 2000 products to thousands of hospitals nationwide.[*] The market is very competitive and subject to many ever-changing government regulations. The DSS is used for sales forecasting, pricing analysis, tracking promotion results, and new product analysis. The uses in these marketing

[*]Condensed from Brown (2).

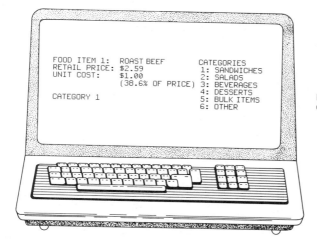

```
FOOD ITEM 1:   ROAST BEEF        CATEGORIES
RETAIL PRICE:  $2.59             1: SANDWICHES
UNIT COST:     $1.00             2: SALADS
               (38.6% OF PRICE)  3: BEVERAGES
                                 4: DESSERTS
CATEGORY 1                       5: BULK ITEMS
                                 6: OTHER
```

Displayed initially to refresh user of current data.

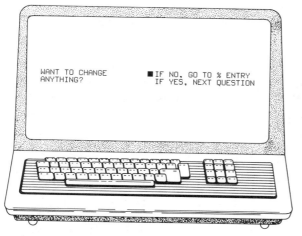

```
WANT TO CHANGE        ■ IF NO, GO TO % ENTRY
ANYTHING?               IF YES, NEXT QUESTION
```

First question asked by the DSS. The system waits at the position of the cursor ■ for user response. If NO is the response, the DSS skips all further change questions and asks for the daily sales percentage only. Note that both lines of the question are displayed and the cursor returns to position ■ so that the user can see the full consequences of his response.

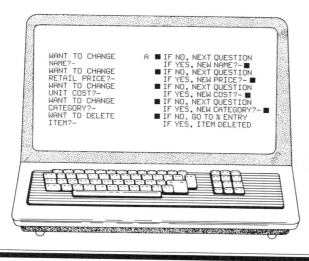

```
WANT TO CHANGE    A ■ IF NO, NEXT QUESTION
NAME?-               IF YES, NEW NAME?-■
WANT TO CHANGE     ■ IF NO, NEXT QUESTION
RETAIL PRICE?-       IF YES, NEW PRICE?-■
WANT TO CHANGE     ■ IF NO, NEXT QUESTION
UNIT COST?-          IF YES, NEW COST?-■
WANT TO CHANGE     ■ IF NO, NEXT QUESTION
CATEGORY?-           IF YES, NEW CATEGORY?-■
WANT TO DELETE     ■ IF NO, GO TO % ENTRY
ITEM?-               IF YES, ITEM DELETED
```

If YES is the response, each attribute of the sales item is reviewed. Again both the question and its consequences are displayed. The cursor first stops at A and if YES is input it then moves to B, awaiting the new value. This is crucial in the DELETE question.

After all (or no) changes have been made to the current attributes of the sales item, the actual days sales percentage is requested. This same process is repeated for all items. Note if there are no changes, the only input by the user is an initial NO to the first change question and then the daily sales percentage.

FIGURE 9.4 Conversational mode for input/output sales data.

areas are an extension of the initial use, which involved financial analysis and business unit management.

System Development

The system was developed using EXPRESS (the software cost about $175,000) and runs on a Prime 2250 computer. Later the system was upgraded to a Prime 750 computer with additional terminals. The development took five months, using extensive prototyping.

Multidimensional Analysis

A major capability of a mainframe (or mini) DSS that is not available on microspreadsheets is an extensive multidimensional analysis. In this case analysis is needed by product, region, price, volume, and so on. Such an analysis can be done quickly because EXPRESS can process information in six dimensions at one time. For example, Abbott could perform sales analysis in hospitals by number and type of beds, by occupancy rate, and by geographical region.

Database

The database is very large because it includes information on over 2000 products, thousands of clients' files, data regarding competition, and the like.

Model Base

Statistical models are the backbone of this DSS, because forecasting is required for many decisions. The statistical analysis is tied to financial planning models. The system uses standard statistical models like moving averages, curve-fitting models, regular and multiple linear regressions, time-series analysis, and factor analysis. Most of the models are embedded in EXPRESS. The model base also includes an electronic order entry system that feeds incoming information in a batch mode for monthly number manipulation.

Decisions Supported

The company's products are divided into several product lines, each with 100–200 items. Each product line has a financial analyst who uses a PC to access the mainframe. Owing to competition and government pressure to contain costs (e.g., through strict ceilings on Medicare payments), hospitals try to pay the lowest possible prices, usually through a bidding system. Therefore the job of the financial analyst responsible for setting prices is extremely difficult and important. The volatile buying patterns add complexity. Thus, the DSS is essential to maintenance of market share.

System Characteristics

1. Besides forecasting, the system is also used for annual budget preparation.
2. "What if" analyses are used extensively to predict the impact of pricing strategies on sales and on profit margins.

3. Decisions regarding which products to "push" and which customers to concentrate on are continuously supported by the DSS.
4. The DSS measures the return on investment on product promotion programs.
5. New product analysis has been changed from mostly subjective to mostly objective because the DSS has been in use.
6. A detailed analysis is performed to determine differences between forecasts and actual sales.

9.13 CASE 12: California Utility Adopts New Strategic Planning Process

In 1976, San Diego Gas and Electric Company (SDG&E) made a commitment to the strategic planning process by installing a planning system to aid management decision making.[*] Like most other utilities SDG&E is grappling with the problems of providing electricity and gas to its customers in a cost-efficient manner. The problems are particularly acute when there is a need for the approval of various regulatory commissions to adjust rates for services.

By 1982, SDG&E had outgrown its existing planning system. To meet its objectives for growth, flexibility, and financial return, SDG&E needed to use available information in a variety of ways. Necessary strategic planning efforts required that the same data be available in many different formats. The existing system failed to meet those requirements.

"Our old planning language was developed in the late 1960s and built in the early 1970s," said Gary Rinehart, manager of decision support services at SDG&E. "The system was great when we bought it; however, it never evolved. Consequently, it could not be used to accommodate our needs in the 1980s."

Rinehart added, "We wanted a system that could handle financial calculations, function under two operating systems (CMS and TSO), run on a mainframe but interface with personal computers, and create a database environment. We also wanted the capability to build our own modeling procedures." SDG&E's search ultimately led to STRATAGEM, a DSS generator from Integrated Planning of Boston, Massachusetts. STRATAGEM was installed on the utility's IBM 3081 in January 1984, operating under the TSO environment.

The planning process at SDG&E can be classified into two categories—period planning and nonperiod planning. Period planning includes annual operating budgets and quarterly projections of the utility's financial future.

Nonperiod planning, done on an ad hoc basis, includes regulatory rate setting, bond and stock offerings, cost of capital analyses, and resource plan analyses.

Using STRATAGEM, SDG&E developed corporate models for each of its planning activities to answer hypothetical, "what if" questions, as well as basic questions about the future, such as, "What will our expected rate of return on gas be next year?"

SDG&E has transferred its entire database and modeling operation from the original system to the new DSS. "Converting from one system to

[*]Condensed from *Public Utilities Fortnightly*, May 2, 1985.

another . . . has forced the company to rethink the whole process of modeling. The old system used line-by-line code. STRATAGEM is matrix-oriented and handles many functions simultaneously. The matrix orientation gives a more global perspective that enables the company to do more advanced planning and analysis, with the same information, than before."

SDG&E uses the DSS generator in three major areas. The financial planning department uses the program to build strategic planning (macroplanning) models. Summarized data is introduced into STRATAGEM, which manipulates collections of individually labeled storage cells (arrays) that contain one data value each. By manipulating the reporting arrays, users can look at the information from different perspectives. Once entered, the information is retained for future analysis.

STRATAGEM is also used to build financial statements and load-forecast models to predict monthly sales based on customer class. Finally, SDG&E uses STRATAGEM for ad hoc development of budget and organizational models.

Rinehart said, "Up to seventy-five SDG&E employees can access the system. The ten major models that make up the corporate model are developed and maintained through different departments in the company. There is a model manager for each, and each manager is responsible for two or three people."

STRATAGEM is also used as SDG&E's executive information system's database (see Chapter 10). "We are defining critical factors for executive work station graphics," Rinehart said. "For example, we provide managers with comparative earnings per share figures of both other California utilities and generic United States utilities, so they can monitor SDG&E's relative performance locally and nationwide. The information is presented graphically," he explained, "so executives who are not familiar with computers do not have to learn complicated languages or functions."

SDG&E's plans for future DSS applications seem limitless.

A primary goal is to make the DSS database the primary source for planning. It could provide a unified corporate database for all SDG&E, high-level, strategic planning models.

Ready-made Systems: A preview

Large numbers of ready-made DSS are available on the market. The systems are general in nature and aim at a specific sector (banking, insurance, hospitals) or a specific functional area (personnel, production, accounting), or a specific task (quality control, investment analysis). Ready-made systems are designed mainly for repetitive tasks of the operational and management control type. The next three cases provide examples of such systems.

9.14   CASE 13: Hewlett Packard (HP) Quality Decision Management

HP Quality Decision Management is an applications software package for analyzing manufacturing processes and product quality.[*] The package provides control and Pareto charts that help production and quality assurance engineers

[*]From HP Publication (9).

identify and prioritize statistically significant product defects and manufacturing process problems. Engineering departments can use data collected on-line to generate scattergrams, histograms, and tabular reports.

The package differs from conventional MIS application packages because of many added-on DSS capabilities. For example, a menu and prompt/response approach allows engineers without programming experience to configure data collection transactions, specify report and graph formats, archive data, and perform system maintenance functions. The database is designed for workstation-oriented production environments. The system provides data collection, validation, and storage to the database. It also allows "what if" analysis, sensitivity analysis, and simulation capabilities. Engineers can statistically analyze the data and output the results in tabular or graphical format.

The HP Quality Decision Management System may be used in the following application areas:

1. *Incoming inspection:* displays of inspection instructions, vendor rating reports, control charts of defect rates, and vendor's quality.
2. *Product test:* manual and automatic online data collection, test procedure display, statistical monitoring of defect levels, and decision support graphics and reports.
3. *Statistical process and product monitoring:* on-line data collection from incoming inspection, manufacturing process and test areas, statistical graphs and reports to monitor manufacturing process quality, correlation between product defect data, and defect cause data (in a real-time environment).

9.15 CASE 14: Equitable Life Insurance— A Ready-made Real Estate Application Via Time Sharing

Introduction

As an option for a company-owned DSS (in-house), it is possible to time share a ready-made DSS. An example of such a situation is provided in this case.*

The Realty Group of this large insurance company buys, sells, and manages hundreds of real estate properties for the insurance company and for clients. The DSS (Tymcom 370) provides the following capabilities:

1. Database management including preparation of ad hoc monthly and quarterly reports and preparation of real estate closing transactions.
2. Cash flow projections (itemized by expense and income categories) for properties that are candidates for acquisitions.
3. Computations of the rate of return on investments and other measures of performance of existing and proposed properties.
4. Access to the corporate database and execution of standard manipulations.
5. User access to the system through telephone lines.

*From *Computerworld*, February 22, 1982, p. 34.

Ready-made DSS for Analyzing Standard & Poor's Corporate Data

Management Decision Systems (Waltham, MA) announced two new mainframe-based software packages. The first is "Easyscan," which analyzes Standard & Poor's "Compustat II" database of corporate financial data. Data for more than 6000 publicly held companies can be scanned, evaluated, and graphically represented with Easyscan. Users define selection based on multiple "and/or" criteria. Once a criterion has been made, it may be saved and recalled for subsequent analysis.

Typical uses include industry analysis—examining the health of a group of firms or an industry as a whole to determine its direction, growth, credit worthiness; competitor analysis; bank customer prospecting; and investor relations. This product is priced at $50,000.

The second product, "The Financial Consolidation and Reporting System," allows corporate consolidations, reorganizations, restatements, acquisitions, and development of other strategic applications for a corporation's subsidiary operations. This product is priced at $120,000.

Condensed from *MIS Week*, February 13, 1985.

System Benefits

This type of DSS provides several advantages. Latest software and hardware technologies are available to the user whose IBM 3033 processors are compatible with Tymcom 370. This system, which is several years old, is being constantly updated for increased capabilities and reduced cost.

1. The major benefits reported are reduction of report turnaround time (by as much as 75 percent), capability of making faster (and more consistent) acquisition decisions, downloading of information from the corporate database to PCs for manipulation by decision makers and comparative analysis of hundreds of managers and properties.
2. Time sharing is mainly appropriate for infrequent use. With the decreased cost of software and hardware and the increased capabilities of microcomputers, there is a trend away from time sharing to in-house computing.

9.16   CASE 15: RealPlan—A Ready-made Commercial Real Estate Investment DSS Utilizing In-House Equipment

With the decreasing cost of software and increasing demands on its use by real estate portfolio managers, time sharing via telephone lines is often an uneconomical choice for implementation of DSS for analysis of commercial real estate investments. Sigma Research Associates (La Jolla, CA) offers a comprehensive DSS for this purpose, called RealPlan, which can be adapted to many different types of in-house hardware configurations.

This DSS performs many of the typical operations required for making real estate acquisition, improvement, and divestment decisions. These include highly detailed income, expense, and cash flow projections. For example, a module is available for projection of income generated by up to 600 tenant spaces for each property, and with complex leases having multiple terms, several types of cost-of-living adjustment formulas, and differing percentage rent clauses. Realplan can also make forecasts of the value of individual properties up to 40 years into the future, and can generate consolidated reports for properties grouped according to type, ownership, or other criteria.

Unique benefits include the following:

1. RealPlan is "portable" to different hardware. This derives from its being programmed almost entirely in FORTRAN 77, a highly standardized and ubiquitous language. Target machines include PRIME, DEC VAX, and IBM 30XX series.
2. RealPlan is highly modular, employing a nucleus of required modules (see Figure 9.5). These can be economically augmented if necessary with additional custom modules for organization-specific types of analyses.
3. A significant advantage of implementing the DSS in-house over using a time-sharing service is that its local database can be more easily integrated with the corporate financial information system, and updating of the local database can be automated. In addition, the DSS's database augments and is accessible by users of the organization's other databases. The DSS's database is tightly integrated with mathematical models employing optimization, sensitivity analysis, and other analytical techniques.
4. Unlike some other types of investments, real estate investment performance is not uncontrollable, but depends heavily on future actions having an impact on the cash flow stream. These include renovation, expansion, refinancing, and divestment.

The portfolio manager creates a table of potential actions for each property. Unlike most other DSS's for this purpose, RealPlan includes an efficient, specialized search algorithm to determine the most advantageous selection and timing of actions included in the action table. Reference 15 includes a discussion of this rather difficult optimization option and other aspects of the RealPlan DSS.

9.17   Summary and Conclusions

The cases presented in this chapter cover a diversity of situations, industries, functional areas, company sizes, construction strategies, and the like. This summary is divided into three parts. First, we discuss the similarity among the cases; then we consider the unique aspects; and finally we summarize the specific decisions supported in each case.

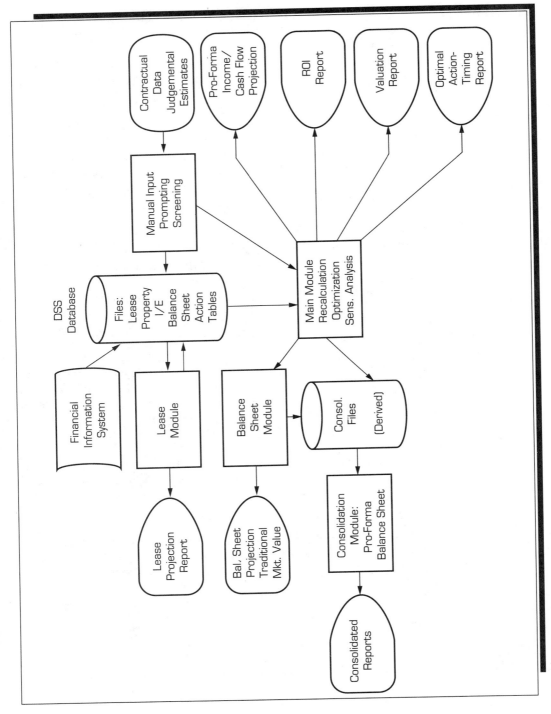

FIGURE 9.5 RealPlan DSS Nucleus.

Similarities

The following characteristics were observed in almost all cases:

1. The typical structure is composed of a database, model base, and dialog.
2. Prototyping was used.
3. Most of the decisions were complex and unstructured.
4. The DSS was used to support ad hoc decisions.
5. The DSS was used to generate periodic reports.
6. The DSS was developed by teams (this characteristic was the result of a choice, because most published material regarding DSS deals with team-built systems).

These similarities reinforce the concept of DSS as presented in Chapters 4 and 5.

Dissimilarities

1. Most early DSS (those constructed during the 1970s [e.g., cases 1, 2, 3, 6, and 7]) were built from scratch, whereas later DSS were constructed with the aid of generators and tools.
2. Several of the DSS were constructed around large databases mainly for report generation and forecasting (cases 1, 2, 3, 4, and 13), whereas others were concerned more with testing policies, scenarios, and decision alternatives (cases 2, 6, 7, 9, and 13). Notice that some cases are in more than one category.
3. Less implementation difficulties were mentioned in the later DSS. This might have been the result of greater user involvement by builders equipped with generators.
4. Cost-benefit analysis was performed only in a few cases (cases 4, 8, and 9). As will be seen in Chapter 20, a monetary analysis is rather difficult to conduct.
5. Optimization is reported in two cases only (cases 1 and 15). This observation is in line with the findings of national surveys (see Chapter 20); most DSS do not include optimization.
6. Complex, multidimensional analysis is reported in only one case (case 11). It requires a very complex and expensive generator (EXPRESS).
7. The vast majority of the systems were not on real-time. Only two (cases 7 and 9) were capable of real-time analysis. Both systems are very expensive. Thus, it seems that real time DSS are not easy to develop.
8. Several of the cases have unique capabilities or applications. For example, case 8 attempts to integrate artificial intelligence technology (see Chapter 19); case 14 includes a distributed DSS environment; and cases 2, 3, and 13 have strong graphics. Finally, a unique application is mentioned in case 3, where over 100 productivity indicators are monitored and analyzed.
9. The users of the DSS were at all organizational levels. Although the majority of users were professionals and analysts, use by top management was also reported (e.g., cases 1, 3, 6, and 8).

10. Integration with executive information system, which is the topic of the next chapter, is discussed in case 12.

Decisions Supported

- ☐ In Case 1: Examination of marketing strategies (pricing, promotion) in response to changing environment and competition.
- ☐ In Case 2: Portfolio reports, data retrieval, correlation analysis.
- ☐ In Case 3: Evaluation of merger possibility, policy analyses, monitoring and analyzing 100 productivity indicators (analysis of productivity improvement proposals).
- ☐ In Case 4: Statistics to support personnel decisions quickly (one hour), evaluation of possible consequences of such decisions ("what if" simulation).
- ☐ In Case 5: Financial aid plans, financial planning, how many students to admit.
- ☐ In Case 6: Forecasting national energy needs, scenario analysis of government policies regarding energy consumption, and developing new energy sources.
- ☐ In Case 7: Production and maintenance planning.
- ☐ In Case 8: Pricing strategy, scheduling, and cost-reduction opportunities examination.
- ☐ In Case 9: Scheduling, dispatching, routing, long-range planning.
- ☐ In Case 10: Short-term scheduling, budgetary and labor control.
- ☐ In Case 11: Sales forecast, product mix analysis, pricing analysis, new product analysis, tracking promotion results.
- ☐ In Case 12: Intermediate and long-term (strategic) planning, financial planning, forecasting sales, competitive analysis.
- ☐ In Case 13: Quality control decisions, vendor analysis, product tests accept/reject, setting QC plans.
- ☐ In Case 14: Real estate closing transactions, and miscellaneous reports (ad hoc and periodicals).
- ☐ In Case 15: Real Estate investment decisions: acquisition, improvement, divestment.

Questions for Discussion

Note: Use only the information provided in the cases to answer the following questions.

1. In the Connoisseur Foods case, what advice would you give regarding DSS implementation?
2. Explain how the iterative process worked in the OPM model (case 2), in the EPLAN (case 6), and in the Conrail case (8).
3. After studying the OPM experience (case 2), what would you conclude about cost-benefit analysis? Is the situation described in the case an exception or a rule? Why?
4. Compare the implementation issues in cases 1 and 2. Discuss the similarities and differences.
5. Prepare a table that lists (only) the content of the database and the model base of the following cases: 2, 3, 6, 8.

6. Prepare a table that summarizes the content of the dialog system in cases 2 and 3.
7. Review the AAIMS case (3) and identify the semistructured and unstructured situations described. List any structured situations.
8. Review the AAIMS case (3). Classify the decisions listed in this case against the DSS classification of Chapter 4, section 11.
9. Given existing technology, which of the limitations and difficulties of a AAIMS (case 3) could be eliminated? Be specific.
10. The RCA case (4) raises an interesting question regarding internal transfer payments for a DSS service in an organization. What do you think about this issue? Should the user pay for the use of DSS? How could charges be determined?
11. List the major contributions of the financial aid model to Wesleyan University (case 5). What DSS capabilities are particularly important in this case?
12. Explain the unstructuredness of the situations for which EPLAN (case 6) is designed.
13. Why is Conrail's DSS based around RAMIS II?
14. Identify the various tools and generators used in the development of Conrail's DSS (case 8).
15. What is a real time DSS? How does it differ from a regular DSS (see FAST, case 9)?
16. The FAST DSS includes optimization capability. Why does one need this type of capability in this case? What does the optimization specifically do?
17. Why is a vehicle-scheduling problem considered to be complex and unstructured (see case 9)?
18. Some people claim that a system such as described in the LS&B case (10) is not really a DSS. Review the case and express an opinion. Be specific.
19. The Abbott Labs DSS (case 11) was developed with a large DSS generator, EXPRESS, that sometimes is described as the "Cadillac" of DSS generators. Why was it necessary to use such an expensive generator?
20. The Abbott Labs case discusses a multidimensional analysis. What is the meaning of such an analysis and how does it differ from a single-dimension analysis?
21. Can the Abbott Labs case be considered a distributed DSS? Why or why not?
22. What competitive advantages can the Abbott Labs DSS provide when the competition is not using such a system?
23. Why was STRATEGEM (see Chapter 6) selected for the San Diego DSS?
24. List all the decisions supported in the San Diego DSS and discuss their nature.
25. What is a ready-made DSS? List some of its major advantages and disadvantages.
26. Why is Hewlett Packard's Quality Decision Management suitable as a ready-made DSS?
27. Why is the Equitable Life system regarded as a ready-made DSS?
28. What DSS capabilities are available on HP's Quality Decision Management System that qualify it as a DSS?
29. Why is a time-sharing mode appropriate for the Equitable Life Insurance Company?
30. Classification Exercise. From the information provided in the cases of this chapter, classify each case according to the following categories:

Category (per Chapter 4)
1. Model-oriented vs. data-oriented.
2. Institutional vs. ad hoc.
3. Procedural vs. nonprocedural.
4. Personal support vs. group support.
5. Sequential interdependent decisions vs. pooled interdependent decisions.

Note: One case may be classified in several categories. Do not make guesses, and write N/A if information is not available. Point to the *main* orientation of the case.
31. Identify the model base in each of the cases.

References and Bibliography

1. Alter, S. L. *Decision Support Systems: Current Practices and Continuing Challenges.* Reading, MA: Addison-Wesley, 1980.
2. Brown, D. C. "The Anatomy of a Decision Support System." *Business Marketing,* June 1985.
3. Carlson, E. D., ed. "Proceedings of a Conference on Decision Support Systems." *Data Base,* Vol. 8, No. 3, Winter 1977.
4. Chandler, J. S. et al. "Decision Support Systems Are for Small Businesses." *Management Accounting,* April 1983.
5. Edelman, F. "Managers, Computer Systems, and Productivity." *MIS Quarterly,* Vol. 5, No. 3, September 1981.
6. Franz, L. S., et al. "An Adaptive DSS for Academic Resource Planning." *Decision Sciences,* April 1981.
7. Hoover, T. B. "Decision Support at Conrail." *Datamation,* June 1983.
8. Hopkins, S. P., et al. "Financial Modeling: Four Success Stories." *EDUCOM Bulletin,* Fall 1982.
9. *HP Quality Decision Management/1000,* San Jose, CA: Hewlett-Packard, Manufacturing Productivity Division, 1984.
10. Keen, P. G. W., and M. S. Scott-Morton. *Decision Support Systems: An Organizational Perspective.* Reading, MA: Addison-Wesley, 1978.
11. Nof, S. Y., and Gurecki, R. "MDSS: Manufacturing Decision Support System." AIIE Spring Conference, May 1980.
12. Oliff, M. D. "FAST Decision Support." *Proceedings of the Decision Sciences Institute,* National Meeting, Toronto, Canada, November 1984.
13. Sol, H. G. "Processes and Tools for Decision Support." *Proceedings of the 1982 IFIP/IIASA Working Conference on DSS,* Amsterdam: North Holland.
14. Sprague, R. H., and E. D. Carlson. *Building Effective Decision Support Systems.* Englewood Cliffs, NJ: Prentice-Hall, 1982.
15. Trippi, R. R. "A Decision Support System for Real Estate Investment Portfolio Management." *Information and Management,* Vol. 15, No. 6, December 1988.

Chapter 10

Executive Information and Support Systems

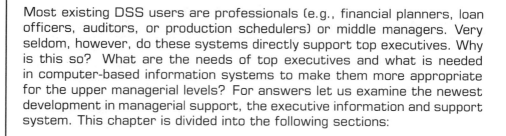

Most existing DSS users are professionals (e.g., financial planners, loan officers, auditors, or production schedulers) or middle managers. Very seldom, however, do these systems directly support top executives. Why is this so? What are the needs of top executives and what is needed in computer-based information systems to make them more appropriate for the upper managerial levels? For answers let us examine the newest development in managerial support, the executive information and support system. This chapter is divided into the following sections:

10.1   Introduction

If we examine the published information about DSS, we will find the following situation: the majority of personal DSS support professionals and middle-level managers. Institutional DSS support mainly planners, analysts, and researchers. Rarely do we see a DSS used directly by top executives. In many cases DSS tools are employed by analysts in finding answers to managers' questions.

Executive support systems (ESS), also known as executive information systems (EIS), is a new technology emerging in response to the situation just described (see Rockart and Treacy [18]). It already has its software and hardware support and is growing rapidly. In a survey conducted by the Center for Information Systems Research (CISR) at MIT, it was found that more than half the EIS systems were used by people with titles of CEO, CFO, and COO. Pilot Executive Software Co. reports (in a private communication) that 76 percent of their systems are used by top-echelon executives. In contrast, several DSS surveys clearly indicate that very few executives use the system directly.

The growth of EIS is evident in a study released in 1986 by MIT's CISR. This study shows that about one-third of large U.S. corporations now have EIS programs installed or underway. This figure has grown to over 50% in 1989 (*Computerworld*, February 27, 1989). In recognition of this fact, the DSS 86-89 International Conferences dedicated about one-third of the papers to EIS (e.g., see Fedorowicz [5]). In addition, starting in 1988, the EIS Institute is organizing national EIS conferences (EIS-88 in Washington, D.C. ; EIS-89 in San Francisco).

10.2   Executive Information System and Executive Support Systems; Definitions

The terms executive information systems (EIS) and executive support systems (ESS) mean different things to different people. In many cases the terms are being used interchangeably.

The following definitions, based on Rockart and Delong (16) and on information provided by Execucom Systems Corp.,* distinguish between EIS and ESS.

Executive Information System (EIS)

EIS is a computer-based system that serves the information needs of top executives. It provides rapid access to timely information and direct access to management reports. It is very user-friendly, supported by graphics, and provides exceptions' reporting and "drill-down" capabilities. It is also easily connected with online information services and electronic mail.

Executive Support System (ESS)

An ESS is a comprehensive support system that goes beyond EIS to include communications, office automation, analysis support and intelligence.

*Major portions of sections 2, 8, 9, 10 and 11 in this chapter were contributed by the staff of Execucom Systems Corp. (Austin TX).

The following statement is provided by Execucom System Corporation (Austin, TX) to demonstrate the differences between the two systems:

> Because EIS serves only the top executives, it does little to improve coordination and control except through the indirect effect of focusing attention throughout the organization on the executive's "critical success factors." The most severe shortcoming of an EIS, however, is that it only helps the executives understand where the organization is today—it does very little to help them visualize where it can be in the future. It delivers *information*, but not *intelligence*. To turn informati n into intelligence, you must understand how it can affect your future.
>
> A computer-based application that supports the executives' planning, analysis, and communications needs in addition to their information needs is an Executive Support System (ESS). And to build an ESS, it is necessary to add DSS capabilities. To understand this, consider Figure 10.1, which characterizes computer applications along two dimensions: the time frame addressed by the data and relationships in the application, and the analysis capabilities of the application.
>
> As this figure illustrates, EIS focuses on the present, usually presenting the executive with information within the budgeting time frame of the organization. Furthermore, it is exclusively a display technology, oriented to presenting static reports and graphs on demand. It offers no analysis capabilities to help executives explain, diagnose, and understand the information presented to them. In addition, an EIS does nothing to help executives forecast the effects of different decisions and plans they might make, or to understand the impact of different situations that might be imposed on the organization from without.

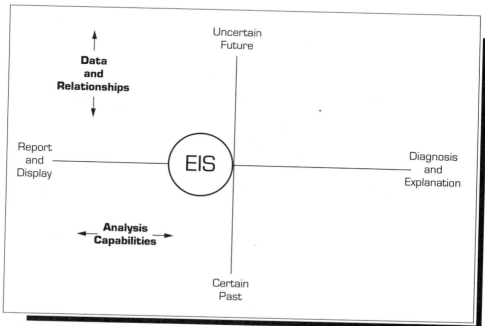

FIGURE 10.1 EIS dimensions.

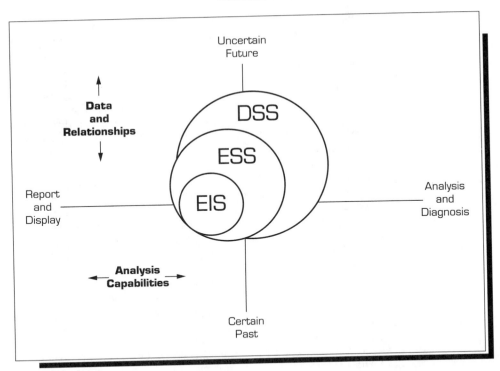

FIGURE 10.2 EIS/ESS/DSS dimensions.

Decision support system (DSS) software is designed to address applications such as strategic planning and budgeting systems that deal with the future of the organization. They offer sophisticated modeling languages and extensive analysis features for forecasting and understanding the effects of change. As Figure 10.2 illustrates, an ESS based on DSS technology can support the executives' investigations of the future, and can offer a greater ability to analyze and truly understand the information presented to them.

As stated earlier, the concepts of EIS and ESS which describe different systems, are mixed up and are used interchangeably in the literature. Furthermore, the term EIS is used in most publications to describe either system. We will use the term ESS only when analytical capabilities are clearly evident in the system.

10.3 Executive Information Needs

Executives need data and information to help them assess their organization's success and the performance of individuals critical to that success. They also need information to support top-level decisions such as:

"Should we spin-off a marginally profitable subsidiary?"

"Should we open another manufacturing plant?"

"How much long-term debt can we afford to risk?"

Such information is available both internally and externally in vast quantities. The data and information are flowing continuously and are ever changing.

The information is collected from two major sources: internal and external. Internal sources are generated from the financial, accounting, personnel, and other internal reports. The external information may come from online databases, newspapers, industry newsletters, personal contacts or government reports, just to mention a few. Such information deals with new technologies, customers, markets, competitors, legislation and the like, and it is becoming an essential competitive tool.* This collection is a part of what is called "environmental scanning." For any large or even midsize organization, the collection and analysis of such information requires a computerized system. Furthermore, there is such a large amount of information that one should be selective in its accumulation and analysis. Therefore, one of the major problems in designing an information system for executives is to correctly determine their information needs. Several studies have been conducted in order to identify these needs. An example is Rockart's study (15). Others have been conducted by McLeod and Jones. In one of their studies (12), the researchers asked five executives to keep careful track of the sources of their information. Furthermore, the executives were asked to assign an importance value to the activity or transaction for which the information was secured. The activities logged by the executive were divided into four categories. Table 10.1 shows the nature of these activities and the percentage of information transactions that were used to support them.

These and similar studies (e.g., Jones and McLeod [8]) clearly show that executives have unique information needs. However, most conventional information systems do not have the capabilities required to support these information needs. (Note: this conclusion is supported by almost all papers in the bibliography.) For example, traditional MIS usually have a slow response time because the information they manage is not oriented to the format, content, or organization of the executive's need. (Companies have been known to dismiss EIS packages that were unable to deliver the desired screen output in

TABLE 10.1 Executive Activities and Information Support.

Nature of Activity (Decision role)	Percentage of Support
Handling disturbances. A disturbance is something that happens unexpectedly and demands immediate attention, but it might take weeks or months to resolve.	42
Entrepreneural activity. Such an activity is intended to make improvements that will increase performance levels. They are strategic and long-term in nature.	32
Resource allocation. Managers allocate resources within the framework of the annual and monthly budgets. Resource allocation is tied with budget and activity planning tasks.	17
Negotiations. The manager attempts to resolve conflicts and disputes, either internal or external to the organization. Such attempts usually involve some negotiations.	3
Other	6

*Note that the distillation and interpretation of the data and information that the executive makes, based on his experience, is what creates the knowledge that give corporations their competitive edge.

How to Find Executives' Information Need

1. Asking senior executives what questions they would ask when they got back from a three-week vacation.
2. Use the critical success factor methodology (discussed in Chapter 2).
3. Interviewing all senior managers to ask what data they think is most important.
4. List the major objectives in the short and long term plans and identify their information requirements.
5. Ask the executives what information they would least like for their competition to see.
6. Either through an interview or through observation, determine what information from current management reports are actually being used by the executive.
7. Simply provide them more immediate, online access to their current management reports, and then ask them how you can better tailor the system to their needs. (Executives are much better at telling you what is wrong with what you have given them than telling you what they need.)

fewer than 20 seconds!) Another reason why many conventional information systems cannot meet the executives' needs is that these systems are primarily designed to meet the needs of the functional areas such as accounting, marketing, manufacturing, or finance. Furthermore, managerial decision making, especially that of a strategic nature, is complex and multidimensional in nature. Conventional MIS is usually designed to deal with fairly structured and much simpler configurations.

Some other deficiencies of conventional systems are that they are *not* usually designed to combine data from different sources, and they store information in unaggregated form.

Thus, there is a clear need for a specially designed support system for executives, whose characteristics are described next.

10.4 Characteristics

The following are desired characteristics of a support system for executives:

☐ Designed to meet the information needs of top executives.
☐ Principally used for tracking and control.
☐ Tailored to the management style of the individual executive.
☐ Contains extensive graphics capabilities so that information can be presented in several ways, and highlights of the implications of the data presented are generated. (See Figure 10.3)
☐ Designed to *rapidly* provide information for decisions made under pressure, that is, timely information is a critical attribute.

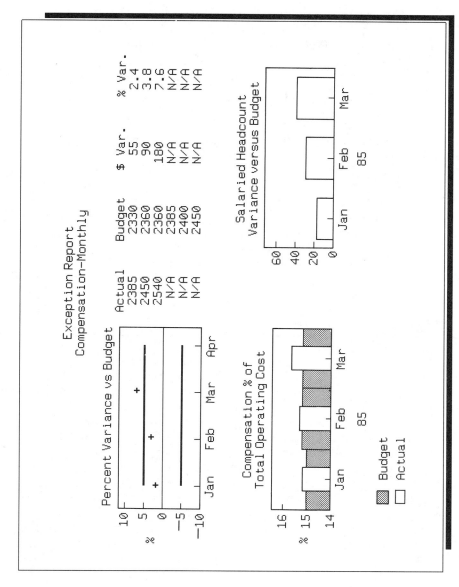

FIGURE 10.3 EIS typical graphic presentation. (*Source:* Courtesy of Pilot Executive Software, Boston, MA.)

□ Keyboard alternatives such as infrared touch pads, mouses, and touch-screen are usually provided for direct manipulation of the system.

□ Exception reporting that highlights deviations from targets is provided.

□ Text and time-series information handling capabilities are provided.

□ Designed to fit the corporate culture and the management style of the corporation.

□ Provides status access, that is, rapid access to current information.

□ Provides "drill-down" for quick access to *detailed information* behind text, numbers, or graphs. That is, the information is organized so that multiple views of the data are possible.

□ Filters, compresses, and tracks critical data.

□ Ease-of-use is critical for reducing initial training and for eliminating reorientation time when the system is used on an occasional basis.

□ Supports open-ended problem explanation since it is impossible to anticipate all situations of interest to the executive.

□ Extensively uses data on the organization's environment (Competitors, customers, industry, markets, government, international.) (Linked to external databases)

10.5   Problem Solving vs. Opportunity Assessment

Decision making is traditionally equated with problem solving. This is especially true for line supervisors and middle managers, because much of their efforts involve solving problems with specific corporate impact. However, when it comes to executives, their focus could be on making decisions that many times do not involve specific problems, but rather deal with planning, strategy formulation, and identifying opportunities. The information needed for solving specific problems and the required computer support could be completely different from the information and computer support needed for opportunity assessment or strategy formulation. Furthermore, the manner in which information is collected, presented, and used can be different in both cases.

EIS is not limited to supporting decisions. In fact, its principal use today is "tracking, control, and communication." Executives usually do not turn to an EIS for an optimum decision or solution. They turn to an EIS to make sure things are going according to plan, to gain a better intuitive grasp of the operation and the market environment, to spot opportunities or emerging trends, and to convey this information to other members of the management team. The information in an EIS might prompt the manager to make a decision, but it is not necessarily the tool that would be used once it was decided that something needs to be done. For instance, executives at GE's Major Appliance Division decided that an immediate marketing response was needed to a competitor's action reported by the EIS. Exactly what that response would be, however, might well have been determined by DSS models and simulation tools.

Timely information is the heart of EIS. That is, it is necessary to continually learn the information needs of the system users and to gain access to the most relevant information very quickly. Therefore, the newest and most innovative software, hardware, and data communication systems are needed to support EIS.

10.6   Software and Hardware

To provide the EIS capabilities discussed earlier, it is necessary to use the latest available software and hardware.

Software.   Commercially available software products typically address one or more of the following functional areas: office automation, electronic mail, information management, remote information access, and information analysis. No single product currently offers extensive features in all of these areas, although some of the more open-ended products permit ESS applications to directly incorporate additional software tools that specialize in some of these areas, such as office automation and E-Mail.

Most of the current generation of EIS require a distributed system that involves at least a minicomputer and PCs with specialized software. A representative list of EIS software products is given in Table 10.2. One of these systems, the Command Center, is described next.

The Command Center.   The Command Center includes sophisticated communications software on both the mainframe and PCs. Consequently, performance is exceptionally fast even over lower-speed communications links (such as 1200-baud dial-up lines). The structure of the Command Center is shown in Figure 10.4. Notice that the Command Center does not have a model base. However, a good EIS package will have an interface that allows it to receive and transmit data to and from DSS, free-standing model(s), or other CBIS. Since data analysis is not a thrust of this product, there is no model base. Another product, the *Executive Edge* (see Section 10), includes extensive modeling capabilities. This is because companies differ in their philosophy and strategy (see Brody [1]).

Hardware.   There are at least four options for hardware configurations for E/S. The simplest is to support the executives from mainframe computers

TABLE 10.2   Representative List of EIS Products.

Product	Vendor
CADET EIS	Southern Electricity International (Atlanta, GA)
Commander EIS	Comshare, Inc. (Ann Arbor, MI)
Command Center	Pilot Executive Software, Inc. (Boston, MA)
CEO	Data General Corp.
DirectLine	Must Software International (Norwalk, CT)
Executive Edge	EXECUCOM Systems Corp. (Austin, TX)
EASEL	Interactive Images, Inc. (Woburn, MA)
METAPHOR	Metaphor Computers, Inc. (Mountain View, CA)
OPN	Lincoln National Information (Fort Wayne, CA)
PC/Forum	Forum Systems (Santa Barbara, CA)
Probus Toolkit	Decision Technology (Stamford, CT)
Resolve	Metapraxis (United Kingdom)
RediMaster	American Information Systems, Inc. (Wellsboro, PA)

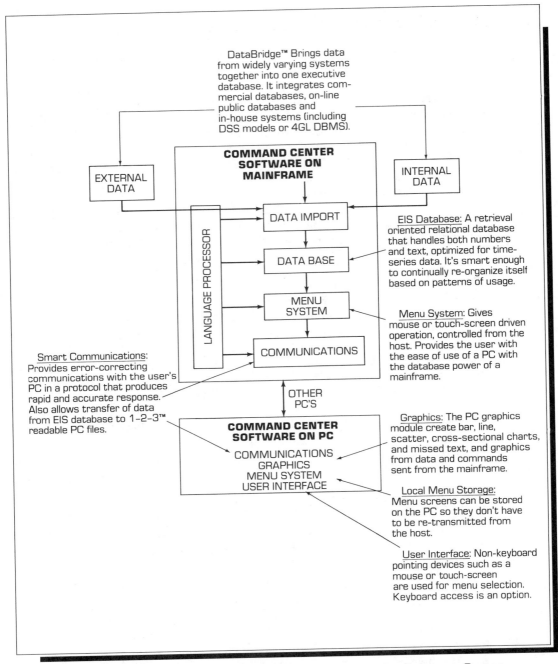

DataBridge™ Brings data from widely varying systems together into one executive database. It integrates commercial databases, on-line public databases and in-house systems (including DSS models or 4GL DBMS).

COMMAND CENTER SOFTWARE ON MAINFRAME

EXTERNAL DATA

INTERNAL DATA

LANGUAGE PROCESSOR

DATA IMPORT

DATA BASE

MENU SYSTEM

COMMUNICATIONS

EIS Database: A retrieval oriented relational database that handles both numbers and text, optimized for time-series data. It's smart enough to continually re-organize itself based on patterns of usage.

Menu System: Gives mouse or touch-screen driven operation, controlled from the host. Provides the user with the ease of use of a PC with the database power of a mainframe.

Smart Communications: Provides error-correcting communications with the user's PC in a protocol that produces rapid and accurate response. Also allows transfer of data from EIS database to 1-2-3™ readable PC files.

OTHER PC'S

COMMAND CENTER SOFTWARE ON PC

COMMUNICATIONS
GRAPHICS
MENU SYSTEM
USER INTERFACE

Graphics: The PC graphics module create bar, line, scatter, cross-sectional charts, and missed text, and graphics from data and commands sent from the mainframe.

Local Menu Storage: Menu screens can be stored on the PC so they don't have to be re-transmitted from the host.

User Interface: Non-keyboard pointing devices such as a mouse or touch-screen are used for menu selection. Keyboard access is an option.

FIGURE 10.4 Command center. (*Source:* Courtesy of Pilot Executive Software, Boston, MA.)

using graphics terminals. In general, this approach is difficult to implement successfully because the options for implementing the user interface are much more limited than is acceptable for executive users. A second configuration is to have personal computers connected to a mainframe or a minicomputer. In this situation, the PCs handle the interface and some of the data reduction functions, while the large system handles the data management and the bulk of the analysis. The third option involves PCs only. In this case information is downloaded onto standalone LANs, and then it is delivered to PCs. The fourth configuration, while not prevalent today, seems to be the configuration of the future. In this system, workstations are used in a network, so that the interface is handled on high-speed graphics display devices, and so that the data management and analysis can be distributed over the network. This "ideal" environment offers the potential of providing maximum performance and flexibility.

The key to the hardware decision is to try to match the actual delivery system with the computational philosophy of the organization. This ensures that the support of whatever system is installed will be within the capabilities of the organization itself. It also makes it easier to implement an ESS that will mesh with the corporate culture of the implementing organization.

Organizations that go with a PC-only EIS are typically smaller than organizations that use a distributed micro/mainframe solution. They have fewer executives to serve, and manage smaller EIS information bases, and so can deliver acceptable levels of performance via smaller personal computers. Larger organizations tend to prefer the micro/mainframe products such as Executive Edge, Command Center, or Commander EIS, because these tools leverage their existing investment in minicomputer/mainframe technology and databases. Larger organizations require the additional horsepower and connectivity of a shared computer to deliver acceptable response time for complex queries and analyses, to permit shared access to large information bases, and to connect executives in a geographically distributed E-Mail network.

The usefulness of PC-only systems will increase with the increased desktop horsepower. These systems will also benefit from the transparent connectivity that will be available through advances in communications and database technology. The growth in distributed database software, peer-to-peer communications, and standardized network protocols should eventually permit a LAN-based or PC-based EIS solution to offer all of the capabilities of today's micro/-mainframe solutions.

10.7 Information for Motivation

An example of information that could be provided by an EIS is the "information for motivation" concept developed by Kogan (10).

Five types of information were identified by Kogan[*] as essential for many senior managers. They are based on the concept of critical success factors (CSF), and are listed as follows:

- □ *Key Problems Narratives.* These reports highlight overall performance, key problems, and causes within an organization. Explanatory text is often combined with tables, graphs, or tabular information.
- □ *Highlight Charts.* These summary displays show high-level information based on the user's own judgment. Because they are designed from

---

[*]Much of the material in this section was condensed from Kogan (10) with permission.

the user's perspective, these displays quickly highlight areas of concern, visually signaling the state of organizational performance against CSF.

□ *Top-level Financials.* These displays provide high-level information on the overall financial health of the company in the form of absolute numbers and comparative performance ratios.

□ *Key Factors.* These displays provide specific measures of CSF, called key performance indicators (KPI), at the corporate level. The displays are often used on an exceptional basis to examine specific measures of CSF that are flagged as problems on the highlights chart.

□ *Detail KPI Responsibility Reports.* These displays indicate the detailed performance of individuals or business units in those areas critical to the success of the company.

Kogan suggested a process, called "information for motivation," for developing an EIS. This process consists of seven steps, as shown in Figure 10.5.

The seven steps are listed as follows.

Step 1: *Determine Success Factors.* Success factors are those items important to achieving the organization's goals. Success factors can be *strategic* or *operational* and are derived mainly from three sources:

□ Environmental factors
□ Organizational factors
□ Industry factors

Strategic success factors form the basis for reviewing and/or developing an organization's strategic plan. Operating success factors are used to create the EIS to track progress in day-to-day operations.

Step 2: *Review or Modify the Organization's Strategic Plan.* This review will establish the high-priority changes that senior management wants to implement.

Step 3: *Select Strategic Success Factors.* Strategic success factors are those few success factors of the greatest importance to the execution of the organization's strategies. They identify the areas of performance that must receive continuous management attention to assure implementation of the organization's strategies.

All strategic success factors must meet the following requirements:

□ They must be controllable.
□ They must be simple.
□ They must be convertible into measurable information.

Step 4: *Determine the Critical Individuals Who Should Be Motivated As Sponsors of EIS.* These individuals usually are top executives ultimately responsible for achieving strategic success and also certain lower-level managers designated to undertake specific steps to implement strategy.

Step 5: *Select Key Performance Indicators.* Key performance indicators are selected for each strategic and operational success factor. They are used to mea-

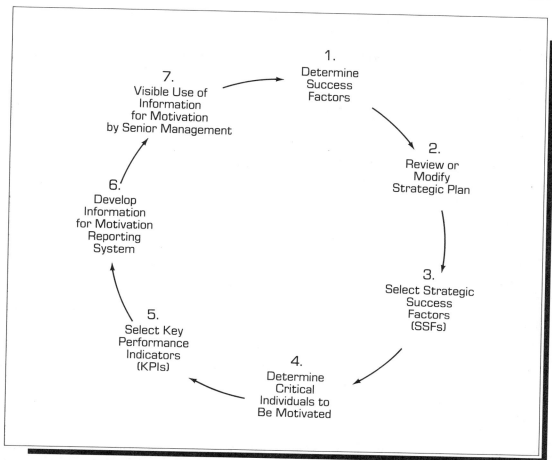

FIGURE 10.5 Information for motivation process.

sure the critical individuals' short-term progress toward achievement of strategic success. Key Performance Indicators must be explicit enough to motivate managers and help them understand that their actions influence strategic success.

    □ Responsibility Reporting
    —Responsibility reporting systems focus primarily on financial data and not on operating data or other aspects of corporate strategy.
    —The level-by-level roll up of responsibility reporting systems can obscure the performance of critical individuals in middle management.
    □ Management by Objectives
    —Some management-by-objectives systems establish performance indicators on the basis of negotiation between subordinates and superiors rather than through a clear top-down communication of corporate goals and strategy.
    —Management-by-objectives systems usually do not provide frequent reporting of performance information.

—Management-by-objectives systems usually are not automated and do not contain "what if" capabilities or a comprehensive database.
   □ Key Factor Reporting System
   —Most key factor reporting systems do not distinguish between strategic and operating information.
   —Priorities are not recognized.
   —Many key factor reporting systems provide too much information to senior management.

"Information for Motivation" differs from the traditional approaches in that it provides senior executives with only the most essential information. In summary, "Information for Motivation" offers eight unique elements:

□ Communicates the organization's strategy and goals in a top-down fashion.
□ Supplies only relevant information to senior management.
□ Ensures that the information used to monitor progress toward achieving corporate goals is consistent throughout the organization.
□ Focuses on individuals whose performance is critical to the organization's success.
□ Motivates managers to become more productive by recognizing their accomplishments.
□ Conveys information that can be used, on a regular basis, to measure and analyze managerial productivity.
□ Fits manager's style and requirements by providing management with a customized information system.
□ Implements and makes measurement practical through the use of state-of-the-art computer technology, to help executives and managers analyze the causes of performance variances and explore alternative solutions.

10.8   Integrating EIS and DSS

In a general sense, EIS is really part of the decision support field. That is, it is designed to support the top management decision process. However, in a functional sense, EIS and DSS are two different but complementary applications, and indeed they complement each other in an ESS. The differences are simple but profound. Fundamentally, EIS is a structured, automated tracking system that operates continuously to keep management abreast of what is happening in all important areas (both inside and outside the corporation). Furthermore, EIS's major role is to provide *communication*. That is, communication capabilities are *essential* in EIS but not in a DSS.

Although EIS can be considered a DSS for executives, it is distinct from traditional DSS. EIS delivers to managers information they need in their day-to-day job responsibilities. The information is typically presented in a structured, easy-to-access manner with only limited capability for ad hoc analysis. EIS tends to be used to usually perform structured, somewhat repetitive analysis, exceptions tracking, and reporting, as opposed to the unique ad hoc analysis of the traditional DSS.*

Another way to contrast EIS with the traditional DSS is to examine their objectives. EIS attempts to provide managers with enough information so that they can *ask* intelligent questions about some aspect of their business. Traditional DSS tools can then be used, usually by staff assistants and analysts, to *answer* these questions.

EIS is designed very differently from DSS (see Figure 10.6). For example, a good EIS must offer a high-speed, nontechnical method for managers to investigate business dynamics (i.e., to understand where and why things are happening so tactical changes and course corrections can be made). This is the area that distinguishes EIS from a reporting system. Any summary coming up on an EIS screen must offer instant access to the supporting detail. Otherwise it is just a glorified slide show. In addition, the supporting detail must be meaningful (e.g., time-series orientation with graphic and numerical content or written narratives from those "in the know"). In this fashion, the simple analysis or investigation can be quickly and easily accomplished by the nontechnical manager. In contrast, raw data tend not to provide executives with quick or meaningful answers to their questions.

DSS overlaps this process when more complex analysis is required to understand *why* things are happening the way they are. These appraisals are done as needed, usually require evaluation of much raw data, consume more time, and almost always require an analyst who is technically proficient with the tools at hand. The evaluation may require one analyst for one day or many analysts over several months.

An EIS can be integrated with a DSS and/or other computer-based information systems. For example, it is very common for EIS to be used as a source for PC-based modeling products. For example, at a large drug company, brand managers download from Pilot's Command Center the previous day's orders of their products. The download creates a Lotus-readable file on their PC disk. They then exit to the PC and run a Lotus DSS model against the data to predict where they will be at the end of the month. The results of this model are then uploaded to the EIS. So by 11A.M. senior managers can get on their EIS and see where each brand manager thinks he or she is going to be at the end of the month. This is a good example of the complementary nature of EIS and DSS. Another example of such integration is the system at Hardee's, a national restaurant chain. (See description in Chapter 1.)

---

*While this is the usual case, both DSS and EIS may center on the investigation and understanding of problems that are not necessarily predictable, structured, or repetitive. For this reason, successful EIS are generally characterized by the same open-endedness that DSS are.

**Executives have an even higher motivation to learn why things are happening than do analysts. For this reason, they need to have the results of both models and expert systems available to them in their support system, otherwise, they will continue to rely on people to provide them with explanations in the time frames that they are used to rather than the time frames that can be handled with computerized technology. For such an integration see the discussion in Chapter 19.

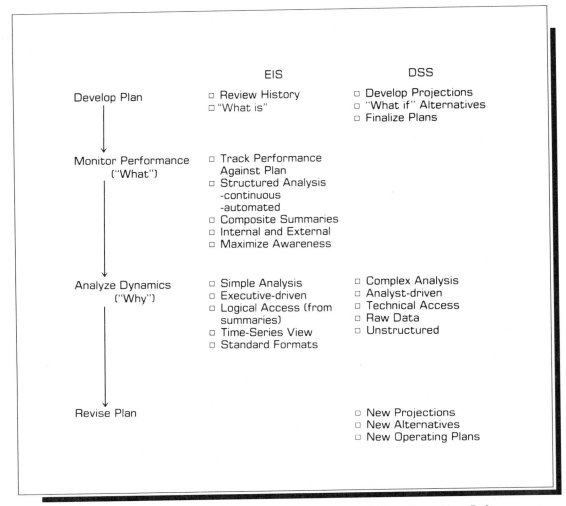

FIGURE 10.6 EIS/DSS interrelationship. (*Source:* Courtesy of Pilot Executive Software, Boston, MA.)

Finally, an EIS can be integrated with DSS and with an Expert System to create a powerful management support system. An example of such integration is the Executive Edge which is described in Section 10.10.

10.9 System Development

Like any other system, EIS can be developed in house, or it can be purchased. If developed in house it can be programmed from scratch, or it can be developed with special productivity tools. For example, Interactive Images (Woburn, MA) sells an EIS generator called EASEL.

In addition, several vendors that develop DSS generators are adapting their products so they can be used to build EIS. Of special interest are Execucom Systems (Austin, TX), which combines its IFPS/Plus with VantagePoint software in its Executive Edge product, and Information Resources (Waltham, MA) which modified its DSS generators (Express and PC Express) so they can be used to construct EIS. Combining DSS generators with EIS development software is especially useful in building integrated DSS/EIS systems.

Another approach is an attempt to modify an existing information system to serve EIS goals. Several companies attempted to turn their DSS into a dual purpose (DSS/EIS) system. This usually does not work. The reason is that a DSS that is productive for an analyst may be counterproductive for the executive. All the design criteria and the capabilities are completely different as well. These systems are designed differently and they perform different functions.

Another interesting issue is who is going to be the EIS developer. In contrast with DSS that can be built by the information system people and even by end users, EIS and ESS are usually constructed by vendors or information system consultants. The following are some explanations to this situation: First of all, it typically takes more personnel to create an EIS than to maintain it over time. Temporary consultants can make up this difference. Second, outside consultants bring a level of objectivity which might be required to identify the real needs of executives in the organization. Insiders often have too many preconceptions and too much historical perspective to correctly identify the critical success factors affecting the organization today. Executives may also be more reluctant to open up and discuss their real information problems with a member of the in-house MIS staff than with an outside consultant. Third, and perhaps most important, is that the area of computer-based executive support is too new for any established application paradigms or—probably—any extensive in-house expertise. The chances of being successful will go up appreciably if one works with experienced outside consultants who have already developed several successful executive support applications for other organizations. Experienced consultants will know the pitfalls to avoid, such as how to properly condition the expectations of the executive users. They can also ensure that the first prototype shown to the executives is both immediately useful and delivered in a reasonably short time period. Fourth, the executive user generally has many other tasks to perform and cannot take much time out of his/her already busy schedule to do the development, whereas the DSS developer's tasks are primarily oriented around the analysis of data, and so the development of the DSS is a normal part of the job. Fifth, the data requirements of an EIS typically span multiple parts of an organization, and the data itself may reside on different computer systems. The procedural difficulties that this raises can only be solved by a trained technical analyst. Sixth, the analytical underpinnings to a good EIS are sometimes quite detailed and complex. Once again, although this may be something the executives could do, it is not something they should be doing given the competing demands on their time. Seventh, the interface issues and the presentation techniques on which the system is based require the attention of professionals skilled in the communication of information. Anything less might result in information displays that could mislead. Finally, the organizational impacts of EIS can be significant. If these issues are not handled well, the EIS can easily be destroyed by political problems.

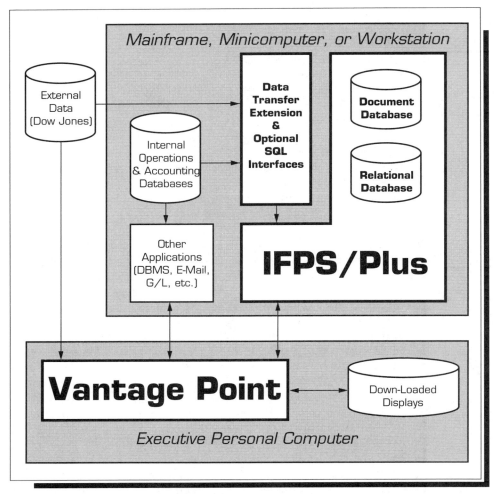

FIGURE 10.7 The Executive Edge.

10.10   The Executive Edge

The Executive Edge (from Execucom Systems Corp., Austin, TX) is an excellent example of an ESS.

As shown in Figure 10.7, Executive Edge includes Execucom's DSS generator, IFPS/Plus, along with a PC software tool called VantagePoint. IFPS/Plus provides database management for storing ESS-specific information, and some unique executive-oriented analysis capabilities (more about this follows). VantagePoint is a tool for producing a PC-style user interface that can front-end any interactive application on a remote minicomputer or mainframe. VantagePoint provides Executive Edge applications with a high level of ease-of-use, plus an open-ended ability to incorporate virtually any source of computer-based information or functionality into the executive support application.

The Executive Edge is equipped with an artificial intelligence capability to provide explanations and to answer "drill-down" questions. This capability, which is provided by IFPS/Plus, is described in Chapter 19 (integration of MSS).

Executive Edge is designed to address the ESS needs of large organizations. Its open-ended architecture is of particular value to companies with existing investments in computer-based information and operational systems. Furthermore, the inclusion of a full-featured DSS capability (IFPS/Plus) means that it can also be used as the foundation of management support applications, management information applications, and analyst-oriented decision support applications.

10.11 Executive Workstations

With few exceptions the current generation of EIS is based on PC technology (combined with mainframe analysis). This technology, however, places limitations on the timeliness of information and the ways in which the information can be combined and displayed. Newer workstation technology offers the potential to overcome some of these limitations. A workstation combines a high performance CPU, a bit-mapped graphics and windowing interface, a multitasking operating system, and network connections. The hardware functionality of a workstation is important for an EIS because it enhances the ways in which an executive can interact with the system, diminishes the time required to respond to an executive's request, and enlarges the types and number of tasks that can be performed by the system.

Figure 10.8 exemplifies the type of display environment provided by this newer technology. Each of the windows and icons in this display represents a separate active task rather than multiple views of a single task. By now, it is clear that this type of display environment, when combined with a pointing device, allows for more intuitive and obvious human/machine interaction. Not only is this type of interface simpler to use, but the display also enables the executive to browse and examine information from a variety of sources and a variety of views simultaneously. In this way the executive can detect and discover problems and relationships that might not be detected in a single window and single-tasked display.

Of course, multiwindowed displays can result in information overload. Here is where the multitasking functionality of a workstation comes into play. Simply put, multitasking means that the system can work on multiple tasks at the same time. A good example of a multitasking system is the "Trader's Workstation" (Leinweber [11]). The trader can work on an interactive analysis of selected stocks, while the workstation performs other activities in the background. At the same time the trader is doing his/her analysis, the machine is monitoring the movement of selected stocks looking for interesting changes in prices and volumes, as well as automatically carrying out various buy/sell transactions for the trader. Both of these latter activities are under the guidance of expert systems. Multitasking offers the same potential for an "Executive Workstation." Not only will it allow the executive to browse and examine information in an interactive fashion but, when combined with various software

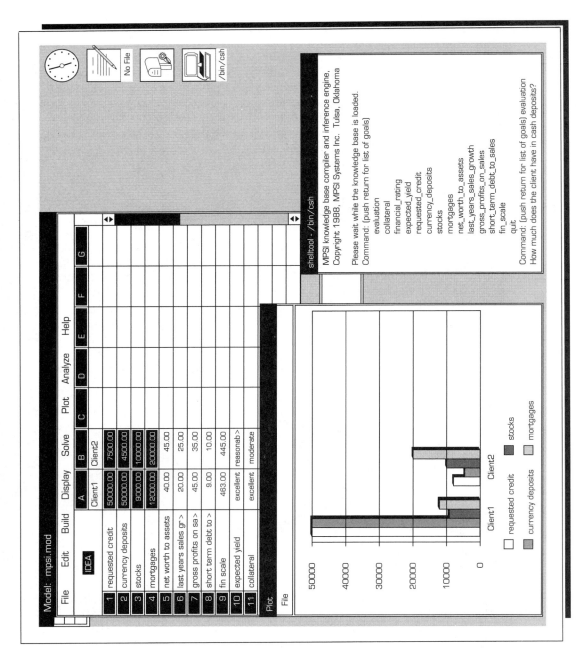

FIGURE 10.8 MPSI's Advisor. (*Source:* Courtesy of MPSI Systems, Inc.)

(e.g., expert systems), it will also enable the system to automatically monitor events in the background and inform the executive when important patterns or changes have occurred, and it will enable the system to communicate important results to other members of the management team with minimal effort and intervention on the part of the executive.

While the stand-alone features of a workstation are certainly important, equally important are its network interconnections. As several studies have indicated, an EIS must provide information in a timely, flexible, and transparent fashion. Communication links between PCs and mainframes are notoriously slow. This is why so much of the data required for an EIS must be downloaded. It is through downloading that response times are made reasonable. But this also means that the system is much less flexible and cannot respond in a timely fashion to unanticipated requests. When an unanticipated request is made, the system must again rely on the communication link to download the data. This is not a problem in a network of workstations. In a network, the data can (and usually do) reside virtually anywhere. When a user issues a request for information, there is little need to specify the location of the information. This is left to the software and hardware of the network. Given the speed of most networks, it usually appears to the user as if the data were located on his or her local workstation. In fact the window on the lower right in Figure 10.8 is actually a display of an expert system running on an entirely different workstation on the network. To the user, however, the window looks like every other window in the display.

Currently, most workstations are used in the realms of science and engineering. The experiences in these domains indicate that workstation technology provides a wide-ranging environment that aids a number of programming and communication tasks. With this technology, the increase in productivity is usually multifold. The increases occur because many of the tasks traditionally performed by the user are now relegated to the workstation. They also occur because these environments encapsulate the user and protect him or her from making obvious mistakes. This is done by building context information into all of the areas of the system with which the user interacts. Then, whenever an action occurs, it can be compared to expected actions or permissible actions, and the user can be notified appropriately. Workstations are beginning to work their way into the business and financial arenas (e.g., the Trader's Workstation). There is every reason to expect that the impact on the productivity of executives and other managers will be the same as on that of engineers.

10.12   EIS Implementation

The implementation of EIS could be different than the implementation of DSS (Chapter 20) because it involves executives. De Long and Rockart (2) offer the following list of factors that they feel are critical for the successful implementation of EIS:

1. *A committed and informed executive sponsor.* There must be an executive who has both a realistic understanding of the capabilities (and limitations) of EIS, and who really wants the system so badly that he or she

is willing to put considerable time and energy into seeing that a system gets developed. There should also be commitment of company resources for a long period.

2. *An operating sponsor.* Because the executive sponsor usually lacks sufficient time to devote to the project, it appears very worthwhile to have an "operating sponsor" designated to manage the details of implementation from the user's side.

3. *Clear link to business objective(s).* The EIS must help in solving business problems or meet a need that is addressed most effectively with information systems (IS) technology. There should be a clear benefit to using the technology. It must provide something that would not otherwise be available, such as very rapid access to external databases, superb graphical displays, or data with textual annotations.

4. *Appropriate IS resources.* The quality of the EIS project manager on the IS side is most critical. This person should have not only technical knowledge, but also business knowledge and the ability to communicate effectively with senior management.

5. *Appropriate technology.* The choice of hardware and software has a major bearing on the acceptance or rejection of a system. One of the early barriers to executive support systems has been the lack of hardware and software that could meet the demands of highly variable executive work styles and environments. Things are improving, however, as more and more products are being designed specifically for the EIS market.

6. *Management of data problems.* The physical and technical ability to provide reliable access to data can be a major issue in EIS development. Aggregating, accessing, and managing databases in a corporation with multiple divisions can be the biggest physical roadblock to the EIS implementation.

7. *Management of organizational resistance.* Political resistance to EIS is one of the most common causes of implementation failure. An EIS alters information flows, and this always has the potential to significantly shift power relationships in a company.

8. *Management of spread and system evaluation.* An installation that is successful and used regularly by the executive sponsor will almost inevitably produce demand by peers or subordinates for access to a similar system. For further discussion of EIS implementation see: Raths, D., "The Politics of EIS," *Infoworld*, May 15, 1989.

10.13   Summary and Conclusion

For an information system to be classified as an EIS, it must possess the following features:

1. It must be consistently utilized by executives.
2. It must include exception and "drill-down" capabilities.
3. It should provide easy access to the current status and projected trends of the business.

4. It should fit the management style of the user.
5. It should contain extensive graphics support.

Executive information and support systems are a development of major importance to management for the following reasons. First, EIS uses the latest technology to improve management's productivity. Second, EIS acts as an executive's filter, causing information to be compressed and summarized in a manner dictated by each user. Third, EIS is designed to match the personal information preference of the executive. Finally, the system goes beyond advanced technology to provide added value based on an understanding of management's role.

EIS supports managerial problem solving. However, it also supports opportunity analysis, or it may simply put an executive in a better position to understand the operations of his or her organization.

The emergence of EIS may be signaling a new era in the organizational use of computers. EIS enables more top managers and their staff to use computers to access and analyze data. It can be seen as an important management support system, complementing DSS and ES or integrating with them.

Questions for Review and Discussion

1. If a DSS is employed in finding answers to management questions, what is the EIS used for?
2. Prepare a table that shows the major differences between DSS and EIS.
3. Discuss the concept of status access and contrast it with ad hoc analysis.
4. Review the five types of information essential to senior management. Relate these to a fast-food company and to a hospital. (Be specific and imaginative in your response.)
5. Prepare a table that shows the differences between a traditional reporting system and an EIS. Use Kogan's list, but add to it from your own experience.
6. American Can Company announced in early 1986 that it was interested in acquiring a company in the health maintenance organization (HMO) field. Two decisions are involved in this act: (1) the decision to acquire an HMO, and (2) the decision of which one to acquire. How can a DSS and EIS be used in such a situation?
7. Why is a typical office automation system insufficient for providing executives' needs?
8. Compare the structure of EIS with that of a typical DSS and comment on the differences.
9. Why is it necessary to include both a mainframe and PCs in an EIS?
10. It is said that EIS supports unstructured decisions. It is also said that EIS is used to perform structured, somewhat repetitive analyses. Use Simon's phases of the decision-making process to reconcile these statements.
11. What is the difference between EIS and ESS?
12. Why can't a conventional MIS fulfill the information needs of executives?
13. Why is it advisable to use vendors or consultants to build an EIS?
14. List a few approaches that can be used to discover the information needs of executives.
15. List the major benefits of executive workstations.

CASE: Fisher-Price's
Integrated Executive Information System[*]

Introduction

Fisher-Price is a manufacturing, marketing, and distribution company with three distinct business groups, Infant, Traditional, and Promotional Products. Headquartered in East Aurora, New York, Fisher-Price is one of the major manufacturers in the highly competitive U.S. toy industry and has a substantial international business in Canada and Europe. Since fiscal 1983, a depressed sales year, real growth in the U.S. market (nominal U.S. sales adjusted for price increases) for Fisher-Price has been 17% per year. The strong gains in real sales growth reflect the successful change in strategic orientation facilitated by the alignment of the information systems strategy with a new business strategy.

Fisher-Price has successfully integrated various management information and support systems into their strategic business plans. Their information systems (IS) objective has been to develop innovative uses of computer and communication technologies for strategic advantage and, where necessary, defensive competitive action. Operationally, they have developed sophisticated decision support systems (DSS) and an executive information system (EIS) in response to their long-range plan to bring the sales force and all levels of management into the 1990s.

The success and direction of the EIS at Fisher-Price has been due to the synergistic effect of several driving forces. The president of Fisher-Price and the vice presidents of IS and Sales and Marketing have been prime EIS sponsors and users since inception. The EIS development team, which included executives, an executive staff, and systems analysts, had thorough knowledge of the business of the firm, technical and interpersonal skills, and the ability to organize data from internal and external sources. Finally and most important is the integral link between their time-based strategic goals and the EIS. A senior project analyst was assigned to handle the daily details associated with operation of the EIS.

Fisher-Price Redefines Its Business Orientation

During the early 1980s, Fisher-Price's business orientation shifted from being manufacturing-driven to market-driven with a focus on market demand responsiveness. The business redefinition necessitated the real-time capture, access, and reporting of internal and market data for planning, analyzing, and monitoring the performance of products, categories, customers, and the total business. This scenario initiated the development and integration of an executive information system (EIS). Custom developed applications systems were developed to interface with the electronic data interchange (EDI) networks of General Electric Information Service Company (GEIS-CO) and McDonnell-Douglas. The EDI system enables Fisher-Price to pick-up hundreds of files on a one-to-one relationship eliminating their customers' need to dial Fisher-Price directly. Through these third-party networks, Fisher-Price is able to transfer information and documents electronically with their retailers, which collapses the time required for receipt and entry of purchase orders. Retail customers also are invoiced electronically to reduce paperwork and errors, a benefit to both Fisher-Price and their retailers. The EIS synthesizes data that is received via EDI into meaningful formats to support tracking and control activities and strategic planning. In addition, Fisher-

[*]This case was written by Linda Volonino (Canisus College, Buffalo, NY) and Gerry Drinkard (Fisher-Price, East Aurora, NY). A modified version of the case appears in *DSS-89 Transactions*. The case is reproduced with permission of the authors and the Institute of Management Sciences.

TABLE 10.3 Objectives and Expected Benefits of the EIS.

1. To provide all levels of management and the sales force with the appropriate up-to-date information.
2. To provide management with enhanced control reporting on customer and territory experience.
3. To develop accounting reports that accurately reflect transactional level summary totals and appropriately meet management planning, monitoring, and control needs.
4. To reduce dependence on Customer Service personnel to answer questions. This would reduce the number of Customer Service personnel and decrease telephone charges.
5. To reduce requests for systems to perform ad hoc reporting.
6. To reduce paper and printing expenditures together with handling and mailing costs.

Price is attempting to monitor inventory at the retail level through the receipt of point of sale (POS) information received through EDI.

Prior to EIS development, the management information systems environment was deficient, characterized by a lack of credible information systems technology and generally computer-illiterate management and clerics. Therefore, there were simultaneous and complementary transformations in the IS department's systems support orientation and Fisher-Price's business orientation. By integrating and coordinating IS planning with strategic planning, Fisher-Price has achieved better materials/inventory management and control systems, improved forecasting systems, quicker response to the marketplace, and better business relationships with key retail customers.

The Initiation of the EIS

Fisher-Price considers itself a "marketing company that also does manufacturing." Thus, sales is the most important critical success factor. However, during the design of a sophisticated sales information system, it was recognized that there is a strong tie between sales and other success factors. Therefore, the IS people proposed to expand the Sales Information System into a comprehensive EIS.

By 1985, IS management had directionally sold general management on their initial project plan of attack for the EIS. The proposed objectives and expected benefits of the EIS are listed in Table 10.3. Before development of the EIS, software, hardware, personnel, and training costs were estimated. Potential benefits of the EIS were assessed subjectively using intuitive feelings of improved decision making, particularly strategic decision making.

Recognizing the need for a comprehensive system to support each of the managerial levels as well as the sales and marketing people, the systems analysts worked concurrently with the president and general management to define what information was required from their immediate subordinates. The president was very computer-knowledgeable and became a prime EIS advocate and user. Knowing what he required to do his job helped significantly in the development of the EIS. When the IS staff began interviewing at the sales force level, their managers had already defined what they needed from the sales people in order to perform effectively.

In summary, the primary goal at the preliminary stage of EIS development was to provide information about customers, products, sales, shipments, and orders. Thus, initially their EIS plan took on the connotation of a sales system.

The Structure of the EIS

The internal structure of the EIS is shown in Figure 10.9. Three modules, SIL, DISTRIBUTION, and PLANNING, are fully functional. The EIS menu concept is being expanded into a more macrolevel menu concept with the inclusion of a HUMAN RESOURCE MODULE (human resource information is currently being entered) and a RETAIL module that is soon to be started.

The Sales-Info-Link (SIL) Module

Numerous screens and reports can be generated from the "Executive Window," "Product/Category Window," and "Customer Reporting Window" selections listed on the SIL main menu. The Executive Window and a sample screen of the month-to-date and year-to-date status for the U.S. toy industry are shown in Figure 10.10.

Summary level records by the hundreds are tunnelled through menus, each with help screen backgrounds, to provide each level of management with the information appropriate to their status in real-time at any level of aggregation. Five levels of information are available, the individual product, product category, business group, sales person, and customer levels for each geographical region. Various levels of detail can be accessed because it is left to the user to define his information and reporting needs. Documentation and a table of contents sit behind every screen and are accessible by simply typing HELP. The system is so user-friendly that if an executive makes a mistake, it will roll him or her back to a point from which he or she automatically knows how to proceed: the opening menu.

The Distribution Module

Aggressive growth was promoting the need for responsive system support for the sales force who had been selling products without information on product availability. With the recognition that the sales force required significant amounts of product

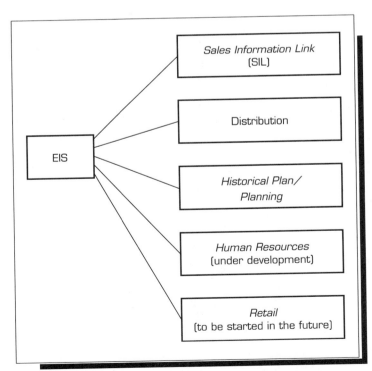

FIGURE 10.9 Fisher-Price's Executive Information System.

```
U.S.                        S A L E S - I N F O - L I N K               03/23/90
                             **  EXECUTIVE WINDOW  **                    HST1 0
-------------------------------------------------------------------------------
                  ----------- MTD INQUIRIES ------------  ( --- OPTIONAL --- )
                     1.   MTD/YTD Status                   BS
                     2.   Monthly Sales By Day             BS MO YR
                     3.   Summary - All Bus Seg

                  ------------ YTD INQUIRIES ------------
                     4.   Act vs Plan - Shpmts             BS YR CF
                     5.   Act vs Plan - Orders             BS YR CF
               *     6.   Ord & Shpmt (Reg, C/O)           BS YR CF
               *     7.   Current Yr vs Last Yr            BS
               *     8.   Sales Detail                     BS YR CF
               *     9.   Summary - All Bus Seg               CF
               *    10.   Summary - All Mkt Grp               YR CF
-------------------------------------------------------------------------------
   * Sales Totalled By Product Line
                        (---------------------- OPTIONAL ----------------------)
         SELECTION < >       BS  < >  MO  < >  YR  < >  CF  < >

                  XMIT Options:    Help (H)   Quit (Q)
   A                                                            XMIT  <  >
```

```
U.S.                            M.T.D. & Y.T.D                     THRU 11/16/89
TOY BUSINESS                        STATUS                          <HST1 0>
-------------------------------------------------------------------------------

000's
                     ----------- MONTH TO DATE -----------
            (----------- SHIPMENT DOLLARS ----------- )   (--------ORDER DOLLARS--------)
             MTD     PLAN     IR-1   A-TEAM               MTD      PLAN      IR-1
REGULAR    18,737   38,830   35,871  36,500             14,086-   11,000   12,872
C/O            96    1,000                                  53-
TOTAL      18,833   39,830   35,871                     14,139-   11,000   12,872

-------------------------------------------------------------------------------
(---- TODAY'S STATUS ----)    (CALENDAR YR COMPARISON)      (------FISCAL YTD -----)
       SHPMT   ASSIGN        SHPMTS   CUR YR   LST YR       SHPMTS   124,243
REG     772    7,210          MTD     18,833   23,215       ORDERS    19,584
C/O              8            YTD    345,197  250,615
                             TOT              262,943       (------ UNFILLED -----)
(------- LAST MONTH -------)  ORDERS                        M/E       53,757
TOT SHPMT     47,361          MTD     14,139   19,279       C-Y/E     73,063
PLAN         58,952          YTD    387,795  269,594        F-Y/E     75,938
IR-0         10,871          TOT             281,213        LST-YR    18,980
-------------------------------------------------------------------------------

                  XMIT Options:    Help (H)   Quit (Q)
   A                                                            XMIT  <  >
```

FIGURE 10.10 Executive Window and Sample Screen of M.T.D. & Y.T.D. Status.

availability and distribution information, the DISTRIBUTION MODULE was developed and added to the EIS.

Another factor contributing to the development of this module was the need for distribution resource planning (DRP). The trend toward *quick response* in the retail trade increased Fisher-Price's need to strictly monitor production and coordinate quick response with distribution. In retailing, quick response means receiving products when they are needed for sale, comparable to the JIT concept. Currently, neither retailers nor manufacturers want finished goods inventory. Storage limitations at Fisher-Price would be exceeded within a short time period without a planned flow of shipments. Because their products are high volume/low value, distribution costs are approximately 3 percent to 5 percent of the cost of the product. DRP has enabled Fisher-Price to move product efficiently. Therefore, sales/production/distribution coordination are extremely important.

The Historical Planning Module

The HISTORICAL PLANNING module was appended to the EIS to support and monitor short- and long-range planning and forecasting. These activities require information regarding the anticipated changes in demographics and tastes. Projected sales of each product are stored in the corporate database for comparison with actual sales to date. Since many of their promotional products have short product life cycles, it is critical to monitor their performance in the highly competitive toy market. This information helps research and development planning by indicating when new products are necessary and what types of products are expected to be in demand.

The Human Resources Module

This module will include information about all management employees, their skills and potential development. It will be used to identify managers when needed and to deal with any issue involving changes in human resources. In addition, the module will have information on all other employees and statistics about salaries, fringe benefits, and recruiting strategies.

The Retail Module

This module will provide information about customers and sales which are not included in the SIL. The emphasis here will be on the retail level. Consumer behavior information, retail requirement, and competitors' strategies aiming at the retailers will be included.

Integration with Other Computer-based Information Systems

Fisher-Price has integrated various management information systems into their strategic plans, but has not integrated all of these systems into the EIS. For example, at the core of their marketing information system is ADDATA, a marketing tool that runs on its Burroughs mainframe and provides storage and retrieval capabilities along with forecasting modules to support the monitoring and planning needs of the marketing managers. On the Control Data mainframe, a decision support system built with APEX 4 is used to support operations research functions. Fisher-Price also has a CAD/CAM system. The company investigated the use of expert systems, but was unable to find a suitable expert system application at the present. The various departments can download data from the corporate database of the EIS into their departmental systems, but they are not directly integrated with the EIS. A similar interface is available between the EIS and the systems. (For the difference between a direct integration and an interface see Chapter 19.) Of special interest are the ties with the EDI described earlier. This integration is shown in Figure 10.11.

Benefits and Impacts of the EIS

Previously, clerks had prepared information that arrived a month late. This created a 30-day blind side for the marketing, production, and distribution managers. With the EIS, information is available the same day it is created, online in a real-time environment. The EIS has literally hundreds of possible screens to satisfy information requirements for anticipated and unanticipated queries and reporting. This has driven

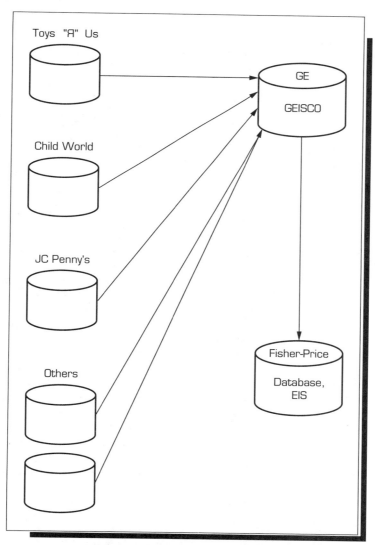

FIGURE 10.11 Electronic Data Interchange System (EDI).

managers to become daily hands-on users of the EIS. Executive analysis changed from "analysis of what had occurred 30 days ago" to "analysis of today." Additional impacts on the corporate environment and culture are summarized in Table 10.4.

The EIS enables senior-level managers to investigate Fisher-Price's business dynamics by providing quick, flexible access to timely information. It gives managers the time for analysis that they previously did not have. It collapses time—a critical factor to Fisher-Price. The overall impression of the EIS is that it is sufficient for executives to operate effectively in their highly competitive industry.

TABLE 10.4 Key Environmental and Cultural Situations Before and After EIS Introduction.

Before EIS Introduction: 1970s and Early 1980s	After EIS Introduction: Mid and Late 1980s
Environment	**Environment**
Redefinition of the business occurring	Orientation toward the importance of sales and marketing
Strategy change from manufacturing-driven to market-driven	Market-driven strategy in effect
Aggressive growth promoting the need for responsive system support because the boundaries of the capabilities of the people had been exceeded	Inertia of the business (1983) necessitated better surveillance of products and customers
Business vocabulary that was provincial in nature	Online-reporting
Hardcopy reporting	Solid transaction level systems in place
Systems that had been developed over a 20-year period	Computer-literate people and IS technology in place
No corporate database	Top-down system planning and support: Systems analysts actively helped users define their information needs
Bottom-up systems approach: Systems analysts did not proactively help users define their information needs	
Culture	**Culture**
Predominantly one of *dependence* on IS personnel and other groups for information, because managers and the work force were non–computer literate and there was very limited IS technology in place. The impacts of this dependence included:	*Independence* from IS personnel and clerics because of quick, easy data access and computer literacy. Impacts of this independence include:
Mistrust of data due to the lack of timeliness and inconsistency leading to redundant work because each manager requested the development of his or her own reports	Data was trusted and considered credible
	Reduced need for clerical staff
Use of the clerical staff to get, prepare, and route data and reports	Information accessed directly by top managers without the assistance of intermediaries
A need to balance data obtained from various data stores and systems	Broader online, "friendly" access to timely information
	Solid bonding of client areas with the systems' capabilities
Emphasis on maintaining the strong franchise through extensive product testing	More time available for detailed analysis
	Much more professional sales force
	Emphasis on leveraging the strong consumer franchise through improved customer support

In response to the question of what it is that executives look at, the answer is "Most executives look at what they are interested in, but they have all information available." Thus, the EIS supports the intuitive process. More specifically, the EIS is used to examine the distinctions between *what was* budgeted and *what is* occurring and to provide consistency in measuring performance. It is used by the sales, marketing research, financial department managers and executives for forecasting and surveillance. This is crucial because popular toys such as Rubik's Cube, Atari, and Cabbage Patch dolls siphon off toy sales from Fisher-Price. Promotional products require diligent scanning due to their potential for a very short product life cycle. However, the EIS is not just a control reporting system that flags deviations from the norm.

Conclusion

Fisher-Price has improved its competitiveness by integrating an EIS into the strategic plans. The EIS and EDI systems provide Fisher-Price's top managers with the speed and flexibility to respond to their rapidly changing markets. They have established excellence in all the marketing and manufacturing basics by clarifying the business and information systems strategies, making a commitment to quality, improving inventory management and materials handling, upgrading the manufacturing process, shortening the product-development cycle, and marketing aggressively abroad. This excellence has been achieved through continuous learning about how to compete better through information systems and technology.

QUESTIONS

1. Why is EIS so important for Fisher-Price?

2. What are some of the reasons that made this EIS a success?

3. Why was a sophisticated "sales information system" insufficient even though "sales" is the most important success factor?

4. Comment on the internal structure of this EIS.

5. Describe the major information delivered by the SIL.

6. The EIS is connected to other computerized systems. Describe these connections and their purpose.

7. Describe the *benefits* of the EIS.

8. How can EIS be improved? To answer this question refer to some of the attributes of advanced EIS described in this chapter.

CASE: Kraft's ESS

Kraft's Grocery Products Group (GPG) recently implemented an executive information system based on Commander EIS software from Comshare of Ann Arbor, Michigan.* This new system has given the group's top decision makers the highly analyzed,

---

*Condensed from "Implementing an EIS," *Information Center*, February, 1988.

refined, and summarized data they need to steer their organization into an even more successful future in a very competitive marketplace. The idea of EIS came from the development of a mainframe-based profit-planning system, which utilized Comshare's decision support generator—System W. System W's ability to direct interface, execution of monthly data analysis, and distributed modeling capability fulfilled a very real information need by providing GPG with an integrated database for monthly analysis of operating results by product line and by region. It also gave GPG planners the ability to develop annual operating and long-term strategic plans.

Commander was chosen as the delivery vehicle for EIS because it would provide direct interface to Kraft's profit-planning system. Therefore, no separate mainframe database would be required to feed the EIS. In addition, its compatibility with current touch screen and PC-mouse technology meant GPG executives could easily learn to use the EIS without memorizing computer commands or worrying about keystrokes. The Execu-View portion of Commander can integrate EIS with System W, which means the narrative analysis could be integrated into reporting flow by its Workstation Manager feature, thus enabling analysts to provide narrative explanations of variances right beside the variance data.

The system was implemented in three phases—offering hard-coded reporting through Commander EIS, online interactive database access through Execu-View, and external access to a public newswire database. The hard-coded reporting portion of the EIS was structured to provide three views of the profit-planning database—total group, regional, and brand group level. "Hot spot" functionality added to the hard-coded reports using Commander Builder allows GPG executives to toggle between the three views of the database in order to access deeper levels of detail in the current view (referred to as the "drill-down" approach). When fully detailed information is needed, the Execu-View portion of the GPG EIS is intended to give executives all of the multidimensional capabilities of System W. Execu-View provides access to the 100 detail variables and products tracked by the profit-planning system under System W by taking snapshots of models from the mainframe and downloading them to the user's PC. Perhaps the most encouraging feedback had been the many requests for bringing more information into the EIS and the extensive use of Execu-View to go beyond the data provided by the Commander reporting portion of the system.

Since much of an executive's office time is spent in meetings, the time he or she has to spend with critical data is usually early morning or late evening hours. This resulted in future implementation of a remote communications link to allow executives to access the EIS from their homes. In addition, further plans like providing executives with goal-seeking capabilities, front-end interfaces to internal and external database, and an electronic mail system are being explored.

QUESTIONS

1. Why was the Commander EIS software selected?
2. List some of the benefits of Kraft's ESS.
3. List some of the features of the user interface that made this system a success.
4. Explain why it is easy to provide narrative explanations of variances right beside the variance data.
5. Analysis is done on three levels: corporate, region, and product. How does the ESS help such analysis?
6. What is meant by "multidimensional capabilities"?
7. Why is the company planning a remote communications link?

References and Bibliography

1. Brody, H. "Computers Invade the Executive Suite." *High Technology Business*, February 1988.
2. DeLong, D. W., and J. F. Rockart. "Identifying the Attributes of Successful Executive Support System Implementation." In Fedorowicz (5).
3. *EIS Conference Report*. Newsletter, McLean, VA: AUI Data Graphics, 1988.
4. El Sawy, O. A., ed. *DSS 87 Transactions*. 7th Annual Conference on DSS. San Francisco: Institute of Management Sciences, June 1987.
5. Fedorowicz, J., ed. *DSS 86 Transactions*. 6th Annual Conference on DSS. Washington, D.C.: Institute of Management Sciences, April 1986.
6. Friend, D. "Executive Information Systems: Successes, Failures, Insights and Misconceptions." In Fedorowicz (5).
7. "Implementing an EIS: Two Stories." *Information Center*, February 1988.
8. Jones, J. W., and R. McLeod. "The Structure of Executive Information Systems: An Exploratory Analysis." *Decision Sciences*, Spring 1986.
9. Jordon, M. L. "Executive Information System—Make Life Easy For the Lucky Few." *Computerworld*, February 29, 1988.
10. Kogan, J. M., "Information for Motivation; A Key to Executive Information System That Translates Strategy Into Results for Management." In Fedorowicz (5).
11. Leinweber, D. "Finance." In *Expert Systems and AI: Applications and Management*. T. C. Bartee, ed. Indianapolis: H. W. Sams, 1988.
12. McLeod, R. Jr., and J. W. Jones. "Making Executive Information Systems More Effective." *Business Horizons*, September–October, 1986.
13. Paller, A. "EIS Applications Catching on With Feds." *Government Comp. News*, June 1988.
14. Rinaldi, D., and Jastrzembski. "Executive Information Systems, Put Strategic Data at Your CEO's Fingertips." *Computerworld*, October 27, 1986.
15. Rockart, J. F. "Chief Executives Define Their Own Data Needs." *Harvard Business Review*, January–February, 1982.
16. Rockart, J. F., and D. DeLong. *Executive Information Systems*. Homewood, IL: Dow Jones-Irwin, 1988.
17. Rockart, J. F., and D. W. DeLong. "Executives Support Systems and the Nature of Executive Work." Report #WP B5, Center for Information Systems Search, MIT, April 1986.
18. Rockart, J. F., and M. E. Treacy. "The CEO Goes On-Line." *Harvard Business Review*, January–February, 1982.
19. Siragusa, G. "The Executive Workstation—Fancy Phone or Productivity Tool?" *Administrative Management*, February 1986.
20. Williams, M. W. "The EIS-Man Cometh." *Chief Information Officer*, June 1988.

Chapter 11

Applied Artificial Intelligence

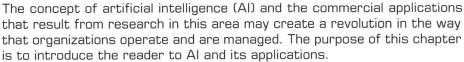

The concept of artificial intelligence (AI) and the commercial applications that result from research in this area may create a revolution in the way that organizations operate and are managed. The purpose of this chapter is to introduce the reader to AI and its applications.

Expert systems, which is a main topic of this book, is one of the applied areas of AI. Furthermore, another applied area, natural language processing, can be integrated into MSS, making them most useful.

This chapter covers the following topics:

11.1 Introduction

The past few years have witnessed an increased interest in applied AI. The topic is enjoying tremendous publicity. Many major periodicals have published cover stories on the topic or have dedicated special issues to AI. Dozens of books on AI have appeared on the market. Many AI newsletters are also being published regularly, and conferences and conventions are being held worldwide on this topic. To a certain extent, AI has become a sensation. The number of AI vendors in the United States broke the 200 mark in March 1985 (see Dickens and Newquist [14]), and it approached 400 in late 1989.

The commercial applications of AI are projected to reach $10 billion by the early 1990s. Major management consulting firms (e.g., A.D. Little and Arthur Andersen) are deeply involved in applied AI. Many research institutions in the United States and all over the world are also heavily involved in AI research projects.

These developments may have a significant impact on many organizations, both private and public, and on the manner in which organizations are being managed. AI technologies already have a major impact on MSS.

11.2 Definitions

Artificial intelligence is a term that encompasses many definitions.* The various topics in the following sections attempt to define and explain the major areas that fall within applied AI. Most experts would agree that AI is concerned with two basic ideas. First, it involves studying the thought processes of humans (to understand what intelligence is); second, it deals with representing those processes via machines (computers, robots, etc.).

A well-publicized definition of AI is as follows: Behavior by a machine that, if performed by a human being, would be called intelligent.

A thought-provoking definition is provided by E. Rich (29): "Artificial Intelligence is the study of how to make computers do things at which, at the moment, people are better."

Let us explore the meaning of "intelligent behavior." Listed below are several abilities considered as signs of intelligence derived from various definitions of intelligence):

☐ Learn or understand from experience.
☐ Make sense out of ambiguous or contradictory messages.
☐ Respond quickly and successfully to a new situation (different responses, flexibility).
☐ Use reason in solving problems and directing conduct effectively.
☐ Deal with perplexing situations.

---

*For a list of 16 definitions, see Dicken and Newquist (14).

□ Understand and infer in ordinary, rational ways.
□ Apply knowledge to manipulate the environment.
□ Acquire and apply knowledge.
□ Think and reason.
□ Recognize the relative importance of different elements in a situation.

An interesting test designed to find out if a computer exhibits intelligent behavior was designed by Alan Turing of the United Kingdom.

The Turing Test. According to this test, a computer could be considered to be thinking only when a human interviewer, conversing with both an unseen human being and an unseen computer, could not determine which is which.

The definitions of AI presented previously concentrated on the comparison between the abilities of humans and the abilities of computers. The following definitions of AI focus on decision making and problem solving, topics that are the core of this book.

Symbolic Processing. Symbolic processing (see Chapter 12 Section 4) is an essential characteristic of artificial intelligence as reflected in the following definition: "Artificial intelligence is that branch of computer science dealing with symbolic, nonalgorithmic methods of problem solving."

This definition focuses on two characteristics of computer programs:

□ *Numeric vs. Symbolic*—Computers were originally designed specifically to process numbers. People, however, tend to think symbolically; our intelligence seems to be based, in part, on our mental ability to manipulate symbols, rather than just numbers.
□ *Algorithmic vs. Nonalgorithmic*—An *algorithm* is a step-by-step procedure with well-defined starting and ending points, guaranteed to reach a solution to a specific problem. Computer architecture readily lends itself to this step-by-step approach. Many human reasoning processes, however, tend to be nonalgorithmic; in other words, our mental activities consist of more than just following logical, step-by-step procedures.

Much AI research continues to be devoted to symbolic and nonalgorithmic processing techniques in an attempt to emulate the human reasoning processes more and more by a computer.

Heuristics and Artificial Intelligence. Heuristics are included as a key element of AI in the following definition: "Artificial intelligence is the branch of computer science that deals with ways of representing knowledge using symbols rather than numbers and with rules-of-thumb, or heuristics, methods for processing information" (Encyclopedia Britannica).

People frequently use heuristics, consciously or otherwise, to make decisions. By using the heuristics one does not have to rethink completely what to do every time a problem is encountered.

Pattern Matching (Recognition). Another definition of AI focuses on pattern-matching techniques: "Artificial intelligence works with pattern-matching methods which attempt to describe objects, events, or processes in terms of their qualitative features and logical and computational relationships."

Computers can be used to collect information about objects, events, or processes; and, of course, computers can process large amounts of information more efficiently than people can. People, however, instinctively do some things that have been very difficult to program into a computer: they recognize relationships between things; they sense qualities, and spot patterns that explain how various items relate to each other.

Newspaper photographs are nothing more than collections of minute dots, yet without any conscious effort, people discover the patterns that reveal faces and other objects in those photos. Similarly, one of the ways that humans make sense of the world is by recognizing the relationships and patterns that help give meaning to the objects and events that they encounter.

If computers are to become more intelligent, they must be able to make the same kinds of associations among the qualities of objects, events, and processes that come so naturally to people.

In summary, the goal of AI is to develop systems that behave intelligently. More specifically, AI is the attempt to create computer hardware and software capable of emulating human reasoning.

11.3   Brief History of AI

The history of AI can be divided into a variety of ages (see Winston and Prendergast [35]).

First are prehistoric times. Thousands of years ago people were irresistibly drawn to the idea of creating intelligence outside the human body. Several examples date back to Greek mythology (e.g., Daedalus, the creator of artificial wings, also attempted to create artificial people). Many other examples can be found in different cultures.

The first recognizable milestone for AI was the year 1884. At that time a scientist named Charles Babbage first experimented with machines that he hoped would exhibit some intelligence. The Countess of Lovelace (for whom the ADA programming language is named) was Babbage's main sponsor. She was besieged by the press, who wondered if Babbage's machines would ever be as smart as people. At that time, she intelligently denied that it would ever be possible, because she knew this application would not occur in the near future and, therefore, should not be mentioned.

The prehistoric times extended to about 1960, because people who wanted to work on the computational approach of understanding intelligence did not have sufficiently powerful computers.

Toward the end of this period there were several attempts to associate computers and intelligence. In 1950 Dr. Claude Shannon (from Bell Labs) suggested that computers would be able to play chess. The field of cybernetics (e.g., the work of Norbert Wiener) also points to the functional similarities between humans and machines.

The Dartmouth Conference—The Beginning of the "Dawn Age." The AI revolution started in 1956 at a conference conducted by Dartmouth College. At this conference the name "artificial intelligence" was suggested by John McCarthy, one of the organizers of the conference. The participants of this conference are considered the pioneers of AI. Among them were Marvin Minsky (founder of the AI Lab at MIT), Claude Shannon (from Bell Labs), Nathaniel Rochester (of IBM), Allen Newell (first president of the American Association of Artificial Intelligence), and Herbert Simon (a Nobel Prize recipient, from Carnegie Mellon University). The conference generated much enthusiasm and some participants predicted that in 10 years computers would be as smart as people. That turned out to be a hopelessly romantic prediction.

The *dawn age* was sparked by certain successes. A program for solving geometric analogy problems like those that appear on intelligence tests was developed. Another development was a program that did symbolic integration, spawning today's MACSYMA* and other mathematical manipulation systems. These two examples, analogy and integration, are particularly important because they introduced ideas that have become extraordinarily popular in the creation of expert systems. Unfortunately, the success of the dawn age created unrealistic expectations about the ease with which creating intelligent computers might happen.

The next period can be described as the *dark age* (1965–1970) because little happened. There was a dry spell because the tremendous enthusiasm generated by the dawn age led many people to believe that the enterprise of creating intelligent computers would be a simple task. Computer scientists searched for a kind of philosopher's stone, a mechanism that when placed in a computer would require only the addition of data to become truly intelligent. The dark ages were largely fueled by overexpectations.

Then we have a *renaissance* (1970–1975). During this period, AI researchers began to make systems like MYCIN that caught people's attention. Such systems were the foundations of today's excitement.

The renaissance was followed by the *age of partnerships* (1975–1980), a period when researchers in AI began to admit that there were other researchers, particularly linguists and psychologists, with whom people working in AI could form fruitful liaisons.

The present age can be described as the *age of entrepreneurs*, or the commercialization of AI. Currently, attempts are being made to take AI out of the lab and apply it in the real world.

AI's basic theory and technical capabilities have been around since the 1950s in university computer research labs and in the minds of a few academicians. What is new is the commercial availability of hardware and software that make it possible to develop economically justifiable AI applications for a wide range of end-user organizations previously served only by more traditional data processing methods. The pivotal software tool for AI was Lisp (List Processing Programming Language), developed by John McCarthy in 1957. Unlike the programming languages with which we are most familiar—BASIC, FORTRAN, COBOL, Pascal, and APL, to mention a few—Lisp deals with complex objects

---

*MACSYMA is an ES that solves complex algebraic and calculus problems. Using symbolic processing, MACSYMA's solutions could otherwise only be approximated by numerical methods.

such as rules, sentences, and names, not just numbers. Therefore Lisp lends itself to the development of flexible systems that can accommodate ambiguities and complex interrelationships among data.

The pivotal hardware tool for users of Lisp was the "Lisp machine," or symbolic processor: a computer system that has a logical architecture specifically designed to efficiently and effectively support AI program development and execution.

The emergence of AI as a viable commercial technology can also be attributed to the recent development of semiconductor devices, computer architectures, and other technological developments. Twenty years ago computer hardware was expensive in relation to humans doing similar tasks. Today the opposite is true. In addition, AI takes up a lot of memory, but memory is now relatively inexpensive. Numerical processing techniques and software that could make the most efficient use of computer hardware have become the dominant technology. The ideal systems design goal behind numerical processing is to make the computer more productive. New computer designs were necessary to provide economical processing of data structures more complex than numbers. The idea behind AI, or logical processing, is to make people more productive.

Artificial intelligence differs from traditional computer software engineering and simple automation in several ways. The latter produces predefined actions according to preprogrammed instructions. In contrast, the actions of an AI system may differ from situation to situation in a way not predefined but determined from a collection of facts, assumptions, and general procedures for decision making—much as a human would act. An AI system may, in fact, react correctly to specific situations that were not considered by the system designers, but for which the system possesses the necessary basic information from which to construct an appropriate response. AI systems can easily be suited for non-quantitative applications because of extended abilities to deal with symbolic information. What makes AI attractive for commercial use are the characteristics that give it advantages over human intelligence. These characteristics are discussed next.

11.4   Artificial vs. Natural (Human) Intelligence

The potential value of artificial intelligence can be better understood by contrasting it with natural, or human, intelligence.* AI has several important commercial advantages:

> ☐ AI is *permanent*. Natural intelligence is perishable from a commercial standpoint in that workers can change their place of employment or forget information. AI, however, is as permanent as computer systems and programs.

*Adapted from Kaplan (18). For further discussion, see Feldman in BYTE (4).

□ AI offers *ease of duplication*. Transferring a body of knowledge from one person to another usually requires a lengthy process of apprenticeship; even so, expertise can never be completely duplicated. However, when knowledge is embodied in a computer system, it can be copied from that computer and easily moved to another computer, sometimes across the globe.

□ AI can be *less expensive* than natural intelligence. There are many circumstances in which buying computer services costs less than having corresponding human power carry out the same tasks.

□ AI, being a computer technology, is *consistent and thorough*. Natural intelligence is erratic because people are erratic; they do not perform consistently.

□ AI can be *documented*. Decisions made by a computer can be easily documented by tracing the activities of the system. Natural intelligence is difficult to reproduce, because a person may reach a conclusion but at some later date be unable to recreate the reasoning process that led to that conclusion or even to recall the assumptions that were a part of the decision.

Some advantages of natural intelligence over AI are as follows:

□ Natural intelligence is *creative*, whereas AI is rather uninspired. The ability to acquire knowledge is inherent in human beings, but with AI, tailored knowledge must be built into a carefully constructed system.

□ Natural intelligence enables people to benefit by and *use sensory experience* directly, whereas most AI systems must work with symbolic input.

□ Perhaps most important, human reasoning is able to make use at all times of a very wide *context of experience* and bring that to bear on individual problems, whereas AI systems typically gain their power by having a very narrow focus.

The advantages of natural intelligence over AI result in many limitations of expert systems. These limitations are discussed in detail in Chapter 12.

11.5 Human Problem Solving—An Information Processing Approach

In Chapter 2 we directed our attention to a managerial decision- making process that was quantitative or numerical in nature. Such a process is used in DSS. In applying AI and ES, we consider a different approach to problem solving and decision making. This approach is based on the belief of AI researchers that problem solving can be understood as information processing; it is based on a cognitive approach that uses a qualitative description of the ways in which people are similar, and the manner in which people think. For an overview of the entire subject see Mayer [22]. Of special interest to AI is the Newell- Simon model of human information processing.

The Newell-Simon Model

Allen Newell and Herbert A. Simon (24) proposed a model of human problem solving that makes use of the analogy between computer processing and human information processing. This model helps us understand how AI works and what its limitations are. The human information processing system consists of the following subsystems: a perceptual subsystem, a cognitive subsystem, a motor subsystem, and an external memory. Figure 11.1 illustrates the memories and processors included in each subsystem.

The Perceptual Subsystem.   External stimuli are the input for the human information processing system. These stimuli enter through sensors like our eyes and ears. The perceptual subsystem consists of these sensors along with buffer memories that briefly store incoming information, while it awaits processing by the cognitive subsystem.

The Cognitive Subsystem.   The senses are constantly placing a huge amount of information in the buffer memories. Whenever there is a need to make a decision, the cognitive system selects the appropriate information. Like a central processing unit (CPU) in a computer, the cognitive processor obtains the information necessary to make this decision from the sensory buffers and transfers it to the short-term memory. The processor works in cycles, which are analogous to the "fetch-execute" cycles of the computer. During each cycle the processor obtains information from a memory, evaluates it, and then stores the information in another memory.

The processor contains three parts: the elementary processor; the short-term memory; and the interpreter, which interprets part or all of the program of instructions for problem solving. The program used by an individual will depend on a number of variables such as the task and the intelligence of the problem solver.

In the simplest tasks, the cognitive system merely serves as a point for transferring information from sensory inputs to motor outputs. Habitual tasks, such as reaching to turn off a light switch, are like that. The performer needs to coordinate the action, but there is little or no "deep thought" involved. In fact, the "thinking" that occurs during such behavior is impossible to recover.

More complex tasks involve more information. That, in turn, calls for more elaborate processing. To accomplish these tasks, the cognitive processor will draw on a second memory system: long-term memory.

Long-term and External Memories.   Long-term memory consists of a large number of stored symbols with a complex indexing system. There are competing hypotheses about what the elementary symbols are and how they arrange themselves. In the simplest memory model, related symbols are associated with one another. In a more elaborate model, symbols are organized into temporal scripts. Another view is that memory consists of clusters of symbols called "chunks." A chunk is a unit of stored information—it can be a digit, a symbol, or a word associated with a set or pattern of stimuli. Chunks are hierarchically organized collections of still smaller chunks. In this conception, memory is a vast network of chunks. It requires only a few hundred milliseconds to read

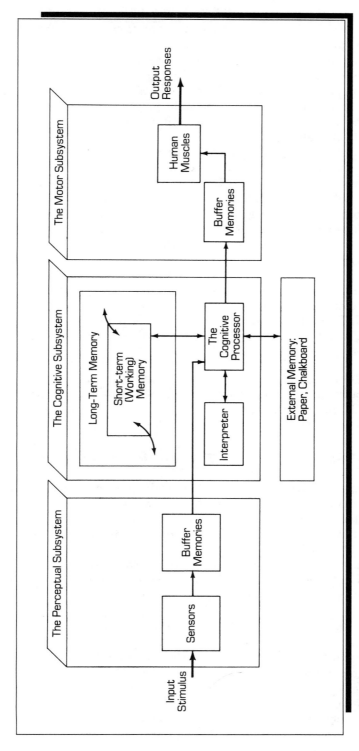

FIGURE 11.1 The Newell-Simon model of human information processing. (*Source:* Adapted from Newell and Simon [24].)

(recall) from long-term memory, but the write time (commitment to memory) is fairly long (say $5N$ to $10N$ seconds, for N symbols, where N = number of symbols involved).

Human beings can support the decision-making process with another memory, the external one. The external memory consists of external media like a pad of paper or a chalkboard. The processing, retrieval, and storage of data by computers can be thousands and millions of times faster than that of humans. Humans are also limited in their ability to generate, integrate, and interpret probabilistic data.

The three memories are shown in Figure 11.1. The long-term memory has essentially unlimited capacity. The short-term memory is quite small. It holds only five to seven chunks. However, only about two chunks can be retained while another task is being performed. This suggests that part of the short-term memory is used for input and output processing. This is one of the major limitations of the human as compared with a computer. The limits of the short-term memory can be expanded, for example, through analogies, associations, or the use of graphics. A graph may provide, in a few chunks, the same information as a large number of data items would. This is why graphics play a very important role in the support of managerial decision making.

The human operates according to this model in serial fashion, rather than in parallel. This means that a human can perform only one information processing task at a time, whereas a computer may operate in either serial or parallel designs.

Motor Output.   After scanning and searching memories, the processor sends information to the motor subsystem. Motor processors initiate actions of muscles and other internal human systems. This, in turn, results in some observable activity, such as talking.

Information Processing Via a Production System

To describe how humans process symbolic information, AI researchers created a "programming language" called a *production system*. Production systems consist of two parts: (1) production rules, or "if-then" statements, and (2) a working memory. Production rules (or simply productions) are applied to working memory. If they succeed, then they ordinarily contribute some new information to memory. The production system provides an extremely powerful model for human thought because it is discrete, simple, and flexible. Indeed, many expert systems could be described as production systems.

A cognitive psychologist using a production system model can easily integrate external behavior with internal mental activity. Events in the world produce stimuli that impinge on us. We sense stimuli and store them in buffers. Some stimuli are transferred to working memory. The transferred stimuli activate the *if* portion of a production rule. The *then* portion of the production rule indicates appropriate actions. The actions are implemented by the motor system and are observed as responses.

Production systems are only one way of describing information processing. Other approaches are being used especially to describe complex processes. For details see Bonnet [9].

Now that the reader is familiar with the definition of AI and the issue of information processing by humans and computers, we proceed to describe the content of the AI field.

11.6 The Artificial Intelligence Field

The development of machines that exhibit intelligent characteristics involves many different sciences and technologies, such as linguistics, psychology, philosophy, computer hardware and software, mechanics, hydraulics, and optics. The intersection between psychology and AI centers on the areas known as cognition and psycholinguistics. Philosophy and AI come together in the areas of logic, philosophy of language, and philosophy of mind. Intersections with linguistics include computational linguistics, psycholinguistics, and sociolinguistics. Mutual interactions between electrical engineering and AI include image processing, control theory, pattern recognition, and robotics.

Lately there have been contributions from management and organization theory (e.g., decision making, implementation), statistics, mathematics, management science (heuristic programming, fuzzy logic, cost-effectiveness), and MIS.

The various disciplines that participate in the AI field overlap and interact. Thus, it is difficult to classify the AI field according to these disciplines. A much more practical classification scheme is achieved by considering the outputs; that is, the applied areas of commercial applications. The major areas are: expert systems, natural language processors, speech understanding, robotics, computer vision and other sensory systems, and intelligent computer-aided instruction. These are discussed next.

11.7 Expert Systems

Expert systems are computerized advisory programs that attempt to imitate or substitute the reasoning processes and knowledge of experts in solving specific types of problems. Expert systems are of great interest to business and scientific communities because of their potential to enhance productivity and to augment work forces in many specialty areas where human experts are becoming increasingly difficult to find and retain. Current applications are restricted to relatively limited and narrowly scoped areas of expertise (termed *domains*).

Human experts specialize in relatively narrow problem-solving areas or tasks. Typically, human experts possess these characteristics: they solve problems quickly and fairly accurately, explain what they do, judge the reliability of their own conclusions, know when they are stumped, and communicate smoothly with other experts. They can also learn from experience, change their points of view to suit a problem, transfer knowledge from one domain to another, and reason on many levels. Finally, they use tools, such as rules of thumb, mathematical models, and detailed simulations.

An expert system is a computer program that attempts to behave like a human expert in some useful ways. Today's state of the art is that expert systems can solve simple problems and provide limited explanations.

Currently, there are several hundred serious expert systems in the commercial world. By dropping the qualifier *serious*, the number jumps to many thousands. The reason is that creating a simple, illustrative expert system is now a fairly simple and inexpensive venture. The topic of ES is covered in Chapters 12–17.

11.8   Natural Language Processing

Natural language technology gives computer users the ability to communicate with the computer in their native language. This technology allows for a conversational style interface, as opposed to the use of computer jargon and commands. Limited success in this area is typified by current systems, which can recognize and interpret written sentences relating to very restricted topics. Although this ability can be used to great advantage with some applications, a general natural language processing (NLP) system is not yet possible.

The field of natural language processing is divided into two subfields:

□ Natural language *understanding*, which investigates methods of allowing the computer to comprehend instructions given in ordinary English so that computers can understand people more easily.
□ Natural language *generation*, which strives to have computers produce ordinary English language so that people can understand computers more easily.

Our interest in this book is in the former.

NLP is an attempt to allow computers to interpret normal statements expressed in a natural human language, such as English or Japanese. The process of speech recognition (see Section 9), in contrast, attempts to translate the human voice into individual words and sentences understandable by the computer. Combining speech recognition and NLP will be required to realize the capability of the computer to converse in a manner normal to humans.

The topic of NLP is revisited in Chapter 18.

11.9   Speech Understanding

Speech understanding or recognition is the recognition and understanding by a computer of spoken language.

Speech understanding is a process that allows one to communicate with a computer by speaking to it. (The term *speech recognition* is sometimes applied only to the first part of the process: recognizing the words that have been spoken without necessarily interpreting their meanings. The other part of the process, in which the meaning of the speech is ascertained, is called *speech understanding*. It may be possible to understand the meaning of a spoken sentence without actually recognizing every word.) This topic is interrelated with NLP and is described in Chapter 18.

11.10 Robotics and Sensory Systems

Sensory systems, such as vision systems, tactile systems, and signal processing systems when combined with AI define a broad category of systems generally referred to as *robotics* (see Aleksander and Burnett [1]).

Robotics

A *robot* is an electromechanical device that can be programmed to perform manual tasks. The Robotic Industries Association formally defines a robot as "a reprogrammable multifunctional manipulator designed to move materials, parts, tools, or specialized devices through variable programmed motions for the performance of a variety of tasks."

Not all of robotics is considered to be part of AI. A robot that performs only the actions that it has been preprogrammed to perform is considered to be a "dumb" robot, possessing no more intelligence than, say, a dishwasher. An "intelligent" robot includes some kind of sensory apparatus, such as a camera, that collects information about the robot's operation and its environment. The intelligent part of the robot allows it to *respond* to changes in its environment, rather than just to follow instructions "mindlessly."

Robots combine sensory systems with mechanical motion to produce machines of widely varying intelligence and abilities. The research and application areas under the sensory systems umbrella include machines that sense, move, and manipulate their environment. Assembly line operations, particularly those that are highly repetitive or hazardous, are beginning to be performed by robots. The major advantages of robots over humans are summarized in Table 11.1.

The difference between the automatic machine and an intelligent robot is that the robot senses its environment and modifies its behavior as a result of the information gained. The intelligent robot is thought to have humanlike capabilities and attributes. For example, some robots are distinguished from regular automation by their ability to deal with uncertainty.

An *intelligent robot* is a system that flexibly connects perception to action. Humans can be viewed as superintelligent robots for the following reasons:

TABLE 11.1 Robots' Advantages over Humans.

1. More reliable work 　　95 percent uptime 　　works three shifts 　　no vacations 　　no coffee breaks	4. More consistent, accurate work 　　improve quality 　　reduce scrap 　　production predictable 　　efficient use of capital 　　self-diagnosis of errors 　　improve work methods
2. Work at lower cost 　　no workman's compensation 　　no retirement benefits 　　no insurance plans	
3. Environmentally insensitive 　　in poor climatic conditions 　　in high noise environments 　　in hazardous locations	5. Work only for the organization 　　no moonlighting 　　no espionage for competition 　　no sabotage 　　no theft 　　no featherbedding

Source: Adapted from *AI Scan Report,* Department of the Treasury, IRS, 1983.

First, we can see and feel. Consequently we can cope with uncertain positions and changing environments. Second, we have graceful arms capable of fast, accurate motion, together with fantastic hands capable of grasping all sorts of objects. Third, we think about what we do. We note and avoid unexpected obstacles. We can select appropriate tools, design jigs, and place sensors. We plan how to fit things together, succeeding even when the geometrics are awkward and the fits are tight. We recover from errors and accidents.

Most of today's industrial robots are clumsy and far from being intelligent. For the most part they cannot see, feel, move gracefully, or grasp flexibly, and they cannot think at all. These industrial robots move through repetitive sequences like gripping, welding, or spraying paint at predetermined times, almost completely uninformed about what is going on around them in the factory. However, the goal of building *intelligent* robots is slowly being attained. Someday, somewhere, robots will behave in ways similar to humans.

For a while the general pace of building and using robots has been slow, and outside of Japan, there has been little rush to accept and exploit the technology produced by artificial intelligence. Now the picture is changing. Small companies are growing rapidly by supplying industry with products in which sensory systems (particularly vision) are a productivity- multiplying component. Large companies like IBM are considered established suppliers in the field.*

As stated earlier robots can perform routine tasks endlessly with great precision and very low error rates. They require a stable environment for this, however. Their predetermined movements generally cannot vary from piece to piece. An exception exists for recent vision systems that can tell the robot where something is located and how to find it. For these vision systems, the environment must be very simple and uncluttered. The pieces must not be moving, except in a predefined manner, or the robot will not be able to find them. The domain of the robot is, thus, quite limited.

Despite these limitations, some industrial robots are able to sense their environment, discover the location of their work piece, and perform their task without human intervention. They are able to measure part tolerances to very small dimensions (1 mm), determine orientation and size (and other measurements), and even determine which of several part types the current part is. This ability enables the replacement of human labor in a number of applications at a lower cost, while maintaining a high level of accuracy and a consistency not formerly attainable. Robots are now widely used in the automobile and steel industries in Japan, the United States, and Europe.

Several representative applications of robots and sensory systems are listed as follows:

> □ *Forms Processing.* Many organizations process a tremendous number of paper forms. Although the increased use of magnetic and other auto-mated media is expected to reduce the volume of paper forms, many organizations will have a significant amount of paper to process for some time. Sensory systems can impact both the physical handling of forms and the retrieval of data from a form. These capabilities exist today,

*For a survey of companies in the robotics area, see Dicken and Newquist (14).

although most are rather limited. Improvements in these areas present opportunities for more effective and less expensive handling of forms.

□ *Production Control and Inspection.* Sensory systems are becoming widely used in a number of industrial processes. As the abilities of these systems become more advanced, a number of opportunities will arise for their use. Labor intensive activities could, in some cases, be executed by advanced sensory systems when it is cost-effective to do so. One example might be quality control inspection of products.

□ *Surveillance.* Intelligent surveillance systems could possibly provide increased security at a decreased cost. For example, equipment that can detect intruders (with low false alarm rates) and take intelligent actions to protect itself and neutralize threats may have valuable commercial applications. Screening activities like those conducted by the U.S. Customs Service, for example, might also use advanced sensory systems.

The application of AI and sensory systems in areas like those just discussed presents implications concerning employment and the composition of the work force. Successful application of these technologies may require a reduction in staffing and the retraining of the remaining personnel.

Where will this new wave of automation go? How far? How fast? We all would like to know the answers to these questions, but it would be too speculative to try to answer them. Instead, we can attempt to answer specific questions:

□ Why is it relatively easy to build humanless parts- fabrication factories and relatively hard to build humanless device-assembly factories?

□ What are the industrial tasks that require humanlike sensing, reasoning, and dexterity? Is it advisable to eliminate or change those tasks by redesigning factories from scratch? (so that the task could be done by robots)?

Robot Fred Keeps His Guard Up

He can "see" through walls, detect body heat and motion 150 feet in any direction, and can warn of fire or flood. But Fred the robot was having more than a little difficulty navigating over the cracks in the sidewalks of New York as he took a promotional stroll through Wall Street. Marketed by Denning Mobile Robotics of Woburn, MA, Fred is designed to replace human guards on patrol in warehouses, shopping malls, prisons and other places where a mute guard might be needed. Denning President Warren George, who guided the four-foot-tall, 485-pound, black robot with a joy stick as he staggered over the pavement to the amusement of tourists and other passers-by, said: "We should have put on its soft tires. It's too bumpy out here." A robot like Fred is already patrolling the World Trade Center in Boston and is being marketed nationwide at a cost of $69,000. John Parker, a human security guard at Morgan Guaranty, was skeptical that the electronic upstart could do his job. "It won't be any good if it can't shoot," he said.

- What can be done by exploiting special lighting arrangements? How far have we gone with the simple vision systems that count each visual point as totally black or totally white, with no shades of gray?
- Is the robot itself important? Can we improve productivity with robots alone, or must we think instead about improving whole manufacturing systems?

These and similar questions may be related to DSS and ES; however, they will not be discussed here. The interested reader is referred to Winston and Predergast (35).

11.11 Visual Recognition

The most advanced AI sensory system is visual recognition. *Visual recognition* has been defined as the addition of some form of computer intelligence and

How Does Computer Vision Work?

The process of visual recognition is composed of several parts. First, a sensor (e.g., a camera, videotape or TV camera, or a light scanner) surveys an object in a particular scene or setting. While the scanning process is being performed, the object's image is broken down by the system into pixels. Once the camera has broken the image into its corresponding pixel count or makeup, the second part of the system, the computer, determines the object's highlights according to the pixels. Depending on the object, this could be the thread of a screw, the curved outline of a bottle, or the concavity of a coffee cup. For each individual object a number of factors are always considered, including shape, size, outline, edge, and apparent dimensionality (since most cameras still view only in two dimensions).

Next, computer memory comes into play. After the characteristics of the object are identified, they are compared, cross-referenced, and correlated to image characteristics previously entered into the system's memory. For object recognition, this allows the computer a fairly high degree of accuracy in matching an unknown object to one stored in memory. For quality control and production line purposes, this memory matching allows the computer to separate out those particular objects of a given type (molded fittings, for instance) that do not match up to specifications that were previously programmed into the system. The computer can then specify the removal or reworking of the errant object. This process can be so precise as to notice gradual misalignment in tools or imperceptibly misplaced screw holes that a human observer would never notice. In addition, an artificial vision system does not suffer from eye strain or fatigue, which improves its efficiency in some applications of an order of magnitude above that of its human counterparts.

decision making to digitized visual information received from a machine sensor. The combined information is then utilized to perform, or control, such operations as robotic movement, conveyor speeds, and production line quality. The basic objective of computer (or robot) vision is to interpret pictures rather than generate pictures (which preoccupies computer graphics). What "interpreting pictures" means differs depending on the application it is adapted to. For example, in interpreting pictures taken by satellite, it may be sufficient to roughly identify regions of crop damage. On the other hand, robot vision systems may find it necessary to precisely identify assembly components to correctly affix the components to the item being assembled.

Research in vision systems may enhance the abilities of automated systems to handle the manipulation of unlike objects in multiple orientations, such as forms lying on a table, or parts moving on a conveyor belt. Optical recognition systems, for example, can retrieve handwritten or typed data from a form and reformat it for storage. For more information about machine vision, see Ballard and Brown (6).

11.12   Intelligent Computer-aided Instruction

Overview and Representative Systems

Computer-aided instruction (CAI) refers to machines that can tutor humans. To a certain extent, such a machine can be viewed as an expert system. However, the major objective of an expert system is to render advice, whereas the purpose of CAI is to teach.

The major advantages of CAI are

- □ individualized, self-adjusted level of material.
- □ remedial or accelerated progress.
- □ immediate feedback (with explanations).
- □ consistency of teaching.
- □ updated material.
- □ no location restrictions.
- □ variety of presentations.

Computer-assisted instruction has been in use for many years, bringing the power of the computer to bear on the educational process. Now AI methods are being applied to the development of intelligent computer-assisted instruction (ICAI) systems in an attempt to create computerized "tutors" that shape their teaching techniques to fit the learning patterns of individual students.

There have been two main directions in the application of AI to computerized teaching. The first is an attempt to bring AI techniques (especially problem solving, knowledge representation, and natural languages) to bear on producing intelligent tutoring systems that can behave with subtlety and more knowledge than traditional computer-assisted instruction systems (see Sleeman and Brown (32) for a compendium of the pioneering and current efforts). This is clearly a difficult AI applications problem that to be solved will require substantial progress in all areas of AI. The other major AI direction in education involves students exploring rich environments from which they can learn on their own initiative, with the environment acting as a constraint that indirectly focuses their learning. A well-known environment is the LOGO "turtle graphics" programming system, from which students can learn about programming and geometry. Other environments are now being built for the exploration of less "mathematical" subjects. (For an overview of intelligent instructional systems, see *Expert Systems*, special issue, vol. 5, no. 4., 1988.) A representative list of intelligent CAI is given in Table 11.2. Two such systems are BUGGY and GUIDON.

BUGGY.   Developed at Bolt, Beranek and Newman (Cambridge, MA) to diagnose a student's problems with basic mathematics, BUGGY identifies and explains a student's misconceptions about arithmetic. BUGGY is based on the assumption that many students who have difficulty solving problems are not unable to follow procedures but rather are following incorrect procedures. BUGGY provides a student with a series of arithmetic problems, finds error patterns in the student's responses, and analyzes those patterns to determine the cause of the errors.

GUIDON.   Using the production rule knowledge base from MYCIN, GUIDON instructs medical students in the diagnosis and treatment of bacteriological infections. Developed at Stanford University, GUIDON conducts an interactive dialog to present symptomatic evidence that can help students analyze problems. Because it is compatible with many rule-based systems, GUIDON can be adapted to create instructional programs for other knowledge bases.

TABLE 11.2   Some ICAI Systems.

ICAI System	Training Area	Knowledge Representation
ALGEBRA	Applied Algebra	Rules
BP	Programming in BASIC	Rules
BUGGY	Arithmetic Subtraction	Procedural Networks
EXCHECK	Logic and Set Theory	Rules with Logic Interpreters
GUIDON	Infectious Diseases	Rules and Meta-knowledge
INTEGRATE	Symbolic Integration	Adaptive Rules
LMS	Algebraic Procedures	Rules
MENO	Programming in Pascal	Semantic Networks
QUADRATIC	Quadratic Equations	Adaptive Rules
SCHOLAR	South American Geography	Semantic Networks
SOPHIE	Electronic Troubleshooting	Semantic Networks with Circuitry Simulator
SPADE	Programming in LOGO	Rules
STEAMER	Steamship Propulsion	Device Model, Frames
WEST	Arithmetic Expressions	Rules
WHY	Causes of Rainfall	Scripts
WUSOR	Logical Relationships	Genetic Graphs (Networks)

Source: Andriole (3).

CAI applications are not limited to schools. As a matter of fact this type of AI application has found a sizable niche in the military and corporate sectors. Certain CAI systems can be considered expert systems, whereas others exhibit only a few ES characteristics. As will be seen later, many expert systems can be used as tutors in addition to being advisors.

CAI systems are being used today for various tasks such as problem solving, simulation, discovery learning, drill and practice, games, and testing. For further information, see Bork (10).

Even though CAI programs are user-interactive and employ some AI technologies (like natural language interface), there is some debate about whether the programs themselves are really examples of AI. Often these programs are databases structured to respond to specific inputs with specific answers within the predetermined structure. CAI systems are being developed and improved and are slowly penetrating many organizations and schools.

Expert Systems and ICAI

Expert systems, through their explanation capabilities, are used for training. See the special issue of *IEEE Expert* Summer 1987, "Expert systems that teach."

Learning

Until recently, machine learning (for the purpose of improving performance) has not been a major concern for AI. Most AI researchers initially felt that it was necessary to concentrate on how to make a computer program do something before figuring out how the program can learn to improve its performance. Machine learning has now begun to take on an ever-increasing significance in AI.

Early examples of machine learning were provided by checkers and chess playing programs. These programs improved their performance with experience. Learning is done by using analogy, by discovery, through special procedures, by observing, or by analyzing examples. Learning can improve the performance of AI products like experts systems and robotics.

Learning is a "support" area of AI, because it is an investigation into basic principles underlying intelligence rather than an application itself. The following are some observations concerning learning:

1. Learning systems demonstrate interesting learning behavior, some of which (e.g., the checkers playing program) obviously challenge the performance of humans.
2. Although human-level learning capabilities are sometimes matched, there is no attempt to make general claims about being able to learn as well as humans, or in the same way humans do (the checker playing program learns quite differently from humans).
3. Learning systems are not anchored in any formal bedrock. Thus, their implications are not well understood. Many of them have been exhaustively tested but exactly why they succeed or fail is not precisely clear.
4. The one common thread running through most AI approaches to learning (and distinguishing them from non-AI learning approaches) is that

learning in AI involves the manipulation of structures rather than numerical parameters.

11.13 Other Areas

AI has been developed in several other commercial areas (see Winston and Prendergast [35]). Some interesting examples are listed as follows:

Automatic Programming

In simple terms, *programming* is the process of telling the computer exactly what you want it to do. Developing a computer program frequently requires a great deal of time. A program or a system (a group of interrelated programs) must be designed, written, tested, debugged, and evaluated, all as part of the program development process.

The goal of automatic programming is to create special programs that act as "intelligent" tools to assist programmers and expedite each phase of the programming process. The ultimate aim of automatic programming is a computer system that could develop programs by itself, in response to and in accordance with the specifications of a program developer.

Intelligent Workstations

Intelligent workstations help to increase the productivity of engineers and computer programmers by providing them with a computerized environment that helps them do their jobs faster. For example, Daisy System Corp. produces workstations for electronic design. The stations allow the engineer to sit in front of a high-performance graphics terminal that "speaks" engineering language and utilizes special symbols. The station allows for simulated "what if" experimentation with both the logic design and the layout design of electronic products. Similar workstations are manufactured by Apollo, Inc. Other workstations are being used to support computer programmers by providing each programmer with an "electronic helper." Intelligent workstations for managers are now in a developmental stage. They will support the various activities that managers perform. (See Chapter 10.)

Summarizing News

Computer programs can read stories in newspapers or other documents and make summaries in English or several other languages. For further discussion, see Chapter 18.

Translation from One Language to Another

Computer programs are able to translate words and simple sentences from one language to another. For example, a package called LOGOS is used for English to German (and German to English) translations.

Translation between natural languages, which often results in illogical or humorous results, will improve as techniques evolve for resolving the ambiguities and inconsistencies within languages. Accuracy will then increase and the time required for translation will decrease.

Translation can have important commercial applications. For example, in the tourist industry an expert system can be responsive to tourists who ask questions in several languages. It may also be helpful in diplomatic and educational situations.

11.14   Summary and Conclusions

Artificial intelligence is not in itself a commercial field, but a science and a technology. It is a collection of concepts and ideas that are appropriate for research but that cannot be marketed. However, AI provides the scientific foundation for several growing commercial technologies,* the most important of which are natural language processors, robotics and sensory systems (especially vision and speech recognition), computer-aided instruction, and expert systems.

The Fifth-Generation Project (FGP)

Artificial intelligence is often referred to as the fifth- generation of computer technology. The Japanese plan to create their fifth-generation computer to leapfrog the leaders in this field. If successful, it will represent a highly significant event in human history. They are determined to shed the imitator image and make a revolutionary push. The Japanese plan to create a computer that can talk, listen, learn, and make sophisticated decisions. That means an extensive utilization of AI techniques.

Some of the objectives of this fifth-generation computer are as follows:

☐ Provide a high intelligence level to cooperate with people.
☐ Assist people to discover and develop unknown fields.
☐ Offer vast knowledge bases.
☐ Aid in management.
☐ Solve social problems.
☐ Acquire new perceptions by simulating unknown situations.
☐ Offer significant software productivity improvement.
☐ Reduce time and cost to develop computerized systems by a factor of 10.

Ultimately, the computer is to have the capability to recognize continuous speech, possess super vision, make intelligent decisions, perform self-repair, and augment the decision maker in general.

---

*For an assessment see D. B. Davis. "Artificial Intelligence Goes to Work." *High Technology,* April 1987.

The most limiting factor keeping computer systems from being the *predominant* tool in any organization is the absence of a natural dialog between the human and the computer. Keyboards, unnatural command phrases, and intricate software instructions intimidate many potential users, especially at the middle and higher levels of management. The development of NLP and especially speech recognition can remove this obstacle, making the computer as usable a tool on every manager's desk as the telephone.

This chapter defined and briefly described applied AI technologies, their development, and major applications.

We are now experiencing a natural growth of AI from its academic and research roots to productive applications within industry and society. The effects of this growth could change the way in which management and organizations operate. For example, the Fifth-Generation Project (see the accompanying box) could result in a breakthrough in computer technology. Productivity, effectiveness, efficiency, and quality of life all can be improved. Organizations must be prepared to face the new challenges and responsibilities that AI brings. Of all these exciting concepts, the area that could affect management and organizations the most is expert systems. The topic of expert systems will be explored in the following six chapters.

Key Words

artificial intelligence	intelligent work	programming
chunk of information	stations	language
computer-aided	logical processing	robotics
instructions	machine language	sensory systems
expert systems	natural language	speech recognition
fifth-generation	natural language	symbolic processing
computers	processing (NLP)	Turing test
fifth-generation	numerical processing	vision (visual)
project	pattern recognition	recognition
image processing	(matching)	

Questions for Review

1. Define artificial intelligence.
2. Describe the following periods in the history of AI: prehistoric, dawn, dark, renaissance, entrepreneur.
3. What are the Turing test?
4. Describe the major components of the Newell-Simon model.
5. List the major advantages of artificial over natural intelligence.
6. List the major disadvantages of artificial compared with natural intelligence.
7. What are the major differences between traditional computer programs and AI?
8. List the major academic fields that contributed to the development of AI.
9. List the major AI products (areas).
10. Define expert systems.
11. Define natural language processing (NLP).
12. List the four memories of the human information system.

13. Distinguish between a natural language and a programming language.
14. What is a robot? How does it relate to AI?
15. List the major advantages of a robot over a human.
16. What is the difference between an automatic machine and an intelligent robot?
17. Define visual recognition as it applies to computer technology.
18. Define speech recognition and understanding.
19. What are the two major directions of computer- aided instruction (CAI)?
20. List the major benefits of CAI.
21. How might a manager use an "intelligent" workstation?

Questions for Discussion

1. Inflated expectations were a major problem with AI in the past. Why? Is this a problem today? Why or why not?
2. What are the major factors that can help push AI from the lab to the real world?
3. Compare and contrast numerical vs. symbolic processing techniques.
4. What are the major advantages of a human over a robot? What are the managerial implications of robotics' limitations?
5. A robot replaces a bartender in a night club in San Francisco. Compare the situation before and after the replacement. Would you go to such a place? Be imaginative in your response.
6. Why is visual recognition one of the most advanced areas of AI? What are the major advantages of the machine vision? The major disadvantages?
7. "Speech understanding or even recognition could increase the number of managers using the computer directly tenfold." Do you agree? Why or why not.
8. The virtues of CAI are being debated by many proponents and opponents. Prepare a table that lists some of the advantages of CAI. Find at least two journal articles that represent both sides in the debate.
9. Why is learning so important in AI systems? How can a chess-playing machine "learn"? How can an expert system "learn"?
10. Can the concept of an intelligent workstation be applied to managerial work (i.e., can we have an executive workstation that makes executives more productive)?

References and Bibliography

1. Aleksander, I., and P. Burnett. *Reinventing Man: The Robot Becomes Reality*. New York: Holt, Rinehart and Winston, 1984.
2. Allen, J. *Natural Language Understanding*. The Benjamin/Cumming Pub. 10, 1987.
3. Andriole, S. J., ed. *Applications in Artificial Intelligence*. Princeton, NJ: Petrocelli Books, 1984.
4. "Artificial Intelligence." Special issue of *BYTE*, April 1985.
5. Atkinson, M. L. "Computer-Assisted Instruction: Current State of the Art." *Computers in the Schools*, Spring 1984.
6. Ballard, D. H., and C. Brown. *Computer Vision*. Englewood Cliffs, NJ: Prentice-Hall, 1982.
7. Barr, A., and E. A. Feigenbaum. *The Handbook of Artificial Intelligence: Volume 1*. Los Altos, CA: William Kaufmann, 1981.
8. Barr, A., and E. A. Feigenbaum. *The Handbook of Artificial Intelligence: Volume 2*. Los Altos, CA: William Kaufmann, 1982.
9. Bonnet, A. *Artificial Intelligence*. Englewood Cliffs, NJ: Prentice-Hall, 1986.

10. Bork, A. *Learning with Computers*. Bedford, MA: Digital Press, 1981.

11. Breger, W. S., and A. M. Farley. "Artificial Intelligence Approaches to Computer-Based Instruction." *Journal of Computer-Based Instruction*, May 1980.

12. Cercone, N., and G. Mc Calb. "Artificial Intelligence: Underlying Assumptions and Basic Objectives." *Journal of the American Society for Information Science*, September 1984.

13. Cohen, P. R., and E. A. Feigenbaum. *The Handbook of Artificial Intelligence: Volume 3*. Los Altos, CA: William Kaufmann, 1982.

14. Dicken, H. K., and H. P. Newquist, eds. *AI Trends '85*, Scottsdale, AZ: DM Data, 1985 (Annual report on the AI industry).

15. *Environmental Scan Report on Artificial Intelligence*. U.S. Dept. of the Treasury, IRS, December 1983.

16. Feigenbaum, E. A., and P. McCorduck. *The Fifth Generation Computer*. Reading, MA: Addison-Wesley, 1983.

17. Hunt, V. D. *Robotics Source Book*. New York: Elsevier, 1988

18. Kaplan, S. J. "The Industrialization of Artificial Intelligence: From By-Line to Bottom Line." *The AI Magazine*. Summer 1984.

19. Kearsley, G., ed. *Artificial Intelligence and Instruction: Applications and Methods*. Reading, MA: Addison-Wesley, 1987.

20. Kearsley, G., et al. "Two Decades of Computer-Based Instruction Projects: What Have We Learned?" *T.H.E. Journal*, January 1983.

21. Lugar, G. F., *Artificial Intelligence and the Design of Expert Systems*. Addison-Wesley, 1989.

22. Mayer, R. E. *Thinking, Problem Solving, Cognition*. New York: W H. Freeman, 1983.

23. Mishkoff, H. *Understanding Artificial Intelligence*. Dallas, TX: Texas Instruments, 1985.

24. Newell, A., and H. A. Simon. *Human Problem Solving*. Englewood Cliffs, NJ: Prentice-Hall, 1972.

25. O'Shea, T., and M. Eisenstadt. *Artificial Intelligence: Tools, Techniques and Applications*. New York: Harper & Row, 1984.

26. Polson, M. C., and J. Richardson, eds. *Foundations of Intelligent Tutoring Systems*. L. Erlbaum Assoc. New Jersey, 1988.

27. Ralston, D. W. *Principles of AI and Expert Systems Development*. New York: McGraw-Hill, 1988.

28. Reitman, W., ed. *Artificial Intelligence Applications for Business*. Norwood, NJ: ABLEX, 1984.

29. Rich, E. *Artificial Intelligence*. New York: McGraw-Hill, 1983.

30. Schoen, S., and W. Sykes. *Putting AI to Work, Evaluating and Implementing Business Applications*. New York: Wiley, 1987.

31. Seaman, J. "Artificial Intelligence." *Computer Decisions*, August 1984.

32. Sleeman, D., and J. S. Brown. *Intelligent Tutoring Systems*. New York: Academic Press, 1982.

33. Waltz, D. L. "Artificial Intelligence: An Assessment of the State-of-the-Art and Recommendation for Future Directions." *The AI Magazine*, Fall 1984.

34. Waterman, D. *A Guide to Expert Systems*. Reading, MA: Addison-Wesley, 1986.

35. Winston, P. H., and K. A. Prendergast, eds. *The AI Business*. Cambridge, MA: MIT Press, 1984.

Chapter 12

Fundamentals of Expert Systems

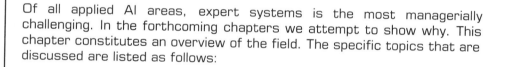

Of all applied AI areas, expert systems is the most managerially challenging. In the forthcoming chapters we attempt to show why. This chapter constitutes an overview of the field. The specific topics that are discussed are listed as follows:

12.1   Introduction

The name *expert systems* was derived from the term "knowledge-based expert systems." An expert system is a system that employs human knowledge captured in a computer to solve problems that ordinarily require human expertise. Well-designed systems imitate the reasoning processes of experts in solving specific problems. They can be used by nonexperts to improve their problem-solving capabilities. Expert systems (ES)* can also be used by experts as knowledgeable assistants. ES are used to propagate scarce knowledge resources for improved, consistent results. Ultimately, such systems could function better than any single human expert in making judgments in a specific, usually narrow expertise area (referred to as a *domain*). This possibility may have a significant impact both on advisory professionals (financial analysts, lawyers, tax advisers, etc.) and on organizations and management.

The purpose of this chapter is to introduce the fundamentals of expert systems. A brief history is presented followed by an actual case. The case leads to a presentation of the basic ideas of ES as well as to its capabilities, structure, and the process of its construction. Finally, various types of ES, their benefits, and their limitations are discussed.

12.2   History of Expert Systems

As stated earlier, ES is a branch of applied AI, and indeed, ES were developed by the AI community as early as the mid-1960s. This period of AI research was dominated by a belief that a few laws of reasoning coupled with powerful computers would produce expert or even superhuman performance. An attempt in this direction was the general-purpose problem solver.

General-purpose Problem Solver

The general-purpose problem solver (GPS) is a procedure developed by Newell and Simon (15) from their Logic Theory Machine, in an attempt to create an "intelligent" computer. Thus it can be viewed as a predecessor to ES. GPS tries to work out the steps needed to change a certain initial situation into a desired goal state. For each problem, GPS is given a set of "operators" that change the world in various ways, a statement of what "preconditions" each operator needs to be true before it can be applied, and a list of "postconditions" that will be true after the operator has been used. It also has an optional set of heuristics for operators to try first. In ES terms, these form a rule base.

GPS attempts to find operators that reduce the difference between a goal and current states. Sometimes, the operators cannot operate on the current states (their preconditions are not suitable). In such cases, GPS sets itself a subgoal: to change the current state into one that is suitable for the operators. Many such subgoals may have to be set before GPS can solve a problem.

GPS, like several other similar programs, did not fulfill its inventors' dreams, but these programs did produce extremely important side benefits. For

*ES is both a singular and plural abbreviation (expert system, expert systems).

example, Prolog is based on Robinson's work on automatic theorem proving.[*] Lisp compilers and "garbage collectors" (which are discussed later) are also based on work in the general problem-solving methodology area.

The shift from general-purpose to special-purpose programs occurred in the mid-1960s with the development of DENDRAL,[**] by E. Feigenbaum, at Stanford University. At that time it was also recognized that the problem-solving mechanism is only a small part in a complete, intelligent computer system.

The construction of DENDRAL (one of the first two expert systems ever built) led to the following conclusions:

□ General problem solvers are too weak to be used as the basis for building high-performance ES.

□ Human problem solvers are good only if they operate in a very narrow domain.

□ Expert systems need to be constantly updated for new information. Such updating can be done efficiently with rule-based representation.

□ The complexity of problems requires a considerable amount of knowledge about the problem area.

By the mid-1970s, several expert systems had begun to emerge. Recognizing the central role of knowledge in these systems, AI scientists worked at developing comprehensive knowledge representation theories and associated general-purpose decision-making procedures and inferences. Within a few years it became apparent that these efforts had limited success for reasons similar to those that doomed the first general problem solvers. "Knowledge," as a target of study, is too broad and diverse; efforts to solve knowledge-based problems in general were premature. On the other hand, several different approaches to knowledge representation proved sufficient for the expert systems that employed them. A key insight was learned at that time: *the power of an ES is derived from the specific knowledge it possesses, not from the particular formalisms and inference schemes it employs.* In short, an expert's knowledge per se seems both necessary and nearly sufficient to develop an expert system.

Figure 12.1 displays some of the developmental lines within the ES field. The field spans two decades, and because most projects continue for many years, the temporal positions shown in the figure are only approximate. Several of those that do appear will be described later in some detail.

By the beginning of the 1980s, ES technology, first limited to the academic scene, began to appear as commercial applications. Notable were XCON and XSEL (developed from R-1, at Digital Equipment Corporation, see Chapter 17) and CATS-1 (at General Electric). CATS-1 will be described soon.

In addition to building ES, a substantial effort was made to develop tools for speeding up the construction of ES. These tools, which are described in Chapter 15, include programming tools like EMYCIN and AGE, knowledge acquisition tools like EXPERT and KAS, and tools for learning from experience such as META-DENDRAL and EURISKO.

[*]See Robinson, J. A. " The Generalized Resolution Principle." In: *Machine Intelligence 3*, D. Michie, ed. New York: Elsevier, 1986.

[**]All the systems referred to in this chapter are described in Appendix A.

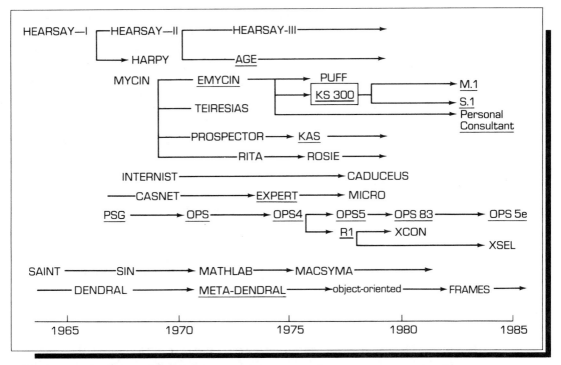

FIGURE 12.1 Evolution of selected expert systems and expert systems development tools. (Underlines indicate development languages.) (*Source*: Modified from Hayes-Roth et al. [11].)

Such tools became commercially available starting in 1983. Most of the early developed tools required special hardware (e.g., Lisp machines), but recently developed software can run on regular computers including microcomputers (e.g., M.1, EXSYS, and Personal Consultant—see Chapter 15). These latest developments could have a major impact on the rate of ES development and implementation.

12.3 The Case of CATS-1 (DELTA)

The Problem. General Electric's top locomotive field service engineer, David I. Smith, has been with the company for more than 40 years. He was the top expert in troubleshooting diesel electric locomotive engines. Approaching retirement, Smith was traveling throughout the country to places where locomotives were in need of repair, to determine what was wrong and to advise young engineers about what to do. Being very busy, he had little time to train a successor. Should Smith retire, GE would have to rely on a younger, less experienced generation of engineers, some of whom, being less loyal to the company, could move to another employer as soon as they were trained.

The Traditional Solution. GE's traditional approach to such a situation was to create teams that paired senior and junior engineers. The pairs worked together for several months or years, and by the time the older engineers finally did retire, the young engineers had absorbed enough of their senior's expertise to carry on troubleshooting or other tasks. This practice proved to be a good short-term solution, but GE still wanted a more effective and dependable way of disseminating expertise among its engineers, and preventing valuable knowledge from retiring with the worker. Furthermore, having railroad service shops throughout the country requires extensive travel, or moving the locomotives to an expert, because it is not economically feasible to have an expert in each shop.

The Expert System. In 1980, GE decided to build an ES by modeling the way a human troubleshooter works. The system builders spent several months interviewing Smith and transferring his knowledge to a computer. The computer programming was prototyped over a three-year period, slowly increasing the information and the number of decision rules stored in the computer. Finally, the system was able to "reason" much the same way an experienced locomotive engineer reasons. The new diagnostic technology enables a novice engineer or a technician to uncover a fault by spending only a few minutes at the computer terminal. The system can also *explain* to the user the logic of its advice, thus serving as a teacher as well. Furthermore, the system can lead users through the required repair procedures, presenting a detailed, computer-aided drawing of parts and subsystems, and providing specific "how to" instructional demonstrations.

The system is based on a flexible, humanlike thought process, rather than rigid procedures expressed in flowcharts or decision trees.

The system, which was developed on a PDP 11/23 but operates on a microcomputer, is currently installed at every railroad repair shop served by GE, thus eliminating delays and boosting maintenance productivity. For further information, see Bonissone and Johnson (4).

12.4 The Basic Concepts of Expert Systems—An Overview

The example above introduces six basic concepts of expert systems: expertise, experts, transferring expertise, reasoning, rules, and explanation capability. These concepts are defined in this section, with the remainder of the chapter devoted to a more detailed description and discussion of them and their integration into an ES.

Expertise. Expertise is the extensive, task-specific knowledge acquired from training, reading, and experience. The following types of knowledge are examples of what expertise includes:

- Facts about the problem area.
- Theories about the problem area.
- Hard-and-fast rules and procedures regarding the general problem area.
- Rules (heuristics) of what to do in a given problem situation (i.e., rules regarding problem solving).
- Global strategies for solving these types of problems.
- Meta-knowledge (knowledge about knowledge).

These types of knowledge enable experts to make better and faster decisions than nonexperts in solving complex problems. It takes a long time to become an expert, and novices become experts only incrementally.

Experts

It is difficult to define what an expert is because we actually talk about degrees or levels of expertise. (The question is: "How much expertise should a person possess before qualifying as an expert?") Nevertheless, it has been said that nonexperts outnumber experts in many fields by a ratio of 100 to 1. Distribution of expertise appears to be of the same shape regardless of the type of knowledge being evaluated. Figure 12.2 represents a typical distribution of expertise. The top tenth (decile) performs three times better than the average, and 30 times better than the lowest tenth. This distribution suggests that the overall effectiveness of human expertise can be significantly increased if we can somehow make top-level expertise available to other decision makers.

The Characteristics of a Human Expert. Typically, human expertise includes a constellation of behavior that involves the following activities:

□ Recognizing and formulating the problem.
□ Solving the problem quickly and properly.
□ Explaining the solution.
□ Learning from experience.
□ Restructuring knowledge.
□ Breaking rules.
□ Determining relevance.
□ Degrading gracefully.

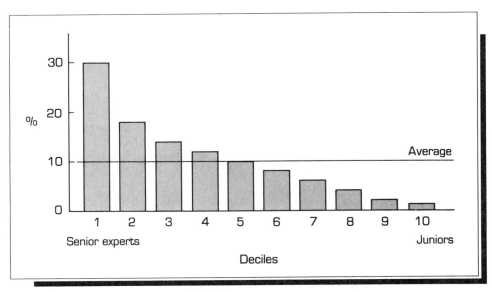

FIGURE 12.2 Distribution of expertise, percent successes achieved per decile. (*Source:* Adapted from Augustine [2].)

Experts can take a problem stated in some arbitrary manner and convert it to a form that lends itself to a rapid and effective solution. Problem-solving ability is necessary, but not sufficient by itself. Experts should be able to explain the results, learn new things about the domain, restructure knowledge whenever needed, break rules whenever necessary (i.e., know the exceptions to the rules), and determine whether their expertise is relevant. Finally, experts "degrade gracefully," meaning that as they get close to the boundaries of their knowledge, they gradually become less proficient at solving problems. All these activities must be done efficiently (quickly, at low cost) and effectively (high-quality results).

To mimic the human expert it is necessary to build a computer that exhibits all these characteristics. To date (1990), work in ES has primarily explored the second, third, and fourth of these activities.

Transfering Expertise. The objective of expert systems is to transfer expertise from the expert to the computer and then on to other humans. This process involves two activities: knowledge acquisition (from experts) and knowledge representation (in the computer). The knowledge is stored in the computer in a component called a *knowledge base*. Two types of knowledge are distinguished: facts and procedures (usually rules) regarding the problem domain.

Reasoning. A unique feature of an expert system is its ability to reason. Given that all the expertise is stored in the knowledge base, the computer is programmed so that it can make inferences from that knowledge. The reasoning is performed in a component called the *inference engine*, which includes procedures regarding problem solving by an approach called symbolic reasoning.

Symbolic Reasoning. When human experts solve problems, particularly the type we consider appropriate for expert systems, they don't do it by solving sets of equations or performing other laborious mathematical computations. Instead, they choose symbols to represent the problem concepts and apply various strategies and rules to manipulate these concepts.[*] An ES also represents knowledge symbolically as sets of symbols that stand for problem concepts. In AI jargon a *symbol* is a string of characters that stands for some real-world concept. Examples of symbols are as follows:

- Product
- Defendant
- 0.8

These symbols can be combined to express relationships between them. When these relationships are represented in an AI program, they are called *symbol structures*. The following are examples of symbol structures:

- (DEFECTIVE product)
- (LEASED-BY product defendant)
- (EQUAL (LIABILITY defendant) 0.8)

[*]According to Waterman (21).

These structures can be interpreted to mean "the product is defective," "the product is leased by the defendant," and "the liability of the defendant is 0.8."

To solve a problem, an ES manipulates these symbols. This is not to say that ES does not do math; rather, the emphasis is on manipulating symbols. The consequence of this approach is that knowledge representation—the choice, form, and interpretation of the symbols used—becomes very important.

Rules. Most commercial ES are rule-based; that is, the knowledge is stored mainly in the form of rules, as are the problem-solving procedures. A simple rule is structured in an If-Then format. A rule in the CATS-1 case may look like this: "*IF*, the engine is idle, and the fuel pressure is less than 38 psi, and the gauge is accurate, *THEN*, there is a fuel system fault." There are about 600 such rules in the CATS-1 system.

Explanation Capability. Another unique feature of an ES is its ability to explain its advice or recommendations and even to justify why a certain action was not recommended. The explanation and justification is done in a subsystem called the justifier, or the explanation subsystem. It enables the system to examine its own reasoning and to explain its operation.

The characteristics and capabilities of ES make them different from conventional systems. For a comparison see Table 12.1.

TABLE 12.1 Comparison of Conventional Systems and Expert Systems.

Conventional Systems	Expert Systems
Knowledge and processing are combined in one sequential program	Knowledge base is clearly separated from the processing (inference) mechanism (i.e., knowledge rules separated from the control)
Program does not make mistakes (programmers do)	Program may make mistakes
Do not (usually) explain why input data are needed or how conclusions were drawn	Explanation is a part of most ES
Changes in the knowledge are tedious	Changes in the rules are easy to accomplish
The system operates only when it is completed	The system can operate with only a few rules (as the first prototype)
Execution is done on a step-by-step (algorithmic basis)	Execution is done by using heuristics and logic
Need complete information to operate	Can operate with incomplete or uncertain information
Effective manipulation of large databases	Effective manipulation of large knowledge bases
Representation and use of data	Representation and use of knowledge
Efficiency is a major goal	Effectiveness is the major goal
Easily deal with quantitative data	Easily deal with qualitative data
Captures, magnifies, and distributes access to numerical data (TPS) or to information (MIS, DSS)	Captures, magnifies, and distributes access to judgment

12.5 The Structure of Expert Systems

Expert systems are composed of two major parts: the development environment and the consultation (run-time) environment (see Figure 12.3). The expert system development environment is used by the ES builder to introduce expert knowledge into the knowledge base. The consulation environment is used by a nonexpert to obtain expert knowledge and advice.

The following components exist in a sophisticated expert system:

☐ Knowledge acquisition (an expert and a knowledge engineer).
☐ Knowledge base.
☐ Inference engine.
☐ Blackboard (workplace).

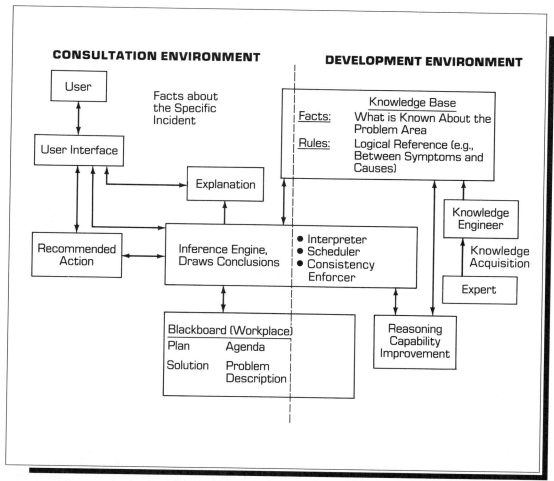

FIGURE 12.3 Structure of an expert system.

□ User interface.
□ Explanation facility (justifier).
□ Knowledge refining system.

Most existing expert systems do not contain the knowledge refinement component. There are also very large variations in the content and capabilities of each component.

A brief description of these components follows.

Knowledge Acquisition Subsystem

Knowledge acquisition is the accumulation, transfer, and transformation of problem-solving expertise from some knowledge source to a computer program for constructing or expanding the knowledge base. Potential sources of knowledge include human experts, textbooks, databases, special research reports, and pictures.

Acquiring the knowledge from experts is a complex task that creates a bottleneck in ES construction. The state of the art today requires a knowledge engineer to interact with one or more human experts in building the knowledge base. Typically, the knowledge engineer helps the expert structure the problem area by interpreting and integrating human answers to questions, drawing analogies, posing counterexamples, and bringing to light conceptual difficulties (see Davis and Lenat [7]). The acquisition process, its supports, and its problems are discussed in Chapter 13.

The Knowledge Base

The information in the knowledge base is everything necessary for understanding, formulating, and solving the problem. It includes two basic elements: (1) facts, such as the problem situation and theory of the problem area; and (2) special heuristics, or rules that direct the use of knowledge to solve problems in a particular domain. (In addition, the inference engine includes *standard* problem-solving and decision-making rules.) The heuristics express the informal judgmental knowledge of an application area. Global strategies, which can be both heuristics and a part of the theory of the problem area, are usually included in the knowledge base. Knowledge, not mere facts, is the primary material of expert systems. The information in the knowledge base is incorporated into a computer program by a process called knowledge representation, which is discussed in Chapter 14.

The Inference Engine

The "brain" of the ES is the inference engine, also known as the *control* structure or the rule interpreter (in rule-based ES). This component is essentially a computer program that provides a methodology for reasoning about information in the knowledge base and in the *blackboard*, and for formulating conclusions. This component makes decisions about how to use the system's knowledge by developing the agenda that organizes and controls the steps taken to solve current problems.

The major elements of the inference engine are as follows:

□ An *interpreter* (rule interpreter in most systems), which executes the chosen *agenda* items by applying the corresponding knowledge base rules.

□ A *scheduler*, which maintains control over the agenda. It estimates the effects of applying inference rules in light of item priorities or other criteria on the agenda.

□ A *consistency enforcer*, which attempts to maintain a consistent representation of the emerging solution.

The Blackboard (Workplace)

The blackboard is an area of working memory set aside for the description of a current problem, as specified by the input data; it is also used for recording intermediate results. The workplace records intermediate hypotheses and decisions. Three types of decisions can be recorded on the blackboard: (1) *plan*—how to attack the problem; (2) *agenda*—potential actions awaiting execution; and (3) *solution*—candidate hypotheses and alternative courses of action that the system has generated thus far.

Example: In a malfunction diagnosis system of a car, the knowledge base includes all the rules and processes relating to car failures. When your car fails, you enter the symptoms of the failure into the computer for storage in the blackboard. As the result of an intermediate hypothesis, the computer may then suggest that you do some additional checks (e.g., see if your battery is connected properly) and ask you to report the results. All this information is recorded in the blackboard.

User Interface

Expert systems contain a language processor for friendly, problem-oriented communications between the user and the computer. This communication could best be carried out in a natural language, and in some cases it is supplemented by menus and graphics.

Explanation Subsystem (Justifier)

The ability to trace responsibility for conclusions to their sources is crucial both in the transfer of expertise and in problem solving. The explanation subsystem can trace such responsibility and explain the ES behavior by interactively answering questions such as the following:

□ *Why* was a certain question asked by the expert system?
□ *How* was a certain conclusion reached?
□ *Why* was a certain alternative rejected?
□ *What* is the plan to reach the solution? For example, what remains to be established before a final diagnosis can be determined?

The Knowledge Refining Program

Human experts can analyze their own performance, learn, and improve it for future consultations. Similarly, such evaluation is necessary in computerized learning so that the program will be able to analyze the reasons for its success or failure. This could lead to improvements resulting in a better knowledge base and more effective reasoning. This component is not available in commercial expert systems at the moment, but it is being researched in experimental ES in several universities.

12.6   The Human Element in Expert Systems

At least two humans, and possibly more, participate in the development and use of an expert system. At a minimum there is an expert and a user. Frequently, there is also a knowledge engineer. The roles of these participants are as follows:

The Expert.   The expert, commonly referred to as the domain expert, is a person who has the special knowledge, judgment, experience, and methods, with the ability to apply these talents to give advice and solve problems. It is the domain expert's job to provide knowledge about how he or she performs the task that the knowledge system will perform. For an advice-giving episode, the expert knows which facts are important and the meaning of relationships among facts. In diagnosing an automobile's electrical system, for example, an expert mechanic knows that fan belts can break and cause the battery to discharge. Directing a novice to check the fan belts and interpreting the meaning of a loose or missing belt are examples of expertise. Sometimes more than one expert is used. Such situations can become difficult if the experts disagree. (This issue is discussed in Chapter 13.)

Usually, the initial body of knowledge, including terms and basic concepts, is documented in textbooks, reference manuals, sets of policies, or a catalog of products. However, this is not sufficient for a powerful ES. The reason why not all expertise is documented is that most experts are unaware of the exact mental process by which they diagnose or solve a problem. Therefore an interactive procedure is needed to acquire additional information from the expert to expand the basic knowledge. This process is fairly complex and usually requires the intervention of a knowledge engineer.

The Knowledge Engineer.   The knowledge engineer helps the human expert(s) structure the problem area by interpreting and integrating human answers to questions, drawing analogies, posing counterexamples, and bringing to light conceptual difficulties. He or she is also the system programmer. The shortage of experienced knowledge engineers is probably the major bottleneck in ES construction. To overcome this bottleneck, ES designers are using productivity tools (e.g., special editors) and research is being conducted on building systems that will bypass the need for knowledge engineers.

The User. Most computer-based systems have evolved in a single user mode. In contrast, an ES has several possible types of users:

□ A nonexpert client seeking direct advice. In such a case the ES acts as a *consultant*.

□ A pupil or a student who wants to learn. In such a case the ES acts as an *instructor*.

□ An ES builder who wants to improve or increase the knowledge base. In such a case the ES acts as a *partner*.

□ An expert. In such a case the ES acts as a *colleague*.

For example, the system can provide a "second opinion," so the expert can validate his or her judgment. An expert can also use the system as an assistant to carry on routine analysis or computations or to search for and classify information.

Users may not be familiar with computers and may lack in-depth knowledge in the problem domain. However, users should have an interest in making better and possibly cheaper and faster decisions by using expert systems. The domain expert and the knowledge engineer should anticipate users' needs and limitations when designing ES.

The capabilities of ES were developed to save users' time and effort. Therefore unlike more traditional computer systems, ES provide *direct* answers to questions, not merely information and support. Further, ES address the need to teach and train nonexperts. In addition, experts can improve their expertise through the use of ES (e.g., by discovering combinations of facts not previously considered). Finally, ES can be used as a knowledge assistant to experts by executing tedious tasks like searches and computations.

12.7 How Expert Systems Work

Three major activities take part in ES construction and use: development, consultation, and improvement.

Development. The development of an expert system involves the construction of the knowledge base by acquiring knowledge from experts and/or from documented sources. As stated earlier, the knowledge is both *declarative* (factual) and *procedural*. In contrast, non-AI computer-based systems include only declarative knowledge. The development activity also includes the construction (or acquisition) of an inference engine, a "blackboard," an explanation facility, and any other required software, such as interfaces. (See Figure 12.3.)

The major participants in this activity are the domain expert, the knowledge engineer, and possibly information systems programmers (especially if there is a need to program from scratch). The knowledge is represented in the knowledge base in such a way that the system can draw conclusions by emulating the reasoning process of human experts.

Consultation. Once the system is developed and validated, it is transferred to the users. When users want advice, they come to the ES. The ES conducts a bidirectional dialog with the user, asking her or him to provide facts about the specific incident. After accepting the user's answers, the ES attempts to reach a conclusion. This effort is made by the inference engine, which "decides" which heuristic search techniques should be used to determine how the rules in the knowledge base are to be applied to the problem. The user can ask for explanations (e.g., why a certain question was asked by the computer, and how certain conclusions were derived). We will show several examples of consultations later on. The quality of inference capability is determined by the knowledge representation method used and by the power of the inference engine.

Because the user is usually a computer novice, the ES must be very easy to use. At the present state of the technology the user must sit by the computer terminal and type in the description of the problem (future ES will use voice input). The ES asks questions, the user answers them; more questions may be asked and answered and, finally, a conclusion is reached.

The consultation environment is also used during the development phase to test the system. At that time users may be asked to participate so that the interface and the explanation facility may be tested in addition to the rules (in a rule-based representation) and the inference.

Improvement. Expert systems are improved several times during their development. After the system is operating in the field, it goes through additional improvements. The improvements include the addition of new rules (to deal with unique cases), modification of rules (to deal with changing conditions, or to correct rules), and deletion of rules that are no longer relevant. The improvement task is similiar to the initial development task. However, this time, the user participates more actively in the process.

12.8 Problem Areas Addressed by Expert Systems

Expert systems can be classified in several ways. One way is a generic categorization that uses the general problem areas they address. For example, diagnosis can be defined as "inferring system malfunctions from observations." Diagnosis is a generic activity executed in medicine, organizational studies, computer operations, and so on. The generic categories of expert systems are listed in Table 12.2. Some ES belong to two or more of these categories. A brief description of each category follows.

Interpretation systems infer situation descriptions from observations. This category includes surveillance, speech understanding, image analysis, signal interpretation, and many kinds of intelligence analysis. An interpretation system explains observed data by assigning them symbolic meanings describing the situation.

Prediction systems include weather forecasting, demographic predictions, economic forecasting, traffic predictions, crop estimates, and military, marketing, or financial forecasting.

Diagnostic systems include medical, electronic, mechanical, and software diagnosis. Diagnosis systems typically relate observed behavioral irregularities to underlying causes.

TABLE 12.2 Generic Categories of Expert Systems

Category	Problem Addressed
Interpretation	Inferring situation descriptions from observations
Prediction	Inferring likely consequences of given situations
Diagnosis	Inferring system malfunctions from observations
Design	Configuring objects under constraints
Planning	Developing plans to achieve goals(s)
Monitoring	Comparing observations to plan vulnerabilities, flagging exceptions
Debugging	Prescribing remedies for malfunctions
Repair	Executing a plan to administer a prescribed remedy
Instruction	Diagnosing, debugging, and correcting student performance
Control	Interpreting, predicting, repairing, and monitoring system behaviors

Design systems develop configurations of objects that satisfy the constraints of the design problem. Such problems include circuit layout, building design, and plant layout. Design systems construct descriptions of objects in various relationships with one another and verify that these configurations conform to stated constraints.

Planning systems specialize in problems of planning like automatic programming. They also deal with short- and long-term planning in areas such as project management, routing, communications, product development, military applications, and financial planning.

Monitoring systems compare observations of system behavior with standards that seem crucial for successful goal attainment. These crucial features correspond to potential flaws in the plan. Many computer-aided monitoring systems exist for topics ranging from air traffic to fiscal management tasks.

Debugging systems rely on planning, design, and prediction capabilities to create specifications or recommendations for correcting a diagnosed problem.

Repair systems develop and execute plans to administer a remedy for some diagnosed problem. Such systems incorporate debugging, planning, and execution capabilities.

Instruction systems incorporate diagnosis and debugging subsystems that specifically address the student as the focus of interest. Typically these systems begin by constructing a hypothetical description of the student's knowledge that interprets his or her behavior. They then diagnose weaknesses in the student's knowledge and identify appropriate remedies to overcome the deficiencies. Finally, they plan a tutorial interaction intended to deliver remedial knowledge to the student.

Control systems adaptively govern the overall behavior of a system. To do this, the control system must repeatedly interpret the current situation, predict the future, diagnose the causes of anticipated problems, formulate a remedial plan, and monitor its execution to ensure success.

Appropriate Tasks. Not all the tasks that one can usually find within each of the preceding 10 categories are suitable for expert systems. Some guidelines for task selection are presented in Chapter 15.

Table 12.3 attempts to answer, in general terms, the question: "What tasks are expert systems right for?"

TABLE 12.3 What Tasks Are Expert Systems Right For?

TOO EASY Use Conventional Software	JUST RIGHT	TOO HARD Requires Human Intelligence
Payroll, Inventory	Diagnosing and troubleshooting	Designing new tools or a cover for a magazine
Simple tax returns	Analyzing diverse data	Stock market predictions
Decision trees	Production scheduling	Discovering new principles
Database management	Equipment layout	Everyday language
Mortgage computations	Advise on tax shelters	"Common sense" problems
Regression analysis	Determine type of statistical analysis	
Facts are known precisely; they are reduced to numbers.	Facts are known but not precisely; they are stated as ideas.	Requires innovation or discovery or "common sense."
Expertise is cheap.	Expertise is expensive but available.	Expertise is not available, or nobody knows enough to be an expert.

(*Source*: Based on Van Horn [19])

12.9 Benefits of Expert Systems

ES can provide major benefits to users. Potential benefits are listed as follows.

Increased Output and Productivity. ES can work faster than humans. For example, XCON has enabled DEC to increase fourfold the throughput of configurating VAX orders. Increased output means fewer workers needed and reduced costs.

Increased Quality. ES can increase quality by providing consistent advice and reducing error rate. For example, XCON reduced the error rate of configuring computer orders from 35 percent to 2 percent.

Reduced Downtime. Many operational ES (e.g., the CATS-1 system described earlier) are used for diagnosing malfunctions and prescribing repair. By using ES it is possible to reduce downtime significantly. For example, one day of lost time on an oil rig can cost as much as $250,000. A system called Drilling Advisor was developed to detect malfunctions in oil rigs. This system saved a considerable amount of money for the company involved.

Capturing Scarce Expertise. The scarcity of expertise becomes evident where there are not enough experts for a task, the expert is about to retire or leave a job, or expertise is required over a broad geographical location. Typical systems that capture scarce expertise are CATS-1, Campbell Soup's ES (see Chapter 17), ACE, and DART (see Appendix A for details).

Flexibility. ES can offer flexibility in providing services and in manufacturing. For example, DEC tries to make each VAX order fit the customer's needs as closely as possible. Before XCON, DEC found it increasingly difficult to do this because of the variety of customer requests.

Equipment Operation. ES make complex equipment easier to operate. For example, STEAMER is an ES intended to train inexperienced workers to operate complex ship engines. Another example is an ES developed for Shell Oil Company (by Intelligent Terminal Ltd., Glasgow, Scotland) to train people to use complex FORTRAN routines.

Using Less Expensive Equipment. In many cases a human must rely on expensive instruments for monitoring and control. ES can perform the same tasks with lower-cost instruments. This is the result of the ES ability to investigate more thoroughly and quickly the information provided by instruments. DENDRAL is an example of such an ES.

Operation in Hazardous Environments. Many tasks require humans to operate in a hazardous environment. The ES may enable humans to avoid such environments. Not only is this characteristic extremely important in military conflicts; it can also enable workers to avoid hot, humid, or toxic environments.

Reliability. ES are reliable. They do not become tired or bored, call in sick, or go on strike, and they do not talk back to the boss. ES also consistently pay attention to all details and do not overlook relevant information and potential solutions.

Response Time. ES respond in some cases much faster than humans, especially when it is necessary to work with a large volume of data.

Integration of Several Experts' Opinions. In certain cases ES forces us to integrate the opinion of several experts and thus may increase the quality of the advice.

Working with Incomplete and Uncertain Information. In contrast to conventional computer systems, ES can, like human experts, work with incomplete information. The user can respond with a "don't know" or "not sure" answer to one or more of the system's questions during a consultation, and the expert system will still be able to produce an answer, although it may not be a certain one. ES do not have to be complete in the same way in which a set of FORTRAN IF-statements do. They can also deal with probabilities, as long as the inference engine can cope with them.

Educational Benefits. ES can provide training. Novices who work with ES become more and more experienced. The explanation facility can also serve as a teaching device, and so can notes that may be inserted in the knowledge base.

Enhances Problem Solving. ES enhance problem solving by allowing the integration of top experts' judgment into analysis. They also increase users' understanding through explanation. ES can be used to support the solution of difficult problems. For example, an ES was developed to help novices use complex statistical computer packages.

Knowledge Transfer to Remote Geographical Locations and to Developing Countries. One of the greatest potential benefits of ES is its ease of transfer across international boundaries. This can be extremely important to developing countries that cannot pay for knowledge delivered by human experts. An example of such a transfer is an eye-care ES developed at Rutgers University (by Kulikowski), in conjunction with the World Health Organization. The program was tested in Egypt and Algeria, where serious eye diseases are prevalent, but eye specialists are rare. The program is rule-based, runs on a micro, and can be operated by a nurse, a physician's assistant, or a general practitioner. The program diagnoses the disease and then recommends a treatment.

Solve Complex Problems in a Narrow Domain.   Expert systems may, one day, solve problems whose complexity exceeds human ability. Already some ES are able to solve problems where the required scope of knowledge exceeds that of any one individual. However, these problems must be in a narrow domain.

12.10 Problems and Limitations of Expert Systems

Available ES methodologies are not straightforward and effective even for applications in the generic categories (see Table 12.2). For applications of even modest complexity, most ES code is generally hard to understand, debug, extend, and maintain. Here are some factors and problems that slow down the commercial spread of ES:

- Knowledge is not always readily available.
- Expertise is hard to extract from humans.
- The approach of each expert to situation assessment may be different, yet correct.
- It is hard, even for a highly skilled expert, to abstract good situational assessments when he or she is under time pressure.
- Users of expert systems have natural cognitive limits. Humans see what they are prepared to see, often only what falls within a narrow attention span.
- ES work well only in a narrow domain, in some cases in very narrow domains.
- Most experts have no independent means of checking whether their conclusions are reasonable.
- The vocabulary that experts use for expressing facts and relations is frequently limited and not understood by others.
- Help is frequently required from knowledge engineers who are rare and expensive, a fact that could make ES construction rather costly.

An interesting way to examine ES limitations is to review the generic areas where ES were found to be successful (Table 12.2) and point out the major difficulties encountered in each category (see Table 12.4).

Last, but not least, is the fact that expert systems may not be able to arrive at conclusions (especially in early stages of system development). For example, even the fully developed XCON cannot fulfill about 2 percent of the orders presented to it. In addition, expert systems do make mistakes (see accompanying box).

TABLE 12.4   Representative Experts' Tasks and Their Difficulties.

Task	Difficulties
Interpretation. Analysis of data to determine their meaning.	□ Data are often "noisy" and full of errors □ Data values may be missing
Diagnosis. Fault-finding in a system based on interpretation of data.	□ Faults can be intermittent □ Symptoms of other faults may interfere □ Data contain errors or are inaccessible □ Diagnostic equipment may be unreliable
Monitoring. Continuously interpreting signals and flag for intervention.	□ When to flag is often context-dependant □ Signal expectations vary with the time/situation
Prediction. Forecasting from past and present.	□ Integration of incomplete information □ Account for multiple possible futures □ Contingencies for uncertainties □ Diversity of data, often contradicting data
Planning. Creating a plan to achieve goals.	□ Many alternative courses of action □ Overwhelming volume of details □ Interactions between plans and subgoals □ Planning context is only approximately known
Design. Making specifications to create objects for satisfying particular requirements.	□ Difficulty in assessing consequences □ Several conflicting constraints □ Interaction among subdesigns

Source: Adopted from Stefik (17).

Expert Systems Make Mistakes

Whereas conventional programs are designed to produce the correct answer every time, expert systems are designed to behave like experts, usually producing correct answers but sometimes producing incorrect ones. John McDermott, describing the development of an ES for configuring VAX-11 computer systems for the Digital Equipment Corporation, neatly summarizes the problem:

> I have hammered on the theme that a knowledge-based program must pass through a relatively lengthy apprenticeship stage and that even after it has become an expert, it will, like all experts, occasionally make mistakes. The first part of this message got through, but I suspect that the second has not. My concern then, is whether this characteristic of expert systems is recognized. Will Digital (or any other large corporation) be emotionally prepared to give a significant amount of responsibility to programs that are known to be fallible?

At first glance it would seem that conventional programs have a distinct advantage over ES in this regard. However, the advantage is an illusion. Conventional programs that perform complex tasks, like those suitable for expert systems, may result in mistakes. But their mistakes will be very difficult to remedy because the strategies, heuristics, and basic assumptions on which these programs are based will not be explicitly stated in the program code. Thus they cannot be easily identified and corrected. ES, like their human counterparts, make mistakes. But unlike conventional programs, they have the potential to learn from their errors. With the help of skillful users, ES can be made to improve their problem-solving abilities on the job. Futhermore, the programming job required to make improvements is much simpler than that required in most conventional systems.

(*Source:* Waterman [21].)

These limitations clearly indicate that today's ES fall short of generally intelligent human behavior. Several of these limitations will diminish or disappear with technological improvements.

12.11   Types of Expert Systems

Expert systems appear in many varieties. The following are some classifications of ES. They are not exclusive (one ES can appear in several categories).

Expert Systems vs. Knowledge Systems

According to this classification, an ES is one whose behavior is so sophisticated that we would call a person who performed in a similar manner an expert. MYCIN and XCON are both good examples. Highly trained professionals diagnose blood diseases (MYCIN) and configure complex computing equipment (XCON). These systems truly attempt to emulate world-class human experts.

In the commercial world, however, systems are emerging that—although competent—perform tasks for which the description "expert" does not truly apply. Such small systems are referred to as *knowledge systems** (also known as advisory systems, intelligent job aid systems, or operational systems). As an example, let us look at a system that gives advice on immunizations recommended for travel abroad. The advice depends on many attributes such as the age, sex, and health of the traveler and the country of destination. One needs to be knowledgeable to give such advice, but one need not be an expert. In this case, practically *all* the knowledge that relates to this advice is documented in a manual available at most public health departments (in only 1 or 2% of the cases is it necessary to consult a physician).

The distinction between the two types may not be so sharp when it comes to reality. Many systems involve both documented knowledge and undocu-

---

*This terminology is not widely accepted as yet. Therefore the terms expert systems and knowledge systems are frequently used interchangeably.

mented expertise. Basically it is a matter of *how much* real expertise is included in the systems that classifies them in one category or the other.

Knowledge systems can be contructed more quickly and cheaply than true expert systems, as demonstrated in Chapter 15.

Rule-based Expert Systems

Many commercial ES are rule-based, because the technology of rule-based systems is relatively well developed. In such systems the knowledge is represented as a series of production rules (see Chapter 13). The classical example of a rule-based ES is MYCIN (which is described in Chapter 17). Many commercial systems can be considered as descendants of MYCIN.

Model-based Systems*

In contrast to rule-based systems where knowledge is based on human expertise and is represented as rules, these systems are based on knowledge of the structure and behavior of the devices they are designed to understand. Model-based systems are especially useful in diagnosing equipment problems. The systems include a model of the device to be diagnosed that is then used to identify the cause(s) of the equipment's failure. Because they draw conclusions directly from knowledge of a device's structure and behavior, model-based expert systems are said to reason from "first principles."

The Hardware Troubleshooting Group in MIT's AI lab assesses the use of model-based ES to diagnose malfunctioning computers. The group uses a computer-repair scenario to contrast the rule-based with the model-based approaches. First, the rule-based approach:

> Consider the likely behavior of an engineer with a great deal of repair experience. He or she simply stares briefly at the console, noting the pattern of lights and error message, then goes over to one of the cabinets, opens it, raps sharply on one of the circuit boards inside, and restarts the machine.

The diagnostic process used in this episode represents the approach that is incorporated in a rule-based expert system. A knowledge engineer formalizes the reasoning process that an expert uses to discover the source of the problem and encodes that procedure in a series of production rules.

A model-based approach, on the other hand, is represented by a scenario such as the following:

> Consider a new engineer who has just completed training. He or she carefully notes the symptoms, gets out a thick book of schematics, and spends the next half hour poring over them. At last he or she looks up, goes over to one of the cabinets, opens it, raps sharply on one of the circuit boards inside, and restarts the machine.

Although in this example the rule-based and model-based approaches resulted in the same actions, the procedures used to arrive at the conclusions were very different. Because the novice engineer in the latter scenario could

*Based on Mishkoff (13).

not rely on his or her expertise to diagnose and repair the computer, he or she had to refer to documentation that explained how the computer worked. Similarly, a model-based system depends on knowledge of the structure and behavior of a device, rather than relying on production rules that represent expertise. Although it remains largely experimental, the model-based approach looks very promising for ES designed for diagnosis and repair.

One especially attractive feature of model-based ES is their "transportability." A rule-based ES that incorporates an expert's knowledge of troubleshooting problems with a particular computer might be of no value for repairing a different kind of computer. On the other hand, if a model-based ES included a thorough working knowledge of digital electronic computer circuits, it theoretically could be used to diagnose the problems of *any* computer.

Classification by Functions

Buchanan and Shortliffe (5) distinguished the following types of ES. One type deals with *evidence gathering*. The system leads the user to a *structured selection* from among a reasonable number of possible outcomes or actions. (A "reasonable" number might be dozens or hundreds; it would not be tens of thousands or more.) This evidence-gathering type of ES is the one being most widely developed today. The problems that are treated by this type of ES are called *"classification problems."* The process of dealing with such problems can be described as follows:

> The system solves problems by precisely classifying what the problem is and then retrieving the solution to this class of problem. For example, the problem of repairing an automobile can be viewed as the problem of precisely classifying the problem: "it is a charging system failure caused by one or more shorted diodes in the alternator." Once the problem is classified precisely, the repair or advice is clear.

Another example of this type of system interrogates a designer about the configuration of a device, selects a design template and tailors it to the designer's needs, builds a source file of the information, and ships it to a CAD/CAM system. That system then prepares a blueprint for engineering. (Such a system was constructed with the aid of software called S.1, see Chapter 15.)

A second type is a *stepwise refinement* system. It deals with a large number of possible outcomes by means of successive levels of detail.

A third type of system is *stepwise assembly*, where the subject domain can have an extremely large number of possible outcomes. Such a system requires a lot of interaction with the user, so that the user's intelligence can help steer the system in the right direction for a solution. A special case of this type is called a *catalog selection*. This system deals with problems like choosing the right chemical, steel, or auto parts from a catalog of choices. Users know the characteristics of the problem but lack the knowledge of the catalog or the relationships between the problem and item in the catalog. This application also generalizes an ES as a front-end to a database.

Ready-made (Turnkey) Systems

ES can be developed to meet the particular needs of a user (custom-made), or they can be purchased as ready-made packages for any user. Ready-made packages are similar to application packages like an accounting general ledger or project management in operations management. Ready-made systems enjoy the economy of mass production and therefore are considerably less expensive than customized systems. They also can be used as soon as they are purchased. Unfortunately, ready-made systems are very general in nature, and the advice they render may not be of value to a user involved in a complex situation. Ready-made systems started to appear on the market in 1983. Most of them are sold for microcomputers only. A few are available for mainframes, usually through an online arrangement.

Ready-made ES are not popular yet. However, as time passes, their performance will improve and they will probably become as widespread as other CBIS application packages. (For further discussion and examples see Chapter 17.)

Real-Time Expert Systems

Real-time computer systems are those systems where there is a strict time limit on the system's response time, which should be *fast enough* for use to control the process being computerized. In other words, the system *always* produces response by the time it is needed.

Real-time computer systems in general have become an integral part of our life. They are being used in a growing number of applications. The complexity of these systems is increasing along three dimensions: (1) the number of functions controlled, (2) the rate at which the functions must be controlled, and (3) the number of factors that must be considered before a decision can be made. For example, oil platform control rooms are being planned which will make available as many as 20,000 signals for just two or three operators. It becomes difficult for a human to interpret and act in a timely manner in such situations.

Expert systems are being developed in order to assist the human operators by reducing the cognitive load on users, or by enabling them to increase their productivity without the cognitive load on them increasing.

Note: Cognitive load refers to the manner in which people perceive and/or process information.

Real-time ES, also known as "online" or "real-time online" systems, obtain information directly from the process they control and take *complete control* over the process, in real-time environment, without human interaction. These systems are especially important for intelligent robots, for quality control and for process control.

12.12   Developing Expert Systems

The process of developing ES is much like developing DSS, for two reasons. First, an iterative approach is used and second there is a distinction between team-built large systems and micro-based small systems. Building large systems requires heavy tools and the support of knowledge engineers. Small systems are constructed on PCs with the aid of development tools. The basic steps in the construction process, shown in Figure 12.4, are fairly standard, regardless

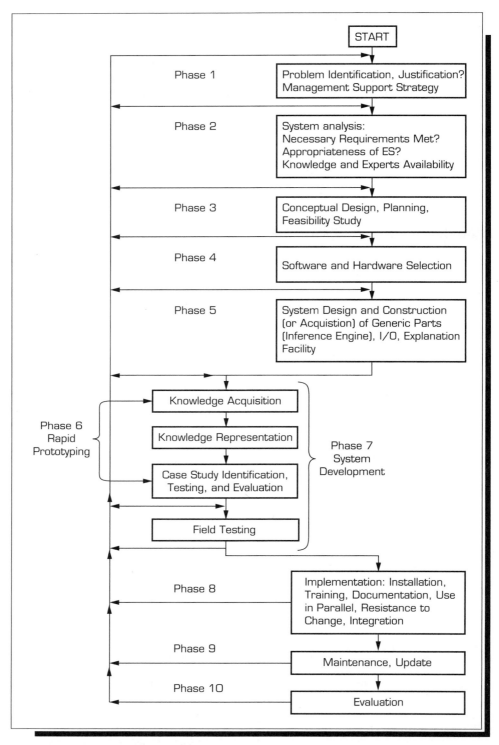

FIGURE 12.4 ES development process.

of the nature of the system built. However, the exact content of each step is occasionally unique.

The development process of ES is described in the next three chapters. Chapter 13 examines step 5 of the process, namely, knowledge acquisition, while Chapter 14 deals with knowledge representation and inferencing. Chapter 15 deals with the remaining steps and covers in great detail ES software development tools.

12.13 **Summary and Conclusions**

Expert systems differ from other computerized systems primarily in their ability to *reason* and to *explain*. In addition, they manipulate symbolic knowledge and can deal with incomplete input information. Furthermore, whereas in other systems pertinent knowledge and the method for utilizing it are intermingled, in ES they are separated. The knowledge base is manipulated by a separate, clearly identifiable control mechanism (the inference engine). Thus ES incorporate data in such a way that new knowledge can be added without extensive reprogramming.

ES face a long but promising road. The technology of ES aims to create means for people to capture, store, distribute, and apply knowledge electronically. Although the early applications have demonstrated the feasibility and economic importance of this work, they also revealed the enormous size of the field for potential applications.

Developing intelligent computers has been a dream of scientists almost since the first computer was built. This dream is now materializing through the use of AI in expert systems. Modeled after human experts, ES use sophisticated problem-solving techniques and vast stores of knowledge to solve complex problems, especially in narrow domains where expertise is well described. In contrast to other computerized decision aids, ES draw conclusions principally through logical or plausible inference, rather than by calculations. The first generation of ES reasons from rules of experience and has been applied mainly in medicine, military applications, engineering, and physical sciences. A limited number of applications have been developed for business (e.g., accounting, finance, strategic planning). Presently, however, we witness the construction of thousands of systems in business.

The future for ES is indeed bright; some of the mechanisms for human intelligence are present. Already machines can perform as well as people—in a limited sense. Moreover, many machines may soon possess sight, touch, hearing, and speech, thus imitating humans' sensory capacities as well as their reasoning abilities.

But whole areas of the human thought process—volition, emotion, the creative uses of error—still lie well outside the computer's capability. Scientists are still far from their ultimate goal—a computer-based analog of the human brain.

At present, a major objective is to build ES of a satisfactory quality in a reasonable time and at a reasonable cost. This objective is attainable with the aid of several tools employed in a systematic process. The process and the tools are described in the following two chapters.

Key Words

blackboard
consultation environment
development
  environment
domain
expertise
expert systems
explanation facility
general-purpose problem
  solver (GPS)

heuristics
inference engine
justifier
knowledge acquisition
knowledge engineer
knowledge refining
knowledge
  representation

knowledge systems
model-based
  systems
ready-made systems
real-time systems
rule-based systems
symbolic reasoning
workplace

Questions for Review

1. List three capabilities of ES.
2. "The power of an ES is derived from the specific knowledge it possesses, not from the particular formulas and inference schemes it employs." Explain this statement.
3. Explain how ES can distribute (or redistribute) the available knowledge in an organization.
4. From Figure 12.2, estimate the percentage of knowledge possessed by the top 30 percent of experts.
5. List the types of knowledge included in "expertise."
6. List and describe the eight activities that human experts perform. Which activities are performed well by current expert systems?
7. What is the difference between knowledge acquisition and knowledge representation?
8. Which component of ES is mostly responsible for the reasoning capability?
9. List and define the major components of an ES.
10. A knowledge base includes facts and rules. Explain the difference between the two.
11. Describe real-time ES.
12. What is the role of a knowledge engineer?
13. List the major components of the inference engine.
14. What are the major activities performed in the "workplace"?
15. What is the function of the justifier?
16. List the four types of potential users of ES.
17. List the 10 generic categories of ES.
18. List some of the limitations of ES.
19. What is a ready-made ES? (Define, give an example.)
20. Why did the general-purpose problem solver (GPS) machine fail?
21. Define the ES development environment and contrast it with the consultation environment.

Discussion Questions

1. It is said that reasoning ability, powerful computers, inference capabilities, and heuristics are necessary but not sufficient for solving real problems. Why?
2. Comprehensive knowledge representation theories and associated general-purpose

systems when added to the capabilities listed in question 1 were helpful but still not sufficient. Why?

3. Review the CATS-1 case. What are the major lessons learned? What kind of ES is CATS-1? (per Table 12.2). What are the major advantages of this system?

4. It is said that a major difference between DSS and ES is that the former can explain a "how" question whereas the latter can also explain a "why" question. Discuss.

5. Explain how the major components of the inference engine relate to the major components of the workplace (blackboard).

6. Define symbolic reasoning and contrast it with nonsymbolic reasoning.

7. Why is it so difficult to build the knowledge-refining component?

8. Explain the relationship between development environment and consultation (run-time) environment.

9. Explain why it is said that ES make mistakes. What kind of mistakes do they make and why? Why is it easier to correct mistakes in ES than in conventional programs?

10. What are the major differences between rule-based and model-based systems?

11. Table 12.2 provides a list of 10 categories of ES. Compile a list of 20 examples, 2 in each category, from the various functional areas in an organization (accounting, finance, production, marketing, personnel, etc.)

12. Review all the limitations discussed in Section 12.10. From what you know, which of these limitations are the most likely to remain as limitations in the year 2100? Why? (See Chapter 22 for some insights.)

13. A ready-made ES is selling for $10,000. Developing one will cost you $50,000. A ready-made suit costs you $100; a tailored one will cost you $500. Develop an analogy between the two situations and describe the markets for the ready-made and the customized products.

Debate: Can an ES Enhance the Image of a Bank?

Listed below is a reporter's opinion regarding ES use by a bank for loan approval. Then a counterargument is given. Read the arguments of both sides and express your opinion. (Can you reconcile the different arguments?)

Against ES*

If you saw that classic science fiction film *2001: A Space Odyssey,* you might remember the astronaut saying, "Open the pod bay door, HAL." That was the computer's name, the HAL 2000. HAL replies, "I'm sorry Dave, I can't do that."

HAL could say things like that. He had artificial intelligence. Well, there's a computer in your future. When you go into the bank to ask for a loan, it might just say to you, "I'm sorry Dave, I can't do that." The First National Bank of Chicago is experimenting with a special artificial intelligence software program that supposedly is able to reason and make decisions just like a real human banker.

*Condensed from an article in *The Orange County Register,* February 17, 1986.

That's how the bank AI programs are supposed to work. Experienced bankers feed all their knowledge and criteria for making loans into a computer. They program the computer with the various criteria they use to make lending decisions. The AI program then has 100 to 150 rules on how to make lending decisions.

When you come in for a loan, the younger or less experienced lending officer types your information into the system. Then the computer asks some questions to clarify a few points. Then it decides whether you get the loan.

Using AI to diagnose illnesses, locate petroleum deposits, or play chess (as many of the programs are designed to do) seems like a sensible thing. But making a loan is based on a list of criteria, such as that the bank wants to "reduce its exposure to risk."

That strikes me as pretty cold, but it's exactly the reason I take a dim view of AI computers in banking. Banks have been trying to shake that cold, impersonal image they had for years by taking out the steel bars at the teller windows and developing a business style that is more sensitive to customers. Now, along comes this cold, calculating computer that will never understand, or be able to take into account, somebody's personal situation. A couple with a new child on the way won't get a home improvement loan for a room addition because the computer says the bank wants to "reduce its exposure" to those kinds of loans.

Computers can't think, they can't feel, and so far, they cannot reason. Don't get me wrong; I like computers, and I use them every day. But it's how they're used that's important. AI programs could be used to find reasons to say "yes" when people want a loan. They could be used to help people solve complex personal financial planning problems. I'd like to see the bankers realize that their AI programs ought to be designed to say, "Sure, Dave, I'd be happy to open the pod bay door."

For ES*

Many banks are busily developing ES that capture the experience of their top loan officers in sizing up loan applicants. These capture not just the formulas loan officers use to analyze the applicant's financial statements and the condition of the applicant's industry, but also all the subjective factors—the loan officers' "sixth sense"—which leads them to grant a loan to an applicant who looks questionable on paper, or to turn down an applicant who looks good. This allows junior loan officers to draw on the expertise of the most successful lenders as advisory systems.

Furthermore, loan officers must have at their fingertips an enormous amount of constantly changing data—on industry conditions, interest rates, tax law, credit ratings of the applicant's customers, and so on. Systems that make available the latest data, coupled with the heuristic rules, are providing a service that easily pays for itself and provides better service to the clients.

There is a concern that lenders would put too much reliance on the dumb system and lose the human element. But from experience so far, the reality

*Per Van Horn (19, p. 194).

seems the opposite. Bankers who are unsure of their ability to make good decisions tend to be too conservative and to turn down potentially good loans. This costs the bank just as much as granting poor loans. So these expert loan advisers allow more people to make better decisions. As a result, banks keep their clients happy and improve their own profitability.

References and Bibliography

1. Alexander, T. "Why Computers Can't Outthink the Experts." *Fortune*, August 20, 1984.
2. Augustine, N. R. "Distribution of Expertise." *Defense System Management*, Spring 1979.
3. Blanning, R. W. "Management Applications of Expert Systems." *Information and Management*, December 1984.
4. Bonissone, P. P., and H. E. Johnson, Jr. "Expert System for Diesel Electric Locomotive Repair." *Human Systems Management*, Vol. 4, 1985.
5. Buchanan, B. G., and E. H. Shortliffe, eds. *Rule-Based Expert Systems*. Reading, MA: Addison-Wesley, 1984.
6. Corcone, N., and G. McCalla. "Artificial Intelligence: Underlying Assumptions and Basic Objectives." *Journal of the American Society for Information Science*, September 1984.
7. Davis, R., and D. B. Lenat. *Knowledge-Based Systems in Artificial Intelligence*. New York: McGraw-Hill, 1983.
8. Feigenbaum, E., and P. McCorduck. *The Fifth Generation*. Reading, MA: Addison-Wesley, 1983.
9. Harmon, P., and D. King. *Expert Systems*. New York: Wiley, 1985.
10. Hayes-Roth, F. "The Knowledge-Based Expert System: A Tutorial." *Computer*, September 1984.
11. Hayes-Roth, F., et al. *Building Expert Systems*. Reading, MA: Addison-Wesley, 1983.
12. Holsapple, C. W., and A. B. Whinston, *Business Expert Systems*. Irwin, Homewood, IL, 1987.
13. Mishkoff, H. C. *Understanding Artificial Intelligence*. Dallas: Texas Instruments, 1986.
14. Naylor, C. *Build Your Own Expert System*. New York: Wiley, 1985 (for micros).
15. Newell, A., and H. Simon. *Human Problem Solving*. Englewood Cliffs, NJ: Prentice-Hall, 1973.
16. Reitman, W., ed. *Artificial Intelligence Applications for Business*. Norwood, NJ: ABLEX 1984.
17. Simon, H. A. *The Sciences of the Artificial*. Cambridge, MA: MIT Press, 1981.
18. Stefik, M., et al. "The Organization of Expert Systems, a Tutorial." *Artificial Intelligence*, March 1982.
19. Van Horn, M. *Understanding Expert Systems*. Toronto: Bantam Books, 1986.
20. Waterman, D. A. *A Guide to Expert Systems*. Reading, MA: Addison-Wesley, 1985.
21. Waterman, D. A. "How Do Expert Systems Differ from Conventional Programs?" *Expert Systems*, January 1986.
22. Weiss, S. M., and C. A. Kulikowsky. *A Practical Guide to Designing Expert Systems*. Totowa, NJ: Rowman and Allanheld, 1984.
23. Winston, P. H., and K. A. Prendergast, eds. *The AI Business*. Cambridge, MA: MIT Press, 1984.
24. Yaghmai, N. S., and J. A. Maxin. "Expert Systems: A Tutorial." *Journal of the American Society for Information Sciences*, September 1984.

APPENDIX A: Systems Cited in this Chapter

System	Vendor	Description
ACE	Bell Laboratories (Whippany, NJ)	It identifies trouble spots in telephone networks and recommends appropriate repair and preventive maintenance. The system analyzes maintenance reports generated on a daily basis by CRAS, a cable repair administration computer program. Once ACE locates the faulty telephone cables, it selects the type of maintenance most likely to be effective. It uses a rule-based knowledge representation scheme controlled by forward chaining.
DART	Stanford University (Stanford, CA)	It assists in diagnosing faults in computer hardware systems using information about the design of the device being diagnosed. The system has been applied to simple computer circuits and the teleprocessing facility of the IBM 4331. DART uses a device-independent inference procedure similar to a type of resolution theorem proving, where the system attempts to generate a proof related to the cause of the device's malfunction.
DENDRAL	Stanford University (Stanford, CA)	It infers the molecular structure of unknown compounds from mass spectral and nuclear magnetic response data. The system uses a special algorithm to systematically enumerate all possible molecular structures; it uses chemical expertise to prune this list of possibilities to a manageable size. Knowledge in DENDRAL is represented as a procedural code.
EURISKO	Stanford University (Stanford, CA)	It learns new heuristics and new domain-specific definitions of concepts in a problem domain. The system can learn by discovery in a number of different problem domains, including VLSI design. EURISKO operates by generating a device configuration, computing its input/output behavior, assessing its functionality, and then evaluating it against other comparable devices.
META-DENDRAL	Stanford University (Stanford, CA)	It helps chemists determine the dependence of mass spectrometric fragmentation on substructural features. It does this by discovering fragmentation rules for given classes of molecules. META-DENDRAL first generates a set of highly specific rules that account for a single fragmentation process in a particular molecule. Then it uses the training examples to generalize these rules. Finally, the system reexamines the rules to remove redundant or incorrect rules.
STEAMER	U.S. Navy in cooperation with Bolt, Beranek, and Newman (Cambridge, MA)	It is an intelligent CAI that instructs Navy personnel in the operation and maintenance of the propulsion plant for a 1078-class frigate. The system can monitor the student executing the boiler light-off procedure for the plant, acknowledge appropriate student actions and correct inappropriate ones. The system works by tying a simulation of the propulsion plant to a sophisticated graphical interface program that displays animated color diagrams of plant subsystems. The student can manipulate simulated components like valves, switches, and pumps, and observe the effects on plant parameters, such as changes in pressure, temperature, and flow. STEAMER uses an object-oriented representation scheme.

Chapter 13

Knowledge Acquisition

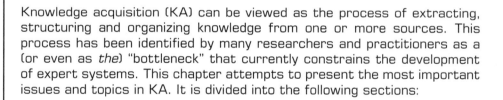

Knowledge acquisition (KA) can be viewed as the process of extracting, structuring and organizing knowledge from one or more sources. This process has been identified by many researchers and practitioners as a (or even as *the*) "bottleneck" that currently constrains the development of expert systems. This chapter attempts to present the most important issues and topics in KA. It is divided into the following sections:

13.1   Knowledge Engineering

The activity of knowledge engineering has been defined by Feigenbaum (7), a pioneer and a major contributor to the AI field, as:

> the art of bringing the principles and tools of AI research to bear on difficult applications problems requiring experts' knowledge for their solutions. The technical issues of acquiring this knowledge, representing it, and using it appropriately to construct and explain lines-of-reasoning are important problems in the design of knowledge-based systems. The art of constructing intelligent agents is both part of and an extension of the programming art. It is the art of building complex computer programs that represent and reason with knowledge of the world.

Knowledge engineering involves the cooperation of human experts in the domain who work with the knowledge engineer to codify and make explicit the rules (or other reasoning procedures) that a human expert uses to solve real problems. Often the expert uses rules applied almost subconsciously. Usually, the program is developed in what may seem a hit-or-miss method. As the rules are refined by using the emerging program, the expertise of the system increases. As more knowledge is incorporated into the program, the level of expertise rises.

Knowledge engineering usually has a synergistic effect. The knowledge possessed by human experts is often unstructured and not explicitly expressed. The construction of an ES aids the expert to articulate what he or she knows. It can also pinpoint variances from one expert to another (if several experts are being used).

A major goal in knowledge engineering is to construct programs that are modular in nature, so that additions and changes can be made in one module without affecting the workings of other modules. (*Note:* this is not necessarily the same as the concept of structural programming. Here, the concept of modularity refers to separation of knowledge structures from control mechanisms.) A second major goal is obtaining a program that can explain why it did what it did, and justify how it did it.

The success of ES depends not only on the knowledge acquired but also on how the knowledge is represented in the computer. The representation determines the manner in which inference (or reasoning) is executed. All these topics are discussed in this and the forthcoming chapter.

The Knowledge Engineering Process

The knowledge engineering process includes the following activities:

Knowledge Acquisition (KA). This activity involves the acquisition of knowledge from human experts, books, documents, sensors, or computer files. The knowledge may be specific to the problem domain and the problem-solving procedures, or it may be general knowledge (e.g., knowledge about business), or it may be metaknowledge (knowledge about knowledge). By the latter, we mean information about how experts use their knowledge to solve problems. The acquired knowledge has to be refined and organized for appropriate representation in the computer. This topic is discussed in Chapter 13.

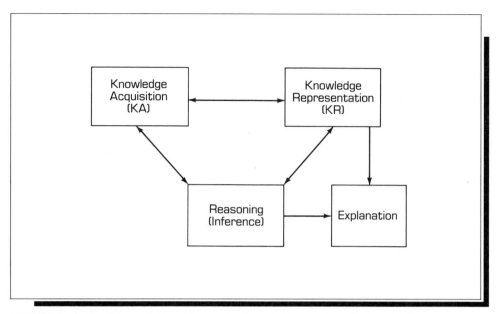

FIGURE 13.1 The interrelationship among knowledge engineering activities.

Knowledge Representation (KR).   This step involves encoding the knowledge in the knowledge base so that appropriate inferences can be made. This topic and the next two are discussed in Chapter 14.

Inference.   This activity involves the design of software that will enable the computer to make inferences based on the knowledge, and then provide advice to the user on specific issues.

Explanation and Justification.   This activity involves the design and programming of an explanation capability; for example, programming the ability to answer questions like *why* a specific piece of information is needed by the computer or *how* a certain conclusion was derived by the computer.
   The interrelationship among these activities is shown in Figure 13.1. Each of these components is influenced by the others and is influencing them as well.

13.2 **The Scope of Knowledge**

Knowledge acquisition is the extraction of knowledge from sources of expertise and its transfer to the knowledge base, and sometimes to the inference engine. Acquisition is actually done throughout the entire development process.
   Knowledge is a collection of specialized facts, procedures, and judgment rules. Some types of knowledge used in ES are shown in Figure 13.2.

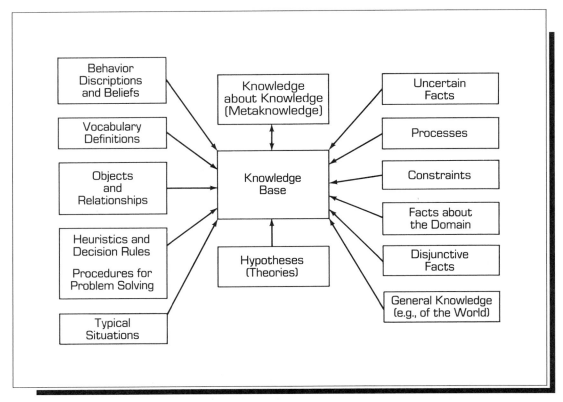

FIGURE 13.2 Types of knowledge to be represented in the knowledge base. (*Source:* Adapted from Fikes and Kehler [8].)

Sources of Knowledge

Knowledge may be collected from many sources. A representative list of sources includes:

> Books, films, computer databases, pictures, maps, flow diagrams, stories, songs, or observed behavior. These sources can be divided into two types: *documented* and *undocumented*. The latter resides in people's minds. Knowledge can be identified and collected by using any of the human senses. Knowledge can also be identified and collected by machines.

The multiplicity of sources and types of knowledge contributes to the complexity of knowledge acquisition. This complexity is only one reason why it is difficult to acquire knowledge, especially from human experts. Other reasons for the difficulties are discussed next.

13.3   Difficulties in KA

Transferring information from one person to another is difficult, in general. There are several mechanisms that can be used to conduct such a transfer: written, oral, sight, and sound—and not one of them is perfect.

Problems exist in transferring knowledge—even in communicating simple messages. Transferring knowledge in ES is even more difficult, for the following reasons:

Transfer via a Machine. The knowledge is transferred first to a machine where it must be organized in a particular manner. The machine requires the knowledge to be expressed explicitly at a lower, *more detailed* level than humans use. Human knowledge exists in a compiled format. A human simply does not remember all the intermediate steps used by his or her brain in transferring or processing knowledge. Thus, there is a mismatch between computers and experts.

The Number of Participants. While in a regular transfer of knowledge there are two participants (a sender and a receiver), in ES there could be as many as four participants (plus a computer). These participants are: the *expert*, the *knowledge engineer*, the *system designer* (builder), and the *user*. Sometimes there are even more participants (e.g., programmers and vendors). These participants have different backgrounds and they use different terminology and possess different skills and knowledge. The expert, for example, may know very little about computers, while the knowledge engineer knows very little about the problem area.

Expressing the Knowledge. The expert is often unaware of the detailed process that he or she uses to arrive at a conclusion. Therefore, the expert may use different rules in reality from what he or she states in an interview.

Structuring the Knowledge. It is necessary to elicit not only the knowledge, but also its structure. This is because it is necessary to *represent* the knowledge in a structured way (e.g., as rules).

Information Processing. In order to solve a problem an expert executes a two-step process. First, information about the external world is inputted into the brain. This information is collected via sensors or it is being retrieved from memory. Second, the expert uses an inductive, deductive, or other problem-solving approach on the preceding information. The result (output) is a recommendation.

This process is *internal* and the knowledge engineer must ask the expert to *introspect* about the process and about the "inner experiences" that are involved in it. It may be very difficult for the expert to express his or her experiences regarding this process, especially when they are made up of sensations, thoughts, sense memories, and feelings.

Representation Mismatch. There is a difference between the way a human expert normally expresses knowledge and the way the knowledge must be represented in the computer.

Other Reasons. Several other reasons add to the complexity of the problem. These include:

□ Lack of time and/or cooperation on the part of the expert.
□ The complexity of testing and refining knowledge.
□ Poorly defined methods for knowledge elicitation.

Many efforts have been made recently in order to overcome some of these problems (For a comprehensive survey, see Gaines [10]). For example, research on knowledge acquisition tools has begun to focus on ways to decrease the representation mismatch between the human expert and the program under development. One form of this research might be characterized as research on learning by being told. The attempt here is to develop programs capable of accepting advice as it would often be given to a human novice. For example, in teaching a novice how to play the card game Hearts, an expert might advise the novice to "avoid taking the queen of spades." A human novice would be able to operationalize this advice by translating it into specific techniques or procedures that would result in not acquiring the queen of spades ("Don't lead the ace or king of spades"). The ability of ES to make this kind of association is currently very limited.

Another method of easing the representation mismatch between an expert and a program is to allow the expert to converse with the system in a natural language. One step in this direction is to develop computer representations for knowledge which are easily represented in their English-language equivalent. This approach has been taken in developing the ROSIE system (see Chapter 15). Other ES development software packages such as EXSYS and VP Expert greatly simplify the syntax of the rules (in a rule-based system) to make them easier for an ES builder to create and understand without special training.

Finally, some of these difficulties may be lessened or eliminated with computer-aided KA (see Section 13.7) and with extensive integration of the KA efforts. (see Gaines [10]).

13.4   The Process of Knowledge Acquisition

The general process of knowledge acquisition is composed of five stages (see Figure 13.3). These stages are (per Hayes-Roth [12]):

1. *Identification.* During this stage the problem and its major characteristics are identified. The problem is broken into subproblems (if necessary), the participants (experts, users, etc.) are identified, and the resources are outlined. The knowledge engineer learns about the situation, and the purpose of the ES is agreed on.
2. *Conceptualization.* The knowledge relevant to the decision situation can be very diversified. Therefore, it is necessary to determine the concepts and relationships used. "Which information is used and how can it be represented in an ES? Are rules a good representation medium? How is certain knowledge to be extracted?" These and many other questions are answered during the conceptualization.
3. *Formalization.* Knowledge is acquired for representation in the knowledge base. The manner in which knowledge is organized and represented could determine the acquisition methodology. For example, in

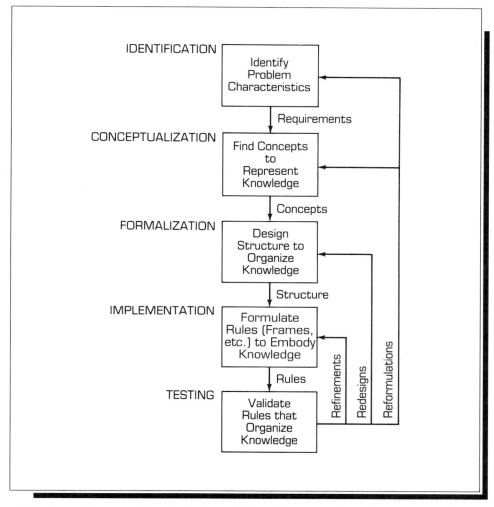

FIGURE 13.3 Stages of knowledge acquisition. (*Source:* Hayes-Roth, F. "The Knowl-edge-Based Expert System: A Tutorial." *Computer*, September 1984, © 1984, IEEE.)

rule-based systems the knowledge must be organized in terms of rules. In this stage knowledge acquisition is actually mixed with knowledge representation. Here the various software and hardware pieces are also examined. This stage is very difficult because it includes the extraction of knowledge from experts.

4. *Implementation.* This stage involves the programming of knowledge into the computer. However, refinements of the knowledge are made with additional acquisitions or changes. A prototype ES is being developed at this stage.

5. *Testing.* In the final stage, the knowledge engineer tests the system by subjecting it to examples. The results are shown to the expert and the rules or the frames are revised if necessary. That is, the validity of the knowledge is examined.

As can be seen in Figure 13.3 each stage involves a circular procedure of iteration and reiteration (i.e., the knowledge engineer reformulates, redesigns, and refines the system constantly). In addition, rules (or other representations of knowledge) are added and deleted periodically. During the entire time, the knowledge engineer works closely with the domain expert.

The execution of these stages can be very lengthy and tedious. Many experts are usually not explicitly aware of conceptualization and modeling. Therefore, the knowledge engineer needs to clarify the identification and conceptualization stages. Representative issues that need to be clarified are shown in Table 13.1.

13.5   Manual Methods of Knowledge Elicitation

The basic model of knowledge engineering portrays teamwork in which a knowledge engineer mediates between the expert and the knowledge base (see Figure 13.4). He or she elicits knowledge from the expert, refines it with the expert, and represents it in the knowledge base. The elicitation of the knowledge from the expert can be done manually or with the aid of computers. In this section we will describe the major manual methods that are being used in KA.

Most of these techniques were borrowed (but frequently modified) from psychology. These methods are classified in different ways and even appear under different names in the literature.

TABLE 13.1   Preliminary and Detailed Issues in KA.

Preliminary Issues

- The basic ("primitive") concepts and terms
- The inputs to the problem; which of them are difficult
- Typical solutions (outputs) to the problem; what are their characteristics?
- Sources of knowledge to be used
- Methods of knowledge acquisition
- Decomposition of the problem (if needed)
- Process to be used
- Implementation strategies (and problems) of proposed solutions

Detailed Issues

- The specific input data; where they come from and how they are organized and which ones are difficult to obtain
- The interrelationship between data items; how they relate to decision rules
- The relative importance and validity of data
- The degreee of certainty of the data (inputs, outputs) and the expert's strength of belief in data, rules, and output
- The underlying assumptions, strategies, and conclusions
- The constraints
- The conflicts, exceptions to rules, and conflict resolutions
- The reasoning process; the types of inferences
- The expert's responses to changes in the system or its environment
- The measures of performance (of the outcome)
- The degree of complexity of the problem
- The relationship to solutions of other experts

Source: Adapted (with additions) from Hart (11) and Wolfgram et al. (27).

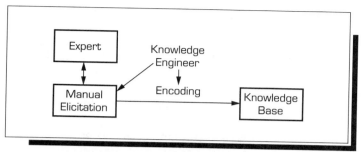

FIGURE 13.4 Manual knowledge elicitation.

The following groups of methods will be discussed in this section:

☐ Interview analysis.
☐ Observations of experts.
☐ Questionnaires and experts' reports.
☐ Analysis of documented knowledge.

Interview Analysis

The most commonly used form of KA is the face to face interview analysis. It is an explicit technique and it appears in several variations. It involves a direct dialogue between the expert and the knowledge engineer (KE). Information is collected with the aid of conventional instruments (such as tape recorders or questionnaires), and it is subsequently transcribed, analyzed, and coded.

Example Problems (Cases).   In this form of interview the expert is presented with a simulated case or better with an actual problem of the sort that the ES will be expected to solve. The expert is asked to "talk" the knowledge engineer through the solution. Sometimes this method is referred to as the *walkthrough* method. One refinement of the example interview begins with no information at all given to the expert. Any facts that the expert requires must be asked for explicitly. By doing this, the expert's path through the domain may be made more evident, especially in terms of defining the input an ES would require.

Here is a simple example of knowledge acquisition in the area of helping novices use the Statistical Analysis System (SAS) computer package (the example was provided by David King of Teknowledge, Inc.). The dialogue between the expert and the KE may look like this:

EXPERT: Yesterday I talked with a typical novice. He couldn't get started because he didn't understand the DATA step. That's generally a first step and people often forget it.
KE: What did this novice need in the DATA step?
EXPERT: Well, he needed one and it was missing. There are about five different kinds of DATA steps. I recommended a simple fixed-field input and suggested he put the data in the deck rather than in a separate file. By doing that, it cuts down on the complexity of the JCL.
KE: JCL?

EXPERT: JCL is Job Control Language, a nasty set of instructions mostly for file handling. If the data are elsewhere, then a line of JCL must be prepared that says where the data file is and how it is formatted.

KE: We may need to talk more about JCL, but for now, let's return to the man yesterday and his need for a DATA step. Why did you suggest a fixed-format DATA step?

EXPERT: Mostly because his data set was simple. Fixed-format requires the person to refine his data and organize it neatly in rows and columns. Free-field input in the DATA step seems easier to novices, but the possibility of error is greater and finding mistakes in a free-field data set is difficult.

KE: When you say that this man's data set was simple, what do you mean?

EXPERT: There were fewer than 100 records, and only about 15 variables. There also were no missing data and no complexity in the cases. Last week I talked with a woman who couldn't decide what a record was. She had scores for people who were in classrooms that were nested in schools. She wanted to study school differences. That's not a simple data set.

By interviewing the expert, the knowledge engineer slowly, step-by-step, learns what is going on. Then he or she builds a representation of the knowledge in the expert's terms.

The process of knowledge acquisition involves uncovering the attributes of the problem to which the expert pays attention (e.g., the DATA step, fixed-field input) and making explicit the thought process (usually expressed as rules) that the expert uses to interpret these attributes.

This type of interview is most common. It appears in several variations. In addition to the "talkthrough" one can ask the expert to "teachthrough," or "readthrough." In a "teachthrough" the expert acts as an instructor and the knowledge engineer as a student. The expert not only tells *what* he or she does, but also explains *why* and, in addition, instructs the knowledge engineer in the skills and strategies needed to perform the task. In a "readthrough" approach the expert is asked to instruct the knowledge engineer *how* to read and interpret the documents which are used for the task.

Protocol Analysis.   Protocol analysis, particularly a set of techniques known as verbal protocol analysis, is a common method by which the knowledge engineer acquires detailed knowledge from the expert. A "protocol" is a record or documentation of the expert's step-by-step information processing and decision-making behavior. In this method, which is very similar to the previous one, but more formal and systematic, the expert is asked to perform a real task and to verbalize his or her thought process. The expert is asked by the knowledge engineer to "think aloud" while performing the task or solving the problem under observation. Usually, a recording is made as the expert thinks aloud, describing every aspect of his information processing and decision-making behavior. This recording then becomes a record or "protocol" of the expert's ongoing behavior. Later, the recording is transcribed for further analysis (e.g., deduce the decision process) and coded by the knowledge engineer. For further details see Ericsson and Simon (6) and Wolfgram et al. (27).

Discussion of Cases in Context of a Repertory System.   The existence of a prototype can often be used to improve the knowledge engineering process.

By taking the expert through example cases, tested on the prototype, the knowledge engineer has an opportunity to see what the expert thinks of the work to date. The principle that applies in this case is that cued recall is generally much more effective than uncued. Given something concrete to criticize, experts may find that they can more easily clarify their own ideas.

Classification Interviews and the Repertory Grid Approach. The purpose of a classification interview is to gain insight into the expert's mental model of the problem domain. The techniques for eliciting this kind of knowledge were derived from psychology. The primary method is called *repertory grid analysis* (RGA).

The RGA is based on Kelly's model of human thinking, called Personal Construct Theory. According to this theory each person is a scientist with his or her own personal model of the world. This scientist classifies and categorizes knowledge and perceptions about his or her world, developing theories about it. Based on these theories he or she is able to anticipate, and then act on the basis of these anticipations.

This model matches our view of an expert at work: it is a description of the development and use of his knowledge, and therefore it is suitable for expert systems as shown by Hart (11).

In an RGA, the expert is presented with triplets of objects from the domain and asked to say what features distinguish any two from the third. Repertory grid analysis may be very time-consuming if the number of domain objects exceeds a half dozen.

The techniques associated with repertory grid analysis are all subject to the criticism that they may serve only to elicit experts' *attitudes* to the objects rather than their knowledge about them.

Multidimensional scaling is another classification technique for evaluating the underlying structure of the expert's knowledge. It too may evaluate only perceptions and thus should be used in conjunction with other methods.

Directed Interviews. In this form of interview, which usually supplements the previous interview methods, the expert and the knowledge engineer discuss the domain and the ways of solving problems within it at a more general level than in the previous two methods. Directed interviews provide the knowledge engineer with an opportunity to clarify matters that remain unclear from previous work. In particular, it would be useful to have the expert describe some of her or his most memorable cases, and the best remembered exceptional occurrences.

Informal Interviews. The above methods attempt to introduce some structure into interviews. However, many KA interviews are being conducted informally, usually as a starting point. This approach saves time and requires less skill. It helps to get quickly to the basic structure of the domain, and is usually followed by a formal technique. (Actually, you do not want too much information too early.)

Observation of the Expert at Work

In some cases it may be possible to observe the expert at work in the field. This is in many ways the most obvious and straightforward approach to knowledge acquisition. The difficulties involved should not, however, be underestimated. For example, most experts advise several people and systems simultaneously. Thus, when observations are being taken, they cover all other activities as well. Therefore large quantities of data are being collected from which only a little is useful. In particular, if recordings and/or video tapings are made, the cost of transcribing large quantities of tape or video should be carefully considered.

Observations can be viewed as a special case of protocols. There are two types of observations: motor and eye-movement. In the first case the expert's *physical* performance of the task (e.g., walking, reaching, talking) is documented. In the second one a record of where the expert fixes his gaze is being made. Observations are used primarily as a way of supporting verbal protocols. They are generally expensive and time consuming.

Questionnaires and Experts' Reports[*]

Sometimes it is possible to elicit knowledge from experts by using a questionnaire or an organized report. Open-ended questionnaires are appropriate for knowledge discovery, where high-level concepts are usually the result. Close-ended (or forced-answer) questionnaires are more structured and easy to fill in, but the knowledge collected is limited. In addition to questionnaires, experts may be asked to log their activities, prepare a one-hour introductory lecture, or produce reports about their problem solving activities.

Experts' reports and questionnaires exhibit a number of problems:

1. They essentially require the expert to act as a knowledge engineer, without a knowledge engineer's training.
2. The reports tend to have a high degree of bias; they typically reflect the expert's opinion concerning how the task "should be done" rather than "how it is really done."
3. Experts will often describe new and untested ideas and strategies they have been contemplating, but still have not included, in their decision-making behavior. The mixing of actual behavior and "ideal future" behavior is endemic.
4. Experts' reports are time-consuming efforts, and the experts lose interest rapidly. The quality of information attained will rapidly decrease as the report progresses.
5. Experts must be proficient in flowcharting or other process-documenting techniques.

Given these caveats, under certain conditions, such as the inaccessibility of an expert to the knowledge engineer, expert reports and questionnaires may provide useful preliminary knowledge discovery and acquisition.

Analysis of Documented Knowledge

The previous methods were designed to extract undocumented knowledge from human experts. However, in many cases knowledge can be acquired from other sources, in addition to, or instead of, human experts. The major advantage of

[*](per Wolfgram et al. [27]).

this approach is that there is no need to use an expert. It is used in *knowledge-based* systems where the concern is to handle a large or complex amount of information rather than world class expertise. Searching through corporate policy manuals or catalogs is an example of such a situation.

At present there are a very few methodologies that deal with knowledge acquisition from documented sources. It has, however, a great potential for automation. Documented knowledge, of almost any type, can be easily (and inexpensively) transferred to a computer's database. The analysis of the knowledge can then be done manually, but it can also be done with the use of AI technologies (perhaps a combination of a speech understanding and expert systems). Thus, expert systems may be used to build other expert systems.

Expert systems already can scan databases and digitize books, journals, and magazines and this capability is increasing. Data stored in another computer system could be retrieved electronically to create or update the knowledge base of the expert system, all without the intervention of a knowledge engineer or an expert.

Potential benefits of automated knowledge acquisition and analysis which are discussed in the forthcoming sections are (1) automated methods that may prove more competent than humans for acquiring and fine-tuning knowledge bases and databases (especially as the amount of information grows and becomes more complex), and (2) automated methods that would significantly reduce the high cost of human resources and time involved in constructing the knowledge base.

Knowledge Transformation

A topic related to the acquisition of documented knowledge is the *transformation* of knowledge among or between expert systems. Such a situation may develop when the knowledge engineer attempts to transfer a specific system from one ES shell to another, combine two or more ES, or build communicating ES. This problem can be difficult, especially when the knowledge bases are written in different representation languages (e.g. rules and frames). When such transformation is completed, the knowledge must be *preserved*. The process should also be efficient and effective. For a suggested process and examples, see Rothman (25).

13.6　Computer-aided Knowledge Acquisition and Induction

The elicitation methods presented earlier are labor intensive. The two major participants are the knowledge engineer, who is difficult to get and is highly paid, and the domain expert, who is usually busy and frequently uncooperative. Therefore, manual elicitation methods are both slow and expensive. In addition, they exhibit some other deficiencies, such as:

□ It is difficult to validate the acquired knowledge.
□ There is frequently weak correlation between verbal reports and mental behavior.

□ In certain situations experts are unable to provide an overall account of how their decisions are made.

□ The quality of the system depends too much on the quality of the expert and the knowledge engineer.

□ The knowledge engineer does not understand, in many cases, the nature of the business.

Therefore, it makes sense to develop KA methods that will reduce or even eliminate the need for these two participants. These methods, which are described as *computer-aided KA*, or automated KA, vary in their objectives. These objectives are:

□ Increase the productivity of knowledge engineering.
□ Reduce the skill level required for KA.
□ Eliminate (or drastically reduce) the need for an expert.
□ Eliminate (or drastically reduce) the need for a knowledge engineer.

The specific methods described in the text vary in their objectives, processes, and degree of success. For example, induction methods, which are discussed next, aim to replace both the expert and the knowledge engineer.

Automated Rule Induction. *Induction* means a process of reasoning from the specific to the general. In ES terminology it refers to the process in which rules are generated by a computer program from example cases.

A rule-induction system is given examples of a problem (called a *training set*) where the outcome is known. When it has been given several examples (the more the better), the rule induction system can create rules that are true for the example cases. The rules can then be used to assess other cases where the outcome is not known. The heart of a rule-induction system is an *algorithm*, which is used to induce the rules from the examples.

An example of a simplified rule induction can be seen in the work of a loan officer in a bank. The requests for loans include information about the applicants such as income level, assets, age, and the number of dependents. These are the *attributes* or characteristics of the applicants. If we log several example cases each with its final decision, we will find a situation that resembles the data in Table 13.2.

From these cases it is easy to infer the following rules:

1. If income is above $69,000, approve the loan.

TABLE 13.2 Cases for Induction

	Attributes				
Applicant	Annual Income ($)	Assets ($)	Age	Number of Dependents	Decision
Mr. White	50,000	100,000	30	3	Yes
Ms. Green	70,000	None	35	1	Yes
Mr. Smith	40,000	None	33	2	No
Ms. Rich	30,000	250,000	42	0	Yes

2. If income is $30,000 or more, the age is at least 40, the assets are above $249,000, and there are no dependents, approve the loan.
3. If income is between $30,000 and $70,000 and assets are at least $100,000, approve the loan.

The Advantages of Rule Induction. One of the leading researchers in the KA field, Donald Michie, has pointed out that only certain types of ES tasks can be accomplished using knowledge acquisition methods like interviews and observations. These are the systems where the domain of knowledge is certain, small, loosely coupled, or modular. As the domain gets bigger and more complex, experts become unable to explain how they operate. However, they can still supply the knowledge engineer with suitable examples of problems and solutions. Using rule induction allows ES to be used in the more complicated, and more commercially rewarding, field. (see: Michie, D. (ed.), "Introductory Readings in Expert Systems," New York: Gordon & Breach, 1984.)

Another advantage is that the builder does not have to be a knowledge engineer. He or she can be the expert or a system analyst. This not only saves time and money, but it also solves the problem of the knowledge engineer, especially if he or she is an outsider unfamiliar with the "business."

Other advantages are

- Machine induction offers the possibility of deducing new knowledge. It may be possible to list all the factors that influence a decision, without understanding their impacts, and to induce a rule that works successfully.
- Once rules are generated they are reviewed by the expert and modified if necessary. A big advantage of rule induction is that it enhances the thinking process of the expert.

Difficulties in Implementation. Several difficulties exist with the implementation of rule induction. They are as follows:

- Some induction programs may generate rules that are not easy for a human to understand, because the way in which they classify a problem's attributes and properties may not be in accordance with the way that a human would do it.
- Rule-induction programs do not select the attributes. An expert still has to be available to specify which attributes are significant: for example, which are the important factors in approving a loan. Rule-induction systems also do not help discover that two attributes may be functionally or causally related, and not independent of each other. Using such redundant attributes can create biased and incorrect rules.
- The search process in rule induction is based on special algorithms that generate efficient decision trees that reduce the number of questions that must be asked before a conclusion is reached. Several alternative algorithms are available and they vary in their processes and capabilities. (e.g., general vs. specific).
- The method is good only for rule-based, classifications-type problems. (However, many problems can be rephrased or split so that they fall into the classification category).

☐ The number of attributes must be fairly small. With more than 15 attributes there may be a need for a large computer. The upper limit on the number of attributes is approached very quickly.

☐ The number of "sufficient" examples that are needed can be very large.

☐ The set of examples must be "sanitized," for example, cases that are exceptions to rules must be removed. (These exceptions can be determined by observing inconsistent rules.)

☐ A major problem with the method, per Hart (11), is that the builder does not know in advance whether the number of examples is sufficient and whether the algorithm is good enough. To be sure of this would presuppose that the builder had some idea of the "solution"; the reason for using induction in the first instance is that the builder *does not know* the solution, but wants to discover it by using the rules.

Software Packages.   Several software packages are available on the market both for PCs and for larger computers. Representative packages are

☐ 1st Class, from Program in Motion, Inc. Wayland, MA (PC).

☐ TIMM, from General Research Corp, Santa Barbara, CA (Larger computer).

☐ Rule Master (PC, and Larger).

☐ EX-Tran 7 (PC, and Larger).

☐ Expert one (Ease); see case 5, Ch. 17 (PC).

☐ WIZARD (PC).

☐ VP Expert (which is introduced later) (PC).

Most of these programs not only generate rules, but also check them for possible logical conflict. Furthermore, some of them can be used as ES shells. That is, they can be used both to generate the rules for the knowledge base and then to construct an ES that uses this knowledge.

An example of a rule induction screen (generated with 1st Class) is shown in Figure 13.5. Another example, using VP Expert, is given in the instructor's manual to this book.

Interactive Induction.   The major objective of rule induction methods and software, as described earlier, is to eliminate or drastically reduce the need for both the expert and the knowledge engineer. The tools are fairly simple so they can be used with little training. However, in many cases it is advisable to use a knowledge engineer even if the rules are induced automatically. The combination of a knowledge engineer supported by a computer is labeled interactive acquisition. An attempt to automate some tasks of the knowledge engineer will be shown in the next section. However, one interesting attempt that combines *induction* and interactive acquisition can be found in a tool called *Auto-Intelligence* (from IntelligenceWare, Inc., Los Angeles, CA). Auto-Intelligence captures the knowledge of an expert through interactive interviews, distills the knowledge and then automatically generates a knowledge base (rule-based). An important part of the interaction with Auto-Intelligence is a structure discovery, during which the *system* interviews the expert *prior* to classifying the information and distilling knowledge by induction.

new_**E**xample. **R**eplicate. **C**hange. **A**ctivate. **M**ove. **D**elete.

Files   Definitions   **Examples**   Methods   Rule   Advisor

[F1 = Help]   14 Examples in SHIPPING   [F9=Definitions]   [F10=Methods]
      (inactive)   weights–>

	MEMO	POUNDS	SPEED	SAT_DEL?	TIME_RQD	SHIP_BY
> 1:	–	up_to_.5	next_day	*	10:30_A.M.	Onite_Let
2:	–	up_to_.5	next_day	*	later	Exp_Mail
3:	–	.5_to_2	next_day	*	later	Exp_Mail
4:	–	.5_to_2	next_day	*	10:30_A.M.	Courier_Pak
5:	–	2_to_20	next_day	*	later	Courier_Pak
6:	–	2_to_20	next_day	*	later	Exp_Mail
7:	–	over_20	next_day	no	*	UPS_nxt_day
8:	–	over_20	next_day	yes	*	Priority_1
9:	–	over_20	next_day	yes	*	Exp_Mail
10:	–	over_20	2nd_day	yes	*	Std_Air
11:	–	over_20	2nd_day	no	*	UPS_2_day
12:	Check this.	over_20	3rd_day	*	*	Priority
13:	–	over_20	6_days	*	*	UPS_Ground
14:	–	*	6_days	*	*	Parcel_Post

How much does the package weigh in pounds?

Edit_rule.   **M**ark!examples.   **P**rint_rule.   **S**tatistics on/off.   line: 4

Files   Definitions   Examples   Methods   **Rule**   Advisor

[F1=Help]   File = SHIPPING   [F9=Definitions] [F10=Methods]
— start of rule —
SPEED??
┌ next_day: POUNDS??
│   ┌ up_to_.5: TIME_RQD??
│   │   10:30_A.M.:———————————— Onite_Let
│   │   later:———————————————— Exp_Mail
│   ├ .5_TO_2: TIME_RQD??
│   │   10:30_A.M.:———————————— Courier-Pak
│   │   later:———————————————— Exp_Mail
│   ├ 2_TO_20: TIME_RQD??
│   │   10:30_A.M.:———————————— Courier-Pak
│   │   later:———————————————— Exp_Mail
│   └ over_20: SAT_DEL??
│   yes: ———————————————— Priority_1
│   &– – – – – – – – – – – – Exp_Mail
│   no: ————————————————— UPS_nxt_day
└ 2nd_day: SAT_DEL??
            yes: ———————————————————— Std_Air
            no: ————————————————————— UPS_2_day

Active examples:	14	Answer's examples:	1	Examples 1	
Answer frequency:	0.07	Answer probability:	0.07	Relative probability:	1.00
Total weight:	14.00	Answer weight:	1.00	Average weight:	1.00

SHIPPING ADVISOR

[F1 = Help]   1st-CLASS Advisor for SHIPPING   [F9=Rule]   [Esc=Stop]

This advisor recommends options for shipping packages.
When do you need it delivered?

> next_day   <
  2nd_day
  3rd_day
  6_day

Three steps to create an expert system with 1st-CLASS: [1] Define a "knowledge base" and
enter examples of how an expert makes decisions (in this case: shipping a package), selecting from a menu. [2] Check the resulting automatically created rule (or create your own).
[3] Test the advisor (part the user sees).

FIGURE 13.5 Rule induction using 1st class (*Source:* Program in Motion Inc.)

Structure is discovered by utilizing special deductive question generation techniques based on repertory grids, multi-dimensional scaling, and data classification. These techniques help experts think about problems locally and piece by piece, thus gradually revealing their expertise. A number of induction techniques are used to extend and generalize knowledge.

Auto-Intelligence builds ES for structured selection or heuristic classification tasks in which an expert makes decisions and selects among a number of choices based on available criteria. Examples of heuristic classification tasks include diagnosis, investment selection, situation assessment, etc. Auto-Intelligence interacts with experts (without knowledge engineers) helping them bypass their cognitive defenses and identify the important criteria and constructs used in decision making. For details, see Parsaye (22).

13.7   Interactive Methods and Tools

There exists a number of KA and encoding tools that greatly reduce the need for the time (and/or skill level) of the knowledge engineer. The knowledge engineer in such a case still plays an important role in the process as shown in Figure 13.6. The figure shows the major tasks of the knowledge engineer (per Gaines [10]). These tasks are:

□ Advise the expert on the process of interactive knowledge elicitation.
□ Manage the interactive knowledge acquisition tools, setting them up appropriately.
□ Edit the unencoded and coded knowledge base in collaboration with the expert. Manage the knowledge encoding tools, setting them up appropriately.
□ Validate the application of the knowledge base in collaboration with the expert.
□ Train the clients in the effective use of the knowledge base in collaboration with the expert by developing operational and training procedures.

This use of interactive elicitation can be combined with manual elicitation and with the use of the interactive tools by the knowledge engineer. The knowledge engineer can:

□ Directly elicit knowledge from the expert.
□ Use the interaction elicitation tools to enter knowledge into the knowledge base.

Several types of tools were developed to support KA. Representative examples are as follows:

Editors and Interfaces.   Using a text editor or a special knowledge-base editor can facilitate the task of entering knowledge into the system and decrease the chance of errors. A good editor provides smooth user interfaces that facilitate instruction and display information conveniently. The editor checks, for example, the syntax and the semantics for completeness and consistency. The

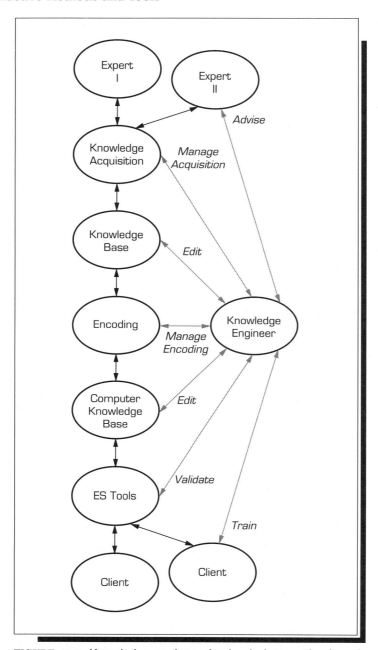

FIGURE 13.6 Knowledge engineers' roles in interactive knowledge acquisition. (*Source*: Adapted from Gaines [10].)

rule editor of EXSYS is an example of one that simplifies rule input and testing. A spelling and a grammar checker can also be used to detect errors.

Explanation Facility. The explanation subsystem serves not only the user but also the knowledge engineer and the expert in refining and improving the knowledge base. In addition to general-purpose devices (such as debugging and trace mechanisms), there are specially constructed explanation facilities. The latter can trace, for example, the chain of reasoning after it has been completed.

Knowledge-base Revision.   Changes in the knowledge base can be made by selecting an appropriate revision from a set of possible ones. To avoid introducing new bugs or direct inconsistencies, one can use such aids as a semantic consistency checker or automated testing.

Expertise Transfer System (ETS).   This is a computer program that interviews experts and helps them to build expert systems. The interviewing methodology is borrowed, similarly to the RGA, from a branch of psychology called Personal Construct Theory. ETS interviews experts to "uncover vocabulary conclusions, problem-solving traits, trait structures, trait weights, and inconsistencies." It has been utilized to construct rapid prototypes (often in less than two hours), to aid the expert in determining if there is sufficient knowledge to solve the problem, and to create knowledge bases for a variety of different ES shells from its own internal representation. A new version of ETS called NeoETS has been developed to expand the capabilities of ETS. The method is limited to classification-type problems. For details see Boose (2).

Pictorial Knowledge Acquisition (PIKA).   PIKA is a graphics editor whose output is a collection of structured graphical objects that can be combined to support a multilevel interface. (see Freiling et al. [9]).

Kriton.   This experimental system attempts to automate the use of the repertory grid approach. It conducts interviews with experts, then it analyzes protocols and documents by interacting with the experts. The expert, based on keyword statistics on articles, selects portions of texts for propositional analysis using the same tools used in protocol analysis. Since documents are normally not as problem-oriented as protocols, the expert adds goal information to the results of the analysis. Should the experiments with the system be successful, the system can replace a knowledge engineer, resulting in a true breakthrough in AI applications. For further details see Diederich et al. (5).

An Example of a Knowledge Acquisition Aid—TEIRESIAS.   This program was developed to assist the knowledge engineer in the creation (or revision) of rules for a specific ES while working with the EMYCIN shell. The program uses a natural language interface to assist the knowledge engineer in testing and debugging new knowledge. It provides an expanded explanation capability. For example, if builders find that a set of knowledge rules leads to an inadequate conclusion, they can have TEIRESIAS show all the rules used to reach that conclusion. With the rule editor, adjustments can easily be made. To expedite the process, TEIRESIAS translates each new rule, which is entered in natural language, into Lisp. Then it retranslates the rule into natural language. The program thus can point out inconsistencies, rule conflicts, and inadequacies.

Integrated Tools.   Most of the preceding tools and many others were designed separately on the assumption that they will be used by a specific ES participant (e.g., the expert) for the execution of a specific task. In reality, however, participants may play multiple roles or even exchange roles. Therefore, there is a trend to integrate the acquisition aids. For an overview of such integration see Gaines (10). Examples of such an integration are Auto-Intelligence, which was described earlier, and KADS, which is described next.

Knowledge Acquisition and Documentation System (KADS). This is a set of techniques developed at the University of Amsterdam. Their purpose is to aid the knowledge engineer in acquiring, structuring, analyzing, and documenting expert knowledge. KADS is known to be very successful in increasing the knowledge engineer's productivity.

13.8   Knowledge Acquisition From Multiple Experts

An important element in the development of an ES is the identification of experts. This is a complicated task in the real world environment, perhaps because often so many support mechanisms are used by practitioners for certain tasks (questionnaires, informal and formal consultations, texts, etc.). Together these support mechanisms contribute to the high quality of professional output. However, this may tend to make it difficult to identify a knowledge "czar" whose estimates, process, or knowledge are clearly superior to what the system and mix of staff, support tools, and consulting skills produce in the rendering of normal client service.

The usual approach to this problem is to build ES for a very narrow domain, where expertise is clearly defined. In such a case it is easy to find one expert. However, whereas many ES were constructed with one expert, an approach that is advocated as a good strategy for ES construction, there could be a need for multiple experts, especially when more serious ES are being constructed or when expertise is not particularly well defined.[*]

The major purposes of using multiple experts are: (1) to broaden the coverage of proposed solutions (i.e., the solutions complement each other) and (2) to combine the strengths of different approaches of reasoning.

When multiple experts are used, there are often differences of opinion and conflicts that have to be resolved. This is especially true when developing expert systems with multiple knowledge sources, since these systems typically address problems that involve the use of subjective reasoning and heuristics. The conflicts can arise owing to a lack of knowledge of a certain aspect of the problem, or owing to statistical uncertainty (e.g., different experts may assign different event outcome probabilities while observing the same evidence). Experts may also follow different lines of reasoning derived from their background and experience, which could lead to conflicting solutions. Multiple lines of reasoning can sometimes be used to combine the strengths of the proposed solutions and/or to assure a complete coverage of the domain.

Other related issues are:

□ Identifying different aspects of the problem and matching them with different experts.
□ Integrating knowledge from various experts.
□ Assimilating conflicting strategies.

[*]Much of the discussion in the remaining portion of this section was extracted from Alexander and Evans (1).

◻ Personalizing community knowledge bases.

◻ Developing programming technologies to support the above issues.

Methods of Integrating the Knowledge of Several Experts

The major approaches to the issue of integration are:

◻ Blend several lines of reasoning through consensus methods.

◻ Use an analytical approach.

◻ Keep the lines of reasoning distinct and select a specific line of reasoning based on the situation.

◻ Decompose the knowledge acquired into specialized knowledge sources (Blackboard Systems).

◻ Automate the process.

Consensus Methods

Consensus can be reached in several ways using methodologies borrowed from behavioral sciences such as group dynamics. Each expert is provided information on the judgment of the other experts within the group and is provided an opportunity to revise his or her judgment based on this information. The interaction could include a face-to-face meeting of the experts, or the experts' identities might be concealed from each other to avoid personality influences.

Analytical Approaches

An analytical approach can be used when the expertise involves numerical values (such as assessment of probabilities). One can use methods borrowed from the literature on multiple-criteria decision making. Several attempts were made to develop a "group probability" as a weighted aggregation of individual probability assessments. For details see Alexander and Evans (1).

Select a Specific Line of Reasoning

According to this procedure, which was developed by LeClair (15), multiple lines of reasoning are allowed to coexist without unwanted interactions that could compromise an expert's advice. Hence, a deduction obtained through one expert's line of reasoning would not be used in the reasoning process of another expert.

Once multiple lines of reasoning are accommodated in the expert system then the system should attempt to select a line of reasoning based on the characteristics of each situation. The goal is not to achieve a consensus solution, but to select the most appropriate solution. LeClair achieves this by introducing information specific to the decision situation; the expert system then *automatically* selects a line of reasoning using this information. The basis for this approach is that each expert's line of reasoning is founded on his or her unique experiences in the problem domain and therefore represents a distinct philosophy regarding the problem domain.

Automated Processes

While the previous method uses an automated approach for selecting a line of reasoning, once multiple lines of reasoning are programmed and accommodated in the knowledge base (using metarules), an attempt is made to automate the entire process. Expert Ease (an early ES shell, which currently sells under the name Expert One) allows for the input of multiple lines of reasoning. Once the multiple lines of reasoning have been input, the system determines the most efficient way (using the theory of entropy or uncertainty reduction) to reach the solution. However, it is difficult to discern what line of reasoning is followed, since the system blends the multiple lines of reasoning together in attempting to find the most efficient route to a solution. Another negative aspect of Expert Ease is that it does not accommodate conflicts in lines of reasoning. When a conflict does occur, it simply avoids the problem by selecting the first occurrence of the conflicting rule.

Blackboard Systems

Blackboard systems maximize independence among knowledge sources by appropriately dividing the problem domain. In this approach expertise is divided among subdomains (one expert for each subdomain) and the experts cooperate to solve the problem. However, the interaction is kept to a minimum. Many experts' systems have been developed using the blackboard system architecture (e.g., see ExperTax, in Chapter 16). The interaction among experts can be done in several ways. For example, conclusions of the different knowledge sources are posted on a "blackboard" and these are available to all knowledge sources. The knowledge sources have a condition and an action part. The condition component specifies the situations under which a particular knowledge source could contribute to an activity. A scheduler or an event manager controls the progress toward a solution in blackboard systems, by determining which knowledge source to schedule next, or which problem subdomain to focus on. For further details see Nii (20).

13.9 Validation and Verification of the Knowledge Base

Knowledge acquisition involves quality control aspects. These appear under the terms "evaluation," "validation," and "verification." These terms are frequently confused, mixed up, or used interchangeably. We use the following definitions (per O'Keefe et al. [21]):

Evaluation. Evaluation is a broad concept. Its objective is to assess an expert system's overall value. In addition to exhibiting acceptable performance levels, ES would be *usable, efficient,* and *cost effective.*

Validation. Validation is the part of evaluation that deals with the *performance* of the system (e.g., as it compares to the expert's). Simply stated, validation refers to building the "right" system, that is, substantiating that a system performs with an acceptable level of accuracy.

Verification. Verification is also part of evaluation. It refers to building the system "right," that is, substantiating that the system correctly implements its specifications.

These activities in the realm of ES are dynamic, since they must be repeated each time that the prototype is changed.

In terms of the knowledge base, it is necessary to assure that we have the *right* knowledge base, that is, that the knowledge is valid. It is also essential to assure that the knowledge base was constructed properly (verification).

The validation and verification of the knowledge base can be done separately as part of the knowledge acquisition process. They can also be done during the system's evaluation step.

In executing these quality control tasks one deals with several activities and concepts. These are listed in Table 13.3.

TABLE 13.3 Measures of Validation. Adapted from Marcot (17).

Measure (Criteria)	Description
Accuracy	How well the system reflects reality. How correct the knowledge is in the knowledge base.
Adaptability	Possibilities for future development, changes.
Adequacy (or Completeness)	The portion of the necessary knowledge that is included in the knowledge base.
Appeal	How well the knowledge base matches intuition and stimulates thought and practicability.
Breadth	How well the domain is covered.
Depth	The degree of the detailed knowledge.
Face Validity	How credible is the knowledge?
Generality	Capability of a knowledge base to be used with a broad range of similar problems.
Precision	Capability of the system to replicate particular system parameters. Consistency of advice. Coverage of variables in knowledge base.
Realism	Accounting for relevant variables and relations. Similarity to reality.
Reliability	The fraction of the ES predictions that are empirically correct.
Robustness	Sensitivity of conclusions to model structure.
Sensitivity	The impact of changes in the knowledge base on quality of outputs.
Technical and Operational Validity	Goodness of the assumed assumptions, context, constraints, and conditions, and their impact on other measures.
Turing test	Ability of a human evaluator to identify if a given conclusion is made by an ES or by a real expert.
Usefulness	How adequate the knowledge is (in terms of parameters and relationships) for solving correctly.
Validity	The knowledge base's capability of producing empirically correct predictions.

Automated Verification and Validation

Automated verification of knowledge is offered in the Auto-Intelligence product described earlier. Verification is conducted by measuring the system's performance and it is limited to classification cases with probabilities. It works as follows: when an ES is presented with a new case to classify, it will assign a confidence factor to each selection. By comparing these confidence factors (which are discussed in the next chapter) with those provided by an expert, one can measure the *accuracy* of the ES as it is reflected in each case. By performing comparisons on many cases one can arrive at an overall measure of performance of the ES. For details see Parsaye (22).

13.10 Knowledge Analysis, Coding, Documentation, and Diagramming

Regardless of the method of acquisition, the collected knowledge must be analyzed, coded, and documented. The manner in which these activities are being done will depend on the methods of acquisition and representation. The following example (based on Wolfgram et al. [27]) illustrates some of the steps in this process. It deals with knowledge acquired with the use of verbal protocols. Four steps are identified:

Transcription. A complete transcription of the verbal report should be made, including not only the expert's utterances, but also those of the knowledge engineer and any other distractions or interferences that may have occurred during the session.

Phrase Indexing. A useful process is to break up the transcription into short phrases, each identified by an index number. Each phrase should correspond to the knowledge engineer's assessment of what constitutes a piece of knowledge, that is, a single task, assertion, or data collection process by the expert.

Knowledge Coding. This activity attempts to classify the knowledge. One useful classification is to distinguish between descriptive and procedural knowledge. *Descriptive knowledge* relates to a specific object. It includes information about the meaning, roles, environment, resources, activities, associations, and outcomes of the object. *Procedural knowledge* relates to the procedures employed in the problem solving process (e.g., information about problem definition, data gathering, solution process, and evaluation criteria). Each piece of knowledge is indexed according to the appropriate category and sub-category.

Documentation. The knowledge should be properly organized and documented. One way of organizing the documentation is to divide it into four parts: comprehensive domain listing, descriptive knowledge, procedural knowledge, and glossary. Certainly, the documented knowledge should be maintained (e.g., use of security measures) and updated properly. The documentation should be done in a consistent manner. Forms can be used for documentation. Several vendors of ES provide their clients with necessary forms.

Knowledge Diagramming

Knowledge diagramming is a graphical approach to improve the process of knowledge acquisition. It consists of hierarchical, top-down descriptions of the major types of knowledge used to describe facts and reasoning strategies for problem-solving in expert systems. These types are: objects, events, performance, and metaknowledge. The diagramming also describes the linkages and interactions among the various types of knowledge. As knowledge is acquired, the diagrams support the analysis and planning of subsequent acquisitions. The process is similar to diagramming in system analysis; by acting as a high-level representation of knowledge, the *productivity* of the builders and the *quality* of the system can be increased.

The hierarchical diagramming ends with a primitive level that cannot be decomposed. The decomposition in all levels is diagrammed providing a partitioned view of events and objects. A special knowledge representation language called KRL (Knowledge Representation Language) is used in the process. Graphical techniques are used to augment the scope, understanding, and modularity of knowledge.

Knowledge diagramming can be used to manage acquisition very effectively when it is being tied to the five-stage model of KA (see Figure 13.3). A special Expert System called INQUEST has been developed using this approach, by Contel Information Management Systems Division (Springfield, VA). For information about this system and knowledge diagramming in general, see Hillman (14).

13.11   Concluding Remarks

Several years ago the objectives of an ideal KA system were outlined by Hill et al. (13) as:

- □ Direct interaction with the expert without intervention by a knowledge engineer.
- □ Applicability to unlimited, or at least a broad class of, problem domains.
- □ Tutorial capabilities to eliminate the need for prior training of the expert.
- □ Ability to analyze work in progress to detect inconsistencies and gaps in knowledge.
- □ Ability to incorporate multiple sources of knowledge.
- □ A human interface (i.e., a natural conversation) that will make the use of the system enjoyable and attractive.
- □ Ability to interface easily with different expert system tools, as appropriate to the problem domain.

In order to attain these objectives it is necessary to automate the KA process. However, automatic KA methods, known also as *machine learning*, are presently very limited in their capabilities. Nevertheless, diligent efforts on the part of researchers, vendors and system builders help in slowly approaching these objectives. Best results can be achieved in acquisition of knowledge that is difficult to acquire manually (e.g., large databases). In the interim, acquisition will continue to be done manually in most cases, but it will be supported by productivity improvement aids. While such improvements are being made it is necessary to recognize the existence of different types of knowledge and the fact that they can be best elicited by different techniques and computerized aids. Furthermore, in some systems it is best to employ several techniques jointly. Unfortunately, this is not a simple task (one day we will see an expert system that will advise us on this matter). Since the knowledge is collected for the purpose of representing it, representation may have a major impact on the selected method(s). Ideally, one should start with preliminary knowledge acquisition (e.g., using informal interviews), then decide on a representation technique based on the type of knowledge collected, and only then determine the elicitation method. Sometimes, the representation method could be changed once the prototype is in progress; however, this is also true of the knowledge acquisition method.

The various representation methods together with the inference techniques are the subject of our next chapter.

Key Words

directed interview	knowledge acquisition	protocol analysis
elicitation of knowledge	knowledge diagramming	repertory grid analysis
expertise transfer system	knowledge engineering	rule induction
(ETS)	knowledge transformation	walkthrough
interactive induction	multidimensional scaling	validation
interview analysis	multiple experts	verification

Questions for Review

1. Define knowledge engineering.
2. List the steps of the knowledge engineering process.
3. Define knowledge acquisition and contrast it with knowledge representation.
4. List several sources of knowledge.
5. List the five stages in the knowledge acquisition process.
6. What is the difference between documented and undocumented knowledge?
7. List four reasons why KA is difficult.
8. Describe the process of protocol analysis.
9. What is the "Repertory Grid Analysis" method?
10. Describe the process of observation of the expert at work.
11. What is the major advantage of using documented knowledge?
12. Briefly discuss three deficiencies of manual KA.
13. Describe the process of automated rule induction.
14. List the major difficulties of KA from multiple experts.
15. List and briefly discuss the five major approaches to KA from multiple experts.
16. Define: evaluation, validation, and verification of knowledge.

Questions for Discussion

1. Discuss the major tasks performed by knowledge engineers. What skills are necessary for the performance of these tasks?
2. Explain the advantage of a knowledge base constructed in a modular fashion.
3. Assume that you are to collect knowledge for one of the following systems:
   a. Advisory system on equal opportunity situation in your organization.
   b. Advisory system on investment in residential real estate.
   c. Advisory system on how to prepare your federal tax return (Form 1040).
   What sources of knowledge would you consider? (Consult Figure 13.2).
4. Why is knowledge acquisition considered by many as the most difficult step in knowledge engineering?
5. Discuss the major advantages of rule induction. Give an example that illustrates the method and point to a situation where you think it will be most appropriate.
6. Discuss the difficulties of knowledge acquisition from several experts. Describe a situation that you are familiar with where there could be a need for several experts.
7. Transfer of knowledge from a human to a machine to a human is said to be a more difficult task than a transfer from a human to a human. Why?
8. Explain the importance of *conceptualization* and list some of the detailed issues that are involved.
9. What are the major advantages and disadvantages of interviews based on example problems?
10. Compare and contrast protocol analysis to interviews based on example cases.
11. What are the major advantages and disadvantages of working with a prototype system for KA?
12. The Repertory Grid Analysis approach has been used in several KA methods. Why is it so popular? What are its major weaknesses?
13. What are the major advantages and disadvantages of the observation method?
14. Discuss some of the problems of KA through the use of expert reports.
15. What are the present and future benefits of KA through an analysis of documented knowledge? What are its limitations?
16. Why are manual elicitation methods so slow and expensive?
17. Why can the case analysis method be used as a basis for knowledge acquisition?
18. What are the advantages of rule induction as an approach to knowledge acquisition?
19. What are the major benefits of Auto-Intelligence (or similar products) over a conventional rule induction package?
20. Discuss how some productivity improvement tools can expedite the work of the knowledge engineer.
21. Give an *example* for which an automated approach to "KA from multiple experts" would be feasible.
22. Explain why it is necessary to both verify and validate the content of the knowledge base. Who should do it?
23. Why is it important to have the knowledge analyzed, coded, and documented in a systematic way?
24. What are the major advantages of acquiring knowledge through a knowledge engineer?

Exercises

1. Fill in the following table with regard to the type of communication between the expert and the knowledge engineer. Use the following symbols: Y = Yes, N = No, H = High, M = Medium, L = Low.

Method	Type of Communication				
	Face—to—face contact	Written communications	Continuing for a long time	Time spent by expert	Time spent by K.E.
Interview analysis					
Observations of experts					
Questionnaires and expert report					
Analysis of documented knowledge					

2. Evaluate the current success of automated rule induction and interactive methods in KA. Use the following table. Then, comment on the major limitation of each method.

Method/tool	Time of expert	Time of knowledge engineer	Skill of knowledge engineer
Rule induction			
Auto-intelligence			
Smart editors			
ETS			

3. Knowledge Acquisition Session.

KNOWLEDGE ENGINEER (KE): You have the reputation for finding the best real-estate properties for your clients. How do you do it?

EXPERT: Well, first I learn about the clients' objectives.

KE: What do you mean by that?

EXPERT: Some people are interested in income, others in price appreciation. There are some speculators, too.

KE: Assume that somebody is interested in price appreciation. What would your advice be?

EXPERT: Well, I will find first how much money the investor can put down and to what degree he or she can subsidize the property.

KE: Why?

EXPERT: The more cash you put as downpayment, the less subsidy you will need. Properties with high potential for price appreciation need to be subsidized for about two years.

KE: What else?

> EXPERT: Location is very important. As a general rule I recommend looking for the lowest-price property in an expensive area.
> KE: What else?
> EXPERT: I compute the cash flow and consider the tax impact by using built-in formulas in my calculator.

Assignment.
  a. List the heuristics cited in this interview
  b. List the algorithms mentioned.

4. Examination of admission records of Pacifica University shows the following admission cases:

Case#	GMAT	GPA	Decision
1	510	3.5	Yes
2	620	3.0	Yes
3	580	3.0	No
4	450	3.5	No
5	655	2.5	Yes

  a. Assume that admission decisions are based only on the scores of GMAT and GPA. Find, by induction, the rules used. Subject all five cases to the rules generated. Make sure that they are consistent with the rules.
  b. Assume that only *two* rules were used. Can you identify these rules?

References and Bibliography

1. Alexander, S. M., and G. W. Evans. "The Integration of Multiple Experts: A Review of Methodologies." In E. Turban and P. Watkins, eds. *Applied Expert Systems*, North-Holland, 1988.
2. Boose, J. H. *Expertise Transfer for Expert Systems Design.* New York: Elsevier, 1986.
3. Brule, J. F., and A. Blount. *Knowledge Acquisition.* New York: McGraw-Hill, 1989.
4. Deal, D. M., and N. O. Heaton. *Knowledge-based Systems.* Chichester, England: Ellis Harwood, 1988.
5. Diederich, J., et al. "Kriton: a knowledge acquisition tool for expert systems." *Int. J. Man-Machine Studies*, January 1987.
6. Ericsson, K. A., and H. A. Simon. *Protocol Analysis, Verbal Reports and Data.* Cambridge, MA: MIT Press, 1984.
7. Feigenbaum, E., and P. McCorduck. *The Fifth Generation.* Reading, MA: Addison-Wesley, 1983.
8. Fikes, R., and T. Kehler. "The Role of Frame-Based Representation in Reasoning." *Communication of ACM*, September 1985.
9. Freiling, M. et al. "Starting a Knowledge Engineering Project: A Step-by-Step Approach." *AI Magazine*, Fall 1985.
10. Gaines, B. R. "Knowledge Acquisition: Developments and Advances." In M. D. Oliff, ed. *Expert Systems and Intelligent Manufacturing.* New York: Elsevier Science, 1988.
11. Hart, A. *Knowledge Acquisition for Expert Systems.* New York: McGraw-Hill, 1986.
12. Hayes-Roth, F., et al. *Building Expert Systems.* Reading, MA: Addison-Wesley, 1983.

13. Hill, R., Berry D. C. Wolfgram, and D. E. Broadbent. "Expert Systems and The Man-Machine Interface." *Expert Systems*, October 1986.
14. Hillman, D. "Bridging an acquisition and representation." *AI Expert*, November 1988.
15. LeClair, S. R. "A Multi-Expert Knowledge System Architecture for Manufacturing Decision Analysis." Unpublished Ph.D. Dissertation, Arizona State University, 1985.
16. McGraw, K. L., and B. K. Harbison. *Knowledge Acquisition, Principles and Guidelines.* Englewood Cliffs, NJ: Prentice-Hall, 1989.
17. Marcot, B. "Testing Your Knowledge Base." *AI Expert*, August 1987.
18. Mittal, S. "Knowledge Acquisition From Multiple Experts." *AI Magazine*, Summer 1985.
19. Nguyen, T. A. , et al. "Knowledge Base Verification." *AI Magazine*, Summer 1987.
20. Nii, P. H. "Blackboard Systems." *AI Magazine*, Vol. 7, No. 3, 1986.
21. O'Keefe, R. M., et al. "Validating Expert System Performance." *IE Expert*, Winter 1987.
22. Parsaye, K. "Acquiring and Verifying Knowledge Automatically." *AI Expert*, May 1988.
23. Prerau, D. S. "Knowledge Acquisition In The Development Of A Large Expert System." *AI Magazine*, Summer 1987.
24. Ralandi, W. P. "Knowledge Engineering in Practice." *AI Expert*, December 1986.
25. Rothman, P. "Knowledge Transformation." *AI Expert*, November 1988.
26. Shachter, R. D., and D. E. Hecherman. "Thinking Backward for Knowledge Acquisitions." *AI Magazine*, Fall 1987.
27. Wolfgram, D. D. , et al. *Expert Systems.* New York: John Wiley & Sons, Inc. 1987.

Chapter 14

Knowledge Representation and Inferencing

A major difference between ES and other CBIS, including DSS, lies in the knowledge representation and in the inference capabilities. These activities include representation of knowledge in the computer, and building an inference mechanism that can infer from the stored knowledge and explain its line of reasoning. The specific topics included in this chapter are as follows:

485

14.1 **Introduction**

Acquired knowledge needs to be organized in the computer so it can be used whenever needed. Specific domain knowledge is stored in a knowledge base while the knowledge that deals with problem-solving processes is stored in the inference engine. Much of the latter is generic and it can be used to solve many different problems, especially if they have a similar structure. For example, in diagnosing malfunctions in a human, a machine, or an organization, we may use the same problem-solving procedures, and all can be constructed with the same inference engine.

Knowledge can be organized in one or more configurations (termed schemes). This is analogous to a database that can be organized as relational, hierarchical, or network. Furthermore, the knowledge in the knowledge base may be organized differently than that in the inference engine.

A variety of knowledge representation schemes have been developed over the years. These representation schemes share two common characteristics. First, they can be programmed with existing computer languages and stored in memory. Second, they are designed so that the facts and other knowledge contained within them can be used in reasoning. That is, the knowledge base contains a data structure that can be manipulated by an inference system that uses search and pattern-matching techniques on the knowledge base to answer questions, draw conclusions, or otherwise perform an intelligent function.

Knowledge representation schemes have generally been categorized as either *declarative* or *procedural*. A declarative scheme is one used to represent facts and assertions. A procedural representation scheme deals with actions or procedures.

Declarative knowledge representation methods include logic, semantic networks, frames, rules and scripts. Procedural knowledge representation schemes include procedures or subroutines and rules. The key to the success of any AI program is the selection of a knowledge representation scheme that best fits the domain knowledge and the problem to be solved. That choice is best left to the knowledge engineer with considerable AI software design experience.

In this chapter we cover four types of knowledge representation: logic, rules, frames, and semantic networks.

The manner in which knowledge is organized determines both the inference or "reasoning" capability of the system and its ability to explain some of its activities. In this chapter we concentrate mainly on inferences and explanation in rule-based systems.

One of the major properties of an expert system is its ability to handle incomplete or fuzzy information. Again, we will treat only rule-based systems in this text.

Finally, the topic of object-oriented programming (OOP) is presented. OOP can be extremely useful in representing knowledge and its role in ES is increasing rapidly.

14.2 Some Concepts of Knowledge Representation and Inferencing

In the following three sections we will discuss several basic concepts that are important for understanding this chapter.

The Knowledge Base and the Inference Engine

In Chapter 12 we described the structure of an expert system and briefly discussed the role of the knowledge base and the inference engine. The relationships between these two components are shown in Figure 14.1. Note that the knowledge base is composed of two parts. The upper part includes knowledge about the domain. For example, rules such as "IF the temperature is above 32°F, THEN it will not snow." The second part is the assertion (or the data) base, which includes facts about the specific situation. For example, "the current temperature is 40°F," or "it is snowing now." The assertion base is a part of what we called in Chapter 12 the *blackboard* or the *workplace*.

As described earlier there is a *complete separation* between what is known about the domain (contained in the knowledge base) and the problem-solving procedures (contained in the inference engine). The content of the building blocks in Figure 14.1 and the manner in which they interact are the subject of the remainder of this chapter.

Object-Attributes-Values

A common way to represent knowledge is to use the object-attributes-values (O-A-V) triplet. Objects may be physical or conceptual. Attributes are the characteristics of the objects. Values are the specific measures of the attributes in a

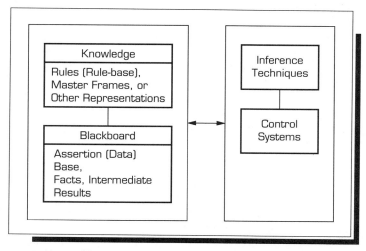

FIGURE 14.1 The knowledge base and the inference engine.

given situation. Table 14.1 presents several O-A-V triplets. An object may have several attributes. An attribute itself may be considered as a new object with its own attributes. For example, in Table 14.1, a bedroom is an attribute of a house but also an object of its own. O-A-V are used both in frame and semantic network representations.

Inheritance

Inheritance is the ability of one object (or attribute) to "inherit" properties of other objects (or attributes) that are related to it. As will be seen later, inheritance can eliminate duplication and redundancy in knowledge representation. For example, a dog and a cat are animals. If we know that an animal needs food it is obvious that both dogs and cats need food. It is not necessary to state it in the knowledge base. Inheritance is used both in frames and in semantic networks.

Deductive and Inductive Reasoning

Two types of reasoning are used in making inferences: deductive and inductive.

Deductive Reasoning. In this case we move from a *general* principal to a *specific* conclusion. Most deductive reasoning involves a major and a minor premise (or known facts) and a specific conclusion.

> *Example 1*: Major premise: A cat has a tail.
>   Minor Premise: Mittens is a cat.
>   Conclusion: Therefore, Mittens has a tail.

> *Example 2*: Major premise: It never snows if the temperature is above 32°F.
>   Minor premise: The temperature today is 40°F.
>   Conclusion: There is no snow today.

Inductive Reasoning. Inductive reasoning uses a number of specific *facts*, in order to draw a *general conclusion*.

> *Example 1*: Premises: Jack smokes a lot.
>   Donna smokes a lot.
>   Jack and Donna are frequently sick.
>   Conclusion: Excessive smoking causes sickness.

TABLE 14.1 Representative O-A-V items

Object	Attributes	Values
House	Bedrooms	2, 3, 4, etc.
House	Color	Green, white, brown
Admission to a university	Grade point average	3.0, 3.5, 3.7, etc.
Inventory control	Level of inventory	15, 20, 30, etc.
Bedroom	Size	9×10', 6×12', etc.

Example 2: Premises: Mary has one head.
Jeff has one head.
Mary and Jeff are human beings.
Conclusion: All human beings have one head.

The interesting thing about inductive reasoning is that the conclusion may be difficult to arrive at (e.g., it took many years to determine that smoking may cause cancer.) Furthermore, the conclusion is never final since new premises may be discovered (it is very difficult to assure that *all* the premises were checked). Therefore, inductive reasoning contains some measure of uncertainty. In example 2, the conclusion is absolutely true only if Mary and Jeff were the only human beings in the world. However, if we add many more people to the list, we may find one person with two heads, which will make the conclusion invalid.

14.3 Object-oriented Programming

Object-Oriented Programming (OOP) is a novel way of thinking about data, procedures, and relationships among them. Some people view OOP as a unique programming language, others claim that this is *not* a programming language. OOP features can be added to most existing programming languages for the purpose of increasing programmers' productivity as well as for making these languages more flexible.[*]

Key Concepts

Several key concepts underline OOP:

Objects. An object can be physical or it can be a concept or an event. It can be anything that we want to describe.

Encapsulation. Data and procedures (or code) are packaged inseparably in a capsule called an object. (See Figure 14.2)

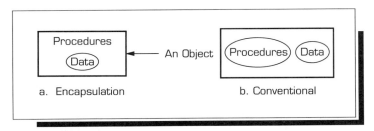

FIGURE 14.2 Encapsulation vs. conventional organization.

---

[*]This section is based in part on Harmon, P., et al. *Expert Systems Tools and Applications*, Wiley, 1988, and on Howard, G. S., "Object-Oriented Programming Explained," *Journal of Systems Management*, July 1988.

Reusability. An object could be made sufficiently general and self-contained so it could be used as a component or a module that can be "plugged in" when a system is programmed.

Inheritance. Objects inherit properties from other objects. (See Section 14.2.)

Multiple Inheritance. Inheritance can be singular or multiple. (See Section 14.8 for a discussion.)

Execution. In contrast to other programming languages that execute programming in a procedural, nonprocedural, functional (such as a Lisp), or logical (such as PROLOG) manner, in OOP a program execution is regarded as a physical model. Such a model simulates the behavior of either a real or an imaginary part of the world.

Messages, Methods, and Responses

Messages. An object can be accessed only by the private code surrounding the object. One reason to access an object is to send messages to it. Each message consists of a *selector*, which tells the object what to do with the message, and an *argument*. The argument is optional and its purpose is to explain, comment, provide instruction, or clarify the content of the message.

Methods. A method is a private procedure in an object that tells us what to do with the message and how to do it. Since each object owns its methods, objects will respond *differently* to the same message. This is a powerful property of OOP. The object, based on the available knowledge, knows which is the most appropriate method to use.

Response. Once a message has been received, the object sends a response to other objects or to the system based on the selected method.

The World of Objects

Each object is considered a small world unto itself. It contains data and methods (procedures). It can receive and send messages. However, objects are related to other objects through a *hierarchy* of classes and subclasses of objects. Such a world is created by a process called *instantiation*.

Instantiation

In OOP, we may create objects by taking a copy of a preexisting object (called the parent), and then telling that object how it is to behave differently from the parent. For example, a parent object may be a "vehicle." By taking this object and adding a property "can fly," the "vehicle" becomes a new object, called "airplane." We refer to the airplane as a child (or offspring). We can create more objects from the "vehicle" (e.g., boat, car, train), and we can create objects from each of the new objects. For example, we can create a sailboat and a motorboat from a boat object. The process of creating new objects is called *instantiation*.

Classes and Inheritance

Organisms are grouped by biologists into classes and subclasses. For example, class "animal" contains subclasses "bird" and "mammal." The classes inherit characteristics from their upper classes. A similar organization is available in OOP, as shown in Figure 14.3.

When an object is created, it contains two parts. The left portion in Figure 14.3 shows the new information unique to those objects. The right side shows pointers that point to the parent. Objects in lower levels inherit data and procedures from an upper level, except that private data and procedures are being added. The ultimate source of data is the object at the top. It is called class of all classes (or master object), and it has neither a parent nor private data. Everything held in common between a set of objects is the *class* of the objects. (See Figure 14.3.)

When a message is sent to an object (say the "sailboat"), it checks its private data and procedures to see how to handle the message. If it cannot find such information, it moves to its parent's private file and so on. This may continue, if needed, to the class of all classes whose data and procedures are shared with everybody else. This shared information is what we called the *class* of the objects.

Benefits

OOP eliminates data dependency problems that exist in conventional programming. Thus, the complexity of information systems is drastically reduced. Programmers' productivity can also be increased.

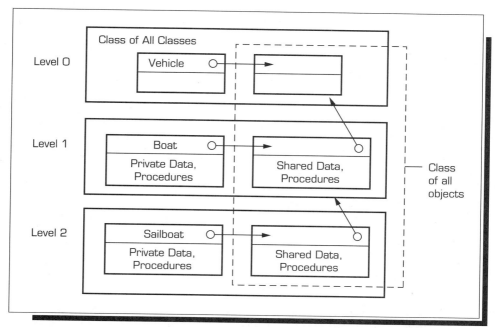

FIGURE 14.3

OOP and Languages

OOP can be written in regular languages such as COBOL or BASIC. However, they are usually programmed with special languages. Some of these are:

Smalltalk. Smalltalk is a programming environment within which the boundaries among operating systems, compilers, editors, utilities, data, and application programs become blurred. Hundreds of classes and methods are provided with an extensive use of icons, windows, and a mouse. Related products are Smalltalk-80 and Smalltalk V.

C + +. This is a C implementation of OOP, specially suited for the Unix environment. A similar product is Objective C.

LOOPS (from Xerox Computer Services). It is a language for object-oriented representation. It also supports rule-based, access-oriented, and procedure-oriented representation methods. Its principal characteristic is the integration of its four programming schemes. For example, rules and rule sets are considered LOOPS objects. The support system contains display-oriented debugging tools, such as break packages and editors.

Other Languages. Many new languages appeared on the market in the late 1980s. For a review see: Retting, M., et al., "Object-oriented programming in AI-New choices," *AI Expert*, January 1989.

Frames

When AI programmers develop OOP environments, they tend to refer to objects as *frames*. Thus, when we talk about frame representation (Section 14.8), we essentially talk about using OOP in building ES.

Access-oriented Programming

In access-oriented programming, gathering or sorting data can cause procedures to be invoked. This complements object-oriented programming. In object-oriented programming, when one object sends a message to another, the receiving object may change its data. Here, when one object changes its data, a message may be sent out. Access programs are composed of two parts: computing and monitoring the computations.

Figure 14.4 shows a simulation of city street traffic (based on Stefik et al. [22]). The program includes objects such as city blocks, cars, emergency vehicles, and traffic lights that exchange messages to simulate traffic interactions. The display controller has objects for traffic icons, viewing transformations, and windows that display different parts of the city connected to the simulation objects by active values. The simulator represents the dynamics of traffic. For example, when a traffic light turns green, it sends messages to start traffic. The user can interact and control the view in the traffic windows. What the access-oriented programming does is connect the simulation model with its numerical

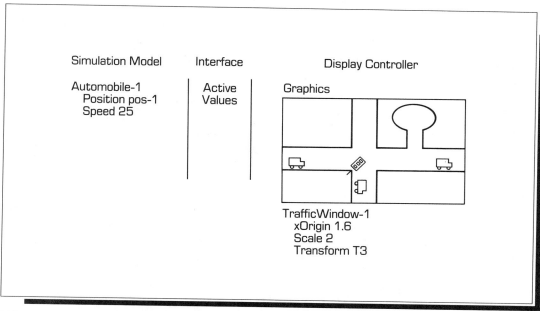

Simulation Model   Interface   Display Controller

Automobile-1
   Position pos-1
   Speed 25

Active
Values

Graphics

TrafficWindow-1
   xOrigin 1.6
   Scale 2
   Transform T3

FIGURE 14.4 Simulation of a city street, ©1986, IEEE.

analysis to the graphical display. For example, when a light turns green, a message is sent to certain vehicles to move. The program computes the initial velocity and position. When the cars move, their position on the display is updated. The user can see the cars actually moving. The access-oriented and object-oriented programming provide the interactive simulation capabilities that are discussed in Chapter 18.

These representation methods are supported by special software (such as LOOPS), and can be combined with a DSS generator and/or ES shells. An example of such a combination is KEE. For further details, see Stefik et al. (22).

14.4 Problem Solving and Search Approaches[*]

The general process of solving any problem involves three major elements: *problem states*, a *goal*, and *operators*. Problem states define the problem situation and existing conditions. The *goal* is the objective to be achieved, a final answer, or a solution. There may be more than one goal. *Operators* are procedures used for changing from one state to another. An operator describes a process whereby some action is taken to change the initial state into another state that more closely approaches the goal. Operators move the problem from one state to the next, following the guidance of a master control strategy, until a goal is reached. An operator could be an algorithmic subroutine.

[*]This section is condensed from Frenzel (11) with permission.

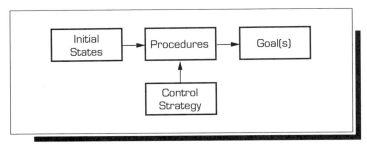

FIGURE 14.5 The relationship between the initial states, procedures, and goal(s) in the search process.

Figure 14.5 shows the relationship between the initial states, procedures, and goals. The initial conditions provide the states that are manipulated by procedures to achieve the goal. A control strategy selects or guides the procedures.

It is important to point out that even though we may treat search as being separate from the knowledge representation scheme, the two are very much interrelated. The selection of a particular knowledge representation method will greatly affect the type of search and control strategy used.

State and Search Space.   To define a problem, visualize a solution, or select a search method, it is often useful to express the problem in graphical terms. This can be done by drawing a graph of the problem showing the various problem states and how they are interconnected. The resulting graph is usually referred to as a state graph or the state space.

State Graph.   Figure 14.6 shows a state graph for a simple problem, attempting to find the best path from one city, the source (S), to another city, the destination or goal (G). The state graph is a map showing the various intermediate towns and cities that would be passed through in reaching the desired destination. In such a problem, there often will be several alternative routes. The problem is to reach the destination in the least amount of time or using the shortest route.

The nodes in a state graph are interconnected by arcs or links. The arcs usually have arrows showing the direction from one state to the next. The arcs represent the application of an operator to a node. The numbers on the arcs represent the distance (or travel time) between nodes.

In practice, it is difficult to represent a state graph such as that in Figure 14.6 in software form. For example, some of the paths through the state graph can be retraced repeatedly. The path "S to node B to node A back to node S" could be repeated over and over again. Such endless loops cannot be tolerated in a computer program and, therefore, some procedure must be followed to eliminate undesired cyclical conditions such as this. This is done by converting the state graph into a *search tree*.

Search Tree.   A *search tree* based on the state graph in Figure 14.6 is illustrated in Figure 14.7. The new tree diagram states the same problem but in a slightly

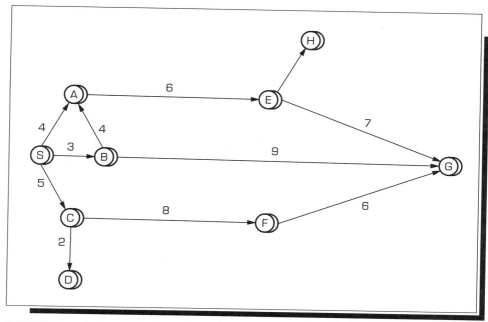

FIGURE 14.6 A state graph showing alternate routes from the start (S) to the goal (G).

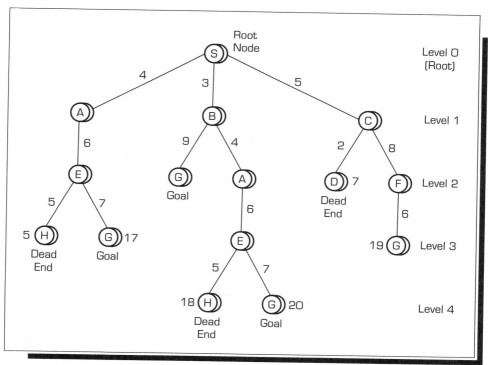

FIGURE 14.7 A search tree.

different format. The network thus formed is more like a hierarchy. Note that some of the nodes are repeated to eliminate the cyclical loop problem described earlier.

A special verbal language has been developed to describe a search tree. For example, the initial state node is called root node. Other nodes branch out from the root. These successor or descendant nodes are also sometimes referred to as children. Working backwards through the tree, nodes are said to have predecessors, ancestors, or parents. Nodes with no children or successors are called leaves. The interconnecting arcs are referred to as branches.

Finally, note in Figure 14.7 that a search tree is divided into various levels that are a function of the hierarchy. These levels describe the *depth* of the tree. The root node is usually designated Level 0, and successive deeper levels are designated sequentially from numbers 1 through the highest level required to represent the state space.

AND/OR Trees.   In the previous discussion of search trees, the branches from a node to its successors represented two or more alternative paths to subgoals. One path or another could lead to the goal. We can call these OR nodes because one branch, OR another, OR another could be the path to the goal.

In some problems, however, the successor nodes might represent problem states that must all be achieved or traversed before the goal is reached. These are referred to as AND nodes. One subgoal AND another subgoal (AND possibly others) must be achieved to solve the problem.

Search Methods

There are two basic approaches to searching a state space. The first is a *blind search* and the second is a *heuristic search*. Both are used in AI applications, but a heuristic search is the primary method of problem solving in AI. Actually, a heuristic search is a blind search that has been given some guidance or direction. (Both approaches were briefly described in Chapters 2 and 3.)

Blind Search.   A blind search is a collection of procedures used to search a state space. Beginning at the root node, operators are used to generate successor states. The search continues until a solution is found. The idea behind a blind search is to examine the *entire* tree in an orderly manner, using all the operators and generating as many successor nodes as possible to find the desired solution.

Starting with the root node, there are several procedures for proceeding through the tree, but these approaches are inefficient, brute-force techniques. In very large problems, a huge number of new states are generated and many alternatives are considered. As a result, it takes a considerable amount of time and effort to find the solution. Very high speed computers make blind search acceptable for some problems. However, there are some other problems that are too large for a blind search; for example, a large traveling salesperson problem (see Chapter 3). Another example is the possible number of moves in a chess game, which is estimated to be 10 to the 120th power. For such cases a heuristic search is more appropriate.

Breadth-First Search. Blind search methods differ primarily in the order in which the various nodes in the tree are examined.

A breadth-first search examines all of the nodes in a search tree, beginning with the root node. The nodes in each level are completely examined before moving on to the next level. A simple breadth-first search is illustrated in Figure 14.8. The numbers inside the node circles designate the sequence in which the nodes are examined. In this instance, the search (follow the broken line) would actually end at node 7 as that is the goal.

A breadth-first search of the state space will always find the shortest path between the initial state and the goal state, with the least number of steps. In a blind search procedure, the process usually starts at the initial state node and works *downward* in the tree from left to right.

Depth-First Search. A depth-first search begins at the root node and works downward to successively deeper levels. An operator is applied to the node to generate the next deeper node in sequence. This process continues until a solution is found or backtracking is forced by reaching a dead end.

A simple depth-first search is illustrated in Figure 14.9. Again, the numbers inside the nodes designate the sequence of nodes generated or searched. This process seeks the deepest possible nodes. If a goal state is not reached in this way, the search process *backtracks* to the next highest level node where additional paths are available to follow. Again this process continues downward and in a left-to-right direction until a goal is discovered. Here the search would actually end at node 13.

When a dead-end node is discovered, such as node 4 in Figure 14.9, the search process *backtracks* so that any additional branching alternative at the

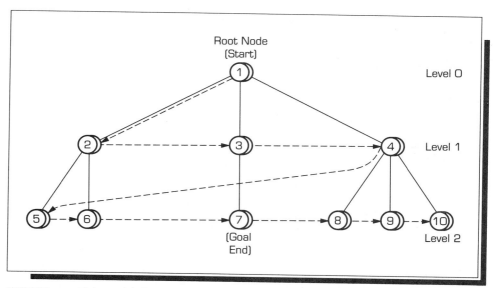

FIGURE 14.8 A breadth-first search.

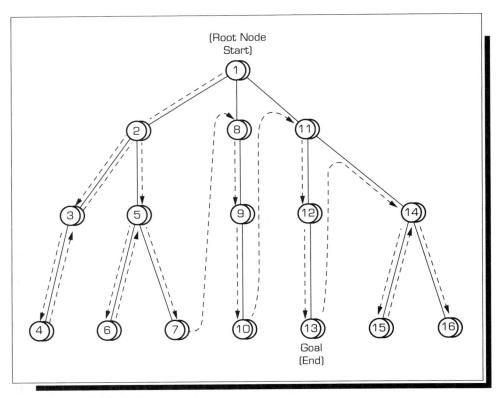

FIGURE 14.9 A depth-first search.

next higher node level is attempted. The search backs up to node 3. It has no alternate paths, so the search *backtracks* to node 2. Here, another path through node 5 is available. The path through node 6 is explored until its depth is exhausted. The backtracking continues until the goal is reached.

The depth-first search guarantees a solution, but the search may be a long one. Many different branches may have to be considered to a maximum depth before a solution is reached. (By setting a "depth bound," it is frequently possible to reduce the search.)

14.5 Propositional Logic and Predicate Calculus

Early attempts at building intelligent systems used propositional (or mathematical) logic as their representation language. It is also referred to as first-order logic. In this approach, knowledge is represented in propositions that make possible logical inferences. For example, the statement

All companies have a president.

is a formal proposition. A proposition (premise) can be either true or false.

The advantage of formal representation is that there is a set of rules, called *rules of inference in logic*, by which facts that are known to be true can be used to derive other facts that *must* also be true. Furthermore, the truth of any new statement can be checked, in a well-specified manner, against the facts that are already known to be true. For example, suppose we add another proposition:

Every brokerage house is a company.

If these two propositions are true then we can conclude, using the rules of inference, that the following must be also true:

All brokerage houses have presidents.

This type of logic is well suited to represent relationships inside a computer's memory because its structure corresponds to the binary language of computer programs.

Example: Let us assume that propositional logic is used to store the following proposition in the computer memory.

Proposition 1: If we raise prices p, revenues r will increase.

The relationship states that if p is true, then r is true. Inside the computer, a true condition is represented as a 1 and a false condition as a 0. So the area of memory corresponding to r will have a 1 stored in it any time the memory cell for p has a 1 stored in it.

What happens if we pose a second proposition to the computer?

Proposition 2: We have raised prices.

The first portion of proposition 1 now has a 1 (true) in it, so the computer searches its memory for a cell that was also changed to a 1, finds r, and reports:

Revenues will increase.

In its domain, propositional logic is effective, but the domain is limited. One reason for this is summarized by the old law that "there is an exception to every rule." For example, consider the following argument:

Proposition 1: Birds can fly.
Proposition 2: An ostrich is a bird.
Inference: Therefore, an ostrich can fly.

It is a perfectly valid, but false, conclusion; ostriches do not cooperate.

Another limitation of propositional logic is that it deals only with complete statements, which can be either true or false. It cannot make assertions about the individual elements that make up the statement. To overcome this problem, AI researchers use a modified form of propositional logic called *predicate calculus*. (The word calculus in this instance specifies a formal logical system and has nothing to do with the branch of mathematics that goes by the same name.)

Predicate Calculus

This is an extension of propositional logic. A predicate makes statements about objects that can be either true or false. This configuration permits the computer to draw conclusions not only in a specific case, but also if some conditions *are changed*. That is, the computer is programmed with general rules, using variables instead of specific values. Predicate calculus is the basis for the AI language called PROLOG.

Note: Propositional and Predicate logic can be much more complex, involving operators such as AND, OR, and IMPLIES. Generally speaking they are used in the theoretical AI world much more than in the applied one.

14.6   Production Rules

Production systems were developed by Newell and Simon (19) for their model of human cognition. The production systems are modular knowledge representation schemes that are finding increasing popularity in many AI applications. The basic idea of these systems is that knowledge is presented as rules, called productions, in the form of condition-action pairs: "IF this *condition* (or premise or antecedent) occurs, THEN some action (or result, or conclusion or consequent) will (or should) occur. For example:

> *Example 1*: IF the stoplight is red AND you have stopped, THEN a right turn is okay.
>
> *Example 2*: (This example from an internal control procedure includes a probability.)
>
> IF the client uses purchase requisition and the purchase orders are approved and purchasing is segregated from receiving, accounts payable, and inventory records, THEN there is strongly suggestive evidence (90% probability) that controls to prevent unauthorized purchases are adequate.

Each production rule in an ES implements an autonomous chunk of expertise that can be developed and modified independently of other rules. When combined and fed to the inference engine, the set of rules behaves synergistically, yielding better results than that of the sum of the results of the individual rules. In reality ES rules are not independent. They quickly become highly interdependent. For example, adding a new rule may conflict with an existing rule, or it may require a revision of attributes and/or rules.

The utility of production rule representation comes from the fact that the conditions for which each rule is applicable are made explicit and, in theory, the interactions between rules are minimized. In addition, they involve simple syntax and are flexible and easy to understand. Moreover, they enhance the explanation facility.

Production systems are useful as mechanisms for controlling the interaction between statements of declarative (factual, explicit) and procedural knowledge (steps to take in solving a problem). Productions have been used in many ES like DENDRAL, MYCIN, and PROSPECTOR, as well as in most commercially available ES development tools.

In addition, rules can be used as descriptive tools for problem-solving heuristics, replacing a more formal analysis of the problem. In this sense, the rules are thought of as incomplete but useful guides to make search decisions that can reduce the size of the problem space being explored. These rules are entered sequentially to an ES by the builder.

Finally, rules can be viewed, in some sense, as a simulation of the cognitive behavior of human experts. According to this view, rules are not just a neat formalism to represent expert knowledge in a computer; rather, they represent a model of actual human behavior.

Rules may appear in different forms. Following are some examples:

IF premise THEN conclusion. IF your income is high, THEN your chance of being audited by the IRS is high.

Conclusion IF Premise. Your chance of being audited is high IF your income is high.

Inclusion of ELSE. IF your income is high or your deductions are unusual, THEN your chance of being audited by the IRS is high, ELSE your chance of being audited is lower.

More Complex Rules. IF credit rating is high and salary is more than $30,000, or assets are more than $75,000, and pay history is not "poor," THEN approve a loan up to $10,000, and list the loan in category "B." The action part may include additional information: THEN "approve the loan" and "refer to an agent."

The IF side of a rule may include dozens of IFs. The THEN side may include several parts as well.

Knowledge Rules and Inference Rules

There are two types of rules in ES: knowledge and inference. Knowledge declarative rules state all the facts and relationships about a problem. Inference procedural rules, on the other hand, advise on how to solve a problem, given that certain facts are known.

Example: Assume you are in the business of buying and selling gold. Knowledge rules may look like this:

Rule 1: IF international conflict begins
   THEN the price of gold goes up.

Rule 2: IF inflation rate declines
   THEN the price of gold goes down.

Rule 3: IF the international conflict lasts more than seven days and IF it is
         in the Middle East
   THEN buy gold.

Inference rules may look like this:

Rule 1: IF the data needed are not in the system
   THEN request it from the user.

Rule 2: IF more than one rule applies
   THEN deactivate any rules that add no new data.

The following inference rule is designed to determine if an AND/OR node is satisfied:

Rule 3: Determine if the node is satisfied without recourse to subgoals. If so, announce that the node is satisfied. Otherwise determine if the node is an AND node or an OR node, and then:

3a: If the node is an AND node, use the AND procedure to determine if the node is satisfied.

3b: If the node is an OR node, use the OR procedure to determine if the node is satisfied.

These types of rules are also called metarules, or rules about rules. They pertain to other rules (or even to themselves).

The knowledge engineer separates the two types of rules: *knowledge rules* go to the knowledge base, whereas *inference rules* become part of the inference engine. Note that the inference rules are not domain specific.

Inferencing With Rules

Modus Ponens. Most rule-based systems use an inference strategy called modus ponens. According to this strategy, in a production rule whose structure is "IF A, THEN B," if we know that A is true, it is valid to conclude that B is also true. Similarly, if B is known to be true, then it is valid to conclude that A is true. Also, if A is false, then B is false.

The inference mechanism in most commercial expert systems uses this approach. The use of this approach is reflected in the search approach using the rule interpreter. Basically two control strategies are used: forward and backward chaining. They will be described in Sections 14.11–14.13.

Example: Look at Rule 1.

Rule 1: IF international conflict begins, THEN the price of gold goes up.

Let us assume that the ES knows that an international conflict just started. This information is stored in the "facts" (assertion) portion of the knowledge base. This means that the premise (IF side) of the rule is *true*. Using modus ponens, the conclusion (consequent) is then accepted as *true*. We say that Rule 1 *fires*. A rule *fires* only when all of its parts are satisfied (being either true or false). Then, the conclusion drawn is stored in the assertion base. In our case the conclusion (the price of gold goes up) is added to the assertion base, and it could be used to satisfy the premise of other rules. The true (or false) values for either portion of the rules can be obtained by querying the user or by firing other rules. Testing a rule premise or conclusion can be as simple as matching a symbolic pattern in the rule to a similar pattern in the assertion base. This is a *pattern matching*.

Every rule in the rule base (Figure 14.1) can be checked to see if its premise or conclusion can be satisfied by previously made assertions. This process may be done in one of two directions, *forward* or *backward*, and it will continue until no more rules can fire, or until a *goal* is achieved. These control strategies are discussed in Sections 14.11–14.13.

Rule representation is very popular because of its simplicity and the ease with which inferencing and explanation is made. However, as we will see later, it has several limitations. For this reason we use two other representation methods: semantic networks and frames. The latter is becoming very popular.

14.7   Semantic Networks

Networks are a natural and efficient way to organize knowledge. They are composed of nodes and links. Nodes describe facts like physical objects, concepts,

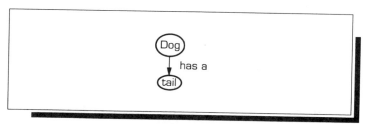

FIGURE 14.10 "Has [is] a" link.

or situations, whereas links (arcs) define the relevant relationships among the facts. Each node may point to a subnode that represents more detailed levels. One of the most common relationships in semantic networks is the "is a" (or "has a") link, which allows facts (e.g., dogs have tails) to be attached to classes of objects (e.g., dogs) and then inherited by specific objects in the class (e.g., poodle). This is shown in Figure 14.10, where dog and tail are the nodes and "has a" is the relationship.

The ability to point directly to relevant facts is particularly salient with respect to the "is a" and other links, which establish a property inheritance hierarchy in the network. For example, the network segment in Figure 14.11 might be interpreted to mean that because poodles are dogs, and dogs have tails, then a poodle has a tail.

Semantic nets are easy-to-understand means of representing nonrule knowledge. Semantic net notation is based on associations between concepts. The notion of an "associative memory" has been traced as far back as Aristotle.

Semantic nets are best depicted diagrammatically, as shown in Figure 14.12. In this diagram, we see "nodes" (Sharon, pet, food) connected by "links" or "arcs." Each node is named. Each link bears the name of a relation (is a, has, is, owns, needs). For example,

Sharon "is a" human means Sharon is a member of the class of humans.

Vertebrate "has" backbone means backbone is a part of vertebrates.

Other kinds of links (owns, needs) may be chosen as the problem dictates.

Much of the earlier popularity of semantic nets arose from the processing power afforded by the "is a" link in building hierarchies of concepts. In our diagram, we do not have to attach to each of Sharon, Morris, Lassie, and

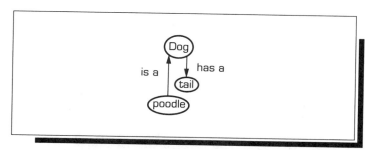

FIGURE 14.11 Links and nodes.

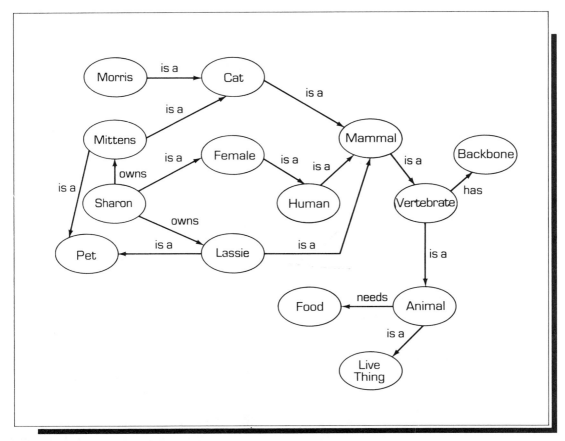

FIGURE 14.12 A semantic net.

Mittens the fact that they need food or that they are alive. We can deduce that because animals need food and because vertebrates are animals, then vertebrates need food. Similarly, mammals need food and so do Sharon and Mittens.

This ability of a node to "inherit" characteristics of other related nodes is very helpful in describing knowledge.

For example, Sharon inherits everything known specifically about female, who inherits from human, and so on. The reasoning mechanism of networks is based on matching network structures. For example, if we want to know what Sharon owns, we can construct a network segment such as in Figure 14.13. This

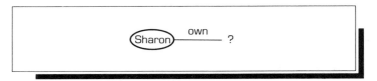

FIGURE 14.13 Network Segment.

segment is matched against the knowledge base (by a search of "own" links that are connected to Sharon). If a link is found the answer is given: "Sharon owns Mittens and Lassie"; otherwise the answer would have been "Sharon owns nothing." Searching semantic networks for a specific object is difficult. Therefore, semantic networks seem to be more popular in other AI applications (e.g., natural language processing) than in ES. Nevertheless, a number of ES rely on network formalisms, among them very large systems like INTERNIST and PROSPECTOR.

14.8   Frames

Definition

A *frame* is a data structure that includes all the knowledge about a particular object. This knowledge is organized in a special hierarchical structure that permits a diagnosis of knowledge independence.[*] Frames are basically an application of object-oriented programming for AI and ES.

Each frame describes one *object*. In order to describe what frames are and how the knowledge is organized in a frame it is necessary to use a special terminology. This terminology is listed in Table 14.2.

Hierarchy of Frames

Frames are arranged in hierarchies. This arrangement permits inheritance. Figure 14.14 shows a set of vehicles. The vehicles are organized in a tree. The *root* of the tree is at the top, where the highest level of abstraction is represented. Frames at the bottom (called *leaves* of the tree) represent actual *instances*. When specific, actual values are placed in a frame, an *instance* of the frame is created. The hierarchy permits inheritance of characteristics. Each frame usually inherits the characteristics of all related frames of *higher levels*. These characteristics are expressed in the internal structure of the frame.

TABLE 14.2   Frame's Terminology

Default
Demons
Facets
Hierarchy of Frames
If - needed
Instance - of
Instantiation
Master Frame
Object
Slots
Values (Entries)

---

[*]The discussion of this section is based, in part, on Arcidiacono (1).

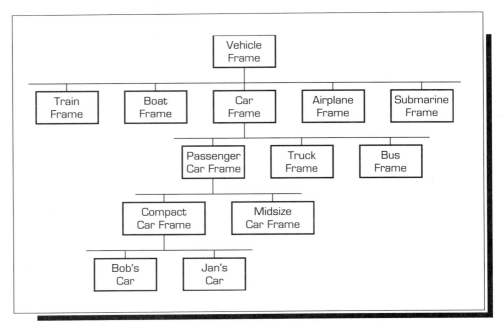

FIGURE 14.14 Hierarchy of frames describing vehicles.

Content of a Frame

A frame includes two basic elements: slots and facets.

Slots. This is a set of attributes that describes the *object* represented by the frame. For example, for a car frame, a size or a color will be in the slots.

Facets. Each slot contains one or more facets. The facets (sometimes called subslots) describe some knowledge or procedures about the attribute in the slot. Facets may take many forms, such as

- □ *Values.* These describe the attributes such as blue color.
- □ *Default.* This facet is used if the slot is empty—that is, without any description. For example, in a car frame a default value for an engine size slot may be six cylinders (V6). That is, since we do not know how many cylinders, we assume automatically, that it is six.
- □ *Range.* The range indicates what kind of information can appear in a slot (e.g., integer numbers only, two decimal points).
- □ *IF added.* This facet contains procedural information. It specifies an *action* to be taken when a value in the slot is *added* (or modified). Such procedural attachments are called *demons*.
- □ *IF needed.* The IF needed facet is used in a case when no slot value is given. It triggers, much like the if added situation, a procedure that goes out and gets or computes a value.
- □ *Other.* Slots may contain frames, rules, semantic networks, or any type of information.

Types of Frames

Two types of frames exist: Parents and children. This is identical to what we described in Section 14.3, regarding OOP. Placing values in the slots of a parent frame *instantiates* (creates an instance of) the child's frame. An example is shown in Figure 14.15.

The root frame has the most general characteristic; it is a master frame equivalent to the class of classes in OOP. Frames further down inherit all the characteristics (e.g., the slots and the facets) from frames in their ancestral lines.

Frames can inherit slots from multiple frames, not just from one ancestral line. For example, Jan's car can be related to Jan's properties frame. Figure 14.16 shows a generic arrangement and relationship of frames.

Inferencing with Frames

Reasoning with frames is much more complicated than reasoning with rules. The slot provides a mechanism for a kind of reasoning called *expectation-driven processing*. Empty slots (i.e., unconfirmed expectations) can be filled, subject to certain conditions, with data that confirm the expectations. Thus, frame-based reasoning is based on looking for confirmation of expectations and is often just filling in slot values.

Perhaps the simplest way to specify slot values is by default. The default value is attached loosely to the slot so as to be easily displaced by a value that meets the assignment condition. In the absence of information, however, the default value remains attached and expressed.

Name: Compact car	
Slots	**Facets**
Owner	check registration list
Color	list, per manufacturer
No. of cylinders	
Range:	4 or 6
If needed	ask owner
Make	
Range:	list of all manufacturers
If needed	ask owner
Model	use frame corresponding to make
Vintage (year)	
Range:	1950–1989
If needed	ask owner

a. Parent Frame

Name: Jan's Car instance of: compact car frame	
Slots	**Facets**
Owner	Jan
Color	Blue
No. of cylinders	6
Make	Honda
Model	Accord
Vintage (year)	1989

b. Child Frame

FIGURE 14.15 Parent and child frames.

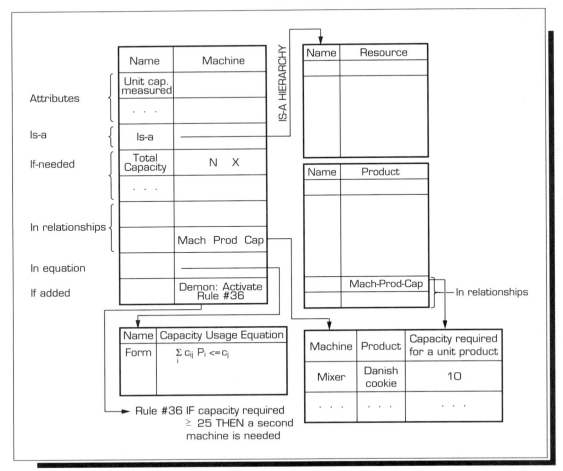

FIGURE 14.16 (*Source:* Blanning, R.W., "The application of AI to model management." Working paper, Owen graduate school of management, Vanderbilt University, 1988.)

Certain procedures can be attached to slots and used to derive slot values. For example, slot-specific heuristics are procedures for deriving slot values in a particular context. An important aspect of such procedures is that they can be used to direct the reasoning process. In addition to filling in slots, they can be triggered when a slot is filled.

Using Frames

A frame representation is based on the theory that previous situational experiences create certain expectations about objects and events associated with new situations. Frames provide frameworks within which new information can be interpreted. For example, based on previous experience, a chair is generally expected to be a kind of furniture with arms, legs, and a back. The expectations represent things that are always true about chairs and provide the context within which other objects can be interpreted. These expectations are represented as slots.

Obviously before a frame can be used it must be identified as applicable to the current situation. Generally speaking, this can be done by matching the frame system against the facts in the knowledge base. The selected frame will be the one with the greatest number of lower-level slots filled in. Then an attempt is made to fill in higher-level slots and if this fails, another frame is selected. For example, a "room" with very short walls and no windows or artificial light might better fit the "broom cupboard" frame than a "room" frame.

An example of a system that uses a frame-based representation is RLL (Representation Language Language), which helps a knowledge engineer design, construct, use, and modify an ES. Like other programs that help knowledge engineers build ES, RLL begins with a store of primitives and a collection of types of slots, control mechanisms, and inheritance schemes.

14.9   Multiple Knowledge Representation

Knowledge representation should be able to support the tasks of acquiring and retrieving knowledge as well as of the subsequent reasoning. Factors that must be taken into account in evaluating knowledge representations for these three tasks include

1. The naturalness, uniformity, and understandability of the representation.
2. The degree to which knowledge is explicit (declarative) or embedded in procedural code.
3. The modularity and flexibility of the knowledge base.
4. The efficiency of knowledge retrieval and the heuristic power of the inference procedure (*heuristic power* is defined as the reduction of the search space achieved by heuristic mechanism).

No single knowledge representation method is ideally suited by itself for all tasks (see Table 14.3). When using several sources of knowledge simultaneously, the goal of uniformity may have to be sacrificed in favor of exploiting the benefits of multiple knowledge representations, each tailored to a different subtask. The necessity of translating among knowledge representations becomes a problem in such cases. Nevertheless, some recent ES shells use two or more knowledge representation schemes.

A rather successful combination of knowledge representation methods is that of production rules and frames. By themselves, production rules do not provide a totally effective representation facility for many ES applications. In particular, their expressive power is inadequate for defining terms and for describing domain objects and static relationships among objects.

The major inadequacies of production rules are in areas that are effectively handled by frames. A great deal of success, in fact, has been achieved by integrating frame and production rule languages to form hybrid representation facilities that combine the advantages of both components. Systems such as KEE and ART have shown how a frame language can serve as a powerful foundation

TABLE 14.3 The Advantages and Disadvantages of Different Representations.

Scheme	Advantages	Disadvantages
Production rules	Simple syntax, easy to understand, simple interpreter, highly modular, flexible (easy to add to or modify)	Hard to follow hierarchies, inefficient for large systems, not all knowledge can be expressed as rules, poor at representing structured descriptive knowledge
Semantic networks	Easy to follow hierarchy, easy to trace associations, flexible	Meaning attached to nodes might be ambiguous, exception handling is difficult
Frames	Expressive power, easy to set up slots for new properties and relations, easy to create specialized procedures, easy to include default information and detect missing values	Difficult to program, difficult for inference, lack of inexpensive software
Formal logic	Facts asserted independently of use, assurance that all and only valid consequences are asserted (precision), completeness	Separation of representation and processing, inefficient with large datasets, very slow with large knowledge base

for a rule language. The frames provide a rich structural language for describing the objects referred to in the rules and a supporting layer of generic deductive capability about those objects that does not need to be explicitly dealt with in the rules. Frame taxonomies can also be used to partition, index, and organize a system's production rules. This capability makes it easier for the domain expert to construct and understand rules, and for the system designer to control when and for what purpose particular collections of rules are used by the system.

More recently, knowledge representation researchers have become increasingly concerned with the need to formally understand the representational adequacy of various knowledge representation schemes. When various knowledge representations are "recast" in terms of logic, they can be compared and the strengths and weaknesses of logic for knowledge representations can be better understood. These investigations have already led to a better understanding of knowledge representation and to the development of logic that can handle incompleteness and default reasoning.

14.10 Inference Techniques

There are several ways in which people reason and solve problems. An interesting way to view the problem-solving process is one in which people draw on "sources of power." Lenat (16) identified nine such sources:

1. Formal Methods—formal reasoning methods (e.g., logical deduction).
2. Heuristic Reasoning—"IF, THEN" rules.
3. Focus—common sense related toward more or less specific goals.
4. Divide and Conquer—divide complex problems into subproblems.
5. Parallelism—neural processors (perhaps a million) operating in parallel.
6. Representation—ways of organizing pieces of information.

7. Analogy—being able to associate and relate concepts.
8. Synergy—the whole being greater than the sum of its parts.
9. Serendipity—luck, or "fortuitous accidents."

These methods range from purely deductive reasoning best handled by computer systems to inductive reasoning that is more difficult to computerize. Lenat believes that the future of AI lies in finding ways to tap those sources that have only begun to be exploited.

Here are some inference approaches used in expert systems.

Reasoning by Analogy.   This approach (which is natural to humans but still difficult to accomplish mechanically) assumes that when a question is asked, the answer can be derived by analogy. For example, if you ask, "What are the working hours of engineers in the company?" the computer may reason that engineers are white-collar employees. Because the computer *knows* that white-collar employees work 9 to 5, it will infer that engineers work 9 to 5. This is an area of much research and many new developments should be forthcoming.

Analogical Thinking.   Similar to the preceding is analogical thinking (for an overview see Eliot [8]). Here the problem solver uses *prior experience* to solve a current problem. The use of this technique has not been exploited yet in the AI field.

Formal Reasoning.   This approach involves syntactic manipulation of data structures to deduce new facts, following prescribed rules of inference. A typical example is the mathematical logic used in proving theorems in geometry. Another example is the approach of predicate calculus, which is an effective symbolic representation and deductive technique.

Generalization and Abstraction.   This approach can be successfully used with both logical and semantic representation of knowledge. For example, if we know that *all* companies have presidents and that *all* brokerage houses are considered companies, then we can infer and generalize that any brokerage house will have a president.

Similarly, if we know that in a certain company all engineers are on a monthly salary, as are the accountants and the systems analysts, eventually the computer might conclude that *all* professionals in the company are on a monthly salary.

Procedural Reasoning.   This approach uses mathematical models or simulation to solve problems.

Metalevel Reasoning.   This approach involves "knowledge about what you know" (e.g., about the importance and relevance of certain facts). It could play a major role in developing future ES.

Which approach to use, and how successful the inference will be is greatly dependent on which knowledge representation method is used. For example, reasoning by analogy can be more successful with semantic networks than with frames.

14.11 Forward and Backward Chaining—An Overview

There are two approaches for controlling inference in rule-based ES: forward chaining and backward chaining (each of which have several variations). We shall provide an intuitive description of these two approaches in this section; a detailed discussion is given in Sections 12 and 13.

Example 1

Suppose you want to fly from Denver to Tokyo and there are no direct flights between the two cities. Therefore you try to find a chain of connecting flights starting from Denver and ending in Tokyo. There are two basic ways to search for this chain of flights:

1. Start with all the flights that arrive at Tokyo and find the city where each flight originated. Then look up all the flights arriving at those cities and find where they originated. Continue the process until you find Denver. Because you are working backward from your goal (Tokyo), this search process is called *backward chaining*.
2. List all flights leaving Denver and mark their destination (intermediate) cities. Then look up all the flights leaving these intermediate cities and find where they land; continue the process until you find Tokyo. In this case, you are working forward from Denver toward your goal, so this search process is called *forward chaining*.

This example also demonstrates the importance of heuristics in expediting the search process. Going either backward or forward, you can use rules to make the search more efficient. For example, in the backward approach you can look at flights that go only eastward. Depending on the goals of your trip (e.g., minimize cost, minimize travel time, maximize stopovers), you can develop additional rules to expedite the search even further.

Example 2

Suppose your car will not start. Is it because you are out of gas? Or is it because the starter is broken? Or is it because of some other reason? Your task is to find out why the car won't start. From what we already know (the *consequence:* "The car won't start"), we go *backward* trying to find the *condition* that caused it. This is a typical application of ES in the area of diagnosis (i.e., the conclusion is known and the causes are sought).

A good example of forward chaining is a situation in which a water system is overheating. In this case the goal is to predict the most likely result. Again, reviewing the rules and checking additional evidence, you can finally find the answer. In forward chaining, start with a *condition*, or a symptom, which is given as a fact.

As will be shown later, the search process in both cases goes through a set of knowledge rules. Determining which rules are true and which are false, the search will end in a finding (we hope). The word *chaining* signifies the linking of a set of pertinent rules.

The search process is directed by an approach sometimes referred to as *rule interpreter*, which works as follows:

□ *Forward chaining*: If premise clauses match the situation, then the process attempts to assert the conclusion.
□ *Backward chaining*: If the current goal is to determine the fact in the conclusion, then the process attempts to determine whether or not the premise clauses match the situation.

Details of these two methods are given in the next two sections.

14.12 Backward Chaining

Backward chaining is a *goal-driven* approach in which you start from an expectation of what is to happen (hypothesis), then seek evidence that supports (or contradicts) your expectation. Often this entails formulating and testing intermediate hypotheses (or subhypotheses).

Hypothesis: Total sales are down because of the cold weather.

Subhypothesis: Sales are relatively lower in the northern states.

Now, segregate the northern states and compare the sales with that of the remaining states so that the hypothesis can either be accepted or rejected.

On a computer, goal-driven reasoning works the same way. The program starts with a goal to be verified as either true or false. Then it looks for a rule that has that goal in its *conclusion*. It then checks the *premise* of that rule in an attempt to satisfy this rule. It checks the assertation base first. If the search there fails, the ES will look for another rule whose conclusion is the same as that of the premise of the first rule. An attempt is then made to satisfy the second rule. The process continues until all the possibilities that apply are checked or until the first rule is satisfied.

Example: Here is an example of an investment decision. The following variables are involved:

$$A = \text{Have } \$10,000$$
$$B = \text{Younger than } 30$$
$$C = \text{Education at college level}$$
$$D = \text{Annual income of at least } \$40,000$$
$$E = \text{Invest in securities}$$
$$F = \text{Invest in growth stocks}$$
$$G = \text{Invest in IBM stocks}$$

Each of these variables can be answered as true (yes) or false (no).

The facts: Let us assume that an investor has $10,000 (i.e., A is true) and she is 25 years old (B is true). She would like advice on investing in IBM stocks. (Yes or No for the *goal*)

The rules: Let us assume that our knowledge base includes the five following rules:

> R1: IF a person has $10,000 and she has a college degree, THEN she should invest in securities.
>
> R2: IF a person's annual income is at least $40,000 and she has a college degree, THEN she should invest in growth stocks.
>
> R3: IF a person is younger than 30 and if she is investing in securities, THEN she should invest in growth stocks.
>
> R4: IF a person is younger than 30, THEN she has a college degree.
>
> R5: IF one wants to invest in growth stocks, THEN the stocks should be IBM.

These rules can be written as

> R1: IF A and C THEN E.
>
> R2: IF D and C THEN F.
>
> R3: IF B and E THEN F.
>
> R4: IF B THEN C.
>
> R5: IF F THEN G.

Our goal is to find whether or not to invest in IBM stocks.

Starting Point. In backward chaining we start by looking for a rule that includes the goal (G) in its *conclusion* (then) part. Since Rule 5 is the only one that qualifies, we start with it. If several rules include G, then the inference engine will have a procedure as to how to handle the situation.

Step 1. Try to accept/reject G. The ES goes now to the *assertion base* to see if G is there. At the present time, all we have in the assertation base is

> A is true.
>
> B is true.

Therefore, the ES will proceed to step 2.

Step 2. R5 says that if it is *true* that we invest in growth stocks (F), THEN we should invest in IBM (G). If we can conclude that the premise of R5 is true or false, then we have solved our problem. However, we do not know if F is true. What shall we do now? Note that F, which is the *premise* of R5, is also the *conclusion* of R2 and R3. Therefore, to find out if F is true, we must check these two rules.

Step 3. We try R2 first (arbitrarily); if both D and C are true, then F is true. Now we have a problem. D is not a conclusion of any rule, nor is it a fact. The computer can then either move to another rule or try to find if D is true by asking the investor for whom the consultation is given if her annual income is above $40,000.

What the ES will do depends on the procedures in the inference engine. Usually a user is going to be asked for an additional information *only* if the information is not available or it cannot be deduced.

We abandon R2 and return to the other rule, R3. This action is called *backtracking* (i.e., knowing that we are in a dead end, we try something else. The computer must be preprogrammed to handle backtracking).

Step 4. Go the R3, test B and E. We know that B is true, because it is a given fact. To prove E, we should go to R1, where E is the conclusion.

Step 5. Examine R1. It is necessary to find if A and C are true. A is true because it is a given fact. To test C, it is necessary to test rule R4 (where C is the conclusion).

Step 6. Rule R4 tells us that C is true (because B is true). Therefore, C becomes a fact (added to the assertion base).

Step 7. If C is true, then E is true, which validates F, which validates our goal (i.e., the advice is to invest in IBM). A negative response to any of the preceding would result in a "do not invest in IBM stocks."

Notice that during the search the ES moved from the *THEN* part to the *IF* part to the *THEN* part, et cetera. This is a typical search pattern in *backward chaining*. As will be seen next, the forward chaining starts with the *IF* part, moves to the *THEN* part, then to another *IF*, and so on. Some systems allow a change in the direction of the search during midcourse, that is, they will go from a *THEN* to *THEN* (or from *IF* to *IF*) if needed.

For another example of backward chaining, see Appendix A.

14.13 Forward Chaining

Forward chaining is a *data-driven* approach. In this approach we start from available information as it comes in, or from a basic idea, then try to draw conclusions.

The computer analyzes the problem, looking for the facts that match the IF portion of its if-then rules. For example, if a certain machine is not working, the computer checks the electricity flow to the machine. As each rule is tested, the program works its way toward a conclusion.

Example: Let us use the same example that we introduced in backward chaining. Here we reproduce the rules:

R1: IF A and C THEN E.
R2: IF D and C THEN F.
R3: IF B and E THEN F.
R4: IF B THEN C.
R5: IF F THEN G.

Start: Since it is known that A and B are true, the ES starts with one of them (takes A first), looking for a rule that includes an A in the IF side of the rule. In our case, this is R1. It includes E in its conclusion.

Step 1. Attempt to verify E. Since A is known (fact, in the assertion base) it is necessary to test C in order to conclude about E. The system tries to find C in the assertion base. Since C is not there, the ES moves to a rule where C is in the THEN side. This is R4.

Step 2. Test R4; C is true because it is matched against B, which is known to be true, in the assertion base. Therefore, C is added to the assertion base as being true.

Step 3. Now R1 fires and E is established to be true. This leads to R3 where E is in the IF side.

Step 4. Since B and E are known to be true (they are in the assertion base), then R3 fires, and F is established to be true in the assertion base.

Step 5. Now R5 fires (since F is in its IF side) which establishes G as true. That is, the expert systems will recommend an investment in IBM.

We have seen that a deduction-oriented antecedent-consequent rule system can run forward or backward, but which one is the better? The answer depends on the purpose of the reasoning and the shape of the search space. For example, if the goal is to discover all that can be deduced from a given set of facts, the system should run forward. In some cases the two strategies can be mixed.

The execution of the forward and/or the backward chaining is done with the aid of a *rule interpreter*. Its function is to examine production rules to determine which one(s) are capable of being fired and then to fire the rule. The *control strategy* of the rule interpreter (e.g., the backward chaining) determines how the appropriate rules are found and when to apply them.

14.14   The Inference Tree

The inference tree (also goal tree, or logical tree) provides a schematic view of the inference process. It is similar to a decision tree. Note that each rule is composed of a premise and a conclusion. In building the inference tree the premises and conclusions are shown as nodes. The branches connect the premises and the conclusions. The operators AND and OR are used to reflect the structure of the rules. There is no deep significance to the construction of such trees, except that they provide a better insight into the structure of the rules.

Figure 14.17 presents the logical tree of the example that we used in the previous two sections.

By using the tree, we can visualize the process of inference and a movement along the branches of the tree. This is called *tree traversal*. To traverse an AND node, we must traverse all the nodes below it. To traverse an OR node, it is enough to traverse just one of the nodes below.

The inference tree is constructed upside down: the root is at the top and the branches point downward. The tree ends with "leaves" at the bottom. (It can also be constructed from the left to the right, much like a decision tree.)

Inference trees are composed basically of clusters of goals like those in Figure 14.18. Each goal may have subgoals (children) and a supergoal (parent). The top goal (root goal) does not have a parent; the bottom goals ("leaves") are facts or dead ends, and they do not have children.

Single inference trees are always a mixture of AND nodes and OR nodes; they are often called AND/OR trees. (More complicated trees involve several goals, and additional parts of a rule such as ELSE.) The AND node signifies a situation in which a goal is satisfied only when *all* its immediate subgoals are satisfied. The OR node signifies a situation in which a goal is satisfied when *any* of its immediate goals is satisfied. When enough subgoals are satisfied to achieve the primary goal, the tree is said to be *satisfied*. The inference engine contains procedures for expressing this process as a backward and/or forward chaining. These procedures are organized as a set of instructions involving inference rules.

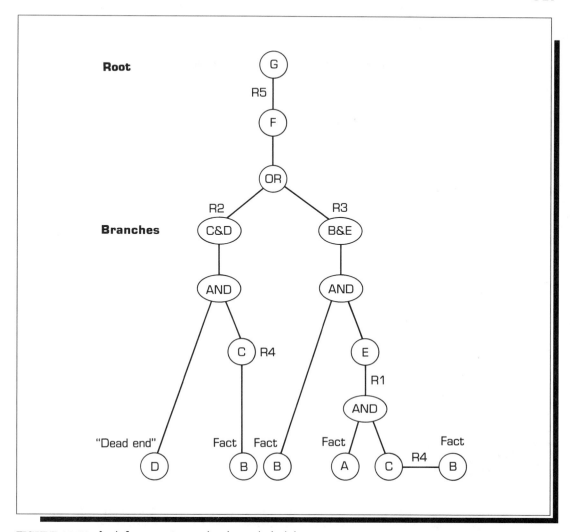

FIGURE 14.17 An inference tree—backward chaining.

These procedures aim at satisfying the inference tree and collectively contribute to the process of goal (problem) reduction. For further discussion see Winston (24).

The inference tree has another big advantage; it provides a guide for answering the *why* and *how* questions in the explanation process.

Notes: The *how* question is a question asked by users when they want to know how a certain conclusion has been reached. The computer follows the logic in the inference tree, identifies the goal (conclusion) involved in it and the AND/OR branches, and reports the immediate subgoals.

The *why* question is asked by users when they want to know why the computer requests certain information as input. To deal with why questions, the computer identifies the goal involved with the computer-generated query and reports the immediate subgoals.

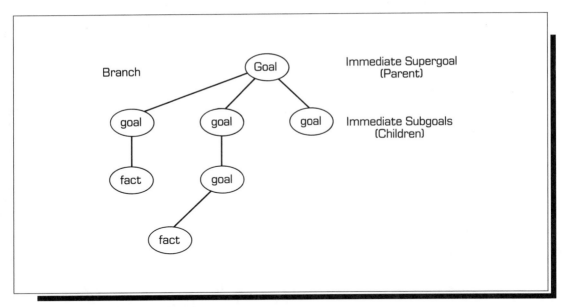

FIGURE 14.18 Goals and subgoals.

A similar graphical presentation to an inference tree is the inference net. An inference net shows the inference process together with the rules that are being used. For further details, see Winston (24, Chapter 6).

14.15 Explanation, Self Knowledge, and Metaknowledge

An *explanation* is an attempt by an ES to clarify its reasoning, actions, or recommendations. The part of an ES that provides explanations is called an *explanation facility* (or *justifier*).

Human experts are often asked to explain their views, recommendations, or decisions. If ES are to mimic humans in performing highly specialized tasks, they need to justify and explain their actions as well.

The specific purposes of the explanation facility are to:

☐ Make the system more intelligible to the user.
☐ Uncover the shortcomings of the rules and knowledge base ("debugging" the systems by the *knowledge engineer*).
☐ Explain situations that were unanticipated by the user.
☐ Satisfy psychological and/or social needs by helping a user feel more assured about the actions of the ES.
☐ Clarify the assumptions underlying the system's operations, both to the user and the builder.
☐ Conduct sensitivity analyses. Using the explanation facility, the user can predict and test the effects of a change on the system.

Explanation in rule-based ES is usually associated with some form of tracing the rules that are fired during the course of a problem-solving session. This is about the closest to real explanation that today's systems can come, given that their knowledge is usually represented almost exclusively as rules that do not include basic principles necessary for a human- type explanation.

Programs like MYCIN replay the exact rule used when asked for an explanation. A DIGITALS ADVISOR, written by Swartout, is a slight improvement over this. Instead of feeding back the rule verbatim, the ADVISOR determines the generic principle that the rule is based on (at that point in the consultation) and displays that general principle.

In developing large ES, the need for a good explanation facility is essential. Large ES always include more facts and rules than one can easily remember. Often a new rule added during ES development will interact with other rules and data in unanticipated ways and will make the ES display strange behavior.

The *Why* and *How* Explanations

Most existing explanation facilities provide two basic types of explanation: the *why* and the *how*.

The *Why* Explanation. A typical *why* question is posed by the user to the computer after the computer asks the user to provide some information. For example, in an investment example (Section 14.12) we may have the following dialog:

COMPUTER: What is your annual income?
CLIENT: Why do you want to know?
COMPUTER: In checking R2, I need to know if your income is above $40,000. If this is true, I will conclude that because you have a college degree, you should invest in growth stocks.

Note: The ES asked for this input because it was unable to find it in the conclusion part of any rule! In the example cited, the computer actually backtracked to another rule and successfully arrived at a final conclusion.

The *How* Explanation. The typical *how* question is posed by users when they would like to know how a certain conclusion or recommendation was reached. Simple systems are limited to the final conclusion. More complex systems can handle intermediate conclusions as well. The system can explain why a certain rule was fired. That is, it shows the chain of rules used to reach the conclusion. In the investment problem the *how* explanation may look like this:

COMPUTER: Invest in IBM stocks.
CLIENT: How? (conclusion was reached)
COMPUTER: Given that you have $10,000 to invest and you are younger than 30, then according to Rule 4 you have a college degree. If this is the case, then according to R1 you should invest in securities. For a young investor like you, according to R3, you should invest in growth stocks if you are going to invest at all. Finally, in your case, according to R5, if you need to invest in growth stocks, then IBM is your best bet.

The *why* and *how* explanations can show the rules as they are written (usually as a reply to a "List" or some other command).

Other Explanations.   Some sophisticated ES can provide other explanations. For example, some systems provide a limited *why not* capability. Let us assume that the system selected IBM as a growth stock. The user may ask: "*Why not GE?*" and the system may answer: "Because the annual growth rate of GE is only 7 percent, whereas that of IBM is 11 percent, using Rule 78."

Note: This example illustrates a possible connection between the ES and a regular database. In order to provide explanation the computer may need to go to a database.

Explanation in nonrule-based systems is much more difficult than in rule-based ones because the inference procedures are more complex. For an overview of the explanation topic see Moore et al. (17).

Metaknowledge.   The system's knowledge about how it reasons is called *metaknowledge*, or knowledge about knowledge. The inference rules presented earlier are a special case of metaknowledge.

Explanation can be viewed as another aspect of metaknowledge. In the future, metaknowledge will allow ES to do even more. They will be able to create the rationale behind individual rules by reasoning from first principles. They will tailor their explanations to fit the requirements of their audience. And they will be able to change their own internal structure through rule correction, knowledge-base reorganization, and system reconfiguration.

There are different methods for generating explanations. An easy way to do them is to preinsert pieces of English text in the system. For example, each question that could be asked by the user may have an answer text associated with it. This is called a *static* explanation.

There are several problems with static explanations. For example, all questions and answers must be anticipated in advance. For large systems this is very difficult. The system also has essentially no idea about what it is saying. In the long run, the program may be modified without changing the text, thus causing inconsistency.

A better form of explanation is a *dynamic* explanation, which is reconstructed according to the execution pattern of the rules. In this method the system reconstructs the reasons for its actions as it evaluates rules.

Most existing explanations fail to meet some of the objectives and requirements listed earlier. The following are some thoughts on this topic (according to Kidd and Cooper [14]).

The explanation facility of most ES consists of printing out a trace of the rules being used. Explanation is not treated as a task that requires intelligence in itself. If ES are to provide satisfactory explanations, future systems must include not only knowledge of how to solve problems in their respective domains but also knowledge of how to effectively communicate to users their understanding of this problem-solving process. Obviously, the relative balance of these two types of knowledge will vary according to the primary function of the system. Constructing such knowledge bases will involve formalizing the heuristics used in providing good explanations.

With current ES, much of the knowledge vital to providing a good explanation (e.g., knowledge about the system's problem-solving strategy) is not expressed explicitly in the rules. Rather, it is implicit in the ordering of certain rule clauses or the way certain hypotheses are linked (i.e., there is a mass of implicit knowledge underpinning each rule and the way groups of rules are structured). Kidd and Cooper have recorded dialogues between experts and their clients in various domains and have found that rules of the form "IF . . . THEN . . . BECAUSE . . . " are used extensively in explanations. Explanations can also be supported graphically.

The purely rule-based representation may be difficult to grasp, expecially when the relationships between the rules are not made explicit in the explanation. Kidd and Cooper developed an explanation facility that can show the inference tree and the parts of it that are relevant to specific queries.

14.16 Dealing with Uncertainty (Inexact Reasoning)

One of the basic assumptions made in the previous sections was that every rule can have only two truth values (i.e., it is either *true* or *false*). In this sense, our previous discussion forced us to be exact about the truth of statements.

However, human knowledge is often inexact. Sometimes one is only partially sure about the truth of a statement and still has to make educated guesses to solve problems. Some concepts or words are inherently inexact. For instance, how can we exactly determine if someone is tall? The concept *tall* has a built-in form of inexactness. Moreover, one sometimes has to make decisions based on partial or incomplete data.

One source of uncertainty occurs when the user cannot provide a definite answer when prompted for a response. For example, when asked to provide a choice between responses B or C, the user may respond that he or she is 30 percent sure of B and 70 percent sure of C.

Another source of uncertainty stems from imprecise knowledge. In many situations, a set of symptoms can help indicate a particular diagnosis without being conclusive.

To deal with inexact concepts, it is necessary to understand how people process uncertain knowledge. (See Hink and Woods [13].) We also use inexact logic and inexact inference. The need for inexact inference methods arises from the fact that we may often have many inexact pieces of data and knowledge that we have to combine.

There exist several approaches to deal with uncertainty, none of which is clearly superior in all cases to all others. Most of these approaches are related to mathematical and statistical theories such as Bayesian Statistics, Dempster and Shafer's belief functions and fuzzy sets (per Zadeh).

Three ways of representing uncertain information in ES are presented here:

□ Subjective probabilities.
□ Certainty factors.
□ Fuzzy logic.

A fourth approach, the use of neural computing, is extremely promising but it is still in a research stage (see Chapter 22).

Subjective Probabilities

The most straightforward approach provides a subjective probability for each proposition. If E is the evidence (sum of all information available to the system), then each proposition P has associated with it a value representing the probability that P holds in the light of all the evidence E, derived by using Bayesian inference. Bayes's Theorem provides a way of computing the probability of a particular event given some set of observations we have made. The main point here is not how this value is derived, but that what we know or have inferred about a proposition is represented by a single value for its likelihood.

Two criticisms may be advanced against this approach. The first is that the single value does not tell us much about its precision, which may be very low when the value is derived from uncertain evidence. To say that the probability of a proposition being true in a given situation is 0.5 (in a range of 0 to 1) usually refers to an *average* figure that is true within a given range. For example, 0.5 plus or minus 0.001 is completely different than 0.5 plus or minus 0.3, yet both may be reported as 0.5. The second criticism is that the single value combines the evidence for and against a proposition without indicating how much there is of each.

The subjective probability expresses the "degree of belief," or how strongly a value or a situation is believed to be true.

Combining Probabilities

There exist several methods of combining probabilities. Three common approaches will be illustrated via an example.
Example: Given

R1: IF inflation is low, THEN stock prices are high (Probability = 0.70).
R2: IF the dollar exchange is strong, THEN stock prices are high (Probability = 0.90).

1. If the two probabilities are independent of each other, one can use a joint probability approach, i.e., multiply the two probabilities. Thus, the probability that stock prices are high is: $0.70 \times 0.90 = 0.63$.
Alternatively, some ES simply average out the probabilities:

$$\frac{0.70 + 0.90}{2} = 0.80$$

2. If the two probabilities are *dependent* on each other, then Bayes' Theorem can be used. (A difficult procedure that is usually not applicable to most expert systems.)

Certainty Factors (CF) in Rule-Based Systems

In this approach there are two separate values for the validity of each proposition. One is a measure of *belief* in P (probability) given E (event or evidence), and the other is a measure of *disbelief* in P given E. The belief and disbelief measures are independent and so cannot be combined as probabilities although they have the same interpretation at their extremes; that is, if the measure of belief (MB) in P is 1, then this means there is conclusive evidence that P is true. The two measures are combined into a single assessment of P given E, resulting in what is called a *certainty factor* (CF[P,E]), which is defined as

$$CF[P,E] = MB[P,E] - MD[P,E]$$

where MD = measure of disbelief. This method like the previous one is subject to the criticism about precision, because both belief measures are point values.

Measuring Certainty Factors

The value of certainty factors is measured by different scales. For example,

- ☐ In EMYCIN the range is from −1 (complete disbelief), to 1 (completely true).
- ☐ In EXSYS and M.1 the range is from −100 to 100 (in EXSYS there is an additional 0 to 10 option).
- ☐ In Personal Consultant, the range is from −1000 to +1000.
- ☐ In INSIGHT 2 and VP Expert, the range is from 0 to 100.

Combining Certainty Factors

Certainty factors can be combined in several ways. Before using any ES shell make sure that you understand how CF are combined (for an overview see Kopcso et al. [15]). The most acceptable way of combining CF in rule-based systems is the approach used in EMYCIN. According to this approach, we distinguish between the following two cases:

Combining Several CF in One Rule

1. Given a rule with an AND operator:

    IF inflation is above 5 percent, CF = 50 percent (A)
    and IF unemployment rate is above 7 percent, CF = 70 percent (B)
    and IF bond prices decline, CF = 100 percent (C)
    THEN stock prices decline

    For this type of rule, for the conclusion to be true, all IFs must be true. However, since several CFs are involved, the CF of the conclusion will be the *minimum* CF on the IF side:

    CF (A,B,and C) = minimum [CF(A), CF(B), CF(C)]

    In our case CF for stock prices to decline will be 50 percent.
2. Given a rule with an OR operator:

    IF inflation is low, CF = 70 percent
    or IF bond prices are high, CF = 85 percent
    THEN stock prices will be high

In this case it is sufficient that only *one* of the IFs is true for the conclusion to be true. Thus, if *both* IFs are believed to be true (at their certainty factor) then the conclusion will have a CF with the *maximum* of the two.

$$CF \ (A \ or \ B) = maximum \ [CF \ (A), \ CF \ (B)]$$

In our case: CF = 0.85 for stock prices to be high.
Note: Both cases hold for any number of IFs.

Combining Two or More Rules. *Example:* Let's assume there are two rules:

> R1: IF the inflation rate is less than 5 percent, THEN stock market prices go up. CF = 0.7

> R2: IF unemployment is less than 7 percent, THEN stock market prices go up. CF = 0.6

Now, let's assume it is predicted that next year the inflation rate will be 4 percent and unemployment will be 6.5 percent (i.e., we assume that the premises of the two rules are true). The combined effect is to be computed in the following way:

$$CF(R1,R2) = (CF(R1) + CF(R2)[1 - CF(R1)]$$

Example: Given CF(R1) = 0.7 AND CF(R2) = 0.6, then:
CF(R1,R2) = 0.7 + 0.6(1 - 0.7) = 0.7 + 0.6(0.3) = 0.88

That is, the ES will tell us that there is an 88 percent chance that stock prices will increase.

Note: If we just added the CFs of R1 and R2, their combined certainty would be greater than 1. We modify the amount of certainty added by the second certainty factor by multiplying it by (1 − the first certainty factor). Thus the greater the first CF, the less certainty is added by the second. But additional factors always add some confidence. For a third rule to be added, the following formula may be used:

$$CF(R1,R2,R3) = CF(R1,R2) + CF(R3[1 - CF(R1,R2)])$$

Example: Assuming a third rule is added:
R3: IF bond price increases, THEN stock prices go up. CF = 0.85

Now, assuming all rules are true in their IF part, the chance that stock prices will go up is:

CF(R1,R2,R3) = 0.88 + 0.85(1 - 0.88) = 0.88 + 0.85(.12) = 0.982

Note: CF(R1,R2) was computed earlier as 0.88.

Fuzzy Logic

Some AI programs exploit the technique of approximate reasoning. This technique, which uses the mathematical theory of fuzzy sets (e.g., see Zadeh [25] and Negotia [18]), simulates the process of normal human reasoning by allowing the computer to behave less precisely and logically than conventional computers do.

Uncertainty and approximations, often the nemesis of managers, are being deliberately programmed into computers. Does this mean that they are going to be as confused in their "thinking" as people sometimes are? Quite the contrary. They will make more intelligent decisions. Software programs are being developed that use a natural language, with heavy emphasis on qualifying adjectives and adverbs like "usually," "highly unlikely," "not very," "probable," and "marginal."

The thinking behind this is that decision making isn't always a matter of black and white, true or false; it often involves gray areas and the term "maybe." In fact, creative decision-making processes are unstructured, playful, contentious, and rambling.

Fuzzy thinking can be advantageous for the following reasons:

□ *It provides flexibility.* Rigid thinking can often lead to unsatisfactory conclusions. This is because you've locked yourself into a set pattern. Make allowances for the unexpected, and you can shift your strategy whenever necessary.

□ *It gives you options.* If you're confronted with a number of possibilities, you'll need to consider them all. Then, using facts *and* intuition ("highly unlikely," or "very good"), you can make an educated guess. Even computers are learning to use such rules of thumb.

□ *It frees the imagination.* At first you may feel that something simply can't be done—all the facts conspire against it. Why not try asking yourself, "What if . . . ?" Follow another avenue and see where you end. You may end up making a better decision.

□ *It's more forgiving.* When you're forced to make black or white decisions, you cannot afford to be wrong, because when you're wrong, you lose. The other way is more forgiving. If you figure something is 80 percent gray, but it turns out to be 90 percent gray, you're not going to be penalized very much.

□ *It allows for observation.* Literal-minded computers have been known to come up with some peculiar results. For example, when one user instructed her computer to come up with information on smoking in the workplace, the computer diligently churned out an article on a salmon-processing plant. A little fuzzy logic might have helped the computer make a more intelligent choice.

An example for a fuzzy set that describes a tall person may look like this: suppose people are asked to define the minimum height that a person must attain before being considered as "tall." The answers could range, say, from 5' 10" to 6' 2". The distribution of answers may look like this:

Height	Proportion voted for
5' 10'	.05
5' 11'	.10
6'	.60
6' 1'	.15
6' 2'	.10

In contrast to certainty factors that include two values (e.g., the degree of belief and disbelief), fuzzy sets use a spectrum of possible values. Fuzzy logic has not been used much in ES in the past because it is more complex to develop, it requires more computing power, and it is more difficult to explain to users.

Fuzzy Logic in Rule-based Systems

In a regular rule-based system, a production rule has no concrete effect at all unless the data completely satisfy the antecedent of the rule. The operation of the system proceeds sequentially, with one rule "firing" at a time; if two rules are simultaneously satisfied, a conflict-resolution policy is needed to determine which one takes precedence. In a fuzzy rule- based system, in contrast, *all* rules are executed during each pass through the system, but with strengths ranging from "not at all" to "completely," depending on the relative degree to which their fuzzy antecedent propositions are satisfied by the data. If the antecedent is satisfied exceptionally well, the result of the rule firing is an assertion exactly matching the consequent proposition of the rule; if the antecedent fuzzy proposition is only partially satisfied, the result is an assertion resembling the consequent but made vague in proportion to the fuzziness of the match; if the antecedent is not satisfied at all, the result of the rule firing is a null proposition that puts no restrictions on the possible values of the variables in the consequent.

Acquisition of Inexact Knowledge

Whereas researchers are busy studying sophisticated methods involving numerical values to express uncertainty, experts and users in the field are not using them much (e.g., see Kidd and Cooper [14]). From interviews with dozens of users and developers, it becomes fairly clear that the whole issue of degree of belief is completely ignored (i.e., users assume complete certainty), or they use an ordinal system of preference (i.e., they use ranking). At best, users would prefer to use qualitative statements such as "most likely," "likely," or "unlikely." In such a case it is necessary to translate this scale to some numerical value. The translation is found in practice to be very difficult and inaccurate. For this reason, one can find several numerical scales for measuring probabilities, sometimes in one software package. For example, EXSYS offers three scales: 0 or 1, 0 to 10, and −100 to +100. The whole issue of uncertainty adds to the complexity of knowledge acquisition described earlier.

The acquisition of knowledge in the form of fuzzy production rules can be facilitated by the use of linguistic variables. The domain of a linguistic variable consists of words and phrases from a quasi-natural language. Any phrase that obeys the syntax of this language can be defined in terms of an abstract-ordered "universe of discourse"; each legal phrase is associated with a specific fuzzy subset of this universe of discourse.

14.17   Some Topics in Knowledge Engineering

Monotonic vs. Nonmonotonic Reasoning

Most existing ES deal with static or monotonic situations. In such cases, if one can prove a statement from more basic facts, the statement remains true regardless of what other information is added. However, in real life we deal with situations that are not static: a particular situation (fact) can change as new information is added. These are nonmonotonic situations. Production planning and control is an example that could involve nonmonotonic reasoning.

Shallow and Deep Representation of Knowledge

Rule-based representation is considered to be very limited compared with frames and networks. Therefore the former is classified as shallow (or surface) representation, whereas the latter is considered as providing deep representation.

Frame-based and network-based approaches allow the implementation of "deeper-level" reasoning such as abstraction and analogy. Reasoning by abstraction and analogy is an important expert activity. You can also represent the objects and processes of the domain of expertise at this level. What is important are the relations among objects. Deep-representation ES perform inference using relations represented by networks or frames. The control of frame or semantic-net systems is usually much more involved than with surface systems and is implemented in a way that an explanation is much more difficult to produce.

One type of expertise that has been represented with a deep-level approach is tutoring. The goal is to convey to students a domain knowledge that is best represented at the deep level: concepts, abstractions, analogies, and problem-solving strategies.

Conflict Resolution

Conflict resolution refers to a situation where the computer needs to select a rule from several rules that apply. For example, suppose we have two rules that look like this:

    R1 If a person is old, THEN . . .
    R2 If a person is over 65, THEN . . .

We may instruct the computer to select the second rule because it is more specific.

Similarly, the computer may be instructed to ignore confidence levels if they are below 0.2.

Conflict resolution instructions are stored in the inference engine and they can be found in several ES development tools.

Metarules

Conflict resolution is done in many cases by introducing inference rules. For example, deciding about which rules to use next. In such a case, we deal with metarules or rules about rules.

Inference engines that include metarules are more complex than those that do not. Furthermore, it is worth noting that metarules also make the knowledge base harder to read and understand. This is because one metarule potentially affects the sequence in which all other rules are called; the effect of a metarule is distributed throughout the rest of the knowledge base.

Pattern Matching

A special technique for inferencing, called *pattern matching*, works with semantic networks, frames, or rules. In the AI context, a pattern is a type of standardized, simplified frame. Many of the details that might be present in a specific frame in a knowledge base are not present in a pattern, but patterns can be far more powerful. For example, the specific frame for a car might include its color. A pattern for a car would include only the essential description of the car (e.g., sedan or sport). If an unknown vehicle is compared with the specific frame for a known car, the color stored there would be detected as a difference and could cause an error. The car pattern would identify the unknown vehicle as a car *regardless* of color, provided it fits the rest of the description.

Patterns can take many forms. In the example above, the pattern is a kind of sterotypical frame that could be used to fill in the details of another frame that is incomplete, but otherwise matches the stereotype. Pattern matching also can be used to invoke heuristics and thus limit the amount of time the computer spends searching through its rules of thumb and testing them on a given problem.

Pattern matching also plays an important role in systems using natural language processing, machine vision, and speech recognition.

The quality of development tools is frequently recognized by their pattern matching capability. For example, OPS 5 has a powerful capability permitting quite complex patterns to be efficiently processed and matched.

14.18 Conclusion

Knowledge engineering is the limiting factor in the development of expert systems. It involves multitudes of activities ranging from knowledge acquisition to the creation of the explanation mechanism. The identification of the problem domain and the expert(s) selection triggers the knowledge engineering process. At that time the knowledge engineer and the expert start developing a mutual working environment. This environment is very important because both participants will work together on the knowledge acquisition phase for weeks, months, or even years. The acquired knowledge is coded using one or more methods of representation. Most common ones are production rules and frames. The representation is designed to enable the reasoning capability or the inference. Finally, an explanation capability must be added to increase the effectiveness of the ES.

The technology of ES provides the possibility of inexact reasoning. This is done through the introduction of probabilities, certainty factors, and fuzzy logic. Although few users currently take advantage of this capability, future systems will involve more of this approach, enabling more complicated domains to be the subjects of ES.

There are many initiatives in progress to reduce the problems of knowledge engineering. They range from automated knowledge acquisition to easy rule editors. The most successful attempt is probably the use of development tools that can increase the productivity of ES developers. They are the subject of the next chapter.

Key Words

access-oriented programming	forward chaining	multiple experts
backtracking	frames	multiple inheritance
backward chaining	fuzzy logic	object-oriented programming
blind search	inductive reasoning	O-A-V triplets
breadth-first search	icons	pattern matching
certainty factors	inexact (approximate) reasoning	predicate calculus
classes	inference tree	procedural knowledge
conflict resolution	instantiation	production rules
declarative knowledge	justification	propositional logic
deductive reasoning	knowledge engineering	reusability
deep presentation	knowledge representation	rule induction
demons	metaknowledge	rule interpreter
depth-first search	metarules	rules
encapsulation	modus ponens	semantic networks
explanation facility	monotonic reasoning	shallow presentation
firing a rule		state-space search

Questions For Review

1. What is propositional logic? Give an example.
2. What is a production rule? Give an example.
3. What are the basic parts of a production rule? List several names for each part.
4. Define and contrast declarative and procedural knowledge.
5. List the major knowledge representation methods.
6. Define a semantic network.
7. Define backward chaining and contrast it with forward chaining.
8. Define an inference tree. What is its major purpose?
9. Define conflict resolution.
10. List some of the purposes of the explanation capability.
11. Explanation in current expert systems is done by tracing the rules. Discuss how this is done.
12. What is the *why* question? What is a typical answer to this question?
13. What is the *how* question? What is a typical answer to this question?
14. What is metaknowledge? How is it related to the explanation facility?

15. Define static explanation.
16. Define approximate reasoning.
17. List the three methods of handling inexact reasoning.
 18. List two advantages of fuzzy logic.
19. What is meant when we say that a rule "fires?"
20. List the various methods of knowledge acquisition.
21. What is a state-space search?
22. Describe the modus ponens inference strategy.
23. Describe a frame. Give an example of a "sailboat" frame.
24. What is encapsulation? What is its major advantage?
25. What is an instantiation of a frame?
26. What is a class of OOP?
27. What is the advantage of a state tree over a state graph?
28. List three types of facets of a frame and explain their meaning.

Questions for Discussion

1. Give an example that illustrates the difference between propositional logic and predicate calculus.
2. Give examples of production rules in three different functional areas (e.g., marketing, accounting).
3. Give an example of two knowledge rules and a related inference rule.
4. Why is frame representation considered more complex than production rules representation? What are the advantages of the former over the latter?
5. How is object-oriented programming related to frames?
6. Relate access-oriented to object-oriented programming.
7. Relate metaknowledge to metarules. Explain how metarules work. How do they relate to inference rules?
8. Discuss the major deficiencies of existing explanation facilities. Organize your discussion as a comparison with a potential explanation given by a human.
9. The explanation facility serves the user as well as the developer. Discuss the benefits derived by each.
10. If you had a dialog with a human expert, what other questions besides "Why?" and "How?" would you be likely to ask? Give examples.
11. Discuss some of the reasons that could create uncertainty in ES; provide examples.
12. Discuss the major differences among subjective probability, certainty factors, and fuzzy logic.
13. Discuss some of the difficulties in acquiring knowledge.
14. It is said that multiple knowledge representation can be very advantageous. Why?
15. It is said that DSS provides static explanation while ES provides a dynamic one. Explain.
16. Explain how OOP works with respect to messages.

Exercises

1. Given a set of rules for a question: Should we buy a house or not?
   R1   IF inflation is low
          THEN interest rates are low
          ELSE interest rates are high

R2   IF interest rates are high
           THEN housing prices are high

R3   IF housing prices are high
           THEN do not buy a house
           ELSE buy it

Run a backward chaining with a high inflation rate, and a forward chaining with a low inflation rate. Prepare an inference tree for the backward chaining case.

2. Given an ES with the following rules:

R1   IF interest rate falls
           THEN bond prices decline

R2   IF interest rate increases
           THEN bond prices decline

R3   IF interest rate is unchanged
           THEN bond prices remain unchanged

R4   IF the dollar rises (against other currencies)
           THEN interest rate declines

R5   IF the dollar falls
           THEN interest rate increases

R6   IF bond prices decline
           THEN buy bonds

    a. A client just observed that the dollar exchange rate is falling. He wants to know whether or not to buy bonds. Run a forward and a backward chaining and submit a report to him.

    b. Prepare an inference tree for the backward chaining in part "a".

    c. A second client observed that the interest rates are unchanged. She asks for advice on investing in bonds. What will the ES tell her? Use forward chaining.

3. Assume you plan to drive from New York to Los Angeles to arrive midafternoon for an appointment. To arrive fresh, you want to drive no more than two hours the day you arrive, but on other days, you're willing to drive eight to ten hours. One logical way to approach this problem is to start at Los Angeles, your goal, and work backward. You would first find a place about two hours from Los Angeles for your final stopover before arrival, then plan the rest of your trip by working backward on a map until your route is planned completely. You have a limited number of days to complete the trip.

How would you analyze the problem starting from New York? What are the major differences? Which approach would you use? Why?

4. Given rules:

R1   IF inflation is high
           THEN unemployment is high

R2   IF inflation is high and the interest rate is high
           THEN stock prices are low

R3   IF the gold price is high or dollar exchange is low
           THEN stock prices are low

R4   IF gold price is high
           THEN unemployment is high

Conduct the following computations; list the rules used.

    a. The CF for high inflation is 0.8 and for high interest rates is 0.6. Find the CF for stock prices.

    b. The CF for a high gold price is 0.5, and the CF for a low dollar exchange rate is 0.7. Find the CF for stock prices.

    c. Given all the information in a. and b., figure the CF for low stock prices; for high stock prices.

d. Figure the CF for a high unemployment rate given that the inflation rate is high and the gold price is high. (Use the data in a. and b.)

5. Given three rules:

R1 IF blood test results = 'yes'

THEN there is 0.8 evidence

R2 IF in malaria zone = 'yes'

THEN there is 0.5 evidence that disease is 'Malaria'

R3 IF bit by flying bug is True

THEN there is 0.3 evidence that disease is 'Malaria'

What certainty factors will be computed for having Malaria by the expert system if:

a. the first two rules are considered

b. all three rules are considered

6. Given an expert system with six rules pertaining to interpersonal skills for a job applicant

RULE 1

IF: The applicant answers questions in a straightforward manner

THEN: He is easy to converse with

RULE 2

IF: The applicant seems honest

THEN: He answers questions in a straightforward manner

RULE 3

IF: The applicant has items on his resume that are found to be untrue.

THEN: He does not seem honest

ELSE: He seems honest

RULE 4

IF: The applicant is able to get an appointment with the executive assistant

THEN: He is able to strike up a conversation with the executive assistant

RULE 5

IF: The applicant struck up a conversation with the executive assistant and the applicant is easy to converse with

THEN: He is amiable

RULE 6

IF: The applicant is amiable

THEN: He has adequate interpersonal skills

RULE 7

IF: The applicant has adequate interpersonal skills

THEN: He will get the job

a. It is known that the applicant answers questions in a straightforward manner. Run a backward chaining analysis to find if the applicant will get the job or not.

b. Assume that the applicant does not have any items on his resume that are found to be untrue and he is able to get an appointment with the executive assistant. Run a *forward* chaining analysis to find out if he will get the job.

c. We just discovered that the applicant was able to get an appointment with the executive assistant. It is also known that he is honest.

Does he have interpersonal skills, or not?

Note: a, b, and c are *independent* incidents.

7. Given rules:

R1 If you study hard, then you will receive an A in the course. CF = 0.82

R2 If you understand the material, then you will receive an A in the course. CF = 0.85.

R3 If you are very smart, then you will receive an A in the course. CF = 0.90.

a. What is the chance of getting an A in the course if you study hard and understand the material?

b. What is the chance of getting an A in the course if all premises of the rules are true?

8. Construct a semantic network for the following situation: Mini is a robin; it lives in a nest which is on a pine tree in Ms. Wang's backyard. Robins are birds, they can fly and they have wings. They are an endangered species and they are protected by government regulations.

9. Write a frame that will describe the object Robin, as described in the previous question.

10. Prepare a set of frames of an organization, given the following information:
    Company: 1050 employees, 130 million annual sales, and Jan Fisher is the president
    Departments: accounting, finance, marketing, production, personnel
    Production Department: 5 lines of production
    Product: computers
    Annual budget: $50,000 + $12,000 × no. of computers produced
    Materials: $6,000 per unit produced
    Working days: 250
    No. of supervisors: 1 for each 12 employees
    Range of no. of employees: 400–500 per shift (2 shifts per day). Overtime or part time on a third shift is possible.

11. Write a narrative of Figure 14.12.

APPENDIX A: Example of Goal-Directed Search

In this example, the program identifies a goal that is to answer the question in the upper box. Then it scans the rules to find which ones will give the answer to this question (i.e., the "value" of A). Rule 3 is the one chosen because its consequent gives the answer to the question. But to apply this rule, the program will need three pieces of information: A1, B, and A2. The program will check if these pieces of information are in the assertation base. If they are not, the new goal becomes to find the value of A1, B, and A2 by using rules R1 and R2, and asking the user for the value of B. The same procedure is then applied to rules 1 and 2 until all the information necessary to apply the rules is found in the knowledge base. The value of it is then determined (see THEN below).

RULE 1

IF   System makes use of specially designed forms
       AND
       Anticipation controls are present

THEN The methods used to ensure that all data are initially recorded and identified are good.

RULE 2

IF   System makes use of batch control totals
       AND
       The batch totals are reconciled by the control group
       OR
       The batch totals are reconciled by the computer

THEN The controls that insure that the input are reconciled are good.

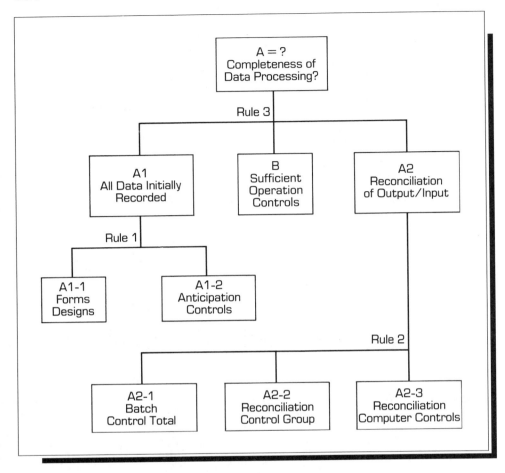

RULE 3

IF   The methods used to ensure that all data are initially recorded and identified are good

AND

The operation controls are sufficient

AND

The controls that insure that the input and output are reconciled are good

THEN The quality of the system of controls to ensure the completeness of data
processed by the computer is good.

Source: Bedard et al. (2).

References and Bibliography

1. Arcidiancono, T. "Computerized Reasoning." *PC Tech Journal*, May 1988.
2. Bedard, J., et al. "Decision Support Systems and Auditing." Working paper #49,
   Center for Accounting Research, University of Southern California, 1983.

3. Brachman, R. J., and H. J. Levesque. *Readings in Knowledge Representation*. Palo Alto, CA: Morgan- Kaufman, 1985.

4. Buchanan, G., and E. H. Shortliffe, eds. *Rule-Based Expert Systems*. Reading, MS: Addison-Wesley, 1984.

5. Cercone, N., and G. McGalla. "Artificial Intelligence: Underlying Assumptions and Basic Objectives." *Journal of the Amerian Society for Information Science*, September 1984.

6. Cox, B. J. *Object-Oriented Programming: An Evolutionary Approach*. Reading, MA: Addison-Wesley, 1986.

7. Davis, R., and D. B. Lenat. *Knowledge-Based Systems in Artificial Intelligence*. New York: McGraw-Hill, 1983.

8. Eliot, L. B. "Analogical Problem Solving and Expert Systems." *IEEE Expert*, Summer 1986.

9. Feigenbaum, E., and P. McCorduck. *The Fifth Generation*. Reading, MA: Addison-Wesley, 1983.

10. Fikes, R., and T. Kehler. "The Role of Frame-Based Representation in Reasoning." *Communications of ACM*, Vol. 28, No. 9, September 1985.

11. Frenzel, L. *Crash Course in AI and Expert Systems*, Indianapolis, IN: H. W. Sams, 1987.

12. Frenzel, L. *Understanding Expert Systems*, Indianapolis, IN: H. W. Sams, 1987.

13. Hink, R. F., and D. L. Woods. "How Humans Process Uncertain Knowledge," *AI Magazine*, Fall 1987.

14. Kidd, A. L., and M. B. Cooper. "Man-Machine Interface Issues in the Construction and Use of an Expert System." *International Journal of Man-Machine Studies*, Vol. 22, 1985.

15. Kopcso, D. et al. "A Comparison of the Manipulation of Certainty Factors by Individuals and Expert Systems Shells." *Journal of Mgmt. Information Systems*, Vol. 5, No. 1, 1988.

16. Lenat, D. B. "The Ubiquity of Discovery." *Artificial Intelligence*, Vol. 19, No. 2, 1982.

17. Moore, J. D., et al. "Explanation in Expert Systems—A Survey." *Proceedings, The First International Symposium on Business, Finance, and Accounting*, School of Accounting, The University of Southern California, September 1988.

18. Negotia, C. V. *Expert Systems and Fuzzy Systems*. Menlo Park, CA: Benjamin Cummins, 1985.

19. Newell, A., and H. A. Simon. *Human Problem Solving*. Englewood Cliffs, NJ: Prentice-Hall, 1972.

20. "Object-oriented Programming," *BYTE*, August 1986.

21. Prerau, D. S. "Selection of an Appropriate Domain for an Expert System." *AI Magazine*, Summer 1985.

22. Stefik, M. J., et al. "Integrated Access-Oriented Programming into a Multiparadigm Environment." *IEEE Software*, January 1986.

23. Van Horn, M. *Understanding Expert Systems*. Toronto: Baton Books, 1986.

24. Winston, P. H. *Artificial Intelligence*. 2nd ed. Reading, MA: Addison-Wesley, 1984.

25. Zadeh, L. A. *The Management of Uncertainty in Expert Systems*. Proceedings, First Symposium on Application of Expert Systems in Emergency Management Operation, FEMA/NBS, Washington, D.C., April 1985.

Chapter 15

Building Expert Systems: Process, Tools, and Strategy

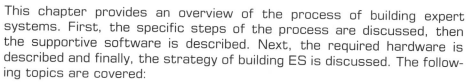

This chapter provides an overview of the process of building expert systems. First, the specific steps of the process are discussed, then the supportive software is described. Next, the required hardware is described and finally, the strategy of building ES is discussed. The following topics are covered:

537

15.1 Introduction

Most early commercial expert systems demonstrated many potential benefits that materialize when expertise can be automated. These early projects also revealed extraordinary levels of effort. Building an ES required special-purpose computing hardware and highly trained personnel. Most of the well-known systems, such as XCON, MYCIN, and DENDRAL,* took many person-years of effort to construct at a cost of several million dollars. Three events changed this picture radically. First, software tools for knowledge engineering are accelerating ES development. Second, special-purpose AI computers are adding general-purpose capabilities and at the same time ES software is being developed to run on general-purpose computers. Thus, the cost of hardware and/or software is being continuously reduced. Third, it is now apparent that less complex and powerful ES are also valuable.

This chapter deals with three topics: Process, tools, and strategy.

Process. The general process of building ES was introduced in the last section of Chapter 12. Here (in Sections 15.2–15.10) we discuss in detail the various steps of the process.

Tools. A variety of software tools are available for expediting the construction of expert systems. These are discussed in Sections 15.11–15.15 together with the hardware support (Section 15.16).

Strategy. Three dimensions of strategy are discussed (Section 15.17). First, the organization's strategy toward building ES; second, user-built vs. team constructed systems; and finally, the mainframe environment.

The various development phases that follow were described in Chapter 12, Figure 12.4.

15.2 Selection of Problems (Phases 1 and 2)

The ES development process starts with the identification of an appropriate problem domain and a specific task. This step can be very short or very long, depending on the magnitude and complexity of the problem. A related issue is who selects the ES project.

The selection of the problem area in the case of large systems may require a formal feasibility study. A framework for such a study was proposed by Waterman (25). According to this proposal, a study should be composed of three parts: *necessary requirements, justification,* and *appropriateness.*

Necessary Requirements for ES Development

Waterman listed seven requirements that are *all necessary* to make ES development possible:

1. The task does not require common sense.
2. The task requires only cognitive, not physical, skills.

---

*Most of the systems and tools referred to in this chapter are described in the Appendices and/or in Chapter 17.

3. At least one genuine expert, who is willing to cooperate, exists.
4. The experts involved can articulate their methods of problem solving.
5. The experts involved must agree on the knowledge and the solution approach to the problem.
6. The task is not too difficult.
7. The task is well understood, and is defined clearly.

Additional requirements are:

8. The task definition is fairly stable.
9. Conventional (algorithmic) computer solution techniques are not satisfactory.
10. Incorrect or nonoptimal results can be tolerated.
11. The domain must be well bounded and narrow.
12. Data and test cases are available.
13. The vocabulary has no more than a couple of hundred concepts.

Justification for ES Development

Waterman lists the following factors, at least one of which must be present, to justify the ES:

1. The solution to the problem has a high payoff. (The task is important.)
2. The ES can preserve scarce human expertise so it will not be lost.
3. The expertise is needed in many locations.
4. The expertise is needed in hostile or hazardous environments.

Other factors to consider are as follows:

5. The expertise improves performance and/or quality.
6. The system can be used for training.
7. The ES solution can be derived faster than that which a human can provide.
8. The ES is more consistent and/or accurate than a human.

Appropriateness of the ES

Waterman suggests that the following factors be considered in determining when it is appropriate to develop an ES:

1. *The nature of the problem.* The problem should have a symbolic structure, and heuristics should be available for its solution. In addition it is desirable that the task be decomposable for development.
2. *The complexity of the task.* The task should be neither too easy nor too difficult for a human expert.
3. *The scope of the problem.* The task problem should be of a manageable size; it also should have some practical value.

Checklists.   Several checklists were developed to assist in finding candidate applications.

TABLE 15.1 A Checklist for Task Selection.

A. Are the answers to your problem or your decisions determined at random?
  1. Yes
  2. No
B. How important is accuracy in the answers or decisions? What is the consequence of a wrong answer or decision?
  1. I need total accuracy. The consequences of a wrong answer or decision are catastrophic.
  2. Accuracy is important. I can tolerate occasional wrong answers, but I need the right answers most of the time.
  3. Although accuracy is still important, I can tolerate initial errors as long as I can adapt the system to new or changing circumstances.
C. How complete is the set of examples describing your problem or decision?
  1. My set of examples is 100 percent complete, and covers every possible case that could arise.
  2. My set of examples is almost complete. I think it covers most cases that will arise.
  3. My set of examples covers only a small number of the possible situations that could occur.
  4. My set of examples covers a fair number of the possible situations that could occur.
D. How well will the people who will use the system be able to detect wrong answers?
  1. The people who will use the system are capable of spotting wrong answers. They can compensate for flaws or gaps in the set of examples.
  2. The people who will use the system will not be able to detect wrong answers.

Source: Expert-Ease (now called Expert One), a software program, from Human Edge, Palo Alto, CA.

  1. An elaborate method with four separate checklists is suggested by Sagle and Wick (23), who use a weighing point system.
  2. A two-page, "one-minute knowledge engineer" checklist is offered in *EDP Analyzer*, March 1987.
  3. A computerized checklist built into Expert-Ease is shown in Table 15.1. This simple checklist helps the user to decide whether the task is appropriate for an ES. For instance, if the answer to A is yes, then ES is not appropriate. A good ES candidate will be one with an answer such as: A-2, B-3, C-1 or 2, and D-1. Based on the user's answers, the ES tells the user if the task selected is appropriate.

The choice of problem area should also take into consideration the generic areas discussed in Chapter 12 where ES has proved to be successful.

15.3 Selecting the Expert(s) (Phase 2)

Source of Expertise. Documented knowledge contributes a major part of the knowledge base in many existing ES, particularly in small systems. Documented knowledge can be found in the following sources:

  ☐ *Textbooks*—General and specific facts and rules.
  ☐ *Databases*—Empirical data, real-time information, case studies, facts and rules.
  ☐ *Other Sources*—Manuals, memos, reports, films, pictures, audio, and video sources.

TABLE 15.2   Attributes of a Good Expert.

☐ The expert should be thoroughly familiar with the domain, including
  —Task expertise built up over a long period of task performance.
  —Knowledge of the organizations that will be developing and using the ES.
  —Knowledge of the user community.
  —Knowledge of technical and technological alternatives.

☐ The expert's knowledge and reputation must be such that if the ES is able to capture a portion of the expert's expertise, the system's output will have credibility and authority.

☐ The expert will commit a substantial amount of time to the development of the system, including temporary relocation to the development site, if necessary.

☐ The expert is capable of communicating his or her knowledge, judgment, and experience.

☐ The expert should be cooperative, easy to work with, and eager to work on the project.

☐ The expert should have an interest in computer systems, even if he or she is not a computer specialist.

Source: Goyal et al. (6), with permission of Learned Information, Inc., Medford, NJ

Undocumented knowledge is found in the minds of human experts. Appendix A and Table 15.2 list some characteristics of human experts. Human experts possess knowledge that is much more complex than what we find in documented sources. It is based on experience, it frequently involves common sense, and in many cases it can be expressed in terms of heuristics.

The Selection. ES use both documented sources and human experts as sources of knowledge. The more human expertise is needed, the longer and more complicated the acquisition process will be.

Several issues may surface in executing this step:

☐ Who selects the expert(s).
☐ How to motivate the expert to cooperate.
☐ How to identify an expert (what characteristics an expert should exhibit).
☐ What to do if several experts exist (see Chapter 13).

15.4   Conceptual Design and Feasibility (Phase 3)

Although a preliminary feasibility study was developed during the problem selection step, it is necessary to formalize the *conceptual design* and the *feasibility study* before the system can be developed. Activities in this phase include:

A *conceptual design* of an ES is like an architectural sketch of a house. It gives you a general idea of what the system will look like, its purpose, and its anticipated capabilities. Conceptual design is interrelated with the *feasibility study*. The feasibility study of ES is similar in structure to a feasibility study of any information system. A proposed outline is shown in Table 15.3 (for details consult books on system analysis and design).

The larger the system the more *formal* the step must be, since *approval* by top management is required.

TABLE 15.3 Elements of a feasibility study.

Economic (Financial) Feasibility	Cost of system development (itemized)
	Cost of maintenance
	Payback (anticipated)
	Cash flow analysis
	Needs assessment
Technical Feasibility	Interface requirements
	Networking issues
	Availability of knowledge and data
	Security of confidential knowledge
	Knowledge representation scheme
	Hardware/software availability/compatibility
Operational Feasibility	Availability of human and other resources
	Priority as compared to other projects
	Project management (plan, timing, etc.)
	Organizational and implementation issues
	Management and user support
	Availability of expert(s) and knowledge engineer(s)
	Legal and other constraints

At the end of this phase the builder should have a fairly good idea about what the system is going to look like.

15.5 Selecting Software and Hardware (Phases 4 and 5)

Once an appropriate problem is selected and its feasibility determined, a decision must be made regarding the software tools needed to build the system. ES tools contain various facilities for representing knowledge and conducting a consultation, as well as browsing and debugging aids, editors, explanation facilities, and so on.

In principle, the selection of a tool is based on a match between the varieties of knowledge to be represented and the built-in features of the tool. In practice this selection process is complex for several reasons:

- It is difficult to make the transition from problems to tools. At issue is the difference between the problem and the problem-solving strategy. The same problem can be approached very differently by different experts. It is often hard at the onset to know what methods the expert will use to solve the problem.
- Practically speaking, tool selection is affected by whatever tool one may already own and the degree of familiarity with ES tools. Stretching a known piece of software to its limit may be more practical than acquiring and learning the ins and outs of a new, more powerful tool. (By analogy, in the world of statistical packages, BMD is well known for its flexibility in handling analysis of variance. However, if your data set is embedded in SPSS, you might choose to remain in SPSS rather than pay the cost of transferring the data, learning about BMD, and so on.)

□ Currently, tools on the market are more similar than they are different. Among commercially available software are many rule-based knowledge engineering tools. Lately, there appeared several tools for frames and hybrid representations, most of which run on standard hardware and even on PCs.

The various software tools are described in Sections 15.10–15.14.

The major issues involved in the selection of ES development software are summarized in Table 15.4.

The selection of hardware is a problem only when large systems are constructed. Small systems are being developed and implemented on PCs. Even large systems can be developed on existing minicomputers. For further discussion of this issue, see Sections 15.16 and 15.18.

Evaluation Procedures

Several methodologies were proposed for evaluation of ES software. Generally speaking, these methods develop a set of attributes against which existing packages are compared. In addition, in-depth evaluations of popular packages appear periodically in various magazines. One problem is that most of these evaluations are subjective while the capabilities of the packages are being changed rapidly with the appearance of new versions. The following references can be reviewed for both proposed methodologies and actual evaluations:

TABLE 15.4   Issues in ES Software Selection

□ Can the tool be easily obtained and installed?
This includes cost factors, legal arrangements, and compatibility with existing hardware.

□ How well is the tool supported? Will later upgrades of the tool be backward-compatible? Is the current version of the system fairly stable?

□ Has the tool been used successfully in a variety of application domains?

□ How difficult will it be to expand, modify, or add a front or a back end to the tool? Is a source code available or is the system sold only as a black box?

□ Is it simple to incorporate Lisp (or other language) functions to compensate for necessary features that are not built-in?

□ What kind of knowledge representation schemes does the tool provide? rules? networks? frames? others? How well do these match the intended application (for example, production rules are particularly attractive when expert knowledge is in the form of empirical associations; networks are attractive for representing complex interrelations among concepts).

□ Can the tool handle the expected form of application data: continuous, error-filled, inconsistent, uncertain, time-varying, etc.?

□ Do the inference mechanisms provided match the problem?

□ Does the allowable granularity of knowledge match what is needed by the problem?

□ Does the expected speed of the developed system match the problem if real-time use is required?

□ Is there a delivery (consultation) vehicle available if many copies of the application will be needed?

Source: Goyal et al. (6), with permission of Learned Information, Inc., Medford, NJ

□ Gevarter (5)
□ Harmon et al. (8)
□ Holsapple and Whinston (11)
□ Mettrey (16)
□ Rosenthal (20)

Figure 15.1 shows the various attributes and capabilities which could be used to assess the various packages.

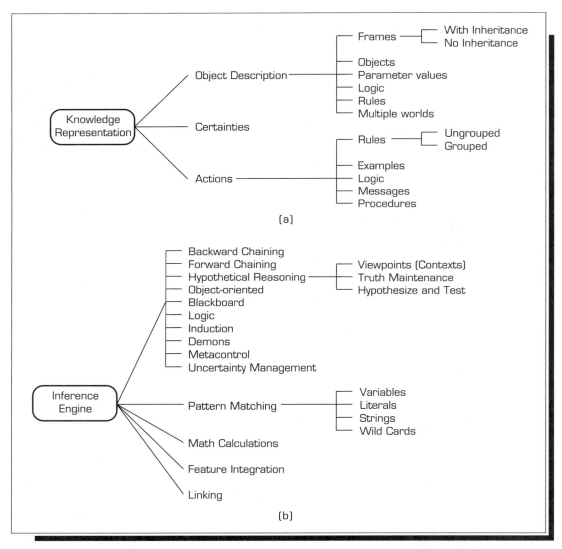

(a)

(b)

FIGURE 15.1 Attributes and capabilities of ES software. (*Source:* Gevarter [5]. (U.S. Government work not protected by U.S. copyright.)

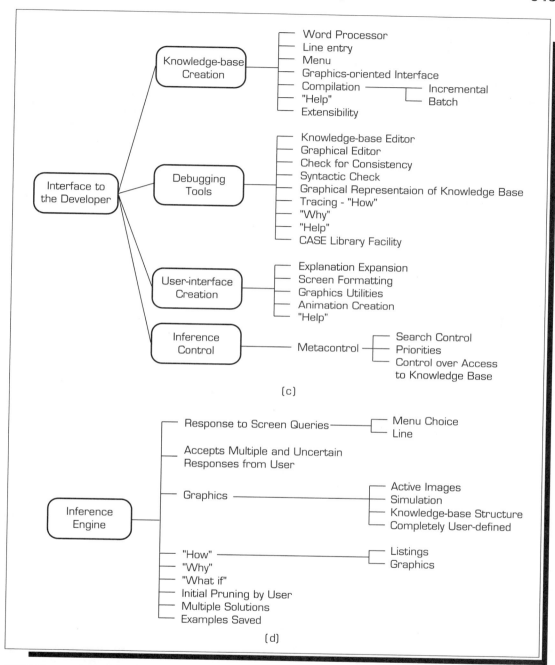

FIGURE 15.1 (*continued*)

15.6 Knowledge Acquisition, Representation, and Inferencing (Phases 5 and 6)

Once the problem, the expert, and the tools are determined, it is possible to start the knowledge acquisition process. The construction process continues with the creation (or acquisition) of the inference engine and the explanation facility. Then the acquired knowledge is programmed in the knowledge base as described in the previous two chapters.

15.7 Rapid Prototyping (Phase 6)

Prototyping has been crucial to the development of many ES. A prototype in ES refers to a small-scale system. It includes representing the knowledge captured in a manner that enables quick inference, and the creation of the major components of an ES on a rudimentary basis. For example, in a rule-based system, the prototype may include only 50 rules. However, this small number of rules is sufficient to produce consultations of a limited nature.

The prototype helps the builder to decide on the structure of the knowledge base before spending a large amount of time on building more rules. Developing the prototype has other advantages as well:

☐ Accelerated process of knowledge acquisition.
☐ Easier for experts to criticize existing programs or provide exceptions to the rules.
☐ Selling the system to the skeptics becomes easier.
☐ Getting more support from top management.
☐ Helping sustain the expert's interest.
☐ Providing an idea of the value of the software and the hardware.
☐ Providing an idea of the degree of the expert's cooperation.
☐ Providing information about the initial definition of the problem domain, the need for the ES, and the like.
☐ Demonstrating the capabilities of the ES.

Rapid prototyping is essential in large systems because the cost of poorly structured and then not used ES can be very high.

The Prototyping Process.   The rapid-prototyping process is shown in Figure 15.2.

We start with the *design* of a small system. The designer determines what aspect (or segment) to prototype, how many rules to use in the first cut, et cetera. Then the knowledge is acquired for the first cut and represented in the ES. Next, a test is conducted. The test can be done using historical or hypothetical cases. The expert is asked to judge the results. The knowledge representation methods, the software and the hardware effectiveness are also determined. Finally, a potential user may be invited to test the system. The results are analyzed by the knowledge engineer and if improvement is needed the system is redesigned. Usually the system goes through several iterations

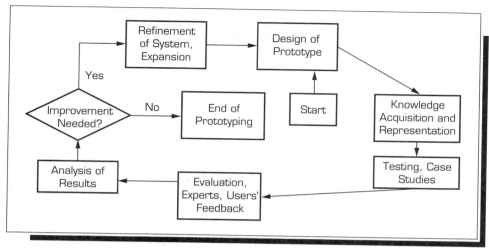

FIGURE 15.2 Rapid prototyping.

with appropriate refinements. This process continues until the system is ready to test in the field. For details on the prototyping process see Redin (19) and Cholawsky (3).

15.8   Evaluation for Performance and Improvements (Phases 6 and 7)

The prototype, and later on improved versions of the system, are being tested and evaluated for performance both in the lab and in the field. This evaluation is initially done in a simulated environment. The system is exposed to test problems (e.g., historical cases or sample cases provided by users). There is a close link between the evaluation and the refinements (improvements) of the ES. The evaluation reveals cases not handled by the system's rules. As a result, new rules are added or old ones are modified. Such changes may have unexpected negative effects on parts of the system. For example, there could be a conflict (inconsistency of rules). A good development tool provides a rapid consistency check for the rules in the knowledge base.

Evaluation for performance deals not only with identification of cases that cannot be handled by the systems, but also with the issue of the quality of the advice rendered. This can be a very difficult activity because we may lack standards for comparison. ES often give advice in areas where there is no "gold standard," so a simple comparison to judge accuracy is impossible. As a result of these characteristics, ES are being evaluated in less formal and more experimental ways.

A principal method used to evaluate ES is to compare its performance to an accepted criterion, such as a human expert's decision. This approach is called the *"modified Turing test,"* in which managers are shown two solutions to a problem—one the result of human judgment, the other of an ES, without knowing which is which—and are asked to compare them.

Difficulties in Evaluating ES

The following issues should indicate the difficulties that stand in the way of evaluation studies:

1. What characteristics should be evaluated? The performance of the system has been the main characteristic of interest. However, the system's discourse or ease-of-use may also be key to its acceptance.

2. How should performance be evaluated? Owing to the nature of expert system applications, it is sometimes hard to define a "gold standard" against which to compare the system's performance. For example, a match between the conclusions of the system and the expert may be hard to obtain. Indeed, different experts may disagree on certain details or both the problem and the expert may be wrong. In evaluating performance, should one look only at the conclusion or should the program's line of reasoning be evaluated as well? What form should the evaluation take when the system provides multiple (as opposed to unique) answers?

3. How should the test problems be selected? The fact that the realism of real world exceptions and irrelevancies can seriously affect the performance of an expert system is well known. However, in certain areas, the supply of realistic studies may be very limited. In the case of PROSPECTOR, for instance, there is only a small number of known ore deposits to draw on, and the time between initial and final characterizations of the deposit could be long. Similar problems occur with rare diseases and other cases when sampling costs are high.

4. How should one evaluate the program's mistakes? In judgmental areas, it is interesting to observe the type of mistakes an expert system may make. One is reminded that the work of Piaget on developmental psychology was prompted by the patterns of mistakes (not the correct responses) in IQ tests by children. The same search for error patterns occurs in intelligent tutoring systems but the implications for evaluation studies appear to be unexplored. Clearly, this issue also relates to the requirement that expert systems "degrade gracefully."

(*Source:* Assad and Golden [2].)

There are several problems with this approach. First, the open-endedness of many management problems may make it difficult to describe them to an independent evaluator. The problems may be so complex that even experienced managers may disagree on their proper interpretation and solution. Second, ES used by teams of managers should probably be evaluated by teams of managers; hence they may be more difficult to evaluate (because of possible disagreements). Despite these difficulties, an ES might be useful even if it only reduces the time needed to perform existing tasks without reduction in quality. Such time reduction may provide a good initial criterion for ES evaluation.

In business settings ES can often be evaluated by experimentation. If, for example, preventive maintenance is to be performed on several identical machines, then an expert system's advice about frequencies of maintenance could be implemented in some of the machines while the rest are scheduled according to the vendor's recommendations. The relative breakdown rates and repair and maintenance costs under the two methods can then be compared to find which one is superior.

An Iterative Process of Evaluation. Each time the system is exposed to a new case or whenever there are changes in the environment, the system needs a refinement. Such a refinement, in a rule-based system, is likely to produce more rules.

XCON, for example, grew from a couple of hundred to over 10,000 rules in about six years. Each time a substantial refinement is made, an evaluation should follow. The growth pattern of ES is thus similar to that of DSS as an iterative approach is used. The reader should be careful with the terminology, however. In ES, prototyping refers to the initial pilot system. In DSS it is sometimes interchangeable with the entire iterative process.

Evaluation occurs during and after each iteration. Performance is recorded as the system improves its use either in a simulated or in the real-life environment. However, development and the evaluation will continue as long as improvements are achieved. Here is a difference between what we labeled in Chapter 12 as ES vs. knowledge systems. Development of ES (with human experts) takes much longer than development of knowledge systems, where most of the knowledge is documented. Therefore the latter will reach stabilization much faster.

15.9   Implementation (Phase 8)

The implementation of ES is a lengthy and complex process which is described in detail in Chapter 20. Here we will briefly touch on two subjects.

Acceptance by the User and User's Training

Even if an ES is more accurate than a human expert, it does not necessarily mean that the system will be accepted by the user. The acceptance of ES will depend on several factors. Important here are behavioral and psychological considerations. Therefore it is important that the development of specific ES be communicated as widely as possible to foster a climate of acceptability for ES among the people who will design and use them.

Installation Approaches

The expert system is ready to be fielded when it reaches an acceptable level of stability and quality. For example, in rule-based systems this may occur when the system can handle 75 percent of the cases and exhibit less than a 5 percent error rate. The installation approach depends on the situation. For example, one may use the ES in parallel with a human expert for six months. For other approaches the reader can consult any book on computer system development and Chapter 20.

15.10 Documentation, Maintenance Plans, and Security (Phase 9)

Many ES never reach finalization; they are continually being developed. Knowledge systems, in contrast, reach maturity and stability fairly fast. From then on, only *minor* improvements will be made. In either case developing documentation and maintenance plans are crucial, just as they are for any other computerized systems. Security is a heightened concern in ES because such systems are no longer akin to computer software templates having only the capacity to manipulate numbers; they may also contain the accumulated proprietary knowledge of a firm. Communicating and distributing the end product, protecting the software, and at the same time providing an environment that does not constrain unauthorized users in its application is a practical problem. Although the value of such a system may diminish over time if it is not continuously updated and maintained, the implications of the system's misappropriation or unauthorized use or transfer are more significant than with many other software products. Accordingly, organizational and hardware and/or software controls assume increased importance in the design and distribution of expert systems.

15.11 Software Classification

It is helpful to identify several levels of software (and sometimes hardware) that have been involved in ES and their construction. The classification of levels is similar to that used with DSS, as developed by Sprague and Carlson (25).

The collection of software is divided here into three major groups: specific expert systems, shells, and tools.* The analogy between DSS and ES can be seen in Table 15.5.

Building tools can be used to build shells or to build specific ES. ES shells are used to build specific ES (sometimes in conjunction with building tools).

The three levels of technology are shown in Figure 15.3.

To illustrate the concept of technology levels, let us examine the history of the development of the MYCIN family. The MYCIN family originated with a rule-based ES for the diagnosis and treatment of infectious blood diseases. Its general methodology gave rise to a shell called EMYCIN and a related programming aid, TEIRESIAS, that could assist in the knowledge acquisition process in EMYCIN. PUFF, an expert system for interpreting respirameter data and diagnosing pulmonary diseases, was the first actual application built with EMYCIN. KS 300 combined many of the best features of EMYCIN and TEIRESIAS and has supported numerous commercial specific ES. Two of these—WAVES and

TABLE 15.5 DSS vs. ES Technology Levels.

Level of Technology	DSS	ES
Low	Tools	Tools
Intermediate	Generators	Shells (skeletal or development kits)
High	Specific DSS	Specific ES

*Tools appear under several names: hybrid environment, knowledge engineering environment, building tools, development tools, etc. Frequently these names include shells.

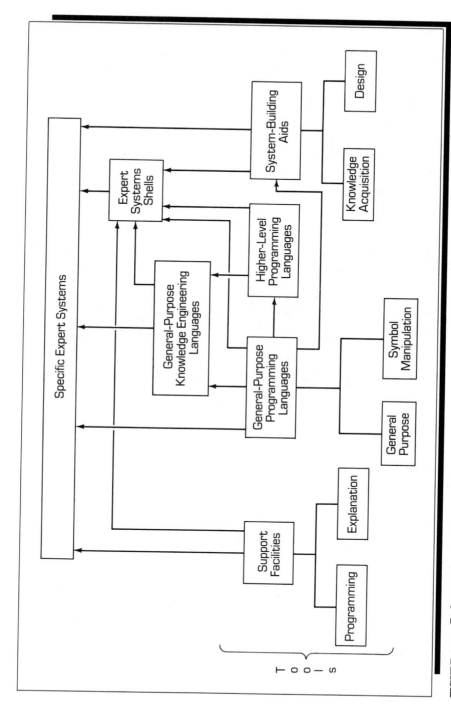

FIGURE 15.3 Software for building expert systems.

the Drilling Advisor—illustrate the breadth of systems that can be built with it. WAVES is an ES that assesses a data analysis problem for a geophysicist and prescribes the best way to process the data using selected modules from a million-line FORTRAN analysis package. The Drilling Advisor, on the other hand, determines the most likely cause for a stuck oil drill bit and prescribes expert corrective and preventive measures. KS 300 was further developed to S.1 and M.1, which are enhanced commercial domain independent shells (from Teknowledge, Inc.); Texas Instruments is also selling a subset of EMYCIN called Personal Consultant.

Specific Expert Systems.   Specific ES are the final products that advise a specific user on a specific issue. Examples of specific ES are a consultation system that diagnoses a malfunction in a locomotive, and systems that advise on tax shelters or on buying software. Most specific ES are custom made, but some are ready made. Ready made ES can be used by any end-user with a specific problem (e.g., any taxpayer looking for a tax shelter). Such systems are available for sale "off the shelf" in computer stores. Specific ES can be used for only a very restricted application in one company, or one segment of a company, or even a part of a piece of equipment (e.g., a diagnostic system for finding malfunctions in the electrical system of GE's model D-1 locomotives). ES can also be used by an entire industry (e.g., airlines or telephone companies). Specific ES are constructed with the other two categories of software: tools and shells, which are presented next.

Shell (Skeletal) Systems.   Rather than building an ES from scratch, it is often possible to borrow extensively from a previously built specific ES. This strategy resulted in several software tools that are described as shell (skeletal) systems. The shells are ES stripped of their knowledge component, leaving only a shell—the explanation and inference mechanisms.

Tools.   Tools provide skilled programmers with a rapid prototyping environment in which they can build shells or specific ES. ART, for example (a package from Inference Corporation), contains modules from which an inference engine can be assembled. One module provides a procedure for handling measures of uncertainty, while another module provides a Bayesian procedure for handling probabilities. The knowledge engineer builds an inference engine and then proceeds to use that engine in conjunction with a knowledge base to build an expert system. Shells and tools differ in their degree of focus. Tools are more flexible, but less focused. They place more responsibility on the knowledge engineer. Shells address a narrower application area, and provide a more focused approach.

Shells and tools can be general or they can aim at specific industries or even applications. For example, ARBIE and IN-ATE are designed for building ES for electronic equipment diagnosis, REVEAL is aimed at financial applications, and PICON is targeted at process control applications.

15.12   Tools: Languages and Other Packages

The software packages that can be classified as tools are divided into several basic categories as follows:

General-purpose Programming Languages

Numerous programming languages are oriented toward artificial intelligence. The most important are the symbol-manipulation languages like Lisp and PROLOG. Commercial versions of these languages and their variants are available for a wide range of computers. These languages are available now for both micros and larger computers. ES can also be programmed with traditional problem-oriented programming languages such as FORTRAN, Pascal, or C.

Non-AI Languages. Some ES development tools are written in non-AI languages; for example, TIMM is written in FORTRAN 77, INSIGHT 2 in Turbo Pascal, and EXSYS in C. Some specific ES were also completely programmed in such languages. Why? A most likely reason is that no other language is available for the hardware on which the ES is to run. Another likely reason is that some ES must run in the field on a PC. Implementation of AI languages *may* require more memory, and may not give programmers the fine control they need to conserve memory. Therefore the AI language may be too restrictive. ES written in non-AI languages may run much faster on micros than if they were written in an AI language. Finally, the interface of ES with databases, DSS, or any CBIS can be much easier if the ES is written in a conventional language.

There are ways to circumvent these problems, such as recoding from one language to another. Programmers can design their ES with AI languages like PROLOG or Lisp. Once they are satisfied the system works, they can translate the code into Pascal, FORTRAN, or C.

Languages like FORTRAN suffer from a disadvantage in that they can manipulate effectively only a small range of ES data types (e.g., numbers, logical values), whereas in writing ES the programmer needs to handle objects like rules, semantic nets, and explanations. The latter can be conveniently programmed with Pascal (or its variants). However, Pascal is inefficient for the following reason: In programming ES, it is sometimes necessary to build and split rules or construct nets continuously. In the course of such operations the computer's memory is filled, temporarily, with a large quantity of intermediate results. To avoid running out of memory, these results must be removed. In Pascal, the programmer must write instructions to do so. In AI languages, the memory is cleaned automatically by a process called garbage collection.

AI Languages. The AI or symbolic manipulation languages provide an effective way to present AI type objects. The two major languages in this case are Lisp and PROLOG. Using these languages the programming and debugging procedures can frequently be done much faster. The major characteristics of these languages are described next.

Lisp. Lisp (for List Processor, see Winston and Horn [27]) is one of the oldest general-purpose languages (developed at MIT by J. McCarthy in 1958) still in active use. Lisp's applications include artificial intelligence, natural language processing, robotics, and educational and psychological programming. Lisp's unique features give the programmer the power to develop software that goes far beyond the limitations of other general-purpose languages like BASIC and Pascal.

Specifically, Lisp is oriented toward symbolic computation; the programmer can assign values to terms like "financial" and "liquidity." Although they have no direct meaning in Lisp, the Lisp program can conveniently manipulate such symbols and their relationships. Lisp programs also have the ability to modify themselves. In a limited sense, this means that a computer can be programmed to "learn" from its past experiences.

Lisp allows programmers to represent objects like rules and nets as "lists" — as sequences of numbers, character strings, or other lists. It provides them with operations for splitting lists apart, and for making new lists by joining old ones. Conventionally, Lisp programmers write lists as bracketed sequences of their elements. They often draw them as box-and-arrow diagrams. The accompanying illustration shows a list that represents the sentence "PC is a computer."

In most programming situations, lists will contain other lists or sublists as elements.

Here is a simple example of Lisp code, a recursive definition of a function that sums two integers:

```
(defun sum (A B)
  (cond ((eq A O) B)
    (t (sum (minus 1 A)(plus 1 B)))))
```

This definition says, "If you have two numbers and the first [A] is 0, then the other [B] is their total. If the first is not 0, then try for the sum (A − 1, B + 1)." In this example, *sum* is a newly defined function, whereas the remaining functions (e.g., defun, cond, minus 1, t) are predefined. Lisp programs consist of many such functions.

The Lisp code is usually executed directly by a Lisp interpreter. In some versions the source program is compiled to increase efficiency.

There are numerous variations of Lisp. Most notable are COMMON Lisp, IQLISP, INTERLISP, MACLISP, ZETALISP, GOLDEN COMMON Lisp, and FRANZLISP (Unix-based). Each of these may have several subvariants.

PROLOG.   Although Lisp is the most popular AI language in the United States, PROLOG (for Programming in LOGIC) is the most popular AI language in Japan and probably in Europe (see Clocksin and Mellish [4]).

The basic idea is to express statements in logic as statements in programming language, and the proof of theorem using these statements could be thought of as a way of executing those statements. Thus logic itself could be used directly as a programming language. For example, the statements "All dogs are animals" and "Lassie is a dog," and the theorem "Lassie is an animal" could be expressed formally in PROLOG as:

PROLOG	Meaning
animal (X):- dog(X)	(X is an animal if X is a dog)
dog (Lassie)	(Lassie is a dog)
?-animal (Lassie)	(Is Lassie an animal?)

PROLOG can then be run to try to prove the theorem, given the two statements. Clearly, it will come to the conclusion that the theorem is true.

There are three basic types of statements in PROLOG:

:-P	means P is a goal (or predicate) to be proven
P.	means P is an assertion or a fact
P:-Q,R,S	means Q, R, and S imply P

To define a goal, several clauses may be required. As mentioned earlier, one of the techniques of knowledge representation is first-order logic. Because PROLOG is based on a subset of first-order logic (predicate calculus), it can use this format of knowledge representation. PROLOG has the additional advantage of having a very powerful inference engine in place. Therefore the algorithm used in PROLOG is more powerful than the simple pattern-matching algorithms commonly used with Lisp in production-rule representations of knowledge.

PROLOG's basis in logic provides its distinctive flavor. Because a PROLOG program is a series of statements in logic, it can be understood declaratively; that is, it can be understood quite separately from considerations of how it will be executed. Traditional languages can be understood only procedurally; that is, by considering what happens when the program is executed on a computer. Representative variants of PROLOG include MPROLOG, ARITY PROLOG, QUINTUS PROLOG, and Turbo PROLOG.

Lisp has been and still is the favorite AI language in the United States. This is to a large extent due to the existence of sophisticated programming environments and specialized AI workstations. This situation is changing as more sophisticated implementations of PROLOG supported by improved environments are appearing in the market.

PROLOG allows a program to be formulated in smaller units, each with a natural declarative reading; by contrast, the size and multiple nesting of function definitions in Lisp are barriers to readability. In addition, PROLOG's built-in pattern-matching capability is an extremely useful device.

PROLOG, however, has certain deficiencies. For example, the use of built-in input/output predicates creates symbols that have no meaning in logic.

The arguments for (and against) Lisp and PROLOG are likely to go on for some time. In the meantime some attempts are being made to combine the two. One such example is a product called POPLOG.

POPLOG is a programming environment that combines PROLOG, Lisp, and POP-11 (POP-11 is an extension of PROLOG) into a single package that is friendlier than its components and, when compiled, runs faster than PROLOG, Lisp, and POP-11 (it is marketed by Systems Designers Software, Inc., Woburn, MA).

Symbolic vs. Other Languages

Generally speaking, most rule-based and rule-induction development tools are written in conventional languages such as C and PASCAL. Most hybrid tools, on the other hand, are written in symbolic languages. Representing complex knowledge, handling complex search and reasoning techniques, prototyping, and running complex systems can currently be executed more efficiently and effectively if written in AI languages, especially in Lisp (e.g., see Graham [7]). Some vendors offer their products both in AI language and a conventional one (for example, ART is available both in Lisp and in C). Conventional languages offer an easy interface with other CBIS as well as compatibility with a wide range of existing hardware. Therefore, the future of symbolic languages is uncertain. For further discussion see Harmon et al. (8).

Higher-level Languages

The ease of creating new functions in Lisp is very important for ES design. It makes Lisp an excellent base for higher-level languages that address problems specific to the domain being modeled. For example, XPLAIN was programmed in a powerful higher-level language called XLMS (Experimental Linguistic Memory System), which is an extension of Lisp. XLMS aided in the generation of clear, nonredundant explanations from the program—which was one of the major goals of the XPLAIN system. The XPLAIN system itself is used for constructing the explanation subsystem in a shell or in a specific ES. Incidentally, this example demonstrates that there could be several layers of tools within what was classified on one level. Another example of such a higher-level language is Xerox Corporation's LOOPS.

General-purpose Knowledge Engineering (Representation) Languages

Several general-purpose languages were developed specifically for knowledge engineering. Generally they are more flexible and less constrained than shell systems. On the other hand, they may lack sophisticated facilities for input and/or output processes, for knowledge-base construction, and for explanation. Therefore, their programming environment is not as comprehensive as the one provided by the shell programs. Unlike the shell programs, which are restricted to generic applications (e.g., diagnosis), these programs are unrestricted. Because they are not as closely tied to particular frameworks, they allow for a wider variety of control structures. They can thus be applied to a broader range of tasks, although the process of applying them may be more difficult than with shell systems.

Four pioneering languages are listed in this category: HEARSAY-III, ROSIE, OPS-5, and RLL. For further discussion, information, and references, see Hayes-Roth et al. (10).

System-building Aids

System-building aids consist of programs that help acquire and represent the domain expert's knowledge and programs that help the design and construction of specific ES. Two major categories of tools exist: design aids and knowledge acquisition aids. Representative systems in each category are:

□ Design aids: AGE, TIMM, EXPERT EASE
□ Knowledge acquisition: TEIRESIAS, ROGET, SEEK

For further details see Hayes-Roth et al. (10) and Waterman (26).

Support Facilities

Support facilities are tools used by programmers to increase productivity. Four typical categories have been identified by Waterman (26): debugging aids (e.g., for tracing rules used), knowledge-base editors (e.g., for checking the consistency of added rules, for knowledge extraction, and for syntax checking), input/output facilities (e.g., menus and natural language processors), and explanation facilities.

Natural Language Processors.   ES can be integrated with natural language tools to provide a friendlier interface. See Chapter 18 for details.

Explanation Facility.   Users should be able to ask for information on how a system is solving their problem. For example, a *why* question by users causes the system to explain why certain information has been requested from the users. This may include printing out the rule that the system is currently considering. A *how* question causes the system to explain how a particular conclusion was obtained. This includes specifying which rules were used to make the conclusion (i.e., display reasoning that leads to the conclusion).

The combination of the *why* and *how* questions provides users with a great deal of insight into how the system reaches its conclusions. This helps them fully accept (or have a valid reason to reject) the system's conclusions. These capabilities can also provide excellent tutorial sessions to the user during the consultation.

15.13   Shell (Skeletal) Systems

In a rule-based shell all the domain-specific knowledge is represented explicitly as rules. This structure makes possible the replacement of the original knowledge base by a new knowledge base for a different task, greatly simplifying the construction of specific ES (see Figure 15.4). Although there are several difficulties in using skeletal systems, there has been significant success in many cases. Shells are essentially integrated packages of software that provide a set of capabilities to build specific ES quickly, easily, and at low cost.

Most of the well-known shells developed in the 1970s (e.g., EMYCIN, KAS, and EXPERT), are located mainly at universities and/or research institutions, and have certain drawbacks. First, they run on mainframes or minicomputers; thus they are costly to use. Second, they usually embody only one reasoning mechanism and knowledge representation, while sophisticated applications often require a combination of representation techniques. Finally, they are poorly documented and maintained. The commercial tools presented next are derived from these shells, but they are designed to eliminate these drawbacks.

Rule-based and Hybrid Shells

Most shells can be classified either as rule-based or as hybrid.

Rule-based.   These are the oldest and the simplest shells, many of which originated from EMYCIN.

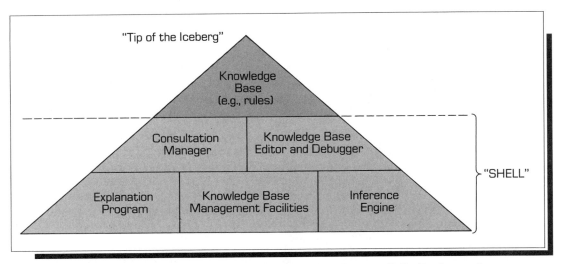

FIGURE 15.4 How do some systems get built so fast? (*Source:* B.G. Buchanan in Texas Instruments First Satellite Program.)

Examples of rule-based systems are:

Small size:	Exsys, Insight 2 +, Personal Consultant Easy, VP Expert
Medium size:	Exsys Professional, GURU, KES 2.2, Nexpert, Personal Consultant Plus
Large size:	IBM's ESE, S.1, AES, IMPACT, SYNTEL, ADS
Induction:	1st Class, TIMM

For a typical rule-based shell (EXSYS), see Appendix D.

Hybrid Systems.   Hybrid systems (tools or environments) are defined (per Harmon et al. [8]), as development systems that support *several* different ways of representing knowledge and handling inferences. They use frames, object-oriented programming, semantic networks, rules and metarules, different types of chaining (forward, backward and bidirectional), nonmonotonic reasoning, a rich variety of inheritance techniques, and more. These systems permit a programming environment that allows for building complex specific systems or complex tools. Hybrid tools were developed initially for large computers and AI workstations. They are available now on PCs. Representative packages are:

Large systems:	ART, KEE and Knowledge Craft
PC Systems:	Goldworks II, Nexpert Object, Keystone, KEE/PC, Personal Consultant Plus and DAI-SOGEN

For additional information on all types of shells see appendices at the end of this chapter, Gevarter (5), Harmon et al. (8), and Rosenthal (20).

15.14 *Commercial Knowledge Engineering Tools*

Building tools, shells, and other software are frequently referred to as knowledge engineering (KE) tools. KE tools are now responsible for about 85 percent of the fielded ES, and this proportion is likely to increase in the future (according to the August 1986 issue of *Expert System Strategies*). By the end of 1990, small shells, such as EXSYS and INSIGHT 2, will have already been sold to thousands of customers each.

Working with KE tools makes ES more economically justifiable, especially when the products are being developed on PCs. Furthermore, the cost of throwing away unsuccessful systems is low. Several commercial KE development tools for mainframes and minis appeared on the market in the early 1980s. They were followed by a host of micro-based packages starting in 1984. Some of these systems can be used to construct simple ES, especially knowledge systems (per our definition), sometimes even without the services of knowledge engineers. Many commercial systems evolved from shell systems through enhancements aimed at increasing usability and generality. This latest development could have a significant effect on the practice of ES. Let us examine a similar phenomenon, the widespread use of end-user computing and spreadsheets.

Desktop computers did not become widely accepted until it was no longer necessary for the user to "program" them or until the programming task became fairly easy. The emergence of user-friendly software like electronic spreadsheets, word processing packages, relational databases, DBMS, and fourth-generation DSS generators stimulated the rapid expansion of the desktop computer industry. The movement of KE tools into practical applications is analogous to the development of end-user computing. Until now, most ES have required well-trained engineers to be in the loop between the machine and the application. As long as this is the case, the diffusion of ES will be slow. Only when user-friendly application software is available to bridge the gap between the user and the application will the use of software become widespread, especially in the personal computing market. The same is true for DSS; for example, millions of individuals are using Lotus 1-2-3 to support their decision capabilities.

Until recently, the critical element missing in the ES arena has been software that would support non-AI–trained industry specialists to build knowledge systems for their specific applications without outside consulting help. Such tools are now emerging and the development of these tools could fuel the proliferation of ES into many more practical applications.

Representative commercial shells and other tools are listed in Appendix B. For further details of these packages, see Harmon et al., (8), Waterman (26), Lehner and Barth (14), and Assad and Golden (2).

Problems with Commercial Development Tools

The increased availability of development tools (including shells) does not mean that all ES will be constructed using this approach. There are several problems with some of the development tools that make their use inappropriate in many cases. One reason is that applying a particular tool to someone else's problem really means looking for someone with a problem that matches the software. This match may not exist. Other difficulties arise when the ES is being integrated with other computer systems. For example, Archibald et al. (1) report that Shell Research Ltd. had to reprogram an ES with PROLOG after the system was initially programmed with the SAGE shell. The reason in this case was that a need have been developed to incorporate conventional system tools into the knowledge base to perform such tasks as database management, screen handling, and substantial numerical calculation. Furthermore, SAGE's inference system is strictly backward chaining. This meant that it was not possible to volunteer information and allow the consequences of the new data to propagate through the inference networks. Finally, the ES constructed with shells may not be as user-friendly as needed. For example, it may provide only limited graphical representation.

And indeed, Arthur D. Little, Inc. — a major management consulting company using the powerful KEE package — finds KEE applicable in only about 50 percent of the large ES. In the other 50 percent they either supplement KEE with additional programming or they program from scratch. The better commercial packages are aiming for about 90 percent tool-based design and development. In other words, 90 percent of the cases will not require any additional programming.

15.15 **Building Expert Systems with Tools**

Several software tools (including shells) may simplify the construction of ES.[*] In fact, most knowledge engineers build ES by using some commercial KE development software, adding only a problem-specific knowledge base. Over the past 20 years, these tools have evolved, bottom-up, from low-level languages to high-level KE aids. Now, however, commercial quality software tools are becoming available.

A KE tool reflects a certain knowledge engineering viewpoint and a specific methodology for building ES. It includes a problem-solving paradigm. It may, for example, reflect a preference for building diagnostic ES by capturing an expert's empirical symptom-problem associations. A specific paradigm constitutes a strategy for using knowledge to solve a class of problems.

Each paradigm implies certain design properties for the knowledge system architecture, and a knowledge engineering tool generally builds these properties directly into its knowledge-base structure and inference engine.

A shell such as EXSYS supports the construction of ES with rule-based, backward-chaining architecture. This may appear restrictive because the design constrains what a knowledge engineer can do and what the specific ES can do. On the other hand, a shell like EXSYS exploits its knowledge-system–designed constraints to improve the quality and power of the assistance it gives. Because it "knows" how knowledge is stored within the knowledge base, the detailed operation of the inference engine, and the organization and control of problem-solving activities, the KE tool can simplify development tasks considerably. There is an analogy here to any focused software. A spread-

---

[*]The discussion in this section is based on Hayes-Roth (9) and (10).

sheet, for example, constrains the user to rows and columns, which makes programming a natural and easy process; that is, constraints may be very useful.

Building an ES with KE tools involves the following steps:

1. The builder employs the tool's development engine (see Figure 15.5) to load the knowledge base.
2. The knowledge base is tested on sample problems using the inference engine. The test may suggest additions and changes that could result in an improved knowledge base. This is basically a prototyping step done with the aid of the editor and debugging tools.
3. The process is repeated until the system is operational.
4. The development engine is removed and the specific ES is ready for its users.

15.16 Hardware Support

The choice of software packages is frequently determined by the hardware used and its processing and memory power, which could be a significant constraint on many ES developments. Efficient Lisp execution requires very specialized hardware architectures, which have been commercially available for only the last few years under the name "Lisp Machines." Although Lisp implementations exist for a wide variety of conventional computers (including micros), performance could be marginal for many large-scale or complex commercial

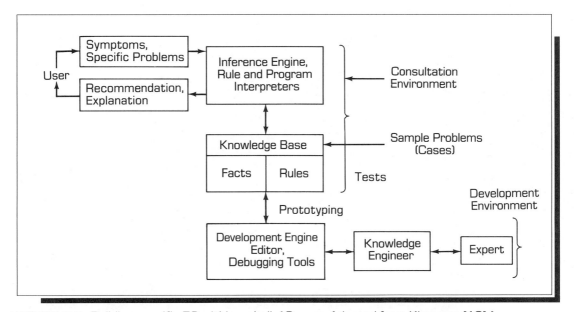

FIGURE 15.5 Building specific ES within a shell. (*Source:* Adapted from Kinnucan [12].)

applications. The development of dedicated AI workstations, together with progress in semiconductor devices and new computer architectures, have set the stage for rapid movement of AI workstations into the real world.

The dedicated AI machines have processors whose machine code is especially designed to obey instructions useful to Lisp: "check that this is a number"; "split this list here." These machines are generally known as "Lisp machines" and will support a single user, or a small number of users, with a complete programming environment, including editors, Lisp debuggers, and a network interface.

AI workstations were also found to be useful in facilitating the development of software that is not related to AI.

The major features found on LISP machines are:

1. Single-user or a small number of users (vs. time sharing in a regular computer).
2. Designed to maximize the efficiency of symbolic processing.
3. Very high-speed processing (allows more search in a limited time) when Lisp programs are used.
4. Large memory. AI programs usually require more random access memory (RAM) and more storage space on the disk drive than other programs do. These are provided by the AI workstation. For example, Symbolics 3670 provides 30 megabytes of RAM, and 474 megabytes on its disk drive (external memory). This memory is *not* shared.
5. High resolution that permits display of more text at one time.
6. Specialized keyboard. About two dozen extra keys are provided to improve programmers' productivity and increase the speed of use.
7. A mouse device is provided for faster, nonkeyboard communication.

Special software is available for these machines. Included are programming languages (Lisp, PROLOG), ES development tools, editors, debuggers, and screen windows.

For ES to be more cost-effective, it is necessary to reduce the cost of hardware usage. This could be done, for instance, with a bus-centered architectural design, which allows for resource sharing. In addition, it provides an efficient means to augment existing non-AI application software with powerful AI tools. For example, a Lisp machine equipped with both Lisp and Unix processors (with full-communication, bus-centered systems) can also furnish an environment for PROLOG and/or Unix-based software and for DSS software applications. This will enable dedicated AI workstations to be used also for general-purpose computing—a considerable cost reduction to the user.

Some commercial vendors are moving away from Lisp and PROLOG, porting their tools to conventional languages like C. Another approach is to develop the ES on a special hardware, using Lisp or PROLOG, then run the ES consultation on a less powerful AI computer or on a standard computer.

ES can run on regular (non-AI dedicated) computers. Actually, at the present time, all ES microprograms run on regular computers. In general, mainframes or large minicomputers are usually adequate for both AI and other languages, provided that enough memory is available. However, the typical situation where such machines show their limits is when lots of users are running the same program at the same time. There is usually not enough memory to hold more than 5 or 10 copies of a Lisp or PROLOG program.

Latest Developments. The Lisp machines are designed for running Lisp much faster than conventional machines. If properly used, the advantages of the Lisp machines can be very substantial. Furthermore, data input, type-checking, and other programmer's duties can be dramatically improved (for a complete description see Graham [7]). Indeed, Symbolic's top machines (now using the Ivory chip) and Texas Instruments' Explorer II with its new graphics and color capabilities, can help in both building and running ES.

However, the latest technological developments may change the role of the dedicated AI workstations in favor of conventional machines that are enhanced with innovations. Examples of these are:

1. Reduced instruction set computers (RISC). These machines, which are still in their infancy, show a tremendous suitability for Lisp development and delivery. According to Somel (24), the Sun 4 may excel in Lisp performance.
2. Both Symbolic and TI are combining their CPUs with Mac II. For example, MicroExplorer (from TI) is a combination of Mac II and Explorer. TI's Lisp chip is integrated with Mac II. Thus, it is possible to run programs concurrently on the two processors and enjoy the best of both machines (e.g., Mac's superb user interface and Explorer's symbolic processing power). Furthermore, the merger permits sharing resources (such as memory, display, hard disks), which reduces costs.

15.17 A Strategy for ES Development

Expert systems are getting considerable attention in organizations. Now that we are familiar with the technique and its development process, we can present the strategy for ES development.

ES in a Mainframe Environment (Based on Schwartz [21])

Most ES work is being done on micros. Four reasons account for this situation:

1. There are many more PCs and PC users.
2. The ES development tools for the PC are much superior.
3. It is easy to buy a low-cost shell and experiment with the technology.
4. The MIS backlog plagues almost every mainframe shop.

Therefore, any movement toward mainframe intelligence must be accomplished by a careful understanding, nurturing, and support.

On the other hand, ES technology can greatly improve the operation of many mainframe-based information systems. One of the major issues in developing a mainframe ES is where the computerized corporate knowledge base should reside. This knowledge provides, in many cases, the competitive edge of the corporation and it originates in the heads of experts who usually use PCs and not a mainframe. However, there is a considerable amount of information in the corporate database, on the mainframe. Experts need to access this information, or even build the ES on the mainframe. Therefore, it makes sense to *connect* the PC's with the mainframe. PC users must be able to use ES on mainframes via their PCs; that is, it is necessary to develop *distributed ES*. Several products enable such a connection. For example:

- ☐ ADS (from Aion Corp., Palo Alto, CA).
- ☐ Application Expert (from Cullinet, Westwood, MA).
- ☐ ESE and AS/400 (from IBM, White Plains, NY) known also as "Knowledge Tool."
- ☐ KEE (from IntelliCorp, Mountain View, CA).
- ☐ S.1 (from Teknowledge, Palo Alto, CA).

For additional information and suggested processes see Schwartz (21).

Large, complex ES should be considered as an organizational project. ES like those used by AIG (see Chapter 17) for writing insurance policies cost millions of dollars to develop and can significantly change the competitiveness of corporations. Obviously such a project is of concern to top management and requires its involvement. Furthermore, in such a case vendor participation might be a necessity. An ES group needs to be established that will assume complete responsibility and control over the project. The director of the ES group selects the experts, deals with their motivation (e.g., by giving them rewards), and centralizes the entire operation.

Smaller ES are being constructed on PCs. Typically an individual gets interested in ES and buys the software and perhaps gets some training. Then she or he starts building an ES in one area. Success may lead to some additional systems. All in all an observer can see several systems being prototyped in an informal way.

Small ES can also be developed by a centralized unit, such as the ES group described earlier, in a formal manner. Pacific Bell, for example, created a five-person group that develops 10 to 20 ES each year.

Developing Small Expert Systems

Small expert systems, like small DSS, are going through an abbreviated process. They are usually developed with ES shells. Several suggestions were made for the short process. For example, Paul Harmon, in the January 1986 issue of *Expert Systems Strategies*, advocates the following seven-step process:

Phase 1: Problem identification, cost-effective analysis, arrange management support.
Phase 2: Task and knowledge identification.
Phase 3: Develop small prototype.
Phase 4: Develop system (add knowledge as needed).
Phase 5: Test with actual users.
Phase 6: Port to field, train users.
Phase 7: Update and maintain system.

Another process is suggested by Harmon et al. (8) who list the following six phases:

1. Select a tool and implicitly commit yourself to a particular consultation paradigm.
2. Identify a problem and then analyze the knowledge to be included in the system.
3. Design the system on paper with flow diagrams, matrices, and a few rules.
4. Develop a prototype of the system using a tool. This includes creating a knowledge base and testing it by running a number of consultations.
5. Expand, test, and revise the system until it does what you want it to do.
6. Maintain and update as needed.

The relatively low cost that is involved in small systems enables shortcuts that can save development time.

Another strategy is used by du Pont (see boxed material). Their approach is to deploy ES via massive training for user groups. At first, this approach seems to be similar to user-built DSS, where training is given in Lotus 1-2-3 or similar software, and users are expected to build their own systems. However, there is one major difference. The users of ES cannot be the builders. The builder of the ES can be the knowledge engineer, the expert (if the shells are easy to work with), an information center or information systems employee, an industrial engineer, or a management scientist, but not the user. The user in many cases

The du Pont Strategy

Some companies are using micro-based shells to create expert systems for internal use. One particularly active firm is du Pont. According to Ed Mahler, the AI program director at du Pont, his group has helped build about 200 expert systems in the last year alone. "We are a catalyst group," Mahler says. "We train end-users on three development packages: 1st Class, Insight 2 Plus, and TIMM." Mahler's group now runs at least one training session a week with 20 participants apiece. In 1987, Mahler expects to train 800 users; by the end of the year, he thinks 2000 expert systems will have been built at the du Pont facility.

"We're getting everybody to do it," Mahler says, "from systems analysts to factory-floor mechanics to executives, technicians, and even some support people." The expert systems these people are building can have anywhere from 40 to 500 rules, which is a fairly modest number for expert systems. Rules, generally expressed in if/then statements, are the foundation on which the knowledge base (the actual information used) is built. Constructing an expert system takes roughly one hour for every rule—from conception to a usable program.

Source: Personal Computing, December 1986

is not even known at the time of construction. The individual might be a new employee who will start work tomorrow, or a present employee who is being retrained. Thus, someone other than the user must assume responsibility for the development of ES. Who will assume it depends on many factors ranging from the philosophy of the company to the purpose of the specific ES.

15.18   Some Concepts, Capabilities, and Design Issues

The builder, the user, and those who approve the acquisition or construction of ES should be aware of the following important concepts and capabilities.

User Interface and Ease of Use

To move ES applications from the sciences and engineering into managerial fields, a simple and natural user interface is highly desirable. Two different aspects of a user interface should be addressed. The first aspect is *ease of learning*. Because of the complex subject matter, built-in teaching aids are required to instruct new users of the system. Infrequent usage tends to force even experienced users to relearn the system after periods of disuse. To support ease of learning and enhance the usability of expert systems, the system should provide simple point-and-select prompting techniques whenever possible. This allows the user to select from a list of alternatives instead of memorizing numerous commands. Also desirable is the HELP facility that allows the ES builder to anticipate and respond to questions that the user may ask.

The second important aspect of a user interface is its *ease of use*. Frequent users of the system can increase their efficiency by minimizing keystrokes. For example, selections from lists can be made by typing only the first letter or by pointing. All system functions should be available through clearly labeled function keys. These same ease-of-use features also help reduce the typing skills required to use the system.

The system normally operates in a question-and-answer dialog with users, leading them through a consultation by asking appropriate questions. The exact wording of the questions can be controlled by the ES builder. A HELP facility should be provided in case the user cannot understand the question being asked. The ES builder can supply a second, more helpful version of all prompts, which can be accessed by the user via a function key.

One of the features that increases ease of use is a window-oriented system, which shows rules being tested, intermediate conclusions, and other pertinent data as the system is working. This displayed information can be very useful in debugging and refining the system. Many of the ES developmental tools have such a capability. KEE, GoldWorks, Nexpert Object, and Personal Consultant Plus are good examples.

Real-Time Expert Systems

Most ES deal with a static world; few attempt continuous, online operation and real-time processing. The environment in such systems is dynamic and may be too complex for obtaining information by querying a human operator. This means that conclusions are based on facts obtained directly from the system being monitored and not from human-interpreted inputs. Several other complexities exist both in the design and the operation of such systems. An example of such a system is IBM's Yorktown Expert System for MVS operation. This system, called YES/MVS, is described in Chapter 17.

15.19 Conclusions

The construction of ES is a lengthy process that requires a prototyping approach. It is an iterative process involving continuous testing, evaluating, and improving. A major problem with the process is knowledge acquisition, which constitutes a bottleneck in the spread of large ES.

To shorten the development process and make ES economically feasible, many tools have been developed. These tools, which are available at different levels of technology, can be used independently, or they can be combined. The major tool concept is the shell, which represents an ES minus its knowledge base. The shell, when upgraded and improved with special capabilities, can be used to build specific ES rapidly and inexpensively.

Although much attention has been given to software tools, the hardware issue is also important. Efficiency can be greatly improved in many complex cases, when specially designed AI workstations (or so-called Lisp machines) are used. These machines are combined now with Mac II for greater effectiveness and economy.

Despite the shortcomings of existing KE development tools, it is likely that they will be used extensively in the future. With increasing ease of use, these tools could minimize or even eliminate the need for knowledge engineers in many simple, specific ES (particularly in knowledge systems). The ability of users to build their own systems could have an impact analogous to the impact of spreadsheet technology: namely, a significant increase in the number of end-users who will build and apply knowledge systems on a routine basis.

Key Words

AI workstations	"garbage collection"	rapid prototyping
consultation (delivery)	Lisp	real-time expert systems
environment	Lisp machines	shells (skeletal programs)
development environment	POPLOG	technology levels
explanation facility	PROLOG	

Questions for Review

1. Why did early ES take many person-years to construct?
2. What is included in a conceptual design of ES?
3. List the steps in the ES development life cycle (refer to Chapter 12).
4. List some of the criteria that can be used to justify ES.
5. List some guidelines for selecting a problem domain.

6. List the major guidelines for selecting experts.
7. List the various technology levels of ES software.
8. Define ES shells and discuss their use.
9. Explain the difference between a shell and a tool.
10. What is rapid prototyping used for?
11. Define a general-purpose language; give two examples.
12. List the major characteristics of Lisp.
13. What is POPLOG?
14. What is the difference between EMYCIN and MYCIN?
15. List some of the difficulties in evaluating expert systems.
16. List five advantages of dedicated AI workstations.

Questions for Discussion

1. Discuss some of the difficulties in using development tools for solving real life problems.
2. Most ES shells are geared to deal with diagnosis and prescription of a treatment. Why is this so?
3. Compare the major characteristics of Lisp and PROLOG. How do they differ from each other?
4. Comment on the following statement: "Constraints in software development tools may be very helpful."
5. Review the process of building a specific ES with KE tools. Compare it with building any information system with tools (such as a spreadsheet or a DSS generator).
6. Discuss the advantages and disadvantages of AI workstations as compared with standard computers. Distinguish between micros and larger computers.
7. Why is it so difficult to evaluate ES?
8. Distinguish between user's acceptance and acceptance by a designer.
9. Why are "windows" so important for ES and other CBIS?
10. Why is it important to select an appropriate problem area? (Give five major reasons.)
11. Why is the security issue so important in ES?
12. Compare the technology levels of ES and DSS. Comment on the differences.
13. Discuss the role of the explanation facility. Why is it so important?

EXERCISE 1: A Feasibility Study for Expert Systems

Assume that the president of a company or the commander of a military base asks you to prepare a feasibility study for the introduction of an expert system in the organization. Prepare a report that will include the following information:

a. Identification of a problem area. Go through the process proposed in this chapter.
b. Identify the expert(s) to be involved, describe their capabilities and willingness to participate.
c. What software and hardware will you use in this project and why?
d. Who is going to be included in the development team and why?
e. Timetable for development and implementation.
f. List of the potential difficulties during the construction period.
g. List of managerial problems (related to the *use* of the system) that could appear if the expert system is introduced.
h. Prepare construction and operating budgets.
i. List the interfaces (if needed) with other computer-based information systems.

EXERCISE 2: Starting an ES Project.

a. Think of a specific problem that could be aided by (or even replaced with) an expert system. Preferably the problem would be one about which you can obtain the required knowledge from an expert; however, if this is not possible, you may choose a problem in which the knowledge is obtained from published materials. Problems in which you are the expert should be selected only as a last resort. Describe the problem task in general terms.

b. How is this task normally performed without the aid of an expert system? Who is responsible for the final judgment? What sort of training and/or experience does this person normally have?

c. Identify the generic category that best describes your problem task and explain why.

CASE 1: Development of an Expert System at a Major Oil Refinery

Background

This case study describes the development of an expert system at a major West Coast oil refinery.* The intent here is not to describe the actual programming steps and development hurdles. Rather, it is to describe the reasoning that went into deciding why and how the system should be developed.

Management Support

By far the single biggest reason that development began on the ES was because corporate management is convinced of ES long-term applicability. While the oil industry has been undergoing considerable restructuring (including cutbacks in manpower and capital expenses), management at this company has been approving funding for applied research in artificial intelligence. In this specific case, funding was approved before any specific expert system applications were even considered.

On a local level, considerable enthusiasm was generated for expert systems largely through simple PC-based systems that belonged to refinery engineers. In particular, a "wine-taster" PC-based expert system (this system recommends wines based on meal selection and cost constraints) convinced a number of superintendents that a computerized expert system could improve operating decisions.

Selecting an Application

Selection of an application was based on a few key concepts. First, the system should be applied to a process where there is a strong economic incentive for improved knowledge propagation. Second, the process should lend itself to improvement through descriptive instructions rather than mathematically precise solutions. Third, corporate experts should be available who could be "tapped" for decision rules. Finally, the potential should exist to extend the application to a sensor-integrated expert system in the future.

*Developed by Ted Oakes, an MBA student, Graduate School of Business Administration, University of Southern California, 1985.

The refinery process selected as the object of a computer-based expert system was the catalytic reforming process. In this process, low-octane gasoline components are converted under pressure to high-octane components and hydrogen. Because high lead levels are no longer an environmentally acceptable method for improving gasoline octane, the reforming process is rapidly becoming a more critical process in the refining industry. This process is having a growing impact on refinery profitability.

The process is conceptually simple. What generally leads to operating success is not the implementation of sophisticated operating strategies. Rather, it is reacting to and correcting occasional abnormalities. Many of the abnormalities tend to resurface, but only after months or years. For this reason, an expert system is a more appropriate tool than a computerized plant model.

This oil company is an industry leader in catalytic reforming technology. It markets and licenses this technology to other refineries throughout the world. As an industry leader, it employs a number of experts in this process who have person-decades of experience in troubleshooting catalytic reforming process problems. In addition, a number of these experts are within five years of mandatory retirement. An expert system is seen as a means by which their expertise can be preserved.

Finally, this particular process plant is operated with the assistance of a sophisticated direct digital control computer system. Therefore, it may be possible to take advantage of the many process sensor signals already being transmitted into computer signals.

Selection of the Expert System Development Software

Selection of the software was based primarily on the grounds of previous corporate experience, a desire to quickly develop a working prototype, and hardware considerations.

Although this company has never before explicitly embarked on an expert system development project, many research staff members have experimented with them in the course of their everyday work. In particular, a number of "mini" expert systems have been developed on personal computers.

Several advantages were seen to developing a PC-based system. First, because of the accessibility of personal computers throughout the corporation, a PC-based system would be easy to implement corporatewide. Not only is the equipment available in most of the company's refineries, but generally there are knowledgeable PC users as well. By using PCs it would be possible to easily "customize" the software for each individual refinery. PCs are considered highly reliable. They are not subject to communication problems or system downtime. If a PC breaks, a substitute can be readily found.

The expert system shell EXSYS was adopted for this application. It was selected primarily because research members had already used it on a periodic basis. It was viewed as a "user-friendly" and "developer-friendly" tool that could be used by a novice engineer with minimal training. Its cost is relatively low ($395), and it is a fairly powerful shell. It includes a built-in rule editor and it can construct systems of up to 5000 rules.

Progress to Date

In four months, a prototype system has been developed. The system embodies decision rules from a research department catalytic reforming expert. It was submitted to plant engineers who assessed the usefulness of the system and attempted to customize it for site-specific applications. After approximately two months of on-site evaluation, the system will be modified to incorporate actual day-to-day problem decision rules. The current goal is to have a system available for corporatewide use in another five months.

QUESTIONS

1. Review the manner in which the ES started and comment on it.
2. Review the initial development process in light of the steps suggested in this chapter and comment.
3. Discuss the importance of a PC as a delivery vehicle for the system.
4. How will the ES be related in the future to other existing computer-based systems?
5. Review the criteria used for selecting the domain. Comment.
6. Review the shell selection criteria and comment.

References and Bibliography

1. Archibald, I. G., et al. "Bridging the Generation Gap: Expert Systems." *R & D Management*, February 1985.
2. Assad, A. A., and B. L. Golden. "Expert System, Microcomputers, and Operations Research." *Computers and Operations Research*, Vol. 13, No. 213, 1986.
3. Cholawski, E. M. "Beating the Prototype Blues." *AI Expert*, December 1988.
4. Clocksin, W. F., and C. S. Mellish. *Programming in PROLOG*. New York: Springer, 1981.
5. Gevarter, W. B. "The Nature and Evaluation of Commercial Expert Systems Building Tools." *Computer*, May 1987.
6. Goyal, S. K., et al. "COMPASS: An Expert System for Telephone Switch Maintenance." *Expert Systems*, July 1985.
7. Graham, P. "Anatomy of a Lisp Machine." *AI Expert*, December 1988.
8. Harmon, P., et al. *Expert Systems Tools and Applications*. New York: Wiley, 1988.
9. Hayes-Roth, F. "Knowledge-Based Expert Systems." *Computer*, October 1984.
10. Hayes-Roth, F., et al. *Building Expert Systems*. Reading, MA: Addison-Wesley, 1983.
11. Holsapple, C. W., and A. B. Whinston. *Building Expert Systems* (using GURU). Homewood, IL: Irwin, 1987.
12. Kinnucan, P. "Software Tools Speed Expert System Development." *High Technology*, March 1985.
13. Kulikowski, C., and S. Weiss. *A Practical Guide to Designing Expert Systems*. Totowa, NJ: Rowman and Allanheld, 1985.
14. Lehner, P. E., and S. W. Barth. "Expert Systems on Microcomputers." *Expert Systems*, October 1985.
15. Leibowitz, J. "Useful Approach for Evaluating Expert Systems." *Expert Systems*, April 1986.
16. Mettrey, W. "An Assessment of Tools for Building Large Knowledge-Based Systems." *AI Magazine*, Winter 1987.
17. Prerau, D. "Selection of an Appropriate Domain for an Expert System." *AI Magazine*, Summer 1985.
18. Rauch-Hindin, W. B. *A Guide to Commercial AI*. Englewood Cliffs, NJ: Prentice-Hall, 1988.
19. Redin, P. "Developing ES on PC's—A Methodology." *AI Expert*, October 1987.
20. Rosenthal, S. "You Don't Have to be an Expert to Use Expert Systems." *PC Week*, December 19, 1988.
21. Schwartz, T. *Expert Systems in a Mainframe Environment*. Special Report, Intelligent Systems and Analyst, New York, 1988.

22. Shanteau, J. "Psychological Characteristics of Expert Decision Makers." *Proceedings, Symposium on Expert Systems and Audit Judgment*, School of Accounting, University of Southern California, Los Angeles, February 17–18, 1986.

23. Slagle, J., and M. Wick. "A Method for Evaluating Candidate Expert Systems Application." *AI Magazine*, Winter 1988.

24. Somel, J. "AI on Your Personal Computer?" *AI Expert*, December 1988.

25. Sprague, R. H., Jr., and E. D. Carlson. *Building Effective Decision Support Systems*. Englewood Cliffs, NJ: Prentice-Hall, 1982.

26. Waterman, D. *A Guide to Expert Systems*. Reading, MA: Addison-Wesley, 1986.

27. Winston, P. H., and B. K. Horn. *Lisp*. 2nd ed. Reading, MA: Addison-Wesley, 1985.

APPENDIX A: Some Characteristics of Expert Decision Makers

1. A highly developed *perceptual attention* ability—experts can "see" what others cannot.

2. An awareness of the difference between *relevant* and *irrelevant* information—experts know how to concentrate on what's important.

3. An ability to *simplify* complexities— experts can "make sense out of chaos."

4. A strong set of *communication skills*— experts know how to demonstrate their expertise to others.

5. A knowledge of when to make *exceptions*— experts know when and when *not* to follow decision rules.

6. A strong sense of *responsibility* for their choices—experts are not afraid to stand behind their decisions.

7. A *selectivity* about which problems to solve—experts know which problems are significant and which are not.

8. An outward *confidence* in their decisions —experts believe in themselves and their abilities.

9. An ability to *adapt* to changing task conditions—experts avoid rigidity in decision strategies.

10. A highly developed *content knowledge* about their area—experts know a lot and keep up with the latest developments.

11. A greater *automaticity* of cognitive processes—experts can do habitually what others have to work at.

12. An ability to *tolerate stress*—experts can work effectively under adverse conditions.

13. A capability to be more *creative*—experts are better able to find novel solutions to problems.

14. An inability to *articulate* their decision processes—experts make decisions "on experience."

Source: Shanteau (22).

APPENDIX B: ES Products

Product	Developer	Description
AGE	Stanford University (Stanford, CA)	System-building design tool for aiding in designing a rule-language, selecting a framework, and assembling the expert system.
ART, ART-IM	Inference Corp. (Culver City, CA)	Sophisticated tool for building complex ES; enables reasoning about possible solutions in parallel and in real-time.
EMYCIN	Stanford University (Stanford, CA)	The classical ES shell. Created from MYCIN by removing the medical knowledge base. It allows the MYCIN inference engine and explanation capabilities to be applied to other problem domains.
EXPERT	Rutgers University (New Brunswick, NJ)	Programming system for building ES of the classification type. First developed for diagnostic problems and then extended to many others.
Expert-Ease (Expert One)	Intelligent Terminals Ltd. (Glasgow, Scotland)	A PC-based system-building aid that helps a domain expert construct a rule-based ES. The expert defines the problem in terms of features or factors that lead to particular results, and the system queries the expert for examples describing conditions leading to each result. From the examples, the system learns a procedure for solving the problem and generates a decision tree representing that procedure.
EXSYS and EXSYS Professional	EXSYS, Inc. (Albuquerque, NM)	A rule-based ES shell for the PC. It includes a rule editor and explanation facility. It is very user-friendly, inexpensive, and has interfaces to DBMS and Lotus 1-2-3.
Ex-Tran 7	Turing Institute Ltd. (Scotland)	Inductive generator for creation of rules from examples (similar to Expert-Ease, but more powerful and expensive).
1st Class	Programs in motion (Wayland, MA)	Powerful rule-induction shell for the PC. Using a decision tree approach simplifies the process. Can handle 32 attributes in 255 examples. Deals also with uncertainty. Can be used to build small ES.
GoldWorks and GoldWorks II	Gold Hill Computers (Cambridge, MA)	Hybrid shell that runs on micros (836 chip) with extensive OOP, frames, rules and assertations. SQL and extensive interface to Lotus, dBase VI, C, networks and graphics. Includes Golden Common LISP. Very user friendly.
GURU	MBDS (Lafayette, IN)	A micro-based integrated package that includes an ES shell, natural language processor, DBMS, spreadsheet, communication software, and word processor. It can be viewed as a DSS generator plus ES shell.

(continued)

APPENDIX B (continued)

Product	Developer	Description
HEARSAY-III	Information Science Institute, University of Southern Calif. (Marina del Rey, CA)	Generalized program for developing ES prototypes. It assists users in developing methods for knowledge representation. Based on the concept of the blackboard (workplace).
If(then)	If/then solutions (San Francisco, CA)	A tutorial for ES accompanying Lotus 1-2-3. It also provides micros and templates for building small ES (with Lotus). Perfect for Lotus users. Good for initial prototyping.
Insight 2; (level 5)	Information Builders (New York, NY)	A rule-based shell for the PC. It includes editing facilities and interfaces with CBIS.
KAS	Syntelligence, Inc. (Sunnyvale, CA)	A powerful shell for rule-based diagnostic system (developed from PROSPECTOR). It is basically a knowledge acquisition and representation system that uses semantic network and probabilistic production rules.
KEE and KEE/PC	Intellicorp. (Mountain View, CA)	A powerful language for frame-based representation. It also supports rule-based, procedure-oriented, and object-oriented representation methods. Its principal characteristics include forward and backward chaining for its rule interpreter. Its support environment includes a graphics-oriented debugging package and an expanation facility that uses graphic displays to indicate inference chains.
KES	Software A & E (Reston, VA)	This program includes an inference engine and a knowledge base parser that establishes and checks rule relationships.
Knowledge Craft	Carnegie Group (Pittsburgh, PA)	Based on a semantic net and includes powerful OOP. Very flexible (has OPS 5, Prolog, and CRL). Extensive use of meta-information. Runs on workstations and minicomputers.
M.1	Teknowledge, Inc. (Palo Alto, CA)	Micro-based ES shell for rule-based representation. Its principal characteristics include a backward chaining control scheme and an English-like language syntax. The support environment contains graphics-oriented interactive debugging tools for tracing system operation, facilities for explaining the system's reasoning process, and mechanisms for automatically querying the user when the database lacks required information.
Nexpert Object	Neuron Data Palo Alto, CA	This is a sophisticated structured rule-based tool that provides limited OOP. It has superb graphics and user interface. It is written in C and it runs on PCs and workstations. It runs on MAC and IBM PCs (and compatibles).

Product	Developer	Description
OPS 5	Verac Corp. (OPS 5e) (San Diego, CA) Digital Equipment Corp. (OPS 5) (Maynard, MA)	A knowledge engineering language for rule-based representation. Its principal characteristics include a design that supports generality in both data representation and control structures, a powerful pattern-matching capability, and an efficient, forward-chaining interpreter for matching rules against the data. The support environment contains editing and debugging packages, including a mechanism to help determine why a rule didn't fire when the programmer thought it should.
Personal Consultant (EASY, PLUS)	Texas Instruments (Austin, TX)	It provides a sophisticated, structured rule environment. The plus product provides limited OOP. An add-on package, PC Images, provides excellent graphics and active images. Another add-on, PC Online, provides support for multiple interfaces to data acquisition and DSS. It runs both on PCs and on workstations.
PICON	Lisp Machines Inc. (LMI) (Andover, MA)	A system-building aid for developing process control ES. It supports object-oriented, frame-based, and rule-based representation methods and combines both forward and backward chaining control schemes. Knowledge acquisition from a domain expert is accomplished through a graphics-oriented interface that helps transfer structural information, process descriptions, and heuristics into the knowledge base. PICON also provides an explanation facility and the ability to dynamically update the expertise contained in the system.
REVEAL	Reveal Software, Inc. (Muttontown, NY)	A large-scale software product designed to make the technique of KE accessible in an environment that is equally supportive of DSS. Provides synergy to ES and DSS through their integration.
RLL	Stanford University (Stanford, CA)	RLL (Representation-Language, Language), which is an ES whose task domain is the construction, use, and modification of ES. The system contains several construction tools, organized in a library, such as control mechanisms and methods of inference. Users pick the ES configuration and RLL combines the necessary tools into a representation language that can be used to build a knowledge base. RLL is a programming language, but in one sense it is also an ES. It has knowledge about ES programming in general, and about its own subroutines in particular.

(continued)

APPENDIX B (continued)

Product	Developer	Description
ROGET	Stanford University (Stanford, CA)	System-building aid that helps a domain expert design a knowledge base for a diagnosis-type ES. It interacts with the expert, asking pertinent questions that identify types of subproblems the ES must solve, the results or solutions the system must produce, the evidence or data required to solve the problem, and the relationships between the data or facts of a case and its solution.
ROSIE	Rand Corp. (Santa Monica, CA)	A general-purpose, rule-based system with an English-like syntax for facilitating the creation of the knowledge base. Helpful for complex ES that cannot be built with a shell; can be used to build shells. Several add-on capabilities are available.
RULEMASTER	Radian Corp. (Austin, TX)	A system-building aid for developing rule-based ES. It consists of an extensible language for expressing rules, and a rule induction system that creates rules from sets of examples. Its principal characteristics include the induction of rules from examples, hierarchical structuring of generated rules, the capability to access external data and processes via programs written in any Unix-supported language, and automatic generation of explanations as complete English sentences.
SEEK	Rutgers University (New Brunswick, NJ)	A system-building aid that gives advice about refinement during the development of a diagnostic-type ES. It helps refine rules represented in the EXPERT language. SEEK suggests possible ways to generalize or specialize rules by looking for regularities in the rules' performance on a body of stored cases with known conclusions.
S.1	Teknowledge, Inc. (Palo Alto, CA)	A rule-based shell for complex ES in the areas of structured selection and catalog selection.
TEIRESIAS	Stanford University (Palo Alto, CA)	A system-building aid that facilitates the interactive transfer of knowledge from a domain expert to a knowledge base. The system interacts with the user in a restricted subset of English to acquire new rules about the problem domain. TEIRESIAS also assists with knowledge-base debugging, using mechanisms for explanation and simple consistency checking.

APPENDIX B

Product	Developer	Description
TIMM	General Research (Santa Barbara, CA)	A system-building aid that helps a domain expert construct an ES. The expert provides a list of all possible decisions that can be made and the names and values of factors to consider in arriving at a decision. The system then asks for examples of factors and their values that lead to each of the decisions and uses these examples to infer a set of IF-THEN rules for reaching the same decisions. TIMM supports the use of certainty values to represent probabilistic information.
VP Expert	Paperback Software (Berkeley, CA)	See instructor's manual.

APPENDIX C: Additional Commercial Expert Systems Shells and Tools (See *AI Expert*, Sept. 1989)

For Large Computers
- ES Consultation Environment (ESCE/VM), from IBM
- ES Development Environment (ESDE/VM), from IBM
- OPS 83, from Production Systems Technologies

For Microcomputers
- Advisor, from Ultimate Media, Inc.
- AION Systems, from AION Development Corp.
- DAISY, from Lithp Systems
- ESP Advisor, from Expert Systems International
- EXPER OPS 5, from ExperTeligence, Inc.
- EXPERT 4, from Elsevier-Biosoft
- KDS, from KDS Corp.
- Micro Expert, from ISIS Systems, Ltd.
- NEXUS, from Helix Products & Marketing, Inc.
- X1, from Expertech, Ltd.
- NSYS, from California Intelligence
- MacSMARTS, from Cognitions Technology Corp.
- Instant Expert, from Human Intellect System
- VP Expert, from Paperback Software, Inc.
- Arity Expert, from Arity Corp.
- Crystal, from Intelligent Environment
- Decision Expert, from Digital Equipment Corp.
- I-CAT, from Automated Reasoning Corp.

APPENDIX D: EXSYS Knowledge Base Development

All EXSYS expert system development is done within a single program, the EXSYS Rule Editor. This program provides rapid menu prompted rule entry, rule consistency checking and knowledge base execution. All rules are compiled as they are entered allowing immediate switching to run mode. Likewise, one can return to the edit mode from the run mode with a single keystroke. This ability to switch rapidly between modes without having to wait for file loading or compiling greatly increases the efficiency of the development cycle. A separate Runtime program with the inference engine is available for distribution of completed systems to end users.

Chapter 16

Major Case Studies

There is growing evidence for the development and use of expert systems in many organizations all over the world. It is estimated that thousands of dedicated AI workstations were sold by late 1989. ES are being prototyped on microcomputers in many companies and universities. Unfortunately, most of these efforts are not being made public, because companies regard ES as giving them a confidential, competitive advantage. In Chapters 16 and 17 we present several application cases; in this chapter we present two cases in greater detail; in Chapter 17 we present condensed versions of the other cases.

The first case in this chapter describes a large-scale system (with more than 1000 rules) that was developed by a team of knowledge engineers and experts in the tax area. This system was developed from scratch over a period of two years with six person-years of work. The second case represents a user-developed system which was constructed with a shell on a microcomputer.

We decided to present two different aspects of ES construction in these cases. The first case deals with the process of building expert systems, as described in Chapter 15. The major emphasis is on knowledge acquisition, system structure, prototyping, and testing and evaluation. The second case illustrates a student's project that was successfully implemented in a hospital.

Case 1: Coopers & Lybrand's Expert System (ExperTAX)

16.1   The Problem

Tax accrual, the process of identifying tax-book differences and explaining differences between statutory and effective tax rates, is an audit task requiring specialized training, great expertise, and considerable time.[*] Tax accrual is executed in connection with tax services provided by a CPA firm. The client's tax strategy, timely filing issues, and planning opportunities are also identified during the course of the audit.

Many accounting firms have developed questionnaires, forms, or checklists that facilitate the gathering of information necessary to conduct the tax accrual and tax planning functions. These questionnaires are usually completed by staff accountants in the field and may be brought back to the office or left in the field for analysis. At the client's location, an audit manager conducts the accrual analysis, and a tax manager, either in the office or at the client's location, reviews the analysis and identifies tax planning issues and opportunities. If these issues or opportunities are significant, the case is referred to more experienced personnel, such as the tax and audit partners, for further analysis and/or interaction with the client.

The process as described seems rather efficient. Knowledge is leveraged to the field by the use of specialized questionnaires. Information is gathered by staff accountants and utilized by audit and tax managers not only to conduct the tax accrual computation, but also to corroborate their tax accounting practices and identify tax planning opportunities. Senior experts are brought in on a timely basis when they are clearly needed.

The problem is that practical realities limit the efficiency of the process. Tax accrual questionnaires are perceived by audit personnel to be long, complicated documents. On the other hand, tax professionals are concerned that such questionnaires attempt to simplify and standardize rather complex situations. Audit staff assigned to the task are concerned primarily with the tax accrual computation and may not be aware of the detailed tax planning implications of some of the information collected. Other questions clearly address tax issues that are beyond their audit expertise and, although perhaps important to the tax planning function, may not be directly relevant to the task at hand.

After all the required information has been collected, its analysis by both the audit and tax managers on a timely basis is a complex task. Although the tax accrual computation requires some time, identifying tax planning issues and opportunities is a much more demanding task. Reviewing the issues may require several rounds of on-site information gathering to complete the questionnaires and answer follow-up questions. In the process of this review, the

---

[*]Condensed from a paper by D. Shpilberg and L.E. Graham, delivered in a conference on Expert Systems in Auditing Judgment at the University of Southern California, Los Angeles, March 1986, with permission.

tax and audit reviewers must focus their expert attention on both simple and complex issues. The physical timing of this task creates considerable stress on tax planning efficiency, sometimes necessitating late hours and emergency meetings to meet critical deadlines.

16.2 The Expert System and Its Objectives

ExperTAX* is an ES developed by Coopers & Lybrand (New York, NY), one of the Big Eight CPA firms to address the stated problem. The specific objectives of the system are: (1) actively guiding staff-accountants through the information-gathering process, and (2) efficiently directing them to the relevant issues and pointing out the specific importance of the information requested. This will motivate the accountants to obtain the data and educate them on the potential ramifications of the information requested. Such a system would improve the staff accountants' productivity as well as the quality of the information they gathered; it would also accelerate their training process.

Once the issue of efficient collection of relevant information has been dealt with, processing the information on a timely basis in adequate depth and by the appropriate experts becomes the knowledge bottleneck. Better information does not by itself alleviate the problems associated with the audit and tax managers' reviews. If anything, it increases their need for larger blocks of time close to year-end to examine adequately all the known facts and identify the relevant issues.

Thus, to improve the process meaningfully, the ES should be capable of analyzing and synthesizing the information to identify relevant issues to be brought to the attention of the audit and tax managers. If the ES routinely uncovered and described most of the basic tax accrual and planning issues so that the attention of the experts could be directed to the higher-level issues, the process would be more efficient.

ExperTAX functions as an "intelligent" questionnaire, guiding the user through the information-gathering process. It asks only questions that are relevant to the client situation, is capable of sifting through issues that require clarification, and requests additional information when needed. It is also capable of explaining to the user why a question is being asked and why the response is relevant. In addition, it keeps track of any relevant questions still unanswered and documents all the questions asked, answers given, and user-generated "marginal notes."

16.3 Understanding the Expert System's Tasks

The current operating environment for the tax accrual process and related functions is summarized in Table 16.1. As can be seen from the table, the process consists of various phases and involves a number of professionals of differing backgrounds. To aid in the conduct of the process, several supporting

*ExperTAX is a registered trademark of Coopers & Lybrand International (US).

TABLE 16.1 Current Tax Accrual Process.

Task	Person(s) Responsible	Site	Support Instruments	Duration (hrs)	Cumulative Elapsed Time (days)	Output	Level of Expertise	Type of Expertise
Audit Strategy/Planning								
1. Prepare tax strategy summary	In-charge accountant (ICA) or audit manager	Client/Office	Prior-year information (summary, questionnaire, tax returns), preliminary financials, client discussion	1	2	Completed tax strategy summary	Medium	Audit and tax
2. Review tax strategy summary and identify accrual issues and alternate tax strategies	Audit and tax managers and partners	Office	Completed tax strategy summary	2	10	Memoranda, possible client discussion	High	Audit and tax
Preliminary Fieldwork								
3. Complete TAX questionnaire	ICA	Client	Prior-year information, preliminary financials, client discussion			TAX questionnaire responses, notes, schedules	Medium	Audit and tax
4. Review data for tax accrual issues	Audit manager	Office	Prior-year information, completed TAX			Memoranda	High	Audit
5. Review data for tax planning/ compliance issues and develop alternative tax strategies	Audit manager, tax manager, and audit and tax partners	Office	Prior-year information, completed TAX			Memoranda, client discussions	High	Tax
Year-End Fieldwork								
6. Gather tax accrual data, compute accrual, and update questionnare	ICA	Client	Memoranda, financial statement data, updated TAX			Financial statement numbers, tax return schedules	Medium	Audit

| 7. Perform a final review of tax accrual and TAX | Audit manager Tax manager | Client Client/Office | Tax accrual work papers, updated TAX | Memoranda | High | Audit and tax |
| 8. Make a final identification of issues and alternative strategies | Engagement managers and partners | Office | Updated TAX questionnaire | Reports to clients, memoranda | Very high | Audit and tax |

583

PHOTO 16.1 TI's Explorer™ II color system.

instruments are used and interim reports are produced. All these factors and their interactions have to be considered if an effective ES is to be developed.

The ES would help improve the tax accrual process if it could reduce the time devoted to specific tasks, reduce the time elapsed from start to finish, maintain the quaility of the output, and reduce the time demands and pressures on high-level expertise.

To improve data gathering, the ES would have to animate the questionnaire functions, asking only relevant questions and explaining the reasons for the required information in the context of the client's situation. The process would allow more specialized questions to be asked, improve the average quality of the intial responses, and significantly reduce the time spent both by staff accountants and by experts.

16.4 Selection of Experts

To cover all areas of the tax accrual and tax planning specialties, several types of experts are required:

1. Experts who know what information should be collected and the most efficient order in which to answer relevant questions.
2. Experts who know what questions to ask and why, and what follow-up questions may be needed to clarify a particular issue.
3. Experts who are skilled in summarizing results and preparing information for analysis.
4. Experts who can construct viable alternative strategies based on information provided to them.

Actual expert resources for the current system include the following:

1. Audit and tax specialists to design and maintain support tools (questionnaires) used in the field.
2. Engagement auditors to gather data.
3. Managers and partners who review data and make recommendations.
4. Tax auditors and consultants specializing in various areas of tax planning. These experts are often used by managers as expert resources and partners on engagements.

All together, 20 experts participated in this project, investing about 1000 hours of their time. (*Note:* The experts contributed their knowledge as part of their regular job. No special compensations were made to the contributors.)

16.5 Knowledge Acquisition

In early exchanges with the experts, they described their tasks in holistic terms (i.e., "focus on the main issues," "analyze all the relevant data," "base our analysis on experience," "react to the particular characteristics of the client"). They described the process in terms that criticized the shortcomings of questionnaires and emphasized the value of unstructured, yet careful, analysis. However, the evidence clearly suggests that most analysis is based on the information gathered through the existing questionnaires and, on some occasions, through additional requests for specific data.

A Role-playing Experiment. To bring structure to the knowledge acquisition process and to facilitate the understanding of its dynamics, a simulation (role-playing) experiment was conducted. An experienced auditor provided a real case for which the tax accrual process had recently been completed. He provided all the basic paperwork and tax return information that had been used to process the case. Two other experienced auditors, one in audit and one in tax, were asked to identify the specific information required to conduct a complete tax accrual process for the client in question.

A conference room with a long table in the middle was divided by a curtain. All the case information was gathered and deposited on the left side of the table, including the forms and questionnaires deemed relevant. A staff accountant with no previous practice experience in the tax accrual process was selected at random and asked to sit at the left side of the table. Two experienced audit and tax people were given blank questionnaires and forms and were asked to sit at the right side of the table, separated by the curtain from the staff accountant and the case data.

The staff accountant was informed that it was his responsibility to conduct a successful tax accrual process for the client. He was told that he currently had all the necessary information in front of him, and more important, the resource of a panel of experts behind the curtain. The experts were told that it was their responsibility to guide the staff accountant toward the successful completion of the tax accrual process. They were instructed to actively guide him with verbal advice and to answer questions when asked. They were unable to go to the other side of the curtain to explain; only verbal communication was allowed.

The process was videotaped with two cameras and observed by the knowledge engineering team. Several variations of the process were conducted for a total of 12 hours over three days. At the end of the experiment, the knowledge engineering team had a clear picture of the basic structure of the knowledge base and the minimum requirements for the user screen interface.

Specific conclusions derived are as follows:

1. The expert system had to probe continuously for information, deciding which questions to ask and in what order. In addition, it must have the ability to explain "why" a question is being asked and reveal some of the implications associated with the answers.
2. The data-gathering process should be conducted first. The analysis of the data gathered should be executed only on demand, after part or all of the data have been gathered. The system also needs to produce written reports detailing the information gathered and documenting the accrual process and planning issues raised.

16.6   Selecting Software and Hardware

Software

Several ES shells ranging in price from $150 to $15,000 were identified and studied. First-cut prototypes were developed in those considered most promising. Several proved easy to use and versatile enough to accommodate some version of the desired prototype. However, they all failed to satisfy the technical specifications deemed essential for ExperTAX. For example, screen design was not flexible enough to support the level of dialog interaction required; response time was judged to be unbearably slow; the facility to explain the system's reasoning was rudimentary at best. In some, the size of the knowledge base was severely restricted, or the quality of displayed and printed output was unacceptable.

It was thus decided that the system would have to be custom designed using a suitable programming language. Common Lisp was selected because it is relatively mature and versatile and is rapidly becoming the standard Lisp dialect for artificial intelligence work in the United States. From among the Common LISP implementation vehicles available for the IBM PC, Gold Hill Computers' Golden Common Lisp was selected for the project.

Hardware

IBM PC ATs were used during the prototyping phase, but the product was designed to run on an IBM PC XT or compatible unit with 640 kilobytes of memory. The disk storage requirement for the knowledge base is under ten megabytes. To enhance the quality of the user interface, a high-resolution color monitor is supported as optional equipment. A laser printer is the preferred output vehicle for printed reports.

The reason for selecting the IBM PC (or compatible) is that much of the consultation with the ES is expected to take place at clients' locations. Most of these clients have IBM PCs (or compatibles), and only a few have Lisp machines. The builders felt that if the clients' machines are used to support the ES, the chance for successful implementation of the ES would be noticeably enhanced.

16.7   The Structure of the System

The ES is based around a Q-Shell ES shell.[*] It is a rule-base program especially designed to accommodate the requirements of the tax accrual and planning process as conducted at Coopers & Lybrand. Although it was designed for a single purpose, the shell has proven to be a flexible programming environment for other kinds of questionnaire-driven ES.

The ES is composed for four components: knowledge base, inference engine, user interface, and knowledge-base maintenance facility. A brief description of each follows.

[*]Q-Shell is a trademark of Coopers and Lybrand International (US).

The Knowledge Base

The ExperTAX knowledge base stores information as "frames." Frames are classified by the *context* of the knowledge (e.g., inventory, receivables) and by the *type* of knowledge they represent (e.g., questions, issues, facts, rules). Several kinds of information are attached to each frame. Some information relates to how and when to use the frame, some is used to determine what should happen next, and some determines what to display or print. A frame can include several rules.

There are two types of frames in the ExperTAX knowledge base: question frames and issue frames. They differ in the number and type of attributes (also called slots), procedures, and facts associated with them.

The question frames include the following attributes: questions, preconditions (rules), possible answers (rules), marginal note instructions, and why messages. The attributes include attached procedures that can evaluate facts and fire rules, display information, request additional facts, and transfer control to other frames. Figure 16.1 presents a typical question frame.

The issue frames are simpler than the question frames. They include only a rule and a display attribute. The attached procedures evaluate facts, and fire and issue displays. Figure 16.2 presents a typical issue frame.

The frames are further classified by sections, which are groups of frames that share an execution sequence. The number of frames in a section and the number of sections in the knowledge base are restricted only by the storage limitation of the hardware and software environment.

What is client's bad-debt write-off method for TAX purposes?
   S = Specific charge-off
   R = Reserve method

Summary: Bad debt write-off method

Precondition: (QZ1 IS A): Accrual or Cash Basis IS Accrual

Possible Answers:
   S = Specific charge-off
      (clarifying explanation required)
   R = Reserve method
      Follow-up Questions:
      QA19—Bad-debt reserve method
      QA20—Difference between BOOK and TAX reserve
      QA21—Bad-debt recoveries to reserve

WHY Message:

In a typical environment, the Reserve method over time will result in larger tax deductions than the Specific charge-off method.

FIGURE 16.1 Question frame.

> The IRS has indicated it will not allow the taxpayer using the completed contract method of accounting also to elect LIFO. See proposed long-term contract regulations, which are contrary to Peninsula Steel Products and Equipment Co. v. Comm., 78 TC 1029 (1982).
>
> Rule:
>   (QA2 IS C): LT Contract TAX method IS Completed Contract
>   AND
>   (QB14 IS L): Method of accounting for inventory IS
>   LIFO
>   OR
>   (QB14 IS B): Method of accounting for inventory IS
>   Both LIFO and FIFO
>
> Issue on Plan List

FIGURE 16.2 Issue frame.

The Inference Engine

The ExperTAX inference engine is of the forward chaining type. It incorporates a frame manager, a facts database, and a rule interpreter.

The ExperTAX inference engine keeps track of the inference chain created by the successive firings of rules, allowing for the display of specific reasoning associated with conclusions. The inference engine permits interruption and resumption of the inference process at any stage and backtracking of the process for alternative fact evaluation.

User Interface

Q-Shell's user interface controls the screen display used for communicating with the user and the printer commands necessary for formatting and issuing reports.

The screen layout consists of three active horizontal windows. The top window displays information identifying the section being analyzed. The middle window displays long and short forms of the questions being asked, the precondition that fired the current rule, and the valid answers. The lower window presents clarification messages (*why* messages) when requested and types in "marginal note" information when requested by the system or the users. Figure 16.3 presents a sample screen display.

The user interface operates through a system of nested menus that allow the user substantial control of the inference process. At virtually any point in the process, the user can return to a menu that allows for an orderly interruption of the process or for the resumption of the process at a different session or frame.

The printed reports generated by the user interface include lists of all issues identified by ExperTAX, audit trails of all questions asked and answers received,

Any Inventory: Yes

Does the client include any of the following items in inventory for TAX purposes?

Real Estate
Materials and supplies not held for sale (e.g., office supplies)
Deferred cost under the Completed Contract method
Consigned goods to which the client does not have title

Summary: Noninventory items

QB3   Answer one of: (Y N)

The items mentioned above may be treated as inventory items for BOOK purposes but may not be treated as such for TAX purposes (Ref. Atlantic Coast Reality v. Comm., Rev. Rul. 59-329, REg. 1.471-1).

F1 - Note F2 - Skip F3 - Why F5 - Back

FIGURE 16.3 Screen display.

notes taken during the sessions, and specialized forms issued when additional documentation is required. Figure 16.4 presents a sample of an issues report.

Knowledge Base Maintenance System

Q-Shell's knowledge base maintenance system is an independent software system designed to update, modify, and expand the knowledge base. The system includes a frame editor, logic evaluator, and rule interaction display.

The frame editor permits the user to state the different components of a frame in simple English. It edits the information entered for consistency and completeness and helps the user correct omissions or inconsistencies.

The following planning ideas and issues should be reviewed to determine their applicability to the client. Some may be inappropriate owing to immateriality. Others may represent issues that should be examined closely.

□ The IRS has indicated that it will not allow the taxpayer who is using the Completed Contract method of accounting to also elect LIFO. See proposed long-term contract regulations, which are contrary to Peninsula Steel Products and Equipment Co. v. Comm., 78 TC 1029 (1982).
□ Etc.

FIGURE 16.4 Issues report.

The logic evaluator checks for possible conflicts in logic between the rules in the frame being edited and the rules contained in currently valid frames. If an inconsistency is discovered, the evaluator suggests editorial actions to resolve the situation.

The rule interaction display allows the user to dynamically observe all the frames affected by changes in the frame being edited. This permits the user to better visualize the changes in operating procedure that could be implicit in modifications of a frame with several complex rules or follow-up routines.

16.8   Prototyping

After initial interactive knowledge acquisition sessions were conducted with the computer (excluding simulation sessions), a functional prototype of ExperTAX was built. This prototype was then used in all following working sessions with experts. After each session, additions were introduced.

Although the final version of ExperTAX closely resembles the original prototype developed, it nevertheless incorporates a few significant changes deemed relevant by the experts as a result of the interactive knowledge acquisition sessions. The friendly and productive programming environment provided by Q-shell in particular, and Lisp in general, made it feasible to expediently modify ExperTAX to accommodate new perceived user needs as the knowledge acquisition process progressed. The construction process extended to an approximately two-year span for a total of six person-year efforts.

16.9   **Testing and Evaluation**

The testing and evaluation was done by a group of practice partners and managers in different offices. They were asked to test the system for a representation set of their clients. A knowledge engineer supervised the process and ensured that all relevant comments made during the sessions were noted. The practice partners and managers familiarized themselves with ExperTAX by running random exercises and evaluating the system's responses. Once they were satisfied with the overall performance, they processed several client cases whose tax accrual and planning process had recently been completed and compared the system's responses with their personal evaluations of the cases. Some issues were raised as to the clarity of the wording of specific questions, explanation, or recommendations. These issues were brought back to the experts who contributed those areas to the knowledge base, and appropriate modifications of the knowledge base were made.

Whereas the knowledge base validation was by no means exhaustive, it did suggest a procedure to be followed for the ongoing monitoring of the system's performance. For example, it is clear that practitioners in the field will continually face situations that might not be directly addressed by the system. In some cases, it will be desirable to enhance the knowledge base to handle the situation. This decision will be evaluated by the group within the organization responsible for maintaining the knowledge base. The knowledge maintenance group will be able to conduct a continuous validation of the knowledge base and an ongoing evaluation of its performance, as well as respond to changes in the environment that dictate modifications to its frames, rules, or facts.

16.10   **ExperTAX at Work: A Sample Session**

The first thing ExperTAX does is present a menu that allows the user to make a selection from a series of options. Although there are several possible choices nested in various menus, they basically deal with a choice between starting to work with a new client or continuing a job for a regular client.

To illustrate, assume we are starting with a new client, Artificial Company, a highly successful manufacturer of smart computers. ExperTAX would start by asking some questions from the preliminary session of its knowledge base. It would quickly find out that Artificial accounts for its transactions on an accrual basis, is a privately held company, and is interested in tax minimization strategies. That general information would help ExperTAX structure its search procedures and access frame sections so as to minimize unnecessary paths and then load into memory those subsets of the knowledge base that contain rules more likely to be fired.

If we join an ExperTAX session where inventory issues related to the write-down of obsolete goods are being aired, the middle window on the ExperTAX screen displays the following question:

> How does the client value these obsolete goods?
>   C = Cost
>   S = Selling price less direct cost of disposition
> Summary: Net realizable value method

The user always has the option of answering the question, asking why the question is being asked, or ignoring it altogether. The user elects to answer C. The middle window of ExperTAX changes its display to the following:

> Net realizable value method: Cost
>   Do the obsolete goods include any excess inventory items that are sold under an agreement that allows the client to repurchase the items at a predetermined price?
>   Summary: Thor Power Sham Transaction

At this point, the user elects to press the "Why" key. The lower window displays the following statement (the middle screen is still displaying the question):

> The IRS has held that a sale of items under an agreement to repurchase at a predetermined price is not a sale and thus the excess inventory must be continued to be valued at cost.

Having read the explanation, the user answers the question and continues in similar manner until ExperTAX finishes the section and returns to the selection menu.

Once the user has finished the inventory section, he or she might elect to continue with another section, to look at the issues raised so far, or to print those issues and the accompanying documentation. If the user elects to look at the issues raised, they would appear in the middle window, one at a time, together with the specific answers that triggered them. For example:

> LIFO inventory may not be valued for tax purposes using the lower-of-cost-or-market method!! The IRS may terminate the taxpayer's LIFO election if LIFO inventory is valued at lower-of-cost-or-market. See Rev. Proc. 79-23. In limited situations, a taxpayer may be able to change to the Cost method and preclude the IRS from terminating its LIFO election. See Rev. Proc. 84–74. Market write-downs are required to be included in income under the provisions of Sec. 472(d) when LIFO is elected.[*]
>
> Reasoning:
>
> Method of accounting for inventory: LIFO
>
> Inventory valuing: Lower of cost, or market
>
> [*] These issues require a change in accounting method for which approval must be requested within 180 days of the beginning of the taxable year.

Once the user has answered all revelant sections, a complete printed report is generated. The report lists all issues raised, segmented by type (e.g., accrual, planning). It also lists all questions asked and responses received during the session and all notes taken by the user, whether voluntarily or because of prompts by the system to further explain an answer.

The ExperTAX report would then be used by the audit and tax managers or partners in charge of the engagement to prepare the final tax accrual and issue their tax planning recommendations to the client.

16.11 System Implementation and Release

It is uncertain, because of the competitive environment of the industry, whether the ExperTAX package will be sold commercially or remain with the developer.

Commercializing and distributing the product, protecting software, and providing an environment that does not constrain authorized users in its application are potential problems for the implementers of the ExperTAX system. However, the system does provide a practical application of an ES to a current subject area.

Latest developments. Since the release of ExperTAX in the fall of 1986, Coopers & Lybrand has dropped the paper versions of the questionnaire that was the forerunner of ExperTAX. Firm policy is now to use ExperTAX where applicable. To expand the applicability of the product across specialized industry lines, insurance, oil and gas, and other industry-specific modules have been developed and implemented. These industry modules are not trivial. It is reported that the insurance industry module is as large in terms of questions and rules as ExperTAX itself.

Maintenance on the knowledge base of the product is currently performed by nonprogrammers in the National Tax group, but enhancements and new features are continually added to the basic Q-Shell. Since inception, several updated versions of the product are released each year.

For further description of the system see Shpilberg, Graham and Scatz, "ExperTAX: An Expert System for Corporate Tax Planning," *Expert Systems*, July 1986.

Questions for Discussion

1. Prepare a diagram that shows the development process of ExperTAX. Discuss the various steps in the process.
2. Using as many as 20 experts did not create a problem (such as contradicting opinions). Explain why.
3. Discuss the major advantages of ExperTAX.
4. Discuss the nature of the potential users of the system. Who will use it most and why?
5. Review the role-playing procedures. Describe the experiment and discuss its objectives and results.
6. Review and discuss the reasons for not using a commercial ES shell. Do you agree? Why or why not?
7. Should a client be told that an expert system was used in the process? Why or why not?
8. Discuss the advantage of multiple windows in this case.
9. The testing and evaluation process described in this case is unique. Can it be applied to other ES? Can it be used generally or does it apply only to certain types of ES? Be specific.

Case 2: Expert Telephone Configuration System (EXTELCSYS)

This case illustrates a *student project* executed in EXSYS. We selected this project because it deals with a real-life situation and because it was implemented successfully by the developer.

16.12 Introduction

Tripler Army Medical Center Expert Telephone Configuration System (EXTELCSYS) is designed to aid Tripler Information Management Division personnel, U.S. Army Information Systems Command Signal Battalion Liaison personnel, and telephone users in selecting appropriate telephone equipment and configuring a hospital department, division, or separate service telephone system, to meet users' needs within constraints imposed by Army regulations, the budget, equipment available, and the ongoing hospital renovation project.

The system (using EXSYS) was developed during the summer of 1988.[*] Knowledge required to develop the system rules was acquired from the current personnel and from the system developer (the author of this case). The system was installed on an existing Zenith 248 PC. The liaison office staff uses it to develop, modify, or confirm telephone equipment configurations associated with telephone move and change requests received from Tripler customers.

We expect EXTELCSYS to simplify training required for new personnel as well as expedite processing of telephone moves and changes associated with the hospital renovation project. Future enhancements planned for the system include adding the capability to produce a consolidated listing of all the equipment required, by room number, for an entire department or division telephone system.

16.13 Problem Domain

The Tripler Army Medical Center Information Management Division is responsible for overseeing all aspects of the five components of the Army's Information Mission Area (IMA) within the Medical Center. These include automation, communications, visual information, records management, and printing/publishing. Communications support is provided to the Medical Center by the Army Information Systems Command Signal Battalion-Hawaii. This includes voice, data, and radio communications support. The battalion provides this support on a day-to-day basis through a Signal Liaison office at the hospital composed of an officer, a noncommissioned officer, and two or three enlisted soliders. These liaison office staff receive and process all requests from the Medical Center for communications support. The liaison office staff are required to evaluate each request and determine the best method of providing the support. Their recommendations are then reviewed and approved by the Medical Center Information Management Officer before being forwarded for execution.

By far, the biggest job of the Signal Liaison office staff is to review requests for telephone moves and changes associated with the massive hospital renovation project, which has been ongoing since 1984 and will not be completed until 1992. Because each hospital activity must move one or more times on an interim or permanent basis, hundreds of telephone move or change requests are generated. Two different telephone companies provide service to the hospital. The old sections of the hospital and the outlying buildings are serviced by Hawaiian Telephone Company. The newly renovated sections of the hospital are serviced by Tel-a-Com Hawaii. Telephone configurations are complicated by the two-contractor situation. All of the telephone lines provided by Hawaiian Telephone in the old and outlying areas must be serviced by the new Tel-a-Com Hawaii switch, and all off-post (non-military) and commercial access requires access to trunks provided by Hawaiian Telephone company. Telephone equipment provided by Tel-a-Com Hawaii is made by Rolm Inc., while telephone

[*]This project was developed by Major Gary Gilbert, a graduate student at the University of Southern California.

equipment provided by Hawaiian Telephone is made by GTE. In addition, the Hawaiian Telephone equipment is all analog equipment while the new switch and the majority of the Tel-a-Com Hawaii telephone equipment is digital. Digital instruments will not work on analog lines and vice versa. Many telephone instrument features are available through the new switch; some can be provided with the old equipment while some cannot.

A significant amount of training and experience is required in order to familiarize the Signal Liaison personnel with the complicated hospital telephone system well enough to enable them to do an adequate job of configuring telephones. The Medical Center Information Management Officer must have similar knowledge in order to be able to adequately review proposed telephone configurations to ensure they are within regulatory and budget constraints while also meeting the hospital's needs. Since the Information Management Officer is a Medical Service Corps officer, he or she most likely has very little previous technical communications training.

Because both the Signal Liaison personnel and the Information Management Officer are military, their tenure is limited to the length of their Hawaii assignments, usually four years or less. In addition, military personnel career management practices favor reassigning officers and noncommissioned officers after 18 months to two years in a new job in order to broaden their experience. This results in a significant problem in maintaining sufficient expertise within the Signal Liaison and Information Management staffs to be able to competently configure telephones. Therefore, it is the purpose of this expert system to "capture" and maintain telephone configuration expertise. To save money and to rapidly develop the system an ES shell, EXSYS, has been used.

16.14 Feasibility Study

Necessary Requirements for Expert System Development

Specific requirements that must be validated in order to develop an expert system (using EXSYS) are as follows.

1. The task requires more than simple numeric analysis or application of common sense for solution. For this task, real knowledge about the various Tripler telephone systems, the renovation project, budget and regulatory constraints, and interdepartmental politics along with the ability to make heuristic judgements and/or decisions based on that knowledge is required.
2. The task requires only cognitive skills, rather that physical or mechanical skills, to be able to reason or infer a solution. For this task all technical/mechanical skills are cognitive.
3. A genuine expert is available. The current Signal Liaison Officer, noncommissioned officer, and Information Management Officer (system designer and author of this case) are sufficiently knowledgeable and experienced to be considered "experts" in this narrow area of telephone

communication engineering. All three are scheduled for imminent reassignments.

4. The experts can articulate their methods of problem solving, and in the case of EXSYS can express them in the form of heuristic rules. The telephone configuration process is just application of a variety of "rules" to the specific requirements and constraints of a particular situation.

5. The problem at hand is not so difficult or complex as to warrant it unsolvable by a well-trained human expert. The task is well understood and is clearly defined. The current experienced "experts" previously mentioned solve the telephone configuration problems every day. The problem as defined above in "Problem Domain" is sufficiently narrow in scope.

6. Computer equipment and staff resources or funding are available to complete the project. An IBM/MSDOS compatible personal computer and EXSYS software are available for development and for installation and operation. The available system developer is sufficiently trained to use the EXSYS development tool, and computer-assisted tutorials are available for both development and operational training.

Appropriateness of the EXTELCSYS System

1. Nature of the problem. Heuristic rules are used to configure telephones. The rules often change because of changes in regulations, changes in availability of funds, changes in command policies, and progress in the renovation project. Therefore a rule-based system that can easily be modified is appropriate.

2. Complexity of the task. The task is not overly complex or difficult for a "trained expert." However, the constant turnover of personnel makes it very difficult to maintain staff expertise. Because there are so many variables and the "rules" are subject to interpretation by the individual doing the configuration analysis, the results are not consistent.

3. Scope of the problem. Because this problem is rather narrow and has a small number of rules, it is appropriate for development and installation on a microcomputer through the use of a simple, rule-based, expert system development tool.

Justification for EXTELCSYS Development

1. Improved performance. Since the system will apply the rules in a more consistent manner than do most of the employees, especially new ones, the results obtained should be less likely to omit requirements, and provide for more consistent and efficient telephone configurations.

2. Faster configurations. The system will produce a recommended configuration much faster than the staff members can. Since the Information Management Officer will have more confidence in the configuration recommendations, he can spend less time reviewing them before approving them. This will free up the Signal Liaison staff and Information Management Officer to perform other tasks.

3. Reduced requirements for training. Since the system can be operated by "nonexperts," who can use the explanation capability to learn on the job, training requirements are significantly reduced.

4. Easy maintenance. It is easy to modify the rules, the goals (choices), and the qualifiers in an EXSYS-based system. Therefore, maintenance and updates to the system can be easily performed.

16.15 EXTELCSYS
Conceptual Design and Feasibility

Selection of an Expert. As stated above the currently assigned Signal Liaison Officer, 2LT Anthony Lee; noncommissioned officer, SSG José Rossario; and Information Management Officer, MAJ Gary Gilbert, are sufficiently knowledgeable to be considered experts in this narrowly focused problem area. Together, they have more than 7 years experience with the Tripler telephone system, and more than 30 years of telephone communications work experience.

System Developer. MAJ Gary Gilbert is the system developer and author of this case. He has his Master's degree in management of computer systems applications, 10 years of automation management and computer systems design experience, and 3 years experience at preparing, reviewing, and/or approving telephone configurations at Tripler.

Development Strategy. Rapid prototyping was used to develop the system. At the first cut a 15-rule system was developed. The system was then revised and expanded to include more features and situations, until enough rules were included to provide satisfactory results in at least 90 percent of the specific consultations tested.

Selection of Hardware and Software. The system was developed on a laptop Zenith 184 microcomputer using EXSYS. Once completed, the system was transported and operated on a Zenith 248 microcomputer.

Project Development Costs.

Hardware (currently in place and operational):

Zenith 248 PC with dot matrix printer	$1,900

Software:

EXSYS program	$395
DOS (bundled with hardware)	0
TOTAL	$2,295

Personnel person-hours (military personnel provided):

IMO System Developer/Expert	25
Sig Liaison staff experts	12
TOTAL person-hours	37

Cost/Benefit Analysis. This system will be very inexpensive to fully develop and use in the field, especially since the computer hardware is already in place, and military humanpower will be used for both the developer and knowledge acquisition. Even if those costs are included, the benefits of this system far outweigh the costs. Most significant is the reduction in training requirements and the reduction in time required by the Signal Liaison staff to prepare telephone configurations and by the Information Management officer to review and approve them. If the increase in quality and consistency of the final product is also considered, this system will pay for itself in less than a month.

16.16 Knowledge Acquisition Methodology

In the case of EXTELCSYS, the system developer is also an expert. This is an excellent example of a user-developed system in which the expert is tasked to "capture" his or her own expertise. This type of expert system development often results in a better product than one in which the system developer or knowledge engineer must extract the knowledge from some expert, especially if the expert is uncooperative.

Since pooling knowledge from several experts could result in "synergy," the EXTELCSYS system developer also interviewed the other experts from the Signal Liaison staff to add any additional information to the knowledge base that the developer omitted or did not know. The developer also tested the system with the Signal Liaison staff during and after completion of development to insure that rules were clearly stated, accurate, and not ambiguous.

16.17 Rapid Prototyping Procedures

EXTELCSYS was built using the rapid prototyping methodology. A simple prototype was built using 15 rules and 10 choices. This prototype was able to determine what type of instrument should be installed (digital or analog), what make (Rolm or GTE), what model (multi- or single-line, push-button or rotary dial, etc.), if the line(s) should be capable of receiving incoming calls from offpost (direct inward dial), and how it should be installed (wall-mounted or on a desk) depending on the required location within the Medical Center and a selection of user requirements. A total of seven qualifiers were used in the first prototype. The basic rules, choices, and qualifiers still exist in the final (current) version of the system, although they have been significantly modified.

After the first prototype was tested, new rules, qualifiers, variables, values, choices, et cetera were continually added until all the basic features and/or requirements known to the experts were included. Some features that are automatically included with installation of a new telephone were not included.

The final (1988) system includes 50 rules, 15 qualifiers, 4 mathematical variables, and 35 choices.[*] The user (or the inference engine) can select from 17 different features, including headset, speaker phones, commercial long distance, military long distance (called AUTOVON), internal department and/or hospital-wide intercom, group teleconferencing, computer MODEM, telefax, autoanswering machine, hunt groups (rings the next line in an office when one is busy), pick groups (enables any line in an office to be answered from any telephone), digital radio paging, and a 25-foot extension cord.

16.18   **Training and Implementation Plan**

Implementation of EXTELCSYS involves three steps: (1) transporting the system to the Signal Liaison office Zenith 248 personnel computer; (2) training the Signal Liaison staff on the system; and (3) changing Standing Operating Procedures (SOPs) for processing telephone moves and changes or preparing and reviewing telephone configuration plans.

1. Transporting EXTELCSYS simply requires that a copy of EXSYS "run-time" and the EXTELCSYS rules and text files be loaded on the Zenith 248. Since the system was developed on a Zenith 184 laptop computer, there should be no compatibility problems between the two systems. In fact, the EXTELCSYS has been tested on the Zenith 248 as part of the rapid prototyping process and expert review/testing.
2. The Signal Liaison staff are the primary users. Initial training was conducted by the Information Management Officer. Subsequent training of new personnel will be conducted by the Signal Liaison staff. The EXSYS Help features and the tutorial demos will also be used for refresher or remedial training. The Information Management Officer will train his replacement and cross-train another Information Management Division staff member on both operation and maintenance of the system. EXSYS demo tutorials will also be used to conduct system maintenance training.
3. The Information Management Officer issued instructions to the staff for updating SOPs. A complete EXSYS/EXTELCSYS consultation printout for each recommended telephone instrument configuration is required to be included with all telephone move or change requests which are forwarded to the Information Management Officer by the Signal Liaison staff for approval.

[*]After the completion of the case the system was further developed before it was fielded. It includes over 100 rules in its fielded version.

16.19 Documentation,
Maintenance, and Continued Program Plans

Documentation. EXTELCSYS user documentation consists of the EXSYS user documentation itself, the starting and ending texts (Appendix A), two sample consultation printouts (Appendix B), and printouts of the choices (possible recommendations) and rules (Appendices C–D). The EXSYS "run-time" module also has built-in help modules that can be screen printed or called up by the user during a consultation. System maintenance documentation consists of the EDITXS user documentation, the EDITDEMO tutorials and software, the user documentation listed previously and contained in the appendices, plus the EXTELCSYS rules and text files.

System Maintenance. System maintenance consists of updating the rules, choices, qualifiers, or variables to meet new user needs or changes in procedures, regulations, or equipment available. This will be performed by the Information Management Officer rather than by the Signal Liaison user personnel. This will enable him to maintain control and familiarity with the rules, choices, and qualifiers which are the basis for system recommendations. For this plan to be successful, the Information Management Officer must consult regularly with the Signal Liaison user personnel to ensure that he revises the rules or develops new rules for any situation for which the system does not produce a satisfactory recommendation.

Continued Program Plans. The Information Management Officer will continue to revise and expand EXTELCSYS to incorporate rules and choices for configuring those standard features not included in the current version. Although those features (transfer, call forward, hold, camp-on-busy, park, conference, system speed dial, etc.) are automatically included with each telephone configuration, the user does have an option of including a button for each feature on his or her instrument or using a series of pound sign (#) or star (*) commands to execute them. For the sake of system development expedience, these options were not included in the current version. In addition, the Information Management Officer plans to expand the system to enable Signal Liaison personnel to run EXTELCSYS for an entire department at one time and produce a consolidated listing of all telephone instrument configurations required for a department. The current version must be run individually for each instrument required. This will require increased use of the EXSYS math functions and interface to a database. Finally, the Information Management Officer plans to produce a database of all telephone equipment currently installed or in storage. EXTELCSYS would then be modified to automatically update the database any time a telephone move or change is approved and executed.

16.20 Security and Integrity

EXTELCSYS does not contain any sensitive information; therefore, security of the system is not of great concern. The software is of some value because several person-hours have gone into producing it. However, it can easily be developed again if lost or destroyed. The knowledge base, however, cannot be recreated if the experts are no longer available because they have been reassigned (which will occur shortly). Therefore, security of the system entails carefully backing up the knowledge base rules and text files and storing backups in a secure location away from the work site. Complete copies of the EXTELCSYS files and documentation will be stored in the Tripler Data Processing Center computer magnetic media library and at Tripler's alternate storage site at the Fort Shafter Data Processing Center.

System integrity will be maintained by providing only the EXSYS "run-time" module and the EXTELCSYS rules and text files to the Signal Liaison staff personnel. They will not be provided the EDITXS or EDITDEMO editing software. They will thereby be unable to modify the rules or choices without contacting the Information Management Officer. The Information Management Officer will occasionally require the Signal Liaison staff to provide an expanded consultation printout which includes the rules used by EXSYS to make the recommendations. He will then be able to spot check the rules to make sure no unauthorized changes have been made to the system.

16.21 Problems and Lessons Learned

Conversion of heuristic rules-of-thumb into IF-THEN-ELSE rules is not easy, even when a system such as EXTELCSYS is well suited for a rule-based expert system. It is difficult even if the developer, knowledge engineer, and expert are all the same person; it is even more difficult when they are different persons.

Since the "EDITDEMO" (student) version of the EXSYS was available to the developer during the initial prototype, the knowledge base includes only 50 rules. The full-blown EDITXS is needed in order to expand and include the additional requirements and telephone feature options mentioned above.

Because the EXSYS inference engine uses "backward chaining" exclusively, there are some situations that occur within EXTELCSYS in which user input to EXSYS questions does not result in all the appropriate choices being selected. This usually occurs after the system has determined its own answers to some qualifier without asking the user and then asks the user a question that would allow him or her to add a requirement for a feature that may have been inadvertently omitted earlier. Examples are Rules 34–44 which, before modification, asked the user about MODEM, telefax, or answering machine features. A rule could have been invoked because the user selected an answering machine but not a MODEM or telefax machine. However, when the user saw the qualifier's 15 questions, which included answers pertaining only to MODEMs or telefax machines, he or she may have remembered that a MODEM was needed and selected some answers that pertain to MODEMs. This situation required the rules to be modified.

As with any automated development or editing tool, the developer should save work at regular intervals to avoid loss of significant work effort because the computer or software system "hung." Failure to follow that simple procedure resulted in the developer being required to do extra work more than once.

Maintenance of backup copies of the rules and text files during development can save redoing development work because the master rule or text files become corrupted. This occasionally happens while files are being saved to disk. Again, failure to follow this simple rule resulted in extra work being required during the EXTELCSYS development effort.

16.22 Conclusion

EXTELCSYS provides the Tripler Army Medical Center Information Management Division staff with a workable expert system that reduces the time involved in preparing and reviewing telephone configurations. Expertise previously available only from existing staff members has been preserved.

Questions for Discussion

1. List the factors that created the need for the system.
2. Describe the process of *requesting* equipment and *approving* it. Explain how the ES is going to be used in this process.
3. List some of the *necessary requirements* for this project.
4. What are the project's major justification points?
5. Describe how the rapid prototyping has been executed.
6. Discuss the implementation and training plan. Can it be improved.
7. Briefly summarize the lessons learned.
8. The grade on this paper was an A. What would you do to elevate it to an A+?
9. Using multiple experts in this case was beneficial. How does it differ from a typical case?

APPENDIX A: Starting and Ending Texts

Expert Telephone Configuration System (EXTELCSYS)

Starting Text

Tripler Army Medical Center Expert Telephone Configuration System (EXTELCSYS) is designed to aid information Management Division personnel, Signal Battalion Liaison personnel, and telephone users in configuring an office telephone system to meet their Department, Division, or separate service needs. The system is designed to select an appropriate telephone instrument with features required to perform these functions desired by the user depending on the user's office, clinic, or ward location within the Medical Center installation. It is to be used to plan telephone moves and changes associated with renovation program. In many cases user activities will be converted from the existing rotary dial analog telephone system provided under lease contract from Hawaiian Telephone Company to the digital telephone system being installed by Tel-a-Com Hawaii Corporation. For those activity moves that are only temporary, the existing rotary equipment will be moved or an electronic key pushbutton system may be temporarily leased from Hawaiian Telephone if funds are available.

EXTELCSYS should be run for each new telephone you need and/or for each old telephone you are moving. The system will recommend the type of telephone and associated features which will best fit the needs of the user in the new location.

INSTRUCTIONS: Select ONE or MORE answers to each question EXTELCSYS asks you, and enter the numbers of the selections separated by commas.

Ending Text

EXTELCSYS will now recommend the type of telephone instrument and associated features best suited to the user's needs as provided by the answers you gave to the questions the system asked of you. REMEMBER, this is only a recommendation. If the user is not satisfied he or she may submit a request for exception with justification to the Chief, Information Management Division.

To see why EXTELCSYS made a recommendation, enter the number of the recommendation.

APPENDIX B: Sample Consultation

This appendix contains a sample of EXTELCSYS consultations for which the computer screens have been printed out as they would appear to the user.

The consultation is an example of a telephone installation required for a user located in the old section of the hospital, which is serviced by Hawaiian Telephone using GTE rotary dial equipment. The user is a department chief; therefore certain features and options are automatically approved or provided even if the user does not select them. An example of the logic employed by the system is contained in the choice, "External Keypad." The user did not select push-button dial and a rotary instrument is provided in the old section of the hospital, but the user did select digital paging, which requires a push-button dial; therefore, EXTELCSYS included an external keypad.

Example 1: The user is asked four questions:

1. Instrument location is
  1. in new/renovated section of main hospital
  2. in old section of main hospital
  3. in outlying buildings of Medical Center installation
  4. in an office
  5. in a reception area
  6. in a treatment room
  7. in a patient room
  8. on a desk
  9. mounted on the wall

       10. unknown at this time
       11. in a conference room
       2, 4, 8 = Answer

  2. Feature(s) desired is/are
       1. push-button dial
       2. headset
       3. pick group
       4. external speaker
       5. microphone
       6. commercial long distance
       7. Autovon
       8. off-post dialing
       9. ability to receive calls from off-post
       10. internal (activity) intercom
       11. Group Teleconferencing with speaker phone
       12. Computer MODEM
       13. Telefax machine
       14. Answering machine
       15. 25-foot extension cord
       16. Digital paging
       17. Hunt group
       18. none of the above
       7, 8, 9, 12, 16, 17 = Answer

  3. User is
       1. a Department or Division Chief
       2. not a Department or Division Chief
       3. status unknown
       1 = Answer

  4. Computer MODEM or Telefax machine is
       1. on primary line
       2. on extension line
       3. required to dial off post
       4. required to make Autovon calls
       5. required to make long distance calls
       6. required to receive calls from off post
       7. on post only
       8. operates at speeds greater than 2400 baud
       9. not required
       10. none of the above
       1, 3, 6 = Answer

Results and Sensitivity Analysis

Results. The system's recommendations are shown in Table 16.2. Twelve items are recommended, starting with CF = 100 (Hawaiian Telephone) to CF = 10 for the last item (column "original value"). It is now up to the liaison office staff to determine what to approve.

TABLE 16.2

Values based on −100 to +100 system	Original Value	New
1. Hawaiian Telephone Rotary Instrument	100	−90
2. RJ 11 jack required	80	80
3. Primary line is Priority Autovan (AVP)	70	70
4. Additional line is Direct Inward Dial (DID)	70	70
5. External keypad	60	60
6. Primary line is Direct Inward Dial (DID)	60	None
7. Additional C line	55	55
8. Hunt group	50	50
9. Primary line is extension	50	−20
10. PAX Intercom required	50	50
11. Additional line is an extension line	20	20
12. Department/Division/Activity Intercom	10	10
13. Analog extension required	None	80
14. Rolm single-line digital instrument	None	100

Sensitivity Analysis. By pressing "C" it is possible to change any of the input data. As an illustration we changed the location from the old location to the renovated one. The system asked us more questions and then displayed new recommendations side by side with the original one (column "new" was added). Notice that new items appear on the list and negative values appeared on some of the original items. These items should *not* be included in the package.

APPENDIX C: Sample Choices (out of 35)

Choices

1. Hawaiian Telephone rotary instrument
   Used in rule(s): (0005) (0006) (0007) (0009) (0010) (0011) (0049)
2. Hawaiian Telephone electronic push-button Instrument
   Used in rule(s): (0009) (0010)
3. Rolm single-line digital instrument
   Used in rule(s): (0006) (0024)

APPENDIX D: Sample Rules (out of 50)

Rule 1
IF   Instrument location is in old section of main hospital or in outlying buildings of Medical Center installation
THEN the instrument type is analog
       AND

Equipment make is GTE (Hawaiian Telephone)
AND
Primary line is extension—Probability = 50/100
AND
Primary line is private—Probability = –20/100
ELSE   Equipment make is Rolm
AND
Primary line is private—Probability = 20/100
AND
Primary line is extension—Probability = –20/100

Note: Digital Rolm phones cannot be installed in outlying buildings because existing cables will not support digital system. Digital Rolm phones will not be installed in the old part of the hospital.
Reference TAMC Telephone Switch Installation Contract

Rule 2
IF   Instrument location is in old section of main hospital
AND
Instrument location is in a patient room
THEN Telephones will not be installed in patient rooms located in the old hospital or outlying building

Rule 3
IF   Instrument location is NOT in new renovated section of main hospital or unknown at this time
AND
Instrument location is NOT in old section of main hospital
AND
Instrument location is NOT in outlying buildings of Medical Center installation
THEN Proposed location of instrument must be determined before configuration can be completed

Chapter 17

Expert Systems Applications Cases

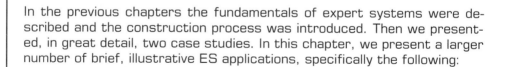

In the previous chapters the fundamentals of expert systems were described and the construction process was introduced. Then we presented, in great detail, two case studies. In this chapter, we present a larger number of brief, illustrative ES applications, specifically the following:

607

Expert systems are being developed and implemented today at an accelerated rate. Many thousands of such systems exist in various stages of development in the United States, Japan, and Europe. The dozen or so minicases presented in this chapter (see Table 17.1 for summary and brief description) are intended to:

□ Reinforce concepts and ideas presented in the previous chapters. Some of this reinforcement takes place through the questions for discussion at the end of the chapter.
□ Show the potential use of ES in various industries and functional areas.
□ Raise some issues concerning the development and use of such systems.
□ Analyze some commonalities and differences among the systems.

There is a major problem in collecting information about successful, commercial ES. Because such systems may give their users a significant competitive advantage, companies do not like to share information about their ES. Furthermore, many of the serious ES are still being developed and the monetary results are not clear. The developers of such systems are reluctant to give any information that would increase expectations in their own organizations. Finally, several systems presented in the literature as ES are merely MIS or at best DSS.

TABLE 17.1 List of Cases.

Case	Functional Area	Developing or User Organization	Brief Description
1. MYCIN	Medical	Stanford University	Diagnosing infections, prescribing treatment
2. XCON	Operations management	Digital Equipment Corp. (DEC)	Configures computer orders
3. YES/MVS	Operations management	IBM	Scheduling and adjustments, real time systems
4. ISIS-II	Operations management	Westinghouse Corp.	Intelligent jobs' scheduling, factory automation
5. PROSPECT	Marketing	USC (student project)	Selecting method for contacting customers
6. COMPASS	Maintenance and repair	General Telephone	Analyze maintenance reports
7. AIG/DIC	Insurance	American International Group	Underwriting complex insurance policies
8. Hostages	Police management	University of Arizona	Advice on how to handle hostage-taking incidents
9. Loan analysis	Banking, loans	The ABC Bank	Estimating the chances of approving large loans
10. CARGEX	Transportation	Lufthansa (Germany)	Cargo configuration, scheduling
11. Management Edge	Management, personnel	The Human Edge, Inc.	Management situations, personnel
12. La-Courtier	Investment	Cognitive Systems, Inc.	Advice on trading stocks

Case 1: MYCIN

Each year two million people get sick while in hospitals recovering from something else; and perhaps 50,000 of them die. The cause is hospital-borne infections. These may develop unnoticed, and when discovered they need to be diagnosed quickly. MYCIN, which is considered the granddaddy of ES, was developed to aid physicians in diagnosing meningitis and other bacterial infections of the blood and to prescribe treatment. Specifically, the system's objective is to aid physicians during a critical 24–48-hour period after the detection of symptoms, a time when much of the decision making is imprecise because all the relevant information is not yet available. Early diagnosis and treatment can save a patient from brain damage or even from death.

MYCIN was developed at Stanford Medical School in the 1970s by Dr. Edward H. Shortliffe. The program's record of correct diagnoses and prescribed treatments has equaled the performance of top human experts.

MYCIN introduced several features that have become the hallmarks of ES:

□ *The knowledge representation is rule based.* The knowledge base consists of about 500 "IF-THEN" inference rules. For example:

IF   1. The infection that requires therapy is meningitis, and
          2. The patient has evidence of serious skin or soft tissue infection, and
          3. Organisms were not seen on the stain of the culture, and
          4. The type of infection is bacterial

THEN There is evidence that the organism (other than those seen on cultures or smears) that might be causing the infection is *Staphylococcus coagpos* (0.75), or *Streptococcus* (0.5).

□ *Probabilistic Rules.* Many of the rules include a *chance* option that allows the system to reach plausible conclusions from uncertain evidence. The chance figures in the rules are expressed as certainty factors.

□ *Backward Chaining Method.* The program executes an exhaustive *backward chaining* search for a diagnosis, augmented by a numerical heuristic function. In its output it *rank orders* competing hypotheses. For an example of the reasoning process, see Figure 17.1.

□ *Explanation.* MYCIN can explain its reasoning. The user (a physician) can interrogate it in various ways—by inquiring *why* the ES asked a particular question or *how* it reached an intermediate or final conclusion. Because each rule is a semi-independent package of knowledge, the user can easily trace the rules that led to a certain question or conclusion.

□ *User-Friendly system.* MYCIN is very easy to use. The required training is minimal. The entire dialogue is conducted in plain English.

Using MYCIN

In a typical consultation session, the physician conducts an interactive dialog with MYCIN about a particular patient. He or she provides information (e.g.,

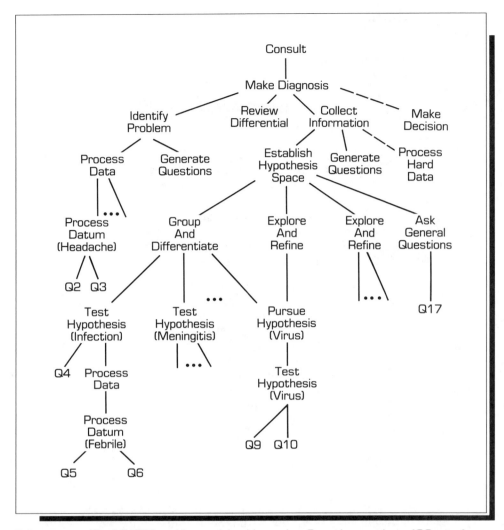

FIGURE 17.1 The MYCIN problem-solving hierarchy. Question numbers (Q2, etc.) correspond to questions asked in the consultation. Solid lines show tasks actually done, dashed lines show those that might be done. (*Source:* Adapted from Bennett and Englemore [1].)

symptoms, patient's characteristics) and responds to questions generated by the ES. The user can also apply *certainty factors* to qualify the answers. MYCIN examines approximately 100 potential diagnoses. Once the diagnosis is completed, a drug treatment is prescribed.

Because physicians have the final responsibility for treatment, transparency in the system is essential. By typing RULE, the user obtains an English-language explanation of the last rule executed. Typing WHY triggers a back-trace of the inference process that fired the system's last question. Repeated use of RULE and WHY activates further backtracing. A sample consultation with MYCIN is shown in Table 17.2.

TABLE 17.2 Interacting with MYCIN.

MYCIN, an ES for medical diagnosis, works on the assumption that a possible disease exists for the case at hand and then tries to find evidence that supports or contradicts its hypothesis. It gathers this evidence from the physician working on a case, starting with the initial choice of a possible disease. An example of dialog follows:

MYCIN: What is the infection?
Physician: Endarteritis [an inflammation of the inner layer of an artery that can be caused by a number of agents].
MYCIN: Is organism-1 a rod or a coccus? [This question will narrow the range of possible agents for the disease.]
Physician: Rod.

MYCIN then asks additional questions about laboratory test results to help determine what organisms might be causing the disease. When it has reached its conclusion, it will recommend a particular drug therapy to combat the organism or organisms involved. So that the physician will trust MYCIN's conclusions, the program is designed to answer questions about its reasoning. For example:

Physician: How did you decide that organism-1 is *E. coli*?
MYCIN: I used rule 084 to conclude that organism-1 is *E. coli.* This gave a cumulative certainty factor of 0.51. [The physician can question further, either by looking at the text of the rule involved, or by questioning its antecedents.]

Case 2:   XCON (Expert VAX System Configuration), Digital Equipment Corp. (DEC)

DEC has always offered its customers a wide range of minicomputer system configurations.[*] It is not uncommon to have thousands of customer orders on hand, each one involving different needs and specifications. This wide range of combinations creates a complex business environment involving many interdependent decisions and tasks for processing the orders, scheduling the necessary manufacturing and other operations, and distributing computer system orders to the customer in a timely manner.

Until XCON became available, the computer system configuration task was accomplished manually. Technical editors in manufacturing reviewed all customer orders for technical correctness and order completeness. This was an extremely difficult task, requiring many knowledgeable people. Traditional work methods did not yield the accurate, cost-effective, fast response that XCON provides.

Most of the computer system orders that customers send to DEC have unique specifications (many line items per order). The development of XCON represented a very significant tool for managing the complexity of DEC's business. A dramatic increase in productivity of the technical editors has occurred, owing to the effective use of XCON in the manufacturing environment. XCON is a rule-based system with several thousand rules, implemented in OPS-5, a general-purpose, rule-based language. Like other rule-based languages, OPS-5 provides a rule memory, a global working memory, and an interpreter that tests the rules to determine which ones are satisfied by

[*]For more information, see O'Connor (7) and McDermott (6).

the descriptions in the working memory. On each cycle the interpreter selects a satisfied rule and applies it. Because applying a rule results in changes to working memory, different subsets of rules are satisfied on successive cycles. OPS-5 does not impose any organization on rule memory; all rules are evaluated in every cycle. When more than one rule is satisfied in a given cycle, the interpreter uses a few general conflict resolution strategies to decide which rule to apply.

When XCON was first installed for the configuration of the VAX 11/750 and 11/780 computers, the system had limited capability and knowledge. Therefore much interaction was required with the technical editors to increase the system's expertise. The results, however, are astonishing. Traditionally trained manufacturing technical editors required 20–30 minutes to configure each system order. In contrast, XCON can configure extremely complex system orders in less than a minute. It also provides additional functions and capabilities not formerly performed by the traditional technical editors, such as (1) defining the exact cable length for all cables required between each system component, and (2) providing the vector addresses calculation for the computer bus options.

By 1985 all VAX family system orders in U.S. and European plant operations were configured by XCON. As the workload increased in the system manufacturing plants, no additional technical editors were hired because of the increase in productivity and capacity provided by XCON.

In the past, a large portion of the system orders scheduled for the factory floor had numerous configuration errors and lacked completeness; with XCON, VAX orders have accurate configurations 98 percent of the time (compared with 65 percent in the manual system). Manufacturing operation benefits from accurate system configurations include (1) an increased through-put order rate, (2) fewer shipments delayed because of system configuration errors, and (3) better use of materials on hand.

When numerous line item changes occur on customer orders already scheduled in the manufacturing process, XCON provides a tool to save time, increase output per person, and lower manufacturing costs.

Redeployment of DEC's highly skilled senior technicians has occurred, allowing them to address more technically difficult tasks. Cost savings to DEC are estimated at about $15 million each year. Plant management, extremely satisfied with the emerging artificial intelligence methodologies, are participating in this pioneering effort with great enthusiasm.

The company is developing related ES. Figure 17.2 shows the expansion to XSEL, XSITE, and several other related systems.

XSEL.   XSEL is a system that checks orders for consistency, such as making sure that power supplies match the equipment being shipped.

XSITE.   This system provides a site plan for the customer's machine room and lists the equipment needed.

Other systems are ISA, to aid scheduling; IMACS, to aid manufacturing; ILRPS, to aid long-range planning; IPMS, to aid in project management; and ICSR, to aid in customer service.

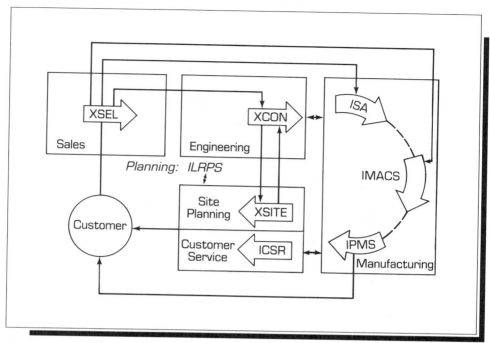

FIGURE 17.2 Expert systems network at DEC.

Managerial Lessons. DEC in 1985 had five years of experience using ES on a daily basis in U.S. and European manufacturing plant operations. During this time the company moved slowly up the learning curve (more than 120,000 computers were configured by 1986), occasionally making mistakes but always learning. The company established an internal Digital AI Training Center to help meet growing training and development needs in the ES area.

The following lessons are worth mentioning:

- Use senior management to nuture, sponsor, and guide the innovation process.
- Identify and limit your "core" ES problem space; keep it to a manageable size.
- Relate the ES to company goals.
- Demonstrate early your prototype ES.
- Manage culture resistance and management expectations persistently.
- Where possible, provide seed funding for new systems.
- Carefully manage the introduction of ES; have a plan and follow it closely.
- Provide educational and training support to ease implementation problems.

Other considerations include the following:

- The level of effort required to develop and extend the system remains fairly constant over the life of the project.

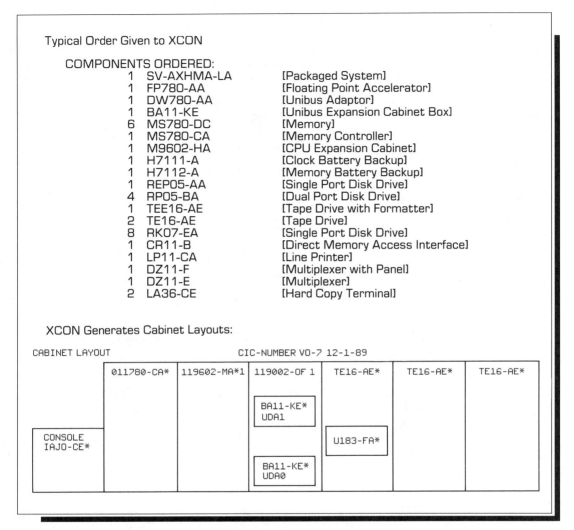

Typical Order Given to XCON

COMPONENTS ORDERED:
1	SV-AXHMA-LA	[Packaged System]
1	FP780-AA	[Floating Point Accelerator]
1	DW780-AA	[Unibus Adaptor]
1	BA11-KE	[Unibus Expansion Cabinet Box]
6	MS780-DC	[Memory]
1	MS780-CA	[Memory Controller]
1	M9602-HA	[CPU Expansion Cabinet]
1	H7111-A	[Clock Battery Backup]
1	H7112-A	[Memory Battery Backup]
1	REP05-AA	[Single Port Disk Drive]
4	RP05-BA	[Dual Port Disk Drive]
1	TEE16-AE	[Tape Drive with Formatter]
2	TE16-AE	[Tape Drive]
8	RK07-EA	[Single Port Disk Drive]
1	CR11-B	[Direct Memory Access Interface]
1	LP11-CA	[Line Printer]
1	DZ11-F	[Multiplexer with Panel]
1	DZ11-E	[Multiplexer]
2	LA36-CE	[Hard Copy Terminal]

XCON Generates Cabinet Layouts:

CABINET LAYOUT   CIC-NUMBER VO-7 12-1-89

FIGURE 17.3 An input-output example for XCON.

□ The developers found they did not have to wait until the system was complete before putting it to use. To expect anything close to perfection during the first few years of system use (especially if the task is complex) is a serious mistake. It took 80,000 orders to uncover some of the inadequacies in XCON's configuration knowledge, and the configuration task is being continually redefined as new products are introduced.

□ The system was not developed from scratch, but by means of an ES building tool (OPS-4 and then OPS-5). This tool allowed developers to create the initial prototype of 250 rules in a little under one person-year of effort.

□ The initial system was built quite rapidly and then expanded and tested while being used. Several changes were made without starting over from scratch.

☐ One unique feature of XCON is that, unlike most other recent ES, it does not use probabilities or certainty factors. A component is either included or omitted.

☐ Unlike diagnostic systems, XCON does not carry on a dialog with the technician as it is being designed. After all the necessary information is inputted, XCON chugs away until the configuration is completed (see Figure 17.3). For a typical configuration, XCON will go through 1000 rules and 250 product descriptions.

☐ Building an expert configurer is a seemingly unending process, requiring incremental growth over long periods of time.

DEC's experience provides a good argument for the use of expert systems. Without the flexibility and modular organization inherent in the rule-based ES approach, developers would have been hard-pressed to maintain the incremental growth needed to support DEC's changing product lines.

Case 3:   YES/MVS, IBM's Real-Time Expert System

This case exemplifies an ES operating in a real-time environment.[*] Real-time situations involve decisions to be made on systems that are already operating; that is, decisions are made and immediately implemented while the system is in operation.

Large, computerized data processing systems and their assorted networks often involve multiple processors and a large number of peripherals, representing a multimillion-dollar investment. Decisions in such systems center around job scheduling, monitoring performance and delays, and making adjustments and maintenance decisions whenever needed.

Typically, the planning and control of such systems rests largely in the hands of a few operators. In addition to routine activities like mounting tapes, operators continually monitor the condition of the computer's operating system—the program that controls all the computer's activities—and initiate queries and/or commands to diagnose maintenance problems and other delays as they arise. These conditions require that the decision be made in a real-time environment.

A group of researchers at the IBM Thomas J. Watson Research Division, Yorktown Heights, NY, have successfully applied ES techniques to problems in managing computer installations and operations, choosing the MVS operating system as the subject. MVS is the most widely used operating system in large mainframe IBM computers.

Most existing ES applications are consultation-oriented; that is, they do not act on their own but run through a session in a batch mode and deal with a static world. Unlike many of the consultation ES, a real time ES must base its conclusions on facts obtained directly from the system being monitored, not from data observed and interpreted by humans—there just is not time for that.

[*]IBM (5).

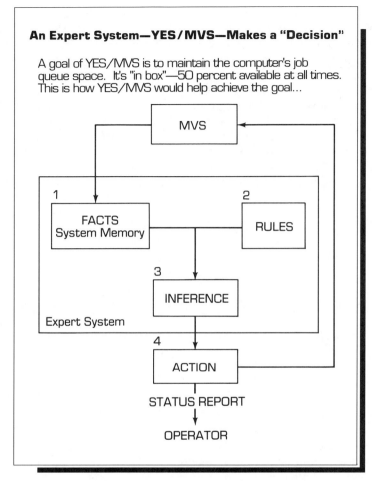

An Expert System—YES/MVS—Makes a "Decision"

A goal of YES/MVS is to maintain the computer's job queue space. It's "in box"—50 percent available at all times. This is how YES/MVS would help achieve the goal...

FIGURE 17.4 YES/MVS. This diagram illustrates how the experiment system YES/MVS makes a "decision". The goal of YES/MVS in this example is to keep 50 percent of the computer's job queue space available at all times. The expert system will combine the facts it has about the system's condition with the rules it possesses to make an inference. It will either use the inference about the system to get more data or to make a "decision" about what to do in order to achieve or maintain the goal.

For example:

1. MVS says queue space is low (FACT)
2. . . . and a RULE says that when space is low, query the printer's state . . .
3. . . . which is an INFERENCE . . .
4. . . . which starts the program over again, by determining that . . .
1. (FACT) a. The printer has a few short jobs
        b. The printer is holding a long job
        c. The printer is limited to printing 30,000 lines
   . . . combining these FACTS with the
2. . . . RULE that is a, b, and c are true, the correct
3. . . . INFERENCE is to raise the printer's line limit . . .
4. . . . an ACTION is initiated; raise the printer's line limit.

The action frees the computer's job queue space, by releasing the large printing job on hold. This achieves the goal (i.e., the system's jobs queue space becomes at lease 50 percent available).

(*Source: IBM Research Highlights* No. 2, 1984; IBM Corp., Princeton, N.J. For further information, see: Ennis, R.L., et al, "A Continuous Real-Time Expert System for Computer Operations." *IBM Journal of Research and Development* (Jan. 1986).)

YES/MVS is a continuous, real-time ES that exerts interactive control over the computer's operating system as an aid to computer operators. It can summarize the system conditions and respond instantly and automatically to needs. The response is done in conjunction with a human who can override the ES. When a potential problem is detected, the operator may ask MVS for additional information and send one or more corrective commands. Written in a version of PROLOG called PSC PROLOG, the system is used on mainframe computers. Figure 17.4 illustrates how the system works.

Case 4:   Intelligent Scheduling and Information System (ISIS-II) at Westinghouse Electric

Scheduling complex work orders on a factory floor should become more efficient and cost-effective if ISIS-II, an ES developed at Westinghouse's Productivity and Quality Center in Pittsburgh, Pa., lives up to its early promise.* ISIS-II (Intelligent Scheduling and Information System) schedules work orders for individual factory work centers. Westinghouse envisions that each work center, or job shop, within its factories will eventually have its own ISIS-II to schedule its orders. Westinghouse co-founded the ISIS project, in conjunction with the Robotics Institute of Carnegie-Mellon University (CMU) in the spring of 1983 in order to learn more about how AI could benefit the company.

ISIS-II uses the KEE software on a dedicated AI computer to generate, compare, and rate alternative job shop schedules. Results are superior to schedules generated with conventional scheduling methods, even when supported by management science models and computers, because ISIS-II can consider all the complex factors and constraints encountered in a job shop situation.

ISIS-II generates a prioritized list of work orders. Each order includes the machine that will process the order, the operation to be performed, and the time and date of operation.

ISIS-II considers five types of constraints (see Table 17.3).

The constraints are represented in the KEE system as rules and are ranked by the order of their importance, which may vary over time.

The machines, production processes, orders, and other aspects of the job shop are represented as frames. ISIS-II's user interface utilizes the Kee system's ActiveImages.

The availability of both rule-based and frame-based components in the KEE package was found to be a major advantage in the development work. The use of ActiveImages for creating a user interface saved a great deal of time and freed the ES builder to work on the more interesting and difficult parts of the application.

ISIS has been highly rated by expert schedulers in a factory environment. The system is also of particular importance to facility design, where it is being used in simulation (or in analytic performance) models for post analysis of facility design output. ISIS can model a manufacturing plant with a high level of detail, from physical machine descriptions to process descriptions to organizational structures and relations (see Figure 17.5).

*Based on Fox and Smith (3).

TABLE 17.3　Scheduling Constraints.

Type of Constraint	Examples of Constraints
Organizational goals and policies	Due date Work-in-process Shop stability Shifts Cost Productivity goals Quality Relative priorities of jobs
Physical constraints	Machine physical constraints (e.g., capabilities and tooling) Setup times Processing time Quality
Causal restrictions	Operation alternatives Machine alternatives Tool requirements Material requirements Personnel requirements Interoperation transfer times
Availability constraints	Resources reservations Machine downtime Shifts Inventories
Preference constraints	Operation preferences Machine preferences Sequencing preferences

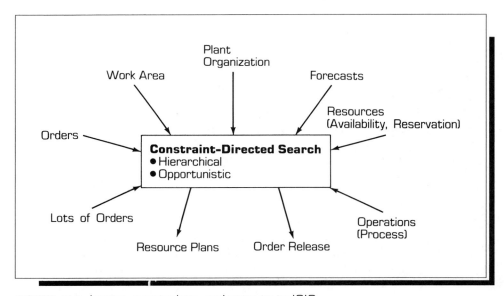

FIGURE 17.5　Inputs, constraints, and outputs to ISIS.

Case 5: **Selecting Marketing Contact Form**

A prototype marketing expert system was developed to help corrugated container sales representatives decide which is the most appropriate form of contact: telephone, mail, or personal sales calls.[*] This system was constructed by using a *rule-induction* approach with a shell called Expert Ease (now it is called Expert One).

The following steps are involved in the construction and use of the system:

> ☐ Step 1 *Listing the Attributes.* This step involves listing all the attributes that are necessary in the development and operation of the ES. Figure 17.6 shows a simplified example of data input during the development of

```
EXPERT-EASE Attribute Listing, Problem: PROSPECT
REASON       :
     R1           :    Respond to a request for quote that
                       does not require inspection.
     R2           :    Request for quote on item that requires
                       inspection.
     Qualify      :

     Present      :
     QandP        :    Qualify and present is your objective.
     Initiate     :
POTENTIAL    :
     SMALL        :    Small-Less than 250 MSF/Month
     MEDIUM       :    Medium-Between 250-500 MSF/Month
     LARGE        :    Large-Greater than 500 MSF/Month
BuyCriteria:
     Design       :    Design is an important criteria for a
                       buy decision.
     Price        :    Price is the most important buying
                       decision and design is not involved.
     QSC          :    Quality, service and company reputation
                       is most important and design is not
                       involved.
     DK           :    Don't know yet what is important to the
                       buyer.
METHOD       :
     TELEPHONE    :
     MAIL         :
     PERSONAL     :
     TandM        :    Telephone and Mail combination
```

FIGURE 17.6 List of attributes

[*]This case was developed as a term paper by Steve Durale, an MBA student at the University of Southern California, Los Angeles (1985).

the program. In this case there are three attributes: reason, potential, and buy criteria. Each attribute can assume different values. The attributes with their values are:

☐ *Reason.* This is the list of six possible reasons why a contact is made. For example, R1 is an abbreviation for "respond to a request for quote that does not require inspection." Some of the reasons are not defined, just listed, because they are terms known to the user.

☐ *Potential.* There are three possible volumes of sales to a client: small, medium, and large.

☐ *Buy Criteria.* Four criteria important for buyers are listed here as examples: design, price, quality, and not sure.

☐ *Method.* Once the decision attributes are listed, it is necessary to list the alternative decisions; in this case four alternative methods of contact are defined: telephone, mail, personal, and telephone combined with mail.

☐ Step 2 *Analyzing Cases* (Example Listing). In this step the computer is presented with different cases. Figure 17.7 shows 17 cases. In each case a combination of three values of each of the three attributes is shown. For example, case 1 involves "qualify" (a reason attribute), "large" number of contacts (for the potential attribute), and "price" (as the most important buying criteria attribute).

When asked to suggest a contact method for such a combination of values, the human expert recommended, in sample case 1, a "personal"

EXPERT-EASE Example Listing, Problem: PROSPECT			
REASON logical	POTENTIAL logical	BuyCriteri logical	METHOD logical
1 Qualify	LARGE	Price	PERSONAL
2 R1	SMALL	Design	PERSONAL
3 R1	SMALL	Price	TELEPHONE
4 Qualify	MEDIUM	DK	TELEPHONE
5 Present	MEDIUM	Price	PERSONAL
6 Present	SMALL	Price	TELEPHONE
7 Qualify	SMALL	DK	TELEPHONE
8 Present	SMALL	Design	PERSONAL
9 R2	SMALL	Price	PERSONAL
10 Present	LARGE	DK	PERSONAL
11 Present	SMALL	QSC	MAIL
12 Initiate	LARGE	DK	PERSONAL
13 Initiate	MEDIUM	DK	TELEPHONE
14 Initiate	SMALL	DK	MAIL
15 R1	MEDIUM	QSC	TandM
16 R1	SMALL	QSC	TandM
17 R1	MEDIUM	Price	PERSONAL

FIGURE 17.7 List of cases.

```
EXPERT-EASE Rule Listing, Problem: PROSPECT
BuyCriteria
        Design : PERSONAL
        Price : POTENTIAL
              SMALL : REASON
                         R1 : TELEPHONE
                         R2 : PERSONAL
                    Qualify : null
                    Present : TELEPHONE
                      QandP : null
                   Initiate : null
              MEDIUM : PERSONAL
              LARGE : PERSONAL
          QSC : REASON
                 R1 : TandM
                 R2 : null
            Qualify : null
            Present : MAIL
              QandP : null
           Initiate : null
          DK : POTENTIAL
              SMALL : REASON
                         R1 : null
                         R2 : null
                    Qualify : TELEPHONE
                    Present : null
                      QandP : null
                   Initiate : MAIL
                :MEDIUM : TELEPHONE
                 LARGE : PERSONAL
```

FIGURE 17.8 Rules as generated by the computer program.

contact. However, instead of interrogating a human expert, cases can be derived from historical files.

□ Step 3 *Rule Listing.* In this step the computer creates the rules.

Figure 17.8 shows an example of rules generated by the computer. The current prototype is sufficient to generate advice. As more cases are added rules are added, or previous rules are modified. The program will identify inconsistencies in the rules as new rules are generated.

The next four figures demonstrate a consultation session between a potential user and the computer. Figure 17.9 shows the first question posed to the user: "What is the value of Buy Criteria?" The user selects item 4 from the menu. Figure 17.10 shows a selection of item 3 for the "potential" question (i.e., there is a potential for large sales). Figure 17.11 asks the reason for the contact. The user selects item 6 (an initial contact).

Following the input information, the computer arrives at a conclusion (Figure 17.12—the use of "Telephone").

```
┌─────────────────────────────────────────────────────────────────────┐
│  EXPERT-EASE   file: PROSPECT    43958 bytes left        1 : REASON   │
├─────────────────────────────────────────────────────────────────────┤
│  What is the value of BuyCriteria?                                    │
│                                                                       │
│     1. Design is an important criterion for a buy decision.           │
│                                                                       │
│     2. Price is the most important buying decision and design is not  │
│        involved.                                                      │
│                                                                       │
│     3. Quality, service, and company reputation is most important and │
│        design is not involved.                                        │
│                                                                       │
│     4. Don't know yet what is important to the buyer                  │
│                                                                       │
│                                                                       │
├─────────────────────────────────────────────────────────────────────┤
│  running PROSPECT                                                     │
│  Enter value 1..4                                                     │
│  >                                                                    │
└─────────────────────────────────────────────────────────────────────┘
```

FIGURE 17.9

Expert Ease can display for the user the rules used to arrived at any appropriate recommendation. At present, the software can take only a small number of attributes and values. All the information is also assumed to be under certainty; that is, no certainty factors or probabilistic values are permitted.

```
┌─────────────────────────────────────────────────────────────────────┐
│  EXPERT-EASE   file: PROSPECT    43958 bytes left        1 : REASON   │
├─────────────────────────────────────────────────────────────────────┤
│  What is the value of POTENTIAL ?                                     │
│                                                                       │
│     1. Small - Less than 250 MSF/Month                                │
│                                                                       │
│     2. Medium - Between 250 - 500 MSF/Month                           │
│                                                                       │
│     3. Large - Greater than 500 MSF/Month                             │
│                                                                       │
│                                                                       │
│                                                                       │
│                                                                       │
├─────────────────────────────────────────────────────────────────────┤
│  running PROSPECT                                                     │
│  Enter value 1..3                                                     │
│  >                                                                    │
└─────────────────────────────────────────────────────────────────────┘
```

FIGURE 17.10

```
┌─────────────────────────────────────────────────────────────────────┐
│ EXPERT-EASE   file: PROSPECT    43958 bytes left        1 : REASON    │
├─────────────────────────────────────────────────────────────────────┤
│ What is the value of REASON ?                                         │
│                                                                       │
│   1. Respond to a request for quote that does not require inspection. │
│                                                                       │
│   2. Request for quote on item that requires inspection.              │
│                                                                       │
│   3. Qualify                                                          │
│                                                                       │
│   4. Present                                                          │
│                                                                       │
│   5. Qualify and present is your objective.                          │
│                                                                       │
│   6. Initiate                                                         │
│                                                                       │
├─────────────────────────────────────────────────────────────────────┤
│ running PROSPECT                                                      │
│ Enter value 1..6                                                      │
│ >                                                                     │
└─────────────────────────────────────────────────────────────────────┘
```

FIGURE 17.11

Case 6: COMPASS: A Telephone Switch Maintenance System

The Problem Domain

COMPASS (Central Office Maintenance Printout Analysis and Suggestion System) analyzes maintenance printouts of telephone company control switching equipment and suggests maintenance actions to be performed.[*]

A central office telephone switch system connects thousands or tens of thousands of telephone lines to one another or external trunks (interconnec-

```
┌─────────────────────────────────────────────────────────────────────┐
│ EXPERT-EASE   file: PROSPECT    43958 bytes left        1 : REASON    │
├─────────────────────────────────────────────────────────────────────┤
│ The value of METHOD is TELEPHONE                                      │
│                                                                       │
├─────────────────────────────────────────────────────────────────────┤
│ do you want to run  PROSPECT again (y or n) ?                         │
│ >                                                                     │
└─────────────────────────────────────────────────────────────────────┘
```

FIGURE 17.12

[*]Based on Goyal et al. (4).

tions among central offices). Such a switch system can produce hundreds of maintenance messages daily. They are analyzed to determine what actions are necessary to maintain the switch.

GTE's COMPASS is an ES developed to perform an analysis of maintenance messages for GTE's No. 2 Electronic Automatic Exchange (EAX). The No. 2 EAX was selected because its technology is stable, widely used, and scheduled to be in use for several years. In addition, the available expertise in No. 2 EAX maintenance and administration is likely to diminish as technicians migrate to work on newer situations.

Presently, a GTE software system called Remote Monitor and Control System (RMCS) monitors the output messages of several telephone switches. The maintaince printouts from RMCS are analyzed to determine what maintenance actions should be taken. A maintenance message describes an error situation that occurred during the telephone call-processing operation of the switch but gives no indication as to where the problem could be. Problem patterns appear only by collecting a series of messages over an extended time. Expertise is required to analyze and act on the printouts of the RMCS. There are several levels of expertise; people with less expertise perform the job less well and more slowly than those with greater expertise. Internal consultants with great expertise are consulted when less expert people cannot solve a problem. The expertise involves judgment and rules of thumb accumulated over many years. In maintaining older switches, corporate expertise is lost as experts migrate to work on newer switches. Thus the need for an expert system now exists and will grow in the future.

A large amount of expertise is required to analyze a No. 2 EAX maintenance printout (see Figure 17.13) and determine and prioritize maintenance actions, including:

☐ Identifying groups of maintenance messages that are likely to be caused by the same switch fault.

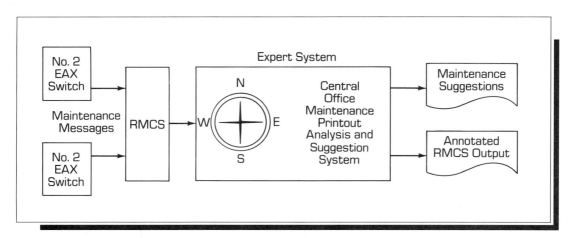

FIGURE 17.13 COMPASS block diagram.

☐ Analyzing the messages in each group, along with any related information, to determine the possible specific faults in the switch that could be causing those maintenance messages.

☐ Estimating the likelihood of recurrence of the possible faults.

☐ Determining the possible maintenance actions that could be suggested to the switchperson to enable these faults to be verified and remedied.

☐ Prioritizing the list of suggested actions by taking into account such considerations as the likelihood of the fault and the ease of performing the corrective action.

☐ Making the system's suggestions known to the user in the most user-friendly way.

COMPASS includes all these areas of expertise.

System Development

The system was developed on a Xerox 1108 AI workstation using the KEE development tool (see Chapter 15). The prototyping, which involved several person-years of effort, lasted about a year (elapsed time). The entire development process is documented in Goyal et al. (4). Some of the lessons learned from the construction of the system were presented in Chapter 15.

Testing and Validation

Initial field use of this system has been successful. In one field trial, COMPASS analyzed the maintenance messages and suggested maintenance actions for four No. 2 EAX switches (two in Texas and two in Florida). These switches service over 100,000 lines of customer phones and trunks. For each switch, COMPASS was run once a day for three to five days. COMPASS found a total of 51 switch problems. During the time allotted for the trial, switch maintenance personnel were able to execute the recommended set of actions for 33 of the 51 problems. In all 33 cases the recommended actions fixed the switch problem. In most cases the problem was fixed by COMPASS's first recommendation (if the first recommendation does not help, a second one is issued, etc.).

In addition to the field trials, COMPASS's analyses, rules, and procedures were examined in detail by a group of four No. 2 EAX switch experts (peers of the project's domain expert). The group strongly endorsed COMPASS. They generally came to the same conclusions as COMPASS, though sometimes by a slightly different procedure. In one test case, they agreed that COMPASS had correctly identified a switch problem that none of these top experts had identified in their analysis.

Results of the field trials and expert analyses convinced telephone switch operating personnel to request that the present version of COMPASS be quickly installed in a field location. It is used to analyze maintenance problems for GTE's No. 2 EAX switches throughout the country. (There are over 150 such switches nationwide.) More important, COMPASS will provide the basis for studying the impact of ES on human resources and for quantifying the costs and benefits of such systems.

Potential COMPASS Advantages, Payoffs, and Expansions

COMPASS affords several potential advantages to users:

☐ It supports better telephone switch performance, yielding higher-quality service to telephone customers.
☐ It increases the productivity of experienced switch maintenance persons.
☐ It upgrades the performance of less experienced personnel.
☐ It provides guaranteed maintenance of existing switches by capturing expertise that may not be available in the future.

COMPASS can perform certain tasks better than the top human experts. For example, COMPASS can analyze a complete situation (which is difficult even for a top human expert), automate present maintenance procedures that involve laborious and error-prone table look-ups and calculations, analyze each situation without bias, and perform equally well any day or any hour.

One of the positive aspects of the COMPASS is the long-term growth potential. It is possible to expand COMPASS to include:

☐ Covering maintenance messages from other types of switches.
☐ Combining RMCS information with information from other local indicators, such as switch alarm systems.
☐ Adding network traffic information to allow analysis on a more global basis.
☐ Learning from experience to upgrade performance, such as learning better values for the frequency of switch faults.

The elapsed time for a typical COMPASS run was (in 1985) about one-half hour (this time is decreasing rapidly with improved technology). Depending on their level of expertise, No. 2 EAX maintenance personnel would take five minutes to two hours to perform a similar analysis (which in many cases is not as accurate or complete as that of COMPASS).

Case 7: AIG's Underwriting System

American International Group, Inc. (New York, NY), is the nation's seventh largest insurance company (more than $11 billion in assets).[*] The company operates in 130 countries, primarily writing custom-made policies for major corporations. Many clients (such as aerospace companies) encounter unusual risk problems. Therefore underwriting the policies requires experienced individuals with flexible thinking capabilities.

Development of the System

The ES was developed at the American Home Inland Marine division, which insures literally "anything that moves," from telecommunications signals to

[*]Based on Shamoon (8)

registered mail. The system was developed by Syntelligence, Inc. (an AI vendor in Sunnyvale, CA), to mimic a top AIG risk manager. The division operates 14 offices nationwide, and the prototype was developed in one office only. Once the system is fully implemented, it will be equivalent to having another top underwriter in each of the 14 offices.

The prototype was initially done on one product (out of nine major products). This product, called DIC, deals with an insurance policy that covers all types of perils, including earthquakes and floods.

The ES was structured with a construction tool called Syntel (developed by Syntelligence, Inc., for building financial expert systems). The software runs on a Xerox 1108 AI workstation.

The development took about a year with numerous iterations, each of which improved the system's performance. By late 1985 the system covered 95 percent of the expert's knowledge, and it was continually being improved. Many knowledge acquisition sessions were required (see accompanying box) to extract the knowledge from the top risk managers.

A Sample of Knowledge Acquisition Dialog

Q = Questions by the knowledge engineer

A = Answers by the expert

Q: How do you determine a premium?

A: I . . .

Q: It doesn't just come out of the air magically. You think about a lot of things, don't you?

A: Yes, I do. I think about flood exposure, earthquake exposure, collapse, burglary.

Q: What do you think about when you think about burglary?

A: I think about the commodity—whether it's liquor and cigarettes or widgets.

Q: If it's liquor or cigarettes, is that good or bad compared with widgets? Which would you rather have and why?

Capabilities

The system is designed to help the company's staff explore how a risk manager should think about insurance or size up risks and price them—which is basically what underwriters do. In contrast to ready-made, off-the-shelf ES (which are presented later), the AIG ES can think as top experts at AIG think. The system advises, for example, whether or not to accept a client and what the premium should be.

The system is also being used as a training device for new underwriters, who work with the machine on actual cases under the supervision of a top expert.

The ES uses the certainty factor approach for assigning weights to the recommendations. In addition, the system takes into account geographical differences. It knows, for example, how AIG experts think about earthquake chances in Los Angeles as compared with San Francisco.

More than 100 AIG people with PCs can tap into the company's mainframe and use the ES.

Facts, Issues, and Lessons

- □ The system cost about $2 million. The company estimates a $2\frac{1}{2}$-year payback period. This estimate is based on saving the salary of 14 senior risk managers (one in each office). At $60,000 a person, the annual savings is $840,000.
- □ Risk managers will not be fired; however, over the next two to three years, the computer will be able to handle a substantially increased volume of business with existing personnel.
- □ Senior managers who were skeptical at the beginning now think the system is great, with lots of potential in it.
- □ Eight experts were interviewed to ensure that expertise in diversified topics is covered.
- □ Once the first product line is operational, the company will prototype the other eight product lines.
- □ Some employees fear that ES will replace the need for human experts. This fear was communicated to management, which is currently seeking a solution.
- □ Expert systems improve corporate decision making by speeding it up and making it more consistent than is normally possible for humans.
- □ Intelligent systems can also be used as tools to train new or junior people in an organization.

Case 8: Expert System in Law Enforcement

The Problem

One of the most difficult decision-making situations may occur when law enforcement officials are involved in stressful circumstances such as responding to hostage-taking incidents.[*] Police officers must make critical, emotionally charged decisions under conditions of high stress and great uncertainty. The vast majority of officers that are involved in such incidents have little experience. Very few trained and experienced officers can be brought fast enough to all places that require them. Therefore, the availability of an expert on a disk in each police station holds great promise.

[*]Based on Vedder and Mason (9)

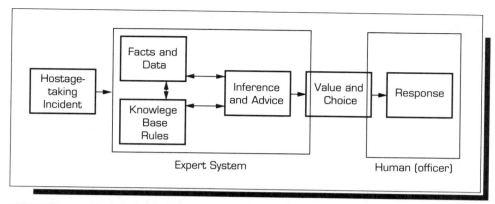

FIGURE 17.14 Model of ES for law enforcement.

Methodology

First, a feasibility study was conducted to make sure that ES is justifiable. Once the criteria were satisfied a model of the situation was developed. This model is shown in Figure 17.14.

As can be seen, the purpose of the ES is to advise the officer what to do. The recommendation is filtered through the human value system and he or she makes the final decision.

The system was developed initially to handle 41 different scenarios, each of which may develop during a hostage-taking incident. Knowledge was solicited from human experts.

System Development

The system is rule-based and it can assist several different decision makers simultaneously. It was developed with a simple rule-based shell and was run on a VAX 11/785 (superminicomputer).

The first prototype was developed fast and its recommendations and rules were evaluated by an expert officer. The officer found the first prototype to be "too academic." For example, the information required by the system took too long to collect. There also was a problem with four different decision makers that needed to coordinate their activities.

The second prototype incorporated many of the suggestions of the evaluator. Yet, the results were far from being satisfactory. Next, the prototype was tested on a simulated hostage-taking incident. A student used the expert system to make decisions that were evaluated, on the scene, by an expert. The system performed fairly well and it is currently been used as a training tool.

The system needs to go through several additional iterations, however, before it would be possible to use it for real incidents. The system should also run on a microcomputer so that it can be used in many locations. While all this is going on it is suggested that you take a break and go to the movies to see "The Three Fugitives."

Case 9: High-Value Loan Analysis

The Problem

ABC Bank (requested anonymity) specializes in loans of over $30,000,000. Such loans are typically for major construction projects. The money for such loans is almost always Federal money and there are extensive regulations on such large loans. Before such a loan can be approved, a lengthy and expensive study must be performed. The study is typically about 3200 pages long, takes six months to complete, and costs about $250,000. The cost of doing the study is recovered by the bank as part of the cost of issuing the loan, however, the $250,000 is recovered ONLY if the bank issues the loan. If after doing the study, it is determined that the loan should not be issued, the bank loses the $250,000. Consequently, there is a great deal of pressure to issue the loan, even if the situation is not as secure as desired.

The Expert System

To solve this problem, the bank had an EXSYS expert system developed by Walter Roberts of Micro Support Inc. of MD. The expert system uses data that can easily be obtained at low cost. A staff member can run the expert system on a laptop computer on site. The results of the expert system are sent to the bank via modem for examination by the chief underwriter. The expert system uses this data to predict if the full study will result in a loan that can or should be issued. The system divides loans into three categories—likely to be issued, unlikely to be issued, and "gray area." The loans that are unlikely to be issued can be dropped prior to expending the time, resources, and dollars on the full study. This has resulted in tremendous savings. Since the system can explain why the loan was rejected, the borrower also knows specifically what would have to be corrected to successfully reapply for the loan. The loans likely to be issued can be pursued with confidence that the costs will be recovered. The "gray area" loans can be examined by human experts. The conclusions of the expert system can be analyzed by the experts to determine if they should proceed with the full study.

In addition, the expert system also determines the most appropriate money source for the potential loan—either the Ginnie Mae, Fannie Mae, Freddie Mac, or private funds—by evaluating the many requirements associated with each loan. The expert system contains 380 rules and was developed over three months. The system used a wide range of analysis techniques including Delphi studies conducted during the knowledge acquisition phase and decision modeling to establish the probability factors used during rule generation.

Case 10: CARGEX—Cargo Expert System

The Problem

The German airline Lufthansa concentrates on airfreight consolidation processes.[*] Worldwide, all airfreight applications are routed into the cargo cen-

---

[*]Condensed from Koenig, W., et al. "Building on an Expert System to Create an active DSS." *HICSS, 1988.*

ter in Frankfurt. A "traditional" EDP system makes automatic loading decisions, as long as:

- ☐ It is some kind of standard freight.
- ☐ Some threshold values on loading an aircraft are not exceeded.

Applications that cannot be handled by this system are routed on the screen to experts who decide:

- ☐ Whether an application is acceptable, and if yes, at what price.
- ☐ On which specific flights the airfreight should be loaded.

Due to the following facts, the last decision is not a trivial one:

1. Aircraft are loaded by both weight and volume. Various aircraft types differ in the optimal ratio of weight to volume. The employment of mixed mode aircraft (e.g., 74M) allows short-term decisions on the distribution of passengers and freight on the passenger deck. It is the task of the consolidator to properly accept new freight into an aircraft so that (1) the amount of chargeable kilograms of freight is maximized, and (2) the total weight/volume ratio of the aircraft is near the optimum.
2. There are various freight types that interact heavily, for example, living animals (which require special handling and cannot be loaded by side in a lot of cases), valuable goods (which require particular loading/unloading procedures), and dangerous chemicals.
3. Although the airline has a one-hub network, there is considerable complexity in each branch out of (and into) Frankfurt. Moreover, in cases of capacity bottlenecks the airline employs trucking between two airports. Freight may also be stored and shipped later in order to achieve better loading configurations. However, some freight types require an immediate transport (e.g., live fish, flowers).
4. There are many qualitative conditions that apply in an actual decision, for example, customer priority (which may overrule other decision parameters in certain cases), assessment of the accuracy of delivery of freight to the airport (which differs between Africa and Europe, for example), and assessment of the level of the actual airfreight market.

The Expert System

CARGEX is an ES constructed to assist making the loading decisions. The user interface of CARGEX is shown in Figure 17.15. The screen is subdivided into three zones, named north, central, and south. The northern part contains a calendar, the required destination of each flight, the specification of the actual season (which influences the market level), and the sender. Moreover, the freight is specified by an airway bill (identification), type of freight, origin of freight, weight, volume, type of container, number of singular pieces, whether or not a split is allowed between various flights, and whether or not it is a must-go freight.

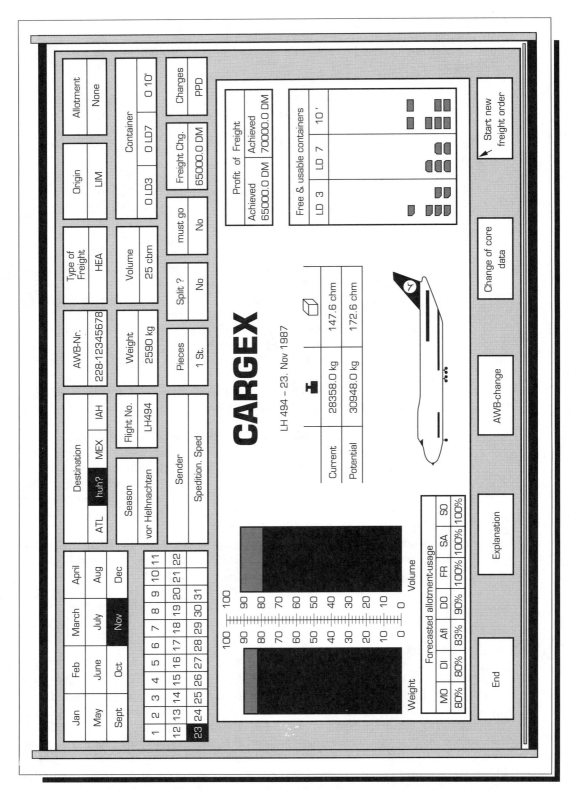

FIGURE 17.15 CARGEX'S screen.

The central part shows both graphically and numerically the actual loading situation of the respective flight, subdivided into weight and volume for the scheduled aircraft. In mixed-mode aircraft, the distribution of the passenger deck is also included in these calculations. Moreover, the usage of various container types for the respective aircraft is shown.

The southern part contains the command line. One can:

☐ Quit the expert system.

☐ Ask for explanations of a proposal, which shows the rules and their hierarchy.

☐ Require investigations (look up of particular airway bills which have to be rescheduled).

☐ Change environmental data.

CARGEX actually supports the segments among Frankfurt, Atlanta, Dallas/Fort Worth, Houston, and Mexico. It contains some 300 rules that are described in about 6000 lines of code. The basic goal of the application of CARGEX is an increased productivity of the consolidation system, which is expressed in two objectives:

☐ Maximize the amount of kilogram chargeable per aircraft. This measure is computed as the sum of the actual weights of the goods and the virtual weights of voluminous goods.

☐ Handle an increasing amount of airfreight business with a substantially smaller increase of consolidation personnel.

CARGEX successfully underwent two field tests at the airline's cargo center in June and December 1987. The tests revealed that in standardized decision situations, which counts for some 90 percent of all cases, CARGEX was able to create a decision quality similar to or in some cases even better than a human expert. Moreover, the consolidation people are convinced that these techniques will help them to handle more applications per period, thus reducing the actual time required for working on really hard problems.

Ready-made (General-purpose) Systems: An Overview

There is an increasing number of software packages that address generic problems troubling people. Such problems range from selecting a wine for complementing a dinner to maintaining software and hardware. Like any other application off-the-shelf packages, these systems have standard features. They do not have a perfect match with specific problems, but they are much cheaper than custom-made systems and can be used instantaneously. Such packages are being developed by vendors of shells or by third-party firms who buy development tools (or shells), develop a knowledge base for a specific application,

TABLE 17.4   Representative Ready-made Expert Systems.

Name	Area	Vendor
FX	Foreign exchange trading	Athena Group, New York, NY
Management Edge, Sales Edge	Management sales, training, advertising	Human Edge, Palo Alto, CA
Negotiation Edge	Personnel, labor relations	Human Edge, Palo Alto, CA
Communications Edge	Management	Human Edge, Palo Alto, CA
Hiring Edge	Personnel management	Human Edge, Palo Alto, CA
Counsellor	Agricultural advice, diagnosis, economic analysis for farmers	ICI Corp., England
Resource 1	Productivity, time management	Resource 1, San Diego, CA
Questware	Selecting PC hardware and software	Dynaquest, Downers Grove, IL
Logician	Electronic design	Daisy Systems, Inc., Atlanta, GA
SMP/Macsyma	Mathematical problem solving	Inference Inc., Los Angeles, CA and Symbolic Inc., Cambridge, MA
Leading-Effectively	Effectiveness, productivity	Thoughtware, Inc., Coconut Grove, FL
Capital-Investment	Capital investment	Palladian, Cambridge, MA
MLES	Manufacturing and logistics	Palladian, Cambridge, MA
Production	An integrated factory management	Carnegie Group, Inc., Pittsburgh, PA
Project-Management	Software project management	Carnegie Group, Inc., Pittsburgh, PA
CAD/CAE/CAM	Automated engineering design	Carnegie Group, Inc., Pittsburgh, PA
Concept	Marketing simulation, consumer behavior, integration DSS/ES	Timeshare Systems, Inc., Minneapolis, MN
PowerPlan	Financial planning	APEX Systems, Inc., Cambridge, MA
Financial-Advisor	Capital budgeting	Palladian, Cambridge, MA
MORE	Selecting potential customers from large lists	American Express, Woburn, MA
TITAN	TI 990 minicomputers	Raidan, Inc., Austin, TX

and then sell it to the end-user. Instead of buying a shell and then developing its own ES using its own experts, the end-user buys computerized expertise. The use of such systems is expanding rapidly in areas ranging from investment (e.g., capital budgeting) and financial planning, to admission decisions in universities. (See Table 17.4 for illustrative examples.)

There is a major limitation to the use of ready-made systems. Since the experts that are employed to build such systems have no idea about the specific circumstances of the end-users, general (and somewhat vague) recommendations tend to be given. Therefore, several of the reviews of these products (especially those that are micro-based) are critical of the ES's value.

On the other hand, these programs, like any other ES, are improving with time, and their quality is expected to rise in the future. Some of the more expensive packages can be modified to fit users' needs more closely as well.

In the following sections we give a brief description of several ready-made packages.

Case 11: Management Edge (from Human Edge, Inc.)

The Management Edge offers a method of understanding and communicating with co-workers, subordinates, and superiors by presenting expert management advice in specific situations.

The program is composed of several steps. First, the user is asked to conduct a self-assessment through a list of 80 statements with which the user can either agree or disagree (see Figure 17.16). This approach is very similar to a standard psychological test like a MMPI (Minnesota Multiphasic Personality Inventory). The administration of the self-assessment enables the computer to "learn" about users and their attitudes and beliefs. Then users can receive advice about (1) a relationship with a subordinate, (2) a relationship with a superior, (3) assessment of the users' managerial skills, and (4) assessment of users' organizations. For each of the four categories, users answer several dozen additional questions.

The assessment given by the system is based on pattern recognition. If the answers of the user show a certain pattern (or profile), a matching assessment

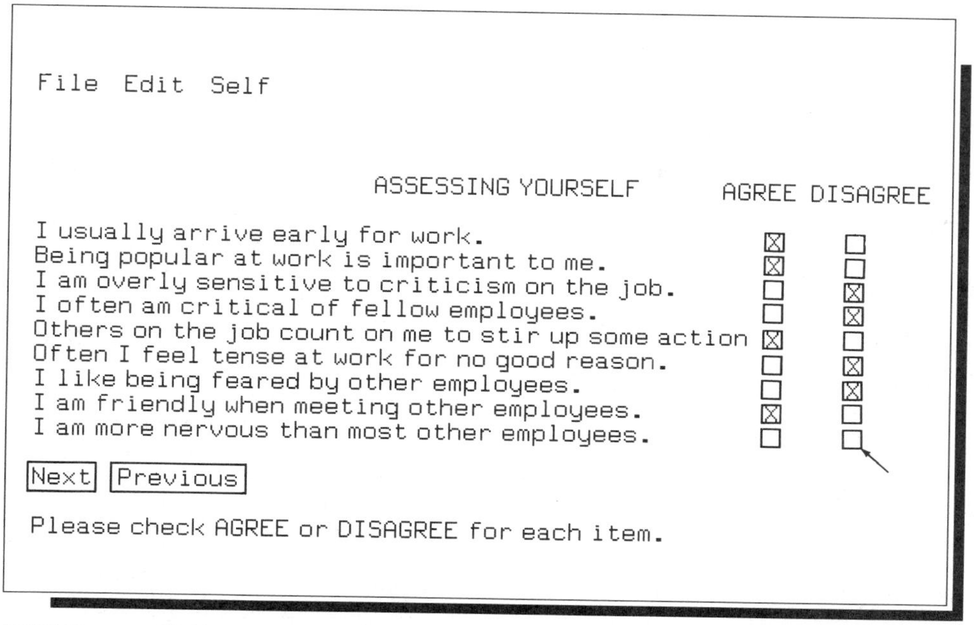

FIGURE 17.16 Self-assessment—sample questions.

```
                                            Agree  Disagree
1. Employee seem to get along very well       ☒       ☐
2. The majority of employees strive to power  ☒       ☐
3. The organization has a goal of high growth ☐       ☒
4. Employees do not socialize among themselves☒       ☐
5. The company can be described as risk-taking☐       ☒
```

FIGURE 17.17 Sample questions concerning an organization.

(or recommendation) is given. There is a limited number of possible computer outputs.

Sample questions for an assessment of the user's organization are shown in Figure 17.17. A typical assessment produced by the computer is shown in Figure 17.18.

```
          * * * * * * * * * * * * * * * * * * *
          *   T H E   M A N A G E M E N T   E D G E    *
          * * * * * * * * * * * * * * * * * * *


                    - - - - - - - - - - - - - - - - - -
                    YOUR ORGANIZATION
                    - - - - - - - - - - - - - - - - - -


You have described your overall organization as stable and
formally organized. Rules and authority tend to be formalized,
and employee responsibilities are well defined. Compliance and
commitment are valued assets. It is likely that you work within
bureaucratic structure. Because of your flexible nature, you will
work well in this organization. Although you might find some
things about a bureaucracy frustrating, in general, you are a
good match for this company.


The organization you work in also values achievement. High
productivity and independent action are emphasized. Individuals
are motivated to succeed through their own hard effort. In this
organization, you will perform to the extent of your capacity. It
is likely that the emphasis placed on achievement will raise your
motivation and productivity. Your reliable and consistent work
habits will help you to succeed in this setting.
```

FIGURE 17.18 The ES output.

Case 12: La-Courtier—Financial Planner

La-Courtier, a system in the financial planning area, stands out as an excellent example of the features that should be expected from most future ready-made, knowledge-based products.[*] La-Courtier is a security portfolio advisory system developed at Cognitive Systems, Inc. (New Haven, CT), for installation in the lobbies of most branches of a major Belgian bank. Its purpose is to provide high-quality investment advice to customers of the bank, without the need for highly paid investment analysis in each branch.

La-Courtier is to be used directly by the bank's customers, whether or not they have used a computer system before. The system, which accepts both conversational French and English input, offers specific recommendations about stock purchases and portfolio distribution and also answers factual questions about the Belgian stock market.

For a new customer, La-Courtier conducts an interview to collect information about the user's financial situation. Then, according to the user's current portfolio distribution practices and current market conditions, La-Courtier gives advice about which stocks to buy or sell.

Although La-Courtier can conduct an interview with a customer and offer investment advice without any prompting from the user, the user may interrupt at any time. The user can then express likes or dislikes or ask questions about an individual stock, the advice given, or investment matters in general. This mixed-initiative user environment is another essential aspect of the meaning of user-friendliness of ES. The system has the expertise to operate in a free-running mode, but its self-determination can always be overridden by the user.

Like a human financial analyst, La-Courtier can give detailed investment advice only if it has a detailed financial profile of the customer. It gives the customer the option of completing a brief or an in-depth financial statement questionnaire, including current investments, assets and liabilities, and cash available for investment.

From this information, La-Courtier may make stock portfolio recommendations or it may determine that, according to its built-in investment policy, the customer's assets are not large enough to warrant investments in the stock market. But the customer can choose to override the system's recommendations. If the customer decides to invest in the stock market despite La-Courtier's recommendations to the contrary, the system will still present recommended stock purchases.

Once a recommendation is made, and it happened to be an electric utility, the customer can say, for example, "I don't want to invest in any utilities." La-Courtier will respond by revising the suggested portfolio to reflect this preference.

One of the more frustrating aspects of traditional query facilities is that they tend to interpret questions too literally and provide insufficient or incomplete answers. ES have the means to discover the real question that is being asked and to provide a meaningful answer. La-Courtier, for example, uses its knowledge of the market to provide helpful answers to ques-

[*]Based on information provided by the developer (6).

tions where a simple yes or no might be adequate. For example, a customer might ask, "Shouldn't I buy SGB?" A simple yes or no could be adequate, but La-Courtier is more likely to respond with a statement like this: "Soc. Gen. de Banque (SGB) would not be a bad investment (it has average market performance); however, Kredietbank would make a better investment in the banking sector."

As another example, assume the database includes only current price and earnings data for the last quarter. Assume also that a customer has asked for a five-year history of price and earnings for SGB. Database query systems are likely to tell the user the question cannot be answered. In contrast, the knowledge-based system is aware that it can't answer the question as asked but can answer some part of it. Its belief system suggests that some part of the total answer is better than no answer at all.

La-Courtier would produce an answer like "I do not yet have historical data available. However, these current data may be useful: the current price-to-earnings ratio for SGB is 6.3."

Miscellaneous Ready-made Expert Systems

Wheat Counsellor. This system, which was developed by ICI in England, advises on the control of disease in winter wheat, including recommendations on which chemicals to use when treating crop diseases. Because ICI markets many agrichemicals, it is in its interest to ensure that farmers use them correctly.

Wheat Counsellor first evaluates the risks of fungal diseases in a crop by asking for information about the variety of wheat being grown, its location, the soil type, local weather, and so on. It then draws on crop-growth data from several organizations, and states the expected loss if no treatement is given. Next, Wheat Counsellor examines the range of fungicides sold by ICI and other manufacturers, and recommends treatment from this range. Finally, it provides costing for these, and states the likely return on investment.

Wheat Counsellor is interesting because it is attached to videotex. The expert system itself runs on a PDP 11. ICI uses a private videotex system called Grapevine, which is similiar to the public British system Prestel. An ordinary telephone is sufficient to connect an adaped television set or other terminal to Grapevine; Wheat Counsellor can then interact with that terminal.

Wheat Counsellor provides the usual explanation facilities. Because it is used by computer-naive users, ICI has taken care to make its output comprehensible.

Capital Investment. This system (by Palladian, Inc.) helps managers make capital investment decisions. Using a wide range of sophisticated financial techniques, the system can help the user evaluate new product proposals, capacity expansion plans, and cost reduction proposals; decide between equipment make/buy and lease/buy situations; and assess major strategic acquisitions and investments.

This Palladian system also explains how it arrives at each step in an analysis. Like expert consultants, the system tests every input assumption and conclusion against an extensive knowledge of general business practice, such as the user's company policies, its accounting and management practices, its historical performance, and its competition.

Finally, the Capital Investment System comes with no user's reference manual, because there is no need for users to operate or understand the system. It can be considered a DSS/ES combination.

Buying Computer Hardware and Software. A system for advising on a purchase of computer software and hardware is available from Dynaquest Corp. The system, called Questware, is being expanded for diagnostic sessions regarding computer systems. The advice is given only online via the telephone lines.

College Admission. MIKE, developed by the Mandell Institute (Storrs, CT), is the automated admissions representative of Brandeis University. Built to expand the pool of high-quality applicants for that school, MIKE is designed to be used by high school seniors who are narrowing their choice of colleges.

MIKE not only explains all the academic and extracurricular programs in which the prospective applicant has an interest, but also uses his video-base to take the student on a tour of the campus. Once he has the student's interest, he will even give feedback concerning the likelihood of admission and type and amount of financial aid. At this point, the student's name and address are taken for transmission to the campus-based computer for follow-up.

A new, enhanced MIKE will be able to do detailed financial aid planning with prospective applicants and their parents and will even output a customized catalogue for students. This catalogue will focus on the areas in which the student showed the greatest interest, in the judgement of MIKE.

Fair-Cost. This sytem, by DM Data, Inc., Scottsdale Ariz, provides an interactive planning aid for strategic planning, system costing, engineering, and purchasing involved in obtaining custom VLSI circuits for electronic systems.

FX: A Foreign Exchange Expert Advisory System. This system, from the Athena Group, New York, NY, advises on foreign exchange trading activity. It supports a number of different analysis techniques and provides probabilistic decision support. Thus it can be considered a DSS/ES combination. The system contains several trading, hedging, and risk-control strategies.

PM and SO. These packages, from the Athena Group, New York, NY, helps stock portfolio management (PM) and stock option (SO) strategies.

PEANUT. PEANUT is an irrigation management ES written with EXSYS and being tested in the southeastern United States. The user supplies soil type, growth stage of the peanut plant, and general information about the soil temperature, the amount of water applied, and the predicted weather. The system responds with a recommendation to irrigate or not, and gives extensive information telling why the decision was reached. It also uses the same input to issue warnings if conditions indicate possible problems with pests. For more information, contact United States Department of Agriculture, Peanut Reasearch Laboratory, Dawson, GA, or USDA, Agricultural Research Services, Temple, TX.

Wines on Disk. This ready-made ES (from Paperback Software, Berkeley, CA) provides advice on how to select American Wines to suit any occasion. The wine inventory includes 600 choices and the expert is Anthony Dias Blue, an internationally acknowledged wine expert.

The ES will advise about the wine's varietal, vineyard, year, price range, rating, and tasting comments. It is available for $39.95 in many liquor stores and vineyards.

Summary and Conclusion

The various case applications discussed in this chapter present a diversified sample of ES developed over the last few years in several organizations. Most of these systems are pure rule-based systems. Some include an explanation facility. Most were constructed with shells or some construction packages. This is where the similiarity among these systems ends. Each system was constructed for a different purpose and therefore exhibits unique characteristics. The questions for discussion that follow are designed to explore some of the similarities and differences among the systems.

Questions for Discussion

1. Discuss the complexity of the job executed by XCON.
2. Consult the ten generic areas of expert systems (Chapter 12), and relate each of the systems in this chapter to one (or more) of the areas.
3. What tasks does XCON perform better or faster than a human?
4. It is said that most knowledge can be presented as rules. Review all the cases in this chapter and identify all the rule-based systems. Also identify the systems that use presentations other than rules (or in addition to rules). Do you think that most knowledge can be represented as rules? Why or why not?
5. Review the eight lessons learned in XCON. Why are they important?
6. What is a real-time expert system? Why is XCON not such a system?
7. Both YES/MVS and ISIS deal with scheduling problems in a manufacturing environment. What are the similarities and differences between the systems?
8. Relate ISIS to the topic of visual simulaton (see Chapter 18).
9. Discuss some of the advantages and disadvantages of rule induction in a shell such as "Expert Ease." Describe a situation in which rules cannot be authored by a computer.
10. Follow the development process of COMPASS. Compare it with the process suggested in Chapter 12. What phases in the process can be identified in this case?
11. Review all the cases and identify those systems constructed with shells. List the shells and review the reasons (whenever possible) why these shells were selected. Which of the systems were constructed from scratch? Why?
12. Identify the iterative approach in the systems in this chapter. Prepare a table that lists the cases where the iterative process is described and explain how the initial prototyping was expanded.

13. Rapid prototyping is an essential approach in developing ES. Why is this so? In what cases is there evidence of rapid prototyping?
14. Most systems described in this chapter were executed in very large corporations or in research institutions. This situation is changing now and an ES can be economically developed in a small business. What caused the change?
15. Several of the systems described in this chapter were developed as a joint venture of two partners. List all the systems that were constructed in this way, identify the nature of the partners, and assess the potential benefits to each of them.
16. Some people believe that the Management Edge is not an expert system. Others say that this is a typical rule-based system and an explanation capability can be easily added. What do you think?
17. What are the similarities between the Management Edge and La-Courtier? What are the differences?
18. Relate the major benefits of ES to the systems described in this chapter. Fill the following table with check marks to designate a capability-system relationship. (Add more benefits and more systems to the table.)

Capabilities

System	Increase Productivity	Increase Quality	Preserve Expertise		
MYCIN XCON PROSPECTOR : : : :					

19. Why may ES help in hostage-taking incidents?
20. Why is the ES currently good only for training and not for actual use (in Case 8)?
21. How can one justify the need for an ES for case 9?
22. Why is EXSYS (small rule-based system) sufficient in this Case (9)?
23. Is CARGEX an ES or ES/DSS? Explain.

References and Bibliography

1. Bennett, J. S., and R. S. Englemore. "SACON: A Knowledge-Based Consultant for Structural Analysis." *IJCA*, Vol. 179, 1979.
2. Buchanan, B. G., and E. H. Shortliffe. *Rule-Based Expert Programs. The MYCIN Experiments of the Stanford Heuristic Programming Project*. Reading, MA: Addison-Wesley, 1981.
3. Fox, M. S., and S. F. Smith. "ISIS—A Knowledge-Based System for Factory Scheduling." *Expert System*, Vol. 1, No. 1, 1984.
4. Goyal, S. K., et al. "COMPASS: An Expert System for Telephone Switch Maintenance." *Expert Systems*, July 1985.
5. IBM. "Artificial Intelligence Topics of IBM." *IBM Research Highlight*, vol. 2, 1984, IBM Research Division Lab., San Jose, CA.
6. McDermott, J. "R1 Revisited: Four Years in the Trenches." *AI Magazine*, Fall 1984.
7. O'Connor, D. E. "Using Expert Systems to Manage Change and Complexity in Manufacturing." In W. Reitman, ed. *Artificial Intelligence Application for Business*. Norwood, NJ: ABLEX, 1984.

8. Shamoon, S. "The 'Expert' That Thinks Like an Underwriter." *Management Technology*, February 1985.

9. Vedder, R. G., and R. O. Mason. "An Expert System Application For Decision Support In Law Enforcement." *Decision Sciences*, Summer 1987.

10. Waterman, D. *A Guide to Expert Systems*. Reading, MA: Addison-Wesley, 1986.

APPENDIX A: Representative List of Commercial ES Applications

Financial Services

- ☐ Claim estimation.
- ☐ Credit analysis.
- ☐ Tax advisor.
- ☐ Financial statement analysis.
- ☐ Financial planning advisor.
- ☐ Retail bank services advisor.

Data Processing and MIS

- ☐ Front-end to statistical analysis package.
- ☐ Front-end to a large software package (several applications).
- ☐ Database management system selection.
- ☐ Software services consultant.

Finance and Administration

- ☐ Legal analysis of contract claims.
- ☐ Loan application assistant for school administrators.
- ☐ Performance evaluation of dealerships.
- ☐ Conflict-of-interest consultant.
- ☐ Inventory management advisor.

Manufacturing

- ☐ Maintenance advisor for multimillion-dollar hydraulic system.
- ☐ Continuous-process manufacturing advisor.
- ☐ Tooling selection for machining (several applications).
- ☐ Drilling advisor for machining.
- ☐ Material selection (chemical).
- ☐ Procedure advisor for oil well drilling operations (several applications).
- ☐ Electrical system fault diagnosis.
- ☐ Gas turbine engine fault diagnosis.
- ☐ Electronic equipment fault diagnosis (several applications).
- ☐ Power supply fault diagnosis.
- ☐ Mechanical equipment fault diagnosis (several applications).

- ☐ Refinery process control.
- ☐ Sensor verification for power generation equipment.

Field Service

- ☐ Software system troubleshooter.
- ☐ Fault diagnosis of electronic systems from event traces (several applications).
- ☐ Fault diagnosis of automotive subsystems (several applications).
- ☐ Computer network fault diagnosis.

Education

- ☐ Problem diagnosis training aid.
- ☐ Speech pathology advisor.
- ☐ Test result interpreter.
- ☐ Worksheet generation based on students' prior performance.
- ☐ Student behavior consultant.
- ☐ Learning disability classification advisor.
- ☐ Textbook selection advisor.

Sales and Marketing

- ☐ Selection of components from an engineering catalog.
- ☐ Qualification of sales leads.

Engineering

- ☐ Design of motor components (outputs engineering drawings).
- ☐ Fastener selection (several applications).
- ☐ Material selection for manufacturing process (several applications).
- ☐ Front-end for complex computer simulation program.
- ☐ Front-end for engineering design package.
- ☐ Engineering change order manager.
- ☐ Weight estimator for evolving designs.
- ☐ Statistical analysis tool selector.
- ☐ Front-end to structural analysis software system.
- ☐ Construction project planning and evaluation.
- ☐ Structural analysis of buildings.
- ☐ Sensor interpretation for drilling.
- ☐ Robot sensor interpretation.

Source: TRANSFER, IJCAI Show Edition, Teknowlege, Inc., August 1985.

Note: For additional list of systems see:

1) Walker T. C., and R. K. MIller, *Expert Systems 1987, An Assessment of Technology and Applications*, SEAI Tech. Pub., 1987, and

2) *The CRI Directory of Expert Systems*, Learned Information Systems, Medford, NJ, 1986.

Chapter 18

User Interface

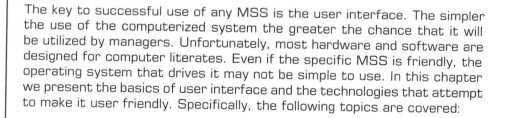

The key to successful use of any MSS is the user interface. The simpler the use of the computerized system the greater the chance that it will be utilized by managers. Unfortunately, most hardware and software are designed for computer literates. Even if the specific MSS is friendly, the operating system that drives it may not be simple to use. In this chapter we present the basics of user interface and the technologies that attempt to make it user friendly. Specifically, the following topics are covered:

645

18.1 Introduction

Most MSS users have limited computer experience.[*] These users are not prepared to learn the computer-oriented details typically required of experienced users and often expect to walk up and use the promised power as easily as they might drive a rented car. But the operating systems and other software supporting MSS applications were developed for users accustomed to carrying out complicated tasks. Meeting the needs of users who demand power without complication has made industry increasingly sensitive to the design of the user interface.

Defining The User Interface. The user interface may be thought of as a surface through which data are passed back and forth between user and computer. Physical aspects of the user interface (Figure 18.1) include the display devices, audio devices that may be used, and input devices such as tablet, joystick, mouse, microphone, or keyboard.

Data displayed on the workstation provide a context for interaction, giving cues for user action (we assume that the user knows how to interpret what is displayed). The user formulates a response and takes an action. Data then pass back to the computer through the interface. In this concept, all aspects of the system that are known to the user are defined at the interface.[**] The quality of the interface, from the user perspective, depends on what the user sees (or senses), what the user must know in order to understand what is sensed, and what actions the user can (or must) take to obtain needed results. The following cyclical process is shown in Figure 18.1:

1. *Presentation language.* This is the information displayed to the user. It can be shown as display menus, windows, or text. It can be static or

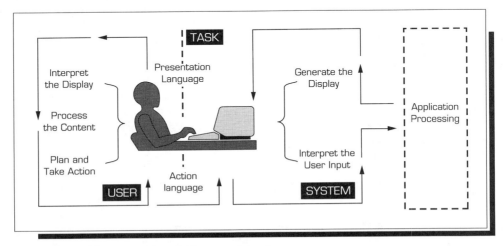

FIGURE 18.1 The two sides of the user interface.

[*]The remainder of this section has been condensed from Bennet (3). Copyright 1986, International Business Machines Corp. Reprinted with permission from *IBM Systems Journal.*
[**]For an overview of interface issues in expert systems see the October 1988 issue of *AI Expert.*

dynamic, numerical or symbolic. It can appear on the CRT as voice or as print.

2. *The user's reaction.* The user interprets the display, processes the content, and plans an action.

3. *The action language.* The user's action can take various shapes. He or she can select an item from the menu, answer a question, move a display window, or type in a command. He or she can use one or more input devices.

4. *The computer.* The computer interprets the user action (input), executes a task (e.g., computation), and generates a display that is basically the presentation language, or the output of the computer.

These elements can be designed and executed in different manners. The presentation/action language combination is referred to as an interactive or (dialog) style.

18.2 Interface Modes (Styles)

Interface modes refer to the interactive communication between the user and a computer. The interface mode determines how information is displayed on the monitor and how information is entered into the computer, as well as the ease and simplicity of learning the system and using it. The topic appears under several names, such as dialog styles, dialog modes, and conversational formats.

The following styles are presented in this section: menu interaction, command language, questions and answers, form interaction, natural language, and object manipulation.

Menu Interaction. The user selects from a list of possible choices (the menu) the one he or she wants to perform, for example, what report to produce or what analysis to run. The choice is made by use of input devices ranging from a remote control infrared device to a keyboard. Menus appear in a logical order, starting with a main menu, and going on to submenus.

Menu items can include commands. They appear in separate submenus, or they are mixed up with noncommand items. The use of Lotus 1-2-3, IFPS, EXSYS, and VP Expert, which were described earlier, involve extensive use of commands that are a part of a menu.

The use of menus may become too tedious and time consuming when complex situations are analyzed since many items appear in several menus and the user must shift back and forth among several menus.

Command Language. The user enters a command such as "run" or "plot." Many commands are composed of a verb-noun combination (e.g., "plot sales"). Some commands can be executed with the function keys (F1 ... F10) on the keyboard. Another way to simplify commands (or even a series of commands), is the use of macros, described in Chapter 6.

Question and Answer. The computer asks the user a question. The user answers the question with a phrase or a sentence. The computer may prompt the user for clarification and/or additional input. The dialog may involve a large number of questions, some of which result from previous answers. A question may involve the presentation of a menu from which the answer is to be selected. In certain MSS the sequence of questioning may be reversed. The user may ask a question and the computer gives an answer.

Form Interaction.   The user enters data or commands into designated spaces (fields) in forms. The headings of the form (or the report or the table) serve as a prompt for the input. The computer may produce some output as a result, and the user may be requested to continue the form interaction process.

Natural Language.   A human-computer dialog, which is similar to a human-human dialog, is referred to as natural language. Such a dialog will be conducted, in the future, using voice as input and output. Today, natural language dialog is done by using the keyboard. The problem of using natural language is essentially the inability of the computer to *understand* natural language (such as English or Japanese). However, as will be seen in Sections 18.3 and 18.4, advances in AI enable limited natural language dialog. For example, natural language processors are being used to access databases (Section 18.5).

Object Manipulation.   Objects, usually represented as icons (or symbols) can be directly manipulated by the user. For example, the user can use the mouse or the cursor to point at an icon, and then use a command to move it, enlarge it, or show the details behind the object.

Several studies were conducted to determine the efficiency and accuracy of the various styles. Majchrzak et al. (14) summarize the research in this area and also evaluate the usability of four of the styles along four dimensions (see Table 18.1. The last three dimensions in the table were added by the author).

TABLE 18.1 Comparison of Interface Modes.

Dimensions	Menu	Fill-in-the blanks	Command	Object Manipulation
Speed	Slow at times	Moderate	Fast	Could be slow
Accuracy	Error-free	Moderate	Many errors	Error-free
Training time	Short	Moderate	Long	Short
Users' preference	Very high	Low	Prefer, if trained (only)	High
Power	Low	Low	Very high	Moderate-high
Flexibility	Limited	Very limited	Very high	Moderate-high
Control	The system	The system	The user	The system and the user

Source: Based in part on Majchrzak et al. (14).

> ## Paperlike Interface
>
> Researchers at IBM are exploring a way to use computers in which people simply write on a flat surface. The user writes with a kind of "electronic ink." Then, handwriting-recognition software instantly translates the writing and other hand-drawn marks, mathematical symbols, and even musical notes into words, numbers, and commands for the computer.

Several other interface modes are being developed (see boxed material). Natural language processing, the subject of the next three sections, when complemented with voice recognition, would probably be the most preferred style by MSS users of the future.

18.3 Natural Language Processing—Overview

Natural language processing (NLP) refers to communicating with a computer in English or whatever language you may speak.[*] Today, we communicate with a computer through special codes or languages. To tell a computer what to do, we type in terse commands by keyboard or enter programs in a special language designed for creating software. In responding to a user, the computer outputs symbols or short cryptic notes of information or direction.

To use a computer properly, you must learn the commands, languages, and jargon. This usually takes considerable time and practice. It is the main reason why computers have been called unfriendly. Menus and icons with pointing devices like light pens, mouse, and touch screens help, of course, but they are not perfectly natural.

Many problems could be minimized or even eliminated if we could communicate with the computer in our own language. No special commands or languages would have to be learned or used. We would simply type in directions, instructions, or information in any convenient form. The computer would be smart enough to interpret the input regardless of its format. An even better alternative would be to give the computer voice instructions.

Natural language processing can also help us to cope with *information overload*. Books and other printed sources, television, radio, and human conversation bombard us daily. There is so much information available to us that we have no good way to absorb it all and use it. As a result, a lot of good information goes to waste.

Information overload is frustrating and wasteful, but there are ways to deal with it. Once information is collected, it can be sorted, categorized, and otherwise organized to provide access to it. The information may be put into a

[*]Major portions of the next three sections are taken from *Crash Course in Artificial Intelligence and Expert Systems*, by Louis E. Frenzel Jr.; Reproduced with the permission of the publisher, Howard W. Sams & Co., ©1986.

database management system or even an expert system. The information may be converted to knowledge and conveniently made available.

Database management systems and expert systems both provide a means of conveniently accessing information and knowledge, but difficult computer techniques often must be used. Special query languages are required to obtain information from a database. Most expert systems have a less than optimum user interface. In both cases, NLP will make such systems much easier to use.

NLP can be viewed as a special type of knowledge-based system. To understand a natural language inquiry, a computer must have knowledge to analyze, then interpret the input. This knowledge may include linguistic knowledge about words, domain knowledge, common sense knowledge, and even knowledge about the users and their goals. NLP must understand grammar and the definitions of words. AI techniques are used to represent the internal knowledge and process the inputs. Several search and pattern-matching techniques may be used along with the knowledge to provide understanding. Once the computer understands the input, it can take the desired action.

In addition to *natural language understanding*, there is also *natural language generation*. Once the computer takes action, it will usually provide some output. In many cases it is desirable to provide that output in natural language. For that reason, the computer must be able to generate appropriate natural language, and the easiest way to do this is to provide "canned" sentences, phrases, paragraphs, or other outputs. When a particular input is detected, an appropriate output response is accessed and delivered. More sophisticated techniques for generating natural language output are also available.

In this chapter we are going to talk about natural language processing software, the programs that understand and generate natural language inputs and outputs. We will also cover the practical applications of such software. Finally, we will consider voice recognition systems.

18.4   Natural Language Processing—Methods

Introduction

NLP is an attempt to allow computers to interpret normal statements expressed in a natural human language, such as English or Japanese. The process of speech recognition (see Section 18.6), in contrast, attempts to translate the human voice into individual words and sentences understandable by the computer. Combining speech recognition and NLP will be required to realize the capability of the computer to converse in a manner normal to humans.

All prior computer languages (excluding 4GLs) have been sets of commands that had to be executed in a specified sequence or according to a procedure defined by the programmer. These are used for manipulating data in files, extracting information from a database, doing word processing, executing spreadsheet calculations, and performing other similar data processing activities. In other words, all those languages involve ways to "write a program" that give relatively explicit instructions and procedures on how to perform the operations.

With NLP, the computer's "understanding" of human statements may or may not be translated into a "program." It could just as easily be translated into another language. The most advanced fourth-generation languages today use the early results of NLP research, but their abilities are still quite limited compared with the ultimate goals of NLP.

Presently two major techniques are used in NLP programs: *Key word search* (pattern matching) and *language processing* (syntactical and semantic analysis). Other methods such as the use of neural computing and the method of conceptual dependency are in research stage and will not be covered here.

The natural language input to a computer comes from the user by way of the keyboard. Future technology, however, will make NLP much more powerful when a voice input/output will be added.

Key Word Analysis (Pattern Matching)

In this process, the NLP program searches through an input sentence looking for key words or phrases. The program is able to identify only selected words and phrases. Once a key word or phrase is recognized, the program responds with specific "canned" responses.

Alternately, the program may actually construct a response based on a partial reply coupled with the key word or selected phrases from the input. The program recognizes very specific inputs that it uses to construct an output response or initiate some other action.

Figure 18.2 shows a flow chart of the basic procedures that a key word NLP program uses to understand input sentences. The flow chart uses standard symbols: a rectangle represents some particular processing action carried out by a subroutine or segment of the program. The diamond symbol represents a decision point with yes and no responses. Let's work through the flow chart to be sure you understand how key word processing works.

The program usually starts by displaying a message on the screen to elicit some input response from the user. The user's response is accepted by the program and stored in an input buffer.

Next, the program scans the input text searching for a key word. The program can tell where one word ends and another begins by looking for spaces and punctuation marks. As each word is identified, it is used in a pattern-matching processing that compares it to a list of prestored words and phrases.

Since you want the program to be able to respond to random natural language input, a considerable number of words with their synonyms and variations will have to be stored if you wish to recognize the input text.

Each word in the input text string is matched against those in the key word directory stored in the program. The diamond element in the flow chart labeled "keyword found?" has two output paths, depending on the outcome of this search. The first possibility is that no key word is located. If that is the case, the program is set up to respond with one or more stock messages (e.g., "please rephrase your message"), then the process continues for all key words. This process may continue for several iterations until an appropriate word is recognized.

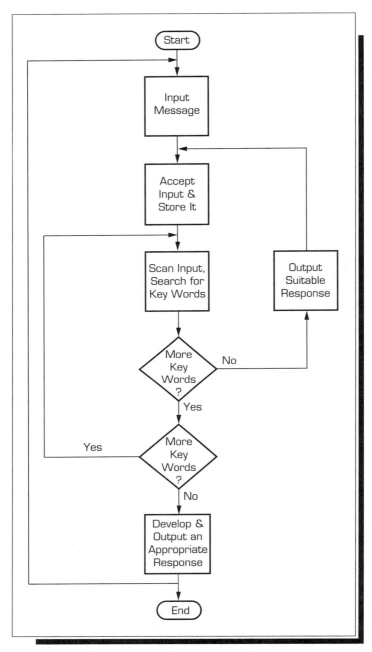

FIGURE 18.2 The process of key word analysis.

When a key word is located, (the second possibility) it is flagged or marked so that it can be used to select an appropriate "canned" response or can be used in an assembled response.

Example. Let's assume that a user requested the computer to *identify* all *employees* who *make* above *$50,000*. The *italicized* words are the key words. The following is a possible dialog between the computer (C) and the user (U).

C: By "identify" do you mean "list"?
U: Yes
C: By "make" do you mean model?
U: No
C: Please rephrase the word *make*
U: I mean whose salaries

Note: Now the word *salaries* has been identified as a key word.

C: By salaries do you mean annual salaries?
U: Yes.

Note: The NLP has now identified all the key words.

Finally, an appropriate output response is selected or developed and sent to the user. An interesting key word matching program is ELIZA. (Ask your teacher to demonstrate it to you). Using ELIZA it is easy to see both the capabilities and the limitations of NLP.

Language Processing (Syntactic, Semantic, and Pragmatic Analysis)

Introduction. While key word pattern matching is a widely used natural language technique, its usefulness is restricted because it simply cannot deal with the large variations in language that naturally occur. For that reason, AI researchers have looked for and developed more sophisticated ways of analyzing an input sentence and extracting meaning from it.

The most obvious and straightforward approach to the problem is to perform a detailed analysis of the syntax and semantics of an input statement. In this way, the exact structure of an input sentence and its meaning can be determined. Of course, this is easier said than done. Even sophisticated systems for analyzing the syntax and semantics fall short of the job, because *there are too many words with multiple meanings* (such as "can," "will," and "class") and an enormous number of ways to put those together to form sentences.

Example: The following is one question rephrased in five different ways:

☐ How many nonstop flights are there from Phoenix to Boston?
☐ Do you have any nonstop flights from Phoenix to Boston?
☐ I would like to go from Phoenix to Boston without any layovers.
☐ What planes leave Phoenix and get to Boston without stopping?
☐ It's important that I find a nonstop Phoenix–Boston flight.

All the phrases just given request the same information, but they are syntactically dissimilar. A NLP can determine, through questions such as "do you mean to say . . ." exactly what the question is.

Definitions. Before we get into the step-by-step details of natural language processors, let's take a look at the individual units of the input we have to work with. First, the basic unit of the English language is the sentence. A sentence expresses a complete thought, asks a question, gives a command, or makes an exclamation. The sentence, of course, is made up of individual units known as words. The words have meaning and when they are linked together in various ways; their relationships represent ideas, thoughts, and visual images.

User Interface

The individual words, besides having a meaning of their own, also fall into various categories known as parts of speech. As you recall from your English language classes, there are eight different parts of speech including: nouns, pronouns, verbs, adjectives, adverbs, prepositions, conjunctions, and interjections. Every word is classified as one of these parts of speech.

Syntax analysis looks at the way a sentence is built, the arrangement of its components and their relationships. Syntactic processes analyze and designate sentences to make the grammatical relationships between words in sentences clear. *Semantics* is concerned with assigning meaning to the various syntactic constituents. *Pragmatics* attempts to relate individual sentences to one another and to the surrounding context. The boundaries separating these levels are not distinct. In particular, sentences need not pass through these levels of interpretation sequentially. Research is continuing into how to integrate information from any level when it is needed.

How Natural Language Processing Works.   Although there are two different types of natural language systems, one in which you type English sentences free-form and another in which you pick words and phrases out of menu windows, the inner workings are fundamentally the same. In simple terms, a natural language system deciphers the parts of speech and action in a common sentence and then translates them into application commands, or into a compiled program language, so that the computer can respond.

Figure 18.3 shows a simplified block diagram of the major elements in a natural language processing program. The five major elements are: the parser, the lexicon, the understander, the knowledge base, and the generator. Let's look at each of these major elements in detail.

The parser. The key element in a natural language system is the parser. It is a piece of software that analyzes the input sentence syntactically. Each word is identified and its part of speech clarified. The parser then maps the words into a structure called a parse tree. The parse tree shows the meanings of all of the words and how they are assembled. This syntactical analysis is the first step toward trying to extract meaning from the sentence.

Recall that a sentence (S) is made up of a subject or noun phrase (NP) and a predicate or verb phrase (VP). We show this as:

$$S = NP + VP$$

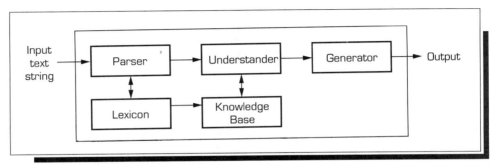

FIGURE 18.3 General block diagram of a natural language understanding program of the syntax/semantic analysis type.

The noun phrase could be a single noun, but it usually breaks down further into several additional parts of speech, such as an article (ART) or determiner (D) like "a", "this", or an adjective (ADJ) and the main noun. We show it like this:

$$NP = D + ADJ + N$$

The noun phrase may even have a prepositional phrase (PP) made up of a preposition (P) such as "of" or "with" and another determiner and a noun:

$$PP = P + D + N$$

The verb phrase (VP) is made up of the verb (V) and often the object of the verb, which is usually another noun (N) and its determiner. A prepositional phrase may also be associated with the verb phrase. It might be represented as:

$$VP = V + D + N + PP$$

Of course, there are many other variations.

The lexicon. In order to perform the semantic analysis, the parser needs a dictionary. This dictionary is called the *lexicon*.

The lexicon contains all of the words that the program is capable of recognizing. The lexicon also contains the correct spelling of each word and its role in a sentence. For words that can have more than one meaning, the lexicon lists all of the various meanings permitted by the system.

The parser and the lexicon work together to pick apart a sentence and then create the parse tree, a new data structure that helps to get at the real meaning of the sentence. But even though the various parts of speech have been identified and the sentence has been fully analyzed syntactically, the computer still does not understand it. As a result, the need for semantic analysis becomes essential.

In operation, the parser is largely a pattern matcher. Once the individual word has been identified, the parser searches through the lexicon, comparing each input word with all of the words stored there. If a match is found, the word is put aside along with the other lexical information, such as part of speech and meaning. The parser then goes on to analyze additional words and ultimately builds the parse tree.

During this process, the parser can also take care of general housekeeping activities such as misspelled words.

Once the parse tree has been constructed, the system is ready for semantic analysis to obtain further meaning.

The understander and knowledge base. Semantic analysis is the function of the understander block in Figure 18.3. The understander works in conjunction with the knowledge base to determine what the sentence means.

In order to determine what is meant by an input sentence, the system must know things about words and how they are put together to form meaningful statements. The knowledge base is the primary means of understanding what has been said.

The purpose of the understander is to use the parse tree to reference the knowledge base. The understander can also draw inferences from the input statement. Many English sentences do not tell the whole story directly, but we are able to infer the meaning from our general knowledge.

The generator. The generator uses the understood input to create a usable output. The understander creates another data structure that represents the meaning and understanding of the sentence and stores it in memory. That data structure can be used to initiate additional action. If the NLP is part of an interface or a front-end, the data structure will be used to create special codes to control another piece of software. It may give the software commands needed to initiate some action. For example, in a DBMS, the generator would write a program in a query language to begin a search for specific information.

In its simplest form, the natural language generator feeds standard pre-stored output responses to the user based on the meaning extracted from the input. However, more sophisticated generators will construct an original response from scratch.

18.5 Applications of Natural Language Processing and Software

Natural language processing programs have been applied in several areas. The most important are:

- □ NLP interfaces.
- □ Abstracting and summarizing text.
- □ Grammar analysis.
- □ Translation of a natural language to another natural language (e.g., English to German).
- □ Translation of a computer language to another computer language.
- □ Speech understanding.

The first application is discussed in this section and the last one in the following section. For information on the other applications see Frenzel (7).

Natural language interfaces. By far the most predominant use of NLP is in interfaces of "front-ends" for other software packages. Such interfaces are used to simplify and improve the communications between the applications program and the user. Many programs are complex and difficult to use. They require learning a special language or set of commands. This takes a lot of time and effort and frequently puts off the user.

The natural language front-end allows the user to operate the applications programs with everyday language. Even the most inexperienced users can take advantage of the applications software.

The reason why NLP can be very helpful is demonstrated in Figure 18.4. The inverted triangle represents the number of people in each language category and their required training. The computer languages are listed on the right side. DSS languages are in the middle of the triangle, ranging from PL/1 and APL to RAMIS II and FOCUS (fourth-generation computer languages). The natural language interface is aimed at users who do not know (or do not want to know) formal computer languages but still want to use the computer. Typical users in this category are managers, doctors, lawyers, and other professionals. It should be noted, however, that only a few existing ES have natural language interfaces

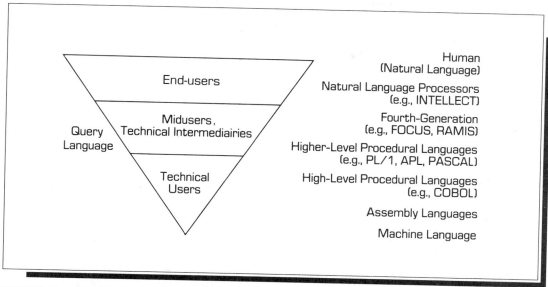

FIGURE 18.4 Market for natural language. (*Source:* Adapted from Harris [8].)

as front-ends; they usually have a *structured* questions and answers dialog. Because natural language front-end systems such as Intellect and Clout have been successfully applied to accessing complex databases, it seems reasonable to assume that they will become an integral part of many MSS.

Natural language front-ends make the software transparent to the user. Because users do not have to learn or worry about special languages or procedures, they can focus on the job, not on the process of getting it done. This will permit computer illiterate managers, executives, and other busy people to use the computer. Further, NLP will help open up the corporate mainframe database to users other than data processing programmers.

Although natural language front-ends are being created for a wide variety of applications programs, their most common use is with DBMS.

To access information, the DBMS must be given instructions to tell it what kind of information to access. Different operations may have to be performed to access the information, including searching and sorting. Some editing is also required to put the information into the final desired output format. This is usually accomplished with a special language called a query language. It is made up of special commands and instructions that are listed sequentially to form a program that will access the data you want in the format you want. This makes most DBMS hard to use.

Today many DBMS software packages include a natural language front-end or offer one as an option.

Natural Language Processing Software for Interfacing

Many NLP software packages are available on the market, both for mainframe and some for micros (for a representative list see Table 18.2). A brief description of some of these products follows:

TABLE 18.2 Representative Natural Language Processors.

Natural Language System	General Function	Specific Area
LADDER	Machine Translation/Interfacing	Ship Identification and Location
SAM	Machine Translation/Interfacing	Generic Story Understanding
ELLIE	Interfacing	Database Management System
SHRDLU	Interfacing	Location and Manipulation of Three-dimensional Figures
EXPLORER	Interfacing	Map Generation and Display, Mainframe
INTELLECT	Interfacing	Database Management, Mainframe
NATURALLINK	Interfacing	Dow Jones Data Retrieval and Display
TEAMS	Generic Interfacing	Database Management
MARKETEER	Interfacing	Market Analysis
POLITICS	Inference Making	Ideological Belief System Simulation
BROKER	Interfacing	Standard & Poor's Data Base Management System
STRAIGHT TALK	Interfacing	Word Processing/Microcomputer Workstations
THEMIS (Spock)	Interfacing	Database Management System, Minicomputers
CLOUT	Interfacing	R:base 5000
K-CHAT	Integrating/interfacing	Knowledge Man, GURU
RAMIS II English	Interfacing	RAMIS II
HAL	Interfacing	Spreadsheet (Lotus 1-2-3)

Source: Andriole, S.J., "The Promise of Artificial Intelligence," *Journal of Systems Management*, July, 1985. (Expanded)

Intellect (from Artificial Intelligence Corp.).

One of the oldest and most widely used natural language front-ends is Intellect, which is a complete natural language interface for large mainframe computers. It is designed primarily to be used with DBMS that operate in the IBM operating systems environments.

In addition to being able to access data in a DBMS, Intellect allows the user to *create* databases using natural language. The built-in lexicon may be modified to fit a particular application. A lexicon editor allows the user to build and maintain special dictionaries for special uses. Unique words and their meanings or synonyms can be added to the lexicon. In this way, you can customize Intellect to the application. Intellect is available in a configuration that uses query languages (e.g., FOCUS) for large DBMS. Intellect allows the user to enter natural English statements and then converts them into the command structure of the query language which, in turn, accesses the desired data.

Spock (from Frey Associates, Inc.).

Spock (previously Themis) is used for Digital Equipment Corporation's VAX family of minicomputers. The system is designed to interface with DEC DBMS/32 database software. Versions are also available to work with other minicomputers which use the Oracle DBMS.

Clout (from Microrim, Inc. Bellevue, WA). Clout by Microrim is a front-end designed to be used with Microrim's popular R:Base 4000 and 5000 relational DBMS. It comes with a basic dictionary of 300 commonly used terms for accessing data and specifying relationships. The user can add up to 500 additional terms. Clout makes it extremely easy to tap the information in the database.

For instance, a user may want to look at some customer files. By using natural language, he can ask questions such as:

"How much does John F. Smith owe on his account?" "What was the date of the last purchase by Mary C. Jones?" "What did she buy?"

The natural language front-end can easily go into the database and find this information.

Clout is a very effective personal computer front-end. However, it works only with Microrim's DBMS. Further, it is strictly for use in retrieving data from the database. It cannot be used for creating new databases. Clout allows users to pose a question similarly to the way they would talk with an associate, rather than by formal commands. Thus a query using Clout could be posed as follows: "Give me the names of all persons with sales records of over $250,000 last year." Without Clout, the query would take this form: "SELECT Name, Sales from Annual Sales, WHERE Sales greater than 250,000 AND Year equals 1989."

An NLP software package has been programmed to look for key words in a sentence. In our query, these would be "names," "sales," "250,000," and "last year." The NLP stores predetermined key words and their synonyms. These will be used to determine the meaning of the query and to select appropriate relationships and data items. In our example, "names" could mean persons, people, executives, salespersons, and last names. The NLP builds a profile of common user terminology. If it cannot match a key word to a stored synonym, the NLP is programmed to ask the user to give another word, or to select from several choices that are probable synonyms. For example, the NLP will ask the user about "names": "Do you mean names of executives?" The user will answer: "No, I mean salespersons."

Although Clout and R:Base are two separate products, there are several products that integrate NLP into DBMS that are sold as one product. Two such products are Q & A and PARADOX.

Q & A (from Symantec Corp., Cupertino, CA). Q&A is a basic file manager that contains modules for building files, accessing the files, and generating an output report in a specific format. It also contains a natural language front-end called "The Intelligent Assistant." The Intelligent Assistant parses common English input questions and converts them into queries that the file manager can understand. A built-in, 600-word vocabulary (more words are being added with every new version) provides the lexical information for understanding the input query.

A unique feature of Q&A is that it paraphrases your input request to ensure that it fully understands what you want. Using a sales example, you may request the following:

"Show the total 1989 sales for the Central Region"

Q&A's Intelligent Assistant may come back with an inquiry that looks like this:

```
SHALL I DO THE FOLLOWING?
    CREATE A REPORT SHOWING THE AMOUNT OF SALES FOR THE
    CENTRAL REGION IN 1989?
    YES — CONTINUE      NO — CANCEL REQUEST
```

Paraphrasing verifies what you want to do. If it is correct, simply type Y for yes and the data access will be completed. A no answer will cancel the request, and then you may change it or rephrase it.

The primary disadvantage of the Q&A system is that it is not a relational database. For that reason, it cannot initiate queries for multiple information items that are contained in separate files. It can only access information in one file at a time. Relational databases, on the other hand, permit several files to be open at a time to access multiple data items. For example, if the sales for widgets is in a separate file from whizbangs, Q&A could not answer the question, "State the total sales of widgets and whizbangs." However, you can get the same information by asking for the sales in separate inquiries.

PARADOX (from Borland International, Inc.). Paradox is a *relational* DBMS with an AI technology based on the "query by example" approach, developed by IBM. It does not have NLP capability but it has an inference capability that allows users to retrieve information from the database with only a most cursory knowledge of its inner details. Users are presented with a graphical representation of an empty record in the database called the "query table," which they fill in with data exemplary of the desired result of the search. By analyzing these entries, Paradox infers which information users are looking for, and takes appropriate action, creating an "answer table" on a screen to display its findings. Users may stipulate which fields should be included in the report and/or make changes in the query table. Paradox provides two major advantages: ease of use and correct interpretation of the user's request. The program uses an "heuristic query optimization" approach to improve the efficiency of the database search.

HAL (from Lotus Development Co., Cambridge, MA). Lotus 1-2-3 is an integrated software package that can be considered a simple DSS generator. Although it became an industry standard, some users find the commands difficult to remember and awkward to use. Therefore, HAL was developed to ease the interface.

HAL provides the user with an alternative way to enter commands. Commands may be entered in sentences that substitute for Lotus 1- 2-3 menu selections. They produce a result that otherwise would require a series of keystroke entries and they add new features to Lotus 1-2-3.

To illustrate the ease of HAL and its flexibility, the boxed material shows a routinely used function of Lotus 1-2-3, the copy command. In order to copy the data that appear in Cell A5 to ten other cells, A6 through A15, the user would have to enter the commands shown if Lotus 1-2-3 is used, or a simple command if HAL is used.

```
Lotus 1-2-3
/
C (for copy)
A5 (for source)
A6.A15 (for destination)
```

The user of HAL could have received the same result by typing *any* of the following sentences:

```
DUPLICATE CELL A5 IN A6.A15
COPY CELL A5 TO A6.A15
COPY A6 DOWN 10
```

Or, if the cursor is located in Cell A5, the user could type:

```
COPY THIS CELL TO A6 THROUGH A15
```

HAL can be used to simplify many tasks related to Lotus (e.g., writing macros, preparing tables, creating a graph, or writing a formula. For details see Holt, J. A., *Cases and applications in Lotus 1-2-3 with HAL,* 2nd ed., Irwin, 1988.

The major benefits of HAL to DSS accrue from five features. First, HAL has a powerful undo command that facilitates "what if" analysis. Second, there is linking that provides automatic data updating with one keystroke. Third, the speed and ease with which graphs can be prepared allow the user to *create* and view graphs to help him or her think about the work, not just use graphs for presentations. Fourth, there is auditing that provides automatic documentation (using precedent trees). Last, the file management capabilities improve Lotus 1-2-3's use as a DSS; the user does not have to specify input data criteria, nor set output ranges. HAL also efficiently handles complicated rearrangements of records and fields and simplifies data extraction. Despite all its benefits HAL can be considered as a "weak" NLP with very limited vocabulary and appropriate syntax.

Note: Many of HAL's capabilities are incorporated in Lotus 3.0.

ES-Natural Language Processors and Databases

As described earlier, NLP are being used as front-ends to databases. Such a combination requires extensive definitions for business terms in the NLP dictionary. ES that already have the knowledge about these terms in its knowledge base can be added, and therefore greatly increase the capabilities of the system.

Figure 18.5 demonstrates a before and after structure of such a combination. Part A shows a typical use of a database using a DBMS; the user must know the DBMS language, which may take weeks of training. Part B adds a NLP, which makes the communication easier, yet it is very limited. The NLP dictionary must be prepared to understand a diversified natural language (e.g., business terminology) and translate it to the DBMS limited commands.

The connection of NLP and DBMS can be very difficult especially when large computers are involved. This is where ES can be of help. As shown in part

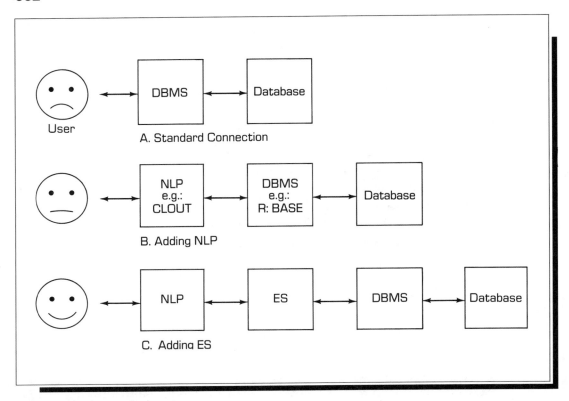

FIGURE 18.5 Integrated systems.

C, an ES is added to improve communication by allowing the NLP to use the knowledge of the ES. A commercial product that combines ES and NLP is Conversational Advisory System (from Cognitive Systems). For further discussion of this topic see Harris (8).

18.6   Speech (Voice) Recognition and Understanding

Speech or voice recognition is the process of having the computer recognize normal human speech. When a speech recognition system is combined with a natural language processing system, the result is an overall system that not only recognizes voice input but also *understands* it.

Speech recognition is a process that allows one to communicate with a computer by speaking to it. The term *speech recognition* is sometimes applied only to the first part of the process: recognizing the words that have been spoken without necessarily interpreting their meanings. The other part of the process, in which the meaning of the speech is ascertained, is called *speech understanding*. It may be possible to understand the meaning of a spoken sentence without actually recognizing every word and vice versa.

For applications of voice processing see K. Gottesman in the Winter 1989 issue of the *Journal of Information Systems Management*.

Advantages of Speech Recognition

The ultimate goal of speech recognition is to allow a computer to understand the natural speech of any human speaker at least as well as a human listener could understand it. In addition to being the most natural method of communication, speech recognition offers several advantages:

- □ *Ease of Access*—Many more people can speak than can type. As long as communication with a computer depends on developing typing skills, many people may not be able to use computers effectively. Although natural language understanding may help reduce the severity of the problem, it will not solve it completely.
- □ *Speed*—Even the most competent typists can speak more quickly than they can type. It is estimated that the average person can speak twice as fast as a proficient typist can type.
- □ *Manual Freedom*—Obviously, communicating with a computer by typing occupies your hands. There are, however, many situations in which computers might be useful to people whose hands are otherwise occupied, such as product assemblers, pilots of military aircraft, and busy executives.
- □ *Remote Access*—Many computers are set up to be accessed remotely by telephone. If a remote database includes speech recognition capabilities, you could retrieve information by issuing verbal commands into a telephone.
- □ *Accuracy*—In typing information one is prone to make mistakes. However, in a spoken language one is also prone to make mistakes (e.g., incomplete sentences or incorrect grammar). The point is that in voice input we have only the second source of errors, while in typing we may have both. AI technology can fix the errors made in the second part more easily than fixing both, especially when the typing mistakes are not in spelling but in codes and names.

Potential areas of speech recognition applications include the following:

- □ *Clinical*—Medical records, services for the handicapped.
- □ *Entertainment and Education*—Voice-controlled toys and interactive video games.
- □ *Manufacturing Process Control*—Machine operation, package sorting.
- □ *Office Automation*—Data entry, automatic dictation, automatic transcription.
- □ *Security*—Voice-print identification, building access.

Classifying Speech Recognizers

Speech recognizers are classified in several different ways. First, there are systems that recognize individual words and others that recognize continuous speech. Second, the systems are further classified as either speaker dependent or speaker independent. Let's see what these terms mean.

Word Recognizers. A word recognizer, as its title implies, is a speech recognition system that identifies individual words. Such systems are capable of recognizing only a small vocabulary of single words or possibly simple phrases. To give commands or data to a computer using one of these systems, you must state the input information in clearly definable single words given one after another.

Continuous Speech Recognizers. These speech recognition units recognize a continuous flow of words. You can speak to them in complete sentences, and your input will be recognized and understood. Continuous speech recognizers are far more difficult to build. The difficulty lies in separating one word from another in a continuous phrase or sentence. When we speak, most of the words slur together in one continuous stream. It is difficult for such a system to know where one word ends and another begins. Far more sophisticated and complex techniques must be used to deal with continuous speech.

Today there are very few practical continuous speech systems in use. Most of them are research and experimental systems made on very large and expensive computers. Many of them do not even operate on real-time. That is, the information spoken is not recognized instantly as it is with word recognition systems. It may take many minutes for only a few seconds of speech to be analyzed and understood.

Speaker Dependent. A speaker-dependent system means that the system has been customized to the voice of a particular individual. Because there are such wide variations in the way that people speak, it is difficult to build computer systems that will recognize anyone's voice. By limiting the system to the voice of one person, the system is not only simpler but also more reliable.

Speaker Independent. Speaker-independent systems mean that anyone can use the system. The speech recognizer is designed to be as versatile as possible so that even though voice characteristics may vary widely from one speaker to another, the system can recognize them. Most speaker independent systems are incredibly complex and costly. They also have very limited vocabularies. Some of the most advanced systems in this area are Speech Recognition System (from Bell Labs) and a system developed at Carnegie-Mellon University. However, both systems can understand only about 1200 words (in 1989). The Bell Labs system is used, for example, for airline reservations via human phone input.

How Speech Recognition Systems Work

All types of speech recognition systems use the same basic techniques. The voice input to the microphone produces an analog speech signal. This speech signal is then converted into binary words compatible with a digital computer by an analog-to-digital converter. The binary version of the input voice is then stored in the system and compared to previously stored binary representations of words and phrases. The computer searches through the previously stored speech patterns and compares them, one at a time, to the current speech input. When a match occurs, recognition is achieved. Once recognition is achieved, the spoken word in binary form is written on a video screen or passed along to a natural language understanding processor for additional analysis.

A Typical Word Recognizer

A typical speaker-dependent word recognizer is shown in Figure 18.6. The voice input is applied to a microphone. The electrical analog signal from the microphone is fed to an amplifier where it is increased in level. The amplifier will contain some kind of automatic gain control (AGC) to provide an output signal in a specific voltage range.

The analog signal representing a spoken word is a complex waveform that contains many individual frequencies. The way to recognize the spoken word is to break that complex input signal into its component parts. This is usually done with a set of filters. A filter is an electronic circuit that passes or rejects frequencies in a certain range. In speech recognition equipment, bandpass filters (BPF) are used. These filters pass frequencies only in a certain frequency range.

The filter output is then fed to analog-to-digital converters (ADC) that translate the output into digital words. The ADCs feed input circuits controlled by a CPU. The digital values are stored in a large memory (RAM).

The computer must first be taught to recognize the input of a particular user. The user speaks all the words in the vocabulary. These words are digitized and stored as templates in the memory.

When the user activates the system, the computer, through a search routine, matches each spoken word against the templates. Once a word is identified a binary or ASCII version is displayed or used in some other manner.

Voice Synthesis

This refers to the technology by which computers "speak." The synthesis of voice by computer differs from a simple playback of a prerecorded voice

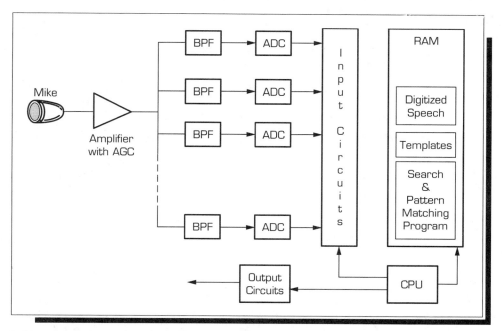

FIGURE 18.6 A speaker-dependent word recognition speech recognizer.

by either analog or digital means. As the term "synthesis" implies, the sounds that make up words and phrases are constructed electronically from basic sound components and can be made to form any desired voice pattern.

Voice synthesis has already come of age. There are several good, commercially available voice synthesis packages that work on limited domains and encompass phonetic rules. The "voices" generated today are generally flat, artificial voices that are obviously different from human voices, yet the improved implementations are easily understandable.

Voice synthesis is not considered to be an AI technology, however, it can be integrated with AI technologies. Voice synthesis is now used in education, dynamic and interactive queries (e.g., in banking), and human interaction with technical instruments.

The quality of synthesized voice is currently very good, but the technology remains somewhat expensive. The anticipated lower cost and improved performance of synthetic voice in the near future will encourage more widespread commercial applications. The opportunities for its use will encompass almost all applications that can provide an automated response to a user, such as inquiries by employees pertaining to payroll and benefits. Several banks already offer a voice service to their customers, informing them about their balance, about which checks were cashed, and so on. Another example is the answer provided for requests for telephone numbers. For an overview of the topic see Lee et al. (12) and Schutzer (18).

While progress in this area is fairly slow the user interface can be currently improved by other approaches. These will be discussed in the next two sections.

18.7 Visual Interactive Modeling (or Decision Making)

One of the most interesting developments in computer graphics is visual interactive modeling (VIM). The technique has been used for DSS in the area of

How Can Visual Interactive Decision Making Help a Manager?

The first exposure to VIM sets the manager on unfamiliar ground. A large color screen lights up with a graphic display that may include moving icons and blinking colors. The first response is usually a comparison with a video game and, indeed, the program creating the display has much in common with game software. The comparison is, however, short-lived. The power of the technique emerges in stages:

1. Managers recognize the screen display as a graphic representing a familiar process or situation.
2. Managers observe the screen carefully, perhaps also several other screen displays, and accept the picture(s) as a sufficiently detailed

image of the real process, with any motion showing realistic process evolution.

3. Managers interact with the model, and observe that the screen image responds in accordance with their understanding of the real system.

4. Through experimentation and observation, managers gain confidence in the visual model and become convinced that the model producing the displays is a valid representation of the real system.

5. Once convinced of the validity of the visual model, managers can begin to ask "what if," and the visual model becomes a powerful decision-making aid.

The power of VIM as a decision-making tool comes from the *confidence* in the model that grows as managers see the model confirm their understanding of the real system. Managerial validation of the model occurs because:

□ A picture is recognizable as a model of the real world more readily than a table of numbers; a street map of a city is easier to recognize as the city than a list of the coordinates of street intersections.

□ A visual model is not a "black box." The interior workings of the model are in full view and nothing has to be taken on trust.

□ Dynamic visual models show the same transient behavior of the process that the manager sees every day, rather than average behavior over a long period of time.

□ VIM enables the manager to interact directly with the model rather than working with a mathematical model through an analyst.

Once confidence in the visual model is achieved, VIM provides the manager with a decision-making environment very much like that of a scientist working in a laboratory. The manager chooses experiments to be conducted, and evaluates them using results provided by the model. Explicit measures of the quality of alternative solutions can be incorporated into the model; for example, in a bus-routing problem it may be desirable to keep the routes as short as possible; after changing stops around, the total length of the routes can be computed and displayed. Optimizing procedures can also be built into the model: when a stop is moved from one route to another, the routes can be redrawn so that the distance traveled is a minimum.

VIM is particularly powerful when decision makers have multiple decision criteria, or where decision criteria are implicit or difficult to formalize. VIM allows decision makers to choose a best solution using whatever criteria they think appropriate. VIM is also a powerful *training* device, allowing exposure to operations that can be very like the real thing—a flight simulator, for example, is an advanced form of VIM application.

(*Source:* Bell et al. [2].)

operations management with unusual success (see Hurrion [10]). The technique appears under the following names: visual interactive problem solving, visual interactive modeling, and visual interactive simulation.

Visual interactive modeling (VIM) uses computer graphic displays to present the impact of different management decisions. It differs from computer graphics in that the user can intervene in the decision-making process and can see the results of the intervention. A visual model is a graphic used as an integral part of decision making or problem solving and not just as a communication device. The VIM displays the effect of different decisions in graphic form on a computer screen.

VIM can represent a static or a dynamic system. Static models display a visual image of the result of one decision alternative at a time. (With computer windows, several results can be compared on one screen.) Dynamic models display systems that evolve over time. The evolution is represented by animation.

One of the most developed areas in dynamic VIM is visual simulation. It is a very important technique for DSS, because simulation is considered a major capability in DSS. Visual interactive simulation (VIS) is a decision simulation in which the end-user watches the progress of the simulation model in an animated form using graphics terminals. The user may interact with the simulation and try different decision strategies.

Conventional Simulation.   Simulation has long been established as a useful method of giving insight into complex DSS problem situations. However, the technique of simulation does not usually allow decision makers to *see* how a solution to a complex problem is developing through time, nor does it give them the ability to interact with it. The simulation technique gives only statistical answers at the end of a set of particular experiments. As a result, decision makers are not an integral part of the simulation development, and their experience and judgment cannot be used to directly assist the study. Thus any conclusions obtained by the model must be taken on trust. If the conclusions do not agree with the intuition or practical judgment of the decision maker, a confidence gap will appear regarding the use of the model. The very nature of simulation studies means that a significant part of the analysis must appear as a "black box." For this reason a solution derived by simulation studies may not be implemented.

Visual Interactive Simulation.   The basic philosophy of VIS is that decision makers will be able to watch a simulation model of their problem situation develop through time. This is achieved by using a visual display unit. Decision makers can also contribute to the validation of that model. They will have more confidence in its use because of their own participation. They are also in a position to use their knowledge and experience to interact with the model in order to explore alternative strategies.

Simulation can be interactive at the design stage, at the model running stage, or both. To gain insight into how systems operate under different conditions, it is important to be able to interact with the model while it is running so that alternative suggestions or directives can be tested.

Visual Interactive Models and DSS

VIM was used with DSS in several operations management decisions (see application case at the end of this chapter and Hurrion [10]). The method consists of priming a visual interactive model of a plant (or company) with its current status. The model is then rapidly run on a computer allowing management to observe how a plant is likely to operate in the future. A similar approach was used to assist in the consensus negotiations among senior managers for the development of their budget plans. A simple example of VIM is the area of waiting lines (queuing). A DSS in such a case usually computes several measures of performance (e.g., waiting time in the system) for the various decision alternatives.

Complex waiting line problems require simulation. The VIM can display the size of the waiting line or the value of the waiting time as it changes during the simulation runs. The VIM can also present graphically the answers to "what if" questions regarding changes in input variables.

The VIM approach was also used in conjunction with artificial intelligence. The integration of the two techniques adds several capabilities that range from the ability to build systems graphically to learning about the dynamics of the system.

General-purpose dynamic VIM software is commercially available for both mainframe (e.g., see Bell et al. [2]) and microcomputers (see Hollocks [9]). Examples are See Why (from BLSL Inc.), Siman (System Modeling Corp.), 1 DDS (Pritsker and Associates, Inc.), PC Model (Simulation Software Systems, Inc.), SIMSOFT (from Microsoft Corp.), and VIG (from NumPlan).

18.8 Hypertext and Hypermedia

User interface may be improved thanks to the technique of Hypertext. Hypertext is an approach for handling text and graphic information by allowing the users to jump from a given topic, whenever they wish, to related ideas. Reading or viewing of information thus becomes open ended, controlled by the user. Hypertext allows users to access information in a nonlinear fashion by following a train of thought. It lets the reader control the level of details and the type of information displayed. Hypertext allows a quick search according to the reader's interest. For example, as you started reading this section the first words were "user interface." Using hypertext you can highlight the words "user interface," then press a button, and the computer would bring up a passage of text related to this topic. When you are finished you can return to the beginning of the section or jump to any other related topic.

Hypertext is still in its developmental stages (for an overview and products see the October 1988 issue of *Byte* magazine). The concept may contribute to improved user interfaces in MSS as will be described next.

Hypertext is a natural companion to expert systems development tools. The reason is that both technologies deal with the *transfer of knowledge*. In hypertext, however, the user controls the tools, and he or she may not do it in the most efficient way. ES can lead and direct the user. For further information see Shafer (19). Several products perform such an integration. For example, *Knowledge Pro* (from Knowledge Garden, Inc., Nassau, NY) integrates hypertext and expert systems. Such an integration enables a powerful knowledge representation including easy access to colors, windows, and mouse control. It lets communication take place between expert and novice, teacher and pupil, consultant and manager. It lets each side react to what the other says. For further information see S. L. Shepard, "AI Meets Hypertext-KnowledgePro and KnowledgeMaker," *Language Technology*, November–December 1987. The VP Expert package includes Hypertext capabilities (see Instructor's manual to this text). Programs in Motion, Inc. (Wayland, MA) is also marketing several products in the 1st Class family which offer ES/hypertext programs.

An example of a hypertext product that can be integrated with an ES is HyperCard.

HyperCard. HyperCard is a graphically based data management software program for the Macintosh (II, SE, and PLUS), from Apple Computer, Inc. HyperCard creates a visual and logical metaphor to the hierarchical structure of data files. It also employs the concept of hypertext in which texts, images, and data are linked to other text, images, and data by buttons. Click on a designated button and the linked items are brought onto the screen. HyperCard's data structure illustrates the logical relationship between data elements in a simple manner. Instead of programs or databases, HyperCard uses stacks. Instead of files, it uses cards. This organization enables presentation of information and knowledge in a way that makes sense to the user. HyperCard is not simple to learn because of the abundance of creative tools. However, once you learn, it can provide you with almost unlimited opportunities. HyperCard extends the Macintosh user interface and makes everybody a programmer. HyperCard is supported by *HyperTalk*, a simple object-oriented language whose syntax reminds one of COBOL. It includes event-oriented scripts that are executed when a certain event occurs. These events go through HyperCard as messages. For further details see D. Goodman, *The Complete HyperCard Handbook*, Bantam Computer, 1987.

HyperCard can be used as an ES knowledge base source. A user can view information that resides in the stacks and cards during ES consultation. Since one can store pictures in HyperCard, it can support regular rule-based systems very nicely. MacSMARTS (from Cognition Technology) permits the user of its ES to enter a HyperCard file, look up the answer to a question, and return to MacSMARTS. A similar approach is executed by Human Intellect Systems, Inc., whose Instant Expert Plus product is tightly integrated with HyperCard. In addition, HyperCard can be used as an extremely user-friendly front-end to an expert system shell. This approach is used in Cognate, an ES shell from Peridom, Inc. For further discussion on how HyperCard can make user interface friendlier see D. Shafer in the July–August 1988 issue of *PC AI*.

Finally, another attachment of HyperCard, HyperCalc, is a spreadsheet stack that can improve modeling capabilities in MSS.

Hypermedia. Hypermedia is a term used to describe documents that could contain several types of media, such as text, graphics, audio, and video. Multimedia can be very useful in constructing knowledge-based applications.[*] Hypermedia may contain several layers of information such as:

- □ *A menu-based natural language interface* to provide a simple and transparent way for users to run the system and query it.
- □ *An object-oriented database* that permits concurrent access to its data structures and operations.
- □ *A relational query interface* that can efficiently support complex queries.
- □ *A hypermedia abstract machine* that lets users link different types of information.
- □ *Media editors* that provide ways to view and edit text, graphics, images, and voice.
- □ *A change management virtual memory* to manage temporary versions, configurations, and transformations of design entities.

By adding control structures on top of hypermedia systems, computer-aided instruction, CAD, CASE, cooperative authoring, and groupware systems can be built.

Work is being done at Texas Instruments aimed at producing widely applicable software tools for dealing with "semistructured" information.

18.9 **Concluding Remarks**

A friendly user interface is the key to successful implementation of MSS. And indeed there is a major drive by software and hardware vendors to improve the interface. There are estimates that over 50 percent of all new developments in computerized systems during the 1990s will be in the area of interface. From the traditional methods of menus and commands interaction there is a move toward object manipulation, natural language processing, and speech understanding. These emerging technologies attempt to make the use of computers as natural and as simple as it can be. Some day users will be able to use the computer with the same ease that they are using the telephone. The computer, then, will act very similar to the way that a human assistant acts. Namely, the manager will ask a question in voice, the computer will go to work and provide an answer, by voice, within seconds. As a matter of fact, such systems will be very fast, very consistent, and very flexible. At that time they will be used by all managers on a routine basis.

[*]This description is based on information provided in the *AI Letter* from Texas Instruments, December 1988.

Key Words

action language	information overload	pattern matching
command language	key word search	pragmatic analysis
continuous speech	lexicon	semantic analysis
form interaction	menu interaction	speech understanding
front-end interface	natural language interface	syntactic analysis
hypermedia	natural language processing	understander
hypertext	object manipulation	voice recognition
interface	parser	word recognizer

Questions for Review and Discussion

1. Define user interface.
2. It is said that the interface is the most important component of an MSS. Explain why.
3. Explain the *process* of user-computer interaction (per Figure 18.1).
4. Define presentation and action languages.
5. Menu interaction is probably the most liked interface style. Explain why.
6. Why is a command language the preferred style of experienced users?
7. Which interface style is used mostly in expert systems and which in DSS? Why is this so?
8. Describe a combination of menus and commands from your own experience.
9. Define a natural language and natural language processing.
10. What are the major advantages of NLP?
11. Distinguish between NLP and natural language generation.
12. Explain how key word search works. What are its major limitations?
13. Obtain an access to ELIZA and run a conversation with it. After about 12–15 questions and answers, stop. What are the major limitations of ELIZA?
14. It is said that language processing is far more effective than key word search. Why?
15. Explain how language processing works (use Figure 18.3).
16. Give an example of how the parser segregates a sentence.
17. Describe the functions of the lexicon.
18. What is the role of the understander and the knowledge base in NLP?
19. The use of NLP as an interface to DBMS is gaining popularity. Explain how NLP increases the accessibility to databases.
20. Obtain an NLP/DBMS software (e.g., Clout and R:Base, Q&A). Try to use it on the database of Chapter 6, Exercise 4. Compare the use of a regular DBMS to the one supported by NLP.
21. Compare Paradox to Q&A. List the major differences.
22. If possible, get a copy of HAL or HAL DEMO. Use HAL with Lotus 1-2-3 to solve the database Exercise 4 in Chapter 6.
23. What is the difference between voice recognition and voice understanding?
24. List the major advantages of voice recognition.
25. Give five examples where voice recognition can be applied today and list the benefit(s) in each case. Be specific.
26. Describe the difference between word and continuous speech recognizers.
27. Why is a speaker-independent system preferred over a speaker-dependent one? Why is it so difficult to build it?
28. It is said that voice synthesis is not AI technology. Why?
29. Describe how hypertext works. What is its major advantage?

30. Expert systems are being coupled with hypertext. What are the advantages of such an integration?

31. Define visual simulation and compare it to conventional simulation.

32. Several computer games, such as Flight Simulation II and GATO, can be considered visual simulation. Explain why.

33. Define visual interactive modeling (VIM).

34. It is said that VIM is particularly helpful in implementing recommendations derived by computers. Explain why.

APPLICATION CASE: Visual Simulation at Weyerhaeuser Co.

Weyerhaeuser Co. (of Tacoma, WA) is a large timber processor. The company developed several applications of VIM (one of which is described here). The company estimates the annual increase in profit contribution to top $7 million, owing to the introduction of VIM.

Log-cutting Decisions[*]

Timber processing involves harvesting trees that are delimbed and topped. The resulting "stems" are crosscut into logs of various lengths. These logs are allocated among different mills, each of which makes a different end product (e.g., plywood, lumber, paper). For each tree there may be hundreds of reasonable cutting and allocating combinations. The cutting and allocation decisions are the *major* determinant of revenues of the company and its profitability. The decisions are made on a stem-by-stem basis, because each tree is physically different from every other tree. Many variables determine the manner in which a stem is cut. Because costs are not affected much by these decisions, the larger the revenue generated, the larger the profit.

Management scientists have developed a theoretical optimization model for the cutting and allocating decisions, using the technique of dynamic programming. However, the employees in the field were reluctant to use solutions that resulted from an unfamiliar, somewhat intimidating, "black box" algorithm. Furthermore, like any other mathematical models, this model too is based on several assumptions that do not always capture reality. Thus, the operators have had a legitimate reason for not following the computer's recommendations. Visual decision simulator allows the operators to deal with the proposed solutions on their own terms. This is done by allowing the operators to simulate on a video display a realistic representation of each stem. The simulator allows the operator to roll, rotate, cut, and allocate each representation of each stem. The simulator allows the operator to roll, rotate, cut, and allocate each stem the way he or she wants on the computer screen, of course. One can *see* the end product and the resultant profit contribution of the suggested solution (see Figure 18.7). He or she then can compare it with the profit resulting from the recommendation of the dynamic programming model. If not satisfied, the operator can recut the same stem repeatedly (on the computer screen, of course) to explore alternate decisions. The final decision, how to cut, is always made by the

[*]Abstracted by permission of Mark R. Lembersky and Uli H. Chi (13).

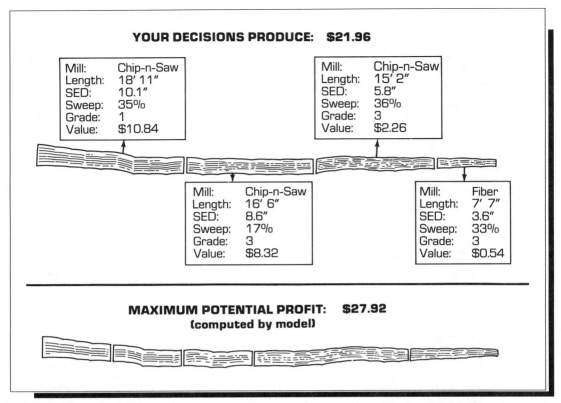

FIGURE 18.7 Display of the economic consequences of the user's decision compared with the model's maximization results. Log information (shown in boxes in the upper part) is available, but not shown, in the lower part.

operator; therefore the system is nonthreatening. Furthermore, the repeated cutting experimentations on the screen have been documented to improve decision-making skills in the field. The system is used also by management to evaluate alternative stem-processing strategies.

QUESTIONS

1. Why is log cutting such a complex problem?
2. Why were the employees reluctant to use the dynamic programming optimization technique?
3. How does visual simulation overcome the deficiencies of the regular optimization model?

References and Bibliography

1. Allen, J. *Natural Language Understanding*. Benjamin-Cummings, Menlo Park, CA: 1987.
2. Bell, P. C., et al. "Visual Interactive Problem Solving—A New Look at Management Problems." *Business Quarterly*, Spring 1984.

3. Bennett, J. L., "Tools for Building Advanced User Interfaces." *IBM Systems Journal*, No. 3/4, 1986.

4. Dos Santos, B. L., and M. L. Bariff. "A Study of User Interface Aids for Decision Support Systems." *Management Science*, 1988.

5. Eisenberg, J., and J. Hill. "Using Natural-Language Systems on Personal Computers." *BYTE*, January 1984.

6. Fersko-Weiss, H. "Natural Language—The Dialogue Has Begun." *Personal Computing*, November 1985.

7. Frenzel, L. *Crash Course in AI and Expert Systems*. Indianapolis: H. Sams, 1987.

8. Harris, L. R. "Natural Language Front Ends." In Winston, P. H., and K. A. Prendergast, eds. *The AI Business*. Cambridge, MA: MIT Press, 1984.

9. Hollocks, B. "Personal Computers and Operations Research—Experience in British Steel." *Journal of Operational Research Society*, April 1982.

10. Hurrion, R. D. "Implementation of Consensus Decision Support Systems." *European Journal of Operations Research*, Vol. 20, 1985.

11. Joost, M. G., et al. "Voice Communication with Computers: A Primer," *Computers and Industrial Engineering*, Vol. 7, No. 2, 1983.

12. Lee, S. M., et al. "Voice Recognition: An Examination of an Evolving Technology and its Use in Organizations." *Computers and Operations Research*, Vol. 14, No. 6, 1987.

13. Lembersky, M. R., and U. H. Chi. "Decision Simulators Speed Implementation and Improve Operations." *Interfaces*, July–August 1984 (see also January–February 1986).

14. Majchrzak, A., et al. *Human Aspects of Computer-Aided Design*. Philadelphia: Taylor and Francis, 1987.

15. Meyer, K., and M. Harper. "User Friendliness." *MIS Quarterly*, March 1984.

16. Popp, G. "The User Interface in Group Decision Support Systems." In *DSS 88 Transactions*, S. Weber, ed. Boston, June 1988.

17. Potter, A. "Direct Manipulation Interfaces." *AI Expert*, October 1988.

18. Schutzer, D. *AI—An Applications Oriented Approach*, New York: Van Nostrand Reinhold, 1987.

19. Shafer, D. "Hypermedia and Expert Systems: A Marriage Made in Hyper Heaven." *Hyperage*, May–June 1988.

20. Shneiderman, B. *Designing The User Interfaces: Strategies For Effective Human-Computer Interaction*. Reading, MA: Addison-Wesley, 1987.

21. Shwartz, S. *Applied Natural Language Processing*. Princeton, NJ: Petrocelli, 1988.

22. Winston, T. W., et al. "Natural Language Query Processing." *AI Expert*, February 1989.

Chapter 19

Management Support Systems Integration

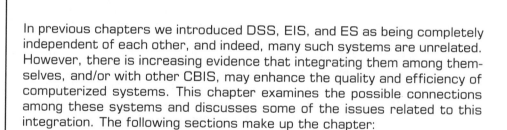

In previous chapters we introduced DSS, EIS, and ES as being completely independent of each other, and indeed, many such systems are unrelated. However, there is increasing evidence that integrating them among themselves, and/or with other CBIS, may enhance the quality and efficiency of computerized systems. This chapter examines the possible connections among these systems and discusses some of the issues related to this integration. The following sections make up the chapter:

19.1   **Introduction**

In the previous chapters we introduced DSS, EIS, and ES as being completely independent systems. In this chapter the issue of integrating these systems is considered.

While there is no doubt that these systems are valuable in many cases as stand-alone systems, great benefits can be derived also when they are integrated with each other or with other computer-based information systems. This chapter begins with a definition of integration and then it proceeds to describe the integration of ES with the three components of DSS: data management, model management, and interfaces—to make them more "intelligent." Next we describe the following combinations of integration:

- ES-DSS*
- ES-EIS
- DSS-EIS
- DSS-EIS-ES
- DSS/EIS/ES with CBIS

Such integration leads to a broad MSS.

19.2   **What is Systems Integration?**

The integration of computer-based systems means that rather than having separate hardware, software, and communications for each independent system, these systems are integrated into one facility. An integration can be at the *development tools level* or it can be at *the application system* level. There exist two general types of integration: functional and physical.

Functional integration implies that different support functions are provided as a single system. For example, working with electronic mail, using a spreadsheet, communicating with external databases, creating graphics representations, and storing and manipulating data, can all be accomplished at the same workstation. The user can access the appropriate facilities through a single, consistent interface, and can switch from one task to another and back again.

Physical integration refers to packaging of the hardware, software, and communications features required to accomplish functional integration. The software integration is determined to a large extent by the hardware integration.

Several physical integration approaches exist. The major ones, per Newman (44), are shown in Figure 19.1 and are summarized next.

Access Approaches

According to this approach, MSS development tools, and/or application programs, can *access* each other or access standard applications or development software. The access can be done based on the hardware configuration.

---

*The integration of DSS with ES is based on a paper titled "Integrating Expert Systems and Decision Support Systems" by E. Turban and P. R. Watkins, which appeared in the June 1986 issue of *MIS Quarterly* (reproduced with the permission of the journal).

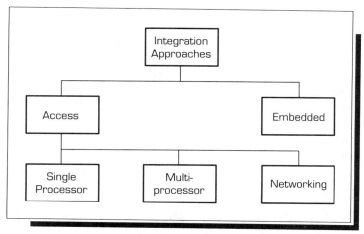

FIGURE 19.1 Integration approaches.

Three subcategories exist here: single processor, multiprocessor, and networking.

Single Processor.   This simple and most common approach relies on different types of software, operating on the same processor. With this approach, traditional programs and databases are callable from the computer memory or from some software package.

An example of such an integration is the availability of Lisp and/or PROLOG on a single processor with conventional languages. HP AI System is a good illustration. This system integrates Lisp, Fortran, C, Pascal, and HP-UX (a version of UNIX). As a result, programmers can edit, compile, test, and debug Fortran, C, and Pascal programs incrementally and interactively, using either Lisp or UNIX, without ever leaving the Lisp editor.

This approach is not so expensive, and the processor can be highly utilized, but it is *not as powerful* as the following approaches.

Multiprocessors.   According to this approach, different softwares are operating on different processors within the same machine. Lisp Machine Inc. was the first vendor to produce a machine with both Lisp and UNIX processors. The different software communicate with each other. While UNIX is being used during the data acquisition, Lisp can be used for data representation and analysis. Texas Instruments is currently using a similar approach by combining an Explorer processor with that of the Macintosh.

This approach is much more expensive than the previous one but it is more flexible and it can assist in faster processing of complex jobs.

Networking.   MSS and/or conventional systems reside in completely different machines but can interface with each other. In such a case the integration requires some kind of networking.

Networking permits easy and quick interface among MSS software and/or between conventional programs. An example of such a connection is General

Motors' MAP. MAP, which is the acronym for Manufacturing Automation Protocol, is supported by powerful AI-dedicated workstations. These machines (which are made by Symbolic Inc., Texas Instruments, and Xerox Corp.) support Transport Control Protocol, Ethernet, Internet Protocol, and SNA, enabling a wide range of networking. TI's Explorer is an example of a dedicated AI workstation that is networked with other systems. Apollo's Domain communication board, for example, is plugged into the TI Explorer. The Domain's virtual demand-paged capabilities allow any computer on the network to store, access, or execute information on any other Domain-network computer, as if it were on its own.

Embedded Systems

In this approach the MSS software (especially ES and sometimes DSS) is embedded in a conventional IS program. This approach can be considered as the "second generation" of integrated ES, DSS, and conventional systems. It embeds value-added ES or DSS capabilities in conventional programs. The users see a single application that they can work with. There is no distinction between the ES, the DSS, and the conventional parts.

An example of an embedded development tool is GURU (from Micro Data Base Systems, Inc.). This package embeds an ES shell and a natural language processor (another AI product) in an environment that supports integrated spreadsheets, text processing, relational DBMS, graphics, report generation, communication, and business computing (for details, see Rauch-Hindin [46]). Another example is the Executive Edge. This tool combines DSS, EIS, and limited ES explanation capabilities. See Chapter 10 and Section 19.14. Embedded systems are usually more efficient than systems that provide an access of ES.

In building integrated systems the physical structure may become an extremely important factor. While embedded systems may seem to be desirable they are more difficult and more expensive to construct. There are many standard components on the market that can support the access approaches, resulting in savings of time and/or money. The selection of an appropriate integration mode is outside the scope of this chapter. However, it certainly should be considered in the design phase of an integrated project.

19.3   Intelligent Databases and Their Management

Tying expert systems to databases, especially large ones, is one of the most critical and rewarding areas of ES integration. There are several goals and several physical modes of such integration.

Organizations, private and public, are continuously collecting data, information, and knowledge (all are referred to here as "information") and storing it in computerized systems. The updating, retrieving, use, and removal of this information become more complicated as the amount increases. At the same time the number of individuals that are interacting with this information increases due to networking, end-user computing, and reduced cost of information processing. Working with large databases is becoming a difficult task that requires considerable expertise. Without database access it is difficult to use ES in large MIS applications, ranging from factory automation to credit card authorization.

Expert systems can make the management of databases simpler. One way to do so is to *enhance* the database management system (DBMS) by providing it with an inference capability. Al-Zobaidie and Grimson (1) provide three possible architectures for such a coupling. They also explain how the efficiency and the functionality of the DBMS can be enhanced. The contribution of ES in such a case can be further increased if it is coupled with a natural language processor (NLP). For a description of a database, DBMS, ES, and NLP integration see Harris (19).

Another purpose of ES-DBMS integration is to improve the *knowledge management* of the ES's knowledge base. As ES becomes increasingly complex and diverse, the need for efficient and effective management of their growing knowledge base is apparent. Al-Zobaidie and Grimson (1) proposed an *enhanced ES* to deal with such situations. The ES will have a special DBMS that can be used to manage its own knowledge base.

A different way of looking at ES-database integration is shown in Figure 19.2.

In addition to the enhanced DBMS and the enhanced ES discussed earlier, it is possible to integrate the ES and the DBMS via a network. Such an integration is discussed by Al-Zobaidie and Grimson (1).

Difficulties in tying ES to large databases has been a major problem even for large corporations (e.g., Boeing Aircraft, American Express). Recognizing the importance of such an integration, several vendors developed software products to support it. Examples of products include Oracle relational DBMS (from Oracle Corp., Belmont, CA), which incorporates some ES functionality in the form of a query optimizer, which selects the most efficient path for database queries to travel. In a distributed database, for example, a query optimizer would recognize that it is more efficient to transfer two records to a machine that holds 10,000 records than vice versa. (The optimization is important to

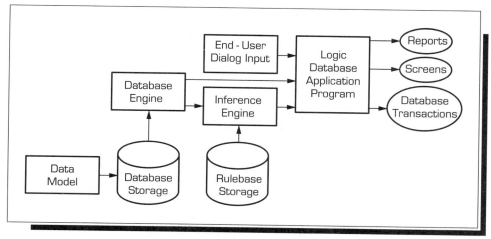

FIGURE 19.2 Intelligent database. (*Source:* Cohen [7].)

users because with such a capability they need to know only a few rules and commands to use the database.) This product will include, in the near future, a knowledge base that will incorporate, for example, rules for selecting which indexes to create or delete.

One of IBM's current main thrusts in commercial AI is providing a knowledge processing subsystem to work with a database, enabling users to extract information from the database and pass it to an expert system's knowledge base in several different knowledge representation structures. Another IBM project is the easy transferability of data from a typical database format (e.g., COBOL) to an ES format (e.g., Lisp) and vice versa. Another example is the KEE Connection (from IntelliCorp). This product translates KEE commands into database queries and automatically keeps track of data that are passed back and forth between KEE's knowledge base and a relational database using the SQL query language. Other benefits of such integration are the ability to use symbolic representation of data, improvements in the construction, operation, and maintenance of the DBMS (see Jarke and Vassiliou [29]), and the benefit for the ES itself, which is derived from the accessiblity to a database.

The integration of ES and databases has been the topic of several international and national conferences, books, and dozens of papers. For further information see Brodie and Mylpoulos (6), Cohen (7), Hsu and Skevington (27), Kerschberg (31), and Schur (49).

Expert Systems as an Interface to Online Databases

Commercial online databases are developed independently of each other, with different command languages, file structures, and access protocols. If one adds to this the complexity of searching, the proliferation of online databases (several thousand), and the lack of standardization, it is not difficult to see why there is a need for extensive knowledge in order to use these databases efficiently. Expert systems are being utilized (usually combined with a natural language processor) as interfaces to such databases. The knowledge base of the ES includes knowledge about search strategy. For example, such a system can advise a casual user on how to conduct a simple search or it can guide the more experienced user in accessing databases whose organization is complex. In all, it can make an online system transparent to the user. Such an integration is extremely important for EIS. For details see Kehoe (30) and Hawkins (20).

19.4   Intelligent Modeling and Model Management

The integration of ES and databases has become a top priority of many organizations. Integrated systems have been moved from the research lab to vendors' products and to fielded systems. Data's major complementary component, however, the quantitative model, is lagging behind in terms of ES integration. The topic attracted significant academic attention in recent years (e.g., see Blanning [4], Fedorowicz and Williams [11], Elam and Konsynski [10], Liang [39], and Vasant and Croker [62]) because the potential benefits could be very substantial. However, it seems that the implementation of integrated ES models is fairly difficult and slow.

Three interrelated subtopics will be investigated: the construction of models (formulation), the use of models (analysis), and the interpretation of the output of models. The quantitative models are primarily in the areas of managerial decision making. More specifically these are mainly: management science, engineering economics, statistical, and financial models.

The Construction of Models (Formulation). The construction of models for decision making involves the simplification of a real world situation so that a *simplified representation* of reality can be made. Models can be normative or descriptive and they are being used in various types of DSS or other CBIS. Finding an appropriate balance between simplification and representation in modeling requires expertise. The definition of the problem to be modeled, the attempt to *select* a prototype model (e.g., linear programming), the data collection, the model validation, and the estimation of certain parameters and relationships are not simple tasks either. For example, data may be tested for suitability to certain statistical distribution (e.g, "does the arrival rate in queuing follow a Poisson distribution"). The user may be guided by such a test, so an appropriate quantitative tool may be selected.

The Use of Models (Analysis). Once models are constructed they can be put to use. The application of models may require some judgmental values (e.g, setting an alpha value in exponential smoothing). Experience is also needed to conduct a sensitivity analysis as well as to determine what constitutes a significant difference ("is project A really superior to B?"). Expert systems can be used to provide the user with the necessary guidelines to the use of models. In addition, the ES can conduct a cause-effect analysis.

Interpretation of the Results. Expert systems can provide interpretation and explanation of the models used and the derived results. For example, an ES can trace anomalies of data. Futhermore, sensitivity analysis may be needed or translation of information to a certain format may be desired.

Current work on ES is done occasionally along the preceding subtopics: the construction and use of models and the interpretation of the results of parts of them. For example, Courtney et al. (8) developed an expert system for problem diagnosis. Zahedi (65) developed a system for model selection. Elam and Konsynski (10) show, via examples, how future model management systems will work when supported by ES.

However, most experimental ES are being developed not according to these categories but according to the type of mathematical model used. Then, some portions of one or more of the above three subtopics are being exercised; for example, interpreting the results of simulation (e.g., see Mellichamp [41]), use of forecasting models, or setting up the queuing model. A representative list of models is given in Table 19.1 with appropriate references.

For a proposed software architecture for an intelligent model management see Liang (39) and Figure 19.3.

TABLE 19.1 Representative Expert Systems in Quantitative Models.

Topic	References
Decision Theory Financial Models	Ko and Lin (34), Lehner and Donnel (38), Turner and Obilichetti (60)
Forecasting	Feng-Yang (12), Kumar and Cheng (35)
Mathematical Programming	Goul et al. (16), Murphy and Stohr (43)
Project Management	Hosley (25), Sathi (48)
Queuing	Hossein et al. (26)
Simulation	Doukidis (9), Ford and Schroer (13),
Statistics	Hand (18), Gale (14)
Strategic Planning	Goul et al. (17), Lee and Lee (37)
System Dynamics	Wu (64)

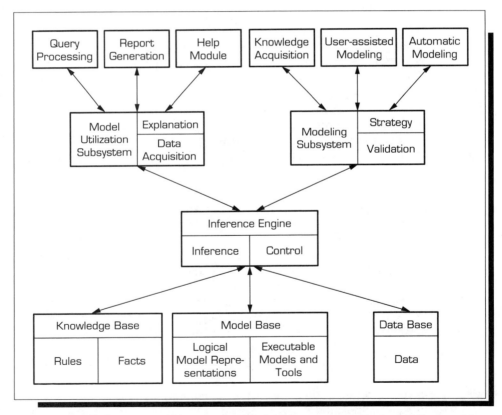

FIGURE 19.3 Software architecture for Model Management System. (*Source:* Liang [39]). The model utilization subsystem (left) directs the effective use of the model. The modeling subsystem (right) helps in increasing the productivity of model building. The inference engine drives the model selection and integration, and the integration of the model base, database, and knowledge base.

Human experts often use quantitative models to support their experience and expertise. For example, an expert may need to forecast the sales of a certain product or to estimate the future cash flow using a corporate planning model. Such a model can stand alone (meaning the expert can run the model on a computer as needed), or it can be part of the DSS system used by several decision makers and experts. In the latter case, the model can be used by the ES itself (e.g., when certain IF-THEN rules call for it).

ES contribution in the area of models and model management can be demonstrated by examining the work of a consultant. A consultant is involved in the following steps:

1. Discussing with the manager (user) the nature of the problem.
2. Identifying and classifying the problem.
3. Constructing a mathematical model of the problem.
4. Solving the model.
5. Conducting sensitivity analyses with the model.
6. Recommending a specific solution.
7. Assisting in implementing the solution.

In this process, the system involves a decision maker, a consultant, and a computer.

If we can codify the knowledge of the consultant in an ES, we can build a DSS/ES capable of the same process. Unfortunately, at this time relatively little is known about the nature of the cognitive skills that consultants use. However, interesting work is being done at Oregon State University, where Goul et al. (16) have developed a DSS/ES system that attempts to replicate the manager-consultant-computer system. In this system:

1. The computer queries the manager to determine the general category of the problem (e.g., an allocation problem vs. inventory management).
2. The computer queries the manager to determine the *exact nature* of the problem (e.g., what kind of allocation problem).
3. Then the computer suggests which management science model to use (e.g., dynamic programming versus linear programming).

The manager can ask the system to define terminology to justify the recommendation made by the machine, and to explain the model used. The decision maker then can formulate the problem using the model, conduct "what if" analysis, or use an alternative model. The ES, in this case, helps in identifying and classifying the managerial problem, acting as a tutor, providing illustrative examples, and selecting the model(s) to be used.

Lehner and Donnel (38) claim that there is a natural synergy between the prescriptive problem structuring techniques used in the DSS model base and the rule-based program architectures used in ES. In particular, the modeling procedures of the model base are suitable for *initial* problem structuring, whereas ES program architectures are suitable for (1) making the problem structure incrementally modifiable, and (2) developing a user interface that uses terms familiar to users.

Expert systems can be used as an *interface* between the user and the model base. Such an integration is demonstrated by BUMP, a statistical ES (18). Large numbers of statistical packages are available on the market. These packages are being used both in industry and in educational institutions to support managerial decision making and research. They contain statistical tests and models that are included in the model base of a DSS. A major dilemma faced by a nonexpert user is to determine which statistical models to use for what purposes. This is where BUMP is brought into action. This ES selects the appropriate statistical procedure, and also guides the novice user in using the not-so-friendly statistical packages (such as MULTIVARIANCE or SPSS) that usually require a trained statistician for their operation.

19.5   Intelligent Interface

Expert systems may be integrated with the interface subsystem so that the human-machine dialogue will be conducted faster and better. Expert systems are being used today as front-ends to many application and development software packages. For example, Conversational Advisory System front-ends several DBMS, and Clout is used as a front-end to R:Base 5000.

For details on this role of ES see: Harris (19), Ishikawa (28), and Chapter 18 of this book.

19.6   Integrating DSS and ES—Overview

In certain problem domains both ES and DSS may have distinct advantages that, when combined, can yield synergetic results. DSS typically gives full control to the decision maker regarding information acquisition, information evaluation, and the final decision. As research has shown, human judgmental biases may be present in complex decisions that are supported by a DSS. An ES, on the other hand, is free from acquisition, evaluation, and judgmental biases, at least in the human sense (*if* the knowledge of the expert(s) is properly represented in the ES and *if* the ES is properly designed). The ES would serve to provide intelligence for a particular domain and would make a tentative decision. The decision maker could also utilize the DSS in the traditional sense and arrive at a tentative decision. The results of the ES and DSS could then be reconciled and evaluated, with a likelihood that the joint effort could produce better results than either approach independently. This approach is not necessarily constrained by the narrowness of the domain of the ES, because an operational DSS can also be domain-specific; for example, DSS for routing vehicles in a textile company, or DSS for determing the allocation of IBM customer engineers to geographic territories.

Although typical DSS support quantitative, mathematical, and computational reasoning, DSS should also be developed to support qualitative analysis based on methodologies such as analogical reasoning, pattern recognition, and content analysis. ES are particulary well suited for these types of methodologies, and thus may provide an important link to the DSS for providing more balance in supporting various types of decision processes.

TABLE 19.2 Summary of Integration Benefits.

	ES Contribution	DSS Contribution
Database and Database Management Systems (DBMS)	□ Improves construction, operation, and maintenance of DBMS (29) □ Improves accessibility to large databases □ Improves DBMS capabilities (29) □ Permits symbolic representation of data	□ A database is provided to the ES (29)
Models and Model Base Management Systems	□ Improves model management (2) □ Helps in selecting models (16, 18) □ Provides judgmental elements to models □ Improves sensitivity analysis (16) □ Generates alternative solutions (47) □ Provides heuristics (21) □ Simplifies building simulation models □ Makes the problem structure incrementally modifiable □ Speeds up trial-and-error simulation (52)	□ Provides initial problem structure (38) □ Provides standard models and computations □ Provides facts (data) to models □ Stores specialized models constructed by experts in the model base
Interface	□ Enables friendlier interface (19, 29, 63) □ Provides explanations (38) □ Provides terms familiar to user (21) □ Acts as a tutor (16) □ Provides interactive, dynamic, visual problem-solving capability (3)	□ Provides presentations to match individual cognitive styles
System Capabilities (Synergy)	□ Provides intelligent advice (faster and cheaper than human) to the DSS or its user □ Adds explanation capability (21) □ Expands computerization of the decision-making process (16, 40)	□ Provides experience in data collection □ Provides experience in implementation (21) □ Provides individualized advice to users to match their decision styles

In the previous sections we discussed the benefits of integrating ES with the *components* of the DSS. These benefits are summarized in Table 19.2 together with the benefits from the overall system integration.

In the forthcoming section we will introduce several models of integration.

19.7 Models of DSS/ES Integration

Several researchers and practitioners proposed models for integrating DSS and ES.

The following models are described in this chapter:

a. Expert systems attached to DSS components.
b. ES as a separate DSS component.

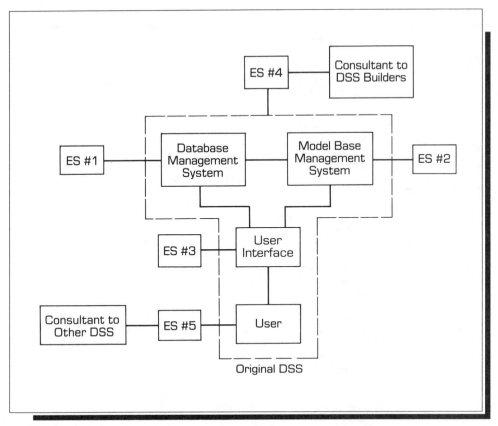

FIGURE 19.4 Integration of ES into all ESS components.

    c. ES sharing in the decision-making process.
    d. ES generating alternative solutions for DSS.
    e. A unified approach.

a. Expert Systems Attached to DSS Components.

This arrangement (per Turban and Watkins [58]) is shown in Figure 19.4. It includes five expert systems:

ES #1. This is the database intelligent component (See Section 19.3).

ES #2. This is the intelligent agent for the model base and its management (See Section 19.4).

ES #3. Improvements to the interface can be made through this system (See Section 19.5).

ES #4. In addition to advice on constructing the various components of the DSS, one can visualize an ES that will give advice on how to structure a DSS, how to glue the various parts together, how to conduct a feasibility study, and how to execute the many activities that are involved in the construction of a DSS.

The same system may be used to advise the builder (or the user) how to change the DSS to fit the needs of the environment, or the specific scenario that the DSS describes.

ES #5. The user who is considered a component of a DSS may solicit the advice of an expert for complex issues such as the nature of the problem, the environmental conditions, or the possible implementation problems. For example, in a DSS designed to examine various proposals for reorganization, the user may ask an expert how the new structure will affect certain groups of employees. Instead of consulting an expert, the user may consult an ES. A user also may want an ES that will guide him or her in how to use the DSS and its output. Another possible situation is for the user to seek advice on which specific DSS to use (if several are available).

Note: This ideal model has not been implemented yet, to the best knowledge of the author. However, an integrated system from the Carnegie Group includes several expert systems, each of which supports a *different* aspect of a DSS. For details see *High Technology Business*, July 1986.

b. ES as a Separate DSS Component

According to this proposal (per Turban and Watkins [58]), ES will be added as a separate component (See Figure 19.5). Notice that the systems share the interface as well as other resources. However, as indicated by King (32), such an integration is also available via a communication link (the networking, as discussed in Section 19.2). There are several possibilities for such an integration.

ES Output as Input to a DSS. DSS users may direct the ES output to the DSS. For example, the ES can be used during the intelligence phase of problem solving to determine the importance of the problem or to identify the problem. Then the problem is transferred to a DSS for possible solution. For an example see Courtney et al. (8).

DSS Output as Input to ES. In many cases the results of a computerized quantitative analysis provided by a DSS are forwarded to an individual or a group of experts for the purpose of evaluation. Therefore, it would make sense to direct the output of a DSS into an ES that would perform the same function as an expert, whenever it is cheaper and/or faster to do so (especially if the quality of the advice is also superior).

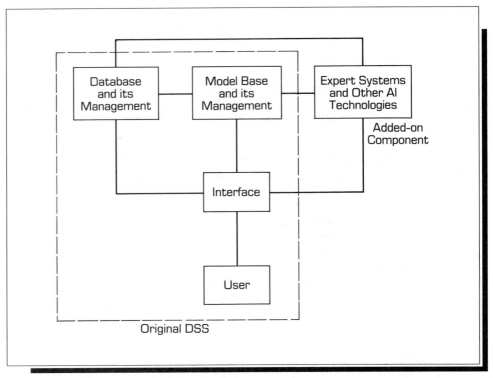

FIGURE 19.5   ES as a separate component of DSS.

Feedback   According to this configuration the output from the ES goes to a DSS, and then the output from the DSS goes back to the original ES (or to another ES).

c. Sharing in the Decision-Making Process

According to this approach, ES can complement DSS in one or more of the steps in the decision-making process. An example for such an approach is proposed by Meador, et al. (40). Decision making is viewed as an eight-step process consisting of:

1. Specification of objectives, parameters, probabilities.
2. Retrieval and management of data.
3. Generation of decision alternatives.
4. Inference of consequences of decision alternatives.
5. Assimilation of verbal, numerical, and graphical information.
6. Evaluation of sets of consequences.
7. Explanation and implementation of decisions.
8. Strategy formulation.

The first seven are typical DSS functions, whereas the last one, which requires judgment and creativity, can be done by an ES. Meador et al. [40] suggest that ES might supplement the DSS by using a built-in associative memory with knowledge of business and inferential rules.

Such an integration may be visualized as follows: The user works with the DSS following the first seven DSS steps. On reaching the strategy formulation phase he or she calls on the ES, which will be a completely separate system although it may share the database and perhaps use some of the capabilities of the model base. To better understand this type of integration, we assume that the ES plays the role of a human expert that the user can call on when in need of expertise in strategy formulation. The expert may give an answer immediately, or may conduct some analysis (e.g., forecasting). Such analysis can be accomplished by using the DSS database and its forecasting model.

d. Generating Alternative Solutions

Reitman (47) points out that most current DSS help users evaluate and choose among potential courses of action (the choice phase of decision making). However, unlike a staff assistant these DSS cannot suggest the alternative courses of action that should be considered (the design phase). He contends that this deficiency in existing DSS might be met by applying concepts and techniques taken from artificial intelligence.

Reitman describes an AI system that plays the game of Go. This system is able to work with nonnumeric data to develop alternative game strategies, evaluate them, and select the best alternative. He provides a detailed description of the strategies employed by the system to find or develop courses of action:

□ Use of a network of experts at various levels of complexity of the game.
□ Successive refinement of problems from general to specific.
□ Assignment of priorities to situations.
□ Use of an "expert and critic" structure.

Reitman demonstrates how the system tests alternatives and how it limits a search to keep the solution to a manageable task.

After describing the Go system, Reitman considers how AI-based DSS might be transferred to systems in a business context. For example, decisions regarding trading futures of commodities appear to be roughly of the same order of complexity as existing AI applications, and therefore appear to be a promising place to begin exploring the practical use of AI-based DSS.

e. A Unified Approach

Teng et al. (56) proposed a unified architecture for the ES/DSS integration. The proposal is shown in Figure 19.6.

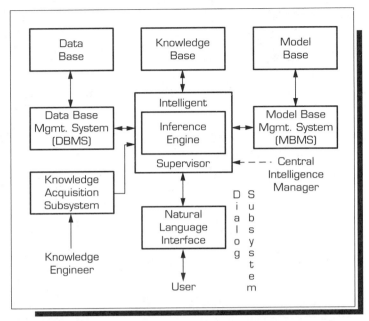

FIGURE 19.6 A unified architecture for an intelligent decision support system. (*Source:* Teng et al. [56].)

According to this proposal the ES is structured between the data and the models. Its basic function is to integrate the two components in an intelligent manner.

19.8   Integrating EIS and DSS

An EIS can be integrated with a DSS. It is especially common for EIS to be used as a source of data for PC-based modeling products. For example, at a large drug company, brand managers download from Pilot's Command Center (an EIS) the previous day's orders of their products. The download creates a Lotus-readable file on their PC disk. They then exit to the PC and run a Lotus DSS model against the data to predict where they will be at the end of the month. The results of this model are then uploaded to the EIS. So, by 11 A.M., senior managers can get on their EIS and see, for example, where each brand manager thinks he or she is going to be at the end of the month.

The integration of EIS and DSS can be accomplished in several ways. Most likely is that the information generated by the EIS is being used as an input to the DSS. More sophisticated systems include feedback to the EIS and even an explanation capability. An integrated EIS/DSS is often called an Executive Support System (ESS) and, with an explanation capability, it can be defined as an "intelligent ESS." A schematic view of such a system is given in Figure 19.7.

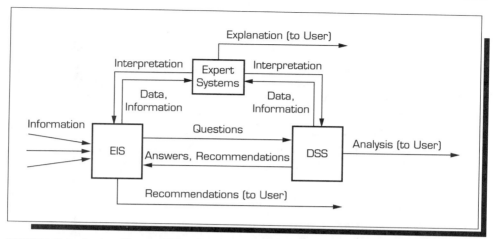

FIGURE 19.7   An intelligent ESS. (*Source:* Turban and Stevenson [57].)

19.9   Integrating ES and EIS

There is very little discussion in the literature on the integration of ES and EIS, or on how to make EIS "smarter." It is simply a very new topic. There are some studies, however, that relate to EIS functions (e.g., use of ES in problem identification). An attempt to set the stage for such an integration is reported by King (33).

Generally speaking, the major contribution of ES to EIS can be in making *interpretation* of the vast amount of information monitored by the EIS; for example, looking at abnormalities or examining potential trends. Another area is the provision of explanations to questions that may be raised by users. Of special interest is the accessibility to commerical databases.

19.10   Integrating MSS Technologies

The Management Process.   The integration of the various MSS tools can best be explored by viewing the managerial support given by such a system. To visualize such support the reader is referred to Chapter 1 Figure 1.7. The major thrust in integrated MSS is the provision of intelligent capabilities by using expert systems.

The Integration of ES

Figure 19.8 shows the potential integration of ES in the EIS/DSS supported process; what we call integrated MSS. The figure presents a potential use of seven different expert systems. Their areas of application are marked from ES 1 to ES 7.

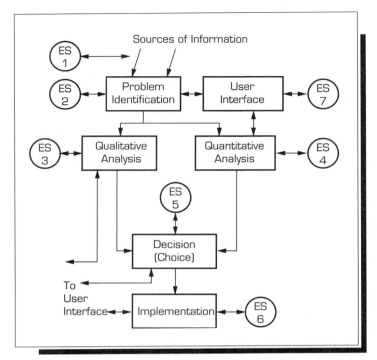

FIGURE 19.8 Integrating ES/ESS/DSS. (*Source:* Turban and Watson [59].)

ES 1. This sytem can help in the design of the flow of information to the executive (e.g., what to monitor, when) and in the *interpretation* of the collected information. Because some of the information is fuzzy, a combination of ES and neural computing can be very helpful. The entire area of scanning, monitoring, forecasting (e.g., trends), and assessment (or interpretation) can be greatly helped by automation in general (e.g., E-mail, etc.) and by ES in particular. Finally, the use of ES with external databases was discussed in Section 19.3.

ES 2. Based on the information collected, a problem (opportunity) identification is made. Expert systems can play an important role in this step both as support for the EIS (e.g., see King [33]) and in helping with a precise definition of the problem (e.g., see Courtney et al. [8]).

ES 3. Qualitative analysis is based on the use of expertise. Here, one can replace experts with ES (with a substantial saving of time and money). For example, an ES can give advice on legal or tax issues that relate to the problem. Another possible use of ES at this time is for supporting qualitative forecasting methods.

ES 4. The support of ES for quantitative analysis was discussed in detail in Section 19.4. Of special importance is the explanation capability of the results of the analysis. The analysis may be executed by staff analysts.

ES 5. A final choice of an alternative can be made by an individual or by a group. Both may need interpretation of information generated during the analysis and the execution of additional predictions. These are two typical generic categories of ES. However, the decision makers can use the ES to help in developing the final design and planning (including an implementation plan) of the proposed action. The role of ES in GDSS can be extremely important; at present we have very little information about this topic.

ES 6. ES were found to be very helpful in increasing the chances of successful implementation. The major benefits could be in the areas of explanation and training.

ES 7. Superb user interface is a key to successful implementation of any management support system. ES can improve the interface, especially when combined with natural language processors. Such an integrated system does not exist at the moment. However, the Executive Edge development tool, which is described in Chapter 10 and in Section 19.14, is the first step in this direction.

19.11 Linkages With Other CBIS

DSS, ES, EIS, or their combinations can be linked or integrated with other CBIS. For example, an EIS can be linked to commercial databases, to customers, or to suppliers. In Chapter 10, Case 1 we exhibited such an integration. DSS is tied in many cases to the corporate database (see the Xerox case in Chapter 5). In other words, MSS in many cases are integrated with the corporate information system. Another example is the link between a DSS and development and application systems. Lotus 1-2-3, for example, can be interfaced with hundreds of different software packages.

Another linkage that was discussed earlier is that of distributed systems. Micro-based DSS can be linked to the corporate IS, and data can be downloaded to the micro level.

DSS or any other MSS might be linked with others of its kind. Expert systems may be "talking" to each other much like experts do. One DSS may feed into another one or provide data to a powerful linear programming package that will conduct optimization and return the result to the DSS.

GDSS is often connected to DSS, so members can conduct analysis during deliberation. It can be tied to the corporate database or it can be connected to decision makers in remote locations.

An important integration takes place under what is described as the automated factory or integrated manufacturing. The *automated factory* is composed of several different machines, material handling facilities, robots, and other components. Orders for work flow in constantly, and therefore it is necessary to continuously plan the operation of the factory. An expert system(s) can be used to execute such planning in conjunction with some DSS and the robots. The planning will attempt to coordinate all activities of the plant, to achieve efficiency in the use of resources, to maximize productivity, to meet delivery dates, et cetera. For further details see "the integrated factory of the future" in Chapter 22.

Another application of ES is in the area of *error recovery*. The automated factory is monitored by several sensors and other detecting devices. The data collected here can be *interpreted* by an ES. Such interpretation will detect errors (or even potential errors) in the operation of any of the components. Next, an ES can *diagnose* the cause of the problem and recommend a *recovery*. A more advanced system could be integrated with robots that will execute the necessary repairs. For futher details see: Turban, E., "Expert Systems-based Robot Technology," *Expert Systems*, forthcoming.

Expert and decision support systems have been connected to CAD/CAM systems, sensory systems, and several manufacturing applications software. For further information see Kusiak (36) and Mellichamp (41).

19.12   Problems and Issues in Integration

Technical Issues

Integration will require compatibility of hardware and software. For example, if an existing ES runs on a Lisp-type machine, and the DSS on a micro, we may face some technical problems, such as the need to use different programming languages. Additionally, if we use generators, shells, and some building blocks there could be problems in finding skilled programmers for developing and combining the different parts. Such technical problems may be lessened in the future as both hardware and software containing DSS/ES capabilities continue to be developed.

Behavioral Issues

Behavioral issues in DSS include consideration of the personal characteristics of decision makers, environmental or task characteristics, and related organizational issues. Behavioral research attempts to (1) enhance the usefulness of information to the decision maker, (2) identify decision makers' information processing tendencies to tailor the database underlying the DSS to specific information processing styles, and (3) to provide insights into environmental and task characteristics that influence the decision. Because ES tend to draw conclusions and make recommendations, mimicking a human advisor, then certain aspects of the ES decision process do not directly benefit from much of the behavioral research accomplished to date in DSS. One reason for this is that ES focus on cognitive processes underlying the notion of expertise. These cognitive processes center on the long-term memory of the expert, and include perception, representation, retrieval, and reasoning. In contrast, MIS and DSS behavioral research has tended to emphasize personalities and abilities.

As discussed earlier, a desirable feature of ES is that it provides an explanation or justification for the decision reached. In practice, explanations of how ES arrive at their conclusions are not very convincing. One possible reason is that the explanations may not be tailored to specific individual users. The DSS behavioral literature concerning individual differences and the tailoring of information supplied by the DSS to individual decision makers could have relevance in tailoring the justification mechanism of ES. This is only one example for suggested research in this area.

Design Issues

Several approaches to the design process for DSS can be borrowed from the construction of ES and vice versa. For example, the iterative DSS design approach is also most suitable for ES construction. According to this approach, one uses a step-by-step dynamic approach to system development, as opposed to the systems life cycle approach commonly used in MIS system development.

Other design issues for expert systems or subsystems pertain to limitations of current ES. One limitation is the fact that constructing a large expert system may require several person-years of effort from an expert in ES design, while ES designers are currently in short supply. The expertise required on the part of the designer is: (1) knowledge of cognitive processes and the appropriate methodologies needed for extracting expertise from expert(s), and (2) programming skills in appropriate languages such as Lisp, PROLOG, and/or the specialty dialects such as frame representation, natural language processors, and assembly languages. Note that these skills need not be provided by a single individual—a team approach is usually used. Typical DSS builders, including programmers and database experts, do not have the level of expertise necessary for building ES.

Thus, the construction time of a DSS, even when constructed with the aid of a DSS generator, can be stretched to an unacceptable length if an ES component is added. Commercially available "inference engines" and shells can reduce this problem by significantly decreasing the design and development time. Another possible relief to the problem is adding on "ready-made" expert systems to a specific DSS for advising in a general area of expertise.

Despite these (and possibly other) integration difficulties, there is evidence that DSS/ES integrated systems are being developed at an increasing rate.

Notes:
1. For design issues of EIS see Chapter 10.
2. For a comprehensive review of research on MSS and their integration see: I. Benbasat and B. R. Nault, "An Evaluation of Empirical Research in Managerial Support Technologies," Research Report, Faculty of Commerce and Business Administration, University of British Columbia, 1988.

19.13 Examples of Integrated Systems

Manufacturing

IBM's Integrated Manufacturing System (55). A system called Logistics Management System (LMS) was developed by IBM for operations management. The system combines ES, simulation, traditional DSS, and computer-based information systems. In addition, the system includes computer-aided manufacturing (CAM) and distributed data processing subsystems. It provides IBM's Burlington plant manufacturing management a tool to assist in resolving crises and in planning. A similar system is used at IBM by financial analysts to simulate long-range financial planning, where an ES provides judgmental information and other pertinent factors.

DSS/Decision Simulation (DSIM) (54).   DSIM is the outcome of combining traditional DSS, statistics, operations research, database management, query languages, and artificial intelligence. AI, especially natural language interfaces and expert systems, provides three things to DSIM:

1. Ease of communication of pertinent information to the computational algorithm or display unit.
2. Assistance in finding the appropriate model, computational algorithm, or data set.
3. A solution to a problem where the computational algorithm(s) alone is not sufficient to solve the problem, a computational algorithm is not appropriate or applicable, and/or the AI creates the computational algorithm.

Marketing

Promoter.   This ES analyzes the effects of promotions and advertisements on sales in the packaged goods industry. It was developed by Management Decision Systems, Inc., and it must be used together with their mainframe EXPRESS DSS generator.

TeleStream.   This ES is used to support salespersons working in distributed houses that are selling thousands of products. The system has two parts: Sales Advisor and Sales Assistant. The Sales Advisor tells the sales person what to offer to the customer. It also tells all about accessories and supplies. The DSS part attempts to maximize management goals (such as profits and low inventories). The Sales Assistant is an interface, which determines the content of the information to be presented to the user and the method of presentation. For details see the *AI Letter*, Texas Instruments, June 1988.

Engineering ES/DSS

This integrated system was designed to boost engineers' productivity at Boeing Co. The DSS portion, called STRUDL (Structural Design Language), is essentially a passive tool whose effectiveness depends on the user's abilities. By supplying the proper data into the formula or the graphic modeling application, a design engineer can gain insight into his or her design prototype's potential. Unfortunately, STRUDL cannot help him or her decide what questions to ask or what data to key in, nor can it give any hints about further actions to take based on the results of an analysis. However, an expert system that assumes the role of teacher/partner was added on to do all this.

Financial Services

A large financial services company already has a system that is close to being a working DSS/ES (50). The company uses the system to match its various services with individual customers' needs (e.g., placing customers' assets into optimal investment packages).

Similar applications are being actively developed by large international accounting firms for combining analytical methods and judgment in auditing, and by other business entities for credit evaluation, strategic planning, and related applications. General Dynamic Corp., for example, is using ES to support project management analysis.

FINEXPERT.[*] This ES/DSS combination is designed to produce financial reports and analysis of corporations. It was developed in France by EXPERTeam in cooperation with Texas Instruments. Linked to a company's standard accounting system, the ES can produce all the standard financial reports and 50 different charts. Then it performs a *financial analysis* that includes financial activity, ratio analysis, risk analysis, profitability, and financial equilibrium. Its report also satisfies the Securities and Exchange Commission's requirements (of publicly held corporations). The system can run simulations and forecasting models, and a sophisticated explanation facility is available. The system is marketed worldwide as a ready-made system. For further details see *AI Letter*, Texas Instruments, April 1989.

American Express. The 300 American Express employees who authorize credit card purchases may access as many as 13 different databases in making their decision. Now, they are being assisted by an expert system.[**]

Inference, Inc. (Los Angeles, Calif.) personnel worked with credit authorizers from American Express's Fort Lauderdale site, the credit authorization manager, and details from case histories, to create the expert system. Figure 19.9 illustrates the credit authorization process with the authorization expert system assistant.

It took one year to build rules, check them, and fix them as necessary. A prototype was unveiled in April 1986 and tested for five months. The expert system was operational in January 1987 with 800 rules.

The only problems experienced with the system so far involve connecting the human credit authorizer's local area networks of IBM PCs with the IBM mainframe in Phoenix, Ariz. Currently, the PCs are hooked through a Sun microsystem workstation to the mainframe, but officials at American Express are hoping to attain a single vendor solution or will have to run the expert system solely on the mainframe.

The benefits of the expert system include expected productivity improvements of 20–30 percent, reduced cases of fraud and unpaid charges, and the ability to keep up with the growing number of transactions without increasing the staff.

[*]A registered trademark of EXPERTeam.
[**]Condensed from: Davis, D. B. "Artificial Intelligence Goes To Work," *High Technology*, April 1987, and from the vendor's literature.

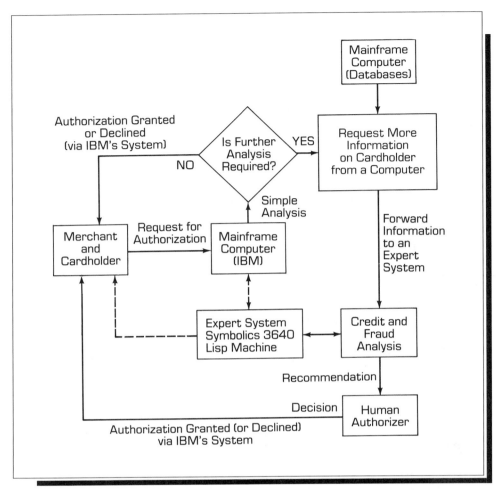

FIGURE 19.9 American Express authorizer's assistant. The merchant requests authorization from the mainframe computer. The computer checks the credit availability and performs a simple analysis (e.g., checking the cardholder's normal charging pattern). If no further analysis is needed, the authorization is either granted or declined. If further analysis is necessary, the computer collects more information about the cardholder from another mainframe computer. The initial and new information is forwarded to a rule-based expert system, which was developed with ART (from Inference Corp.). The expert system may request more information from the cardholder if necessary; then it provides a recomendation to the human authorizer (who uses an IBM 327 X terminal). (*Source:* Based on information provided by Inference Corp. and American Express.)

The Fifth-Generation Project (FGP)

Bonczek et al. (5) cite the efforts of the Fifth-Generation project as an example of the movement toward integrated DSS and ES. Figure 19.10 presents the conceptual diagram of the software system envisioned by the Japanese. As shown there, the key elements of the system are the knowledge base and its

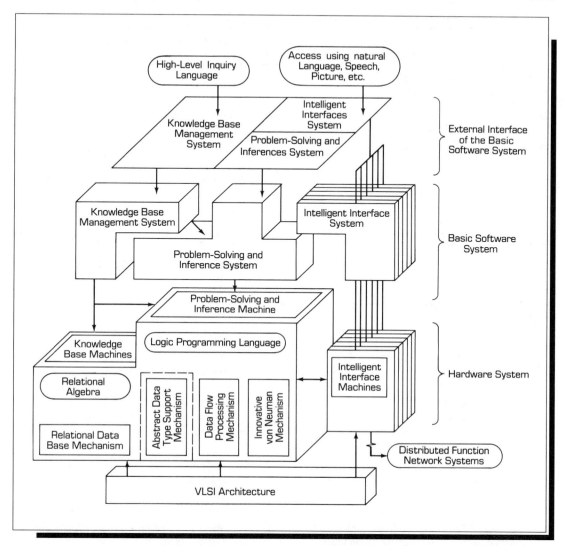

FIGURE 19.10 Basic configuration image of the fifth-generation computer systems. (*Source:* Japan Information Processing Development Center.)

management system, which would incorporate the database, model base, and the DBMS of current DSS. The problem-solving inference system would be the ES aspect, and the intelligent interface system would encompass a natural language interface. In addition, intelligent systemization and utility systems would be developed. The basic application system would then interface with the rest of the components, much like current DSS.

Table 19.3 shows some of the major constituents of a fifth-generation system. As well as being central to the problem-solving and inference system, the core language (a PROLOG derivative) will also be used to write much of the software for the knowledge-base system and the intelligent interface system.

TABLE 19.3 The Components of the Fifth-Generation-Project.

	Knowledge Base Management System	Problem-Solving and Inference System	Intelligent Interface System
External interface to basic software	High-level inquiry language	Core language (PROLOG derivative)	Natural language, speech, pictures, etc.
Basic Software	1. Knowledge representation language 2. Knowledge base support system 3. Knowledge acquisition system 4. External knowledge bases	1. Intelligent programming system 2. Meta-inference system 3. Distributed problem solving	1. Intelligent parser and meaning analyzer 2. Continuous speech recognizer 3. Picture processing system
Hardware	1. Relational database machine 2. Parallel relational operations	1. Data flow machine 2. Abstract data-type mechanism 3. Parallel inference mechanism	1. Image processing machine 2. Speech processing machine

Source: Van Horn (61).

There are two relations between expert systems and the Fifth-Generation project. First, expert systems are seen as a major application of the new computers, which are intended to tackle a range of nonnumeric processing tasks presently untouched by computers. The new architecture and the much faster processing speeds will allow much more sophisticated expert systems to be built and will offer researchers ways of solving some of the more difficult problems inherent in the technology.

The second aspect of the relationship between the Fifth-Generation and expert systems is that expert systems will be an integral part of the new computers. The hardware will be so complicated that it will be impossible for ordinary users to make the best use of it. Their interactions with the computer will be guided by an expert system (or several expert systems), probably using a natural language interface.

Developmental Tools

At the present time the developmental tools of DSS and ES are completely independent. However, there are some indications that such tools can be combined. Some ES developmental tools already possess DSS capabilities. GURU (from Micro Data Base Systems, Inc.) combines an expert system's shell with a database management system, a spreadsheet, graphics, communications, and a word processing package. KEE (from Intellicorp, Menlo Park, CA) includes models for various computations and a system's simulation (regular and visual).

Finally, Executive Edge (Chapter 10 and Section 19.14) permits the construction of EIS/DSS with explanation capabilities.

The Fifth-Generation Project (FGP)

Artificial intelligence is often referred to as the fifth generation of computer technology. The Japanese plan to create their fifth-generation computer to leapfrog the leaders in this field. If successful, it will represent a highly significant event in human history. They are determined to shed the imitator image and make a revolutionary push. The Japanese plan to create a computer that can talk, listen, learn, and make sophisticated decisions. That means an extensive utilization of AI techniques.

Some of the objectives of this fifth-generation computer are to:

☐ Provide high intelligence level to cooperate with people.
☐ Assist people to discover and develop unknown fields.
☐ Offer vast knowledge bases.
☐ Aid in management.
☐ Solve social problems.
☐ Acquire new perceptions by simulating unknown situations.
☐ Offer significant software productivity improvement.
☐ Reduce time and cost to develop computerized systems by a factor of 10.

Ultimately, the computer is to have the capability to recognize continuous speech, possess supervision, make intelligent decisions, perform self-repair, and augment the decision maker in general.

19.14 Execucom's Integrated System

Executive Edge is the first commerical ESS product to exploit the power of ES to improve the executive's ability to analyze information. AI-based analysis capabilities in IFPS/Plus can permit the executive to ask a "drill down" question and receive an automated answer that is similar in scope and focus to the type of answer a technically proficient analyst could produce. The ES in this case is a built-in, rule-based system that embodies much of the expertise that a technical analyst uses when searching a computer application to isolate the primary causes for a particular output.[*]

These rules include such things as the "80/20 Rule" (most of the significance is covered by explaining 80 percent of the output), the importance of offsetting variances (variances of opposite sign but similar scale are equally important), and the effects of scaling (a partially owned operation is only important to the degree to which it is owned).

To illustrate how the explanation facility works with IFPS/Plus and the Executive Edge we present an example.

[*]The origin and some of the theory underlying this system are described in: King, D., "The ERGO Project: A natural language query facility for explaining financial modeling results," *DSS 86 Transactions*, San Francisco, CA, June 1986.

Example: Applying Expert System
Explanation Capabilities in IFPS*

Mainframe IFPS/Plus provides several AI-based (rule-based) explanation commands. These commands give answers in plain English sentences that explain which variables were most important in producing an answer. To illustrate the explanation commands, consider the WHAT IF CONTINUE case of the Simple IFPS Model for computing dividend forecasts, introduced in Chapter 7.

The Why Questions. The following are representative WHY questions you might ask after reviewing the solution in Figure 19.11 .

WHY DID DIVIDENDS GO DOWN IN 1993?
WHY IS NET PROFIT AFTER TAX HIGHER IN 1995 THAN IN 1993?
WHY DO DIVIDENDS PEAK IN 1993?

The IFPS answer to the first question is shown in Figure 19.12. In the case of the third question, the question is wrong; dividends did not peak in 1993.

```
***** WHAT IF CASE 2 *****
3 WHAT IF STATEMENTS PROCESSED

                           1991    1992    1993    1994    1995

         IFPS MODEL FOR COMPUTING DIVIDEND FORECAST

DIVIDENDS                   324   333.7   214.8   221.3   264.4
NET PROFIT AFTER TAX        648   667.4   429.7   442.6   528.8
SALE                       4500    4635    5968    6147    7344
COGS                       3600    3708    5371    5532    6610
TAXES                       252   259.6   167.1   172.1   205.6

  ASSUMPTIONS

TAX RATE                  .2800   .2800   .2800   .2800   .2800
DIVIDEND PAYOUT RATE      .5000   .5000   .5000   .5000   .5000
SALES COST RATE           .8000   .8000   .8000   .8000   .8000
QUANTITY SOLD              1000    1000    1250    1250    1450
SELLING PRICE             4.500   4.635   4.774   4.917   5.065
SELLING PRICE GROWTH RATE 1.030   1.030   1.030   1.030   1.030

ENTER SOLVE OPTIONS

?
```

FIGURE 19.11 Solution of WHAT IF CONTINUE case.

*This section was written by Dr. Paul Gray and is reproduced with his permission.

```
?  WHY DID DIVIDENDS GO DOWN IN 1993

DIVIDENDS WENT DOWN IN 1993 BECAUSE NET PROFIT AFTER TAX
DECREASED
50 DIVIDENDS = DIVIDEND PAYOUT RATE * NET PROFIT AFTER TAX


                                   AMOUNT
                         1992      CHANGE     1993
DIVIDENDS                333.7     -118.9     214.8
NET PROFIT AFTER TAX     667.4     -237.8     429.7
```

FIGURE 19.12 Typical WHY Explanation.

They actually peaked in 1992. IFPS is smart enough to give the correct answer. (Try it!)

With the CONTINUE command, issued subsequent to any WHAT IF or WHAT IF CONTINUE, IFPS steps down one level in the solution tree steucture and examines the variable(s) at that level.

IFPS then produces an explanation of the one independent variable which had the most significant effect on the previous explanation. CONTINUE may be repeatedly issued until the variable being analyzed contains input data only. This situation is demonstrated in Fig. 19.13.

The Outline and Diagram Commands. IFPS provides the OUTLINE and DIAGRAM commands that show the *interrelations* among the variables of a model. For example, the OUTLINE command for the variable DIVIDENDS, in the dividend forecast model, yields the result shown in Figure 19.14.

Here, the indentation shows the hierarchy of variable definition. Variables marked with an asterisk (such as SALES) are defined higher in the hierarchy. The OUTLINE command produces a vertical display of all the direct and indirect inputs to a particular variable where the direct variables are those included in the definition in line 50 and the indirect variables are those, such as sales and initial sales, which have to be evaluated to obtain the direct variables. The DIAGRAM command for DIVIDENDS shows the inputs to the left and outputs to the right of the variable name:

```
DIVIDEND PAYOUT RATE - |- DIVIDENDS - |- NONE
NET PROFIT AFTER TAX - |
```

The WHY, OUTLINE, and DIAGRAM commands can be issued after any question mark and, provided the SOLVE command has been used, IFPS will respond. The WHY question has to be in the form WHY followed by a statement that includes:

   □ A variable name (e.g., DIVIDENDS).
   □ A column reference (e.g., 1994).
   □ A reference to a previous column or a previous case.

```
? WHY DID DIVIDENDS GO DOWN IN 1993

DIVIDENDS went down in 1993 because NET PROFIT AFTER TAX
decreased.

50 DIVIDENDS = DIVIDEND PAYOUT RATE*NET PROFIT AFTER TAX

                                        Amount
                            1992        Change        1993
DIVIDENDS                   333.7       -118.9        214.8
NET PROFIT AFTER TAX        667.4       -237.8        429.7

? CONTINUE

NET PROFIT AFTER TAX went down in 1993 because COGS increased.
This result was partially offset because SALES increased
and TAXES decreased.

60 NET PROFIT AFTER TAX = SALES - COGS - TAXES

                                        Amount
                            1992        Change        1993
NET PROFIT AFTER TAX         667        -238           430
COGS                        3708        1663          5371
SALES                       4635        1333          5968
TAXES                        260        -92.47         167

? CONTINUE

COGS went up in 1993 because SALES and SALES COST RATE
increased.

80 COGS = SALES COST RATE * SALES

                                        Amount
                            1992        Change        1993
COGS                        3708        1663          5371
SALES                       4635        1333          5968
SALES COST RATE             .8000       .1000         .9000

? CONTINUE

Sales went up in 1993 because QUANTITY SOLD increased.

70 SALES = SELLING PRICE * QUANTITY SOLD

                                        Amount
                            1992        Change        1993
SALES                       4635        1333          5968
QUANTITY SOLD               1000         250          1250

? CONTINUE

QUANTITY SOLD DOES NOT DEPEND ON ANY OTHER VARIABLES.

180 QUANTITY SOLD = 1000 FOR 2, 1250 FOR 2, 1450
? CONTINUE
CANNOT CONTINUE FROM THIS POINT
```

FIGURE 19.13 CONTINUE command in a WHY explanation.

```
? OUTLINE DIVIDENDS

50 DIVIDENDS = DIVIDEND PAYOUT RATE*NET PROFIT AFTER TAX

DIVIDENDS
 .DIVIDEND PAYOUT RATE
 .NET PROFIT AFTER TAX
  ..SALES
   ...SELLING PRICE
    ....SELLING PRICE GROWTH RATE
   ...QUANTITY SOLD
  ..COGS
   ...SALES COST RATE
  ..*SALES
  ..TAXES
  ..*SALES
  ..*COGS
   ...TAX RATE
```

FIGURE 19.14 Result of OUTLINE DIVIDENDS Command.

The latter is particularly useful because it allows direct comparison of different WHAT IF cases.

The Explain Command. If your computer is a mainframe or mini made by IBM or DEC, you can use the EXPLAIN command, which automates the explanation commands. To obtain EXPLAIN, type the command in response to a question mark. That is,

 ? explain

The menu screen shown in Figure 19.15 appears.

The EXPLAIN screen presents the essence of the questions being asked in menu form. Like the menu at some Chinese restaurants, you are asked to pick one item from each column. The first column lists the questions you can ask, such as WHY DID or OUTLINE. The second column lists each of the variables in the model. The third column is used for WHY DID and WHY IS questions. The names of the column headings are shown last. After an item is selected from a list, the cursor is automatically moved to the next appropriate list. For example, if the user selects WHY DID, the cursor will automatically be moved to the variables list, and so on. This ensures that a user cannot ask a question that cannot be handled by the system.

It is important to note that this type of automated, AI-based analysis greatly extends the usability and maintainability of an MSS, but is still not a substitute for the human analyst. That is because the complete answer may not be in the numbers available to the ES-based analysis tool. For example, in analyzing a variance in corporate net income, the AI-based tool might be able to isolate an aberrant pattern in the expenses of a particular division as the key contributing

```
MODEL: DIVIDEND

COMMANDS          VARIABLES           DID COMPARISONS       COLUMNS
WHY DID           DIVIDENDS           GO UP                 1991
WHY IS            DIVIDEND PAYOUT     GO DOWN               1992
DEFINITION FOR    NET PROFIT AFTER    CHANGE                1993
VALUE OF          SALES               GO UP SO MUCH         1994
DIAGRAM           COGS                GO UP SO LITTLE       1995
OUTLINE           TAXES               GO DOWN SO MUCH
AGAIN             SELLING PRICE       GO DOWN SO LITTLE
CONTINUE          SELLING PRICE GR    PEAK
CONTINUE DOWN     QUANTITY SOLD       DIP
MSGWAIT           SALES COST RATE
QUIT              TAX RATE            IS COMPARISONS
                                      HIGHER
                                      LOWER
                                      THE SAME AS

===> WHY DID DIVIDENDS GO DOWN IN 1993?
```

FIGURE 19.15 EXPLAIN screen in IFPS.

factor. However, a human analyst will still have to investigate that expense fluctuation to determine if it was actually caused by a flood, or a strike, or some other phenomenon that is not described by the numbers.

19.15 Conclusions

ES can make DSS and EIS a more active, and potentially more valuable, participant in the decision process. Presently DSS is often used to answer the question "what if?" DSS/ES will also be able to answer the question "why?"

Scott-Morton, who pioneered the concept of DSS, made the following remarks regarding the DSS/ES integration:

> DSS as we know them may even become obsolete in the foreseeable future. They are being supplanted by expert decision support systems—EDSS. This next generation of DSS will combine existing DSS technology with the capabilities of AI . . . The messages users input and the computer's response will virtually duplicate everyday human conversation, and the EDSS will be able to supply a variety of alternative solutions to problems ("if that doesn't work, try this . . ."). EDSS will even warn users when they are proceeding under faulty assumptions ("Are you sure your figures for FY 1988 are accurate?") or supplying incomplete information (if the user inputs, "Give me the sales figures for Kansas City," the system will quickly reply, "Do you mean Kansas City, Missouri, or Kansas City, Kansas?"). (50, p. 12)

Despite the great potential of integration, one should not conclude that all future systems will be integrated. On the contrary, most DSS (especially the small ones for personal use) will remain independent, at best sharing certain AI concepts and technologies with ES. Similarly, many ES will operate as independent systems, advising users on specific issues that are completely unrelated to any DSS. Finally, many EIS will function as stand-alone systems.

However, there are several reasons why we believe that MSS integration will be most prevalent. First, there is evidence that some current design efforts are using this approach and several systems already are structured in this fashion. Second, an ES is usually applied to a narrow domain, whereas a DSS or an EIS is usually broader in scope; therefore, it logically follows that several ES may be needed to fully support one DSS or EIS. This seems to be a very expensive arrangement. However, an expert system that specializes in one area (e.g., in a model base) could advise several DSS builders on model base issues (such as selection of a model), thus reducing the cost through sharing. Finally, recent developments in ES software tools could make the construction of a simple ES, in a very narrow domain, an inexpensive and rapid undertaking. Therefore, it would be economically feasible to have several small ES exclusively serving one large, even ad hoc, DSS, or one EIS, or their combination.

While evalutating the potential integration of MSS, one should not forget the potential difficulties of such integration.

As we described earlier, DSS have the flexibility to support the solution of a wide range of semistructured and unstructured problems. ES are developed for very narrow domains. Thus the integration of a *general* problem support system (DSS) and a *specific*, narrow problem support system (ES) poses some difficulties. It is not clear that the expertise in ES is transferable across problem domains such as those potentially supported by a DSS, and thus research needs to be undertaken in this area. Today's ES also fall short of the goal of performing at high levels of general, intelligent behavior. Additional technical, behavioral, and design limitations and issues could provide a fertile ground for DSS/ES integration research. These limitations are spurring development of smarter systems, systems able to reason from what is called "deep knowledge." But it may take several years before such systems are fully developed.

All of which is not to suggest that companies should refrain from integrating MSS, to wait until a trouble-free combination is available. Some experts contend that a state-of-the-art DSS or EIS could be upgraded today into an intelligent system with existing ES technology.

Recent studies from both the Boston-based Yankee Group and International Data Corporation in Framingham, Mass. (50), show that decision support systems are currently being used by only two to three percent of non-DP/MIS executives and managers in U.S. companies. When the integrated MSS attain their full potential, and when executives are able to communicate with the computer by using their voices, these systems will be used by almost all managers and executives.

Questions for Review

1. DSS and ES integration may result in benefits along what three dimensions?
2. List the areas where synergy may result as DSS and ES are integrated.

3. It is said that ES is an intelligent DSS. List the common characteristics of DSS and ES.
4. List the major differences between DSS and ES.
5. What is the difference between functional and physical integration?
6. Summarize the benefits DSS can gain in its database when integrating with ES.
7. How can DSS benefit the knowledge base of an ES?
8. Summarize the benefits that ES can provide to a DSS in the area of models and their management.
9. What is the major capability of BUMP?
10. What is a natural language?
11. What is a natural language processor?
12. Summarize the benefits that ES can provide to a DSS dialog subsystem.
13. What is the difference between embedded and access integration?
14. How can an ES assist the user of a DSS?
15. List the various possibilities of integrating DSS and ES according to the model suggested in Figure 19.5.
16. Give an example of an ES output that can be used as an input to a DSS. Give also an example of the reverse relationship.
17. How can an ES assist in generating alternative courses of action?
18. List some technical issues of integrating DSS and ES.
19. List some behavioral issues of DSS/ES integration.
20. List some design issues that may arise during DSS/ES integration.
21. List the major contributions of ES to Decision Simulation (DSIM).
22. How can ES enhance knowledge management?
23. Why is an ES needed as an interface to commercial databanks?

Questions for Discussion

1. Why may it be difficult to integrate an expert system with an existing information system? Comment on data, people, hardware, and software.
2. "An integration of DSS and ES can result in benefits during the construction (development) of systems and during their operation." Explain this statement and give an example of both cases.
3. DSS is older and more developed than ES. How can the experience in building DSS benefit ES construction?
4. Review the differences listed in Table 1.4 between DSS and ES. Which are the three most important?
5. One ES may be used to consult several DSS. What is the logic of such an arrangement? What problems may result when two or more DSS share an ES?
6. Review the work of Goul and associates (16). Assume they will be successful in developing an ES that will perform as well as a management scientist consultant. What could be the major implications of such a system? Why is it difficult to build it?
7. Compare the work of Goul and associates with that of Hand (18). Specifically, what is the major similarity between BUMP and Goul's system?
8. Why is visual problem solving (or visual modeling) considered an integration of DSS and ES?
9. Explain how the addition of ES capability can improve the chance of successful implementation of a DSS.
10. Compare Figures 19.4 and 19.5. What are the major differences? What are the similarities? Can Figure 19.5 be viewed as a special case of Figure 19.4? Why or why not?

11. Review current journals and identify a system that you believe is an integration of DSS and ES. Analyze this system according to the models suggested in this chapter.

12. Explain why the Fifth-Generation Project is viewed as a DSS-ES integration.

13. Will DSS, as we know them today, become obsolete in the future? (That is, will all DSS be supplemented by ES? See prediction made by Scott-Morton.)

14. In some of our models we suggested that several ES will be included in one MSS. What is the logic of such an arrangement?

15. Modeling involves three activities: Construction, use, and interpretation. Give an example from use of models in an area that you are familiar with and explain how ES can help the process.

CASE 1: The Program Manager's Support System (PMSS)

The PMSS is an integrated MSS developed by the Defense Systems Management College (DSMS).* It is an application of decision support systems technology to the defense acquisition program management environment.

The purpose of the PMSS is to provide a management tool for managers in a program management office (PMO), to assist them in their decision-making process, and to help them execute their project more effectively and efficiently. It makes maximum use of color and graphical presentations. It uses "zoom" to show the last six months of activities. It also has explanation screens.

The PMSS is intended to support the defense program manager and his or her first-echelon staff. The PMSS also can be utilized by other managers in the acquisition community.

The PMSS will:

- Be an integrated software system operable on various hardware systems. The target hardware is low-cost microcomputers; for example, the DOD standard Zenith Z-248. (The system also is being designed to run on minicomputers.)
- Provide a capability to (1) integrate program management functional areas of responsibility, (2) generate program alternatives and impacts caused by various management actions and technical activities, (3) assess these impacts on the program's functional areas, and (4) utilize other decision-making support methodologies.
- Provide educational tools to facilitate the teaching of program management functions at educational institutions involved with defense systems acquisition program management.

The PMSS consists of two major parts, functional modules and the integrated PMSS. Functional modules are software programs that can be used as stand-alone programs to assist in program management areas of responsibility such as planning, acquisition strategy development, program management plan generation, cost estimating, scheduling, Program Objectives Memorandum (POM) development, budget generation, budget execution monitoring, financial management, systems engineering,

*The description of this program is based on Scanlon, K. M., and H. J. Schutt, *The Program Manager's Support (MSS), An Executive Overview and Systems Description*, Defense Systems Management College, Fort Belvior, VA, January 1987, and on a fact sheet No. 9.5, December 1988.

production planning, integrated logistics support planning, test issues identification, Test and Evaluation Master Plan (TEMP) generation, TEMP evaluation and monitoring, configuration management, document generation, document evaluation and monitoring, program office staffing and organization, et cetera. These modules support specific functions of program management operations.

The integrated PMSS consists of a number of integrated functions. The Program Overview function shows, in a color-coded (green, yellow, red) mode, the overall status of a program by the program hierarchical information categories. This provides the program manager an "instant" visual picture of his or her program status and quickly pinpoints program areas that require further management attention. The integrated PMSS, through the Program Impact Advisor function, provides the capability for a program manager to tackle unstructured problems and address "What if?" and "Should I?" questions. This capability integrates the functions of the functional modules so that a program manager can look across his or her entire program and address such questions as "What is the impact on my program if I get a 10 percent cut?" or "What is the impact on my program if the technology I need slips six months?" or "What is the impact on my program if there is a schedule delay?" The integrated PMSS looks across and within all functional areas of responsibility to assess the impact on the program and helps the program manager develop alternatives for recovery.

The PMSS will also provide executive support aids such as a calendar; name, address, and phone listings with dial-up capability; a tickler system; travel status reports; and a briefing presentation aid. Support capabilities such as word processing, spreadsheets, database management, and decision tools can be added by the user, at his or her discretion.

The PMSS permits the integration of the user's experience, judgment, and intuition to allow the user to evaluate available alternatives and, ultimately, aid the user to make better, more timely decisions.

PMSS includes DSS, EIS, and ES capabilities as will be described next.

The DSMC/PMSS Functional Modules In Distribution

1. *Contract Appraisal System (CAPPS)* module. The purpose of the CAPPS module is to help managers keep abreast of, and quantify, project contract status information. The CAPPS provides an analysis of Cost Performance Report (CPR) or Cost/Schedule Status Report (CSSR) data provided by contractors. The module provides performance "exception" indicators, interpretations of the data presented, and automated trend analysis. The CAPPS includes mathematical checks on new data.

2. The *Cost Analysis Strategy Assessment (CASA)* module is a life cycle costing model. It can be used for trade-off analyses, repair-level analyses, production rate and quantity analyses, warranty analyses, spares provisioning, resource projections (e.g., manpower, support equipment), risk and uncertainty analyses, cost driver sensitivity analyses, reliability growth analyses, operational availability analyses, and spares optimization.

3. The computerized *Competition Evaluation Model (CEM)* helps decision-makers determine the economics of using production competition. It compares the benefits with the costs of using a competitive production strategy. This particular model uses standard progress (learning) curve theory as a starting point for analysis.

4. *Software Cost Estimating (SWCE)* module. This module was developed as a template on Symphony (from Lotus Development Corp.). The user can enter any of 14 cost drivers with results shown in terms of estimated effort in man-hours and estimated development time.

5. The *Government Activity Tasking (GAT)* module can assist with the planning, budgeting and tracking of tasks assigned to government activities (as opposed to contracting). This module allows correlation of tasks by funding citation, project, activity, or task.

6. The *Procurement Strategy Module (PSM)* is designed to assist in selecting a procurement strategy that can be pursued during each phase of a specific defense system's life cycle.

7. *Schedule Risk Assessment Management (SCRAM)* module. This module provides the capabilities of (1) developing network schedules of program activities, (2) performing schedule management functions (such as determining program status, identifying critical acitivities, developing work-arounds, etc.), and (3) conducting top-level schedule risk assessment. As a risk management tool, the module will provide estimates of the likelihood of achieving specified program milestones and will assist the manager in developing alternative plans that do meet program objectives.

8. The *Executive Support System (ESS)* module is designed to assist government users with the day-to-day administrative type of functions such as keeping track of appointments and actions due. It contains a calendar function, action item status, telephone and address lists with automatic dialing, and travel status.

9. *The Program Office Organization and Staffing (PROS)* module assists with organization and staffing functions such as turnover rates analysis or travel trends.

The PMSS Functional Modules In Development And Testing

1. The *QuickCost* module is designed to respond quickly to budget questions, such as "What is the impact if we cut the production rate from 500/year to 300/year?" The module shows quantity/rate relationships and the impacts of stretchouts and inflation changes.

2. *Expert Systems for Acquisition Strategies (ESAS)/Procurement Document Generator (PDG)*. The *ESAS* and the PDG were developed for an Army activity that was concerned with nondevelopmental items (NDI) and nonmajor development support equipment. The ESAS module was tailored for that application and cannot be used by program management offices in other weapons systems areas. However, it can be customized to any user's need by the builders. The ESAS is designed to assist managers in writing clear, concise, and consistent acquisition strategy. The system encourages an inexperienced project engineer to think about important issues that are often overlooked. The (PDG) is designed to assist managers in the development and maintenance of procurement documentation. The PDG may be executed in conjunction with the ESAS module.

3. *Parametric Cost Estimating (PACE)*. The objective of this module is to assist managers to develop cost estimates for elements of a weapon system and the conduct of cost trade-off analyses.

4. *Schedule and Resource Allocation (SARA)* Module. This is a planning tool to assist managers in the initial development of, and subsequent changes in, a program schedule and the allocation of resources. A schedule is entered, resource categories are designated (up to 13 can be color coded), resource limitations are entered, and the program schedule is constructed in a Gantt Chart format.

5. *Automated Program Planning and Documentation Module (APPDM)*: The objective of this module is to develop a generic software program to assist managers with planning and documentation activities in all appropriate elements of a defense weapon system acquisition program.
6. *Budget Preparation and Execution (BP&E)* module provides a simulation and tracking tool to assist managers with program budget formulation, monitoring, and decision making.
7. *The Venture Evaluation Review Techniques (VERT)* is a stochastic network module designed to simulate decision environments under risk. The VERT provide accurate risk information in all three risk parameters (time, cost, and performance) simultaneously.
8. *The Document Keyword Search (DOKS)* module provides the capability to index text files and search multiple files based on user-selectable key words. (Using natural language processing.)
9. The *Parametric Cost Estimating Relationships (PACER)* module provides for collecting and documenting Cost Estimating Relationships (CERs) and Cost Factors (CF) to assist in the defense material systems life-cycle cost estimating process.
10. *Small Contract Cost Performance System (SCCPS)* is a modification to the CAPPS module designed to accommodate less than major programs and service contract data.
11. *Test Issues Management Evaluation (TIME)* module is an expert system that will assist the manager in identifying and developing the test issues and criteria for a weapons systems program.

The Integrated PMSS

The Integrated PMSS is an automated, interactive decision support system designed for use on a day-to-day basis. It operates on a database of program information that may be derived from a program's MIS or from direct entry through PMSS.

The PMSS operates on this data to permit the user to ask "What if?" and "Should I?" questions, and to generate alternative courses of action for consideration. By integrating the results with external influences imposed on the program, and by applying experience, judgment, and intuition, the user will be able to evaluate the available alternatives and, ultimately, make better and more timely decisions.

The basic concept of the PMSS is the integration of information from all of a program's functional areas. Various primary PMSS functions allow the user to use and manipulate this integrated information to solve program problems.

The PMSS contains seven components. These are Executive Support, Program Overview, Program Impact Advisor, Functions, Category, Modules, and Utilities. The *Executive Support* contains a calendar, telephone and address lists, action item status, and travel status.

The *Program Overview* component is designed to allow the user to obtain an overall program status report, assess key program areas, and evaluate potential problem areas.

The *Program Impact Advisor* provides the capability to change a program schedule and/or funding, and through an *expert system*, obtain an analysis of the impacts those changes have on the overall program. In addition, modifications to the program are recommended for the user's consideration.

The *Functions* component contains a number of functional capabilities that are used to create or modify program information. The functional areas currently supported include work breakdown structure, PERT networks and critical path display, budget planning and preparation, program evaluation, budget tracking and execution, Gantt milestones, and report generation.

Category gives the user access to the program data via six information categories and the database's hierarchical structure. The Modules component provides the capability to directly access PMSS stand-alone modules and user installed commercial software packages. Finally, the Utilities component includes both system administration and program management utilities such as setting user access, screen colors, data backup, et cetera. The Integrated PMSS is designed to operate on a Zenith Z-248 or compatible with a 40MB hard disk and EGA Graphics.

PMSS Implementation. The implementation of the PMSS is carried through the Program Manager's Decision Support Center which comprises three facilities as shown in Figure 19.16.

A major research objective of the PMSS program is to determine how much of an overall PMSS can be implemented on a stand-alone microcomputer system costing about $10,000–15,000. Hence, one part of the Decision Support Center is a PMSS Laboratory. The purpose of the laboratory is threefold: first, to test the PMSS concept; second, to have a facility to design, build, debug, test, and operate modules of the PMSS; third, to test the microcomputer capabilities and capacities in the PMSS environment. In addition, standard, off-the-shelf software packages will be tested in the laboratory for application in the PMSS environment.

A second part of the Decision Support Center is the Decision Conference Room. It will be used by student groups to solve classroom exercises or by program managers and their staffs to solve real problems. In either case, users bring the technical content of their problems and exercise them by using the PMSS.

The third part is the Defense Acquisition Information Repository (DAIR). The DAIR is the collection of programmatic data on selected defense system programs that provide the necessary database for operation of the modules and PMSS.

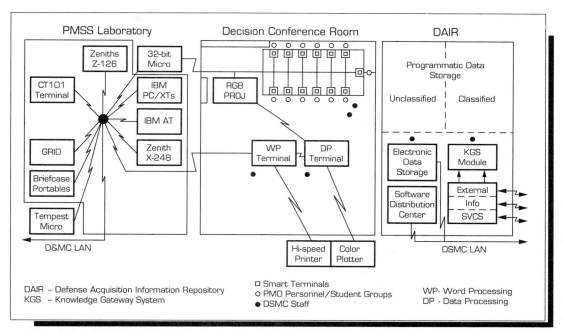

FIGURE 19.16 PMSS implementation.

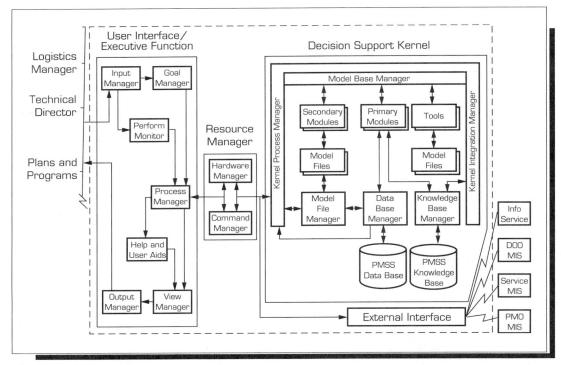

FIGURE 19.17 PMSS software architecture.

PMSS Software Architecture. The PMSS software architecture, delineated in Figure 19.17, consists of a user interface/executive module, a resource manager, a decision support kernel, and an external interface module. The user interface/executive module includes seven submodules: input manager, goal manager, performance monitor, user interface process manager, view manager, output manager, and help and user aids. The resource manager acts as an interface among the user interface/executive, the decision support kernel, and the external interface. It also coordinates and allocates hardware resources and builds actual system commands.

The decision support kernel is the heart of the PMSS. It contains a kernel process manager, kernel integration manager, model base manager (which interfaces with all of the PMSS functional modules), module file manager, knowledge base manager, database manager, module files, and the PMSS data and knowledge bases. An application of artificial intelligence in the decision support kernel to support the program impact analysis function is being developed.

The external interface provides the user the capability to query other automated systems ranging from the program management office's own management information system to external information services such as Defense Technical Information Center (DTIC) and Compuserve. This module contains a knowledge gateway system (KGS) to translate the user's needs into the proper protocol and query the appropriate databases/systems so the user will not have to learn about each. The external interface may also be used to update the PMSS database from the management information systems used by the program management office.

Questions

1. What is the difference between the functional modules and the integrated PMSS?
2. Identify the EIS elements of PMSS.
3. Describe and discuss the role of ES in PMSS.
4. List the major benefits of PMSS.
5. PMSS provides extensive "what if" capabilities. Why are these so important in this case?
6. Most of the 20 modules include extensive formulas and models. As such they can be used independently of PMSS. Why is there a need to provide an integrated PMSS?
7. Identify the ES contribution to CAPPS.
8. How do DSS features improve the effectiveness of CEM?

CASE 2: The Procurement, Assembly, and Distribution (PAD) System

Introduction

The PAD system was developed at the Intelligent Computers Systems Research Institute, University of Miami, FL.* The system, which was prototyped at IBM's PC plant, provides analysis and advice for the procurement of parts, assignment of plants for their assembly, and allocation of finished products to worldwide distribution centers for a five-year planning horizon. The system departs from and adds to typical rule-based ES-type programs in several ways:

1. By including elements of DSS like management science models.
2. By being programmed in OPS–5, the ES can be used on several types of computers in a routine fashion.
3. By covering a set of important, broadly based management problems (as opposed to the usual very specialized programs utilizing specific knowledge in narrow problem areas).

The process of establishing part procurement schedules for alternative vendors under varying company rules and constraints, the time-phased assignment of those schedules to various plants, and the allocation of outputs to distribution centers, make for a complex process in which there are many cascading decision points. Overall the process may be viewed as very large, multidimensional dynamic programming,** which in theory has an optimum solution. But the size of the problem and the uncertainties involved precluded any practical implementation of such a solution. Furthermore, the program is required for a variety of final products, so there is a high premium on flexibility. Finally, the program has to be as self-documenting and explanatory as possible.

*Based on Lynch, J. D. and D. B. Hertz, "The Anatomy of AI: An Industrial Example," paper presented at TIMS/ORSA annual meeting, Atlanta, GA, November 5–6, 1985.
**Dynamic programming is a fairly complex management science tool. For further information, see J. M. Norman, *Elementary Dynamic Programming*, New York: Crane, Russak, 1975.

```
FLEXIBLE EXPERT SYSTEM DEVELOPED FOR
COMPUTER MANUFACTURER

OBJECTIVE:  COST-EFFECTIVE CONFIGURATIONS
            FOR COMPONENT SOURCING,
            ASSEMBLY LOCATIONS, AND
            PRODUCT DISTRIBUTION

            FIVE-YEAR HORIZON, 20 PRODUCTS
            DOMESTIC AND FOREIGN
```

FIGURE 19.18 The PAD system.

The Procurement, Assembly, and Distribution Problem

The problem, as posed by the user, was to develop a flexible ES that would permit management to determine the total cost of an assembled personal computer for any configuration of components, component sourcing, assembly locations, and distribution points using given cost factors and geographic locations. With the ES, management was to be able to determine comparative total costs of alternative parts composition and production configurations and to check the sensitivity of those costs to any changes in input factors. It was required that the program provide context-sensitive operational aids as well as explanations of resulting outputs. Figure 19.18 gives an overview of the system.

System Capabilities

PAD is designed to accommodate both domestic and foreign configurations of component sourcing, assembly, and distribution. The task of establishing the schedules of procurement, assembly, and distribution prior to PAD had been carried out by a team of individuals over several weeks. The end result was one schedule that was difficult to modify. A major objective of the new system was to permit quick modifications and comparisons of a number of alternatives to achieve improved schedules in short time frames (one day or less).

The product part of the knowledge base from which PAD operates contains, for each product (see Figure 19.19):

```
CREATES CUSTOMIZED PRODUCT DEFINITION/
KNOWLEDGE DATABASE

    □ COMPONENT DEFINITION
    □ POTENTIAL SUPPLIER LOCATIONS AND
      BIDDING RULES
    □ ASSEMBLY PLANT AND DEMAND
      LOCATIONS
    □ CONSTRAINTS
```

FIGURE 19.19 The PAD system.

1. Components used.
2. Supplier locations for each component.
3. Assembly plant locations.
4. Distribution points or demand locations.
5. Bills of materials (component quantities per unit).
6. Bid volume ranges for suppliers.

In addition, the cost data included in the knowledge base contains (Figure 19.20):

1. Bids by supplier for each component by volume range (dollars per component unit).
2. Inland freight costs associated with each supplier to international shipping point for each assembly location (dollars per component unit).
3. Customs costs for each component at the international shipping point for each assembly location (dollars per component unit).
4. Procurement administrative costs for each component for each supplier (percentage of component manufacturing costs).
5. International freight costs for each component from each supplier to each assembly location (dollars per component unit).
6. Import surcharge costs for each component from each supplier location at each assembly location (percentage of component manufacturing costs).
7. Duties costs for each component from each supplier location at each assembly location (percentage of component manufacturing costs plus import surcharge costs).
8. Inland freight costs for each component from each supplier from the international receiving point for each assembly location to the assembly plant (dollars per component unit).

The knowledge base also contains the information necessary to determine the costs of an assembly of components delivered to any demand point on a similar basis. To all these are added other cost factors and comments:

1. Capital costs for each component at each supplier location.
2. Nonrecurring support costs for each component at each supplier location.
3. Engineering costs for each component at each supplier location.
4. General comments on each component at each supplier location (e.g., "This supplier has been known to have quality problems with this type of component.").

CREATES FIVE-YEAR COST DATABASE, BASED ON
PRODUCT DEFINITION/KNOWLEDGE DATABASE

- COMPONENT-ASSOCIATED COSTS
- ASSEMBLY-ASSOCIATED COSTS
- CAPITAL COSTS, NONRECURRING SUPPORT
  COSTS, ENGINEERING COSTS

FIGURE 19.20 The PAD system.

Operational Aspects of the PAD Program

The PAD program permits storage of several databases, which may apply to different product programs, or alternatives (in some cases test or hypothetical products or production configurations, or past runs of the program). For a given run, the user specifies the knowledge base of interest, which may be a past run file (past run files contain all user inputs and program outputs from a previous run that may be modified as desired to match current data) or a new file. The system is run in segments, with years 2–5 in a run based on the outputs from year 1.

For year 1, the user specifies (and may subsequently modify): (1) the demand locations to be considered (Figure 19.21); (2) volume for each location (e.g., Europe or the Far East); (3) assembly locations available; (4) percentage of each component's total requirements to be provided by the first, second, and third best sources for each (the knowledge base used will contain these data; for a new knowledge base, component supplier data will have been entered, and the program will have determined a best-cost basis, subject to constraint rules for the particular component and supplier); and (5) that part of (2) that each assembly location will deliver.

During the run, various reports will be available to the user, along with data change entry information. Thus, the user may query the system to determine the cost, at each demand location, for producing the entire world demand from any single assembly locations under various user assumptions as to the component supplier mix for that location. The user may interact with the program during this process and make tests of alternative configurations. The assembly locations may be either predesignated, or chosen by the program under user-specified rules.

For each of the subsequent four years of the program, component sourcing is based on a specified percentage use of the three least-cost component suppliers and user-specified assembly volumes to be shipped to each demand location to satisfy world demand. At any time the user may request sets of cost data by year, by assembly location, or by component. The user choices for years 2–5 may be modified; any given run may be entered into the run file for subsequent analysis or use as a starting point for future runs.

USER SELECTS SPECIFIC KNOWLEDGE
    DATABASE AND COST DATABASE FOR
    ANALYSIS

USER SELECTS DEMAND LOCATION
    ALTERNATIVES

PAD DETERMINES LOWEST-COST
    CONFIGURATION FOR SOURCING, ASSEMBLY
    AND DISTRIBUTION, FOR USER-SPECIFIED
    VOLUME LEVELS

USER MAY RELAX CONSTRAINTS, PAD
    RECONFIGURES

FIGURE 19.21 The PAD system.

```
KEY OUTPUTS IN EXECUTIVE SUMMARY:

   □ FIVE-YEAR DETAIL ON COMPONENT
     SOURCING FOR EACH ASSEMBLY PLANT
   □ FIVE-YEAR DETAIL ON ASSEMBLY COSTS
     AND PRODUCT DISTRIBUTION PLAN

   ANY END RESULT MAY BE USED AS
   STARTING POINT FOR NEW
   RECONFIGURATION ANALYSIS
```

FIGURE 19.22 The PAD system.

Conclusions

After a run session has been completed, the user may request an executive summary (Figure 19.22) containing the following output:

1. Five-year detail component data, showing for each component:
  a. volumes shipped from each supplier location to assembly location.
  b. unit and total cost of shipments.
  c. breakdown of unit costs.
2. Five-year detail assembly data, showing:
  a. volumes shipped from each assembly location to each demand location.
  b. unit and total costs of shipments.
  c. breakdown of unit costs.

PAD is designed to bring together in an interactive program the expertise of purchasing and scheduling analysts in a manner that provides easy use, clear historical information, and rapid simulation of various combinations of supplier choices and volumes, assembly allocations and new assembly plants, and potential costs for volume levels at new and old demand points.

In the hands of an expert, PAD is a flexible analytical instrument with embedded knowledge and rules encoded and structured in the expert's own language. In the hands of a nonexpert, it provides management with assurance that the program demands and key factors in a major cost activity will not be forgotten, as well as the opportunity to examine real and hypothetical alternatives.

QUESTIONS

1. Discuss the complexity of the procurement and distribution problem. Identify narrow domains of the problems for which ES can be suitable.
2. Prepare a diagram that shows the typical DSS and ES components that are integrated in this system.
3. In what way does the DSS part of this system support the ES, and vice versa?
4. List the content of the knowledge base.
5. List the content of the model base.
6. Summarize and discuss the major benefits of the system.

References and Bibliography

1. Al-Zobaidie, A., and J. B. Grimson. "Expert Systems And Database Systems: How Can They Serve Each Other?" *Expert Systems*, Feburary 1987.

2. Basu, A., and A. Dutta. "AI-Based Model Management in DSS." *Computer*, September 1984.

3. Bell, P. C., D. C. Parker, and P. Kirkpatrick. "Visual Interactive Problem Solving—A New Look at Management Problems." *Business Quarterly*, Spring 1984.

4. Blanning, R. W. "The Application of Artificial Intelligence To Model Management." *Proceedings, 21st HICSS*, Hawaii, January 1988.

5. Bonczek, R. H., C. W. Holsapple, and A. B. Whinston. "Developments in Decision Support Systems." In *Advances in Computers*. Vol. 23. M. Yoritz, ed. New York: Academic Press, 1984.

6. Brodie, M. L., and J. Mylpoulos. *On Knowledge Base Management Systems: Integrating Artificial Intelligence and Database Techniques*. New York: Springer-Verlag, 1986.

7. Cohen, B. "Merging Expert Systems and Databases." *AI Expert*, February 1989.

8. Courtney, J. F. Jr., et al. "A Knowledge-based DSS For Managerial Problem Diagnosis." *Decision Sciences*, Summer 1987.

9. Doukidis, G. I. "An Analogy on the Homology of Simulation and Artificial Intelligence." *Journal of Operations Research Society*, August 1987.

10. Elam, J. J., and B. Konsynski. "Using AI Techniques To Enhance The Capabilities of Model Management System." *Decision Sciences*, Summer 1987.

11. Fedorowicz, J., and G. Williams. "Representing Modeling Knowledge In An Intelligent Decision Support System." *Decision Support System*, Vol. 2, No. 1, 1986.

12. Feng-Yang, K. "Combining Expert Systems and the Bayesian Approach To Support Forecasting." *Proceeding, 21st HICSS*, Hawaii, January 1988.

13. Ford, D. R., and B. J. Schroer. "An Expert Manufacturing Simulation System." *Simulation*, May 1987.

14. Gale, W. A. *Artificial Intelligence and Statistics*. Reading, MA: Addison-Wesley, 1986.

15. Goul, M., and F. Tonge. "Project IPMA: Applying Decision Support System Design Principles to Building Expert-Based Systems." *Decision Sciences*, Vol. 18, No. 3, Summer 1987, pp. 448–468.

16. Goul, M., B. Shane, and F. Tonge. "Designing the Expert Component of a Decision Support System." Paper delivered at the ORSA/TIMS meeting, San Francisco, May 1984.

17. Goul, M., et al. "Using a Knowledge-based Decision Support System in Strategic Planning Decisions: An Empirical Study." *Journal of Management Information Systems*, Spring 1986.

18. Hand, D. J. "Statistical Expert Systems: Design." *The Statistician*, Vol. 33, No. 10, October 1984, pp. 351–369.

19. Harris, L. R. "The Natural-language connection; An AI Note." *Information Center*, April 1987.

20. Hawkins, D. T. "Applications of AI and Expert Systems for Online Searching." *ONLINE*, January 1988.

21. Hayes-Roth, F., D. Waterman, and D. Lenat. *Building Expert Systems*. Reading, MA: Addison-Wesley, 1983.

22. Henderson, J. C. "Finding Synergy Between Decision Support Systems and Expert Systems." *Decision Sciences*, Summer 1987,

23. Hogarth, R. M., and S. Makridakis. "Forecasting and Planning: An Evaluation." *Management Science*, Vol. 27, No. 2, February 1981.

24. Holsapple, C. W., and A. B. Whinston. "Management Support Through Aritificial Intelligence." *Human Systems Management*, April 1985.

25. Hosley, W. N. "The Application of Artificial Intelligence Software to Project Management." *Project Management Journal*, August 1987.

26. Hossein, J., et al. "Stochastic Queing Systems, An AI Approach." *1987 DSI Proceedings.*

27. Hsu, C., and C. Skevington. "Integration of Data and Knowledge in Manufacturing Enterprises; A Conceptual Framework." *Journal of Manufacturing Systems*, Vol. 6, April 1987.

28. Ishikawa, H. "KID, Knowledge-based Natural Language Interface For Accessing Database Systems." *IEEE Expert*, Summer 1987.

29. Jarke, M., and Y. Vassiliou, "Coupling Expert Systems with Database Management Systems." In *Artificial Intelligence Applications for Business.* W. Reitman, ed. Norwood, NJ: ABLEX Pub. Co., 1984.

30. Kehoe, C. A. "Interfaces and Expert Systems For Online Retrieval." *Online Review*, December 1985.

31. Kerschberg, G., ed. *Expert Database Systems.* Menlo Park, CA: Benjamin/Cummings, 1986.

32. King, D. "Modeling and Reasoning: Integrating Decision Support with Expert Systems." In J. Leibowitz, ed. *Expert Systems for Business and Management*, Englewood Cliffs, NJ: Prentice-Hall, 1989.

33. King, D. "The Role of Intelligent Agents in Executive and Decision Support." *DSS 89 Transactions*, San Diego, CA, June 1989.

34. Ko, C., and T. W. Lin. "Multiple Criteria Decision Making And Expert Systems." In E. Turban and P. Watkins, eds. *Applied Expert Systems.* Amsterdam: North-Holland, 1988.

35. Kumar, S., and H. Cheng. "An Expert System Framework for Forecasting Method Selection." *Proceedings, 21st HICSS*, Hawaii, January 1988.

36. Kusiak, A., ed. *Artificial Intelligence, Implications for CIM, IFS.* New York, NY: Springer-Verlag 1988.

37. Lee, J. K., and H. G. Lee. "Integration of Strategic Planning and Short-term Planning: An Intelligent DSS Approach By The Post-Model Analysis Approach." *Decision Support Systems*, 1988.

38. Lehner, P. E., and M. L. Donnel. "Building Decision Aids: Exploiting the Synergy Between Decision Analysis and Artificial Intelligence." Paper presented at the ORSA/TIMS National Meeting, San Francisco, May 1984.

39. Liang, T. "Development of a Knowledge-based Model Management System." *Operations Research*, November–December 1988.

40. Meador, C. L., P. G. W. Keen, and M. J. Guyote. "Personal Computer and Distributed Decision Support." *Computerworld*, Vol. 18, No. 19, May 7, 1984.

41. Mellichamp, J. H. "An Expert System for FMS Design." *Simulation*, May 1987.

42. Mintzberg, H. "Planning on the Left Side and Managing on the Right." *Harvard Business Review*, July–August 1976.

43. Murphy, F., and E. Stohr. "An Intelligent Support For Formulating Linear Programming." *Decision Support Systems*, Vol. 2, No. 1, 1986.

44. Newman, W. M. *Designing Integrated Systems for the Office Environment.* New York: McGraw-Hill, 1987.

45. Pedersen, K. "Connecting Expert Systems and Conventional Programming." *AI Expert*, May 1988.

46. Rauch-Hindin, W. "Software Integrates AI, Standard Systems." *Mini-Micro Systems*, October 1986.

47. Reitman, W. "Applying Artificial Intelligence to Decision Support." In *Decision Support Systems.* M. J. Ginzberg, W. Reigman, and E. Stohr, eds. Amsterdam: North Holland, 1982.

48. Sathi, A., et al. "CALLISTO: An Intelligent Project Management System." *AI Magazine*, Winter, 1986.

49. Schur, S. "Intelligent Databases." *Database Programming and Design*, June 1988.

50. Scott-Morton, M. "Expert Decision Support Systems." Paper presented at a special

DSS conference, Planning Executive Institute and Information Technology Institute, New York, May 21–22, 1984.

51. Sen, A., and G. Biswas. "Decision Support Systems: An Expert Systems Approach." *Decision Support Systems*, Vol. 1, 1985.

52. Shannon, R. E. "Expert Systems and Simulation." *Simulation*, June 1985.

53. Stock, M. "Cooperating Expert Systems Distribute AI." *Digital News*, February 9, 1987.

54. Sullivan, G., and K. Fordyce. *Decision Simulation, One Outcome of Combining AI and DSS*. Working paper #42-395, IBM Corporation, Poughkeepsie, NY, 1984.

55. Sullivan, G., and K. Fordyce. "The Role of Artificial Intelligence in Decision Support Systems." Paper delivered at the International Meeting of TIMS, Copenhagen, June 1985.

56. Teng, J. T. C., et al. "A Unified Architecture for Intelligent DSS." *Proceedings, 21st HICSS*, Hawaii, January 1988.

57. Turban, E., and D. H. Stevenson. "The Executive Information System—DSS Connection." *Proceedings DSI 1989*, New Orleans, November 1989.

58. Turban, E., and P. Watkins. "Integrating Expert Systems and Decision Support Systems." *MIS Quarterly*, June 1986.

59. Turban, E., and H. Watson. "Integrating ES, EIS and DSS." *DSS 89 Transactions*, San Diego, CA, June 1989.

60. Turner, M., and B. Obilichetti. "Possible Directions In Knowledge-based Financial Modeling Systems." In *DSS '85 Transactions*, Providence, RI, TIMS, 1985.

61. Van Horn, M. *Understanding Expert Systems*. Toronto: Bantam, 1986.

62. Vasant, D., and A. Croker, "Knowledge-based Decision Support in Business: Issues and a Solution." *IEEE Expert*, Spring 1988.

63. Waltz, D. "Artificial Intelligence: An Assessment of the State-of-the-Art and Recommendations for Future Directions." *AI Magazine*, Vol. 4, Fall 1983.

64. Wu, Wenhua. "An Integrated System Based on the Synergy Between System Dynamics and Artificial Intelligence." *Proceedings*, 1988 International Conference of the Systems Dynamics Society, La Jolla, CA, July 1988.

65. Zahedi, F. "Qualitative Programming for Selection Decisions." *Computer and Operations Research*, Vol. 14, No. 5, 1987, pp. 395–407.

Chapter 20

Implementing Management Support Systems

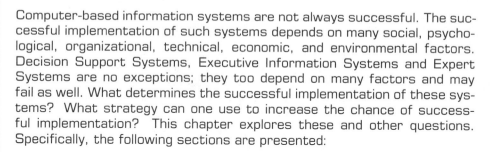

Computer-based information systems are not always successful. The successful implementation of such systems depends on many social, psychological, organizational, technical, economic, and environmental factors. Decision Support Systems, Executive Information Systems and Expert Systems are no exceptions; they too depend on many factors and may fail as well. What determines the successful implementation of these systems? What strategy can one use to increase the chance of successful implementation? This chapter explores these and other questions. Specifically, the following sections are presented:

20.1   Introduction

As with any other computer-based information system, implementing a management support system is not always a success story. Furthermore, a well-designed system may fail in one organization whereas a poorly designed system may succeed in another. *Implementation* is an ongoing process of preparing an organization for the new system and introducing it in such a way as to assure its success.

The implementation issue of MSS is complex because these systems are not merely information systems that collect, manipulate, and distribute information. Rather, they are linked to the process by which managers arrive at decisions. Nevertheless, many of the implementation factors are generic to any information system. Hence much of the discussion in this chapter is based on experience gained in the implementation of information systems and/or management science models. For an overview see Swanson (32).

The successful implementation of MSS is determined by many factors ranging from technological to psychological. The type of systems, the individuals involved, the anticipated results, and the organizational climate can all affect implementation.

This chapter surveys major relevant factors, discusses their impact on implementation, and suggests implementation strategies. Several issues regarding EIS implementation were discussed in Chapter 10.

20.2   Implementation and Success: Definitions

What is Implementation?

Machiavelli astutely noted over 400 years ago that there was "nothing more difficult to carry out, nor more doubtful of success, nor more dangerous to handle, than to initiate a new order of things." The implementation of an MSS is, in effect, the initiation of a new order of things, or in modern language—the introduction of a change.

The definition of implementation is complicated because implementation is a long, involved process with vague boundaries. Implementation can be defined simplistically as getting a newly developed, or significantly changed, system to be used by those for whom it was intended.

According to Lucas (21), the implementation of a computer-based information system is an ongoing process that takes place during the entire development of the system—from the original suggestion through the feasibility study, systems analysis and design, programming, training, conversion, and installation of the system. Other authors refer to implementation as only the final stage in the system's life cycle. The definition of implementation of MSS and ES is more complicated because of the iterative nature of their development. Therefore we accept Lucas's broader definition as a basis for our discussion.

Classification of Implementation

There is a distinction between two classes of implementation. First, the routine repetitive MSS, which include DSS periodical reports and their analyses (e.g., a monthly productivity report). For such situations, implementation means a commitment to routine and frequent use of the system, or *institutionalization*.

Second, for ad hoc decisions, implementation means the one-time use of the system.

Another way to classify implementation is to look at the three types of decisions supported by DSS, as suggested by Sprague and Carlson (31).

DSS for Personal Support.   In this case, the user and the builder (or the user and the Information Center) are usually the only participants. Hence implementation is relatively easy and informal. The participants modify the DSS until success is achieved (unless a decision is reached to abandon the project).

DSS for Group Support.   In this case, because the users are a group, communication within the user group and with the builder(s) is essential. Communication must be formal (e.g., conduct group processes to achieve consensus).

DSS for Organizational Support.   In this case (as in the GLSC example, see Chapter 4), there could be many users over an extended period of time. Therefore several users cannot participate in the construction, or they participate very little. It is necessary to integrate the DSS into the organization. Such integration should be achieved, according to Sprague and Carlson, through user education, installation, and evaluation. These topics are discussed later in this chapter, together with several other related topics like user involvement, resistance to change, management support, and strategies for implementation.

The Implementation Success

The definition of implementation includes the concept of success. A number of possible indicators for a successful information system have been suggested in various implementation studies. Unless a set of success measures is agreed on, it will be difficult to evaluate the quality (or success) of a system. Dickson and Powers (13) suggest four independent success critieria:

1. Ratio of actual project execution time to the estimated time.
2. Ratio of actual cost to develop the project to the budgeted cost for the project.
3. User satisfaction; managerial attitudes toward the system and how well their information needs are satisfied.
4. The impact of the project on the computer operations of the firm.

The success measures of Dickson and Powers, with the exception of user satisfaction, have not been widely adopted in implementation research or in practice. Most organizations have employed one or more of the following measures:

1. The use of the system as measured by the intended and/or the actual use: for example, the number of inquiries made of an online system.
2. User satisfaction like self-report, measured with a questionnaire or by an interview. (see Swanson [32], Chapter 6).

3. Favorable attitudes, either as an objective by itself, or as a good predictor of the use of a system.
4. The degree to which a system accomplishes its original objectives (i.e., whether it supports decisions).
5. Payoff to the organization (through cost reductions, increased sales, etc.).

Because a distinction was made between ad hoc and routine DSS, one should also consider the following success criteria for routine use:

□ The degree of institutionalization of the DSS/ES in the organization. An institutionalized system is regarded as a permanent fixture in the organization with continuing financial support.
□ The integration of MSS as a permanent tool in the decision-making process.

In evaluating the success of expert systems, one can use additional measures:

□ The degree to which the system agrees with a human expert when both of them are presented with the same cases.
□ The adequacy of the explanations provided by the system.
□ The percentage of cases submitted to the system for which advice was not given (the ES itself may decide that it is not qualified to deal with certain cases).
□ The improvement of the ES on the learning curve; or how fast the system reaches maturity.

(For further details see Smith, D. L., "Implementing Real World ES," *AI Expert*, Dec. 1988.)

Success of implementation should be measured on a relative scale. Therefore one can speak only about the *degree* of successful implementation.

20.3 Implementation Failures

The implementation of information systems or mathematical models involves several problems that have been subject to extensive research (see Lucas [21] and Meredith [23]). Indeed, there are stories about millions of dollars invested in designing systems that were never used. But very little evidence is available to substantiate the true extent and magnitude of the problem. Actual information on the subject is a closely held secret in many organizations, especially when millions of dollars have been spent on unimplemented systems.

Meredith (23) believes that there have been many "grandiose failures" of information systems (including DSS). Frequently, the absence of conditions necessary for successful implementation result in what Dickson and Wetherbe (12) call "tactics of counter-implementation." These tactics at managerial levels include (1) diverting resources from the project, (2) deflecting the goals of the project, (3) dissipating the energies of the project, and (4) neglecting the project with the hope it will go away. At an operating level, tactics of counter-implementation take the form of (1) making errors on purpose, (2) using the system for purposes other than it was intended for, (3) failing outright to use the system, and (4) relying on old manual procedures whenever possible.

One DSS researcher, Alter (1), reports that the expected synergy of human and machine in interactive DSS simply hasn't developed and actual instances of managers sitting at a terminal and solving problems are very rare. On investigation, it was found that half the actual DSS users are secretaries or junior analysts. Furthermore, the amount of managerial use of DSS was found to be inversely proportional to the amount of staff help available to the manager.

Another example of frequent implementation failure in large, computer-based systems is that of manufacturing information systems such as Material Requirements Planning (MRP).

Even the *attempt* to implement information systems can trigger a failure. Mohan (24) reports:

> There is considerable evidence that firms . . . experience *severe internal disruptions and change as the new technology* is introduced. In some cases the reactions have been adverse enough to result in temporary rejection of the technology, and a period of three to five years has been necessary for reintroduction.

Thus the initial failure not only postpones progress for a number of years, but it also makes later attempts more likely to fail.

Although there is not any formal data on MSS failures, there are many informal reports on unsuccessful implementation. Why do such systems fail and what are the necessary conditions to minimize failures? These and some other related issues are dealt with in the following sections.

20.4   **Models of Implementation**

The importance of the implementation problem discussed earlier led to extensive research regarding the determinants of successful implementation. The research began several decades ago with studies examining resistance to change, conducted by behavioral scientists. The management science movement has been occupied with this issue since the late 1950s, and MIS researchers have been studying implementation issues for over a decade. Considerable numbers of ideas and theories were accumulated and several models of implementation were proposed for both management science and information systems implementation (see Schultz and Slevin [29], Lucas [21], Swanson [32], and Meredith [23]). None of these models deals specifically with DSS or ES, but many of their elements are directly related to both technologies.

Several dozen factors could determine the degree of success of any MSS project. The words *factor* or *success factor* refer to a condition present in the organization, such as the support of top management or the existence of an Information Center.

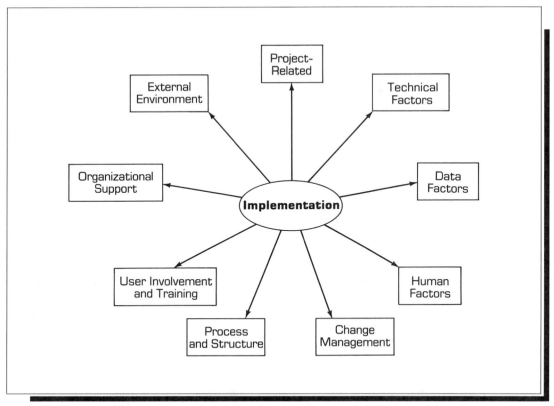

FIGURE 20.1 The determinants of successful implementation.

The success factors of implementation in this chapter are grouped in nine categories (see Figure 20.1). These categories are frequently interrelated. Some factors can be classified under two or more categories. Thus this classification should be regarded as a rough attempt to organize the many factors involved rather than as a strict universal classification. These nine categories are discussed in the following sections.

20.5 Technical Factors

Technical factors relate to the mechanics of the implementation procedure.

Level of Complexity. To maximize the likelihood of successful implementation, the basic rule is to keep the system as simple as possible. The advantages of simplicity for implementation success are many: fewer errors, greater integrity of design, simpler data requirements, easier user training, managerial transparency, ease of control, and speed of installation. Of course, simplicity must be tempered with another desirable system characteristic: completeness of critical aspects. The conflict between simplicity and completeness poses a dilemma for standard (turn-key or ready-made) systems. If systems are oversimplified, a lot of work will be needed to tailor them to specific users. This is one reason why there are so few ready-made MSS on the market.

Cost and Adaptability. System customizing leads to two more conflicting technical factors relevant to implementation: adaptability and cost. If the system cannot be easily altered to accommodate changes, the chances for successful implementation are minimal. Such built-in flexibility requires an iterative design process, which can be lengthy and costly.

System Response Time and Reliability. Situations where the system reacts too slowly, crashes, or is unavailable when needed have been known to create user dissatisfaction. Slow response was observed in several expert systems, especially when standard hardware was used (prior to 1987). The Firestone implementation minicase at the end of the chapter provides an example of this difficulty.

Availability and Accessibility. Certain DSS were not used because they were unavailabile to users or not accessible when needed. For example, lines may form at terminals if there are not enough terminals. Even the perception of inadequate accessibility was found to be a key determinant in implementation (see Culnan [9]).

Inadequate Functions. Limited primary core memory, an imbalance between hardware and software capabilities, poor graphics, user-unfriendliness, and inability to deal quickly with changing situations are all examples of inadequate functions that tend to discourage users.

In addition to the technical issues just pointed out, there are several other related issues, which are listed in Table 20.1.

Technical issues can be classified into two categories: technical constraints, due mainly to the limitations of available technology, and technical problems, which are not the result of the binding technology but are caused by other factors, such as scarcity of resources. The first category of problems may disappear when new technologies are developed. The second category can be solved by increasing available resources (including technical expertise).

A frequently mentioned technical problem is the data problem. This is true for both DSS (see Alter [1]) and ES. In the latter case, the problem is compounded owing to the difficulty of knowledge acquisition.

TABLE 20.1 Technical Implementation Issues.

Lack of equipment
Standardization
Problem with the networks
Mismatch of hardware/software
Low level of technical capacity of the project team
Inappropriate implementation mechanics
Data problems

20.6   Data Problems

All computer-based systems depend on data. A classic expression that sums it up well is "Garbage in, garbage out" (GIGO). MSS are even more dependent on data, because compiled data make up information and knowledge that are the center of any decision-making system.

The major data problems in DSS are summarized in Table 20.2 along with some possible solutions. These problems were observed in large DSS during the mid- to late 1970s. Although some of these problems may be less acute today

TABLE 20.2 Data Problems.

Problem	Typical Cause	Possible Solutions (in some cases)
Data are not correct.	Raw data were entered inaccurately.	Develop a systematic way to ensure the accuracy of raw data.
	Data derived by an individual were generated carelessly.	Whenever derived data are submitted, carefully monitor both the data values and the manner in which the data were generated.
Data are not timely.	The method for generating the data is not rapid enough to meet the need for the data.	Modify the system for generating the data.
Data are not measured or indexed properly.	Raw data are gathered according to a logic or periodicity that is not consistent with the purposes of the analysis.	Develop a system for rescaling or recombining the improperly indexed data.
Too many data are needed.	A great deal of raw data is needed to calculate the coefficients in a detailed model.	Develop efficient ways of extracting and combining data from large-scale data processing systems.
	A detailed model contains so many coefficients that it is difficult to develop and maintain.	Develop simpler or more highly aggregated models.
Needed data simply do not exist.	No one ever stored data needed now.	Whether or not it is useful now, store data for future use. (This may be impractical because of the cost of storing and maintaining data. Furthermore, the data may not be found when they are needed.)
	Required data never existed.	Make an effort to generate the data or to estimate them if they concern the future.

Source: Alter (1), p. 30.

because of developments in software, hardware, and computer networks, they still present potential problem areas for most MSS.

Data must either be available to the system or the system must include a data acquisition subsystem, which is the case with any specific ES. The data issue should be considered in the planning stage of the system life cycle. If too many problems are anticipated, the project should not be undertaken.

20.7 People Factors

The implementation of computer-based information systems in general, and MSS in particular, is impacted by the way people perceive these systems and by how people behave. Two topics are discussed in this section: the user-builder relationship and decision styles. Another topic, resistance to change, is discussed in the next section.

User-builder Relationship

Conventional management science systems have had two participants: a manager and an analyst. Much research has been conducted on the relationship between the two roles and its impact on implementation. Similar roles exist in DSS (user and builder) and in ES (user and knowledge engineer). Therefore the findings of the previous research are probably applicable to the new technologies.

Churchman and Schainblatt (8) have designed a matrix to explain the types of relationships that may exist between the analyst and the manager. Four possible types of relationships are considered, depending on who has the responsibility for implementation (see Table 20.3).

Position A'B' is called the *separate function position*. This position represents the approach that it is the role of the analyst to present a project (or a change) with detailed instructions on how to implement it. The manager then takes the analyst's plan and applies it. The functions of the parties are entirely separate; the job of the manager begins when that of the analyst ends. Obviously, the success of implementation is strongly dependent on the implementation instruction given by the analyst.

TABLE 20.3 Types of Implementation Relationships.

	Analyst Is Responsible B	Analyst Is Not Responsible B'
Manager Is Responsible A	Mutual Understanding	Communication
Manager Is Not Responsible A'	Persuasion	Separate Function

Position A'B is called the *persuasion position*. It holds that successful implementation depends to a great extent on the skill of the analyst in understanding the manager's problems. That is, the obligation of the analyst is to understand the essence of the manager's personality and overcome any resistance by using a persuasion approach.

Cell AB' is called the *communication position*. This position holds that the solutions suggested by the analyst are not accepted because the manager does not "understand" them. Very little empirical evidence was found to support this position.

The fourth position, AB, is called the *mutual understanding position*. Here implementation is considered to be a function of the type of relationship that exists between two responsible parties, and this position represents the most desirable kind of relationship. The ingredients of the relationship have been summarized in the concept of "trust":

- The two parties have faith in each other's recommendations.
- Each party is sensitive to the motivations, aspirations, and values of the other.
- Each party understands his or her own decision-making process, as well as that of the other.
- Continuity of planning and implementation is essential.
- The needs and values of both parties should be considered.

Decision Styles

Different individuals make decisions differently. They may use different approaches to making decisions, a different sequence of the same steps in the process, or they may use the same sequence but emphasize the steps differently.

A popular explanation as to why people make decisions differently is that they possess different cognitive styles. A classic distinction is made between the analytic and heuristic styles discussed earlier. Managers with more analytic styles are usually predisposed to accept a DSS, whereas those with more intuitive styles will tend to reject the DSS. However, the latter will tend to accept the ES, especially if the explanation component is effective.

Other representative decision styles are (1) those with high information needs versus those with low information needs, and (2) those who like details versus those who do not. The decision style is likely to influence a person's willingness to learn about a system and his or her resistance to change.

20.8   Resistance to Change and How to Manage It

Introducing new technologies into organizations will almost always result in some change. The application of an MSS means a change in the manner in which decisions are made, communications are transmitted, control is exercised, and power is allocated. Therefore it is only natural to assume that several behavioral problems related to such changes would develop, together with some kinds of dysfunctions.

Fear of Change

The changes that result from implementing MSS can be social, technical, psychological, structural, or a combination of these factors (see accompanying box).

When managers (or employees) resist the logical arguments presented in defense of a MSS, they may not be resisting the technical aspects of the proposed change as much as the perceived social or psychological ramifications. Managers often feel threatened by modern techniques of analysis and sense that a computerized project may take over or jeopardize their job. This fear of change may originate from various sources: from apprehension that their jobs will be eliminated, that previous performance will prove inefficient relative to the new technique, or that the new technique will result in a downgrading of the status or intrinsic satisfaction of their job. In addition there are also irrational fears relating to computers (computer phobia).

Of course, top management may think that such beliefs are absurd. The important point, however, is that what governs the user's behavior is not so much the real threat as the *perceived* threat.

A good way for the analyst or system introducer to cope with the fear of change is to eliminate the perceived threat. The problem is that some of the

---

The Dimensions of Change[*]

- □ *Rivalries and territorial threats:* The system can increase the power or influence of one department, an individual, or one group over another.
- □ *Fear of obsolescence:* The system can diminish job responsibilities or contribute to a feeling of loss of esteem.
- □ *Group cohesiveness leading to resistance to outsiders:* Systems specialists and/or consultants are resisted because they are not part of the local group and do not "understand the business."
- □ *Cultural factors:* The system is resisted because it does not fit in with present practice or goes against the experience of incumbent managers.
- □ *Job security:* There are concerns that jobs will be eliminated or that job duties will be diminished.
- □ *Information possessiveness:* The system could make information that is presently closely held available to others. Of special concern is the fact that subordinate managers may lose decision autonomy or excuses for poor performance based on a lack of information. Furthermore, having data and information is an element of power and must either be protected if currently present or sought if not possessed.
- □ *Job pattern changes:* The system can change communication patterns with peers, present psychic rewards, and affect work group norms.
- □ *Other:* Fear of the unknown, uncertainties, disruption of stability.
- □ *Invasion (or loss) of privacy:* A perception related to personnel-type CBIS.

[*] *Source:* This material is condensed from Dickson and Wetherbe (12).

perceived threat is probably real (e.g., workers may be laid off and the importance of certain jobs may be reduced). In addition, some of the consequences of the change are uncertain or even unknown.

Users sometimes are afraid of the changes in their actual job responsibilities. If job content and meaning are changed, users may be unsure how they will perform their jobs in the future. They may foresee more responsibility (which many like to avoid), more control, and more accountability than they are used to. Although users may not like their job to become more challenging, neither may they like it to become more routinized than what they were used to.

One possible solution is retraining. This is not an easy task, however. For example, some users think of themselves as complete failures with computer applications and mathematics because they had problems with quantitative methods 30 years ago in school; therefore they will resist training or do poorly in classes. Dealing with resistance to change requires a planned approach or a strategy.

Overcoming Resistance to Change

Several researchers have viewed implementation as a social change process. They observed that the interpersonal and organizational dynamics of the change process had an overwhelming impact that determines the success of DSS implementation.

Therefore, it was suggested that managing change can enhance successful implementation, and several theories were developed on how to do it. A most publicized one is that of Lewin and Schein (see Lewin [20]). They focus on the *process* by which change takes place. The Lewin-Schein theory of change is a concise description of this process. The theory states that change consists of three steps:

□ *Unfreezing:* creating an awareness of the need for change and a climate of receptivity to change.
□ *Moving:* changing the magnitude or direction of the forces that define the initial situation; developing new methods and/or learning new attitudes and behaviors.
□ *Refreezing:* reinforcing the changes that have occurred, thereby maintaining and stabilizing a new equilibrium situation.

Zand and Sorensen (34) applied this change theory directly and demonstrated that success in handling the issues at each step was strongly associated with overall success in a large sample of projects involving the implementation of management science models. The Lewin-Schein theory has been used as a change-planning basis to indicate strategies to handle resistance to change in information systems. For example, Dickson and Wetherbe have made the following suggestions (12):

For the Unfreezing Phase.   In this phase the goals of the change must be established, a supportive climate must be created, and a momentum for change should be built up.

Other activities in this phase include: (1) establishing the nature of the user's problem, (2) making sure the person or group serving as the change agent possesses the proper skills, (3) appointing a person in the user organization to serve as champion for the project and ensuring that this person can provide the needed resources and leverage to support the project, (4) making sure a felt need for the project exists; or taking action to establish such a need, (5) making sure that senior management is supportive of the change and defining the actions necessary on the part of this group to reflect this attitude, (6) making sure that users understand and agree to the project's goals and objectives, (7) identifying measurable checkpoints in the project to see that these objectives are being met, and (8) working out an adequate psychological contract by agreeing on roles during the project for the change agents and the users, and identifying conditions for terminating the relationship.

For the Moving (Change) Phase. Suggested activities in this phase are: (1) determining that actual changes are occurring, (2) ensuring that users are receiving the type of training needed to use the system successfully, (3) measuring to see that the goals of the project are actually being met, (4) responding to any signs of resistance to change, and (5) making sure the change agent has really built up personal credibility with the user.

For the Refreezing Phase. The final stage establishes that the new system has meshed into the user organization and its ongoing practice. Here, one must: (1) make sure that new behavior patterns have been adequately learned, (2) ensure that the user organization can use the system without the system builders' presence, (3) establish that users feel they "own" the system, and (4) make sure that users are committed to using the new system.

This theory of planned change was adapted to DSS by several researchers. For example, Ginzberg (15) and Alter (1) studied the DSS implementation process in its entirety and identified the refreezing phase as being of special importance to CBIS project success or failure. In DSS, the refreezing phase is especially important, because the user must initiate the interaction with the system, and DSS is expected to impact on the decision-making process of users. Furthermore, the relationship between a DSS and its users evolves simultaneously, so the design and implementation of a DSS is an ongoing process.

An important related issue is the role of intermediaries in the refreezing phase, who serve as integrating (change) agents and as human interfaces between the decision makers and the DSS. Thus they can play a major role in implementing DSS.

Organizational Culture or Climate

Sometimes the organizational climate of a company is so hostile to innovation that it is difficult to accomplish any changes. If the attitudes of organizational members are poor toward attempts to introduce computer-based systems or even toward their peers, then introducing any change will be difficult. On the positive side, if there is an openness in the organization so that opinions and values are shared, change can be facilitated. Researchers studying organizational change have spoken of a climate that supports mutual trust between the potential users of the system and its developers (e.g., see Zmud and Cox [36]).

In most cases, the influence of senior management is vital in determining the organizational climate. If the climate is poor, steps must be taken to improve matters in this area before any attempt is made to introduce change. Typical cases, ranging from the introduction of GM Nova model to the introduction of automation in the U.S. Post Office (see Dickson and Wetherbe [12]), have repeatedly shown that there is strong resistance to change in a poor organizational climate. If the organizational culture is conservative and computers are being avoided in general, the chance for success of MSS or ES will be minimal.

Organizational Politics

The process of implementation is inherently change-oriented and organizations tend to resist change. As an organization's growth slows, internal relationships tend to stabilize, division of authority and power is negotiated, and a sense of security and well-being sets in. The implementation of a large-scale DSS or ES may threaten this equilibrium and arouse opposition toward the project.

This is where "politics" frequently enters the picture. The prevalence of politics in organizations, especially large ones, is often underestimated or ignored. Thus the successful implementation of a project may well depend on politics. The MSS team leader may be well advised to become involved, learn the rules, and determine the power centers and cliques. An important question the team leader may eventually have to face is whether or not she or he can remain neutral in the political environment.

20.9   Process Factors

The way in which the process of developing and implementing MSS is managed can greatly influence the success of implementation. Topics that are traditionally included under process factors are:

  □ Top management support.
  □ Management and user commitment.
  □ Institutionalization.
  □ Individual innovation (which is also a behavioral factor).
  □ Length of time user has been using MSS.

Top Management Support

Top management support has long been recognized as one of *the* most important ingredients necessary for the introduction of any organizational change. Meredith (23) cites 19 references that support this phenomenon in CBIS. This phenomenon was also found to be true for DSS (see Alter [1], Sanders and

Courtney [28], and Meador et al. [22]). It is also basically true for ES (see DePree [10]).

If top management advocates and devotes full attention to the system, the chances of implementation success are enhanced. Furthermore, if top management *initiates* the project, the likelihood of implementation success increases markedly.

The support from top management must be meaningful. Top managers must know about the difficulties of the project and the amount of time and resources required to support it. Such support is more likely if the managers have had previous experience with similarly sophisticated projects. It is also helpful if top managers are familiar with the need to accept trade-offs in system designs, and are willing to allow a sufficient time span to implement large-scale MSS.

There is a danger in advocacy when the support comes primarily from one person. If he or she leaves or is transferred, then the support disappears. Clearly, top management support must be broad-based to be meaningful.

Obtaining this support is easier said than done. In some cases top management still views the computer as a tool solely intended for financial and accounting purposes. If the DSS or ES is in any other functional area, it may not have top management's support.

Extensive research has focused on specific means to gain top management support. Essentially, it was felt that top management had to be *sold* on the value of the project in terms of the benefits to be gained. This is not a simple task because of the difficulty in measuring benefits and proving savings.

Management and User Commitment

There is a difference between support and commitment. Support, as described earlier, means understanding of issues, participation, and making contributions. However, there is a major distinction between contribution (participation) and commitment, as demonstrated in the C&P case (see following box).

Ginzberg (15) has shown that two kinds of commitment are required for successful implementation. The first is a commitment to the project itself. The

The C&P Case

A chicken and a pig grew together since childhood and became very friendly. One day they decided to embark on a new venture. The chicken, who was the quick thinker, suggested that they open a restaurant that serves breakfasts. "Can you imagine," the chicken said, "the comparative advantage that we possess having all the ingredients right here, and we can serve the freshest ham-and-eggs meals in the county." The pig, who was a much slower thinker, was at first amazed at the clever idea. However, after some additional thinking he said: "My dear friend, what you are proposing does not seem to be a fair partnership. While you will make a *contribution* to the venture, you want me to make a *commitment*."

second is a commitment to change. Commitment to the project means that during the stages of system development, installation, and use, management must ensure that the problem the system is designed to deal with is understood, and that the system developed solves the right problem. Both users and

The Case of Connoisseur Food Corp.

Management stated that their real goal is not the implementation of isolated systems or models. Rather, it is the institution of new approaches in corporate decision making. Basically, this means that everyone in the organization should use the new approaches where appropriate and should be able to communicate effectively with either superiors or subordinates concerning recommendations based on these methods. It does not mean that everything should be based on models. Rather, it says that when a model-based analysis suggests a particular course of action in resource allocation, it should be possible to reconcile that suggestion with overall considerations in a much more rigid and disciplined manner.

Movement in a number of directions is increasing the degree of diffusion and acceptance of these models. Visible successes have been attained in a number of applications. Quantitative expertise was developed among Connoisseur Foods personnel, particularly with the hiring of MBAs. Managers were learning to approach situations in a more disciplined way.

To date, these efforts have had a definite impact on the way some brand managers think about their markets. They have a much deeper understanding of the market process they are involved in. Previously, they made decisions and monitored their strategies for time intervals of one year. Now they can monitor the quality of a brand's position on a month-to-month basis. For the first time it is possible to see the explicit impact of marketing decisions on the progress of the brand. Furthermore, the organization has become much more aware of the value of DSS because it can now have a much more direct impact on planning decisions, which are an important determinant of sales and profit.

An example of the process of institutionalization can be seen in reviewing the participation of the subsidiaries. The people in the subsidiaries heard about the use of models at the headquarters and felt that this approach might be of value to them. Because the corporate DSS group had had three years of experience with modeling technologies by that time, they felt confident that their personnel could organize and lead the proposed model-building efforts. The result turned out to be one of the most sophisticated applications yet attempted at Connoisseur Foods.

(*Source:* Condensed from Alter [1].)

management must develop this commitment to increase the odds that appropriate actions will be taken at each stage of development. Commitment to change means that management and users are willing to accommodate the change that is likely to be required to implement the system or will be the result of its introduction.

Institutionalization

Institutionalization is a process through which the MSS becomes incorporated as an ongoing part of organizational activities. Institutionalization can occur in several ways: use of the system by successors to the original user, diffusion of the system to other users, changing the work of employees, and changing the structure and processes of the organization. Finally, adding more DSS and ES throughout the organization is evidence of institutionalization. All these changes are expected to be permanent.

Institutionalization clearly points to the successful implementation of CBIS; it also helps to create a supportive organizational culture for future specific DSS and ES, as demonstrated in the case of Connoisseur Food Corp. (see box on previous page).

Individual Innovation

For several decades, scientists from psychology, economics, marketing, and organization theory have studied the conditions under which an individual chooses to try something new. One result is Slevin's theory of *innovation boundary* (29), which suggests that two zones of innovation exist. In one zone individuals will choose to innovate or try new things, whereas in the other (no innovation) they will not. Between the two zones lies the innovation boundary. The idea is shown in Figure 20.2. The formation of the boundary is a function of four variables: current success level (S), target aspiration level (T), cost of innovation (C), and reward of successful performance (R).

Through experimentation and questionnaires it is possible to predict the location of individuals in the zones. It is also possible to analyze the means of transforming an individual from the "no innovation" zone to the "innovation" zone. Figure 20.2 shows situations with (1) a potential move from point A (no innovation) to point B (innovation), and (2) a potential move of the innovation boundary itself in such a way that location A, which was previously in the no innovation zone, will be in the innovation zone. Moving individuals who play key roles in implementations (e.g., via training) into the innovation zone can greatly enhance the success of implementation.

Length of Time User Has Been Using MSS

The length of time that a user has been using DSS was shown to be a critical factor contributing to DSS satisfaction (see Sanders and Courtney [28]). In general, the longer users use DSS or MSS, the more satisfied they become.

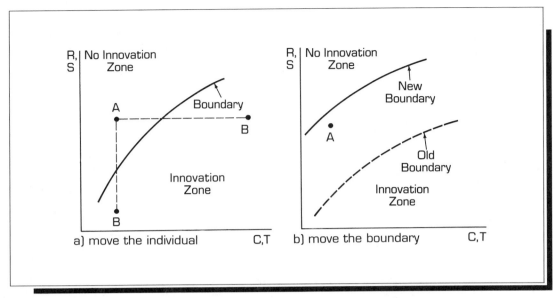

FIGURE 20.2 The innovation boundary. Left: Change in position owing to an increase in aspiration level (T), or a decrease in current success level (S). Right: Change in the boundary owning to a decreased cost (C), or an increased reward (R). In either case the object is to move from no innovation to innovation.

20.10 User Involvement and Training

User Involvement

User involvement refers to participation in the system development process by users or representatives of the user group. It is almost an axiom in MIS literature that user involvement is a necessary condition for successful development of a CBIS (see Ives and Olson [18]). User involvement with DSS is even more crucial. In expert systems, user involvement is less important because the builder may not know who the users are going to be. It is only in the phases of testing and improving the systems that users' involvement becomes important. In building EIS, user involvement is a *must*, since the system is tailored to the users.

Although there is agreement that user involvement is important, determining when it should occur and how much involvement is appropriate are questions that receive inadequate research attention.

In user-developed systems, the user obviously is very much involved. When teams are used the involvement issue becomes fairly complex, as shown in Table 20.4.

User involvement takes on a slightly different meaning with regard to a DSS than with traditional computer applications. In the latter the users (who frequently are nonmanagement employees) are primarily involved in the planning stage and in testing and evaluation. With regard to DSS development, heavy user involvement is advocated *throughout* the developmental process with a considerable amount of direct management participation. Many researchers advocate not only user involvement (management and nonmanagement), but

TABLE 20.4   Examples of User Participation.

1.   Planning Phase
     a.   The user initially suggests that the model be built.
     b.   The user participates in initial discussions prior to building the model.
     c.   The user evaluates the potential cost-benefit ratio for building the model.
     d.   The user defines the goals of the model.
2.   Design Phase
     1.   The user is the team leader in building the model.
     2.   The user obtains necessary data to build the model.
     3.   The user makes suggestions for improving the model.
     4.   The user "smoothes the way/runs interference" during the model design phase.

Source: Brightman and Harris (5).

also user control of (and commitment to) the project, thus requiring continuous involvement and responsibility.

Table 20.5 depicts the results of a study, conducted by Hogue and Watson, regarding management involvement in six phases of the DSS system development life cycle. The results reveal that there is a substantial involvement in all phases of DSS development. Also evident from the data is that top management had almost no involvement in building and testing the decision support system and played only a small role in its demonstration. Middle management was deeply involved with all phases of the development process. The generally low levels of involvement by lower management can be explained by the fact that the systems studied were almost exclusively designed to support middle- and/or top-management decision making.

User involvement should depend on the degree of decision structure. As problems become unstructured, the user should assume *more* responsibility in the DSS development. The end-user's familiarity with the specific complex problem is essential in developing a model that accurately represents reality.

Training

User training is one of the most important determinants of the success of system implementation (see Meredith [23]). Training should not only describe the system and explain why it is being installed, but must also teach users

TABLE 20.5   Management Involvement in the Development of the DSS. Percentage of Companies with Management Involvement at Each Management Level and Development Stage.

Phase in Life Cycle	Management Level			
	Lower	Middle	Top	Any Level
Idea (conceptualization)	0	61.1	61.1	100
Information requirements	0	77.8	61.1	100
Building	11.1	72.2	5.6	77.8
Testing	11.1	72.2	5.6	83.3
Demonstration	11.1	77.8	27.7	88.9
Acceptance of System	0	72.2	66.7	100

Source: Hogue and Watson (16).

how to ask for information and how to use the information they receive. Training must be a continuous process, conducted as new people enter the system, and should take place whenever significant changes are made in the system. Training sessions should include a "critical mass" of users, because dependence on the old system by a number of users could jeopardize the successful implementation of the new one.

Guidelines for successful DSS and ES training programs are similar to other CBIS training guidelines. Zmud (35) argues that for online systems, a terminal training routine is preferred over a formal training program. In most instances, however a formal program is used.

Training for DSS is often provided by the company's Information Center or by vendors (especially for complex DSS generators and for ES). Routine training (e.g., in spreadsheet and word processing) could be provided by the training unit in the personnel department. User training in ES is less important because these systems are much easier to use. Users are also less involved in system development in ES than they would be in DSS. Finally, the EIS training *must* be minimal. Executives will not go online if extensive training is needed.

20.11   Organizational Factors

Organizational factors relate primarily to structural issues. In some situations they can cause MSS to fail. The following topics are briefly discussed in this section:

☐ Competence and technical capabilities of the team's members.
☐ Organization and location of the DSS team and its influence and reputation.
☐ The relationship of the team to other units.
☐ The selection of projects.
☐ Values and ethics.
☐ Adequacy of support services and resources.
☐ Other factors.

The Competence (Skills) of the Team's Members

The participants' skills, especially those of the DSS builder and the technical support, were found to be critical for the success of DSS. Table 20.6 summarizes the findings of Meador et al. (22) regarding the *perceived* importance of these skills in general and the estimated skill level in the respondents' companies. Note that there is a wide gap between what is believed to exist in organizations and what is perceived as important. These results suggest that adjustments in this area could be very beneficial.

Organization of the DSS Team

The organization of the building team can affect implementation. Organization is reflected by the following topics:

TABLE 20.6 Average Rated Importance and Performance of DSS Participants' Skills (scale: 1 = lowest importance, 7 = highest importance).

	Average Rated Importance (perceived)	Average Rated Performance (estimated)
Sensitivity to users' needs	6.23	4.43
Project management skills (planning and control)	5.64	4.42
Implementation planning: Education, motivation, and training of users	5.49	4.24
Expertise in design of analysis-based systems like DSS	5.47	3.57
Intimate knowledge of your department's operations	5.21	3.82
Willingness to work closely with users in designing new systems	5.09	5.84
Leadership ability, administrative experience, sensitivity to political issues	4.78	4.03

Source: Meador et al. (22). Copyright 1984, by the Society for Information Management and the Management Information Systems Research Center at the University of Minnesota.

☐ Team size and composition.
☐ Team leadership.
☐ To whom the team reports.
☐ Who controls the team.
☐ How much status the team possesses.

The responsibility for the development and implementation of DSS is also an important factor. Table 20.7 shows some empirical results for existing DSS. Notice that most DSS development is controlled by users. In contrast to a common belief that the IS department is not involved, this study shows that in about one quarter of all cases, the IS department assumes a major role.

Relationship with MIS, Management Science, and Other Units

Most MSS should be connected with the organization's database. The existing information system must be capable of providing current and historical data. By continuously monitoring the information flow to detect changes in basic model assumptions, managerial priorities, environmental constraints, and other pertinent information, the DSS team leader can significantly increase the likelihood of successful implementation. In addition, the DSS could be related to the operations research/management science department that provides modeling expertise.

The nature of the information system is also important to implementation. Typically, an accounting information system does not provide sufficient data for an MSS.

TABLE 20.7 Responsibility for DSS Development and Implementation.

Department	Development Responsibility (%)	Implementation Responsibility (%)
Respondent department	55.6	64.9
DP, (IS) department	23.7	19.1
Jointly	4.6	5.3
Consultant, vendor	7.7	0.0
Other (head office, outside service)	8.4	10.7
	100.0	100.0

Source: Huff et al. (17).

As noted earlier, the relationship between the IS department or information technology [IT] department and MSS is very sensitive. Initially the IS department was excluded from DSS. This situation is changing, however. Information system departments are being expanded constantly, and in some cases they have taken over the Information Centers. Finally, because many MSS rely on local area networks (LANs) and other networks, and because these networks are usually controlled by the IS department, cooperation between the MSS and the IS department is essential for successful implementation.

Selection of Projects— Organizational Validity and Fit

The concept of organizational validity developed by Schultz and Slevin (29) implies that for a project to be successfully implemented, it must be compatibile with, or "fit," that organization. This fit *must* occur at three levels: individual, small group, and organizational. If a DSS or ES project requires an extraordinary amount of change in individual attitudes, small group dynamics, or organizational structure (i.e., there is no fit), then the probability of successful implementation will be reduced. The authors suggested several methods for measuring the fit. Such information should be acquired in the planning stage and can determine the strategy of MSS development and implementation.

Values and Ethics

Management should consider the ethics and values involved in implementing an MSS project. The following points are of importance:

1. *Goals of the Project.* Because the process of implementation is based on an attempt to attain certain goals, the MSS team should decide whether the ultimate goals desired are ethical. They should also determine whether the goals are ethical to those people who are crucial to the implementation process.

2. *Implementation Process.* Another question the MSS builder should address is whether the implementation process is ethical or even legal. That is, the goals may be ethical whereas the implementation process itself is not; for example, attempting to attain a sales goal via violation of a government antitrust law.

3. *Possible Impact on Other Systems.* The goals and process may both be ethical, but the probable outcome of the implemented project on another system may not be.

Adequacy of Resources

The success of any MSS depends also on the degree to which organizational arrangements facilitate access to the use of the required computerized system and other resources. It depends on factors such as availability of terminals and microcomputers, the quality of the LAN, the accessibility to databases, and the user fees for using the system. Other factors include support and help facilities (e.g., availability of Information Centers), maintenance of software, (see Swanson [32]) and availability of hardware. The use of a mainframe DSS, for example, can provide much broader coverage and, of course, faster response time than a micro DSS would.

Other Organizational Factors

Other organizational factors important in MSS implementation are:

□ The role of the system advocate who initiated the project.
□ Compatibility of the system with organizational and personal goals.

20.12   External Environment

MSS implementation may be affected by factors outside the immediate environment of the decision maker.

The external environment contains legal, social, economic, political, and other factors that could impact on the implementation of MSS either positively or negatively. For example, the current "overselling" of ES can "kill" a good ES. Government regulations regarding telecommunications across international borders may restrict the use of an otherwise international DSS or EIS to a single country. Legal considerations may limit the use of ES because developers may be afraid they could be taken to court if the advice rendered by the ES leads to damages.

The publicity given to the Fifth-Generation Project in Japan is another example of an external environment. This publicity has caused the U.S. government and several private corporations to invest hundreds of millions of dollars in ES. Thus, the U.S.– Japan competition has proven to be very beneficial to the development of ES. Finally, it is possible that some governments may restrict the use of ES if they find that ES cause unemployment to rise.

20.13   Project-related Factors

Most of the factors discussed in the previous sections can be considered elements in the implementation climate. This climate can be viewed as the general conditions surrounding implementation; hence climate is considered more or less equal for all projects—that is, it is independent of any particular project. A favorable climate is very helpful, but not sufficient. Each specific DSS or ES must be evaluated on its own merits, such as its relative importance to the organization and its members. It must also satisfy certain cost-benefit criteria. Such an evaluation involves several dimensions, and requires consideration of several issues. These issues appear, according to Meredith (23), under the following names and terms:

□ An important or major problem exists that needs to be resolved.
□ A real opportunity exists that needs to be evaluated.
□ Urgency of solving the problem.
□ High-profit contribution of the problem area.
□ Contribution of the problem area to growth.
□ Substantial resources tied to the problem area.
□ Demonstrable payoff to result if problem is solved.

Several of these terms will be highlighted in the discussion of the following topics:

□ Expectations and perceived need.
□ Cost-benefit analysis.
□ Operations and resources.
□ Availability of financing.
□ Timing and priority.

Expectations and Perceived Need

Expectations on the part of users as to how a system will contribute to their performance and the resultant rewards can greatly affect which system is utilized (see Robey [27]). Expectations are especially important in flexible systems like DSS and ES (see DeSanctis [11]).

Expectations as to a system's value bear some relationship to how one perceives the need for a system. If users don't expect a system to enable them to do their jobs better and increase organizational efficiency, then user perceived need for the system is likely to be low. Similarly, if users expect that performing well on job tasks supported by the system will not assist them in achieving their goals, they will be unlikely to use the system. Expectations can be affected by training, experience, and attitudes. It is possible, therefore, to use tactics associated with these areas to influence expectations and to deal with causes of implementation problems.

Owing to the tremendous publicity given in the last two years to artificial intelligence in general, and to ES in particular, the general level of expectations both by top management and users may be too high. This can be very dangerous to the success of the first ES in an organization, where the strategy could be to sacrifice potential payoff and speed of success for effectiveness and quality. If people expect quick, large savings from ES, but they do not get it, they will not continue to support such ventures. Therefore expectations must be maintained at realistic levels.

Cost-Benefit Analysis

A DSS or ES proposal can be viewed as an alternative investment. As such, it should show an advantage over other investment alternatives including the option of "do nothing." Effective implementation may depend on the ability to show such advantage.

Each DSS and ES project requires an investment of resources (including money) that can be viewed as the cost of the system, in exchange for some expected benefit(s).

The viability of a project is determined by comparing the costs with anticipated results. This comparison is termed a *cost-benefit* or *cost-effective analysis*. In practice, such an analysis may become rather complicated. The iterative nature of DSS and ES makes it difficult to predict costs and benefits, because the systems are changed constantly. In addition there are several factors, which we will now discuss, that complicate the analysis.

Cost Valuation. The cost of a project seems, at least at first sight, easy to identify and quantify. In practice, it is often difficult to relate costs to projects in a precise manner. Allocation of overhead cost is an example. Should it be allocated by volume, activity level, or value? What about future costs? A well-known "game" is to show the advantages of a certain alternative while neglecting future costs. There are additional accounting complications like the impact of taxation and the selection of a proper interest rate for present value analysis.

Benefit Valuation. The assessment of costs is not easy, but the assessment of benefits is more difficult for the following reasons: First, some benefits are intangible. Second, one frequently cannot precisely relate a benefit to a single cause. Third, results of a certain action may occur over a long period of time. Fourth, a valuation of benefits includes the assessment of both quantity and quality. The latter is difficult to measure, especially when service industries are involved. Fifth, the multiplicity of consequences can pose a major problem for quantification. Some consequences like goodwill, inconvenience, waiting time, and pain are also extremely difficult to measure and evaluate. For an extensive discussion see Money et al. (25) and Sharda et al. (30).

Partial Implementation. Decisions are frequently made on the basis of the return shown if *total* implementation is achieved rather than the more likely 90, or even 70, percent of effective implementation. Clearly this will be misleading to management. One reason for less than 100 percent implementation is that a change introduced at one point in a system usually precipitates compensatory change(s) elsewhere. This may force management to drop some parts of the proposal.

Payback Period. Management may insist on a very short payback period (e.g., two years), which considers only tangible benefits. Ignoring longer-term intangible benefits, such as competitive advantage, may result in the rejection of valuable support systems.

Empirical studies indicate that very few companies conduct a cost-benefit analysis on their DSS (e.g., see Money [25] and Hogue and Watson [16]). Instead, they use a value analysis that includes nonmonetary benefits (see Money et al. [25]).

Operations and Resources

Several practical questions should be answered regarding the project prior to its implementation. For example:

☐ Who will be responsible for executing each portion of the project?
☐ When must each part be completed?
☐ What resources (in addition to money) will be required?
☐ What information is needed?

In brief, a complete planning document for implementation should be prepared. With the answers to these questions, operating procedures, necessary training, and transitions can be planned beforehand so they do not become implementation problems later on. Such planning is difficult to perform owing to the iterative nature of the system development.

Availability of Financing

All required financing, cash flows, identification of sources, and assurances of funds should be planned in advance. Commitments should be secured so that money will be available when needed. Lack of appropriate financing is cited as a major obstacle to implementation of large-scale MSS.

Timing and Priority

Two interrelated factors in project implementation are timing and priority. For example, a DSS builder may find that an issue held to be very important at the time of the feasibility study is not as important at implementation time. Timing and priority are usually uncontrollable factors as far as the DSS team is concerned. It may be possible, however, to anticipate some problems and defer or adjust the study.

20.14 Evaluation

Development of large-scale DSS or ES in an organizational setting often requires a great investment of money, time, and personnel. At the same time, results may be neither measurable nor tangible.[*]

---

[*]The material in this section is condensed from Athappilly (3).

Regardless of how fascinating an MSS is, or how well recommended it is to an organization, there has to be a convincing way of assessing the worth of the MSS and there has to be a formal evaluation quite distinct from the informal assessment of its builders.

Also, the special characteristics of DSS, particularly the cyclic and evolutionary nature of its implementation, and its impact on decision making call for a special approach to its evaluation.

This special approach must be distinct from the usual type of "post implementation audit." Evaluations in that category are cumulative in nature. The intent of these evaluations is only to assess the outcome. In many cases, these cumulative evaluations suffer from "being too little and too late." They do not help the organization by revealing what factors led to those outcomes, and how or why they occurred. Obviously, those evaluations do not give insights into the preventive, curative, or alternative measures that may be adopted to improve the system.

But some evaluations provide useful information in addition to the end-product assessment. They are called *formative evaluations*. In the context of DSS, this formative evaluation has an added dimension, which is its dynamic and evolutionary nature. An example of such evaluation is given in Figure 20.3. The evaluation is conducted in four phases, as shown in the accompanying box.

The DSS evaluation must be an integral part of the DSS development and implementation, encompassing all phases of the DSS development process. The emphasis on decision support must be the focal point of DSS evaluation.

The Success of DSS

In a survey conducted by Meador et al. (22), respondents were asked to rate their agreement with several statements indicating the "success of their DSS." These statements included:

1. The DSS fits in well with our planning methods.
2. The DSS fits in well with our reporting methods.
3. The DSS fits in well with our way of thinking about problems.
4. The DSS has improved our way of thinking about problems.
5. The DSS fits in well with the "politics" of how decisions are made around here.
6. Decisions reached with the aid of the DSS are usually implemented.
7. The DSS has resulted in substantial time savings.
8. The DSS has been cost-effective.
9. The DSS has been valuable relative to its cost.
10. The DSS will continue to be useful to our organization for a number of years.
11. The DSS has so far been a success.

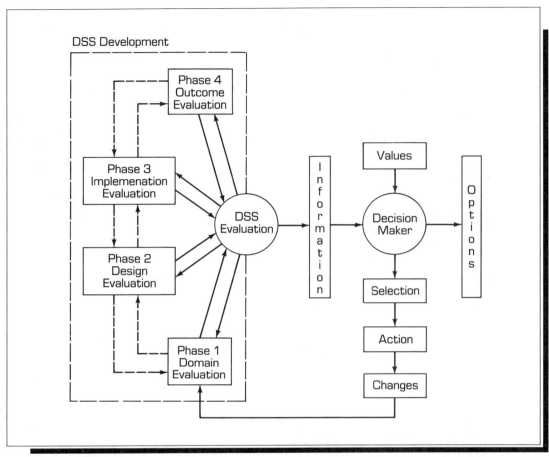

FIGURE 20.3 A dynamic DSS evaluation model. (*Source:* Athappilly [3]. Copyright and reprint permission granted. 1985. Data Processing Management Association.)

A Proposal for DSS Evaluation

A proposal for DSS evaluation is shown in Figure 20.3. The evaluation process is composed of four phases: domain, design, implementation, and outcome.

□ *Domain.* Analysis of the project, its justification, the opportunities, the constraints, and the objectives of the DSS. This phase is nonquantitative and it includes expert judgment.

□ *Design.* Identification of system capabilities, assessment of input data, and suggestions for design. The objective is to select the DSS design and the design of the modifications that result from the iterative process. The evaluation is mainly descriptive, involving resource description, pilot projects, and expert advice.

□ *Implementation.* Providing periodic feedback to the implementors. Detecting drawbacks in the procedural design, providing information about the predefined decisions, and maintaining records and procedures. This evaluation is executed with tools such as event logging and routine reports; it results in suggestions for design modifications.

□ *Outcome(s).* Outcome(s) of the DSS are measured and interpreted during the construction of the DSS and at the end. Comparison with objectives and plans is executed. Variance analysis is performed. Many tools can be used: cost-benefit, value analysis (see Keen [19]), system analysis, rating and weighing, cognitive testing, event logging, and outcome assessment. The result of this phase may be the continuation, modification, or termination of the DSS.

(*Source:* Based on Athappilly [3].)

20.15 Implementation Strategies

During the last twenty-five years there were many suggestions of implementation strategies for management science (e.g., see Schultz and Slevin [29]) and for information systems (e.g., see Lucas [21] and Meredith [23]). Many of the suggestions are generic and can be used as guidelines in implementing DSS and ES as well. The purpose of this section is to summarize strategies that were developed specifically for DSS and ES. (For an implementation strategy of EIS see Chapter 10.)

Implementation Strategies for DSS

The implementation strategies of DSS can be divided into four major categories:

1. Divide the project into manageable pieces.
2. Keep the solution simple.
3. Develop a satisfactory support base.
4. Meet user needs and institutionalize the system.

In general terms, each of these categories may seem obvious. Given a choice, who would want to provide a system that does not meet user needs or that does not have a satisfactory support base? However, a number of distinct strategies exist under each heading. And as outlined in Table 20.8, every one of these strategies has certain advantages and certain pitfalls, just as have the strategies for losing weight.

Implementation Concerns in ES

Most of the factors discussed so far are important for both DSS and ES. The degree of importance, however, differs. For example, DSS are constructed *with* the user, whereas ES are constructed *for* users; therefore user involvement in ES is less important. The following topics are especially important in ES implementation:

TABLE 20.8 Implementation Strategy.

Implementation Strategy	Typical Situation or Purpose	Pitfalls Encountered
1. Divide project into manageable pieces.	To minimize the risk of producing a massive system that doesn't work.	
Use prototypes.	Success of the effort hinges on relatively untested concepts. Test these concepts before committing to a full-fledged version.	Reactions to the prototype system (in an experimental setting) may differ from reactions to a final system in day-to-day use.
Use an evolutionary approach.	Implementer attempts to shorten feedback loops between self and clients and between intentions and products.	Requires users to live with continuing change, which some people find annoying.
Develop a series of tools.	To meet ad hoc analysis needs by providing databases and small models that can be created, modified, and discarded.	Limited applicability. Expense of maintaining infrequently used data.
2. Keep the solution simple.	To encourage use and to avoid scaring away users.	Although generally beneficial, can lead to misrepresentation, misunderstanding, misuse.
Be simple.	Not an issue for inherently simple systems. For other systems or situations, it may be possible to choose between simple and complicated approaches.	Some business problems are not inherently simple. Insisting on simple solutions may result in skirting the real issue.
Hide complexity.	The system is presented as a "black box" that answers questions using procedures not presented to the user.	Use of "black boxes" by nonexperts can lead to misuse of the results because of misunderstanding of the underlying models and assumptions.
Avoid change.	Given a choice of automating existing practice or developing new methods, choose the former.	New systems may have little real impact. Not applicable to efforts purporting to foster change.
3. Develop a satisfactory support base.	One or more components of a user-management support base is missing.	Danger that one support-gaining strategy will be applied without adequate attention to others.
Obtain user participation.	The system effort was not initiated by users. The usage pattern is not obvious in advance.	With multiple users, difficulty of getting everyone involved and incorporating everyone's interests. With sophisticated models, reduced feasibility of user participation in model formulation and interpretation.
Obtain user commitment.	The system has been developed without user involvement. The system is to be imposed on users by management.	It is difficult to obtain commitment without some kind of *quid pro quo* or demonstration that the system will help the user.

TABLE 20.8 (continued)

Implementation Strategy	Typical Situation or Purpose	Pitfalls Encountered
Obtain management support.	To obtain funding for continuation of the project. To obtain management action in forcing people to comply with the system or use it.	Management enthusiasm may not be shared by users, resulting in perfunctory use or disuse.
Sell the system.	Some potential users were not involved in system development and do not use it. System is not used to full potential by the organization.	Often unsuccessful unless real advantages can be demonstrated convincingly.
4. Meet user needs and institutionalize system.	A system is to have many individual users in an ongoing application.	Since strategies under this heading are somewhat incompatible, emphasis on one may exclude another.
Provide training.	The system is not designed in close cooperation with *all* potential users.	Frequent difficulties in estimating the type and intensity of training that is needed. Initial training programs often require substantial reformulation and elaboration.
Provide ongoing assistance.	The system is used by an intermediary rather than a decision maker. The system is used with the help of an intermediary who handles mechanical details.	If the system is used by an intermediary, the decision maker may not understand the analysis in sufficient detail.
Insist on mandatory use.	The system is a medium for integration and coordination in planning. The system purports to facilitate work of individuals.	Difference between genuine use and half-hearted submission of numbers for a plan. Difficulty in forcing people to think in a particular mold.
Permit voluntary use.	Avoid building resistance to a hard sell by allowing voluntary use.	Generally ineffective unless the system meets a genuine felt need or appeals to an individual intellectually or otherwise.
Rely on diffusion and exposure.	It is hoped that enthusiasts will demonstrate the benefits of a system to their colleagues.	Ineffective: perhaps as much an excuse for lack of positive action as it is a real strategy.
Tailor systems to people's capabilities.	People differ in their ability and/or propensity to use analytic techniques.	Not clear how to do so. In practice, systems seem to be built to people's requirements, not their capabilities.

Source: Alter (1), pp. 166–169 (with permission).

- □ Quality of the system.
- □ Cooperation of the expert(s).
- □ Conditions that justify the need for a particular ES.
- □ Removal of the barriers that hinder the applicability of ES.

For further discussion see DePree (10).

Quality of the System.   The success of ES depends on the quality of the system. Buchanan and Shortliffe (6) believe the following seven features should be presented in a good ES:

1. The ES should be developed to fulfill a recognized need.
2. The ES should be easy to use even by a novice.
3. The ES should be able to increase the expertise of the user.
4. The ES should have exploration capabilities.
5. The program should be able to respond to simple questions.
6. The system should be capable of learning new knowledge (i.e., the system should be able to ask questions to gain additional information).
7. The program knowledge should be easily modified (i.e., add, delete, and modify rules).

These features are necessary but far from being sufficient for a successful ES.

The Cooperation of Expert(s).   For an ES to be successfully implemented it must give good advice. Such advice depends, most of all, on the cooperation of the domain expert. Most functioning ES had very little trouble with expert cooperation. The reason was that the experts were researchers, professors, or maintenance experts due to retire soon. The whole idea of ES is challenging, new, and innovative, so experts tend to cooperate. In some systems there was an engagement of several experts, each of whom contributed only a small portion of a large knowledge base.

However, this situation may be different when different types of experts are involved. The following are some questions with regard to experts' cooperation that must be discussed before building an ES:

□ Should the experts be compensated for their contribution (e.g., in the form of royalties, a special reward, or payment)?
□ How can one tell if the experts are telling the truth about the way they solve problems?
□ How can the experts be assured that they will not lose their jobs, or that their jobs will not be deemphasized, once the ES is fully operational?
□ Are the experts concerned about other people in the organization whose jobs may suffer because of the introduction of ES, and what can management do in such a case?

In general, management should use some incentives to influence the experts so that they will cooperate fully with the knowledge engineer. The experts have lots of power, which they can even use to sabotage a system; this power must be recognized and respected.

Conditions That Justify an ES.   Expert systems are more prone to succeed when one or more of the following conditions prompted the need for the system (based on Van Horn [33]):

□ The expert is not always available or is expensive.
□ Decisions must be made under pressure, and missing even a single factor could be disastrous.

Barriers to the Development of Expert Systems

Technical Problems

☐ The cost and size of computers that are large and powerful enough to use for ES.

☐ Lack of availability of knowledge acquisition tools that are flexible and easy enough to use by nonprogrammers.

Conceptual Problems

☐ Integrating knowledge from different fields and reducing it to a common format.

☐ Reconciling experts who disagree or approach the same task in different ways.

☐ Understanding exactly what knowledge is needed to build into an ES for a desired task.

Infrastructure Problems

☐ Scarcity and expense of AI programmers and other skilled experts in the problem area.

☐ Absence of networks of trained users and operators to collect, enter, update, and weed out data.

☐ Time and cost of developing the system in the first place and of using the system, compared with doing the same task without an ES.

(*Source:* Van Horn [33])

☐ There is rapid employee turnover resulting in a constant need to train new people. Such training is costly and time-consuming.

☐ A huge amount of data must be sifted through.

☐ A shortage of experts is holding back development and profitability.

☐ Expertise is needed to augment the knowledge of junior personnel.

☐ There are too many factors—or possible solutions—for a human to keep in mind at once, even when the problem is broken into smaller pieces.

☐ The problem requires a knowledge-based approach and cannot be handled by a conventional computational approach.

☐ Consistency and reliability, not creativity, are paramount.

☐ Factors are constantly changing, and it is very hard for a person to keep on top of them all and find what is needed at just the right time.

☐ One type of expertise (e.g., statistics) must be made available to people in different fields (e.g., accounting, marketing) so they can make better decisions.

For additional conditions see the ES feasibility study, Chapter 15.

Removal of the Barriers That Hinder the Applicability of ES. The accompanying box lists barriers that hinder the applicability of ES. The more these barriers are removed, or the more their impact is lessened, the better is the chance of successful implementation.

20.16   Summary and Conclusions

Many computer-based information systems, including MSS, are being developed and then not implemented, or only partially implemented. The implementation problem is mainly generic in nature. Issues like absence of top management support and fear of change are known as major problems in implementation of any change.

Strategies for dealing with these generic issues have been developed over the years. Some of the most pertinent ones are described here. However, MSS have some unique determinants of success, ranging from data problems in DSS to experts' cooperation in ES. Therefore it is necessary to guarantee the successful implementation of these technologies by dealing with these determinants. For example, users' involvement is extremely important in DSS, and appropriate selection of the problem area is of utmost importance in ES. Most important, the implementation issue should be an integral part of the system's development, and it should be carefully planned and managed.

Questions for Review and Discussion

1. Why would implementing DSS and ES be a more complex process than implementing MIS?
2. Define implementation in a broad sense.
3. Define implementation in a narrow sense.
4. What is meant by institutionalization?
5. List the major criteria for measuring the success of an implemented information system.
6. List several measures of success for an ES.
7. List several technical factors in implementation.
8. What is meant by system response time?
9. List some of the so-called "data problems."
10. What action can you take if too much data are needed for a DSS?
11. List the four possible relationships between a manager and an analyst according to Churchman and Schainblatt.
12. List two actions that can be used to improve the manager-analyst relationship.
13. What is a decision style?
14. What is the difference between analytic and heuristic decision styles?
15. List some of the dimensions of change.
16. What is information possessiveness?
17. What is organizational climate?
18. Why is the support of top management vital to implementation?
19. What actions can be taken by top management to support MSS?
20. How can an individual's innovation boundary impact a MSS implementation?
21. List the activities that indicate user involvement in the planning and design phases.
22. What is the difference between user involvement and user commitment?
23. List specific phases in the DSS life cycle where top management involvement is extensive.
24. What are the major skills needed for DSS builders?
25. List some of the organizational factors that can impact the success of implementation.
26. Why is the issue of "expectation" so important in ES implementation?
27. List some difficulties in evaluating MSS.

Exercises

1. Given below is a DSS success factor questionnaire (developed by Sanders and Courtney [28]). Administer the enclosed questionnaire to 10 users of DSS in your organization. Assign a "5" to a strongly agree, "4" to agree, "3" to neutral, "2" to disagree, and "1" to strongly disagree. Compute the average results and rank the factors in order of their importance.

   Overall Satisfaction

   _____ I have become dependent on DSS.
   _____ As a result of DSS, I am seen as more valuable in this organization.
   _____ I have personally benefited from the existence of DSS in this organization.
   _____ I have come to rely on DSS in performing my job.
   _____ All in all, I think that DSS in an important system for this organization.
   _____ DSS is extremely useful.

   Decision-making Satisfaction

   _____ Utilization of DSS has enabled me to make better decisions.
   _____ As a result of DSS, I am better able to set my priorities in decision making.
   _____ Use of data generated by DSS has enabled me to present my arguments more convincingly.
   _____ DSS has improved the quality of decisions I make in this organization.
   _____ As a result of DSS, the speed at which I analyze decisions has been increased.
   _____ As a result of DSS, more relevant information has been available to me for decision making.
   _____ DSS has led me to greater use of analytical aids in my decision making.

   Comment on the results.

2. **a.** List three complex managerial problems in your company, some of which have been solved and some of which are being solved. Aim at middle and top management-level situations.

   b. List, in detail, the information (data) required for each of the above problems. Be as specific as you can. For example, if the problem is to determine the feasibility of adding a new product, the information may include:

   ☐ cost of the product.
   ☐ project demand (for how many years?).
   ☐ project price.
   ☐ competitors' reaction.
   ☐ resource availability.
   ☐ organizational impact.
   ☐ equipment need.

   c. For each piece of information, answer the following questions:
   1. Is the information quantifiable? How is it measured?
   2. Are data available, or is a subjective assessment needed?
   3. Is the information available in the existing information system?
   4. What portions of it are computerized?
   5. How many people were (are) involved in each decision process? Who are these people (roles and job titles, not names)?
   6. To what extent was (is) a computer used in the decision-making (problem-solving) process?
   7. What commerically available software packages were used in the decision process?

8. Is it possible to use a DSS and/or ES for solving each of the three problems? Why or why not?

3. Review the Louisiana DSS case in Chapter 4. A number of factors have led to the successful development and use of the DSS, called FPS, at the Louisiana National Bank. A key factor was the support and involvement of top management. They requested the system and have been its primary beneficiaries.

Another important factor was the characteristics of the system's sponsor. Gil Urban was patient, low-keyed, and determined to maintain a low profile. Although he had the opportunity to build a power base through FPS, he chose not to do so. Other managers knew this and chose to work with him freely.

The bank offered an excellent organizational environment for the creation of FPS. There was a need for the system, and the bank had a history of innovation. Open communications were encouraged, and the system became a communication vehicle and framework for unified decision making. Bank officers have high morale and pride, which have enabled them to embrace institutional goals over personal goals.

A transitional development and implementation approach was used. The initial version of FPS provided familiar reports and required little additional understanding. Over time, as trust in the system grew, the system slowly and patiently moved managers from the old to new ways of thinking.

Finally, FPS provided a unified planning system. It combined three closely related, but often separated, phases of the planning process: forecasting, analysis, and reporting. FPS allows managers to move from one phase to another in an easy, integrated manner.

a. Identify the major factors that led to the successful implementation of FPS.

b. Why was the "transitional development and implementation approach" successful?

CASE 1: Implementing DSS at Firestone Tire & Rubber Co.

The short-term goal of "the DSS mission" was simply to support senior executives through DSS implementation. The long-range goal of this mission was to expand DSS use throughout Firestone. The DSS strategy was to support the overall corporate strategic plan and provide management with the analytical tools and capabilities to run the company more successfully.

The issues raised in the initial phase of DSS implementation were manifold: corporate accounting and financial functions were largely decentralized. Firestone executives were also unfamiliar with computers—many could not even type—and they were almost impossible to pin down in terms of a training schedule. The need to provide something usable and useful immediately was critical.

The implementation group quickly reached several key decisions. The first was to limit the scope of the user group. Next, it developed a simple, menu-driven approach to get the user on the system. Third, it decided it should start quickly, so it brought in the Dow Jones & Co., Inc., news service, as a vehicle to acquaint users with the terminals and the system. "Start quickly," Bode, the DSS builder, advised, "while interest is high."

The implementation strategy also included the development of a "straw man" database, along with a DSS conceptual design, based on the user interviews conducted by the group. An executive steering committee was set up to assist in the initial design and also to become educated in the potential of DSS. Finally, the implementation group provided online demonstration DSS systems to enable hands-on DSS processing.

DSS training at Firestone consisted of one-on-one coaching sessions, comprehensive documentation with lots of examples, online help features, telephone hotline user support, and online product enhancement announcements.

The implementation has meant some good news and some bad news. The good DSS news was that the company had a solid base system in place, the executive training and acceptance looked promising, and the alignment of DSS and corporate objectives would serve to solidify the company's position in the marketplace.

The bad news was that overexpansion of DSS could impede the system's ability to respond quickly; getting increased volumes of data onto the system is difficult and the responsibility of database administration is an issue that must be resolved. Specifically the company decided that this responsibility should not be that of the management information systems director but that of the vice president for administration.

By the time the system went up, the executives were comfortable with the terminals and the DSS process, their expectations of the implementation were quite realistic, and the users understood the importance of taking the time to learn the system.

Firestone's DSS plans are:

- □ To expand DSS usage in the analysis of data (graphics capabilities and so forth).
- □ To expand user groups along the line of internal strategic interests in the company.
- □ To integrate DSS with other office systems such as word processing functions.

Questions

1. Identify the determinants of success in the Firestone case.
2. Which of these are not discussed in this chapter?
3. Identify the major implementation problems cited in the case.
4. What are some unique features about DSS that one can learn from this case?
5. Why was DSS an appropriate tool in this case?
6. Why was the responsibility for database administration delegated to the V.P. for administration?

CASE 2: Cambell Soup Puts Expert System to Work in Their Kitchens

The process of soup making is highly automated from beginning to end but minor malfunctions do occur. So the Campbell folks decided that expert system approaches could help their repair and maintenance people to anticipate and prevent malfunctions, and to diagnose them faster when they occurred.[*]

Campbell worked with Texas Instruments (TI) Corp. to select the first application for an expert system. The application they chose was the diagnosis of malfunctions that can occur in cooker systems (more formally called "hydrostatic sterilizers").

Source: Condensed from *Computerworld*, September 27, 1982.

Cookers are the working heart of every Campbell canning plant, and the plants are spread throughout the world. The cooker's vital job is to sterilize the food. Elaborate conveyor systems load and unload the cookers. Downtime is expensive and disrupts shipping schedules.

Campbell plant operators and maintenance people are well able to handle day-to-day operation of the cookers, and to correct common malfunctions. Occasionally, though, difficulties arise that demand diagnosis by an expert—someone thoroughly versed in the design, installation, and operation of the cookers.

The Campbell people wanted to capture this expertise in an inexpensive computer system, so that even their smallest plant could have it immediately available. That would also free their experts to concentrate on design improvements and new processes. A secondary objective was to use the system as a training tool for new maintenance personnel.

The system was developed on a TI Professional Computer, a microcomputer system with 512K of memory, a 10MB Winchester disk, and a color graphics display. The ES can be delivered on any IBM PC (or compatible) because PCs are inexpensive, familiar, and easy to use. The system was developed with the Personal Consultant shell (see Chapter 15).

The accompanying box presents an example of an English translation of one of the rules in Campbell's expert system.

"IF the cooker's symptom is TEMPERATURE-DEVIATION, and the problem temperature is T30-INTERMEDIATE-COOLING-SPRAY, and the input and output air signals for TIC-30 are correct, and the valve on TCV-30 is not open,

THEN the problem with the cooker is that TCV-30 is not working properly. Check the instrumentation and the air signal."

Development of Campbell's first expert system took about six months from initial contact with the human expert to field testing. The history of its development is instructive. On November 5, 1984, the Campbell cooker expert met with TI knowledge engineers for the first time. The expert was understandably skeptical, but completely cooperative. The first four days were devoted to teaching the TI people about the normal operation of the cookers, so they could discuss malfunctions intelligently.

On December 10 TI returned to Campbell with a first-draft system that used 32 rules. TI's development philosophy is to get a prototype system up and running as quickly as possible for early evaluation by the clients. It has proven to be the best strategy for eliciting further knowledge. Few people are able to create, but all of us are generous with constructive criticism.

With the wealth of additional knowledge elicited in a three-day review of the prototype with Campbell management, TI enlarged the system to 66 rules, and presented it to Campbell on January 22, 1985. This time, the review produced no great changes. Rather, some of the terms were refined and some detailed steps were added to certain diagnostic procedures.

Also at this point, the system was demonstrated to potential users—a shift supervisor at Campbell's Camden, NJ plant, and several operations and mainte-

*Condensed from the *Artificial Intelligence Letter*, Vol. 1, No. 5, November 1985. Published by Texas Instruments Data Systems Group, Austin, Texas.

nance people at Campbell's Napoleon, OH plant. Their consensus was that the system would be useful to have at the plants. During this trip, Campbell also decided to expand the expert system to cover both start-up and shut-down procedures.

On February 12, TI presented the next refinement of the system to Campbell. It had now grown to 85 rules, plus 12 start-up and shut-down procedures. After a few minor flaws were corrected, Campbell declared this first phase of the system ready. A second phase covering rotary cookers had been added by Campbell after the hydrostatic sterilizer system appeared destined for success.

On March 19, an expert system covering hydrostatic cookers, their startup and shutdown, and rotary cookers was presented. It had now grown to 125 rules. On this visit, the system was demonstrated to a wider circle of Campbell's management, and there was consensus that Campbell's first expert system was nearly ready for field testing. The next month was spent refining the rotary cooker rules and including rules covering a different type of hydrostatic cooker used at only one of Campbell's plants.

By November 1, 1985, the expert system contained 151 rules plus startup and shutdown procedures, and Campbell was fanning out the system to its plants.

Four of the key people in the project—Aldo Cimino and Reuben K. Tyson of Campbell, Richard Herrod and Michael D. Smith of TI— have summarized some of the practical lessons learned or reconfirmed:

- It's more important to put together a prototype fast than to make it complete.
- Extracting knowledge from the human expert is a difficult process for both the expert and the knowledge engineer, and they must guard against discouragement.
- The knowledge engineer must be prepared to accept frequent correction—and the expert must be willing to give it.
- Because experts are seldom aware of all their thinking processes, each review of a developing system is helpful in uncovering additional needed knowledge.
- The expert must be fully cooperative, even if skeptical.
- Strong management commitment to a project of this type is absolutely essential to its success. An expert's time is in short supply and the project must have a high enough priority to assure adequate access to the expert.
- Early demonstration to potential users is important. Without their feedback about perceived deficiencies, and without their support, even a well-conceived system can end up in a closet, collecting dust.
- An expert system must continue to grow, to cover unforeseen situations and equipment modifications. Fortunately, it's fairly easy to add new knowledge to an expert system.

Questions

1. Trace the development process of this system. List all the measures that were taken to ensure successful implementation.
2. Compare the practical lessons listed at the end of this case with the theoretical approach to successful implementation proposed in this chapter. Discuss similarities and differences.
3. Discuss some of the potential benefits of the system.
4. The development of the system was done by an outside vendor, working as a consultant. Discuss the advantages and disadvantages of such an approach from an implementation point of view.
5. Users' involvement in this case occurred about midcourse in the development cycle. This is fairly typical in ES. In DSS, on the other hand, users are involved much earlier.

Explain the logic behind the two practical approaches. Do you agree with it? Why or why not?

6. A close relationship between the expert and the knowledge engineer is essential to successful implementation. Review the case and point out the incidents of interaction between the two and the lessons learned.

7. Why is it so important to complete the first prototype early? How can it enhance implementation?

References and Bibliography

1. Alter, S. L. *Decision Support Systems, Current Practice and Continuing Challenges.* Reading, MA: Addison-Wesley, 1980.

2. Andriole, S. J. *Microcomputer Decision Support Systems: Design, Implementation and Evaluation.* Wellesley, MA, QED Information Science, 1986.

3. Athappilly, K. "Successful Decision Making Starts With DSS Evaluation." *Data Management*, February 1985.

4. Barki, H. "Change, Attitude to Change, and DSS Successes." *Information and Management*, Vol. 95, 1985.

5. Brightman, H. J., and S. E. Harris. "Building Computer Models that Really Work." *Managerial Planning*, January–February 1984.

6. Buchanan, B. G., and E. H. Shortliffe. *Rule-Based Expert Systems: The MYCIN Experiments of the Stanford Heuristic Programming Project.* Reading, MA: 1 Addison-Wesley, 1984.

7. Casimir, R. J. "Characteristics and Implementation of Decision Support Systems." *Information and Management*, Vol. 14, 1988.

8. Churchman, C. W., and A. H. Schainblatt. "The Researcher and the Manager: A Dialectic of Implementation." *Management Science*, Vol. 11, 1965.

9. Culnan, M. J. "The Dimensions of Accessibility to Online Information: Implications for Implementing Office Automation Systems." *ACM Transactions on Office Automation Systems*, February 1984.

10. DePree, R. "Implementing Expert Systems." *Micro User's Guide*, Summer 1988.

11. DeSanctis, G. "An Examination of Expectancy Theory-Model of Decision Support System Use." *Proceedings of the Third International Conference on Information Systems*, Ann Arbor, MI, 1982.

12. Dickson, G. W., and J. C. Wetherbe. *The Management of Information Systems.* New York: McGraw-Hill, 1985.

13. Dickson, G., and R. Powers. "MIS Project Management: Myths, Opinions and Realities." In W. McFarlin, et al., eds. *Information Systems Administration.* New York: Holt, Rinehart and Winston, 1973.

14. Fallik, F. *Managing Organizational Change: Human Factors and Automation.* Taylor & Francis, 1988.

15. Ginzberg, M. J. "Key Recurrent Issues in the MIS Implementation Process." *MIS Quarterly*, Vol. 5, No. 2, 1981.

16. Hogue, J. T., and H.J. Watson. "Current Practices in the Development of Decision Support Systems." *Information and Management*, May 1985.

17. Huff, S. L., et al. "An Empirical Study of Decision Support Systems." *INFOR*, February 1984.

18. Ives, B., and M. H. Olson. "User Involvement in Information System Development: A Review of Research." *Management Science*, Vol. 30, No. 5, May 1984.

19. Keen, P. G. W. "Value Analysis: Justifying Decision Support Systems." *MIS Quarterly*, March 1981.

20. Lewin, K. "Group Decision and Social Change." In *Readings in Social Psychology*, T. M. Newcomb and E. L. Hartley, eds. New York: Holt, Rinehart and Winston, 1947.
21. Lucas, H. C. *Implementation: The Key to Successful Information Systems*. New York: Columbia University Press, 1981.
22. Meador, C. L., M. J. Guyote, and P. G. W. Keen. "Setting Priorities for DSS Development." *MIS Quarterly*, Vol. 8, No. 2, June 1984.
23. Meredith, J. R. "The Implementation of Computer-Based Systems." *Journal of Operational Management*, October 1981.
24. Mohan, L., and A. S. Bean. "Introducing OR/MS into Organizations: Normative Implications of Selected Indian Experience." *Decision Sciences*, Vol. 10, 1979.
25. Money, A., et al. "The Quantification of Decision Support Benefits within the Context of Value Analysis." *MIS Quarterly*, June 1988.
26. Morino, M. M. "Managing and Coping with Change: An IS Challenge." *Journal of Information Systems Management*, Winter 1988.
27. Robey, D. "User Attitudes and MIS Use." *Academy of Management Journal*, Vol. 22, No. 3, September 1979.
28. Sanders, G. L., and J. F. Courtney. "A Field Study of Organizational Factors Influencing DSS Success." *MIS Quarterly*, March 1985.
29. Schultz, R. L., and D. P. Slevin, eds. *Implementing Operations Research/Management Science*. New York: Elsevier, 1975.
30. Sharda, R., et al. "Decision Support Systems Effectiveness: A Review and Empirical Test." *Management Science*, Feb. 1988.
31. Sprague, R. H., Jr., and E. D. Carlson. *Building Effective Decision Support Systems*. Englewood Cliffs, NJ: Prentice-Hall, 1982.
32. Swanson, E. B. *Information System Implementation*. Homewood, IL: Irwin, 1988.
33. Van Horn, M. *Understanding Expert Systems*. Toronto: Bantam Books, 1986.
34. Zand, D. E., and R. E. Sorenson. "Theory of Change and Effective Use of Management Science." *Administrative Science Quarterly*, Vol. 20, No. 4, 1975.
35. Zmud, R. W. "Individual Differences and MIS Success: A Review of the Empirical Literature." *Management Science*, Vol. 25, No. 10, 1979.
36. Zmud, R. W., and J. F. Cox. "The Implementation Process: A Change Process." *MIS Quarterly*, June 1979.

Chapter 21

Organizational and Societal Impacts of Management Support Systems

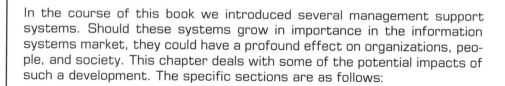

In the course of this book we introduced several management support systems. Should these systems grow in importance in the information systems market, they could have a profound effect on organizations, people, and society. This chapter deals with some of the potential impacts of such a development. The specific sections are as follows:

767

21.1   **Introduction**

Management support systems are important participants in the Information Revolution, a cultural transformation that most people are only now coming to terms with. Unlike preceding, slower revolutions, such as the Industrial Revolution, the Information Revolution is taking place very quickly, impacting upon every facet of our lives. Inherent in this rapid transformation is a host of managerial and social problems, such as the impact on organizational structure, resistance to change, and possible increased unemployment levels. The AI share of the computer industry could reach 20 percent by the year 2000 (see material in box), so its impact can be substantial.

Separating the impacts of MSS from the impact of other computerized systems is a difficult task. Very little published information regarding the impact of these tools exists because the techniques are so new. Therefore some of our discussion relates to CBIS in general rather than to DSS and ES specifically. However, we recognize that DSS, EIS, and especially ES technologies do have some unique organizational, social, and cultural implications. These implications will be highlighted throughout this chapter.

The impacts of MSS have both micro- and macro-implications: they could affect particular individuals and jobs and the work structure of departments and units within the organization (microeffects); they could also have significant long-term effects on total organizational structures, entire industries, communities, and society as a whole (macroeffects).

Figure 21.1 presents a framework for research that shows a complete management system. Such a system stays in equilibrium as long as all its parts are

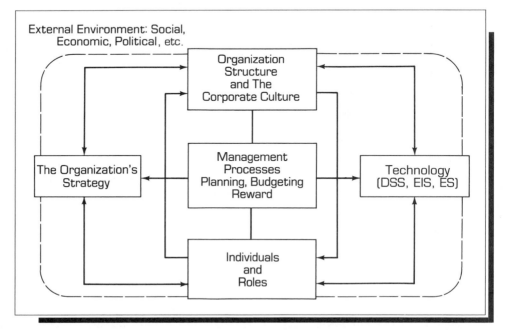

FIGURE 21.1 A framework for organizational and societal impacts of technology. (*Source:* Scott-Morton [34] based on Leavitt [21].)

Where is the AI Market Going?

- □ 1990 $5–10 billion 2–4% of computer industry
- □ 1995 $30–70 billion 2–15% of computer industry
- □ 2000 $50–110 billion 10–20% of computer industry

(*Source:* From A.D. Little Decision Resources 1984 conference on "The Businesses and Technologies of Tomorrow.")

unchanged. However, when there is a change in one of the components, it will impact some of the other components. The major impacts in the future could result from changes in technology, especially computerized systems like DSS and ES.

The purpose of this chapter is to foster a basic understanding of the major set of personal and societal implications of a widespread use of CBIS and MSS. Regardless of the extent to which individual organizations will use MSS, these systems clearly could generate substantial change in the world around us. Consideration of these issues will give insight into how organizations should position themselves to carry out their missions and responsibilities in the world of the not-too-distant future. This chapter attempts to help managers assess

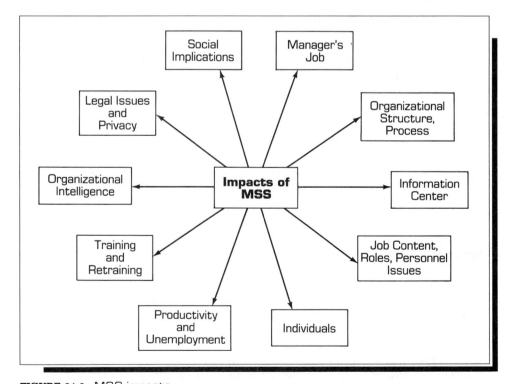

FIGURE 21.2 MSS impacts.

MSS with a balanced view of their likely impact on people and organizations. The chapter has 10 major subdivisions according to the major areas of impact (see Figure 21.2). Another potential impact, on profitability and competitiveness, is not discussed here. See Crescenzi (7) for details.

21.2   Organizational Impacts

The organizational impacts may be felt along several dimensions ranging from structure and degree of centralization to distribution of power. Here we will deal only with a few of the issues. For an overview on the impacts of expert systems see O'Leary and Turban (28). For an overview of computerization impacts on productivity and quality of work see Krout et al. (20).

Structure

Computer-based systems have already created changes in organizational structures. MSS could further enhance these changes in the following ways:

Flatter Organizational Hierarchies.   With the increased productivity of managers provided by DSS and EIS, and the need for fewer experts (owing to ES), it is reasonable to assume that *fewer* managerial levels will exist in many organizations (both staff and line). This trend is already evidenced by the continuation of the "shrinking size of middle-management" phenomena (e.g., see [23], [25], and [31]).

Flatter organizational hierarchies will also result from managers' increased span of control, the reduction in the total number of employees owing to increased productivity, and the ability of lower-level employees to perform higher-level jobs. For example, the Bank of America's reorganization, announced in 1985, resulted in a smaller corporation and a much flatter structure due mainly to the increased use of computers.

Staff-to-Line Ratio.   The ratio of staff to line in most organizations has increased with the replacement of clerical jobs by computers and with the increased need for information systems specialists. The expansion of MSS and especially ES may reverse this trend. Specifically, the number of professionals and specialists could decline in relation to the total number of employees in the organization.

Centralization of Authority

The relationship between computerized systems and the degree of centralization of authority (and power) in the organizations that these systems serve has been extensively debated, especially since the introduction of microcomputers. After analyzing both DSS and ES cases, it is still difficult to establish a clear pattern. For example, the introduction of ES in General Electric's maintenance area increased the power of the decentralized units because they became less dependent on the company's headquarters. The DSS at GLSC Shipping Co., on the other hand, resulted in a highly centralized planning and control system. Computer-based information systems (CBIS) could support either centralization (when a large central computer dominates) or decentralization (when PCs and a distributed processing network dominate) of electronic information processing within an organization. The same concept can be applied to the centralization and decentralization of operations and of management within a computer-using organization.

□ *Centralization.* Large, central computer systems, where large MSS are developed and used, allow upper management to centralize the decision making formerly done at lower levels of the organization.

□ *Decentralization.* Personal computers and data communication networks allow top management to delegate more responsibility to middle managers and to increase the number of branch offices (or other company units) while still providing top management with the ability to control the organization.

Although information systems are usually established after an organizational structure is completed, it is very possible that a new or modified information system will change the organizational structure and/or the degree of decentralization.

Because of the trend toward flatter organizations, centralization may become more popular. However, this trend could be offset by specialization. Whether MSS will result in more centralization or decentralization of business operations and management may depend on top management's philosophy. After all, people still can control the direction in which computers take us.

Power and Status

"Knowledge is power." This fact has been recognized for generations. The latest developments in computerized systems are changing the power structure within organizations. The struggle over who will control the computers and information resources has become one of the most visible conflicts in many organizations, both private and public. Expert systems, for example, may reduce the power of certain professional groups because their knowledge will become public domain. (See Ryan [33].) On the other hand, those individuals who serve on the DSS and ES teams may gain considerable prestige, knowledge, power, and status. In contrast with regular CBIS, the issues at stake could be much more important and visible, because complex decision situations and upper management may be involved. A sophisticated EIS, or a large-scale DSS may control some of the major decisions in an organization, including long-range strategic ones. Expert systems may shift power from professionals to administrators. Future large-scale DSS, especially when combined with ES and networking, could shift power from the finance and marketing units to the systems and engineering units. As a matter of fact, a large financial institution, which was controlled by both the VP for marketing and finance as late as 1983, is now dominated by the VP for information systems and technology. The salaries of the chief information officers (CIOs) in some large corporations (e.g., Bank of

America) are much higher than the salaries of the chief finance, marketing, and operation management officers. An interesting example of this power struggle can be found in the concept of the information center.

21.3 The Information Center and Other Special Units

One of the most interesting changes in organizational structure related to computer technology is the introduction of the information center (IC).[*] The concept of the IC was conceived (by IBM, Canada, see Hammond [13]) as a response to the increased number of end-user requests for new computer applications. This demand created a huge backlog of work in the DP department,[**] and users had to wait several years to get their system installed. This situation is similar to the dilemma telephone companies faced in the 1920s. When it became apparent that most Americans wanted a telephone, AT&T realized that it would need almost as many operators as there were potential users. The solution, of course, was to provide users with the ability to dial their own calls.

The IC is a unit that helps users learn to write their own application programs—to dial their own calls, so to speak. As the rotary dial made customer telephone dialing possible, fourth-generation languages and other MSS tools and generators have been the driving force behind user-driven computing. Sometime in the future, when users will become more educated, and the hardware and software will be easier to use, we can expect that users will refer to the IC only for complex or unusual cases, much as we use the telephone operator today.

Information centers are groups of employees specially trained in the use of MSS building tools (such as DBMS, spreadsheet technology, and ES shells) and applications software. The IC's primary task is to provide fast turnaround on users' requests for information, data analyses, special reports, and other one-time information needs. An IC can also be defined as an organizational unit within a company that provides end-users with proper education, technical support, usable tools, data, and convenient access to computer systems.

In a short time the IC concept has become very popular; there is a large national IC society, a special journal (*Information Center*), and regional and national conferences catering to ICs.

Purposes and Activities

The three main functions of an IC are (1) to provide assistance to end-users in dealing with computing problems, (2) to provide general technical assistance, and (3) to provide general support services. Each function should fulfill the following requirements (per Jacobson H., and Cardullo, J., "Information Centers: Boon or Bane," *Management Technology*, September 1983):

---

[*]Other names for a similar organizational unit are information resource center and users' service center.

[**]The name *data processing* (DP) *department* is still used by many organizations. However, this name is being slowly replaced by new names like *information systems* (IS) *department*.

End-user computing
- Training and education.
- Assisting in software (application) development.
- Developing prototype programs.
- Establishing configuration for standardization.
- Debugging assistance.
- Identifying networking requirements.
- Consulting with the user to determine if a particular application is appropriate for end-user development.
- Providing a formal means for users' communication with management and with the traditional data processing staff.
- Cooperating with database administrators to improve shared-data resources.
- Generating a catalog or library of existing applications for future use.
- Managing software documentation for specific applications (e.g., for specific DSS).

Technical assistance
- Provide guidance in the selection of hardware and system software.
- Help in the selection and evaluation of application packages, DSS and ES generators, and building tools.
- Software installation and updates.
- Assistance in using query and report languages and/or packages.
- Hardware installation and use.
- Communication devices, installation, and use.
- Establishing database (or file) backup, recovery, and archive guidelines.

General support services
- Providing clearinghouse functions for receiving and disseminating information on relevant personal computing issues.
- Establishing a "hotline" for interrupt-driven user requests for information on software, hardware, or application systems.
- Chairing user group meetings on a regular and ad hoc basis.

Staffing

Information centers should be staffed by people with the following attributes:

- Business knowledge (usually MBAs).
- Analytical skills.
- Current software package knowledge (DSS generators, ES shells, and miscellaneous tools).
- Current basic hardware knowledge.
- Knowledge of where to go outside the organization for needed information.
- Patience and enthusiasm.
- Good interpersonal communication skills.
- Programming skills (especially in 4GLs).
- Drive and motivation to complete programs without direct supervision.
- End-user and service orientation.

Problem Areas

The purposes and activities of the IC as described above are a utopian vision: Executives get the information they need *when* they need it; the data processing department is *freed* from mundane programming to work on important projects. As for other managers and professionals in an organization, there is a wealth of information that can be easily tapped for the benefit of the corporation. All this is coordinated at the IC, where users and IC personnel work together to meet everyone's needs. Reality, however, may be quite different. Although many tend to agree that the IC is the best way to control and capitalize on the sweep of new information technology, it is evident that many organizations have also found that the path to the utopian vision is a rocky one. The following are some potential problem areas in IC operations:

- ☐ Opposition from the DP department (power struggle and ego problems).
- ☐ Users do not have enough computer knowledge, yet they set up their own IC. This may result in low-quality service.
- ☐ Corporate management anticipates that the IC will be an expensive new unit with its hardware and software. Because it is difficult to conduct a cost-benefit analysis of an IC, management may be reluctant to establish one.
- ☐ Resistance from noncomputer-oriented users who fear that the IC will help computer-oriented users.
- ☐ Security problems (e.g., more company data in more hands).
- ☐ The struggle regarding whom the IC should report to and who should control it.
- ☐ Lack of senior management support.
- ☐ Staffing the IC with individuals who do not possess the specified attributes discussed earlier. This problem may taper off within the next two to three years.
- ☐ Potential backlog for IC-developed or assisted applications.
- ☐ Proliferation of PCs may have resulted in "uncontrolled" purchases, which may mean supporting multiple vendors' products and incompatibility of equipment.
- ☐ Redundancy of effort if IC operations are not centralized (several IC-like groups may emerge and duplicate one another's efforts).

Despite the problem areas, the information center is becoming an extremely important support for user-developed DSS. It could become a major factor in the development of ES as well.

The Roles of the Information Systems (IS) Department

One of the major purposes of end-user computing is to ease the pressure on the IS department. And indeed, very few of the early DSS were constructed by the IS department. Furthermore, the organization's IS group was initially seen, by DSS builders, as the "enemy." With the introduction of the information center's concepts, it seemed that the role of the IS department in constructing MSS would diminish. However, it is recognized that constructing MSS can provide status and power to the builders, and therefore IS departments may struggle to participate and even control such development projects. Therefore, it is not surprising that Huff et al. (17) found that the IS department had the main development responsibility in 23.7 percent of 133 DSS. The complete findings of the study (conducted in Canada in 1983) are presented in Chapter 20, Table 20.7.

Lately, some ICs have started to move from the user organization to the IS department. This can be a trend in those companies where the information (computer) area becomes very powerful.

The Chesebrough-Pond's Case

A typical example of an information center that uses DSS extensively is Chesebrough-Pond's, Inc., a large, diversified producer of consumer goods (food, apparel, health/beauty).

Chesebrough-Pond's (Trumbull, CT) started an information center in 1981 after conducting a year-long study to determine how to decrease both the high cost of computerized (time-sharing) systems and the long development backlog. Then a users' survey was conducted to determine needs and to set up and prioritize decision analysis criteria.

The initial software selected was
□ EXPRESS (as a comprehensive DSS generator)
□ FOCUS (for data management)
□ FCS/EPS (for financial planning and modeling)

The operating environment was IBM's VM/CMS. The selection of software was based primarily on the following criteria: "what if" capability, reporting capability, ease of use, and the reputation of the vendor. Vendors were selected because they had large user bases (the company decided not to "blaze trails" with an untested vendor). The selectors looked at technical assistance and stable vendorship.

The info center was staffed with analytically skilled people with MBA-type backgrounds, good communication skills, service orientation, self-motivation, and experience. The company decided *not* to use people out of the MIS department. ("These people often are not oriented to the end-user environment.") The center not only responded to people but also played a proactive role (e.g., by showing management the progress of various systems through prototyping and by searching for opportunities for DSS).

The center charges users for the services, encouraging them to retain control over spending. The center does not get involved in MIS development work.

(*Source:* Condensed from *Computerworld*, October 25, 1982.)

Other Special Units: A DSS and/or ES Unit

Another change in organizational structure is the possibility of creating a DSS department, management support department, and/or AI department. Such a department (or a unit) can be an extension of the information center, can replace a management science unit, or can be a completely new entity.

DSS departments exist in several large corporations. For example, Security Pacific Corp. Bank has a 15-person DSS department in its financial services division. Mead has a corporate DSS applications department at the same level as the IS department. Many companies have a small DSS unit.

Several large corporations have created AI departments. For example, FMC Corp. created one of the earliest and largest AI departments (see material in box); Boeing Aerospace operates a large AI department. In both cases the departments are involved in extensive training in addition to their research, consulting, and applications activities.

A related interesting issue is where to place an EIS and who will be responsible for its development.

Artificial Intelligence at FMC Corp.

FMC Corp. (Santa Clara, CA) has made a major commitment to AI. The company is building a 90-person AI center. Major applications are starting in the defense area and moving to the industrial machinery (manufacturing and maintenance) area. Expert systems operate in the area of oil pumping operations, automotive engine design, and tool design. Applications are seen in the operations of chemical plants and machinery manufacturing. Robotics and machine vision technology are being transferred from defense to the manufacturing plants.

To build up the necessary personnel, the company has designed an in-house training program equivalent to a master of science program for the AI specialists.

With a rich application environment and a strong corporate commitment, the company hopes to become an industrial center of excellence in applied AI.

21.4   Job Content and Personnel Issues

One of the major impacts of DSS, and especially of ES, will be on the content of many jobs in both private and public organizations. Job content is important not only because it is related to organizational structure but also because it is interrelated with employee satisfaction, compensation, status, and productivity. The following topics could be important considerations in any large-scale DSS and ES:

The Role of Employees and Managers

DSS and ES could cause major changes in the roles that both managers and employees play. Many experts in organizations will stop providing routine advice, but conduct more research and development instead. For example, at General Electric, technicians using ES perform some tasks previously done by engineers. At Security Pacific Bank, employees at low levels perform some tasks previously done by higher-level employees. Thus, many role definitions will be changed. New jobs will also be created, such as knowledge engineers and MSS builders. On the other hand, some jobs will disappear altogether. For example, an ES that can advise travelers on what immunizations are required when traveling abroad could eliminate the position of the person who currently gives out this information.

The support staff for a manager will generally be information specialists (e.g., employees of the information center or the IS department), whereas today's typical manager would have mainly specialists in functional areas (e.g., finance, law, accounting). The need for functional specialization would decrease mainly owing to the introduction of ES.

The Change in the Experts' Job—The XCON's Experience

Before XCON

Do manual checking, tedious job, very repetitive and boring. Made many mistakes that had to be corrected. Low status.

After XCON

□ Check what XCON is doing.
□ Do the 2 percent that XCON cannot do.
□ Update XCON's knowledge base with new information.
□ High status, the operators are considered the custodians of XCON's pool of configuration knowledge.

Role Ambiguity and Conflict

The changes in the job content would result in opportunities for promotion and employee personal development. But these changes could create problems of role conflict and ambiguity, especially in the short run (e.g., see Katz and Kahn [19]). In addition, there may be considerable resistance to changes in roles, primarily on the part of managers who favor a noncomputerized communications system.

Employee Career Ladders

The increased use of MSS in organizations could have a significant and somewhat unexpected impact on employee career ladders.

Today, many highly skilled professionals have developed their abilities through years of experience. This experience is gained by holding a series of positions that expose the person to progressively more difficult and complex situations. The use of DSS and ES may "block out" a portion of this learning curve. Those tasks of low and medium difficulty that now are part of a professional's experience may be performed in the future with considerable assistance from an ES. However, skilled professionals will still be required for highly complex activities. Several questions remain unaddressed: How will high-level human expertise be acquired with minimal experience in lower-level tasks? What will be the effect on compensation at all levels of employment? How will human resource development programs be structured? What career plans will be offered to employees?

Changes in Supervision

The fact that an employee's work is performed online and stored electronically introduces the possibility for greater "electronic supervision." For professional employees whose work is often measured by completion of long-term deliverables, "remote supervison" implies greater emphasis on deliverables and less on personal contact. This emphasis is especially true if employees work in geographically dispersed locations away from their supervisors. In general, the supervisory process may become more formalized, with greater reliance on procedures and measurable outputs than on informal processes.

For clerical work, this formalization will mean short-term external pacing of work as well as close monitoring of any measurable work, such as number of keystrokes or number of lines typed. Many word processing systems, for example, already monitor work electronically and record the results at a supervisory workstation. Interesting issues could be the use of DSS and especially ES to support supervision. Another interesting issue is the required skill and training of supervisors.

Human/Machine Interface Considerations

Several issues could evolve regarding human/machine interface when MSS are involved. For example, one may ask questions such as: What should computernaïve users of MSS be told that will make them more effective users of these systems? In what ways should the abilities of an AI system resemble the abilities and limitations of its users and in what ways should they not? How can MSS be designed to meet the needs of users with varying degrees of experience and expertise?

Turnover and Retirement

The current professional work force could experience a higher-than-normal retirement rate owing to obsolescence of skills and voluntary early retirement. In addition, certain categories of professionals will exhibit excessive turnover rates either because of lucrative employment opportunities in other companies (if their skills are in demand) or because their jobs will be eliminated.

The following questions need to be addressed: What can be done to lessen these problems? Are we set up to absorb retirees into the nonworking community? How do we address the potential feelings of alienation in displaced workers? How is training to be planned and executed?

Computerized Personal Financial Advice—A Fringe Benefit

An interesting impact of DSS and especially of ES on organizations is the recent trend toward providing computerized personal financial advice as a fringe benefit to managers and other employees. *The Wall Street Journal* described the innovation in detail (June 13, 1986, p. 21). The following is a summary of that description.

For years corporations have paid the cost of financial planning for their top executives. This planning, provided by human experts, costs corporations five to ten thousand dollars per executive. The planner makes recommendations on such issues as tax shelters, retirement planning, investment opportunities, and covering college expenses. But such personalized service is too expensive to be given to all employees. The cheaper alternative is a computerized system.

Several ready-made financial planning DSS are on the market. For example, Consumer Financial Institute, a Newton, MA, unit of Price Waterhouse, sells such services. Owing to the complexity of financial planning, the advice is usually provided on a time-sharing basis, at a cost of $150 to $500 per employee. The major suppliers of such programs are financial service giants such as American Express, E.F. Hutton, and Merrill Lynch. In addition to the time-sharing basis, it is possible to buy the DSS software and subscribe to a regular updating.

Serious packages are available for large computers at a price of $10,000 to over $100,000. There exist several dozen micropackages that cost only several hundred dollars each, but they are very limited in their consultation capabilities.

Some financial planners question the value of computerized advice, especially when provided by a DSS. They say that impersonal questionnaires (which are used to collect data from the participants), cannot assess people's personalities (isolate their degree of risk aversion, for instance). Some of these deficiencies can be solved by expert systems. An interesting product is available from Applied Expert Systems, Inc. (APEX) under the name PlanPower. It is a personal financial planning system that includes several thousand rules that match the financial situation of an individual client with the right financial products and services. The software is sold both to corporations and to independent financial planners at a price of $50,000.

The vendors of the computerized advice claim their products help people understand personal financial planning, leading them to think about their financial affairs and their retirement. One interesting aspect of this program is a comparison of the cost of working versus the cost of retiring. This feature is already used (and even misused) by some companies to persuade older employees to retire early.

About 6 percent of all large U.S. corporations provide this service (in 1989) to employees as a fringe benefit. It is estimated that within five years, roughly a quarter of all large U.S. companies will offer computerized financial planning to their white-collar employees.

Other Considerations

Several other personnel-related issues will surface as a result of using MSS. For example, one may raise the following issues: What will be the impact of MSS on managerial office work?, on job qualifications?, on training requirements?, and on worker satisfaction? How can jobs involving the use of these tools be designed so they present an acceptable level of challenge to users? (An acceptable level of challenge is assumed to be one that is neither prohibitively great nor too small to make the job boring or demeaning.) How might MSS be used to personalize or enrich jobs? What can be done to make sure that the introduction of AI and MSS does not demean jobs or have other negative impacts from the workers' point of view? What principles should be used to allocate functions to people and machines, especially those functions that can be performed equally well by either one? Should cost or efficiency be the sole or major criterion for such allocation? All these and several other issues could be encountered in any system implementation and should be the subject for research by the academic and the business communities.

21.5 Impact on Individuals

Computer systems may affect individuals in various ways. What is a benefit to one individual may be a curse to another. What is an added stress today can be a relief tomorrow. The following are some of the areas where MSS may affect individuals, their perceptions, and behaviors.

Job Satisfaction

Although many managerial jobs may become substantially more "enriched" with MSS, other jobs may become less satisfying in the new, more structured organizational environment. Because MSS, like other technologies, can either help improve jobs or make them less satisfying, designers of these systems should take into account the opportunity to improve the quality of work life rather than just focus on technical quality.

Behavioral scientists (e.g., Argyris [2]), predicted that CBIS would reduce managerial discretion in decision making, and thus create dissatisfied managers. Although such a prediction has not been realized to date, it should be reexamined in light of the introduction of ES. As far as a DSS and EIS are concerned, it could *increase* managerial discretion, owing to the DSS flexibility and adaptability and the capabilities of EIS.

Inflexibility and Dehumanization

A frequent criticism of traditional data processing systems is their negative effect on people's individuality. Such systems are criticized as being impersonal; they dehumanize and depersonalize activities that have been computerized, because they reduce or eliminate the human element present in noncomputerized systems. Many people feel a loss of identity; they feel like "just another number."

One of the major objectives of DSS is to create *flexible* systems that will fit different decision styles and allow individuals to input their opinion and knowledge. DSS, EIS, and ES should also be people-oriented and user-friendly to make them more easily accepted. By having these qualities, MSS can help promote greater personalization and attention to the individual than would otherwise be possible.

21.6 Impact on Productivity and Employment—An Overview

The Industrial Revolution of the eighteenth century saw machines replace muscle power.[*] This was the beginning of automation: the automatic transfer and positioning of work by machines, or the automatic operation and control of a production process by machines. The assembly line operation of an automobile is a typical example of automation. Thus, automation can be viewed as the use of machines to replace some human brain power and manual dexterity.

The impact of computers on employment and productivity is directly related to the use of computers for achieving automation. There can be no doubt that computers have created new jobs and increased productivity, while also causing a significant reduction in some types of job opportunities. Computers used for office information processing or for the numerical control of machine tools are accomplishing tasks formerly performed by clerks and machinists. Jobs created by computers require different types of skills and education than those jobs eliminated by computers. Therefore specific individuals within an organization will become unemployed unless they are retrained for new positions or new responsibilities.

The productivity of many individual workers has been significantly increased by computerization. One worker now does the work of several, and the time required to perform certain tasks has been drastically reduced. Increased productivity has led to lower labor costs and prices, which in turn have increased demand for products and services and, thus, have increased employment. The higher profits caused by increases in productivity also have stimulated more investment in the expansion of production facilities, resulting in further increased employment.

Another point to remember is that the higher standard of living caused by increased productivity generates *more* rather than *less* demand for more types and amounts of goods and services (at least up to a certain limit). "Yesterday's luxuries become today's necessities" is a statement that emphasizes the almost unlimited demand for goods and services our society seems to exhibit. This phenomenon is related to the impact of computers on employment, because a desire to increase the standard of living leads to an expanded demand for goods and services, and results in an increase in employment opportunities.

---

[*]This section is based on O'Brien's work(27).

The computer industry has created a host of new job opportunities for the manufacture, sale, and maintenance of computer hardware, software, and other computer services. Many new jobs (systems analysts, computer programmers, computer operators) have been created. Additional jobs have been created because the computer makes possible the production of complex industrial and technical goods and services that would otherwise be impossible or uneconomical to produce.

The controversy over the effect of computers on employment will continue as long as activities formerly performed by people are computerized. Unemployment figures are more than statistics; office and factory workers whose jobs have been eliminated by computerization are real people with real employment needs. Such people will take little comfort in the fact that computers have many beneficial effects on employment in general. Business firms and other computer-using organizations, labor unions, and government agencies must continue to provide job opportunities for people displaced by computers. This includes transfers to other positions, relocation to other facilities, or training for new responsibilities. Only if society continues to take positive steps to provide jobs for people displaced by computers can we take pride in the increase in employment caused by computer usage. Finally, education, starting at elementary schools and ending at universities, must keep up with technology to prevent massive unemployment.

21.7   Artificial Intelligence, Productivity, and Employment

The previous section presented an overview of the issue of CBIS, productivity, and employment. There is very little information on the relationship of MSS to these topics. However, AI in general, and ES in particular, have the potential of significantly affecting both the productivity and employment of many types of employees. The material in this section summarizes the position of some of the country's top experts with regard to the impact of AI on productivity and unemployment.[*]

Although the impact of AI may take decades to materialize, there is agreement among researchers that AI in general, and ES in particular, will increase the productivity of "knowledge employees."[**] Technology will be relatively inexpensive and thus create substantial shifts in jobs and job contents. However, a major disagreement exists about the potential impact of AI and ES on the aggregate employment (or unemployment) level. The two extreme positions are (1) massive unemployment, versus (2) increased employment (or at worst, no change in the employment level). These positions are supported by two Nobel prize winners: Wassily Leontief, who supports the massive unemployment argument, and Herbert Simon, who counters Leontief. Now, let us examine the major arguments of the opposing parties.

[*]This discussion is based on Nilsson (26). For extended discussion see Partridge (30).

[**]For a comprehensive discussion of knowledge employees and their role in organizations see Holsapple and Whinston (16).

Massive Unemployment

Massive unemployment is predicted because (1) the need for human labor will be significantly reduced; (2) the skill levels of people performing jobs with the help of AI will be low; (3) AI will affect both blue- and white-collar employees, including professionals and managers in all sectors, including services and high-technology companies (in the past, both service industries and the high-technology sector absorbed employees replaced by automation in other sectors); (4) "the signs are already written on the wall"—in the last few years several industries such as banking and insurance have laid off many employees or announced their intention of doing so; (5) industry, government, and services already have a substantial amount of "hidden unemployment"; companies retain many employees who are not needed or not fully utilized for humanitarian reasons, union pressures, or governmental policies; (6) unemployment levels have steadily grown in the last decade in spite of increased computerization; and (7) the per capita amount of goods and services that people can consume is limited, and sooner or later may stop growing.

Survey: Computers Cause Joblessness

NEW YORK—Unemployment is the greatest concern among a polled population in France, Germany, Great Britain, Norway, Spain, and the United States.

And in every one of those countries—except the United States—respondents believed that increased use of computers would worsen the unemployment problem.

The poll further showed Japan as the exception in believing unemployment was "the greatest concern for yourself and your country today."

The poll, entitled "The Impact of Technological Change in the Industrial Democracies," was conducted by Louis Harris International.

There was a large measure of agreement in all the countries polled that the use of computer data banks would facilitate infringement on personal privacy.

The conclusions that the Atlantic Institute made from the data are "unexpected," it said.

According to the institute, France, Britain, Spain, and, to a lesser extent, Italy reflect a high degree of optimism about computer and word processing systems, while Japan and Germany seem to generate considerable and widespread negativism about their use.

The United States, it feels, is a case apart, with Americans already much more attuned to the perceived advantages of the technologies.

The Atlantic Institute for International Affairs, headquartered in Paris, is a private, independent and nongovernment center for research and discussion.

(*Source:* Condensed from *MIS Week*, August 28, 1985.)

Increased Employment Levels

Increased employment levels are predicted because: (1) historically, automation has always resulted in increased employment (in the macro sense); (2) unemployment is worse in unindustrialized countries; (3) work, especially professional and managerial, can always be expanded, so there will be work for everyone; (4) the task of converting to automated factories and offices is complex and may take several generations; (5) many tasks cannot be fully automated (e.g., top management, nursing, marriage counseling, surgery, the performing arts, and the creative arts); (6) machines and people can be fully employed, each where its comparative advantage is strongest; (7) real wages may be reduced, however, because people will have income from other sources (assuming that the government will control the distribution of wealth), they will have enough money to spend, thus creating more jobs; and (8) the cost of goods and services will be so low that the demand for them will significantly increase. Automation will never catch up with the increased demand.

This debate raises a few other questions: Is unemployment really socially undesirable? (People would have more leisure time.) Should the government intervene more in the distribution of income and in the determination of the employment level? Can the "invisible hand" in the economy, which has worked so well in the past, continue to be successful in the future? Will AI make most of us idle but wealthy? (Robots will do the work; people will enjoy life.) Should the issue of income be completely separated from that of unemployment?

Cooperation with the Computer

This issue is especially important in the case of human experts who are about to volunteer their expertise to an ES. The following are examples of some thoughts that may enter an expert's mind:

- □ "The computer may replace me."
- □ "The computer may make me less important."
- □ "Why should I tell the computer my secrets? What will I gain?"
- □ "The computer may find out that I am not as great an expert as people think."

This kind of thinking may cause the expert not to cooperate, or even to give incorrect knowledge to the computer. To deal with such situations, management should motivate (and possibly compensate) experts so that they truly work with knowledge engineers to create a good ES.

21.8   Training, Retraining, and Education

With the increasingly reduced cost of MSS, there will be a corresponding boost in productivity. As a result, MSS could change the ways that people do their jobs—not only blue-collar employees, but supervisors, managers, and technical experts as well. The greater the change, the greater the amount of training/education (retraining) is required.

People react differently to the need for training, according to factors like education, time elapsed since previous educational experience, time since previous training, job security, proximity to retirement, ability to ignore competing commitments, age, family status, and income needs. This situation gives rise to questions like: What kind of employment policies are most conducive to successful training for this new technology? If it is in the national interest to foster rapid, well-integrated technical change, should the government do more to finance and assist the prospective massive training effort? What roles should private and public educational institutions play in this effort? These and other questions are being considered by management, unions, and the government.

Management's Position

The position of management will vary from company to company. Some companies (e.g., the auto industry) have instituted extensive retraining programs. In other cases nothing is being done. Management's position is strongly influenced by the position taken by unions.

The Position of Trade Unions

Most unions respond to technological change with opposition or at best with "unwilling acceptance." Very few unions welcome technological change (see Rosow [32]). However, studies indicate that union opposition is usually followed by adjustment and accommodation. The union is likely to adapt when satisfactory trade-offs can be made. Union accommodation usually occurs under the following circumstances:

- Union leadership sees that the technological change is inevitable.
- Where the membership base is notably larger than the group affected by technology changes.
- Management has given detailed consideration to the union's political circumstances and developed "trade-off" routes into which union response can be channeled.

Among the techniques commonly used to lessen the impact of unemployment are:

- Early-warning systems regarding layoffs linked to business planning (at least six months to one year ahead).
- Work force reduction to be accomplished only by voluntary resignation or early retirement.
- Contractually provided special rights to training and retraining, transfer to other jobs, other functions (including relocation), wage retention after bumping or transfer ("red circling"). For example, the federal government grants two-year pay protection.
- Severance pay, supplemental unemployment benefits, and integration with unemployment insurance programs.

The Position of Government

The federal government was not active in this area until recently. Even now (1989) there is only one concrete program, the Job Training Partnership Act (JTPA), described next.

The Job Training Partnership Act (JTPA).   The JTPA supplements the federal Comprehensive Employment and Training Act (CETA). Although primarily targeted at the economically and culturally disadvantaged, JTPA includes provisions (Title III) for retraining displaced workers. In essence, the act provides block grants to the state, which, in cooperation with the private sector, set up and run local training programs. A main goal of JTPA is to move retraining and job creation more into the private sector, in contrast to CETA, which focused on public-sector support and positions. The JTPA law represents the first time that the federal government, through national legislation, has identified dislocated workers as a pervasive problem.

21.9   Organizational Intelligence and Institutional Knowledge Bases

The availability of MSS technology implies the possible development of very large and complex data- and knowledge bases that require trained expertise to use and maintain. (For a detailed discussion, see Holsapple and Whinston [16]).

Such institutional information bases are now maintained by written documentation and experts in methods of accessing and interpreting information. The information that makes up these knowledge bases is accumulating at an ever-increasing rate. The ability of human experts to work with this knowledge base is becoming strained. In many cases, work is limited to a few individuals who have a tremendous amount of training and experience. The use of ES could greatly facilitate both the maintenance and use of the institutional knowledge bases.

As system integration continues to expand in organizations, the volume of accessible data will grow considerably, demanding powerful filtering and reporting systems that can be used by nonprogrammers. Problem determination and analysis will be much faster than what is now available with the traditional MIS approach.

Some questions that need to be addressed include the following:

□ How will the availability of information affect strategic plans? Do we use information that is now more readily available on a tactical basis just because it's there?

□ How will the communication stream be affected? Will results of decisions be as readily communicated to peers, subordinates, and superiors by managers, who may assume that these people *have* and *take advantage* of the access to MSS?

□ How do we train managers to make *effective* use of these new tools? The tools themselves are only aids; they are not surrogates for native intelligence or sound managerial practices.

□ What needs to be done to assess the current competency of managers and to match the tools to these competencies?

21.10   Legal Implications and Privacy

The introduction of MSS, and especially ES, may compound a host of legal issues already involved in CBIS. Some of the issues surrounding computers and artificial intelligence will be settled, not in the research centers or user communities, but in the courtrooms. The expensive, prolonged litigation of IBM's antitrust case and the restructuring of AT&T are two prominent examples. Questions concerning liability for the actions of intelligent machines in the world of industry, business, and commerce are just now beginning to be considered. The issue of a computer as a form of unfair competition in business has already been raised in a recent dispute over airline reservation system practices.

Beyond the question of resolving disputes over unexpected, and possibly damaging, results, of some DSS and ES, other interesting questions may surface. For example, who will assume liability should an enterprise find itself bankrupt as a result of using MSS? Will the enterprise itself be held responsible for not testing such systems adequately prior to entrusting them with sensitive issues? Will auditing and accounting firms, which are just beginning to use DSS and ES, share the liability for failing to apply adequate auditing tests? Will the manufacturers of such systems be jointly liable?

Some specific issues that may be encountered are listed as follows:

□ What is the value of an "expert" opinion in court, when the expert is a computer?
□ Who is liable for wrong advice (or information) provided by an ES? For example, what happens if a physician accepts a wrong diagnosis made by a computer and performs an act that results in the death of a patient?
□ What happens if a manager enters an incorrect judgment value into DSS or ES and the result is a damage or a disaster?
□ Who owns the knowledge in a knowledge base?
□ Should royalties be paid to experts, and if so how much?
□ Can management force experts to contribute their expertise?

For a discussion of these and other issues see Zeide and Liebowitz (37).

In addition, the issue of privacy, which exists in other CBIS, will surface in DSS and ES and become even more difficult to control because there will be additional databases and knowledge bases on top of the regular corporate database.

Modern computer systems can economically collect, store, integrate, interchange, and retrieve information and knowledge. However, this ability can affect every individual's right to privacy. Confidential information on individuals contained in knowledge bases (e.g., how they are likely to react to certain actions) could be misused and result in invasion of privacy and other injustices. Unauthorized use of such information would seriously invade the privacy of individuals, while errors in data files could seriously hurt their reputation.

The use of ES in the administration and enforcement of laws and regulations may increase public concern regarding privacy of information. These fears, generated by the perceived abilities of ES, whether real or not, will have to be addressed at the outset of almost any ES development efforts.

21.11   Social Implications

The positive and negative social implications of MSS could be far-reaching.[*] DSS and ES already have had many direct beneficial effects on society when used to solve complicated human and social problems, such as medical diagnosis, computer-assisted instruction, government program planning, environmental quality control, and law enforcement. Such problems could not have been solved economically (or solved at all) by other CBIS.

For example, the DSS generator GADS (Chapter 5) was used to build specific DSS in the following areas:

  □ Assigning police officers to territories.
  □ Performing burglary analysis.
  □ Evaluating urban growth policies.
  □ Planning educational institutions.
  □ Planning fire equipment and disaster management.
  □ Controlling traffic.
  □ Planning inspection and maintenance.
  □ Evaluating human service delivery systems.
  □ Planning commuter bus routes.

DSS has been used by the U.S. Coast Guard, pollution control agencies, and many other local and federal government agencies.

Eliminating Unpleasant or Dangerous Work.   DSS and ES, especially when combined with sensors and robots, can reduce or even eliminate the need for a human presence in dangerous or uncomfortable environments.

Opportunities for the Handicapped.   The integration of some AI technologies (speech recognition, vision recognition) into MSS could create new employment opportunities for handicapped people. For example, those who cannot type would be able to use a voice-operated typewriter, and those who cannot travel could work at home. Boeing Aerospace, Inc. is developing several ES that help handicapped employees perform useful tasks.

Working at Home.   Another trend gaining momentum is working at home. This phenomenon, called "cottage industry" in the past, is now referred to as *telecommuting*. Employees work at home on a computer or a terminal linked

[*]For an overview see Partridge (30).

to their place of employment. The first telecommuters to work at home were typists and bookkeepers, but now a growing number of professionals do a significant part of their work at home. (See Cross and Raizman [8].)

Another change for some professionals is that the tools needed to support their work are now available via the nearest telephone line and terminal. Thus employees may work remotely from each other. They may be assigned to work groups without being relocated, thus increasing organizational flexibility in project assignments. The advantages of telecommuting are more flexible hours, less commuting, less need for office and parking space, and the ability of the housebound to hold a job. However, there are some disadvantages to telecommuting: difficulties in supervising work, lack of human interaction, and increased isolation. (For a discussion of these and other negative factors see the March 30, 1986 issue of *The Wall Street Journal* [p. 25]).

Will the spread of MSS result in telecommuting executives? Some people believe that managers must be present at the work site to react to issues, and that face-to-face communication is essential. Others believe that managers will be able to stay at home most of the time in the near future. Certainly, more professionals will do so once MSS and computer networking become institutionalized. Note that some advanced EIS provide easy communication links to executives' cars and homes.

Quality of Life. On a broader scale, MSS have implications for the quality of life in general. Improved organizational efficiency may result in more leisure time, at least for the white-collar work force. The workplace can now be expanded from nine to five at a central location to 24 hours a day at *any* location. This expansion provides flexibility that can significantly improve the quality of leisure time, even if the total amount of leisure time is not increased. For example, not having to commute every day or commuting during nonrush hours, would immediately improve the quality of life for many people! Related to the quality of life are the potential changes in lifestyle.

Negative Effects. The improvement in quality of life may be accompanied by some negative effects. In addition to unemployment and the creation of large economic gaps among people, both DSS and ES may have other negative effects, some of which are common to other CBIS:

- □ *Computer crime.* Fraud and embezzlement by "electronic criminals" is continuously increasing.* With ES there is a possibility of deliberately providing wrong advice (e.g., to advise employees to opt for early retirement in cases in which they really should stay on).
- □ *Too much power.* Integrated information systems that allow greater centralization in decision making and the control of an organization may give some individuals too much power over other people. Power may be used in an unethical manner.
- □ *Blaming the computer phenomenon.* Many people tend to blame the computer to cover up human errors or wrongdoing. People may say "but the

---

*The American Bar Association estimates the losses from theft of tangible and intangible assets (including software), destruction of data, embezzlement of funds, and fraud at as much as $45 billion annually (1).

expert systems told us to do it," to justify some actions (e.g., in personnel administration) that otherwise would be unjustifiable.

Sociological Implications. Several issues could be raised in this area, for example: How do we anticipate the broad social effects of MSS and the things they make possible? What can be done to ensure that people's attitudes toward these techniques are well founded and that their expectations regarding what these systems can and cannot do are accurate? How do we determine the potential positive and negative effects of MSS before they become realities?

Other areas of social impact include changes in the proportion of the work force engaged in service and leisure industries, and the potential changes in the division of labor and sex roles.

But other potential consequences of DSS and ES point in the opposite direction. The widespread use of home terminals, for instance, threatens to have an even more isolating influence than television. If people are encouraged to work and shop from their living rooms, some unfortunate psychological effects in terms of stress and loneliness could develop. Some writers even predict that commercially available AI systems will be heavily used not only in task-oriented ways but as surrogates for human contact as well.

These contrasting examples show that widespread application of MSS could have subtle yet profound and varying influences on society. Moreover, AI could foster a general view of humanity as either "mechanistic" or "nonmechanistic," depending on how it is interpreted by the public. The most common interpretation is that AI presents us as "mere machines," with no free choice or moral responsibility. Because this image could have socially pernicious effects, people should be encouraged to understand that it is fundamentally wrong. An education in computer literacy could reshape perceptions. More generally, we should start thinking now about what the optimal social arrangements might be for a post-industrial information society. Other issues are the knowledge transfer such as the universality of human knowledge and human needs (see Gill [12]).

Social Responsibility. Organizations need to be motivated to utilize MSS to improve the quality of life in general. Organizations should design MSS to minimize their negative effects. This challenge relates not only to companies that produce MSS hardware and software, but also to companies using these technologies (because properly designed systems can be implemented and used in ways that are either positive or negative).

Public Pressure. Increased exposure to the concepts and actual use of MSS will bring some pressure on public agencies and corporations to employ the latest capabilities for solving social problems. At the same time, conflicting public pressures may rise to suppress the use of MSS because of concerns about privacy and "big brother" government.

Computer and Staff Resources. Obvious implications of the introduction of MSS involve the increased need for computer resources and people with computer and AI and DSS skills. MSS may not be the dominant factors in the expected future growth of computer resources, but they will be significant ones.

Depending on the level of involvement in MSS, significant impacts could be expected on the recruitment of personnel and training. It is forecasted that it will be very difficult to find skilled AI practitioners, and especially knowledge engineers, in the next five to ten years.

21.12   The Manager's Job

Computer-based information systems have impacted the manager's job for about two decades. However, this impact was felt mainly at the lower- and middle-managerial levels. MSS will impact the top manager's job as well, because these tools can deal with unstructured decisions. There is no doubt that MSS will save managers a considerable amount of time, freeing them from routine tasks. An ES, for example, can save time currently being spent on checking manuals and directories. Analysis of reports could be expedited by an EIS, and training inexperienced employees could be delegated to a computer-aided instruction system. The Executive Edge (Chapter 10), for example, is a step in this direction.

Allowing the computer to take over routine decisions should not be viewed by managers as a threat but as an opportunity to engage in more creative activities with more "quality" time for the benefit of the organization. Many managers have reported that the computer has finally given them time to "get out of the office and into the field." Thus managers can finally spend enough time pursuing their marketing responsibilities with customers and salespersons, their personnel management responsibilities with subordinates, and their societal responsibilities with various public and government groups. Managers can spend more time on planning activities instead of spending much of their time "putting out fires." MSS can enable many managers to become real managers rather than "paper shufflers."

Another aspect of the management challenge lies in the ability of MSS to *support* the decision process in general, and the strategic planning and control decisions in particular. MSS could change the decision-making process and even decision-making styles. For example, the intelligence phase of decision making will be much shorter. As a result, managers may change their approach to problem solving. Research indicates (e.g., see Mintzberg [24]) that most managers currently work on a large number of problems simultaneously, moving from one to another as they wait for more information on their current problem, or some external event "interrupts" them. MSS would tend to reduce the time to complete any step in the decision-making process. Therefore, managers will work on fewer tasks during the day but complete more of them. The reduction of start-up time associated with moving from task to task could be the most important source of increased managerial productivity.

Another possible impact on the manager's job could be a change in leadership requirements. What are generally considered to be good qualities of leadership may be significantly altered. If face-to-face communication is replaced by electronic mail and computerized conferencing, leadership qualities attributed to physical appearance could be less important (e.g., see Hiltz and Turoff [15]). This may have positive implications for opportunities for women, minorities, and the handicapped in managerial roles.

Even if the manager's job may not change dramatically, the methods that managers use to do their jobs will. For example, an increasing number of CEOs no longer use intermediaries, but work directly with computers (e.g., see Fersko-Weiss [10]). All these issues give rise to questions such as:

□ Is working directly with the computer the best use of a CEO's talent and time?
□ Do we really need "information locks" running the organization, or is it more appropriate to have an office of the CEO, with balanced representation from information systems, finance, and marketing?
□ Interpretation of information is more important than being able to manipulate the information without intermediaries. Are we encouraging the development of this attribute as well as the use of CBIS?

Finally, the proliferation of computers and MSS in organizations will require management involvement in the development and operation of CBIS even if they are not end-users. Proper management involvement requires the knowledgeable and active participation of managers in the planning and control of computer-based information systems. Managers must practice information resource management: the management of hardware, software, people, data, and information resources. Being an involved manager means knowing the answers to such questions as:

□ How do our MSS contribute to the short-term and long-term objectives of this organization?
□ Have we invested too few or too many resources in a specific system?
□ Do we have realistic long-range plans for information systems development and for acquisition of computer resources that will improve the efficiency of our operations and the quality of management decisions?
□ Are MSS development projects being properly managed?

Without a high degree of involvement, managers will not know the answers to such questions and will not be able to control the quality of the CBIS. Management can no longer claim that acquiring knowledge about computer fundamentals and the use of MSS is too difficult or time-consuming.

21.13 Summary and Conclusions

The Information Revolution, like the Industrial Revolution, will have profound, long-lasting cultural, organizational, and social implications. Lifestyles, social customs and patterns, the conduct of business, and daily living will change as new technologies replace older ones. Artificial intelligence concepts and applications will play an increasingly significant role in this process.

In the organizational arena, organizations will be "flatter" (fewer managerial levels), with reduced staff (experts) and increased productivity. ES will generally push toward decentralized operations and control, whereas EIS and sometimes DSS could push toward centralization. Power will shift from experts to top managers and to those who control the MSS. The concept of the information center will continue to spread in organizations, assisting in building personal DSS and small ES. The struggle for control of the IC will continue. Many jobs will change or disappear; others will be created. This situation will impact many personnel policies ranging from career ladders to supervision. These changes will impact individuals in areas like job satisfaction and personal development. The overall impact may be either negative or positive, depending on the individual affected.

The impact on employment (and unemployment) is not clear. Predictions range from massive unemployment to almost full employment. Regardless of the general level of employment, many displaced employees will need training or job placement. This task may be extensive and require a partnership among government, management, unions, and employees. The government needs to become more involved in retraining.

The increased use of MSS means more and improved organizational information. This may have positive implications for organizational knowledge (or intelligence) and negative effects on privacy.

Many social implications are expected; DSS and ES can be used to solve complex social problems, provide assistance and information to citizens, and create opportunities for minorities and the handicapped. Furthermore, quality of life can be improved because of increased productivity, increased leisure time, and the opportunity to work at home. On the negative side, computer crime and deliberate system misuse can hurt both organizations and individuals.

Finally, the manager's job will be expanded and enriched and the thought process and decision-making styles will be changed. Managers will be freed from many routine tasks. In addition, they will be provided with a better mechanism for decision making and problem solving. Therefore, managers' effectiveness and efficiency will increase, along with the welfare of their organizations and the economy as a whole.

Key Words

application backlog	job content	organizational intelligence
cottage industry	Job Training Partnership	quality of life
Federal Privacy Act	Act (JTPA)	role ambiguity
hidden unemployment	knowledge employees	telecommunications
Information Centers	(workers)	workplace

Questions for Review

1. Explain why organizations will have fewer managerial layers (or levels). Give at least two reasons.
2. Why might the ratio of staff to line decrease in the future?
3. How can ES increase the trend toward decentralization?
4. Explain the impact of microcomputers on the degree of decentralization.
5. List the major forces behind user-oriented computing.
6. Describe the potential power shift in organizations due to ES use.
7. List the major activities of the IC.

8. List the major characteristics of the IC staff.
9. List some problems created by IC.
10. Describe some potential changes in jobs and job description in organizations that will use ES extensively.
11. List some issues related to human-computer interactions (interface).
12. List some of the reasons why an expert may not be able to contribute his or her expertise to an ES.
13. List three reasons why ES/AI could result in massive unemployment.
14. List three arguments to counter the arguments in Question 13.
15. What actions can management take to reduce the impact of employee replacement by a computer?
16. What is the Job Training Partnership Act?
17. What is organizational intelligence?
18. List some of the legal implications of ES.
19. List some potential social benefits of DSS.
20. List some potential social benefits of ES.
21. Why could work at home be increased by ES?
22. How can telecommuting improve the quality of our life?
23. List some possible negative effects of MSS.
24. Why will managers in the future work on fewer problems simultaneously?
25. "ES could provide more managerial opportunities for handicapped and minorities." Why or why not?

Questions for Discussion and Exercises

1. Would AI in general and ES in particular humanize or dehumanize managerial activities? List arguments for both points of view. (See Boden [4]).
2. Write a short essay that describes the major similarities and differences between the Industrial and the Information Revolutions.
3. "DSS and ES will increase organizational productivity." Do you agree? Why or why not?
4. Describe the manager of the future working in a place that uses DSS and ES extensively.
5. Should top managers, using ES instead of a human assistant, be paid more or less for their job? Why?
6. Should an IC charge users for help given in building personal DSS?
7. How can an ES increase the span of control of a manager?
8. The following story was published in the November 1974 issue of *Infosystems*:

> I've seen the ablest executives insist on increased productivity by a plant manager, lean on accounting for improved performance, and lay it on purchasing in no uncertain terms to cut its staff. But when these same executives turn to EDP they stumble to an uncertain halt, baffled by the blizzard of computer jargon. They accept the presumed sophistication and differences that are said to make EDP activities somehow immune from normal management demands. They are stopped by all this nonsense, uncertainty about what's reasonable to expect, and what they can insist upon. They become confused and then retreat, muttering about how to get a handle on this blasted situation.

Explain how DSS, EIS and ES can change such a situation.

9. Read the article "The Molting of America" by J. Cook, in *Forbes*, November 22, 1982. Relate the development of MSS to the future of America, as projected in this article. Specifically, consider the national benefits of these techniques.

10. The Department of Transportation in a large metropolitan area developed an expert system that advises an investigator whether or not to open an investigation on a reported car accident. (This system, which includes 300 rules, was developed by Dr. Nagy at George Washington University.)

   a. What do you feel about such a system?

   b. Should the people involved in an accident be informed that an ES decides about the investigation?

   c. What are some of the potential legal implications?

11. Diagnosing infections and prescribing pharmaceuticals are weak points of many practicing physicians (per Dr. Shortliffe, one of the developers of MYCIN). Therefore, society could be well served if MYCIN were used extensively. But few physicians use it.

   a. Why is MYCIN little used by physicians?

   b. Assume that you are a hospital administrator whose physicians are salaried and reporting to you. What can you do to influence and persuade these physicians to use MYCIN?

   c. If the potential benefits to society are so great, can society do something that will increase the use of MYCIN by doctors?

References and Bibliography

1. American Bar Association. *Report on Computer Crime.* American Bar Association, Computer Crime Task Force, White-Collar Crime Committee, Criminal Justice Section. Washington, D.C., June 1984.
2. Argyris, C. "Management Information Systems: The Challenge to Rationality and Emotionality." *Management Science,* February 1971.
3. Ayers, R., and S. Miller. *Robotics: Applications and Social Implications.* New York: Harper & Row, 1983.
4. Boden, M. A. "Impact of Artificial Intelligence." *Futures,* February 1984.
5. Brod, C. *Technostress: The Human Cost of the Computer Revolution.* Reading, MA: Addison-Wesley, 1985.
6. Cook, J. "The Molting of America." *Forbes,* November 22, 1982.
7. Crescenzi, A. D. "Organizational Impacts of Successful DSS." *DSS 87 Transactions,* El Sawy, ed. June 1987.
8. Cross, T. B., and Raizman, M. *Telecommuting: The Future Technology of Work,* Homewood, IL: Dow-Jones/Irwin, 1986.
9. Davis, D. B. "Workplace High Tech Spurs Retraining Efforts." *High-Technology,* November 1984.
10. Fersko-Weiss, H. "Personal Computing at the Top." *Personal Computing,* March 1985.
11. Fossum, E., ed. *Computerization of Working Life.* New York: Wiley, 1983.
12. Gill, K. S. *Artificial Intelligence and Society.* New York: Wiley, 1986.
13. Hammond, L. W. "Management Considerations for an Information Center." *IBM System Journal,* Vol. 21, No. 2, 1982.
14. Hayes, J. E., and D. Michie, eds. *Intelligent Systems: The Unprecedented Opportunity.* New York: Wiley, 1983.
15. Hiltz, S. R., and M. Turoff. *The Network Nation.* Reading, MA: Addison-Wesley, 1979.
16. Holsapple, C. W., and A. B. Whinston. *Business Expert Systems.* Homewood, IL: Irwin, 1987.
17. Huff, S. L., et al. "An Empirical Study of Decision Support Systems." *INFOR,* February 1984.
18. "The Info Center." Special issue of *Data Management,* February 1984.
19. Katz, D., and R. L. Kahn. *The Social Psychology of Organizations,* 4th ed. New York: Wiley, 1986.

20. Krout, R., et al. "Computerization, Productivity and Quality of Work Life." *Communication of the ACM*, February 1989.
21. Leavitt, H. J. "Applying Organizational Change in Industry: Structural, Technological and Humanistic Approaches." In J. G. March, ed. *Handbook of Organizations*. Chicago: Rand McNally, 1965.
22. Linder, J. "Computers, Corporate Culture and Change." *Personnel Journal*, September 1985.
23. Lucas, H. C. Jr. "Organizational Power and the Information Services Department." *Communication of the ACM*, January 1984.
24. Mintzberg, H. *The Nature of Managerial Work*. New York: Harper & Row, 1973.
25. "A New Era for Management." *Business Week*, April 25, 1983.
26. Nilsson, N. J. "Artificial Intelligence, Employment and Income." *AI Magazine*, Summer 1984.
27. O'Brien, A. J. *Computers in Business Management*. 4th ed. Homewood, IL: Irwin, 1985.
28. O'Leary, D., and E. Turban. "The Organizational Impact of Expert Systems." *Human System Management*, Vol. 7, Spring 1987.
29. Olson, M. H., and H. C. Lucas, Jr. "The Impact of Office Automation on the Organization: Some Implications for Research and Practice." *Communications of the ACM*, November 1982.
30. Partridge, D. "Social Implication of AI." in *AI: Principles and Applications*. M. Yazdani, ed. Chapman and Hall, 1986.
31. "The Recovery Skips Middle Managers." *Fortune*, February 6, 1984.
32. Rosow, J. M. "People vs. High Tech: Adapting New Technologies to the Workplace." *Management Review*, September 1984.
33. Ryan, J. "Expert Systems in the Future: The Redistribution of Power." *Journal of System Management*, April 1988.
34. Scott-Morton, M. "DSS Revisited for the 1990s." Paper presented at DSS 1986, Washington, D.C., April 1986.
35. Toffler, A. *The Third Wave*. New York: William Morrow, 1984.
36. Trappl, R., ed. *Artificial Intelligence: Impacts on Science, Society, and Economy*. New York: Elsevier, 1985.
37. Zeide, J. S., and J. Liebowitz. "Using Expert Systems: The Legal Perspective." *IEEE Expert*, Spring 1987.
38. Zuboff, S. *In the Age of the Smart Machine*, New York: Basic Books, 1988.

Chapter 22

The Future of
Management Support
Systems

In the previous chapters the technologies of MSS were presented as they exist today. This chapter explores MSS from a futuristic perspective. The specific sections of this chapter are the following:

797

22.1   Immediate Obsolescence

Developments in the areas of MSS, and especially in the area of ES, are very rapid. At no other time in history have we witnessed such accelerated technological progress. Many commercial MSS products become obsolete as soon as (or even before) they are fully developed. In addition, developments in computer technology have a profound effect on progress in the areas of MSS and on the implementation of these tools. Our objective here is to briefly describe trends in computer technology that are likely to impact the development of MSS. In addition, we attempt to predict the future direction of the technologies from a broad, general view.

22.2   Trends in Computer Technology

Advances in MSS will depend on advances in computer technology.* Large, complex MSS generally require more computer resources than management information systems or management science projects. Computer technology, for example, has been an especially limiting factor for ES implementation. Therefore a brief discussion of trends and advances in computer technology is essential for understanding future trends of MSS. Specifically, three topics are the most relevant: VLSI, parallel processing, and neural computing.

Very Large-Scale Integration (VLSI)

The process of combining electronic components into a single compact device is known as *integration*, and the devices containing multiple electronic components are *integrated circuits* or *chips*. Since the invention of the chip in the late 1950s, computer scientists have been trying to combine more and more components on a single chip, about a quarter of an inch square. Because integration can *increase* processing speeds and *decrease* costs at the same time, advances in integration often are accompanied by the development of more powerful computers.

In the 1970s, the techniques of large-scale integration (LSI) allowed chip manufacturers to combine the functions of several thousand components on a single chip. The modern techniques of VLSI allow several hundred thousand or even several millions of electronic components to be combined on a single chip. Advanced VLSI techniques may allow computers to feature the large memory and high processing speeds essential for many AI applications. For example, the Japanese Fifth-Generation Project hopes to develop computers with memories as large as 1000 gigabytes (1,000,000,000,000 characters) and with processing speeds of up to 1 billion logical inferences per second. Logical inferences per second (LIPS) is a measure of the speed of computers used for AI applications. A logical inference usually consists of from 100 to 1000 computer instructions; therefore a computer operating at 1 billion LIPS could execute from 100 billion to 1000 billion computer instructions per second. In the mid-1980s, by way

---

*Condensed from Mishkoff (17).

of contrast, an exceptionally high-speed computer might operate at a mere 20 million instructions per second.

In 1987, TI developed a custom Lisp processor in sub 2–micrometer CMOS technology using its proprietary VLSI semiconductor design and processing capabilities. The new chip is to provide two to ten times the processing power of the 1987 commercial symbolic processors. Other companies are also developing expert systems on a chip. See boxed material.

Megachip Technologies. Megachip technologies is a concept developed by Texas Instruments. It relates not to a single chip, process or service, but it is a culmination of new requirements for creating, manufacturing and supporting highly sophisticated integrated circuits. A megachip circuit can include over 1,000,000 components (for example, the Intel 486 chip contains 1.2 million components). These chips are being manufactured with the aid of AI technologies and extensive automation.

AT&T Develops Expert System on a Chip

Combining custom hardware design and "fuzzy logic," scientists at AT&T Bell Laboratories have built the first expert system-on-a-chip for real-time response applications such as missile command and control, robotics, and manufacturing operations.

The experimental chip is promising to be significantly faster than conventional expert systems.

There are many expert system applications where a fast and reasonable response is called for but the data aren't precise. The expert system-on-a-chip can handle many of these situations.

The chip's initial use will be for robot arm control. It could, for example, guide a robot hand to a part rolling around on a conveyor belt. It could also decide when and by how much to reduce the temperature during a chemical process.

In developing the chip, the developers build the operating instructions of the expert system into its circuitry rather than writing them in software, which avoids time-consuming retrieval of instructions from external memory. Fuzzy logic reduces the number of rules required to act on problems. Combining these techniques, the researchers achieved a chip speed of 80,000 fuzzy logic inferences per second, which is about 10,000 times faster than conventional expert systems.

Using fuzzy logic, the expert system-on-a-chip accepts vague data, compares them to all the rules in its memory simultaneously, and assigns each rule a weight. The highest weights are given to the rules that best match the data. The decision is based on the combined recommendations of these rules.

(*Source:* Condensed from *Applied AI Reporter.* January 1986.)

Parallel Processing

In 1945, John von Neumann outlined a logical structure of processing information with a computer, specifying a theory of information processing that has permeated the development of computers ever since. In fact, modern computers sometimes are called "von Neumann machines" because the information processing methods they use descended directly from his theories. One important element of the von Neumann machine that has stood the test of time is the concept of *sequential processing*.

Computers, which may seem to be doing many things at once, actually perform actions one at a time, in sequence. One of the goals of advanced computer research is to increase computing speeds, and one method of increasing speed is to abandon the sequential processing model and have more than one process executing at a time. This technique, called *parallel processing*, is shown schematically in Figure 22.1.

Parallel architectures are being considered for future AI machines. This is especially attractive for PROLOG because its structure facilitates parallel search. Parallel processing techniques provide an alternative for computers to solve large problems faster according to the premise that dividing a problem into smaller parts will yield faster results. The underlying concept behind all new parallel architectures is to have small blocks of tightly coupled memory elements divide the algorithm and parallel process its parts concurrently. As a result, larger problems can be solved faster.

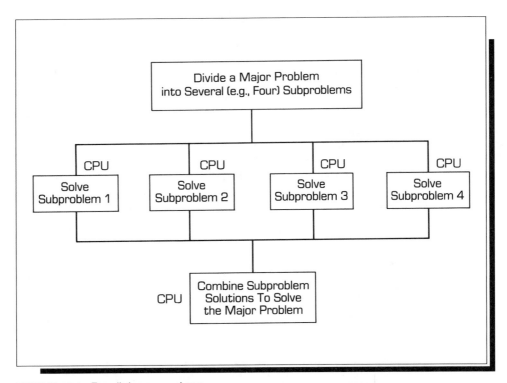

FIGURE 22.1 Parallel processing.

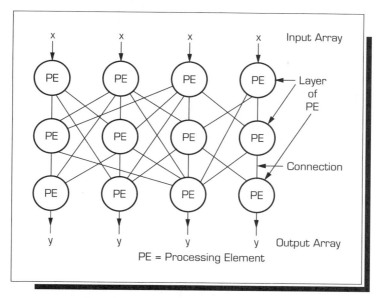

FIGURE 22.2 Neural networks.

Neural Computing

Parallel processing can be executed in several ways. A common distinction is made between coarse-grained architecture and fine-grained computing. Coarse-grained employs a relatively small number (up to a few thousand) of fairly powerful CPUs in parallel. However, as shown in Figure 22.1, the CPUs are independent of each other. Fine-grained approach is used in *neural computing*, which uses relatively simple *interconnected* processors, each of which is capable of executing (currently) only simple tasks (see Figure 22.2). In neural computing it is also possible to use up to several million processors, in parallel. For further information, see Hecht-Nielson (11), Almasi and Gottlieb (1), Perrot (18), and Tank and Hopfield (26). Neural computing (which appears under other names, such as connectionist systems, neural networks, and associative memory technology) employs a nonalgorithmic information processing approach based on models of the brain's functions. The use of neural computing (which will be discussed in more detail in Section 22.11) will help MSS in solving complex problems that are currently unsolvable (or take too long to solve) by existing computing tools.

Other Developments

Several other developments in computer technology can enhance the progress of DSS, ES, and EIS. One important area is computer storage. One emerging technology is the compact disk. For example, a single CD-ROM (computer disk read-only-memory) can hold as many as 550 megabytes of data. (To hold the same amount of information one needs about 1500 regular 5 1/4" floppy disks.) Data are read by a laser beam. The technology is already used to store large public databanks that are very important for some DSS and EIS.

A related technology is the WORM (write once, read many) optical disk. Users record the information once, then it cannot be changed. A WORM disk can store about 200 megabytes. For further information see: "CD-ROM Special Report," *PC World*, April 1987.

Combining parallel processing with VLSI and other developments could significantly advance computer technology. Four large-scale national research efforts are capitalizing on these developments. They are discussed next.

22.3 Large-scale Research Efforts

This section explores several large-scale research efforts that may have profound implications for the future of AI in general and ES (and possibly DSS) in particular.*

The DARPA Strategic Computing Program

In 1983, the Defense Advanced Research Projects Agency (DARPA) announced one of the most ambitious scientific research projects ever attempted: the Strate-

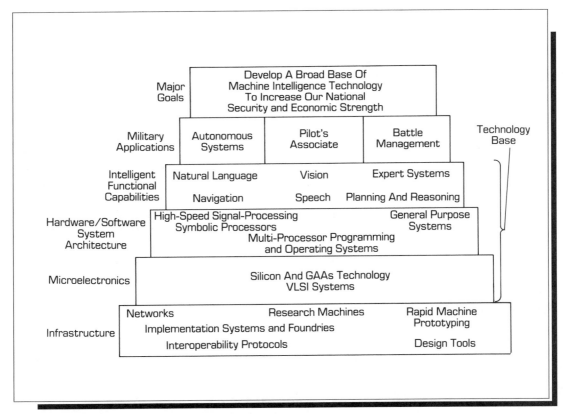

FIGURE 22.3 Structure and goals of the SCP project.

*Much of the material in this section was condensed from Mishkoff (17).

gic Computing Program (SCP). The SCP, which began in 1984, was scheduled to last five years.

The SCP actually contains a number of projects in a wide range of AI and other computing areas, as shown in Figure 22.3. Its ultimate goal is to provide the United States with a broad line of machine intelligence technology and to demonstrate applications of the technology to critical problems in defense. At a later time, we could see a technology transfer from defense to nondefense sectors. This program was extended in 1988 to include neural computing.

The Fifth-Generation Project

The Fifth-Generation Project, which has been mentioned previously, is an ambitious 10-year project announced in 1982 by the Japanese government.

The Japanese have marshalled an impressive array of resources in an attempt to change their image from implementers of technology to developers and innovators (see accompanying box). For the first several years the project has not required private funding; $450 million of financing has been provided by the powerful Ministry of International Trade and Industry. By the time it is complete, the Fifth-Generation Project may require more than $1 billion in a typical Japanese combination of public and private financing. The Institute for New Generation Computer Technology (ICOT) has been established in Tokyo to bring the project to fruition. Forty of the brightest young computer researchers in Japan have been brought together at ICOT. Over 150 other researchers in various locations contribute to the project under contract to ICOT.

Fifth-Generation Technology. The ultimate aim of the project is the development of fifth-generation computers. To achieve this goal, the Japanese have divided the project into the following four parts:

- □ *Data Access.* AI programs typically require large amounts of data. The ability to retrieve information as needed is just as important as the ability to store the information in the first place. The Fifth-Generation Project already has developed a prototype computer, called the Relational Database Machine, that is designed specifically to facilitate the storage and retrieval of information.
- □ *Inference.* An inference engine is an essential component of a knowledge-based system. The Fifth-Generation Project is developing a prototype computer, known as the Personal Sequential Inference Machine, to provide inference capabilities in PROLOG. When ready, the inference machine will be used by researchers as a tool to write programs for other parts of the project.
- □ *Ease of Use.* The Fifth-Generation Project includes research into several areas of AI that investigate ways of making computers easier to use, including computer vision, speech recognition, and natural language processing. In the second year of the project, it was reported that this part was faltering; however, several private Japanese companies now are tackling these problems on their own.
- □ *Intelligent Programming.* Intelligent computer programming tools are being developed to expedite the programming efforts in all phases of the project.

The Japanese—Implementors of Others' Innovations

The United States traditionally has been the greatest source of technological innovation in the world. More recently, the Japanese have founded their own "tradition" in what has been called their "economic miracle"; during the years since World War II, they have become the acknowledged leaders at the implementation of technology. For example:

□ The automobile was first mass-produced in the United States; but by applying American technology and management techniques in innovative ways, Japanese automobile manufacturers have impacted the American automobile industry dramatically and irrevocably.

□ It is becoming increasingly difficult to purchase a high-quality stereo, television, or other electronic device that is not manufactured in Japan.

□ Although hand-held calculators and digital watches were both invented in the United States, creative Japanese competition has driven nearly every American manufacturer out of those markets.

□ The process of electronic miniaturization was created in the United States, first with transistors and then with integrated circuits. Japanese companies are now among the largest producers of chips in the world and may be on the verge of dominating that market.

□ The manufacture of cameras and other optical instruments, previously dominated by Germany, is now dominated by the Japanese.

The Change: The Fifth-Generation Project

If these kinds of trends were to continue, you might expect the Japanese to wait until American manufacturers had commercialized AI successfully and developed a wide range of AI products. Then, if past scenarios were to be adhered to, Japanese companies would develop clever, creative, and inexpensive products based on the mature American technology. But this time, the Japanese have served notice that they are no longer content to create innovative uses for American technology. This time, they intend to develop the technology themselves; this time, they plan to make their own discoveries.

Because the original goals of the project were stated in general, imprecise terms, the evaluation of its progress is difficult. Although some cite the project's small budget and other difficulties as evidence that it will ultimately fail, the Japanese remain confident. Evidence of actual progress since 1986 indicates major difficulties and few achievements. Nevertheless, even skeptics generally concede that the Fifth-Generation Project is having a positive effect on AI research everywhere. The Japanese have shaken up the rest of the computer science community around the world, and that's no small accomplishment.

Knowledge Is Power. Why are the Japanese so intent on supplanting the United States by becoming the world leader in computer technology? What is it about intelligent machines that is leading them to devote so many resources to their development? Why is it so important to be first?

Quite simply, the Japanese believe that knowledge, supplied by a new generation of intelligent machines, is poised to become the basis of a new economic order. They believe that the world is evolving toward a post-industrial society in which the wealth of nations will be measured not in terms of gold or oil but information. The Japanese believe the nation that is first to commercialize AI technology successfully will gain an enormous economic advantage over other nations. First place will not only give that nation an obvious advantage in the computer industry; it will have repercussions throughout a wide range of human affairs.

The United States currently dominates the worldwide processing of information by computers. Because information processing in the United States is a $130 billion industry (annually), it is a dominance that the U.S. can scarcely afford to lose. Yet losing a preeminent position in the computer industry might be just the tip of the iceberg, merely the most obvious of the widespread economic advantages that the Japanese hope the Fifth-Generation Project will provide them. The successful development, implementation, and proliferation of AI technology (according to Feigenbaum and McCorduck [9]) could render all Japanese products so much better than their competitors', thanks to the degree of knowledge that will be brought to bear on their design and manufacture, that the Japanese expect to dominate markets in conventional products, too.

Although many American AI researchers do not believe that the Fifth-Generation Project will be a complete success, no one is prepared to discount its prospects with complete confidence. Even if the goals for the project are realized only in part, the Japanese will have developed technologies that will make their competition as formidable in the information age as it currently is in the industrial age.

The Microelectronics and Computer Technology Corporation (MCC)

The MCC, established in 1983, can be considered a response to the Japanese challenge and threat. It is a consortium of 21 major U.S. corporations in the computer and computer-related industries.* MCC currently is engaged in four long-term projects with a common goal: to provide the technology necessary to make computers faster, more reliable, and capable of performing more complex tasks at a higher level of quality and much lower cost. By concentrating on long-term goals (6 to 10 years) rather than seeking an immediate profit, MCC is free to follow a long-range strategy that might have been difficult for its members to pursue individually; corporations often are under intense stockholder pressure to generate short-term profits, frequently at the expense of long-term goals.

*The corporations are Advanced Micro Devices; Allied Corporation; Bell Communications Research (Bellcore); BMC Industries, Inc.; Boeing Company; Control Data Corporation; Digital Equipment Corporation; Eastman Kodak Company; Gould, Inc.; Harris Corporation; Honeywell, Inc.; Lockheed Corporation; Martin Marietta Corporation; Mostek Corporation; Motorola, Inc.; National Semiconductor Corporation; NCR Corporation; RCA Corporation; Rockwell International Corporation; Sperry Corporation; and 3M.

The programs undertaken by MCC fall into four major areas:

1. *Packaging.* The packaging project aims to advance state-of-the-art semi-conductor packaging and interconnect technology.
2. *Software Technology.* The MCC software technology effort aims to develop new techniques, procedures, and tools that can be used to improve the productivity of the software development process by one or two orders of magnitude.
3. *VLSI/Computer-Aided Design.* MCC's program in the area of VLSI/computer-aided design aims to improve computer-aided design technology and to develop an integrated set of tools that will have particular application to complex systems and the very complex VLSI chips from which they will be built.
4. *Advanced Computer Architecture.* The most complex and ambitious of the MCC programs is a 10-year effort focusing on the following projects:

   □ *AI/Knowledge-Based Systems*—Realize the computer's problem-solving potential by developing new ways to represent human knowledge and thought concepts, as well as new engineering and managerial models and tools to apply human expertise to a wide range of problems.
   □ *Database System Management*—Improve database design and storage methods and capacities to permit more flexible storage and faster retrieval of a broader range of more complex information.
   □ *Human Factors Technology*—Improve the relationship between people and computers by simplifying computer use through techniques like improved voice, character recognition, and natural languages.
   □ *Parallel Processing*—Develop the languages and architectures to allow computers to perform tasks simultaneously instead of sequentially, with corresponding increases in processing speed.

The Alvey Program

This is a British government-backed research effort ($800 million plus $225 million from industry). The main areas of research are: (1) expert systems; (2) VLSI; (3) software engineering; and (4) the interface of human and machine. The primary aim of the Alvey Program is to provide the British information technology industry with a technical lead over foreign rivals. The Alvey Program and the development of ES in the United Kingdom is discussed in a special issue of *R&D Management*, April 1985. The research efforts described in this section could affect several other areas of computer technology that are important to DSS and ES. Some representative areas are discussed next.

22.4   Voice Recognition and Speech Understanding

One of the major obstacles for the wide use of computers by managers and professionals is manual data entry via keyboards. For some it remains a clerical function; to others it is "just a waste of time." The use of menus, icons, touch screens, and the like simplifies the problem, but does not eliminate it.

Whenever human-machine communication will be done in a natural language and by voice, the use of MSS will explode.

Recent efforts of vendors clearly point to this direction. Several companies are developing front-end packages to DSS and ES development tools (such as Lotus 1-2-3 and TI Personal Consultant). Natural language processors to databases are being marketed under fancy names like CLOUT and Q&A (see chapter 18). Once voice is added, these systems could be embraced by 10 times as many additional users.

The technological developments discussed earlier could provide the mechanism that will make speech understanding an integral part of many computer systems. It is only a question of time before it will become a reality. It may happen as early as 1992, or it may occur in the 21st century, but it is coming.

The utilization of voice in computerized systems will complement another development important for MSS: distributed systems and communication networks, a topic that we discuss next.

22.5 Distributed Systems, Local and Global Networks, and Public Databases

Distributed data processing systems (DDP) offer a means of solving complex problems affecting a large physical area like a plant or city. Using Local Area Networks (LANs), different components and participants of a MSS are able to communicate and cooperate with one another. It is reasonable to assume that in the future there will be a larger use of distributed MSS for the following reasons:

1. Hardware technology has been improved so the building of very large distributive networks is becoming technologically and economically feasible.
2. A large number of MSS applications need distributive technology to succeed, or to be more efficient.
3. Understanding the process of group problem solving is helpful in learning how to manage both humans and machines working together.

Of special interest is the future development of distributed AI. A distributed AI is a special case of DDP. Although the two technologies are similar in that the terminal the user is working on does not do all the processing, they are different in the process of execution. A DDP user gains access to other computers for very specific parts of a job (e.g., downloading data from the corporate database). A distributive AI system, on the other hand, will be composed of expert systems, each of which will work on a specific problem part for which it is an "expert."

Distributed AI is one of the key architectural opportunities and requirements for the broad-based introduction of ES technology into mainstream problems and application environments. Such an architecture, which is actively pursued by several vendors (mainly DEC and IBM), makes it possible to achieve answers to the issues of high performance, high availability, and fault tolerance. In addition, distributed AI deals with concurrency in AI computations, coordinating the intelligent behavior of several ES or intelligent robots, and working toward a single goal.

Many real-world information systems are already distributed. Through the intelligent use of distributed AI techniques it is possible to develop an infinitely expandable system that can address the time-critical needs of the real-world environment. For example, expert systems will provide the wisdom for an intelligent distribution of other ES over the network. For further details see Bond and Gasser (2).

Distributed MSS and AI are necessary if the computerized system is to function similarly to a group of people working together. Communication among humans is an important part of developing intelligence. Communication among DSS and ES is necessary not only so they can mimic this human ability, but also so they will not need a human monitor to direct distributed activities.

The developments in communication networks, both local and global, could enhance the spread of MSS. Someday it will be economically and technically feasible to access a computer by voice from almost any place in the world. People will be able to seek the advice of intelligent computers simply by picking up the telephone and asking for it. Advice will be provided on hundreds of topics, both organizational and personal.

Related to these developments are the merging of voice and data. Such a merger can greatly reduce the cost of communication. This can enhance the use of distributed MSS in remote locations.

Networks will promote the use of group DSS. Decision makers will be able to work together on complex problems, even when they are in different locations. Again, the introduction of speech understanding and voice synthesis will enhance the use of such systems because people will be able to participate, using the telephone, while in locations without computers.

There is an increasing availability of external data services. Several thousand commercial databases can be accessed today by computers through telephone lines. Because DSS, EIS, and ES use many external data, the availability of such data at a reasonable cost could encourage the spread of these technologies.

22.6 The DSS of the Future

The intersection of the continued progress in DSS and the developments cited earlier resulted in some important trends in DSS. The following six short-term DSS trends are forecasted by Sprague and McNurlin (22):

1. Personal computer–based DSS will continue to grow mainly for personal support. Integrated micropackages containing spreadsheets will take on more and more functions, eventually encompassing some of the functions previously performed by DSS generators. Newer packages for "creativity support" will become more popular as extensions of analysis and decision making.

2. For institutional DSS that support sequential and interdependent decision making, the trend is toward distributed DSS—close linkages between mainframe DSS languages and generators and the PC-based

facilities. Vendors of both mainframe and PC products are now offering DSS generator versions that run on, and link with, each other.

3. For pooled interdependent decision support, group DSS will become much more prevalent in the next few years. The growing availability of local area networks and group communication services like electronic mail will make this type of DSS increasingly available.

4. Decision support system products will begin to incorporate, and eventually include, the tools and techniques of artificial intelligence work. Many of the self-contained, stand-alone products in AI will prove to be like the stand-alone statistical and management science models of a decade ago— they will need to be embedded in a "delivery system" that facilitates their use. DSS will provide the system for the assimilation of ES knowledge representation, natural language query, voice and pattern recognition, and so on. The result will be "intelligent DSS" that can "suggest," "learn," and "understand" in dealing with managerial tasks and problems. The first area of such integration is adding natural language processors as a front end to database management systems and to DSS generators. See Kandt (13) for discussion.

5. DSS groups will become less like special project "commando teams" and more a part of the support team for a variety of other end-user support, perhaps as a part of an information center.

6. Cutting across all the trends previously given is the continued development of user-friendly capabilities. This, more than any other feature, is what put DSS on the map and promises to put "a computer on every manager's desk." The development of dialog support hardware, such as light pens, mouse devices, touch screens, and high-resolution graphics, will be further advanced by speech recognition and voice synthesis. Dialog support software such as menus, windows, and "help" functions will also continue to advance. The "virtual desktop" dialog pioneered by the Xerox Star, and currently used by Apple's Macintosh computers, embodies many user-friendly features and has set the pace for other personal computers. Users appreciate the ability to quickly move the cursor (via a "mouse"), call up a menu, select an item on the menu, and obtain the results—all in two to three seconds. Selecting spreadsheet commands, storing files, initiating data communications—all can be handled in this manner. Features like these will help support the growing use of DSS by both new and experienced users. For further discussion see Er (8) and Keen (14).

Group DSS

Group decision support systems (GDSS) will become an important topic for research, leading the way to practical applications. As stated earlier, major organizational decisions are being made by groups, and the increased use of telecommuting will increase the use of GDSS. The following observations are made by Gray (10):

> GDSS is still in a laboratory stage. When these systems are installed in industry and government, they behave like shooting stars. They are put in by one senior executive and used during his or her tenure. However, as soon as

that individual is replaced, the system is dismantled or falls into disuse. The classic "not-invented-here" syndrome holds sway. The major problem is that at this point we do not know how to use these systems effectively and how to train people to use them.

It is appropriate therefore that GDSS activity is centered in university research laboratories at this time. One possible outcome of this research is that GDSS may be a solution for which there is no known problem. If so, it is better that we find out now in laboratory settings rather than in the field after massive investment and failure.

Note: There are some exceptions to Gray's observations, mainly in the military and some large corporations. For example, the military is actively using systems to facilitate consensus or at least resolve social choice. One such system is TOPSIS, used by Army Personnel Command, for determining selection board criteria. Other systems are in operation in the Department of Defense for resource allocation (e.g., allocation of computer resources) based on group preferences.

The research topics suggested by Gray are summarized in Table 22.1.

Integration GDSS and ES.   In the near future it will be possible to use an integrated GDSS and ES to call "experts on disks" in a particular subject into a GDSS meeting, and obtain their advice. Expert systems will also assist in group deliberations. Their role can range from rendering advice on a specialized topic, to synthesis of new alternatives to helping resolve conflicts of opinions.

TABLE 22.1   Research Issues in GDSS.

   I.   GDSS DESIGN
- human factors design (e.g., spatial arrangement, public screens, informal communications channels)
- database design
- user interface design
- interface with DSS
- design methodologies

  II.   APPROPRIATENESS OF GDSS
- when should a GDSS be used and when should it not be used
- when is a GDSS preferred to a DSS
- selecting the right GDSS design

 III.   GDSS SUCCESS FACTORS
- measures of success (e.g., reduction in group conflict, degree of consensus, group norms)
- effects of hardware, software, user motivation, and top management support on GDSS's success

 IV.   IMPACT OF GDSS
- communication patterns
- confidence in decision
- costs
- level of consensus
- user satisfaction

  V.   MANAGING THE GDSS
- responsibility for GDSS in organization
- planning requirements for GDSS
- training, maintenance, and other support needed

Source: Based on DeSanctis and Gallupe (5).

DSS Research Directions

A group of leading DSS researchers and practitioners have defined a vision for DSS, and delineated a set of research questions.* They made the following points:

1. Currently DSS are passively responding to "what if" questions when posed. But as discussed earlier, the DSS/ES combination can add a proactive flavor. More active tools can encourage deeper thinking about problem situations.
2. Today's DSS are not creative, but future DSS should be, providing new ways of defining models, structuring problems, managing ambiguity and complexity, solving new classes of decisions in new contexts of decision making. ES can make a major contribution in this direction.
3. DSS has been decision-centered but not decision-paced. Future DSS should also deal with the reasons for selecting particular decision classes for support.
4. Management science, the DSS model source, should play a much larger DSS role by improving the thought quality in decision making. Similar contributions should be forthcoming from cognitive psychology, behavioral theory, information economics, computer science, and political science.
5. The latest advances in computer technology, in particular telecommunications, knowledge-based systems, and advanced data management tools, should be used to build improved DSS.
6. These improved DSS should deal with the more unstructured problems, such as those that impact overall organizational efficiency and effectiveness.
7. The DSS of the future must be able to create alternative courses of action on its own, in addition to judging those alternatives supplied by the decision maker.
8. DSS research must take a much longer-range perspective, dealing with organization effectiveness and strategic planning. This new perspective will be supported by the addition of creativity and innovation capabilities, resulting in a DSS that is proactive in creating change rather than just reactive.
9. Research should be conducted on interactions between individuals and among groups. In particular, social and ethical problems should be addressed.
10. The human component of DSS should be examined in terms of the impact of DSS on learning.
11. The integration of DSS with ES and with other CBIS and different computer technologies (e.g., telecommunications) will be a major research area.
12. The model management concept should be expanded, both theoretically and in software development. Again, ES can make a valuable contribution in such areas as model selection by providing the judgmental elements needed in model construction. (See Kandt [13]).

*Source: J. J. Elam, J. C. Henderson, P. G. W. Keen, and B. Konsynski, *A Vision for Decision Support Systems*, Special Report, University of Texas at Austin, 1986.

13. DSS theory should be enhanced. Theories must be developed on topics such as decision quality measurement, learning, and effectiveness.

14. Theories must also be developed for the areas of organizational decision making and group decision making.

15. DSS applications could be enhanced by the inclusion of values, ethics, and aesthetics. But the problem is how to do it. This will require a broader range of variables, which are difficult to measure or even to define.

16. Human-machine interfaces and their impacts on creativity and learning should be a major thrust of DSS research.

17. Exploration is needed to find the appropriate architectures that enable the decision maker to use ES to improve decision-making capabilities.

18. The organizational impacts of MSS could be significant. Considerable research should be conducted in this area.

22.7   The Future of ES

The present enthusiasm for ES must be placed in perspective before we talk about the future.* The recent interest in this topic can be viewed as an interplay of both technical and social factors. Artificial intelligence research is a young field—in its infancy when compared with other scientific endeavors. It is unrealistic to expect immediate practical results. Yet, as many AI researchers started to deal with real-world problems, they noticed that they were achieving some degree of success in modeling expert behavior. Although many projects began as basic research for knowledge representation, they evolved into realistic schemes for solving highly bounded problems. We already see some definite technical achievement, and the potential for developing even more powerful and imaginative ES is not hard to foresee.

Does this mean that developing ES is now routine? Hardly! The design and building of an ES usually involves quite a difficult and intensive effort. A distinction was made earlier between ES and knowledge systems. Building a system that will use domain knowledge hardly qualifies the resulting system as an ES. However, we can expect more and more ES to be developed, together with a very large number of knowledge systems.

Most early developmental work in AI has taken place on relatively large, time-shared computers. These machines, which are beyond the means of many users, tend also to become heavily loaded with competing applications and therefore limit the applicability of most ES that may be developed. However, we are beginning to see small machines at a relatively modest cost, with large memories (some with virtual memories), more guaranteed (i.e., noncompetitive) CPU time, large amounts of disk space, and high-speed graphics capabilities. Machines with some or all of these characteristics should not only enhance our ability to develop ES, but also increase the possibilities for wider dissemination. (Examples of such machines are the AI VAXstation and the MicroExplorer.)

The state-of-the-art technology in building ES is what is called the *classification model*. A number of generalized tools have been developed to help design

---

*The material in this section was condensed from Weiss and Kulikowski (30), pp. 157–165.

a prototype reasoning classification model. The typical classification model uses production rules and covers a highly bounded problem. Although the classification model may be a proven vehicle for building an ES, the critical task of acquiring the knowledge from the expert and building the computer model remains in the hands of the skilled knowledge engineer.

It is clear that not all problems can be represented by the classification model, and alternative approaches are necessary. Such approaches still present many open research issues because there are only a few comparable schemes with more complex structures that are both as generalizable and practical as the classification model. One may reasonably expect that a particularly fruitful approach toward designing more powerful yet practical ES is to start with the classification model and then consider extensions to some basic model that may be necessary to solve a particular problem. Obviously not all problems will be solvable by this approach.

There are currently many research topics under investigation at various laboratories and institutions that follow this direction. The following four topics could have the greatest impact in advancing the class of problems for which solutions can be offered.

Adding New Types of Knowledge to the System

Not all knowledge can be captured by production rules. Experts use other forms of knowledge in their reasoning. For example, they may use causal information, or mathematical relationships, none of which is easily captured by production rules. The classification model would fall into what is called a "shallow" or "surface" model category, wheras models capturing the other types of knowledge would be described as the "deep" model.

The surface model is relatively easy to represent and design. In contrast, the deeper model is much harder to describe and use. As we try to increase the power and scope of the surface model, we can see its limitations and we will have difficulty in extending the performance of the model. The problem with current state-of-the-art ES models is that there are trade-offs between the two types of models. We acknowledge that the surface model is much easier to specify and use. Also, it is recognized that some problems may be simple enough for the surface model to be adequate. Furthermore, even if we knew how to build the deep model, in the final analysis it might not be worth the effort. However, some problems may not be easily solvable as classification problems, and will need to take advantage of the richer class of information that the expert may use. To date no one has demonstrated generalized approaches or tools for the deeper models that are analogous to those that exist for the classification models. However, the use of OOP has greatly contributed to this area. Another possible contribution could come from neural computing.

Easing the Knowledge Acquisition Task

The ultimate design goal for knowledge acquisition is to allow experts to encode their own knowledge directly into the computer, removing the role of the knowledge engineer from the knowledge acquisition phase. Moreover, experts should spend as little time as possible in encoding their knowledge. However, it is not likely that we will see any revolutionary change in the current balance between knowledge engineering and experts in the near future. Rather, we can expect a gradual evolution in the development of tools to facilitate the building of a knowledge base that will speed up the process of developing an ES.

Improved hardware at lower costs will make ES more practical and more widespread. Improved software, particularly specialized knowledge engineering packages, can ease the task of knowledge representation. But for now, the role of the knowledge engineer, which is of prime importance, cannot be automated. The knowledge engineer is an artist who cannot be reproduced by supplying another individual with high-quality paints and brushes.

Learning from Experience

Most of the practical lessons in the near future are likely to come from applying current ES technology to real world problems. This is also likely to lead to a better understanding of the types of problems we understand well versus those that require further research. This in turn will lead to gradual extensions to the basic classification model and an improved set of developmental tools. One area of great potential, but as yet unfulfilled promise, involves systems that learn from experience. However, today we are far from being ready to supplant the knowledge engineer and the expert with a system that automatically learns rules from experience and automatically improves and expands the ES itself. For a survey and analysis see Rauch-Hindin (20).

Incorporation Time and Location Relationships into the Expert Model

One important issue is the influence of time relationships on decision making. The classification model has no direct statement of time, although the observations used in the model could be made over time. Most classification models assume that all past information is summarized in a current snapshot. This situation can be quite complicated and there is much room for improvement in how time is to be incorporated in these models. Although the snapshot assumption summarizes the past, it is known that this is not the usual way of gathering information. ES of the future will have to handle dynamic situations. Real-time systems deal with dynamic situations and they are more difficult to construct than static systems.

An issue related to time is space. Most of the real-world classification models are one-dimensional. However, in some cases a system must reason with multiple instances of the same item. For example, a car repair ES is a typical classification model. But a car may have many instances of the same object, such as four tires and six cylinders. If these multiple instances can be treated independently, the solutions are straightforward. However, generalized solutions tend to grow more complex with increasing numbers of interactions among the multiple instances (or locations) of objects.

22.8 The Future of EIS and ESS

From a technological standpoint, the capabilities of the current generation of EIS/ESS are achieved by dividing the labor between a PC and a mainframe.* Under this division, the mainframe houses both the corporate data and the DSS or DBMS used to produce the summary results, which are then shipped to the PC. This division of labor capitalizes on the strengths and minimizes the weaknesses of both systems. But, the division also places limitations that can only be overcome by newer hardware platforms.

Executives place substantial requirements on EIS. First, they often ask questions that require complex, real-time analyses for their answers. This is why more and more EIS/ESS are being built on top of mainframe DSS systems, which provide the necessary analytical tools for performing these requisite analyses. But even these systems often lack the ability to respond in real-time. Delay in the delivery of information can mean loss of competitive position, loss of sales and loss of profits. Second, like other infrequent, untrained, or uncooperative users, executives require systems that are "easy to use," "easy to learn", and "easy to navigate". Current EIS/ESS systems generally possess these qualities. However, "ease of use" can also mean that the system has enough intelligence to automatically determine which tasks need to be performed and either performs the tasks directly or guides the user through the tasks. While current systems provide executives with the capabilities to monitor the present state of affairs, the systems typically lack the ability to automate the processes of interpreting or explaining information. The automation of these tasks requires the integration of current EIS/ESS capabilities with those of an expert system. Third, executives tend to have highly individualized workstyles. While the current generation of EIS/ESS can be molded to the needs of the executive, it is very difficult to alter the "look-and-feel" of the system or to alter the basic way in which the user interacts with the system. Finally, any information system is essentially a social system. One of the key elements of an EIS/ESS is the E-mail capabilities that it provides for members of the executive team. In the current generation of systems, however, these capabilities are again limited.

Therefore, the EIS/ESS of the future will look substantially different from today's systems. Like most other systems, EIS/ESS will migrate to the networked world of the technical workstation. These will have at least 10 times the speed and 10 times the memory of today's PCs, will have at least 4–8 times the disk capacity, will possess a very high resolution, bitmapped screen, will be multitasking, and will be connected with other workstations over a high-speed network (e.g., Ethernet). The advantages of such a configuration are that data and programs can be distributed and shared as needed. Individual workstations will have the ability to house and run mainframe versions of most DSS and DBMS software. In fact because of their multitasking capabilities, these programs can be running simultaneously (in separate windows), if need be.

The following list briefly describes some of the features that are likely to appear in the next generation of EIS/ESS:

*This section was condensed from an unpublished work of D. King of Execucom Systems Corp.

□ *A toolbox for building customized systems.* In order to quickly configure a system for an executive, the builder of the system needs a toolbox of graphic and analytical objects that can be easily linked together to produce the system. In the future EIS/ESS systems are likely to provide toolkits like Hypercard for building visual and graphic front ends.

□ *Multimedia support.* The requirement that an EIS/ESS be configurable also requires support of multiple modes of input and output. The current generation basically provides text and graphic output with touch screen, mouse, or keyboard input. The rapid proliferation of databases supporting image data and the slow, but sure, appearance of video as well as voice I/O, will probably mean that future EIS/ESS will be multimedia in nature. For example, in the next generation of systems an executive may be sitting in front of a high-resolution map of the company's sales regions. By touching one of these regions the executive might be presented with an animated display of the regions, revenue and expense figures over the past few years along with a voice summary of the results mailed by the regional sales directors. Not only does this mean that the workstation will have to support the storage and display of multimedia objects but also that the network will support the transfer of these objects.

□ *Merging of analytical systems with desktop publishing.* Many of the reports prepared for executives contain tables, graphs, and text. To support the preparation of these reports, some software companies are now beginning to merge desktop publishing capabilities with various analytical capabilities. Examples are the recent Wingz product from Informix and an earlier program for the McIntosh called Trapeze. In keeping with the multimedia features, coming EIS/ESS are likely to have the capability to at least cut and paste data and graphs from various windows into a document, and to ship that document via E-mail to other executives.

□ *Automated support and intelligent assistance.* Expert systems and other AI technologies (e.g., natural language) are currently being embedded or integrated with existing DSS or DBMS systems. This will clearly add more automated support and assistance to the analytical engines underlying EIS/ESS. However, we are also likely to see other forms of intelligent or automated assistance. One such form is the "agent." We might think of an "agent" as a small, individualized, knowledge-based system designed to carry out a few rudimentary tasks. For example, we might have a mail "agent" that monitors incoming E-mail, and, based on various built-in rules, places the mail in appropriate slots. Thus, instead of thinking of an EIS/ESS as a single program or system, we might think of the system as a society of agents whose actions need to be coordinated. While the concept of an agent may appear a bit foreign, it is currently being touted as the foundation for Apple's Knowledge Navigator—the ultimate ESS of the future.

22.9   Factories of the Future and Intelligent Robots

Most existing automated factories consist of islands of automation linked by material-handling devices under the control of a centralized computer. There are several computerized systems in the factory, but they are usually independent of one another. One computer system may operate the numerically controlled machines, another system is used for production planning and control, yet another one is used for administrative purposes, and finally a computer system may be used for supporting executive decisions. Factories of the future will utilize integrated computerized systems.

Decision support systems, expert systems, CAD/CAM, and intelligent robots will be important components in the factory of the future. DSS, ES, and EIS will provide the brain of the factory. In addition, intelligent robots (directed by ES) will provide the technology for creating higher degrees of factory automation.

The major advantages of the computerized factories will be:

☐ Reduced cost by increasing productivity.
☐ Increased quality of products.
☐ Increased capacity.
☐ Controlled (and minimized) interruptions.
☐ Flexibility in production (i.e., quick, inexpensive move from one product to another).

An Embedded Expert System

Computer hardware advances have made possible an expert system embedded in a microprocessor chip to form an integrated hardware/software package.[*] One example of this is the EEG Analysis System, an ES embedded in a Motorola MC6801 single-chip, eight-bit microcomputer designed to interpret electroencephalograms recorded from renal patients. In an integrated ES, there is no need to distinguish among the ES proper, the language in which the ES is written, and the computer that executes that language. For all practical purposes they are one unit. Such an integrated ES can be embedded in a piece of equipment, such as a complex electronic gear or robot, to form an intelligent system.

The intelligent system concept is actually a merging of ideas about fault-tolerant equipment and ES. Computer hardware size and price reductions have made it feasible for complex equipment to contain its own dedicated computer, and to run an ES that takes care of the equipment in some way. The integrated ES could handle tasks such as monitoring and controlling equipment operation, detecting and diagnosing equipment faults, assisting in correcting the faults, and planning ways to work around the faults until they are corrected. Figure 22.4 illustrates the idea of such an intelligent system.

As the figure implies, the integrated ES is "hard-wired" into the equipment with direct connections to sensor and switches that allow the ES to monitor and, in some cases, control the equipment. For applications where dangerous or unexpected situations are likely to arise, the operator could be taken out of the loop completely.

The intelligent system configuration will be particularly useful when the equipment to be monitored forms a hierarchy of physical units arranged in

[*]Based on Waterman (29).

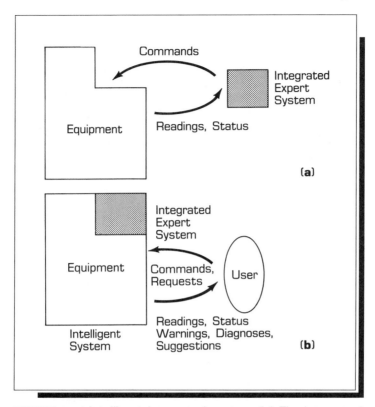

FIGURE 22.4 Intelligent integrated system. (a) The integrated expert system communicates with the equipment; (b) The user communicates with the equipment. (*Source:* Waterman [29], p. 222.)

some network structure. Each unit can then have an attached ES that monitors its own operation and the operation of its component units and suggests how to work around lower-level system components when they are not operational.

It may even be possible to develop the ES in conjunction with the design of the physical unit or equipment. In this case it could influence the design process and result in a more fault-tolerant design. Alternatively, the ES could be developed to work with CAD (computer-aided design) systems to help the equipment designer develop a fault-tolerant design.

An intelligent system has already been developed and put into commercial use. The SPE ES runs on a microprocessor inside CliniScan, Helena Laboratories' scanning densitometer. The ES interprets waves from the densitometer to determine which of several diseases a patient might have.

The Integrated Factory

The integration of the factory of the future is shown schematically in Figure 22.5. The role of the DSS, ES, robots, and EIS in each computerized component of the factory is summarized in Table 22.2.

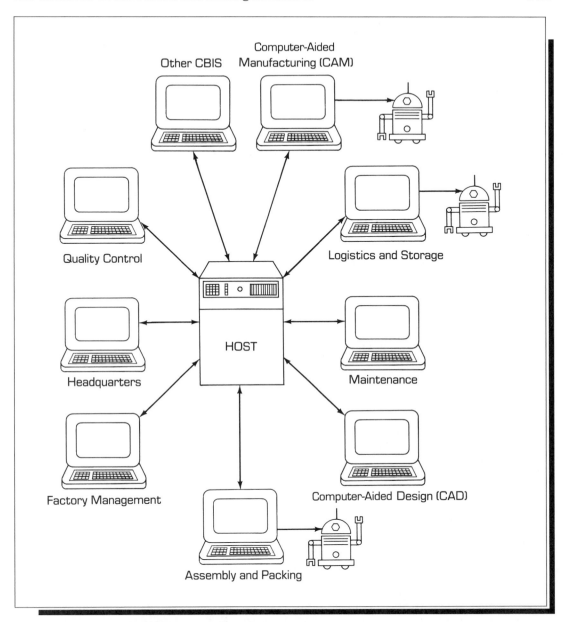

FIGURE 22.5 The integrated factory of the future.

For further information regarding the factory of the future, see Chase and Acquilano (3), Rosenthal (21), the special issues of *Electronic Magazine* October 20, 1983, *Business Week*, March 3, 1986, and B. Gold, "Computerization in Domestic and International Manufacturing", *Calif. Mgt. Review* Winter, 1989.

TABLE 22.2 The Role of DSS, ES, EIS, and Robots in the Factory of the Future.

Function Aided by Computers	Description	Supported by			
		DSS	ES	EIS	Robots
Assembly and packaging	Uses robots to put together parts fabricated on site and purchased from outside. Packages ready for shipment.	X	X		X
Design (CAD)	Creates a design for a product.		X		
Engineering	Designs the tools, molds, and other facilities needed for manufacturing.		X		
Factory Management	Runs the entire production process, coordinates incoming orders, requests components and material, planning and scheduling, overseeing cost control, arranges deliveries.	X	X	X	
Headquarters	Decides what products to make, when, and how much (based on market research, available resources, and strategic planning).	X	X	X	
Logistics and Storage	Purchases and distributes materials, inventory control, removal of materials, management of supplies. Shuttles incoming materials and parts, work in process, and final products.	X	X		X
Maintenance	Monitors equipment and processes, makes adjustments when needed, takes care of emergency breakdowns, fault diagnosis, preventive and corrective maintenance.		X		X
Manufacturing (CAM)	Fabricates metals, plastics, and other materials by molding, machining, welding, etc.		X		X
Quality Control	Tests incoming materials and outgoing products, tests of process in progress, quality assurance.		X		X

22.10 Human-Machine Interaction and Knowledge Codification

What may be the most important factor in increasing the acceptance of MSS is society's changing view of computers with the microcomputer revolution and the advent of personal computers. Professionals particularly see them mostly as aids to increasing their own productivity and creativity. The tasks performed by the computer may be simple, time-saving efforts, such as personal financial planning, or they may be economically productive efforts, such as those in computer-aided design. Whereas a decade ago computers were viewed by the majority of people as a machine to be distrusted and possibly even feared, today computers have become so familiar that *Time* magazine changed the Man of the Year selection for 1982 to be a Machine of the Year. Computer programming has become mandatory for many students in secondary education, and the number of jobs in computer-related industries is growing rapidly.

Not all people will welcome MSS with open arms. Many professionals and managers may feel that their jobs are threatened. This feeling is often cited as a negative factor in assessing the impact of computers on society. It is true that many people, particularly in clerical jobs, have been forced to retrain or become unemployed as new technologies displace old ones. With DSS and ES, still other groups of individuals may feel threatened. Our society has become increasingly more specialized, with new skills and professions dominating many fields. Individuals may be protective of their experience and knowledge, unwilling to share it with others. Their knowledge, particularly if it involves tricks of the trade that have never been explicitly formulated, may be of great economic value to them. Perhaps the greatest benefit of MSS is the potential for formalizing (or codifying) knowledge in areas where knowledge is mostly experimental and not widely disseminated, both because of economic reasons and because people may have no formal structure to give to decision-making knowledge.

Thus one of the most important by-products of ES development will be the codification of knowledge. As developers construct large, sophisticated knowledge bases, a market will develop for the knowledge itself, independent of any associated computer system. Tutoring facilities will be developed to help disseminate this information to students trying to learn about the application domain, and "knowledge decompilers" will be designed to translate the knowledge bases into coherent books or written reports. Because metaknowledge, knowledge about effective strategies and procedures for using the domain knowledge, will be used more extensively in future ES, it too will become an important commodity. From the social point of view, ES are likely, in the next two decades, to help systematize the better-established reasoning procedures used by experts. They will not replace the experts, but rather help people to move into more intellectually challenging activities where the knowledge encoded in an ES is another routine source of information. On the positive side, this ought to spur experts into more creative jobs; but given human nature, this is bound to meet resistance and resentment, just as previous technological innovation has. How far can all this go? Can computers take over? Some provocative discussion is provided in the forthcoming section.

22.11 **Is There a Limit?**

How intelligent can a computer be? It there a limit? To what extent can ES replace experts? It is difficult to answer these questions (for a discussion see Davis [4]). However, several scientists believe that there are major limitations to ES and intelligent MSS, even those in the distant future.

In a challenging book titled *Mind over Machine*, two U.C.-Berkeley professors, Huber Dreyfus and Stuart Dreyfus (6,7) make the following 19 statements:

1. Real-life situations rely on less than 100 percent predictability.
2. Machine intelligence cannot replace human reasoning ability.
3. Humans possess know-how based on practice and past experience. These are not quantifiable into rules.

4. Certain daily skills (e.g., conversing at a party, walking) are too complex to explain with rules.

5. Many daily skills are not innate and must be learned by trial and error or from someone we consider proficient (experience-based knowledge versus knowing how).

6. Computers cannot progress to the expert level of human skill because experts do not rely mainly on rules but rely more on practical understanding and intuition.

7. Experts are able to react to changing and new situations. Computers cannot.

8. Computers can't relate to "world" knowledge. They are restricted to microworlds, isolated domains that cannot be combined and extended to reflect daily life.

9. Computers cannot incorporate human belief systems into decisions.

10. Computers cannot be programmed for context.

11. Computers cannot use common sense rules (i.e., under normal conditions . . .)

12. Computers cannot selectively choose only rules that apply in a particular situation.

13. It is impossible to include all possible exceptions to rules.

14. In real life, no set of rules is complete.

15. People use images, not descriptions, to understand and respond to situations.

16. Computers make inferences only from a list of facts.

17. Computers cannot recognize emotions portrayed visually.

18. Computers cannot anticipate social consequences of situations with simulations.

19. Computers cannot deal with uncertain data.

Another point was raised by Zadeh (31), who advocates the use of fuzzy logic for ES. Zadeh is less impressed about the potential of ES to surpass the ability of human decision makers in the foreseeable future. One of the challenging problems is that of writing programs that allow a machine to understand problems. The ability to understand can be demonstrated by "summarization," as Zadeh says—understanding the meaning of some material (text, data, graphics) and summarizing it. Having a very high-speed computer, capable of performing millions of LIPS, will not help in itself because no one yet knows how to write a program that will enable a machine truly to summarize information.

Furthermore, Zadeh is not at all sure that the AI research community is approaching the problem in a way that is likely to produce the desired ability to understand. Most of the research is based on the use of two-valued yes-no logic; something is either right or wrong, true or false. He advocates the use of fuzzy logic, which humans use most of the time. Two-valued logic cannot deal with fuzzy quantifiers such as "few," "many," "several," "most," and "tall." Most of what is common sense reasoning uses fuzzy logic, he says. Two-valued logic is much too precise and much too confining to serve as a good model for common sense reasoning. "The reason why humans can do many things that present-day computers cannot do well, or perhaps even at all, is because existing computers employ two-valued logic," he says. And the design of the new, very high-speed computers apparently will continue to use the two-valued logic.

The arguments raised by the Dreyfus brothers and Zadeh may not hold for a long time, owing to the development of the neural computing. Should such development be successful, computers may act like humans in a manner that could top our present-day imagination.

Computer Will Understand Body Language

Researchers at Nippon Telegraph & Telephone (Japan) are developing computers that may understand body language. For example, by looking at your face, the computer will know if you look puzzled, unhappy, or even sick.

A digitized image of the user's face is taken by a video camera and it is being analyzed by an expert system. When fully developed the system will be able to "read" not only people's faces, but also other body movements.

When such systems will be commercialized, they could significantly increase the effectiveness of human-machine interface. They will also be helpful in medical diagnosis, personal interviews, and criminal investigations.

(*Source:* Based on a story published in *High Technology Business*, December 1988, by R. C. Wood.)

22.12   Neural Computing

Definitions.   *Neuron:* A brain cell that processes information (similar to a CPU). *Neural Network:* A network of neuron-like processing elements (CPUs), which resembles a nervous system in the brain, and which is composed of cells and lines connecting the cells (see Figure 22.2).

How They Work.   Neural networks consist of many simple, self-adjusting processing elements (PEs) cooperating in a densely interconnected network.

Each PE is responsible for generating a single output signal, dependent on its inputs which is then transmitted to other processing elements. Each input is gated by a weighing factor that determines the amount of influence that the input will have on the output. The strength of these weighing factors is adjusted autonomously by the PE as data is processed.

Thus, information is not stored as a set of values at specific memory locations, but is represented by the strengths of the weighing factors. Information is retrieved by watching the pattern of PE outputs that result from these weighing factors.

A neurocomputer is not programmed. It is *trained* in a manner similar to how a child is taught: by exposing it repeatedly to examples of the problem that it must solve.

Neurocomputing is different than most information systems which are based on von Neumann's process. To use such systems, we must first devise algorithms to solve problems, and then program the computer. The more complex problems must await our ability to devise the algorithms. For example, there is no algorithmic software today for an automobile autopilot, a handwritten character reader, or a spoken language translator. The brain can do all of these. Neural networks is a type of AI system that is also beginning to do these things.

Neural Networks—How They Can Help AI Technology.   AI technology is aimed at mimicking many activities of humans all of which call for use of the brain. It appears that all aspects of AI, including expert systems, NLP, voice/speech, ICAI, robotics, vision, translating language, general problem solving, and games can utilize neural networks.

Our major interest in this book is DSS and ES. For the potential contribution of neural computing to DSS and modeling see Trippi and Turban (27). The potential use in ES is discussed next.

Neural Computing and Expert System.[*]   Several characteristics of conventional AI searches lend themselves to execution or integration with neural computing. They are: use of pattern matching, use of heuristics, search strategies that can be done in parallel (e.g., when a depth-first search is conducted), and incomplete or fuzzy information. Neural network subsystems can help with complex pattern matching, incomplete information, and extremely large numbers of transactions.

The neural computing approach may solve another problem in ES construction, namely, facilitating the knowledge acquisition process by eliminating the need for an expert. In place of the expert's elicited knowledge, the neural network uses a training set of cases. Most proposed neural network–based expert systems have been designed around a "patterns classification" learning paradigm. After the network is trained with training samples, another set of cases is used to validate its performance. Unlike rule induction in conventional expert systems, a trained neural network may stabilize on decision criteria that have little apparent relevance to the problem, and that may even conflict with conventional theory, but that nevertheless produce good results.

Success in training neural networks to make decisions using historical data in areas such as mortgage insurance underwriting and credit approval has been reported by Nestor, Inc. In field tests, their system produced predictive risk assessments on mortgage insurance applications, based on the experience of the company's underwriters. Applications are rated with greater speed and accuracy than could be done with a conventionally implemented ES.

AVCO Corp., for example, has compared the performance of a neural network credit scoring system with its conventional statistical one. The trained neural network significantly increased productivity and quality.

Risk assessment is another example of an ES/neural computing application. This task differs from recognition problems, to which neural networks have been most frequently applied. In the former case, the network is expected to correctly predict an output from an input that is not contained in the set of

---

[*]Based on Trippi and Turban (27).

examples with which it was trained. There are reports (see [27]) regarding successful application of neural computing to the problem of rating bonds. The network was able to categorize bonds with fewer errors than those of conventional approaches (e.g., multiple regression). Standard AI approaches (e.g., rule-based systems) are difficult to apply successfully to this particular problem since the domain lacks a well-defined model or theory.

A potential problem with neural network–implemented expert systems is the difficulty of making the network "relearn" when the input-desired result relationship changes. Thousands of cases may be poorly handled before the network's weights readjust sufficiently to compensate for an external change that may have taken place.

Professor John Hopfield of Cal Tech is experimenting with a computerized system using associative memory technology, pattern recognition, and neural networks. If successful, computers will behave more like the human brain, overcoming many deficiencies of binary computers.*

Human brains are not restricted to specific site storage of information, and the process of calling up information is more general. Humans use two-way information processing rather than one-way, as do conventional computers. Using this system, resistors connect circuits to register multiple values combined with simultaneous memory storage.

The machines developed by Hopfield and researchers from other universities can cope with misinformation by using memory circuits. They can choose the most likely response when fed an ambiguous sequence of voltages hinting at either of two complete memories, choosing the larger of the two memories like human brains. These machines are capable of electronic inspiration and occasionally construct originally stored information. The Hopfield machine matches optimum choices from complex alternatives. Cal Tech is developing this system using optical composite lasers and holographs to recall images of faces.

These developments could refute many of the Dreyfus brothers' statements. The Dreyfus brothers claim that humans are all-knowing when in reality humans make decisions based on past experiences and "gut reactions" to current situations. It is true that intuition can play an important role in decision making, but humans also make mistakes based on their intuition. Computers make mistakes owing to lack of human input, but humans make mistakes too— regardless of intuition.

The biggest problems with Hopfield's experiments are lack of money and insufficient computer storage capacity. Even if his machine is perfected, our ability to make extensive use of this technology is a long way off. The ability of humans to "read" a situation, particularly a societal one, will remain an elusive skill for computers and should probably stay in the human domain.

Great strides, however, can be made with the pattern recognition and neural network ideas. The Cal Tech machine may be capable of generalizing its success achieved in limited situations. However, successes are limited in scope to date and still somewhat unpredictable.

In summary, the Dreyfus brothers' position is based on a comparison of "imperfect" computers with "perfect" humans. Neither of these assumptions is totally accurate. Table 22.3 attempts to refute the 19 points raised earlier,

*Condensed from Maugh (16). For further discussion see *Business Week*, June 2, 1986, pp. 92–96, Kinoshita and Palevsky (15), and Tank and Hopfield (26).

TABLE 22.3 Refuting the Dreyfus Brothers' Statements.

Statement No.	Counterarguments: Why These Statements May Not Hold
1	Certainty factors and fuzzy logic could decrease uncertainty.
2	Future developments in AI, metaknowledge, and learning will improve reasoning.
3	Future expert systems may approach humans' know-how.
4	True, at least in the short run.
5	Limited success of expert systems. More to come.
6	True in complex situations; ES are successful in narrow domains. Deep knowledge technology could change this situation.
7	Limited success of ES. Neural computing could solve the problem.
8	True, only success of neural computing could solve the problem.
9	True; however, advanced ES, DSS, and EIS can solve the problem.
10	Not yet; more storage, higher speed, and better representation techniques will do.
11	True; however, heuristics could be used to discover common-sense rules.
12	Neural networks can help.
13	Humans don't do this either (especially one person).
14	This is true for humans (especially one person) too.
15	Hopfield's laser and holographs can solve the problem (but it will take a long time to be commercialized).
16	Neural computing and AI Pattern Recognition could change this situation.
17	Computer vision will do it, in the far future.
18	Humans cannot do it accurately either.
19	No one really can; however, fuzzy logic can help.

assuming a limited success of neural computing. Related to neural computing is the promising avenue in the development of *optical computers* that could be the next generation of computer technology. These computers process information encoded in light beams. Thus, these computers have the potential of computing at the speed of light. In addition, optical lenses can perform mathematical calculations that are very difficult digitally. Finally, these computers will have a high storage and will be much easier to maintain. Optical computers could provide a major boost to ES development. Commercialization is expected in the early 1990s. For further information, see Miller, R.K. *Optical Computers: The Next Frontier in Computing.* Madison, GA: SEAI Technical Publications, 1986.

22.13 Conclusions

The time appears to be at hand for MSS to be widely used; most of the prerequisite accomplishments are in place. Although this statement might have appeared radical only a few years ago, recent experience strongly supports this view. The process of diffusion will be gradual and systems will appear as DSS,

ES, DSS/ES combinations or their variants, possibly combined with some additional applied AI features and other CBIS.

MSS will make decision making more effective. Faster and better decisions will result in increased welfare of individuals, organizations, and society.

There is no question that hardware cost will continue to decrease. Market trends show that many people, particularly professionals, increasingly view the computer as a problem-solving tool that can be exploited. Societies do not have the luxury of ignoring technological change because we live in a world economy where, if we do not change, the competition from other countries will force change on us. And it is always far better for us to design and control the changes (to whatever extent possible), than for others to do that for us! MSS can serve as intelligent assistants, improving productivity and the quality of decision making. We see, for example, that computer-aided design systems are readily accepted by engineers because these systems perform laborious tasks like assembling engineering drawings, which used to take hours of human time, much of it given to repetitive, mechanical tasks. MSS are a logical extension of the goals of such systems.

The explosion of MSS use will be accompanied by many problems. Some exist today; others could develop tomorrow. These problems will be managerial, technical, social, sociological, psychological, and economic. Wide research efforts are needed to solve them so that we achieve a successful implementation of MSS.

Key Words

associative memory technology	integrated circuits	neural networks
chip	logical inferences per second (LIPS)	optical computers
classification model (for ES)	metaknowledge	parallel processing
deep model (for ES)	Microelectronics and Computer Technology Corporation (MCC)	sequential processing
factory of the future		shallow (surface) model for ES
fault-tolerance	natural language processors	speech recognition
Fifth-Generation Project	neurons	VLSI (very large-scale integration)
human factors technology		

Questions for Discussion

1. Why is it easier for MCC to pursue a long-term strategy than for the individual companies that compose MCC?
2. Why is parallel processing so important for ES development?
3. How can the developments in VLSI and parallel processing assist the developments of DSS and ES?
4. Why are the Japanese so concerned about innovation?
5. Why is Japan called the "master of the implementation of technology"?
6. Read some recent information on the Fifth-Generation Project. Assess the progress of the project.
7. The Japanese divided their project into four components: data access, inference, ease of use, and intelligent programming. Discuss the importance of each area and its potential contribution to DSS, ES, and EIS.

8. Most managers employ intermediaries when using a DSS today. Thinking 25 years into the future, do you still see this as being the case? Why or why not?

9. Human factors technology is recognized as an important factor in computer technology. Find an article in a recent issue of any journal that deals with a human factors issue, then summarize and discuss it.

10. Review Table 22.1 for research topics in group DSS. Then review the literature of the most recent year to find an article on group DSS, summarize and discuss it. How does it fit into Table 22.1?

11. Knowledge acquisition is considered a major (perhaps *the* major) obstacle for wide use of ES. Find a recent article on the topic and discuss it.

12. The expert systems being installed on a chip can be implanted in a robot. What in your opinion could be the impact of such an installation?

13. Review the 19 statements of the Dreyfus brothers. How do you feel about each of them? Prepare a table similar to Table 22.3 for your responses.

14. What are the major potential benefits of using neural computing in MSS?

15. Define neuron and neural networks.

16. It is said that neural computers are not programmed. How do they work?

17. It is said that increased telecommuting may increase the use of GDSS. Why?

Exercises

1. You are trying to identify a specific number in the set of 1 to 16. You can ask questions such as: "is this number in the set 1–8?" The answer can either be yes or no. In either case you will continue to ask more questions until you can identify the number.*
   a. How many questions are needed, in the worst and the best possible cases, in order to identify such a number?
   b. Is the problem suitable for parallel processing? Why or why not?

2. A set of five letters from the alphabet is given to you (say B, E, M, S, and T). Your task is to compose as many words as possible from these letters. One way to do it is to write a computer program that will try to match each combination of these letters to words in a dictionary.
   1. Describe the process that a regular computer will go through.
   2. Is the problem suitable for parallel processing? Why or why not?

References and Bibliography

1. Almasi, G. S., and A. Gottlieb. *Highly Parallel Computing.* Redwood City, CA: Benjamin/Cummings, 1989.
2. Bond, A. H., and L. Gasser. *Reading in Distributed AI.* Morgan Kaufman, 1988.
3. Chase, R. B., and N. J. Acquilano. *Production and Operations Management.* 4th ed. Homewood, IL: Irwin, 1985.
4. Davis, R. "Expert Systems: How Far Can They Go?" Part I, *AI Magazine,* Spring 1989; Part II, Summer 1989.
5. DeSanctis, G., and B. Gallupe. "Group Decision Support Systems: A New Frontier." *Data Base,* Winter 1985.
6. Dreyfus, H., and S. Dreyfus. *Mind Over Machine.* New York: The Free Press, 1986.
7. Dreyfus, H., and S. Dreyfus. "Why Computers May Never Think Like People." *Technology Review,* January 1986.

*This problem and the next were borrowed from the April 15, 1988 issue of *AI Week* (contributed by D. B. Hertz).

8. Er, M. C., "DSS: A Summary of Problems and Future Trends." *Decision Support Systems*, Vol. 4, 1988.
9. Feigenbaum, E. A., and P. McCorduck. *The Fifth-Generation Computer*. Reading, MA: Addison-Wesley, 1983.
10. Gray, P. "Group Decision Support Systems." *Decision Support Systems*, Vol. 3, 1987.
11. Hecht-Nielson, R. "Neurocomputing: Picking the Human Brain." *IEEE Spectrum*, March 1988.
12. Holloway, C., and H. H. Hand. "Who's Running the Store, Anyway? Artificial Intelligence!!!" *Business Horizons*, March-April 1988.
13. Kandt, K. "On Building Future Decision Support Systems." *HICCS 21*, Hawaii, January 1988.
14. Keen, P. G. W. "Decision Support Systems: The Next Decade." *Decision Support Systems*, Vol. 4, 1988.
15. Kinoshita, J., and N. G. Palevsky. "Computers with Neural Networks." *High Technology*, May 1987.
16. Maugh, T. H., II. "The Brain May Yet Meet Its Match in a Computer." *Los Angeles Times*, March 18, 1986.
17. Mishkoff, H. C. *Understanding Artificial Intelligence*. Dallas: Texas Instruments, 1985.
18. Perrot, R. H. *Parallel Programming*. Reading, MA: Addison-Wesley, 1987.
19. Rasmus, D. W. "Artificial Intelligence from A to I." *MacUser*, December 1988.
20. Rauch-Hindin, W. B. *A Guide to Commercial AI*, Englewood Cliffs, NJ: Prentice-Hall, 1988.
21. Rosenthal, S. R. "Progress Toward the Factory of the Future." *Journal of Operations Management*, May 1984.
22. Sprague, R. H., Jr., and B. C. McNurlin. *Information Systems in Practice*. 2nd ed. Englewood Cliffs, NJ: Prentice-Hall, 1989.
23. Sprague, R. H., Jr., and H. Watson, eds. *Decision Support Systems*. 2nd ed. Englewood Cliffs, NJ: Prentice-Hall, 1989.
24. Stefik, M. "The Next Knowledge Medium." *AI Magazine*, Spring 1986.
25. Stevens, L. *The Search for the Perfect Machine*. Hasbrouck, NJ: Hayden, 1985.
26. Tank, D. W., and J. J. Hopfield. "Collective Computation in Neuronlike Circuits." *Scientific American*, Vol. 257, No. 6, 1987.
27. Trippi, R., and E. Turban. "The Contribution of Parallel and Neural Computing to Managerial Decision Making." *Journal of Management Information Systems*, Fall 1989.
28. Van Lamsweerde, A., and P. Dufour. *Current Issues in Expert Systems*. San Diego, Ca: Academic Press, 1987.
29. Waterman, D. *A Guide to Expert Systems*. Reading Mass.: Addison-Wesley, 1986.
30. Weiss, S. M., and C. A. Kulikowski. *A Practical Guide to Designing Expert Systems*. Totowa, NJ: Rowman & Allanheld, 1984.
31. Zadeh, L. A. *The Management of Uncertainty in Expert Systems*. Proceedings, 1st Symposium on Application of Expert Systems in Emergency Management Operations, FEMA/NBS, Washington, DC, April 1985.

Glossary

Algorithm A step-by-step search, where improvement is made in every step until the best solution is found.

Analogical Reasoning Determining the outcome of a problem by the use of analogies. A procedure for drawing conclusions about a problem by using past experience.

Application Software Programs that can perform specific, user-oriented tasks.

Artificial Intelligence (AI) The subfield of computer science that is concerned with symbolic reasoning and problem solving.

Assembly Language Computer language that replaces the binary digits of machine language with abbreviations to indicate processing operations.

Assertion The database or fact part of the knowledge base. It includes rules that are known to be true or false and any other information.

Assertation (See Assertion)

Associative Memory Technology An experimental computer technology that attempts to build computers that will operate like a human brain. The machines possess simultaneous memory storage, and work with ambiguous information. (*See* Neural Computing.)

Backtracking A technique used in tree searches. The process of working backward from a failed objective or an incorrect result to examine unexplored alternatives.

Backward Chaining A search technique used in production ("if-then" rule) systems that begins with the action clause of a rule and works "backward" through a chain of rules in an attempt to find a verifiable set of condition clauses.

Binary Code A system of numbering in base 2, which uses only 1s and 0s as digits. Because of the simple correspondence to the on–off states of electronic switches, the binary number system is used to "code" information and instructions inside a computer.

Blind Search A search approach that makes use of no knowledge or heuristics to help speed up the search process. A time-consuming and arbitrary search process that attempts to exhaust all possibilities.

Breadth–first Search A search technique that evaluates every item at a given level of the search space before proceeding to the next level.

Certainty Factor A percentage supplied by an expert system that indicates the probability that the conclusion reached by the system is correct. Also, the degree of belief of the expert that a certain conclusion will occur if a certain premise is true.

Chip A single device consisting of transistors, diodes, and other components forming a complex circuit on a $\frac{1}{4}''\times\frac{1}{4}''$ section of a wafer sliced from a crystal of silicon.

Chunk of Information A collection of facts stored and retrieved as a single unit. The limitations of working memory are usually defined in terms of the number of chunks that can be handled simultaneously.

831

Classification Model (for ES)   A model used in building expert systems that uses production rules and covers a highly bounded problem.

Cognitive Style (Cognition)   The subjective process through which individuals organize and change information during the decision-making process.

Complete DSS   A strategy for constructing a full-service DSS generator and an organization to manage it. Contrasted with a quick-hit strategy.

Computer-aided Instruction   In general, the use of the computer as a teaching tool. Synonymous with Computer-based Instruction, Computer-assisted Learning, and Computer-based Training.

Computer Graphics   The presentation of data in the form of bar charts, histograms, pie charts, or grids on a display screen or plotter to highlight data variations. Graphics are available in black and white or in color and can be presented in two or three dimensions.

Conflict Resolution (of Rules)   Selecting a procedure from a conflicting set of applicable competing procedures or rules.

Consultation Environment   The part of the expert system that is used by the non-expert to obtain expert knowledge and advice. It includes the workplace, inference engine, explanation facility, the recommended action, and the user interface.

Controllable Variables   Decision variables such as quantity to produce, amounts of resources to be allocated, etc. that can be changed and manipulated by the decision maker.

Cottage Industry   Factory employees who are doing the work in their homes. The modern version of the cottage industry is telecommuting.

CPU   The "brain" of a computer, which includes the circuits that retrieve (fetch) instructions and data from memory and execute the instructions. When the CPU is contained on a single chip, the CPU is called a microprocessor.

Critical Success Factors   A methodology developed at MIT for identifying the factors that are most critical to the success of an organization.

Database   The organizing of files into related units that are then viewed as a single storage concept. The data are then made available to a wide range of users.

Database Management System (DBMS)   The software to establish, update, or query a database.

Decision Room   An arrangement for a group DSS in which terminals are available to some or all participants. The objective is to enhance the decision-making process (e.g., by tabulating secret ballots).

Decision Styles   The manner in which decision makers think and react to problems. It includes their perceptions, cognitive responses, values, and beliefs.

Decision Support Systems (DSS)   Computer-based information systems that combine models and data in an attempt to solve nonstructured problems with extensive user involvement.

Decision Tree   A graphical presentation of a sequence of interrelated decisions to be made under assumed risk.

Declarative Knowledge Representation   Representation of facts and assertions.

Deductive Reasoning   In logic, reasoning from the general to the specific. Conclusions follow premises. Consequent reasoning.

Deep Model (for ES)   A model that captures all the forms of knowledge used by experts in their reasoning.

Default Value   A value given to a symbol or variable automatically if no other value is defined by the programmer or user.

DELPHI   A qualitative forecasting methodology using anonymous questionnaires. Effective for technological forecasting and forecasting involving sensitive issues.

Demon   A procedure that is automatically activated if a specific, predefined state is recognized.

Dependent Variables   Systems' measure of effectiveness.

Depth-first Search A search procedure that explores each branch of a search tree to its full vertical length. Each branch is searched for a solution and if none is found, a new vertical branch is searched to its depth, and so on.

Descriptive Models Models that describe things as they are.

Deterministic Models Models that are constructed under assumed certainty, namely, there is only one possible (and known) result to each alternative course or action.

Development Environment That part of the expert system that is used by the builder. It includes the knowledge base, the inference engine, knowledge acquisition, and improving reasoning capability. The knowledge engineer and the expert are considered a part of this environment.

Dialog Generation and Management System (DGMS) A software management package in a DSS whose functions in the dialog subsystem is similar to that of a DBMS in a database.

Dialog Style The combination of the action languages, the display language, and knowledge base which determines input and provides output. Examples of styles include menu-driven and command language.

Dialog System The hardware and software that provide the user interface for DSS. It also includes the ease-of-use, accessibility, and human–machine interface.

Directory A catalog or dictionary of all the data in a database.

Domain An area of knowledge or expertise.

Domain Expert A person with expertise in the domain in which the expert system is being developed. The domain expert works closely with the knowledge engineer to capture the expert's knowledge in a knowledge base.

DSS Generator Computer software (sometimes with hardware) that provides a set of capabilities to quickly build a specific DSS.

DSS Tools Software elements (such as languages) that facilitate the development of a DSS, or a DSS generator.

Dynamic Models Models whose input data are being changed over time; for example, a five-year profit (loss) projection.

Editor A software tool to aid in modifying a software program.

Effectiveness The degree of goal attainment. Doing the right things.

Efficiency Ratio of output to input. Appropriate use of resources.

Electronic Data Processing (EDP) Processing of data largely performed by electronic devices.

EMYCIN Nonspecific part (called shell) of MYCIN consisting of what is left when the knowledge is removed. EMYCIN becomes a new problem solver by adding the knowledge (using rules) for a different problem domain.

Encapsulation Coupling of data and procedures in object-oriented programming.

End-User Computing Development of one's own information system by a computer user.

English-like Language A computer language that is very similar to the everyday, ordinary English.

Enumeration (Complete) A listing of *all* possible solutions and the comparison of their results in order to find the best solution.

Evolutionary (Iterative) Process A systematic process for system development that is used in DSS. A portion of the system is quickly constructed, then tested, improved, and enlarged in steps. Similar to prototyping.

Exception Reporting A report generated by the system when a function ceases to perform within a prescribed range or limits.

Executive Information Systems (EIS) Computerized systems that are specifically designed to support executive work.

Executive Support System An executive information system that includes some analytical capabilities.

Expert System (ES)   A computer system that applies reasoning methodologies on knowledge in a specific domain in order to render advice or recommendations, much like a human expert. A computer system that achieves high levels of performance in task areas that, for human beings, require years of special education and training.

Expertise   The set of capabilities that underlines the performance of human experts, including extensive domain knowledge, heuristic rules that simplify and improve approaches to problem-solving, metaknowledge and metacognition, and compiled forms of behavior that afford great economy in skilled performance.

Explanation Facility   The component of an expert system that can explain the system's reasoning and justify its conclusions.

Extraction   Capture data from several sources, synthesize them, summarize, find the relevant data, and organize them.

Facet   An attribute or a feature that describes the content of a slot in a frame.

Factory of the Future   Highly automated factory that is managed and controlled by intelligent computers.

Fault-Tolerance   A computing system that continues to operate satisfactorily in the presence of faults.

Feasibility Study   A preliminary investigation to develop plans for construction of a new information system. The major aspects of the study are cost/benefit, technological, human, organizational, and financial.

Federal Privacy Act   Federal legislation (1974) that prohibits governmental agencies from providing information about individuals without the consent of the individuals.

Fifth-generation Languages   Artificial Intelligence languages such as Lisp and PROLOG and their variants.

Fifth-generation Project   The research project in which the Japanese are investigating parallel processing and other advanced computing techniques in an attempt to develop a "fifth generation" of computer systems, which will be both efficient and intelligent.

Firing a Rule   Obtaining information on either the IF or THEN part of a rule, which makes this rule an assertation.

Flexibility in DSS   System ability to react to changes in the environment, tasks, or users of the DSS. It is the ability to modify, adapt, solve problems, and evolve.

Fourth-generation Languages (4GLs)   Nonprocedural, user-oriented languages that enable quick programming by specifying only the desired results.

Frames   A knowledge representation scheme that associates one or more features with an object in terms of various slots and particular slot values.

Front-end Systems   Software systems (sometimes with hardware) that are used to simplify the accessibility to other computerized systems (e.g., to a database).

Fuzzy Logic   Ways of reasoning that can cope with uncertain or partial information; characteristic of human thinking and many expert systems.

Garbage Collection   A technique for recycling computer memory cells no longer in use.

General-purpose Problem Solver   A procedure developed by Newell and Simon in an attempt to create an intelligent computer. Although unsuccessful, the concept itself made a valuable contribution to the AI field.

Generators   Software packages that are designed to expedite the programming efforts that are required to build information systems.

Goal-seeking   The capability of asking the computer what values certain variables must have in order to attain desired goals.

Group DSS   An interactive, computer-based system that facilitates solution of unstructured problems by a set of decision makers working together as a group.

Hardware   The physical equipment of a computer system, including processor, memory, input/output devices, and other components.

Heuristics The informal, judgmental knowledge of an application area that constitutes the "rules of good judgment" in the field. Heuristics also encompass the knowledge of how to solve problems efficiently and effectively, how to plan steps in solving a complex problem, how to improve performance, and so forth.

Hidden Unemployment Refer to cases in which people are considered employed but are working only part of the time. Thus, the same amount of work can be executed by fewer employees.

High-level Languages Computer programming languages that approximate the use of the English language or mathematical functions and can be used on a variety of computers. Examples are: COBOL, PASCAL, FORTRAN, and "C."

Highlight Charts Summary displays that show only important information based on the user's own judgment.

Human Factors Technology Physiological, psychological, and training factors to be considered in the design of hardware and software and the development of procedures to ensure that humans can interface with machines efficiently and effectively.

Hybrid Environment A software package for expediting the construction of expert systems that includes several knowledge representation schemes.

Hypermedia Combination of several types of media such as text, graphics, audio, and video.

Hypertext An approach for handling text and other information by allowing the user to jump from a given topic, whenever he or she wishes, to related topics.

Icon A visual, graphic representation of an object, word, or concept.

Iconic Model A physical, scaled replica.

IF-THEN A conditional rule in which a certain action is taken only if some condition is satisfied.

Implementation The introduction of a change; putting things to work.

Independent Variables Variables in a model that are controlled by the decision maker and/or by the environment and that determine the result of a decision (also called Input Variables).

Inductive Reasoning In logic, reasoning from the specific to the general. Conditional or antecedent reasoning.

Inexact (Approximate) Reasoning Used when the expert system has to make decisions based on partial or incomplete information.

Inference The process of drawing a conclusion from given evidence. To reach a decision by reasoning.

Inference Engine That part of an expert system that actually performs the reasoning function.

Inference Tree A schematic view of the inference process that shows the order in which rules are being tested.

Influence Diagram A diagram that shows the various types of variables (decision, independent, result) in a problem and how they are related to each other.

Information Center Facility with end-user tools that is staffed by end-user oriented specialists who first train and then support business users.

Information for Motivation A process for the development and use of EIS, starting with the determination of success factors and ending with a motivation program based on goal attainment.

Inheritance The process by which one object takes on or is assigned the characteristics of another object higher up in a hierarchy.

Innovation Boundary Theory by Slevin that suggests that a boundary exists between the zones where people will innovate and where they will not.

Inputs The resources introduced into a system for transformation into outputs.

Instantiation The process of assigning (or substituting) a specific value or name to a variable in a frame (or in a logic expression) making it a particular "instance" of that variable.

Institutional MSS One that is a permanent fixture in the organization with continuing financial support. It deals with decisions of a recurring nature.

Institutionalization The process through which an MSS system becomes incorporated as an ongoing part of organizational procedures.

Integrated Circuits Circuits composed of many tiny transistors that have been placed together in a single physical element, typically into a silicon chip.

Integrated Computer Systems Software packages that perform several different functions. For example Lotus 1-2-3 provides modeling capability, database management, and graphics.

Intelligent Computer-aided Instruction (ICAI) Using AI techniques for training or teaching with a computer.

Interactive Visual Decision Making (IVDM) Graphic animation in which systems and processes are presented dynamically to the decision maker. It enables visualization of the results of different potential actions.

Interactive Visual Simulation A special case of IVDM in which a simulation approach is used in the decision-making process.

Interdependent Decisions A series of decisions that are interrelated. Sequential decisions are usually interdependent.

Interface The portion of a computer system that interacts with the user, accepting commands from the computer keyboard and displaying the results generated by other portions of the computer system.

Intermediary A person who uses the computer to fulfill requests made by other people. Example: a financial analyst uses the computer to answer questions for top management.

Iterative Process *See* Evolutionary Process.

Job Content The element that comprises a job.

Justification Facility. *See* Explanation Facility. Also called justifier.

Key Performance Indicators (KPI) Specific measures of the critical success factors (CSF).

Knowledge Understanding, awareness, or familiarity acquired through education or experience. Anything that has been learned, perceived, discovered, inferred, or understood. The ability to use information.

Knowledge Acquisition The extraction and formulation of knowledge derived from various sources, especially from experts.

Knowledge Base A collection of facts, rules, and procedures organized into schemas. The assembly of all of the information and knowledge of a specific field of interest.

Knowledge Engineer An AI specialist responsible for the technical side of developing an expert system. The knowledge engineer works closely with the domain expert to capture the expert's knowledge in a knowledge base.

Knowledge Engineering (KE) The engineering discipline whereby knowledge is integrated into computer systems in order to solve complex problems normally requiring a high level of human expertise.

Knowledge Refining The ability of the program to analyze its own performance, learn, and improve itself for future consultations.

Knowledge Representation A formalism for representing in the computer facts and rules about a subject or a specialty.

Knowledge System Computer systems that embody knowledge, include inexact, heuristic, and subjective knowledge; the results of knowledge engineering.

Lexicon A dictionary.

Linear Programming A mathematical model for optimal solution of resource allocation problems.

Lisp (List Processor) An AI programming language, created by AI pioneer John McCarthy, that is especially popular in the United States.

Lisp Machines (or "AI Workstations") A single-user computer designed primarily to expedite the development of AI programs. Recently these machines were extended to serve several users simultaneously.

Logical Inferences Per Second (LIPS) A means of measuring the speed of computers used for AI applications.

Machine Language A language for writing instructions in a form to be executed directly by the computer. The language is composed of two values: zeros and ones.

Make-Or-Buy An analysis designed to answer the question: should we make a certain product ourselves or buy it? It is the issue of subcontracting products and services.

Management by Exception A control system in which performance is monitored and action is taken only if the performance is outside a designated range.

Management by Objective A procedure by which objectives are determined by an employee and his superior through a negotiated session. These objectives are then used for planning, control, and rewards.

Management Information Systems (MIS) A business information system designed to provide past, present, and future information appropriate for planning, organizing, and controlling the operations of the organization.

Management Science (MS) The application of scientific approach and mathematical models to the analysis and solution of managerial decision problems.

Mathematical Model A system of symbols and expressions representing a real situation.

Metaknowledge Knowledge in an expert system about how the system operates or reasons. More generally, knowledge about knowledge.

Metarules A rule that describes how other rules should be used or modified.

Microcomputers A complete computer system based on a microprocessor.

Microelectronics Miniaturization of electronic circuits and components.

Microelectronics and Computer Technology Corporation (MCC) A consortium of American companies involved in AI and other advanced computer research.

Model Base A collection of preprogrammed quantitative models (e.g., statistical, financial, optimization) organized as a single unit.

Model Base Management System (MBMS) A software to establish, update, combine, etc. a model base.

Model Building Blocks Preprogrammed software elements that can be used to build computerized models. For example, a random number generator can be used in the construction of a simulation model.

Modeling Tools Software programs that enable the building of mathematical models quickly. A spreadsheet and a planning language are modeling tools.

Modus Ponens An inference rule type which from "A implies B", justifies B by the existence of A.

Monotonic Reasoning A reasoning system based on the assumption that once a fact is determined it cannot be altered during the course of the reasoning process.

Monte Carlo Simulation A mechanism that uses random numbers in order to predict the behavior of an event whose probabilities are known.

Multiple Experts A case in which two or more experts are used as the source of knowledge for an expert system.

MYCIN Early rule-based expert system, developed by Dr. Edward H. Shortliffe, that helps to determine the exact identity of an infection of the blood and that helps to prescribe the appropriate antibiotic.

Natural Language A natural language is a language spoken by humans on a daily basis, such as English, French, Japanese, or German.

Natural Language Processors (NLP) An AI-based user interface that allows the user to carry on a conversation with a computer-based system in much the same way as he or she would converse with another human.

Neural Computing Networks An experimental computer design that aims at building intelligent computers that will operate much like the human brain.

Nonprocedural Languages The programmer specifies only the desired results rather than the detailed steps of how to get there.

Normative Prescribes how a system should operate.

Numerical Processing The traditional use of computers to manipulate numbers.

Object-Oriented Programming A language for representing objects and processing those representations by sending messages and activating methods.

Operations Research *See* Management Science.

Optimization Identification of the best possible solution.

Organizational Culture (Climate) The aggregate attitudes in the organization concerning a certain issue (such as technology, computers, and DSS).

Outputs The result of a transformation process in a system.

Parallel Processing An advanced computer processing technique that allows the computer to perform multiple processes at the same time, in "parallel."

Parsing The process of breaking down a character string of natural language input into its component parts so that it can be more readily analyzed, interpreted, or understood.

Pattern Recognition (Matching) The technique of matching an external pattern to one stored within a computer's memory, used in inference engines, image processing, and speech recognition. For example: the process of classifying data into predetermined categories.

Planning Language A software package designed to expedite the construction of a financial and/or operational computerized planning system.

Predicate Calculus A logical system of reasoning used in AI programs to indicate relationships among data items. The basis for the computer language PROLOG.

Principle of Choice The criterion for making a choice among alternatives.

Problem Solving Problem solving is a process in which one starts from an initial state and proceeds to search through a problem space in order to identify a desired goal.

Procedural Knowledge (contrasted with Declarative Knowledge) Information about courses of action.

Procedural Languages The programmer must define the procedures that the computer is to follow.

Production Rules A knowledge representation method in which knowledge is formalized into "rules" containing an IF part and a THEN part (also called a condition and an action).

Productivity The ratio of outputs (results) to inputs (resources).

PROLOG A high-level computer language designed around the concepts of predicate calculus.

Propositional Logic A formal logical system of reasoning in which conclusions are drawn from a series of statements according to a strict set of rules.

Protocols A set of instructions governing the format and control of data in moving from one medium to another.

Prototyping A strategy in system development in which a scaled down system or portion of a system is constructed in a short time, tested, and improved in several iterations.

Query Language A language provided as part of a DBMS for easy access to data in the database.

Quick Hit A strategy for DSS development in which a specific DSS is constructed for a specific purpose without much planning for future DSS.

Random Number A number sampled from a uniform distribution in an unbiased manner (each number has exactly the same chance of being selected).

Rapid Prototyping In expert systems development, a prototype is an initial version of an expert system, usually a system with 25 to 200 rules, that is quickly developed to test the effectiveness of the overall knowledge representation and inference mechanisms being employed to solve a particular problem.

Ready-Made Expert System Mass-produced packages that may be purchased from software companies. These are very general in nature.

Real-Time In synchronization with the actual occurrence of events; results are given rapidly enough to be useful in directly controlling a physical process or guiding a human user.

Refreezing A step in the process of dealing with resistance to change in which reinforcement of the change occurs.

Relational Database A database whose records are organized into tables that can be processed by either relational algebra or relational calculus.

Repertory Grid Technique A tool used by psychologists to represent a person's view of a problem in terms of its elements and constructs.

Report Generation The ability to use a few commands to generate an entire report. At the extreme, one command can generate an entire report patterned according to a template.

Risk Analysis Analysis of decision situations in which results are dependent on events whose probabilities of occurrence are assumed to be known.

Robotics The science of using a machine (a robot) to perform manual functions without human intervention.

Role Ambiguity A situation in which the role to be performed by an employee is not clear. Lack of job description and changing conditions often result in role ambiguity.

ROMC (Representation, Operations, Memory Aids, Mechanism Control) A systematic approach for developing large-scale DSS. It is a user-oriented approach for articulating system performance requirements.

Rule A formal way of specifying a recommendation, directive, or strategy, expressed as IF premise THEN conclusion.

Rule Induction Rules are created by a computer from examples of problems where the outcome is known. These rules are generalized to other cases.

Run-time System The part of an expert system shell that provides a consultation by interfacing with a user and an *existing knowledge base* and inference engine.

Satisfice A process during which one seeks a solution that will satisfy a set of constraints. In contrast to optimization, which seeks the best possible solution; when one satisfices, one simply seeks a solution that will work. (Good enough)

Scenario A statement of assumptions and configurations concerning the operating environment of a particular system at a particular time.

Schema A data structure for knowledge representation. Examples of schemas are frames and rules.

Semantic Networks A knowledge representation method consisting of a network of nodes, standing for concepts or objects, connected by arcs describing the relations between the nodes.

Semantics The meaning in language. The relationship between words and sentences.

Semistructured Decisions Decisions in which some aspects of the problem are structured and others are unstructured.

Sensitivity Analysis A study of the effect of a change in one or more input variables on a proposed solution.

Sensory System Any system that monitors the external environment for a computer.

Sequential Processing The traditional computer processing technique of performing actions one at a time, in a sequence.

Shallow (Surface) Model for ES A model that does not capture all of the forms of knowledge used by experts in their reasoning. Contrasted with the Deep Model.

Shell A kind of expert system development tool consisting of two stand-alone pieces of software: a rule set manager and an inference engine capable of reasoning with rules set built with the rule set manager. A shell is a complete expert system stripped of its specific knowledge.

Simulation An imitation of reality.

Slot A sub-element of a frame of an object. A particular characteristic, specification, or definition used in forming a knowledge base.

Software A collection of programs and routines that support the operation of the computer system.

Specific DSS A system that actually accomplishes a specific task. It is similar to "application software" in conventional MIS.

Specific Expert Systems An expert system that advises users on a specific issue.

Speech Understanding An area of AI research that attempts to allow computers to recognize words or phrases of human speech.

Spreadsheet (Electronic) Computer technology that is similar to columns-and-rows worksheets used by accountants. It is a modeling tool.

State Space Search Looking for a solution by systematically searching through the various situations (states) of a problem.

Status Access Rapid access, provided by a computer, to current information.

Strategic Models Planning models, usually for the long run, that encompass the corporate strategies for development and growth.

Structured Decisions Standard or repetitive decision situations for which solution techniques are already available.

Suboptimal Best for a subsystem of the total system.

Symbolic Processing Use of symbols, rather than numbers, combined with rules-of-thumb (or heuristics), in order to process information and solve problems.

Syntax The manner in which words are assembled to form phrases and sentences. Putting words in a specific order.

System A set of elements that is considered to act as a single, goal-oriented entity.

System Analysis The investigation and recording of existing systems and the conceptual design and feasibility study of new systems.

System Design Specification of appropriate hardware and software components required to implement an information system.

System Development Life Cycle (SDLC) A systematic process for constructing large information systems in an effective manner.

Telecommunication The transfer of information over distance by means of telephone, radio, or other transmission.

Telecommuting Employees work at home, usually using a computer or a terminal that is linked to their place of employment.

Template A piece of presentation knowledge that indicates the visual layout of a report's contents and the sources of values that can appear in particular locations.

Templates (for Spreadsheets) Preprogrammed, reusable spreadsheet models with built-in titles and formulas, developed for specific applications.

Time-series analysis A technique that analyzes historical data over a period of a few years and then makes a forecast.

Turing Test A test that is designed to measure the degree of a computer's "intelligence."

Uncertainty In the context of expert systems, uncertainty refers to a value that cannot be determined during a consultation. Many expert systems can accommodate uncertainty. That is, they allow the user to indicate if he or she does not know the answer.

Uncontrollable Variations Factors that affect the result of a decision but are not under the control of the decision maker. These can be internal (technology, policies) or external (legal, climate).

Unfreezing The first phase in the treatment of resistance to change, creating an awareness of the need for a change.

Unstructured Decisions   Complex decisions for which no standard solutions exist.

User-Friendly   Term used to describe a facility designed to make interaction with a computer system easy and comfortable for the user.

User Interface (or "Human Interface")   The component of a computer system that allows bidirectional communication between the system and its user.

Visual Simulation   *See* Interactive Visual Simulation.

VLSI (Very-Large-Scale Integration)   The process of combining several hundred thousand electronic components into a single integrated circuit (chip).

Voice Recognition   The ability of a computer to understand the meaning of spoken words (sentences as input).

Voice Synthesis   A transformation of computer output to an audio (voice); for example, a telephone number given as a response to a request from 411.

"What If" Analysis   The capability of "asking" the computer what the effect will be of changing some of the input data.

Workplace (or Blackboard)   A globally accessible database used in expert systems for recording intermediate, partial results of problem solving.

Index

RANDOM
HOUSE
LARGE
PRINT

"Immensely readable . . . a multistranded narrative account of the most devastating pandemic the world has ever known, as well as a history of twentieth-century science and medicine . . . He describes how the influenza virus attacks the body with a clarity that lays the conceptual groundwork for much that would ensue. . . . And as a piece of social history, **The Great Influenza** is invaluable. It shows the courage and cowardice of individuals under great pressure; it shows how institutions, captive to the ethics of the time, can rise to the occasion or abjectly fall. . . . It's a lesson to ponder in our times."　　　　　　　　　**—The Seattle Times**

"Magisterial . . . evocative . . . unusual literary panache . . . impressively up-to-date understanding . . . very artfully constructed [with phrases] repeated like Wagner's leitmotifs . . . The fact is that flu is one of the most formidable infections confronting humankind. The virus mutates constantly as it circulates among birds, pigs, and human beings, so each new flu season now challenges experts . . . His message for our time is clear."　　　　　**—The New York Review of Books**

"Compelling and timely."　　　　**—The Boston Globe**

"Barry writes like an angel. . . . Through a vision of the scientists of the day he brings back the tension and excitement, the despair and the sorrow . . . yes I have indulged myself and read the book twice. . . . Barry's writing . . . manage[s] to capture the science of virology. . . . This book is a wake-up call."　**—Nature**

"Hypnotizing, horrifying, almost incomprehensible . . . energetic, lucid prose . . . His important story stands solidly and eloquently on its own as a work of history and a cautionary tale." —**The Providence Journal**

"History brilliantly written . . . **The Great Influenza** is a masterpiece." —**Baton Rouge Advocate**

"A medical thriller . . . It combines popular history and popular science in a way that reminds one of David McCullough's great books on the Johnstown flood and the building of the Panama Canal and the Brooklyn Bridge. **The Great Influenza** might be the most interesting such concoction since . . . well, since the same author's **Rising Tide: The Great Mississippi Flood of 1927 and How It Changed America.**"
—**Arkansas Times**

"What distinguishes Mr. Barry's account is its thoroughness and the writer's command of both the science and the politics that conspired to spread the disease . . . compelling . . . The storytelling is vivid . . . masterly detail." —**The Dallas Morning News**

"Majestic, spellbinding treatment of a mass killer . . . With the same terrorizing flair of Richard Preston's **Hot Zone,** the author follows the disease . . . as if from Weegee's camera."
—**Kirkus Reviews** (starred review)

"Barry puts the pandemic into a context of medical, national, and world history. . . . His well-researched and well-written account raises the obvious question: Could it happen again? And the answer is: Of course it could." **—Los Angeles Times**

"Barry provides enormous insight into the very nature of science . . . **The Great Influenza** is a must read for its unnerving relevance to today's scientific challenges of emerging and reemerging infectious diseases and the society's tragic confrontations with war and terrorism . . . alarming similarities to today . . . gripping."
—Ronald Atlas, former president
of the American Society of
Microbiology, **ASM News**

"Terrifying . . . The lessons of 1918 couldn't be more relevant." **—Newsweek**

"An enthralling symphony of a book, whose every page compels." **—Booklist** (starred review)

penguin books

THE GREAT

INFLUENZA

■ The Story of the Deadliest
Pandemic in History

JOHN M. BARRY

RANDOM HOUSE
LARGE PRINT

Cover photograph: Science History Images/Alamy Stock Photo
Cover design by studio ormus

Photograph credits appear on page 925.

The Library of Congress has established a
Cataloging-in-Publication record for this title.

ISBN: 978-0-593-34646-4

www.penguinrandomhouse.com/large-print-format-books

FIRST LARGE PRINT EDITION

Printed in the United States of America

10 9 8 7 6 5 4 3 2 1

This Large Print edition published in accord with
the standards of the N.A.V.H.

To my darling Anne
and to the spirit that was Paul Lewis

Contents

THE GREAT INFLUENZA

PROLOGUE

THE GREAT WAR had brought Paul Lewis into the navy in 1918 as a lieutenant commander, but he never seemed quite at ease when in his uniform. It never seemed to fit quite right, or to sit quite right, and he was often flustered and failed to respond properly when sailors saluted him.

Yet he was every bit a warrior, and he hunted death.

When he found it he confronted it, challenged it, tried to pin it in place like a lepidopterist pinning down a butterfly, so he could then dissect it piece by piece, analyze it, and find a way to confound it. He did so often enough that the risks he took became routine.

Still, death had never appeared to him as it did now, in mid-September 1918. Row after row of men confronted him in the hospital ward, many of them bloody and dying in some new and awful way.

He had been called here to solve a mystery that dumbfounded the clinicians. For Lewis was a scientist. Although a physician he had never practiced on a patient. Instead, a member of the very first generation of American medical scientists, he had spent his life in the laboratory. He had already built an extraordinary career, an international reputation, and he was still young enough to be seen as just coming into his prime.

A decade earlier, working with his mentor at the Rockefeller Institute in New York City, he had proved that a virus caused polio, a discovery still considered a landmark achievement in the history of virology. He had then developed a vaccine that protected monkeys from polio with nearly 100 percent effectiveness.

That and other successes had won him the position of founding head of the Henry Phipps Institute, a research institute associated with the University of Pennsylvania, and in 1917 he had been chosen for the great honor of giving the annual Harvey Lecture. It seemed only the first of many honors that would come his way. Today, the children of two prominent scientists who knew him then and who crossed paths with many Nobel laureates say their fathers each told them that Lewis was the smartest man they had ever met.

The clinicians now looked to him to explain the

violent symptoms these sailors presented. The blood that covered so many of them did not come from wounds, at least not from steel or explosives that had torn away limbs. Most of the blood had come from nosebleeds. A few sailors had coughed the blood up. Others had bled from their ears. Some coughed so hard that autopsies would later show they had torn apart abdominal muscles and rib cartilage. And many of the men writhed in agony or delirium; nearly all those able to communicate complained of headache, as if someone were hammering a wedge into their skulls just behind the eyes, and body aches so intense they felt like bones breaking. A few were vomiting. Finally the skin of some of the sailors had turned unusual colors; some showed just a tinge of blue around their lips or fingertips, but a few looked so dark one could not tell easily if they were Caucasian or Negro. They looked almost black.

Only once had Lewis seen a disease that in any way resembled this. Two months earlier, members of the crew of a British ship had been taken by ambulance from a sealed dock to another Philadelphia hospital and placed in isolation. There many of that crew had died. At autopsy their lungs had resembled those of men who had died from poison gas or pneumonic plague, a more virulent form of bubonic plague.

Whatever those crewmen had had, it had not spread. No one else had gotten sick.

But the men in the wards now not only puzzled Lewis. They had to have chilled him with fear also, fear both for himself and for what this disease could do. For whatever was attacking these sailors was not only spreading, it was spreading explosively.

And it was spreading despite a well-planned, concerted effort to contain it. This same disease had erupted ten days earlier at a navy facility in Boston. Lieutenant Commander Milton Rosenau at the Chelsea Naval Hospital there had certainly communicated to Lewis, whom he knew well, about it. Rosenau too was a scientist who had chosen to leave a Harvard professorship for the navy when the United States entered the war, and his textbook on public health was called "The Bible" by both army and navy military doctors.

Philadelphia navy authorities had taken Rosenau's warnings seriously, especially since a detachment of sailors had just arrived from Boston, and they had made preparations to isolate any ill sailors should an outbreak occur. They had been confident that isolation would control it.

Yet four days after that Boston detachment arrived, nineteen sailors in Philadelphia were hospitalized with what looked like the same disease. Despite their immediate isolation and that of everyone with whom they had had contact, eighty-seven sailors were hospitalized the next day. They and their contacts were again isolated. But two days later, six hundred men were hospitalized with this strange disease. The hospital ran out of empty beds, and hospital staff began falling ill. The navy then began sending hundreds more sick sailors to a civilian hospital. And sailors and civilian workers were moving constantly between the city and navy facilities, as they had in Boston. Meanwhile, personnel from Boston, and now Philadelphia, had been and were being sent throughout the country as well.

That had to chill Lewis, too.

Lewis had visited the first patients, taken blood, urine, and sputum samples, done nasal washings, and swabbed their throats. Then he had come back again to repeat the process of collecting samples and to study the symptoms for any further clues. In his laboratory he and everyone under him poured their energies into growing and identifying whatever pathogen was making the men sick. He needed to find the pathogen. He needed to find the cause of the disease. And even more he needed to make a curative serum or a preventive vaccine.

Lewis loved the laboratory more than he loved anyone or anything. His work space was crammed; it looked like a thicket of icicles—test tubes in racks, stacked petri dishes, pipettes—but it warmed him, gave him as much and perhaps more comfort than did his home and family. But he did not love working like this. The pressure to find an answer did not bother him; much of his polio research had been conducted in the midst of an epidemic so extreme that New York City had required people to obtain passes to travel. What did bother him was the need to abandon good science. To succeed in preparing either a vaccine or a serum, he would have to make a series of guesses based on at best inconclusive results, and each guess would have to be right.

He had already made one guess. If he did not yet know precisely what caused the disease, nor how or whether he could prevent it or cure it, he believed he knew what the disease was.

He believed it was influenza, although an influenza unlike any known before.

Lewis was correct. In 1918 an influenza virus emerged—probably in the United States—that would spread around the world, and one of its earliest appearances in lethal form came in Philadelphia. Before that worldwide pandemic faded away in 1920, it would kill more people than any other outbreak of disease in human history. Plague in the 1300s killed a far larger proportion of the population—more than one-quarter of Europe—but in raw numbers influenza killed more than plague then, more than AIDS today.

The lowest estimate of the pandemic's worldwide death toll is twenty-one million, in a world with a population less than one-third today's. That estimate comes from a contemporary study of the disease and newspapers have often cited it since, but it is almost certainly wrong. Epidemiologists today estimate that influenza likely caused at least fifty million deaths worldwide, and possibly as many as one hundred million.

Yet even that number understates the horror of the disease, a horror contained in other data. Normally influenza chiefly kills the elderly and infants, but in the 1918 pandemic roughly half of those who died were young men and women in the prime of their life, in their twenties and thirties. Harvey Cushing, then a brilliant young surgeon who would go on to great fame—and who himself fell desperately ill with influenza and never fully recovered from what was likely a complication—would call these victims "doubly dead in that they died so young."

One cannot know with certainty, but if the upper estimate of the death toll is true as many as 8 to 10 percent of all young adults then living may have been killed by the virus.

And they died with extraordinary ferocity and speed. Although the influenza pandemic stretched over two years, perhaps two-thirds of the deaths occurred in a period of twenty-four weeks, and more than half of those deaths occurred in even less time, from mid-September to early December 1918. Influenza killed more people in a year than the Black Death of the Middle Ages killed in a century; it killed more people in twenty-four weeks than AIDS has killed in twenty-four years.

The influenza pandemic resembled both of those scourges in other ways also. Like AIDS, it killed

those with the most to live for. And as priests
had done in the bubonic plague, in 1918, even in
Philadelphia, as modern a city as existed in the
world, priests would drive horse-drawn wagons
down the streets, calling upon those behind doors
shut tight in terror to bring out their dead.

Yet the story of the 1918 influenza virus is not
simply one of havoc, death, and desolation, of a society fighting a war against nature superimposed on
a war against another human society.

It is also a story of science, of discovery, of how
one thinks, and of how one changes the way one
thinks, of how amidst near-utter chaos a few men
sought the coolness of contemplation, the utter
calm that precedes not philosophizing but grim,
determined action.

For the influenza pandemic that erupted in 1918
was the first great collision between nature and
modern science. It was the first great collision between a natural force and a society that included individuals who refused either to submit to that force
or to simply call upon divine intervention to save
themselves from it, individuals who instead were
determined to confront this force directly, with a
developing technology and with their minds.

In the United States, the story is particularly one
of a handful of extraordinary people, of whom Paul
Lewis is one. These were men and some very few
women who, far from being backward, had already

developed the fundamental science upon which much of today's medicine is based. They had already developed vaccines and antitoxins and techniques still in use. They had already pushed, in some cases, close to the edge of knowledge today.

In a way, these researchers had spent much of their lives preparing for the confrontation that occurred in 1918 not only in general but, for a few of them at least, quite specifically. In every war in American history so far, disease had killed more soldiers than combat. In many wars throughout history, war had spread disease. The leaders of American research had anticipated that a major epidemic of some kind would erupt during the Great War. They had prepared for it as much as it was possible to prepare. Then they waited for it to strike.

The story, however, begins earlier. Before medicine could confront this disease with any promise of effect, it had to become scientific. It had to be revolutionized.

Medicine is not yet and may never be fully a science—the idiosyncrasies, physical and otherwise, of individual patients and doctors may prevent that—but, up to a few decades before World War I, the practice of medicine had remained quite literally almost unchanged from the time of Hippocrates more than two thousand years earlier. Then, in Europe first, medical science changed and, finally, the practice of medicine changed.

But even after European medicine changed, medicine in the United States did not. In research and education especially, American medicine lagged far behind, and that made practice lag as well.

While for decades European medical schools had, for example, required students to have a solid background in chemistry, biology, and other sciences, as late as 1900, it was more difficult to get into a respectable American college than into an American medical school. At least one hundred U.S. medical schools would accept any man—but not woman—willing to pay tuition; at most 20 percent of the schools required even a high school diploma for admission—much less any academic training in science—and only a single medical school required its students to have a college degree. Nor, once students entered, did American schools necessarily make up for any lack of scientific background. Many schools bestowed a medical degree upon students who simply attended lectures and passed examinations; in some, students could fail several courses, never touch a single patient, and still get a medical degree.

Not until late—very late—in the nineteenth century, did a virtual handful of leaders of American medical science begin to plan a revolution that transformed American medicine from the most backward in the developed world into the best in the world.

William James, who was a friend of—and whose

son would work for—several of these men, wrote that the collecting of a critical mass of men of genius could make a whole civilization "vibrate and shake." These men intended to, and would, shake the world.

To do so required not only intelligence and training but real courage, the courage to relinquish all support and all authority. Or perhaps it required only recklessness.

In **Faust,** Goethe wrote,

> 'Tis writ, "In the beginning was the Word."
> I Pause, to wonder what is here inferred.
> The Word I cannot set supremely high:
> A new translation I will try.
> I read, if by the spirit, I am taught,
> This sense, "In the beginning was the
>   Thought. . . ."

Upon "the Word" rested authority, stability, and law; "the Thought" roiled and ripped apart and created—without knowledge or concern of what it would create.

Shortly before the Great War began, the men who so wanted to transform American medicine succeeded. They created a system that could produce people capable of thinking in a new way, capable of challenging the natural order. They, together with the first generation of scientists they had trained—Paul Lewis and his few peers—formed a cadre who stood on alert, hoping against but expecting and preparing for the eruption of an epidemic.

When it came, they placed their lives in the path of the disease and applied all their knowledge and powers to defeat it. As it overwhelmed them, they concentrated on constructing the body of knowledge necessary to eventually triumph. For the scientific knowledge that ultimately came out of the influenza pandemic pointed directly—and still points—to much that lies in medicine's future.

■ Part I
THE WARRIORS

CHAPTER ONE

ON SEPTEMBER 12, 1876, the crowd overflowing the auditorium of Baltimore's Academy of Music was in a mood of hopeful excitement, but excitement without frivolity. Indeed, despite an unusual number of women in attendance, many of them from the uppermost reaches of local society, a reporter noted, "There was no display of dress or fashion." For this occasion had serious purpose. It was to mark the launching of the Johns Hopkins University, an institution whose leaders intended not simply to found a new university but to change all of American education; indeed, they sought considerably more than that. They planned to change the way in which Americans tried to understand and grapple with nature. The keynote speaker, the English scientist Thomas H. Huxley, personified their goals.

The import was not lost on the nation. Many newspapers, including the **New York Times,** had reporters covering this event. After it, they would print Huxley's address in full.

For the nation was then, as it so often has been, at war with itself; in fact it was engaged in different wars simultaneously, each being waged on several fronts, wars that ran along the fault lines of modern America.

One involved expansion and race. In the Dakotas, George Armstrong Custer had just led the Seventh Cavalry to its destruction at the hands of primitive savages resisting encroachment of the white man. The day Huxley spoke, the front page of the **Washington Star** reported that "the hostile Sioux, well fed and well armed" had just carried out "a massacre of miners."

In the South a far more important but equally savage war was being waged as white Democrats sought "redemption" from Reconstruction in anticipation of the presidential election. Throughout the South "rifle clubs," "saber clubs," and "rifle teams" of former Confederates were being organized into infantry and cavalry units. Already accounts of intimidation, beatings, whippings, and murder directed against Republicans and blacks had surfaced. After the murder of three hundred black men in a single Mississippi county, one man, convinced that words from the Democrats' own mouths would convince the world of their design, pleaded with the **New York Times,** "For God's sake publish the testimony of the Democrats before the Grand Jury."

Voting returns had already begun to come in—there was no single national election day—and two months later Democrat Samuel Tilden would win the popular vote by a comfortable margin. But he would never take office as president. Instead the Republican secretary of war would threaten to "force a reversal" of the vote, federal troops with fixed bayonets would patrol Washington, and southerners would talk of reigniting the Civil War. That crisis would ultimately be resolved through an extra-constitutional special committee and a political understanding: Republicans would discard the voting returns of three states—Louisiana, Florida, South Carolina—and seize a single disputed electoral vote in Oregon to keep the presidency in the person of Rutherford B. Hayes. But they also would withdraw all federal troops from the South and cease intervening in southern affairs, leaving the Negroes there to fend for themselves.

The war involving the Hopkins was more muted but no less profound. The outcome would help define one element of the character of the nation: the extent to which the nation would accept or reject modern science and, to a lesser degree, how secular it would become, how godly it would remain.

Precisely at 11:00 A.M., a procession of people

advanced upon the stage. First came Daniel Coit
Gilman, president of the Hopkins, and on his arm
was Huxley. Following in single file came the governor, the mayor, and other notables. As they took
their seats the conversations in the audience quickly
died away, replaced by expectancy of a kind of declaration of war.

Of medium height and middle age—though
he already had iron-gray hair and nearly white
whiskers—and possessed of what was described as
"a pleasant face," Huxley did not look the warrior.
But he had a warrior's ruthlessness. His dicta included the pronouncement: "The foundation of mo-
rality is to have done, once and for all, with lying."
A brilliant scientist, later president of the Royal
Society, he advised investigators, "Sit down before
a fact as a little child, be prepared to give up every
preconceived notion. Follow humbly wherever and
to whatever abysses nature leads, or you shall learn
nothing." He also believed that learning had purpose, stating, "The great end of life is not knowledge but action."

To act upon the world himself, he became a
proselytizer for faith in human reason. By 1876 he
had become the world's foremost advocate of the
theory of evolution and of science itself. Indeed,
H. L. Mencken said that "it was he, more than
any other man, who worked that great change in
human thought which marked the Nineteenth
Century." Now President Gilman gave a brief and

simple introduction. Then Professor Huxley began to speak.

Normally he lectured on evolution, but today he was speaking on a subject of even greater magnitude. He was speaking about the process of intellectual inquiry. The Hopkins was to be unlike any other university in America. Aiming almost exclusively at the education of graduate students and the furtherance of science, it was intended by its trustees to rival not Harvard or Yale—neither of them considered worthy of emulation—but the greatest institutions of Europe, and particularly Germany. Perhaps only in the United States, a nation ever in the act of creating itself, could such an institution come into existence both so fully formed in concept and already so renowned, even before the foundation of a single building had been laid.

"His voice was low, clear and distinct," reported one listener. "The audience paid the closest attention to every word which fell from the lecturer's lips, occasionally manifesting their approval by applause." Said another, "Professor Huxley's method is slow, precise, and clear, and he guards the positions which he takes with astuteness and ability. He does not utter anything in the reckless fashion which conviction sometimes countenances and excuses, but rather with the deliberation that research and close inquiry foster."

Huxley commended the bold goals of the Hopkins, expounded upon his own theories of education—theories that soon informed those of William James and John Dewey—and extolled the fact that the existence of the Hopkins meant "finally, that neither political nor ecclesiastical sectarianism" would interfere with the pursuit of the truth.

In truth, Huxley's speech, read a century and a quarter later, seems remarkably tame. Yet Huxley and the entire ceremony left an impression on the country deep enough that Gilman would spend years trying to edge away from it, even while simultaneously trying to fulfill the goals Huxley applauded.

For the ceremony's most significant word was one not spoken: not a single participant uttered the word "God" or made any reference to the Almighty. This spectacular omission scandalized those who worried about or rejected a mechanistic and necessarily godless view of the universe. And it came in an era in which American universities had nearly two hundred endowed chairs of theology and fewer than five in medicine, an era in which the president of Drew University had said that, after much study and experience, he had concluded that only ministers of the Gospel should be college professors.

The omission also served as a declaration: the Hopkins would pursue the truth, no matter to what abyss it led.

In no area did the truth threaten so much as in the study of life. In no area did the United States lag behind the rest of the world so much as in its study of the life sciences and medicine. And in that area in particular, the influence of the Hopkins would be immense.

By 1918, as America marched into war, the nation had come not only to rely upon the changes wrought largely, though certainly not entirely, by men associated with the Hopkins; the United States Army had mobilized these men into a special force, focused and disciplined, ready to hurl themselves at an enemy.

The two most important questions in science are "What can I know?" and "How can I know it?"

Science and religion in fact part ways over the first question, what each can know. Religion, and to some extent philosophy, believes it can know, or at least address, the question "Why?"

For most religions the answer to this question ultimately comes down to the way God ordered it. Religion is inherently conservative; even one proposing a new God only creates a new order.

The question "why" is too deep for science. Science instead believes it can only learn "how" something occurs.

The revolution of modern science and especially medical science began as science not only focused on this answer to "What can I know?" but more important, changed its method of inquiry, changed its answer to "How can I know it?"

This answer involves not simply academic pursuits; it affects how a society governs itself, its structure, how its citizens live. If a society does set Goethe's "Word . . . supremely high," if it believes that it **knows** the truth and that it need not question its beliefs, then that society is more likely to enforce rigid decrees, and less likely to change. If it leaves room for doubt about the truth, it is more likely to be free and open.

In the narrower context of science, the answer determines how individuals explore nature—how one does science. And the way one goes about answering a question, one's methodology, matters as much as the question itself. For the method of inquiry underlies knowledge and often determines what one discovers: how one pursues a question often dictates, or at least limits, the answer.

Indeed, methodology matters more than anything else. Methodology subsumes, for example, Thomas Kuhn's well-known theory of how science advances. Kuhn gave the word "paradigm" wide usage by arguing that at any given point in time, a particular paradigm, a kind of perceived truth, dominates the thinking in any science. Others have applied his concept to nonscientific fields as well.

According to Kuhn, the prevailing paradigm tends to freeze progress, indirectly by creating a mental obstacle to creative ideas and directly by, for example, blocking research funds from going to truly new ideas, especially if they conflict with the paradigm. He argues that nonetheless researchers eventually find what he calls "anomalies" that do not fit the paradigm. Each one erodes the foundation of the paradigm, and when enough accrue to undermine it, the paradigm collapses. Scientists then cast about for a new paradigm that explains both the old and the new facts.

But the process—and progress—of science is more fluid than Kuhn's concept suggests. It moves more like an amoeba, with soft and ill-defined edges. More important, method matters. Kuhn's own theory recognizes that the propelling force behind the movement from one explanation to another comes from the methodology, from what we call the scientific method. But he takes as an axiom that those who ask questions constantly test existing hypotheses. In fact, with a methodology that probes and tests hypotheses—regardless of any paradigm—progress is inevitable. Without such a methodology, progress becomes merely coincidental.

Yet the scientific method has not always been used by those who inquire into nature. Through most of known history, investigators trying to penetrate the natural world, penetrate what we call science, relied upon the mind alone, reason alone. These investigators believed that they could know a thing if their knowledge followed logically from what they considered a sound premise. In turn they based their premises chiefly on observation.

This commitment to logic coupled with man's ambition to see the entire world in a comprehensive and cohesive way actually imposed blinders on science in general and on medicine in particular. The chief enemy of progress, ironically, became pure reason. And for the bulk of two and a half millennia—twenty-five hundred years—the actual treatment of patients by physicians made almost no progress at all.

One cannot blame religion or superstition for this lack of progress. In the West, beginning at least five hundred years before the birth of Christ, medicine was largely secular. While Hippocratic healers—the various Hippocratic texts were written by different people—did run temples and accept pluralistic explanations for disease, they pushed for material explanations.

Hippocrates himself was born in approximately 460 B.C. **On the Sacred Disease,** one of the more famous Hippocratic texts and one often attributed to him directly, even mocked theories that attributed epilepsy to the intervention of gods. He and his followers advocated precise observation, then theorizing. As the texts stated, "For a theory is a composite memory of things apprehended with sense perception." "But conclusions which are merely verbal cannot bear fruit." "I approve of theorizing also if it lays its foundation in incident, and deduces its conclusion in accordance with phenomena."

But if such an approach sounds like that of a modern investigator, a modern scientist, it lacked two singularly important elements.

■   ■   ■

First, Hippocrates and his associates merely observed nature. They did not probe it.

This failure to probe nature was to some extent understandable. To dissect a human body then was inconceivable. But the authors of the Hippocratic texts did not test their conclusions and theories. A theory must make a prediction to be useful or scientific—ultimately it must say, **If this, then that**—and testing that prediction is the single most important element of modern methodology. Once that prediction is tested, it must advance another one for testing. It can never stand still.

Those who wrote the Hippocratic texts, however, observed passively and reasoned actively. Their careful observations noted mucus discharges, menstrual bleeding, watery evacuations in dysentery, and they very likely observed blood left to stand, which over time separates into several layers, one nearly clear, one of somewhat yellowy serum, one of darker blood. Based on these observations, they hypothesized that there were four kinds of bodily fluids, or "humours": blood, phlegm, bile, and black bile. (This terminology survives today in the phrase "humoral immunity," which refers to elements of the immune system, such as antibodies, that circulate in the blood.)

This hypothesis made sense, comported with observations, and could explain many symptoms. It explained, for example, that coughs were caused by the flow of phlegm to the chest. Observations of people coughing up phlegm certainly supported this conclusion.

In a far broader sense, the hypothesis also conformed to the ways in which the Greeks saw nature: they observed four seasons, four aspects of the environment—cold, hot, wet, and dry—and four elements—earth, air, fire, and water.

Medicine waited six hundred years for the next major advance, for Galen, but Galen did not break from these teachings; he systematized them, perfected them. Galen claimed, "I have done as much for medicine as Trajan did for the Roman Empire when he built the bridges and roads through Italy. It is I, and I alone, who have revealed the true path of medicine. It must be admitted that Hippocrates already staked out this path. . . . He prepared the way, but I have made it possible."

Galen did not simply observe passively. He dissected animals and, although he did not perform autopsies on humans, served as a physician to gladiators whose wounds allowed him to see deep beneath the skin. Thus his anatomic knowledge went far beyond that of any known predecessor. But he remained chiefly a theoretician, a logician; he imposed order on the Hippocratic body of work, reconciling conflicts, reasoning so clearly that, if one accepted his premises, his conclusions seemed inevitable. He made the humoral theory perfectly logical, and even elegant. As the historian Vivian Nutton notes, Galen raised the theory to a truly conceptual level, separating the humours from direct correlation with bodily fluids and making them invisible entities "recognizable only by logic."

Galen's works were translated into Arabic and underlay both Western and Islamic medicine for nearly fifteen hundred years before facing any significant challenge. Like the Hippocratic writers, Galen believed that illness was essentially the result of an imbalance in the body. He also thought that balance could be restored by intervention; a physician thus could treat a disease successfully. If there was a poison in the body, then the poison could be removed by evacuation. Sweating, urinating, defecating, and vomiting were all ways that could restore balance. Such beliefs led physicians to recommend violent laxatives and other purgatives, as well as mustard plasters and other prescriptions that punished the body, that blistered it and theoretically restored balance. And of all the practices of medicine over the centuries, one of the most enduring—yet least understandable to us today—was a perfectly logical extension of Hippocratic and Galenic thought, and recommended by both.

This practice was bleeding patients. Bleeding was among the most common therapies employed to treat all manner of disorders.

Hippocrates and most of those who followed him—even deep into the nineteenth century—also believed that natural processes must not be interfered with. The various kinds of purging were meant to augment and accelerate natural processes, not resist them. Since pus, for example, was routinely seen in all kinds of wounds, pus was seen as a necessary part of healing. Until the late 1800s, physicians routinely would do nothing to avoid the generation of pus, and were reluctant even to drain it. Instead they referred to "laudable pus."

Similarly, Hippocrates scorned surgery as intrusive, as interfering with nature's course; further, he saw it as a purely mechanical skill, beneath the calling of physicians who dealt in a far more intellectual realm. This intellectual arrogance would subsume the attitude of Western physicians for more than two thousand years.

This is not to say that for two thousand years the Hippocratic texts and Galen offered the only theoretical constructs to explain health and disease. Many ideas and theories were advanced about how the body worked, how illness developed. And a rival school of thought gradually developed within the Hippocratic-Galenic tradition that valued experience and empiricism and challenged the purely theoretical.

It is impossible to summarize all these theories in a few sentences, yet nearly all of them did share certain concepts: that health was a state of equilibrium and balance, and that illness resulted either from an internal imbalance within the body or from external environmental influences such as an atmospheric miasma, or from some combination of both.

But in the early 1500s three men began to challenge at least the methods of medicine. Paracelsus declared he would investigate nature "not by following that which those of old taught, but by our own observation of nature, confirmed by . . . experiment and by reasoning thereon."

Vesalius dissected human corpses and concluded that Galen's findings had come from animals and were deeply flawed. His **De humani corporis fabrica,** likely illustrated by a student of Titian, became a cornerstone of the Renaissance.

Fracastorius, an astronomer, mathematician, botanist, and poet, meanwhile hypothesized that diseases had specific causes and that contagion "passes from one thing to another and is originally caused by infection of the imperceptible particle." One medical historian called his body of work "a peak maybe unequalled by anyone between Hippocrates and Pasteur."

The contemporaries of these three men included Martin Luther and Copernicus, men who changed the world. In medicine the new ideas of Paracelsus, Vesalius, and Fracastorius did not change the world. In the actual practice of medicine they changed nothing at all.

But the approach they called for did create ripples while the scholasticism of the Middle Ages that stultified nearly all fields of inquiry was beginning to decay. In 1605 Francis Bacon in **Novum Organum** attacked the purely deductive reasoning of logic, calling "Aristotle . . . a mere bondservant to his logic, thereby rendering it contentious and well nigh useless." He also complained, "The logic now in use serves rather to fix and give stability to the errors which have their foundation in commonly received notions than to help the search after truth. So it does more harm than good."

In 1628 Harvey traced the circulation of the blood, arguably perhaps the single greatest achievement of medicine—and certainly the greatest achievement until the late 1800s. And Europe was in intellectual ferment. Half a century later Newton revolutionized physics and mathematics. Newton's contemporary John Locke, trained as a physician, emphasized the pursuit of knowledge through experience. In 1753 James Lind conducted a pioneering controlled experiment among British sailors and demonstrated that scurvy could be prevented by eating limes—ever since, the British have been called "limeys." David Hume, after this demonstration and following Locke, led a movement of "empiricism." His contemporary John Hunter made a brilliant scientific study of surgery, elevating it from a barber's craft. Hunter also performed model scientific experiments, including some on himself—as when he infected himself with pus from a gonorrheal case to prove a hypothesis.

Then in 1798 Edward Jenner, a student of Hunter's—Hunter had told him "Don't think. Try."—published his work. As a young medical student Jenner had heard a milkmaid say, "I cannot take the smallpox because I have had cowpox." The cowpox virus resembles smallpox so closely that exposure to cowpox gives immunity to smallpox. But cowpox itself only rarely develops into a serious disease. (The virus that causes cowpox is called "vaccinia," taking its name from vaccination.)

Jenner's work with cowpox was a landmark, but not because he was the first to immunize people against smallpox. In China, India, and Persia, different techniques had long since been developed to expose children to smallpox and make them immune, and in Europe at least as early as the 1500s laypeople—not physicians—took material from a pustule of those with a mild case of smallpox and scratched it into the skin of those who had not yet caught the disease. Most people infected this way developed mild cases and became immune. In 1721 in Massachusetts, Cotton Mather took the advice of an African slave, tried this technique, and staved off a lethal epidemic. But "variolation" could kill. Vaccinating with cowpox was far safer than variolation.

From a scientific standpoint, however, Jenner's most important contribution was his rigorous methodology. Of his finding, he said, "I placed it upon a rock where I knew it would be immoveable before I invited the public to take a look at it."

But ideas die hard. Even as Jenner was conducting his experiments, despite the vast increase in knowledge of the body derived from Harvey and Hunter, medical practice had barely changed. And many, if not most, physicians who thought deeply about medicine still saw it in terms of logic and observation alone.

In Philadelphia, twenty-two hundred years after Hippocrates and sixteen hundred years after Galen, Benjamin Rush, a pioneer in his views on mental illness, a signer of the Declaration of Independence, and America's most prominent physician, still applied logic and observation alone to build "a more simple and consistent system of medicine than the world had yet seen."

In 1796 he advanced a hypothesis as logical and elegant, he believed, as Newtonian physics. Observing that all fevers were associated with flushed skin, he concluded that this was caused by distended capillaries and reasoned that the proximate cause of fever must be abnormal "convulsive action" in these vessels. He took this a step further and concluded that **all** fevers resulted from disturbance of capillaries, and, since the capillaries were part of the circulatory system, he concluded that a hypertension of the entire circulatory system was involved. Rush proposed to reduce this convulsive action by "depletion," i.e., venesection—bleeding. It made perfect sense.

He was one of the most aggressive of the advocates of "heroic medicine." The heroism, of course, was found in the patient. In the early 1800s praise for his theories was heard throughout Europe, and one London physician said Rush united "in an almost unprecedented degree, sagacity and judgment."

A reminder of the medical establishment's acceptance of bleeding exists today in the name of the British journal **The Lancet,** one of the leading medical journals in the world. A lancet was the instrument physicians used to cut into a patient's vein.

But if the first failing of medicine, a failing that endured virtually unchallenged for two millennia and then only gradually eroded over the next three centuries, was that it did not probe nature through experiments, that it simply observed and reasoned from observation to a conclusion, that failing was—finally—about to be corrected.

What can I know? How can I know it?

If reason alone could solve mathematical problems, if Newton could think his way through physics, then why could not man reason out the ways in which the body worked? Why did reason alone fail so utterly in medicine?

One explanation is that Hippocratic and Galenic theory did offer a system of therapeutics that seemed to produce the desired effect. They seemed to work. So the Hippocratic-Galenic model lasted so long not only because of its logical consistency, but because its therapies seemed to have effect.

Indeed, bleeding—today called "phlebotomy"— can actually help in some rare diseases, such as polycythemia, a rare genetic disorder that causes people to make too much blood, or hemachromatosis, when the blood carries too much iron. And in far more common cases of acute pulmonary edema, when the lungs fill with fluid, it could relieve immediate symptoms and is still sometimes tried. For example, in congestive heart failure excess fluid in the lungs can make victims extremely uncomfortable and, ultimately, kill them if the heart cannot pump the fluid out. When people suffering from these conditions were bled, they may well have been helped. This reinforced theory.

Even when physicians observed that bleeding weakened the patient, that weakening could still seem positive. If a patient was flushed with a fever, it followed logically that if bleeding alleviated those symptoms—making the patient pale—it was a good thing. If it made the patient pale it worked.

Finally, a euphoric feeling sometimes accompanies blood loss. This too reinforced theory. So bleeding both made logical sense in the Hippocratic and Galenic systems and sometimes gave physicians and patients positive reinforcement.

Other therapies also did what they were designed to do—in a sense. As late as the nineteenth century—until well after the Civil War in the United States—most physicians and patients still saw the body only as an interdependent whole, still saw a specific symptom as a result of an imbalance or disequilibrium in the entire body, still saw illness chiefly as something within and generated by the body itself. As the historian Charles Rosenberg has pointed out, even smallpox, despite its known clinical course and the fact that vaccination prevented it, was still seen as a manifestation of a systemic ill. And medical traditions outside the Hippocratic-Galenic model—from the "subluxations" of chiropractic to the "yin and yang" of Chinese medicine—have also tended to see disease as a result of imbalance within the body.

Physicians and patients wanted therapies to augment and accelerate, not block, the natural course of disease, the natural healing process. The state of the body could be altered by prescribing such toxic substances as mercury, arsenic, antimony, and iodine. Therapies designed to blister the body did so. Therapies designed to produce sweating or vomiting did so. One doctor, for example, when confronted with a case of pleurisy, gave camphor and recorded that the case was "suddenly relieved by profuse perspiration." His intervention, he believed, had cured.

Yet a patient's improvement, of course, does not prove that a therapy works. For example, the 1889 edition of the **Merck Manual of Medical Information** recommended one hundred treatments for bronchitis, each one with its fervent believers, yet the current editor of the manual recognizes that "none of them worked." The manual also recommended, among other things, champagne, strychnine, and nitroglycerin for seasickness.

And when a therapy clearly did not work, the intricacies—and intimacies—of the doctor-patient relationship also came into play, injecting emotion into the equation. One truth has not changed from the time of Hippocrates until today: when faced with desperate patients, doctors often do not have the heart—or, more accurately, they have too much heart—to do nothing. And so a doctor, as desperate as the patient, may try anything, including things he or she knows will not work as long as they will not harm. At the least, the patient will get some solace.

One cancer specialist concedes, "I do virtually the same thing myself. If I'm treating a teary, desperate patient, I will try low-dose alpha interferon, even though I do not believe it has ever cured a single person. It doesn't have side effects, and it gives the patient hope."

Cancer provides other examples as well. No truly scientific evidence shows that echinacea has any effect on cancer, yet it is widely prescribed in Germany today for terminal cancer patients. Japanese physicians routinely prescribe placebos in treatment. Steven Rosenberg, a National Cancer Institute scientist who was the first person to stimulate the immune system to cure cancer and who led the team that performed the first human gene therapy experiments, points out that for years chemotherapy was recommended to virtually all victims of pancreatic cancer even though not a single chemotherapy regimen had ever been shown to prolong their lives for one day. (At this writing, investigators have just demonstrated that gemcitabine can extend median life expectancy by one to two months, but it is highly toxic.)

Another explanation for the failure of logic and observation alone to advance medicine is that unlike, say, physics, which uses a form of logic—mathematics—as its natural language, biology does not lend itself to logic. Leo Szilard, a prominent physicist, made this point when he complained that after switching from physics to biology he never had a peaceful bath again. As a physicist he would soak in the warmth of a bathtub and contemplate a problem, turn it in his mind, reason his way through it. But once he became a biologist, he constantly had to climb out of the bathtub to look up a fact.

In fact, biology is chaos. Biological systems are the product not of logic but of evolution, an inelegant process. Life does not choose the logically best design to meet a new situation. It adapts what already exists. Much of the human genome includes genes which are "conserved"; i.e., which are essentially the same as those in much simpler species. Evolution has built upon what already exists.

The result, unlike the clean straight lines of logic, is often irregular, messy. An analogy might be building an energy efficient farmhouse. If one starts from scratch, logic would impel the use of

certain building materials, the design of windows
and doors with kilowatt-hours in mind, perhaps
the inclusion of solar panels on the roof, and so on.
But if one wants to make an eighteenth-century
farmhouse energy efficient, one adapts it as well as
possible. One proceeds logically, doing things that
make good sense given what one starts with, given
the existing farmhouse. One seals and caulks and
insulates and puts in a new furnace or heat pump.
The old farmhouse will be—maybe—the best one
could do given where one started, but it will be irregular; in window size, in ceiling height, in building materials, it will bear little resemblance to a new
farmhouse designed from scratch for maximum
energy efficiency.

For logic to be of use in biology, one has to apply
it from a given starting point, using the then-extant
rules of the game. Hence Szilard had to climb out
of the bathtub to look up a fact.

Ultimately, then, logic and observation failed
to penetrate the workings of the body not because
of the power of the Hippocratic hypothesis, the
Hippocratic paradigm. Logic and observation failed
because neither one tested the hypothesis rigorously.

Once investigators began to apply something
akin to the modern scientific method, the old hypothesis collapsed.

By 1800 enormous advances had been made in
other sciences, beginning centuries earlier with a

revolution in the use of quantitative measurement. Bacon and Descartes, although opposites in their views of the usefulness of pure logic, had both provided a philosophical framework for new ways of seeing the natural world. Newton had in a way bridged their differences, advancing mathematics through logic while relying upon experiment and observation for confirmation. Joseph Priestley, Henry Cavendish, and Antoine-Laurent Lavoisier created modern chemistry and penetrated the natural world. Particularly important for biology was Lavoisier's decoding of the chemistry of combustion and use of those insights to uncover the chemical processes of respiration, of breathing.

Still, all these advances notwithstanding, in 1800 Hippocrates and Galen would have recognized and largely agreed with most medical practice. In 1800 medicine remained what one historian called "the withered arm of science."

In the nineteenth century that finally began to change—and with extraordinary rapidity. Perhaps the greatest break came with the French Revolution, when the new French government established what came to be called "the Paris clinical school." One leader of the movement was Xavier Bichat, who dissected organs, found them composed of discrete types of material often found in layers, and called them "tissues"; another was René Laennec, inventor of the stethoscope.

Meanwhile, medicine began to make use of other

objective measurements and mathematics. This too was new. Hippocratic writings had stated that the physician's senses mattered far more than any objective measurement, so despite medicine's use of logic, physicians had always avoided applying mathematics to the study of the body or disease. In the 1820s, two hundred years **after** the discovery of thermometers, French clinicians began using them. Clinicians also began taking advantage of methods discovered in the 1700s to measure other bodily functions precisely.

By then in Paris, Pierre Louis had taken an even more significant step. In the hospitals, where hundreds of charity cases awaited help, using the most basic mathematical analysis—nothing more than arithmetic—he correlated the different treatments patients received for the same disease with the results. For the first time in history, a physician was creating a reliable and systematic database. Physicians could have done this earlier. To do so required neither microscopes nor technological prowess; it required only taking careful notes.

Yet the real point at which modern medicine diverged from the classic was in the studies of pathological anatomy by Louis and others. Louis not only correlated treatments with results to reach a conclusion about a treatment's efficacy (he rejected bleeding patients as a useless therapy), he and others also used autopsies to correlate the condition of organs with symptoms. He and others dissected organs, compared diseased organs to healthy ones, learned their functions in intimate detail.

What he found was astounding, and compelling, and helped lead to a new conception of disease as something with an identity of its own, an objective existence. In the 1600s Thomas Sydenham had begun classifying diseases, but Sydenham and most of his followers continued to see disease as a result of imbalances, consistent with Hippocrates and Galen. Now a new "nosology," a new classification and listing of disease, began to evolve.

Disease began to be seen as something that invaded solid parts of the body, as an independent entity, instead of being a derangement of the blood. This was a fundamental first step in what would become a revolution.

Louis's influence and that of what became known as "the numerical system" could not be overstated. These advances—the stethoscope, laryngoscope, ophthalmoscope, the measurements of temperature and blood pressure, the study of parts of the body—all created distance between the doctor and the patient, as well as between patient and disease; they objectified humanity. Even though no less a personage than Michel Foucault condemned this Parisian movement as the first to turn the human body into an object, these steps had to come to make progress in medicine.

But the movement was condemned by contemporaries also. Complained one typical critic, "The practice of medicine according to this view is entirely empirical, is shorn of all rational induction, and takes a position among the lower grades of experimental observations and fragmentary facts."

Criticism notwithstanding, the numerical system began winning convert after convert. In England in the 1840s and 1850s, John Snow began applying mathematics in a new way: as an epidemiologist. He had made meticulous observations of the patterns of a cholera outbreak, noting who got sick and who did not, where the sick lived and how they lived, where the healthy lived and how they lived. He tracked the disease down to a contaminated well in London. He concluded that contaminated water caused the disease. It was brilliant detective work, brilliant epidemiology. William Budd borrowed Snow's methodology and promptly applied it to the study of typhoid.

Snow and Budd needed no scientific knowledge, no laboratory findings, to reach their conclusions. And they did so in the 1850s, before the development of the germ theory of disease. Like Louis's study that proved that bleeding was worse than useless in nearly all circumstances, their work could have been conducted a century earlier or ten centuries earlier. But their work reflected a new way of looking at the world, a new way of seeking explanations, a new methodology, a new use of mathematics as an analytical tool.*

At the same time, medicine was advancing by borrowing from other sciences. Insights from physics allowed investigators to trace electrical impulses through nerve fibers. Chemists were breaking down the cell into its components. And when investigators

---

* The effort to correlate treatments and results has not yet triumphed. A "new" movement called "evidence-based medicine" has emerged recently, which continues to try to determine the best treatments and communicate them to physicians. No good physician today would discard the value of statistics, of evidence accumulated systematically in careful studies. But individual doctors, convinced either by anecdotal evidence from their own personal experience or by tradition, still criticize the use of statistics and probabilities to determine treatments and accept conclusions only reluctantly. Despite convincing studies, for example, it took years before cancer surgeons stopped doing radical mastectomies for all breast cancers.

A related issue involves the methodology in "clinical studies"— i.e., studies using people. To stay with cancer as an example, Vince DeVita, former director of the National Cancer Institute; Samuel Hellman, a leading oncologist; and Steven Rosenberg, chief of the Surgery Branch of the National Cancer Institute coauthor a standard reference for physicians on cancer treatments. DeVita and Rosenberg believe that carefully controlled randomized studies—experiments in which random chance determines the treatment given a patient—are necessary to find out what treatment works best. Yet Hellman has argued in **The New England Journal of Medicine** that randomized trials are unethical. He believes that physicians must always use their best judgment to determine treatment and cannot rely on chance, even when the effectiveness of a treatment is unknown, even to answer a question about what treatment works best, even when the patient has given fully informed consent.

began using a magnificent new tool—the microscope equipped with new achromatic lenses, which came into use in the 1830s—an even wider universe began to open.

In this universe Germans took the lead, partly because fewer French than Germans chose to use microscopes and partly because French physicians in the middle of the nineteenth century were generally less aggressive in experimenting, in creating controlled conditions to probe and even manipulate nature. (It was no coincidence that the French giants Pasteur and Claude Bernard, who did conduct experiments, were not on the faculty of any medical school. Echoing Hunter's advice to Jenner, Bernard, a physiologist, told one American student, "Why think? Exhaustively experiment, then think.")

In Germany, meanwhile, Rudolf Virchow—both he and Bernard received their medical degrees in 1843—was creating the field of cellular pathology, the idea that disease began at the cellular level. And in Germany great laboratories were being established around brilliant scientists who, more than elsewhere, did actively probe nature with experiments. Jacob Henle, the first scientist to formulate the modern germ theory, echoed Francis Bacon when he said, "Nature answers only when she is questioned."

And in France, Pasteur was writing, "I am on the edge of mysteries and the veil is getting thinner and thinner."

Never had there been a time so exciting in medicine. A universe was opening.

Still, with the exception of the findings on cholera and typhoid—and even these won only slow acceptance—little of this new scientific knowledge could be translated into curing or preventing disease. And much that was being discovered was not understood. In 1868, for example, a Swiss investigator isolated deoxyribonucleic acid, DNA, from a cell's nucleus, but he had no idea of its function. Not until three-quarters of a century later, at the conclusion of some research directly related to the 1918 influenza pandemic, did anyone even speculate, much less demonstrate, that DNA carried genetic information.

So the advances of science actually, and ironically, led to "therapeutic nihilism." Physicians became disenchanted with traditional treatments, but they had nothing with which to replace them. In response to the findings of Louis and others, in 1835 Harvard's Jacob Bigelow had argued in a major address that in "the unbiased opinion of most medical men of sound judgment and long experience . . . the amount of death and disaster in the world would be less, if all disease were left to itself."

His address had impact. It also expressed the chaos into which medicine was being thrown and the frustration of its practitioners. Physicians were abandoning the approaches of just a few years earlier and, less certain of the usefulness of a therapy, were becoming far less interventionist. In Philadelphia in the early 1800s Rush had called for wholesale bloodletting and was widely applauded. In 1862 in Philadelphia a study found that, out of 9,502 cases, physicians had cut a vein "in one instance only."

Laymen as well were losing faith in and becoming reluctant to submit to the tortures of heroic medicine. And since the new knowledge developing in traditional medicine had not yet developed new therapies, rival ideas of disease and treatment began to emerge. Some of these theories were pseudoscience, and some owed as little to science as did a religious sect.

This chaos was by no means limited to America. Typical was Samuel Hahnemann, who developed homeopathy in Germany, publishing his ideas in 1810, just before German science began to emerge as the dominant force on the Continent. But nowhere did individuals feel freer to question authority than in America. And nowhere was the chaos greater.

Samuel Thomson, founder of a movement bearing his name that spread widely before the Civil War, argued that medicine was simple enough to be comprehended by everyone, so anyone could act as a physician. "May the time soon come when men and women will become their own priests, physicians, and lawyers—when self-government, equal rights and moral philosophy will take the place of all popular crafts of every description," argued his movement's publication. His system used "botanic" therapeutics, and he charged, "False theory and hypothesis constitute nearly the whole art of physic."

Thomsonism was the most popular layman's medical movement but hardly the only one. Dozens of what can only be called sects arose across the countryside. A Thomsonian rhyme summed up the attitude: "The nest of college-birds are three, / **Law, Physic and Divinity;** / And while these three remain combined, / They keep the world oppressed and blind / . . . Now is the time to be set free, / From priests' and Doctors' slavery."

As these ideas spread, as traditional physicians failed to demonstrate the ability to cure anyone, as democratic emotions and anti-elitism swept the nation with Andrew Jackson, American medicine became as wild and democratic as the frontier. In the 1700s Britain had relaxed licensing standards for physicians. Now several state legislatures did away with the licensing of physicians entirely. Why should there be any licensing requirements? Did physicians know anything? Could they **heal** anyone? Wrote one commentator in 1846, "There is not a greater aristocratic monopoly in existence, than this of regular medicine—neither is there a greater humbug." In England the title "Professor" was reserved for those who held university chairs, and, even after John Hunter brought science to surgery, surgeons often went by "Mister." In America the titles "Professor" and "Doctor" went to anyone who claimed them. As late as 1900, forty-one states licensed pharmacists, thirty-five licensed dentists, and only thirty-four licensed physicians. A typical medical journal article in 1858 asked, "To What Cause Are We to Attribute the Diminished Respectability of the Medical Profession in the Esteem of the American Public?"

By the Civil War, American medicine had begun to inch forward, but only inch. The brightest lights involved surgery. The development of anesthesia, first demonstrated in 1846 at Massachusetts General Hospital, helped dramatically, and, just as Galen's experience with gladiators taught him much anatomy, American surgeons learned enough from the war to put them a step ahead of Europeans.

In the case of infectious and other disease, however, physicians continued to attack the body with mustard plasters that blistered the body, along with arsenic, mercury, and other poisons. Too many physicians continued their adherence to grand philosophical systems, and the Civil War showed how little the French influence had yet penetrated American medicine. European medical schools taught the use of thermometers, stethoscopes, and ophthalmoscopes, but Americans rarely used them and the largest Union army had only half a dozen thermometers. Americans still relieved pain by applying opiate powders on a wound, instead of injecting opium with syringes. And when Union Surgeon General William Hammond banned some of the violent purgatives, he was both court-martialed and condemned by the American Medical Association.

After the Civil War, America continued to churn out prophets of new, simple, complete, and self-contained systems of healing, two of which, chiropractic and Christian Science, survive today. (Evidence does suggest that spinal manipulation can relieve musculoskeletal conditions, but no evidence supports chiropractic claims that disease is caused by misalignment of vertebrae.)

Medicine had discovered drugs—such as quinine, digitalis, and opium—that provided benefits, but, as one historian has shown, they were routinely prescribed indiscriminately, for their overall effect on the body, not for a specific purpose; even quinine was prescribed generally, not to treat malaria. Hence Oliver Wendell Holmes, the physician father of the Supreme Court justice, was not much overstating when he declared, "I firmly believe that if the whole materia medica, as now used, could be sunk to the bottom of the sea, it would be all the better for mankind—and all the worse for the fishes."

There was something else about America. It was such a practical place. If it was a nation bursting with energy, it had no patience for dalliance or daydreaming or the waste of time. In 1832, Louis had told one of his most promising protégés—an American—to spend several years in research before beginning a medical practice. The student's father was also a physician, James Jackson, a founder of Massachusetts General Hospital, who scornfully rejected Louis's suggestion and protested to Louis that "in this country his course would have been so singular, as in a measure to separate him from other men. We are a business doing people. . . . There is a vast deal to be done and he who will not be doing must be set down as a drone."

In America the very fact that science was undermining therapeutics made institutions uninterested in supporting it. Physics, chemistry, and the practical arts of engineering thrived. The number of engineers particularly was exploding—from 7,000 to 226,000 from the late nineteenth century to just after World War I—and they were accomplishing extraordinary things. Engineers transformed steel production from an art into a science, developed the telegraph, laid a cable connecting America to Europe, built railroads crossing the continent and skyscrapers that climbed upward, developed the telephone—with automobiles and airplanes not far behind. The world was being transformed. Whatever was being learned in the laboratory about biology was building basic knowledge, but with the exception of anesthesia, laboratory research had only proven actual medical practice all but useless while providing nothing with which to replace it.

Still, by the 1870s, European medical schools required and gave rigorous scientific training and were generally subsidized by the state. In contrast, most American medical schools were owned by a faculty whose profits and salaries—even when they did not own the school—were paid by student fees, so the schools often had no admission standards other than the ability to pay tuition. No medical school in America allowed medical students to routinely either perform autopsies or see patients, and medical education often consisted of nothing more than two four-month terms of lectures. Few medical schools had any association with a university, and fewer still had ties to a hospital. In 1870 even at Harvard a medical student could fail four of nine courses and still get an M.D.

In the United States, a few isolated individuals did research—outstanding research—but it was unsupported by any institution. S. Weir Mitchell, America's leading experimental physiologist, once wrote that he dreaded anything "removing from me the time or power to search for new truths that lie about me so thick." Yet in the 1870s, after he had already developed an international reputation, after he had begun experiments with snake venom that would lead directly to a basic understanding of the immune system and the development of antitoxins, he was denied positions teaching physiology at both the University of Pennsylvania and Jefferson Medical College; neither had any interest in research, nor a laboratory for either teaching or research purposes. In 1871 Harvard did create the first laboratory of experimental medicine at any American university, but that laboratory was relegated to an attic and paid for by the professor's father. Also in 1871 Harvard's professor of pathologic anatomy confessed he did not know how to use a microscope.

But Charles Eliot, a Brahmin with a birth defect that deformed one side of his face—he never allowed a photograph to show that side—had become Harvard president in 1869. In his first report as president, he declared, "The whole system of medical education in this country needs thorough reformation. The ignorance and general incompetency of the average graduate of the American medical Schools, at the time when he receives the degree which turns him loose upon the community, is something horrible to contemplate."

Soon after this declaration, a newly minted Harvard physician killed three successive patients because he did not know the lethal dose of morphine. Even with the leverage of this scandal, Eliot could push through only modest reforms over a resistant faculty. Professor of Surgery Henry Bigelow, the most powerful faculty member, protested to the Harvard Board of Overseers, "[Eliot] actually proposes to have written examinations for the degree of doctor of medicine. I had to tell him that he knew nothing about the quality of the Harvard medical students. More than half of them can barely write. Of course they can't pass written examinations. . . . No medical school has thought it proper to risk large existing classes and large receipts by introducing more rigorous standards."

Many American physicians were in fact enthralled by the laboratory advances being made in Europe. But they had to go to Europe to learn them. Upon their return they could do little or nothing with their knowledge. Not a single institution in the United States supported any medical research whatsoever.

As one American who had studied in Europe wrote, "I was often asked in Germany how it is that no scientific work in medicine is done in this country, how it is that many good men who do well in Germany and show evident talent there are never heard of and never do any good work when they come back here. The answer is that there is no opportunity for, no appreciation of, no demand for that kind of work here. . . . The condition of medical education here is simply horrible."

In 1873, Johns Hopkins died, leaving behind a trust of $3.5 million to found a university and hospital. It was to that time the greatest gift ever to a university. Princeton's library collection was then an embarrassment of only a few books—and the library was open only one hour a week. Columbia was little better: its library opened for two hours each afternoon, but freshmen could not enter without a special permission slip. Only 10 percent of Harvard's professors had a Ph.D.

The trustees of Hopkins's estate were Quakers who moved deliberately but also decisively. Against the advice of Harvard president Charles Eliot, Yale president James Burrill Angell, and Cornell president Andrew D. White, they decided to model the Johns Hopkins University after the greatest German universities, places thick with men consumed with creating new knowledge, not simply teaching what was believed.

The trustees made this decision precisely because there was no such university in America, and precisely because they recognized the need after doing the equivalent of market research. A board member later explained, "There was a strong demand, among the young men of this country, for opportunities to study beyond the ordinary courses of a college or a scientific school. . . . The strongest evidence of this demand was the increased attendance of American students upon lectures of German universities." The trustees decided that quality would sell. They intended to hire only eminent professors and provide opportunities for advanced study.

Their plan was in many ways an entirely American ambition: to create a revolution from nothing. For it made little sense to locate the new institution in Baltimore, a squalid industrial and port city. Unlike Philadelphia, Boston, or New York, it had no tradition of philanthropy, no social elite ready to lead, and certainly no intellectual tradition. Even the architecture of Baltimore seemed exceptionally dreary, long lines of row houses, each with three steps, crowding against the street and yet virtually no street life—the people of Baltimore seemed to live inward, in backyards and courtyards.

In fact, there was no base whatsoever upon which to build . . . except the money, another American trait.

The trustees hired as president Daniel Coit Gilman, who left the presidency of the newly organized University of California after disputes with state legislators. Earlier he had helped create and had led the Sheffield Scientific School at Yale, which was distinct from Yale itself. Indeed, it was created partly because of Yale's reluctance to embrace science as part of its basic curriculum.

At the Hopkins, Gilman immediately recruited an internationally respected—and connected—faculty, which gave it instant credibility. In Europe, people like Huxley saw the Hopkins as combining the explosive energy and openness of America with the grit of science; the potential could shake the world.

To honor the Hopkins upon its beginnings, to honor this vision, to proselytize upon this new faith, Thomas Huxley came to America.

The Johns Hopkins would have rigor. It would have such rigor as no school in America had ever known.

The Hopkins opened in 1876. Its medical school would not open until 1893, but it succeeded so brilliantly and quickly that, by the outbreak of World War I, American medical science had caught up to Europe and was about to surpass it.

■   ■   ■

Influenza is a viral disease. When it kills, it usually does so in one of two ways: either quickly and directly with a violent viral pneumonia so damaging that it has been compared to burning the lungs; or more slowly and indirectly by stripping the body of defenses, allowing bacteria to invade the lungs and cause a more common and slower-killing bacterial pneumonia.

By World War I, those trained directly or indirectly by the Hopkins already did lead the world in investigating pneumonia, a disease referred to as "the captain of the men of death." They could in some instances prevent it and cure it.

And their story begins with one man.

CHAPTER TWO

NOTHING ABOUT the boyhood or youth of William Henry Welch suggested his future.

So it is apt that the best biography of him begins not with his childhood but with an extraordinary eightieth-birthday celebration in 1930. Friends, colleagues, and admirers gathered for the event not only in Baltimore, where he lived, but in Boston, in New York, in Washington; in Chicago, Cincinnati, and Los Angeles; in Paris, London, Geneva, Tokyo, and Peking. Telegraph and radio linked the celebrations, and their starting times were staggered to allow as much overlap as time zones made possible. The many halls were thick with scientists in many fields, including Nobel laureates, and President Herbert Hoover's tribute to

Welch at the Washington event was broadcast live over American radio networks.

The tribute was to a man who had become arguably the single most influential scientist in the world. He had served as president of the National Academy of Sciences, president of the American Association for the Advancement of Science, president of the American Medical Association, and president or dominant figure of literally dozens of other scientific groups. At a time when no government funds went to research, as both chairman of the Executive Committee of the Carnegie Institution of Washington and president—for thirty-two years—of the Board of Scientific Directors of the Rockefeller Institute for Medical Research (now Rockefeller University), he had also directed the flow of money from the two greatest philanthropic organizations in the country.

And yet Welch had been no great pioneer even in his own field of medical research—no Louis Pasteur, no Robert Koch, no Paul Ehrlich, no Theobald Smith. He had generated no brilliant insights, made no magnificent discoveries, asked no deep and original questions, and left no significant legacy in the laboratory or in scientific papers. He did little work—a reasonable judge might say he did no work—so profound as to merit even membership in, much less the presidency of, the National Academy of Sciences.

Nonetheless, these hundreds of the world's

leading scientists had measured him as coldly and objectively as they measured everything and found him worthy. They had gathered to celebrate his life, if not for his science, then for what he had done for science.

In his lifetime the world had changed radically, from horse and buggy to radio, airplanes, even the first television. Coca-Cola had been invented and rapidly spread across the country before 1900, by the 1920s Woolworth's had over fifteen hundred stores, and a technocratic makeover of America had accompanied the Progressive Age, culminating in 1930 in a White House conference on children that proclaimed the superiority of experts to parents in child raising, because "it is beyond the capacity of an individual parent to train her child to fit into the intricate, interwoven, and interdependent social and economic system we have developed."

Welch had of course played no role in those changes. But he had played a large and direct role in an equivalent makeover of medicine and especially American medicine.

He had served first as a kind of avatar, his own experience embodying and epitomizing that of many in his generation. Yet he was no simple symbol or representative. Like an Escher drawing, his life both represented that of others and simultaneously defined the lives of those who followed him, and those who followed them, and those who followed them, down to the present.

For if he did no revolutionary science, he lived a revolutionary life. He was personality and theater; he was impresario, creator, builder. Like an actor on a live stage, his life was a performance given once, leaving its impact upon his audience, and only through them echoing in time and place. He led the movement that created the greatest scientific medical enterprise, and possibly the greatest enterprise in any of the sciences, in the world. His legacy was not objectively measurable, but it was nonetheless real. It lay in his ability to stir other men's souls.

Welch was born in 1850 in Norfolk, Connecticut, a small town in the northern part of the state that remains even today a hilly and wooded retreat. His grandfather, great-uncle, father, and four uncles were physicians. His father also served a term in Congress and in 1857 addressed the graduates of Yale Medical School. In that speech he demonstrated a significant grasp of the latest medical developments, including a technique that would not be mentioned at Harvard until 1868 and the striking new "cell theory with its results in physiology and pathology," a reference to the work of Rudolf Virchow, who had then published only in German-language journals. He also declared, "All positive knowledge obtained . . . has resulted from the accurate observation of facts."

Yet if it seemed foreordained that Welch would become a physician, this was not the case. Years

later he told the great surgeon Harvey Cushing, a
protégé, that in his youth medicine had filled him
with repugnance.

Perhaps part of that repugnance came from his
circumstances. Welch's mother died when he was
six months old. His sister, three years older, was sent
away, and his father was distant both emotionally
and physically. Throughout Welch's life he would
be closer to his sister than to any other living soul;
over the years their correspondence revealed what
intimacies he was willing to share.

His childhood was marked by what would become
a pattern throughout his life: loneliness masked by
social activity. At first he sought to fit in. He was
not isolated. Neighbors included an uncle and cousins his age with whom he played routinely, but he
longed for greater intimacy and begged his cousins
to call him "brother." They refused. Elsewhere, too,
he sought to fit in, to belong. At the age of fifteen,
submitting to evangelical fervor, he formally committed himself to God.

He attended Yale, where he found no conflict between his religious commitment and science. While
the college had begun teaching such practical arts
as engineering, it kept a measured distance from the
scientific ferment of these years immediately following the Civil War, purposely setting itself up as a
conservative, Congregationalist counterbalance to
the Unitarian influence at Harvard. But if Welch's
intellectual interests developed only after college,

his personality had already formed. Three attributes in particular stood out. Their combination would prove powerful indeed.

His intelligence did shine through, and he graduated third in his class. But the impression left on others came not from his brilliance but from his personality. He had the unusual ability to simultaneously involve himself passionately in something yet retain perspective. One student described him as "the only one who kept cool" during heated discussions, and he would carry this trait through the rest of his life.

There was something about him that made others want him to think well of them. Hazing of freshmen was brutal at the time, so brutal that a classmate was advised to keep a pistol in his room to prevent sophomores from abusing him. Yet Welch was left entirely alone. Skull and Bones, perhaps the single most secret society in the United States, which marks its members powerfully with the embrace of the establishment, inducted him, and he would remain deeply attached to Bones his entire life. Perhaps that satisfied his desire to belong. At any rate, his earlier desperation to fit in was replaced by a self-sufficiency. His roommate on parting left him an extraordinary note: "I ought to try to express my great indebtedness for the kindness which you always manifested toward me, the pure example you set me, . . . I feel now more deeply the truth of what I often said to others if not to you—that I was utterly unworthy of such a chum as yourself. I often pitied you, to think that you had to room with me, your inferior in ability, dignity and every noble and good quality."

It is the kind of note that a biographer might interpret as homoerotic. Perhaps it was. At least one other man would later devote himself to Welch with what could only be called ardor. Yet for the rest of Welch's life he also seemed somehow, in some indefinable way, to generate similar if less intense sentiments in others. He did so without effort. He charmed without effort. He inspired without effort. And he did so without his reciprocating any personal connection, much less attachment. A later age would call this "charisma."

His class rank entitled him to give an oration at commencement. In an undergraduate essay entitled "The Decay of Faith," Welch had decried mechanistic science, which viewed the world as a machine "unguided by a God of justice." Now, in 1870, a decade after Darwin published **Origin of Species,** in his oration Welch attempted to reconcile science and religion.

He found it a difficult task. Science is at all times potentially revolutionary; any new answer to a seemingly mundane question about "how" something occurs may uncover chains of causation that throw all preceding order into disarray and that threaten religious beliefs as well. Welch personally was experiencing the pains that many in the last half of the

nineteenth century experienced for the first time as
adults as science threatened to supplant the natural
order, God's order, with an order defined by mankind, an order that promised no one knew what,
an order that, as Milton wrote in **Paradise Lost,**
"Frighted the reign of Chaos and old night."

Taking a step backward from what his father
had said a dozen years before, Welch rejected the
personal God of Emerson and the Unitarians, reiterated the importance of revealed truth in Scripture,
argued that revelation need not submit to reason,
and spoke of that which "man could never discover
by the light of his own mind."

Welch would ultimately devote his life to discovering all the world with his own mind, and to
spurring others to do the same. But not yet.

He had studied classics and he had hoped to teach
Greek at Yale. Yale did not, however, offer him a position, and he became a tutor at a new private school.
That school closed, Yale still offered him nothing,
and, with no immediate prospects for employment,
with his family importuning him to become a physician, he returned to Norfolk and apprenticed to
his father.

It was an old-fashioned practice. Nothing his father did reflected his knowledge of the newest medical concepts. Like most American physicians, he
ignored objective measurements such as temperature
and blood pressure, and he even mixed prescriptions

without measuring dosages, often relying on taste. This apprenticeship was not a happy time for Welch. In his own later accounts of his training, he passed over it as if it had never occurred. But sometime during it, his views of medicine changed.

At some point he decided that if he was going to become a physician, he would do so in his own way. Routinely those preparing for medicine apprenticed for six months or a year, and then attended medical school. He had served his apprenticeship. But in the next step he took, he marked out a new course. Welch returned to school all right, but he did not attend medical school. He learned chemistry.

Not only did no medical school in the United States require entering students to have either any scientific knowledge or a college degree, neither did any American medical school emphasize science. Far from it. In 1871, a senior professor at the Harvard Medical School argued, "In an age of science, like the present, there is more danger that the average medical student will be drawn from what is practical, useful, and even essential by the well-meant enthusiasm of the votaries of the applicable sciences, than that he will suffer from the want of knowledge of these. . . . [We] should not encourage the medical student to while away his time in the labyrinths of Chemistry and Physiology."

Welch had a different view. Chemistry seemed to him a window into the body. By then Carl

Ludwig, later Welch's mentor, and several other leading German scientists had met in Berlin and determined to "constitute physiology on a chemico-physical foundation and give it equal scientific rank with physics."

It was highly unlikely that Welch knew of that determination, but his instincts were the same. In 1872 he entered Yale's Sheffield Scientific School to study chemistry. He considered the facilities there "excellent . . . certainly better than in any medical school, where chemistry as far as I can learn is very much slighted."

After half a year of grounding, he began medical school at the College of Physicians and Surgeons in New York City, which was not yet connected to Columbia University. (He disdained Yale's medical school; fifty years later he was asked to give a speech on Yale's early contributions to medicine and replied that there hadn't been any.) It was a typical good American medical school, with no requirements for admission and no grades in any course. As elsewhere, faculty salaries came directly from student fees, so faculty wanted to maximize the number of students. Instruction came almost entirely through lectures; the school offered no laboratory work of any kind. This, too, was typical. In no American school did students use a microscope. In fact, Welch's work in one course won him the great prize of a microscope; he cherished it but did not know how to use it, and no professor offered to instruct him. Instead he enviously watched them work, commenting, "I can only admire without understanding how to use its apparently complicated mechanism."

But unlike in many other schools, students at the College of Physicians and Surgeons could examine cadavers. Pathological anatomy—using autopsies to decipher what was happening within organs—enthralled Welch. New York City had three medical schools. He took the course in pathological anatomy at all three.

Then he completed his school's single requirement for an M.D. He passed a final examination. Welch called it "the easiest examination I ever entered since leaving boarding school."

Shortly before Welch took this test, Yale finally offered him the position he had so earnestly sought earlier—professor of Greek. He declined it.

To his father he wrote, "I have chosen my profession, am becoming more and more interested in it, and do not feel at all inclined to relinquish it for anything else."

He was interested indeed.

He was also beginning to be recognized. Francis Delafield, one of his professors, had studied pathological anatomy in Paris with Pierre Louis and, like Louis, kept detailed records of hundreds of autopsies. Delafield's was the best work in America, the most precise, the most scientific. Delafield now brought Welch into his fold and allowed him the extraordinary privilege of entering his own autopsy findings into Delafield's sacred notes.

Yet huge gaps in Welch's knowledge remained. He still did not know how to use his microscope. Delafield, an expert in microscopic technique who had made his own microtome (a device for cutting exquisitely thin slices of tissue), would sit for hours with one eye glued to the lens, smoking a pipe, while Welch watched impotently. But Delafield did let Welch perform a huge number of autopsies for someone in his junior position. From each one he tried to learn.

That knowledge did not satisfy him. His best professors had studied in Paris, Vienna, and Berlin. Although Welch still intended to practice clinical medicine—not a single physician in the United States then made a living doing research—he borrowed from family and friends and, having run through all that his American professors could teach him, on April 19, 1876, a few months before Huxley spoke at the inauguration of the Johns Hopkins University, Welch sailed for Europe to continue his scientific education. Simon Flexner, Welch's protégé and a brilliant scientist in his own right, declared this trip "a voyage of exploration that was in its results perhaps the most important ever taken by an American doctor."

He was hardly alone in seeking more knowledge in Germany, where the best science was then being done. One historian has estimated that between

1870 and 1914, fifteen thousand American doctors studied in Germany or Austria, along with thousands more from England, France, Japan, Turkey, Italy, and Russia.

The overwhelming majority of these physicians were interested solely in treating patients. In Vienna professors established a virtual assembly line to teach short courses on specific aspects of clinical medicine to foreign doctors, especially Americans. These Americans took the courses partly out of desire to learn and partly to gain an edge over competitors at home.

Welch himself expected to have to practice medicine to make a living, and he recognized how helpful to such a career studying in Germany could be. He assured his sister and brother-in-law as well as his father, all of whom were helping support him financially, "The prestige and knowledge which I should acquire by a year's study in Germany would decidedly increase my chance of success. The young doctors who are doing well in New York are in a large majority those who have studied abroad."

But his real interest lay with the tiny minority of Americans who went to Germany to explore a new universe. He wanted to learn laboratory science. In America he had already acquired a reputation as knowing far more than his colleagues. In Germany he was refused acceptance into two laboratories because he knew so little. This inspired rather than depressed him. Soon he found a place to start and excitedly wrote home, "I feel as if I were only just initiated into the great science of medicine. My previous experiences compared with the present are like the difference between reading of a fair country and seeing it with one's own eyes. To live in the atmosphere of these scientific workshops and laboratories, to come into contact with the men who have formed and are forming the science of today, to have the opportunity of doing a little original investigation myself are all advantages, which, if they do not prove fruitful in later life, will always be to me a source of pleasure and profit."

Of Leipzig's university, he said, "If you could visit the handsome and thoroughly equipped physiological, anatomical, pathological and chemical laboratories and see professors whose fame is already world-wide, with their corps of assistants and students hard at work, you would realize how by concentration of labor and devotion to study Germany has outstripped other countries in the science of medicine."

He focused on learning how to learn and stayed constantly alert to technique, to anything offering another window into the new world, anything that allowed him to see more clearly and deeply. "The chief value" of his work with one scientist was "in teaching me certain important methods of handling fresh tissues, especially in isolating particular elements." Of another scientist whom he disliked, he said, "What is of greater importance, I have acquired a knowledge of methods of preparing and mounting specimens so that I can carry on investigations hereafter."

By now he was attracting attention from his mentors, who included some of the leading scientists in the world, but they left a more distinct impression upon him. One was Carl Ludwig, whom he called "my ideal of a scientific man, accepting nothing upon authority, but putting every scientific theory to the severest test. . . . I hope I have learned from Professor Ludwig's precept and practice that most important lesson for every man of science, not to be satisfied with loose thinking and half-proofs, not to speculate and theorize but to observe closely and carefully."

Julius Cohnheim, another mentor, taught him a new kind of curiosity: "Cohnheim's interest centers on the explanation of the fact. It is not enough for him to know that congestion of the kidney follows heart disease. . . . He is constantly inquiring why does it occur under these circumstances. . . . He is almost the founder and certainly the chief representative of the so-called experimental or physiological school of pathology."

Welch began to analyze everything, including his most deeply held beliefs. Five years earlier he had condemned the concept of a world ruled other than by a God of justice. Now he told his father that he embraced Darwin: "That there is anything irreligious about the doctrine of evolution I cannot see. . . . In the end our preconceived beliefs must change and adapt themselves. The facts of science never will change."

He also analyzed the means by which German science had achieved such stature. Its three most important elements, he decided, were the thorough preparation required of students by German medical schools, the schools' independent financing, and the support of research by the government and universities.

In 1877, a year after the Johns Hopkins University opened, its president, Daniel Gilman, laid plans to assemble the greatest medical school faculty in America, one to rival any in Europe. The decision to launch a national—indeed international—search was itself revolutionary. With the exception of the University of Michigan, located in tiny Ann Arbor, every medical school in the United States filled its faculty exclusively from the ranks of local physicians. To perform the search Gilman chose the perfect man: Dr. John Shaw Billings.

Billings lay behind America's first great contribution to scientific medicine: a library. This library grew out of the detailed medical history of the Civil War ordered by the army surgeon general. The army also created a medical "museum," which was actually a library of specimens.

Both the museum and the history were remarkable. In 1998 scientists at the Armed Forces Institute of Pathology, a direct descendant of this museum, used specimens preserved in 1918 to determine the genetic makeup of the 1918 influenza virus. And the medical history was extraordinarily precise and useful. Even Virchow said he was "constantly astonished at the wealth of experience therein found. The greatest exactness in detail, careful statistics even in the smallest matters, and a scholarly statement embracing all sides of medical experience are here united."

Billings did not write that history, but it did inspire him to create a medical library of comparable quality. He built what one medical historian judged "probably the greatest and most useful medical library in the world." By 1876 it already held eighty thousand volumes; ultimately it grew into today's National Library of Medicine.

But he did more than collect books and articles. Knowledge is useless unless accessible. To disseminate knowledge, Billings developed a cataloging system far superior to any in Europe, and he began publishing the **Index Medicus,** a monthly bibliography of new medical books and articles appearing in the Americas, Europe, Japan. No comparable bibliography existed anywhere else in the world.

And no one else in the world had a better sense of what was going on in all the world's laboratories than Billings.

He traveled to Europe to meet possible candidates for the Hopkins faculty, including established scientists of international renown. But he also sought out young men, the next generation of leaders. He had heard of Welch, heard of his potential, heard that he had exposed himself not to one or two of the great scientists but to many, heard that he seemed to know everyone in Germany, including—even before they emerged as arguably the two greatest medical scientists of the nineteenth or early twentieth century—Robert Koch and Paul Ehrlich. (In fact, when Koch, then unknown, first made his dramatic demonstration of the life cycle of anthrax, Welch was in the same laboratory.)

Billings met with Welch in an ancient Leipzig beer hall, a hall that itself belonged to myth. On the wall were murals depicting the sixteenth-century meeting of Faust and the Devil, for the meeting had supposedly occurred in that very room. Billings and Welch talked passionately of science deep into the night, while the murals endowed their words with conspiratorial irony. Billings spoke of the plans for the Hopkins: unheard-of admission standards for students, labs that filled great buildings, the most modern hospital in the world, and of course a brilliant faculty. They talked also about life, about each other's goals. Welch knew perfectly well he was being interviewed. In response, he opened his soul.

After the dinner Billings told Francis King, president of the yet-to-be-built Johns Hopkins Hospital, that Welch "should be one of the first men to be secured, when the time came."

■   ■   ■

That time would not come for a while. The Hopkins had begun as a graduate school only, without even any undergraduate students, although it quickly expanded to include a college. Further expansion abruptly became problematic since its endowment was chiefly in Baltimore & Ohio Railroad stock. The country had been wallowing in depression for four years when the B&O and the Pennsylvania Railroad cut wages 10 percent, sparking violent strikes by railroad workers in Maryland that soon spread to Pittsburgh, Chicago, St. Louis, and farther west. B&O stock collapsed, and the plans to open the medical school had to be put off. There were no new faculty posts at the Hopkins to fill.

So in 1877 Welch returned to New York desperate for "some opportunity" in science "and at the same time making a modest livelihood." Failing to find one, he returned to Europe. In 1878 he was back in New York.

At no time in history had medicine been advancing so rapidly. The thousands who flocked to Europe were proof of American physicians' intense interest in those advances. Yet in the United States neither Welch nor anyone else could support himself by either joining in that great march or teaching what had been learned.

Welch proposed to a former mentor at the College of Physicians and Surgeons that he teach a laboratory course. The school had no laboratory and wanted none. No medical school in the United

States used a laboratory for instruction. The school rejected his suggestion but did offer to let Welch lecture—without salary—in pathology.

Welch turned to Bellevue, a medical school with a lesser reputation. It let him offer his course and provided three rooms for it, equipped only with empty kitchen tables. There were no microscopes, no glassware, no incubators, no instruments. Facing the empty rooms, discouraged, he wrote, "I cannot make much of a success out of the affair at present. I seem to be thrown entirely upon my own resources for equipping the laboratory and do not think that I can accomplish much."

He was also worried. His entire compensation would come from student fees, and the three-month course was not required. He confided to his sister, "I sometimes feel rather blue when I look ahead and see that I am not going to be able to realize my aspirations in life. . . . There is no opportunity in this country, and it seems unlikely there ever will be. . . . I can teach microscopy and pathology, perhaps get some practice and make a living after a while, but that is all patchwork and the drudgery of life and what hundreds do."

He was wrong.

In fact he would catalyze the creation of an entire generation of scientists who would transform American medicine, scientists who would confront influenza in 1918, scientists whose findings from that epidemic still echo today.

CHAPTER THREE

WELCH'S COURSE quickly became extraordinarily popular. Soon students from all three of New York City's medical schools were lining up for it, attracted as Welch had been to this new science, to the microscope, to experimentation. And Welch did not simply teach; he inspired. His comments always seemed so solid, well grounded, well reasoned. A colleague observed, "He would leak knowledge." And the excitement! Each time a student fixed a specimen on a slide and looked through a microscope, an entire universe opened to him! To some, discovering that universe, entering into it, beginning to manipulate it, was akin to creating it; they must have felt almost godlike.

The College of Physicians and Surgeons had to offer a laboratory course to compete. It beseeched Welch to teach it. He declined out of loyalty to Bellevue but recommended the hiring of T. Mitchell Prudden, an American he had known—and considered a rival for the Hopkins job—in Europe. It was the first of what would be uncounted job offers that he engineered. Meanwhile one of his students recalled "his serious, eager look, his smiling face, his interest in young men which bound them to him. He was always ready to drop any work in which he was engaged and answer even trivial questions on any subject—in fact he was never without an answer for his knowledge was encyclopedic. I felt instinctively that he was wasted at Bellevue, and was destined to have a larger circle of hearers."

But despite the throngs of motivated students taking the two courses, neither Prudden nor Welch prospered. Two years went by, then three, then four. To cobble together a living, Welch did autopsies at a state hospital, served as an assistant to a prominent physician, and tutored medical students before their final exams. As he passed his thirtieth birthday he was doing no real science. He was making a reputation and it was clear if he chose to concentrate on practice he could become wealthy. Little medical research was being done in America—although the little that was done was significant—but even that little he had no part of. In Europe science was marching from advance to advance, breakthrough to breakthrough. The most important of these was the germ theory of disease.

Proving and elaborating upon the germ theory would ultimately open the way to confronting all infectious disease. It would also create the conceptual framework and technical tools that Welch and others later used to fight influenza.

Simply put, the germ theory said that minute living organisms invaded the body, multiplied, and caused disease, and that a specific germ caused a specific disease.

There was need for a new theory of disease. As the nineteenth century progressed, as autopsy findings were correlated with symptoms reported during life, as organs from animals and cadavers were put under a microscope, as normal organs were compared to diseased ones, as diseases became more defined, localized, and specific, scientists finally discarded the ideas of systemic illness and the humours of Hippocrates and Galen and began looking for better explanations.

Three theories stood as rivals to the germ theory.

The first involved "miasma." Several variations of this concept existed, but they basically argued that many diseases were caused by some kind of putrefaction in the atmosphere, or by some climactic influence, or by noxious fumes from decaying organic materials. (In China the wind was originally regarded as a demon that caused illness.) Miasmas seemed a particularly good explanation of epidemics, and the unhealthiness of swamp regions seemed to support the theory. In 1885, when Welch considered the germ theory as proven, the New York City Board of Health warned that "laying of all telegraph wires under ground in one season . . . would prove highly detrimental to the health of the city . . . through the exposure to the atmosphere of so much subsoil, saturated, as most of it is, with noxious gases. . . . Harlem Flats [had] a sufficient supply of rotting filth to generate fetid gases adequate to the poisoning of half the population." As late as the 1930s one prominent and highly regarded British epidemiologist continued to advocate the miasma theory, and after the 1918 influenza pandemic, climatic conditions were scrutinized in a search for correlations.

The "filth" theory of disease was almost a corollary of the miasma theory. It also suited Victorian mores perfectly. Fear of "swamp gas"—often a euphemism for the smells of fecal matter—and installation of indoor toilets were all part of the Victorian drive to improve sanitation and simultaneously to separate the human body from anything Victorians found distasteful. And filth often is associated with disease: lice carry typhus; contaminated water spreads typhoid and cholera; rats through their fleas spread plague.

Both the miasma and filth theories had

sophisticated adherents, including public health officials and some extremely gifted scientists, but the most scientific rival of the germ theory explained disease in terms purely of chemistry. It saw disease as a chemical process. This theory had much to recommend it.

Not only had scientists used chemistry as a lens that brought much of biology into focus, but some chemical reactions seemed to mimic the actions of disease. For example, advocates of the chemical theory of disease argued that fire was a chemical process and a single match could set off a chain reaction that ignited an entire forest or city. They hypothesized that chemicals they called "zymes" acted like a match. A zyme started a series of chemical reactions in the body that could launch the equivalent of fermentation—infection. (The chemical theory of disease, without the name, has in fact largely been validated. Scientists have clearly demonstrated that chemicals, radiation, and environmental factors can cause disease, although usually only through long-term or massive exposure and not, as the zymote theory hypothesized, by suddenly igniting a cascade of reactions.)

Ultimately this theory evolved to suggest that zymes could reproduce in the body; thus they acted as both catalysts and living organisms. In fact, this more sophisticated version of the zymote theory essentially describes what is today called a virus.

Yet these theories left many scientists unsatisfied.

Disease often seemed to germinate, grow, and spread. Did there not then have to be a point of origin, a seed? Jacob Henle in his 1840 essay "On Miasmata and Contagia" first formulated the modern germ theory; he also offered evidence for the theory and laid out criteria that, if met, would prove it.

Then, in 1860, Pasteur proved that living organisms, not a chemical chain reaction, caused fermentation, winning converts to the germ theory. The most important early convert was Joseph Lister, who immediately applied these findings to surgery, instituting antiseptic conditions in the operating room and slashing the percentage of patients who died from infections after surgery.

But the work of Robert Koch was most compelling. Koch himself was compelling. The son of an engineer, brilliant enough to teach himself to read at age five, he studied under Henle, was offered research posts, but became a clinician to support his family. He did not, however, stop investigating nature. Working alone, he conducted a series of experiments that met the most rigid tests and discovered the complete life cycle of the anthrax bacillus, showing that it formed spores that could lie dormant in the soil for years. In 1876 he walked into the laboratory of Ferdinand Cohn, one of Welch's mentors, and presented his findings. They brought him instant fame.

He subsequently laid down what came to be

known as "Koch's postulates," although Henle had earlier proposed much the same thing. The postulates state that before a microorganism can be said to cause a given disease, first, investigators had to find the germ in every case of the disease; second, they had to isolate the germ in pure culture; third, they had to inoculate a susceptible animal with the germ and the animal then had to get the disease; and, fourth, the germ had to be isolated from the test animal. Koch's postulates became a standard almost immediately. (Meeting the standard is not simple; finding a test animal that suffered the same symptoms as humans when infected with a human pathogen, for example, is not always possible.)

In 1882 Koch's discovery of the tubercle bacillus, the cause of tuberculosis, shook the scientific world and further confirmed the germ theory. Tuberculosis was a killer. Laymen called it "consumption," and that name spoke to the awfulness of the disease. It consumed people. Like cancer, it attacked the young as well as the old, sucked the life out of them, turned them into cachectic shells, and then killed them.

It would be difficult to overstate the importance of Koch's discovery to the believers in bacteriology. In New York, one of Welch's friends came running into his bedroom with a newspaper account of the discovery. Welch jumped out of bed and together they rushed to tell another friend. Almost immediately afterward, Welch felt the excitement directly. He demonstrated Koch's discovery to his class, copying Koch's method, his class watching steam rise from the plate while he stained sputum from a consumption patient with carbol-fuchsin, the stain binding to the bacillus so that it became visible on a slide. Here was the newest and greatest of discoveries! Students looked at the slide through the microscope, saw what Koch had seen, and were electrified, many recalling the moment vividly years later. One of those students was Hermann Biggs, who became a giant in his own right; at that moment he decided to spend his life in bacteriology.

But for Welch, reproducing Koch's finding must have been bittersweet. He knew the Germans, knew nearly all of these men adventuring into the unknowns of science. Yet here he was only keeping track of their work, doing none himself.

Then, in 1883, Koch achieved the first great triumph of science over disease. Earlier in the nineteenth century, two cholera epidemics had devastated Europe and the United States. As a new epidemic in Egypt threatened the borders of Europe, France dispatched investigators in this new field of bacteriology to track down the cause of the disease. Germany dispatched Koch.

Before this, medicine's great successes had come about almost serendipitously, beginning with an observation. With smallpox Jenner started out by taking seriously the experiences of country folk inoculating themselves. But not here. In this case the target had been fixed in advance. Both the French and Koch rationally designed an approach, then turned the general tools of the laboratory and bacteriology to a particular target.

The French failed. Louis Thuillier, the youngest member of the expedition, died of cholera. Despite the bitter and nationalistic rivalry between Pasteur and Koch, Koch returned with the body to France and served as a pallbearer at Thuillier's funeral, dropping into the grave a laurel wreath "such as are given to the brave."

Koch then returned to Egypt, isolated the cholera bacillus, and followed it to India to explore his findings in greater depth. John Snow's earlier epidemiological study in London had proved only to some that contaminated water caused the disease. Now, in conjunction with Koch's evidence, the germ theory seemed proven in cholera—and by implication the germ theory itself seemed proven.

Most leading physicians around the world, including in the United States, agreed with a prominent American public health expert who declared in 1885: "What was theory has become fact."

But a minority, both in the United States and Europe, still resisted the germ theory, believing that Pasteur, Koch, and others had proven that germs existed but not that germs **caused** disease—or at least that they were the sole cause of disease.*

The most notable critic was Max von Pettenkofer, who had made real and major scientific contributions. He insisted that Koch's bacteria were only one of many factors in the causation of cholera. His dispute with Koch became increasingly bitter and passionate. With a touch of both Barnum and a tightrope walker about him, Pettenkofer, determined to prove himself right, prepared test tubes thick with lethal cholera bacteria. Then he and several of his students drank them down. Amazingly, although two students developed minor cases of cholera, all survived. Pettenkofer claimed victory, and vindication.

It was a costly claim. In 1892 cholera contaminated the water supply of Hamburg and Altona, a smaller adjacent city. Altona filtered the water, and its citizens escaped the disease; Hamburg did not filter the water, and there 8,606 people died of cholera. Pettenkofer became not only a mocked but a reviled figure. He later committed suicide.

---

* The critics made some valid points. Clearly the attacking organism does not entirely determine whether someone gets sick. The same organism can attack two people, kill one, and not cause any symptoms in the other. An individual's genes, immune system, environment, and even such factors as stress all affect susceptibility.

As late as 1911 the head of the school training French army doctors in public health said that germs alone were "powerless to create an epidemic." But that particular view was by then an idiosyncratic, not simply minority, opinion.

There was still no cure for cholera, but now science had demonstrated—the dead in Hamburg were the final evidence—that protecting the water supply and testing for the bacteria would prevent the disease. After that only an isolated and discredited group of recalcitrants continued to reject the germ theory.

By then Welch had arrived at the Hopkins. It had not been an easy journey to Baltimore.

When the offer finally came in 1884, Welch had become comfortable in New York, and wealth was his for the asking. Virtually every student who had ever passed through his course had the utmost respect for him, and by now many were physicians. He had already made a reputation; that and his charm entered him into society as much as he desired.

His closest friend was his preparatory school roommate Frederick Dennis, wealthy son of a railroad magnate and also a physician who had studied in Germany. At every opportunity Dennis had advanced Welch's career, extolling his talents to editors of scientific journals, using his society connections to help him in New York, occasionally even subsidizing him indirectly. Indeed, Dennis behaved more like a lover trying to win affection than a friend, even a close friend.

But Dennis had always demanded a kind of fealty. Welch had heretofore been willing to give it. Now Dennis demanded that Welch stay in New York.

When Welch did not immediately agree, Dennis orchestrated an elaborate campaign to keep him there. He convinced Welch's father to advise him to stay, he convinced Andrew Carnegie to donate $50,000 for a laboratory at Bellevue, and he convinced Bellevue itself to pledge another $45,000; that would match any laboratory in Baltimore. And not only Dennis urged Welch to stay. A prominent attorney whose son had studied under Welch warned him that going to Baltimore would be "the mistake of your life. It is not in a century that a man of your age has acquired the reputation which you have gained." Even the president of the United States Trust Company sent a message that "however bright the prospect is in Baltimore it is darkness compared with the career" before him in New York.

The pressure was not without effect. Dennis did get Welch to set conditions that, if met, would cause him to stay. For Welch had his own doubts. Some related to his own fitness. He had done almost no real science in the years since returning from Germany. He had only talked for years about how his need to make a living prevented him from conducting original research.

The Hopkins expected more than talk. It had been open for eight years and, tiny as it was, had earned an international reputation. Welch confessed to his stepmother, "Such great things are expected of the faculty at the Johns Hopkins in the way of achievement and of reform of medical education in this country that I feel oppressed by the weight of responsibility. A reputation there will not be so cheaply earned as at Bellevue."

Yet precisely for that reason the Hopkins offered, he wrote, "undoubtedly the best opportunity in this country." Declining would reveal him as a hypocrite and a coward. Meanwhile in New York, the conditions he had set were not met, although Dennis considered them to have been.

Welch accepted the Hopkins offer.

Dennis was furious. His friendship with Welch had been, at least on Dennis's side, of great emotional depth and intensity. Now Dennis felt betrayed.

Welch confided to his stepmother, "I grieve that a life-long friendship should thus come to an end, but . . . [i]t looks almost as if Dr. Dennis thought he had a lien upon my whole future life. When he appealed to what he had done for me I told him that was a subject which I would in no way discuss with him."

Later Dennis sent Welch a letter formally breaking off their friendship, a letter written with enough intensity that in the letter itself he asked Welch to burn it after reading.

For Welch too the breaking off of the friendship was intense. He would not have another. Over much of the next half century, Welch's closest collaborator would be his protégé Simon Flexner. Together they would achieve enormous things. And yet Flexner too was kept distant. Flexner himself wrote that after Welch's estrangement from Dennis, "Never again would he allow any person, woman or colleague, close. . . . The bachelor scientist moved on a high plane of loneliness that may have held the secret of some of his power."

For the rest of his life Welch would remain alone. More than just alone, he would never dig in, never entrench himself, never root.

He never married. Despite working with others in ways that so often bind people together as comrades, with the single possible exception of the great and strange surgeon William Halsted—and that exception only a rumored possibility*—he had no known intimate relationship, sexual or otherwise, with either man or woman. Although he would live in Baltimore for half a century, he would never own a home there nor even have his own apartment; despite accumulating considerable wealth, he would live as a boarder, taking two rooms in the home of the same landlady, then moving with his landlady when she moved, and allowing his landlady's daughter to inherit him as a boarder. He would take

---

* Halsted had known Welch well in New York; both of them were trying to apply science to medicine. But Halsted began studying cocaine and became addicted. His life collapsed and he moved to Baltimore to be close to Welch. Once Halsted ended his addiction, Welch gave him a chance at the Hopkins, where he linked surgery to physiological research and became the most influential surgeon in the country and arguably the world. Halsted did marry, but he was eccentric and erratic and became addicted to morphine. It was unclear if Welch knew of this addiction.

nearly every dinner in one of his gentlemen's clubs, retreating to a world of men, cigars, and the conversations of an evening for the rest of his life. And he would, observed a young colleague, "deliberately break off relationships which seemed to threaten too strong an attachment."

But if he lived on the surface of ordinary life, his life was not ordinary. He was free, not just alone but free, free of entanglements of people, free of encumbrances of property, utterly free.

He was free to do extraordinary things.

At the Hopkins—it became simply "Hopkins" gradually, over several decades—Welch was expected to create an institution that would alter American medicine forever. When he accepted this charge in 1884, he was thirty-four years old.

The Hopkins went about achieving its goal both directly and indirectly. It served as home, however temporary, to much of the first generation of men and women who were beginning the transformation of American medical science. And its example forced other institutions to follow its path—or disappear.

In the process Welch gradually accumulated enormous personal power, a power built slowly, as a collector builds a collection. His first step was to return to Germany. Already he had worked under Cohn, to whom Koch had brought his anthrax studies, Carl Ludwig, and Cohnheim, three of the leading scientists in the world, and had met the young Paul

Ehrlich, his hands multicolored and dripping with dyes, whose insights combined with his knowledge of chemistry would allow him to make some of the greatest theoretical contributions to medicine of all.

Now Welch visited nearly every prominent investigator in Germany. He had rank now, for he happily reported that the Hopkins "already has a German reputation while our New York medical schools are not even known by name." He could entertain with stories, recite a Shakespeare sonnet, or bring to bear an enormous and growing breadth of scientific knowledge. Even those scientists so competitive as to be nearly paranoid opened their laboratories and their private speculations to him. His combination of breadth and intelligence allowed him to see into the depths of their work as well as its broadest implications.

He also learned bacteriology from two Koch protégés. One gave a "class" whose students were scientists from around the world, many of whom had already made names for themselves. In this group too he shined; his colleagues gave him the honor of offering the first toast of appreciation to their teacher at a farewell banquet. And Welch learned the most from Koch himself, the greatest name in science, who accepted him into his famous course—given only once—for scientists who would teach others bacteriology.

Then, back in Baltimore, years before its hospital or medical school actually opened, even without patients and without students, the Hopkins began to precipitate change. For although the Hopkins medical hospital did not open until 1889, and the medical school until 1893, its laboratory opened almost immediately. That alone was enough.

In just its first year, twenty-six investigators not on the Hopkins faculty used the laboratories. Welch's young assistant William Councilman—who later remade Harvard's medical school in the Hopkins's image—kept them supplied with organs by riding his tricycle to other hospitals, retrieving the organs, and carrying them back in buckets suspended from the handlebars. Many of these guests or graduate students were or became world-class investigators, including Walter Reed, James Carroll, and Jesse Lazear, three of the four doctors who defeated yellow fever. Within a few more years, fifty physicians would be doing graduate work at the same time.

And the Hopkins began assembling a faculty. Its institutional vision combined with Welch himself allowed it to recruit an extraordinary one. Typical was Franklin Mall.

Mall had gotten his medical degree from the University of Michigan in 1883 at age twenty-one, gone to Germany and worked with Carl Ludwig, done some graduate work at the Hopkins, and had already made a mark. He expected—required—the highest conceivable standards, and not just from his students. Victor Vaughan, dean of the Michigan medical school and second only to Welch in his influence on American medical education, considered the school's chemistry lab the best in America and comparable to the best in the world. Mall dismissed it as "a small chemical lab" and called his Michigan education equal to that of a good high school.

When Welch offered Mall a job, Mall was at the University of Chicago where he was planning the expenditure of $4 million, an enormous sum—John D. Rockefeller was the major donor to Chicago—to do what Welch was attempting, to build a great institution. Mall responded to Welch's offer by proposing instead that Welch leave the Hopkins for Chicago at a significant increase in salary.

By contrast, the Hopkins was desperate for resources but Welch rejected Mall's proposal and replied, "I can think of but one motive which might influence you to come here with us and that is the desire to live here and a belief in our ideals and our future. . . . They will not appeal to the great mass of the public, not even to the medical public, for a considerable time. What we shall consider success, the mass of doctors will not consider a success."

Mall considered the alternatives. At Chicago he had already, as he told Welch, "formulated the biological dept, got its outfit for $25,000 and have practically planned its building which will cost $200,000," all of it funded, with more to come from Rockefeller. At the Hopkins there was a medical school faculty and, by now, a hospital, but no money yet with which to even open the school. (Its medical school finally opened only when a group of women, many of whom had also recently founded Bryn Mawr College, offered a $500,000 endowment provided that the medical school would accept women. The faculty and trustees reluctantly agreed.) But there was Welch.

Mall wired him, "Shall cast my lot with Hopkins. . . . I consider you the greatest attraction. You make the opportunities."

Yet it was not Welch's laboratory investigations that attracted, that made opportunities. For, unknown to Gilman and Billings, who hired him, and even to Welch himself, he had a failing.

Welch knew the methods of science, all right, could grasp immediately the significance of an experimental result, could see and execute the design of further experiments to confirm a finding or probe more deeply. But he had had those abilities during his six years in New York, when he did no science. He had told himself and others that the demands of making a living had precluded research.

Yet he had no family to support and others did magnificent science under far greater burdens. No scientist had faced more adverse conditions than George Sternberg, an autodidact whom Welch called "the real pioneer of modern bacteriologic work in this country . . . [who] mastered the technique and literature by sheer persistence and native ability."

In 1878, as Welch met Billings in the same beer hall where legend had Faust meeting the Devil, Sternberg was an army medical officer in combat with the Nez Perce Indians. From there he traveled by stagecoach for four hundred and fifty miles—enduring day after day after day of the stink of sweat, of bone-shattering bumps that shot up the spine, of choking on the dust—only to reach a train, then by train for another twenty-five hundred miles of steaming discomfort, jostling elbows, and inedible food. He endured all this to attend a meeting of the American Public Health Association. While Welch was bemoaning his lack of facilities in New York, Sternberg was building a laboratory largely at his own expense at a frontier army post. In 1881 he became the first to isolate the pneumococcus, a few weeks before Pasteur and Koch. (None of the three recognized the bacteria's full importance.) Sternberg also first observed that white blood cells engulfed bacteria, a key to understanding the immune system. He failed to follow up on these observations, but many of his other achievements were remarkable, especially his pioneering work taking photographs through microscopes and his careful experiments that determined both the temperature at which various kinds of bacteria died and the power of different disinfectants to kill them. That information allowed the creation of antiseptic conditions in both laboratory and public health work. Sternberg began that work too in a frontier post.

Meanwhile, in New York City Welch was swearing that if only he were free of economic worries his own research would flower.

In Baltimore his work did not flower. For there, even with talented young investigators helping him, his failing began to demonstrate itself.

His failing was this: in science as in the rest of his life, he lived upon the surface and did not root. His attention never settled upon one important or profound question.

The research he did was first-rate. But it was only first-rate—thorough, rounded, and even irrefutable, but not deep enough or provocative enough or profound enough to set himself or others down new paths, to show the world in a new way, to make sense out of great mysteries. His most important discoveries would be the bacteria now called **Bacillus welchii,** the cause of gas gangrene, and the finding that staphylococci live in layers of the skin, which meant that a surgeon had to disinfect not only the skin surface during an operation but layers beneath it. These were not unimportant findings, and, even in the absence of any single more brilliant success, if they had represented a tiny piece of a large body of comparable work, they might have added up to enough to rank Welch as a giant.

Instead they would be the only truly significant

results of his research. In the context of an entire lifetime, especially at a time when an entire universe lay
naked to exploration, this work did not amount
to much.

The greatest challenge of science, its art, lies in
asking an important question and framing it in a
way that allows it to be broken into manageable
pieces, into experiments that can be conducted that
ultimately lead to answers. To do this requires a certain kind of genius, one that probes vertically and
sees horizontally.

Horizontal vision allows someone to assimilate
and weave together seemingly unconnected bits of
information. It allows an investigator to see what
others do not see, and to make leaps of connectivity
and creativity. Probing vertically, going deeper and
deeper into something, creates new information.
Sometimes what one finds will shine brilliantly
enough to illuminate the whole world.

At least one question connects the vertical and
the horizontal. That question is "So what?" Like a
word on a Scrabble board, this question can connect
with and prompt movement in many directions. It
can eliminate a piece of information as unimportant or, at least to the investigator asking the question, irrelevant. It can push an investigator to probe
more deeply to understand a piece of information.
It can also force an investigator to step back and
see how to fit a finding into a broader context. To see
questions in these ways requires a **wonder,** a deep

wonder focused by discipline, like a lens focusing the sun's rays on a spot of paper until it bursts into flame. It requires a kind of conjury.

Einstein reportedly once said that his own major scientific talent was his ability to look at an enormous number of experiments and journal articles, select the very few that were both correct and important, ignore the rest, and build a theory on the right ones. In that assessment of his own abilities, Einstein was very likely overly modest. But part of his genius was an instinct for what mattered and the ability to pursue it vertically and connect it horizontally.

Welch had a vital and wide curiosity, but he did not have this deeper wonder. The large aroused him. But he could not see the large in the small. No question ever aroused a great passion in him, no question ever became a compulsion, no question ever forced him to pursue it until it was either exhausted or led him to new questions. Instead he examined a problem, then moved on.

In his first years at the Hopkins he would constantly refer to his work, refer to his need to return to the laboratory. Later he abandoned the pretense and ceased even attempting to do research. Yet he never fully accepted his choice; to the end of his life he would sometimes express the wish that he had devoted himself to the laboratory.

Nonetheless, despite this lack of scientific achievement, Welch did not live one of those lives that began with great promise and ended in bitterness

and disappointment. Despite his minimal production in the laboratory, people like Mall were drawn
to him. As a prominent scientist said, "Everyone
agrees that Welch himself was the great attraction at
the Pathological. . . . [H]is example, his intelligence,
and his comprehensive knowledge formed the keystone of the arch of scientific medicine in America."
For William Welch's real genius lay in two areas.

First, he had not only knowledge but judgment. He
had an extraordinary ability to hear someone describe his or her experiments, or read a paper, and
immediately define the crucial points still obscure,
the crucial series of experiments needed to clarify
them. It was as if, although he could not himself
conjure, he knew the techniques of conjuring and
could teach others conjury.

He had an equally extraordinary ability to judge
people, to identify those with the promise to do
what he had not done. He largely chose the medical school faculty, and he chose brilliantly. All were
young when appointed. Welch was thirty-four;
William Osler, a Canadian and arguably the most
famous clinical physician of the modern era, forty;
William Halsted, a surgeon who changed the way
surgeons thought, thirty-seven; Howard Kelly,
a gynecologist and pioneer in radiation therapy,
thirty-one; J. J. Abel, a chemist and pharmacolo-
gist who would discover adrenaline and help revolutionize pharmacopoeia, thirty-six; W. H. Howell,

a physiologist, thirty-three; and Mall, thirty-one. (Howell, Abel, and Mall had been graduate students at the Hopkins.)

Second, Welch inspired. He inspired unconsciously, simply by being himself. In the early days of the school, Welch was heavy but not yet fat, short, with bright blue eyes that flashed above a dark beard called an "imperial"—a mustache and pointed goatee. He dressed conservatively but well in dark clothes and often carried a derby hat in his hand. Despite his bulk, his hands and feet were conspicuously small and made him appear almost delicate. But his most singular quality was not physical. He seemed so centered and comfortable with himself that he gave comfort to those around him. He exuded confidence without arrogance, smugness, or pomposity. In his disputes—and he had many with those outsiders who resisted changes—he never raised his voice, never seemed to feel, according to a man who watched him for decades, "the exuberant joy of putting an opponent down."

Everything about him was positive. His intelligence and the depth and breadth of his knowledge stimulated his teaching as well. He walked into the classroom without notes or preparation, often not knowing what subject he was to lecture on, and in an instant began discoursing lucidly and logically in ways that provoked thought and excitement. He was paternal without being paternalistic. Physicians sent him pathology samples for analysis and paid a hefty fee. His assistants did the work; he wrote up the results and gave them the money. He loved to eat and hosted lavish dinners at his club, the Maryland Club, often inviting junior colleagues or graduate students; one of them called these dinners among his "rosiest memories" because of Welch's conversation, his ability to make students feel "the richness of the world"—the world of art and literature as well as science.

The total effect, said Simon Flexner, "made for an atmosphere of achievement . . . The desire to be like Welch, the desire to win his approval, these were the principal incentives of the eager young men who crowded his lab."

Finally, a certain mystery clung to Welch. Although this was not part of his genius it explained part of his impact. For all his cordiality he remained distant. The cordiality itself was a barrier others could not penetrate. He paid little, and decreasing, attention to students until they did something significant enough to get his attention. He seemed casual, even sloppy. He would get so animated in conversation that his cigar ash would routinely drop onto his coat, where it would lie unnoticed. He was never on time. His desk would be piled with months of unanswered correspondence. Younger colleagues gave him a nickname, a nickname that spread from the Hopkins to younger scientists everywhere. They called him, never to his face, "Popsy."

It was a comfortable, paternal, and warm

nickname. But if he gave comfort, he took comfort from no one. Although he helped all whom he deemed worthy, although he surrounded himself with people, he neither encouraged nor allowed anyone to confide personal troubles to him. And he confided in no one. Mall once wrote his sister that he longed for a real friendship with Welch, not just an acquaintanceship. Even Mall would not get it. Welch took vacations alone in Atlantic City, where he enjoyed its tackiness.

The students had a chant: "Nobody knows where Popsy eats / Nobody knows where Popsy sleeps / Nobody knows whom Popsy keeps / But Popsy."

The Hopkins medical school sat on the city's outskirts atop a hill, miles from the main campus of the university and downtown. The main building, the Pathological Laboratory, was ugly and squat, two stories of stone, with six tall windows on each floor, and square chimneys towering above the building itself. Inside, an amphitheater for autopsies hollowed out the building, and students on the top floor could peer down over railings; a long narrow room lined each floor, a pathology laboratory on the first floor, a bacteriology laboratory on the second.

Even without the school, once the hospital opened in 1889, with sixteen buildings on fourteen acres, a small community began to develop. People breakfasted together and lunched together every day, and often met in the evening. Every Monday night a slightly more formal group of thirty to forty people gathered, including faculty, students who already had an M.D. or Ph.D., and clinicians. They would discuss current research or cases, and comments routinely generated new questions. Senior faculty sometimes dined in evening clothes at the "high table" in a bay window overlooking the grounds. The younger men played poker together, entertained each other, and went to the "Church" together—Hanselmann's restaurant and bar, at Wolfe and Monument, where they drank beer. A Harvard professor compared the Hopkins to a monastery. Harvey Cushing said, "In the history of medicine there was never anything quite like it." And they did have a mission.

Elias Canetti, a Nobel laureate in literature, observed in his book **Crowds and Power** that large movements were often generated by what he called "crowd crystals, . . . the small, rigid groups of men, strictly delimited and of great constancy, which serve to precipitate crowds. Their structure is such that they can be comprehended and taken in at a glance. Their unity is more important than their size. Their role must be familiar; people must know what they are there for. . . . The crowd crystal is **constant. . . .** Its members are trained in both action and faith. . . . The clarity, isolation, and constancy of the crystal form an uncanny contrast with the excited flux of the surrounding crowd."

In the same way that precipitates fall out of

solution and coalesce around a crystal, individuals with extraordinary abilities and a shared vision had now coalesced about Welch at the Hopkins. Together, with a handful of others around the country, they intended to precipitate a revolution.

CHAPTER FOUR

AMERICAN MEDICAL EDUCATION needed a revolution. When the Hopkins medical school did at last open in 1893, most American medical schools had still not established any affiliation with either a teaching hospital or a university, most faculty salaries were still paid by student fees, and students still often graduated without ever touching a patient. Nor did Welch exaggerate when he said that, other than the Hopkins, no American "medical school requires for admission knowledge approaching that necessary for entrance into the freshman class of a respectable college. . . . [S]ome require no evidence of preliminary education whatever."

By contrast, the Hopkins itself, not student fees, paid faculty salaries, and it required medical students to have not only a college degree but fluency in French and German and a background of science courses. Indeed, these requirements were so rigorous that Welch and Osler worried that the Hopkins would attract no students.

But students did come. They came flocking. Motivated and self-selected, they flocked to a school where students did not simply listen to lectures and take notes. They trooped through hospital rooms and examined patients, made diagnoses, heard the crepitant rales of a diseased lung, felt the alien and inhuman marble texture of a tumor. They performed autopsies, conducted laboratory experiments, and they explored: they explored organs with scalpels, nerves and muscles with electric currents, the invisible with microscopes.

Those at the Hopkins were hardly alone in seeking reform. The need had been recognized for decades. Leaders at a few other medical schools—especially Vaughan at Michigan, William Pepper Jr. at the University of Pennsylvania, William Councilman (Welch's assistant until 1892) at Harvard, others at Northwestern, at New York's College of Physicians and Surgeons, at Tulane—were advancing the same values that Welch and the Hopkins were, and they were doing so with equal urgency. The American Medical Association had pushed reform since its inception, and individual physicians sought better training as well; the thousands who studied in Europe proved that.

But relatively little change had occurred in the bulk of medical schools, and even at Harvard, Penn, and elsewhere, change had often come only after violent infighting, with continual rear-guard actions fought by reluctant faculty. William Pepper had made Penn good enough that the Hopkins raided its faculty, yet after sixteen years of fighting he spoke not of achievement but of "long and painful controversy."

Even where change had occurred, a gap between the Hopkins and elsewhere still remained. Harvey Cushing trained at Harvard and came to Baltimore as Halsted's assistant. Nothing in Boston had prepared him for the difference. He found the Hopkins "strange. . . . The talk was of pathology and bacteriology of which I knew so little that much of my time the first few months was passed alone at night in the room devoted to surgical pathology looking at specimens with a German textbook at hand."

The Hopkins did not limit its influence to medicine. Half a century after it opened, of 1,000 men starred in the 1926 edition of **American Men of Science,** 243 had Hopkins degrees; second was Harvard with 190. Even Harvard's Charles Eliot conceded that the Harvard Graduate School "started feebly" and "did not thrive, until the example of Johns Hopkins. . . . And what was true of Harvard was true of every other university in the land."

But in medicine the Hopkins made its chief mark. As early as 1900 Welch noted that at the Harvard-run Boston City Hospital "they have only Hopkins men there, and want no others." By 1913 a European acknowledged that research in the United States in his field rivaled that done in any European country and gave credit "to one man—Franklin P. Mall at the Johns Hopkins University." Of the first four American Nobel laureates in physiology or medicine, the Hopkins had trained three, while the fourth had received his highest degree in Europe.

In patient care its impact was similar. As with all medical schools, most of its graduates became practicing physicians. And within thirty-five years after opening, more than 10 percent of **all** Hopkins graduates had become full professors, with many younger graduates on track to do so. Many of these men transformed entire medical schools at other universities—people like Councilman and Cushing at Harvard, William MacCallum at Columbia, Eugene Opie at Washington University, Milton Winternitz at Yale, George Whipple (a Nobel laureate) at Rochester.

Howard Kelly, for all his strangeness—a fundamentalist who preached to prostitutes on street corners of whom one student said, "The only interest he manifested in my classmates was whether they were saved"—revolutionized gynecology and pioneered radiation therapy. And no individual had more impact on patient care than William Halsted, who introduced rubber gloves into surgery, who insisted upon preparation and thought prior to every step. He took such care that William Mayo once joked that his patients were healed by the time he finished, but the Mayo brothers also stated that they owed him a tremendous debt. So did all of American surgery: of seventy-two surgeons who served as residents or assistant residents under him, fifty-three became professors.

In the meantime, Henry James described the Hopkins as a place where, despite "the immensities of pain" one thought of "fine poetry . . . and the high beauty of applied science. . . . Grim human alignments became, in their cool vistas, delicate symphonies in white. . . . Doctors ruled, for me, so gently, the whole still concert."

Behind this still concert lay Welch, the impresario. By the first decade of the twentieth century, Welch had become the glue that cemented together the entire American medical establishment. His own person became a central clearinghouse of scientific medicine. Indeed, he became **the** central clearinghouse. As founding editor of the **Journal of Experimental Medicine,** the first and most important American research journal, he read submissions that made him familiar with every promising new idea and young investigator in the country.

He became a national figure, first within the profession, then within science, then in the larger world, serving as president or chairman of nineteen different major scientific organizations, including the American Medical Association, the American Association for the Advancement of Science, and the National Academy of Sciences. Stanford president Ray Wilbur neither flattered nor overstated when in 1911 he wrote him, "Not to turn to you for information in regard to the best men to fill vacancies in our medical school would be to violate all the best precedents of American medical education." Welch had, said one colleague, "the power to transform men's lives almost by the flick of a wrist."

But his use of power in placing people in positions—or for that matter using it for such things as defeating antivivisection legislation, which would have prevented using animals as experimental models and thus crippled medical research—was trivial in its impact compared to his application of power to two other areas.

One area involved completing the reform of all medical education. The example of the Hopkins had forced more and faster reforms at the best schools. But too many medical schools remained almost entirely unaffected by the Hopkins example. Those schools would learn a harsh lesson, and soon.

Welch's second interest involved starting and directing the flow of tens of millions of dollars into laboratory research.

In Europe governments, universities, and wealthy donors helped support medical research. In the United States, no government, institution, or philanthropist even began to approach a similar level of support. As the Hopkins medical school was opening, American theological schools enjoyed endowments of $18 million, while medical school endowments totaled $500,000. The difference in financial support as well as educational systems largely explained why Europeans had achieved the bulk of medical advances.

Those advances had been extraordinary, for medicine in the late nineteenth and early twentieth centuries was experiencing arguably its most golden age—including anytime since. The germ theory had opened the door to that progress. Finally investigators began using that door.

In 1880 Pasteur—who observed, "Chance favors the prepared mind"—was trying to prove he had isolated the cause of chicken cholera. He inoculated healthy chickens with the bacteria. They died. Then chance intervened. He had put aside a virulent culture for several days, then used it to inoculate more chickens. They lived. More significant, those same chickens survived when exposed to other virulent cultures. Crediting Jenner for the idea, he tried to weaken, or "attenuate," his word, cultures and use them to immunize birds against lethal bacteria. He succeeded.

He began applying these techniques to other infections. With anthrax he was not the first to experiment with weakened cultures, but his work was both definitive and very public. While a gallery of newspapermen and officials watched, he inoculated cattle, then exposed them to anthrax; the inoculuated ones lived, while the controls died. Three years later 3.3 million sheep and 438,000 cattle were vaccinated against anthrax in France. He also saved the life of a boy bitten by a rabid dog by giving him gradually stronger injections of fluid containing the pathogen. The next year, 1886, an international fund-raising drive created the Pasteur Institute. Almost immediately the German goverment funded research institutes for Koch and a few other outstanding investigators, and research institutes were founded in Russia, Japan, and Britain.

Meanwhile, public health measures were containing cholera and typhoid, and in Germany, Richard Pfeiffer, Koch's greatest disciple, and Wilhelm Kolle immunized two human volunteers with heat-killed typhoid bacilli. In Britain Sir Almroth Wright advanced upon this work and developed a vaccine against typhoid.

All these advances **prevented** infectious disease. But no physician could yet **cure** a patient who was dying of one. That was about to change.

One of the deadliest of childhood diseases was diphtheria. Usually it killed by choking its victims to death—by generating a membrane that closed the breathing passages. In Spain the disease was called **el garrotillo,** "the strangler."

In 1884, German scientist Friedrich Loeffler isolated the diphtheria bacillus from throats of patients, grew it on a special medium (laboratories today still use "Loeffler's serum slope" to grow the bacteria from suspected cases), and began careful experiments in animals that took several years. His work suggested that the bacteria themselves did not kill; the danger came from a toxin, a poison, that the bacteria excreted.

In 1889 Pasteur's protégés Émile Roux and Alexandre Yersin grew broth thick with diphtheria bacteria and used compressed air to force the broth through a filter of unglazed porcelain. (The filter was designed by Charles Chamberland, a physicist working with Pasteur; though only a tool, the filter itself would prove to be immensely important.) No bacteria or solids could pass through the porcelain. Only liquid could. They then sterilized this liquid. It still killed. That proved that a soluble toxin did the killing.

Meanwhile, an American physiologist named Henry Sewall at the University of Michigan was studying snake venom, which chemically resembles many bacterial toxins. In 1887 he immunized pigeons against rattlesnake poison.

If pigeons could be immunized, humans likely could be too. As they had with cholera, French and German scientists raced one another, building upon Sewall's and one another's advances, studying both diphtheria and tetanus. In December 1890, Koch protégés Emil Behring, who would later win the Nobel Prize, and Shibasaburo Kitasato showed that serum—the fluid left after all solids are removed from blood—drawn from one animal made immune to tetanus could be injected into a different animal and protect it from disease.

The paper shook the scientific world. Work on diphtheria at a level of intensity heretofore unknown proceeded in laboratories. Over the Christmas holiday in 1891 in Berlin, the first attempt to cure a person of diphtheria was made. It succeeded.

Scientists had discovered a way not simply to prevent a disease. They had found a way to cure disease. **It was the first cure.**

Over the next few years work continued. In 1894, Émile Roux of the Pasteur Institute read his paper summarizing experiments with diphtheria antitoxin before the International Congress on Hygiene in Budapest.

Many of the greatest scientists in the world sat in the audience. As Roux finished, these men, each renowned in his own right, began to clap, then stood on their seats, their hands making thunderous sounds, their voices shouting applause in half a dozen languages, their hats thrown to the ceiling. Welch then reported American experiences confirming the work of both the French and Germans. And each delegate returned to his home with a bottle of this marvelous curative agent in his possession.

In the keynote speech at the next meeting of the Association of American Physicians, an association created to foster scientific medicine, Welch said, "The discovery of the healing serum is entirely the result of laboratory work. In no sense was the discovery an accidental one. Every step leading to it can be traced, and every step was taken with a definite purpose and to solve a definite problem. These studies and resulting discoveries mark an epoch in the history of medicine."

His comment was a declaration not of war but of victory. Scientific medicine had developed technologies that could both prevent and cure diseases that had previously killed in huge numbers, and killed gruesomely.

And if French and German scientists had found the antitoxin, Americans William Park, chief of the laboratory division of the New York City Health Department, and Anna Williams, his deputy and perhaps the leading female bacteriologist in this country—possibly anywhere—transformed it into something that every doctor in the developed world had easy access to. They were an odd couple: he with an original and creative mind but staid, even stolid, extremely precise and well organized; she, wild, risk taking, intensely curious, a woman who took new inventions apart to see how they worked. They complemented each other perfectly.

In 1894 they discovered a way to make a toxin five hundred times as potent as that used by Europeans. This lethality made a far more efficient stimulator of antitoxin and slashed the cost to one-tenth what it had been. Park then broke the production process into tasks that ordinary workers, not scientists, could perform and turned part of the laboratory into a virtual factory. It soon became by far the cheapest, most efficient, and reliable producer of the antitoxin in the world. Diphtheria-antitoxin production today is still based on their methods.

The lab distributed it free in New York and sold it elsewhere. Park used the money to subsidize basic research and make the city laboratories into arguably the best medical research institution in the country at the time. Its annual reports soon contained, according to one historian of medicine, "a body of research of which any Institute in the world would be proud."

And the antitoxin suddenly became available around the world. Diphtheria fatality rates quickly fell by almost two-thirds, and country doctors began to perform miracles. It was only the first miracle of what promised to be many.

As the use of this antitoxin was becoming widespread, Frederick Gates, an intellectually curious Baptist minister who had a gift for seeing opportunities to exploit and was an assistant to John D. Rockefeller, picked up a medical textbook written by William Osler called **The Principles and Practice of Medicine,** a textbook that would go through many editions and find a readership among both physicians and informed laymen. In it

Osler traced the evolution of medical ideas, explored controversies, and, most significant, admitted uncertainty and ignorance.

Gates had started working for Rockefeller as a philanthropic adviser, but nothing limited him to eleemosynary concerns. He organized several Rockefeller business ventures, pulling, for example, a $50 million profit out of the Mesabi iron range in Minnesota. Rockefeller himself used a homeopathic physician, and Gates had also read **The New Testament of Homeopathic Medicine,** written by Samuel Hahnemann, founder of the movement. Gates decided that Hahnemann "must have been, to speak charitably, little less than lunatic."

Osler's book impressed Gates in very different ways for it presented a paradox. First, it showed that medical science had immense promise. But it also showed that that promise was far from being realized. "It became clear to me that medicine could hardly hope to become a science," Gates explained, "until . . . qualified men could give themselves to uninterrupted study and investigation, on ample salary, entirely independent of practice. . . . Here was an opportunity, to me the greatest, which the world could afford, for Mr. Rockefeller to become a pioneer."

Meanwhile, John D. Rockefeller Jr. talked about the idea of funding medical research with two prominent physicians, L. Emmett Holt and Christian Herter, both former students of Welch. Both eagerly endorsed the idea.

On January 2, 1901, Rockefeller Sr.'s grandchild John Rockefeller McCormick, also the grandchild of Cyrus McCormick, died of scarlet fever in Chicago.

Later that year the Rockefeller Institute for Medical Research was incorporated. It would change everything.

Welch declined the offer to head the new institute, but he assumed all the duties of launching it, chairing both the institute board itself and its board of scientific directors. That scientific board included Welch's old friend T. Mitchell Prudden, Holt, Herter, two other prominent scientists who had been students of Welch, and Harvard's Theobald Smith. Smith, one of the leading bacteriologists in the world, had been Welch's first choice for director but had declined because he had done most of his research on animal diseases—for example, developing a vaccine to prevent hog cholera—and thought it would be more politic to have a director who had investigated human disease.

So Welch offered the position to Simon Flexner, who had left the Hopkins to take a highly prestigious professorship at the University of Pennsylvania's medical school. (Flexner had rejected an offer of an $8,000 salary from Cornell to take the position at Penn at $5,000.) But his appointment had been contentious, and at the meeting where he was chosen, one faculty member said that accepting the Jew as a professor did not involve accepting him as a man. Daily he fought with other faculty over both personal and substantive issues.

Flexner accepted Welch's offer, and a raise. But the launching of the institute remained firmly under Welch's control. In this, Flexner said, Welch "accepted no assistance, not even clerical. Every detail was attended to with his own hand, every letter handwritten."

The European research institutes were either dedicated to infectious disease or designed to allow freedom to individuals such as Pasteur, Koch, and Ehrlich. The Rockefeller Institute saw medicine itself as its field; from its earliest existence, scientists there studied infectious disease, but they also laid the groundwork in surgery for organ transplants, established links between viruses and cancer, and developed a method to store blood.

At first the institute gave modest grants to scientists elsewhere, but in 1903 it opened its own laboratory, in 1910 its own hospital. And Flexner began to come into his own.

There was a roughness about Simon Flexner, something left over from the streets, from his growing up the black sheep in an immigrant Jewish family in Louisville, Kentucky. Older and younger brothers were brilliant students, but he quit school in the sixth grade. Sullen and flirting with delinquency, he was fired even by an uncle from a menial job in a photography studio. Next he worked for a dry-goods dealer who defrauded people and fled the city. A druggist fired him. His father gave him a tour of the city jail to try to frighten him into obedience, then arranged a plumbing apprenticeship, but the plumber balked when Simon's old principal warned him "not to have anything to do with Simon Flexner."

At the age of nineteen Flexner got another job with a druggist, washing bottles. The shop had a microscope and the druggist forbade him to touch it. He ignored the order. Flexner hated any kind of tedium, and taking orders. What the microscope showed him was not at all tedious.

Abruptly his mind engaged. He was fascinated. He began making sudden impossible leaps. In a single year he finished a two-year program at the Louisville College of Pharmacy and won the gold medal for best student. He began working for his older brother Jacob, another druggist who also had a microscope; now Simon did not have sneak to use it. Simultaneously he went to a medical school—at night. Flexner later recalled, "I never made a physical examination. I never heard a heart or lung sound."

But he did get an M.D. His younger brother Abraham had graduated from the Hopkins, and Simon sent some of his microscopic observations to Welch. Soon Simon was studying at the Hopkins himself.

Welch took to him though they were opposites. Flexner was small and wiry, almost wizened, and no one ever called him charming. He had an edgy insecurity and said, "I have never been educated in any branch of learning. There are great gaps in my knowledge." To fill the gaps, he read. "He read," his brother Abraham said, "as he ate." He devoured books, read everything, read omnivorously, from English literature to Huxley and Darwin. He felt he had to learn. His insecurities never fully left him. He talked of "sleepless nights and days of acute fear . . . a maddening nervousness which prevented me from having a quiet moment."

Yet others recognized in him extraordinary possibilities. Welch arranged a fellowship for him in Germany, and four years later he became professor of pathology at the Hopkins. Often he went into the field: to a mining town to study meningitis, to the Philippines to study dysentery, to Hong Kong to study plague. Nobel laureate Peyton Rous later called Flexner's scientific papers "a museum in print, only they stir with life; for he experimented as well as described."

He never lost his street toughness but his sharp hard edges did become rounded. He married a woman who was herself extraordinary enough to captivate Bertrand Russell (sixty letters from him were in her papers) and whose sister was a founder of Bryn Mawr. The famed jurist Learned Hand became a close friend. And he left his mark on the Rockefeller Institute.

Emerson said that an institution is the lengthened

shadow of one man, and the institute did reflect Simon Flexner. Raymond Fosdick, later president of the Rockefeller Foundation, talked of the "steely precision of his reason. His mind was like a search-light that could be turned at will on any question that came before him." A Rockefeller researcher said he had "a logic far beyond that of most men, final as a knife."

But in place of the comfort and monastic pur-pose and intimacy that Welch gave the Hopkins, Flexner made Rockefeller sharp, edgy, cold. Once, when the usefulness ended of horses that had been immunized against a disease, then bled over and over to produce antiserum, he never considered turning them out to pasture; he considered only either selling them for slaughter "to manufacturers or they can be bled further, with the idea of sacrific-ing them"—bleeding them to death for a final har-vest of serum. He could dismiss a person as easily, ridding the institute of what he termed "unoriginal" men as soon as he made that determination. The room most feared in the institute was Flexner's of-fice. He could be brutal there, and several prominent scientists were afraid of him. Even at Flexner's me-morial service, a Nobel laureate said, "Individuals were as nothing to Dr. Flexner compared with the welfare of the institute."

He sought attention for the institute from the press and credit from the scientific community. His own work created controversy. Shortly after the Rockefeller Institute was established, a meningitis epidemic struck the eastern United States. Desperate measures were used to fight the infection. Diphtheria antitoxin was tried, and some physicians even tried the ancient practice of bleeding patients. At the Hopkins, Cushing tried draining pus-filled fluid from the spinal canal.

At the Rockefeller Institute, the meningitis epidemic seemed a particular challenge. Rockefeller and Gates wanted results. Flexner wanted to produce them.

Ten years earlier William Park, who had perfected diphtheria antitoxin, had developed a serum against meningococci. In every laboratory test his serum had worked. But it had had no effect on people. Now two Germans developed a similar serum, but they injected it directly into the spinal column instead of into veins or muscle. Normally the mortality rate from the disease was 80 percent. In 102 patients they cut the mortality to 67 percent, suggestive but not a statistically significant improvement.

Still, Flexner's instincts told him it meant something. He repeated the German experiments. His patients died at a 75 percent rate. Instead of discarding the approach, however, he persisted; he began a long series of experiments, both in the laboratory, to improve the serum's potency, and physiologically, searching for the best way to administer it to monkeys. After three years of work, he settled upon the method: first, to insert a needle intrathecally—under a thin membrane lining the spinal cord—and withdraw 50 ccs of spinal fluid, and then to inject 30 ccs of serum. (Unless fluid was withdrawn first, the injection could increase pressure and cause paralysis.) It worked. In 712 people the mortality rate fell to 31.4 percent.

Physicians from Boston, San Francisco, Nashville—all confirmed the work, with one noting, "Remarkable results were obtained in the use of this serum by the country practitioners."

Not all accepted Flexner's role. Later, in a bacteriology textbook, Park implied that Flexner had contributed little to the development of the serum. Flexner responded with an angry visit to Park's lab; a shouting matching ensued. There would be further disputes between the two, public enough that newspapers reported on one.

Ultimately Flexner cut the death rate for patients infected by the meningococcus, the most common cause of bacterial meningitis, to 18 percent. According to a recent **New England Journal of Medicine** study, today with antibiotics patients at Massachusetts General Hospital, one of the best hospitals in the world, suffering from bacterial meningitis have a mortality rate of 25 percent.

He and the institute received massive amounts of publicity. He liked it and wanted more. So did Gates and Rockefeller. In the first decade of the institute especially, whenever someone there seemed on the edge of something exciting, Flexner hovered about.

His constant attention seemed to demand results, and he routinely urged investigators to publish, writing, for example, "In view of the rapidity with which publications are appearing from Belgium and France, I advise the publication of your present results. Please see me about this promptly."

The pressure did not all come from Flexner. It simply flowed down through him. At a 1914 dinner Gates declared, "Who has not felt the throbbing desire to be useful to the whole wide world? The discoveries of this institute have already reached the depths of Africa with their healing ministrations. . . . You announce a discovery here. Before night your discovery will be flashed around the world. In 30 days it will be in every medical college on earth."

The result was a publicity machine. Highly respected investigators mocked the institute for, said one who himself spent time there, "frequent ballyhoo of unimportant stuff as the work of genius" because of "administrators and directors impelled by the desire for institutional advertising."

Yet Flexner also had a large vision. In his own work, he had what Welch lacked: the ability to ask a large question and frame it in ways that made answering it achievable. And when he judged an investigator original, an asset to the institute, he gave his full support. He did so with Nobel laureates Alexis Carrel and Karl Landsteiner, both of whose work was recognized early, but he also gave freedom and support to young investigators who had not yet made their mark. Peyton Rous, whose undergraduate and medical degrees both came from the Hopkins, would win the Nobel Prize for his discovery that a virus could cause cancer. He made that finding in 1911. The prize did not come until 1966. Initially the scientific community mocked him; it took that long for his work first to be confirmed, then appreciated. Yet Flexner always stood by him. Thomas Rivers, a Hopkins-trained scientist at Rockefeller who defined the difference between viruses and bacteria, recalled, "I am not saying Flexner wasn't tough or couldn't be mean—he could, believe me—but he also was tender with people."

Even in a formal report to the board of scientific directors, thinking of Rous perhaps, or perhaps Paul Lewis, an extraordinarily promising young scientist working directly with Flexner, Flexner said, "The ablest men are often the most diffident and self-deprecatory. They require in many cases to be reassured and made to believe in themselves." When another scientist Flexner had faith in wanted to switch fields, Flexner told him, "It will take two years for you to find your way. I won't expect anything from you until after that."

And finally, Flexner believed in openness. He welcomed disagreement, expected friction and interaction, wanted the institute to become a living thing. The lunchroom was as important to Flexner as the laboratory. There colleagues working in different areas exchanged ideas. "Rous was a brilliant conversationalist, Jacques Loeb, Carrel," recalled Michael Heidelberger, then a junior investigator. Although Rous and Carrel won the Nobel Prize, Loeb may have been the most provocative. "These were really remarkable sessions sometimes. They were a great inspiration."

Each Friday especially mattered; investigators routinely presented their most recent work in a casual setting, and colleagues made comments, suggested experiments, added different contexts. It was a place of excitement, of near holiness, even though some men—Karl Landsteiner, for instance, another Nobel laureate—almost never made presentations. Flexner actively sought out individualists who did not fit in elsewhere, whether they be loners or prima donnas. The mix was what mattered. Flexner, Rous said, made the institute "an organism, not an establishment."

And Flexner's impact, like Welch's, was extending far beyond anything he did personally in the laboratory, or for that matter, in the Rockefeller Institute itself.

Even before the institute had exerted wide influence, American medical science was attaining world class. In 1908 the International Congress on Tuberculosis was held in Washington. Robert Koch came from Germany, great and imperious, prepared to pass judgment and issue decrees.

At a meeting of the section on pathology and

bacteriology, which Welch headed, Park read a paper stating that "it is now absolutely established that quite a number of children have contracted fatal generalized tuberculosis from bacilli" in cow's milk. Koch insisted Park was wrong, that no evidence supported the idea that cattle gave tuberculosis to man. Theobald Smith then rose and supported Park. Arguments broke out all over the room. But the congress as a whole was convinced; a few days later, it passed a resolution calling for preventive measures against the spread of tuberculosis from cattle to man. Koch snapped, "Gentlemen, you may pass your resolutions, but posterity will decide!"

One delegate noted, "Dr. Koch isolated the tubercle bacillus; today, science isolated Dr. Koch."

Science is not democratic. Votes do not matter. Yet this vote marked the coming of age of American medicine. It was by no means due solely to the Hopkins. Neither Park nor Smith had trained or taught there. But the Hopkins and the Rockefeller Institute were about to fit two more pieces into place that would give American medicine a true claim to scientific leadership.

CHAPTER FIVE

Tᴀ ᴍᴇɴ ᴡʜᴏ ᴄʀᴇᴀᴛᴇᴅ the Rockefeller
Institute always intended to have a small affili-
ated hospital built to investigate disease. No patient
would pay for treatment and only those suffering
from diseases being studied would be admitted. No
other research institute in the world had such a facility. That much William Welch, Simon Flexner,
Frederick Gates, and John D. Rockefeller Jr. did intend. But they did not plan to have what Rufus Cole,
the hospital's first director, all but forced upon them.

Tall, mustached, and elegant, with an ancestor who
arrived at Plymouth, Massachusetts, in 1633, Cole did
not appear to be a forceful man, did not seem someone capable of confronting Flexner. But he always
remained true to those things that he had thought

out, and his thinking was powerful. Then he yielded only to evidence, not to personality, and advanced his own ideas calmly and with tenacity. His longtime colleague Thomas Rivers called him "a modest man, a rather timid man," who "would go out of his way to dodge" a confrontation. But, Rivers added, "He was considered the brightest man that ever graduated from Hopkins at the time he graduated. . . . If you get him mad, get him in a corner and kind of back him up, . . . [y]ou would find, generally to your sorrow, that the old boy wasn't afraid to fight."

Cole had wide interests and late in life wrote a two-volume, 1,294-page study of Oliver Cromwell, the Stuarts, and the English Civil War. But at the institute lunch table he focused. Heidelberger recalled, "He would sit there and listen to whatever was going on, and then he'd ask a question. Sometimes the question seemed almost naive for a person who was supposed to know as much as he did, but the result always was to bring out things that hadn't been brought out before and to get much deeper down into the problem than one had before. Dr. Cole was really quite remarkable in that way."

His father and two uncles were doctors, and at the Hopkins his professor Lewellys Barker had established laboratories next to patient wards to study disease, not just conduct diagnostic tests. There Cole had done pioneering research. He came away from that experience with ideas that would influence the conduct of "clinical" research—research using patients instead of test tubes or animals—to this day.

Flexner saw the hospital as a testing ground for ideas generated by laboratory scientists. The scientists would control experimental therapies. The doctors treating the patients would do little more than play the role of a technician caring for a lab animal.

Cole had other ideas. He would not allow the hospital and its doctors to serve, said Rivers, as a "handmaiden. He and his boys were not going to test Noguchi's ideas, Meltzer's ideas, or Levens's ideas. Cole was adamant that people caring for patients do the research on them."

In a letter to the directors Cole explained that the clinicians should be full-fledged scientists conducting serious research: "One thing that has most seriously delayed the advancement of medicine has been the physical and intellectual barrier between the laboratory and the wards of many of our hospitals. Clinical laboratories most often exist merely to aid diagnosis. I would therefore urge that the hospital laboratory be developed as a true research laboratory, and that moreover [the doctors] of the hospital be permitted and urged to undertake experimental work."

This was no simple question of turf or bureaucratic power. Cole was setting an enormously important precedent. He was calling for—demanding—that physicians treating patients undertake rigorous research involving patients with disease. Precedents for this kind of work had been seen elsewhere, but not in the systematic way Cole envisioned.

Such studies not only threatened the power of the scientists doing purely laboratory research at the institute but, by implication, also changed the doctor-patient relationship. They were an admission that doctors did not know the answers and could not learn them without the patients' help. Since any rigorous study required a "control," this also meant that random chance, as opposed to the best judgment of the physician, might dictate what treatment a patient got.

Timid of nature or not, Cole would not yield. Flexner did. As a result, the Rockefeller Institute Hospital applied science directly to patient care, creating **the** model of clinical research—a model followed today by the greatest medical research facility in the world, the Clinical Center at the National Institutes of Health in Bethesda, Maryland. That model allowed investigators to learn. It also prepared them to act.

The Rockefeller Institute Hospital opened in 1910. By then the best of American medical science and education could compete with the best in the world. But an enormous gap existed in the United States between the best medical practice and the average, and an unbridgeable chasm separated the best from the worst.

In effect, there were outstanding generals, colonels, and majors, but they had no sergeants, corporals, or privates; they had no army to lead, at least not a reliable one. The gap between the best and the average had to be closed, and the worst had to be eliminated.

Physicians already practicing were unreachable. They had on their own either chosen to adopt scientific methods or not. Thousands had. Simon Flexner himself received his M.D. from a terrible medical school but had more than compensated, confirming Welch's observation: "The results were better than the system."

But the system of medical education still needed massive reform. Calls for reform had begun in the 1820s. Little had been accomplished outside a handful of elite schools.

Even among elite schools change came slowly. Not until 1901 did Harvard, followed soon by Penn and Columbia, join the Hopkins in requiring medical students to have a college degree. But even the best schools failed to follow the Hopkins's lead in recruiting quality faculty, instead choosing professors in clinical medicine from among local physicians. The official history of Penn's medical school conceded, "Inbreeding of a faculty could hardly go farther." Harvard's clinical professors were actually selected by a group of doctors who had no status at Harvard and met at the Tavern Club to make their decisions, which were usually based on seniority. Not until 1912 would Harvard select a clinical professor from outside this group.

Pressure did come from within the profession to improve. Not only those at the Hopkins, Michigan,

Pennsylvania, Harvard, and other leading medical schools devoted themselves to reform. So did a large number of individual physicians and surgeons. In 1904 the American Medical Association finally formed a Council on Medical Education to organize the reform movement. The council began inspecting all 162 medical schools—more than half of all the medical schools in the world—in the United States and Canada.

Three years later the AMA council issued a blistering—but confidential—report. It concluded that at the better schools improvement was occurring, although, despite enormous effort by many reformers, not at a rapid enough pace. But the worst schools had barely changed at all. Faculty still owned most of them, most still had no connection to a university or hospital and no standards for admission, and tuition still funded faculty salaries. One school had graduated 105 "doctors" in 1905, none of whom had completed any laboratory work whatsoever; they had not dissected a single cadaver, nor had they seen a single patient. They would wait for a patient to enter their office for that experience.

The report had some effect. Within a year, fifty-seven medical schools were requiring at least one year of college of their applicants. But that still left two-thirds of the schools with lower or no requirements, and it did not address the content of the education itself.

Unable to confront its own membership again—

in 1900 the AMA had only eight thousand members out of one hundred ten thousand doctors and feared antagonizing the profession—the AMA gave its report to the Carnegie Foundation, insisted that it remain confidential, and asked for help. In turn, the Carnegie Foundation commissioned Simon Flexner's brother Abraham to survey medical education. Although not a doctor, Flexner had been an undergraduate at the Hopkins—he said that even among undergraduates "research was the air we breathed"—and had already demonstrated both a ruthless, unforgiving judgment and a commitment to advancing model educational institutions. In his first job after college, he had taught in a Louisville high school—where he failed his entire class of fifteen students—and had experimented with new ways of teaching. Later he would create the Institute for Advanced Study at Princeton, and personally recruit Albert Einstein to it.

Abraham Flexner began his study by talking at length to Welch and Franklin Mall. Their views influenced him, to say the least. He stated, "The rest of my study of medical education was little more than an amplification of what I had learned during my initial visit to Baltimore."

In 1910, the same year the Rockefeller Institute Hospital opened, his report **Medical Education in the United States and Canada** appeared. It soon came to be known simply as "The Flexner Report."

According to it, few—very, very few—schools

met his standards, or any reasonable standard. He dismissed many schools as "without redeeming features of any kind . . . general squalor . . . clinical poverty. . . . [O]ne encounters surgery taught without patient, instrument, model, or drawing; recitations in obstetrics without a manikin in sight—often without one in the building." At Temple, at Halifax University, at the Philadelphia College of Osteopathy, the dissecting rooms "defy description. The smell is intolerable, the cadavers now putrid." At North Carolina Medical College Flexner quoted a faculty member saying, "'It is idle to talk of real laboratory work for students so ignorant and clumsy. Many of them, gotten through advertising, would make better farmers.'"

Flexner concluded that more than 120 of the 150-plus medical schools in operation should be closed.

It was the Progressive Era. Life was becoming organized, rationalized, specialized. In every field "professionals" were emerging, routing the ideas of the Jacksonian period, when state legislatures deemed that licensing even physicians was antidemocratic. Frederick Taylor was creating the field of "scientific management" to increase efficiencies in factories, and Harvard Business School opened in 1908 to teach it. This rationalization of life included national advertising, which was now appearing, and retail chains, which were stretching across the continent; United Drug Stores, the largest, had 6,843 locations.

But the Flexner report did not merely reflect the Progressive Era. Nor did it reflect the context in which one Marxist historian tried to place scientific medicine, calling it "a tool developed by members of the medical profession and the corporate class to . . . legitimize" capitalism and shift attention from social causes of disease. Noncapitalist societies, including Japan, Russia, and China, were adopting scientific medicine as well. The report reflected less the Progressive Era than science. Not surprisingly, progressives failed in a similar effort to standardize training of lawyers. Anyone could read a statute; only a trained specialist could isolate a pathogen from someone sick.

The Progressive Era was, however, also the muckraking era. Flexner's report raked muck and created a sensation. Fifteen thousand copies were printed. Newspapers headlined it and investigated local medical schools. Flexner received at least one death threat.

The impact was immediate. Armed now with the outcry Flexner had generated, the AMA's Council on Medical Education began rating schools as "Class A" and fully satisfactory; "Class B," which were "redeemable"; or "Class C," which were "needing complete reorganization." Schools owned and operated by faculty were automatically rated C.

Less than four years after Flexner's report was

issued, thirty-one states denied licensing recognition to new graduates of Class C institutions, effectively killing the schools outright. Class B schools had to improve or merge. Medical schools at such universities as Nebraska, Colorado, Tufts, George Washington, and Georgetown kept a tenuous hold on AMA approval but survived. In Baltimore three Class B schools consolidated into the present University of Maryland medical school. In Atlanta, Emory absorbed two other schools. Medical schools at such institutions as Southern Methodist, Drake, Bowdoin, and Fordham simply collapsed.

By the late 1920s, before the economic pressure of the Depression, nearly one hundred medical schools had closed or merged. The number of medical students, despite a dramatic increase in the country's population, declined from twenty-eight thousand in 1904 to fewer than fourteen thousand in 1920; in 1930, despite a further increase in the country's population, the number of medical students was still 25 percent less than in 1904.

Later, Arthur Dean Bevan, leader of the AMA reform effort, insisted, "The AMA deserved practically all the credit for the reorganization of medical education in this country. . . . 80% of the Flexner report was taken from the work of the Council on Medical Education." Bevan was wrong. The AMA wanted to avoid publicity, but only the leverage of the publicity—indeed, the scandal—Flexner generated could force change. Without the report, reform would have taken years, perhaps decades. And Flexner influenced the direction of change as well. He defined a model.

The model for the schools that survived was, of course, the Johns Hopkins.

Flexner's report had indirect impact as well. It greatly accelerated the flow, already begun, of philanthropic funds into medical schools. Between 1902 and 1934, nine major foundations poured $154 million into medicine, nearly half the total funds given away to all causes. And this understates the money generated, because the gifts often required the school to raise matching funds. This money saved some schools. Yale, for example, was rated a weak Class B school but it launched a fund-raising drive and increased its endowment from $300,000 to almost $3 million; its operating budget leaped from $43,000 to $225,000. The states also began pouring money into schools of state universities.

The largest single donor remained the Rockefeller Foundation. John D. Rockefeller himself continued to see a homeopathic physician.

Welch had turned the Hopkins model into a force. He and colleagues at Michigan, at Penn, at Harvard, and at a handful of other schools had in effect first formed an elite group of senior officers of an army; then, in an amazingly brief time, they had revolutionized American medicine, created and expanded the officer corps, and begun training their army, an army of scientists and scientifically grounded physicians.

On the eve of America's entry into World War I, Welch had one more goal. In 1884, when the Hopkins first offered Welch his position, he had urged the establishment of a separate school to study public health in a scientific manner. Public health was and is where the largest numbers of lives are saved, usually by understanding the epidemiology of a disease—its patterns, where and how it emerges and spreads—and attacking it at its weak points. This usually means prevention. Science had first contained smallpox, then cholera, then typhoid, then plague, then yellow fever, all through large-scale public health measures, everything from filtering water to testing and killing rats to vaccination. Public health measures lack the drama of pulling someone back from the edge of death, but they save lives by the millions.

Welch had put that goal aside while he focused on transforming American medicine, on making it science-based. Now he began to pursue that goal again, suggesting to the Rockefeller Foundation that it fund a school of public health.

There was competition to get this institution, and others tried to convince the foundation that though creating a school of public health made good sense, putting it in Baltimore did not. In 1916, Harvard president Charles Eliot wrote bluntly to the foundation—and simultaneously paid Welch a supreme compliment—when he dismissed the entire Hopkins medical school as "one man's work in a new and small university. . . . The more I consider the project of placing the Institute of Hygiene at Baltimore, the less suitable expedient I find it. . . . In comparison with either Boston or New York, it conspicuously lacks public spirit and beneficent community action. The personality and career of Dr. Welch are the sole argument for putting it in Baltimore—and he is almost 66 years old and will have no similar successor."

Nonetheless, that "sole argument" sufficed. The Johns Hopkins School of Hygiene and Public Health was scheduled to open October 1, 1918. Welch had resigned as a professor at the medical school to be its first dean.

The study of epidemic disease is, of course, a prime focus of public health.

Welch was sick the day of the scheduled opening, and getting sicker. He had recently returned from a trip to investigate a strange and deadly epidemic. His symptoms were identical to those of the victims of that epidemic, and he believed he too had the disease.

The army Welch had created was designed to attack, to seek out particular targets, if only targets of opportunity, and kill them. On October 1, 1918, the abilities of that army were about to be tested by the deadliest epidemic in human history.

■ Part II
THE SWARM

CHAPTER SIX

HASKELL COUNTY, KANSAS, lies west of Dodge City, where cattle drives up from Texas reached a railhead, and belongs geographically to and, in 1918, not far in time from, the truly Wild West. The landscape was and is flat and treeless, and the county was, literally, of the earth. Sod houses built of earth were still common then, and even one of the county's few post offices was located in the dug-out sod home of the postmaster, who once a week collected the mail by riding his horse forty miles round trip to the county seat in Santa Fe, a smattering of a few wooden buildings that was already well on its way to becoming the ghost town it would be in another ten years—today only its cemetery remains as a sign of its existence. But other towns nearby did have life. In Copeland, Stebbins Cash Store sold groceries, shoes, dry goods, dishes, hardware, implements, paints, and oils, while in Sublette, in the absence of a bank, S. E. Cave lent money on real estate for 7.5 percent.

Here land, crops, and livestock were everything, and the smell of manure meant civilization. Farmers lived in close proximity to hogs and fowl, with cattle, pigs, and poultry everywhere. There were plenty of dogs too, and owners made sure to teach their dogs not to chase someone else's cattle; that could get them shot.

It was a land of extremes. It was dry enough that the bed of the Cimarron River often lay cracked and barren of water, dry enough that the front page of the local newspaper proclaimed in February 1918, "A slow rain fell all day, measuring 27 one hundredths. It was well appreciated." Yet torrential rains sometimes brought floods, such as the one in 1914 that drowned ranchers and wiped out the first and largest permanent business in the area, a ranch that ran thirty thousand head of cattle. In summer the sun bleached the prairie, parching it under a heat that made light itself quiver. In winter unearthly gales swept unopposed across the plains for hundreds of miles, driving the wind chill past fifty degrees below zero; then the country seemed as frozen and empty as the Russian steppes. And storms, violent storms, from tornadoes to literally blinding blizzards, plagued the region. But all these extremes of nature came every season. Another extreme of nature came only once.

Epidemiological evidence suggests that a new influenza virus originated in Haskell County, Kansas, early in 1918. Evidence further suggests that this virus traveled east across the state to a huge army base, and from there to Europe. Later it began its sweep through North America, through Europe, through South America, through Asia and Africa, through isolated islands in the Pacific, through all the wide world. In its wake followed a keening sound that rose from the throats of mourners like the wind. The evidence comes from Dr. Loring Miner.

Loring Miner was an unusual man. A graduate of the oldest university in the West, Ohio University in Athens, Ohio, a classicist enamored of ancient Greece, he had come in 1885 to this region. Despite a background so unlike those of his fellow frontiersmen, he had taken to the country and done well.

Miner was a big man in many ways: physically large, with angular features and a handlebar mustache, gruff, someone who didn't suffer fools—especially when he drank, which was often. A certain rebelliousness was part of his bigness as well. He hadn't seen the inside of a church in years. Periodically he reread the classics in Greek, but he ate peas with his knife. And in thirty years on that prairie he had built a small empire apart from medicine. In the Odd Fellows he was a past noble grand, he had chaired the county Democratic Party, had been county coroner, was county health officer. He owned a drugstore and grocery and expected his patients to buy from him, and he married into the family of the largest landowners in western Kansas. Even in Haskell there was a social order, and now, during the war, his wife used her social standing as head of the county Red Cross Woman's Work Committee. When she asked for something few said no to her, and most women in the county did Red Cross work—real work, hard work, almost as hard as farmwork.

But Miner also personified Welch's comment that the results of medical education were better than the system. Although an isolated country doctor who began practicing before the establishment of the germ theory of disease, he had quickly accepted it, kept up with the astounding advances in his profession, built a laboratory in his office, learned how to use the new antitoxins for diphtheria and tetanus. By 1918 one of his sons had also become a doctor with a fully scientific education, and was already in the navy. He prided himself on his own scientific knowledge and puzzled over problems. His patients said they'd rather have him drunk than someone else sober.

His practice ranged over hundreds of square miles. Perhaps that was what Miner liked about it, the great expanse, the extremes, the lonely wind that could turn as violent as a gunshot, the hours spent making his way to a patient, sometimes in a horse and buggy, sometimes by car, sometimes by train—conductors would hold the train for him, and in winter stationmasters would violate the rules and let him wait inside the office by the stove.

But in late January and early February 1918, Miner had other concerns. One patient presented with what seemed common symptoms, although with unusual intensity—violent headache and body aches, high fever, nonproductive cough. Then another. And another. In Satanta, in Sublette, in Santa Fe, in Jean, in Copeland, on isolated farms.

Miner had seen influenza often. He diagnosed the disease as influenza. But he had never seen influenza like this. This was violent, rapid in its progress through the body, and sometimes lethal. This influenza killed. Soon dozens of his patients—the strongest, the healthiest, the most robust people in the county—were being struck down as suddenly as if they had been shot.

Miner turned all his energies to this disease. He drew blood and obtained urine and sputum samples, and used the laboratory skills his son had helped him improve. He searched all his medical texts and journals. He called his few colleagues in that part of the state. He contacted the U.S. Public Health Service, which offered him neither assistance nor advice. Meanwhile he likely did what little he could, trying diphtheria antitoxin with no effect, perhaps even trying tetanus antitoxin—anything that might stimulate the body's immune system against disease.

The local paper, the **Santa Fe Monitor,** apparently worried about hurting morale in wartime, said little about deaths but on inside pages reported, "Mrs. Eva Van Alstine is sick with pneumonia. Her little son Roy is now able to get up. . . . Ralph Lindeman is still quite sick. . . . Goldie Wolgehagen is working at the Beeman store during her sister Eva's sickness. . . . Homer Moody has been reported quite sick. . . . Mertin, the young son of Ernest Elliot, is sick with pneumonia. . . . We are pleased to report that Pete Hesser's children are recovering nicely. . . . Mrs J. S. Cox is some better but is very weak yet. . . . Ralph McConnell has been quite sick this week."

By now the disease overwhelmed Miner with patients. He pushed everything else aside, slept sometimes in his buggy while the horse made its own way home—one advantage over the automobile— through frozen nights. Perhaps he wondered if he was being confronted with the Plague of Athens, a mysterious disease that devastated the city during the Peloponnesian Wars, killing possibly one-third the population.

Then the disease disappeared. By mid-March the schools reopened with healthy children. Men and women returned to work. And the war regained its hold on people's thoughts.

The disease still, however, troubled Miner deeply.

It also frightened him, not only for his own people but for the people beyond. Influenza was neither a "reportable" disease—not a disease that the law required physicians to report—nor a disease that any state or federal public health agency tracked.

Yet Miner considered his experience so unusual, and this eruption of the disease so dangerous, that he formally warned national public health officials about it.

Public Health Reports was a weekly journal published by the U.S. Public Health Service to alert health officials to outbreaks of all communicable diseases, not only in North America and Europe but anywhere in the world—in Saigon, Bombay, Madagascar, Quito. It tracked not just deadly diseases such as yellow fever and plague but far lesser threats; especially in the United States, it tracked mumps, chickenpox, and measles.

In the first six months of 1918, Miner's warning of "influenza of severe type" was the only reference in that journal to influenza anywhere in the world. Other medical journals that spring carried articles on influenza outbreaks, but they all occurred after Haskell's, and they were not issued as public health warnings. Haskell County remains the first outbreak in 1918 suggesting that a new influenza virus was adapting, violently, to man.

As it turned out, the death rate in Haskell as a percentage of the entire county's population was only a fraction of what the death rate for the United States would be later that year, when influenza struck in full force.

People suffering from influenza shed virus—expel viruses that can infect others—for usually no more than seven days after infection and often even less. After that, although they may continue to cough and sneeze, they will not spread the disease. As sparsely populated and isolated as Haskell was, the virus infecting the county might well have died there, might well have failed to spread to the outside world. That would be so except for one thing: this was wartime.

The same week that Homer Moody and a dozen others in Jean, Kansas, fell ill, a young soldier named Dean Nilson came home to Jean on leave from Camp Funston, located three hundred miles away within the vast Fort Riley military reservation. The **Santa Fe Monitor** noted, "Dean looks like soldier life agrees with him." After his leave, of course, he returned to the camp. Ernest Elliot left Sublette, in Haskell County, to visit his brother at Funston just as his child fell ill; by the time Elliot returned home, the child had pneumonia. Of nearby Copeland on February 21, the paper said, "Most everybody over the country is having lagrippe or pneumonia." On February 28 it reported that John Bottom just left Copeland for Funston: "We predict John will make an ideal soldier."

Camp Funston, the second-largest cantonment in the country, held on average fifty-six thousand green young troops. The camp was built at the confluence of the Smoky Hill and Republican Rivers, where they form the Kansas River. Like all the other training camps in the country, Funston had been thrown together in literally a few weeks in 1917. There the army prepared young men for war.

It was a typical camp, with typical tensions between army regulars and men who had until recently been civilians. When Major John Donnelly was stopped by military police for speeding, for example, he defended himself to the commanding general: "I have, on a few occasions, corrected (enlisted) personnel along the road parallel to that camp for failure to salute; cases that I could not conscientiously overlook, there being no excuse whatever for their failure to do so. This, like my attempted correction of this guard, may not have been taken in the proper spirit, resulting in a feeling of insubordinate revenge and animosity towards me by members of this organization."

There were also the usual clashes of egos, especially since Camp Funston and Fort Riley had different commanding officers. These clashes ended when Major General C. G. Ballou, who commanded the cantonment, sent a missive to Washington. He had developed what he described as a "training ground for specialists" at Smoky Hill Flat. In fact, Smoky Hill Flat was the best of three polo fields on the base. The commanding officer of Fort Riley, only a colonel, established the post dump beside it. The general requested and received authority "to exercise command over the entire reservation of Fort Riley," and the colonel was relieved of his command.

Funston was typical in another way. The winter of 1917–18 was one of record cold, and, as the army itself conceded, at Funston as elsewhere "barracks and tents were overcrowded and inadequately heated, and it was impossible to supply the men with sufficient warm clothing."

So army regulations—written for health reasons—detailing how much space each man should have were violated, and men were stacked in bunks with insufficient clothing and bedding and inadequate heating. That forced them to huddle ever more closely together around stoves.

Men inducted into the army from Haskell County trained at Funston. There was a small but constant flow of traffic between the two places.

On March 4 a private at Funston, a cook, reported ill with influenza at sick call. Within three weeks more than eleven hundred soldiers were sick enough to be admitted to the hospital, and thousands more—the precise number was not recorded—needed treatment at infirmaries scattered around the base. Pneumonia developed in 237 men, roughly 20 percent of those hospitalized, but only thirty-eight men died. While that was a higher death toll than one would normally expect from influenza, it was not so high as to draw attention, much less than the death rate in Haskell, and only a tiny fraction of the death rate to come.

All influenza viruses mutate constantly. The timing of the Funston explosion strongly suggests that the influenza outbreak there came from Haskell; if Haskell was the source, whoever carried it to Funston brought a mild version of the virus, but it was a version capable of mutating back to lethality.

Meanwhile Funston fed a constant stream of men to other American bases and to Europe, men whose business was killing. They would be more proficient at it than they could imagine.

CHAPTER SEVEN

No ONE WILL EVER KNOW with absolute certainty whether the 1918–19 influenza pandemic actually did originate in Haskell County, Kansas. There are other theories of origin, including France, Vietnam, and China. But Frank Macfarlane Burnet, a Nobel laureate who lived through the pandemic and spent most of his scientific career studying influenza, later concluded that the evidence was "strongly suggestive" that the 1918 influenza pandemic began in the United States, and that its spread was "intimately related to war conditions and especially the arrival of American troops in France." Numerous other scientists agree with him. And the evidence does strongly suggest that Camp Funston experienced the first major outbreak of influenza in America; if so, the movement of men from an influenza-infested Haskell to Funston also strongly suggests Haskell as the site of origin.

Regardless of where it began, to understand what happened next, one must first understand viruses and the concept of the mutant swarm.

Viruses are themselves an enigma that exist on the edges of life. They are not simply small bacteria. Bacteria consist of only one cell, but they are fully alive. Each has a metabolism, requires food, produces waste, and reproduces by division.

Viruses do not eat or burn oxygen for energy. They do not engage in any process that could be considered metabolic. They do not produce waste. They do not have sex. They make no side products, by accident or design. They do not even reproduce independently. They are less than a fully living organism but more than an inert collection of chemicals.

Several theories of their origin exist, and these theories are not mutually exclusive. Evidence exists to support all of them, and different viruses may have developed in different ways.

A minority view suggests that viruses originated independently as the most primitive molecules capable of replicating themselves. If this is so, more advanced life forms could have evolved from them.

More virologists think the opposite: that viruses began as more complex living cells and evolved—or, more accurately, devolved—into simpler organisms.

This theory does seem to fit some organisms, such as the "rickettsia" family of pathogens. Rickettsia used to be considered viruses but are now thought of as halfway between bacteria and viruses; researchers believe they once possessed but lost activities necessary for independent life. The leprosy bacillus also seems to have moved from complexity—doing many things—toward simplicity—doing fewer. A third theory argues that viruses were once **part** of a cell, an organelle, but broke away and began to evolve independently.

Whatever the origin, a virus has only one function: to replicate itself. But unlike other life forms (if a virus is considered a life form), a virus does not even do that itself. It invades cells that have energy and then, like some alien puppet master, it subverts them, takes them over, forces them to make thousands, and in some cases hundreds of thousands, of new viruses. The power to do this lies in their genes.

In most life forms, genes are stretched out along the length of a filament-like molecule of DNA, deoxyribonucleic acid. But many viruses—including influenza, HIV, and the coronavirus that causes SARS (severe acute respiratory syndrome)—encode their genes in RNA, ribonucleic acid, an even simpler but less stable molecule.

Genes resemble software; just as a sequence of bits in a computer code tells the computer what to do—whether to run a word processing program, a computer game, or an Internet search—genes tell the cell what to do.

Computer code is a binary language: it has only two letters. The genetic code uses a language of four letters, each representing the chemicals adenine, guanine, cytosine, and thymine (in some cases uracil substitutes for thymine).

DNA and RNA are strings of these chemicals. In effect they are very long sequences of letters. Sometimes these letters do not form words or sentences that make any known sense: 97 percent of human DNA contains no genes; called "nonsense" or "junk" DNA, its function is still unknown.

But when the letters spell out words and sentences that do make sense, then that sequence is by definition a gene.

When a gene in a cell is activated, it orders the cell to make particular proteins. Proteins can be used like bricks as building blocks of tissue. (The proteins that one eats generally do end up building tissue.) But proteins also play crucial roles in most chemical reactions within the body, as well as in carrying messages to start and stop different processes. Insulin, for example, is a hormone but also a protein; it helps regulate the metabolism and it particularly affects blood glucose levels.

When a virus successfully invades a cell, it inserts its own genes into the cell's genome, and the viral genes seize control from the cell's own genes. The cell's internal machinery then begins producing what the viral genes demand instead of what the cell needs for itself.

So the cell turns out hundreds of thousands of viral proteins, which bind together with copies of the viral genome to form new viruses. Then the new viruses escape. In this process the host cell almost always dies, usually when the new viral particles burst through the cell surface to invade other cells.

But if viruses perform only one task, they are not simple. Nor are they primitive. Highly evolved, elegant in their focus, more efficient at what they do than any fully living being, they have become nearly perfect infectious organisms. And the influenza virus is among the most perfect of these perfect organisms.

Louis Sullivan, the first great modern architect, declared that form follows function.

To understand viruses, or for that matter to understand biology, one must think as Sullivan did, in a language not of words, which simply name things, but in a language of three dimensions, a language of shape and form.

For in biology, especially at the cellular and molecular levels, nearly all activity depends ultimately upon form, upon physical structure—upon what is called "stereochemistry."

The language is written in an alphabet of pyramids, cones, spikes, mushrooms, blocks, hydras, umbrellas, spheres, ribbons twisted into every imaginable Escher-like fold, and in fact every shape imaginable. Each form is defined in exquisite and absolutely precise detail, and each carries a message.

Basically everything in the body—whether it belongs there or not—either carries a form on its surface, a marking, a piece that identifies it as a unique entity, or its entire form and being comprises that message. (In this last case, it is pure information, pure message, and it embodies perfectly Marshall McLuhan's observation that "the medium is the message.")

Reading the message, like reading braille, is an intimate act, an act of contact and sensitivity. Everything in the body communicates in this way, sending and receiving messages by contact.

This communication occurs in much the same way that a round peg fits into a round hole. When they fit together, when they match each other in size, the peg "binds" to the hole. Although the various shapes in the body are usually more complex than a round peg, the concept is the same.

Within the body, cells, proteins, viruses, and everything else constantly bump against one another and make physical contact. When one protuberance fits the other not at all, each moves on. Nothing happens.

But when one complements the other, the act becomes increasingly intimate; if they fit together well enough, they "bind." Sometimes they fit as loosely as the round peg in the round hole, in which case they may separate; sometimes they fit more snugly, like a skeleton key in a simple lock on a closet door; sometimes they fit with exquisite precision, like a variegated key in a far more secure lock.

Then events unfold. Things change. The body reacts. The results of this binding can be as dramatic, or destructive, as any act of sex or love or hate or violence.

There are three different types of influenza viruses: A, B, and C. Type C rarely causes disease in humans. Type B does cause disease, but not epidemics. Only influenza A viruses cause epidemics or pandemics, an epidemic being a local or national outbreak, a pandemic a worldwide one.

Influenza viruses did not originate in humans. Their natural home is in wild aquatic birds, and many more variants of influenza viruses exist in birds than in humans. But the disease is considerably different in birds and humans. In birds, the virus infects the gastrointestinal tract. Bird droppings contain large amounts of virus, and infectious virus can contaminate cold lakes and other water supplies.

Massive exposure to an avian virus can infect man directly, but an avian virus cannot go from person to person. It cannot, that is, unless it first changes, unless it first adapts to humans.

This happens rarely, but it does happen. The virus may also go through an intermediary mammal, especially swine, and jump from swine to man. Whenever a new variant of the influenza virus does adapt to humans, it will threaten to spread rapidly across the world. It will threaten a pandemic.

Pandemics often come in waves, and the cumulative "morbidity" rate—the number of people who get sick in all the waves combined—often exceeds 50 percent. One virologist considers influenza so infectious that he calls it "a special instance" among infectious diseases, "transmitted so effectively that it exhausts the supply of susceptible hosts."

Influenza and other viruses—not bacteria—combine to cause approximately 90 percent of all respiratory infections, including sore throats.*

Coronaviruses (the cause of the common cold as well as SARS), parainfluenza viruses, and many other viruses all cause symptoms akin to influenza, and all are often confused with it. As a result, sometimes people designate mild respiratory infections as "flu" and dismiss them.

But influenza is not simply a bad cold. It is a quite specific disease, with a distinct set of symptoms and epidemiological behavior. In humans the virus directly attacks only the respiratory system, and it becomes increasingly dangerous as it

---

* Nonetheless, people today often demand antibiotics from physicians and the physicians too often accommodate them. But antibiotics have no effect whatsoever on viruses. Administering them serves only to increase resistance to antibiotics by bacteria: bacteria that survive exposure to antibiotics become immune to them.

penetrates deeper into the lungs. Indirectly it affects many parts of the body, and even a mild infection can cause pain in muscles and joints, intense headache, and prostration. It may also lead to far more grave complications.

The overwhelming majority of influenza victims usually recover fully within ten days. Partly because of this, and partly because the disease is confused with the common cold, influenza is rarely viewed with concern.

Yet even when outbreaks are not deadly as a whole, influenza strikes so many people that even the mildest viruses almost always kill. Currently in the United States, even without an epidemic or pandemic, the Centers for Disease Control estimates that influenza kills from 3,000 to 56,000 Americans a year, depending chiefly on the virulence of that year's virus.

It is, however, not only an endemic disease, a disease that is always around. It also arrives in epidemic and pandemic form. And pandemics can be more lethal—sometimes much, much more lethal—than endemic disease.

Throughout known history there have been periodic pandemics of influenza, usually several a century. They erupt when a new influenza virus emerges. And the nature of the influenza virus makes it inevitable that new viruses emerge.

■   ■   ■

The virus itself is nothing more than a membrane—a sort of envelope—that contains the genome, the genes that define what the virus is. It is usually spherical (it can take other shapes), about 1/10,000 of a millimeter in diameter, and it looks something like a dandelion with a forest of two different-shaped protuberances—one roughly like a spike, the other roughly like a tree—jutting out from its surface.

These protuberances provide the virus with its actual mechanism of attack. That attack, and the defensive war the body wages, is typical of how shape and form determine outcomes.

The protuberances akin to spikes are hemagglutinin. When the virus collides with the cell, the hemagglutinin brushes against molecules of sialic acid that jut out from the surface of cells in the respiratory tract.

Hemagglutinin and sialic acid have shapes that fit snugly together, and the hemagglutinin **binds** to the sialic acid "receptor" like a hand going into a glove. As the virus sits against the cell membrane, more spikes of hemagglutinin bind to more sialic acid receptors; they work like grappling hooks thrown by pirates onto a vessel, lashing it fast. Once this binding holds the virus and cell fast, the virus has achieved its first task: "adsorption," adherence to the body of the target cell.

This step marks the beginning of the end for the

cell, and the beginning of a successful invasion by the virus.

Soon a pit forms in the cell membrane beneath the virus, and the virus slips through the pit to enter entirely within the cell in a kind of bubble called a "vesicle." (If for some reason the influenza virus cannot penetrate the cell membrane, it can detach itself and then bind to another cell that it **can** penetrate. Few other viruses can do this.)

By entering the cell, as opposed to fusing with the cell on the cell membrane—which many other viruses do—the influenza virus hides from the immune system. The body's defenses cannot find it and kill it.

Inside this vesicle, this bubble, shape and form shift and create new possibilities as the hemagglutinin faces a more acidic environment. This acidity makes it cleave in two and refold itself into an entirely different shape. The refolding process somewhat resembles taking a sock off a foot, turning it inside out, and sticking a fist in it. The cell is now doomed.

The newly exposed part of the hemagglutinin interacts with the vesicle, and the membrane of the virus begins to dissolve. Virologists call this the "uncoating" of the virus and "fusion" with the cell. Soon the genes of the virus spill into the cell, then penetrate to the cell nucleus, and the viral genes begin issuing orders. The cell begins to produce viral proteins instead of its own. Within a few hours these proteins are packaged with new copies of the viral genes.

Meanwhile, the spikes of neuraminidase, the other protuberance that jutted out from the surface of the virus, are performing another function. Electron micrographs show neuraminidase to have a boxlike head extending from a thin stalk, and attached to the head are what look like four identical six-bladed propellers. The neuraminidase breaks up the sialic acid remaining on the cell surface. This destroys the acid's ability to bind to influenza viruses.

This is crucial. Otherwise, when new viruses burst from the cell they could be caught as if on fly paper; they might bind to and be trapped by sialic acid receptors on the dead cell's disintegrating membrane. The neuraminidase guarantees that new viruses can escape to invade other cells. Again, few other viruses do anything similar.

From the time an influenza virus first attaches to a cell to the time the cell bursts generally takes about ten hours, although it can take less time or, more rarely, longer. Then a swarm of between 100,000 and 1 million new influenza viruses escapes the exploded cell.

The word "swarm" fits in more ways than one.

Whenever an organism reproduces, its genes try to make exact copies of themselves. But sometimes mistakes—mutations—occur in this process.

This is true whether the genes belong to people,

plants, or viruses. The more advanced the organism, however, the more mechanisms exist to prevent mutations. A person mutates at a much slower rate than bacteria, bacteria mutate at a much slower rate than a virus—and a DNA virus mutates at a much slower rate than an RNA virus.

DNA has a kind of built-in proofreading mechanism to cut down on copying mistakes. RNA has no proofreading mechanism whatsoever, no way to protect against mutation. So viruses that use RNA to carry their genetic information mutate much faster—from 10,000 to 1 million times faster—than any DNA virus.

Different RNA viruses mutate at different rates as well. A few mutate so rapidly that virologists consider them not so much a population of copies of the same virus as what they call a "quasi species" or a "mutant swarm."

These mutant swarms contain trillions and trillions of closely related but different viruses. Even the viruses produced from a single cell will include many different versions of themselves, and the swarm as a whole will routinely contain almost every possible permutation of its genetic code.

Most of these mutations interfere with the functioning of the virus and will either destroy the virus outright or destroy its ability to infect. But other mutations, sometimes in a single base, a single letter, in its genetic code will allow the virus to adapt rapidly to a new situation. It is this adaptability that explains why these quasi species, these mutant swarms, can move rapidly back and forth between different environments and also develop extraordinarily rapid drug resistance. As one investigator has observed, the rapid mutation "confers a certain randomness to the disease processes that accompany RNA [viral] infections."

Influenza is an RNA virus. So are HIV and the coronavirus. And of all RNA viruses, influenza and HIV are among those that mutate the fastest. The influenza virus mutates so fast that 99 percent of the 100,000 to 1 million new viruses that burst out of a cell in the reproduction process are too defective to infect another cell and reproduce again. But that still leaves between 1,000 and 10,000 viruses that **can** infect another cell.

Both influenza and HIV fit the concept of a quasi species, of a mutant swarm. In both, a drug-resistant mutation can emerge within days. And the influenza virus reproduces rapidly—far faster than HIV. Therefore it adapts rapidly as well, often too rapidly for the immune system to respond.

An INFECTION is an act of violence; it is an invasion, a rape, and the body reacts violently. John Hunter, the great physiologist of the eighteenth century, defined life as the ability to resist putrefaction, resist infection. Even if one disagrees with that definition, resisting putrefaction certainly does define the ability to live.

The body's defender is its immune system, an extraordinarily complex, intricate, and interwoven combination of various kinds of white blood cells, antibodies, enzymes, toxins, and other proteins. The key to the immune system is its ability to distinguish what belongs in the body, "self," from what does not belong, "nonself." This ability depends, again, upon reading the language of shape and form.

The components of the immune system—white blood cells, enzymes, antibodies, and other elements—circulate throughout the body, penetrating everywhere. When they collide with other cells or proteins or organisms, they interact with and read physical markings and structures just as the influenza virus does when it searches for, finds, and latches on to a cell.

Anything carrying a "self" marking, the immune system leaves alone. (It does, that is, when the system works properly. "Autoimmune diseases" such as lupus or multiple sclerosis develop when the immune system attacks its own body.) But if the immune system feels a "nonself" marking—either foreign invaders or the body's own cells that have become diseased—it responds. In fact, it attacks.

The physical markings that the immune system feels and reads and then binds to are called "antigens." The word refers to, very simply, anything that stimulates the immune system to respond.

Some elements of the immune system, such as so-called natural killer cells, will attack anything that bears any nonself-marking, any foreign antigen. This is referred to as "innate" or "nonspecific" immunity, and it serves as a first line of defense that counterattacks within hours of infection.

But the bulk of the immune system is far more targeted, far more focused, far more specific. Antibodies, for example, are in effect floating receptors that recognize and bind to a single target antigen. So antibodies bearing these receptors will recognize and bind **only** to, for example, a virus bearing that antigen. They will not bind to any other invading organism.

One link between the nonspecific and specific immune response is a particular and rare kind of white blood cell called a dendritic cell. Dendritic cells attack bacteria and viruses indiscriminately, engulf them, then "process" their antigens and "present" those antigens—in effect they chop up an invading microorganism into pieces and display the antigens like a trophy flag.

The dendritic cells then travel to the spleen or the lymph nodes, where large numbers of other white blood cells concentrate. There these other white blood cells learn to recognize the antigen as a foreign invader and begin the process of producing huge numbers of antibodies and killer white cells that will attack the target antigen and anything attached to the antigen.

The recognition of a foreign antigen also sets off a parallel chain of events as the body releases enzymes. Some of these affect the entire body, for example, raising its temperature and causing fever. Others directly attack and kill the target. Still others serve as chemical messengers, summoning white blood cells to areas of invasion or dilating capillaries so killer cells can exit the bloodstream at the point of attack. Swelling, redness, and fever are all side effects of the release of these chemicals.

All this together is called the "immune response," and once the immune system is mobilized, it is formidable indeed. But all this takes time. The delay can allow infections to gain a foothold in the body, even to advance in raging cadres that can kill.

In the days before antibiotics, an infection launched a race to the death between the pathogen and the immune system. Sometimes a victim would become desperately ill; then, suddenly and almost miraculously, the fever would break and the victim would recover. This "resolution by crisis" occurred when the immune system barely won the race, when it counterattacked massively and successfully.

But once the body survives an infection, it gains an advantage. For the immune system epitomizes the saying that that which does not kill you makes you stronger.

After it defeats an infection, specialized white cells (called "memory T cells") and antibodies that bind to the antigen remain in the body. If any invader carrying the same antigen attacks again, the immune system responds far more quickly than the first time. When the immune system can respond so quickly that a new infection will not even cause symptoms, people become immune to the disease.

Vaccinations expose people to an antigen and mobilize the immune system to respond to that disease. In modern medicine some vaccines contain only the antigen, some contain whole killed pathogens, and some contain living but weakened ones.

They all alert the immune system and allow the body to mount an immediate response if anything bearing that antigen invades the body.

The same process occurs in the body naturally with the influenza virus. After people recover from the disease, their immune systems will very quickly target the antigens on the virus that infected them.

But influenza has a way to evade the immune system.

The chief antigens of the influenza virus are the hemagglutinin and neuraminidase protruding from its surface. But of all the parts of the influenza virus that mutate, the hemagglutinin and neuraminidase mutate the fastest. This makes it impossible for the immune system to keep pace.

By no means do the antigens of all viruses, even all RNA viruses, mutate rapidly. Measles is an RNA virus and mutates at roughly the same rate as influenza. Yet measles antigens do not change. Other parts of the virus do, but the antigens remain constant. (The most likely reason is that the part of the measles virus that the immune system recognizes as an antigen plays an integral role in the function of the virus itself. If it changes shape, the virus cannot survive.) So a single exposure to measles usually gives lifetime immunity.

Hemagglutinin and neuraminidase, however, can shift into different forms and still function. The result: their mutations allow them to evade the immune system but do not destroy the virus. In fact, they mutate so rapidly that even during a single epidemic both the hemagglutinin and neuraminidase often change.

Sometimes the mutations cause changes so minor that the immune system can still recognize them, bind to them, and easily overcome a second infection from the same virus.

But sometimes mutations change the shape of the hemagglutinin or neuraminidase enough that the immune system can't read them. The antibodies that bound perfectly to the old shapes do not fit well to the new one.

This phenomenon happens so often it has a name: "antigen drift."

When antigen drift occurs, the virus can gain a foothold even in people whose immune system has loaded itself with antibodies that bind to the older shapes. Obviously, the greater the change, the less efficiently the immune system can respond.

One way to conceptualize antigen drift is to think of a football player wearing a uniform with white pants, a green shirt, and a white helmet with a green **V** emblazoned on it. The immune system can recognize this uniform instantly and attack it. If the uniform changes slightly—if, for example, a green stripe is added to the white pants while everything else remains the same—the immune system will continue to recognize the virus with little difficulty. But if the uniform goes from green shirt and white pants to white shirt with green pants, the immune system may not recognize the virus so easily.

Antigen drift can create epidemics. One study found nineteen discrete, identifiable epidemics in the United States in a thirty-three-year period—more than one every other year. Each one caused between ten thousand and forty thousand "excess deaths" in the United States alone—an excess over and above the death toll usually caused by the disease. As a result influenza kills more people in the United States than any other infectious disease, including AIDS.

Public health experts monitor this drift and each year adjust the flu vaccine to try to keep pace. But they will never be able to match up perfectly, because even if they predict the direction of mutation, the fact that influenza viruses exist as mutating swarms means some will always be different enough to evade both the vaccine and the immune system.

But as serious as antigen drift can be, as lethal an influenza as that phenomenon can create, it does not cause great pandemics. It does not create firestorms of influenza that spread worldwide such as those in 1889–92, in 1918–19, in 1957, and in 1968, and to a lesser extent in 2009.

Pandemics generally develop only when a radical change in the hemagglutinin, or the neuraminidase, or both, occurs. When an entirely new gene coding for one or both replaces the old one, the shape of the new antigen bears little resemblance to the old one.

This is called "antigen shift."

To use the football-uniform analogy again, antigen shift is the equivalent of the virus changing from a green shirt and white pants to an orange shirt and black pants.

When antigen shift occurs, the immune system cannot recognize the antigen at all. Few people in the world will have antibodies that can protect them against this new virus, so the virus can spread through a population at an explosive rate.

Hemagglutinin occurs in eighteen known basic shapes, neuraminidase in nine, and they occur in different combinations with subtypes. Virologists use these antigens to identify what particular virus they are discussing or investigating. "H1N1," for example, is the name given the 1918 virus, currently found in swine. An "H3N2" virus is circulating among people today.

Antigen shift occurs when a virus that normally infects birds attacks humans directly or indirectly. Since 1997, two different avian viruses, H5N1 and H7N9, have directly infected more than 2,300 people, killing more than 1,000 and threatening another 1918-like pandemic.

Birds and humans have different sialic-acid receptors, so a virus that binds to a bird's sialic-acid receptor will not normally bind to—and thus infect—a human cell. In Hong Kong what most

likely happened was that the eighteen people who
got sick were subjected to massive exposure to the
virus. The swarm of these viruses, the quasi species, likely contained a mutation that could bind to
human receptors, and the massive exposure allowed
that mutation to gain a foothold in the victims. Yet
the virus did not adapt itself to humans; all those
who got sick were infected directly from chickens.

But the virus can adapt to man. It can do so
directly, with an entire animal virus jumping to
humans and adapting with a simple mutation. It
can also happen indirectly. For one final and unusual attribute of the influenza virus makes it particularly adept at moving from species to species.

The influenza virus not only mutates rapidly but
also has a "segmented" genome. This means that its
genes do not lie along a continuous strand of its nucleic acid, as do genes in most organisms, including
most other viruses. Instead, influenza genes are carried in unconnected strands of RNA. Therefore, if
two different influenza viruses infect the same cell,
"reassortment" of their genes becomes very possible.

Reassortment mixes some of the segments of the
genes of one virus with some from the other. It is
like shuffling two different decks of cards together,
then making up a new deck with cards from each
one. This creates an entirely new hybrid virus, which
increases the chances of a virus jumping from one
species to another.

If the Hong Kong chicken influenza had infected

someone who was simultaneously infected with a human influenza virus, the two viruses might easily have reassorted their genes. They might have formed a new virus that could pass easily from person to person. And the lethal virus might have adapted to humans.

The virus may also adapt indirectly, through an intermediary. Some virologists theorize that pigs provide a perfect "mixing bowl," because the sialic-acid receptors on their cells can bind to both bird and human viruses. Whenever an avian virus infects swine at the same time that a human virus does, reassortment of the two viruses can occur. And an entirely new virus can emerge that can infect man. In 1918 veterinarians noted outbreaks of influenza in pigs and other mammals, and pigs today still get influenza from a direct descendant of the 1918 virus. But it is not clear whether pigs caught the disease from man or man caught it from pigs.

And Dr. Peter Palese at Mount Sinai Medical Center in New York, one of the world's leading experts on influenza viruses, considers the mixing-bowl theory unnecessary to explain antigen shift: "It's equally likely that co-infection of avian and human virus in a human in one cell in the lung [gives] rise to the virus. . . . There's no reason why mixing couldn't occur in the lung, whether in pig or man. It's not absolute that there are no sialic acid receptors of those types in other species. It's not absolute that the avian receptor is really that different from the human, and, with one single amino acid change, the virus can go much better in another host."*

Antigen shift, this radical departure from existing antigens, led to major pandemics long before modern transportation allowed rapid movement of people. There is mixed opinion as to whether several pandemics in the fifteenth and sixteenth centuries were influenza, although most medical historians believe that they were, largely because of the speed of their movement and the number of people who fell ill. In 1510 a pandemic of pulmonary disease came from Africa and "attacked at once and raged all over Europe not missing a family and scarce a person." In 1580 another pandemic started in Asia, then spread to Africa, Europe, and America. It was so fierce "that in the space of six weeks it afflicted almost all the nations of Europe, of whom hardly the twentieth person was free of the disease," and some Spanish cities were "nearly entirely depopulated by the disease."

There is no dispute, though, that other pandemics in the past were influenza. In 1688, the year of the Glorious Revolution, influenza struck England, Ireland, and Virginia. In these places "the people

* In 2001 Australian scientist Mark Gibbs advanced a theory that the influenza virus can also "recombine" its genes. Recombination means taking part of one gene and combining it with part of another gene. It is like cutting all the cards of two decks in pieces, taping the pieces together randomly, then assembling the first fifty-two for a new deck. Recombination has been demonstrated, but most virologists are skeptical of Gibbs's hypothesis.

dyed . . . as in a plague." Five years later, influenza spread again across Europe: "all conditions of persons were attacked. . . . [T]hose who were very strong and hardy were taken in the same manner as the weak and spoiled, . . . the youngest as well as the oldest." In January 1699 in Massachusetts, Cotton Mather wrote, "The sickness extended to allmost all families. Few or none escaped, and many dyed especially in Boston, and some dyed in a strange or unusual manner, in some families all weer sick together, in some towns allmost all weer sick so that it was a time of disease."

At least three and possibly six pandemics struck Europe in the eighteenth century, and at least four struck in the nineteenth century. In 1847 and 1848 in London, more people died from influenza than died of cholera during the great cholera epidemic of 1832. And in 1889 and 1890, a great and violent worldwide pandemic—although nothing that even approached 1918 in violence—struck again. In the twentieth century, three pandemics struck. Each was caused by an antigen shift, by radical changes in either the hemagglutinin or the neuraminidase antigens, or both, or by changes in some other gene or genes.

Influenza pandemics generally infect from 15 to 40 percent of a population; any influenza virus infecting that many people and killing a significant percentage would be beyond a nightmare. In recent years public health authorities have at least twice identified a new virus infecting humans but successfully prevented it from adapting to man. To prevent the 1997 Hong Kong virus, which killed six of eighteen people infected, from adapting to people, public health authorities had every single chicken then in Hong Kong, 1.2 million of them, slaughtered.

An even greater slaughter of animals occurred in the spring of 2003 when a new H7N7 virus appeared in poultry farms in the Netherlands, Belgium, and Germany. This virus infected eighty-two people and killed one, and it also infected pigs. So public health authorities killed nearly thirty million poultry and some swine.

In 2004, H5N1, which had never fully disappeared, returned with a vengeance. At this writing it has infected approximately four hundred people around the world in five years, and it has killed approximately 60 percent of them. It threatened, and it still threatens, to cause another pandemic. In total, hundreds of millions of poultry were slaughtered in an attempt to contain it. Nonetheless it has become endemic worldwide.

This costly and dreadful slaughter was done to prevent what happened in 1918. It was done to stop either of these influenza viruses from adapting to, and killing, man. Meanwhile, in 2009 an entirely unexpected virus, one combining genes from viruses which had previously infected birds, swine, and humans, has launched the next pandemic.

■   ■   ■

One more thing makes influenza unusual. When a new influenza virus emerges, it is highly competitive, even cannibalistic. It usually drives older types into extinction. This happens because infection stimulates the body's immune system to generate all its defenses against all influenza viruses to which the body has ever been exposed. When older viruses attempt to infect someone, they cannot gain a foothold. They cease replicating. They die out. So, unlike practically every other known virus, only one type—one swarm or quasi species—of influenza virus dominates at any given time. This itself helps prepare the way for a new pandemic, since the more time passes, the fewer people's immune systems will recognize other antigens.

Not all pandemics are lethal. Antigen shift guarantees that the new virus will infect huge numbers of people, but it does not guarantee that it will kill large numbers. The twentieth century saw three pandemics.

The most recent new virus attacked in 1968, when the H3N2 "Hong Kong flu" spread worldwide with high morbidity but very low mortality—that is, it made many sick, but killed few. The "Asian flu," an H2N2 virus, came in 1957; while nothing like 1918, this was still a violent pandemic. Then of course there was the H1N1 virus of 1918, the virus that created its own killing fields.

Part III
THE TINDERBOX

CHAPTER NINE

IN THE SPRING OF 1918 death was no stranger to the world. Indeed, by then the bodies of more than five million soldiers had already been fed into what was called "the sausage factory" by generals whose stupidity was matched only by their brutality.

German generals, for example, had decided to bleed France into submission by matching it death for death at Verdun, believing that Germany's greater population would leave it victorious. The French later replied with their own massive offensive, believing that their **élan vital** would triumph.

Only slaughter triumphed. Finally one French regiment refused orders to make a suicidal charge. The mutiny spread to fifty-four divisions, stopped only by mass arrests, the conviction of twenty-three thousand men for mutiny, with four hundred sentenced to death and fifty-five actually executed.

Yet nothing expressed the brutality of this war as did a sanitation report on the planned eradication of rats in the trenches to prevent the spread of disease. A major noted, "Certain unexpected problems are involved in the rat problem. . . . The rat serves one useful function—he consumes the corpses on No Man's Land, a job which the rat alone is willing to undertake. For this reason it has been found desirable to control rather than eliminate the rat population."

All of Europe was weary of the war. Only in the United States Anglophiles and Francophiles, most of them concentrated on the East Coast and many of them holding positions of power or influence, were not weary. Only in the United States Anglophiles and Francophiles still regarded war as glorious. And they put intense pressure on President Woodrow Wilson to enter the war.

The war had begun in 1914. Wilson had withstood this pressure. A German submarine had sunk the **Lusitania** in 1915 and he had not gone to war despite outrage in the press, instead winning a German commitment to limit submarine warfare. He had resisted other justifications for war. He could fairly campaign for reelection in 1916 on the slogan "He Kept Us Out of War." And he warned, "If you elect my opponent, you elect a war."

On election night he went to bed believing he

had lost, but woke up reelected by one of the narrowest margins in history.

Then Germany took a great gamble. On January 31, 1917, giving only twenty-four hours' notice, it announced unrestricted submarine warfare against neutral and merchant vessels. It believed that it could starve Britain and France into submission before the United States—if the United States did at last declare war—could help. The action utterly outraged the nation.

Still Wilson did not go to war.

Then came the Zimmermann note: captured documents revealed that the German foreign minister had proposed to Mexico that it join Germany in war against the United States and reconquer parts of New Mexico, Texas, and Arizona.

Wilson's critics sputtered in fury at his pusillanimity. In a famous essay, pacifist and socialist Randolph Bourne, who later died in the influenza epidemic, lamented, "The war sentiment, begun so gradually but so perseveringly by the preparedness advocates who come from the ranks of big business, caught hold of one after another of the intellectual groups. With the aid of [Theodore] Roosevelt, the murmurs became a monotonous chant, and finally a chorus so mighty that to be out of it was at first to be disreputable and finally almost obscene. And slowly a strident rant was worked up against Germany."

On April 2, three weeks after the disclosure of

the note, after his cabinet unanimously called for war, Wilson finally delivered his war message to Congress. Two days later he explained to a friend, "It was necessary for me by very slow stages and with the most genuine purpose to avoid war to lead the country on to a single way of thinking."

And so the United States entered the war filled with a sense of selfless mission, believing glory still possible, and still keeping itself separate from what it regarded as the corrupt Old World. It fought alongside Britain, France, Italy, and Russia not as an "ally" but as an "Associated Power."

Anyone who believed that Wilson's reluctant embrace of war meant that he would not prosecute it aggressively knew nothing of him. He was one of those rare men who believed almost to the point of mental illness in his own righteousness.

Wilson believed in fact that his will and spirit were informed by the spirit and hope of a people and even of God. He talked of his "sympathetic connection which I am sure that I have with" all American citizens and said, "I am sure that my heart speaks the same thing that they wish their hearts to speak." "I will not cry 'peace' so long as there is sin and wrong in the world," he went on. "America was born to exemplify that devotion to the elements of righteousness which are derived from the revelations of Holy Scripture."

He is probably the only American president to have held to this belief with quite such conviction, with no sign of self-doubt. It is a trait more associated with crusaders than politicians.

To Wilson this war was a crusade, and he intended to wage total war. Perhaps knowing himself even more than the country, he predicted, "Once lead this people into war, and they'll forget there ever was such a thing as tolerance. To fight you must be brutal and ruthless, and the spirit of ruthless brutality will enter into the very fibre of our national life, infecting Congress, the courts, the policeman on the beat, the man in the street."

America had never been and would never be so informed by the will of its chief executive, not during the Civil War with the suspension of habeas corpus, not during Korea and the McCarthy period, not even during World War II. He would turn the nation into a weapon, an explosive device.

As an unintended consequence, the nation became a tinderbox for epidemic disease as well.

Wilson declared, "It isn't an army we must shape and train for war, it is a nation."

To train the nation, Wilson used an iron fist minus any velvet glove. He did have some legitimate reasons for concern, reasons to justify a hard line.

For reasons entirely unrelated to the war, America was a rumbling chaos of change and movement, its very nature and identity shifting. In 1870 the United States numbered only forty million souls, 72 percent of whom lived in small towns or on farms.

By the time America entered the war, the population had increased to roughly 105 million. Between 1900 and 1915 alone, fifteen million immigrants flooded the United States; most came from Eastern and Southern Europe, with new languages and religions, along with darker complexions. And the first census after the war would also be the first one to find more people living in urban areas than rural.

The single largest ethnic group in the United States was German-American and a large German-language press had been sympathetic to Germany. Would German-Americans fight against Germany? The Irish Republican Army had launched an uprising against British rule on Easter, 1916. Would Irish-Americans fight to help Britain? The Midwest was isolationist. Would it send soldiers across an ocean when the United States had not been attacked? Populists opposed war, and Wilson's own secretary of state, William Jennings Bryan, three times the Democratic nominee for president, had resigned from the cabinet in 1915 after Wilson responded too aggressively for him to Germany's torpedoing the **Lusitania.** Socialists and radical unionists were strong in factories, in mining communities in the Rockies, in the Northwest. Would they, drafted or not, defend capitalism?

The hard line was designed to intimidate those reluctant to support the war into doing so, and to crush or eliminate those who would not. Even before entering the war, Wilson had warned Congress,

"There are citizens of the United States, I blush to admit, . . . who have poured the poison of disloyalty into the very arteries of our national life. . . . Such creatures of passion, disloyalty, and anarchy must be crushed out."

He intended to do so.

His fire informed virtually everything that happened in the country, including fashion: to save cloth, a war material—everything was a war material—designers narrowed lapels and eliminated or shrank pockets. And his fury particularly informed every act of the United States government. During the Civil War, Lincoln had suspended the writ of habeas corpus, imprisoning hundreds of people. But those imprisoned presented a real threat of armed rebellion. He left unchecked extraordinarily harsh criticism. Wilson believed he had not gone far enough and told his cousin, "Thank God for Abraham Lincoln. I won't make the mistakes that he made."

The government compelled conformity, controlled speech in ways, frightening ways, not known in America before or since. Soon after the declaration of war, Wilson pushed the Espionage Act through a cooperative Congress, which balked only at legalizing outright press censorship—despite Wilson's calling it "an imperative necessity."

The bill gave Postmaster General Albert Sidney Burleson the right to refuse to deliver any periodical he deemed unpatriotic or critical of the administration. And, before television and radio, most of the political discourse in the country went through the mails. A southerner, a narrow man and a hater, nominally a populist but closer to the Pitchfork Ben Tillman wing of the party than to that of William Jennings Bryan, Burleson soon had the post office stop delivery of virtually all publications and any foreign-language publication that hinted at less-than-enthusiastic support of the war.

Attorney General Thomas Gregory called for still more power. Gregory was a progressive largely responsible for Wilson's nominating Louis Brandeis to the Supreme Court, a liberal and the court's first Jew. Now, observing that America was "a country governed by public opinion," Gregory intended to help Wilson rule opinion and, through opinion, the country. He demanded that the Librarian of Congress report the names of those who had asked for certain books and also explained that the government needed to monitor "the individual casual or impulsive disloyal utterances." To do the latter, Gregory pushed for a law broad enough to punish statements made "from good motives or . . . [if] traitorous motives weren't provable."

The administration got such a law. In 1798, Federalist President John Adams and his party, under pressure of undeclared war with France, passed the Sedition Act, which made it unlawful to "print, utter, or publish . . . any false, scandalous, or malicious writing" against the government. But that law inflamed controversy, contributed to Adams's reelection defeat, and led to the only impeachment of a Supreme Court justice in history, when Samuel Chase both helped get grand jury indictments of critics and then sentenced these same critics to maximum terms.

Wilson's administration went further, yet engendered little opposition. The new Sedition Act made it punishable by twenty years in jail to "utter, print, write or publish any disloyal, profane, scurrilous, or abusive language about the government of the United States." One could go to jail for cursing the government, or criticizing it, even if what one said was true. Oliver Wendell Holmes wrote the Supreme Court opinion that found the act constitutional—after the war ended, upholding lengthy prison terms for the defendants—arguing that the First Amendment did not protect speech if "the words used . . . create a clear and present danger."

To enforce that law, the head of what became the Federal Bureau of Investigation agreed to make a volunteer group called the American Protective League an adjunct to the Justice Department, and authorized them to carry badges identifying them as "Secret Service." Within a few months the APL would have ninety thousand members. Within a year, two hundred thousand APL members were operating in a thousand communities.

In Chicago a "flying squad" of league members and police trailed, harassed, and beat members of the Industrial Workers of the World. In Arizona, league members and vigilantes locked twelve hundred IWW members and their "collaborators" into boxcars and left them on a siding in the desert across the state line in New Mexico. In Rockford, Illinois, the army asked the league for help in gaining confessions from twenty-one black soldiers accused of assaulting white women. Throughout the country, the league's American Vigilance Patrol targeted "seditious street oratory," sometimes calling upon the police to arrest speakers for disorderly conduct, sometimes acting more . . . directly. And everywhere the league spied on neighbors, investigated "slackers" and "food hoarders," demanded to know why people didn't buy—or didn't buy more—Liberty Bonds.

States outlawed the teaching of German, while an Iowa politician warned that "ninety percent of all the men and women who teach the German language are traitors." Conversations in German on the street or over the telephone became suspicious. Sauerkraut was renamed "Liberty cabbage." The **Cleveland Plain Dealer** stated, "What the nation demands is that treason, whether thinly veiled or quite unmasked, be stamped out." Every day the **Providence Journal** carried a banner warning, "Every German or Austrian in the United States unless known by years of association should be treated as a spy." The Illinois Bar Association declared that lawyers who defended draft resisters were "unpatriotic" and "unprofessional." Columbia University president Nicholas Murray Butler, a national leader of the Republican Party, fired faculty critical of the government and observed, "What had been tolerable became intolerable now. What had been wrongheadedness was now sedition. What had been folly was now treason."

Thousands of government posters and advertisements urged people to report to the Justice Department anyone "who spreads pessimistic stories, divulges—or seeks—confidential military information, cries for peace, or belittles our effort to win the war." Wilson himself began speaking of the "sinister intrigue" in America carried on "high and low" by "agents and dupes."

Even Wilson's enemies, even the supposedly internationalist Communists, distrusted foreigners. Two Communist parties initially emerged in the United States, one with a membership of native-born Americans, one 90 percent immigrants.

Judge Learned Hand, one of Simon Flexner's closest friends, later observed, "That community is already in the process of dissolution where each man begins to eye his neighbor as a possible enemy, where nonconformity with the accepted creed, political as well as religious, becomes a mark of disaffection; where denunciation, without specification or backing, takes the place of evidence; where orthodoxy chokes freedom of dissent."

But American society hardly seemed to be

dissolving. In fact it was crystallizing around a single focal point; it was more intent upon a goal than it had ever been, or might possibly ever be again.

Wilson's hard line threatened dissenters with imprisonment. The federal government also took control over much of national life. The War Industries Board allocated raw materials to factories, guaranteed profits, and controlled production and prices of war materials, and, with the National War Labor Board, it set wages as well. The Railroad Administration virtually nationalized the American railroad industry. The Fuel Administration controlled fuel distribution (and to save fuel it also instituted daylight savings time). The Food Admininstration—under Herbert Hoover—oversaw agricultural production, pricing, and distribution. And the government inserted itself in the psyche of America by allowing only its own voice to be heard, by both threatening dissenters with prison and shouting down everyone else.

Prior to the war Major Douglas MacArthur had written a long proposal advocating outright censorship if the nation did fight. Journalist Arthur Bullard, who was close to Wilson confidant Colonel Edward House, argued for another approach. Congress's rejection of censorship settled the argument in Bullard's favor.

Bullard had written from Europe about the war for **Outlook, Century,** and **Harper's Weekly.** He pointed out that Britain was censoring the press and had misled the British people, undermining trust in the government and support for the war. He urged using facts only. But he had no particular affection for truth per se, only for effectiveness: "Truth and falsehood are arbitrary terms. . . . There is nothing in experience to tell us that one is always preferable to the other. . . . There are lifeless truths and vital lies. . . . The force of an idea lies in its inspirational value. It matters very little if it is true or false."

Then, probably at the request of House, Walter Lippmann wrote Wilson a memo on creating a publicity bureau on April 12, 1917, a week after America declared war. One outgrowth of the Progressive Era, of the emergence of experts in many fields, was the conviction that an elite knew best. Typically, Lippmann later called society "too big, too complex" for the average person to comprehend, since most citizens were "mentally children or barbarians. . . . Self-determination [is] only one of the many interests of a human personality." Lippmann urged that self-rule be subordinated to "order," "rights," and "prosperity."

The day after receiving the memo, Wilson issued Executive Order 2594, creating the Committee on Public Information—the CPI—and named George Creel its head.

Creel was passionate, intense, handsome, and wild. (Once, years after the war and well into middle age, he literally climbed onto a chandelier in a ballroom and swung from it.) He intended to create "one white-hot mass . . . with fraternity, devotion, courage, and deathless determination."

To do so, Creel used tens of thousands of press releases and feature stories that were routinely run unedited by newspapers. And those same publications instituted a self-censorship. Editors would print nothing that they thought might hurt morale. Creel also created a force of "Four Minute Men"— their number ultimately exceeded one hundred thousand—who gave brief speeches before the start of meetings, movies, vaudeville shows, and entertainment of all kinds. Bourne sadly observed, "[A]ll this intellectual cohesion—herd-instinct—which seemed abroad so hysterical and so servile comes to us here in highly rational terms."

Creel began intending to report only facts, if carefully selected ones, and conducting only a positive campaign, avoiding the use of fear as a tool. But this soon changed. The new attitude was embodied in a declaration by one of Creel's writers that, "Inscribed in our banner even above the legend Truth is the noblest of all mottoes—'We Serve.'" They served a cause. One poster designed to sell Liberty Bonds warned, "I am Public Opinion. All men fear me! . . . [I]f you have the money to buy and do not buy, I will make this No Man's Land for you!" Another CPI poster asked, "Have you met this Kaiserite? . . . You find him in hotel lobbies, smoking compartments, clubs, offices, even homes. . . . He is a scandal-monger of the most dangerous type. He repeats all the rumors, criticism, and lies he hears about our country's part in the war. He's very plausible. . . . People like that . . . through their vanity or curiosity or **treason** they are helping German propagandists sow the seeds of discontent. . . ."

Creel demanded "100% Americanism" and planned for "every printed bullet [to] reach its mark." Simultaneously, he told the Four Minute Men that fear was "an important element to be bred in the civilian population. It is difficult to unite a people by talking only on the highest ethical plane. To fight for an ideal, perhaps, must be coupled with thoughts of self-preservation."

"Liberty Sings"—weekly community events— spread from Philadelphia across the country. Children's choruses, barbershop quartets, church choirs—all performed patriotic songs while the audiences sang along. At each gathering, a Four Minute Man began the ceremonies with a speech.

Songs that might hurt morale were prohibited. Raymond Fosdick, a student of Wilson's at Princeton and board member (and later president) of the Rockefeller Foundation, headed the Commission on Training Camp Activities. This commission banned such songs as "I Wonder Who's Kissing Her Now" and "venomous parodies" such as "Who Paid the Rent for Mrs. Rip Van Winkle While Mr. Rip Van Winkle Was Away?" along with "questionable jokes and other jokes, which while apparently harmless, have a hidden sting—which leave the poison of discontent and worry and anxiety in the minds of the soldiers and cause them to fret about home. . . . [T]he songs and jokes were the culmination of letter writing propaganda instigated by the Huns in which they told lying tales to the men of alleged conditions of suffering at home."

And Wilson gave no quarter. To open a Liberty Loan drive, Wilson demanded, "Force! Force to the utmost! Force without stint or limit! the righteous and triumphant Force which shall make Right the law of the world, and cast every selfish dominion down in the dust."

That force would ultimately, if indirectly, intensify the attack of influenza and undermine the social fabric. A softer path that Wilson also tried to lead the nation down would mitigate—but only somewhat—the damage.

The softer path meant the American Red Cross.

If the American Protective League mobilized citizens, nearly all of them men, to spy upon and attack anyone who criticized the war, the American Red Cross mobilized citizens, nearly all of them women, in more productive ways. The International Red Cross had been founded in 1863 with its focus on war, on the decent treatment of prisoners as set forth in the first Geneva Convention. In 1881 Clara Barton founded the American Red Cross, and the next year the United States accepted the guidelines of the convention. By World War I, all the combatants were members of the International Red Cross. But each national unit was fully independent.

The American Red Cross was a quasi-public institution whose titular president was (and is) the president of the United States. Officially chartered by Congress to serve the nation in times of emergency, the American Red Cross grew even closer to the government during the war. The chairman of its Central Committee was Wilson's presidential predecessor William Howard Taft, and Wilson had appointed its entire "War Council," the real ruling body of the organization.

As soon as the United States entered World War I, the American Red Cross declared that it would "exert itself in any way which . . . might aid our allies. . . . The organization seeks in this great world emergency to do nothing more and nothing less than to coordinate the generosity and the effort of our people toward achieving a supreme aim."

There was no more patriotic organization. It had full responsibility for supplying nurses, tens of thousands of them, to the military. It organized fifty base hospitals in France. It equipped several railroad cars as specialized laboratories in case of disease outbreaks—but reserving them for use only by the military, not by civilians—and stationed them "so that one may be delivered at any point [in the country] within 24 hours." (The Rockefeller

Institute also outfitted railroad cars as state-of-the-art laboratories and placed them around the country.) It cared for civilians injured or made homeless after several explosions in munitions factories.

But its most important role had nothing to do with medicine or disasters. Its most important function was to bind the nation together, for Wilson used it to reach into every community in the country. Nor did the Red Cross waste the opportunity to increase its presence in American life.

It had already made a reputation in several disasters: the Johnstown flood in 1889, when a dam broke and water smashed down upon the Pennsylvania city like a hammer, killing twenty-five hundred people; the San Francisco earthquake in 1906; major floods on the Ohio and Mississippi Rivers in 1912. It had also served American troops in the Spanish-American War and during the insurrection in the Philippines that followed.

Still, the American Red Cross began the Great War with only 107 local chapters. It finished with 3,864 chapters.

It reached into the largest cities and into the smallest villages. It made clear that to participate in Red Cross activities was to join the great crusade for civilization, and especially for American civilization. And it used subtlety and social pressure to all but compel participation. It identified the most prominent and influential man in a city, a person whom others could refuse only with difficulty, and asked him to chair the local Red Cross chapter; it appealed to him, told him how important he was to the war effort, how needed he was. Almost invariably he agreed. And it asked the leading hostess, the leader of "society" in cities—in Philadelphia, Mrs. J. Willis Martin, who started the nation's first garden club and whose family and husband's family were as established as any on the Main Line—or whatever passed for "society" in small towns—in Haskell County, Mrs. Loring Miner, whose father was the largest landowner in southwest Kansas—to chair a woman's auxiliary.

In 1918 the Red Cross counted thirty million Americans—out of a total population of 105 million—as active supporters. Eight million Americans, nearly 8 percent of the entire population, served as production workers in local chapters. (The Red Cross had more volunteers in World War I than in World War II despite a 30 percent increase in the nation's population.) Women made up nearly all this enormous volunteer workforce, and they might as well have worked in factories. Each chapter received a production quota, and each chapter produced that quota. They produced millions of sweaters, millions of blankets, millions of socks. They made furniture. They did everything requested of them, and they did it well. When the Federal Food Administration said that pits from peaches, prunes, dates, plums, apricots, olives, and cherries were needed to make carbon for gas masks, newspapers reported, "Confectioners and restaurants in various cities have begun to serve nuts and fruit at cost in order to turn in the pits and shells, a patriotic service. . . . Every American man, woman or child who has a relative or friend in the army should consider it a matter of personal obligation to provide enough carbon making material for his gas mask." And so Red Cross chapters throughout the country collected thousands of tons of fruit pits— so many they were told, finally, to stop.

As William Maxwell, a novelist and **New Yorker** editor who grew up in Lincoln, Illinois, recalled, "[M]other would go down to roll bandages for the soldiers. She put something like a dish towel on her head with a red cross on the front and wore white, and in school we saved prune pits which were supposed to be turned into gas masks so that the town was aware of the war effort. . . . At all events there was an active sense of taking part in the war."

The war was absorbing all of the nation. The draft, originally limited to men aged twenty-one to thirty, was soon extended to men aged eighteen to forty-five. Even with the expanded base, the government declared that all men in that age group would be called within a year. **All** men, the government said.

The army would require as well at least one hundred thousand officers. The Student Army Training Corps was to provide many of that number: it would admit "men by voluntary induction, . . . placing them on active duty immediately."

In May 1918 Secretary of War Newton Baker wrote the presidents of all institutions "of Collegiate Grade," from Harvard in Cambridge, Massachusetts, to the North Pacific College of Dentistry in Portland, Oregon. He did not ask for cooperation, much less permission. He simply stated, "Military instruction under officers and non-commissioned officers of the Army will be provided in every institution of college grade which enroll 100 or more male students. . . . All students over the age of 18 will be encouraged to enlist. . . . The commanding officer . . . [will] enforce military discipline."

In August 1918 an underling followed Baker's letter with a memo to college administrators, stating that the war would likely necessitate "the mobilization of all physically-fit registrants under 21, within 10 months from this date. . . . The student, by voluntary induction, becomes a soldier in the United States Army, uniformed, subject to military discipline and with the pay of a private . . . on full active duty." Upon being activated, nearly all would be sent to the front. Twenty-year-olds would get only three months' training before activation, with younger men getting only a few months more. "In view of the comparatively short time during which most of the student-soldiers will remain in college and the exacting military duties awaiting them, academic instruction must necessarily be modified along the lines of direct military value."

Therefore the teaching of academic courses was to end, to be replaced by military training. Military officers were to take virtual command of each college in the country. High schools were "urged to intensify their instruction so that young men 17 and 18 years old may be qualified to enter college as quickly as possible."

The full engagement of the nation had begun the instant Wilson had chosen war. Initially the American Expeditionary Force in Europe was just that, a small force numbering little more than a skirmish line. But the American army was massing. And the forging of all the nation into a weapon was approaching completion.

That process would jam millions of young men into extraordinarily tight quarters in barracks built for far fewer. It would bring millions of workers into factories and cities where there was no housing, where men and women not only shared rooms but beds, where they not only shared beds but shared beds in shifts, where one shift of workers came home—if their room could be called a home—and climbed into a bed just vacated by others leaving to go to work, where they breathed the same air, drank from the same cups, used the same knives and forks.

That process also meant that through both intimidation and voluntary cooperation, despite a stated disregard for truth, the government controlled the flow of information.

The full engagement of the nation would thus provide the great sausage machine with more than one way to grind a body up. It would grind away with the icy neutrality that technology and nature share, and it would not limit itself to the usual cannon fodder.

CHAPTER TEN

WHILE AMERICA still remained neutral, William Welch, then president of the National Academy of Sciences, and his colleagues watched as their European counterparts tried to perfect killing devices.

Technology has always mattered in war, but this was the first truly scientific war, the first war that matched engineers and their abilities to build not just artillery but submarines and airplanes and tanks, the first war that matched laboratories of chemists and physiologists devising or trying to counteract the most lethal poison gas. Technology, like nature, always exhibits the ice of neutrality however heated its effect. Some even saw the war itself as a magnificent laboratory in which to test and improve not just the hard sciences but theories of crowd behavior, of scientific management of the means of production, of what was thought of as the new science of public relations.

The National Academy had itself been created during the Civil War to advise the government on science, but it did not direct or coordinate scientific research on war technologies. No American institution did. In 1915 astronomer George Hale began urging Welch and others in the NAS to take the lead in creating such an institution. He convinced them, and in April 1916 Welch wrote Wilson, "The Academy now considers it to be its plain duty, in case of war or preparation for war, to volunteer its assistance and secure the enlistment of its members for any services we can offer."

Wilson had been a graduate student at the Hopkins when Welch had first arrived there and immediately invited him, Hale, and a few others to the White House. There they proposed to establish a National Research Council to direct all war-related scientific work. But they needed the president to formally request its creation. Wilson immediately agreed, although he insisted the move remain confidential.

He wanted confidentiality because any preparation for war set off debate, and Wilson was about to use all the political capital he cared to in order to create the Council of National Defense, which was to lay plans for what would become, after

the country entered the war, the virtual government takeover of the production and distribution
of economic resources. The council's membership
was comprised of six cabinet secretaries, including the secretaries of war and the navy, and seven
men outside the government. (Ironically, considering Wilson's intense Christianity, three of the seven
were Jews: Samuel Gompers, head of the American
Federation of Labor; Bernard Baruch, the finan-
cier; and Julius Rosenwald, head of Sears. Almost
simultaneously, Wilson appointed Brandeis to the
Supreme Court. All this marked the first significant
representation of Jews in government.)

But Wilson's silent approval was enough. Welch,
Hale, and the others formed their new organization,
bringing in respected scientists in several fields, scientists who asked other colleagues to conduct specific pieces of research, research that fitted in with
other pieces, research that together had potential
applications. And medicine, too, had become a
weapon of war.

By then a kind of organizational chart had developed in American scientific medicine. This chart
of course did not exist in any formal sense, but it
was real.

At the top sat Welch, fully the impresario, capable of changing the lives of those upon whom his
glance lingered, capable as well of directing great
sums of money to an institution with a nod. Only

he held such power in American science, and no one else has held such power since.

On the rung below him were a handful of contemporaries, men who had fought beside him to change medicine in the United States and who had well-deserved reputations. Perhaps Victor Vaughan ranked second to him as a builder of institutions; he had created a solid one at Michigan and been the single most important voice outside the Hopkins demanding reform of medical education. In surgery the brothers Charles and William Mayo were giants and immensely important allies in forcing change. In the laboratory Theobald Smith inspired. In public health Hermann Biggs had made the New York City Department of Health probably the best municipal health department in the world, and he had just taken over the state health department, while in Providence, Rhode Island, Charles Chapin had applied the most rigorous science to public health questions and reached conclusions that were revolutionizing public health practices. And in the U.S. Army, Surgeon General William Gorgas also had developed an international reputation, continuing and expanding upon George Sternberg's tradition.

Both the National Research Council and the Council of National Defense had medical committees that were controlled by Welch himself, Gorgas, Vaughan, and the Mayo brothers, all five of whom had already served as president of the American Medical Association. But conspicuous by his absence was Rupert Blue, then the civilian surgeon general and head of the U.S. Public Health Service (USPHS). Welch and his colleagues so doubted his abilities and judgment that they not only blocked him from serving on the committees but would not allow him even to name his own representative to them. Instead they picked a USPHS scientist they trusted. It was not a good sign that the head of the public health service was so little regarded.

From the beginning of their planning, these men focused on the biggest killer in war—not combat, but epidemic disease. Throughout the wars in history more soldiers had often died of disease than in battle or of their wounds. And epidemic disease had routinely spread from armies to civilian populations.

This was true not just in ancient times or in the American Civil War, in which two men died from disease for every battle-related death (counting both sides, one hundred eighty-five thousand troops died in combat or of their wounds, while three hundred seventy-three thousand died of disease). More soldiers had died of disease than combat even in the wars fought since scientists had adopted the germ theory and modern public health measures. In the Boer War that raged from 1899 to 1902 between Britain and the white settlers of South Africa, ten British troops died of disease for each combat-related death. (The British also put nearly a quarter of the Boer population in concentration camps, where 26,370 women and children died.) In the Spanish-American War in 1898, six American soldiers died of disease—nearly all of them from typhoid—for every one killed in battle or who died of his wounds.

The Spanish-American War deaths especially were entirely unnecessary. The army had expanded in a matter of months from twenty-eight thousand to two hundred seventy-five thousand, and Congress had appropriated $50 million for the military, but not a penny went to the army medical department; as a result, a camp of sixty thousand soldiers at Chickamauga had not a single microscope. Nor was army surgeon general Sternberg given any authority. Military engineers and line officers directly rejected his angry protests about a dangerously unsanitary camp design and water supply. Their stubbornness killed roughly five thousand American young men.

Other diseases could be equally dangerous. When even normally mild diseases such as whooping cough, chickenpox, and mumps invade a "virgin" human population, a population not previously exposed to them, they often kill in large numbers—and young adults are especially vulnerable. In the Franco-Prussian War in 1871, for example, measles killed 40 percent of those who fell ill during the siege of Paris, and a measles epidemic erupted in the U.S. Army in 1911, killing 5 percent of all the men who caught the disease.

Those facts were of deep concern to Welch, Vaughan, Gorgas, and the others. They committed themselves to ensuring that the best medical science be available to the military. Welch, sixty-seven years old, short, obese, and out of breath, put a uniform on, devoted much time to army business, and took a desk in Gorgas's personal office that he used whenever in Washington. Vaughan, sixty-five years old and equally obese at 275 pounds, put a uniform on and became head of the army's Division of Communicable Disease. Flexner at age fifty-four put a uniform on. Gorgas had them all commissioned majors, the highest rank then allowed (regulations were changed and they all later became colonels).

They thought not only about caring for soldiers wounded in combat. They thought not only about finding a source for digitalis, which was imported from Germany (Boy Scouts gathered foxglove in Oregon and tests found it produced a suitable drug), or surgical needles (these too were all imported, so they set up a U.S. factory to produce them), or discovering the most efficient way to disinfect huge amounts of laundry (they asked Chapin to look into this).

They thought about epidemic disease.

The single man who had the chief responsibility for the performance of military medicine was Surgeon General of the Army William Crawford Gorgas. The army gave him little authority with which to work—not much more than Sternberg had had. But he was a man able to accomplish much in the face of not only benign neglect but outright opposition from those above him.

Naturally optimistic and cheerful, devout, son of a Confederate officer who became president of the University of Alabama, Gorgas took up medicine ironically in pursuit of another aim: a military career. After he failed to get an appointment to West Point, it seemed his only way into the army, and he took it despite his father's bitter opposition. He soon became entirely comfortable in medicine and preferred to be addressed as "Doctor" rather than by rank, even as he rose to "General." He loved learning and set aside a fixed amount of minutes each day for reading, rotating his attention among fiction, science, and classical literature.

Gorgas had a distinct softness around his eyes that made him appear gentle, and he treated virtually everyone with whom he came into contact with dignity. His appearance and manner belied, however, his intensity, determination, focus, and occasional ferocity. In the midst of crisis or obstacles his public equanimity made him a center of calm, the kind that calmed and gave confidence to others. But in private, after encountering obtuseness if not outright stupidity in his superiors, he slammed drawers, hurled inkwells, and stormed out of his office, muttering threats to quit.

Like Sternberg, he spent much of his early career at frontier posts in the West, although he also took Welch's course at Bellevue. Unlike Sternberg, he did not personally do any significant laboratory research. But he was every bit as tenacious, every bit as disciplined.

Two experiences epitomized both his abilities and his determination to do his job. The first came in Havana after the Spanish-American War. He did not belong to Walter Reed's team investigating yellow fever. Their work in fact did not convince him that the mosquito carried the disease. Nonetheless he was given the task of killing mosquitoes in Havana. He succeeded in this task—despite doubting its usefulness—so well that in 1902 yellow fever deaths there fell to zero. **Zero.** And malaria deaths fell by 75 percent. (The results convinced him that the mosquito hypothesis was correct.) An even more significant triumph came when he later took charge of clearing yellow fever from the construction sites along the Panama Canal. In this case his superiors rejected the mosquito hypothesis, gave him the barest minimum of resources, and tried to undermine his authority, his effort, and him personally, at one point demanding that he be replaced. He persisted—and succeeded—partly through his intelligence and insight into the problems disease presented, partly through his ability to maneuver bureaucratically. In the process he also earned a reputation as an international expert on public health and sanitation.

He became surgeon general of the army in 1914 and immediately began massaging congressmen and senators for money and authority to prepare in case the country went to war. He wanted no repeat of Sternberg's Spanish-American experience. Believing his work done, in 1917 he submitted his resignation to join a Rockefeller-sponsored international health project. When the United States entered the war, he withdrew his resignation.

Then sixty-three years old, white-haired, with a handlebar mustache, and thin—as a boy he had been almost fragile, and he remained thin despite an appetite for food that rivaled Welch's—he took as his first task surrounding himself with the best possible people, while simultaenously trying to inject his and their influence into army planning. His War Department seniors did not consult his department on the sites for its several dozen new cantonments, but army engineers did pay close attention to the medical department in the actual design of the training camps. They too wanted no repeat of the mistakes that had killed thousands of soldiers in 1898.

But only in one other area did the army medical department receive even a hearing from War Department leadership. That was its massive campaign against venereal disease, a campaign supported strongly by a political union of progressives, many of whom believed in perfecting secular society, and from Christian moralists. (The same political odd couple would soon unite to enact Prohibition.) Gorgas's office recognized "to what extremes the

sexual moralist can go. How unpractical, how in-
tolerant, how extravagant, even how unreasoning,
if not scientifically dishonest, he can be." But it also
knew that one-third of all workdays lost to illness
in the army were caused by venereal disease. That
loss the military would not tolerate.

The medical corps told enlisted men to mastur-
bate instead of using prostitutes. It produced posters
with such slogans as "A Soldier who gets a dose is
a traitor." It examined enlisted men twice a month
for venereal disease, required any men infected to
identify the person with whom or the building in
which they had had sex, docked the pay of soldiers
or sailors sick with venereal disease, and also made
them subject to court-martial. With support from
the most senior political leadership, the military
by law prohibited prostitution and the sale of alcohol within five miles of any base—and the military had seventy bases with ten thousand or more
soldiers or sailors scattered around the country.
The health boards of twenty-seven states passed
regulations allowing detention of people suffering venereal infection "until they are no longer a
danger to the community." Eighty red-light districts were shut down. Even New Orleans had to
close down its legendary Storyville, where prostitution was legal, where Buddy Bolden, Jelly Roll
Morton, Louis Armstrong, and others had invented
jazz in the whorehouses. And New Orleans mayor
Martin Behrman was no reformer; he headed a

political machine so tight it was called simply "the Ring."

But if Gorgas had the power to act decisively on venereal disease, if engineers listened to his sanitary experts in designing water supplies, the army paid him little heed on anything else. On no subject where he had only science behind him, science without political weight, could he get even a hearing from army superiors. Even when an American researcher developed an antitoxin for gangrene, Gorgas could not convince them to fund testing at the front. So Welch arranged for the Rockefeller Institute to pay the expenses of a team of investigators to go to Europe, and for the British army to test the antitoxin in British hospitals. (It worked, although not perfectly.)

In many ways, then, Gorgas, Welch, Vaughan, and their colleagues operated as a team independent of the army. But they could not operate independently in regard to epidemic disease, and they could not operate either independently or alone as camps filled with hundreds of thousands—in fact, millions—of young men.

When the war began there were one hundred forty thousand physicians in the United States. Only 776 of them were serving in the army or navy.

The military needed tens of thousands of physicians, and it needed them immediately. It would make no exceptions for scientists. Most would volunteer anyway. Most wanted to participate in this great crusade.

Welch and Vaughan joined the military, despite their being one hundred pounds overweight and past the regular army's mandatory retirement age, and they were not alone. Flexner joined at age fifty-four. Flexner's protégé Paul Lewis at Penn, Milton Rosenau at Harvard, and Eugene Opie at Washington University joined. All around the country laboratory scientists were joining.

And to avoid losing scientists piecemeal either as volunteers or to the draft, Flexner suggested to Welch that the entire Rockefeller Institute be incorporated into the army. Welch carried the idea to Gorgas, and Gorgas's deputy wired Flexner, "[U]nit will be arranged as you desire." And so the Rockefeller Institute became Army Auxiliary Laboratory Number One. There would be no auxiliary laboratory number two. Men in uniforms marched down laboratory and hospital corridors. An army adjutant commanded the technicians and janitors, maintained army discipline among them, and drilled them on parade on York Avenue. Lunch became "mess." A mobile hospital unit on wheels with buildings, wards, labs, laundry, and kitchen was rolled into the front yard of the institute from Sixty-fourth to Sixty-sixth Streets to treat soldiers with intractable wounds. Sergeants saluted scientists who—except for two Canadians who became privates—received officer rank.

This was no mere cosmetic change to allow life to go on as usual.* At Rockefeller the fiber of the work was rewoven. Nearly all research shifted to something war-related, or to instruction. Alexis Carrel, a Nobel laureate in 1912 who pioneered the surgical reattachment of limbs and organ transplantation as well as tissue culture—he kept part of a chicken heart alive for thirty-two years—taught surgical techniques to hundreds of newly militarized physicians. Others taught bacteriology. A biochemist studied poison gas. Another chemist explored ways to get more acetone from starch, which could be used both to make explosives and to stiffen the fabric that covered airplane wings. Peyton Rous, who had already done the work that would later—decades later—win him a Nobel Prize, redirected his work to preserving blood; he developed a method still in use that led to the first blood banks being established at the front in 1917.

The war also consumed the supply of practicing physicians. Gorgas, Welch, and Vaughan had already laid plans for this. In December 1916 they had, through the Council of National Defense, asked state medical associations to secretly grade physicians. Roughly half of all practicing physicians

---

* During the Vietnam War many physician-scientists joined the Public Health Service to avoid the draft. But their work did go on as usual. They were assigned to the National Institutes of Health, which enjoyed some of its most productive years in history because of the influx of talent.

were judged incompetent to serve. So when America did enter the war, the military first examined every male graduate of medical school in 1914, 1915, and 1916, seeking, as Vaughan said, the "best from these classes." This would supply approximately ten thousand doctors. Many of the best medical schools also sent much of their faculty to France, where the schools functioned as intact units, staffing and unofficially lending their names to entire military hospitals.

Yet these moves could not begin to satisfy the need. By the time the Armistice was signed, thirty-eight thousand physicians would be serving in the military, at least half of all those under age forty-five considered fit for service.

The military, and especially the army, did not stop there. In April 1917 the army had fifty-eight dentists; in November 1918 it had 5,654. And the military needed nurses.

There were too few nurses. Nursing had, like medicine, changed radically in the late nineteenth century. It too had become scientific. But changes in nursing involved factors that went beyond the purely scientific; they involved status, power, and the role of women.

Nursing was one of the few fields that gave women opportunity and status, and that they controlled. While Welch and his colleagues were revolutionizing American medicine, Jane Delano, Lavinia Dock—both of whom were students in Bellevue's nursing program while Welch was exposing medical students there to new realities—and others were doing the same to nursing. But they fought not with an entrenched Old Guard in their own profession so much as with physicians. (Sometimes physicians, threatened by intelligent and educated nurses, waged a virtual guerrilla war; in some hospitals physicians replaced labels on drug bottles with numbers so nurses could not question a prescription.)

In 1912, before becoming surgeon general, Gorgas had anticipated that if war ever came, the army would need vast numbers of nurses, many more than would likely be available. He believed, however, that not all of them would have to be fully trained. He wanted to create a corps of "practical nurses," who lacked the education and training of "graduate nurses."

Others were also advancing this idea, but they were all men. The women who ran nursing would have none of it. Jane Delano had taught nursing and had headed the Army Nurse Corps. Proud and intelligent as well as tough, driven, and authoritarian, she had then just left the army to establish the Red Cross nursing program, and the Red Cross had all responsibility for supplying nurses to the army, evaluating, recruiting, and often assigning them.

She rejected Gorgas's plan, telling her colleagues it "seriously threatened" the status of professional nursing and warning, "Our Nursing Service would be of no avail with these groups of women unrelated to us, organized by physicians, taught by physicians, serving under their guidance." She told the Red Cross bluntly that "if this plan were put through I should at once sever my connection with the Red Cross . . . [and] every member of the State and Local Committee would go out with me."*

The Red Cross and the army surrendered to her. No training of nursing aides commenced. When the United States entered the war it had 98,162 "graduate nurses," women whose training probably exceeded that of many—if not most—doctors trained before 1910. The war sucked up nurses as it sucked up everything else. In May 1918 roughly sixteen thousand nurses were serving in the military. Gorgas believed that the army alone needed fifty thousand.

After Gorgas again pleaded with the Red Cross "to carry out the plans already formulated," after learning confidential information about the desperation

---

* It would seem nurses needed their status protected. In the summer of 1918, the Treasury Department informed the secretary of war that army nurses taken captive, unlike soldiers, were not entitled to pay while they were prisoners of war. Outrage later forced a reversal of this policy.

in combat hospitals, Delano reversed herself, supported Gorgas, and tried to convince her colleagues of the need for "practical" nurses.

Her professional colleagues rebuffed them both. They refused to participate in organizing any large training program of such aides, and agreed only to establish an Army Nursing School. By October 1918 this new nursing school had produced not a single fully trained nurse.

The triumph of the nursing profession at large over the Red Cross and the United States Army, an army at war, was extraordinary. That the victors were women made it more extraordinary. Ironically, this triumph reflected as well a triumph of George Creel's Committee on Public Information over the truth, for Creel's propaganda machine had prevented the public from learning just how profound the need for nurses was.

In the meantime the military's appetite for doctors and nurses only grew. Four million American men were under arms with more coming, and Gorgas was planning for three hundred thousand hospital beds. The number of trained medical staff he had simply could not handle that load. So the military suctioned more and more nurses and physicians into cantonments, aboard ships, into France, until it had extracted nearly all the best young physicians. Medical care for civilians deteriorated rapidly. The doctors who remained in civilian life were largely either incompetent young ones or those over forty-five years of age, the vast majority of whom had been trained in the old ways of medicine. The shortage of nurses would prove even more serious. Indeed, it would prove deadly, especially in civil society.

All this added kindling to the tinderbox. Still more kindling would come.

CHAPTER ELEVEN

WILSON HAD DEMANDED that "the spirit of ruthless brutality . . . enter into the very fibre of national life." To carry out that charge Creel had wanted to create "one white-hot mass," a mass driven by "deathless determination." He was doing so. This was truly total war, and that totality truly included the medical profession.

Creel's spirit even injected itself into **Military Surgeon,** a journal published by the army for its physicians, which said, "Every single activity of this country is directed towards one single object, the winning of the war; nothing else counts now, and nothing will count ever if we don't win it. No organization of any kind should be countenanced that has not this object in immediate view and is likely to help in the most efficient way. . . . Thus the medical sciences are applied to war, the arts are applied in perfecting camouflage, in reviving the spirits of our soldiers by entertainment, etc."

This medical journal, this journal for physicians whose goal was to save life, also declared, "The consideration of human life often becomes quite secondary. . . . The medical officer has become more absorbed in the general than the particular, and the life and limb of the individual, while of great importance, are secondary to measures pro bono publico." And this same journal expressed its opinion of what constituted pro bono publico when it quoted approvingly advice from Major Donald McRae, a combat veteran who said, "If any enemy wounded are found (in the trench) they should be bayonetted, if sufficient prisoners [for interrogation] have been taken."

Gorgas did not share the views of the journal's editors. When the investigator funded by Rockefeller found his gangrene antitoxin effective, he wanted to publish his results—which could help the Germans. Both Gorgas and Secretary of War Newton Baker agreed that he should do so, and he did. Welch told Flexner, "I was very glad that both the Secretary and Surgeon General without any hesitation took this position."

But Gorgas had more important things to do than police the editors of **Military Surgeon**. He was focusing upon his mission, and he was pursuing it with the obsessiveness of a missionary. For Gorgas had a nightmare.

The U.S. Army had exploded from a few tens of thousands of soldiers before the war to millions in a few months. Huge cantonments, each holding roughly fifty thousand men, were thrown together in a matter of weeks. Hundreds of thousands of men occupied them before the camps were completed. They were jammed into those barracks that were finished, barracks designed for far less than their number, while tens of thousands of young soldiers lived through the first winter in tents. Hospitals were the last buildings to be constructed.

These circumstances not only brought huge numbers of men into this most intimate proximity but exposed farm boys to city boys from hundreds of miles away, each of them with entirely different disease immunities and vulnerabilities. Never before in American history—and possibly never before in any country's history—had so many men been brought together in such a way. Even at the front in Europe, even with the importation there of labor from China, India, and Africa, the concentration and throwing together of men with different vulnerabilities may not have been as explosive a mix as that in American training camps.

Gorgas's nightmare was of an epidemic sweeping through those camps. Given the way troops moved from camp to camp, if an outbreak of infectious disease erupted in one, it would be extraordinarily difficult to isolate that camp and keep the disease from spreading to others. Thousands, possibly tens of thousands, could die. Such an epidemic might spread to the civilian population as well. Gorgas intended to do all within his power to prevent his nightmare from becoming real.

By 1917 medical science was far from helpless in the face of disease. It stood in fact on the banks of the river Styx. If it was able to wade into those waters and pull only a few people back from that crossing, in its laboratories lay the promise of much more.

True, science had so far developed only a single one of the "magic bullets" envisaged by Paul Ehrlich. He and a colleague had tried nine hundred different chemical compounds to cure syphilis before retesting the 606th one. It was an arsenic compound; this time they made it work, curing syphilis without poisoning the patient. Named Salversan, it was often called just "606."

But science had achieved considerable success in manipulating the immune system and in public health. Vaccines prevented a dozen diseases that devastated livestock, including anthrax and hog cholera. Investigators had also gone far beyond the first success against smallpox and were now developing vaccines to prevent a host of diseases as well as antitoxins and serums to cure them. Science had triumphed over diphtheria. Sanitary and public health measures were containing typhoid, cholera, yellow fever, and bubonic plague, and vaccines against typhoid, cholera, and plague also appeared. Antitoxin for snake bites went into production. An antiserum for dysentery was found. A tetanus antitoxin brought magical results—before its widespread use, in 1903 in the United States 102 people died out of every 1,000 treated for tetanus; ten years later universal use of the antitoxin lowered the death rate to 0 per 1,000 treated. Meningitis had been checked, if not conquered, largely by Flexner's antiserum. In 1917 an antitoxin for gangrene was developed; although it was not nearly as effective as other antitoxins, scientists could improve it as they had improved others, over time. The possibilities of manipulating the immune system to defeat infectious disease seemed to hold enormous promise.*

At the management level Gorgas was taking action, too. He saw to it that many of the new army doctors assigned to the cantonments were trained at the Rockefeller Institute by some of the best

---

* When antibiotics first appeared in the late 1930s and 1940s, they performed like magic, and much of this research was abandoned; in the early 1960s, public health officials were declaring victory over infectious disease. Now, with dozens of strains of bacteria developing resistance to drugs, with viruses gaining resistance even faster, with such diseases as tuberculosis, once considered conquered, making comebacks, investigators have returned to searching for ways to stimulate the immune system against everything from infections to cancer.

scientists in the world. He began stockpiling huge quantities of vaccines, antitoxins, and sera. He did not rely for these products on drug manufacturers; they were unreliable and often useless. In 1917, in fact, New York State health commissioner Hermann Biggs tested commercial products for several diseases and found them so poor that he banned all sales from all drug manufacturers in New York State. So Gorgas assigned production to people he could rely upon. The Army Medical School would make enough typhoid vaccine for five million men. The Rockefeller Institute would produce sera for pneumonia, dysentery, and meningitis. The Hygienic Laboratory in Washington, which ultimately grew into the National Institutes of Health, would prepare smallpox vaccine and antitoxins for diphtheria and tetanus.

He also transformed several railroad cars into the most modern laboratory facilities—the equipping of these cars was paid for not by the government but by the Rockefeller Institute and the American Red Cross—and stationed these rolling laboratories at strategic points around the country, ready, as Flexner told Gorgas's deputy for scientific matters, Colonel Frederick Russell, to "be sent to any one of the camps at which pneumonia or other epidemic disease prevails."

Also, even before construction began on the cantonments, Gorgas created a special unit for "the prevention of infectious disease." He assigned the very best men to it. Welch, who had already toured

British and French camps and was alert to possible weak points, headed this unit, and its five other members were Flexner, Vaughan, Russell, Biggs, and Rhode Island's Charles Chapin. Each of them had international renown. They laid out precise procedures for the army to follow to minimize the chances of an epidemic.

Meanwhile, as troops were pouring into the camps in 1917, Rockefeller Institute colleagues Rufus Cole, Oswald Avery, and others who had turned their focus to pneumonia issued a specific warning: "Although pneumonia occurs chiefly in endemic form, small and even large epidemics are not unknown. It was the most serious disease which threatened the construction of the Panama Canal"—more so even than yellow fever, as Gorgas well knew—"and its prevalence in regions where large numbers of susceptible workers are brought together renders it of great importance. . . . Pneumonia [seems] especially likely to attack raw recruits. The experience among the small number of troops in the Mexican border, where pneumonia occurred in epidemic form [in 1916], should be a warning of what is likely to happen in our national army when large numbers of susceptible men are brought together during the winter months."

Gorgas's army superiors ignored the advice. As a result, the army soon suffered a taste of epidemic disease. It would be a test run, for both a virus and medicine.

■   ■   ■

The winter of 1917–18 was the coldest on record east of the Rocky Mountains, barracks were jam-packed, and hundreds of thousands of men were still living in tents. Camp hospitals and other medical facilities had not yet been finished. An army report conceded the failure to provide warm clothing or even heat. But most dangerous was the overcrowding.

Flexner warned that the situation "was as if the men had pooled their diseases, each picking up the ones he had not had, . . . greatly assisted by the faulty laying out of the camps, poor administration, and lack of adequate laboratory facilities." Vaughan protested impotently and later called army procedures "insane. . . . How many lives were sacrificed I can not estimate. . . . The dangers in mobilization steps followed were pointed out to the proper authorities before there was any assembly, but the answer was: 'The purpose of mobilization is to convert civilians into trained soldiers as quickly as possible and not to make a demonstration in preventive medicine.'"

In that bitterly cold winter, measles came to the army's barracks, and it came in epidemic form. Usually, of course, measles infects children and causes only fever, rash, cough, runny nose, and discomfort. But like many other children's diseases—especially viral diseases—when measles strikes adults, it often strikes hard. (Early in the twenty-first century, measles is still causing one million deaths a year worldwide.)

This outbreak racked its victims with high fever, extreme sensitivity to light, and violent coughs. Complications included severe diarrhea, meningitis, encephalitis (inflammation of the brain), violent ear infections, and convulsions.

As infected soldiers moved from camp to camp, the virus moved with them, rolling through camps like a bowling ball knocking down pins. Vaughan reported, "Not a troop train came into Camp Wheeler [near Macon, Georgia] in the fall of 1917 without bringing from one to six cases of measles already in the eruptive stage. These men . . . distributed its seeds at the encampment and on the train. No power on earth could stop the spread of measles under these conditions."

Camp Travis outside San Antonio held 30,067 men. By Christmas, 4,571 men had come down with the disease. Funston had an average troop strength of over fifty-six thousand; three thousand were sick enough to require hospitalization. At Greenleaf in South Carolina, Devens in Massachusetts, the numbers were comparable. The 25,260 troops at Camp Cody in New Mexico were free of measles until soon after the arrival of men from Funston. Then measles began roaring through Cody, too.

And some young men began to die.

Investigators could develop neither a vaccine to prevent measles nor a serum to cure it, but most deaths were coming chiefly from secondary infections, from bacteria invading the lungs after the virus had weakened their defenses. And investigators at Rockefeller and elsewhere struggled to find a way to control these bacterial infections. They made some progress.

Meanwhile the army issued orders forbidding men from crowding around stoves, and officers entered barracks and tents to enforce it. But especially for the tens of thousands who lived in tents in the record cold, it was impossible to keep men from crowding around stoves.

Of all the complications of measles, the most deadly by far was pneumonia. In the six months from September 1917 to March 1918, before the influenza epidemic struck, pneumonia struck down 30,784 soldiers on American soil. It killed 5,741 of them. Nearly all these pneumonia cases developed as complications of measles. At Camp Shelby, 46.5 percent of all deaths—**all** deaths from all diseases, all car wrecks, all work accidents, all training mishaps combined—were a result of pneumonia following measles. At Camp Bowie, 227 soldiers died from disease in November and December 1917; 212 of them died of pneumonia after measles. The average death rate from pneumonia in twenty-nine cantonments was twelve times that of civilian men of the same age.

In 1918 the Republican-controlled Senate held hearings on the Wilson administration's mistakes in mobilizing the military. Republicans had despised Wilson since 1912, when he reached the White House despite winning only 41 percent of the vote. (Former Republican president and then third-party candidate Teddy Roosevelt and incumbent Republican president William Howard Taft split the GOP vote, and Socialist Eugene Debs also won 6 percent.) Mobilization failures seemed a perfect opportunity to embarrass him. And there was personal bitterness in the attacks: Congressman Augustus Peabody Gardner, son-in-law of Senate Majority Leader Henry Cabot Lodge, had resigned from Congress and enlisted, only to die of pneumonia in camp.

Gorgas was summoned to explain the measles fiasco. His testimony and his report on the epidemic to the chief of staff made front-page news. Like his mentor Sternberg during the typhoid debacle twenty years earlier, he lacerated his War Department colleagues and superiors for rushing troops to cantonments under living conditions that failed to meet minimum public health standards, for overcrowding, for exposing recruits to measles who had no immunity, for using untrained "country boys" to care for desperately sick men in poorly equipped hospitals and sometimes without hospitals at all. And he stated that the War Department seemed to consider the Medical Department of the army unimportant. "I was never in their confidence, no," he said in response to one senator's question.

He had hoped his testimony would force the army

to give him more power to protect troops. Perhaps it did; the army initiated courts-martial at three cantonments. But his testimony also isolated him. He confided to his sister that, in the War Department, "All my friends seem to have deserted me and everybody is giving me a kick as I pass by."

Meanwhile, Welch visited one of the worst-hit camps, a camp where measles itself had left but where victims with complications still lingered. He told Gorgas that the mortality rate for troops developing pneumonia after measles "is stated to be 30% but more now in hospital will die. A good statistician needed in hospital—registrar not competent." To give the men in the hospital a better chance to survive, he continued, "Have Colonel Russell send directions for Avery's medicine for pneumococcus type work."

He was referring to the Rockefeller Institute's Oswald Avery, one of the Canadians there who had been inducted into the army as only a private. Private or not, he soon would be, if he was not already, the world's leading investigator of pneumonia. And conclusions Avery would reach would have import far—very, very far—beyond that subject. His findings would create a scientific revolution that would change the direction of all genetic research and create modern molecular biology. But that would come later.

Osler called pneumonia "the captain of the men of death." Pneumonia was the leading cause of death around the world, greater than tuberculosis, greater than cancer, greater than heart disease, greater than plague.

And, like measles, when influenza kills, it usually kills through pneumonia.

CHAPTER TWELVE

MEDICAL DICTIONARIES define pneumonia as "an inflammation of the lungs with consolidation." This definition omits mention of an infection, but in practice pneumonia is almost always caused by some kind of microorganism invading the lung, followed by an infusion of the body's infection-fighting weapons. The resulting inflamed mix of cells, enzymes, cell debris, fluid, and the equivalent of scar tissue thickens and leads to the consolidation; then the lung, normally soft and spongy, becomes firm, solid, inelastic. The disease kills usually when either the consolidation becomes so widespread that the lungs cannot transfer enough oxygen into the bloodstream, or the pathogen enters

the blood-stream and carries the infection throughout the body.

Pneumonia maintained its position as the leading cause of death in the United States until 1936.
It and influenza are so closely linked that modern international health statistics, including those
compiled by the United States Centers for Disease
Control, routinely classify them as a single cause
of death. Even now, early in the twenty-first century, with antibiotics, antiviral drugs, oxygen, and
intensive-care units, influenza and pneumonia combined routinely rank as the fifth or sixth—it varies year to year, usually depending on the severity
of the influenza season—leading cause of death in
the United States and the leading cause of death
from infectious disease.

Influenza causes pneumonia either directly, by a
massive viral invasion of the lungs, or indirectly—
and more commonly—by destroying certain parts
of the body's defenses and allowing so-called secondary invaders, bacteria, to infest the lungs virtually unopposed. There is also evidence that the
influenza virus makes it easier for some bacteria to
invade the lung not only by generally wiping out
defense mechanisms but by specifically facilitating
some bacteria's ability to attach to lung tissue.

Although many bacteria, viruses, and fungi can invade the lung, the single most common cause of

pneumonia is the pneumococcus, a bacterium that can be either a primary or a secondary invader. (It causes approximately 95 percent of lobar pneumonias, involving one or more entire lobes, although a far lesser percentage of bronchopneumonias.) George Sternberg, while working in a makeshift laboratory on an army post in 1881, first isolated this bacterium from his own saliva, inoculated rabbits with it, and learned that it killed. He did not recognize the disease as pneumonia. Neither did Pasteur, who discovered the same organism later but published first, so scientific etiquette gives him priority in the discovery. Three years later a third investigator demonstrated that this bacterium frequently colonized the lungs and caused pneumonia, hence its name.

Under the microscope the pneumococcus looks like a typical streptococcus, a medium-size elliptical or round bacterium usually linked with others in a chain, although the pneumococcus usually is linked only to one other bacterium—and is sometimes called a diplococcus—like two pearls side by side. When exposed to sunlight it dies within ninety minutes, but it survives in moist sputum in a dark room for ten days. It can be found occasionally on dust particles. In virulent form, it can be highly infectious—in fact it can itself cause epidemics.

As early as 1892 scientists tried to make a serum to treat it. They failed. In the next decades, while investigators were making enormous advances against other diseases, they made almost no progress against pneumonia. This was not through lack of trying. Whenever researchers made any progress against diphtheria, plague, typhoid, meningitis, tetanus, snake bite, and other killers, they immediately applied the same methods against pneumonia. Still nothing even hinted at success.

Investigators were working at the very outermost edge of science. Gradually they improved their ability to produce a serum that protected an animal, but not people. And they struggled to understand how this serum worked, advancing hypotheses that might eventually lead to therapies. Sir Almroth Wright, who was knighted for developing a typhoid vaccine, speculated that the immune system coated invading organisms with what he called "opsonins," which made it far easier for white blood cells to devour the invader. His insight was correct, but he was wrong in the conclusions he drew from this insight.

Nowhere was pneumonia more severe than among workers in South Africa's gold and diamond mines. Epidemic conditions were virtually constant and outbreaks routinely killed 40 percent of the men who got sick. In 1914 South African mine owners asked Wright to devise a vaccine against pneumonia. He claimed success. In fact he not only failed, his vaccinations could kill. This and other errors earned Wright the mocking nickname "Sir Almost Right" from competing investigators.

But by then two German scientists had found a

clue to the problem in treating or preventing pneumonia. In 1910 they distinguished between what they
called "typical" pneumococci and "atypical" pneumococci. They and others tried to develop this clue.

Yet as the Great War began so little progress had
been made against pneumonia that Osler himself
still recommended venesection—bleeding: "We employ it nowadays much more than we did a few years
ago, but more often late in the disease than early. To
bleed at the very onset in robust, healthy individuals in whom the disease sets in with great intensity
and high fever is, I believe, a good practice."

Osler did not claim that bleeding cured pneumonia, only that it might relieve certain symptoms. He
was wrong. The 1916 edition of his textbook also
stated, "Pneumonia is a self-limited disease, which
can neither be aborted nor cut short by any known
means at our command."

Americans were about to challenge that conclusion.

When Rufus Cole came to the Rockefeller Institute
to head its hospital, he decided to focus most of his
own energies and those of the team he put together
on pneumonia. It was an obvious choice, since it
was the biggest killer.

To cure or prevent pneumonia required, as with
all other infectious diseases at the time, manipulating the body's own defenses, the immune system.

In the diseases scientists could defeat, the
antigen—the molecules on the surfaces of invading

organisms that stimulated the immune system to respond, the target the immune response aimed at—did not change. In diphtheria the dangerous part was not even the bacteria itself but a toxin the bacteria produced.

The toxin was not alive, did not evolve, and had a fixed form, and the production of antitoxin had become routine. Horses were injected with gradually increasing doses of virulent bacteria. The bacteria made the toxin. In turn, the horse's immune system generated antibodies that bound to and neutralized the toxin. The horse was then bled, solids removed from the blood until only the serum remained, and this was then purified into the antitoxin that had become so common and lifesaving.

An identical process produced tetanus antitoxin, Flexner's serum against meningitis, and several other sera or antitoxins. Scientists were vaccinating the horse against a disease, then extracting the horse antibodies and injecting them into people. This borrowing of immune-system defenses from an outside source is called "passive immunity."

When vaccines are used to stimulate people's own immune systems directly, so that they develop their own defenses against bacteria or viruses, it is called "active immunity."

But in all the diseases treated successfully so far, the antigens, the target the immune system aimed at, remained constant. The target stayed still; it did not move. And so the target was easy to hit.

The pneumococcus was different. The discovery of "typical" and "atypical" pneumococci had opened a door, and investigators were now finding many types of the bacteria. Different types had different antigens. Sometimes also the same type was virulent, sometimes not, but why one killed and another caused mild or no disease was not yet a question anyone was designing experiments to answer. That lay out there for the future, a sort of undertow pulling at the data. The focus was far more immediate: finding a curative serum, a preventative vaccine, or both.

By 1912, Cole at Rockefeller had developed a serum that had measurable if not dramatic curative power against a single type of pneumococcus. He happened to read a paper by Avery on an entirely different subject—secondary infections in victims of tuberculosis. Although narrow and hardly a classic, the paper still made a deep impression on Cole. It was solid, thorough, tight, and yet was deeply analytical, showing an awareness of the potential implications of the conclusions and possible new directions for research. It also demonstrated Avery's knowledge of chemistry and ability to carry out a fully scientific laboratory investigation of illness in patients. Cole wrote Avery a note offering him a job at the institute. Avery did not reply. Cole sent a second note. Still he received no reply. Finally Cole visited Avery and raised the salary offer. Later he realized Avery rarely read his mail. It was typical of Avery; his focus was always on his experiments. Now he accepted. Soon after the Great War started, but before America's entry into it, Avery also began working on pneumonia.

Pneumonia was Cole's passion. For Avery it would become an obsession.

Oswald Avery was a short thin fragile man, a tiny man really, who weighed at most 110 pounds. With his large head and intense eyes, he looked like someone who would have been laughed at as an "egghead," if that word had been in use then, and bullied in a schoolyard as a boy. If that was the case, it appeared to have left no scars; he seemed friendly, cheerful, even outgoing.

Born in Montreal, he grew up in New York City the son of a Baptist minister who preached at a church in the city. He had a good many talents. At Colgate University he tied for first prize in an oratory contest with classmate Harry Emerson Fosdick, who became among the most prominent preachers of the early twentieth century (Fosdick's brother Raymond ultimately headed the Rockefeller Foundation; John Rockefeller Sr. built Riverside Church for Harry). Avery also played cornet well enough to have performed in concert with the National Conservatory of Music—a concert conducted by Antonin Dvořák—and he often drew ink caricatures and painted landscapes.

Yet for all his outward friendliness and sociability,

Avery spoke himself of what he called "the true inwardness of research."

René Dubos, an Avery protégé, recalled, "To a few of us who saw him in every day life, however, there was often revealed another aspect of his personality, . . . a more haunting quality, . . . a melancholy figure whistling gently to himself the lonely tune of the shepherd song in **Tristan and Isolde.** An acute need for privacy, even if it had to be bought at the cost of loneliness, conditioned much of Avery's behavior."

If the phone rang Avery would talk animatedly, as if happy to hear from the caller, but when he hung up, Dubos recalled, "It was as if a mask dropped, his smile replaced with a tired and almost tortured expression, the telephone pushed away on the desk as a symbol of protest against the encroaching world."

Like Welch, he never married, nor was he known to have had an emotional or intimate relationship with anyone of either sex. Like Welch, he could be charming and the center of attention; he did comic impersonations so well that one colleague called him "a natural born comedian." Yet he resented any kind of intrusion upon himself, resented even attempts by others to entertain him.

Everything else about him was the opposite of Welch. Welch read widely, had curiosity about everything, traveled throughout Europe, China, and Japan, and seemed to embrace the universe. Welch often sought relaxation in elaborate dinners and almost daily retreated to his club. And Welch as a very young man was recognized as marked for great things.

Avery was none of those things. He was certainly not considered a brilliant young investigator. When Cole hired him, he was almost forty years old. By forty Welch was moving in the highest circles of science internationally. By forty those of Avery's contemporaries who would leave any significant scientific legacy had already made names for themselves. Yet Avery, like much younger investigators at Rockefeller, was essentially on probation and had made no particular mark. Indeed, he had made no mark—but not from want of ambition, nor from lack of work.

While Welch constantly socialized and traveled, Avery had almost no personal life. He fled from one. He almost never entertained and rarely went out to dinner. Although he was close to and felt responsible for his younger brother and an orphaned cousin, his life, his world, was his research. All else was extraneous. Once the editor of a scientific journal asked him to write a memorial piece about Nobel laureate Karl Landsteiner, with whom he had worked closely at Rockefeller. In it Avery said nothing whatsoever about Landsteiner's personal life. The editor asked him to insert some personal details. Avery refused, stating that personal information would help the reader understand nothing that mattered, neither Landsteiner's achievements nor his thought processes.

(Landsteiner likely would have approved Avery's treatment. When he was notified he'd won the Nobel Prize, he continued working in his laboratory all day, got home so late that his wife was asleep, and did not wake her to give her the news.)

The research mattered, Avery was saying, not the life. And the life of research, like that of any art, lay within. As Einstein once said, "One of the strongest motives that lead persons to art or science is a flight from the everyday life. . . . With this negative motive goes a positive one. Man seeks to form for himself, in whatever manner is suitable for him, a simplified and lucid image of the world, and so to overcome the world of experience by striving to replace it to some extent by this image. This is what the painter does, and the poet, the speculative philosopher, the natural scientist, each in his own way. Into this image and its formation, he places the center of gravity of his emotional life, in order to attain the peace and serenity that he cannot find within the narrow confines of swirling personal experience."

With the possible exception of his love for music, Avery seemed to have no existence outside the laboratory. For years he shared the same apartment with Alphonse Dochez, another bachelor scientist who worked closely with him at Rockefeller, and a shifting cast of more temporary scientist-roommates who left when they got married or changed jobs. Avery's roommates lived normal lives, going out, going away for a weekend. When they came home, there would be Avery, ready to begin a lengthy conversation that lasted deep into the night about an experimental problem or result.

But if Avery had little personal life, he did have ambition. His desire to make a mark after so long in the wilderness led him to publish two papers soon after he arrived at Rockefeller. In the first, based on only a few experiments, he and Dochez formulated "a sweeping metabolic theory of virulence and immunity." In the second, Avery again reached well beyond his experimental evidence for a conclusion.

Both were quickly proved wrong. Humiliated, he was determined never to suffer such embarrassment again. He became extraordinarily careful, extraordinarily cautious and conservative, in anything he published or even said outside his own laboratory. He did not stop speculating—privately—about the boldest and most far-reaching interpretations of an experiment, but from then on he published only the most rigorously tested and conservative conclusions. From then on, Avery would only—in public—inch his way forward. An inch at a time, he would ultimately cover an enormous and startling distance.

When one inches along progress comes slowly, but it can still be decisive. Cole and Avery worked together precisely the way Cole had hoped for when he organized the Rockefeller hospital. More important, the work produced results.

In the laboratory Avery and Dochez took the

lead. They worked in simple laboratories with simple equipment. Each room had a single deep porcelain sink and several worktables, each with a gas outlet for a Bunsen burner and drawers underneath. The tabletop space was filled with racks of test tubes, simple mason jars, petri dishes—droppers for various dyes and chemicals, and tin cans holding pipettes and platinum loops. On the same tabletop investigators performed nearly all their work: inoculating, bleeding, and dissecting animals. Also on the tabletop was a cage for the occasional animal kept as a pet. In the middle of the room were incubators, vacuum pumps, and centrifuges.

First they replicated earlier experiments, partly to familiarize themselves with techniques. They exposed rabbits and mice to gradually increasing dosages of pneumococci. Soon the animals developed antibodies to the bacteria. They drew blood from them, allowed solids to settle out, siphoned off the serum, added chemicals to precipitate remaining solids, then purified the serum by passing it through several filters. Others had done the equivalent. They succeeded in curing mice with the serum. Others had done that, too. But the mice were not people.

In a way, they weren't really mice either. Scientists had to keep as many factors constant as possible, limit variables, to make it easier to understand precisely what caused an experimental result. So mice were inbred until all mice in a given strain had virtually identical genes, except for sex differences. (Male mice were and are generally not used in experiments because they sometimes attack each other; the death or injury of a single mouse for any reason can distort experimental results and ruin weeks of work.) These mice were fully alive but also model systems, with as much of the complexity, diversity, and spontaneity of life eliminated as possible; they were bred to be as close to a test tube as a living thing can be.*

But if scientists were curing mice, no one anywhere had made any progress in curing people. Experiment after experiment had failed. Elsewhere other investigators trying similar approaches quit, convinced by their failures that their theories were wrong or that their techniques were not good enough to yield results—or they simply grew impatient and moved on to easier problems.

Avery did not move on. He saw snatches of evidence suggesting he was right. He persisted, experimenting repeatedly, trying to learn from each failure. He and Dochez grew hundreds of cultures of pneumococci, changing the strains, learning more and more about its metabolism, changing the composition of the media in which the bacteria grew. (Soon Avery became one of the best in the world at figuring out what medium would most effectively

---

* The same genetic lines of laboratory mice used by Avery are still in use today; the mice have been inbred since at least 1909 to be a useful tool. As one scientist at the National Cancer Institute says, "I can cure cancer in a mouse one hundred percent of the time. If you can't do that, you may as well hang it up."

grow different bacteria.) His background in both chemistry and immunology began paying off, and they used every piece of information as a wedge, pounding it into the problem, cracking or prying open other secrets, improving techniques, and, finally, gradually inching past the work that others had done.

They and others identified three fairly uniform and common strains of pneumococci, which they called simply Type I, Type II, and Type III. Other pneumococci were designated as Type IV, a catchall for dozens of other strains (ninety have been identified) that appeared less often. The first three types gave them a far more specific target for an antiserum, which they made. When they exposed different cultures of pneumococci to the serum, they discovered that the antibodies in the serum would bind only to its matching culture and not to any other. The binding was even visible in a test tube without a microscope; the bacteria and antibodies clumped together. The process was called "agglutination" and was a test for specificity.

But many things that work in vitro, in the narrow universe of a test tube, fail in vivo, in the nearly infinite complexity of life. Now they went through the cycle of testing in rabbits and mice again, testing different strains of the bacteria in animals for killing potential, testing how well they generated antibodies, how well the antibodies bound to them. They tried injecting massive dosages of killed bacteria, thinking it might spark a large immune response, then using the serum generated by that technique. They tried mixing small doses of living bacteria and massive doses of dead ones. They tried live bacteria. In mice they ultimately achieved spectacular cure rates.

At the same time, Avery's understanding of the bacteria deepened. It deepened enough that he forced scientists to change their thinking about the immune system.

One of the most puzzling aspects of pneumococci was that some were virulent and lethal, some were not. Avery thought he had a clue to the answer to this question. He and Dochez focused on the fact that some pneumococci—but only some—were surrounded by a capsule made of polysaccharides, a sugar, like the hard shell of sugar surrounding the soft insides of M&M candy. Avery's very first paper on the pneumococcus, in 1917, dealt with these "specific soluble substances." He would pursue this subject for more than a quarter of a century. As he tried to unravel this puzzle, he began calling the pneumococcus, this killing bacterium, the "sugar-coated microbe." His pursuit would yield a momentous discovery and a deep understanding of life itself.

Meanwhile, with the rest of the Western world already at war, Cole, Avery, Dochez, and their colleagues were ready to test their immune serum in people.

CHAPTER THIRTEEN

Even when Cole first tried the new serum on patients it showed promise. He and Avery immediately devoted themselves to refining their procedures in the laboratory, in the methods of infecting horses and producing serum, in the way they administered it. Finally they began a careful series of trials with a finished product. They found that giving large dosages of serum—half a liter—intravenously cut the death rate of Type I pneumonias by more than half, from 23 percent to 10 percent.

It was not a cure. Pneumonias caused by other types of pneumococci did not yield so easily. And, as Avery and Cole stated, "Protection in man is inferior to protection in mice."

But of all pneumonias, those caused by Type I pneumococci were the single most common. Cutting the death rate by more than half in the single most common pneumonia was progress, real progress, enough progress that in 1917 the institute published a ninety-page monograph by Cole, Avery, Dochez, and Henry Chickering, another young Rockefeller scientist, entitled "Acute Lobar Pneumonia Prevention and Serum Treatment."

It was a landmark work, for the first time explaining step by step a way to prepare and use a serum that could cure pneumonia. And it very much anticipated outbreaks of the disease in army cantonments, noting, "Pneumonia bids fair in the present war to lead all diseases as a cause of death."

In October 1917, Gorgas told army hospital commanders that, "in view of the probability that pneumonia will be one of the most important diseases amongst the troops," they must send even more doctors to the Rockefeller Institute to learn how to prepare and administer this serum. Avery, still a private, was already diverting time from his research to teach bacteriology to officers who would be working in cantonments. Now he and his colleagues also taught this serum therapy. His students, rather than call him "Private," addressed him respectfully as "Professor"—a nickname already occasionally given him. His colleagues shortened it to "Fess," which stuck with him for the rest of his life.

Simultaneously Cole, Avery, and Dochez were

developing a vaccine to prevent pneumonia caused by Types I, II, and III pneumococci. After proving it worked in animals, they and six other Rockefeller researchers turned themselves into guinea pigs, testing its safety in humans by giving each other massive doses. All of them had negative reactions to the vaccine itself; three had severe reactions. They decided that the vaccine was too dangerous to administer in those dosages but planned another experiment with lower doses administered once a week for four weeks, which gave recipients time to gradually build up immunity.

This vaccine came too late for any large-scale impact on the measles epidemic, but at Camp Gordon outside Atlanta, a vaccine against the strain of pneumococcus causing most of the pneumonias there was tested on one hundred men with measles, with fifty men vaccinated and fifty used as controls. Only two of those vaccinated developed this pneumonia, compared to fourteen unvaccinated men.

Meanwhile, Cole wrote Colonel Frederick Russell, who during his own scientific career in the army had significantly improved typhoid vaccine, about "the progress we have already made in the matter of prophylactic vaccination against pneumonia." But, Cole added, "The manufacture of large amounts of vaccine will be a big matter, much more difficult than the manufacture of typhoid vaccine. . . . I have been getting an organization together so that the large amounts of media necessary could be prepared, and so the vaccine could be made on a large scale."

Cole's organization was ready for a large test in March 1918, just as influenza was first surfacing among soldiers in Kansas. The vaccine was given to twelve thousand troops at Camp Upton on Long Island—that used up all the vaccine available—while nineteen thousand troops served as controls, receiving no vaccine. Over the next three months, not a single vaccinated soldier developed pneumonia caused by any of the types of pneumococci vaccinated against. The controls suffered 101 cases. This result was not absolutely conclusive. But it was more than suggestive. And it was a far better result than was being achieved anywhere else in the world. The Pasteur Institute was also testing a pneumonia vaccine, but without success.

If Avery and Cole could develop a serum or vaccine with real effectiveness against the captain of death . . . If they could do that, it would be the greatest triumph medical science had yet known.

Both the prospect of finally being able to defeat pneumonia and its appearance in the army camps only intensified Gorgas's determination to find a way to limit its killing. He asked Welch to create and chair a special board on the disease. Gorgas wanted the board run, literally, out of his own office; Welch's desk was in Gorgas's personal office.

Welch demurred and called Flexner. Both men

agreed that the best man in the country, and probably in the world, to chair the board was Rufus Cole. The next day Flexner and Cole got on a train to Washington to meet Gorgas and Welch at the Cosmos Club. There they picked the members of the pneumonia board, a board to be supported by all the knowledge and resources of Gorgas, Welch, Flexner, and the institutions they represented.

They chose well. Each person selected would later be elected to membership in the National Academy of Sciences, arguably the most exclusive scientific organization in the world.

Avery would of course lead the actual laboratory investigations and stay in New York. Most of the others would work in the field. Lieutenant Thomas Rivers, a Hopkins graduate and Welch protégé, would become one of the world's leading virologists and succeed Cole as head of the Rockefeller Institute Hospital. Lieutenant Francis Blake, another Rockefeller researcher, would become dean of the Yale Medical School. Captain Eugene Opie, regarded as one of the most brilliant of Welch's pathology students, was already dean of the Washington University Medical School when he joined the army. Collaborating with them, although not actual board members, were future Nobel laureates Karl Landsteiner at Rockefeller and George Whipple at the Hopkins. Years later another Rockefeller scientist recalled, "It was really a privilege to be on the pneumonia team."

On a routine basis—if such urgency could be routine—Cole traveled to Washington to discuss the latest findings with Welch and senior army medical officers in Gorgas's office. Cole, Welch, Victor Vaughan, and Russell had also been conducting a series of the most rigorous inspection tours of cantonments, checking on everything from the quality of the camp's surgeons, bacteriologists, and epidemiologists right down to the way camp kitchens washed dishes. Any recommendations they made were immediately ordered to be carried out. But they did not simply dictate; many of the camp hospitals and laboratories were run by men they respected, and they listened to ideas as well.

Late that spring, Cole reported to the American Medical Association one of his conclusions about measles: that it "seems to render the respiratory mucous membrane especially susceptible to secondary infection." He also believed that these secondary infections, like measles itself, "occur chiefly in epidemic form. . . . Every new case of the infection adds not only to the extent but also to the intensity of the epidemic."

On June 4, 1918, Cole, Welch, and several other members of the pneumonia board appeared in Gorgas's office once more, this time with Hermann Biggs, New York State health commissoner; Milton Rosenau, a prominent Harvard scientist who was then a navy lieutenant commander; and L. Emmett Holt, one of those instrumental in the founding of the Rockefeller Institute. This time the discussion was wide-ranging, focusing on how to minimize the possibility of something worse than the measles epidemic. They were all worried about Gorgas's nightmare.

They were not particularly worried about influenza, although they were tracking outbreaks of the disease. For the moment those outbreaks were mild, not nearly as dangerous as the measles epidemic had been. They well knew that when influenza kills, it kills through pneumonia, but Gorgas had already asked the Rockefeller Institute to gear up its production and study of pneumonia serum and vaccine, and both the institute and the Army Medical School had launched major efforts to do so.

Then the conversation turned from the laboratory to epidemiological issues. The inspection tours of the camps had convinced Welch, Cole, Vaughan, and Russell that cross-infections had caused many of the measles-related pneumonia deaths. To prevent such a problem from recurring, Cole suggested creating contagious-disease wards with specially trained staffs, something the best civilian hospitals had. Welch pointed out that the British had isolation hospitals with entirely separate organizations and rigid discipline. Another possible solution to cross-infection involved using cubicles in hospitals—creating a warren of partitions around hospital beds.

They also discussed overcrowding in hospitals and isolation of troops. Since 1916 the Canadian army had segregated all troops arriving in Britain for twenty-eight days, to prevent their infecting any trained troops ready to go to the front. Welch advised establishing similar "detention camps for new recruits where men are kept for 10–14 days."

They all recognized the difficulty of convincing the army to do this, or of convincing the army to end the even more serious problem of overcrowding in barracks.

Still, another army medical officer injected one piece of good news. He said that the problem of overcrowding in the hospitals themselves had been eliminated. Every hospital in the army had at least one hundred empty beds as of May 15, with a total of twenty-three thousand beds empty. Every single epidemiological statistic the army collected showed improved overall health. He insisted that facilities and training were adequate.

Time would tell.

Man might be defined as "modern" largely to the extent that he attempts to control, as opposed to adjust himself to, nature. In this relationship with nature, modern humanity has generally been the aggressor, and a daring one at that, altering the flow of rivers, building upon geological faults, and, today, even engineering the genes of existing species.

Nature has generally been languid in its response, although contentious once aroused and occasionally displaying a flair for violence.

By 1918 humankind was fully modern, and fully scientific, but too busy fighting itself to aggress against nature. Nature, however, chooses its own moments. It chose this moment to aggress against man, and it did not do so prodding languidly. For the first time, modern humanity, a humanity practicing the modern scientific method, would confront nature in its fullest rage.

■ Part IV
IT BEGINS

CHAPTER FOURTEEN

IT IS IMPOSSIBLE to prove that someone from Haskell County, Kansas, carried the influenza virus to Camp Funston. But the circumstantial evidence is strong. In the last week of February 1918, Dean Nilson, Ernest Elliot, John Bottom, and probably several others unnamed by the local paper traveled from Haskell, where "severe influenza" was raging, to Funston. They probably arrived between February 28 and March 2, and the camp hospital first began receiving soldiers with influenza on March 4. This timing precisely fits the incubation period of influenza. Within three weeks eleven hundred troops at Funston were sick enough to require hospitalization.

Only a trickle of people moved back and forth

between Haskell and Funston, but a river of soldiers moved between Funston, other army bases, and France. Two weeks after the first case at Funston, on March 18, influenza surfaced at both Camps Forrest and Greenleaf in Georgia; 10 percent of the forces at both camps would report sick. Then, like falling dominoes, other camps erupted with influenza. In total, twenty-four of the thirty-six largest army camps experienced an influenza outbreak that spring. Thirty of the fifty largest cities in the country, most of them adjacent to military facilities, also suffered an April spike in "excess mortality" from influenza, although that did not become clear except in hindsight.

At first it seemed like nothing to worry about, nothing like the measles outbreak with its pneumonic complications. Only in Haskell had influenza been severe. The only thing at all worrisome was that the disease was moving.

As Macfarlane Burnet later said, "It is convenient to follow the story of influenza at this period mainly in regard to the army experiences in America and Europe."

After the pandemic, outstanding epidemiologists searched military and civilian health records in the United States for any signs of uncommon influenza activity prior to the Funston outbreak. They found none. (The warning published about Haskell misstated the date, incorrectly putting it after Funston.)

In France there had been some localized flare-ups of influenza during the winter, but they did not seem to spread and behaved like endemic, not epidemic, disease.

The first unusual outbreaks in Europe occurred in Brest in early April, where American troops disembarked. In Brest itself, a French naval command was suddenly crippled. And from Brest the disease did spread, and quickly, in concentric circles.

Still, although many got sick, these outbreaks were, like those in the United States, generally mild. Troops were temporarily debilitated, then recovered. For example, an epidemic erupted near Chaumont involving U.S. troops and civilians: of 172 marines guarding headquarters there, most fell ill and fifty-four required hospitalization—but all of them recovered.

The first appearance in the French army came April 10. Influenza struck Paris in late April, and at about the same time the disease reached Italy. In the British army the first cases occurred in mid-April; then the disease exploded. In May the British First Army alone suffered 36,473 hospital admissions and tens of thousands of less serious cases. In the Second Army, a British report noted, "At the end of May it appeared with great violence. . . . The numbers affected were very great. . . . A brigade of artillery had one-third of its strength taken ill within forty-eight hours, and in the brigade ammunition column only fifteen men were available for duty one day out of a strength of 145." The British Third Army suffered equally. In June troops returning from the Continent introduced the disease into England.

But again the complications were few and nearly all the troops recovered. The only serious concern—and it was serious indeed—was that the disease would undermine the troops' ability to fight.

That seemed the case in the German army. German troops in the field suffered sharp outbreaks beginning in late April. By then German commander Erich von Ludendorff had also begun his last great offensive—Germany's last real chance to win the war.

The German offensive made great initial gains. From near the front lines Harvey Cushing, Halsted's protégé, recorded the German advance in his diary: "They have broken clean through. . . ." "The general situation is far from reassuring. . . . 11 P.M. The flow of men from the retreating Front keeps up." "Haig's most disquieting Order to the Army . . . ends as follows: 'With our backs to the wall, and believing in the justice of our cause, each one of us must fight to the end. The safety of our homes and the freedom of mankind depend alike upon the conduct of every one of us at this moment.'"

But then Cushing noted, "The expected third phase of the great German offensive gets put off from day to day." "When the next offensive will come off no one knows. It probably won't be long postponed. I gather that the epidemic of grippe which hit us rather hard in Flanders also hit the Boche worse, and this may have caused the delay."

Ludendorff himself blamed influenza for the loss of initiative and the ultimate failure of the offensive: "It was a grievous business having to listen every morning to the chiefs of staff's recital of the number of influenza cases, and their complaints about the weakness of their troops."

Influenza may have crippled his attack, stripped his forces of fighting men. Or Ludendorff may have simply seized upon it as an excuse. British, French, and American troops were all suffering from the disease themselves, and Ludendorff was not one to accept blame when he could place it elsewhere.

In the meantime, in Spain the virus picked up its name.

Spain actually had few cases before May, but the country was neutral during the war. That meant the government did not censor the press, and unlike French, German, and British newspapers—which printed nothing negative, nothing that might hurt morale—Spanish papers were filled with reports of the disease, especially when King Alphonse XIII fell seriously ill.

The disease soon became known as "Spanish influenza" or "Spanish flu," very likely because only Spanish newspapers were publishing accounts of the spread of the disease that were picked up in other countries.

It struck Portugal, then Greece. In June and July, death rates across England, Scotland, and Wales surged. In June, Germany suffered initial sporadic outbreaks, and then a full-fledged epidemic swept across all the country. Denmark and Norway began suffering in July, Holland and Sweden in August.

The earliest cases in Bombay erupted on a transport soon after its arrival May 29. First seven police sepoys who worked the docks were admitted to the police hospital; then men who worked at the government dockyard succumbed; the next day employees of the Bombay port fell ill, and two days later men who worked at a location that "abuts on the harbor between the government dockyard and Ballard Estate of the Port Trust." From there the disease spread along railroad lines, reaching Calcutta, Madras, and Rangoon after Bombay, while another transport brought it to Karachi.

Influenza reached Shanghai toward the end of May. Said one observer, "It swept over the whole country like a tidal wave." A reported half of Chungking lay ill. It jumped to New Zealand and then Australia in September; in Sydney it sickened 30 percent of the population.

But if it was spreading explosively, it continued to bear little resemblance to the violent disease that had killed in Haskell. Of 613 American troops admitted to the hospital during one outbreak in France, only one man died. In the French army, fewer than one hundred deaths resulted from forty thousand hospital admissions. In the British fleet, 10,313 sailors fell ill, temporarily crippling naval operations, but only four sailors died. Troops called it "three-day fever." In Algeria, Egypt, Tunisia, China, and India it was "everywhere of a mild form."

In fact, its mildness made some physicians wonder if this disease actually was influenza. One British army report noted that the symptoms "resembled influenza" but "its short duration and absence of complications" created doubt that it was influenza. Several different Italian doctors took a stronger position, arguing in separate medical journal articles that this "febrile disease now widely prevalent in Italy [is] not influenza." Three British doctors writing in the journal **The Lancet** agreed; they concluded that the epidemic could not actually be influenza, because the symptoms, though similar to those of influenza, were too mild, "of very short duration and so far absent of relapses or complications."

That issue of **The Lancet** was dated July 13, 1918.

In March and April in the United States, when the disease began jumping from army camp to army camp and occasionally spreading to adjacent cities, Gorgas, Welch, Vaughan, and Cole showed little concern about it, nor did Avery commence any laboratory investigation. Measles was still lingering, and had caused many more deaths.

But as influenza surged across Europe, they began to attend to it. Despite the articles in medical journals about its generally benign nature, they had heard of some worrisome exceptions, some hints that perhaps this disease wasn't always so benign after all, that when the disease did strike hard, it was unusually violent—more violent than measles.

One army report noted "fulminating pneumonia, with wet hemorrhagic lungs"—i.e., a rapidly escalating infection and lungs choked with blood—"fatal in from 24 to 48 hours." Such a quick death from pneumonia is extraordinary. And an autopsy of a Chicago civilian victim revealed lungs with similar symptoms, symptoms unusual enough to prompt the pathologist who performed the autopsy to send tissue samples to Dr. Ludwig Hektoen, a highly respected scientist who knew Welch, Flexner, and Gorgas well and who headed the John McCormick Memorial Institute for Infectious Diseases. The pathologist asked Hektoen "to look at it as a new disease."

And in Louisville, Kentucky, a disturbing anomaly appeared in the influenza statistics. There deaths were not so few, and—more surprisingly—40 percent of those who died were aged twenty to thirty-five, a statistically extraordinary occurrence.

In France in late May, at one small station of 1,018 French army recruits, 688 men were ill enough to be hospitalized and forty-nine died. When 5 percent of an entire population—especially of healthy young adults—dies in a few weeks, that is frightening.

By mid-June, Welch, Cole, Gorgas, and others were trying to gather as much information as possible about the progression of influenza in Europe. Cole could get nothing from official channels but did learn enough from such people as Hans Zinsser, a former (and future) Rockefeller investigator in the army in France, to become concerned. In July, Cole asked Richard Pearce, a scientist at the National Research Council who was coordinating war-related medical research, to make "accurate information concerning the influenza prevailing in Europe" a priority, adding, "I have inquired several times in Washington at the Surgeon General's office"— referring to civilian Surgeon General Rupert Blue, head of the U.S. Public Health Service, not Gorgas—"but no one seems to have any definite information in regard to the matter." A few days later Cole showed more concern when he advised Pearce to put more resources into related research.

In response Pearce contacted several individual laboratory scientists, such as Paul Lewis in Philadelphia, as well as clinicians, pathologists, and epidemiologists, asking if they could begin new investigations. He would act as a clearinghouse for their findings.

Between June 1 and August 1, 200,825 British soldiers in France, out of two million, were hit hard enough that they could not report for duty even in the midst of desperate combat. Then the disease was gone. On August 10, the British command declared the epidemic over. In Britain itself on August 20, a medical journal stated that the influenza epidemic "has completely disappeared."

The **Weekly Bulletin** of the Medical Service of the American Expeditionary Force in France was less willing than the British to write off the influenza epidemic entirely. It did say in late July, "The epidemic is about at an end . . . and has been throughout of a benign type, though causing considerable noneffectiveness."

But it went on to note, "Many cases have been mistaken for meningitis. . . . Pneumonias have been more common sequelae in July than in April."

In the United States, influenza had neither swept through the country, as it had in Western Europe and parts of the Orient, nor had it completely died out.

Individual members of the army's pneumonia commission had dispersed to perform studies in several locations, and they still saw signs of it. At Fort Riley, which included Camp Funston, Captain Francis Blake was trying to culture bacteria from the throats of both normal and sick troops. It was desultory work, far less exciting than what he was accustomed to, and he hated Kansas. He complained to his wife, "No letter from my beloved for two days, no cool days, no cool nights, no drinks, no movies, no dances, no club, no pretty women, no shower bath, no poker, no people, no fun, no joy, no nothing save heat and blistering sun and scorching winds and sweat and dust and thirst and long and stifling nights and working all hours and lonesomeness and general hell—that's Fort Riley Kansas." A few weeks later, he said it was so hot they kept their cultures of bacteria in an incubator so the heat wouldn't kill them. "Imagine going into an incubator to get cool," he wrote.

He also wrote, "Have been busy on the ward all day—some interesting cases. . . . But most of it influenza at present."

Influenza was about to become interesting.

For the virus had not disappeared. It had only gone underground, like a forest fire left burning in the roots, swarming and mutating, adapting, honing itself, watching and waiting, waiting to burst into flame.

CHAPTER FIFTEEN

THE 1918 INFLUENZA PANDEMIC, like many other influenza pandemics, came in waves. The first spring wave killed few, but the second wave would be lethal. Three hypotheses can explain this phenomenon.

One is that the mild and deadly diseases were caused by two entirely different viruses. This is highly unlikely. Many victims of the first wave demonstrated significant resistance to the second wave, which provides strong evidence that the deadly virus was a variant of the mild one.

The second possibility is that a mild virus caused the spring epidemic, and that in Europe it encountered a second influenza virus. The two viruses infected the same cells, "reassorted" their genes, and

created a new and lethal virus. This could have occurred and might also explain the partial immunity some victims of the first wave acquired, but at
least some scientific evidence directly contradicts
this hypothesis, and most influenza experts today
do not believe this happened.

The third explanation involves the adaptation of
the virus to man.

In 1872 the French scientist C. J. Davaine was
examining a specimen of blood swarming with anthrax. To determine the lethal dose he measured
out various amounts of this blood and injected it
into rabbits. He found it required ten drops to kill
a rabbit within forty hours. He drew blood from
this rabbit and infected a second rabbit, which also
died. He repeated the process, infecting a third rabbit with blood from the second, and so on, passing
the infection through five rabbits.

Each time he determined the minimum amount
of blood necessary to kill. He discovered that the
bacteria increased in virulence each time, and after
going through five rabbits a lethal dose fell from
10 drops of blood to 1/100 of a drop. At the fifteenth passage, the lethal dose fell to 1/40,000 of a
drop of blood. After twenty-five passages, the bacteria in the blood had become so virulent that less
than 1/1,000,000 of a drop killed.

This virulence disappeared when the culture was
stored. It was also specific to a species. Rats and

birds survived large doses of the same blood that killed rabbits in infinitesimal amounts.

Davaine's series of experiments marked the first demonstration of a phenomenon that became known as "passage." This phenomenon reflects an organism's ability to adapt to its environment. When an organism of weak pathogenicity passes from living animal to living animal, it reproduces more proficiently, growing and spreading more efficiently. This often increases virulence.

In other words, it becomes a better and more efficient killer.

Changing the environment even in a test tube can have the same effect. As one investigator noted, a strain of bacteria he was working with turned deadly when the medium used to grow the organism changed from beef broth to veal broth.

But the phenomenon is complex. The increase in killing efficiency does not continue indefinitely. If a pathogen kills too efficiently, it will run out of hosts and destroy itself. Eventually its virulence stabilizes and even recedes. Especially when jumping species, it can become less dangerous instead of more dangerous. This happens with the Ebola virus, which does not normally infect humans. Initially Ebola has extremely high mortality rates, but after it goes through several generations of human passages, it becomes far milder and not particularly threatening.

So passage can also weaken a pathogen. When Pasteur was trying to weaken or, to use his word, "attenuate" the pathogen of swine erysipelas, he succeeded only by passing it through rabbits. As the bacteria adapted to rabbits, it lost some of its ability to grow in swine. He then inoculated pigs with the rabbit-bred bacteria, and their immune systems easily destroyed it. Since the antigens on the weak strain were the same as those on normal strains, the pigs' immune systems learned to recognize—and destroy—normal strains as well. They became immune to the disease. By 1894, veterinarians used Pasteur's vaccine to protect 100,000 pigs in France; in Hungary over 1 million pigs were vaccinated.

The influenza virus is no different in its behavior from any other pathogen, and it faces the same evolutionary pressures. When the 1918 virus jumped from animals to people and began to spread, it may have suffered a shock of its own as it adapted to a new species. Although it always retained hints of virulence, this shock may well have weakened it, making it relatively mild; then, as it became better and better at infecting its new host, it turned lethal.

Macfarlane Burnet won his Nobel Prize for work on the immune system, but he spent the bulk of his career investigating influenza, including its epidemiological history. He noted an occasion when passage turned a harmless influenza virus into a lethal one. A ship carrying people sick with influenza visited an isolated settlement in east Greenland. Two months after the ship's departure, a severe influenza epidemic erupted, with a 10 percent mortality rate;

10 percent of those with the disease died. Burnet was "reasonably certain that the epidemic was primarily virus influenza" and concluded that the virus passed through several generations—he estimated fifteen or twenty human passages—in mild form before it adapted to the new population and became virulent and lethal.

In his study of the 1918 pandemic, Burnet concluded that by late April 1918 "the essential character of the new strain seems to have been established." He continued, "We must suppose that the ancestral virus responsible for the spring epidemics in the United States passaged and mutated. . . . The process continued in France."

Lethality lay within the genetic possibilities of this virus; this particular mutant swarm always had the potential to be more pestilential than other influenza viruses. Passage was sharpening its ferocity. As it smoldered in the roots, adapting itself, becoming increasingly efficient at reproducing itself in humans, passage was forging a killing inferno.

On June 30, 1918, the British freighter **City of Exeter** docked at Philadelphia after a brief hold at a maritime quarantine station. She was laced with deadly disease, but Rupert Blue, the civilian surgeon general and head of the U.S. Public Health Service, had issued no instructions to the maritime service to hold influenza-ridden ships. So she was released.

Nonetheless, the condition of the crew was so frightening that the British consul had arranged in advance for the ship to be met at a wharf empty of anything except ambulances whose drivers wore surgical masks. Dozens of crew members "in a desperate condition" were taken immediately to Pennsylvania Hospital, where, as a precaution against infectious disease, a ward was sealed off for them. Dr. Alfred Stengel, who had initially lost a competition for a prestigious professorship at the University of Pennsylvania to Simon Flexner but who did get it when Flexner left, had gone on to become president of the American College of Physicians. An expert on infectious diseases, he personally oversaw the sailors' care. Despite Stengel's old rivalry with Flexner, he even called in Flexner's protégé Paul Lewis for advice. Nonetheless, one after another, more crew members died.

They seemed to die of pneumonia, but it was a pneumonia accompanied, according to a Penn medical student, by strange symptoms, including bleeding from the nose. A report noted, "The opinion was reached that they had influenza."

In 1918 all infectious disease was frightening. Americans had already learned that "Spanish influenza" was serious enough that it had slowed the German offensive. Rumors now unsettled the city that these deaths too came from Spanish influenza. Those in control of the war's propaganda machine wanted nothing printed that could hurt morale. Two physicians stated flatly to newspapers that the men had not died of influenza. They were lying.

The disease did not spread. The brief quarantine had held the ship long enough that the crew members were no longer contagious when the ship docked. This particular virulent virus, finding no fresh fuel, had burned itself out. The city had dodged a bullet.

By now the virus had undergone numerous passages through humans. Even while medical journals were commenting on the mild nature of the disease, all over the world hints of a malevolent outbreak were appearing.

In London the week of July 8, 287 people died of influenzal pneumonia, and 126 died in Birmingham. A physician who performed several autopsies noted, "The lung lesions, complex or variable, struck one as being quite different in character to anything one had met with at all commonly in the thousands of autopsies one has performed during the last twenty years. It was not like the common broncho-pneumonia of ordinary years."

The U.S. Public Health Service's weekly **Public Health Reports** finally took notice, at last deeming the disease serious enough to warn the country's public health officials that "an outbreak of epidemic influenza . . . has been reported at Birmingham, England. The disease is stated to be spreading rapidly and to be present in other locations." And it warned of "fatal cases."

Earlier some physicians had insisted that the disease was not influenza because it was too mild. Now others also began to doubt that this disease was influenza—but this time because it seemed too deadly. Lack of oxygen was sometimes so severe that victims were becoming cyanotic—part or all of their bodies were turning blue, occasionally a very dark blue.

On August 3 a U.S. Navy intelligence officer received a telegram that he quickly stamped SECRET and CONFIDENTIAL. Noting that his source was "reliable," he reported, "I am confidentially advised . . . that the disease now epidemic throughout Switzerland is what is commonly known as the black plague, although it is designated as Spanish sickness and grip."

Many histories of the pandemic portray the eruption of deadly disease—the hammer blow of the second wave—as sudden and simultaneous in widely separated parts of the world, and therefore deeply puzzling. In fact the second wave developed gradually.

When water comes to a boil in a pot, first an isolated bubble releases from the bottom and rises to the surface. Then another. Then two or three simultaneously. Then half a dozen. But unless the heat is turned down, soon enough all the water within the pot is in motion, the surface a roiling violent chaos.

In 1918 each initial burst of lethality, isolated though it may have seemed, was much like a first bubble rising to the surface in a pot coming to boil. The flame may have ignited in Haskell and set off the first burst. The outbreak that killed 5 percent of **all** French recruits at one small base was another. Louisville was still another, as were the deaths on the **City of Exeter** and the outbreak in Switzerland. All these were bursts of lethal disease, violent bubbles rising to the surface.

Epidemiological studies written relatively soon after the pandemic recognized this. One noted that army cantonments in the United States saw "a progressive increase in cases reported as influenza beginning with the week ending August 4, 1918, and of the influenzal pneumonia cases beginning with the week ending August 18. If this was really the beginning of the great epidemic wave we should expect that if these series of data were plotted out on a logarithmic scale the increase from week to week would plot out as a straight line following the usual logarithmic rise of an epidemic curve. . . . This condition is substantially fulfilled with the curve of rise plotting out on logarithmic paper as a practically straight line."

The report also found "definite outbreaks of increasing severity" occurring during the summer in

1. William Henry Welch, the single most powerful individual in the history of American medicine and one of the most knowledgeable. A wary colleague said he could "transform men's lives almost with the flick of a wrist." When Welch first observed autopsies of influenza victims, he worried, "This must be some new kind of infection or plague."

2. Welch and John D. Rockefeller Jr. (on the right) together created the Rockefeller Institute for Medical Research (now Rockefeller University), arguably the best scientific research institution in the world. Simon Flexner (on the left), a Welch protégé, was the institute's first head; he once said that no one could run an institution unless he had the capacity to be cruel.

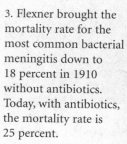

3. Flexner brought the mortality rate for the most common bacterial meningitis down to 18 percent in 1910 without antibiotics. Today, with antibiotics, the mortality rate is 25 percent.

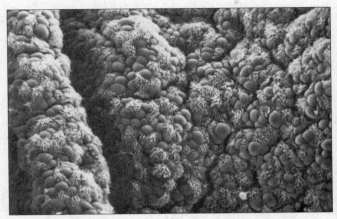

4. A dense jungle-like growth of epithelial cells covers a healthy mouse trachea.

5. Only seventy-two hours after infection the influenza virus transforms the same area into a barren and lifeless desert. White blood cells are patrolling the area, too late.

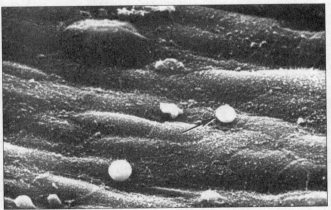

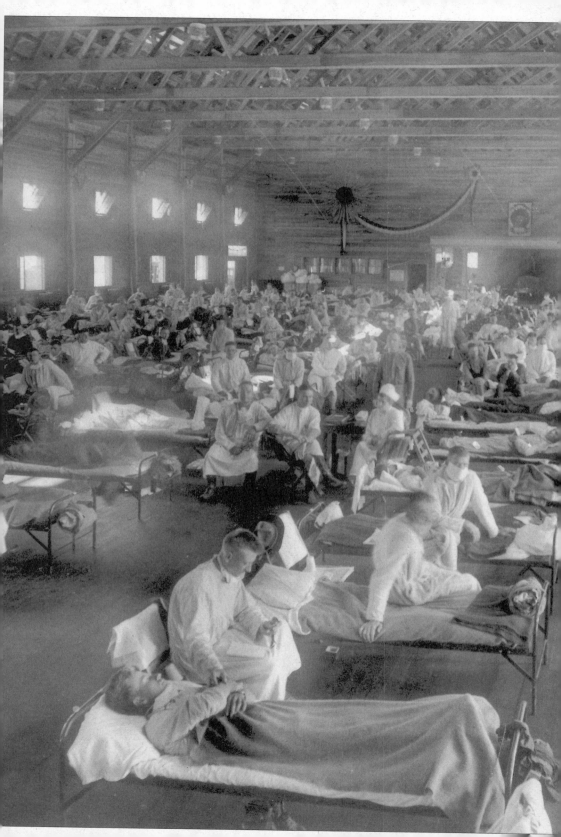

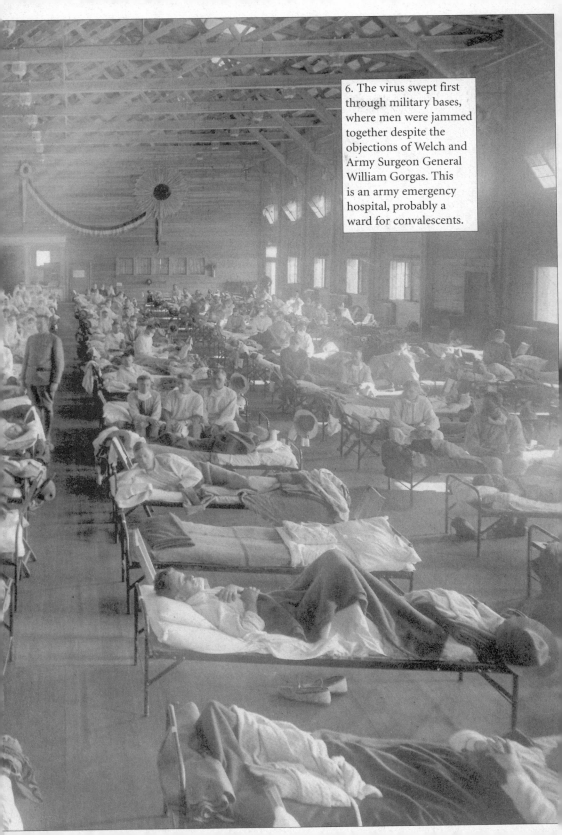

6. The virus swept first through military bases, where men were jammed together despite the objections of Welch and Army Surgeon General William Gorgas. This is an army emergency hospital, probably a ward for convalescents.

7. Army Surgeon General William Gorgas was determined that this would be the first war in which fewer American soldiers died of disease than from combat.

8. Rupert Blue, the civilian surgeon general and head of the U.S. Public Health Service, was a master bureaucrat but failed to heed warnings of, seek advance information about, or prepare for the epidemic.

9. Massachusetts was the first state to suffer huge numbers of civilian deaths. This is a hospital in Lawrence.

Preparing to Bury City's Influenza Victims

DIGGING TRENCH GRAVES FOR EPIDEMIC VICTIMS

10. In Philadelphia the number of dead quickly overwhelmed the city's ability to handle bodies. It was forced to bury people, without coffins, in mass graves and soon began using steam shovels to dig the graves.

11.

Posters and handouts spread warnings and advice. They also spread terror.

12.

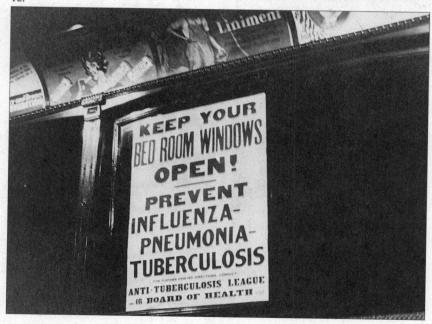

13. The two messages in this photograph—the policeman's protective mask and patriotism—epitomized a conflict of interest in public officials.

14. All New York City workers wore masks. Note the absence of traffic on the street and pedestrians on the sidewalk. The same silent streets were seen everywhere. In Philadelphia a doctor said, "The life of the city had almost stopped."

15. Oswald T. Avery as a private, when the Rockefeller Institute became Army Auxiliary Laboratory Number One.

16. Avery in later life. Persistent and tenacious, he said, "Disappointment is my daily bread. I thrive on it." Welch asked him to find the cause of influenza. His work on influenza and pneumonia would ultimately lead him to one of the most important scientific discoveries of the twentieth century.

17. William Park, who made New York City's municipal laboratories a premier research institution. His rigorous scientific discipline, when teamed with the more creative temperament of Anna Williams [below], led to dramatic advances, including the development of a diphtheria antitoxin still in use. The National Academy of Sciences hoped they could develop a serum or vaccine for influenza.

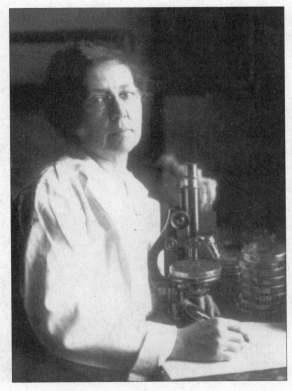

18. Anna Wessel Williams was probably the leading female bacteriologist in the world. A lonely woman who never married, she told herself she would "rather [have] discontent than happiness through lack of knowledge," and wondered "if it would be worthwhile to make the effort to have friends and if so how I should go about it." From her earliest memories, she dreamed "about going places. Such wild dreams were seldom conceived by any other child."

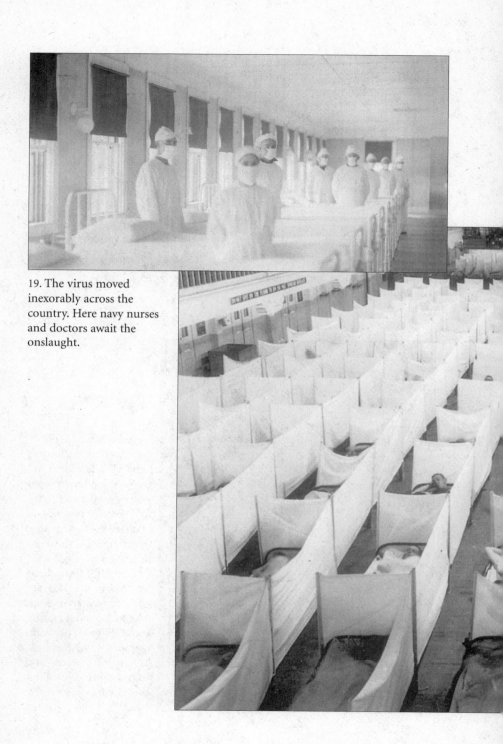

19. The virus moved inexorably across the country. Here navy nurses and doctors await the onslaught.

20. Military commanders tried to protect healthy men; at Mare Island in San Francisco sheets were hung in barracks to screen men from each other's breathing.

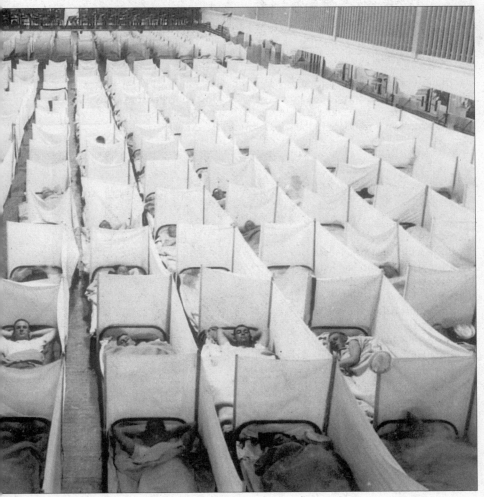

21. In most cities all public meetings were banned, all public gathering places—churches, schools, theaters, and saloons—closed. Most churches simply canceled services but this one in California met outdoors, a technical violation of the closing order but a response to the congregation's need for prayer.

22. Rufus Cole, the Rockefeller Institute scientist who had led the successful effort to develop a pneumonia vaccine and treatment just before the outbreak of the epidemic. He also made the Rockefeller Institute Hospital a model for the way clinical research is conducted, including at the National Institutes for Health.

23.

Seattle, like many other places, became a masked city. Red Cross volunteers made tens of thousands of masks. All police wore them. Soldiers marched through the city's downtown wearing them.

24.

25.

26. More than one scientist called Paul A. Lewis "the brightest man I ever met." As a young investigator in 1908 he proved polio was caused by a virus and devised a vaccine that was 100 percent effective in protecting monkeys. It would be half a century before a polio vaccine could protect man. He too was one of the prime investigators searching for the cause of influenza, and a cure or preventative. Ultimately his ambition to investigate disease would cost him his life.

27. In the late 1920s Richard Shope, Lewis's protégé, unearthed a crucial clue in the search for the cause of influenza. While Lewis went to Brazilian jungles to investigate yellow fever, Shope continued his pursuit of influenza. He was the first to prove a virus caused the disease.

both the United States and Europe, which "indistinguishably blend with the great Fall wave."

In early August the crew of a steamship proceeding from France to New York was hit so hard with influenza "that all of the seamen were prostrate on it and it had to put into Halifax," according to an epidemiologist in Gorgas's office, where it remained until enough crew members were well enough to proceed to New York.

On August 12 the Norwegian freighter **Bergensfjord** arrived in Brooklyn after burying four men at sea, dead of influenza. It carried two hundred people still sick with the disease; ambulances transported many of them to a hospital.

Royal Copeland, head of the New York City health department, and the port health officer jointly stated there was "not the slightest danger of an epidemic" because the disease seldom attacks "a well-nourished people." (Even had he been right, a study by his own health department had just concluded that 20 percent of city schoolchildren were malnourished.) He took no action whatsoever to prevent the spread of infection.

A navy bulletin warned of two steamships from Norway and one from Sweden arriving in New York City with influenza cases aboard on August 14 and 15. On August 18, New York papers described outbreaks on board the **Rochambeau** and **Nieuw Amsterdam;** men from both ships had been taken to St. Vincent's Hospital.

On August 20 even Copeland conceded that influenza, though mild and—he claimed—certainly not in epidemic form, was present in the city.

The lethal variant of the virus was finding its home in humans. Now, almost simultaneously, on three continents separated by thousands of miles of ocean—in Brest, in Freeport, Sierra Leone, and in Boston—the killing, rolling boil was about to begin.

Nearly 40 percent of the two million American troops who arrived in France—791,000 men—disembarked at Brest, a deepwater port capable of handling dozens of ships simultaneously. Troops from all over the world disembarked there. Brest had already seen a burst of influenza in the spring as had many other cities, albeit as in most of those other places that influenza had been mild. The first outbreak with high mortality occurred in July, in a replacement detachment of American troops from Camp Pike, Arkansas. They occupied an isolated camp and the outbreak initially seemed contained. It was not. By August 10, the same day the British army declared the influenza epidemic over, so many French sailors stationed at Brest were hospitalized with influenza and pneumonia that they overwhelmed the naval hospital there—forcing it to close. And the death rate among them began soaring.

The August 19 **New York Times** took note of another outbreak: "A considerable number of American negroes, who have gone to France on horse transports, have contracted Spanish influenza on shore and died in French hospitals of pneumonia."

Within another few weeks all the area around Brest was in flames. American troops continued pouring into and then out of the city, mixing with French troops also training in the vicinity. When soldiers of both armies left the vicinity, they dispersed the virus en masse.

Freetown, Sierra Leone, was a major coaling center on the West African coast, servicing ships traveling from Europe to South Africa and the Orient. On August 15 the HMS **Mantua** arrived there with two hundred crew suffering from influenza. Sweating black men loaded tons of coal into her, guided by several crew.

When the laborers returned to their homes, they carried more than their wages. Soon influenza spread through the force of men who coaled the ships. And this influenza was not mild. On August 24, two natives died of pneumonia while many others were still sick.

On August 27, the HMS **Africa** pulled into port. She too needed coal, but five hundred of the six hundred laborers of the Sierra Leone Coaling Company did not report to work that day. Her crew helped coal her, working side by side with African laborers. She carried a crew of 779. Within a few weeks, nearly six hundred were sick. And fifty-one were dead—7 percent of the entire crew died.

The transport HMS **Chepstow Castle,** carrying troops from New Zealand to the front, coaled at Freetown on August 26 and 27; within three weeks, out of her 1,150 men, influenza struck down nine hundred of them. The death toll on her was thirty-eight.

The **Tahiti** coaled at the same time; sixty-eight men aboard her died before she reached England, the same day as the **Chepstow Castle.** After docking, crew of the two ships suffered eight hundred more cases and 115 more deaths.

In Sierra Leone itself, officials soon after estimated that influenza killed 3 percent of the entire African population, nearly all of them dying within the next few weeks. More recent evidence suggests that the death toll was most likely considerably more than that, possibly double that figure—or higher.

Across the Atlantic, at Commonwealth Pier in Boston, the navy operated a "receiving ship." The name was a misnomer. It was actually a barracks where as many as seven thousand sailors in transit ate and slept in what the navy itself called "grossly overcrowded" quarters.

On August 27, two sailors reported to sick bay with influenza. On August 28, eight more sailors reported ill. On August 29, fifty-eight men were admitted.

As in Brest and Freetown and aboard ship, men began to die. Fifty of the men were quickly transferred to the Chelsea Naval Hospital, where Lieutenant Commander Milton Rosenau and his young assistant, Lieutenant John J. Keegan, worked.

The sailors were in better than good hands. While Keegan would later become dean of the University of Nebraska Medical School, Rosenau was one of the giants of the day. Strong, solid, and thick-necked, he looked as intimidating and determined as a wrestler staring down an opponent. Yet he was uniformly polite and supportive, and people enjoyed working under him. A prime mover in creating the U.S. Public Health Service Hygienic Laboratory and later the president of the Society of American Bacteriologists, he was best known for his textbook, **Preventive Medicine and Hygiene,** which was referred to as "The Bible" for both army and navy medical officers. Only a few weeks earlier, he had met with Welch, Gorgas, and Vaughan to discuss how to prevent or contain any new epidemic.*

* Rosenau and Flexner had had a running but friendly competition for years. In 1911 Rosenau had shown that Flexner had made an important mistake. Two years later Rosenau won the American Medicine Gold Medal in 1913 for "proving" that stable flies transmitted poliomyelitis. Flexner proved that finding to be in error in 1915. Yet each respected the other, and they got along well. Shortly before the war, with Harvard still underfunding medical research, Flexner wrote him, "I am astonished and pained to learn that you have so small a budget for your lab," and promptly arranged for a Rockefeller grant to him. Their cooperation was routine, for example when Rosenau asked Flexner earlier in 1918, "Please send Chelsea Naval Hospital at once sufficient antimeningitis serum for 4 patients."

Rosenau and Keegan immediately isolated the men and did everything possible to contain the disease, working backward from each victim to trace and isolate people with whom the patients had had contact. But the disease was too explosive. They turned their attention to bacteriological analysis, seeking the pathogen so they could prepare a vaccine or serum. Their findings did not satisfy them, and within a few weeks they began using human volunteers from the navy brig in the first experiments in the world to determine if a virus caused the disease.

Long before that, any hopes of containing the disease had collapsed. On September 3 a civilian suffering from influenza was admitted to the Boston City Hospital. On September 4 students at the Navy Radio School at Harvard, in Cambridge across the Charles River from Boston proper, fell ill.

And then came Devens.

CHAPTER SIXTEEN

CAMP DEVENS sat on five thousand acres in rolling hills thirty-five miles northwest of Boston. It included fine farmland along the Nashua River, as well as what had been until recently heavily forested land cut down now to tree stumps. Like the other cantonments in the country it was thrown together with amazing speed, at the rate of 10.4 buildings a day. In August 1917 it opened with fifteen thousand men although the camp was incomplete—its sewage was still being discharged directly into the Nashua River.

Like most other camps, it had suffered from measles and pneumonia. The medical staff was first rate. An inspection of the Devens hospital had given it an excellent review down to its kitchen, noting, "The mess officer is well informed and alert."

In fact the Devens medical staff was so good that Frederick Russell was preparing to rely on it to launch several major new scientific investigations. One involved correlating the existence of streptococci in the mouths of healthy soldiers with streptococcal infections of the throat. Another sought an explanation for the far higher morbidity rates of pneumonia among blacks over whites. Still another involved measles. Late in the summer at Devens, Major Andrew Sellards had passed infectious material from a recent measles case through a porcelain filter to isolate the virus, had inoculated four monkeys with it, and on August 29 began inoculating a series of human volunteers.

The only problem at Devens was that it was built to hold a maximum of thirty-six thousand men. On September 6, Devens held just over forty-five thousand men. Still, the camp hospital could accommodate twelve hundred and it was caring for only eighty-four patients. With enough medical personnel to run several simultaneous research efforts, with a highly competent clinical staff, with a virtually empty hospital, Devens seemed ready for any emergency.

It wasn't.

A week before any reported illness in the harbor, Boston public health authorities worried: "A sudden and very significant increase reported the third week of August in the cases of pneumonia occurring in the army cantonment at Camp Devens in the district seems to justify a suspicion that an influenza epidemic may have started among the soldiers there."

While the eruption at Devens might still have come from the Navy Commonwealth Pier facility, it might also have developed independently. It might even have spread to Boston from Devens. At any rate, on September 1, four more soldiers at Devens were diagnosed with pneumonia and admitted to the hospital. In the next six days, twenty-two more new cases of pneumonia were diagnosed. None of these, however, were considered to be influenza.

On September 7, a soldier from D Company, Forty-second Infantry, was sent to the hospital. He ached to the extent that he screamed when he was touched, and he was delirious. He was diagnosed as having meningitis.

The next day a dozen more men from his company were hospitalized and suspected of having meningitis. It was a reasonable diagnosis. Symptoms did not resemble those of influenza, and a few months earlier the camp had suffered a minor epidemic of meningitis, and the doctors—lacking any false pride—had even called Rosenau for help. He had come himself, along with six bacteriologists; they had worked nearly around the clock for five days, identifying and quarantining 179 carriers of the disease. Rosenau had left the camp impressed with army medicine; even though he and his staff had done much of the work, he had advised navy superiors that the same effort would not have been possible in the navy.

Now, over the next few days, other organizations began reporting cases of influenza-like disease. The medical staff, good as it was, did not at first connect these various cases to one another or to the outbreak on Commonwealth Pier. They made no attempt to quarantine cases. In the first few days no records of influenza cases were even kept because they "were looked upon as being examples of the epidemic disease which attacked so many of the camps during the spring." In the overcrowded barracks and mess halls, the men mixed. A day went by. Two days. Then, suddenly, noted an army report, "Stated briefly, the influenza . . . occurred as an explosion."

It exploded indeed. In a single day, 1,543 Camp Devens soldiers reported ill with influenza. On September 22, 19.6 percent of the entire camp was on sick report, and almost 75 percent of those on sick report had been hospitalized. By then the pneumonias, and the deaths, had begun.

On September 24 alone, 342 men were diagnosed with pneumonia. Devens normally had twenty-five physicians. Now, as army and civilian medical staff poured into the camp, more than two hundred and fifty physicians were treating patients. The doctors, the nurses, the orderlies went to work at 5:30 A.M. and worked steadily until 9:30 P.M., slept, then went at it again. Yet on September 26 the medical staff was so overwhelmed, with doctors and nurses not only ill but dying, they decided to admit no more patients to the hospital, no matter how ill.

The Red Cross, itself by then overwhelmed by the spread of the disease to the civilian population, managed to find twelve more nurses to help and sent them. They were of little help. Eight of the twelve collapsed with influenza; two died.

For this was no ordinary pneumonia. Dr. Roy Grist, one of the army physicians at the hospital, wrote a colleague, "These men start with what appears to be an ordinary attack of LaGrippe or Influenza, and when brought to the Hosp. they very rapidly develop the most vicious type of Pneumonia that has ever been seen. Two hours after admission they have the Mahogany spots over the cheek bones, and a few hours later you can begin to see the Cyanosis extending from their ears and spreading all over the face, until it is hard to distinguish the coloured men from the white."

Blood carrying oxygen in arteries is bright red; without oxygen in veins it is blue. Cyanosis occurs when a victim turns blue because the lungs cannot transfer oxygen into the blood. In 1918 cyanosis was so extreme, turning some victims so dark—the entire body could take on color resembling that of the veins on one's wrists—it sparked rumors that the disease was not influenza at all, but the Black Death.

Grist continued, "It is only a matter of a few hours then until death comes. . . . It is horrible. One can stand it to see one, two or twenty men die, but to see these poor devils dropping like flies . . . We have been averaging about 100 deaths per day. . . . Pneumonia means in about all cases death. . . . We have lost an outrageous number of Nurses and Drs., and the little town of Ayer is a sight. It takes special trains to carry away the dead. For several days there were no coffins and the bodies piled up something fierce. . . . It beats any sight they ever had in France after a battle. An extra long barracks has been vacated for the use of the Morgue, and it would make any man sit up and take notice to walk down the long lines of dead soldiers all dressed and laid out in double rows. . . . Good By old Pal, God be with you till we meet again."

Welch, Cole, Victor Vaughan, and Fredrick Russell, all of them colonels now, had just finished a tour of southern army bases. It was not their first such tour, and as before, knowing that an army barracks offered explosive tinder, they had been inspecting camps to find and correct any practice that might allow an epidemic to gain a foothold. They also spent much time discussing pneumonia. After leaving Camp Macon in Georgia, they had retired for a few days of relaxation to Asheville, North Carolina, the most fashionable summer retreat in the South. The Vanderbilts had built one of the most elaborate estates in the country there, and not many miles away Welch's old colleague William Halsted had built a virtual castle in the mountains (today Halsted's home is a resort called the High Hamptons).

At the Grove Park Inn, one of the most elegant settings in the city, they listened to a concert. Welch lit a cigar. A bellboy promptly told him smoking was not allowed. He and Cole withdrew to the veranda and began talking. Another bellboy asked them to please be quiet during the concert. Welch left in disgust.

Meanwhile Russell wrote Flexner, "We are all well. Welch, Vaughan, and Cole, and I have had a very profitable trip and have begun to believe that immunity"—in this he was referring to efforts to manipulate the immune system—"is the most important thing in pneumonia, as in other infectious diseases. It makes a good working hypothesis and one we will try to follow up by working in the lab, wards, and in the field this fall and winter. Bonne chance."

The group returned to Washington on a Sunday morning relaxed and in good spirits. But their mood changed abruptly as they stepped off the train. An escort had been waiting for them and his anxiety quickly communicated itself. He was taking them to the surgeon general's office—immediately. Gorgas himself was in Europe. His deputy barely looked up

as they opened the door: "You will proceed immediately to Devens. The Spanish influenza has struck
that camp."

They arrived at Devens eight hours later in a cold
and drizzling rain. The entire camp was in chaos, the
hospital itself a battlefield. The war had come home
indeed. As they entered the hospital, they watched
a continuous line of men filing in from the barracks
carrying their blankets or being themselves carried.

Vaughan recorded this sight: "hundreds of young
stalwart men in the uniform of their country coming into the wards of the hospital in groups of ten
or more. They are placed on the cots until every
bed is full and yet others crowd in. The faces wear
a bluish cast; a distressing cough brings up the
blood-stained sputum."

Care was almost nonexistent. The base hospital,
designed for twelve hundred, could accommodate at
most—even with crowding "beyond what is deemed
permissible," according to Welch—twenty-five
hundred. It now held in excess of six thousand.
All beds had long since been filled. Every corridor,
every spare room, every porch was filled, crammed
with cots occupied by the sick and dying. There
was nothing antiseptic about the sight. And there
were no nurses. When Welch arrived, seventy out
of two hundred nurses were already sick in bed
themselves, with more falling ill each hour. Many
of them would not recover. A stench filled the

hospital as well. Bed linen and clothing were rank with urine and feces from men incapable of rising or cleaning themselves.

Blood was everywhere, on linens, clothes, pouring out of some men's nostrils and even ears while others coughed it up. Many of the soldiers, boys in their teens, men in their twenties—healthy, normally ruddy men—were turning blue. Their color would prove a deadly indicator.

The sight chilled even Welch and his colleagues. It was more chilling still to see corpses littering the hallways surrounding the morgue. Vaughan reported, "In the morning the dead bodies are stacked about the morgue like cord wood." As Cole recalled, "They were placed on the floor without any order or system, and we had to step amongst them to get into the room where an autopsy was going on."

In the autopsy room they saw the most chilling sights yet. On the table lay the corpse of a young man, not much more than a boy. When he was moved in the slightest degree fluid poured out of his nostrils. His chest was opened, his lungs removed, other organs examined carefully. It was immediately apparent this was no ordinary pneumonia. Several other autopsies yielded similar abnormalities.

Cole, Vaughan, Russell, the other members of this scientific team were puzzled, and felt an edge of fear. They turned to Welch.

He had studied with the greatest investigators in the world as a young man. He had inspired a generation of brilliant scientists in America. He had visited and seen diseases in China, the Philippines, and Japan that were unknown in the United States. He had read scientific journals in many languages for years, heard back-channel gossip from all the leading laboratories in the world. Surely he would be able to tell them something, have some idea.

He did not reassure. Cole stood beside him, thinking he had never seen Welch look nervous before, or excited in quite this way. In fact Cole was shaken: "It was not surprising that the rest of us were disturbed but it shocked me to find that the situation, momentarily at least was too much for Dr. Welch."

Then Welch said, "This must be some new kind of infection or plague."

Welch walked out of the autopsy room and made three phone calls, to Boston, New York, and Washington. In Boston he spoke to Burt Wolbach, a Harvard professor and chief pathologist at the great Boston hospital the Brigham, and asked him to perform autopsies. Perhaps there was a clue to this strange disease there.

But Welch also knew that any treatment or prevention for this would have to come from the laboratory. From the Rockefeller Institute in New York he summoned Oswald Avery. Avery had been refused a commission in the Rockefeller army unit because he was Canadian, but on August 1 he had become an American citizen. By coincidence, the same day Welch called him, Avery was promoted from private to captain. More important, he had already begun the investigations that would ultimately revolution-ize the biological sciences; influenza would confirm him in this work.

Later that day both Avery and Wolbach arrived and immediately began their respective tasks.

The third call Welch made was to Washington, to Charles Richard, the acting army surgeon general while Gorgas was at the front. Welch gave a detailed description of the disease and his expectations of its course at Devens and elsewhere. For this was going to spread. He urged that "immediate provi-sion be made in every camp for the rapid expansion of hospital space."

Richard responded instantly, sending orders to all medical personnel to isolate and quarantine all cases and segregate soldiers from civilians outside the camps: "It is important that the influenza be kept out of the camps, as far as practicable. . . . Epidemics of the disease can often be prevented, but once established they cannot well be stopped." But he also conceded the difficulty: "There are few diseases as infectious as influenza. . . . It is probable that patients become foci of infection before the active symptoms. . . . No disease which the army surgeon is likely to see in this war will tax more severely his judgement and initiative."

He also warned both the army adjutant general and chief of staff, "New men will almost surely contract the disease. In transferring men from Camp Devens a virulent form of the disease will almost surely be conveyed to other stations. . . . During the epidemic new men should not be sent to Camp Devens, nor should men be sent away from that camp."

The next day, with reports already of outbreaks in other camps, Richard tried to impress upon the chief of staff the lethality of the disease, relating what Welch had told him: "The deaths at Camp Devens will probably exceed 500. . . . The experience at Camp Devens may be fairly expected to occur at other large cantonments. . . . With few exceptions they are densely populated, a condition which tends to increase the chance for 'contact' infection and the virulence and mortality of the disease. . . . It may be expected to travel westward and involve successively military stations in its course." And he urged that the transfer of personnel from one camp to another be all but eliminated except for the most "urgent military necessities."

Gorgas had fought his own war, to prevent epidemic disease from erupting in the camps. He had lost.

On August 27, the same day the first sailors at Commonwealth Pier fell ill, the steamer **Harold Walker** had departed Boston, bound for New

Orleans. En route fifteen crew members had fallen ill; in New Orleans the ship unloaded its cargo and put three crewmen ashore. The three men died. By then the **Harold Walker** had proceeded to Mexico.

On September 4, physicians at the New Orleans naval hospital made the first diagnosis of influenza in any military personnel in the city; the sailor had arrived in New Orleans from the Northeast. That same date a second patient also reported ill with influenza; he was serving in New Orleans. Forty of the next forty-two patients who entered the hospital had influenza or pneumonia.

On September 7 three hundred sailors from Boston arrived at the Philadelphia Navy Yard. Many of them, mixing with hundreds of other sailors, were almost immediately transferred to the navy base in Puget Sound. Others had already gone from Boston to north of Chicago to the Great Lakes Naval Training Station, the largest facility of its kind in the world.

On September 8 at the Newport Naval Base in Rhode Island, more than one hundred sailors reported sick.

The virus was reaching south along the coast, jumping inland to the Midwest, spanning the nation to the Pacific.

Meanwhile, at the Chelsea Naval Hospital, Rosenau and his team of physicians were also overwhelmed—and well aware of the larger implications. Even before Avery arrived, he and Keegan had begun the first effort in the country, and possibly in the world, to create an immune serum that would work against this new mortal enemy. Simultaneously Keegan sent off a description of the disease to the **Journal of the American Medical Association,** warning that it "promises to spread rapidly across the entire country, attacking between 30 and 40 percent of the population, and running an acute course."

Keegan was incorrect only in that he limited his estimate to "the entire country." He should have said "the entire world."

This influenza virus, this "mutant swarm," this "quasi species," had always held within itself the potential to kill, and it had killed. Now, all over the world, the virus had gone through roughly the same number of passages through humans. All over the world, the virus was adapting to humans, achieving maximum efficiency. And all over the world, the virus was turning lethal.

Around the world from Boston, in Bombay, which like so many other cities had endured a mild epidemic in June, the lethal virus exploded almost simultaneously. There it quickly began killing at a rate more than double that of a serious epidemic of bubonic plague in 1900.

As the virus moved, two parallel struggles emerged.

One encompassed all of the nation. Within each

city, within each factory, within each family, into each store, onto each farm, along the length of the track of the railroads, along the rivers and roads, deep into the bowels of mines and high along the ridges of the mountains, the virus would find its way. In the next weeks, the virus would test society as a whole and each element within it. Society would have to gather itself to meet this test, or collapse.

The other struggle lay within one tight community of scientists. They—men like Welch, Flexner, Cole, Avery, Lewis, Rosenau—had been drafted against their will into a race. They knew what was required. They knew the puzzle they needed to solve. They were not helpless. They had some tools with which to work. They knew the cost if they failed.

But they had very little time indeed.

■ Part V
EXPLOSION

CHAPTER SEVENTEEN

ON SEPTEMBER 7, THREE hundred sailors arrived from Boston at the Philadelphia Navy Yard. And what happened in Philadelphia from that point would prove—too often—to be a model for what would happen elsewhere.

Philadelphia was already typical in its war experiences. Every city was being flooded by people, and in Philadelphia shipbuilding alone had added tens of thousands of workers. In a few months a great marsh had been transformed into the Hog Island shipyard, the largest shipyard in the world, where thirty-five thousand workers toiled among furnaces and steel and machinery. Nearby the New York Shipbuilding yard worked eleven thousand five hundred men, and a dozen other shipyards each worked from three thousand to five thousand more. And the city was thick with other great industrial plants: several munitions factories each employed several thousands at a single location, the J. G. Brill Company turned out a streetcar an hour and employed four thousand, Midvale Steel had ten thousand workers, Baldwin Locomotive, twenty thousand.

Overcrowded before the war, with jobs sucking ever more workers into the city and the population swelling to 1.75 million, Philadelphia literally teemed with people. In 1918 a national publication for social workers judged living conditions in its slums, where most tenements still had outhouses servicing dozens of families, worse than on the Lower East Side of New York. Blacks endured even more squalid conditions and Philadelphia had the largest African American population of any northern city, including New York or Chicago.

Housing was so scarce that Boy Scouts canvassed the area seeking rooms for newly arrived women with war jobs. Two, three, and four entire families would cram themselves into a single two- or three-room apartment, with children and teenagers sharing a bed. In rooming houses laborers shared not just rooms but beds, often sleeping in shifts just as they worked in shifts. In those same tenements, the city's own health department had conceded that during the winter of 1917–18 "the death rate . . .

has gone up owing to the high cost of living and scarcity of coal."

The city offered the poor social services in the form of Philadelphia Hospital, known as "Blockley," a poorhouse, and an asylum. But it offered nothing else, not even an orphanage. The social elite and progressives ran whatever charitable activities that did exist. Even normal services such as schools were in short supply. Of the twenty largest cities in America, Philadelphia, the city of Benjamin Franklin and the University of Pennsylvania, spent less on education than all but one. In all of South Philadelphia, home to hundreds of thousands of Italians and Jews, there would be no high school until 1934.

All this made Philadelphia fertile ground for epidemic disease. So did a city government incapable of responding to a crisis. Muckraker Lincoln Steffens called Philadelphia "the worst-governed city in America." He may well have been right.

Even Tammany's use of power in New York was haphazard compared to that of the Philadelphia machine, which had returned to power in 1916 after a reformer's single term in office. Philadelphia's boss was Republican state senator Edwin Vare. He had bested and mocked people who considered themselves his betters, people who despised him, people with such names as Wharton, Biddle, and Wanamaker.

A short, thick-chested, and thick-bellied man—

his nickname was "the little fellow"—Vare had his base in South Philadelphia. He had grown up there before the incursion of immigrants, on a pig farm in a then-rural area called "the Neck." He still lived there despite enormous wealth. The wealth came from politics.

All city workers kicked back a portion of their salary to Vare's machine. To make sure none ever missed a payment, city workers received their salary not where they worked or in City Hall—a classic and magnificent Victorian building, with curved shoulders and windows reminiscent of weeping willow trees—but across the street from City Hall in Republican Party headquarters. The mayor himself kicked back $1,000 from his pay.

Vare was also the city's biggest contractor, and his biggest contract was for street cleaning, a contract he had held for almost twenty years. At a time when a family could live in comfort on $3,000 a year, in 1917 he had received over $5 million for the job. Not all of that money stayed in Vare's pockets, but even the part that left passed through them and paid a toll. Yet the streets were notoriously filthy, especially in South Philadelphia—where the need was greatest, where everything but raw sewage, and sometimes even that, ran through the gutters, and where the machine was strongest.

Ironically, the very lack of city services strengthened the machine since it provided what the city did not: food baskets to the poor, help with jobs and favors, and help with the police—the commissioner and many magistrates were in Vare's pocket. People paid for the favors with votes which, like a medieval alchemist, he transmuted into money.

The machine proved so lucrative that Edwin Vare and his brother William, a congressman, became philanthropists, giving so much to their church at Moyamensing Avenue and Morris Street that it was renamed the Abigail Vare Memorial Methodist Episcopal Church, after their mother. Not many churches are named after mere mortals, but this one was.

Yet nothing about the machine was saintly. On primary election day in 1917, several Vare workers blackjacked two leaders of an opposing faction, then beat to death a policeman who intervened. The incident outraged the city. Vare's chief lieutenant in 1918 was Mayor Thomas B. Smith. In his one term in office he would be indicted, although acquitted, on three entirely unrelated charges, including conspiracy to murder that policeman. That same election, however, gave Vare absolute control over both the Select and Common Councils, the city's legislature, and broad influence in the state legislature.

Director of the Philadelphia Department of Public Health and Charities was Dr. Wilmer Krusen, a political appointee who served at the mayor's pleasure and whose term automatically expired with the mayor's. Krusen, a decent man whose son would become a surgeon at the Mayo Clinic, was as good an appointment as the machine made. But he lacked background in, commitment to, or understanding of public health issues. And he was by nature someone who thought most problems disappeared on their own. He was not someone to rush into a thing.

He certainly would exert no pressure whatsoever on the machine to advance the public health. Although a gynecologist, he refused even to help the military in its massive national campaign against prostitution. Even New Orleans had succumbed to pressure to close Storyville, where prostitution was legal, but no pressure could make Philadelphia, where prostitution remained illegal, in any way hinder its flesh industry. So, according to a military report, the navy "actually took control of police affairs" outside its installations.

The city government was choking on corruption, with lines of authority split among Vare, precinct captains—turned—entrepreneurs, and the mayor. It did not wish to act, nor could it if it chose to.

Four days after the arrival of the sailors from Boston at the Navy Yard, nineteen sailors reported ill with symptoms of influenza.

Lieutenant Commander R. W. Plummer, a physician and chief health officer for the Philadelphia naval district, was well aware of the epidemic's rage on Commonwealth Pier and at Devens and its spread to the civilian population in Massachusetts. Determined to contain the outbreak, he ordered the immediate quarantine of the men's barracks and the meticulous disinfecting of everything the men had touched.

In fact, the virus had already escaped, and not only into the city. One day earlier 334 sailors had left Philadelphia for Puget Sound; many would arrive there desperately ill.

Plummer also immediately called in Paul Lewis.

Lewis had been expecting such a call.

He loved the laboratory more than he loved anyone or anything, and he had the full confidence of Welch, Theobald Smith, and Flexner. Lewis had won their confidence by his extraordinary performance as a young scientist under each of them in turn. He had already achieved much, and he held the promise of much more. He also knew his own worth, not in the sense that it made him smug but in that it gave him responsibility, making his promise at least as much burden as ambition. Only an offer to become the founding head of the new Henry Phipps Institute—Phipps had made millions at U.S. Steel with Andrew Carnegie, then, like Carnegie, had become a prominent philanthropist—which was associated with the University of Pennsylvania, had lured him to Philadelphia from the Rockefeller Institute. He was modeling Phipps after the institute, although Phipps would focus much more narrowly on lung disease, particularly tuberculosis.

No one needed to tell Lewis the urgency of the situation. He knew the details of the British sailors who had died in early July, and he had very likely tried to culture bacteria from them and prepare a serum. Soon after learning that influenza had appeared in the Navy Yard, Lewis arrived there.

It was up to him to take charge of what would normally be the step-by-step, deliberate process of tracking down the pathogen and trying to develop a serum or vaccine. And there was no time for normal scientific procedures.

The next day eighty-seven sailors reported ill. By September 15, while Lewis and his assistants worked in labs at Penn and at the navy hospital, the virus had made six hundred sailors and marines sick enough to require hospitalization, and more men were reporting ill every few minutes. The navy hospital ran out of beds. The navy began sending ill sailors to the Pennsylvania Hospital at Eighth and Spruce.

On September 17, five doctors and fourteen nurses in that civilian hospital suddenly collapsed. None had exhibited any prior symptoms whatsoever. One moment they felt normal; the next, they were being carried in agony to hospital beds.

Navy personnel from Boston had been transferred elsewhere as well. As Philadelphia was erupting, so was the Great Lakes Naval Training Station, thirty-two miles above Chicago. Teddy Roosevelt had created the base in 1905, declaring that it would become the largest and best naval training station in the world. With forty-five thousand sailors it was the largest, and it had begun to generate a proud history. The "Seabees" naval construction battalions were born there, and during the war Lieutenant John Philip Sousa created fourteen regimental bands there; sometimes all fifteen hundred musicians played en masse on Ross Field, a spectacle for tens of thousands who flocked to hear them. As the influenza virus swept through the base, there would be no massing of anyone, musicians or otherwise. At this base, influenza ripped through the barracks very much like an explosion.

Robert St. John had just been inducted into the navy there when he became one of the early victims. Given a cot in a drill hall where soon thousands of men—in that one hall—would lie unattended, he later recalled, "No one ever took our temperatures and I never even saw a doctor." He did make his first friend in the navy, a boy on the next cot who was too ill to reach for water. St. John himself barely had the strength to help him drink from his canteen. The next morning an orderly pulled the blanket over his friend's head, and two sailors put the body on a stretcher and carried it away. By then the medical department had already reported that "33 caskets to Naval Medical Supply Depot required." They would soon require far more than that.

One nurse at Great Lakes would later be haunted by nightmares. The wards had forty-two beds; boys lying on the floor on stretchers waited for the boy on the bed to die. Every morning the ambulances arrived and stretcher bearers carried sick sailors in and bodies out. She remembered that at the peak of the epidemic the nurses wrapped more than one living patient in winding sheets and put toe tags on the boys' left big toe. It saved time, and the nurses were utterly exhausted. The toe tags were shipping tags, listing the sailor's name, rank, and hometown. She remembered bodies "stacked in the morgue from floor to ceiling like cord wood." In her nightmares she wondered "what it would feel like to be that boy who was at the bottom of the cord wood in the morgue."

The epidemic was sweeping through the Philadelphia naval installations with comparable violence, as it had in Boston. Yet in Philadelphia, despite the news out of Boston, despite the Great Lakes situation, despite events at its own Navy Yard, Philadelphia public health director Wilmer Krusen had done absolutely nothing.

Not all the city's public health figures remained oblivious to the threat. The day after the first sailor fell ill, Dr. Howard Anders, a prominent public health expert who despised and had no faith in the Vare machine, wrote Navy Surgeon General William Braisted to ask would "the navy (federal) authorities directly come in, under this threat of influenza invasion, and insist upon safeguarding its men and collaterally the whole population of Philadelphia . . . ?" (Braisted declined.)

Krusen publicly denied that influenza posed any threat to the city. He seemed to believe that, for he made no contingency plans in case of emergency, stockpiled no supplies, and compiled no lists of medical personnel who would be available in an emergency, even though 26 percent of Philadelphia's doctors and even a higher percentage of nurses were in the military. Indeed, despite building pressure from Lewis, from Anders, from physicians all over the city, from faculty at Penn and Thomas Jefferson Medical College—which refused to release six doctors who wanted to volunteer for military service just as the epidemic erupted—not until September 18, a full week after the disease appeared in the city, did Krusen even schedule a meeting with Plummer, Lewis, and several others.

In Krusen's fifth-floor office at City Hall they acquainted each other with the facts. In Massachusetts nearly one thousand had already died, with tens of thousands ill, and the Massachusetts governor had just issued a plea for doctors and nurses from neighboring regions. In Philadelphia hundreds of sailors were hospitalized. Few signs of disease had surfaced among civilians, but Lewis reported that as yet his research had not found an answer.

Even if Lewis succeeded in making a vaccine, it would take weeks to produce in sufficient quantities. Thus, only drastic action could prevent the spread of influenza throughout the city. Banning public meetings, closing businesses and schools, imposing an absolute quarantine on the Navy Yard and on civilian cases—all these things made sense. A recent precedent existed. Only three years earlier Krusen's predecessor—during the single term of the reform mayor—had imposed and enforced a strict quarantine when a polio epidemic had erupted, a disease Lewis knew more about than anyone in the world. Lewis certainly wanted a quarantine.

But Plummer was Lewis's commanding officer. He and Krusen wanted to wait. Both feared that taking any such steps might cause panic and interfere with the war effort. Keeping the public calm was their goal. Those polio restrictions had been imposed when the country wasn't fighting a war.

The meeting ended with nothing decided except to monitor developments. Krusen did promise to start a mass publicity campaign against coughing, spitting, and sneezing. Even that would take days to organize. And it would conflict with the downplaying of danger by Krusen and navy officials.

In Washington, Gorgas, who likely had heard from Lewis, was unsatisfied with these developments. By then influenza had erupted in two more cantonments, Camp Dix in New Jersey and Camp Meade in Maryland, that sandwiched the city. Lewis was in very close contact with the Philadelphia Tuberculosis Society, and Gorgas asked it to print and distribute twenty thousand large posters warning of influenza and stating a simple precaution that might help in at least a small way: "When

obliged to cough or sneeze, always place a hand-
kerchief, paper napkin, or fabric of some kind before
the face."

Meanwhile the **Evening Bulletin** assured its
readers that influenza posed no danger, was as old
as history, and was usually accompanied by a great
miasma, foul air, and plagues of insects, none of
which were occurring in Philadelphia. Plummer
assured reporters that he and Krusen would "confine this disease to its present limits, and in this we
are sure to be successful. No fatalities have been
recorded among Navy men. No concern whatever
is felt by either the military and naval physicians or
by the civil authorities."

The next day two sailors died of influenza. Krusen
opened the Municipal Hospital for Contagious
Diseases to the navy, and Plummer declared, "The
disease has about reached its crest. We believe
the situation is well in hand. From now on the disease will decrease."

Krusen insisted to reporters that the dead were not
victims of an epidemic; he said that they had died
of influenza but insisted it was only "old-fashioned
influenza or grip." The next day fourteen sailors
died. So did the first civilian, "an unidentified
Italian" at Philadelphia General Hospital at South
Thirty-fourth and Pine.

The following day more than twenty victims
of the virus went to a morgue. One was Emma
Snyder. She was a nurse who had cared for the first

sailors to come to Pennsylvania Hospital. She was twenty-three years old.

Krusen's public face remained nothing but reassuring. He now conceded that there were "a few cases in the civilian population" and said that health inspectors were looking for cases among civilians "to nip the epidemic in the bud." But he did not say how.

On Saturday, September 21, the Board of Health made influenza a "reportable" disease, requiring physicians to notify health officials of any cases they treated. This would provide information about its movement. For the board to act on a Saturday was extraordinary in itself, but the board nonetheless assured the city that it was "fully convinced that the statement issued by Director Krusen that no epidemic of influenza prevails in the civil population at the present time is absolutely correct. Moreover, the Board feels strongly that if the general public will carefully and rigidly observe the recommendations [to] avoid contracting the influenza an epidemic can successfully be prevented."

The board's advice: stay warm, keep the feet dry and the bowels open—this last piece of advice a remnant of the Hippocratic tradition. The board also advised people to avoid crowds.

Seven days later, on September 28, a great Liberty Loan parade, designed to sell millions of dollars of war bonds, was scheduled. Weeks of organizing had gone into the event, and it was to be the greatest parade in Philadelphia history, with thousands marching in it and hundreds of thousands expected to watch it.

These were unusual times. The Great War made them so. One cannot look at the influenza pandemic without understanding the context. Wilson had realized his aims. The United States was waging total war.

Already two million U.S. troops were in France; it was expected that at least two million more would be needed. Every element of the nation, from farmers to elementary school teachers, was willingly or otherwise enlisted in the war. To Wilson, to Creel, to his entire administration, and for that matter to allies and enemies alike, the control of information mattered. Advertising was about to emerge as an industry; J. Walter Thompson—his advertising agency was already national, and his deputy became a senior Creel aide—was theorizing that it could engineer behavior; after the war the industry would claim the ability to "sway the ideas of whole populations," while Herbert Hoover said, "The world lives by phrases" and called public relations "an exact science."

Total war requires sacrifice and good morale makes sacrifices acceptable, and therefore possible. The sacrifices included inconveniences in daily life. To contribute to the war effort, citizens across the country endured the "meatless days" during the week, the one "wheatless meal" every day. All these sacrifices were of course voluntary, completely voluntary—although Hoover's Food Administration could effectively close businesses that did not "voluntarily" cooperate. And if someone chose to go for a drive in the country on a "gasless Sunday," when people were "voluntarily" refraining from driving, that someone was pulled over by hostile police.

The Wilson administration intended to make the nation cohere. Wilson informed the head of the Boy Scouts that selling bonds would give "every Scout a wonderful opportunity to do his share for the country under the slogan, 'Every Scout to Save a Soldier.'" Creel's one hundred fifty thousand Four Minute Men, those speakers who opened virtually every public gathering including movie and vaudeville shows, inspired giving. And when inspiration alone failed, other pressures could be exerted.

The preservation of morale itself became an aim. For if morale faltered, all else might as well. So free speech trembled. More than in the McCarthy period, more than during World War II itself, more than in the Civil War—when Lincoln was routinely vilified by opponents—free speech trembled indeed. The government had the two hundred thousand members of the American Protective League, who reported to the Justice Department's new internal security agency headed by J. Edgar Hoover and spied on neighbors and coworkers. Creel's organization advised citizens, "Call the bluff of anyone who says he has 'inside information.' Tell him that it's his patriotic duty to help you find the source of what he's saying. If you find a disloyal person in your search, give his name to the Department of Justice in Washington and tell them where to find him."

Socialists, German nationals, and especially the radical unionists in the Industrial Workers of the World got far worse treatment. The **New York Times** declared, "The IWW agitators are in effect, and perhaps in fact, agents of Germany. The Federal authorities should make short work of these treasonable conspirators against the United States." The government did just that, raiding union halls, convicting nearly two hundred union men at mass trials in Illinois, California, and Oregon, and applying relentless pressure against all opponents; in Philadelphia on the same day that Krusen first discussed influenza with navy officials, five men who worked for the city's German-language paper **Tageblatt** were imprisoned.

What the government didn't do, vigilantes did. There were the twelve hundred IWW members locked in boxcars in Arizona and left on a siding in the desert. There was IWW member Frank Little, tied to a car and dragged through streets in Butte, Montana, until his kneecaps were scraped off, then hung by the neck from a railroad trestle. There was Robert Prager, born in Germany but who had tried to enlist in the navy, attacked by a crowd outside St. Louis, beaten, stripped, bound in an American flag, and lynched because he uttered a positive word about his country of origin. And, after that mob's leaders were acquitted, there was the juror's shout, "I guess nobody can say we aren't loyal now!" Meanwhile, a **Washington Post** editorial commented, "In spite of excesses such as lynching, it is a healthful and wholesome awakening in the interior of the country."

Socialist Eugene Debs, who in the 1912 presidential election had received nearly one million votes, was sentenced to ten years in prison for opposing the war, and in an unrelated trial Wisconsin congressman Victor Berger was sentenced to twenty years for doing the same. The House of Representatives thereupon expelled him and when his constituents reelected him anyway, the House refused to seat him. All this was to protect the American way of life.

Few elites in America enjoyed more luxuries than did Philadelphia society, with its Biddles and Whartons. Yet the **Philadelphia Inquirer** reported approvingly that at "a dinner on the Main Line a dozen men were gathered at the table, and there was some criticism of the way the government was handling things. The host rose and said, 'Gentlemen, it is not my business to tell you what to say but there are four Secret Service agents here this evening.' It was a tactful way of putting a stop to conversation for which he did not care."

Meanwhile, Treasury Secretary William McAdoo believed that during the Civil War the government had made a "fundamental error" not selling bonds to average citizens: "Any great war must necessarily be a popular movement. It is a crusade; and, like all crusades, it sweeps along on a powerful stream of romanticism. [Lincoln's treasury secretary Salmon] Chase did not attempt to capitalize the emotions of the people. We went direct to the people, and that means to everybody—to businessmen, workmen, farmers, bankers, millionaires, schoolteachers, laborers. We capitalized on the profound impulse called patriotism. It is the quality of coherence that holds a nation together; it is one of the deepest and most powerful of human motives." He went still further and declared, "Every person who refuses to subscribe or who takes the attitude of let the other fellow do it, is a friend of Germany and I would like nothing better than to tell it to him to his face. A man who can't lend his govt $1.25 a week at the rate of 4% interest is not entitled to be an American citizen."

The Liberty Loan campaign would raise millions of dollars in Philadelphia alone. The city had a quota to meet. Central to meeting that quota was the parade scheduled for September 28.

Several doctors—practicing physicians, public health experts at medical schools, infectious disease experts—urged Krusen to cancel the parade.

Howard Anders tried to generate public pressure to stop it, telling newspaper reporters the rally would spread influenza and kill. No newspaper quoted his warning—such a comment might after all hurt morale—so he demanded of at least one editor that the paper print his warning that the rally would bring together "a ready-made inflammable mass for a conflagration." The editor refused.

Influenza was a disease spread in crowds. "Avoid crowds" was the advice Krusen and the Philadelphia Board of Health gave. To prevent crowding the Philadelphia Rapid Transit Company had just limited the number of passengers in streetcars.

Army camps had already become so overwhelmed by influenza that on September 26 Provost Marshal Enoch Crowder canceled the next scheduled draft call. That same day, Massachusetts governor Samuel McCall formally pleaded for federal help and for doctors, nurses, and supplies from neighboring states.

If influenza was only beginning its assault on Philadelphia, it was already roaring full speed through the Navy Yard. Fourteen hundred sailors were now hospitalized with the disease. The Red Cross was converting the United Service Center at Twenty-second and Walnut into a five-hundred-bed hospital for the sole use of the navy. Krusen saw those reports and heard from those who wanted to cancel the parade, all right, but he did not seem to be listening. All he did was forbid the entertainment of soldiers or sailors by any organization or private party in the city. But military personnel could still visit stores, ride streetcars, go to vaudeville shows or moving picture houses.

In Philadelphia on September 27, the day before the parade, hospitals admitted two hundred more people—123 of them civilians—suffering from influenza.

Krusen felt intense and increasing pressure to cancel the parade, pressure coming from colleagues in medicine, from the news out of Massachusetts, from the fact that the army had canceled the draft. The decision whether to proceed or not was likely entirely his own. Had he sought guidance from the mayor, he would have found none. For a magistrate had just issued an arrest warrant for the mayor, who was now closeted with his lawyer, distracted and impossible to reach. Earlier, for the good of the city and the war effort, an uneasy truce had been forged between the Vare machine and the city's elite. Now Mrs. Edward Biddle, president of the Civic Club, married to a descendant of the founder of the Bank of the United States, resigned from a board the mayor had appointed her to, ending that truce, adding to the chaos in City Hall.

Krusen did hear some good news. Paul Lewis believed he was making progress in identifying the pathogen, the cause of influenza. If so, work on a serum and a vaccine could proceed rapidly. The press headlined this good news, although it did not report that Lewis, a careful scientist, was unsure of his findings.

Krusen declared that the Liberty Loan parade and associated rallies would proceed.

None of the anxiety of the moment was reported in any of the city's five daily papers, and if any reporter questioned either Krusen or the Board of Health about the wisdom of the parade's proceeding, no mention of it appeared in print.

On September 28, marchers in the greatest parade in the city's history proudly stepped forward. The paraders stretched at least two miles, two miles of bands, flags, Boy Scouts, women's auxiliaries, marines, sailors, and soldiers. Several hundred thousand people jammed the parade route, crushing against one another to get a better look, the ranks behind shouting encouragement over shoulders and past faces to the brave young men. It was a grand sight indeed.

Krusen had assured them they were in no danger.

The incubation period of influenza is twenty-four to seventy-two hours. Two days after the parade, Krusen issued a somber statement: "The epidemic is now present in the civilian population and is assuming the type found in naval stations and cantonments."

To understand the full meaning of that statement, one must understand precisely what was occurring in the army camps.

CHAPTER EIGHTEEN

DEVENS HAD BEEN STRUCK by surprise. The other cantonments and navy bases were not. Gorgas's office had issued immediate warnings of the disease, and medical staffs around the country took heed. Even so, the virus reached first and with most lethality into these military posts, invading the close cluster of young men in their barracks beds. Camp Grant was neither the worst hit, nor the least. Indeed, except for one particular and individual tragedy, it was quite typical.

The camp sprawled across rolling but mostly level country on the Rock River outside Rockford, Illinois. The soil there was rich and lush, and its first commandant had planted fifteen hundred acres on the base with sweet corn and "hog corn," hay, wheat and winter wheat, potatoes, and oats. Most recruits there came from northern Illinois and Wisconsin, farm boys with straw-colored hair and flushed cheeks who knew how to raise the crops and produced them in plenty.

It was a remarkably orderly place, given the haste with which it had been built. It had neat rows of wooden barracks, and more rows and rows of large barrack-tents, eighteen men to each. All the roads were dirt and in the late summer dust filled the air, except when rain turned the roads to mud. The hospital was situated at one end of the camp and had two thousand beds, although the most patients it had cared for at one time was 852; several infirmaries were also scattered throughout the base.

In June 1918, Welch, Cole, Russell, and Richard Pearce of the National Research Council—who rarely left Washington, usually being too busy coordinating research efforts—had inspected the camp and come away impressed. Welch judged Grant's chief medical officer, Lieutenant Colonel H. C. Michie, "capable and energetic," the hospital laboratory "excellent," the pathologist "a good man," while Joe Capps, a friend of Cole, was "of course an excellent chief of service" at the hospital itself. The veterinarian, who was responsible for several hundred horses and assorted livestock, had also impressed them favorably.

During that June visit they had all discussed pneumonia. Capps had started clinical experiments with a serum developed by Preston Kyes that differed from Cole's. Kyes was a promising University of Chicago investigator of whom Welch had said, "It is worth while for us to keep our eye on him." Capps and Cole exchanged information. Capps also spoke of seeing a disturbing trend toward a "different type of pneumonia . . . clinically more toxic and fatal . . . at autopsy often massive areas of consolidation . . . and also areas of hemorrhagic alveoli."

Then he demonstrated for them an innovation he had experimented with: the wearing of gauze masks by patients with respiratory disease. Welch called the mask "a great thing . . . an important contribution in prevention of spray infections." He encouraged Capps to write an article for the **Journal of the American Medical Association** and advised Pearce to conduct studies of the masks' effectiveness. Cole agreed: "This is a very important matter in connection with the prevention of pneumonia."

Welch also came away from that inspection, the last one of that tour, recommending two things. It confirmed in him his desire to have new arrivals at all camps assigned for three weeks to specially constructed detention camps; these men would eat, sleep, drill—and be quarantined—together to avoid any cross-infections with men already in camp. Second, he wanted Capps's use of masks extended to all camps.

Capps did write the **JAMA** article. He reported

finding the masks so successful that after less than three weeks of experimenting he had abandoned testing and simply started using them as "a routine measure." He also made the more general point that "one of the most vital measures in checking contagion" is eliminating crowding. "Increasing the space between beds in barracks, placing the head of one soldier opposite the feet of his neighbor, stretching tent flags between beds, and suspending a curtain down the center of the mess table, are all of proved value."

To prevent a few arriving individuals from infecting an entire camp, he also repeated Welch's recommendation to isolate transferred troops. Grant had such a "depot brigade," a separate quarantine barracks for new recruits and transfers. Its stairways were built on the outside so guards could enforce the quarantine. But officers did not stay in the depot brigade; only enlisted men did.

Capps's article appeared in the August 10, 1918, issue of **JAMA.**

On August 8, Colonel Charles Hagadorn took command of Camp Grant. A short, brooding officer and a West Point graduate, still a bachelor at fifty-one years of age, he had devoted his life to the army and his men. He had also prepared for war all his life, studying it constantly and learning from experience as well as reading and analysis; one report "accredited [him] one of the most brilliant line experts of the regular army." He had fought the Spanish in Cuba, fought guerrillas in the Philippines, and chased Pancho Villa in Mexico just a year before. Sometimes he gave what seemed impulsive and even inexplicable orders, but they had a curve of reason behind them. He was determined to teach his soldiers to survive, and to kill. Not to die. He cared about his troops and liked being surrounded by them.

One problem that confronted him seemed to have little to do with war. The camp was over capacity. Only thirty thousand troops had been present when Welch had visited in June. Now the strength was in excess of forty thousand with no expectation of any decrease. Many men were forced into tents and winter—winter in northern Illinois, one year after a record cold—was only a few weeks away.

Army regulations defined how much space each soldier had in the barracks. These regulations had little to do with comfort and much to do with public health. In mid-September Hagadorn decided to ignore the army regulations on overcrowding and move even more men from tents into barracks. Already the nights were cold, and they would be more comfortable there.

But by then Gorgas's office had issued warnings about the epidemic and influenza had reached the Great Lakes Naval Training Station one hundred miles away. At Camp Grant, doctors watched for the first case. They even had an idea where it might occur. Dozens of officers had just arrived from Devens.

The camp senior medical staff confronted Hagadorn over his plan to increase crowding. Although no record exists of the meeting, these physicians were men whom Welch and Cole held in the highest regard, and in outstanding civilian careers they gave rather than took orders. The meeting had to have been contentious. For God's sake, they would have warned him, scattered cases of influenza had already appeared in Rockford.

But Hagadorn believed that disease could be controlled. In addition to his combat record, he had been chief of staff in the Canal Zone and had seen Gorgas control even tropical diseases there. Besides, he had tremendous confidence in his medical staff. He had more confidence in his doctors than they had in themselves, perhaps reminding them they had avoided even the measles epidemic that had plagued so many cantonments. On September 4 the camp's own epidemiologist had filed a report noting, "The epidemic diseases at this camp were at no time alarming. . . . Cases of Measles, Pneumonia, Scarlet fever, Diphtheria, Meningitis and the Smallpox occurred sporadically. None of these diseases ever assumed epidemic form."

And this was only influenza. Still, Hagadorn made a few concessions. On September 20 he issued several orders to protect the camp's health. To prevent the rise of dust, all roads would be oiled.

And out of concern for influenza he agreed to a virtual quarantine: "Until further notice from these Headquarters, passes and permission to be absent from Camp . . . will not be granted to Officers or enlisted men, except from this office, and then only for the most urgent reasons."

But he issued one more order that day as well. It must have been particularly galling for Michie and Capps to see him use their authority to justify it: "There must as a military necessity be a crowding of troops. The Camp Surgeon under the circumstances authorizes a crowding in barracks . . . beyond the authorized capacity. . . . This will be carried out at once as buildings are newly occupied."

September 21, the day after Hagadorn issued his order, several men in the Infantry Central Officers Training School—the organization with officers from Devens—reported ill. They were immediately isolated in the base hospital.

It did little good. By midnight 108 men from the infantry school and the unit next to it were admitted to the hospital. There each patient had a gauze mask placed over his mouth and nose.

The two units were isolated from the rest of the camp, and men in the units were partly isolated from each other. Every bed had sheets hung around it, and twice a day each man was examined. All public gatherings—movies, YMCA functions, and the like—were canceled, and the men were ordered not "to mingle in any manner with men of other organizations at any time. . . . No visitors will be permitted in the area involved. . . . Any barracks from which several cases are reported will be quarantined; its occupants will not be permitted to mingle in any way with the occupants of other barracks in the same organization."

Guards enforced the orders strictly. But people infected with influenza can infect others before they feel any symptoms. It was already too late. Within forty-eight hours every organization in the camp was affected.

The next day hospital admissions rose to 194, the next 371, the next 492. Four days after the first officer reported sick, the first soldier died. The next day two more men died, and 711 soldiers were admitted to the hospital. In six days the hospital went from 610 occupied beds to 4,102 occupied, almost five times more patients than it had ever cared for.

There were too few ambulances to carry the sick to the hospital, so mules pulled ambulance carts until the mules, exhausted, stopped working. There were too few sheets for the beds, so the Red Cross ordered six thousand from Chicago. There were too few beds, so several thousand cots were crammed into every square inch of corridor, storage area, meeting room, office, and veranda.

It wasn't enough. Early on the medical detachment members had moved into tents so their own barracks could be transformed into a five-hundred-bed—or cot—hospital. Ten barracks scattered throughout the camp were also converted into hospitals. It still wasn't enough.

All training for war, for killing, ceased. Now men fought to stop the killing.

Healthy soldiers were consumed with attending, in one way or another, the sick. Three hundred and twenty men were sent to the hospital as general support staff, then 260 more were added. Another 250 men did nothing but stuff sacks with straw to make mattresses. Several hundred others unloaded a stream of railroad cars full of medical supplies. Hundreds more helped transport the sick or cleaned laundry—washing sheets, making masks—or prepared food. Meanwhile, barely in advance of a threatening thunderstorm, one hundred carpenters worked to enclose thirty-nine verandas with roofing paper to keep the rain off the hundreds of patients exposed to the elements. The gauze masks Capps was so proud of, the masks Welch had praised, were no longer being made; Capps ran out of material and personnel to make them.

The medical staff itself was collapsing from overwork—and disease. Five days into the epidemic five physicians, thirty-five nurses, and fifty orderlies were sick. That number would grow, and the medical staff would have its own death toll.

Seven days into the epidemic soldiers still capable of work converted nine more barracks into hospitals. There were shortages of aspirin, atropine, digitalis, glacial acetic acid (a disinfectant), paper bags, sputum cups, and thermometers—and thermometers that were available were being broken by men in delirium.

Forty more nurses arrived for the emergency, giving the hospital 383. It needed still more. All visitors to the base and especially to the hospital had already been prohibited "except under extraordinary circumstances." Now those extraordinary circumstances had become common, with visitors pouring in, Michie noted, "summoned by danger of death telegrams. . . ." Four hundred thirty-eight telegrams had been handled the day before.

That number was still climbing, and rapidly. To handle what soon became thousands of telegrams and phone calls each day, the Red Cross erected a large tent, floored, heated, wired for electricity, with its own telephone exchange and rows of chairs that resembled an auditorium where relatives waited to see desperately ill soldiers. More personnel were needed to escort these visitors to the sick. More personnel and more laundry facilities were needed just to wash the gown and mask that every visitor donned.

The hospital staff could not keep pace. Endless rows of men coughing, lying in bloodstained linen, surrounded by flies—orders were issued that "formalin should be added to each sputum cup to keep the flies away"—and the grotesque smells of vomit, urine, and feces made the relatives in some ways more desperate than the patients. They offered bribes to whoever seemed healthy—doctor, nurse, or orderly—to ensure care for their sons and lovers. Indeed, visitors begged them to accept bribes.

Michie responded sternly: "Devoting special personal care to any one patient whose condition is not critical is prohibited and the ward personnel is instructed to report any civilian or other person to the commanding officer who makes a special request that a certain patient be given special attention."

And there was something else, something still worse.

The same day that the first Camp Grant soldier died, 3,108 troops boarded a train leaving there for Camp Hancock outside Augusta, Georgia.

They left as a civilian health official several hundred miles away from Camp Grant demanded the quarantine of the entire camp, demanded that even escorts of the dead home be prohibited. They left with the memory of the trains carrying troops infected with measles, when Gorgas and Vaughan had protested uselessly that troops had "distributed its seeds at the encampment and on the train. No power on earth could stop the spread of measles under these conditions." They left after the provost general had had the foresight to cancel the next draft. And they left after Gorgas's office had urged that all movement of troops between infected and uninfected camps cease.

The army did order no "transfer of any influenza contacts" between camps or to bases under quarantine. But even that order came days later, at a time when each day's delay could cost literally thousands of lives. And the order also stated that "movements of officers and men not contacts will be effected promptly as ordered." Yet men could appear healthy while incubating influenza themselves, and they could also infect others before symptoms appeared.

The men leaving Grant on that train were jammed into the cars with little room to move about, layered and stacked as tightly as if on a submarine as they moved deliberately across 950 miles of the country. They would have been excited at first, for movement creates its own excitement, and then tedium would have set in, the minutes dragging out, the hours melding the passage into a self-contained world ten feet across and seven feet high, smelling of cigarette smoke and sweat, with hundreds of men in each car in far closer quarters than in any barracks, and with far less ventilation.

As the country rolled by men would have leaned out windows to suck in a wisp of air the way they sucked on cigarettes. And then one soldier would have broken into a coughing fit, another would have begun pouring out sweat, another would have suddenly had blood pouring out of his nose. Other men would have shrunk from them in fear, and then still others would have collapsed or erupted in fever or delirium or begun bleeding from their nose or possibly their ears. The train would have filled with panic. At stops for refueling and watering, men would have poured out of the train seeking any escape, mixed with workers and other civilians, obeyed reluctantly when officers ordered them back into the cars, into this rolling coffin.

When the train arrived, over seven hundred men—nearly one-quarter of all the troops on the train—were taken directly to the base hospital, quickly followed by hundreds more; in total, two thousand of the 3,108 troops would be hospitalized with influenza. After 143 deaths among them the statistics merged into those of other troops from Camp Hancock—Hancock, to which this shipment of virus was sent—and became impossible to track. But it is likely that the death toll approached, and possibly exceeded, 10 percent of all the troops on the train.

Hagadorn had become all but irrelevant to the running of the camp. Now he yielded on every point to the medical personnel, did everything they asked, made every resource available to them. Nothing seemed even to slow the disease.

On October 4, for the first time more than one hundred men at Camp Grant died in a single day. Nearly five thousand were ill, with hundreds more falling ill each day. And the graph of contagion still pointed nearly straight up.

Soon, in a single day, 1,810 soldiers would report

ill. At some other army camps even more soldiers would collapse almost simultaneously; indeed, at Camp Custer outside Battle Creek, Michigan, twenty-eight hundred troops would report ill—in a **single** day.

Before the epidemic, Capps had begun testing Preston Kyes's pneumonia serum, prepared from chickens. Kyes had reasoned that since chickens were not susceptible to the pneumococcus, infecting them with highly virulent pneumococci might produce a very powerful serum. Capps had planned a series of "very carefully controlled" experiments. But now, with nothing else to try, he administered the serum to all as it arrived—it was in short supply. It seemed to work. Two hundred and thirty-four men suffering from pneumonia received the serum; only 16.7 percent died, while more than half of those who did not receive it died. **But it was in short supply.**

Desperate efforts were being made to protect troops from the disease, or at least prevent complications. Germicidal solutions were sprayed into the mouths and noses of troops. Soldiers were ordered to use germicidal mouthwash and to gargle twice a day. Iodine in glycerin was tried in an attempt to disinfect mouths. Vaseline containing menthol was used in nasal passages, mouths washed with liquid albolene.

Despite every effort, the death toll kept rising. It

rose so high that staff grew weary, weary of paperwork, weary even of identifying the dead. Michie was forced to issue orders warning, "The remains are labeled by placing an adhesive plaster bearing the name, rank, organization around the middle of the left forearm. It is the duty of the Ward Surgeon to see that this is done before the remains leave the ward. . . . A great deal of difficulty has been experienced in reading names on death certificates . . . Either have these certificates typewritten or . . . plainly printed. Any neglect on the part of responsible persons will be interpreted as a neglect of duty."

Michie also instructed all personnel, "The relatives and friends of persons dying at this hospital must not be sent to the base hospital morgue. . . . The handling of the effects of the deceased has grown into an enormous task."

Simultaneously, in that important fight to sustain the country's morale, the **Chicago Tribune** reported good news from Camp Grant. "Epidemic Broken!" blared the paper's headlines. "The small army of expert workers under the command of Lt. Col. H. C. Michie has battled the pneumonia epidemic to a standstill . . . deaths occurred among the pneumonia patients, but more than 100 fighting men pulled through the crisis of their illness . . . 175 patients have been released after winning their fight."

■   ■   ■

At that point Grant's death toll was 452. It showed no sign of slowing. Hoping to have some slight effect on it, hoping to prevent cross-infections, Michie and Capps reiterated their orders to place patients outside: "The crowding of patients in the wards must be reduced to the minimum. . . . The verandas must be used to the greatest advantage."

Perhaps that reminded Hagadorn of his earlier order authorizing overcrowding. Perhaps then too he got word of the hundreds of young men who had died on the train to Georgia, which, like the barracks overcrowding, he had ordered because of "military necessity." Perhaps these things caused him such personal pain that it explained why he abruptly ordered the withholding of the names of all soldiers who died from influenza. Perhaps somehow that allowed him to block the deaths from his mind.

A day later the death toll at the camp broke five hundred, with thousands more still desperately ill. "How far the pandemic will spread will apparently depend only upon the material which it can feed upon," wrote one army physician. "It is too early to foretell the end or to measure the damage which will be done before the pandemic disappears."

Many of the dead were more boys than men, eighteen years old, nineteen years old, twenty years old, twenty-one years old, boys filled with their lithe youth and sly smiles. Hagadorn, the bachelor, had made the army his home, his soldiers his family, the young men about him his life.

On October 8 Michie reported the latest death toll to Colonel Hagadorn in his headquarters office. The colonel heard the report, nodded, and, after an awkward moment, Michie rose to leave. Hagadorn told him to close the door.

Death was all about him, in the papers on his desk, in the reports he heard, literally in the air he breathed. It was an envelope sealing him in.

He picked up his phone and ordered his sergeant to leave the building and take with him all personnel in the headquarters and stand for inspection outside.

It was a bizarre order. The sergeant informed Captain Jisson and Lieutenant Rashel. They were puzzled but complied.

For half an hour they waited. The pistol shot, even from inside the building, came as a loud report.

Hagadorn was not listed as a casualty of the epidemic. Nor did his sacrifice stop it.

CHAPTER NINETEEN

TWO DAYS AFTER Philadelphia's Liberty Loan parade, Wilmer Krusen had issued that somber statement, that the epidemic in the civilian population "was assuming the type found in naval stations and cantonments."

Influenza was indeed exploding in the city. Within seventy-two hours after the parade, every single bed in each of the city's thirty-one hospitals was filled. And people began dying. Hospitals began refusing to accept patients—with nurses turning down $100 bribes—without a doctor's or a police order. Yet people queued up to get in. One woman remembered her neighbors going "to the closest hospital, the Pennsylvania Hospital at 5th and Lombard, but when they got there there were lines and no doctors available and no medicine available. So they went home, those that were strong enough."

Medical care was making little difference anyway. Mary Tullidge, daughter of Dr. George Tullidge, died twenty-four hours after her first symptoms. Alice Wolowitz, a student nurse at Mount Sinai Hospital, began her shift in the morning, felt sick, and was dead twelve hours later.

On October 1, the third day after the parade, the epidemic killed more than one hundred people—117—in a single day. That number would double, triple, quadruple, quintuple, sextuple. Soon the daily death toll from influenza alone would exceed the city's average **weekly** death toll from all causes—all illnesses, all accidents, all criminal acts combined.

On October 3, only five days after Krusen had let the parade proceed, he banned all public meetings in the city—including, finally, further Liberty Loan gatherings—and closed all churches, schools, theaters. Even public funerals were prohibited. Only one public gathering place was allowed to remain open: the saloon, the key constituency of the Vare machine. The next day the state health commissioner closed them.

The first temporary facility to care for the sick was set up at Holmesburg, the city's poorhouse. It was called "Emergency Hospital #1"; the Board of Health knew more would follow. Its five hundred beds were filled in a day. Ultimately there would be twelve similar large hospitals run with city help, three of them located in converted Republican Clubs in South Philadelphia. It was where people had always gone for help.

In ten days—**ten days**!—the epidemic had exploded from a few hundred civilian cases and one or two deaths a day to hundreds of thousands ill and hundreds of deaths each day.

Federal, municipal, and state courts closed. Giant placards everywhere warned the public to avoid crowds and use handkerchiefs when sneezing or coughing. Other placards read "Spitting equals death." People who spat on the street were arrested—sixty in a single day. The newspapers reported the arrests—even while continuing to minimize the epidemic. Physicians were themselves dying, three one day, two another, four the next. The newspapers reported those deaths—on inside pages with other obituaries—even while continuing to minimize the epidemic. Health and city workers wore masks constantly.

What should I do? people wondered with dread. **How long will it go on?** Each day people discovered that friends and neighbors who had been perfectly healthy a week—or a day—earlier were dead.

And city authorities and newspapers continued to minimize the danger. The **Public Ledger** claimed nonsensically that Krusen's order banning all public gatherings was not "a public health measure" and reiterated, "There is no cause for panic or alarm."

On October 5, doctors reported that 254 people

died that day from the epidemic, and the papers quoted public health authorities as saying, "The peak of the influenza epidemic has been reached." When 289 Philadelphians died the next day, the papers said, "Believing that the peak of the epidemic has passed, health officials are confident."

In each of the next two days more than three hundred people died, and again Krusen announced, "These deaths mark the high water mark in the fatalities, and it is fair to assume that from this time until the epidemic is crushed the death rate will constantly be lowered."

The next day 428 people died, and the daily death toll would keep climbing for many days yet— approaching double even that figure.

Krusen said, "Don't get frightened or panic stricken over exaggerated reports."

But Krusen's reassurances no longer reassured.

One could not listen to Paul Lewis speak on any subject and not sense the depth of his knowledge and his ability to see into a problem, envision possible solutions, and understand their ramifications. Other scientists in the city did not defer to him, but they looked to him.

He had been working on this problem for three weeks now. He hardly ever left his laboratory. Nor did his assistants, except for the ones who fell ill. Every scientist in Philadelphia was spending every waking minute in the laboratory as well.

The laboratory was his favorite place anyway, more even than home. Normally, everything in his work gave him peace; the laboratory gave him peace, including the mysteries that he embraced. He settled into them like a man casting off into an impenetrable ocean fog, a fog that made one feel both alone in and part of the world.

But this work did not give him peace. It wasn't the pressure exactly. It was that the pressure forced him off rhythm, forced him to abandon the scientific process. He developed a hypothesis and focused on it, but the shorthand process by which he arrived at it made him uncomfortable.

So did hearing the news of the deaths. The youth and vitality and promise of the dead horrified. The waste of their promise horrified. He worked harder.

Arthur Eissinger, president and "honor man" of Penn's class of 1918, died. Dudley Perkins, a Swarthmore football hero, died. Nearly two-thirds of the dead were under forty.

It was a common practice in 1918 for people to hang a piece of crepe on the door to mark a death in the house. There was crepe everywhere. "If it was a young person they'd put a white crepe at the door," recalled Anna Milani. "If it was a middle-aged person, they'd put a black crepe, and if it was an elderly one, they put a gray crepe at the door signifying who died. We were children and we were excited to find out who died next and we were looking at the door, there was another crepe and another door."

There was always another door. "People were dying like flies," Clifford Adams said. "On Spring Garden Street, looked like every other house had crepe over the door. People was dead there."

Anna Lavin was at Mount Sinai Hospital: "My uncle died there. . . . My aunt died first. Their son was thirteen. . . . A lot of young people, just married, they were the first to die."

But the most terrifying aspect of the epidemic was the piling up of bodies. Undertakers, themselves sick, were overwhelmed. They had no place to put bodies. Gravediggers either were sick or refused to bury influenza victims. The director of the city jail offered to have prisoners dig graves, then rescinded the offer because he had no healthy guards to watch them. With no gravediggers, bodies could not be buried. Undertakers' work areas were overflowing, they stacked caskets in halls, in their living quarters—many lived above their businesses.

Then undertakers ran short of coffins. The few coffins available suddenly became priceless. Michael Donohue's family operated a funeral home: "We had caskets stacked up outside the funeral home. We had to have guards kept on them because people were stealing the caskets. . . . You'd equate that to grave robbing."

There were soon no caskets left to steal. Louise Apuchase remembered most vividly the lack of coffins: "A neighbor boy about seven or eight died and they used to just pick you up and wrap you up in a sheet and put you in a patrol wagon. So the mother and father **screaming,** 'Let me get a macaroni box' [for a coffin]—macaroni, any kind of pasta, used to come in this box, about 20 pounds of macaroni fit in it—'please please let me put him in the macaroni box, don't take him away like that. . . .'"

Clifford Adams remembered "bodies stacked up . . . stacked up out to be buried. . . . They couldn't bury them." The bodies backed up more and more, backed up in the houses, were put outside on porches.

The city morgue had room for thirty-six bodies. Two hundred were stacked there. The stench was terrible; doors and windows were thrown open. No more bodies could fit. Bodies lay in homes where they died, as they died, often with bloody liquid seeping from the nostrils or mouths. Families covered the bodies in ice; even so, the bodies began to putrefy and stink. Tenements had no porches; few had fire escapes. Families closed off rooms where a body lay, but a closed door could not close out the knowledge and the horror of what lay behind the door. In much of the city, a city more short of housing than New York, people had no room that could be closed off. Corpses were wrapped in sheets, pushed into corners, left there sometimes for days, the horror of it sinking in deeper each hour, people too sick to cook for themselves, too sick to clean themselves, too sick to move the corpse off the bed, lying alive on the same bed with the corpse. The dead lay there for days, while the living lived with them, were horrified by them, and, perhaps most horribly, became accustomed to them.

Symptoms were terrifying. Blood poured from noses, ears, eye sockets; some victims lay in agony; delirium took others away while living.

Routinely two people in a single family would die. Three deaths in a family were not uncommon. Sometimes a family suffered even more. David Sword lived at 2802 Jackson Street. On October 5 the sixth member of his family died of influenza, while the **North American** reported that three other family members in the hospital "may also die of the plague."

The plague. In the streets people had been whispering the word. The word slipped, somehow, once, by accident, into that newspaper. The "morale" issue, the self-censorship, the intent by editors to put every piece of news in the most positive possible context, all meant that no newspaper used that word again. Yet people did not need newspapers to speak of the Black Death. Some bodies were turning almost black. People had seen them, and they had lost faith in what they read anyway. One young medical student called in to treat hundreds of patients recalled, "The cyanosis reached an intensity that I have never seen since. Indeed the rumor got about that the Black Death had returned." The newspapers quoted Dr. Raymond Leopold, sounding reasonable: "There is abundant reason for such a rumor. . . . It is true that many bodies have assumed a dark hue and have given off a pronounced odor after death." But he gave his assurance, "There is no truth in the black plague assertion."

He was of course correct. But how many trusted the newspapers anymore? And even if the Black Death had not come, a plague had and, with it, so had terror.

The war had come home.

Long before Hagadorn's suicide, long before the marchers in Philadelphia began to parade down the city streets, influenza had seeded itself along the edges of the nation.

On September 4 it had reached New Orleans, with the three seamen—who soon died—carried to the hospital off the **Harold Walker** from Boston. On September 7 it had reached the Great Lakes Naval Training Station, with sailors transferred from Boston. In the next few days ports and naval facilities on the Atlantic and Gulf Coasts—in Newport, New London, Norfolk, Mobile, and Biloxi—also reported this new influenza. On September 17, 1918, "the extensive prevalence of an influenza-like disease" was reported in Petersburg, Virginia, outside Camp Lee. That same day, the several hundred sailors who had departed Philadelphia earlier for Puget Sound arrived; eleven men had to be carried from the ship on stretchers to a hospital, bringing the new virus to the Pacific.

The virus had spanned the country, establishing itself on the Atlantic, in the Gulf, on the Pacific, on the Great Lakes. It had not immediately erupted in epidemic form, but it had seeded itself. Then the seeds began to sprout into flowers of flame.

The virus followed rail and river into the interior of the continent, from New Orleans up the Mississippi River into the body of the nation, from Seattle to the East, from the Great Lakes training station to Chicago and from there along the railroad lines in many directions. From each original locus, fingers reached out unevenly, like sparks shooting out, often jumping over closer points to farther ones— from Boston to Newport, for example, and only then reaching backward to fill in Brockton and Providence and places in between.

On September 28, when the Liberty Loan paraders marched through Philadelphia streets, there were as yet only seven cases reported in Los Angeles, two in San Francisco. But the virus would get there soon enough.

In Philadelphia, meanwhile, fear came and stayed. Death could come from anyone, anytime. People moved away from others on the sidewalk, avoided conversation; if they did speak, they turned their faces away to avoid the other person's breathing. People became isolated, increasing the fear.

The impossibility of getting help compounded the isolation. Eight hundred fifty Philadelphia doctors and more nurses were away in the military. More than that number were sick. Philadelphia General Hospital had 126 nurses. Despite all precautions, despite wearing surgical masks and gowns, eight doctors and fifty-four nurses—43 percent of the staff—themselves required hospitalization. Ten nurses at this single hospital died. The Board of Health pleaded for help from retired nurses and doctors if they remembered "even a little" of their profession.

When a nurse or doctor or policeman did actually come, they wore their ghostly surgical masks, and people fled them. In every home where someone was ill, people wondered if the person would die. And someone was ill in every home.

Philadelphia had five medical schools. Each one dismissed its classes, and third- and fourth-year students manned emergency hospitals being set up in schools and empty buildings all over the city. The Philadelphia College of Pharmacy closed as well, sending its students out to help druggists.

Before University of Pennsylvania medical students went out to man the hospitals, they listened to a lecture from Alfred Stengel, the expert on infectious diseases who had treated the crew of the **City of Exeter** what seemed so long ago. Stengel reviewed dozens of ideas that had been advanced in medical journals. Gargles of various disinfectants. Drugs. Immune sera. Typhoid vaccine. Diphtheria antitoxin. But Stengel's message was simple: **This doesn't work. That doesn't work. Nothing worked.**

"His suggestion for treatment was negative," Isaac Starr, one of those Penn students who became an internationally known cardiologist, recalled. "He had no confidence in any of the remedies that had been proposed."

Stengel was correct. Nothing they were yet doing worked. Starr went to Emergency Hospital #2 at Eighteenth and Cherry Streets. He did have help, if it could be called that, from an elderly physician who had not practiced in years and who brought Starr into touch with the worst of heroic medicine. Starr wouldn't forget that, the ancient arts of purging, of venesection, the ancient art of opening a patient's vein. But for the most part he and the other students elsewhere were on their own, with little help even from nurses, who were so desperately needed that in each of ten emergency hospitals supplied by the Red Cross only a single qualified nurse was available to oversee whatever women came as volunteers. And often the volunteers reported for their duty once and, from either fear or exhaustion, did not come again.

Starr had charge of an entire floor of an emergency hospital. He thought at first his patients had "what appeared to be a minor illness . . . with fever but little else. Unhappily the clinical features of many soon changed." Most striking again was the cyanosis, his patients sometimes turning almost black. "After gasping for several hours they became delirious and incontinent, and many died struggling to clear their airways of a blood-tinged froth that sometimes gushed from their nose and mouth."

Nearly one-quarter of all the patients in his hospital died **each day.** Starr would go home, and when he returned the next day, he would find that between one-quarter and one-fifth of the patients in the hospital had died, replaced by new ones.

Literally hundreds of thousands of people in Philadelphia were falling ill. Virtually all of them, along with their friends and relatives, were terrified that, no matter how mild the symptoms seemed at first, within them moved an alien force, a seething, spreading infection, a live thing with a will that was taking over their bodies—and could be killing them. And those who moved about them feared—feared both for the victims and for themselves.

The city was frozen with fear, frozen quite literally into stillness. Starr lived twelve miles from the hospital, in Chestnut Hill. The streets were silent on his drive home, silent. They were so silent he took to counting the cars he saw. One night he saw no cars at all. He thought, "The life of the city had almost stopped."

■ Part VI
THE PESTILENCE

CHAPTER TWENTY

THIS WAS INFLUENZA, only influenza.

This new influenza virus, like most new influenza viruses, spread rapidly and widely. As a modern epidemiologist already quoted has observed, **Influenza is a special instance among infectious diseases. This virus is transmitted so effectively that it exhausts the supply of susceptible hosts.** This meant that the virus sickened tens of millions of people in the United States—in many cities more than half of all families had at least one victim ill with influenza; in San Antonio the virus made more than half the entire population ill—and hundreds of millions across the world.

But this was influenza, only influenza. The overwhelming majority of victims got well. They endured, sometimes a mild attack and sometimes a severe one, and they recovered.

The virus passed through this vast majority in the same way influenza viruses usually did. Victims had an extremely unpleasant several days (the unpleasantness multiplied by terror that they would develop serious complications) and then recovered within ten days. The course of the disease in these millions actually convinced the medical profession that this was indeed only influenza.

But in a minority of cases, and not just in a tiny minority, the virus manifested itself in an influenza that did not follow normal patterns, that was unlike any influenza ever reported, that followed a course so different from the usual one for the disease that Welch himself had initially feared some new kind of infection or plague. If Welch feared it, those who suffered with the disease were terrified by it.

Generally in the Western world, the virus demonstrated extreme virulence or led to pneumonia in from 10 to 20 percent of all cases. In the United States, this translated into two to three million cases. In other parts of the world, chiefly in isolated areas where people had rarely been exposed to influenza viruses—in Eskimo settlements of Alaska, in jungle villages of Africa, in islands of the Pacific—the virus demonstrated extreme virulence in far more than 20 percent of cases. These numbers most likely translate into several hundred million severe cases around the world in a world with a population less than one-third that of today.

This was still influenza, only influenza. The most common symptoms then as now are well known. The mucosal membranes in the nose, pharynx, and throat become inflamed. The conjunctiva, the delicate membrane that lines the eyelids, becomes inflamed. Victims suffer headache, body aches, fever, often complete exhaustion, cough. As one leading clinician observed in 1918, the disease was "ushered in by two groups of symptoms: in the first place the constitutional reactions of an acute febrile disease—headache, general aching, chills, fever, malaise, prostration, anorexia, nausea or vomiting; and in the second place, symptoms referable to an intense congestion of the mucous membranes of the nose, pharynx, larynx, trachea, and upper respiratory tract in general, and of the conjunctivae." Another noted, "The disease began with absolute exhaustion and chill, fever, headache, conjunctivitis, pain in back and limbs, flushing of face. . . . Cough was often constant. Upper air passages were clogged." A third reported, "In nonfatal cases . . . the temperature ranged from 100 to 103F. Nonfatal cases usually recovered after an illness of about a week."

Then there were the cases in which the virus struck with violence.

■   ■   ■

To those who suffered a violent attack, there was often pain, terrific pain, and the pain could come almost anywhere. The disease also separated them, pushed them into a solitary and concentrated place.

In Philadelphia, Clifford Adams said, "I didn't think about anything. . . . I got to the point where I didn't care if I died or not. I just felt like that all my life was nothing but when I breathe."

Bill Sardo in Washington, D.C., recalled, "I wasn't expected to live, just like everybody else that had gotten it. . . . You were sick as a dog and you weren't in a coma but you were in a condition that at the height of the crisis you weren't thinking normally and you weren't reacting normally, you sort of had delusions."

In Lincoln, Illinois, William Maxwell felt "time was a blur as I was lying in that little upstairs room and I . . . had no sense of day or night, I felt sick and hollow inside and I knew from telephone calls my aunt had, I knew enough to be alarmed about my mother. . . . I heard her say, 'Will, oh no,' and then, 'if you want me to . . .' The tears ran down her face so she didn't need to tell me."

Josey Brown fell ill working as a nurse at the Great Lakes Naval Training Station and her "heart was racing so hard and pounding that it was going to jump out" of her chest and with terrible fevers she was "shaking so badly that the ice would rattle and would shake the chart attached to the end of the bed."

Harvey Cushing, Halsted's protégé who had already attained prominence himself but had yet to make his full reputation, served in France. On October 8, 1918, he wrote in his journal, "Something has happened to my hind legs and I wobble like a tabetic"—someone suffering from a long and wasting illness, like a person with AIDS who needs a cane—"and can't feel the floor when I unsteadily get up in the morning. . . . So this is the sequence of the grippe. We may perhaps thank it for helping us win the war if it really hit the German Army thus hard [during their offensive]." In his case what seemed to be the complications were largely neurological. On October 31, after spending three weeks in bed with headache, double vision, and numbness of both legs, he observed, "It's a curious business, unquestionably still progressing . . . with considerable muscular wasting. . . . I have a vague sense of familiarity with the sensation—as if I had met [it] somewhere in a dream." Four days later: "My hands now have caught up with my feet—so numb and clumsy that shaving's a danger and buttoning laborious. When the periphery is thus affected the brain too is benumbed and awkward."

Cushing would never fully recover.

And across the lines lay Rudolph Binding, a German officer, who described his illness as "something like typhoid, with ghastly symptoms of intestinal poisoning." For weeks he was "in the grip of the fever. Some days I am quite free; then again

a weakness overcomes me so that I can barely drag
myself in a cold perspiration onto my bed and blankets. Then pain, so that I don't care whether I am
alive or dead."

Katherine Anne Porter was a reporter then, on
the **Rocky Mountain News.** Her fiancé, a young
officer, died. He caught the disease nursing her, and
she, too, was expected to die. Her colleagues set her
obituary in type. She lived. In "Pale Horse, Pale
Rider" she described her movement toward death:
"She lay on a narrow ledge over a pit she knew to
be bottomless . . . and soft carefully shaped words
like oblivion and eternity are curtains hung before
nothing at all. . . . Her mind tottered and slithered
again, broke from its foundation and spun like a
cast wheel in a ditch. . . . [S]he sank easily through
deeps under deeps of darkness until she lay like a
stone at the farthest bottom of life, knowing herself
to be blind, deaf, speechless, no longer aware of the
members of her own body, entirely withdrawn from
all human concerns, yet alive with a peculiar lucid-
ity and coherence; all notions of the mind, . . . all
ties of blood and the desires of the heart, dissolved
and fell away from her, and there remained of her
only a minute fiercely burning particle of being that
knew itself alone, that relied upon nothing beyond
itself for its strength; not susceptible to any appeal
or inducement, being itself composed entirely of
one single motive, the stubborn will to live. This
fiery motionless particle set itself unaided to resist

destruction, to survive and to be in its own madness of being, motiveless and planless beyond that one essential end."

Then, as she climbed back from that depth, "Pain returned, a terrible compelling pain running through her veins like heavy fire, the stench of corruption filled her nostrils, the sweetish sickening smell of rotting flesh and pus; she opened her eyes and saw pale light through a coarse white cloth over her face, knew that the smell of death was in her own body, and struggled to lift her hand."

These victims came with an extraordinary array of symptoms, symptoms either previously unknown entirely in influenza or experienced with previously unknown intensity. Initially, physicians, good physicians, intelligent physicians searching for a disease that fitted the clues before them—and influenza did not fit the clues—routinely misdiagnosed the disease.

Patients would writhe from agonizing pain in their joints. Doctors would diagnose dengue, also called "breakbone fever."

Patients would suffer extreme fever and chills, shuddering, shivering, then huddling under blankets. Doctors would diagnose malaria.

Dr. Henry Berg at New York City's Willard Parker Hospital—across the street from William Park's laboratory—worried that the patients' complaints of "a burning pain above the diaphragm" meant cholera. Noted another doctor, "Many had vomiting; some became tender over the abdomen indicating an intra-abdominal condition."

In Paris, while some physicians also diagnosed cholera or dysentery, others interpreted the intensity and location of headache pain as typhoid. Deep into the epidemic Parisian physicians still remained reluctant to diagnose influenza. In Spain public health officials also declared that the complications were due to "typhoid," which was "general throughout Spain."

But neither typhoid nor cholera, neither dengue nor yellow fever, neither plague nor tuberculosis, neither diphtheria nor dysentery, could account for other symptoms. No known disease could.

In **Proceedings of the Royal Society of Medicine,** a British physician noted "one thing I have never seen before—namely the occurrence of subcutaneous emphysema"—pockets of air accumulating just beneath the skin—"beginning in the neck and spreading sometimes over the whole body."

Those pockets of air leaking through ruptured lungs made patients crackle when they were rolled onto their sides. One navy nurse later compared the sound to a bowl of Rice Krispies, and the memory of that sound was so vivid to her that for the rest of her life she could not tolerate being around anyone who was eating Rice Krispies.

Extreme earaches were common. One physician

observed that otitis media—inflammation of the middle ear marked by pain, fever, and dizziness—"developed with surprising rapidity, and rupture of the drum membrane was observed at times in a few hours after the onset of pain." Another wrote, "Otitis media reported in 41 cases. Otologists on duty day and night and did immediate paracentesis [insertion of a needle to remove fluid] on all bulging eardrums. . . ." Another: "Discharge of pus from the external ear was noted. At autopsy practically every case showed otitis media with perforation. . . . This destructive action on the drum seems to me to be similar to the destructive action on the tissues of the lung."

The headaches throbbed deep in the skull, victims feeling as if their heads would literally split open, as if a sledgehammer were driving a wedge not into the head but from inside the head out. The pain seemed to locate particularly behind the eye orbit and could be nearly unbearable when patients moved their eyes. There were areas of lost vision, areas where the normal frame of sight went black. Some paralysis of ocular muscles was frequently recorded, and German medical literature noted eye involvement with special frequency, sometimes in 25 percent of influenza cases.

The ability to smell was affected, sometimes for weeks. Rarer complications included acute—even fatal—renal failure. Reye's syndrome attacked the liver. An army summary later stated simply, "The symptoms were of exceeding variety as to severity and kind."

It was not only death but these symptoms that spread the terror.

This was influenza, only influenza. Yet to a layperson at home, to a wife caring for a husband, to a father caring for a child, to a brother caring for a sister, symptoms unlike anything they had seen terrified. And the symptoms terrified a Boy Scout delivering food to an incapacitated family; they terrified a policeman who entered an apartment to find a tenant dead or dying; they terrified a man who volunteered his car as an ambulance. The symptoms chilled laypeople, chilled them with winds of fear.

The world looked black. Cyanosis turned it black. Patients might have few other symptoms at first, but if nurses and doctors noted cyanosis they began to treat such patients as terminal, as the walking dead. If the cyanosis became extreme, death was certain. And cyanosis was common. One physician reported, "Intense cyanosis was a striking phenomenon. The lips, ears, nose, cheeks, tongue, conjunctivae, fingers, and sometimes the entire body partook of a dusky, leaden hue." And another: "Many patients exhibited upon admission a strikingly intense cyanosis, especially noticeable in the lips. This was not the dusky pallid blueness that one is accustomed to in a failing pneumonia, but rather [a] deep blueness." And a third: "In cases with bilateral lesions the cyanosis was marked, even to an indigo blue color. . . . The pallor was of particularly bad prognostic import."

Then there was the blood, blood pouring from the body. To see blood trickle, and in some cases spurt, from someone's nose, mouth, even from the ears or around the eyes, had to terrify. Terrifying as the bleeding was, it did not mean death, but even to physicians, even to those accustomed to thinking of the body as a machine and to trying to understand the disease process, symptoms like these previously unassociated with influenza had to be unsettling. For when the virus turned violent, blood was everywhere.*

In U.S. Army cantonments, from 5 percent to 15 percent of all men hospitalized suffered from epistaxis—bleeding from the nose—as with hemorrhagic viruses such as Ebola. There are many reports that blood sometimes spurted from the nose with enough power to travel several feet. Doctors had no explanation for these symptoms. They could only report them.

"15% suffered from epistaxis. . . ." "In about one-half the cases a foamy, blood-stained liquid ran from the nose and mouth when the head was

* Many mechanisms can cause bleeding in mucous membranes, and the precise way the influenza virus does this is unknown. Some viruses also attack platelets—which are necessary for clotting—directly or indirectly, and elements of the immune system may inadvertently attack platelets as well.

lowered. . . ." "Epistaxis occurs in a considerable number of cases, in one person a pint of bright red blood gushing from the nostrils. . . ." "A striking feature in the early stages of these cases was a bleeding from some portion of the body. . . . Six cases vomited blood; one died from loss of blood from this cause."

What was this?

"One of the most striking of the complications was hemorrhage from mucous membranes, especially from the nose, stomach, and intestine. Bleeding from the ears and petechial hemorrhages in the skin also occurred."

One German investigator recorded "hemorrhages occurring in different parts of the interior of the eye" with great frequency. An American pathologist noted: "Fifty cases of subconjunctival hemorrhage [bleeding from the lining of the eye] were counted. Twelve had a true hemoptysis, bright red blood with no admixture of mucus. . . . Three cases had intestinal hemorrhage. . . ."

"Female patients had a hemorrhagic vaginal discharge which was at first considered to be coincident menstruation, but later was interpreted as hemorrhage from the uterine mucosa."

What was this?

Never did the virus cause only a single symptom. The chief diagnostician in the New York City Health Department summarized, "Cases with intense pain look and act like cases of dengue . . . hemorrhage from nose or bronchi. . . . Expectoration is usually profuse and may be bloodstained . . . paresis or paralysis of either cerebral or spinal origin . . . impairment of motion may be severe or mild, permanent or temporary . . . physical and mental depression. Intense and protracted prostration led to hysteria, melancholia, and insanity with suicidal intent."

The impact on the mental state of the victims would be one of the most widely noted sequelae.

During the course of the epidemic, 47 percent of all deaths in the United States, nearly half of all those who died from all causes combined—from cancer, from heart disease, from stroke, from tuberculosis, from accidents, from suicide, from murder, and from all other causes—resulted from influenza and its complications. And it killed enough to depress the average life expectancy in the United States by more than ten years.

Some of those who died from influenza and pneumonia would have died if no epidemic had occurred. Pneumonia was after all the leading cause of death. So the key figure is actually the "excess death" toll. Investigators today believe that in the United States the 1918–19 epidemic caused an excess death toll of about 675,000 people. The nation then had a population between 105 and 110 million, while it was approaching 300 million in 2006. So a comparable figure today would be approximately 1,750,000 deaths.

And there was something even beyond the gross numbers that gave the 1918 influenza pandemic terrifying immediacy, brought it into every home, brought it into homes with the most life.

Influenza almost always selects the weakest in a society to kill, the very young and the very old. It kills opportunistically, like a bully. It almost always allows the most vigorous, the most healthy, to escape, including young adults as a group. Pneumonia was even known as "the old man's friend" for killing particularly the elderly, and doing so in a relatively painless and peaceful fashion that even allowed time to say good-bye.

There was no such grace about influenza in 1918. It killed the young and strong. Studies worldwide all found the same thing. Young adults, the healthiest and strongest part of the population, were the most likely to die. Those with the most to live for—the robust, the fit, the hearty, the ones raising young sons and daughters—those were the ones who died.

In South African cities, those between the ages of twenty and forty accounted for 60 percent of the deaths. In Chicago the deaths among those aged twenty to forty almost quintupled deaths of those aged forty-one to sixty. A Swiss physician "saw no severe case in anyone over 50." In the "registration area" of the United States—those states and cities that kept reliable statistics—breaking the population into five-year increments, the single greatest number of deaths occurred in men and women aged twenty-five to twenty-nine, the second greatest number in those aged thirty to thirty-four, the third greatest in those aged twenty to twenty-four. And more people died in **each** of those five-year groups than the total deaths among **all** those over age sixty.

Graphs that correlate mortality rates and age in influenza outbreaks always—always, that is, except for 1918–19—start out with a peak representing infant deaths, then fall into a valley, then rise again, with a second peak representing people somewhere past sixty-five or so. With mortality on the vertical and age on the horizontal, a graph of the dead would like like a U.

But 1918 was different. Infants did die then in large numbers, and so did the elderly. But in 1918 the great spike came in the middle. In 1918 an age graph of the dead would look like a W.

It is a graph that tells a story of utter tragedy. Even at the front in France, Harvey Cushing recognized this tragedy and called the victims "doubly dead in that they died so young."

In the American military alone, influenza-related deaths totaled just over the number of Americans killed in combat in Vietnam. One in every sixty-seven soldiers in the army died of influenza and its complications, nearly all of them in a ten-week period beginning in mid-September.

But influenza of course did not kill only men in the military. In the United States it killed fifteen times as many civilians as military. And among young adults still another demographic stood out. Those most vulnerable of all to influenza, those most likely of the most likely to die, were pregnant women. As far back as the year 1557, observers connected influenza with miscarriage and the death of pregnant women. In thirteen studies of hospitalized pregnant women during the 1918 pandemic, the death rate ranged from 23 percent to 71 percent. Of the pregnant women who survived, 26 percent lost the child. And these women were the most likely group to already have other children, so an unknown but enormous number of children lost their mothers.

The most pregnant word in science is "interesting." It suggests something new, puzzling, and potentially significant. Welch had asked Burt Wolbach, the brilliant chief pathologist at the great Boston hospital known as "the Brigham," to investigate the Devens cases. Wolbach called it "the most interesting pathological experience I have ever had."

The epidemiology of this pandemic was **interesting.** The unusual symptoms were **interesting.** And the autopsies—and some symptoms revealed themselves only in autopsy—were **interesting.** The damage this virus caused and its epidemiology presented a deep mystery. An explanation would come—but not for decades.

In the meantime this influenza, for it was after all only influenza, left almost no internal organ untouched. Another distinguished pathologist noted that the brain showed "marked hyperemia"— blood flooding the brain, probably because of an out-of-control inflammatory response—adding, "the convolutions of the brain were flattened and the brain tissues were noticeably dry."

The virus inflamed or affected the pericardium— the sac of tissue and fluid that protects the heart— and the heart muscle itself, noted others. The heart was also often "relaxed and flabby, offering strong contrast to the firm, contracted left ventricle nearly always present in post-mortem in patients dying from lobar pneumonia."

The amount of damage to the kidneys varied but at least some damage "occurred in nearly every case." The liver was sometimes damaged. The adrenal glands suffered "necrotic areas, frank hemorrhage, and occasionally abscesses. . . . When not involved in the hemorrhagic process they usually showed considerable congestion."

Muscles along the rib cage were torn apart both by internal toxic processes and by the external stress of coughing, and in many other muscles pathologists noted "necrosis," or "waxy degeneration."

Even the testes showed "very striking changes . . . encountered in nearly every case. . . . It was difficult to understand why such severe toxic lesions of the muscle and the testis should occur. . . ."

And, finally, came the lungs.

Physicians had seen lungs in such condition.

But those lungs had not come from pneumonia patients. Only one known disease—a particularly virulent form of bubonic plague called pneumonic plague, which kills approximately 90 percent of its victims—ripped the lungs apart in the way this disease did. So did weapons in war.

An army physician concluded, "The only comparable findings are those of pneumonic plague and those seen in acute death from toxic gas."

Seventy years after the pandemic, Edwin Kilbourne, a highly respected scientist who has spent much of his life studying influenza, confirmed this observation, stating that the condition of the lungs was "unusual in other viral respiratory infections and is reminiscent of lesions seen following inhalation of poison gas."

But the cause was not poison gas, and it was not pneumonic plague. It was only influenza.

CHAPTER TWENTY-ONE

IN 1918 IN PARTICULAR, influenza struck so suddenly that many victims could remember the precise instant they knew they were sick, so suddenly that throughout the world reports were common of people who toppled off horses, collapsed on the sidewalk.

Death itself could come so fast. Charles-Edward Winslow, a prominent epidemiologist and professor at Yale, noted, "We have had a number of cases where people were perfectly healthy and died within twelve hours." The **Journal of the American Medical Association** carried reports of death within hours: "One robust person showed the first symptom at 4:00 P.M. and died by 10:00 A.M." In **The Plague of the Spanish Lady: The Influenza**

Pandemic of 1918–1919, writer Richard Collier recounted this: In Rio de Janeiro, a man asked medical student Ciro Viera Da Cunha, who was waiting for a streetcar, for information in a perfectly normal voice, then fell down, dead; in Cape Town, South Africa, Charles Lewis boarded a streetcar for a three-mile trip home when the conductor collapsed, dead. In the next three miles six people aboard the streetcar died, including the driver.

Lewis stepped off the streetcar and walked home.

It was the lungs that had attracted attention from pathologists first. Physicians and pathologists had many times seen lungs of those dead of pneumonia. Many of the deaths from influenzal pneumonia did look like these normal pneumonias. And the later in the epidemic a victim died, the higher was the percentage of autopsy findings that resembled normal pneumonia, bacterial pneumonia.

Those who died very quickly, a day or even less after the first symptoms, however, most likely died of an overwhelming and massive invasion of the virus itself. The virus destroyed enough cells in the lung to block the exchange of oxygen. This alone was unusual and puzzling. But the lungs of the men and women who died two days, three days, four days after the first symptom of influenza bore no resemblance to normal pneumonias at all. They were more unusual, more puzzling.

In April a Chicago pathologist had sent lung-tissue

samples to the head of a research institute and asked him "to look over it as a new disease." British pathologists in France had commented on strange autopsy findings in the spring. Capps had mentioned unusual findings in the lungs to Welch, Cole, and other members of the inspection party in June. The lungs Welch himself had seen in the Devens autopsy room had made him fear that the disease was a new one.

The respiratory tract serves a single purpose: to transfer oxygen from the air into red blood cells. One can picture the entire system as an inverted oak tree. The trachea—the windpipe—carries air from the outside world into the lungs and is the equivalent of the tree trunk. This trunk then divides into two great branches, each called a "primary bronchus," which carry oxygen into the right and left lungs. Each primary bronchus subdivides into smaller and smaller bronchi, smaller branches, as they enter the lungs until they become "bronchioles."(Bronchi have cartilage, which helps give the lung a kind of architectural structure; bronchioles do not have cartilage.)

Each lung itself subdivides into lobes—the right lung has three, the left only two. The lobes subdivide into a total of nineteen smaller pockets. Within these pockets, sprouting like leaves from the smaller bronchi and the bronchioles, are clusters of tiny sacs called alveoli. They are much like tiny but porous balloons, and the average person has

300 million of them. The alveoli play a role comparable to that which leaves play in photosynthesis. In the alveoli, the actual transfer of oxygen into the blood takes place.

The right side of the heart pumps blood without oxygen into the lungs, where it passes into capillaries, the smallest blood vessels, so small that individual blood cells often move in single file. Capillaries surround the alveoli, and oxygen molecules slip through the membrane of the alveolar tissue and attach to the hemoglobin of the red blood cells as they circulate past them. After picking up oxygen, the blood returns to the left side of the heart, where it is pumped through arteries throughout the body. (The body's entire blood supply moves through the lungs each minute.)

In arteries, red blood cells carry oxygen and are bright red; in veins, such as those visible on one's wrist, the same cells without oxygen are bluish. When the lungs fail to oxygenate the blood, part of the body, and in some cases the entire body, can turn blue, causing cyanosis. Lack of oxygen, if extended for any length of time, damages and ultimately kills other organs in the body.

Healthy lung tissue is light, spongy, and porous, much lighter than water, and a good insulator of sound. A physician percussing the chest of a healthy patient will hear little. When normal lung tissue is manipulated, it "crepitates": as the air in the alevoli

escapes, it makes a crackling noise similar to rub-
bing hairs together.

A congested lung sounds different from a healthy
one: solid tissue conducts breathing sounds to the
chest wall, so someone listening can hear "rales,"
crackling or wheezing sounds (although it can also
sound either dull or hyperresonant). If the congestion is dense enough and widespread enough, the
lung is "consolidated."

In bronchopneumonia, bacteria—and many
kinds of bacteria can do this—invade the alveoli
themselves. Immune-system cells follow them there,
and so do antibodies, fluid, and other proteins and
enzymes. An infected alveolus becomes dense with
this material, which prevents it from transferring
oxygen to the blood. This "consolidation" appears
in patches surrounding the bronchi, and the infection is usually fairly localized.

In lobar pneumonia, entire lobes become consolidated and transformed into a liverlike mass—hence
the word "hepatization" to describe it. A hepatized
lobe can turn various colors depending on the stage
of disease; gray hepatization, for example, indicates
that various kinds of white blood cells have poured
into the lung to fight an infection. A diseased lung
also includes the detritus of dissolved cells, along
with various proteins such as fibrin and collagen
that are part of the body's efforts to repair damage.
(These repair efforts can cause their own problems.

"Fibrosis" occurs when too much fibrin interferes with the normal functioning of the lung.)

Roughly two-thirds of all bacterial pneumonias and an even higher percentage of lobar pneumonias are caused by a single group of bacteria, the various subtypes of the pneumococcus. (The pneumococcus is also the second leading cause of meningitis.) A virulent pneumococcus can spread through an entire lobe within a matter of hours. Even today, in 20 to 30 percent of the cases of lobar pneumonia, bacteria also spread through the blood to infect other areas of the body, and many victims still die. Some cyanosis is not unusual in lobar pneumonia, but most of the lung often still looks normal.

In 1918 pathologists did see at autopsy the normal devastation of the lungs caused by the usual lobar and bronchopneumonias. But the lungs from those who died quickly during the pandemic, the lungs that so confused even Welch, those lungs were different. Said one pathologist, "Physical signs were confusing. Typical consolidation was seldom found." And another: "The old classification by distribution of the lesions was inappropriate." And another: "Essentially toxic damage to alveolar walls and exudation of blood and fluid. Very little evidence of bacterial action could be found in some of these cases."

At a discussion reported in the **Journal of the American Medical Association,** several pathologists concurred, "The pathological picture was striking, and was unlike any type of pneumonia ordinarily seen in this country. . . . The lung lesions, complex and variable, struck one as being quite different in character to anything one had met with at all commonly in the thousands of autopsies one had performed during the last 20 years."

Normally when the lungs are removed they collapse like deflated balloons. Not now. Now they were full, but not of air. In bacterial pneumonias, normally the infection rages inside the alveoli, inside the tiny sacs. In 1918, while the alveoli were also sometimes invaded, the spaces between the alveoli were filled. This space, which makes up the bulk of the volume of the lung, was filled with the debris of destroyed cells and with every element of the immune system, from enzymes to white blood cells. And it was filled with blood.

One more observer concluded that "the acute death" he saw evidence of in the lungs "is a lesion which does not occur in other types of pulmonary infection. In influenza it is the lesion of characterization."

Victims' lungs were being ripped apart as a result of, in effect, collateral damage from the attack of the immune system on the virus. Since the respiratory tract must allow outside air to pass into the innermost recesses of the body, it is extremely well defended. The lungs became the battleground between the invaders and the immune system. Nothing was left standing on that battleground.

The immune system begins its defense far in advance of the lungs, with enzymes in saliva that destroy some pathogens (including HIV, which makes its home in most bodily fluids, but not in saliva, where enzymes kill it). Then it raises physical obstacles, such as nasal hairs that filter out large particles and sharp turns in the throat that force inhaled air to collide with the sides of breathing passageways.

Mucus lines these passageways and traps organisms and irritants. Underneath the layer of mucus lies a blanket of "epithelial cells," and from their surfaces extend "cilia," akin to tiny hairs which, like tiny oars, sweep upward continuously at from 1,000 to 1,500 beats a minute. This sweeping motion moves foreign organisms away from places they can lodge and launch an infection, and up to the larynx. If something does gain a foothold in the upper respiratory tract, the body first tries to flush it out with more fluid—hence the typical runny nose—and then expel it with coughs and sneezes.

These defenses are as physical as raising an arm to block a punch and do no damage to the lungs. Even if the body overreacts, this usually does no serious harm, although an increased volume of mucus blocks air passages and makes breathing more difficult. (In allergies these same symptoms occur because the immune system does overreact.)

There are more aggressive defenses. Macrophages

and "natural killer" cells—two kinds of white blood cells that seek and destroy all foreign invaders, unlike other elements of the immune system that attack only a specific threat—patrol the entire respiratory tract and lungs. Cells in the respiratory tract secrete enzymes that attack bacteria and some viruses (including influenza) or block them from attaching to tissue beneath the mucus, and these secretions also bring more white cells and antibacterial enzymes into a counterattack; if a virus is the invader, white blood cells also secrete interferon, which can block viral infection.

All these defenses work so well that the lungs themselves, although directly exposed to outside air, are normally sterile.

But when the lungs do become infected, other defenses, lethal and violent defenses, come into play. For the immune system is at its core a killing machine. It targets infecting organisms, attacks with a complex arsenal of weapons—some of them savage weapons—and neutralizes or kills the invader.

The balance, however, between kill and overkill, response and overresponse, is a delicate one. The immune system can behave like a SWAT team that kills the hostage along with the hostage taker, or the army that destroys the village to save it.

In 1918 especially, this question of balance played a crucial role in the war between virus and immune system, and between life and death. The virus was often so efficient at invading the lungs that the immune system had to mount a massive response to it. What was killing young adults a few days after the first symptom was not the virus. The killer was the massive immune response itself.

The virus attaches itself normally to epithelial cells, which line the entire respiratory tract like insulation in a tube all the way to the alveoli. Within fifteen minutes after influenza viruses invade the body, their hemagglutinin spikes begin binding with the sialic-acid receptors on these cells. One after another these spikes attach to the receptors, each one a grappling hook binding the virus tighter and tighter to the cell. Generally about ten hours after the virus invades a cell, the cell bursts open, releasing between 1,000 and 10,000 viruses capable of infecting other cells. At even the lowest reproduction rate—1,000 times 1,000 times 1,000, and so on—one can easily understand how a victim could feel perfectly healthy one moment and collapse the next, just as the fifth or sixth generation of viruses matures and infects cells.

Meanwhile, the virus is also attacking the immune system directly, undermining the body's ability to protect itself; the virus inhibits the release of interferon, and interferon is usually the first weapon the body employs to fight viral infection. In 1918 the ability to inhibit the immune system was so obvious that researchers, even while overwhelmed by the pandemic, noticed that influenza victims had weakened immune responses to other stimuli; they used objective tests to prove it.

Even mild influenza viruses can utterly and entirely denude the upper respiratory tract of epithelial cells, leaving it bare, stripping the throat raw. (The repair process begins within a few days but takes weeks.)

Once an infection gains a foothold, the immune system responds initially with inflammation. The immune system can inflame at the site of an infection, causing the redness, heat, and swelling there, or it can inflame the entire body through fever, or both.

The actual process of inflammation involves the release by certain white blood cells of proteins called "cytokines." There are many kinds of white cells; several kinds attack invading organisms, while other "helper" cells manage attacks, and still others produce antibodies. There are even more kinds of cytokines. Some cytokines attack invaders directly, such as interferon, which attacks viruses. Some act as messengers carrying orders. Macrophages, for example, release "GM CSF," which stands for "granulocyte-macrophage colony-stimulating factor"; GM CSF stimulates the production in the bone marrow of more macrophages as well as granulocytes, another kind of white blood cell. Some cytokines also carry messages to parts of the body not normally considered belonging to the immune system; several cytokines can affect the hypothalamus, which acts like the body's thermostat. When these cytokines bind to receptors in the hypothalamus, body temperature goes up; the entire body becomes inflamed. (Fever is part of the immune response; some pathogens do not grow well at higher temperatures.) In influenza, fever routinely climbs to 103, and can go higher.

But cytokines themselves also have toxic effects. The typical symptoms of influenza outside the respiratory tract, the headache and body ache, are caused not by the virus but by cytokines. A side effect of cytokines' stimulating the bone marrow to make more white cells, for instance, is likely what aches in the bone.

Cytokines can cause more serious and permanent damage as well. "Tumor necrosis factor," to give one example, is a cytokine that gets its name from its ability to kill cancer cells—tumors exposed to TNF in the laboratory simply melt away; it also helps raise body temperature and stimulates antibody production. But TNF is extraordinarily lethal, and not just to diseased cells. It can destroy healthy ones as well. In fact, it can kill the entire body. TNF is a toxin and a major cause of toxic shock syndrome, and it is not the only toxic cytokine.

Routinely, the body fights off the influenza virus before it gains a solid foothold in the lungs themselves. But in 1918 the virus often succeeded in infecting epithelial cells not only in the upper respiratory tract but all the way down the respiratory tract into the innermost sanctuaries of the lungs, into the epithelial cells of the alveoli. This was viral pneumonia.

The immune system followed the virus into the lungs and there waged war. In this war the immune system held nothing back. It used all its weapons. And it killed. It killed particularly with "killer T cells," a white blood cell that targets the body's own cells when they are infected with a virus, and it killed with what is sometimes referred to as a "cytokine storm," a massive attack using every lethal weapon the body possesses.

The same capillaries that moved blood past the alveoli delivered this attack. The capillaries dilated, pouring out fluid, every kind of white blood cell, antibodies, other elements of the immune system, and cytokines into the lung. Then these cytokines and other enzymes virtually obliterated the capillaries. Even more fluid poured into the lung. The cells that line the alveoli were damaged, if they survived the virus itself. Pink glassy membranes, called hyaline membranes, formed on the insides of the alveoli. Once these membranes formed, "surfactant"—a slippery, soap-like protein that reduces surface tension and eases the transfer of oxygen into red blood cells—disappeared from the alveoli. More blood flooded the lungs. The body started producing fiberlike connective tissue. Areas of the lung became enmeshed in cell debris, fibrin, collagen, and other materials. Proteins and fluid filled the space between cells.

Macfarlane Burnet, the Nobel laureate, described what was happening inside the lungs: "acute inflammatory injection . . . very rapid necrosis of most of the epithelial lining of the bronchial tree down to and especially involving the smallest bronchioles. . . . Essentially toxic damage to alveolar walls and exudation of blood and fluid . . . [C]ontinued exudation of fluid in areas where blocking of smaller bronchi had occurred would produce eventually airless regions."

The immune system changes with age. Young adults have the strongest immune system in the population, most capable of mounting a massive immune response. Normally that makes them the healthiest element of the population. Under certain conditions, however, that very strength becomes a weakness.

In 1918 the immune systems of young adults mounted massive responses to the virus. That immune response filled the lungs with fluid and debris, making it impossible for the exchange of oxygen to take place. The immune response killed.

The influenza outbreak in 1997 in Hong Kong, when a new virus jumped from chickens to humans, killed only six people and it did not adapt to man. More than a million chickens were slaughtered to prevent that from happening, and the outbreak has been much studied. In autopsies pathologists noticed extremely high cytokine levels, discovered even that the bone marrow, lymphoid tissue, spleen—all involved in the immune response—and other organs were themselves under attack from an immune system turned renegade. They believed that this "syndrome [was] not previously described with influenza." In fact, investigators in 1918 had seen the same thing.

This was still influenza, only influenza.

In the 1970s physicians began to recognize a pathological process in the lungs that could have many causes but, once the process began, looked the same and received the same treatment. They called it ARDS, which stands for acute respiratory distress syndrome. Almost anything that puts extreme stress on the lung can cause ARDS: near drowning, smoke inhalation, inhaling toxic fumes (or poison gas) . . . or influenzal viral pneumonia. Doctors today looking at pathology reports of lungs in 1918 would immediately designate the condition as ARDS.

One pulmonary expert describes ARDS as "a burn inside the lungs." It is a virtual scorching of lung tissue. When viral pneumonia causes the condition, the immune system toxins designed to destroy invaders are what, in effect, flame in the lung, scorching the tissue.

Whatever the causes of ARDS, even today there is no way of stopping the process of disintegration in the lung once it begins. The only care is supportive, keeping the victim alive until he or she can recover. This requires all the technology of modern intensive-care units. Still, even with the best modern care, even with for example dramatically more efficient and effective administration of oxygen than in 1918, the mortality rate for ARDS patients in different studies ranges from 40 to 60 percent. Without intensive care—and hospitals have few beds in intensive-care units—the mortality rate would approach 100 percent.

(In 2003 a new coronavirus that causes SARS, "severe acute respiratory syndrome," appeared in China and quickly spread around the world. Coronaviruses cause an estimated 15 to 30 percent of all colds and, like the influenza virus, infect epithelial cells. When the coronavirus that causes SARS does kill, it often kills through ARDS, although since the virus replicates much more slowly than influenza, death from ARDS can come several weeks after the first symptoms.)

In ARDS, death can come from many causes. Organs outside the lungs fail because they get too little oxygen. The lungs can so fill with fluid that the right ventricle of the heart cannot empty it, so the victim drowns. The strain of trying to pump blood out of the lung can cause heart failure. Or the victim can simply die from exhaustion: he or she must breathe so rapidly to get enough oxygen that muscles become exhausted. Breathing just stops.

ARDS by no means accounts for all the influenza deaths in 1918 and 1919, or even for a majority of them. It explains only those who died in a few days, and it explains why so many young healthy people died. Although influenza almost certainly killed some people in ways that had little to do with the lungs—for example, someone whose already weak heart could not stand the additional strain of fighting the disease—the overwhelming majority of non-ARDS deaths came from bacterial pneumonias.

The destruction of the epithelial cells eliminated the sweeping action that clears so much of the respiratory tract of bacteria, and the virus damaged or exhausted other parts of the immune system as well. That gave the normal bacterial flora of the mouth unimpeded entry into the lungs. Recent research also suggests that the neuraminidase on the influenza virus makes it easier for some bacteria to attach to lung tissue, creating a lethal synergy between the virus and these bacteria. And in the lungs, the bacteria began to grow.

Bacterial pneumonias developed a week, two weeks, three weeks after someone came down with influenza, including even a seemingly mild case of influenza. Often influenza victims seemed to recover, even returned to work, then suddenly collapsed again with bacterial pneumonia.

It is impossible to know what percentage of the dead were killed by a viral pneumonia and how many died from bacterial pneumonias which can also progress to ARDS. Generally speaking, epidemiologists and historians who have written about this pandemic have assumed that the overwhelming majority of deaths came from secondary invaders, from bacterial pneumonias that can be fought with antibiotics.

The conclusion of the army's pneumonia commission, however, is chilling in terms of implications for today. This commission, comprised of half a dozen of the finest scientists in America, both conducted autopsies and reviewed pathology reports of others; it found signs of what would today be called ARDS in almost half the autopsies. A separate study limited to the pathology of the disease, conducted by Milton Winternitz, a Welch protégé and later dean of the Yale Medical School, reached the same conclusion.

That overstates the proportion of victims who died from ARDS because the army study looked only at deaths among soldiers, men who were young and otherwise healthy, the group most likely to have been killed by their own immune systems. In the total population, viral pneumonias and ARDS would not account for as high a percentage of the deaths. Most deaths almost certainly did come from secondary bacterial infections, but probably not quite so many as has been assumed. That should, however, be small comfort for those who worry about the next influenza pandemic.

The 1957 pandemic was far milder than 1918, but even then 25 percent of the fatalities had viral pneumonia only; three-quarters of the deaths came from complications, generally bacterial pneumonia, even in that golden age of antibiotics. Since then, bacterial resistance has become a major problem in medicine. Today the mortality rate for a bacterial pneumonia following influenza is still roughly 7 percent, and in some parts of the United States, 35 percent of pneumococcal infections are resistant to the antibiotic of choice. When **Staphylococcus aureus**, a bacterium that has become particularly troubling in hospitals because of its resistance to antibiotics, is the secondary invader, the death rate—today—rises to as high as 42 percent. That is higher than the general death rate from bacterial pneumonias in 1918.

■ Part VII
THE RACE

CHAPTER TWENTY-TWO

NATURE CHOSE to rage in 1918, and it chose the form of the influenza virus in which to do it. This meant that nature first crept upon the world in familiar, almost comic, form. It came in masquerade. Then it pulled down its mask and showed its fleshless bone.

Then, as the pathogen spread from cantonments to cities, as it spread within cities, as it moved from city to town to village to farmhouse, medical science began moving as well. It began its own race against the pathogen, moving more rapidly and with more purpose than it ever had.

Scientists did not presume to think that they would or could control this rage of nature. But they did not abandon their search for ways to control the damage of this rage. They still tried to save lives.

Worldwide their struggle, their race, commenced. In the United States that struggle would be fought by Welch, Gorgas, Cole, and their colleagues, as well as by the institutions they had built and the men and women they had trained. Neither these institutions nor these men and women had ever been tested like this. They had never imagined they would be tested like this. But any possibility of affecting the course of the disease lay in their hands.

To save lives they needed the answer to at least one of three questions. It was possible that even a single rough approximation of an answer would give them enough knowledge to intervene, to interrupt the disease at some critical juncture. But it was also possible they could learn detailed answers to all three questions and still remain helpless, utterly helpless.

First, they needed to understand the epidemiology of influenza, how it behaved and spread. Scientists had already learned to control cholera, typhoid, yellow fever, malaria, bubonic plague, and other diseases by understanding their epidemiology even before developing either a vaccine or cure.

Second, they needed to learn its pathology, what it did within the body, the precise course of the disease. That too might allow them to intervene in some way that saved lives.

Third, they needed to know what the pathogen

was, what microorganism caused influenza. This
could allow them to find a way to stimulate the immune system to prevent or cure the disease. It was
also conceivable that even without knowing the precise cause, they could develop a serum or vaccine.

The easiest question to answer for influenza was
its epidemiology. Although some respected investigators still believed in the miasma theory—they
thought influenza spread too fast for person-to-per-
son contact to account for it—most believed correctly it was an airborne pathogen. Breathing it
in could cause the disease. They did not know
the exact, precise details, that for example when the
virus floats in the air it can infect someone else for
anywhere from an hour to a day after it is exhaled (the
lower the humidity, the longer the virus survives).
But they did know that it was "a crowd disease,"
spread most easily in crowds.

They also had an accurate estimate that someone with influenza "sheds" the virus—can infect
others—usually from the third to the sixth day
after he or she is infected.

They also believed, correctly, that people could
catch influenza not only by inhaling it but by
hand-to-mouth or -nose contact. They rightly
thought, for instance, that a sick person could cover
his mouth with his hand when he coughed, then
several hours later shake hands, and the second person could then rub his chin in thought or touch
his nose or stick a piece of candy in his mouth and

infect himself. Similarly, someone sick could cough into a hand, touch a hard surface such as a doorknob, and spread it to someone else who turns the doorknob and later brings a hand to face. (In fact, the virus can remain infectious on a hard surface for days.)

Knowledge of influenza's epidemiology, then, was of little use. Only rigorous and ruthless isolation and quarantine could even slow it down. No scientist and no public health official had the political power to take such action. Some local authorities might take some action, but no national figure could. Even within the army, Gorgas's urgent and desperate calls to end the transfer of troops were ignored.

Scientists were also learning too well about the pathology of the disease and its natural course. They were learning chiefly that they could do almost nothing to intervene in serious cases, in the cases that progressed to viral pneumonia and ARDS; even administering oxygen seemed to have no effect.

They believed they could, however, possibly save lives if they could prevent or treat the slower moving pneumonias caused by what they were fairly quickly suspecting to be secondary invaders. Some preventive measures involved only giving proper guidance, such as to rest in bed after influenza infection, or giving good care, which was becoming more and more impossible as the numbers of the sick rose, as nurses and doctors themselves succumbed.

But if they could find the pathogen . . . They had tools, they could manipulate the immune system, they could prevent and cure some pneumonias—including the most common pneumonias. The conquest of bacterial pneumonias seemed tantalizingly within the reach of science, tantalizingly at the very edge of scientists' reach—or just beyond it. If they could just find the pathogen . . .

All the energies of science rose to that challenge.

William Welch himself would not rise to it. From Camp Devens he had returned directly to Baltimore, neither stopping in New York City nor going on to report to the surgeon general's office in Washington. Others could perform that duty, and on the phone he had said what he had to say.

In the meantime Welch wasn't feeling very well. No doubt he tried to shrug off the discomfort. He had, after all, had an exceedingly difficult trip. Just before going to Devens he, Cole, and Vaughan had concluded their latest round of camp inspections and had just begun to relax for a few days in Asheville, North Carolina. He had even contemplated resigning his commission. Then they had been abruptly ordered to the surgeon general's office on a Sunday, gone straight on to Devens, and there discovered this terrible disease.

So he had every reason to be tired and out of sorts. Likely he told himself something akin to that. The rattling of the train would have disturbed him, exacerbating the first signs of a headache. Large a man as he was, he had difficulty getting comfortable on a train anyway.

But as the train moved south he felt worse and worse, perhaps suffering a sudden violent headache and an unproductive cough, cough in which nothing came up, and certainly with a fever. He would have looked at himself clinically, objectively, and made a correct diagnosis. He had influenza.

No record exists of his precise clinical course. All of Baltimore, all of the East Coast, was erupting in flames. The virus struck the Hopkins itself so hard that the university closed its hospital to all but its own staff and students. Three Hopkins medical students, three Hopkins nurses, and three Hopkins doctors would die.

Welch did not go to the hospital. Almost seventy years old, forty years older than those who were dying in the greatest numbers, having just left the horror at Devens and knowing the enormous strain on and therefore the likely poor care even at the Hopkins facility, he later said, "I could not have dreamed of going to a hospital at that time."

Instead, he went to bed immediately in his own rooms, and stayed there. He knew better than to push himself now: pushing oneself after infection with this disease could easily open the path for a secondary invader to kill. After ten days in bed at home, when he felt well enough to travel at all, to recuperate more he withdrew entirely to his beloved

Hotel Dennis in Atlantic City, the odd tacky place that was his haven.

In the midst of the chaos that was everywhere, he returned to this familiar place that gave him comfort. What had he always liked about it? Perhaps the life that roared through it. Quiet resorts bored him: he described Mohonk, a mountain resort ninety miles above New York City, as "a kind of twin-lakes-resort with Miss Dares sitting in rockers on the broad piazza, . . . where it seems as if nine o'clock will never come so that one could go decently to bed . . . [C]olored neckties are not allowed." But Atlantic City! and "the most terrifying, miraculous, blood-curdling affair called the Flip-flap railroad . . . just built on a long pier out over the ocean . . . [Y]ou go down from a height of about 75 feet . . . with the head down and the feet up, so that you would drop out of the car, if it was not for the tremendous speed. As you go round the circle the effect is indescribable. . . . Crowds stand around and say they would not try it for $1000."

Yes, the life that roared through Atlantic City—the young men and women and their frolicking, the sensuality of sweat and surf and salt, the vibrancy and thrust of flesh about the ocean and boardwalk, all that—made one feel as if one were not merely observing but partaking. But now Atlantic City was quiet. It was October, off-season, the resorts quiet. And here, as everywhere, was influenza. Here, as everywhere, there was a shortage

of doctors, a shortage of nurses, a shortage of hospitals, a shortage of coffins, its schools closed, its
places of public amusement closed, its Flip-flap
railroad closed.

He stayed in bed for several more weeks, recu-
perating. The disease, he told his nephew, "seems to
have localized itself in my intestinal, rather than the
respiratory tract, which is probably fortunate." He
also insisted that his nephew, later a U.S. senator,
make certain if any symptoms of influenza appeared
at all in his family that the victim stay in bed "until
the temperature has been normal for three days."

He had planned to attend a meeting on the disease at the Rockefeller Institute, but almost two
weeks after arriving in Atlantic City, a month after
first becoming ill, he canceled; he had not recovered
enough to attend. He would play no further role
in medical science for the course of the epidemic.
He would not participate in the search for a solution. He had of course done no laboratory work in
years, but he had often proved an extraordinarily
useful conduit, knowing everyone and everything,
a cross-pollinator recognizing how the work of one
investigator might complement the work of another,
and directly or indirectly putting the two in touch.
Now he would not play even that role.

Coincidentally, both Flexner and Gorgas arrived
in Europe on unrelated business just as influenza
erupted in America. The generation who had transformed American medicine had withdrawn from

the race. If anything was to be done in the nature of a scientific breakthrough, their spiritual descendants would do the doing.

Welch had left Massachusetts with Burt Wolbach performing more autopsies, Milton Rosenau already beginning experiments on human volunteers, and Oswald Avery beginning bacteriological investigations. Other outstanding scientists had also already engaged this problem—William Park and Anna Williams in New York, Paul Lewis in Philadelphia, Preston Kyes in Chicago, and others. If the country was lucky, very lucky indeed, one of them might find something soon enough to help.

For all the urgency, investigators could not allow themselves to be panicked into a disorderly approach. Disorder would lead nowhere. They began with what they knew and with what they could do.

They could kill pathogens outside the body. An assortment of chemicals could disinfect a room, or clothes, and they knew precisely the amount of chemicals needed and the duration of exposure necessary to fumigate a room. They knew how to disinfect instruments and materials. They knew how to grow bacteria, and how to stain bacteria to make them visible under microscopes. They knew that what Ehrlich called "magic bullets" existed that could kill infectious pathogens, and they even had started down the right pathways to find them.

Yet in the midst of crisis, with death everywhere,

none of that knowledge was useful. Fumigation and disinfecting required too much labor to work on a mass scale, and finding a magic bullet required discovering more unknowns than was then possible. Investigators quickly recognized they would get no help from materia medica.

Medicine had, however, if not entirely mastered at least knew how to use one tool: the immune system itself.

Investigators understood the basic principles of the immune system. They knew how to manipulate those principles to prevent and cure some diseases. They knew how to grow and weaken or strengthen bacteria in the laboratory, and how to stimulate an immune response in an animal. They knew how to make vaccines, and they knew how to make antiserum.

They also understood the specificity of the immune system. Vaccines and antisera work only against the specific etiological agent, the specific pathogen or toxin causing the disease. Few investigators cared how elegant their experiments were as friends, families, and colleagues fell ill. But to have the best hope of protecting with a vaccine or curing with a serum, investigators needed to isolate the pathogen. They needed to answer a first question, the most important question—indeed, at this point the only question. What caused the disease?

■   ■   ■

Richard Pfeiffer believed he had found the answer to that question a quarter century earlier. One of Koch's most brilliant disciples, scientific director of the Institute for Infectious Disease in Berlin, and a general in the German army, he was sixty years old in 1918 and by then had become somewhat imperious. Over his career he had addressed some of the great questions of medicine, and he had made enormous contributions. By any standard he was a giant.

During and after the 1889–90 influenza pandemic—with the exception of 1918–19, the most severe influenza pandemic in the last three centuries—he had searched for the cause. Carefully, painstakingly, he had isolated tiny, slender, rod-shaped bacteria with rounded ends, although they sometimes appeared in somewhat different forms, from people suffering from influenza. He often found the bacteria the sole organism present, and he found it in "astonishing numbers."

This bacteria clearly had the ability to kill, although in animals the disease produced did not quite resemble human influenza. Thus, the evidence against it did not fulfill "Koch's postulates." But human pathogens often either do not sicken animals or cause different symptoms in them, and many pathogens are accepted as the cause of a disease without fully satisfying Koch's postulates.

Pfeiffer was confident that he had found the cause of influenza. He even named the bacteria

Bacillus influenzae. (Today this bacteria is called **Hemophilus influenzae.**)

Among scientists the bacteria quickly became known as "Pfeiffer's bacillus," and, given his deserved reputation, few doubted the validity of his discovery.

Certainty creates strength. Certainty gives one something upon which to lean. Uncertainty creates weakness. Uncertainty makes one tentative if not fearful, and tentative steps, even when in the right direction, may not overcome significant obstacles.

To be a scientist requires not only intelligence and curiosity, but passion, patience, creativity, self-sufficiency, and courage. It is not the courage to venture into the unknown. It is the courage to accept—indeed, embrace—uncertainty. For as Claude Bernard, the great French physiologist of the nineteenth century, said, "Science teaches us to doubt."

A scientist must accept the fact that all his or her work, even beliefs, may break apart upon the sharp edge of a single laboratory finding. And just as Einstein refused to accept his own theory until his predictions were tested, one must seek out such findings. Ultimately a scientist has nothing to believe in but the process of inquiry. To move forcefully and aggressively even while uncertain requires a confidence and strength deeper than physical courage.

All real scientists exist on the frontier. Even the

least ambitious among them deal with the unknown, if only one step beyond the known. The best
among them move deep into a wilderness region
where they know almost nothing, where the very
tools and techniques needed to clear the wilderness,
to bring order to it, do not exist. There they probe in
a disciplined way. There a single step can take them
through the looking glass into a world that seems
entirely different, and if they are at least partly correct their probing acts like a crystal to precipitate
an order out of chaos, to create form, structure, and
direction. A single step can also take one off a cliff.

In the wilderness the scientist must create . . .
everything. It is grunt work, tedious work that
begins with figuring out what tools one needs and
then making them. A shovel can dig up dirt but
cannot penetrate rock. Would a pick then be best,
or would dynamite be better—or would dynamite
be too indiscriminately destructive? If the rock is
impenetrable, if dynamite would destroy what one
is looking for, is there another way of getting information about what the rock holds? There is a stream
passing over the rock. Would analyzing the water
after it passes over the rock reveal anything useful?
How would one analyze it?

Ultimately, if the researcher succeeds, a flood of
colleagues will pave roads over the path laid, and
those roads will be orderly and straight, taking an
investigator in minutes to a place the pioneer spent
months or years looking for. And the perfect tool

will be available for purchase, just as laboratory mice can now be ordered from supply houses.

Not all scientific investigators can deal comfortably with uncertainty, and those who can may not be creative enough to understand and design the experiments that will illuminate a subject—to know both where and how to look. Others may lack the confidence to persist. Experiments do not simply work. Regardless of design and preparation, experiments—especially at the beginning, when one proceeds by intelligent guess-work—rarely yield the results desired. An investigator must make them work. The less known, the more one has to manipulate and even force experiments to yield an answer.

Which raises another question: How does one know when one knows? In turn this leads to more practical questions: How does one know when to continue to push an experiment? And how does one know when to abandon a clue as a false trail?

No one interested in any truth will torture the data itself, ever. But a scientist can—and should—torture an experiment to get data, to get a result, especially when investigating a new area. A scientist can—and should—seek any way to answer a question: if using mice and guinea pigs and rabbits does not provide a satisfactory answer, then trying dogs, pigs, cats, monkeys. And if one experiment shows a hint of a result, the slightest bump on a flat line of information, then a scientist designs the next experiment to focus on that bump, to create conditions more likely to get more bumps until they either become consistent and meaningful or demonstrate that the initial bump was mere random variation without meaning.

There are limits to such manipulation. Even under torture, nature will not lie, will not yield a consistent, reproducible result, unless it is true. But if tortured enough, nature will mislead; it will confess to something that is true only under special conditions—the conditions the investigator created in the laboratory. Its truth is then artificial, an experimental artifact.

One key to science is that work be **reproducible.** Someone in another laboratory doing the same experiment will get the same result. The result then is reliable enough that someone else can build upon it. The most damning condemnation is to dismiss a finding as "not reproducible." That can call into question not only ability but on occasion ethics.

If a reproducible finding comes from torturing nature, however, it is not useful. To be useful, a result must be not only reproducible but . . . perhaps one should call it **expandable.** One must be able to enlarge it, explore it, learn more from it, use it as a foundation to build structures upon.

These things become easy to discern in hindsight. But how does one know when to persist, when to continue to try to make an experiment work, when to make adjustments—and when finally to abandon a line of thought as mistaken or incapable of solution with present techniques?

How does one know when to do either?

The question is one of judgment. For the distinguishing element in science is not intelligence but judgment. Or perhaps it is simply luck. George Sternberg did not pursue his discovery of the pneumococcus, and he did not pursue his discovery that white blood cells devoured bacteria. He did not because doing so would have deflected him from his unsuccessful pursuit of yellow fever. Given his abilities, had he focused on either of those other discoveries, his name would be well known instead of forgotten in the history of science.

Judgment is so difficult because a negative result does not mean that a hypothesis is wrong. Nor do ten negative results, nor do one hundred negative results. Ehrlich believed that magic bullets existed; chemical compounds could cure disease. His reasoning led him to try certain compounds against a certain infection. Ultimately he tried more than nine hundred chemical compounds. Each experiment began with hope. Each was performed meticulously. Each failed. Finally he found the compound that did work. The result was not only the first drug that could cure an infection; it confirmed a line of reasoning that led to thousands of investigators following the same path.

How does one know when one knows? When one is on the edge, one cannot know. One can only test.

Thomas Huxley advised, "Surely there is a time to submit to guidance and a time to take one's own way at all hazards."

Thomas Rivers was one of the young men from the Hopkins on the army's pneumonia commission. He would later—only a few years later—define the differences between viruses and bacteria, become one of the world's leading virologists, and succeed Cole as head of the Rockefeller Institute Hospital. He gave an example of the difficulty of knowing when one knows when he spoke of two Rockefeller colleagues, Albert Sabin and Peter Olitsky. As Rivers recalled, they "proved polio virus would grow only in nervous tissue. Elegant work, absolutely convincing. Everyone believed it."

Everyone believed it, that is, except John Enders. The virus Sabin and Olitsky were working with had been used in the laboratory so long that it had mutated. That particular virus **would** grow only in nervous tissue. Enders won a Nobel Prize for growing polio virus in other tissue, work that led directly to a polio vaccine. Sabin's career was hardly ruined by his error; he went on to develop the best polio vaccine. Olitsky did well, too. But had Enders pursued his intuition and been wrong, much of his own career would have been utterly wasted.

Richard Pfeiffer insisted he had discovered the cause, the etiological agent, of influenza. His confidence was so great he had even named it **Bacillus influenzae.** He had tremendous stature, half a rung below Pasteur, Koch, and Ehrlich. Surely his reputation stood higher than that of any American investigator before the war. Who would challenge him?

His reputation gave his finding tremendous weight. Around the world, many scientists believed it. Indeed, some accepted it as an axiom: without the bacteria there could be no influenza. "No influenza bacilli have been found in cases here," wrote one European investigator. Therefore the disease was, he concluded, "not influenza."

CHAPTER TWENTY-THREE

LABORATORIES EVERYWHERE had turned to influenza. Pasteur's protégé Émile Roux, one of those who had raced German competitors for a diphtheria antitoxin, directed the work at the Pasteur Institute. In Britain virtually everyone in Almroth Wright's laboratory worked on it, including Alexander Fleming, whose later discovery of penicillin he first applied to research on Pfeiffer's so-called influenza bacillus. In Germany, in Italy, even in revolution-torn Russia, desperate investigators searched for an answer.

But by the fall of 1918 these laboratories could function only on a far-reduced scale. Research had been cut back and focused on war, on poison gas or defending against it, on preventing infection of

wounds, on ways to prevent diseases that incapacitated troops such as "trench fever," an infection related to typhus that was not serious in itself but had
taken more troops out of the line than any other
disease. Laboratory animals had become unavailable; armies consumed them for testing poison gas
and similar purposes. The war had also sucked into
itself technicians and young researchers.

Laboratories in both Europe and the United
States were affected, but Europeans suffered far
more, with their work limited by shortages not
only of people but of everything from coal for heat
to money for petri dishes. At least those resources
Americans had. And if the United States still lagged
behind Europe in the number of investigators, it no
longer lagged in the quality of investigators. The
Rockefeller Institute had already become arguably
the best research institute in the world; out of a mere
handful of scientists working there then, one man
had already won the Nobel Prize and two would win
it. In the most relevant area of work, in pneumonia,
the Rockefeller Institute had a clear lead over the
rest of the world. And Rockefeller scientists were
hardly the only Americans doing world-class work.

For Welch, Michigan's Victor Vaughan, Harvard's
Charles Eliot, Penn's William Pepper, and the
handful of colleagues who had pushed so hard
for change had succeeded. They had transformed
American medical science. If that transformation
had only just occurred, if it had only recently risen

to the level of Europe, it also had the vitality that comes from recent conversion. And the nation at large was not so exhausted as Europe. It was not exhausted at all.

As influenza stretched its fingers across the country and began to crush out lives in its grip, virtually every serious medical scientist—and many simple physicians who considered themselves of scientific bent—began looking for a cure. They were determined to prove that science could indeed perform miracles.

Most of them, simply, were not good enough to address the problem with any hope of success. They tried anyway. Their attempt was heroic. It required not just scientific ability but physical courage. They moved among the dead and dying, reached swabs into mouths and nasal passages of the desperately ill, steeped themselves in blood in the autopsy room, dug deep into bodies, and struggled to grow from swabbings, blood, and tissue the pathogen that was killing more humans than any other in history.

A few of these investigators, possibly as few as a few dozen, were smart enough, creative enough, knowledgeable enough, skilled enough, and commanded enough resources that they were not on a fool's errand. They could confront this disease with at least the hope of success.

In Boston, Rosenau and Keegan continued to study the disease in the laboratory. The bulk of the army's pneumonia commission had been ordered to Camp Pike, Arkansas, where, even as Welch arrived at Devens, they began investigating "a new bronchopneumonia." The Rockefeller team whom Welch had brought to Devens headed back to New York, where they added Martha Wollstein, a respected bacteriologist also associated with the Rockefeller Institute, to the effort; she had studied the influenza bacillus since 1905. In Chicago at the Memorial Institute for Infectious Diseases, Ludwig Hektoen dove into the work. And at the Mayo Clinic, E. C. Rosenow did the same. The only civilian government research institution, the Public Health Service's Hygienic Laboratory, and its director George McCoy joined in.

But of all those working on it in the United States, perhaps the most important were Oswald Avery at Rockefeller, William Park and Anna Williams at the New York City Department of Public Health, and Paul Lewis in Philadelphia.

Each of them brought a different style to the problem, a different method of doing science. For Park and Williams, the work would come as close to routine as something could be in the midst of such extreme crisis; their efforts would have no impact on their own lives in any personal sense, although they would help direct research on influenza down the path that ultimately yielded the right answer. For Avery the work would confirm him in a direction that he would follow for decades, decades first of enormous frustration but then of momentous discovery—in fact a discovery that opened the door to an entire universe even now just beginning to be explored. For Lewis, although he could not have known it, his work on influenza would mark a turning point in his own life, one that would lead to a great tragedy, for science, for his family, and for himself.

It was not a good time to confront a major new threat in the Bureau of Laboratories of the New York City Department of Public Health, the bureau Park ran and in which Williams worked. For they had a special problem: New York City politics.

On January 1, 1918, Tammany Hall reclaimed control of the city. Patronage came first. Hermann Biggs, the pioneer who had built the department, had left a year earlier to become state health commissoner; Biggs had been untouchable because he had treated a top Tammany leader who had protected the entire department during prior Tammany administrations. His successor was not untouchable. Mayor John Hylan replaced him two weeks after taking control. But most jobs in the Department of Health were not patronage positions, so to create vacancies Tammany began to smear the best municipal health department in the world. Soon Hylan demanded the firing of division chiefs and the removal of highly respected physicians on the advisory board.

Even the new Tammany-appointed health

commissioner balked at that and resigned, leaving the department leaderless. The mayor was standing on the sidewalk outside City Hall when a crony introduced Royal Copeland to him, said he was a loyal Tammany man, and suggested the mayor name him the new health commissioner. But Copeland, dean of a homeopathic medical school, was not even an M.D.

Nonetheless the mayor agreed to appoint him. The three men then climbed the steps to his office, and Copeland was sworn in.

The best municipal public health department in the world was now run by a man with no belief in modern scientific medicine and whose ambitions were not in public health but in politics. If Tammany wanted vacancies to fill with loyalists, that is what he would give them. (Copeland once explained his loyalty to Tammany in simple terms: "Man is a social animal and cannot work without cooperation. Organization is a necessity and my organization is Tammany." A few years later Tammany would repay his loyalty by carrying him to the United States Senate.) So he continued the machine's efforts to disassemble the department. One of the best division heads was first threatened with criminal charges, and when that failed, he was hauled to a civil-service hearing on charges of "neglect of duty, inefficiency, and incompetency."

Park had run the department's laboratory division since 1893, had never involved himself in politics, and was himself untouchable. He continued to do excellent science in the midst of this turmoil; soon after Avery and Cole and others at Rockefeller developed their serum against Types I and II pneumococcus, Park developed a procedure for "typing" the pneumococcus so simple that any decent laboratory could perform it within thirty minutes, allowing nearly immediate use of the right serum for treatment.

But now he had to defend the department. He helped organize a defense, and the defense became national. Criticism rained down on Tammany from the city, the state, from Baltimore, Boston, Washington. Welch and nearly every major figure in medicine attacked Tammany. Rupert Blue, the head of the U.S. Public Health Service, publicly called upon the mayor to desist.

Tammany backed off, and Copeland embarked on a public relations campaign to repair the damage to himself and his "organization," relying on patriotism to stifle criticism. By late summer the frenzy had died down, but what had been the best public health department in the world was demoralized. The internationally respected director of the Bureau of Public Health Education resigned. The deputy commissioner of health, in office twenty years, resigned, and the mayor replaced him with his personal physician.

On September 15, New York City's first influenza death occurred. By then the disease had long since begun leaking out of the army and navy bases into the civilian population of Massachusetts.

In two polio epidemics in the preceding decade, public health officials had all but closed down the city. But now Copeland did nothing. Three days later, as hospitals began filling with influenza cases, he made influenza and pneumonia reportable diseases, while simultaneously stating that "other bronchial diseases and not the so-called Spanish influenza are said to be responsible for the illness of the majority of persons who were reported to be ill with influenza. . . ."

A few days more and even Copeland could no longer deny reality. People could see disease all about them. Finally he warned, "The health department is prepared to compel patients who may be a menace to the community to go to hospitals." He also assured all concerned "that the disease is not getting away from the control of the health department but is decreasing."

Park knew better. As a student in Vienna in 1890 he had watched that influenza pandemic kill one of his professors and wrote, "We mourn for him and for ourselves." And for several months now he and others in his laboratory had followed the progress of the disease. He was well aware of the transformation of the **City of Exeter** into a floating morgue and of serious cases in July and August on ships arriving in New York harbor. Those cases did one good thing:

they relieved the laboratory of political pressure and allowed him and it to concentrate on work.

In late August he and Anna Williams began devoting all their energies to the disease. In mid-September they were called to Camp Upton in Long Island. The disease had just reached there, and few deaths had occurred—yet—but already a single barracks, filled with soldiers from Massachusetts, had two thousand cases.

Park and Williams had collaborated now for a quarter of a century, and they complemented each other perfectly. He was a quiet brown-eyed man with a somewhat reserved, even aristocratic, bearing. He had a claim to the social elite; his father's ancestors arrived in America in 1630, his mother's in 1640. He also felt a calling. Three great-aunts had been missionaries and were buried in Ceylon, a cousin to whom he was very close became a minister, and Park himself had considered becoming a medical missionary.

He had a serious purpose and curiosity per se did not drive that purpose. His seeking of knowledge in the laboratory served his purpose only to the extent, as he saw it, that it served God's purpose. He donated his salary as professor of bacteriology at New York University to the laboratory, or at least into the hands of some of his professional workers who struggled on city salaries. He also involved himself directly with patients, often working the diphtheria wards at the city-run Willard Parker Hospital across the street from his laboratory. The hospital was a new, gleaming place, thirty-five iron bedsteads to each ward, with water closets and bathtubs of marble with porcelain lining, the polished hardwood floors washed every morning with a 1:1,000 solution of bichloride of mercury, the same solution in which patients themselves bathed at discharge and admission.

Methodical, somewhat stolid, he was a master bureaucrat in the best sense of the word; he had run the health department's Bureau of Laboratories for decades and had always looked for ways to make the system work. What drove him was the desire to bring laboratory research to patients. He was a pragmatist. Goethe observed that one searches where there is light. Some scientists try to create new light to shine on problems. Park was not one such; his forte was making exhaustive explorations with existing light.

It was his and Williams's work that had led to mass production of inexpensive diphtheria antitoxin. It was his work that had marked America's acceptance as a scientific equal of Europe, when that international conference had endorsed his views on tuberculosis over Koch's. His scientific papers were exact if not quite elegant, and he matched his precision with a deeply probing and careful mind.

It was that precision, and the missionary's sense of right and wrong, that had led to his public feud over meningitis serum a few years earlier with Simon

Flexner and the Rockefeller Institute. In 1911 Park had created the Laboratory for Special Therapy and Investigation, at least in part to rival the Rockefeller Institute. He was a few years older now, but no mellower. He and Flexner remained "pretty acid" about each other, noted one scientist who knew them both well, with "no love lost between them," but despite their animosity both of them cooperated with the other whenever called upon, and neither held back information.

(This openness was a far cry from the atmosphere at some other laboratories, including the Pasteur Institute. Pasteur himself had once advised a protégé not to share information with outsiders, saying, "Keep your cadavers to yourself." When Anna Williams visited there, she was refused any information on a pneumonia antiserum until it was published, and also had to promise that after she left, she would say nothing about anything else she had seen until it was published. Even in publication Pasteur scientists did not tell everything. As Biggs wrote Park, "Marmorek has taught her how it's done—it is secret of course. In the usual way, he omitted the essential thing in his article.")

If Park was almost stolid, Anna Williams injected a certain wildness and creativity into the laboratory. She loved going up in airplanes with stunt fliers—a reckless act in pre–World War I airplanes—and loved sudden fast turns and out-of-control drops. She loved to drive and was always speeding; when traffic was stalled, she often simply pulled into the opposite side of the road and proceeded, and she had a string of traffic tickets to prove it. Once she took a mechanic's course and decided to take her Buick engine apart—but failed to put it back together. In her diary she wrote, "From my earliest memories, I was one of those who wanted to go places. When I couldn't go, I would have my dreams about going. And, such wild dreams were seldom conceived by any other child."

Despite—or more likely because of—her wildness, she had established herself as the premier woman medical scientist in America. Her achievement came at a price.

She was unhappy. She was also lonely. At the age of forty-five, she wrote, "I was told today that it was quite pathetic that I had no one particular friend." She and Park had worked together for decades but they maintained a careful distance. To her diary she confided, "There are degrees to everything, including friendship. . . . [T]here is no sentimentality about my friendships and little sentiment." Religion gave her no relief. She wanted too much from it. She told herself that Jesus knew that his anguish was momentary and that in exchange he was going to save the world. "This knowledge . . . if we were sure, oh! what would we not be willing to undergo." Of course she had no such knowledge. She could only recall "all the good things I have been taught . . . [and] act as if they were true."

Yet in the end, although jealous of those who lived a normal life, she still preferred "discontent rather than happiness through lack of knowledge." Instead she did content herself with the fact that "I have had thrills." Analyzing herself, she confided in her diary that what mattered to her more were "love of knowledge," "love of appreciation," "love of winning," "fear of ridicule," and "power to do, to think new things."

These were not Park's motives, but she and Park made a powerful combination. In science, at least, she had had thrills indeed.

She was fifty-five years old in 1918. Park was the same age. There were no thoughts of thrills on the long drive and rough roads from Manhattan to Camp Upton, even though Park indulged her and let her drive. At the camp the military doctors, knowing what was happening at Devens, begged for advice.

Park and Williams were experts on vaccine therapy. Even during the polio epidemics they had done excellent science, if only to prove the negative; Park had tried to develop but instead proved the ineffectiveness of several treatments. This time they felt hopeful; their work with streptococci and pneumococci, like that of the Rockefeller Institute's, was promising. But as yet Park and Williams had no advice to give; they could only swab the throats and nasal passages of the sick at Upton, return to their laboratory, and proceed from there.

They also got material from another source, which Williams never forgot. It was her first influenza autopsy; the body was that of, she later wrote, "a fine-looking youth from Texas" who shared her last name. She stood staring at his fine features wondering about him, wondering even if he was some distant relative, and noting, "Death occurring so quickly it left little or no marks of disease anywhere except for the lungs."

She could not have looked at his perfect form, perfect but for death, and not wondered just what the country was about to endure. The drive back to New York, the car filled with swabbings from mucosal membranes, sputum, and tissue samples of a mysterious and lethal disease, likely alternated between intense conversation and silence, conversation as they planned their experiments and silence knowing the silence of the laboratory that awaited them.

There was in fact nothing like Park's laboratory in the world. From outside on the street, Park could look up with pride on the six-story building, the floors of laboratories, knowing that his successes had built them. Entirely dedicated to diagnostic testing, production of sera and antitoxins, and medical research, his creation sat at the foot of East Sixteenth Street with the teeming wharves of the East River just beyond.

Streetcars, horse-drawn carriages, and automobiles clattered past, and the smell of manure still mixed with that of gasoline and oil. There was all the sweat and ambition and failure and grit and money of New York City, all that made the city what it was and is.

Inside the building Park oversaw a virtual industry. More than two hundred workers reported to him, nearly half of them scientists or technicians in one laboratory or another, each one with lab tables laid out in horizontal rows, gas burners in virtually constant use on each table, glassware stacked on shelves above the tables as well as filling shelves along the walls, the rooms often hissing with steam and humidity from the autoclaves used to sterilize.

No other laboratory anywhere, not in any institute, not in any university, not sponsored by any government, not run by any pharmaceutical company, had the combination of scientific competence, epidemiological and public health expertise, and ability to carry out directed research—to focus all resources on one question and not be deflected from that search no matter how enticing or important a finding might be—intent on immediate practical results.

His laboratory could also function in extreme crisis. It had done so before: preventing outbreaks of cholera and typhoid, triumphing over diphtheria, helping in meningitis epidemics. It had done so not only in New York City but all over the country; when requested, Park had sent teams to fight outbreaks of disease elsewhere.

And one other ability made the department unique. If a solution was found, it could produce serum and vaccines in industrial quantities as quickly as—and of better quality than—any drug manufacturer in the world. Indeed, it had been so successful making antitoxins that drug makers and city physicians had combined to use all their political power to limit that production. But now Park could quickly gear back up. Because of the assignment to produce serum for the army, he had just quadrupled the number of horses he could infect and then bleed.

So it was not surprising that soon after Park returned from Camp Upton, he received a telegram from Richard Pearce, head of the National Research Council's section on medicine. Pearce was grabbing at any information he could get from the French, the British, even the Germans, and distributing it to investigators everywhere. He was also breaking the questions about influenza into pieces and asking each of a handful of investigators to focus on a single piece. From Park he wanted to know "the nature of the agent causing the so-called Spanish influenza . . . [and] pure cultures of the causative organism if obtainable. . . . Will your lab undertake the necessary bacteriological studies and make reports as quickly as possible to the undersigned?"

Park instantly wired back, "Will undertake work."

■   ■   ■

It was as if the laboratory had gone to war, and Park was confident of victory. As he reviewed every published and unpublished scrap of data on the disease from laboratories around the world, he was unimpressed and dismissed most of it with near contempt. Certain his lab could do better, believing that others' sloppiness at least partly contributed to their failure to understand the disease, he laid extraordinarily ambitious plans. In addition to finding the pathogen, in addition to finding a vaccine or serum or both, in addition to producing that drug in huge quantities, in addition to communicating to others the precise procedures to follow so they could produce it, he intended still more. He intended to make the most thorough study of any disease outbreak ever, selecting a large sample of people and, as many of them inevitably became ill, monitoring them through the most sophisticated possible laboratory and epidemiological means. The workload would be enormous, but he believed that his department could handle it.

But within days, almost within hours, the disease began to overwhelm the department. Park had already compensated for the loss of labor to the war by analyzing every system and maximizing efficiency (installing, for example, a vacuum pump that in fifteen minutes could fill three thousand tubes with individual vaccine doses), and even changing accounting methods. But now, as influenza struck first one janitor or technician or scientist at a time, then four at a time, then fifteen at a time, the laboratory reeled. Not so long before, when the Health Department had tracked a typhus outbreak to ground, four of his workers had died of typhus—most likely from laboratory infection. Now people in Park's own lab were again sick, some dying.

Influenza had humbled him, and quickly. He abandoned both his arrogance about the work of others and his own ambitious plans. Now he was trying to get just one thing right, the important thing. **What was the pathogen?**

Meanwhile, the world seemed to shift underfoot. To Park and Williams and to others in other laboratories racing to find an answer, it must have seemed as if they could see this great catastrophe approaching but had to remain frozen in place, all but incapable of doing anything to defeat or avoid it. It was almost as if one's foot were caught under rocks in a tidal pool while the tide came in—the water rising to the knees, to the waist, one sucking in a deep breath, then doubling over to try to pry one's foot loose and straightening to feel the water at one's neck, the swell of a wave passing over one's head. . . .

New York City was panicking, terrified.

Copeland tried to reassure the public by announcing a strict quarantine, though no quarantine was actually implemented. There were literally hundreds of thousands of people sick simultaneously, many of them desperately sick. The death toll ultimately reached thirty-three thousand for New York City alone, and that understated the number considerably, since statisticians later arbitrarily stopped counting people as victims of the epidemic even though people were still dying of the disease at epidemic rates—still dying months later at rates higher than anywhere else in the country.

It was impossible to get a doctor, and perhaps more impossible to get a nurse. Reports came in that nurses were being held by force in the homes of patients too frightened and desperate to allow them to leave. Nurses were literally being kidnapped. It did not seem possible to put more pressure on the laboratory. Yet more pressure came.

The pressure pushed Park to abandon more than his ambitious plans. He had always been meticulous, had never compromised, had built much of his scientific reputation on exposing the flawed work of others, always moving forward carefully, basing his own experiments upon well-established premises and with as few assumptions as possible. "On the basis of experimental facts," he had always said, "we are justified in . . ."

Now Park had no leisure for justification. If he was to have any impact on the course of the epidemic he would have to guess—and guess right. So those in his laboratory would, he reported, "study closely only the more dominant types that were demonstrated by our procedure. . . . We recognized that our methods . . . did not take into account . . . heretofore undescribed organisms that might have an etiologic relationship to these infections."

The laboratory had only two constants. One was an endless supply of samples, of swabbings, blood, sputum, and urine from live patients and organs from the dead. "We had plenty of material, I am sorry to say," Williams observed laconically.

And they had their routine. Only the need to keep to discipline saved the laboratory from utter chaos. There was nothing even faintly exciting about this work; it was pure tedium, and pure boredom. And yet every step involved contact with something that could kill, and every step involved passion. Technicians took sputum samples from patients in the hospital and immediately—they could not wait even an hour, or bacteria from the patient's mouth could penetrate into the sputum and contaminate it—began working with it. The steps began with "washing": placing each small lump of balled mucus in a bottle of sterile water, removing it and repeating the process five times, then breaking up the mucus, washing it more, passing a platinum loop—a thin circle of platinum, like something one uses to blow bubbles—through it to transfer it to a test tube, taking another loop and repeating the step half a dozen times. Each step took time, time while people died, but they had no choice. They needed each step, needed to dilute the bacteria to prevent too many colonies from growing in the same medium. Then they took more time, more steps, isolating each of these growths.

Everything mattered. The most tedious tasks mattered. Washing glassware mattered. Contaminated glassware could ruin an experiment, waste time, cost lives. In the course of this work, 220,488 test tubes, bottles, and flasks would be sterilized. Everything mattered, and yet no one knew who would report to work each day, who would not—and who would suddenly be carried across the street to the hospital—and if someone failed to come into work it was nearly impossible to keep track of such simple jobs as removing growing cultures from incubators.

There were dozens of ways to grow bacteria but often only one way to grow a particular kind. Some grow only without oxygen, others only with it in plentiful supply. Some require alkaline media, others acid. Some are extremely delicate, others stable.

Every step, every attempt to grow the pathogen, meant effort, and effort meant time. Every hour incubating a culture meant time. They did not have time.

Four days after accepting the task from Pearce, Park wired, "The only results so far that are of real importance have been obtained in two fatal cases, one a man coming from Brooklyn Navy Yard and one a doctor from the naval hospital in Boston. Both developed an acute septic pneumonia and died within a week of the onset of the first infection. In both cases the lungs showed a beginning pneumonia and in smears very abundant streptococci. . . . There were absolutely no influenza bacilli in either of the lungs."

The failure to find the "influenza bacillus" maddened Park. His best hope to produce a vaccine or serum would be to find a known pathogen, and the most likely suspect was the one Pfeiffer had named **Bacillus influenzae.** Pfeiffer had been and still was confident it caused the disease. Park would not hesitate to rule **B. influenzae** out if he did not find good evidence for it, but he had the utmost respect for Pfeiffer. Working in these desperate circumstances, he wanted to confirm rather than reject Pfeiffer's work. He wanted the answer to be Pfeiffer's bacillus. That would give them a chance, a chance to produce something that saved thousands of lives.

B. influenzae was a particularly difficult bacteria to isolate. It is tiny, even by the standards of bacteria, and usually occurs singly or in pairs rather than in large groups. It requires particular factors, including blood, in culture medium for it to grow. It grows only within a very narrow range of temperatures, and its colonies are minute, transparent, and without structure. (Most bacteria form distinctive colonies with a particular shape and color, distinctive enough that they can sometimes be identified just by looking at the colony in the same way that some ants can be identified by the form of their anthill.) **B. influenzae** grows only on the surface of the medium, since it depends heavily upon oxygen. It is also difficult to stain, hence difficult to see under the microscope. It is an easy target to miss unless one is specifically looking for it and unless one uses excellent technique.

While others in the lab searched for other organisms, Park asked Anna Williams to concentrate on finding Pfeiffer's. Anna Williams found it. She found it constantly. Ultimately, once she perfected her technique, she would find it in 80 percent of all samples from the Willard Parker Hospital, in every single sample from the Marine Hospital, in 98 percent of the samples from the Home for Children.

As much as Park wanted Williams to be right, he would not let his desire corrupt his science. He went a step further, to "the most delicate test of identity . . . agglutination."

"Agglutination" refers to a phenomenon in which antibodies in a test tube bind to the antigen of the bacterium and form clumps, often large enough to be visible to the naked eye.

Since the binding of antibodies to an antigen is **specific,** since the antibodies to the influenza bacillus will bind to only that bacterium and to no other, it is a precise confirmation of identity. The agglutination tests proved without doubt that Williams had found Pfeiffer's influenza bacillus.

Less than a week after first reporting his failure to find it, Park wired Pearce that **B. influenzae** "would seem to be the starting point of the disease." But he was well aware that his methods had been less than thorough, adding, "There is of course the possibility that some unknown filterable virus may be the starting point."

The report had consequences. Park's laboratory began the struggle to produce an antiserum and vaccine to Pfeiffer's bacillus. Soon they were culturing liters and liters of the bacteria, transporting it north, and injecting it into the horses on the Health Department's 175-acre farm sixty-five miles north of the city.

But the only way to know for certain that **B. influenzae** caused the disease was to follow Koch's postulates: isolate the pathogen, use it to re-create the disease in an experimental animal, and then re-isolate the pathogen from the animal. The bacillus did kill laboratory rats. But their symptoms did not resemble influenza.

The results, suggestive as they were, did not fully satisfy Koch's postulates. In this case the necessary experimental animal was man.

Human experiments had begun. In Boston, Rosenau and Keegan were already trying to give the disease to volunteers from a navy brig.

None of the volunteer subjects had yet gotten sick. One of the doctors conducting the study did. In fact he died of influenza. In a scientific sense, however, his death demonstrated nothing.

CHAPTER TWENTY-FOUR

WHILE PARK TRIED to produce an antiserum or vaccine against the disease in New York, Philadelphia was already approaching collapse. Its experience would soon be echoed in many cities around the country.

There Paul Lewis was searching for the answer as well. Few, including Park, were more likely to find it. The son of a physician, Lewis grew up in Milwaukee, went to the University of Wisconsin, and finished his medical training at Penn in 1904. Even before leaving medical school he knew he intended to spend his life in the laboratory, and he quickly acquired both a pedigree and a well-deserved reputation. He started as a junior investigator working on pneumonia under Welch, Osler, Biggs, and several others who comprised the Rockefeller Institute's Board of Scientific Advisers. Lewis impressed them all. Most impressed was Theobald Smith, one of the world's leading bacteriologists, for whom Lewis then worked in Boston. Later Smith recommended Lewis to Simon Flexner, saying that Harvard lacked the resources to allow Lewis to develop fully and that "[h]is heart lies in research."

From Smith there could come no higher compliment. Lewis deserved it. He seemed born for the laboratory. At least that was the only place where he was happy; he loved not only the work itself but the laboratory environment, loved disappearing into the laboratory and into thought. "Love" was not too strong a word; his passions lay in the lab. At Rockefeller, Lewis had started off pursuing his own ideas, but when a polio epidemic erupted, Flexner asked him to work with him on it. He agreed. It was a perfect match. Their polio work was a model combination of speed and good science. They not only proved that polio was a viral disease, still considered a landmark finding in virology, but they developed a vaccine that protected monkeys from polio 100 percent of the time. It would take nearly half a century to develop a polio vaccine for humans. In the course of this research Lewis became one of the leading experts in the world on viruses.

Flexner pronounced Lewis "one of the best men in the country, . . . a very gifted fellow." That may have been an understatement. Richard Shope worked closely with him in the 1920s, knew many of the world's best scientists (including Flexner, Welch, Park, Williams, and many Nobel laureates)—and himself became a member of the National Academy of Sciences. He called Lewis the smartest man he ever knew. Joseph Aronson, a prize-winning University of Pennsylvania scientist who had also done research at the Pasteur Institute, named his son after Lewis and, like Shope, said Lewis was the brightest man he had ever met.

When the war began, Pearce, the National Research Council official, told Lewis what he told only four or five other scientists in the country: to expect to be asked "for special service in connection with epidemic disease."

Lewis was ready. He received a navy commission and told Flexner he had "no onerous routine duties." His laboratory abilities were far more important. He was still cooperating with Cole and Avery on the development of pneumonia serum, and he was also, as he told Flexner, experimenting with dyes "as regards their capacity to inhibit the growth" of the bacteria that cause tuberculosis. The idea that dyes might kill bacteria was not original with him, but he was doing world-class work in the area and his instincts were right about its importance. Twenty years later a Nobel Prize would go to Gerhard Domagk for turning a dye into the first antibiotic, the first of the sulfa drugs.

But now the city did not need laboratory

breakthroughs that deepened understanding. It needed instant successes. Lewis had reached his conclusions about polio with tremendous speed—roughly a year, and they had been both sound and pioneering conclusions. But now he had only weeks, even days. Now he was watching bodies literally pile up in the hospital morgue at the Navy Yard, in the morgues of civilian hospitals, in undertaking establishments, in homes.

He remembered Flexner's work on meningitis during an epidemic of that disease. Flexner had solved that problem and the success had made the reputation of the Rockefeller Institute. Knowing that Flexner had succeeded then made a solution to this seem possible. Perhaps Lewis could do the same.

He considered whether a filter-passing organism caused influenza. But to look for a virus Lewis would have to look in darkness. That was science, the best of science—at least to look into the gloaming was—but he was not now engaged only in science. Not right now. He was trying to save lives **now.**

He had to look where there was light.

First, light shone on a kind of blunt-force use of the immune system. Even if they could not find the pathogen, even if they could not follow normal procedures and infect horses with the pathogen and then prepare the blood from horses, there was one animal that was suffering from the disease that was scorching its way across the earth. That animal was man.

Most people who contracted the disease survived. Even most people who contracted pneumonia survived. It was quite possible that their blood and their serum held antibodies that would cure or prevent disease in others. Lewis and Flexner had had some success using this approach with polio in 1910. In Boston, Dr. W. R. Redden at the navy hospital also remembered, as he reported, "the experimental evidence presented by Flexner and Lewis with convalescent serum from poliomyelitis." Now Redden and a colleague drew blood from those who had survived an influenza attack, extracted the serum, and injected it into thirty-six pneumonia patients in a row, beginning October 1. This was not a scientific experiment with controls, and in a scientific sense the results proved nothing. But by the time they reported the results in the October 19 **JAMA,** thirty patients had recovered, five were still undergoing treatment, and only one had died.

Experiments began in Philadelphia using both the whole blood and serum of survivors of influenza as well. These too were not scientific experiments; they were desperate attempts to save lives. If there was any sign this procedure worked, the science could follow later.

Lewis let others conduct that blunt-force work. It took no truly special skills, and others could do it as well as he. He spent his time on four things. He did not do these things sequentially. He did them simultaneously, moving down different paths—setting up experiments to test each hypothesis—at the same time.

First, he tried to develop an influenza vaccine using the same methods he had used against polio. This was a more sophisticated version of the blunt-force approach of transfusing the blood or serum of influenza survivors. For he at least suspected a virus might cause influenza.

Second, he stayed in the laboratory following a shimmer of light. As Park had reasoned, so Lewis reasoned. Research could find bacteria. Pfeiffer had already pointed an accusing finger at one bacillus. Lewis and everyone in his laboratories were working hours and days without relief, taking only a few hours off for sleep, running procedure after procedure—agglutination, filtration, transferring culture growths, injecting laboratory animals. His team too searched for bacteria. They took more swabs from the throats and noses of the first victims, exposed the medium to it, and waited. They worked intensively, twenty-four hours a day in shifts, and then they waited, frustrated by the time it took bacteria to grow in the cultures, frustrated by the number of cultures that became contaminated, frustrated by everything that interfered with their progress.

In the first fifteen cases, Lewis found no **B. influenzae.** Ironically, the disease had exploded so quickly, spreading to hospital staff, that Lewis had little except sputum samples to work with: "The hospitals were so depleted [of staff] . . . I have had no autopsy material" except from four "badly decomposed" bodies, almost certainly too long dead to be of any use.

Then, like Park and Williams, Lewis adjusted his techniques and did begin to find the bacillus regularly. He gave this information to Krusen, the health commissioner. The **Inquirer** and other newspapers, desperate to say something positive, declared that he had found the cause of influenza and "armed the medical profession with absolute knowledge on which to base their campaign against the disease."

Lewis had no such absolute knowledge, nor did he believe he had it. True, he had isolated **B. influenzae.** But he had also isolated a pneumococcus and a hemolytic streptococcus. Some instinct pointed him another direction. He began third and fourth lines of inquiry. The third involved shifting his dye experiments from trying to kill tuberculosis bacteria to trying to kill pneumococci.

But death surrounded him, enveloped him. He turned his attention back to helping produce the only thing that might work **now.** After the emergency, if anything seemed to work he could always return to the laboratory and do careful, deliberate experimentation to understand it and prove its effectiveness.

So he chose as his targets the bacteria he and others had found. From the first instant he had seen the dying sailors, he had known he would have to begin work on it **now.** For even if he had guessed right, even if what he was doing could succeed, it would take time to succeed. So, in his laboratory and in other laboratories around the city, the investigators no longer investigated. They simply tried to produce. There was no certainty that anything they produced would work. There was only hope.

He started by preparing medium using beef peptone broth with blood added, and then growing cultures of the pathogens they had isolated from cases—**B. influenzae,** Types I and II of the pneumococcus, and hemolytic streptococcus. He personally prepared small batches of vaccine including these organisms and gave it to sixty people. Of those sixty, only three people developed pneumonia and none died. A control group had ten pneumonias and three deaths.

This seemed more than just promising. It was not proof. Many factors could explain the results, including random chance. But he could not wait for explanations.

His laboratory had no ability to produce the immense quantities of vaccine needed. It required an industrial operation. They needed vats to grow these things in, not petri dishes or laboratory flasks. They needed vats like those in a brewery.

He handed off this task to others in the city, including those who ran the municipal laboratory. It would take time to grow enough for tens of thousands of people.

The whole process, even in its most accelerated state, would take at least three weeks. And it would take time once they made the vaccine to administer it to thousands and thousands of people in a series of injections of increasing doses spaced several days apart. In all that time, the disease would be killing.

Meanwhile, Lewis began work on still a fifth line of inquiry, making a serum that could cure the disease. This work was trickier. They could make a vaccine with a shotgun approach, combining several organisms and protecting against all of them. (Today vaccines against diphtheria, pertussis—whooping cough—and tetanus are combined in a single shot; a single shot protecting against measles, mumps, and rubella is routinely given to children; and today's flu shots contain vaccines against several subtypes of influenza viruses, while the anti-pneumonia vaccine is a direct descendant of the work done at the Rockefeller Institute in 1917.

A serum had to aim at only one specific target; if it worked at all, it would work only against a single organism. To make a serum that worked, Lewis would have to pick a single target. If he had to aim at a single target, he had to choose the bacillus Pfeiffer had discovered, **B. influenzae.** It was still by far the most likely cause of the disease.

Developing a serum against this organism would likely be difficult. While Lewis was still at the Rockefeller Institute, Flexner himself had tried to do this in collaboration with Martha Wollstein.

Wollstein—a fine scientist, although Flexner never treated her with the respect he gave to others—had experimented with **B. influenzae** almost continuously since 1906. But Flexner and she had made no progress whatsoever. They had not only failed to develop a serum that could help man; they had failed to cure any laboratory animals.

Lewis never understood precisely where Flexner had gone wrong in that attempt, although it certainly would have been the subject of many talks in the famous lunchroom where solutions to so many scientific problems were suggested. Now he had no opportunity to think deeply about the problem, think all the way through it, come up with a hypothesis with explanatory power, and test it.

Lewis could only hope that Flexner failed because his technique was faulty. That was quite possible. Flexner had sometimes been a little sloppy in the laboratory. He had once even conceded, "Technically, I am not well-trained in the sense of meticulous and complete accuracy."

So now Lewis hoped some technical error—perhaps in the preparation of the medium, perhaps in too rough a usage for the killed bacteria, perhaps somewhere else—accounted for Flexner's problems. It might have. For example, many years later a young graduate student entered a laboratory and saw a renowned Harvard professor at the sink washing glassware while his technician was performing a complex task at the workbench. The student asked

him why the technician was not washing the glassware. "Because," the professor replied, "I always do
the most important part of the experiment, and in
this experiment the most important thing is the
cleanliness of the glassware."

Lewis turned all his attention in effect to washing
the glassware, to the most mundane tasks, making certain there would no mistakes in the work
itself, at the same time applying any knowledge
about Pfeiffer's bacillus that had been learned since
Flexner's failure.

Lewis knew full well that little of what he was
doing was good science. It was all, or nearly all, based
on informed guesswork. He only worked harder.

As he worked, the society about him teetered on
the edge of collapse.

CHAPTER TWENTY-FIVE

WHEN WELCH had first seen autopsies of victims at Devens he had walked out of the morgue and made three calls: to a Harvard pathologist, asking him to conduct further autopsies; to Gorgas's office, warning of the coming of an epidemic; and to Oswald Avery at the Rockefeller Institute, asking him to get on the next train from New York. He hoped Avery could identify the pathogen killing the men at Devens.

Avery immediately left his own lab, walked the few blocks home for a change of clothes, then went to Grand Central, that magnificent and uplifting building. For the length of his train ride through the Connecticut countryside, through the teeming train stations of New Haven, Providence, and

Boston, up to Devens, he began to prepare, reviewing the best approaches to this problem.

Welch had told him of his concern that, despite clinical symptoms that looked like influenza, this might be a new disease. Avery's first step would still be to look for the presence of **B. influenzae,** everyone's chief suspect as the cause of influenza. Avery knew a fair amount about Pfeiffer's bacillus, including that it was exceptionally difficult to grow and that its chemistry made it difficult to stain and hence see in a smear under the microscope. The chemistry and metabolism of the bacteria interested him. He wondered how to make it grow better, how to make it easier to find, how to make it easier to identify. For he always did everything, down to washing the glassware, with precision and discipline.

Late that afternoon Avery arrived at the camp and immediately began laboratory tests. He was all but impervious to the chaos about him, impervious to the bodies of young men lying naked or in bloody sheets he had to step over—as Welch, Cole, Vaughan, Russell, and the others of that party had—to reach the autopsy room.

From the first he encountered difficulties, getting puzzling results from the Gram test. In this test, bacteria are stained with crystal violet, treated with iodine, washed with alcohol, and then stained again with a contrasting dye. Bacteria retaining the violet color are called "Gram-positive." Those that do not are "Gram-negative." The result of the Gram test is comparable to a witness identifying an assailant as white or black; the answer simply eliminates some possible suspects.

Unlike other investigators, Avery found no Gram-negative bacteria. **B. influenzae** is Gram-negative. The test eliminated **B. influenzae** as even a possibility. It eliminated all Gram-negative bacteria as possibilities. He repeated the experiment; again he found no Gram-negative bacteria, none at all.

Avery soon solved this particular puzzle. He discovered that all the liquid in the laboratory bottles labeled "alcohol" was actually water. Soldiers had apparently drunk the alcohol and replaced it with water. When he got alcohol, the test results came in as expected. He found Gram-negative bacteria.

Now he began his hunt in earnest. He began it with dead bodies, those of the men who had died most recently, some of whom so recently that their bodies remained warm to the touch. He felt the soggy sponginess of the still-warm lungs and respiratory tract with his gloved hands, seeking out areas of the most obvious infection from which to cut tissue samples, dipping into pockets of pus, seeking the organism responsible for the killing. Perhaps he was a little afraid, this tiny man surrounded by dead young soldiers, but he had courage and he was not hunting rabbits. He had no interest in hunting rabbits.

Smears across slides turned up several possible

pathogens, all of them potential killers. He needed to know which one did the killing.

He stayed at Devens long enough to grow cultures of bacteria. Like Park and Lewis, Avery had initial difficulty but began to find Pfeiffer's bacillus. He discovered it in twenty-two of thirty dead soldiers and gave Welch his results. Meanwhile Burt Wolbach, the Harvard pathologist whom Welch had also asked to help at Devens, made a stronger statement: "Every case showed the influenza bacillus, in many instances pure cultures from one or more lobes. . . . Mixed cultures, usually pneumococcus, where bronchial dilation was marked. . . . Pure cultures of influenza bacillus in the more recent stages and therefore usually in the upper lobes." In an article in **Science,** another respected investigator also wrote, "The causative agent is believed to be the bacillus of Pfeiffer."

On September 27, Welch, Cole, and Victor Vaughan wired the surgeon general from Devens, "It is established that the influenza at Camp Devens is caused by the bacillus of Pfeiffer."

But it was not so established, at least not to Avery. Although he respected Wolbach, not to mention Park, Williams, and Lewis, all of whom were reaching the same conclusion at about the same time, he based conclusions only upon his own findings. And his findings did not convince him yet. In seven of the autopsies he found no sign of any bacterial invasion whatsoever, despite the devastation of the lungs. Also, although he found potentially lethal bacteria without any sign of Pfeiffer's in only a single instance, in roughly half the cases he was finding both Pfeiffer's and other organisms, including the pneumococcus, hemolytic streptococcus, and staphylococcus aureus, which although a lethal organism rarely caused pneumonia.

He could interpret these findings several ways. They might mean that Pfeiffer's **B. influenzae** did not cause the disease. But that was only one possible conclusion. Pfeiffer's might well be the cause of the disease, and, after it infected the victim, other bacteria took advantage of a weakened immune system to follow its lead. This would not be unusual. Finding several pathogens might even actually strengthen the case for Pfeiffer's. Pfeiffer's grew poorly in laboratory cultures whenever other bacteria, especially the pneumococcus or hemolytic streptococcus, were also present. So its existence at all in cultures with these other organisms might indicate that **B. influenzae** had been present in enormous numbers in the victim.

Methodically he ran through all this in his mind. By early October, he was back at Rockefeller hearing reports from dozens of other investigators around the country and the world that they too were finding the influenza bacillus. But there were also reports of failures to find **B. influenzae.** It would be easy to dismiss the failures to find it as failures of technique; Pfeiffer's was after all one of the most

difficult organisms to grow. Still, Avery's own findings alone left too many unanswered questions for
him to reach a conclusion, crisis or not. Unlike Park,
Williams, and Lewis, Avery was not ready to reach
even a tentative conclusion. Yes, Pfeiffer's might
cause influenza. Oh yes it might. But he was not
convinced. From Avery came no reports of finding
influenza's cause, no phone calls or telegrams that
he was sending cultures with which to infect horses
and produce serum or vaccine.

He was pushing himself harder than he ever had
at Devens—and he always pushed hard. He ate in
the laboratory, ran dozens of experiments simultaneously, barely slept, bounced ideas by telephone off
Rosenau and others. He bore into his experiments
like a drill, breaking them apart and examining
every fractured crack in the data for a clue. But if he
pushed himself to work, he would not push himself
toward a conclusion.

He was not convinced.

Oswald Avery was different. Pressure troubled
him less than having to force the direction of his
work, and that he could not pursue the trail wherever it led, could not move at his own pace, could
not take the time to **think.** Make-do solutions
were foreign to his nature. He worked on the vertical. He dove deeply into a thing, to the deepest
depths, following down the narrowest pathways
and into the tiniest openings, leaving no loose ends.

In every way his life was vertical, focused, narrow, controlled.

He prepared . . . **everything,** wanting to control every effect. Even the drafts of his rare talks show marks denoting what words to emphasize, where to change the tone of his voice, where to use nuance. Even in casual conversation it sometimes seemed each word, indeed each hesitation, was carefully prepared, weighed, and perhaps staged. His personal office, adjacent to his laboratory, reflected focus as well. René Dubos, a prominent scientist, called it "small and bare, as empty as possible, without the photographs, mementos, pictures, unused books, and other friendly items that usually adorn and clutter a work place. The austerity symbolized how much he had given up all aspects of his life for the sake of utter concentration on a few chosen goals."

For in digging deep, Avery did not wish to be disturbed. He was not rude or unkind or ungenerous. Far from it. Young investigators who worked under him uniformly became his most loyal admirers. But he burrowed in, deeper and deeper into the world of his own making, a world—however narrow—that he could define and over which exert some control.

But narrow did not mean small. There was nothing small about his thinking. He used information like a springboard, a jumping-off point that allowed his mind to roam freely, indeed to race freely—even carelessly—to speculate. Colin MacLeod, like Dubos a brilliant Avery protégé, said that whenever an experiment yielded unexpected information Avery's "imagination was now fired. . . . He would explore theoretical implications exhaustively."

Dubos put it another way. He believed Avery uncomfortable in and possibly incapable of handling the chaos of social interaction. But he believed Avery comfortable with and capable of confronting the chaos of nature. Avery could do so because of his "uncanny sense of what was truly important" and "imaginative vision of reality. . . . He had the creative impulse to compose those facts into meaningful and elegant structures. . . . His scientific compositions had, indeed, much in common with artistic creations which do not imitate actuality but transcend it and illuminate reality."

Years after the pandemic, Avery's colleague and friend Alphonse Dochez received the Kober Medal, an award Avery himself had received earlier. In a tribute, Avery described Dochez's work ethic. He could have been describing his own: "[R]esults . . . are not random products of chance observations. They are the fruit of years of wise reflection, objective thinking, and thoughtful experimentation. I have never seen his laboratory desk piled high with Petri dishes and bristling with test tubes like a forest wherein the trail ends and the searcher becomes lost in dense thickets of confused thought. . . . I have never known him to engage in purposeless rivalries or competitive research. But often have I seen him sit calmly, lost in thought, while all around him others with great show of activity were flitting about like particles in Brownian motion; then, I have watched him rouse himself, smilingly saunter to his desk, assemble a few pipettes, borrow a few tubes of media, perhaps a jar of ice, and then do a simple experiment which answered the question."

But now, in the midst of a killing epidemic, everything and everyone around him—including even the pressure from Welch—shouldered thought aside, shouldered perspective and preparation aside, substituting for it what Avery so disdained: Brownian motion—the random movement of particles in a fluid. Others hated influenza for the death it caused. Avery hated it for that, too, but for a more personal assault as well, an assault upon his integrity. He would not yield to it.

When Avery experimented, a colleague said, "His attitude had many similarities with the hunter in search of his prey. For the hunter, all the components—the rocks, the vegetation, the sky—are fraught with information and meanings that enable him to become part of the intimate world of his prey." Avery had a hunter's patience. He could lie in wait for an hour, a day, a week, a month, a season. If the prey mattered enough, he could wait through an entire season and then another and then another. But he did not simply wait; he wasted not a single hour, he plotted, he observed, he learned. He learned his prey's escape routes and closed them off; he found better and better vantage points; he bracketed the field through which the prey passed and kept tightening that field until, eventually, the prey had to pass through a noose. And he could lay traps: studying pneumococci by scratching it into the skin, for example, where the immune system could easily control the infection, but which still gave him the opportunity to experiment with the bacteria outside a test tube. He advised, "Whenever you fall, pick up something." And he often said, "Disappointment is my daily bread. I thrive on it."

He would not be rushed. There was pressure on him, pressure on everyone. But he would not be rushed. At Rockefeller he was hardly the only one devoting all his energies to influenza. Martha Wollstein, who had years before collaborated with Flexner on an unsuccessful effort to develop a serum for Pfeiffer's, was searching for antibodies in the blood of recovered patients. Dochez was making an intensive study of throats. Many others were working on the disease. But they had made little progress. Rufus Cole reported to Gorgas's office in mid-October, "We have been compelled to take care of the cases of influenza arising in the Hospital and Institute and these patients have occupied all of our space." Because of the time treating the patients took, he added, "I do not think we can add very much, so far, to the knowledge concerning the disease."

Everywhere the pressure was intense. Eugene

Opie, another Hopkins product who was now a lieutenant colonel on the army's pneumonia commission, had been at Camp Pike in Arkansas when the epidemic broke out. He had gone there because, during the measles epidemic, Pike had had the highest rate of pneumonia of any cantonment in the country. Now of course his orders were to work entirely on influenza. Frederick Russell, speaking for Gorgas, demanded "daily . . . a statement of your findings, as you interpret them." Every **day** he was to report. If he found anything that gave the faintest hint of progress, Gorgas wanted to know it—instantly—so it could be shared. Opie would find no shortage of experimental material. Camp Pike held sixty thousand troops. At the crest of the epidemic thirteen thousand of them would be hospitalized simultaneously.

Investigators struggled to find something— anything—that could help, that could contain the explosion. Though no one had found anything certain, in Philadelphia following Lewis's methods, in New York following Park's, in Chicago following those developed at the Mayo Clinic, laboratories were producing enough vaccines and serum for hundreds of thousands and perhaps millions of people, while from Boston a huge and much-publicized shipment of vaccine was rushed across the country to San Francisco. On October 3, Gorgas's office in Washington offered all headquarters personnel the antipneumococcal vaccine that Cole and Avery had such hopes for, the one vaccine that had been tested—and with such success—that spring at Camp Upton.

Even in the midst of this death, this pressure, Avery would not be rushed. More and more reports came in that investigators around the world could not find the influenza bacillus. This in itself proved nothing. It was almost a test of a bacteriologist's skill to grow Pfeiffer's in the laboratory. At Camp Dodge in Iowa, for example, bacteriologists found Pfeiffer's **B. influenzae** in only 9.6 percent of the autopsied cases. An official army report blamed them: "The low incidence was undoubtedly due to poor technique in handling cultures. . . . [B]acteriologic methods . . . of this camp . . . were not to be depended upon." The laboratory chief at Camp Grant, whom Welch himself had pronounced "excellent" just three months before the epidemic struck, found Pfeiffer's bacillus in only six of 198 autopsies. Even so, his own report said, "We are inclined to take the stand that this study does not prove the lack of association between the Pfeiffer's bacillus and the epidemic owing to the irregular technique followed."

Perhaps that was the case, perhaps technical errors prevented those at Dodge and Grant and elsewhere from identifying the bacillus. Or perhaps Pfeiffer's was not present to be identified.

In his usual methodical way Avery took the step most likely to settle the question. There was no drama to this step. He poured his energies into perfecting the tool, to find ways to make it easier to grow **B. influenzae.** If he succeeded, then everyone could learn whether the inability to find the bacillus was because of incompetence or the absence of the bacteria.

He filled his laboratory with petri dishes, prepared the culture media in dozens of different ways, isolated the different factors, and observed in which dishes the bacteria seemed to grow best. Then he pushed each element that seemed to encourage growth. A hypothesis lay behind each individual experiment. He had learned, for example, that the pneumococcus inhibited the growth of Pfeiffer's. So he wanted to prevent any pneumococci from growing. He already knew as much about the chemistry and metabolism of the pneumococcus as did any person living. He added a chemical, sodium oleate, to the medium to block pneumococcal growth. It worked. In cultures with sodium oleate the pneumococcus did not grow, and Pfeiffer's grew better.

Over a period of weeks he made significant progress. Pfeiffer's also required blood in the culture medium to grow, which was not so unusual. But blood serum inactivated the sodium oleate. So he centrifuged out only red blood cells and used them. And his experiments suggested that blood added to the culture at roughly body temperature inhibited growth. Avery found that **heated** blood, adding blood to media at nearly 200 degrees Fahrenheit, allowed the **B. influenzae** to flourish.

He promptly published the recipe for his preparation, which became known as "chocolate agar," in the **Journal of the American Medical Association,** writing, "It is possible that technical difficulties in the isolation and growth of this microorganism may be in part responsible for the discordant results obtained in different laboratories. . . . The use of this medium has led to an increase in positive findings of B. influenzae in actual cases of the disease and in convalescents."

With this information any reasonably competent scientist could grow and identify the bacteria. At least now they would know that if Pfeiffer's was not found it was because it was not there.

Avery himself still would not be rushed, would not discuss a conclusion he was not yet ready to support. But based on Avery's work Cole told Russell, "I feel less and less inclined to ascribe the primary infection to the influenza bacilli—although that possibility cannot be excluded until the real cause of the infection is demonstrated. . . . I am very hopeful that the anti-pneumococcus vaccination can be pushed rapidly. While the anti-influenzal vaccination"—by this he meant vaccine against **B. influenzae**—"seems to me still doubtful we have very good evidence that the anti-pneumococcus vaccination is going to prove to be of a great help." He added, "It seems to me the influenza epidemic gives an opportunity for developing this in a way that could not have otherwise been done."

There was nothing easy about making either the antipneumococcus serum, which in tests had just cured twenty-eight of twenty-nine patients suffering infection with Type I pneumococcus, or the vaccine. It took two months to prepare the vaccine properly, two months of a difficult process: making 300-liter batches of broth—and the pneumococci themselves dissolved too often in ordinary broth, which meant adding chemicals that later had to be removed—concentrating it, precipitating some of it out with alcohol, separating out the additives, standardizing it. Avery and other Rockefeller investigators did make one important advance in production: by adjusting the amount of glucose in the media they increased the yield tenfold. But they could still move only twenty-five liters a day through centrifuges. It mocked the need.

In the meanwhile the killing continued.

■ Part VIII
THE TOLLING OF THE BELL

CHAPTER TWENTY-SIX

WHILE SCIENCE was confronting nature, society began to confront the effects of nature. For this went beyond the ability of any individual or group of individuals to respond to. To have any chance in alleviating the devastation of the epidemic required organization, coordination, implementation. It required leadership and it required that institutions follow that leadership.

Institutions are a strange mix of the mass and the individual. They abstract. They behave according to a set of rules that substitute both for individual judgments and for the emotional responses that occur whenever individuals interact. The act of creating an institution dehumanizes it, creates an arbitrary barrier between individuals.

Yet institutions are human as well. They reflect the cumulative personalities of those within them, especially their leadership. They tend, unfortunately, to mirror less admirable human traits, developing and protecting self-interest and even ambition. Institutions almost never sacrifice. Since they live by rules, they lack spontaneity. They try to order chaos not in the way an artist or scientist does, through a defining vision that creates structure and discipline, but by closing off and isolating themselves from that which does not fit. They become bureaucratic.

The best institutions avoid the worst aspects of bureaucracy in two ways. Some are not really institutions at all. They are simply a loose confederation of individuals, each of whom remains largely a free agent whose achievements are independent of the institution but who also shares and benefits from association with others. In these cases the institution simply provides an infrastructure that supports the individual, allowing him or her to flourish so that the whole often exceeds the sum of the parts. (The Rockefeller Institute was such an institution.) Other institutions avoid the worst elements of bureaucracy by concentrating on a clearly defined purpose. Their rules have little to do with such procedural issues as a chain of command; instead rules focus on how to achieve a particular result, in effect offering guidance based on experience. This kind of institution even at its best can still stultify creativity, but such institutions can execute, can do a routine thing efficiently. They resemble professionals trying to do their jobs and duty; they accomplish their tasks.

In 1918 the institution of the federal government had more force than it had ever had—and in some ways more force than it has had since. But it was aiming all that force, all its vital energy, in another direction.

The United States had entered the war with little preparation in April 1917, and mobilizing the country took time. By the summer of 1918, however, Wilson had injected the government into every facet of national life and had created great bureaucratic engines to focus all the nation's attention and intent on the war.

He had created a Food Administration to control and distribute food, a Fuel Administration to ration coal and gasoline, a War Industries Board to oversee the entire economy. He had taken all but physical control over the railroads and had created a federally sponsored river barge line that brought commerce back to life on the Mississippi River, a commerce that had been killed by competition from those railroads. He had built many dozens of military installations, each of which held at least tens of thousands of soldiers or sailors. He had created industries that made America's shipyards teem with hundreds of thousands of laborers launching hundreds of ships, dug new coal mines to produce coal for the factories that weaned America's military from British and French weapons and munitions—for, unlike in World War II, America was no arsenal of democracy.

He had created a vast propaganda machine, an internal spy network, a bond-selling apparatus extending to the level of residential city blocks. He had even succeeded in stifling speech, in the summer of 1918 arresting and imprisoning—some for prison terms longer than ten years—not just radical labor leaders and editors of German-language newspapers but powerful men, even a congressman.

He had injected the government into American life in ways unlike any other in the nation's history. And the final extension of federal power had come only in the spring of 1918, after the first wave of influenza had begun jumping from camp to camp, when the government expanded the draft from males between the ages of twenty-one and thirty to those between the ages of eighteen and forty-five. Only on May 23, 1918, had Provost Marshal Enoch Crowder, who oversaw the draft, issued his "work or fight" order, stating that anyone not employed in an essential industry would be drafted—an order that caused major league baseball to shorten its season and sent many ballplayers scurrying for jobs that were "essential"—and promising that "all men within the enlarged age would be called within a year." **All** men, the government had said, with orders for an estimated thirteen million to register September 12. Crowder bragged about doing "in a day what the Prussian autocracy had been spending nearly fifty years to perfect."

All this enormous and focused momentum would not be turned easily.

It would not be turned even by the prospect of peace. In mid-August, as the lethal wave of the epidemic was gathering itself, Austria had already inquired about peace terms, an inquiry that Wilson rebuffed utterly. And as the epidemic was gathering full momentum, peace was only weeks away. Bulgaria had signed an armistice on September 29. On September 30, Kaiser Wilhelm had granted parliamentary government to the German nation; that same day Ludendorff had warned his government that Germany must extend peace feelers or disaster—immediate disaster—would follow. German diplomats sent out those feelers. Wilson ignored them. The Central Powers, Germany and her allies, were simultaneously breaking off one from one another and disintegrating internally as well. In the first week of October, Austria and Germany separately sent peace feelers to the Allies, and on October 7, Austria delivered a diplomatic note to Wilson formally seeking peace on any terms Wilson chose. Ten days later—days of battle and deaths—the Austrian note remained unanswered.

Earlier Wilson had spoken of a "peace without victory," believing only such a peace could last. But now he gave no indication that the war would soon be over. Although a rumor that the war had ended sent thrills through the nation, Wilson quickly renounced it. Nor would he relent. He was not now fighting to the death; he was fighting only to kill. **To fight you must be brutal and ruthless,** he had said. **Force!** he had demanded. **Force to the utmost! Force without stint or limit! The righteous and triumphant Force which shall make Right the law of the world, and cast every selfish dominion down in the dust.**

Reflecting his will, there was no letup in the ferocity and wrath of the Liberty Loan rallies, no letup in the frenzied pressure to produce in coal mines and shipyards, no letup among editorials or for that matter news stories exhorting people to insist upon total and complete German capitulation. Especially within the government itself, there was no letup. Instead Wilson pressed, pressed with all his might—and that meant all the nation's might—for total victory.

If Wilson and his government would not be turned from his end even by the prospect of peace, they would hardly be turned by a virus. And the reluctance, inability, or outright refusal of the American government to shift targets would contribute to the killing. Wilson took no public note of the disease, and the thrust of the government was not diverted. The relief effort for influenza victims would find no assistance in the Food Administration or the Fuel Administration or the Railroad Administration.

From neither the White House nor any other senior administration post would there come any leadership, any attempt to set priorities, any attempt to coordinate activities, any attempt to deliver resources.

The military, especially the army, would confront the virus directly. Gorgas had done all that he could have, all that anyone could have, to prepare for an emergency. But the military would give no help to civilians. Instead it would draw further upon civilian resources.

The same day that Welch had stepped out of the autopsy room at Devens and called Gorgas's office, his warning had been relayed to the army chief of staff, urging that all transfers be frozen unless absolutely necessary and that under no circumstances transfers from infected camps be made: **The deaths at Camp Devens will probably exceed 500. . . . The experience at Camp Devens may be fairly expected to occur at other large cantonments. . . . New men will almost surely contract the disease.**

Gorgas's superiors ignored the warning. There was no interruption of movement between camps whatsoever; not until weeks later, with the camps paralyzed and, literally, tens of thousands of soldiers dead or dying, did the army make any adjustments.

One man did act, however. On September 26, although many training camps had not yet seen any influenza cases at all, Provost Marshal Enoch Crowder canceled the next draft (he would also cancel the draft after this one). It had been scheduled to send one hundred forty-two thousand men to the cantonments.

It was a bold move, made despite the unquenched appetite of General John J. Pershing, in charge of the American Expeditionary Force, for men. In France, Pershing was pressing forward, earlier that same day launching a major offensive in the Meuse-Argonne region. As the Americans charged out of their trenches, the Germans shredded their ranks. General Max von Gallwitz, the commander facing them, entered into his official record, "We [have] no more worries."

Despite this, Crowder had acted immediately and likely saved thousands of lives, but he did not cancel the draft to save lives. He did so because he recognized that the disease was utterly overwhelming and creating total chaos in the cantonments. There could be no training until the disease passed. He believed that sending more draftees into this chaos would only magnify it and delay the restoration of order and the production of soldiers. In **Murder in the Cathedral,** T. S. Eliot could call it "the greatest treason: to do the right thing for the wrong reason." The men who lived because of Crowder might disagree with the poet.

But Crowder's decision and the efforts of the Gorgas-led army medical corps would be the only bright spots in the response of the federal government. Other army decisions were not such good ones. Pershing still demanded fresh troops, troops to replace those killed or wounded in battle, troops to replace those killed by or recovering from influenza, troops to replace those who simply needed relief from the line. All the Allied powers were desperate for fresh American boys.

The army had to decide whether to continue to transport soldiers to France during the epidemic. They had information about the costs. The army knew the costs well.

On September 19 the acting army surgeon general, Charles Richard—Gorgas was in Europe—wrote General Peyton March, the commander of the army, urging him that "organizations known to be infected, or exposed to the disease, be not permitted to embark for overseas service until the disease has run its course within the organization."

March acknowledged the warning from Gorgas's deputy but did nothing. The chief medical officer at the port of embarkation in Newport News, Virginia, rephrased—more emphatically—the same warning: "The condition [on a troopship] is almost that of a powder magazine with troops unprotected by previous [influenza] attack. The spark will be applied sooner or later. On the other hand with troops protected by previous attack the powder has been removed." He too was ignored. Gorgas's office urged quarantining troops heading overseas for one week before departure, or eliminating overcrowding on board. March did nothing.

Meanwhile the **Leviathan** was loading troops. Once the pride of the German passenger fleet, built as the **Vaterland,** she was the largest ship in the world and among the fastest in her class. She had been in New York when America entered the war, and her captain could not bring himself to sabotage or scuttle her. Alone among all German ships confiscated in the United States, she was taken undamaged. In mid-September, on her voyage back from France she had buried several crew and passengers at sea, dead of influenza. Others arrived in New York sick, including Assistant Secretary of the Navy Franklin Roosevelt, who was taken ashore on a stretcher, then by ambulance to his mother's home on East Sixty-fifth Street, where he stayed for weeks too ill to speak with even his closest adviser, Louis Howe, who kept in almost hourly touch with his doctors.

The **Leviathan** and, over the course of the next several weeks, other troopships would ferry approximately one hundred thousand troops to Europe. Their crossings became much like that of the train that carried three thousand one hundred soldiers from Camp Grant to Camp Hancock. They became death ships.

Although the army had ignored most of the pleadings from its own medical corps, it did remove all men showing influenza symptoms before sailing. And to contain influenza on board, troops were quarantined. Military police carrying pistols enforced the quarantine—aboard the **Leviathan,** 432 MPs did so—sealing soldiers into separate areas of the ship behind shut watertight doors, sardining them into cramped quarters where they had little to do but lie on stacked bunks or shoot craps or play poker in the creases of open space available. Fear of submarines forced the portholes shut at night, but even during the day the closed doors and the massive overcrowding made it impossible for the ventilation system to keep pace. Access to the decks and open air was limited. The sweat and smells of hundreds of men—each room generally held up to four hundred—in close quarters quickly became a stench. Sound echoed off the steel bunks, the steel floors, the steel walls, the steel ceiling. Living almost like caged animals, they grew increasingly claustrophobic and tense. But at least they were safe, they thought.

For the plan to keep men quarantined in isolated groups had a flaw. They had to eat. They went to mess one group at a time, but they breathed the same air, their hands went from mouths to the same tables and doors that other soldiers had touched only minutes before.

Despite the removal before departure of men showing influenza symptoms, within forty-eight hours after leaving port, soldiers and sailors struck down with influenza overwhelmed the sick bay, stacked one on top of the other in bunks, clogging every possible location, coughing, bleeding, delirious, displacing the healthy from one great room after another. Nurses themselves became sick. Then the horrors began.

Colonel Gibson, commander of the Fifty-seventh Vermont, wrote of his regiment's experience on the **Leviathan:** "The ship was packed . . . [C]onditions were such that the influenza could breed and multiply with extraordinary swiftness. . . . The number of sick increased rapidly, Washington was apprised of the situation, but the call for men for the Allied armies was so great that we must go on at any cost. . . . Doctors and nurses were stricken. Every available doctor and nurse was utilized to the limit of endurance. The conditions during the night cannot be visualized by anyone who had not actually seen them . . . [G]roans and cries of the terrified added to the confusion of the applicants clamoring for treatment and altogether a true inferno reigned supreme."

It was the same on other ships. Pools of blood from hemorrhaging patients lay on the floor and the healthy tracked the blood through the ship, making decks wet and slippery. Finally, with no room in sick bay, no room in the areas taken over for makeshift sick bays, corpsmen and nurses began laying men out on deck for days at a time. Robert Wallace aboard the **Briton** remembered lying on deck when a storm came, remembered the ship rolling, the ocean itself sweeping up the scuppers and over him and the others, drenching them, their clothes, their blankets, leaving them coughing and sputtering. And each morning orderlies carried away bodies.

At first the deaths of men were separated by a few hours: the log of the **Leviathan** noted, "12:45 P.M. Thompson, Earl, Pvt 4252473, company unknown died on board. . . . 3:35 P.M. Pvt O Reeder died on board of lobar pneumonia. . . ." But a week after leaving New York, the officer of the day was no longer bothering to note in the log "died on board," no longer bothering to identify the military organization to which the dead belonged, no longer bothering to note a cause of death; he was writing only a name and a time, two names at 2:00 A.M., another at 2:02 A.M., two more at 2:15 A.M., like that all through the night, every notation in the log now a simple recitation of mortality, into the morning a death at 7:56 A.M., at 8:10 A.M., another at 8:10 A.M., at 8:25 A.M.

The burials at sea began. They quickly became sanitary exercises more than burials, bodies lying next to one another on deck, a few words and a name spoken, then one at a time a corpse slipped overboard into the sea. One soldier aboard the **Wilhelmina** watched across the waves as bodies dropped into the sea from another ship in his convoy, the **Grant:** "I confess I was near to tears, and that there was tightening around my throat. It was death, death in one of its worst forms, to be consigned nameless to the sea."

•   •   •

The transports became floating caskets. Meanwhile, in France, by any standard except that of the cantonments at home, influenza was devastating troops. In the last half of October during the Meuse-Argonne offensive, America's largest of the war, more Third Division troops were evacuated from the front with influenza than with wounds. (Roughly the same number of troops were in the United States and Europe, but influenza deaths in Europe were only half those in America. The likely explanation is that soldiers at the front had been exposed to the earlier mild wave of influenza and developed some immunity to it.) One army surgeon wrote in his diary on October 17 that because of the epidemic, "Some hospitals are not even working. Evacuation 114 had no medical officer but hundreds of pneumonias, . . . dying by the score."

Shipping more men who required medical care into this maelstrom made little sense. It is impossible to state how many soldiers the ocean voyages killed, especially when one tries to count those infected aboard ship who died later on shore. But for every death at least four or five men were ill enough to be incapacitated for weeks. These men were a burden rather than a help in Europe.

Wilson had made no public statement about influenza. He would not shift his focus, not for an instant. Yet people he trusted spoke to him of the disease, spoke particularly of useless deaths on the transports. Chief among them was certainly Dr. Cary Grayson, a navy admiral and Wilson's personal physician, as he had been personal physician to Teddy Roosevelt and William Howard Taft when they were president. Highly competent and highly organized, Grayson had become a Wilson confidant who strayed into the role of adviser. (After Wilson's stroke in 1919, he would be accused of virtually running the country in concert with Wilson's wife.) He also had the confidence of and excellent relationships with Gorgas and Welch. It was likely that army medical staff had talked to Grayson, and Grayson had been urging army chief of staff General Peyton March to freeze the movement of troops to Europe. March had refused.

Grayson convinced Wilson to summon March to the White House on October 7 to discuss the issue. Late that night Wilson and March met. Wilson said, "General March, I have had representations sent to me by men whose ability and patriotism are unquestioned that I should stop the shipment of men to France until this epidemic of influenza is under control. . . . [Y]ou decline to stop these shipments."

March made no mention of any of the advice he had received from Gorgas's office. He insisted that every possible precaution was being taken. The troops were screened before embarking and the sick winnowed out. Some ships even put ashore in Halifax, Nova Scotia, those who fell seriously ill before the actual Atlantic crossing began. If American divisions stopped arriving in France, whatever the reason, German morale might soar. True, some men had died aboard ship, but, March said, "Every such soldier who has died just as surely played his part as his comrade who died in France."

The war would end in a little over a month. The epidemic had made virtually all training in cantonments impossible. A parliament—not the kaiser—had already taken over the German government and sent out peace feelers, while Germany's allies had already collapsed, capitulated, or, in the case of Austria, asked for peace on any terms Wilson dictated. But March insisted, "The shipment of troops should not be stopped for any cause."

March later wrote that Wilson turned in his chair, gazed out the window, his face very sad, then gave a faint sigh. In the end, only a single military activity would continue unaffected in the face of the epidemic. The army continued the voyages of troopships overseas.

If Wilson did nothing about influenza in the military but express concern about shipping troops to Europe, he did even less for civilians. He continued to say nothing publicly. There is no indication that he ever said anything privately, that he so much as inquired of anyone in the civilian arm of the government as to its efforts to fight the disease.

Wilson had appointed strong men to his administration, powerful men, and they took decisive actions. They dominated the nation's thought, and they dominated the nation's economy. But none of those appointees had any real responsibility for health. Surgeon General Rupert Blue, head of the United States Public Health Service, did. And Blue was not a strong man.

A square-faced man with a square thick athletic body, an amateur boxer, Blue was physically strong all right, even deep into middle age. But he was not strong in ways that mattered, in leadership. In a field that was largely new when he entered it, a field in which colleagues were cutting new paths into the wild in dozens of directions, he had broken no ground, demonstrated no professional courage, nor had he even showed real zeal. If he was by no means unintelligent, he lacked either real intellectual rigor or the creativity to ask important questions, and he had never manifested any truly special talents in or insights into public health.

As far as scientific public health issues went, the real leaders of the medical profession considered him a lightweight. Welch and Vaughan had not even trusted him to name the Public Health Service's representative to the National Research Council, and so they themselves had picked a PHS scientist they respected. Cary Grayson thought so little of him that he began to build an alternative national public health organization. (He abandoned his effort when Tammany took over the New York City Department of Health.) Blue became surgeon general simply by carrying out assigned tasks well, proving himself an adept and diplomatic maneuverer, and seizing his main chance. That was all.

After finishing his medical studies in 1892, Blue had immediately joined the Public Health Service and remained there his entire professional life. His assignments had moved him from port to port, to Baltimore, Galveston, New Orleans, Portland, New York, Norfolk, where he worked in hospitals and quarantine stations and on sanitation issues. His opportunity came with an outbreak of bubonic plague in San Francisco in 1903. Another PHS officer, a highly regarded scientist, had engaged in a running battle with local government and business leaders, who denied plague existed in the city. Blue did not prove that it did—Simon Flexner did that, demonstrating the plague bacillus in the laboratory, as part of a scientific team brought in to settle the question—but Blue did win grudging cooperation from local authorities in efforts to control the disease. This was no easy task, and he both oversaw the killing of rats and kept, according to one laudatory report, "all interests in the State . . . harmonized."

This success won him powerful friends. (He was not successful enough, however, to prevent plague spreading from rats to wild rodent populations; today plague exists in squirrels, prairie dogs, and other animals in much of the Pacific Coast and inland to Arizona, New Mexico, and Colorado.) When plague resurfaced in San Francisco in 1907 he was called back. Another success won him more powerful friends. In 1912 he rose to surgeon general. That same year Congress expanded the Public Health Service's power. From that position he pushed for national medical insurance, which the medical profession then advocated, and in 1916 he became president of the American Medical Association. In his presidential address he declared, "There are unmistakable signs that health insurance will constitute the next great step in social legislation."

Wilson did not bother to choose a new surgeon general, but when the war began he did make the Public Health Service part of the military. It had consisted chiefly of several quarantine stations that inspected incoming ships, the Marine Hospital Service, which cared for merchant seamen and some federal workers, and the Hygienic Laboratory. Now it became responsible for protecting the nation's health, if only so the nation could produce more war matériel. Blue did not grow with the job.

In advance of the epidemic, Gorgas had used all means possible to protect the millions of soldiers from disease. His counterpart Navy Surgeon General William Braisted had done little to match Gorgas, but he was supporting work by such men as Rosenau in Boston and Lewis in Philadelphia.

Blue by contrast did, literally, less than nothing; he blocked relevant research. On July 28, 1918, Blue rejected a request from George McCoy, director of the Hygienic Laboratory, for $10,000 for pneumonia research designed to complement the efforts of the Rockefeller Institute. Although Congress in 1912 had given the agency authority to study "diseases of man and conditions affecting the propagation thereof," Blue determined that McCoy's "investigation is not immediately necessary to the enforcement of the law."

Blue knew of the possibility of influenza in the United States. On August 1, the **Memphis Medical Monthly** published comments by him warning of it. Yet he made no preparations whatsoever to try to contain it. Even after it began to show evidence of lethality, even after Rufus Cole prodded his office to collect data, neither he nor his office attempted to gather information about the disease anywhere in the world. And he made no effort whatsoever to prepare the Public Health Service for a crisis.

Many of those under him were no better. The Commonwealth Pier outbreak began late in August, and by September 9 newspapers were reporting that influenza victims filled "all the hospital beds at the forts at Boston harbor," Camp Devens had thirty-five hundred influenza cases, and Massachusetts hospitals were filling with civilians. Yet the local Public Health Service officer later insisted, "The first knowledge of the existence of the disease reached this officer September 10th."

The virus had reached New Orleans on

September 4; the Great Lakes Naval Training Station on September 7; New London, Connecticut, on September 12.

Not until September 13 did the Public Health Service make any public comment, when it said, "Owing to disordered conditions in European countries, the bureau has no authoritative information as to the nature of the disease or its prevalence." That same day Blue did issue a circular telling all quarantine stations to inspect arriving ships for influenza. But even that order advised delaying infected vessels only until "the local health authorities have been notified."

Later Blue defended himself for not taking more aggressive action. **This was influenza, only influenza,** he seemed to be saying, "It would be manifestly unwarranted to enforce strict quarantine against . . . influenza."

No quarantine of shipping could have succeeded anyway. The virus was already here. But Blue's circular indicated how little Blue had done—in fact he had done nothing—to prepare the Public Health Service, much less the country, for any onslaught.

The virus reached Puget Sound on September 17.

Not until September 18 did Blue even seek to learn which regions of the United States the disease had penetrated.

On Saturday, September 21, the first influenza death occurred in Washington, D.C. The dead man was John Ciore, a railroad brakeman who had been exposed to the disease in New York four days earlier. That same day Camp Lee outside Petersburg, Virginia, had six deaths, while Camp Dix in New Jersey saw thirteen soldiers and one nurse die.

Still Blue did little. On Sunday, September 22, the Washington newspapers reported that Camp Humphreys (now Fort Belvoir), just outside the city, had sixty-five cases.

Now, finally, in a box immediately adjacent to those reports, the local papers finally published the government's first warning of the disease:

Surgeon General's Advice to Avoid Influenza
Avoid needless crowding. . . .
Smother your coughs and sneezes. . . .
Your nose not your mouth was made to breathe
    thru. . . .
Remember the 3 Cs, clean mouth, clean skin, and
    clean clothes. . . .
Food will win the war. . . . [H]elp by choosing and
    chewing your food well. . . .
Wash your hands before eating. . . .
Don't let the waste products of digestion
    accumulate. . . .
Avoid tight clothes, tight shoes, tight gloves—seek
    to make nature your ally not your prisoner. . . .
When the air is pure breathe all of it you
    can—breathe deeply.

Such generalizations hardly reassured a public that knew that the disease was marching from army camp to army camp, killing soldiers in large numbers. Three days later a second influenza death occurred in Washington; John Janes, like the first Washington victim, had contracted the disease in New York City. Also that day senior medical personnel of the army, navy, and Red Cross met in Washington to try to figure out how they could aid individual states. Neither Blue nor a representative of the Public Health Service attended the meeting. Twenty-six states were then reporting influenza cases.

Blue had still not laid plans for an organization to fight the disease. He had taken only two actions: publishing his advice on how to avoid the disease and asking the National Academy of Sciences to identify the pathogen, writing, "In view of the importance which outbreaks of influenza will have on war production, the Bureau desires to leave nothing undone. . . . The Bureau would deem it a valuable service if the Research Council arrange for suitable laboratory studies . . . as to the nature of the infecting organism."

Crowder canceled the draft. Blue still did not organize a response to the emergency. Instead, the senior Public Health Service officer in charge of the city of Washington reiterated to the press that there was no cause for alarm.

Perhaps Blue considered any further action outside the authority of the Public Health Service. Under him the service was a thoroughly bureaucratic institution, and bureaucratic in none of the good ways. Only a decade earlier he had been stationed in New Orleans, when the last yellow-fever epidemic to strike the United States had hit there, and the Public Health Service had required the city to pay $250,000—in advance—to cover the federal government's expenses in helping to fight that epidemic. Only a few weeks earlier, he had rejected the request from the service's own chief scientist for money to research pneumonia in concert with Cole and Avery at the Rockefeller Institute.

But governors and mayors were demanding help, beseeching everyone in Washington for help. Massachusetts officials in particular were begging for help from outside the state, for doctors from outside, for nurses from outside, for laboratory assistance from outside. The death toll there had climbed into the thousands. Governor Samuel McCall had wired governors for any assistance they could offer, and on September 26 he formally requested help from the federal government.

Doctors and nurses were what was needed. Doctors and nurses. And especially nurses. As the disease spread, as warnings from Welch, Vaughan, Gorgas, dozens of private physicians, and, finally, at last, Blue poured in, Congress acted. Without the delay of hearings or debate, it appropriated

$1 million for the Public Health Service. The money was enough for Blue to hire five thousand doctors for emergency duty for a month—if he could somehow find five thousand doctors worth hiring.

Each day—indeed, each hour—was showing the increasingly explosive spread of the virus and its lethality. Blue, as if suddenly frightened, now considered the money too little. He had not complained to Congress about the amount; no record exists of his having asked for more. But the same day Congress passed the appropriation, he privately appealed to the War Council of the Red Cross both for more money and for its help.

The Red Cross did not get government funds or direction, although it was working in close concert with the government. Nor was its charge to care for the public health. Yet even before Blue asked, it had already allocated money to fight the epidemic and had begun organizing its own effort to do so— and do so on a massive scale. Its nursing department had already begun mobilizing "Home Defense Nurses," fully professional nurses, all of them women, who could not serve in the military because of age, disability, or marriage. The Red Cross had divided the country into thirteen divisions, and the nursing committee chief of each one had already been told to find all people with any nursing training, not only professionals or those who had dropped out of nursing schools—for the Red Cross checked with all nursing schools—but down to and including anyone who had ever taken a Red Cross course in caring for the sick at home. It had already instructed each division to form at least one mobile strike force of nurses to be ready to go to areas most in need. And before anyone within the government sought aid, the War Council of the Red Cross had designated a "contingent fund for the purpose of meeting the present needs in coping with the epidemic of Spanish influenza." Now the council agreed instantly to authorize expenditure of far more money than was in the contingency fund.

Finally, Blue began to organize the Public Health Service as well. Doctors and nurses were what was needed, doctors and nurses. But by then the virus had spanned the country, establishing itself on the perimeter, on the coasts, and it was working its way into the interior, to Denver, Omaha, Minneapolis, Boise. It was penetrating Alaska. It had crossed the Pacific to Hawaii. It had surfaced in Puerto Rico. It was about to explode across Western Europe, across India, across China, across Africa as well.

Science, then as now a journal written by scientists for their colleagues, warned, "The epidemics now occurring appear with electric suddenness, and, acting like powerful, uncontrolled currents, produce violent and eccentric effects. The disease never spreads slowly and insidiously. Wherever it occurs its presence is startling."

October, not April, would be the cruelest month.

CHAPTER TWENTY-SEVEN

NOTHING COULD HAVE STOPPED the sweep of influenza through either the United States or the rest of the world—but ruthless intervention and quarantines might have interrupted its progress and created occasional firebreaks.

Action as ruthless as that taken in 2003 to contain the outbreak of a new disease called severe acute respiratory syndrome, SARS, could well have had effect.* Influenza could not have been contained as SARS was—influenza is far more contagious. But any interruption in influenza's spread could have had significant impact. For the virus was growing weaker over time. Simply delaying its arrival in a

* For more about SARS, see page 734.

community or slowing its spread once there—just such minor successes—would have saved many, many thousands of lives.

There was precedent for ruthless action. Only two years earlier several East Coast cities had fought a polio outbreak with the most stringent measures. Public health authorities wherever polio threatened had been relentless. But that was before the United States entered the war. There would be no comparable effort for influenza. Blue would not even attempt to intrude upon war work.

The Public Health Service and the Red Cross still had a single chance to accomplish something of consequence. By early October the first fall outbreaks and the memory of those in the spring had already suggested that the virus attacked in a cycle; it took roughly six weeks from the appearance of the first cases for the epidemic to peak and then abate in civilian areas, and from three to four weeks in a military camp with its highly concentrated population. After the epidemic abated, cases still occurred intermittently, but not in the huge numbers that overwhelmed all services. So Red Cross and Public Health Service planners expected the attack would be staggered just as the arrival of the virus was staggered, peaking in different parts of the country at different times. During the peak of the epidemic, individual communities would not be able to cope; no matter how well organized they were they would be utterly overwhelmed. But if the Red Cross and

Public Health Service could concentrate doctors, nurses, and supplies in one community when most needed, they might be able to withdraw the aid as the disease ebbed and shift it to the next area in need, and the next.

To manage this, Blue and Frank Persons, director of civilian relief and head of the new influenza committee of the Red Cross, divided the labor. The Public Health Service would find, pay, and assign all physicians. It would decide when and where to send nurses and supplies, to whom nurses would report, and it would deal with state and local public health authorities.

The Red Cross would find and pay nurses, furnish emergency hospitals with medical supplies wherever local authorities could not, and take responsibility for virtually everything else that came up, including distributing information. The Red Cross did stipulate one limit on its responsibility: it would not meet requests from military camps. This stipulation was immediately forgotten; even the Red Cross soon gave the military precedence over civilians. Meanwhile, its War Council ordered each one of its 3,864 chapters to establish an influenza committee even—indeed, especially—where the disease had not yet hit. It gave instructions on the organization of those committees, and it stated "each community should depend upon its own resources to the fullest extent."

Persons had one model: Massachusetts. There

James Jackson, the Red Cross division director for New England, had done an amazing job, especially considering that the region was struck without warning by what was originally an unknown disease. While chapters made gauze masks—the masks that would soon be seen everywhere and would become a symbol of the epidemic—Jackson first tried to supply nurses and doctors himself. When he failed, he formed an ad hoc umbrella organization including the state Council of National Defense, the U.S. Public Health Service, state and local public health authorities, and the Red Cross. These groups pooled their resources and allocated to towns as needed.

Jackson had brought in nurses from Providence, New Haven, New York, even from Halifax and Toronto. He had succeeded at least somewhat in alleviating the personnel shortage. But Massachusetts had been lucky. When the epidemic erupted there, no other locality needed help. In the fourth week of the epidemic, Jackson reported, "We have not yet reached the point where any community has been able to transfer its nurses or supplies. In Camp Devens . . . forty nurses ill there with many cases of pneumonia."

He also advised Red Cross headquarters in Washington: "The most important thing in this crisis is more workers to go into the homes quickly and aid the family. Consequently I have telegraphed to all my chapters twice regarding the mobilization of women who have had First Aid and Home Nursing training or any others who are willing to volunteer their services."

And he confided, "The Federal public health service has been . . . unable to handle adequately the entire situation. . . . [They] have not been on the job."

It was October when he sent that wire. By then everyone needed nurses, or they were about to, and they knew it. By then everyone needed doctors, or they were about to, and they knew it. And they needed resources. The biggest task remained finding doctors, nurses, and resources. They needed all three.

Even in the face of this pandemic, doctors could help. They could save lives. If they were good enough, if they had the right resources, if they had the right help, if they had time.

True, no drug or therapy could alleviate the viral infection. Anyone who died directly from a violent infection of the influenza virus itself, from viral pneumonia progressing to ARDS, would have died anyway. In 1918, ARDS had virtually a 100 percent mortality rate.

But there were other causes of death. By far the most common was from pneumonia caused by secondary bacterial infections.

Ten days, two weeks, sometimes even longer than two weeks after the initial attack by the virus, after victims had felt better, after recovery had seemed to begin, victims were suddenly getting seriously ill again. And they were dying. The virus was stripping their lungs all but naked of their immune system; recent research suggests that the virus made it easier for some kinds of bacteria to lodge in lung tissue as well. Bacteria were taking advantage, invading the lungs, and killing. People were learning, and doctors were advising, and newspapers were warning, that even when a patient seemed to recover, seemed to feel fine, normal, well enough to go back to work, still that patient should continue to rest, continue to stay in bed. Or else that patient was risking his or her life.

Half a dozen years earlier medicine had been helpless here, so helpless that Osler in his most recent edition of his classic text on the practice of medicine had still called for bleeding of patients with pneumonia. But now, for some of those who developed a secondary bacterial infection, something could be done. The most advanced medical practice, the best doctors, could help—if they had the resources and the time.

Avery, Cole, and others at the Rockefeller Institute had developed the vaccine that had showed such promising result in the test at Camp Upton in the spring, and the Army Medical School was producing this vaccine in mass quantities. Avery and Cole had also developed the serum that slashed the mortality for pneumonias caused by Types I and II pneumococcus, which accounted for two-thirds or more of lobar pneumonias in normal circumstances. These were not normal circumstances; bacteria that almost never caused pneumonia were now making their way unopposed into the lungs, growing there, and thriving there. But Types I and II pneumococci were still causing many of the pneumonias, and in those cases this serum could help.

Other investigators had developed other vaccines and sera as well. Some, like the one developed by E. C. Rosenow at the Mayo Clinic and used in Chicago, were useless. But others may have done some good.

Physicians also had other assets to call upon. Surgeons developed new techniques during the epidemic that are still in use to drain empyemas, pockets of pus and infection that formed in the lung and poisoned the body. And doctors had drugs that alleviated some symptoms or stimulated the heart; major hospitals had X-rays that could aid in diagnosis and triage; and some hospitals had begun administering oxygen to help victims breathe—a practice neither widespread nor administered nearly as effectively as it would be, but worth something.

Yet for a doctor to use these resources, any of them, that doctor had to have them—and also had to have time. The physical resources were hard to come by, but time was harder. There was no time. For that Rockefeller serum needed to be administered with precision and in numerous doses. There was no time. Not with patients overflowing wards, filling cots in hallways and on porches, not with doctors themselves falling ill and filling those cots. Even if they had resources, they had no time.

And the doctors found by the Public Health Service had neither resources nor time. Nor was it simple to find the doctors themselves. The military had already taken at least one-fourth—in some areas one-third—of all the physicians and nurses. And the army, itself under violent attack from the virus, would lend none of its doctors to civilian communities no matter how desperate the circumstances.

That left approximately one hundred thousand doctors in a labor pool to draw from—but it was a pool limited in quality. The Council of National Defense had had local medical committees secretly grade colleagues; those committees had judged roughly seventy thousand unfit for military service. Most of that number were unfit because they were judged incompetent.

The government had had a plan to identify the best of those remaining. As part of the mobilization of the entire nation, in January 1918 the Council of National Defense had created the "Volunteer Medical Service." This service tried to enlist every doctor in the United States, but it particularly wanted to track the younger physicians who were women or had a physical disability—in other words, those mostly likely to be good doctors who were not subject to and rejected by the draft.

The mass targeting succeeded. Within eight months, 72,219 physicians had joined this service. They had joined, however, only to prove their patriotism, not as a commitment to do anything real—for membership required of them nothing concrete, and they received an attractive piece of paper suitable for framing and office display.

But the plan to identify and have access to good doctors within this group collapsed. The virus was penetrating everywhere, doctors were needed everywhere, and no responsible doctor would abandon his (or, in a few instances, her) own patients in need, in desperate need. In addition, the federal government was paying only $50 a week—no princely sum even in 1918. Out of one hundred thousand civilian doctors, seventy-two thousand of whom had joined the Volunteer Medical Service, only 1,045 physicians answered the pleas of the Public Health Service. While a few were good young doctors who had not yet developed a practice and were waiting to be drafted, many of this group were the least competent or poorest trained doctors in the country. Indeed, so few doctors worked for the PHS that Blue would later return $115,000 to the Treasury from the $1 million appropriation he had considered so insufficient.

The Public Health Service sent these 1,045 doctors to places where there were no doctors at all, to places so completely devastated by the disease that any help, any help at all, was embraced. But they sent them with almost no resources, certainly without Rockefeller vaccines and serum or the training to make or administer them, certainly without X-rays, certainly without oxygen and the means to administer it. The huge caseloads overwhelmed them, weighed them down, kept them moving.

They diagnosed. They treated with all manner of materia medica. Yet in reality they could do nothing but advise. The best advice was this: stay in bed. And then the doctors moved on to the next cot or the next village.

What could help, more than doctors, were nurses. Nursing could ease the strains on a patient, keep a patient hydrated, resting, calm, provide the best nutrition, cool the intense fevers. Nursing could give a victim of the disease the best possible chance to survive. Nursing could save lives.

But nurses were harder to find than doctors. There were one-quarter fewer to begin with. The earlier refusal of the women who controlled the nursing profession to allow the training of large numbers either of nursing aides or of what came to be called practical nurses prevented the creation of what might have been a large reserve force. The plan had been to produce thousands of such aides; instead the Army School of Nursing had been established. So far it had produced only 221 student nurses and not a single graduate nurse.

Then, just before the epidemic struck, combat had intensified in France, and with it, so had the army's need for nurses. The need had in fact become so desperate that on August 1, Gorgas, just to meet existing requirements, transferred one thousand nurses from cantonments in the United States to hospitals in France and simultaneously issued a call for "one thousand nurses a week" for eight weeks.

The Red Cross was the route of supply for nurses to the military, especially the army. It had already been recruiting nurses for the military with vigor. After Gorgas's call, it launched an even more impassioned recruiting campaign. Each division, each chapter within a division, was given a quota. Red Cross professionals knew that their careers were at risk if they did not meet it. Already recruiters had a list of all nurses in the country, their jobs and locations. Those recruiters now pressured nurses to quit jobs and join the military, pressured doctors to let office nurses go, made wealthy patients who retained private nurses feel unpatriotic, pushed private hospitals to release nurses.

The drive was succeeding; it was removing from civilian life a huge proportion of those nurses mobile enough, unencumbered by family or other responsibilities, to leave their jobs. The drive was succeeding so well that it all but stripped hospitals of their workforce, leaving many private hospitals around the country so short-staffed that they closed, and remained closed until the war ended. One Red Cross recruiter wrote, "The work at National Headquarters has never been so difficult and is now overwhelming us. . . . [We are searching] from one end of the United States to the other to rout out every possible nurse from her hiding place. . . . There will be no nurses left in civil life if we keep on at this rate."

The recruiter wrote that on September 5, three days before the virus exploded at Camp Devens.

CHAPTER TWENTY-EIGHT

PHILADELPHIA STAGGERED under the influenza attack, isolated and alone. In Philadelphia no sign surfaced of any national Red Cross and Public Health Service effort to help. No doctors recruited by the Public Health Service were sent there. No nurses recruited by the Red Cross were sent there. Those institutions gave no help here.

Each day people discovered that friends and neighbors who had been perfectly healthy a week—or a day—earlier were dead. **What should I do?** People were panicked, desperate. **How long will it go on?**

The mayor, arrested in the early days of the epidemic and then himself ill, had done absolutely nothing. A review of five daily newspapers—the

Press, Inquirer, Bulletin, Public Ledger, and **North American**—did not find even a single statement about the crisis from the mayor. The entire city government had done nothing. Wilmer Krusen, head of the city health department, no longer had the confidence of anyone. Someone had to do **something.**

Paul Lewis felt the pressures, felt the death all about him. He had felt at least some pressure since the sailors from the **City of Exeter** had been dying what seemed so long ago. In early September, with the virus killing 5 percent of all Philadelphia navy personnel who showed any symptoms of influenza at all, that pressure had intensified. Since then he and everyone under him had hardly left their laboratories to go home. Finding **B. influenzae** had begun his real work, not concluded it.

Never had he been so consumed with the laboratory. He had started his experiments with the pneumococcus. He had begun to explore the possibility that a filterable virus caused influenza. He had continued to look at the influenza bacillus. He and others had developed a vaccine. He was trying to make a serum. All of these he did simultaneously. For the one thing he did not have was time. No one had time.

If Lewis had a scientific weakness, it was that he too willingly accepted guidance from those he respected. Once when he asked for more direction from Flexner, Flexner had rebuffed him, saying, "I much prefer that you arrange plans. . . . I have not planned specifically for your time, but much prefer to leave the direction of it to you." Lewis respected Flexner. He respected Richard Pfeiffer as well.

In the overwhelming majority of cases he was now finding Pfeiffer's **B. influenzae** in swabs from living patients, in autopsied lungs. He was not finding it alone, necessarily, or always. It was not certain proof, but more and more he was coming to believe that this bacterium did in fact cause disease. And, under the pressure of time, he abandoned his investigation into the possibility that a filterable virus caused influenza.

Yet he loved this. Although he hated the disease he loved this. He believed he had been born to do this. He loved working deep into the night amid rows of glassware, monitoring the growth of bacteria in a hundred flasks and petri dishes, running a dozen experiments in staggered fashion; coordinating them like the conductor of a symphony. He even loved the unexpected result that could throw everything off.

The only thing Lewis disliked about his position as head of an institute was charming the fine families of Philadelphia out of philanthropic donations, attending their parties and performing as their pet scientist. The laboratory was where he had always belonged. Now he was in it hours and hours each day. He believed he had spent too much time mixing with the fine families of Philadelphia.

In fact, those fine families of the city deserved more respect. They were about to take charge.

The writer Christopher Morley once said that Philadelphia lies "at the confluence of the Biddle and Drexel families." In 1918 that description was not far wrong.

Of all the major cities in the United States, Philadelphia had a real claim to being the most "American." It certainly had the largest percentage of native-born Americans of major cities and, compared to New York, Chicago, Boston, Detroit, Buffalo, and similar cities, the lowest percentage of immigrants. Philadelphia was not unusual in that its oldest and wealthiest families controlled the charities, the social service organizations—including the local Red Cross—and the Pennsylvania Council of National Defense. But now, with the city government all but nonexistent, it was unusual in that these families considered it their duty to use the Council of National Defense to take charge.

Nationally that organization had been the vehicle through which, before the war, Wilson had laid plans to control the economy, using it to assemble data from across the country on factories, transportation, labor, and natural resources. But each state had its own council, which were often dominated by his political enemies. Once the war started, Wilson created new federal institutions, sidestepped this organization, and it lost power. The Pennsylvania council, however, retained extraordinary, although almost entirely unofficial, influence over everything from railroad schedules to profits and wages at every large company in the state, even though it too was run by Wilson's enemies. It held this power chiefly because it was headed by George Wharton Pepper.

No one had better bloodlines. His great-great-grandfather had led the state militia in the Revolutionary War, his wife was a descendant of Benjamin Franklin, and a statue of his uncle William, who had worked closely with Welch to reform medical education and brought Flexner to the University of Pennsylvania, today sits astride the grand stairway of the Free Library in downtown Philadelphia. George Wharton Pepper had ability as well. An attorney who sat on the boards of half a dozen of the country's largest companies, he was not ruthless, but he knew how to command. An indication of his stature had come a few months earlier when he received one of three honorary degrees awarded by Trinity College in Hartford, Connecticut; his fellow honorees were J. P. Morgan and former president of the United States and soon-to-be chief justice of the Supreme Court William Howard Taft.

The Philadelphia office of the state Council of National Defense was run by Judge J. Willis Martin. His wife, Elizabeth, had organized the country's first garden club and was largely responsible for making Rittenhouse Square a green spot in the city.

She also headed the council's Women's Division as well as Emergency Aid, the most important private social agency in the city.

Nearly all the social agencies were run by women, strong women of intelligence and energy and born to a certain rank, but excluded from all pursuits beside charity. The mayor had created a committee of society women to respond to emergencies; it included Pepper's wife along with Mrs. John Wanamaker; Mrs. Edward Stotesbury, whose husband was the city's leading banker and head of Drexel & Co.; and Mrs. Edward Biddle, president of the Civic Club and whose husband was descended from Nicholas Biddle, creator of the first Bank of the United States, which to his nemesis Andrew Jackson embodied the sinister monied power of the nation. These women despised the Vare machine and had cooperated only to show unity during the war. But with city officials doing nothing whatsoever about the epidemic, the women resigned, effectively dissolving the committee. As Elizabeth Martin wrote the mayor, "Your committee has no real purpose. . . . I therefore hereby sever my connection with it."

Now, in place of the city government, Pepper, the Martins, and their colleagues summoned the heads of a dozen private organizations on October 7 to the headquarters of Emergency Aid at 1428 Walnut Street. There the women took charge, with Pepper adding his weight to theirs. To sell war bonds, they had already organized nearly the entire city, all

the way down to the level of each block, making
each residential block the responsibility of "a logical leader no matter what her nationality"—i.e., an
Irishwoman in an Irish neighborhood, an African
American woman in an African American neighborhood, and so on.

They intended to use that same organization now
to distribute everything from medical care to food.
They intended to inject organization and leadership into chaos and panic. In conjunction with the
Red Cross—which here, unlike nearly everywhere
else in the country, allowed its own efforts to be
incorporated into this larger Emergency Aid—they
also appealed for nurses, declaring, "The death toll
for one day in Philadelphia alone was greater than
the death toll from France for the whole American
Army for one day."

The state Council of National Defense had already
compiled a list of every physician in Pennsylvania,
including those not practicing. Martin's ad hoc committee beseeched each one on the list for help. The
committee had money, and access to more money,
to pay for the help. It set up a twenty-four-hour
telephone bank at Strawbridge & Clothier, which
donated use of its phone lines; newspapers and placards urged people to call "Filbert 100" twenty-four
hours a day for information and referrals. It transformed kitchens in public schools—which were
closed—into soup kitchens that prepared meals for
tens of thousands of people too ill to prepare their

own. It divided the city into seven districts and, to conserve physicians' time, dispatched them according to geography, meaning that doctors did not see their own patients.

And it became a place that volunteers could come to. Nearly five hundred people offered to use their own cars either as ambulances or to chauffeur doctors—they were supplied with green flags that gave them right-of-way over all other vehicles. The organizers of the Liberty Loan drive diverted another four hundred cars to help. Thousands of individuals called the headquarters and offered to do what was needed.

Krusen had not attended the October 7 meeting of the private groups and had been slow to act before. Now he changed. Perhaps the deaths finally changed him. Perhaps the fact that someone else was taking charge forced him to move. But he seemed suddenly not to care about the Vares, or selling war bonds, or bureaucracy, or his own power. He just wanted to stop the disease.

He ceded to the group control over all nurses, hundreds of them, who worked for the city. He seized—in violation of the city charter—the city's $100,000 emergency fund and another $25,000 from a war emergency fund and used the money to supply emergency hospitals and hire physicians, paying them double what the Public Health Service was offering. He sent those physicians to every police station in South Philadelphia, the hardest-hit section. He wired the army and navy asking that no Philadelphia physicians be drafted until the epidemic abated, and that those who had already been drafted but had not yet reported to duty be allowed to remain in Philadelphia, because "the death rate for the past week [was] the largest in records of city."

The U.S. Public Health Service still had no presence in Philadelphia and had done nothing for it. Now Rupert Blue did the only thing he would do for the city in its distress: he wired the surgeon general of the navy to "heartily endorse" Krusen's request. The deaths spoke far more loudly than Blue. The military did allow Philadelphia to keep its doctors.

Krusen also cleaned the streets. The streets of South Philadelphia literally stank of rot and excrement. Victorians had considered it axiomatic that filthy streets per se were linked to disease. The most modern public health experts—Charles Chapin in Providence, Biggs in New York, and others—flatly rejected that idea. But Dr. Howard Anders, who earlier had been ignored by the press when he warned that the Liberty Loan parade would spread influenza, was given page one by the **Ledger** on October 10 to state, "Dirty streets, filth allowed to collect and stand until, germ-laden and disease-breeding, it is carried broadcast with the first gust of wind—there you have one of the greatest causes of the terrible epidemic." Other Philadelphia doctors agreed: "The condition of the streets spreads the epidemic."

So Krusen sent trucks and men down them with their water sprays and sweepers almost daily, doing the job Vare had been paid for many times but had never done. Krusen, Emergency Aid, and the Catholic Church teamed up to do one more thing, the most important thing. They began to clear the bodies.

The corpses had backed up at undertakers, filling every area of these establishments and pressing up into living quarters; in hospital morgues overflowing into corridors; in the city morgue overflowing into the street. And they had backed up in homes. They lay on porches, in closets, in corners of the floor, on beds. Children would sneak away from adults to stare at them, to touch them; a wife would lie next to a dead husband, unwilling to move him or leave him. The corpses, reminders of death and bringers of terror or grief, lay under ice at Indian-summer temperatures. Their presence was constant, a horror demoralizing the city; a horror that could not be escaped. Finally the city tried to catch up to them.

Krusen sent police to clear homes of bodies that had remained there for more than a day, piling them in patrol wagons, but they could not keep up with the dying and fell further behind. The police wore their ghostly surgical masks, and people fled them, but the masks had no effect on the viruses, and by mid-October thirty-three policemen had died, with many more to follow. Krusen opened a "supplementary morgue" at a cold-storage plant at Twentieth and Cambridge Streets; he would open five more supplementary morgues. He begged military embalmers from the army. Pepper and Martin convinced the Brill Company, which made streetcars, to build thousands of simple boxes for coffins, and they gathered students from embalming schools and morticians from as far as 150 miles away. More coffins came by rail, guarded by men with guns.

And graves were dug. First the families of the dead picked up shovels and dug into the earth, faces streaked with sweat and tears and grit. For gravediggers would not work. The city's official annual report notes that "undertakers found it impossible to hire persons willing to handle the bodies, owing to the decomposed nature of the same." When Anna Lavin's aunt died, "They took her to the cemetery. My father took me and the boy, who also had the flu, and he was wrapped—my father carried him—wrapped in a blanket to the cemetery to say the prayer for the dead. . . . The families had to dig their own graves. That was the terrible thing."

Pepper and Martin offered ten dollars a day to anyone who would touch a corpse, but that proved inadequate, and still the bodies piled up. Seminary students volunteered as gravediggers, but they still could not keep pace. The city and archdiocese turned to construction equipment, using steam shovels to dig trenches for mass graves. Michael Donohue, an undertaker, said, "They brought a steam shovel in to Holy Cross Cemetery and actually excavated. . . .

They would begin bringing caskets in and doing the committal prayers right in the trench and they'd line them up right in, one right after another, this was their answer to helping the families get through things."

The bodies that were choking homes and lying in stacks in mortuaries were ready to go, finally, into the ground.

To collect them, Archbishop Denis Dougherty, installed in office only a few weeks earlier—later he became the first cardinal from the archdiocese— sent priests down the streets to remove bodies from homes. They joined the police and a few hardy others who were doing the same.

Sometimes they collected the bodies in trucks. "So many people died they were instructed to ask for wooden boxes and put the corpse on the front porches," recalled Harriet Ferrell. "An open truck came through the neighborhood and picked up the bodies. There was no place to put them, there was not room."

And sometimes they collected the bodies in wagons. Selma Epp's brother Daniel died: "[P]eople were being placed on these horse-drawn wagons and my aunt saw the wagons pass by and he was placed on the wagon; everyone was too weak to protest. There were no coffins in the wagon, but the people who had died were wrapped in a sort of sackcloth and placed in the wagon. One was on top of the other, there were so many bodies. They were drawn by horses and the wagons took the bodies away."

No one could look at the trucks and carts carrying bodies—bodies wrapped in cloth stacked loosely on other bodies wrapped in cloth, arms and legs protruding, bodies heading for cemeteries to be buried in trenches—or hear the keening of the mourners and the call for the dead, and not think of another plague—the plague of the Middle Ages.

Under the initial burst of energy the city seemed at first to rally, to respond with vigor and courage now that leadership and organization seemed in place.

But the epidemic did not abate. The street cleaning accomplished nothing, at least regarding influenza, and the coroner—Vare's man—blamed the increasing death toll on the ban by the state public health commissioner on liquor sales, claiming alcohol was the best treatment for influenza.

In virtually every home, someone was ill. People were already avoiding each other, turning their heads away if they had to talk, isolating themselves. The telephone company increased the isolation: with eighteen hundred telephone company employees out, the phone company allowed only emergency calls; operators listened to calls randomly and cut off phone service of those who made routine calls. And the isolation increased the fear. Clifford Adams recalled, "They stopped people from communicating, from going to churches, closed the schools, . . . closed all the saloons. . . . Everything was quiet."

Very likely half a million—possibly more—Philadelphians fell sick. It is impossible to be more precise: despite the new legal requirement to report cases, physicians were far too busy to do so, and by no means did physicians see all victims. Nor did nurses.

People needed help and, notwithstanding the efforts of Emergency Aid, the Council of National Defense, and the Red Cross, help was impossible to get.

The **Inquirer** blared in headlines: "Scientific Nursing Halting Epidemic."

But there were no nurses.

The log of a single organization that sent out nurses noted without comment, "The number of calls received, 2,955, and calls not filled, 2,758." **Calls received, 2,955; calls not filled, 2,758.** And the report pointed out that even those numbers—93 percent of the calls unfilled, 7 percent filled—was an understatement, since the "'calls received' . . . does not represent the number of nurses required, for many of the calls were for several nurses to go to one place; two of the calls being for 50 nurses each."

Those nurses were needed, needed desperately. One study of fifty-five flu victims who were not hospitalized found that not one was ever seen by a nurse or a doctor. Ten of the fifty-five patients died.

■   ■   ■

It now seemed as if there had never been life before the epidemic. The disease informed every action of every person in the city.

The archbishop released nuns for service in hospitals, including Jewish hospitals, and allowed them to violate rules of their orders, to spend overnight away from the convent, to break vows of silence. They did not make a dent in the need.

By then many of those who had earlier rushed forward to volunteer had withdrawn. The work was too gruesome or too arduous, or they themselves fell ill. Or they too were frightened. Every day newspapers carried new and increasingly desperate pleas for volunteers.

On the single **day** of October 10, the epidemic alone killed 759 people in Philadelphia. Prior to the outbreak, deaths from all causes—all illnesses, all accidents, all suicides, and all murders—averaged 485 a **week.**

Fear began to break down the community of the city. Trust broke down. Signs began to surface of not just edginess but anger, not just finger-pointing or protecting one's own interests but active selfishness in the face of general calamity. The hundreds of thousands sick in the city became a great weight dragging upon it. And the city began to implode in chaos and fear.

Pleas for volunteers became increasingly plaintive, and increasingly strident. Under the headline "Emergency Aid Calls for Amateur Nurses," newspapers printed Mrs. Martin's request: "In this desperate crisis the Emergency Aid calls on all . . . who are free from the care of the sick at home and who are in good physical condition themselves . . . to report at 1428 Walnut Street as early as possible Sunday morning. The office will be open all day and recruits will be enrolled and immediately sent out on emergency work."

Krusen declared, "It is the duty of every well woman in the city who can possibly get away from her duties to volunteer for this emergency."

But who listened to him anymore?

Mrs. Martin called for help from "all persons with two hands and a willingness to work."

Few came.

On October 13, the Bureau of Child Hygiene publicly begged for neighbors to take in, at least temporarily, children whose parents were dying or dead. The response was almost nil.

Elizabeth Martin pleaded, "We simply must have more volunteer helpers. . . . We have ceased caring for ordinary cases of the disease. . . . These people are almost all at the point of death. Won't you ask every able-bodied woman in Philadelphia whether or not she has any experience in nursing to come to our help?"

Few replied.

The need was not only for medical care but for care itself. Entire families were ill and had no one to feed them. Krusen pleaded publicly: "Every healthy woman in the city who can possibly be spared from her home can be used in fighting the epidemic."

But by now the city had heard enough pleas, and had withdrawn into itself. There was no trust, no trust, and without trust all human relations were breaking down.

The professionals had continued to do their duty. One physician at Philadelphia Hospital, a woman, had said she was certain she was going to die if she remained, and fled. But that was a rarity. Doctors died, and others kept working. Nurses died, and others kept working. Philadelphia Hospital had twenty student nurses from Vassar. Already two had died, but the others "have behaved splendidly. . . . They say they will work all the harder."

Other professionals did their jobs as well. The police performed with heroism. Before the epidemic they had too often acted like a private army that owed its allegiance to the Vare machine. They had stood almost alone in the country against the navy's crackdown on prostitution near military facilities. Yet when the police department was asked for four volunteers to "remove bodies from beds, put them in coffins and load them in vehicles," when the police knew that many of those bodies had decomposed, 118 officers responded.

But citizens in general had largely stopped responding. Many women had reported to an emergency hospital for a single shift. They had never returned. Some had disappeared in the middle of a shift. On October 16 the chief nurse at the city's largest hospital told an advisory council, "[V]olunteers in the wards are useless. . . . [T]hey are afraid. Many people have volunteered and then refused to have anything to do with patients."

The attrition rate even where volunteers did not come into contact with the sick—in the kitchens, for example—was little better. Finally Mrs. Martin turned bitter and contemptuous: "Hundreds of women who are content to sit back . . . had delightful dreams of themselves in the roles of angels of mercy, had the unfathomable vanity to imagine that they were capable of great spirit of sacrifice. Nothing seems to rouse them now. They have been told that there are families in which every member is ill, in which the children are actually starving because there is no one to give them food. The death rate is so high and they still hold back."

Susanna Turner, who did volunteer at an emergency hospital and stayed, who went there day after day, remembered, "The fear in the hearts of the people just withered them. . . . They were afraid to go out, afraid to do anything. . . . You just lived from day to day, did what you had to do and not think about the future. . . . If you asked a neighbor for help, they wouldn't do so because they weren't taking any chances. If they didn't have it in their house, they weren't going to bring it in there. . . . You didn't have the same spirit of charity that you do with a regular time, when someone was sick you'd go and help them, but at that time they helped themselves. It was a horror-stricken time."

The professionals were heroes. The physicians and nurses and medical students and student nurses who were all dying in large numbers themselves held nothing of themselves back. And there were others. Ira Thomas played catcher for the Philadelphia Athletics. The baseball season had been shortened by Crowder's "work or fight" order, since sport was deemed unnecessary labor. Thomas's wife was a six-foot-tall woman, large-boned, strong. They had no children. Day after day he carried the sick in his car to hospitals and she worked in an emergency hospital. Of course there were others. But they were few.

"Help out?" said Susanna Turner. "They weren't going to risk it, they just refused because they were so panic-stricken, they really were, they feared their relatives would die because so many did die—they just dropped dead." No one could buy things. Commodities dealers, coal dealers, grocers closed "because the people who dealt in them were either sick or afraid and they had reason to be afraid."

During the week of October 16 alone, 4,597 Philadelphians died from influenza or pneumonia, and influenza killed still more indirectly. That would be the worst week of the epidemic. But no one knew that at the time. Krusen had too often said the peak had passed. The press had too often spoken of triumph over disease.

Even war industries, despite the massive propaganda campaigns telling workers victory depended upon their production, saw massive absences. Anna Lavin said, "We didn't work. Couldn't go to work. Nobody came into work." Even those who weren't sick "stayed in. They were all afraid."

Between 20 and 40 percent of the workers at Baldwin Locomotive, at Midvale Steel, at Sun Shipbuilding, each plant employing thousands, were absent. At virtually every large employer, huge percentages of employees were absent. Thirty-eight hundred Pennsylvania Railroad workers were out. The Baltimore and Ohio Railroad set up its own emergency hospitals along its tracks. The entire transportation system for the mid-Atlantic region staggered and trembled, putting in jeopardy most of the nation's industrial output.

The city was breaking apart. Orphans were already becoming a problem. Social service agencies that tried but fell short in their efforts to deliver food and transport people to hospitals began to plan for the orphans as well.

CHAPTER TWENTY-NINE

WHAT WAS HAPPENING in Philadelphia was happening everywhere. In that densely populated city, Isaac Starr had counted not a single other car on the road in his twelve-mile drive from the city center home. And on the other side of the world, the same experiences—the deaths, the terror, the reluctance to help, the silence—were replicated. Alfred Hollows was in Wellington, New Zealand: "I was detailed to an emergency hospital in Abel Smith Street. It was a hall . . . staffed by women volunteers." They had sixty beds. "Our death rate was really quite appalling—something like a dozen a day—and the women volunteers just disappeared, and weren't seen again. . . . I stood in the middle of Wellington City at 2 P.M. on a weekday afternoon, and there was not a soul to be seen—no trams running, no shops open, and the only traffic was a van with a white sheet tied to the side, with a big red cross painted on it, serving as an ambulance or hearse. It was really a City of the Dead."

In New York City at Presbyterian Hospital, each morning on rounds Dr. Dana Atchley was astounded, and frightened, to see that, for what seemed to him an eternity, every single patient—every one—in the critical section had died overnight.

The federal government was giving no guidance that a reasoning person could credit. Few local governments did better. They left a vacuum. Fear filled it.

The government's very efforts to preserve "morale" fostered the fear, for since the war began, morale—defined in the narrowest, most shortsighted fashion—had taken precedence in every public utterance. As California senator Hiram Johnson said in 1917, "The first casualty when war comes is truth."

It was a time when the phrase "brisk fighting" meant that more than 50 percent of a unit was killed or wounded; a time when the memoir of a nurse at the front, published in 1916, was withdrawn by her publisher after America entered the war because she told the truth about gruesome conditions; a time when newspapers insisted, "There is plenty of gasoline and oil for automobile use," even while gas stations were ordered to close "voluntarily" at night and Sundays and a national campaign was being waged against driving on "gasless Sundays"—and police pulled over motorists who did not "voluntarily" comply.

Newspapers reported on the disease with the same mixture of truth and half-truth, truth and distortion, truth and lies with which they reported everything else. And no national official ever publicly acknowledged the danger of influenza.

But in the medical community, deep concern had arisen. Welch of course had initially feared that it might be a new disease, although he soon recognized it as influenza. Many serious pathologists in Germany and Switzerland considered the possibility of plague. The director of the laboratory at Bellevue Hospital wondered in the **Journal of the American Medical Association** if "the world is facing" not a pandemic of an extraordinarily lethal influenza but instead a mild version of plague, noting, "The similarity of the two diseases is enforced by the clinical features, which are remarkably alike in many respects, and by the pathology of certain tissues other than the lungs."

What pathologists said in medical journals physicians muttered to one another, while laymen and -women watched a husband or wife turning almost black. And a great chill settled over the land, a chill of fear.

Meanwhile, William Park sat in his laboratory amid petri dishes, dissected mice, and cultures of pathogens, and quoted Daniel Defoe's **Journal of the Plague Year:** "In the whole the face of things, as I say, was much altered; sorrow and sadness sat upon every face; and though some parts were not yet over-whelmed, yet all looked deeply concerned; and as we saw it apparently coming on, so every one looked on himself and his family as in the utmost danger."

As terrifying as the disease was, the press made it more so. They terrified by making little of it, for what officials and the press said bore no relation-ship to what people saw and touched and smelled and endured. People could not trust what they read. Uncertainty follows distrust, fear follows uncer-tainty, and, under conditions such as these, terror follows fear.

When influenza struck in Massachusetts, the nearby **Providence Journal** reported; "All the hos-pital beds at the forts at Boston harbor are occupied by influenza patients. . . . There are 3,500 cases at Camp Devens." Yet the paper asserted, "Such re-ports may actually be reassuring rather than alarm-ing. The soldier or sailor goes to bed if he is told to, just as he goes on sentry duty. He may not think he is sick, and he may be right about it, but the mili-tary doctor is not to be argued with and at this time the autocrat is not permitting the young men under his charge to take any chance."

As the virus infested the Great Lakes Naval Training Station, the Associated Press reported,

"To dispel alarm caused throughout the country by exaggerated stories . . . Captain W. A. Moffat, commandant, gave out the statement today that while there are about 4,500 cases of the disease among the 45,000 blue jackets at the station, the situation in general is much improved. The death rate has been only one and one half per cent, which is below the death rate in the east."

That report was meant to reassure. It is unlikely that it did so, even though it omitted the fact that quarantines were being imposed upon the training station, the adjoining Great Lakes Aviation Camp, and the nearby Fort Sheridan army cantonment, which, combined, amounted to the largest military concentration in the country. And military authorities of course assured both civilians nearby as well as the country at large that "the epidemic is on the wane."

Over and over in hundreds of newspapers, day after day, repeated in one form or another was Rupert Blue's reassurance: "There is no cause for alarm if precautions are observed."

They read the words of Colonel Philip Doane, the officer in charge of health at the country's shipyards, who told the Associated Press, "The so-called Spanish influenza is nothing more or less than old-fashioned grippe."

Those words, too, ran in hundreds of newspapers. But people could smell death in them. Then they came to know that death.

Immediately outside Little Rock lay Camp Pike, where eight thousand cases were admitted to the hospital in four days and the camp commandant stopped releasing the names of the dead. "You ought to see this hospital tonight," wrote Francis Blake, one of four members of the army's pneumonia commission at Pike. "Every corridor and there are miles of them with a double row of cots and every ward nearly with an extra row down the middle with influenza patients and lots of barracks about the camp turned into emergency infirmaries and the Camp closed. . . . There is only death and destruction."

The camp called upon Little Rock for nurses, doctors, linens, and coffins, all while within the city the **Arkansas Gazette** declared in headlines, "Spanish influenza is plain la grippe—same old fever and chills."

Outside Des Moines, Iowa, at Camp Dodge, also, influenza was killing hundreds of young soldiers. Within the city a group called the Greater Des Moines Committee, businessmen and professionals who had taken charge during the emergency, included the city attorney who warned publishers—and his warning carried the sting of potential prosecution—"I would recommend that if anything be printed in regard to the disease it be confined to simple preventive measures—something constructive rather than destructive." Another committee member, a physician, said, "There is no question that by a right attitude of the mind these people have kept themselves from illness. I have no doubt that many persons have contracted the disease through fear. . . . Fear is the first thing to be overcome, the first step in conquering this epidemic."

The Bronxville, New York, **Review Press and Reporter** simply said nothing at all about influenza, absolutely nothing, until October 4, when it reported that the "scourge" had claimed its first victim there. It was as if the scourge had come from nowhere; yet even the paper recognized that, without its printing a word, everyone knew of it. And even as the epidemic rooted itself in Bronxville, the paper condemned "alarmism" and warned, "Fear kills more than the disease and the weak and timid often succumb first."

Fear, that was the enemy. Yes, fear. And the more officials tried to control it with half-truths and outright lies, the more the terror spread.

The Los Angeles public health director said, "If ordinary precautions are observed there is no cause for alarm." Forty-eight hours later he closed all places of public gatherings, including schools, churches, and theaters.

The Illinois superintendent of public health had—privately, in a confidential meeting with other Illinois public health officials and Chicago politicians—suggested they close all places of business to save lives. Chicago Public Health Commissioner John Dill Robertson violently rejected that suggestion as unwarranted and very damaging to morale. In his official report on the epidemic, he bragged, "Nothing was done to interfere with the morale of the community." Later he explained to other public health professionals, "It is our duty to keep the people from fear. Worry kills more people than the epidemic."

The mortality rate at Cook County Hospital for all influenza cases—not just those who developed pneumonia—was 39.8 percent.

Literary Digest, one of the largest-circulation periodicals in the country, advised, "Fear is our first enemy."

"Don't Get Scared!" was the advice printed in virtually every newspaper in the country, in large, blocked-off parts of pages labeled "Advice on How to Avoid Influenza."

The **Albuquerque Morning Journal** issued instructions on "How to Dodge 'Flu.'" The most prominent advice was the usual: "Don't Get Scared." Almost daily it repeated, "Don't Let Flu Frighten You to Death," "Don't Panic."

In Phoenix the **Arizona Republican** monitored influenza from a distance. On September 22 it declared "Dr. W. C. Woodward of the Boston Health Department assumed an optimistic attitude tonight. . . . Dr. Woodward said the increase in cases today was not alarming." At Camp Dix "the camp medical authorities asserted they have the epidemic under control." And the paper noted the first influenza deaths in New Orleans two days before the New Orleans daily newspaper the **Item** mentioned any death in the city.

But after the first case appeared in Phoenix itself, the **Republican** fell silent, utterly silent, saying nothing about influenza anyplace in the country until the news was such that it could no longer keep silent. Its competitor the **Gazette** competed in reassurances, quoting local physician Herman Randall saying, "Ten people sit in the same draught, are exposed to the same microbes. Some will suffer and perhaps die, while the others go scot free. . . . The people during an epidemic who are most fearful are usually, on the testimony of physicians, the first ones to succumb to the disease." And in Phoenix, even after the war ended, the "Citizens' Committee" that had taken over the city during the emergency continued to impose silence, ordering that "merchants of the city refrain from mentioning the influenza epidemic directly or indirectly in their advertising."

Meanwhile, Vicks VapoRub advertisements in hundreds of papers danced down the delicate line of reassurance while promising relief, calling the epidemic, "Simply the Old-Fashioned Grip Masquerading Under a New Name."

Some papers experimented in controlling fear by printing almost nothing at all. In Goldsboro, North Carolina, recalls a survivor, "The papers didn't even want to publish the lists of names [of the dead]. . . . The information about who was dying had to come up through the grapevine, verbally, from one person to the other."

A historian studying Buffalo County, Nebraska, expressed puzzlement that "[t]he county newspapers manifested a curious reticence regarding the effects of influenza, perhaps most evident in the **Kearney Hub.** It may be surmised that the editors played down the severity of the problem to discourage the onset of general panic in the face of what was a thoroughly frightening situation." As late as December 14 that paper was telling people not to "get panicky," telling them city officials were "not inclined to be as panicky as a great many citizens."

How could one not get panicky? Even before people's neighbors began to die, before bodies began to pile up in each new community, every piece of information except the newspapers told the truth. Even while Blue recited his mantra—**There is no cause for alarm if proper precautions are taken**—he was calling upon local authorities to "close all public gathering places, if their community is threatened with the epidemic. This will do much toward checking the spread of the disease." Even if Colonel Doane had said **Influenza is nothing more or less than old-fashioned grippe,** newspapers also quoted him saying, "Every person who spits is helping the Kaiser."

And even while Blue and Doane, governors and mayors, and nearly all the newspapers insisted that this was influenza, only influenza, the Public Health Service was making a massive effort to distribute advice—nearly useless advice. It prepared ready-to-print plates and sent them to ten thousand newspapers, most of which did print them. It prepared—the Red Cross paid for printing and distribution—posters and pamphlets, including six million copies of a single circular. Teachers handed them out in schools; bosses stacked them in stores, post offices, and factories; Boy Scouts stuffed them into tens of thousands of doorways; ministers referred to them on Sundays; mailmen carried them to rural free delivery boxes; city workers pasted posters to walls.

But a Public Health Service warning to avoid crowds came too late to do much good, and the only advice of any real use remained the same: that those who felt sick should go to bed immediately and stay there several days after all symptoms disappeared. Everything else in Blue's circulars was so general as to be pointless. Yet all over the country, newspapers printed again and again: "Remember the 3 Cs, clean mouth, clean skin, and clean clothes. . . . Keep the bowels open. . . . Food will win the war. . . . [H]elp by choosing and chewing your food well."

The **Journal of the American Medical Association** knew better. It dismissed the public reassurances and warned, "The danger to life from influenza in this epidemic is so grave that it is imperative to secure from the individual patient the most complete isolation." And it attacked "current advice and instructions to the public from the official and other sources"—Blue's advice, the advice from local public health officials downplaying everything—as useless and dangerous.

"Don't Get Scared!" said the newspapers.

Meanwhile people read—those in the West seeing it before the virus reached them—the Red Cross appeals published in newspapers, often in half-page advertisements that said: "The safety of this country demands that all patriotic available nurses, nurses' aids [**sic**] or anyone with experience in nursing place themselves at once under the disposal of the Government. . . . Physicians are urgently requested to release from attendance on chronic cases and all other cases which are not critically ill every nurse working under their direction who can possibly be spared for such duty. Graduate nurses, undergraduates, nurses' aids, and volunteers are urged to telegraph collect at once . . . to their local Red Cross chapter or Red Cross headquarters, Washington, D.C."

"Don't Get Scared!" said the papers.

Be not afraid.

But not everyone was ready to trust in God.

In 2001 a terrorist attack with anthrax killed five people and transfixed America. In 2002 an outbreak of West Nile virus killed 284 people nationally in six months and sparked headlines for weeks, along with enough fear to change people's behavior. In 2003 SARS killed over eight hundred people around the world, froze Asian economies, and frightened millions of people in Hong Kong, Singapore, and elsewhere into wearing masks on the streets.

In 1918 fear moved ahead of the virus like the bow wave before a ship. Fear drove the people, and the government and the press could not control it. They could not control it because every true report had been diluted with lies. And the more the officials and newspapers reassured, the more they said, **There is no cause for alarm if proper precautions are taken,** or **Influenza is nothing more or less than old-fashioned grippe,** the more people believed themselves cast adrift, adrift with no one to trust, adrift on an ocean of death.

So people watched the virus approach, and feared, feeling as impotent as it moved toward them as if it were an inexorable oncoming cloud of poison gas. It was a thousand miles away, five hundred miles away, fifty miles away, twenty miles away.

In late September they saw published reports, reports buried in back pages, reports in tiny paragraphs, but reports nonetheless: eight hundred cases among midshipmen at Annapolis . . . in New York State coughing or sneezing without covering the face was now punishable by a year in jail and a $500 fine . . . thirty cases of influenza among students at the University of Colorado—but, of course, the Associated Press reassured, "None of the cases, it was said, is serious."

But then it **was** serious: four hundred dead in a day in Philadelphia . . . twenty dead in Colorado and New Mexico . . . four hundred now dead in Chicago . . . all social and amusement activities suspended in El Paso, where seven funerals for soldiers occurred in a single day (it would get much worse) . . . a terrible outbreak in Winslow, Arizona.

It was like being bracketed by artillery, the barrage edging closer and closer.

In Lincoln, Illinois, a small town thirty miles from Springfield, William Maxwell sensed it: "My first intimations about the epidemic was that it was something happening to the troops. There didn't seem to be any reason to think it would ever have anything to do with us. And yet in a gradual remorseless way it kept moving closer and closer. Rumors of the alarming situation reached this very small town in the midwest. . . . It was like, almost like an entity moving closer."

In Meadow, Utah, one hundred miles from Provo, Lee Reay recalled, "We were very concerned in our town because it was moving south down the highway, and we were next." They watched it kill in Payson, then San-taguin, then Nephi, Levan, and Mills. They watched it come closer and closer. They put up a huge sign on the road that ordered people to keep going, not to stop in Meadow. But the mailman stopped anyway.

Wherever one was in the country, it crept closer—it was in the next town, the next neighborhood, the next block, the next room. In Tucson the **Arizona Daily Star** warned readers not to catch "Spanish hysteria!" "Don't worry!" was the official and final piece of advice on how to avoid the disease from the Arizona Board of Health.

Don't get scared! said the newspapers everywhere. **Don't get scared!** they said in Denver, in Seattle, in Detroit; in Burlington, Vermont, and Burlington, Iowa, and Burlington, North Carolina; in Greenville, Rhode Island, and Greenville, South Carolina, and Greenville, Mississippi. And every time the newspapers said, **Don't get scared!** they frightened.

The virus had moved west and south from the East Coast by water and rail. It rose up in great crests to flood cities, rolled in great waves through the towns, broke into wild rivers to rage through villages, poured in swollen creeks through settlements, flowed in tiny rivulets into isolated homes. And as in a great flood it covered everything, varying in depth but covering everything, settling over the land in a great leveling.

Albert Camus wrote, "What's true of all the evils in the world is true of plague as well. It helps men to rise above themselves."

One who rose was Dr. Ralph Marshall Ward, who had abandoned medicine for cattle ranching. Leaving medicine had not been a business decision.

An intellectual, particularly interested in pharmacology, he was a prominent physician in Kansas City with an office and pharmacy in the Stockyard Exchange Building down by the bottoms. But Kansas City was a major railhead, with the yards near his office. Most of his practice involved treating railroad workers injured in accidents. He performed huge numbers of amputations, and seemed always to work on mangled men, men ripped into pieces by steel. To have a practice with so much human agony ripped him into pieces as well.

He had too much of doctoring, and, from treating cowboys hurt on cattle drives north to Kansas City, he had learned enough about the cattle business that he decided shortly before the war to buy a small ranch more than a thousand miles away, near San Benito, Texas, close to the Mexican border. On the long trip south, he and his wife made a pact never to utter a word that he had been a doctor. But in October 1918, influenza reached him. Some ranch hands got ill. He began treating them. Word spread.

A few days later his wife woke up to a disturbing and unrecognizable sound. She went outside and saw out there in the gloaming people, hundreds of people, on the horizon. They seemed to cover that horizon, and as they came closer, it was clear they were Mexicans, a few of them on mules, most on foot, women carrying babies, men carrying women, bedraggled, beaten down, a mass of humanity, a mass of horror and suffering. She yelled for her husband, and he came out and stood on the porch. "Oh my God!" he said.

The people had come with nothing. But they knew he was a doctor so they had come. The Wards later told their granddaughter it was like the hospital scene in **Gone With the Wind,** with rows of wounded and dying laid out on the ground in agony. These people had come with nothing, had nothing, and they were dying. The Wards took huge pots outside to boil water, used all their resources to feed them, treated them. Out on the empty harsh range near the Mexican border, they had no Red Cross to turn to for help, no Council of National Defense. They did what they could, and when it was over they went back to Kansas City; he had already gone back to being a doctor.

There were other men and women like the Wards. Physicians, nurses, scientists did their jobs, and the virus killed them, killed them in such numbers that each week **JAMA** was filled with literally page after page after page after page after page of nothing but brief obituaries in tiny compressed type. Hundreds of doctors dying. Hundreds. Others helped too.

But as Camus knew, evil and crises do not make all men rise above themselves. Crises only make them discover themselves. And some discover a less inspiring humanity.

As the crest of the wave that broke over Philadelphia

began its sweep across the rest of the country, it was accompanied by the same terror that had silenced the streets there. Most men and women sacrificed and risked their lives only for those they loved most deeply: a child, a wife, a husband. Others, loving chiefly themselves, fled in terror even from them.

Still others fomented terror, believing that blaming the enemy—Germany—could help the war effort, or perhaps actually believing that Germany was responsible. Doane himself charged that "German agents . . . from submarines" brought influenza to the United States. "The Germans have started epidemics in Europe, and there is no reason why they should be particularly gentle to America."

Others around the country echoed him. Starkville, Mississippi, a town of three thousand in the Mississippi hill country, was built around a sawmill, cotton farms—not the rich, lush plantations of the Delta but harsh land—and Mississippi A&M College (now Mississippi State University). It served as headquarters for Dr. M. G. Parsons, the U.S. Public Health Service officer for northeastern Mississippi, who proudly informed Blue that he had succeeded in getting local newspapers to run stories he made up that "aid in forming a proper frame of mind" in the public. That frame of mind was fear. Parsons wanted to create fear, believing it "prepared the public mind to receive and act on our suggestions."

Parsons got the local press to say, "The Hun

resorts to unwanted murder of innocent noncombatants. . . . He has been tempted to spread sickness and death thru germs, and has done so in authenticated cases. . . . Communicable diseases are more strictly a weapon for use well back of the lines, over on French or British, or American land." Blue neither reprimanded Parsons for fomenting fear nor suggested that he take another tack. Another story read, "The Germs Are Coming. An epidemic of influenza is spreading or being spread, (we wonder which)."

Those and similar charges created enough public sentiment to force Public Health Service laboratories to waste valuable time and energy investigating such possible agents of germ warfare as Bayer aspirin. Parsons's territory bordered on Alabama, and there a traveling salesman from Philadelphia named H. M. Thomas was arrested on suspicion of being a German agent and spreading influenza—death. Thomas was released, but on October 17, the day after influenza had killed 759 people in Philadelphia, his body was found in a hotel room with his wrists cut—and his throat slit. Police ruled it suicide.

Everywhere, as in Philadelphia, two problems developed: caring for the sick, and maintaining some kind of order.

In Cumberland, Maryland, a gritty railroad and industrial city in the heart of a coal-mining region—where one actually **could** throw a stone across the Potomac River into West Virginia—to prevent the spread of the disease, schools and churches had already been closed, all public gathering places had been closed, and stores had been ordered to close early. Nonetheless, the epidemic exploded on October 5. At noon that day the local Red Cross chairman met with the treasurer of the Red Cross's War Fund and the head of the local Council of National Defense. Their conclusion: "The matter seemed far beyond control. . . . Reports were spreading fast that 'this one' or 'that one' had died without doctor or nurse and it was a panic indeed."

They decided to convert two large buildings on Washington Street to emergency hospitals. From there a handful of women took over, meeting barely an hour after the men had. Each woman had a task: to gather linens or bathroom supplies or cooking utensils or flour. They worked fast. The next morning the hospitals filled with patients.

In Cumberland, 41 percent of the entire population got sick. But the emergency hospitals had only three nurses. The organizers begged for more: "We notified the Bd of Health we must have more nurses if we were to go on. . . . [Nurses] promised. However this help never materialized and up to date . . . 93 admissions, 18 deaths. The question of orderlies is difficult. They are just not to be found."

Back in Starkville, Parsons met with the president of the college, the army commander of the students—all the students had been inducted into the army—and physicians. "We had an open discussion of the dangers and best actions to take and they assured me everything possible would be done," he wired Blue. He asked for and received fifteen thousand pamphlets, posters, and circulars, more than the combined population of Starkville, Columbus, and West Point. But he, and they, accomplished little. Of eighteen hundred students, well over half would get influenza. On October 9 Parsons "found unbelievable conditions with everybody in power stunned." At that moment eight hundred students were sick and 2 percent of all students had already died, with many deaths to come. Parsons found "influenza is all thru the region, in town, hamlet, and single home. People are pretty well scared, with reason. . . ." In West Point, a town of five thousand, fifteen hundred were ill simultaneously. Parsons confessed, "Panic incipient."

In El Paso a U.S. Public Health Service officer reported to Blue, "I have the honor to inform you that from Oct 9th to date there have been 275 deaths from influenza in El Paso among civilians. This does not include civilians who are employed by the government and who died at the base hospital of Fort Bliss, nor does it include soldiers . . . [W]hole city in a panic."

In Colorado, towns in the San Juan Mountains did not panic. They turned grimly serious. They had time to prepare. Lake City guards kept the town entirely free of the disease, allowing no one to enter. Silverton, a town of two thousand, authorized closing businesses even before a single case surfaced. But the virus snuck in, with a vengeance. In a single week in Silverton, 125 died. The town of Ouray set up a "shot gun quarantine," hiring guards to keep miners from Silverton and Telluride out. But the virus reached Ouray as well.

It had not reached Gunnison. Neither tiny nor isolated, Gunnison was a railroad town, a supply center for the west-central part of the state, the home of Western State Teachers College. In early October—far in advance of any cases of influenza—Gunnison and most neighboring towns issued a closing order and a ban on public gatherings. Then Gunnison decided to isolate itself entirely. Gunnison lawmen blocked all through roads. Train conductors warned all passengers that if they stepped foot on the platform in Gunnison to stretch their legs, they would be arrested and quarantined for five days. Two Nebraskans trying simply to drive through to a town in the next county ran the blockade and were thrown into jail. Meanwhile, the nearby town of Sargents suffered six deaths in a single day—out of a total population of 130.

Early in the epidemic, back on September 27— it seemed like years before—the Wisconsin newspaper the **Jefferson County Union** had reported the truth about the disease, and the general in charge of the Army Morale Branch decreed the report "depressant to morale" and forwarded it to enforcement officials for "any action which may be deemed appropriate," including criminal prosecution. Now, weeks later, after weeks of dying and with the war over, the **Gunnison News-Chronicle,** unlike virtually every other newspaper in the country, played no games and warned, "This disease is no joke, to be made light of, but a terrible calamity."

Gunnison escaped without a death.

In the United States, the war was something **over there.** The epidemic was **here.**

"Even if there was war," recalled Susanna Turner of Philadelphia, "the war was removed from us, you know . . . on the other side. . . . This malignancy, it was right at our very doors."

People feared and hated this malignancy, this alien thing in their midst. They were willing to cut it out at any cost. In Goldsboro, North Carolina, Dan Tonkel recalled, "We were actually almost afraid to breathe, the theaters were closed down so you didn't get into any crowds. . . . You felt like you were walking on eggshells, you were afraid even to go out. You couldn't play with your playmates, your classmates, your neighbors, you had to stay home and just be careful. The fear was so great people were actually afraid to leave their homes. People were actually afraid to talk to one another. It was almost like don't breathe in my face, don't look at me and breathe in my face. . . . You never knew from day to day who was going to be next on the death list. . . . That was the horrible part, people just died so quickly."

His father had a store. Four of eight salesgirls died. "Farmers stopped farming and the merchants stopped selling merchandise and the country really more or less just shut down holding their breath. Everyone was holding their breath." His uncle Benny was nineteen years old and had been living with him until he was drafted and went to Fort Bragg, which sent him home when he reported. The camp was refusing all new draftees. Tonkel recalls his parents not wanting to allow Benny back in the house. "'Benny, we don't know what to do with you,'" they said. "'Well, what can I tell you. I'm here,'" his uncle replied. They let him in. "We were frightened, yes absolutely, we were frightened."

In Washington, D.C., William Sardo said, "It kept people apart. . . . It took away all your community life, you had no community life, you had no school life, you had no church life, you had nothing. . . . It completely destroyed all family and community life. People were afraid to kiss one another, people were afraid to eat with one another, they were afraid to have anything that made contact because that's how you got the flu. . . . It destroyed those contacts and destroyed the intimacy that existed amongst people. . . . You were constantly afraid, you were afraid because you saw so much death around you, you were surrounded by death. . . . When each day dawned you didn't know whether you would be there when the sun set that day. It wiped out entire families from the time that the day began in the morning to bedtime at night—entire families were gone completely, there wasn't any single soul left, and that didn't happen just intermittently, it happened all the way across the neighborhoods, it was a terrifying experience. It justifiably should be called a plague because that's what it was. . . . You were quarantined, is what you were, from fear, it was so quick, so sudden. . . . There was an aura of a constant fear that you lived through from getting up in the morning to going to bed at night."

In New Haven, Connecticut, John Delano recalled the same isolating fear: "Normally when someone was sick in those days the parents, the mothers, the fathers, would bring food over to other families, but this was very weird. . . . Nobody was coming in, nobody would bring food in, nobody came to visit."

Prescott, Arizona, made it illegal to shake hands. In Perry County, Kentucky, in the mountains where men either dug into the earth for coal or scratched upon the earth's surface trying to farm despite topsoil only a few inches deep, a county of hard people, where family ties bound tightly, where men and women were loyal and would murder for pride or honor, the Red Cross chapter chairman begged for help, reporting "hundreds of cases up in mountains that they were unable to reach." They were unreachable not just because the county had almost no roads; streambeds in dry weather substituted for them, and when the streambeds filled, transport became impossible. It was more: "People starving to death not from lack of food but because the well were panic stricken and would not go near the sick; that in the stricken families the dead were lying uncared for." Doctors were offered $100 to come out and stay there one hour. None came. Even one Red Cross worker, Morgan Brawner, arrived in the county Saturday and left Sunday, himself terror stricken. He had reason to fear: in some areas the civilian mortality rate reached 30 percent.

In Norwood, Massachusetts, a historian years later interviewed survivors. One man, a newsboy in 1918, remembered that his manager would "tell me to put the money on the table and he'd spray the money before he'd pick it up." Said another survivor; "There wasn't much visiting. . . . We stayed by ourselves." And another: "[H]e'd bring, you know, whatever my father needed and leave it on the doorstep. No one would go into each other's houses." And another: "Everything came to a standstill. . . . We weren't allowed out the door. We had to keep away from people." And another: "A cop, a big burly guy . . . came up to the house and nailed a big white sign and on the sign it said INFLUENZA in red letters. And they nailed it to the door." A sign made a family even more isolated. And another survivor: "I'd go up the street, walk up the street with my hand over my eyes because there were so many houses with crepe draped over the doors." And still another: "It was horrifying. Not only were you frightened you might come down with it, but there was the eerie feeling of people passing away all around you."

In Luce County, Michigan, one woman was nursing her husband and three boys when she "came down with it herself," reported a Red Cross worker. "Not one of the neighbors would come in and help. I stayed there all night, and in the morning telephoned the woman's sister. She came and tapped on the window, but refused to talk to me until she had gotten a safe distance away. . . . I could do nothing for the woman . . . except send for the priest."

Monument and Ignacio, Colorado, went further than banning all public gatherings. They banned customers from stores; the stores remained open, but customers shouted orders through doors, then waited outside for packages.

Colorado Springs placarded homes with signs that read "Sickness."

In no industry did workers hear more about patriotism, about how their work mattered to the war effort as much as that of soldiers fighting at the front, than in shipbuilding. Nor were workers in any industry more carefully attended to. In all plants common drinking cups were immediately destroyed, replaced by tens of thousands of paper

cups. Hospital and treatment facilities were arranged in advance, influenza vaccine supplied, and
it was perhaps the only industry in which nurses
and doctors remained available. As a result, claimed
a Public Health Service officer, "There is no reason
to believe that many men were absent from work
through panic or fear of the disease, because our
educational program took care to avoid frightening
the men. The men were taught that they were safer
at work than any where else."

They were also of course not paid unless they
came to work. But at dozens of shipyards in New
England, the absentee records were striking. At
the L. H. Shattuck Company, 45.9 percent of
the workers stayed home. At the George A. Gilchrist
yard, 54.3 percent stayed home. At Freeport
Shipbuilding, 57 percent stayed home. At Groton
Iron Works, 58.3 percent stayed home.

Twenty-six hundred miles away was Phoenix,
Arizona. At the beginning of the epidemic its newspapers had behaved as did those everywhere else,
saying little, reassuring, insisting that fear was more
dangerous than the disease. But the virus took its
time there, lingered longer than elsewhere, lingered
until finally even the press expressed fear. On
November 8 the **Arizona Republican** warned,
"The people of Phoenix are facing a crisis. The
[epidemic] has reached such serious proportions that
it is the first problem before the people. . . . Almost
every home in the city has been stricken with the

plague. . . . Fearless men and women [must] serve in the cause of humanity."

The war was three days from ending, and several false peaces had been announced. Still, for that newspaper to call influenza "the first problem" while the war continued was extraordinary. And finally the city formed a "citizens' committee" to take charge.

In Arizona, citizens' committees were taken seriously. A year earlier fifteen hundred armed members of a "Citizens Protective League" had put 1,221 striking miners into cattle cars and boxcars and abandoned them without food or water on a railroad siding in the desert, across the New Mexico line. In Phoenix another "citizens' committee" had been going after "bond slackers," hanging them in effigy on main streets. One man refused to buy a bond because of religious reasons. Nonetheless he was hung in effigy with a placard reading, "H. G. Saylor, yellow slacker. . . . Can, but won't buy a liberty bond!" Saylor was lucky. The committee also seized Charles Reas, a carpenter, tied his hands behind his back, painted his face yellow, put a noose around his neck, and dragged him through downtown Phoenix streets wearing a sign that read "with this exception we are 100%."

The influenza citizens' committee took similar initiatives. It deputized a special police force and also called upon all "patriotic citizens" to enforce anti-influenza ordinances, including requiring every person in public to wear a mask, arresting anyone who spit or coughed without covering his mouth, dictating that businesses (those that remained open) give twelve hundred cubic feet of air space to each customer, and halting all traffic into the city and allowing only those with "actual business here" to enter. Soon the **Republican** described "a city of masked faces, a city as grotesque as a masked carnival."

And yet—ironically—influenza touched Phoenix only lightly compared to elsewhere. The panic came anyway. Dogs told the story of terror, but not with their barking. Rumors spread that dogs carried influenza. The police began killing all dogs on the street. And people began killing their own dogs, dogs they loved, and if they had not the heart to kill them themselves, they gave them to the police to be killed. "At this death rate from causes other than natural," reported the **Gazette,** "Phoenix will soon be dogless." Back in Philadelphia Mary Volz lived near a church. She had always "loved to hear the church bells ringing, they were so jubilantly ringing." But now every few minutes people carried a casket into the church, left, "and there would be another casket." Each time the bells rang. "The bells were my joy and then this 'BONG! BONG! BONG!' I was terrified, lying sick in bed hearing 'BONG! BONG! BONG!' Is the bell going to bong for me?"

The war was over there. The epidemic was here.

The war ended. The epidemic continued. Fear settled over the nation like a frozen blanket. "Some say the world will end in fire," wrote Robert Frost in 1920. ". . . ice / Is also great / and would suffice."

An internal American Red Cross report concluded, "A fear and panic of the influenza, akin to the terror of the Middle Ages regarding the Black Plague, [has] been prevalent in many parts of the country."

CHAPTER THIRTY

WIRES POURED INTO the Red Cross and the Public Health Service demanding, pleading, begging for help. From Portsmouth, Virginia: "Urgently need two colored physicians wire prospects obtaining same." From Carey, Kentucky: "Federal coal mines request immediate aid influenza. . . . Immediately rush answer." From Spokane, Washington; "urgent need of four nurses to take charge other nurses furnished by local Red Cross chapter."

The demands could not be met. Replies went back: "No colored physicians available." "It is almost impossible to send nurses all being needed locally." "Call for local volunteers with intelligence and practical experience."

The failure to meet demand was not from lack of trying. Red Cross workers went from house to house searching for anyone with nursing experience. And when they knew of a skilled nurse, the Red Cross tracked her down. Josey Brown was a nurse watching a movie in a St. Louis theater when the lights went on, the screen went blank, and a man appeared onstage announcing that anyone named Josey Brown should go to the ticket booth. There she found a telegram ordering her to the Great Lakes Naval Training Station.

The **Journal of the American Medical Association** repeatedly—sometimes twice in the same issue—published an "urgent call on physicians for help in localities where the epidemic is unusually severe. . . . This service is just as definite a patriotic privilege as is that of serving in the Medical Corps of the Army or Navy. . . . As the call is immediate and urgent it is suggested that any physician who feels that he can do some of this work telegraph to the Surgeon General, USPHS, Washington, D.C."

There were never enough.

Meanwhile, physicians attempted everything— **everything**—to save lives. They could relieve some symptoms. Doctors could address pain with everything from aspirin to morphine. They could control coughing at least somewhat with codeine and, said some, heroin. They gave atropine, digitalis, strychnine, and epinephrine as stimulants. They gave oxygen.

Some treatment attempts that went beyond symptomatic relief had solid science behind them, even if no one had ever applied that science to influenza. There was Redden's approach in Boston based on Lewis's experiments with polio. That approach, with variations, was tried over and over again around the world.

And there were treatments less grounded in science. They sounded logical. They were logical. But the reasoning was also desperate, the reasoning of a doctor ready to try anything, the reasoning that mixed wild ideas or thousands of years of practice and a few decades of scientific method. First-rate medical journals rejected articles about the most outlandish and ridiculous so-called therapies, but they published anything that at least seemed to make sense. There was no time for peer review, no time for careful analysis.

JAMA published the work of a physician who claimed, "Infection was prevented in practically 100% of cases when [my] treatment was properly used." His approach had logic to it. By stimulating the flow of mucus, he hoped to help one of the first lines of defense of the body, to prevent any pathogen from attaching itself to any mucosal membrane. So he mixed irritating chemicals in powder form and blew them into the upper respiratory tract to generate large flows of mucus. The theory was sound; perhaps while mucus was actually flowing, it did some good.

One Philadelphia doctor had another idea, logical but more reaching, and wrote in **JAMA** that "when the system is saturated with alkalis, there is poor soil for bacterial growth." Therefore he tried to turn the entire body alkaline. "I have uniformly employed, and always with good results, potassium citrate and sodium bicarbonate saturation by mouth, bowel and skin. . . . Patients must be willing to forego [**sic**] the seductive relief by acetylsalicylic acid [aspirin]. . . . My very successful experience in this epidemic cannot be dismissed as accidental or unique. . . . I urge its immediate trial empirically. Further investigation in laboratory or clinic may follow later."

Physicians injected people with typhoid vaccine, thinking—or simply hoping—it might somehow boost the immune system in general even though the specificity of the immune response was well understood. Some claimed the treatment worked. Others poured every known vaccine into patients on the same theory. Quinine worked on one disease: malaria. Many physicians gave it for influenza with no better reasoning than desperation.

Others convinced themselves a treatment cured regardless of results. A Montana physician reported to the **New York Medical Journal** of his experimental treatment: "The results have been favorable." He tried the treatment on six people; two died. Still he insisted, "In the four cases that recovered the results were immediate and certain."

Two University of Pittsburgh researchers reasoned no better. They believed they had improved on the technique Redden had adopted from Flexner and Lewis. They treated forty-seven patients; twenty died. They subtracted seven deaths, arguing that the victims received the therapy too late. That still left thirteen dead out of forty-seven. Yet they claimed success.

One physician gave hydrogen peroxide intravenously to twenty-five patients in severe pulmonary distress, believing that it would get oxygen into the blood. Thirteen recovered; twelve died. This physician, too, claimed success: "The anoxemia was often markedly benefited, and the toxemia appeared to be overcome in many cases."

Many of his colleagues tried similarly outlandish treatments and likewise claimed success. Many of them believed it.

Homeopaths believed that the epidemic proved their superiority to "allopathic" physicians. The **Journal of the American Institute for Homeopathy** claimed that influenza victims treated by regular physicians had a mortality rate of 28.2 percent—an absurdity: if that were so, the United States alone would have had several million deaths—while also claiming that twenty-six thousand patients treated by homeopaths, chiefly with the herbal drug gelsemium, had a mortality rate of 1.05 percent, with many homeopaths claiming no deaths whatsoever among thousands of patients.

But the results were self-reported, making it far too easy to rationalize away those under their care who did die—to remove, for instance, from their sample any patient who, against their advice, took aspirin, which homeopaths considered a poison.

It was no different elsewhere in the world. In Greece one physician used mustard plasters to create blisters on the skin of influenza victims, then drained them, mixed the fluid with morphine, strychnine, and caffeine, and reinjected it. "The effect was apparent at once, and in 36 to 48 or even 12 hours the temperature declined and improvement progressed." But the mortality rate of his 234 patients was 6 percent.

In Italy one doctor gave intravenous injections of mercuric chloride. Another rubbed creosote, a disinfectant, into the axilla, where lymph nodes, outposts of white blood cells scattered through the body, lie beneath the skin. A third insisted that enemas of warm milk and one drop of creosote every twelve hours for every year of age prevented pneumonia.

In Britain the War Office published recommendations for therapy in **The Lancet.** They were far more specific than any guidance in the United States, and likely did relieve some symptoms. For sleep, twenty grains of bromide, opiates to relax cough, and oxygen for cyanosis. The recommendations warned that venesection was seldom beneficial, that alcohol was invaluable, but that little could be gained by giving food. For headache: antipyrin and salicylic acid—aspirin. To stimulate the heart: strychnine and digitalis.

In France, not until mid-October did the Ministry of War approach the Académie des Sciences for help. To prevent disease, some physicians and scientists advised masks. Others insisted arsenic prevented it. For treatment, the Pasteur Institute developed an antipneumococcus serum drawn as usual from horses, as well as a serum derived from the blood of patients who had recovered. (Comparisons proved the Cole and Avery serum far superior.) Anything that might lower fever was urged. Stimulants were recommended for the heart. So were "revulsions" that purged the body. Methylene blue, a dye used to stain bacteria to make them more visible under the microscope, was tried despite its known toxicity in the hopes of killing bacteria. Other doctors injected metallic solutions into muscle, so the body absorbed them gradually, or intravenously. (One doctor who injected it intravenously conceded that the treatment was "a little brutal.") Cupping was recommended—using a flame to absorb oxygen and thus create a vacuum in a glass container, then placing it on the body, in theory to draw out poisons. One prominent physician called for "prompt bleeding" of more than a pint of blood at the first signs of pulmonary edema and cyanosis, along with acetylsalicylic acid. He was hardly alone in prescribing bleeding. One physician who recommended a return to "heroic medicine" explained that the more the doctor did, the more the body was stimulated to respond. In disease as in war, he said, the fighter must seize initiative.

Across the world hundreds of millions—very likely tens of millions in the United States alone—saw no doctor, saw no nurse, but tried every kind of folk medicine or fraudulent remedy available or imaginable. Camphor balls and garlic hung around people's necks. Others gargled with disinfectants, let frigid air sweep through their homes, or sealed windows shut and overheated rooms.

Advertisements filled the newspapers, sometimes set in the same small type as—and difficult to distinguish from—news articles, and sometimes set in large fonts blaring across a page. The one thing they shared: they all declared with confidence there **was** a way to stop influenza, there **was** a way to survive. Some claims were as simple as a shoe store's advertising, "One way to keep the flu away is to keep your feet dry." Some were as complex as "Making a Kolynos Gas Mask to Fight Spanish Influenza When Exposed to Infection."

They also all played to fear. "How to Prevent Infection from Spanish Influenza. . . . The Surgeon General of the U.S. Army urges you to keep your mouth clean. . . . [use] a few drops of liquid SOZODONT." "Help Your Health Board Conquer Spanish Influenza by Disinfecting Your

Home . . . Lysol Disinfectant." "For GRIP . . . You Are Safe When You Take Father John's Medicine." "Influ-BALM Prevents Spanish Flu." "Special Notice to the Public. Telephone inquiries from Minneapolis physicians and the laity and letters from many parts of America are coming into our office regarding the use of Benetol, . . . a powerful bulwark for the prevention and treatment of Spanish influenza. . . ." "Spanish influenza—what it is and how it should be treated: . . . Always Call a Doctor/ No Occasion for Panic. . . . There is no occasion for panic—influenza itself has a very low percentage of fatalities. . . . Use Vicks VapoRub."

By the middle of October, vaccines prepared by the best scientists were appearing everywhere. On October 17 New York City Health Commissioner Royal Copeland announced that "the influenza vaccine discovered by Dr. William H. Park, director of the City Laboratories, had been tested sufficiently to warrant its recommendation as a preventive agency." Copeland assured the public that "virtually all persons vaccinated with it [were] immune to the disease."

In Philadelphia on October 19, Dr. C. Y. White, a bacteriologist with the municipal laboratory, delivered ten thousand dosages of a vaccine based on Paul Lewis's work, with tens of thousands of dosages more soon to come. It was "multivalent," made up of dead strains of several kinds of bacteria, including the influenza bacillus, two types of pneumococci, and several strains of other streptococci.

That same day a new issue of **JAMA** appeared. It was thick with information on influenza, including a preliminary evaluation of the experience with vaccines in Boston. George Whipple, another Welch product and later a Nobel laureate, concluded, "The weight of such statistical evidence as we have been able to accumulate indicates that the use of the influenza vaccine which we have investigated is without therapeutic benefit." By "therapeutic" Whipple meant that the tested vaccines could not cure. But he continued, "The statistical evidence, so far as it goes, indicates a probability that the use of this vaccine has some prophylactic value."

He was hardly endorsing Copeland's statement, but at least he provided some hope.

The Public Health Service made no effort to produce or distribute any vaccine or treatment for civilians. It received requests enough. It had nothing to offer.

The Army Medical School (now the Armed Forces Institute of Pathology) in Washington did mount a massive effort to make a vaccine. They needed one. At the army's own Walter Reed Hospital in Washington, the death rate for those with complicating pneumonia had reached 52 percent. On October 25 the vaccine was ready. The surgeon general's office informed all camp physicians, "The value of vaccination against certain of the more important organisms giving rise to pneumonia may be considered to be established. . . . The Army now has available for all officers, enlisted men, and civilian employees of the Army, a lipo vaccine containing pneumococcus Types I, II, and III."

The army distributed two million doses of this vaccine in the next weeks. This marked an enormous production triumph. Earlier a prominent British scientist had pronounced it impossible for the British government to produce even forty thousand doses on short notice. But the vaccine still protected only against pneumonias caused by Types I and II pneumococci, and it came too late; by then the disease had already passed through nearly all cantonments. When civilian physicians from New York to California begged for the vaccine from the army, the reply came back that the army had in fact produced "a vaccine for the prevention of pneumonia, but none is available for distribution." The army feared a recrudescence among troops; it had good reason to fear one.

The Army Medical School had also produced a vaccine against **B. influenzae,** but of this Gorgas's office spoke more cautiously: "In view of the possible etiologic importance of the bacillus influenzae in the present epidemic, a saline vaccine has been prepared by the Army and is available to all officers, enlisted men, and civilian employees of the Army. The effectiveness of bacillus influenzae vaccine . . . is still in the experimental stage."

That army statement was not a public one. Nor really was a cautionary **JAMA** editorial: "Unfortunately we as yet have no specific serum or other specific means for the cure of influenza, and no specific vaccine for its prevention. Such is the fact, all claims and propagandists in the newspapers and elsewhere to the contrary notwithstanding. . . . Consequently the physician must keep his head and not allow himself to make more promises than the facts warrant. This warning applies especially to health officers in their public relations." Nearly every issue contained a similar warning: "Nothing should be done by the medical profession that may arouse unwarranted hope among the public and be followed by disappointment and distrust of medical science and the medical profession."

JAMA represented the American Medical Association. AMA leaders had worked for decades to bring scientific standards and professionalism to medicine. They had only recently succeeded. They did not want to destroy the trust only recently established. They did not want medicine to become the mockery it had been not so long before.

In the meantime physicians continued to try the most desperate measures. Vaccines continued to be produced in great numbers—eighteen different kinds in Illinois alone. No one had any real idea whether any would work. They had only hope.

But the reality of the disease was expressed in a recitation of events during the epidemic at Camp

Sherman, Ohio, the single camp with the highest death rate. Its doctors precisely followed the standard treatment for influenza Osler had recommended in the most recent edition of his textbook—aspirin, rest in bed, gargles, and "Dover's powders," which were a combination of ipecac to induce vomiting and opium to relieve pain and cough. For complicating but standard pneumonias they followed "the usual recommendations for diet, fresh air, rest, mild purgation and elimination. . . . All cases were digitalized"—digitalis given in maximum possible dosages to stimulate the heart—"and reliance placed on soluble caffeine salt for quick stimulation. Strychnin in large doses hypodermically had a distinct value in the existing asthenia."

Then, however, they reported their helplessness in the far too common "acute inflammatory pulmonary edema," what today would be called ARDS. "This presented a new problem in therapy. The principles of treatment employed in pulmonary edema incident to dilation of the heart, though seemingly not indicated by the condition in question, were employed. Digitalis, a double caffeine salt, morphin [**sic**], and venesection"—bleeding again—"were without significant value. . . . Oxygen was of temporary value. Posture accomplished drainage but did not influence the end result. Pituitary solution, hypodermically, was suggested by the similarity of this condition to the results of gassing. No benefits were gained by its use."

They tried everything, everything they could think of, until they finally took pity and stopped, abandoning some of the more brutal—and useless—treatments they had tried "on account of [their] heroic character." By then they had seen enough of heroism from dying soldiers. They were finally willing to let them go in peace. Against this condition they could only conclude, "No especial measure was of avail."

No medicine and none of the vaccines developed then could prevent influenza. The masks worn by millions were useless as designed and could not prevent influenza. Only preventing exposure to the virus could. Nothing today can cure influenza, although vaccines can provide significant—but nowhere near complete—protection, and several antiviral drugs can mitigate its severity.

Places that isolated themselves—such as Gunnison, Colorado, and a few military installations on islands—escaped. But the closing orders that most cities issued could not prevent exposure; they were not extreme enough. Closing saloons and theaters and churches meant nothing if significant numbers of people continued to climb onto streetcars, continued to go to work, continued to go to the grocer. Even where fear closed down businesses, where both store owners and customers refused to stand face-to-face and left orders on sidewalks, there was still too much interaction to break the chain of infection. The virus was too efficient, too explosive, too good at what it did. In the end the virus did its will around the world.

It was as if the virus were a hunter. It was hunting mankind. It found man in the cities easily, but it was not satisfied. It followed him into towns, then villages, then individual homes. It searched for him in the most distant corners of the earth. It hunted him in the forests, tracked him into jungles, pursued him onto the ice. And in those most distant corners of the earth, in those places so inhospitable that they barely allowed man to live, in those places where man was almost wholly innocent of civilization, man was not safer from the virus. He was more vulnerable.

In Alaska, whites in Fairbanks protected themselves. Sentries guarded all trails, and every person entering the city was quarantined for five days. Eskimos had no such luck. A senior Red Cross official warned that without "immediate medical assistance the race" could become "extinct."

Neither Red Cross nor territorial government funds were available. The governor of Alaska came to Washington to beg Congress for $200,000—compared to the $1 million given to the Public Health Service for the entire country. A senator asked why the territory couldn't spend any of the $600,000 in its treasury. The governor replied, "The people of Alaska consider that the money raised by taxes from the white people of Alaska should be spent for the improvements of the Territory. They need the money in roads a great deal. . . . They want to have the Indians in Alaska placed more on a parity with the Indians of other parts of the United States, where they are taken care of by the United States government."

He got $100,000. The navy provided the collier USS **Brutus** to carry a relief expedition. At Juneau the party divided and went in smaller boats to visit villages.

They found terrible things. Terrible things. In Nome, 176 of 300 Eskimos had died. But it would get worse. One doctor visited ten tiny villages and found "three wiped out entirely; others average 85% deaths. . . . Survivors generally children . . . probably 25% this number frozen to death before help arrived."

A later relief expedition followed, funded by the Red Cross, dividing itself in the Aleutian Islands into six groups of two doctors and two nurses each, then boarding other ships and dispersing.

The first group disembarked at a fishing village called Micknick. They arrived too late. Only half a dozen adults survived. Thirty-eight adults and twelve children had died. A small house had been turned into an orphanage for fifteen children. The group crossed the Naknek River to a village with a seafood cannery. Twenty-four adult Eskimos had lived there before the epidemic. Twenty-two had died; a twenty-third death occurred the day after the relief expedition arrived. Sixteen children, now orphans, survived. On Nushagak Bay the Peterson Packing Company had established a headquarters and warehouse. Nurses went hut to hut. "The epidemic of influenza had been most severe at this place, few adults living. On making a search Drs. Healy and Reiley found a few natives bedfast. . . . The doctors worked most faithfully but help arrived too late and five of the patients died."

There was worse. Another rescue team reported, "Numerous villages were found but no sign of life about except for packs of half-starved, semiwild dogs." The Eskimos there lived in what was called a "barabara." Barabaras were circular structures two-thirds underground; they were built like that to withstand the shrieking winds that routinely blew at hurricane force, winds that ripped conventional structures apart. One rescuer described a barabara as "roughed over with slabs of peat sod, . . . entrance to which is gained through a tunnel of from four to five feet in height, this tunnel being its only means of light and ventilation, in most cases; about the sides of these rooms are dug shelves and in these shelves, on mattresses of dried grasses and furs, the people sleep."

Entire family groups, a dozen people or more, lived in this one room. "On entering these barabaras, Dr. McGillicuddy's party found heaps of dead bodies on the shelves and floors, men, women, and children and the majority of the cases too far decomposed to be handled."

The virus probably did not kill all of them directly. But it struck so suddenly, with such simultaneity, it left no one well enough to care for any others, no one to get food, no one to get water. And those who could have survived, surrounded by bodies, bodies of people they loved, might well have preferred to go where their family had gone, might well have wanted to no longer be alone.

And then the dogs would have come.

"It was quite impossible to estimate the number of dead as the starving dogs had dug their way into many huts and devoured the dead, a few bones and clothing left to tell the story."

All the relief party could do was tie ropes around remains, drag them outside, and bury them.

On the opposite edge of the continent the story was the same. In Labrador man clung to existence with tenacity but not much more permanency than seaweed drying on a rock, vulnerable to the crash of surf at high tide. The Reverend Henry Gordon left the village of Cartwright in late October and returned a few days later, on October 30. He found "not a soul to be seen anywhere, and a strange, unusual silence." Heading home, he met a Hudson's Bay Company man who told him "sickness . . . has struck the place like a cyclone, two days after the

Mail boat had left." Gordon went from house to house. "Whole households lay inanimate on their kitchen floors, unable even to feed themselves or look after the fire."

Twenty-six of one hundred souls had died. Farther up the coast, it was worse.

Of 220 people at Hebron, 150 died. The weather was already bitter cold. The dead lay in their beds, sweat having frozen their bedclothes to them. Gordon and some others from Cartwright made no effort to dig graves, consigning the bodies to the sea. He wrote, "A feeling of intense resentment at the callousness of the authorities, who sent us the disease by mail-boat, and then left us to sink or swim, filled one's heart almost to the exclusion of all else. . . ."

Then there was Okak. Two hundred sixty-six people had lived in Okak, and many dogs, dogs nearly wild. When the virus came it struck so hard so fast people could not care for themselves or feed the dogs. The dogs grew hungry, crazed with hunger, devoured each other, and then wildly smashed through windows and doors, and fed. The Reverend Andrew Asboe survived with his rifle beside him; he personally killed over one hundred dogs.

When the Reverend Walter Perret arrived, only fifty-nine people out of 266 still lived. He and the survivors did the only work there was. "The ground was frozen hard as iron, and the work of digging was as hard as ever work was. It took about two weeks to do it, and when it was finished it was 32 feet long, 10 feet wide, and eight feet deep." Now began the task of dragging the corpses to the pit. They laid 114 bodies in the pit, each wrapped in calico, sprinkled disinfectants over them, and covered the trench, placing rocks on top to prevent the dogs from tearing it up.

In all of Labrador, at least one-third of the total population died.

The virus pierced the ice of the Arctic and climbed the roadless mountains of Kentucky. It also penetrated the jungle.

Among Westerners the heaviest blows fell upon young adults densely packed together, civilian or military. Metropolitan Life Insurance found that 6.21 percent of **all** coal miners—not just those with influenza—whom it insured between the ages of twenty-five and forty-five died; in that same age group, 3.26 percent of **all** industrial workers it insured died—comparable to the worst rates in the army camps.

In Frankfurt the mortality rate of all those hospitalized with influenza—not all those with pneumonia—was 27.3 percent. In Cologne the mayor, Konrad Adenauer, who would become one of Europe's great statesmen, said the disease left thousands "too exhausted to hate."

In Paris the government closed only schools, fearing that anything else would hurt morale. The death rate there was 10 percent of influenza victims and 50 percent of those who developed any complications. "These cases," noted one French physician, "were remarkable for the severity of the symptoms and the rapidity with which certain forms progressed to death." Although the symptoms in France were typical of the disease elsewhere, deep into the epidemic physicians seemed to purposely misdiagnose it as cholera or dysentery and rarely reported it.

And populations whose immune systems were naive, whose immune systems had seen few if any influenza viruses of any kind, were not just decimated but sometimes annihilated. This was true not only of Eskimos but of all Native Americans, of Pacific Islanders, of Africans.

In Gambia, 8 percent of the Europeans would die, but from the interior one British visitor reported, "I found whole villages of 300 to 400 families completely wiped out, the houses having fallen in on the unburied dead, and the jungle having crept in within two months, obliterating whole settlements."

Even when the virus mutated toward mildness, it still killed efficiently in those whose immune systems had rarely or never been exposed to influenza. The USS **Logan** reached Guam on October 26. Nearly 95 percent of American sailors ashore caught the disease, but only a single sailor died. The same virus killed almost 5 percent of the entire native population in a few weeks.

In Cape Town and several other cities in South

Africa, influenza would kill 4 percent of the entire population within four weeks of the first reported cases. Thirty-two percent of white South Africans and 46 percent of the blacks would be attacked; 0.82 percent of white Europeans would die, along with at least 2.72 percent—likely a far, far higher percentage—of black Africans.

In Mexico the virus swarmed through the dense population centers and through the jungles, overwhelming occupants of mining camps, slum dwellers and slum landlords, and rural peasants alike. In the state of Chiapas, 10 percent of the entire population—not 10 percent of those with influenza—would die.

The virus ripped through Senegal, Sierra Leone, Spain, and Switzerland, leaving each devastated and keening with a death toll that in some areas exceeded 10 percent of the overall population.

In Brazil—where the virus was relatively mild, at least compared with Mexico or for that matter Chile—Rio de Janeiro suffered an attack rate of 33 percent.

In Buenos Aires, Argentina, the virus attacked nearly 55 percent of the population.

In Japan it attacked more than one-third of the population.

The virus would kill 7 percent of the entire population in much of Russia and Iran.

In Guam, 10 percent of the population would die. Elsewhere the mortality exceeded even that. In the Fiji Islands, 14 percent of the population would die **in the sixteen days between November 25 and December 10.** It was impossible to bury the dead. Wrote one observer, "day and night trucks rumbled through the streets, filled with bodies for the constantly burning pyres."

A very few—very few—isolated locations around the world, where it was possible to impose a rigid quarantine and where authorities did so ruthlessly, escaped the disease entirely. American Samoa was one such place. There not a single person died of influenza.

Across a few miles of ocean lay Western Samoa, seized from Germany by New Zealand at the start of war. On September 30, 1918, its population was 38,302, before the steamer **Talune** brought the disease to the island. A few months later, the population was 29,802. **Twenty-two percent of the population died.**

Huge but unknown numbers died in China. In Chungking one-half the population of the city was ill.

And yet the most terrifying numbers would come from India. As elsewhere, India had suffered a spring wave. As elsewhere, this spring wave was relatively benign. In September influenza returned to Bombay. As elsewhere, it was no longer benign.

Yet India was not like elsewhere. There influenza would take on truly killing dimensions. A serious epidemic of bubonic plague had struck there in

1900, and it had struck Bombay especially hard. In 1918 the peak daily influenza mortality in Bombay almost doubled that of the 1900 bubonic plague, and the case mortality rate for influenza reached 10.3 percent.

Throughout the Indian subcontinent, there was only death. Trains left one station with the living. They arrived with the dead and dying, the corpses removed as the trains pulled into station. British troops, Caucasians, in India suffered a case mortality rate of 9.61 percent. For Indian troops, 21.69 percent of those who caught influenza died. One hospital in Delhi treated 13,190 influenza patients; 7,044 of those patients died.

The most devastated region was the Punjab. One physician reported that hospitals were so "choked that it was impossible to remove the dead quickly enough to make room for the dying. The streets and lanes of the city were littered with dead and dying people. . . . Nearly every household was lamenting a death and everywhere terror reigned."

Normally corpses there were cremated in burning ghats, level spaces at the top of the stepped riverbank, and the ashes given to the river. The supply of firewood was quickly exhausted, making cremation impossible, and the rivers became clogged with corpses.

In the Indian subcontinent alone, it is likely that close to twenty million died, and quite possibly the death toll exceeded that number.

Victor Vaughan, Welch's old ally, sitting in the office of the surgeon general of the army and head of the army's Division of Communicable Diseases, watched the virus move across the earth. "If the epidemic continues its mathematical rate of acceleration, civilization could easily," he wrote in hand, "disappear . . . from the face of the earth within a matter of a few more weeks."

■ **Part IX**

LINGERER

CHAPTER THIRTY-ONE

Vaughan believed that the influenza virus came close to threatening the existence of civilization. In fact, some diseases depend upon civilization for their own existence. Measles is one example. Since a single exposure to measles usually gives lifetime immunity, the measles virus cannot find enough susceptible individuals in small towns to survive; without a new human generation to infect, the virus dies out. Epidemiologists have computed that measles requires an unvaccinated population of at least half a million people living in fairly close contact to continue to exist.

The influenza virus is different. Since birds provide a natural home for it, influenza does not depend upon civilization. In terms of its own survival, it did not matter if humans existed or not.

Twenty years before the great influenza pandemic, H. G. Wells published **War of the Worlds,** a novel in which Martians invaded the earth. They loosed upon the world their death ships, and they were indomitable. They began to feed upon humans, sucking the life force from them down to the marrow of the bone. Man, for all his triumphs of the nineteenth century, a century in which his achievements had reordered the world, had become suddenly impotent. No force known to mankind, no technology or strategy or effort or heroism that any nation or person on earth had developed, could stand against the invaders.

Wells wrote, "I felt the first inkling of a thing that presently grew quite clear in my mind, that oppressed me for many days, a sense of dethronement, a persuasion that I was no longer a master, but an animal among the animals. . . . The fear and empire of man had passed away."

But just as the destruction of the human race seemed inevitable, nature intervened. The invaders were themselves invaded; the earth's infectious pathogens killed them. Natural processes had done what science could not.

With the influenza virus, natural processes began to work as well.

At first those processes had made the virus more

lethal. Whether it first jumped from an animal host to man in Kansas or in some other place, as it passed from person to person it adapted to its new host, became increasingly efficient in its ability to infect, and changed from the virus that caused a generally mild first wave of disease in the spring of 1918 to the lethal and explosive killer of the second wave in the fall.

But once this happened, once it achieved near-maximum efficiency, two other natural processes came into play.

One process involved immunity. Once the virus passed through a population, that population developed at least some immunity to it. Victims were not likely to be reinfected by the same virus, not until it had undergone antigen drift. In a city or town, the cycle from first case to the end of a local epidemic in 1918 generally ran six to eight weeks. In the army camps, with the men packed so densely, the cycle took usually three to four weeks.

Individual cases continued to occur after that, but the explosion of disease ended, and it ended abruptly. A graph of cases would look like a bell curve—but one chopped off almost like a cliff just after the peak, with new cases suddenly dropping to next to nothing. In Philadelphia, for example, in the week ending October 16 the disease killed 4,597 people. It was ripping the city apart, emptying the streets, sparking rumors of the Black Death. But new cases dropped so precipitously that only ten days later, on October 26, the order closing public places was lifted. By the armistice on November 11, influenza had almost entirely disappeared from that city. The virus burned through available fuel. Then it quickly faded away.

The second process occurred within the virus. It was only influenza. By nature the influenza virus is dangerous, considerably more dangerous than the common aches and fever lead people to believe, but it does not kill routinely as it did in 1918. The 1918 pandemic reached an extreme of virulence unknown in any other widespread influenza outbreak in history.

But the 1918 virus, like all influenza viruses, like all viruses that form mutant swarms, mutated rapidly. There is a mathematical concept called "reversion to the mean"; this states simply that an extreme event is likely to be followed by a less extreme event. This is not a law, only a probability. The 1918 virus stood at an extreme; any mutations were more likely to make it less lethal than more lethal. In general, that is what happened. So just as it seemed that the virus would bring civilization to its knees, would do what the plagues of the Middle Ages had done, would remake the world, the virus mutated toward its mean, toward the behavior of most influenza viruses. As time went on, it became less lethal.

This first became apparent in army cantonments in the United States. Of the army's twenty largest cantonments, the first five attacked saw roughly

20 percent of all soldiers who caught influenza develop pneumonia. And 37.3 percent of the soldiers who developed pneumonia died. The worst numbers came from Camp Sherman in Ohio, which suffered the highest percentage of soldiers killed and was one of the first camps hit: 35.7 percent of influenza cases at Sherman developed pneumonia. And 61.3 percent of those pneumonia victims died. Sherman doctors carried a stigma for this, and the army investigated but found them as competent as elsewhere. They did all that was being done elsewhere. They were simply struck by a particularly lethal strain of the virus.

In the last five camps attacked, hit on average three weeks later, only 7.1 percent of influenza victims developed pneumonia. And only 17.8 percent of the soldiers who developed pneumonia died.

One alternative explanation to this improvement is that army doctors simply got better at preventing and treating pneumonia. But people of scientific and epidemiological accomplishment looked hard for any evidence of that. They found none. The army's chief investigator was George Soper, later handpicked by Welch to oversee the nation's first effort to coordinate a comprehensive program of cancer research. Soper reviewed all written reports and interviewed many medical officers. He concluded that the only effective measure used against influenza in any of the camps had been to isolate both individual influenza victims and, if necessary, entire commands that became infected: these efforts "failed when and where they were carelessly applied" but "did some good. . . . when and where they were rigidly carried out." He found no evidence that anything else worked, that anything else affected the course of the disease, that anything else changed except the virus itself. The later the disease attacked, the less vicious the blow.

Inside each camp the same thing held true. Soldiers struck down in the first ten days or two weeks died at much higher rates than soldiers in the same camp struck down late in the epidemic or after the epidemic actually ended.

Similarly, the first cities invaded by the virus—Boston, Baltimore, Pittsburgh, Philadelphia, Louisville, New York, New Orleans, and smaller cities hit at the same time—all suffered grievously. And in those same places, the people infected later in the epidemic were not becoming as ill, were not dying at the same rate, as those infected in the first two to three weeks.

Cities struck later in the epidemic also usually had lower mortality rates. In one of the most careful epidemiological studies of the epidemic in one state, the investigator noted that, in Connecticut, "one factor that appeared to affect the mortality rate was proximity in time to the original outbreak at New London, the point at which the disease was first introduced into Connecticut. . . . The virus was most virulent or most readily communicable when it first reached the state, and thereafter became generally attenuated."

The same pattern held true throughout the country and, for that matter, the world. It was not a rigid predictor. The virus was never completely consistent. But places hit later tended to be hit more easily. San Antonio suffered one of the highest attack rates but lowest death rates in the country; the virus there infected 53.5 percent of the population, and 98 percent of all homes in the city had at least one person sick with influenza. But there the virus had mutated toward mildness; only 0.8 percent of those who got influenza died. (This death rate was still double that of normal influenza.) The virus itself, more than any treatment provided, determined who lived and who died.

A decade after the pandemic, a careful and comprehensive scientific review of findings and statistics not only in the United States but around the world confirmed, "In the later stages of the epidemic the supposedly characteristic influenza lesions were less frequently found, the share of secondary invaders was more plainly recognizable, and the differences of locality were sharply marked. . . . [I]n 1919 the 'water-logged' lungs"—those in which death came quickly from ARDS—"were relatively rarely encountered."

Despite aberrations, then, in general in youth the virus was violent and lethal; in maturity it mellowed. The later the epidemic struck a locality, and the later within that local epidemic someone got sick, the less lethal the influenza. The correlations are not perfect. Louisville suffered a violent attack in both spring and fall. The virus was unstable and always different. But a correlation does exist between the timing of the outbreak in a region and lethality. Even as the virus mellowed, it still killed. It still killed often enough that in maturity it would have been, except for its own younger self, the most lethal influenza virus ever known. But timing mattered.

The East and South, hit earliest, were hit the hardest. The West Coast was hit less hard. And the middle of the country suffered the least. In Seattle, in Portland, in Los Angeles, in San Diego, the dead did not pile up as in the East. In St. Louis, in Chicago, in Indianapolis, the dead did not pile up as in the West. But if the dead did not pile up there as they had in Philadelphia and New Orleans, they still did pile up.

By late November, with few exceptions the virus had made its way around the world. The second wave was over, and the world was exhausted. And man was about to become the hunter.

But the virus, even as it lost some of its virulence, was not yet finished. Only weeks after the disease seemed to have dissipated, when town after town had congratulated itself on surviving it—and in some places where people had had the hubris to believe they had defeated it—after health boards and emergency councils had canceled orders to close theaters, schools, and churches and to wear masks, a third wave broke over the earth.

The virus had mutated again. It had not become radically different. People who had gotten sick in the second wave had a fair amount of immunity to another attack, just as people sickened in the first wave had fared better than others in the second wave. But it mutated enough, its antigens drifted enough, to rekindle the epidemic.

Some places were not touched by the third wave at all. But many—in fact most—were. By December 11, Blue and the Public Health Service issued a bulletin warning that "influenza has not passed and severe epidemic conditions exist in various parts of the country. . . . In California, increase; Iowa, a marked increase; Kentucky, decided recrudescence in Louisville and larger towns, and in contrast to earlier stage of epidemic disease now affects many schoolchildren; Louisiana, disease again increased in New Orleans, Shreveport, [in] Lake Charles height reached equalled last wave; . . . St. Louis 1,700 cases in three days; Nebraska very serious; Ohio recrudescences in Cincinnati, Cleveland, Columbus, Akron, Ashtabula, Salem, Medina . . . ; in Pennsylvania, conditions are worse than the original outbreak in Johnstown, Erie, Newcastle. The state of Washington shows a sharp increase. . . . West Virginia reports recrudescence in Charleston."

By any standard except that of the second wave, this third wave was a lethal epidemic. And in a few isolated areas—such as Michigan—December and January were actually worse than October. In Phoenix for three days in a row in mid-January, the new cases set a record exceeding any in the fall. Quitman, Georgia, issued twenty-seven epidemic ordinances that took effect December 13, 1918, after the disease had seemingly passed. Savannah on January 15 ordered theaters and public gathering places closed—for a third time—with even more rigid restrictions than before. San Francisco had gotten off lightly in the fall wave, as had the rest of the West Coast, but the third wave struck hard.

In fact, of all the major cities in the country, San Francisco had confronted the fall wave most honestly and efficiently. That may have had something to do with its surviving, and rebuilding itself after, the massive earthquake of only a dozen years before. Now on September 21 public health director William Hassler quarantined all naval installations, even before any cases surfaced in them or in the city. He mobilized the entire city in advance, recruiting hundreds of drivers and volunteers and dividing the city into districts, each with its own medical personnel, phones, transport and supply, and emergency hospitals in schools and churches. He closed public places. And far from the usual assurances that the disease was ordinary "la grippe," on October 22 the mayor, Hassler, the Red Cross, the Chamber of Commerce, and the Labor Council jointly declared in a full-page newspaper ad, "Wear a mask and save your life!" claiming that it was "99% proof against influenza." By October 26, the Red Cross had distributed one hundred thousand masks. Simultaneously, while local facilities geared up to produce vaccine, thousands of doses of a vaccine made by a Tufts scientist were raced across the continent on the country's fastest train.

In San Francisco, people felt a sense of control. Instead of the paralyzing fear found in too many other communities, it seemed to inspire. Historian Alfred Crosby has provided a picture of the city under siege, and his picture shows citizens behaving with heroism, anxious and fearful but accepting their duty. When schools closed, teachers volunteered as nurses, orderlies, telephone operators. On November 21, every siren in the city signaled that masks could come off. San Francisco had—to that point—survived with far fewer deaths than had been feared, and citizens believed that the masks deserved the credit. But if anything helped, it would have been the organization Hassler had set in place in advance.

The next day the **Chronicle** crowed that in the city's history "one of the most thrilling episodes will be the story of how gallantly the city of Saint Francis behaved when the black wings of war-bred pestilence hovered over the city."

They thought that **they** had controlled it, that

they had stopped it. They were mistaken. The masks were useless. The vaccine was useless. The city had simply been lucky. Two weeks later, the third wave struck. Although at its peak it killed only half as many as did the second wave, it made the final death rates for the city the worst on the West Coast.

With the exception of a few small outposts that isolated themselves, there was by early in 1919 only one place the virus had missed.

Australia had escaped. It had escaped because of a stringent quarantine of incoming ships. Some ships arrived there with attack rates as high as 43 percent and fatality rates among **all** passengers as high as 7 percent. But the quarantine kept the virus out, kept the continent safe, until late December 1918 when, with influenza having receded around the world, a troopship carrying ninety ill soldiers arrived. Although they too were quarantined, the disease penetrated—apparently through medical personnel treating troops.

By then the strain had lost much of its lethality. In Australia the death rates from influenza were far less than in any other Westernized nation on earth, barely one-third that of the United States, not even one-quarter that of Italy. But it was lethal enough.

When it struck in January and February, the war had been over for more than two months. Censorship had ended with it. And so in Australia the newspapers were free to write what they wanted. And, more than in any other English-language newspaper, what they wrote of was terror.

"We are told by some that the influenza is a return of the old 'Black death,'" reported one Sydney newspaper. Another quoted the classic, Daniel Defoe's **Journal of the Plague Year**—a work of fiction—for advice on precautions to take to prevent "the influenza plague." And headlines of terror ran day after day after day after day: "How They Fought Plagues in the Old Days," "The Pneumonic Plague," "Fighting the Plague," "Plagues in the Past," "The Pagans and the Plague," "Did the Plague Start in NSW?" "Catholic Chaplains in Plague Stricken Camps," "Catholics as Plague Fighters."

The pandemic itself—even in this its most mild incarnation in the developed world—was terrifying enough that those who lived through it as children remembered it not as influenza at all, but as plague. One Australian historian in the 1990s was recording oral histories. She was struck when people she interviewed mentioned "Bubonic Plague," and she explored the issue further.

One subject told her, "I can recall the Bubonic Plague, people dying by the hundreds around us that was come back from the First World War."

Another: "We had to get vaccinated. . . . And I bear the scar today where I was inoculated against the Bubonic Plague."

Another: "I can remember the Plague. There were

doctors going around in cabs with gowns and masks over their faces."

Another: "They all wore masks . . . after the war and how they used to be worried here in Sydney . . . about the Plague."

Another: "We were quarantined, our food was delivered to the front door. . . . We didn't read about the Bubonic Plague. We lived it."

Another: "[T]hey called it the Bubonic Plague. But in France they called it bronchial pneumonia. See that's what they said my brother died from. . . ."

Another: "The Plague. The Bubonic Plague. Yes, I can remember that. . . . I always understood it was the same kind of flu that swept Europe, the Black Death in the Middle Ages. I think it was the same kind of thing, it was carried by fleas on rats."

Another: "Bubonic Plague . . . I think it might have been called a form of influenza towards the finish. . . . The Bubonic Plague was a thing that stuck in my mind . . ."

Yet this was after all only influenza, and the influenza that struck Australia in 1919 was weaker than it was anywhere else in the world. Perhaps the measure of the extraordinary power of the 1918 virus was this: in Australia, without a censored press, the memory that stuck in the mind was not of influenza at all. It was of the Black Death.

The virus was still not finished. All through the spring of 1919 a kind of rolling thunder moved

above the earth, intermittent, unleashing sometimes a sudden localized storm, sometimes even a
lightning bolt, and sometimes passing over with
only a rumble of threatened violence in the distant
and dark sky.

It remained violent enough to do one more thing.

CHAPTER THIRTY-TWO

THE OVERWHELMING MAJORITY of victims, especially in the Western world, recovered quickly and fully. This was, after all, only influenza.

But the virus sometimes caused one final complication, one final sequela. The influenza virus affected the brain and nervous system. All high fevers cause delirium, but this was something else. An army physician at Walter Reed Hospital investigating serious mental disturbances and even psychoses that seemed to follow an attack of influenza specifically noted, "Delirium occurring at the height of the disease and clearing with the cessation of fever is not considered in this report."

The connection between influenza and various mental instabilities seemed clear. The evidence was almost entirely anecdotal, the worst and weakest kind of evidence, but it convinced the vast majority of contemporary observers that influenza could alter mental processes. What convinced them were observations such as these:

From Britain: ". . . profound mental inertia with intense physical prostration. Delirium has been very common. . . . It has varied from mere confusion of ideas through all grades of intensity up to maniacal excitement."

From Italy: ". . . influenzal psychoses of the acute period . . . as a rule subside in two or three weeks. The psychosis, however, may pass into a state of mental collapse, with stupor which may persist and become actual dementia. In other cases . . . depression and restlessness . . . to [which] can be attributed the large number of suicides during the pandemic of influenza."

From France: ". . . frequent and serious mental disturbances during convalescence from and as a result of influenza. . . . The mental disturbances sometimes took on the form of acute delirium with agitation, violence, fear and erotic excitation and at other times was of a depressive nature . . . fear of persecution."

From different U.S. Army cantonments: ". . . The mental condition was either apathetic or there was an active delirium. Cerebration was slow. . . . The patient's statements and assurances were unreliable, a moribund person stating he felt very well. . . . In other cases, apprehensiveness was most striking."

". . . The mental depression of the patient is often out of all proportion to the other symptoms."

". . . Nervous symptoms appeared early, restlessness and delirium being marked."

". . . melancholia, hysteria, and insanity with suicidal intent."

". . . Toxic involvement of the nervous system was evident in all the more severe cases."

". . . Many patients lay in muttering delirium which persisted after the temperature was normal."

". . . Symptoms referable to the central nervous system were seen at times, as twitching of the muscles of the fingers, forearms, and face, . . . an active, even maniacal occasional delirium, or more usually the low mumbling type."

". . . Infectious psychosis was seen in 18 cases, from simple transient hallucinations to maniacal frenzy with needed mechanical restraint."

Contemporary observers also linked influenza to an increase in Parkinson's disease a decade later. (Some have theorized that the patients in Oliver Sacks's **The Awakening** were victims of the 1918 influenza pandemic.) Many believed that the virus could cause schizophrenia, and in 1926, Karl Menninger studied links between influenza and schizophrenia. His study was considered significant enough that the **American Journal of Psychiatry** identified it as a "classic" article and reprinted it in 1994. Menninger spoke of the "almost un-equalled neurotoxicity of influenza" and noted that two-thirds of those diagnosed with schizophrenia after an attack of influenza had completely recovered five years later. Recovery from schizophrenia is extremely rare, suggesting that some reparable process had caused the initial symptoms.

In 1927 the American Medical Association's review of hundreds of medical journal articles from around the world concluded: "There seems to be general agreement that influenza may act on the brain. . . . From the delirium accompanying many acute attacks to the psychoses that develop as 'post-influenzal' manifestations, there is no doubt that the neuropsychiatric effects of influenza are profound and varied. . . . The effect of the influenza virus on the nervous system is hardly second to its effect on the respiratory tract."

In 1934 a similar comprehensive review by British scientists agreed: "There would appear to be no doubt that influenza exerts a profound influence on the nervous system."

In 1992 an investigator studying the connection between suicide and the war instead concluded, "World War I did not influence suicide; the Great Influenza Epidemic caused it to increase."

A 1996 virology textbook said, "A wide spectrum of central nervous system involvement has been observed during influenza A virus infections in humans, ranging from irritability, drowsiness, boisterousness, and confusion to the more serious manifestations of psychosis, delirium, and coma."

The 1997 Hong Kong virus that killed six of the eighteen people infected provided some physical evidence. Autopsies of two victims showed "edematous brains." "Edema" means "swelling." "Most remarkably, bone marrow, lymphoid tissue, liver, and spleen of both patients were heavily infiltrated with [macrophages]. . . . One patient even had such cells on the meninges"—the membranes surrounding the brain and spinal cord—"and in the white matter of the cerebrum." The most likely reason for these macrophages to have infiltrated the brain was to follow the virus there, and kill it. And that 1997 pathology report echoes some from 1918: "**In cases accompanied by delirium, the meninges of the brain are richly infiltrated by serous fluid and the capillaries are injected. . . . Necropsy in the fatal cases demonstrated congestive lesions with small meningeal hemorrhages and especially in islands of edema in the cortical substance surrounding greatly dilated small vessels . . . hemorrhages into gray matter of the cord . . . [brain] tissue cells were altered in these zones of . . . edema."**

In 2002 Robert Webster, one of the world's leading experts on the virus at St. Jude Children's Hospital in Memphis, observed, "These viruses do from time to time get across to central nervous systems and play hell." He recalled a child in

Memphis who was an excellent student, got influenza, and became "a vegetable. I've seen enough examples in my lifetime to believe . . . influenza can get into the brain. It's tenuous but real. Put the virus into chickens, it can go up the olfactory nerve and the chicken's dead."

The 1918 virus did seem to reach the brain. The war fought on that battlefield could destroy brain cells and make it difficult to concentrate, or alter behavior, or interfere with thinking, or even cause temporary psychosis. If this occurred in only a minority of cases, the virus's impact on the mind was nonetheless real.

But that impact would, by terrible coincidence, have a profound effect indeed.

In January 1919 in France, Congressman William Borland of Kansas died, the third congressmen to be killed by the virus. That same month also in Paris, "Colonel" Edward House, Wilson's closest confidant, collapsed with influenza—again.

House had first gotten influenza during the first wave in March 1918, was confined to his home for two weeks, went to Washington and relapsed, and then spent three weeks in bed at the White House. Although a spring attack often conferred immunity to the virus, after the Armistice he was struck down a second time. He was in Europe then, and on November 30 he got up for the first time in ten days and met with French premier Georges Clemenceau for fifteen minutes. Afterward he noted, "Today is the first day I have taken up my official work in person for over a week. I have had influenza 10 days and have been exceeding miserable. . . . So many have died since this epidemic has scourged the world. Many of my staff have died and poor Willard Straight among them."

Now, in January 1919, he was attacked still a third time. He was sick enough that some papers reported him dead. House wryly called the obituaries "all too generous." But the blow was heavy: more than a month after his supposed recovery he wrote in his diary, "When I fell sick in January I lost the thread of affairs and I am not sure that I have ever gotten fully back."

There were affairs of some magnitude to attend to in Paris in early 1919.

Representatives of victorious nations, of weak nations, of nations hoping to be born from the splinters of defeated nations, had all come there to set the terms of peace. Several thousand men from dozens of countries circled around the edges of decision making. Germany would play no role in these decisions; Germany would simply be dictated to. And among this host of nations, this virtual Tower of Babel, a Council of Ten of the most powerful nations supposedly determined the agenda. Even within this tight circle was a tighter one, the "Big Four"—the United States, France, Britain, and

Italy. And in reality only three of those four nations mattered. Indeed, only three men mattered.

French premier Georges Clemenceau, known as "the Tiger," negotiated with a bullet in his shoulder, put there by an assassination attempt during the peace conference on February 19. Prime Minister Lloyd George of Great Britain faced such political problems at home he was described as "a greased marble spinning on a glass table top." And there was Wilson, who arrived in Europe the most popular political figure in the world.

For weeks and then months the meetings dragged on, and tens of thousands of pages of drafts and memos and understandings went back and forth between ministers and staff. But Wilson, Clemenceau, and George did not much need these thousands of pages. They were not simply ratifying what foreign ministers and staffs had worked out, nor were they simply making decisions on options presented to them. They were themselves doing much of the actual negotiating. They were bargaining and wheedling, they were demanding and insisting, and they were rejecting.

Often only five or six men would be in a room, including translators. Often, even when Clemenceau and George had others present, Wilson represented the United States alone, with no staff, no secretary of state, no Colonel House, who by now had been all but discarded as untrustworthy by Wilson.

Interrupted only by Wilson's relatively brief return to the United States, discussions were interminable. But they were deciding the future of the world.

In October, at the peak of the epidemic in Paris, 4,574 people had died there of influenza or pneumonia. The disease had never entirely left that city. In February 1919, deaths in Paris from influenza and pneumonia climbed back up to 2,676, more than half the peak death toll. Wilson's daughter Margaret had influenza in February; she was kept in bed in Brussels at the American legation. In March another 1,517 Parisians died, and the **Journal of the American Medical Association** reported that in Paris "the epidemic of influenza which had declined has broken out anew in a most disquieting manner. . . . The epidemic has assumed grave proportions, not only in Paris but in several of the departments."

That month Wilson's wife, his wife's secretary, Chief White House Usher Irwin Hoover, and Cary Grayson, Wilson's personal White House physician and perhaps the single man Wilson trusted the most, were all ill. Clemenceau and Lloyd George both seemed to have mild cases of influenza.

Meanwhile the sessions with George and Clemenceau were often brutal. In late March Wilson told his wife, "Well, thank God I can still fight, and I'll win."

On March 29, Wilson said, "M. Clemenceau called me pro-German and left the room."

Wilson continued to fight, insisting, "The only principle I recognize is that of the consent of the governed." On April 2, after the negotiations for the day finished, he called the French "damnable"—for him, a deeply religious man, an extreme epithet. He told his press spokesman Ray Stannard Baker, "[W]e've got to make peace on the principles laid down and accepted, or not make it at all."

The next day, April 3, a Thursday, at three P.M., Wilson seemed in fine health, according to Cary Grayson. Then, very suddenly at six o'clock, Grayson saw Wilson "seized with violent paroxysms of coughing, which were so severe and frequent that it interfered with his breathing."

The attack came so suddenly that Grayson suspected that Wilson had been poisoned, that an assassination attempt had been made. But it soon became obvious the diagnosis was simpler, if only marginally more reassuring.

Joseph Tumulty, Wilson's chief of staff, had stayed in Washington to monitor political developments at home. Grayson and he exchanged telegrams daily, sometimes several times a day. But the information of the president's illness was too sensitive for a telegram. Grayson did wire him, "The President took very severe cold last night; confined to bed." Simultaneously he also wrote a confidential letter to be hand-delivered: "The President was taken violently sick last Thursday. He had a fever of over 103 and profuse diarrhoea. . . . [It was] the beginning of an attack of influenza. That night was one of the worst through which I have ever passed. I was able to control the spasms of coughing but his condition looked very serious."

Donald Frary, a young aide on the American peace delegation, came down with influenza the same day Wilson did. Four days later he died at age twenty-five.

For several days Wilson lay in bed, unable to move. On the fourth day, he sat up. Grayson wired Tumulty, "Am taking every precaution with him. . . . Your aid and presence were never needed more."

Wilson for the first time was well enough to have visitors. He received American commissioners in his bedroom and said, "Gentlemen, this is not a meeting of the Peace Commission. It is more a Council of War."

Just before getting sick Wilson had threatened to leave the conference, to return to the United States without a treaty rather than yield on his principles. He repeated that threat again, telling Grayson to order the **George Washington** to be ready to sail as soon as he was well enough to travel. The next day Gilbert Close, his secretary, wrote his wife, "I never knew the president to be in such a difficult frame of mind as now. Even while lying in bed he manifested peculiarities."

Meanwhile the negotiations continued; Wilson, unable to participate, was forced to rely on House as his stand-in. (Wilson had even less trust in Secretary of State Robert Lansing, whom he largely ignored, than in House.) For several days Wilson continued to talk about leaving France, telling his wife, "If I have lost the fight, which I would not have done had I been on my feet, I will retire in good order, so we will go home."

Then, on April 8, Wilson insisted upon personally rejoining the negotiations. He could not go out. Clemenceau and George came to his bedroom, but the conversations did not go well. His public threat to leave had infuriated Clemenceau, who privately called him "a cook who keeps her trunk ready in the hallway."

Grayson wrote that despite "that ill-omened attack of influenza, the insidious effects of which he was not in good condition to resist, . . . [the president] insisted upon holding conferences while he was still confined to his sickbed. When he was able to get up he began to drive himself as hard as before—morning, afternoon, and frequently evening conferences."

Herbert Hoover, not part of the American peace delegation but a large figure in Paris because he had charge of feeding a desolated and barren Europe, said, "Prior to that time, in all matters with which I had to deal, he was incisive, quick to grasp essentials, unhesitating in conclusions, and most willing to take advice from men he trusted. . . . [Now] others as well as I found we had to push against an unwilling mind. And at times, when I just had to get decisions, I suffered as much from having to mentally push as he did in coming to conclusions." Hoover believed Wilson's mind had lost "resiliency."

Colonel Starling of the Secret Service noticed that Wilson "lacked his old quickness of grasp, and tired easily." He became obsessed with such details as who was using the official automobiles. When Ray Stannard Baker was first allowed to see Wilson again, he trembled at Wilson's sunken eyes, at his weariness, at his pale and haggard look, like that of a man whose flesh has shrunk away from his face, showing his skull.

Chief Usher Irwin Hoover recalled several new and very strange ideas that Wilson suddenly believed, including one that his home was filled with French spies: "Nothing we could say could disabuse his mind of this thought. About this time he also acquired a peculiar notion he was personally responsible for all the property in the furnished place he was occupying. . . . Coming from the President, whom we all knew so well, these were very funny things, and we could but surmise that something queer was happening in his mind. One thing was certain: he was never the same after this little spell of sickness."

Grayson confided to Tumulty, "This is a matter that worries me."

"I have never seen the President look so worn and tired," Ray Baker said. In the afternoon "he could not remember without an effort what the council had done in the forenoon."

Then, abruptly, still on his sickbed, only a few days after he had threatened to leave the conference unless Clemenceau yielded to his demands, without warning to or discussion with any other Americans, Wilson suddenly abandoned principles he had previously insisted upon. He yielded to Clemenceau everything of significance Clemenceau wanted, virtually all of which Wilson had earlier opposed.

Now, in bed, he approved a formula Clemenceau had written demanding German reparations and that Germany accept all responsibility for starting the war. The Rhineland would be demilitarized; Germany would not be allowed to have troops within thirty miles of the east bank of the Rhine. The rich coal fields of the Saar region would be mined by France and the region would be administered by the new League of Nations for fifteen years, and then a plebiscite would determine whether the region would belong to France or Germany. The provinces of Alsace and Lorraine, which Germany had seized after the Franco-Prussian War, were moved from Germany back to France. West Prussia and Posen were given to Poland—creating the "Polish corridor" that separated two parts of Germany. The German air force was eliminated, its army limited to one hundred thousand men, its colonies stripped away—but not freed, simply redistributed to other powers.

Even Lloyd George commented on Wilson's "nervous and spiritual breakdown in the middle of the Conference."

Grayson wrote, "These are terrible days for the President physically and otherwise."

As Grayson made that notation, Wilson was conceding to Italy much of its demands and agreeing to Japan's insistence that it take over German concessions in China. In return the Japanese offered an oral—not written—promise of good behavior, a promise given not even to Wilson personally or, for that matter, to any chief of state, but to British Foreign Secretary Alfred Balfour.

On May 7 the Germans were presented with the treaty. They complained that it violated the very principles Wilson had declared were inviolate. Wilson left the meeting saying, "What abominable manners. . . . This is the most tactless speech I have ever heard."

Yet they had not reminded Wilson and the world that he had once said that a lasting peace could be achieved only by—and that he had once called for—"A peace without victory."

Wilson also told Baker, "If I were a German, I think I should never sign it."

Four months later Wilson suffered a major and debilitating stroke. For months his wife and Grayson would control all access to him and become arguably the de facto most important policy makers in the country.

In 1929 one man wrote a memoir in which he said that two doctors believed Wilson was suffering from arteriosclerosis when he went to Paris. In 1946 a physician voiced the same opinion in print. In 1958 a major biography of Wilson stated that experts on arteriosclerosis questioned Grayson's diagnosis of influenza and believed Wilson had instead suffered a vascular occlusion—a minor stroke. In 1960 a historian writing about the health of presidents said, "Present-day views are that [Wilson's disorientation] was based on brain damage, probably caused by arteriosclerotic occlusion of blood vessels." In 1964 another historian called Wilson's attack "thrombosis." In a 1970 article in the **Journal of American History,** titled "Woodrow Wilson's Neurological Illness," another historian called it "a little stroke."

Only one historian, Alfred Crosby, seems to have paid any attention to Wilson's actual symptoms—including high fever, severe coughing, and total prostration, all symptoms that perfectly fit influenza and have no association whatsoever with stroke—and the on-site diagnosis of Grayson, an excellent physician highly respected by such men as Welch, Gorgas, Flexner, and Vaughan.

Despite Crosby, the myth of Wilson's having suffered a minor stroke persists. Even a prize-winning account of the peace conference published in 2002 observes, "Wilson by contrast had aged visibly and the tic in his cheek grew more pronounced. . . . [It] may have been a minor stroke, a forerunner of the massive one he was to have four months later."

There was no stroke. There was only influenza. Indeed, the virus may have contributed to the stroke. Damage to blood vessels in the brain were often noted in autopsy reports in 1918, as they were in 1997. Grayson believed influenza was a cause of Wilson's "final breakdown." An epidemiological study published in 2004 demonstrates definite linkage between influenza and stroke.

It is of course impossible to say what Wilson would have done had he not become sick. Perhaps he would have made the concessions anyway, trading every principle away to save his League of Nations. Or perhaps he would have sailed home as he had threatened to do just as he was succumbing to the disease. Then either there would have been no treaty or his walkout would have forced Clemenceau to compromise.

No one can know what would have happened. One can only know what did happen.

Influenza did visit the peace conference. Influenza did strike Wilson. Influenza did weaken him physically, and—precisely at the most crucial point of negotiations—influenza did at the least drain from him stamina and the ability to concentrate. That much is certain. And it is almost certain that influenza affected his mind in other, deeper ways.

Historians with virtual unanimity agree that the harshness toward Germany of the Paris peace treaty helped create the economic hardship, nationalistic reaction, and political chaos that fostered the rise of Adolf Hitler.

It did not require hindsight to see the dangers. They were obvious at the time. John Maynard Keynes quit Paris calling Wilson "the greatest fraud on earth." Later he wrote, "We are at the dead season of our fortunes. . . . Never in the lifetime of men now living has the universal element in the soul of man burnt so dimly." Herbert Hoover believed that the treaty would tear down all Europe, and said so.

Soon after Wilson made his concessions a group of young American diplomatic aides and advisers met in disgust to decide whether to resign in protest. They included Samuel Eliot Morison, William Bullitt, Adolf Berle Jr., Christian Herter, John Foster Dulles, Lincoln Steffens, and Walter Lippmann. All were already or would become among the most influential men in the country. Two would become secretary of state. Bullitt, Berle, and Morison did resign. In September, during the fight over ratifying the treaty, Bullitt revealed to the Senate the private comments of Secretary of State Robert Lansing that the League of Nations would be useless, that the great powers had simply arranged the world to suit themselves.

Berle, later an assistant secretary of state, settled for writing Wilson a blistering letter of resignation:

"I am sorry that you did not fight our fight to the finish and that you had so little faith in the millions of men, like myself, in every nation who had faith in you. Our government has consented now to deliver the suffering peoples of the world to new oppressions, subjections and dismemberments—a new century of war."

Wilson had influenza, only influenza.

CHAPTER THIRTY-THREE

ON SEPTEMBER 29, 1919, Sir William Osler began coughing. One of the original "Four Doctors" in a famous portrait of the founding faculty of the Johns Hopkins Medical School, a portrait that symbolized the new primacy of science in American medicine, he was and still is regarded as one of the greatest clinicians in history. A man of wide interests, a friend of Walt Whitman, and author of the textbook that ultimately led to the founding of the Rockefeller Institute for Medical Research, Osler was then at Oxford.

Osler had already suffered one great loss with the death of his only child in the war. Now he suffered as well from a respiratory infection he diagnosed as influenza. In Oxford that fall, influenza was

prevalent enough that the dons considered post-
poning the school term. To his sister-in-law, Osler
wrote, "For two days I felt very ill & exhausted
by the paroxysms" of coughing. He seemed to recover, but on October 13 his temperature rose
to 102.5. He wrote a friend he had "one of those
broncho-pneumonias so common after influenza."
He tried to work on a talk about Whitman and also
wrote Welch and John D. Rockefeller Jr. about giving a grant to his alma mater, McGill University.
But on November 7, he felt "a stab and then fire-
works" on his right side. Twelve hours later he began
coughing again: "A bout arrived which ripped
all pleural attachments to smithereens, & with it
the pain."

After three weeks his physicians took him off morphine, gave him atropine, and said they were encouraged. On December 5 he received a local anesthetic
and a needle was inserted into his lungs to drain
fourteen ounces of pus. He gave up working on his
Whitman talk and felt certain now of the end, jok-
ing, "I've been watching this case for two months
and I'm sorry I shall not see the post mortem."

His wife did not like the joke. His pessimism
was crushing her: "[W]hatever he says always does
come true—so how can I hope for anything but
a fatal ending?" She tried to remain optimistic as
the disease dragged on. But one day she found him
reciting a Tennyson poem: "Of happy men that
have the power to die, / And grassy barrows of

the happier dead. / Release me, and restore me to the ground. . . ."

He had turned seventy in July. A birthday tribute to him, a **Festschrift**—a collection of scientific articles in his honor—arrived on December 27, entitled **Contributions to Medical and Biological Research, Dedicated to Sir William Osler.** Publication had been delayed because Welch was editing them. Welch never did anything on time.

His most recent biographer believes that had he been at the Johns Hopkins Hospital instead, he would have received better care. Physicians would have used X-rays, electrocardiograms, earlier surgical intervention to drain an empyema, a pocket of pus from the lung. They might have saved him.

He died December 29, 1919, his last words being, "Hold up my head."

He had always held his head high.

If finally it seemed past, yet it wasn't past. In September 1919, as Osler was dying, Blue predicted that influenza would return: "Communities should make plans now for dealing with any recurrences. The most promising way to deal with a possible recurrence is, to sum it up in a single word, 'preparedness.' And now is the time to prepare."

On September 20, 1919, many of the best scientists in the country met to try to reach a consensus on the cause of the disease or course of therapy. They could not, but the **New York Times** stated that the conference marked the beginning of a joint federal, state, and city effort to prevent a recurrence. Two days later the Red Cross distributed its own confidential battle plan internally: "Proposed Staff Organization for Possible Influenza Emergency / Confidential / Note: No publicity is to be given this bulletin until . . . the first indication of a recurrence of influenza in epidemic form, but until such time there should be no public statement by a Red Cross Chapter or Division office."

By February 7, 1920, influenza had returned with enough ferocity that the Red Cross declared, "Owing to the rapid spread of influenza, the safety of the country demands, as a patriotic duty, that all available nurses or anyone with experience in nursing, communicate with the nearest Red Cross chapters or special local epidemic committees, offering their services."

In eight weeks in early 1920, eleven thousand influenza-related deaths occurred in just New York City and Chicago, and in New York City more cases would be reported on a single day than on any one day in 1918. In Chicago, Health Commissioner John Dill Robertson, who had been so concerned about morale in 1918, organized three thousand of the most professional nurses into regional squads that could range over the entire city. Whenever an influenza case developed, that victim's home was tagged.

The year 1920 would see either (sources differ)

the second or third most deaths from influenza and pneumonia in the twentieth century. And it continued to strike cities sporadically. As late as January 1922, for example, Washington State's health director, Dr. Paul Turner, while refusing to admit the return of influenza, declared, "The severe respiratory infection which is epidemic at this time throughout the state is to be dealt with the same as influenza. . . . Enforce absolute quarantine."

Only in the next few years did it finally fade away in both the United States and the world. It did not disappear. It continued to attack, but with far less virulence, partly because the virus mutated further toward its mean, toward the behavior of most influenza viruses, partly because people's immune systems adjusted. But it left a legacy.

Even before the epidemic ended, New York City Health Commissioner Royal Copeland estimated that twenty-one thousand children in the city had been made orphans by the epidemic. He had no estimate of children who lost only one parent. Berlin, New Hampshire, a tiny town, had twenty-four orphaned children, not counting, said a Red Cross worker, "in one street sixteen motherless children." Vinton County, Ohio, population thirteen thousand, reported one hundred children orphaned by the virus. Minersville, Pennsylvania, in the coal regions, had a population of six thousand; there the virus had orphaned two hundred children.

In March 1919 a senior Red Cross official advised district officers to help wherever possible on an emergency basis, because "the influenza epidemic not only caused the deaths of some six hundred thousand people, but it also left a trail of lowered vitality . . . nervous breakdown, and other sequella [sic] which now threaten thousands of people. It left widows and orphans and dependent old people. It has reduced many of these families to poverty and acute distress. This havoc is wide spread, reaching all parts of the United States and all classes of people."

Months after "recovering" from his illness, the poet Robert Frost wondered, "What bones are they that rub together so unpleasantly in the middle of you in extreme emaciation . . . ? I don't know whether or not I'm strong enough to write a letter yet."

Cincinnati Health Commissioner Dr. William H. Peters told the American Public Health Association meeting almost a year after the epidemic that "phrases like 'I'm not feeling right,' 'I don't have my usual pep,' 'I'm all in since I had the flu' have become commonplace." Cincinnati's public health agencies had examined 7,058 influenza victims since the epidemic had ended and found that 5,264 needed some medical assistance; 643 of them had heart problems, and an extraordinary number of prominent citizens who had had influenza had died suddenly early in 1919. While it was hardly a sci-entific sample, Peters believed that few victims had escaped without some pathological changes.

Throughout the world similar phenomena were noted. In the next few years a disease known as "encephalitis lethargica" spread through much of the West. Although no pathogen was ever identified and the disease itself has since disappeared—indeed, there is no incontrovertible evidence that the disease, in a clearly definable scientific sense, ever existed—physicians at the time did believe in the disease, and a consensus considered it a result of influenza.

There were other aftershocks impossible to quantify. There was the angry emptiness of a parent or a husband or a wife. Secretary of War Newton Baker—who had been criticized for being a pacifist when Wilson appointed him—particularly took to heart charges that War Department policies had in effect murdered young men. In several cases troops from Devens were transferred to a post whose commander protested receiving them because of the epidemic. The protests were futile, the troops came, and so did influenza. The father of one boy who died at such a camp wrote Baker, "My belief is that the heads of the War Department are responsible." Baker replied in a seven-page, single-spaced letter, a letter of his own agony.

The world was still sick, sick to the heart. The war itself . . . The senseless deaths at home, on top of all else . . . Wilson's betrayal of ideals at Versailles, a betrayal that penetrated the soul . . . The utter failure of science, the greatest achievement of modern man, in the face of the disease . . .

In January 1923 John Dewey wrote in the **New Republic,** "It may be doubted if the consciousness of sickness was ever so widespread as it is today. . . . The interest in cures and salvations is evidence of how sick the world is." He was speaking of a consciousness that went beyond physical disease, but physical disease was part of it. He was speaking of the world of which F. Scott Fitzgerald declared "all Gods dead, all wars fought, all faiths in man shaken."

The disease has survived in memory more than in any literature. Nearly all those who were adults during the pandemic have died now. Now the memory lives in the minds of those who only heard stories, who heard how their mother lost her father, how an uncle became an orphan, or heard an aunt say, "It was the only time I ever saw my father cry." Memory dies with people.

The writers of the 1920s had little to say about it. Mary McCarthy got on a train in Seattle on October 30, 1918, with her three brothers and sisters, her aunt and uncle, and her parents. They arrived in Minneapolis three days later, all of them sick—her father had pulled out a gun when the conductor tried to put them off the train—met by her grandparents wearing masks. All the hospitals were full and so they went home. Her aunt and uncle recovered but her father, Roy, thirty-eight years old, died on November 6, and her mother, Tess, twenty-nine years old, died November 7. In **Memories of a Catholic Girlhood** she spoke of how deeply being an orphan affected her, made her desperate to distinguish herself, and she vividly remembered the train ride across two-thirds of the country, but she said almost nothing of the epidemic.

John Dos Passos was in his early twenties and seriously ill with influenza, yet barely mentioned the disease in his fiction. Hemingway, Faulkner, Fitzgerald said next to nothing of it. William Maxwell, a **New Yorker** writer and novelist, lost his mother to the disease. Her death sent his father, brother, and him inward. He recalled, "I had to guess what my older brother was thinking. It was not something he cared to share with me. If I hadn't known, I would have thought that he'd had his feelings hurt by something he was too proud to talk about. . . ." For himself, "[T]he ideas that kept recurring to me, perhaps because of that pacing the floor with my father, was that I had inadvertently walked through a door that I shouldn't have gone through and couldn't get back to the place I hadn't meant to leave." Of his father he said, "His sadness was of the kind that is patient and without hope." For himself, "the death of my mother . . . was a motivating force in four books."

Katherine Anne Porter was ill enough that her obituary was set in type. She recovered. Her fiancé did not. Years later her haunting novella of the disease and the time, "Pale Horse, Pale Rider," is one of the best—and one of the few—sources for what life was like during the disease. And she lived through it in Denver, a city that, compared to those in the east, was struck only a glancing blow.

But the relative lack of impact it left on literature may not be unusual at all. It may not be that much unlike what happened centuries ago. One scholar of medieval literature says, "While there are a few vivid and terrifying accounts, it's actually striking how little was written on the bubonic plague. Outside of these few very well-known accounts, there is almost nothing in literature about it afterwards."

People write about war. They write about the Holocaust. They write about horrors that people inflict on people. Apparently they forget the horrors that nature inflicts on people, the horrors that make humans least significant. And yet the pandemic resonated. When the Nazis took control of Germany in 1933, Christopher Isherwood wrote of Berlin: "The whole city lay under an epidemic of discreet, infectious fear. I could feel it, like influenza, in my bones."

Those historians who have examined epidemics and analyzed how societies have responded to them have generally argued that those with power blamed the poor for their own suffering, and sometimes tried to stigmatize and isolate them. (The case of "Typhoid Mary" Mallon, an Irish immigrant in effect imprisoned for twenty-five years, is a classic instance of this attitude; if she had been of another class, the treatment of her might well have been different.) Those in power, historians have observed, often sought security in imposing order, which gave them some feeling of control, some feeling that the world still made sense.

In 1918 what might be considered a "power elite" did sometimes behave according to such a pattern. Denver Health Commissioner William Sharpley, for example, blamed the city's difficulties with influenza on "foreign settlements of the city," chiefly Italians. The **Durango Evening Herald** blamed the high death toll among Utes on a reservation on their "negligence and disobedience to the advice of their superintendent and nurses and physicians." One Red Cross worker in the mining regions of Kentucky took offense at uncleanliness: "When we reached the miserable shack it seemed deserted. . . . I went on in and there lying with her legs out of the bed and her head thrown way back on a filthy pillow was the woman, stone dead, her eyes staring, her mouth yawning, a most gruesome sight. . . . The mother of the woman's husband came in, an old woman living in an indescribable shack some 300 feet away. . . . I can still smell the terrible odor and will never forget the nauseating sight. The penalty for filth is death."

Yet, despite such occasional harshness, the 1918 influenza pandemic did not in general demonstrate a pattern of race or class antagonism. In

epidemiological terms there was a correlation between population density and hence class and
deaths, but the disease still struck down everyone.
And the deaths of soldiers of such promise and
youth struck home with everyone. The disease
was too universal, too obviously not tied to race
or class. In Philadelphia, white and black certainly
got comparable treatment. In mining areas around
the country, whether out of self-interest or not,
mine owners tried to find doctors for their workers. In Alaska, racism notwithstanding, authorities
launched a massive rescue effort, if too late, to save
Eskimos. Even the very Red Cross worker so nause-
ated by filth continued to risk his own life day after
day in one of the hardest-hit areas of the country.

During the second wave, many local governments collapsed, and those who held the real power
in a community—from Philadelphia's bluebloods
to Phoenix's citizens' committee—took over. But
generally they exercised power to protect the entire
community rather than to split it, to distribute resources widely rather than to guarantee resources
for themselves.

Despite that effort, whoever held power, whether
a city government or some private gathering of the
locals, they generally failed to keep the community
together. They failed because they lost trust. They
lost trust because they lied. (San Francisco was a
rare exception; its leaders told the truth, and the
city responded heroically.) And they lied for the

war effort, for the propaganda machine that Wilson had created.

It is impossible to quantify how many deaths the lies caused. It is impossible to quantify how many young men died because the army refused to follow the advice of its own surgeon general. But while those in authority were reassuring people that this was influenza, only influenza, nothing different from ordinary "la grippe," at least some people must have believed them, at least some people must have exposed themselves to the virus in ways they would not have otherwise, and at least some of these people must have died who would otherwise have lived. And fear really did kill people. It killed them because those who feared would not care for many of those who needed but could not find care, those who needed only hydration, food, and rest to survive.

It is also impossible to state with any accuracy the death toll. The statistics are estimates only, and one can only say that the totals are numbing.

The few places in the world that then kept reliable vital statistics under normal circumstances could not keep pace with the disease. In the United States, only large cities and twenty-four states kept accurate enough statistics for the U.S. Public Health Service to include them in their database, the so-called registration area. Even in them, everyone from physicians to city clerks was trying to survive or help

others survive. Record keeping had low priority,
and even in the aftermath little effort was made to
compile accurate numbers. Many who died never
saw a doctor or nurse. Outside the developed world,
the situation was far worse, and in the rural regions
of India, the Soviet Union—which was engaged
in a brutal civil war—China, Africa, and South
America, where the disease was often most virulent,
good records were all but nonexistent.

The first significant attempt to quantify the
death toll came in 1927. An American Medical
Association–sponsored study estimated that 21 million died. When today's media refers to a death toll
of "more than 20 million" in stories on the 1918
pandemic, the source is this study.

But every revision of the deaths since 1927 has
been upward. The U.S. death toll was originally put
at 550,000. Now epidemiologists have settled on
675,000 out of a population of 105 million. In the
year 2004, the U.S. population exceeds 291 million.

Worldwide, both the estimated toll and the
population have gone up by a far greater percentage.

In the 1940s Macfarlane Burnet, the Nobel laureate who spent most of his scientific life studying influenza, estimated the death toll at 50 to
100 million.

Since then various studies, with better data and statistical methods, have gradually moved the estimates
closer and closer to his. First several studies concluded
that the death toll on the Indian subcontinent alone

may have reached 20 million. Other new estimates were presented at a 1998 international conference on the pandemic. And in 2002 an epidemiological study reviewed the data and concluded that the death toll was "in the order of 50 million, . . . [but] even this vast figure may be substantially lower than the real toll." In fact, like Burnet, it suggested that as many as 100 million died.

Given the world's population in 1918 of approximately 1.8 billion, the upper estimate would mean that in two years—and with most of the deaths coming in a horrendous twelve weeks in the fall of 1918—in excess of 5 percent of the people in the world died.

Today's world population is 6.3 billion. To give a sense of the impact in today's world of the 1918 pandemic, one has to adjust for population. If one uses the lowest estimate of deaths—the 21 million figure—that means a comparable figure today would be 73 million dead. The higher estimates translate into between 175 and 350 million dead. Those numbers are not meant to terrify—although they do. Medicine has advanced since 1918 and would have considerable impact on the mortality rate (see pages 726–729). Those numbers are meant simply to communicate what living through the pandemic was like.

Yet even those numbers understate the horror of the disease. The age distribution of the deaths brings that horror home.

In a normal influenza epidemic, 10 percent or fewer of the deaths fall among those aged between sixteen and forty. In 1918 that age group, the men and women with most vitality, most to live for, most of a future, accounted for more than half the death toll, and within that group the worst mortality figures fell upon those aged twenty-one to thirty.

The Western world suffered the least, not because its medicine was so advanced but because urbanization had exposed its population to influenza viruses, so immune systems were not naked to it. In the United States, roughly 0.65 percent of the total population died, with roughly double that percentage of young adults killed. Of developed countries, Italy suffered the worst, losing approximately 1 percent of its total population. The Soviet Union may have suffered more, but few numbers are available for it.

The virus simply ravaged the less developed world. In Mexico the most conservative estimate of the death toll was 2.3 percent of the entire population, and other reasonable estimates put the death toll over 4 percent. That means somewhere between 5 and 9 percent of all young adults died.

And in the entire world, although no one will ever know with certainty, it seems more than just possible that 5 percent—and in the less developed countries approaching 10 percent—of the world's young adults were killed by the virus.

■   ■   ■

In addition to the dead, in addition to any lingering complications among survivors, in addition to any contribution the virus made to the sense of bewilderment and betrayal and loss and nihilism of the 1920s, the 1918 pandemic left other legacies.

Some were good ones. Around the world, authorities made plans for international cooperation on health, and the experience led to restructuring public health efforts throughout the United States. The New Mexico Department of Public Health was created; Philadelphia rewrote its city charter to reorganize its public health department; from Manchester, Connecticut, to Memphis, Tennessee, and beyond, emergency hospitals were transformed into permanent ones. And the pandemic motivated Louisiana Senator Joe Ransdell to begin pushing for the establishment of the National Institutes of Health, although he did not win his fight until a far milder influenza epidemic in 1928 reminded Congress of the events of a decade earlier.

All those things are part of the legacy left by the virus. But the disease left its chief legacy in the laboratory.

■ Part X
ENDGAME

CHAPTER THIRTY-FOUR

By World War I, the revolution in American medicine led by William Welch had triumphed. That revolution had radically transformed American medicine, forcing its teaching, research, art, and practice through the filter of science.

Those in the United States capable of doing good scientific research remained a small, almost a tiny, cadre. The group was large enough to be counted in the dozens, and, counting the most junior investigators, by the mid-1920s it reached several dozen dozens, but no more.

They all knew each other, all had shared experiences, and nearly all had at least some connection to the Hopkins, the Rockefeller Institute, Harvard, or to a lesser extent the University of Pennsylvania, the

University of Michigan, or Columbia. The group was so small that it still included the first generation of revolutionaries, with Welch and Vaughan and Theobald Smith and a few others still active. Then came their first students, men only a few years younger: Gorgas, who had reached mandatory retirement age from the army days before the war ended—the army could have allowed him to remain, but he had no friends among army superiors—and who then shifted to international public health issues for a Rockefeller-funded foundation; Flexner and Park and Cole in New York; Milton Rosenau in Boston; Frederick Novy at Michigan; and Ludwig Hektoen in Chicago. Then came the next half generation of protégés: Lewis in Philadelphia; Avery, Dochez, Thomas Rivers, and others at Rockefeller; George Whipple in Rochester, New York; Eugene Opie at Washington University in St. Louis; and a few dozen more. It was only in the next generation, and the next, that the numbers of true researchers began to multiply enormously and spread throughout the country.

The bonds that held these men together were not of friendship. Some of them—Park and Flexner, for example—had no love for each other, many had happily embarrassed a rival by finding flaws in his work, and they had no illusions about one another's virtues. The profession had grown large enough for maneuvering within it. If one listened closely, one could hear: "The appointment of Dr. Opie as the primary key man in this plan would be a fatal mistake." Or, "Jordan seems at first a rather dazzling possibility, but I am a little afraid . . . that he is not a man who can be absolutely certain to stand up for his convictions in a tight place." Or, "Of the names you suggest, I would distinctly prefer Emerson but I fear he would be particularly unacceptable to Russell and Cole, and perhaps to the [Rockefeller] Foundation group in general, as I have the impression that he has been somewhat at outs with them."

Yet these men also recognized that whatever each other's flaws might be, each of them also had strengths, remarkable strengths. Their work was good enough that, even if in error, one could often find in that error something new, something important, something to build upon. It was an exclusive group and, despite rivalries and dislikes, almost a brotherhood, a brotherhood that included a very few women, literally a handful, and in bacteriology these very few women did not extend far beyond Anna Williams and Martha Wollstein.*

All of these scientists had worked frenetically in their laboratories from the first days of the disease, and none of them had stopped. In those most

* Florence Sabin was the leading female medical scientist in the United States, the first woman to graduate from the Hopkins Medical School, the first woman full professor at any medical school in the country (at the Hopkins), and the first woman elected to the National Academy of Sciences. Sabin was not a bacteriologist or involved in influenza research, and hence is not a part of this story.

desperate of circumstances, the most desperate circumstances in which they—and arguably any scientist—ever worked, most of them had willingly, hopefully, accepted less evidence than they would normally have to reach a conclusion. For of course as Miguel de Unamuno said, the more desperate one is, the more one hopes. But for all their frenzy of activity, they had still always avoided chaos, they had always proceeded from well-grounded hypotheses. They had not, as Avery said with contempt, poured material from one test tube into another. They had not done the wild things that had no basis in their understanding of the workings of the body. They had not given quinine or typhoid vaccine to influenza victims in the wild hope that because it worked against malaria or typhoid it might work against influenza. Others had done these things and more, but they had not.

They also recognized their failures. They had lost their illusions. They had entered the first decades of the twentieth century confident that science, even if its victories remained limited, would triumph. Now Victor Vaughan told a colleague, "Never again allow me to say that medical science is on the verge of conquering disease." With the contempt one reserves for one's own failings, he also said, "Doctors know no more about this flu than fourteenth-century Florentine doctors had known about the Black Death."

But they had not quit. Now this scientific

brotherhood was beginning its hunt. It would take longer than they knew.

So far each laboratory had been working in isolation, barely communicating with the others. Investigators had to meet, to trade ideas, to trade laboratory techniques, to discuss findings not yet published or that one investigator thought unimportant that might mean something to another. They had to try to piece together some way to make concrete progress against this pestilence. They had to sift through the detritus of their failures for clues to success.

On October 30, 1918, with the epidemic on the East Coast fading to manageable proportions, Hermann Biggs organized an influenza commission of leading scientists. Biggs had a proud history, having made the New York City municipal health department the best in the world, but, fed up with Tammany politics, had left to become state commissioner of public health. His commission included Cole, Park, Lewis, Rosenau, epidemiologists, and pathologists. Welch, still recovering in Atlantic City, was too ill to attend. Biggs opened the first meeting by echoing Vaughan: "[T]here has never been anything which compares with this in importance . . . in which we were so helpless."

But unlike Vaughan he was angry, declaring their failures "a serious reflection upon public health administration and work and medical science that we should be in the situation we now are." They had seen the epidemic coming for months. Yet public health officials and scientists both had done nothing to prepare. "We ought to have been able to obtain all the scientific information available now or that can be had six months from now before this reached us at all."

He was determined that they would now address this problem and solve it.

It would not be so easy. And even in that first meeting the problems presented themselves. They knew virtually nothing about this disease. They could not even agree upon its nature. The pathology was too confusing. The symptoms were too confusing.

Even this late Cole still wondered if it was influenza at all: "All who have seen cases in the early stage think we are dealing with a new disease. . . . One great difficulty for us is to find what influenza is and how to make the diagnosis. . . . We have been going over all case histories during this epidemic and it is almost as difficult to see which is influenza—a very complex picture."

A navy scientist observed, "In several places there has been a similarity of symptoms with the bubonic plague."

A Harvard investigator dismissed their observations: "It is the same old disease and does not change a bit in its character."

But it did change, changed constantly, from mild cases of influenza from which victims recovered quickly to cases with strange symptoms never associated with influenza, from sudden violent viral pneumonias or ARDS to secondary invaders causing bacterial pneumonias. All these conditions were being seen. Lewellys Barker, Cole's mentor at the Hopkins, noted, "The pneumonia specimens which came in from different areas are very different. Those from Devens are entirely different from those from Baltimore and they differ from several other camps. The lesions are quite different in different localities."

They reached no consensus about the disease and moved on to discuss the likely pathogen. There too they could reach not even a tentative conclusion. Investigators had found Pfeiffer's influenza bacillus, yes, but Cole reported that Avery had also discovered **B. influenzae** in 30 percent of healthy people at the Rockefeller Institute. That proved nothing. It might be commonly found now because of the epidemic and be an unusual finding in nonepidemic times. Besides, as they all knew, many healthy people carried pneumococci in their mouths and did not get pneumonia. And in the lungs of epidemic victims they had also found pneumococci, streptococci, staphylococci, and other pathogens. Park asked about the chances that a filterable virus caused the disease. Rosenau was conducting experiments pursuing that question.

They knew so little. So little. They knew only that isolation worked. The New York State Training School for Girls had quarantined itself, even requiring people delivering supplies to leave them outside. It had had no cases. The Trudeau Sanatorium in upstate New York had similar rules. It had no cases. Across the continent, a naval facility in San Francisco on an island that enforced rigid quarantine. It had no cases. All that proved was that the miasma theory, which none of them believed in anyway, could not account for the disease.

Yet they ended with agreement. They agreed on lines of approach, on the work that needed to be done. Only on that—in effect on how little they knew—they could agree.

They intended to proceed down two paths: one exploring the epidemiology of the disease, the other tracing clues in the laboratory. The first task in both lines of attack was to cut through the fog of data that was coming in.

They planned precise epidemiological investigations: correlating public health measures and deaths; performing extremely detailed studies in selected areas, for example, isolating small communities where they would account for the seventy-two hours before every single person who suffered from influenza felt the first symptoms; taking detailed personal histories of both victims and those who had not been attacked; looking for linkages with other diseases, with earlier influenza attacks, with diet.

The epidemiological studies would have the ancillary benefit of exciting and transforming another emerging field of medicine. In November 1918 the American Public Health Association created a Committee on Statistical Study of the Influenza Epidemic, funded largely by the Metropolitan Life Insurance Company. One committee member called this "an opportunity to show what statistics, especially vital statistics, and its methods can do for preventive medicine," while a colleague saw it as the "possible vindication of the theory of probabilities and the method of random sampling." In January 1919 the surgeons general of the army, the navy, and the Public Health Service also joined with the Census Bureau to form an influenza committee that grew into a permanent statistical office. Yet at the same time, an epidemiologist present at the first meeting of the Biggs group said, "I realize the problem has got to be solved ultimately in the laboratory."

Gorgas had had one goal: to make this war the first one in American history in which battle killed more troops than disease. Even with one out of every sixty-seven soldiers in the army dying of influenza, and although his superiors largely ignored his advice, he just barely succeeded—although when navy casualties and influenza deaths were added to the totals, deaths from disease did exceed combat deaths.

Gorgas had largely triumphed over every other disease. U.S. soldiers almost entirely escaped malaria, for example, even while it struck down tens of thousands of French, British, and Italians.

Now two million men were returning from Europe. After other wars, even in the late nineteenth century, returning troops had carried diseases home. British, French, and Russian troops had spread cholera after the Crimean War; Americans troops had spread typhoid, dysentery, and smallpox after the Civil War; Prussians had brought smallpox home from the Franco-Prussian War; and Americans had returned from the Spanish-American War carrying typhoid.

One of Gorgas's last acts was to set in motion plans to prevent any such happenings this time. Soldiers were kept isolated for seven days before they boarded ships home, and were deloused before embarking. Soldiers would be bringing no disease home.

Meanwhile, the most massive scientific inquiry ever undertaken was taking shape. Biggs's commission met three more times. By the last meeting, every member would be serving on other commissions as well. The American Medical Association, the American Public Health Association, the army, the navy, the Public Health Service, the Red Cross, and the Metropolitan Life Insurance Company all launched major studies in addition to those already begun, each of them designed to complement and not overlap with the others. At every meeting of every medical specialty, of every public health organization, in every issue of every medical journal, influenza dominated the agenda. In Europe it was the same.

Every major laboratory in the United States continued to focus on the disease. Lewis in Philadelphia kept after it, as did others at the University of Pennsylvania. Rosenau in Boston led a team of Harvard researchers. Ludwig Hektoen and Preston Kyes at the University of Chicago stayed after it. Rosenow at the Mayo Clinic in Minnesota continued to work on it. Every member of the army's pneumonia commission returned to civilian research and continued to investigate influenza. The Metropolitan Life Insurance Company gave grants to university scientists and actually subsidized both the city of New York and the federal government, giving grants for research by Park and Williams in their New York laboratories and by George McCoy of the Public Health Service's Hygienic Laboratory.

The army also made "every effort to collect . . . specimens representing pulmonary lesions due to the present influenza epidemic," not only from army camps but from civilian sources. These specimens would prove enormously important more than three-quarters of a century later, when Jeffrey Taubenberger would extract the 1918 influenza virus from them and successfully sequence its genome.

At the Rockefeller Institute, Cole put "every available man" to work on it. He also put Martha

Wollstein on it. When Captain Francis Blake, who had been part of the army's pneumonia commission, visited his old colleagues at the institute at Christmas, he found everyone "working tooth and nail on this influenza business with monkeys and everything else." A week later, out of the army and back at Rockefeller, he said, "I shall be so glad when we can get all this business off our hands and finished up and I can do something else for a change, as it seems as though I have done nothing but work on, and eat, and dream about and live with pneumonia and influenza for six months."

He would not be free of it any time soon.

Slowly, over a period of months, a body of knowledge began to form. Investigators began to learn about the firestorm that had roared around the world and was continuing to smolder.

First, they confirmed what they had suspected: the lethal fall disease was a second wave of the same disease that had hit in the spring. They based their conclusion on the fact that those exposed to the spring wave had substantial immunity to the later one. The army had the best records. These records involved chiefly young men, so they were not useful in answering some questions. But they could speak to immunity, and clearly demonstrated it. Camp Shelby, for example, was home to the only division in the United States that remained in the United States from March through the fall. In April 1918 influenza sickened 2,000 of 26,000 troops there enough to seek treatment, many more probably had lesser or subclinical infections, and all 26,000 men were exposed to the disease. During the summer, 11,645 new recruits arrived. In October influenza "scarcely touched" the old troops but decimated the recruits. In Europe in the spring, influenza hit the Eleventh Regiment Engineers, making 613 men out of a command of 1,200 ill and killing two, but protecting them from the lethal wave: in the fall the regiment suffered only 150 "colds" and a single death. Camp Dodge had two units of seasoned troops; influenza had struck one group in the spring, and only 6.6 percent of this organization caught influenza in the fall; the other group escaped the spring wave, but 48.5 percent of them had influenza in the fall. And there were many other examples.

Statistics also confirmed what every physician, indeed every person, already knew. In the civilian population as well, young adults had died at extraordinary, and frightening, rates. The elderly, normally the group most susceptible to influenza, not only survived attacks of the disease but were attacked far less often. This resistance of the elderly was a worldwide phenomenon. The most likely explanation is that an earlier pandemic (later analysis of antibodies proved it was not the 1889–90 one), so mild as to not attract attention, resembled the 1918 virus closely enough that it provided protection.

Finally, a door-to-door survey in several cities also

confirmed the obvious: people living in the most crowded conditions suffered more than those with the most space. It also seemed—although this was not scientifically established—that those who went to bed the earliest, stayed there the longest, and had the best care also survived at the highest rates. Those findings meant of course that the poor died in larger numbers than the rich. (Questions about race and the epidemic yielded contradictory information.)

But nearly everything else about the disease remained unsettled. Even the interplay between the germ theory of disease and other factors was at issue. As late as 1926, a respected epidemiologist still argued a version of the miasma theory, claiming "a correlation between . . . influenza and cyclic variation in air pressure."

In the laboratory, however, the fog remained dense. The pathogen remained unknown. Enormous resources were being poured into this research everywhere. In Australia, Macfarlane Burnet lived through the epidemic as a teenager, and it burned itself into his consciousness. As he said soon after receiving the Nobel Prize, "For me as for many others interested in bacteriology and infectious disease, the outstanding objective in medicine for years was . . . influenza."

Yet all this work had not penetrated the fog.

The problem did not lie in any lack of clues. The problem lay in distinguishing the few clues that led in the right direction from all those that led in the wrong direction. This was not bubonic plague. That was among the easiest pathogens to discover: the bacteria that caused it swarmed in the buboes. This was only influenza.

As the second wave of influenza had broken upon the world, thousands of scientists had attacked the problem. In Germany and France they had attacked it, in Britain and Italy, in Australia and Brazil, in Japan and China. But as 1919 wore away, then 1920, as the disease drifted toward mildness, one at a time these thousands began to peel off. They found the problem too difficult to conceptualize—to figure out a way to address it—or the techniques seemed too inadequate to address it, or it lay too far from their old interests or knowledge base. After two years of extraordinary—and continuing—efforts by many of the world's best investigators, in 1920 Welch made a frustrating prediction: "I think that this epidemic is likely to pass away and we are no more familiar with the control of the disease than we were in the epidemic of 1889. It is humiliating, but true."

Hundreds of investigators did continue to pursue the question but they could agree on little. Everything was in dispute. And central to those disputes were the old team of William Park and Anna Williams on one side, Paul Lewis and many of those at the Rockefeller Institute on another.

Lewis's research would end in irony and tragedy.

The Rockefeller Institute would discover most of its own investigators in error.

But Oswald Avery would not be in error. Avery would make the most profound discovery of them all.

CHAPTER THIRTY-FIVE

THE GREATEST QUESTIONS remained the simplest ones: What caused influenza? What was the pathogen? Was Pfeiffer right when he identified a cause and named it **Bacillus influenzae?** And if he was not right, then what did cause it? What was the killer?

The pursuit of this question is a classic case of how one does science, of how one finds an answer, of the complexity of nature, of how one builds a solid scientific structure.

All through the epidemic bacteriologists had had mixed results looking for **B. influenzae.** People as skilled as Park and Williams in New York, Lewis in Philadelphia, and Avery had all been unable to isolate it from the first cases they studied. Then they adjusted their techniques, changed the medium in which they grew it, added blood heated to a particular temperature to the medium, changed the dyes used for staining, and they found it. Park and Williams soon found it so consistently that Park assured the National Research Council it was the etiological agent—the cause of the disease. The Public Health Service believed it to be the cause. Lewis, despite initial misgivings, thought it the cause.

At Rockefeller, Martha Wollstein had studied Pfeiffer's bacillus since 1906. After several years of work she still had not considered her experiments sufficiently "clean cut and stable to signify Pfeiffer's is the specific inciting agent." But she had continued to study the bacillus, and in the midst of the pandemic she had become convinced **B. influenzae** did cause the disease. She had been so confident that the vaccine she prepared included **only** Pfeiffer's bacillus. Her work convinced her Rockefeller colleagues as well; they all took her vaccine, even though they were among the few in the country with access to the Rockefeller antipneumococcus vaccine, which had proven itself effective.

Midway through the pandemic, failure to find Pfeiffer's seemed a mark not of good science but of incompetence. When one army bacteriologist failed to find it on "blood agar plates from 159 of the first patients," the army sent another scientist to the camp to undertake "an investigation of the bacteriologic methods employed in the laboratory of the base hospital." Typical of the institution Gorgas had built, it was a true investigation, not a witch-hunt, and it concluded that this particular laboratory had done "a splendid piece of work. If the influenza bacillus had been present . . . it would have been found." But that conclusion did not come out until long after the epidemic had passed.

In the meantime the existence of such an investigation told other army bacteriologists that inability to find **B. influenzae** meant they did not know their job. Simultaneously, Avery published the new techniques he had developed that made it much easier to grow the organism. Bacteriologists began to find what they were looking for. At Camp Zachary Taylor, bacteriologists had been unable to find Pfeiffer's bacillus. Now they reported, "More latterly Avery's oleate medium was used with very gratifying results." They found the bacteria everywhere: in 48.7 percent of samples of blood taken directly from the heart, in 54.8 percent of lungs, in 48.3 percent of spleens. At Camp Dix, "in every case studied the influenza bacillus was found either in the lungs or in the upper respiratory tract or nasal sinuses."

In camp after camp, bacteriologists fell into line. Bacteriologists at Camp MacArthur in Texas were not alone in their determination "to obtain the highest possible incidence of B. influenzae," and they found it in 88 percent of lungs. But they did so not through any irrefutable laboratory tests; they simply looked through a microscope and identified the bacteria by appearance. Such observations are subjective and not proof, only indications.

At Camp Sherman, where the mortality rate had been the highest in the country and the reputations of camp doctors had been called into question, the final report on the epidemic exemplified the tension. In a section written by the bacteriologist, the report said, "The persistent absence of influenza bacilli in the diverse materials examined militated against attributing the epidemic to the Pfeiffer organism." But the section written by the pathologist in effect accused the bacteriologist of incompetence. The pathologist said he had observed pathogens through the microscope that he believed **were** "Pfeiffer's organism" and that "all the bacteria which were present in this epidemic were not discovered as a result of the cultural methods used."

Civilian investigators isolated Pfeiffer's with similar regularity. Yet even with all the findings of Pfeiffer's **B. influenzae,** the picture remained confusing. For rarely—even though Avery's medium inhibited the growth of pneumococci and hemolytic streptococci, both of which had often been found in influenza cases—was Pfeiffer's found alone.

And sometimes **B. influenzae** was still not being found at all. Investigators were especially failing to find it in the lungs of victims who died quickly. In at least three camps—Fremont in California and Gordon and Wheeler in Georgia—the failure to find Pfeiffer's in an overwhelming majority of cases simply meant that the bacteriologists, instead of exposing themselves to possible criticism, diagnosed victims of the epidemic as suffering from "other respiratory diseases" instead of influenza. In some cases even the most experienced investigators found the bacillus rarely. In Chicago, D. J. Davis had studied Pfeiffer's for ten years, but found it in only five of sixty-two cases. In Germany, where Pfeiffer himself remained one of the most powerful figures in medical science, some researchers could not isolate the bacillus either, although he continued to insist it caused the disease.

These reports created increasing doubt about the Pfeiffer's influenza bacillus. Scientists did not doubt the word of those who found it. They did not doubt that the bacillus could cause disease and kill. But they began to doubt what finding it proved.

There were other questions. In the midst of the epidemic, under the greatest pressures, many bacteriologists had compromised the quality of their work in the hope of getting quick results. As one scientist said, "It requires at least three weeks of concentrated labor to investigate and identify the various species of streptococci from a single drop of normal sputum smeared on one plate of our culture medium. How then is it possible for two workers to investigate the bacteriology of the respiratory tract of, say, 100 cases of influenza and of

50 normal individuals in one year, except in the most slipshod manner?"

Park and Williams were anything but slipshod. They had been among the first to proclaim **B. influenzae** the likely cause of the epidemic. In mid-October, Park still held to that position, declaring, "The influenza bacilli have been found in nearly every case of clear-cut infectious influenza. In the complicating pneumonias, they have been found associated with either the hemolytic streptococcus or pneumococci. In one case the bronchopneumonia was due entirely to the influenza bacillus. The results of the Department of Health of the City of New York have closely agreed with those reported from Chelsea Naval Hospital."

They had prepared and distributed a vaccine based largely upon their conviction.

But even Park and Williams had made compromises. Now, as the epidemic waned, they continued their investigations with great deliberateness. They had always been best at testing hypotheses, looking for flaws, improving upon and expanding others' more original work. Now, chiefly to learn more about the organism in the hope of perfecting a vaccine and serum—but also to test their own hypothesis that **B. influenzae** caused influenza—they started an extensive series of experiments. They isolated the bacillus from one hundred cases and succeeded in growing twenty pure cultures of it. They then injected these cultures into rabbits, waited long enough for the rabbits to develop an immune response, then drew the rabbits' blood, centrifuged out the solids, and followed the other steps to prepare serum. When the serum from each rabbit was added in test tubes to the bacteria used to infect that rabbit, the antibodies in the serum agglutinated the bacteria—the antibodies bound to the bacteria and formed visible clumps.

They had expected that result, but not their next ones. When they tested these different sera against other cultures of Pfeiffer's, agglutination occurred only four of twenty times. The serum did not bind to the Pfeiffer's in the other sixteen cultures. Nothing happened. They repeated the experiments and got the same results. All the bacterial cultures were definitely Pfeiffer's bacillus, definitely **B. influenzae**. There was no mistake in that. All twenty of their sera would bind to and agglutinate bacteria from the same culture used to infect that particular rabbit. But only four of the twenty different sera would bind to any bacteria from another culture of Pfeiffer's.

For a decade scientists had tried to make vaccine and antiserum for Pfeiffer's influenza bacillus. Flexner himself had tried soon after Lewis left the institute. No one had succeeded.

Park and Williams believed they now understood why. They thought Pfeiffer's resembled the pneumococcus. There were dozens of strains of pneumococci. Types I, II, and III were common enough that a vaccine and serum had been made that could protect somewhat against all three, though with truly good effect only against Types I and II. So-called Type IV wasn't a type at all: it was a grab-bag designation of "other" pneumococci.

As they explored Pfeiffer's further, they became more and more convinced that **B. influenzae** similarly included dozens of strains, each different enough that an immune serum that worked against one would not work against the others. In fact, Williams found "ten different strains in ten different cases."

In early 1919, Park and Williams reversed their position. They stated, "This evidence of multiple strains seems to be absolutely against the influenza bacillus being the cause of the pandemic. It appears to us impossible that we should miss the epidemic strain in so many cases while obtaining some other strain so abundantly. The influenza bacilli, like the streptococci and pneumococci, are in all probability merely very important secondary invaders."

The influenza bacillus, they now said, did not cause influenza. Anna Williams wrote in her diary, "More and more, evidence points to a filterable virus being the cause."

Many others were also beginning to think that a filterable virus caused the disease. William MacCallum at the Hopkins wrote, "In Camp Lee we found practically no influenza bacilli. . . . At the Hopkins Hospital influenza bacilli was rarely found. . . . Since a great many different bacteria have been found producing pneumonia, often in complex mixtures, it would require very special evidence to prove that one of these is the universal cause of the primary disease. And since this particular organism is by no means always present it seems that the evidence is very weak. Indeed, it appears probable that some other form of living virus not recognizable by our microscopic methods of staining, and not to be isolated or cultivated by methods currently in use, must be the cause of the epidemic."

But the subject remained controversial. No evidence pointed toward a filterable virus except negative evidence—the absence of proof of anything else. And the theory that a virus caused influenza had already been tested by excellent scientists. During the very first outbreak of the second wave in the United States, Rosenau had suspected a filterable virus. Indeed, he had suspected it at least since 1916. His instincts led him to conduct extensive and careful experiments with sixty-two human volunteers from the navy brig in Boston. He collected sputum and blood from living victims and emulsified lung tissue of the dead, diluted the samples in a saline solution, centrifuged them, drained off the fluid, and passed them through a porcelain filter, then tried various methods to communicate the disease to the volunteers. He used every imaginable method of injection, inhalation, dripping into nasal and throat passages, even into the eyes, using massive life-risking dosages. None of the volunteers got sick. One of the physicians conducting the experiments died.

In Germany a scientist had also tried, spraying the throats of volunteers with filtered nasal secretions, but none of the subjects got influenza. In Chicago a team of investigators failed to infect human volunteers with filtered secretions of influenza victims. Navy investigators in San Francisco failed.

Only one researcher in the world was reporting success in transmitting the disease with a filtrate: Charles Nicolle of the Pasteur Institute. But Nicolle's entire series of experiments involved fewer than a dozen people and monkeys. He tried four separate methods of transmitting the disease and claimed success for three of them. First he dripped filtrate into the nasal passages of monkeys and reported they got influenza. This was possible, although monkeys almost never get human influenza. He injected a filtrate into the mucosal membranes around the eyes of monkeys and reported they got influenza. This was theoretically possible, but even less likely. He also claimed to have given two human volunteers influenza by filtering the blood from an ill monkey and injecting the filtrate subcutaneously—under the men's skin. Both of the men may have gotten influenza. Neither of them could have gotten it by the method Nicolle claimed. Nicolle was brilliant. In 1928 he won the Nobel Prize. But these experiments were wrong.

So, lacking other candidates, many scientists remained convinced Pfeiffer's did cause the disease,
including most of those at the Rockefeller Institute.
So did Eugene Opie, Welch's first star pupil at the
Hopkins, who had gone to Washington University
in St. Louis to model it after the Hopkins, and had
led the laboratory work of the army's pneumonia
commission. In 1922 he and several other commission members published their results in a book called
Epidemic Respiratory Disease. One coauthor was
Thomas Rivers, who by then had already begun
working on viruses; in 1926 he defined the difference between viruses and bacteria—creating the
field of virology and becoming one of the world's
leading virologists. But he spent his first five years
after the war continuing to research Pfeiffer's, writing many papers on it even while beginning his viral
researches. He recalled, "We managed to get influenza bacilli out of every person that had an attack
of influenza. . . . We found it and quickly jumped
to the conclusion that the influenza bacillus was the
cause of the pandemic."

What it came down to was that nearly all investigators believed their own work. If they had found
the influenza bacillus in abundance, they believed
it caused influenza. If they had not found it, they
believed it did not cause influenza.

Only a very few saw beyond their own work and
were willing to contradict themselves. Park and

Williams were among these few. In doing so they demonstrated an extraordinary openness, an extraordinary willingness to look with a fresh eye at their own experimental results.

Park and Williams had convinced themselves—and many others—that the influenza bacillus did not cause influenza. Then they moved on. They stopped working on influenza, partly out of conviction, partly because the New York City municipal laboratory was losing the funding to do true research. And they were getting old now.

Through the 1920s, investigators continued to work on the problem. It was, as Burnet said, the single most important question in medical science for years.

In England, Alexander Fleming had, like Avery, concentrated on developing a medium in which the bacillus could flourish. In 1928 he left a petri dish uncovered with staphylococcus growing in it. Two days later he discovered a mold that inhibited the growth. He extracted from the mold the substance that stopped the bacteria and called it "penicillin." Fleming found that penicillin killed staphylococcus, hemolytic streptococcus, pneumococcus, gonococcus, diphtheria bacilli, and other bacteria, but it did no harm to the influenza bacillus. He did not try to develop penicillin into a medicine. To him the influenza bacillus was important enough that he used penicillin to help grow it by killing any contaminating bacteria in the culture. He used penicillin as he said, "for the isolation of influenza bacilli." This "special selective cultural technique" allowed him to find "B. influenzae in the gums, nasal space, and tonsils from practically every individual" he investigated.

(Fleming never did see penicillin as an antibiotic. A decade later Howard Florey and Ernst Chain, funded by the Rockefeller Foundation, did, and they developed Fleming's observation into the first wonder drug. It was so scarce and so powerful that in World War II, U.S. Army teams recovered it from the urine of men who had been treated with it, so it could be reused. In 1945, Florey, Chain, and Fleming shared the Nobel Prize.)

In 1929 at a major conference on influenza, Welch gave his personal assessment: "Personally I do feel there is very little evidence that [**B. influenzae**] can be the cause. But when such leading investigators as Dr. Opie, for example, feel that the evidence is altogether in favor of Pfeiffer's, and take the further exasperating position that the failure of other bacteriologists to find it was due to error in technique, to lack of skill, one cannot say there is not room for further investigation. . . . The fact has always appealed to me that influenza is possibly an infection due to an unknown virus . . . with this extraordinary effect of reducing the resistance so that the body, at least the respiratory tract, becomes such that any organisms are able to invade and produce acute respiratory trouble and pneumonia."

In 1931, Pfeiffer himself still argued that, of all organisms yet described, the pathogen he had called **Bacillus influenzae** and that informally bore his name had "the best claim to serious consideration as the primary etiologic agent, and its only competition is an unidentified filterable virus."

Avery continued to work on the influenza bacillus for several years after the pandemic. As his protégé René Dubos said, "His scientific problems were almost forced on him by his social environment." By that he meant that the Rockefeller Institute influenced his choice of problems. If something mattered to Flexner and Cole, Avery worked on it.

And he made remarkable progress, proving that passage in animals did make the bacillus more lethal and, far more important, isolating the factors in blood that **B. influenzae** needed to grow, initially identifying them as "X" and "V." It was extraordinary work, work that marked a milestone in understanding the nutritional needs and metabolism of all bacteria.

But as the likelihood of the influenza bacillus causing influenza began to fade, the pressure on him to work on it faded also. Although he had initially inclined toward the view that it caused influenza, he became one of the increasing number of scientists who believed **B. influenzae** had been misnamed. He had no inherent interest in the organism and had never abandoned his work on the pneumococcus. Far from it. And the epidemic had driven home more than ever the lethal nature of pneumonia. Pneumonia had done the killing. It remained the captain of the men of death. Pneumonia was the target. He returned to his work on the pneumococcus full-time. He would study it for the rest of his scientific life.

In fact, as first months and then years passed, Avery seemed to limit his entire world to the research he himself engaged in. He had always focused. Now his focus tightened. Even Dubos said, "I was often surprised and at times almost shocked by the fact that his range of scientific information was not as broad as could have been assumed from his fame and from the variety and magnitude of his scientific achievement." Another time Dubos observed, "He made little effort to follow modern trends in science or other intellectual fields, but instead focused his attention on subjects directly related to the precise problem he had under study. In the lab he was limited to a rather narrow range of techniques, which he rarely changed and to which he added little."

His interests increasingly narrowed to one interest, the one thing he was trying to comprehend: the pneumococcus. It was as if his mind became not only a filter but a funnel, a funnel that concentrated all the light and information in all the world on one point only. And at the bottom of this funnel he did not simply sit, sifting through data. He used its edges to dig deeper and deeper into the earth, tunneling so deep that the only light present was that which he carried with him. He could see nothing but what lay before him.

And, more and more, he began to narrow his focus even further, to a single aspect of the pneumococcus—to the polysaccharide capsule, the M&M-like sugar shell surrounding it. The immune system had great difficulty attacking pneumococci surrounded by capsules. Encapsulated pneumococci grew rapidly and unimpeded in the lungs; they killed. Pneumococci without capsules were not virulent. The immune system easily destroyed them.

At the lunch tables at the institute, sitting in the comfortable chairs, pulling apart baguettes of French bread, drinking an endless supply of coffee, scientists learned from one another. The tables were of eight, but usually one senior person would dominate a discussion. Avery spoke little, even as he grew in stature and seniority; yet he dominated in his own way, asking pointed questions about problems that confronted him, searching for any ideas that might help.

Constantly he tried to recruit people whose knowledge complemented his own. He wanted a biochemist, and, beginning in 1921, over and over he tried to lure Michael Heidelberger, a brilliant young biochemist, away from the laboratory of Nobel laureate Karl Landsteiner. Heidelberger recalled, "Avery would come upstairs from his lab and show me a little vial of dirty-looking dark gray stuff and say, 'See, my boy, the whole secret of bacterial specificity is in this little vial. When are you going to work on it?'"

Inside the vial were dissolved capsules. Avery had isolated the material from the blood and urine of pneumonia patients. He believed that it held the secret to using the immune system to defeat pneumonia. If he could find that secret . . . Eventually Heidelberger did join Avery. So did others. And Avery settled into an unchanging routine. He lived on East Sixty-seventh Street and his laboratory was on Sixty-sixth and York. Every morning he walked in at the same time wearing what seemed the same gray jacket, took the elevator to his sixth-floor office, and traded the jacket for a light tan lab coat. Only if he was doing something unusual, if there was a special occasion, would he ever wear a white lab coat.

But there was nothing routine in this work. He conducted most experiments at the lab benches, actually wooden desks originally designed for an office. His equipment remained simple, almost primitive. Avery disliked gadgetry. When he experimented, remembered a colleague, he was "intensely focused . . . His movements were limited, but of extreme precision and elegance; his whole being appeared to be identified with the sharply defined aspect of the reality that he was studying. Confusions seemed to vanish, . . . perhaps simply because everything seemed so organized around his person."

Each experiment created its own world, with possibilities for joy and despair. He would leave cultures in an incubator overnight, and each morning he and his young colleagues would converge on the incubator not knowing what they would find. Quiet as he was, reserved as he was, he was always tense then, his expression simultaneously eager and fearful.

In 1923 he and Heidelberger turned the scientific world on its head by proving that the capsules did generate an immune response. The capsules were pure carbohydrate. Until then investigators had believed that only a protein or something containing proteins could stimulate the immune system to respond.

The finding only spurred Avery and his colleagues on. More than ever he concentrated on the capsule, forsaking practically everything else. He believed it to be the key to the specific reaction of the immune system, the key to making an effective therapy or vaccine, the key to killing the killer. And he believed that much of what he discovered about the pneumococcus would be applicable to all bacteria.

Then, in 1928, Fred Griffith in Britain published a striking and puzzling finding. Earlier Griffith had discovered that all known types of pneumococci could exist with or without capsules. Virulent pneumococci had capsules; pneumococci without capsules could be easily destroyed by the immune system.

Now he found something much stranger. He killed virulent pneumococci, ones surrounded by capsules, and injected them into mice. Since the bacteria were dead, all the mice survived. He also injected living pneumococci that had no capsules, that were not virulent. Again the mice lived. Their immune systems devoured the unencapsulated pneumococci. But then he injected dead pneumococci surrounded by capsules and living pneumococci without capsules.

The mice **died.** Somehow the living pneumococci had acquired capsules. Somehow they had changed. And, when isolated from the mice, they continued to grow with the capsule—as if they had inherited it.

Griffith's report seemed to make meaningless years of Avery's work—and life. The immune system was based on specificity. Avery believed that the capsule was key to that specificity. But if the pneumococcus could change, that seemed to undermine everything Avery believed and thought he had proved. For months he dismissed Griffith's work as unsound. But Avery's despair seemed overwhelming. He left the laboratory for six months, suffering from Graves' disease, a disease likely related to stress. By the time he returned, Michael Dawson, a junior colleague he had asked to check Griffith's results, had confirmed them. Avery had to accept them.

His work now turned in a different direction. He had to understand how one kind of pneumococcus was transformed into another. He was now almost sixty years old. Thomas Huxley said, "A man of science past sixty does more harm than good." But now, more than ever, Avery focused on his task.

In 1931, Dawson, then at Columbia University but still working closely with Avery, and an assistant succeeded in changing—in a test tube—a pneumococcus that lacked a capsule into one that had a capsule. The next year people in Avery's own laboratory managed to use a cell-free extract from dead encapsulated pneumococci to do the same thing, to make bacteria without capsules change into ones with capsules.

One after another the young scientists in his laboratory moved on. Avery kept on. By the late 1930s he was working with Colin MacLeod and Maclyn McCarty, and they now turned all their energies to understanding how this happened. If Avery had demanded precision before, now he demanded virtual perfection, irrefutability. They grew huge amounts of virulent Type III pneumococci, and spent not just hours or days but months and years breaking the bacteria down, looking at each constituent part, trying to understand. The work was of the utmost tedium, and it was work that yielded failure after failure after failure after failure.

Avery's name was appearing on fewer and fewer papers. Much of that was because he put his name on papers of people in his laboratory only if he had physically performed an experiment included in the research the paper detailed, no matter how much he had contributed conceptually to the work, or how often he had talked over ideas with the investigator. (This was highly generous of Avery; usually a laboratory chief puts his or her name on virtually every paper anyone in his laboratory writes. Dubos recalled that he worked under Avery for fourteen years, that Avery influenced nearly all his work but only four times did Avery's name appear on his papers. Another young investigator said, "I had always felt so deeply that I was an associate of Avery that . . . with great astonishment I realized for the first time that we had never published a joint paper.")

But Avery was also publishing less because he had little to report. The work was extraordinarily difficult, pushing the limits of the technically possible. **Disappointment is my daily bread,** he had said. **I thrive on it.** But he did not thrive. Often he thought of abandoning the work, abandoning all of it. Yet every day he continued to fill nearly every waking hour with thinking about it. Between 1934 and 1941 he published nothing. **Nothing.** For a scientist to go through such a dry period is more than depressing. It is a refutation of one's abilities, of one's life. But in the midst of that dry spell, Avery told a young researcher there were two types of investigators: most "go around picking up surface nuggets, and whenever they can spot a surface nugget of gold they pick it up and add it to their collection. . . . [The other type] is not really interested in the surface nugget. He is much more interested in digging a deep hole in one place, hoping to hit a vein. And of course if he strikes a vein of gold he makes a tremendous advance."

By 1940 he had gone deep enough to believe he would find something, something of value. Between 1941 and 1944, he again published nothing. But now it was different. Now what he was working on excited him as nothing else had. He was gaining confidence that he would reach his destination. Heidelberger recalled, "Avery would come and talk about his work on the transforming substance. . . . There was something that told him that this transforming substance was something really fundamental to biology, . . . to the understanding of life itself."

Avery loved an Arab saying: "The dogs bark, the caravan moves on." He had nothing to publish because his work was being done chiefly by subtraction. But it was moving on. He had isolated whatever transformed the pneumococcus. Now he was analyzing that substance by eliminating one possibility after another.

First, he eliminated proteins. Enzymes that deactivated proteins had no effect on the substance. Then he eliminated lipids—fatty acids. Other enzymes that destroyed lipids had no effect on the ability of this substance to transform pneumococci. He eliminated carbohydrates. What he had left was rich in nucleic acids, but an enzyme isolated by Dubos that destroys ribonucleic acid had no effect on the transforming substance either. Each of these steps had taken months, or years. But he could see it now.

In 1943 he nominally retired and became an emeritus member of the institute. His retirement changed nothing. He worked exactly as he always had, experimenting, pushing, tightening. That year he wrote his younger brother, a physician, about extraordinary findings and in April informed the institute's Board of Scientific Directors. His findings would revolutionize all biology, and his evidence seemed beyond solid. Other scientists who had found what he had found would have published already. Still he would not publish. One of his junior colleagues asked, "Fess, what more do you want?"

But he had been burned so long ago in that very first work at Rockefeller, when he had published a sweeping theory encompassing bacterial metabolism, virulence, and immunity. He had been wrong, and he never forgot the humiliation. He did more work. Then, finally, in November 1943 he, MacLeod, and McCarty submitted a paper titled "Studies on the Chemical Nature of the Substance Inducing Transformation of Pneumococcal Types. Induction of Transformation by a Desoxyribonucleic Acid Fraction Isolated from Pneumoccus Type III" to the **Journal of Experimental Medicine,** the journal founded by Welch. In February 1944 the journal published the paper.

DNA, deoxyribonucleic acid, had been isolated

in the late 1860s by a Swiss investigator. No one knew its function. Geneticists ignored it. The molecule seemed far too simple to have anything to do with genes or heredity. Geneticists believed that proteins, which are far more complex molecules, carried the genetic code. Avery, MacLeod, and McCarty wrote, "The inducing substance has been likened to a gene, and the capsular antigen which is produced in response to it has been regarded as a gene product."

Avery had found that the substance that transformed a pneumococcus from one without a capsule to one with a capsule was DNA. Once the pneumococcus changed, its progeny inherited the change. He had demonstrated that DNA carried genetic information, that genes lay within DNA.

His experiments were exquisite, elegant, and irrefutable. A Rockefeller colleague conducted confirming experiments on Pfeiffer's **B. influenzae.**

Among historians of science, there has been some controversy over how much immediate impact Avery's paper had, largely because one geneticist, Gunther Stent, wrote that it "had little influence on thought about the mechanisms of heredity for the next eight years." And Avery's conclusions were not immediately accepted as true by the broad scientific community.

But they were accepted as true by the scientists who mattered.

■   ■   ■

Prior to Avery's discovery—and proof—that DNA carried the genetic code, he was being seriously considered for the Nobel Prize for his lifetime of contributions to knowledge of immunochemistry. But then came his revolutionary paper. Instead of guaranteeing him the prize, the Nobel Committee found it too revolutionary, too startling. A prize would endorse his findings and the committee would take no such risk, not until others confirmed them. The official history of the organization that gives the prize states, "Those results were obviously of fundamental importance, but the Nobel Committee found it desirable to wait until more became known. . . ."

Others were determined to make more known.

James Watson, with Francis Crick the codiscoverer of the structure of DNA, wrote in his classic **The Double Helix** that "there was general acceptance that genes were special types of protein molecules" until "Avery showed that hereditary traits could be transmitted from one bacterial cell to another by purified DNA molecules. . . . Avery's experiments strongly suggested that future experiments would show that all genes were composed of DNA. . . . Avery's experiment made [DNA] smell like the essential genetic material. . . . Of course there were scientists who thought the evidence favoring DNA was inconclusive and preferred to believe that genes were protein molecules. Francis, however, did not worry about these skeptics. Many were cantankerous fools who always backed the wrong horses, . . . not only narrow-minded and dull, but also just stupid."

Watson and Crick were not the only investigators seeking the great prize, the greatest prize, the key to heredity and possibly to life, who immediately grasped the significance of Avery's work. Erwin Chargaff, a chemist whose findings were crucial to Watson and Crick's understanding enough about the DNA molecule to determine its structure, said, "Avery gave us the first text of a new language, or rather he showed us where to look for it. I resolved to search for this text."

Max Delbruck, who was trying to use viruses to understand heredity, said, "He was very attentive to what we were doing and we were very attentive to what he was doing. . . . [I]t was obvious that he had something interesting there."

Salvador Luria, who worked with Delbruck—Watson was a graduate student under him—similarly rejected Stent's contention that Avery's findings were ignored. Luria recalled having lunch with Avery at the Rockefeller Institute and discussing the implications of his work with him: "I think it is complete nonsense to say that we were not aware."

Peter Medawar observed, "The dark ages of DNA came to an end in 1944 with" Avery. Medawar called the work "the most interesting and portentous biological experiment of the twentieth century."

Macfarlane Burnet was, like Avery, studying infectious diseases, not genes, but in 1943 he visited

Avery's laboratory and left astounded. Avery, he said, was doing "nothing less than the isolation of a pure gene in the form of desoxyribonucleic acid."

In fact, what Avery accomplished was a classic of basic science. He started his search looking for a cure for pneumonia and ended up, as Burnet observed, "opening . . . the field of molecular biology."

Watson, Crick, Delbruck, Luria, Medawar, and Burnet all won the Nobel Prize.

Avery never did.

Rockefeller University—the former Rockefeller Institute for Medical Research—did name a gate after him, the only such honor accorded to anyone. And the National Library of Medicine has produced a series of online profiles of prominent scientists; it made Avery the first to be so honored.

Oswald Avery was sixty-seven years old when he published his paper on "the transforming principle." He died eleven years later in 1955, two years after Watson and Crick unfolded DNA's structure. He died in Nashville where he had gone to live to be near his brother, his family. Dubos compared his death to that of Welch, in 1934, and quoted Simon Flexner on Welch's exit from the stage: "While his body suffered, his mind struggled to maintain before the world the same placid exterior that had been his banner and his shield. Popsy, the physician who had been so greatly beloved, died as he had lived, keeping his own counsel and essentially alone."

CHAPTER THIRTY-SIX

IN THE FIRST YEARS after the pandemic, Paul Lewis continued to head the Henry Phipps Institute at the University of Pennsylvania.

Yet Lewis was not a happy man. He was one of those who continued to believe that **B. influenzae** caused the disease and continued to work on it after the epidemic passed. There was irony in that, since he had initially been reluctant to embrace its etiological role, suspecting instead a filterable virus. Perhaps the chief reason for his stubbornness was his own experience. He had not only found the bacillus with consistency, but he had produced a vaccine that seemed to work. True, the navy had administered a vaccine prepared according to his methods to several thousand men and it had proven ineffective, but he had not made that vaccine himself. A smaller batch that he had personally prepared and tested—during the peak of the epidemic, not in its later stages when many vaccines seemed to be working only because the disease itself was weakening—had given solid evidence of effectiveness. Only three of sixty people who received the vaccine developed pneumonia, and none died; a control group had ten pneumonias and three deaths.

Those results deceived him. In the past he had not always made the right scientific judgment—no investigator does—but this may have been his first significant scientific error. And it seemed to mark the beginning of a downhill slope for him.

That was not obvious at first. He had already built an international reputation. The German scientific journal **Zeitschrift für Tuberkulose** translated and reprinted his work. In 1917 he was invited to give the annual Harvey Lecture on tuberculosis, a great honor; Rufus Cole, for example, would not receive that invitation for another decade. Eighty-five years later, Dr. David Lewis Aronson, a scientist—whose father, a prize-winning scientist, had worked in the best European laboratories and considered Lewis the smartest man he ever met and gave his son Lewis's name—recalled reading that speech: "You could see Lewis's mind working, the depth of it, and vision, going well beyond what was going on at the time."

Lewis's views had broadened indeed. His interests now included mathematics and biophysics, and, with no resources of his own, he asked Flexner to "arrange for the support" of a physicist Lewis wanted to lure into medicine to examine fluorescent dyes and "the disinfectant power of light and the penetrating power of light for animal tissues." Flexner did so, and Flexner continued to be impressed by Lewis's own work, replying by return mail when Lewis sent him a paper, saying that he would publish it in the **Journal of Experimental Medicine,** calling it "interesting and important."

Yet Lewis's life after the war began pulling him away from the laboratory, frustrating him. Henry Phipps, the U.S. Steel magnate who had given his name to the institute Lewis headed, had not endowed it generously. Lewis's own salary had risen well enough, from $3,500 a year when he started in 1910 to $5,000 just before the war. Flexner still considered him vastly underpaid and saw to it that, immediately after the war, the University of California at Berkeley offered him a professorship. Lewis declined, but Penn raised his salary to $6,000, a substantial income at that time.

But if his own salary was more than adequate, he needed to fund an entire institute, even if a small one. He needed money for centrifuges, glassware, heating, not to mention "dieners"—the word still in use for technicians—and young scientists. He needed to raise the money for all that himself. As a result Lewis more and more found himself drawn into the social milieu of Philadelphia, raising money,

being charming. More and more he was becoming a
salesman, selling both the institute and himself. He
hated it. He hated the time it took from the laboratory, the drain of his energies, the parties. And the
country was in the midst of a deep recession, with
four million soldiers suddenly thrown back onto the
job market, with the government no longer building ships and tanks, with Europe desolate and unable to buy anything. Raising money was more than
just difficult.

In 1921 the University of Iowa approached him.
They wanted to become a first-class research institution, and they wanted him to run the program,
to build the institution. The state would supply the
money. Flexner was more than just a mentor to
Lewis, and Lewis confided in him that the Iowa job
seemed "heavy, safe and of limited inspiration. You
know very well that I do not thrive on routine." And
at Phipps, "Some of the work underway has great
potential I believe. . . . You will see that I am trying
to convince myself that I have a right to gamble here
as against a rather dull safe outlook at Iowa City. A
word from you would be much appreciated."

Flexner advised him to accept the offer: "All I
have heard of the medical situation at Iowa City
is favorable, . . . a pretty sharp contrast to the
[situation] in Philadelphia. It is definite and has
the elements of permanency. . . . I have no doubt
under the influence of your vigorous guidance, the
department—although quite large—over which

you would preside would become so notable that the
State would stand back of you in any enlargement."

He did not tell Lewis how well he thought the
job might suit him, how extraordinary his gifts for
a job like that were. But Flexner did tell a senior
colleague that Lewis "might really come to exercise
a real influence in medical teaching and research."
There was perhaps some of what Welch had in him,
that Lewis had "quite unusual gifts of exposition."
He had broad knowledge, perhaps he even leaked
knowledge, and, whether he realized it or not, he
could inspire. Indeed, Flexner believed he could
"be master of the field."

The University of Pennsylvania countered the
offer: it gave him a new title, raised his salary to
$8,000, guaranteed it for five years, and guaran-
teed funding for the institute itself for two years.
He stayed. Flexner congratulated "you and the
University especially on your new honor. Will the
new chair add to your University responsibility?"

It would. Partly for that reason Lewis remained
restless. He had rejected the Iowa position because,
though it might allow him to build a major institution, it would keep him out of the laboratory.
Now he found himself in much the same situation
at Penn. He detested maneuvering with or around
deans and he continued to play the role of social
creature. Scientists were the new thing, Faustian
figures able to create worlds and fashionable to
show off on the Main Line. Lewis hated being

shown off. There was tension at home with his wife as well. How much of that came from his research frustrations, how much because his wife liked the Philadelphia society that he wanted no part of, how much because his wife simply wanted more of him, it is impossible to know.

One research project in particular seemed to be going well, and he wanted to attend to it, and give up everything else. He envied not only Avery's ability to concentrate on one thing but also his opportunity to do so. For Lewis everything seemed to press upon him. Indeed, everything seemed ready to explode.

In 1922 Iowa offered him the position again. This time he accepted. He felt a responsibility to leave Phipps in good shape and recruited Eugene Opie from Washington University to replace him. Opie had if anything an even greater reputation than his own.

Flexner had always respected Lewis, yet there had always been a gap between them. They had been getting closer. At one point Flexner wrote him, "Some time do let me take a little trouble for you." Lewis confided in return, "You have stood in the light of 'father' to me." Now, when Opie agreed to replace Lewis at Phipps, Flexner seemed to see Lewis in a new light, capable not only as a scientist but as someone who could play another game well, telling him, "Opie surprised me. I supposed him a fixture in St. Louis. If you prepared the way for so good a man at the Phipps Institute, you may well feel gratified."

Lewis did not feel gratified. He remained restless and discontented. What he really wanted was to be shut of everything, everything except the laboratory. Perhaps without quite realizing it, he had been moving toward a crisis. Again he told Flexner that what he really wanted more than anything was to work at his laboratory bench. He was shut of Philadelphia. Now he had to get himself shut of Iowa.

In January 1923 he wrote Flexner, "It is quite clear to me today that I am entitled again for a short time at least to cultivate my personal interests. . . . I am giving up my place here and all of my plans for a future in Philadelphia. . . . I have written to President Jessop, of the University of Iowa, telling him of my change of plan and that that is also in the discard. . . . I am going to try my best to develop the opportunity for a year of study in some place as far removed from any question of 'affairs or position' as possible. . . . I cannot make it too plain that for the coming year I am seeking no position in the conventional sense of the word. What I really want is . . . the rehabilitation of a more or less vacant mind."

He was quitting everything, walking away from position, prestige, and money, walking into the wilderness with no guarantee of anything, stripping himself naked at the age of forty-four with a wife and two children. He was free.

■   ■   ■

Where he had been happiest in his life, where he had done the best science, had been at the Rockefeller Institute. The institute had created a Division of Animal Pathology in Princeton, close to Philadelphia. Theobald Smith, the same man who had rejected Welch's offer to become the first head of the Rockefeller Institute itself, had left Harvard and now headed this division. Smith had also been Lewis's first mentor, and had recommended him so many years before to Flexner. Lewis explored with Smith the possibility of going to Princeton. Smith first wanted assurances that Lewis wanted "to go to work again and . . . that all this advertising business had not gone to [his] head." Lewis eagerly gave them.

Flexner had urged him to take the Iowa job but replied, "I shall be rejoiced to see you return to the lab where you so naturally belong and in which you will do your best, most lasting, and effective work. It seems to me a crying pity that men who have given years to the necessary preparation for a lab career should be so ruthlessly drawn away from it and made to fill executive positions." He also told Lewis that Smith was "very pleased with the prospect of having you associated with him again."

Lewis asked for no salary whatsoever, just full access to the laboratories for a year. Flexner gave him $8,000, his salary at Phipps, and a budget for laboratory equipment, filing cabinets, 540 animal cages for breeding and experimenting, and three assistants. He told Lewis he would expect nothing whatsoever from him for the year, and then they could talk again about the future.

Lewis was ecstatic: "To start with Dr. Smith again on any possible basis, takes me back to 1905—on I hope certainly a new higher level. . . . You will not find me lacking in effort. . . . I am most fortunate and happy in being able to regard myself as entirely in the hands of you two men who, without distinction, and excepting only my parents, have given me the means and the education and the direction. Few have such a chance to renew their youth. My only hope is that I continue to deserve your confidence."

Princeton then was still surrounded by farms and countryside. It was peaceful, almost bucolic. The Rockefeller facility was not far from the campus of Princeton University, which was still transforming itself from the finishing school for gentlemen that F. Scott Fitzgerald described to the intellectual center that it would not fully become until a decade later, when Flexner's brother Abraham started the Institute for Advanced Study with Einstein as its first member. But if the setting was bucolic, if crops grew and assorted animals—not simply guinea pigs or rabbits but cattle, pigs, and horses—grazed only yards from the laboratories, the Rockefeller part of Princeton brewed intensity. Smith was continuing to produce world-class work. Just being around him energized Lewis. For the first time since he left the Rockefeller Institute, he felt at home. Yet he was alone. His wife and children stayed in Philadelphia. He was alone to work, alone to go to the laboratory in the middle of the night, alone with his thoughts.

In nearly a year, however, he produced nothing. Flexner and he did discuss his future. He was forty-five years old. His next move would likely be his last one. He could still return to the University of Pennsylvania if he chose. He did not so choose, telling Flexner, "I can only repeat that I am free of any entanglement there, even of sentiment." The University of Iowa had also extended its offer once again and once again raised the salary. But what he wanted was to stay at Rockefeller. He had made little progress on the tuberculosis project he had brought with him from Philadelphia, but, more important, he had, he assured himself as much as Flexner, rejuvenated himself. He informed Flexner that, despite the higher salary at Iowa, "My only interest in 'position' is [here]."

Lewis's presence fitted perfectly into Flexner's own plans. Flexner explained, "I have always believed that our departments should not be one- man affairs." In New York a dozen or more extraordinary investigators led groups of younger researchers, each group working on a major problem. The Princeton location had not developed similarly; beyond Smith's own operation, it had not filled out.

Flexner told Lewis, "Your coming . . . [offers] the first chance to make a second center there."

Further, Smith would turn sixty-five that year. Flexner and Smith and even Welch hinted to Lewis that he might succeed Smith when he retired. Flexner suggested that Lewis stay one more year under a temporary arrangement, and then they would see.

Lewis told Flexner, "I am secure as I never was before." He believed he was home. It would be his last home.

If Lewis was going to build a department, he needed a young scientist—someone with more than just laboratory skills, someone with ideas. His contacts in Iowa urged him to try a young man they thought would make a mark.

Richard Shope was the son of a physician who was also a farmer. He had gotten his medical degree at the University of Iowa, then spent a year teaching pharmacology at the medical school and experimenting on dogs. An outstanding college track athlete, tall, a man's man at ease with himself—something Lewis never quite seemed to be—Shope always maintained contact with the wild, with the forest, with hunting, not only in the laboratory but with a gun in his hands. His mind had a certain wildness, too, like a small boy playing with a chemistry set hoping for an explosion; he had more than an inquiring mind, he had an original one.

Years later Thomas Rivers, the virologist who not only succeeded Cole as head of the Rockefeller Institute Hospital but served as president of four different scientific associations, said, "Dick Shope is one of the finest investigators I have ever seen. . . . A stubborn guy, and he is tough, . . . Dick would no sooner start to work on a problem than he would make a fundamental discovery. It never made one bit of difference where he was." In World War II, Rivers and Shope landed on Guam soon after combat troops secured it (in Okinawa they would come under fire) to investigate tropical diseases that might threaten soldiers. While there, Shope occupied himself by isolating an agent from a fungus mold that mitigated some viral infections. Ultimately he was elected to membership in the National Academy of Sciences.

Yet even with Shope's help, Lewis's work did not go well. It was not for lack of intelligence on Lewis's part. Shope knew Welch, Flexner, Smith, Avery and many Nobel laureates well, yet he considered Lewis a notch above; like Aronson, the prize-winning scientist who had worked at the Pasteur Institute and knew Lewis at Penn, Shope considered Lewis the smartest person he ever met.

Lewis had reached some tentative conclusions in Philadelphia about tuberculosis. He believed that three, and possibly four, inherited factors affected the natural ability of guinea pigs to produce antibodies—i.e., to resist infection. He had planned to unravel precisely what the nature of these factors was. This was an important question, one that potentially went far beyond tuberculosis to a deep understanding of the immune system.

But when he and Shope repeated the Philadelphia experiments they got different results. They examined every element of the experiments to see what might explain the differences and repeated them again. Then they repeated the process and the experiments again. Again they got differing results, results from which it was impossible to draw a conclusion.

Nothing in science is as damning as the inability of an outside experimenter to reproduce results. Now Lewis himself could not reproduce the results he had gotten in Philadelphia, results he had depended upon. Much less could he build upon and expand them. He had run into a wall.

He began plugging away at it. Shope too plugged away at it. Both of them had the tenacity to stay after a thing. But they made no progress.

More distressing to Smith and Flexner, who watched closely, was the way Lewis was approaching the problem. His failures seemed to confuse him. Unlike Avery, who broke his problems down into smaller ones that could be solved and who learned from each failure, Lewis seemed simply to be applying brute force, huge numbers of experiments. He sought to add other scientists with particular expertise to his team, but he did not define what precise role new people would play. Unlike Avery, who recruited people with specific skills to attack a specific question, Lewis seemed simply to want to throw resources at the problem, hoping someone would solve it.

He seemed desperate now. Desperate men can be dangerous, and even feared, but they are rarely respected. He was losing their respect, and with that would go everything.

As Lewis approached the end of his third year in Princeton, Smith confided his disappointment to Flexner: "He is perhaps aiming higher than his training and equipment warrant and this results in a demand to surround himself with technically trained chemists, etc. This is what Carrel"—Alexis Carrel at the Rockefeller Institute in New York, who had already received the Nobel Prize—"is doing but Carrel has another type of mind and gets results from his organization. A closely-knit group requires that the ideas come from the head man."

Nor did Lewis seem to recognize as worth pursuing potentially promising side questions his experiments raised. His explanation for his failures, for example, was that the diet of the guinea pigs was different in Princeton than it had been in Philadelphia. This was potentially significant, and it was possible he was correct. The relationship between diet and disease had been noted before but chiefly in terms of outright diet deficiencies that directly caused such diseases as scurvy and pellagra.

Lewis was thinking about far more subtle and indirect linkages between diet and disease, including infectious disease. But instead of pursuing this line of inquiry, Lewis continued to pound away at his old one. He did so without result. He reported to the Board of Scientific Directors, "I have planned no change in my line of work for the coming year."

Flexner wanted to hear something different. Lewis was making himself a marked man, marked in no good way. It wasn't Lewis's failures that did so; it was the manner in which he was failing—dully, without imagination, and without the gain of knowledge elsewhere. Lewis had shown enough, or failed to show enough, that Flexner had already made one judgment. When Smith retired, Lewis would not replace him.

Flexner wrote him a chilling letter. In a draft Flexner was brutal: "There is no obligation expressed or implied in the Institute's relation to you, or your relation to the Institute, beyond this service year period. . . . As the Iowa chair is still open and you are very much wanted to fill it, and the University of Iowa would make a supreme effort to secure you, I believe it due you to be minutely informed just what the position the Board of Scientific Directors has taken with reference to you. . . . There was doubt expressed about your future in general."

Flexner did not send that letter. It was too harsh even for him. Instead he simply informed Lewis that the board was "unequivocally opposed to the appointment of one primarily a human pathologist"—which Lewis was—"to the directorship of the Department of Animal Pathology," and that therefore he would not replace Smith. But he also warned Lewis that the board would not elevate him to the rank of a "member" of the institute, the equivalent of a tenured full professor. He would remain only an associate. His appointment expired in six months, in mid-1926, and the board would give him a three-year appointment into 1929. Perhaps he should accept the Iowa offer after all.

In **Faust,** Goethe wrote, "Too old am I to be content with play, / Too young to live untroubled by desire."

Lewis was too old to play, too young to be untroubled by desire. Reading Flexner's letter had to have been a crushing blow. He had expected to be told he would succeed Smith. He had been certain he would be elevated to the rank of "member" of the institute. From the laboratory, he drew his identity, and yet now the laboratory gave him not sustenance but cold rebuff. The two men he most admired in the world, two men he had thought of as scientific fathers—one of whom he regarded as almost a father—had judged that he lacked something, lacked a thing that would entitle him to join their brotherhood, to become a member.

By now Lewis's family had moved to Princeton, but his marriage was no better. Perhaps the fault lay entirely within him, within what was now not so much a failing ambition as a failing love.

He declined the Iowa job once again. He had always been willing to gamble. Now he gambled on proving himself to Flexner and Smith.

For the next year and a half, he worked, at first feverishly but then . . . Something in him made him withdraw. His son Hobart, then fourteen years old, was having difficulties emotionally and difficulties in school, although a change of schools seemed to help. And Lewis had a car accident that broke his concentration.

He accomplished little. Again his failures were not like those that Avery would confront for nearly a decade. Avery was attacking the most fundamental questions of immunology and, ultimately, genetics. From each failed experiment he learned, perhaps not much but something. And what he was learning went beyond how to fine-tune an experiment. What he was learning from his failures had large ramifications that applied to entire fields of knowledge. One could argue that none of Avery's experiments failed.

Lewis was simply foundering. He had spent hour after hour in the laboratory. It had always been his favorite place, his place of rest, of peace. It gave him no peace now. He began to avoid it. His marriage was no better; his wife and he barely communicated. But he found other things to do, gardening, carpentry, things he had never attended to before. Perhaps he hoped getting away would clear his mind, allow him to see through the fog of data. Perhaps he thought that. But his mind never seemed to go back to the problem.

In August 1927, he confessed to Flexner, "I feel I have not been very productive—certainly I feel that I have had a meager return for a lot of hard work—but some way everything I have touched in the hope it would go faster than the very slow jobs I have been on for so long has either been a wash-out or turned into some other big [problem]."

Then he said something even more striking. He was no longer going to the laboratory: "I am spending most of my time on an old house and garden I have gotten hold of."

Flexner replied, for him, gently. Lewis was now more than a year into his three-year contract extension. Flexner warned that his tuberculosis work "has been under way as your major problem for four years. The outcome, even if continued many years longer, is uncertain and the yield of side issues, often the most fruitful of all, has been small. I do not believe in sticking to a rather barren subject. One of the requisites of an investigator is a kind of instinct which tells him quite as definitely when to drop, as well as when to take up a subject. Your time can be more promisingly employed along another major line."

Lewis rejected the advice.

■   ■   ■

On September 30, 1918, J. S. Koen, a veterinarian with the federal Bureau of Animal Industry, had been attending the National Swine Breeders Show in Cedar Rapids. Many of the swine were ill, some of them deathly ill. Over the next several weeks he tracked the spread of the disease, the deaths of thousands of swine, and concluded they had influenza—the same disease killing humans. Farmers attacked his diagnosis; it could cost them money. Nonetheless, a few months later he published his conclusion in the **Journal of Veterinary Medicine:** "Last fall and winter we were confronted with a new condition, if not a new disease. I believe I have as much to support this diagnosis in pigs as the physicians have to support a similar diagnosis in man. The similarity of the epidemic among people and the epidemic among pigs was so close, the reports so frequent, that an outbreak in the family would be followed immediately by an outbreak among the hogs, and vice versa, as to present a most striking coincidence if not suggesting a close relation between the two conditions."

The disease had continued to strike swine in the Midwest. In 1922 and 1923, veterinarians at the Bureau of Animal Industry transmitted the disease from pig to pig through mucus from the respiratory tract. They filtered the mucus and tried to transmit the disease with the filtrate. They failed.

Shope observed swine influenza during a trip home to Iowa. He began investigating it. Lewis helped him isolate a bacillus virtually identical to **B. influenzae** and named it **B. influenzae suis.** Shope also replicated the experiments by the veterinarians and began to move beyond them. He found this work potentially very interesting.

Lewis's own work, however, continued to founder. Flexner and Smith had kept their assessments of it confidential. As far as the rest of the world—even including Shope—knew, they held him in the highest regard. In June 1928, for the fourth time, the University of Iowa made Lewis still another offer, an outstanding offer. Flexner urged him to accept. Lewis replied that his "compelling" interest remained at Princeton.

Flexner called Smith to discuss "our future Lewis problem." They could not understand him. Lewis had produced nothing in five years. They in fact did have the highest regard for him—just no longer for his laboratory skills. Flexner still believed that Lewis had true gifts, broad and deep vision, an extraordinary ability to communicate and inspire. Flexner still believed that Lewis could become a dominant figure in medical teaching and research. Of that field, he could still be master.

Lewis had shown at least some of what Welch had. Perhaps he had much of it. And perhaps in the end he also lacked what Welch lacked, the creativity and organizational vision to actually run a major laboratory investigation.

Two days after Flexner and Smith talked, Flexner sat down with Lewis. He was blunt. But he assured Lewis the bluntness "was a conclusion placed before [you] in all kindness." The prospect of Lewis's becoming a member of the institute was a distant dream. His research had been "sterile" for the past five years. Unless it yielded something solid and important in the next year, he would not be reappointed even to a temporary position. He was approaching fifty years of age and Flexner told him, "The chances of [your] changing in the direction of more fertile ideas [are] small." He also said Lewis had not acted with "energy and determination." He had not **fought.** Then, most painfully, Flexner said he was "not essentially of the investigator type."

Flexner urged him—indeed, all but ordered him—to take the Iowa position. It was an extraordinary offer: $10,000 a year salary—more than double the median income for physicians—and a free hand in organizing a department. Flexner assured him that he still believed he had great gifts. Great gifts. He could still make a huge contribution, a significant and important contribution. At Iowa he could become a major figure, inspire respect, and be far happier.

Lewis listened quietly and said little. He did not remonstrate or argue. He was almost passive, yet firm. There was a cold, unreachable center within him. Regarding Iowa, that was settled. He would reject the offer. He had no interest in anything but the laboratory. He hoped in the next year to justify reappointment.

After the conversation Flexner was frustrated, frustrated and angry. "I put all the pressure I could upon him but without avail," he wrote Smith. "My notion is our obligations to Lewis are now fulfilled and that unless a great change takes place it will be our duty to act decisively next spring. He has been a real disappointment to me. . . . I left no doubt as to the risk he takes, and he left me no doubt that he understands and accepts that risk."

A few months before Flexner's brutal conversation with Lewis, Hideyo Noguchi had gone to Ghana to investigate yellow fever. Noguchi was as close to a pet as Flexner had. They had first met almost thirty years earlier, when Flexner was still at Penn and gave a speech in Tokyo. Uninvited, Noguchi had followed him to Philadelphia, knocked on his door, and announced he had come to work with him. Flexner found a position for him, then took him to the Rockefeller Institute. There Noguchi had developed an international reputation, but a controversial one.

He had done real science with Flexner, for example, identifying—and naming—neurotoxin in cobra venom. And he had claimed even more significant breakthroughs on his own, including the ability to grow polio and rabies viruses. (He could not have grown them with his techniques.) Rivers,

also at Rockefeller and the first person to demonstrate that viruses were parasites on living cells,
questioned those claims. Noguchi responded by
telling him that a man who had done research for
a long time had scars that he could never get rid
of. Later Rivers discovered a significant unrelated
mistake in his own work and confessed to Noguchi
that he planned to retract his paper. Noguchi advised against it, saying it would take fifteen years
for anyone else to find out he was wrong. Rivers
was astounded, later saying, "I don't think Noguchi
was honest."

Noguchi's most important claim, however, was to
have isolated the pathogen that caused yellow fever. It
was a spirochete, he said, a spiral-shaped bacterium.
Years before, Walter Reed had seemed to prove that
a filterable virus caused the disease. Reed was long
dead, but others attacked Noguchi's findings. In response to one such attack, Noguchi wrote Flexner,
"[H]is objections were very unreasonable. . . . I am
not certain whether these Havana men are really
interested in scientific discussion or not."

Noguchi did not lack courage. And so he went to
Ghana to prove himself correct.

In May 1928 he died there, of yellow fever.

Noguchi's death came one month before Flexner
and Lewis had their conversation. It attracted international attention, made the front pages of newspapers around the world, inspired glowing tributes
in all the New York papers. For Noguchi, it was a

Viking funeral, a blazing glory that obliterated all questions about the quality of his science.

The entire Rockefeller Institute reeled from the loss. Despite any scientific controversies, Noguchi had been buoyant, enthusiastic, always helpful, universally liked. Both Flexner and Lewis suffered in particular. Noguchi had been, literally, like a son to Flexner. Lewis had known him well, very well, going back to his first happy days in New York.

Noguchi's death also left open the question of whether he had in fact isolated the pathogen that caused yellow fever. The institute wanted that question answered.

Shope volunteered to do it. He was young and believed himself invulnerable. He wanted action. He wanted to investigate yellow fever.

Flexner refused to allow him to go. Shope was also only twenty-eight years old, with a wife and an infant son. It was too dangerous.

Then Lewis volunteered. The scientific question remained, and it was a major one. Who was more qualified to investigate it than he? He had proven himself expert at cultivating bacteria and, even more important, he had proven that polio was a viral disease. Noguchi notwithstanding, it seemed a virus did cause yellow fever. And, important as the question was, it also had built-in limits; it was the kind of narrow and focused science that Flexner still had faith in Lewis to answer.

Lewis's wife, Louise, objected. The laboratory had

taken him away from her and their two children enough. She was already furious at him for once again declining the Iowa position. But **this** . . . this was something else.

Lewis had never listened to her. They had not had a real marriage for a long time. For him, this solved every problem. If he succeeded, he would restore himself in Flexner's eyes. Five years before he had resigned from the Phipps Institute and simultaneously withdrawn his acceptance of the Iowa offer without any other prospects. All that he had done in order to do the one thing he loved, return to the laboratory. He was willing to gamble again. He was energized again. And he was more desperate than ever.

Instead of Ghana, however, he would go to Brazil. A particularly virulent strain of yellow fever had surfaced there.

In late November 1928, Flexner came to Princeton to see Lewis off. Flexner's attitude toward him had already seemed to change. He was willing again to talk about the future. He also wanted, he said, to "learn about Shope's Iowa work." Shope had recently observed an extraordinarily violent influenza epizootic—an epidemic in animals—in swine. The overall mortality of the entire local pig population had reached 4 percent; in some herds mortality had exceeded 10 percent. That very much sounded like the influenza pandemic in humans a decade earlier.

A month later Lewis sailed for Brazil. On January 12, 1929, Frederick Russell, the colonel who had organized much of the army's scientific work for Gorgas and who now worked for a Rockefeller-sponsored international health organization, received a cable saying Lewis had arrived and was well. The institute relayed the news to his wife, who had been so angry at Lewis's departure that she had wanted nothing to do with the Rockefeller Institute and returned to Milwaukee, where both she and Lewis had grown up. Each week Russell was to receive news of Lewis and send it on to her.

Lewis located his laboratory in Belem, a port city on the Para River, seventy-two miles from the ocean but the main port of entry into the Amazon Basin. Europeans settled there in 1615, and a rubber boom in the nineteenth century had filled the city with Europeans while Indians went back and forth into the interior in dugout canoes. It was steamy, equatorial, and received as much precipitation as any area in the world.

On February 1, Lewis wrote Flexner, "Arrived here on Tuesday and went right to work. . . . [H]ave been setting up my own shop here, awaiting materials, having additional screening prepared, etc. . . . Should be started at something by early next week I hope."

He seemed the old Lewis, energetic and confident. And each week Russell received a two-word wire: "Lewis well." He received them through

February, March, April, and May. But if Lewis was well, he sent no word about his research; he gave no sign that work was going well.

Then, on June 29, Russell sent a note hand-delivered by messenger to Flexner: "The following message from Rio de Janeiro, regarding Dr. Paul Lewis, was sent to me today, with the request that it be delivered to you. 'Lewis's illness began on June 25th. Doctors state it to be yellow fever. Condition of June 28th, temperature 103.8, pulse 80. . . .' The Foundation is sending the message to Dr. Theobald Smith and also to Mrs. Lewis at Milwaukee."

Even as Russell sent that note to Flexner, Lewis was in agony. He had vomited violently, the nearly black vomit of the severe cases; the virus attacked the mucosa in his stomach, which bled, giving the vomit the dark color; it attacked the bone marrow, causing violent aching. An intense, searing head-ache gave him no rest, except perhaps when he was delirious. He had seizures. His colleagues packed him in ice and tried to keep him hydrated, but there was little else they could do.

The next day another wire came: "Lewis condition critical. Anuria supervened Saturday."

His kidneys were failing and he was producing no urine. All the toxins that the body normally rid itself of were now building up in his system. Later that same day, Russell received a second wire: "Lewis on fourth day of illness. Marked renal involvement."

He was becoming jaundiced, taking on the classic color that gave the disease its name. Symptom by symptom, step by step his body was failing.

June 30, 1929, was a Sunday. All day Lewis suffered, writhed in delirium. He went into a coma. It was his only relief. It was the fifth day of his illness. There would not be a sixth.

Shortly before midnight Dr. Paul A. Lewis found release.

An unsigned wire to Russell reported, "Typical yellow fever. Probably laboratory infection. Wire instructions regarding body."

Shope walked down Maple Street on the edge of the Princeton campus to inform Lewis's wife, who had come back from Milwaukee, and son Hobart, now a college student who had remained in Princeton.

Lewis's widow gave simple and explicit instructions. She was returning immediately to Milwaukee and wanted the body shipped directly there, where those who cared about Paul were. She specifically stated that she wanted no memorial service held at the Rockefeller Institute, in either New York or Princeton.

There was none.

Shope accompanied the body to Wisconsin. The business manager of the Rockefeller Institute asked him, "I wonder if you could arrange when you arrive to order some flowers for the service for Dr. Lewis."

The flowers came, with a card signed "the Board of Scientific Directors of the Rockefeller Institute."

Lewis's daughter, Janet, wrote the thank-you note, addressing it "Dear Sirs." Her mother could not bring herself to have any contact with the institute, particularly a thank-you note. The institute paid Lewis's salary to her through June 1930 and also paid his son Hobart's college tuition. (Like his grandfather and aunt Marian, the first woman to graduate from Rush Medical College in Chicago, he became a physician—but a clinician, not a scientist.)

In the next report to the Board of Scientific Directors of the Rockefeller Institute—a board which now included Eugene Opie, whom Lewis had recruited as his successor at Phipps—Flexner noted that one scientist's resignation "which is much regretted, left the study of light phenomena unprovided for."

Lewis had originally suggested that work to Flexner. Flexner mentioned a "recrudescence of poliomyelitis." Lewis had proved that a filterable virus caused that disease.

Flexner went through item after item concerning the institute. He pointed out "a pressing problem was the one in connection with the still unfinished work of Dr. Noguchi." He made no mention of Paul A. Lewis, no mention of Dr. Lewis at all.

Later Flexner received Lewis's autopsy report and news that researchers at the institute in New York had succeeded in transmitting Lewis's virus—they called it "P.A.L."—to monkeys and were continuing experiments with it. Flexner wrote in reply, "Thank you for sending me the report on the comparison of the Rivas and P.A.L. strains of yellow fever virus. At your convenience I should like to talk over the report with you. Dr. Cole thinks white paint and some other improvements desirable in your animal quarters. Has he spoken with you about them?"

Lewis had worked with deadly pathogens his entire adult life and had never infected himself. Since Noguchi's death everyone working with yellow fever took special care.

In the five months Lewis worked in Brazil he did not report any details of his research and his laboratory notes provided almost no information about it. He died from a laboratory accident. Somehow he gave yellow fever to himself.

Shope later told his sons a rumor that Lewis, who smoked often, had somehow contaminated a cigarette with the virus and smoked it. The virus entered the bloodstream through a cut on his lip. David Lewis Anderson recalls that his father, Lewis's friend in Philadelphia, also blamed cigarettes for Lewis's death.

Three years earlier Sinclair Lewis, no relation, won the Pulitzer Prize for his bestselling novel **Arrowsmith,** a novel about a young scientist at a fictionalized version of the Rockefeller Institute.

Everyone in medical science, especially at the institute, knew that novel. In it, the main character's wife dies from smoking a cigarette contaminated by a deadly pathogen.

Flexner wrote an obituary of Lewis for **Science** in which he referred to "the important observations made by him in association with Sewall Wright on the hereditary factors in research in tuberculosis." Lewis's work with Wright had been carried out in Philadelphia; Flexner made no mention of anything Lewis had done in the five years since his return to the institute.

Meanwhile, Shope returned to Iowa to explore further this swine influenza, to observe still another epidemic among pigs.

In 1931, two years after Lewis's death, Shope published three papers in a single issue of the **Journal of Experimental Medicine.** His work appeared in good company. In that same issue were articles by Avery, one of the series on the pneumococcus that would lead to his discovery of the transforming principle; by Thomas Rivers, the brilliant virologist; and by Karl Landsteiner, who had just won the Nobel Prize. All of these scientists were at the Rockefeller Institute.

Each of Shope's articles was about influenza. He listed Lewis as the lead author on one. He had found the cause of influenza, at least in swine. It was a virus. We now know that the virus he found in swine descended directly from the 1918 virus, the virus that made all the world a killing zone. It is still unclear whether humans gave the virus to swine, or swine gave it to humans, although the former seems more likely.

By then the virus had mutated into mild form, or the swine's immune systems had adjusted to it, or both, since the virus alone seemed to cause only mild disease. Shope did demonstrate that with **B. influenzae** as a secondary invader it could still be highly lethal. Later he would show that antibodies from human survivors of the 1918 pandemic protected pigs against this swine influenza.

Shope's work was momentous and provocative. As soon as his articles appeared, a British scientist named C. H. Andrewes contacted him. Andrewes and several colleagues had been expending all their efforts on influenza, and they found Shope's articles compelling. Andrewes and Shope became close friends; Shope even took him hunting and fishing where he had vacationed since he was six years old, at Woman Lake, Minnesota.

In England in 1933, during a minor outbreak of human influenza, Andrewes, Patrick Laidlaw, and Wilson Smith, largely following Shope's methodology, filtered fresh human material and transmitted influenza to ferrets. They found the human pathogen. It was a filter-passing organism, a virus, like Shope's swine influenza.

Had Lewis lived, he would have coauthored the

papers with Shope, and even added breadth and experience to them. He would have helped produce another of the seminal papers in virology. His reputation would have been secure. Shope was not perfect. For all his later accomplishments in influenza and in other areas, some of his ideas, including some of those pertaining to influenza, were mistaken. Lewis, if energized and once again painstaking, might have prevented those errors. But no matter.

Shope was soon made a member of Rockefeller Institute. Lewis would likely have also been made a member. He would have been invited into the inner sanctum. He would have maintained his membership in the community of those who do science. He would have belonged there. He would have had all that he wanted.

William Park, Oswald Avery, and Paul Lewis each approached science in his own way.

Park, a man who almost became a medical missionary, saw it as a means to a larger end; he saw it as a tool to relieve suffering. Disciplined and methodical, his interest lay chiefly in immediate results that he could apply to his purpose. His contributions, particularly those made with Anna Williams, were enormous; their improvement of diphtheria antitoxin alone doubtless saved hundreds of thousands of lives over the past century. But his purpose also limited him, narrowed him, and limited the kind of findings he and those under him would make.

Avery was driven and obsessive. Part artist and part hunter, he had vision, patience, and persistence. His artist's eye let him see a landscape from a new perspective and in exquisite detail, the hunter in him told him when something, no matter how seemingly trivial, was out of place, and he wondered. The wonder moved him to the sacrifice of all else. He had no choice but to sacrifice. It was his nature. Cutting a Gordian knot gave him no satisfaction. He wanted to unfold and understand mysteries, not cut through them. So he tugged at a thread and kept tugging, untangling it, following where it led, until he unraveled an entire fabric. Then others wove a new fabric for a different world. T. S. Eliot said any new work of art alters slightly the existing order. Avery accomplished that all right, and far more.

Paul Lewis was a romantic, and a lover. He wanted. He wanted more and loved more passionately than Park or Avery. But as is true of many romantics, it was the idea of the thing as much or more than the thing itself that he loved. He loved science, and he loved the laboratory. But it did not yield to him. The deepest secrets of the laboratory showed themselves to Lewis when he was guided by others, when others opened a crack for him. But when he came alone to the laboratory, that crack closed. He could not find the right loose thread to tug at, the way to ask the question. To him the laboratory presented a stone face, unyielding to his pleadings. And whether his death was a suicide or a true accident, his failure to win what he loved killed him. One could consider Lewis, in a way meaningful only to him, the last victim of the 1918 pandemic.

AFTERWORD

EVENTS HAVE OVERTAKEN this book. When I began work on it early in 1997, my plan was to use the events of 1918 as a narrative vehicle and a probe to explore several questions that did not necessarily even involve influenza. Chiefly, I wanted to see how American society reacted to an immense challenge, a war nature had launched against humanity imposed on a war humans had launched against one another. I wanted to explore how individuals who had at least some power to deal with this challenge reacted, whether they be politicians or scientists, and what effects their decisions had on society. And I wanted to see what lessons we might take from such an investigation.

The continued threat of a new, possibly lethal

pandemic has made those questions more relevant than ever. Between 1959 and 1997, only two people suffered documented infections by avian viruses; neither victim died. But in 1997, an H5N1 avian influenza virus, the so-called bird flu, killed six of eighteen people in Hong Kong. Millions of fowl were slaughtered in an unsuccessful effort to wipe it out, and it reemerged with a vengeance in 2003. Since then, H5N1 and more recently an H7N9 avian virus have been infecting humans at previously unknown rates. Between 2003 and 2017—the latest numbers as I write this—these viruses have infected 2,342 people and killed 1,053 of them—a case fatality rate of 44.9 percent. The case fatality rate is high because both viruses bind only to cells deep in the lung, so the starting point for the disease is, in effect, viral pneumonia. Deaths have occurred in places as far apart as Azerbaijan, Egypt, and China.

Almost all victims have been infected through direct contact with birds (a very few occurred within families), but every time the virus infects a person, it has another opportunity to develop the capacity to bind to human cells in the upper respiratory tract, as do seasonal influenza viruses. This would allow it to pass easily from person to person. If that happens, the case fatality rate would drop—most victims would start with ordinary influenza, not a viral pneumonia—but another pandemic would occur.

In 1918 such a virus did infect humans. Since

the original publication of this book, scientists have found evidence (the question is not settled) that seven of the eight segments of the 1918 virus are of avian origin, and the virus jumped species to humans probably after a reassortment (see 112) with another virus in which it acquired a human hemagglutinin gene—the gene which allows the virus to bind to and thus infect cells. And even that eighth segment had recent avian roots. This reassortment would have occurred when the avian virus infected a mammal—human, horse, pig, whatever—that was simultaneously infected by another influenza virus carrying that gene.

In 1918, the world population was 1.8 billion, and the pandemic probably killed 50 to 100 million people, with the lowest credible modern estimate at 35 million. Today the world population is 7.6 billion. A comparable death toll today would range from roughly 150 to 425 million.

Chiefly because antibiotics would slash the toll from secondary bacterial infections, if a virus caused a 1918-like pandemic today, modern medicine could likely prevent significantly more than half of those deaths—assuming adequate supplies of antibiotics, which is quite an assumption—but tens of millions would still die. And a severe influenza pandemic would hit like a tsunami, inundating intensive-care units even as doctors and nurses fall ill themselves and generally pushing the health care system to the point of collapse and possibly beyond it. Hospitals, like every other industry, have gotten more efficient by cutting costs, which means virtually no excess capacity—on a per capita basis the United States has far fewer hospital beds than a few decades ago. Indeed, during a routine influenza season, usage of respirators rises to nearly 100 percent; in a pandemic, most people who needed a mechanical respirator probably would not get one. (The strain influenza puts on health care was driven home to me in a personal way on my book tour. In Kansas City, a flare-up of ordinary seasonal influenza forced eight hospitals to close emergency rooms, yet this was only a tiny fraction of the pressure a pandemic would exert.) This and similar problems—such as if a particular secondary bacterial invader is resistant to antibiotics, or shortages of such seemingly trivial items as hypodermic needles or bags to hold IV fluids (a severe shortage of these bags is a major problem as I write this)—could easily moot many medical advances since 1918.

Disease impact would also ripple through the economy to disastrous effect. With everyone from air traffic controllers to truck drivers out sick, just-in-time inventory systems would crash, supply chains would collapse, for lack of some part production lines would shut down, while schools and day-care facilities might close for weeks, and an overburdened "last mile" would limit the ability of people to work from home.

With the emergence of H5N1, the threat of just

such a scenario got the attention of large companies and governments; businesses began working on supply chains and continuity plans; government in developed countries began pouring money into pandemic preparedness, including basic research, vaccine production, and stockpiling certain drugs. In addition, since manufacturing and distributing a vaccine would take months at best, and since no antiviral drugs are very effective, they also asked public health officials to devise policies to mitigate the impact of a pandemic using non-pharmaceutical interventions, or NPIs—i.e., what to do without drugs. Since most of these were based on an analysis of events in 1918, I was asked to join in the effort that brought together people with backgrounds in history, laboratory science, public health, international relations, mathematical modeling, and politics. My involvement continued for several years, and I worked with others through the National Academy of Sciences, national security entities, other state and federal agencies, think tanks, and officials in the Bush and Obama White Houses.

Planners prepared for a Category 5 hurricane. The 2009 H1N1 swine flu pandemic, not even a tropical storm, threw them off-balance. This pandemic, the mildest ever known, taught new lessons, including some that required rethinking NPI policy.

The 2009 pandemic killed "only" an estimated 150,000 to 575,000 worldwide, with probably about 12,000 U.S. deaths. (However, if one looks at the

2009 pandemic in terms of total years of life lost, not just deaths, it was much more severe: the average age of victims was only forty, and 80 percent of victims were younger than sixty-five. In seasonal influenza, only 10 percent of deaths occur in those under sixty-five.) By comparison, ordinary seasonal influenza kills up to 650,000 people worldwide annually, and in the United States the disease kills between 3,000 and 56,000 a year, depending mainly on the virulence of the virus and to a lesser extent on the efficacy of that year's vaccine.

The 2009 experience should reassure no one. It seems likely that throughout history many such outbreaks occurred but escaped notice; only modern surveillance and molecular biology allowed us to recognize it as a pandemic. When the **Washington Post** asked Tom Frieden, then head of the Centers for Disease Control and Prevention, what scared him the most, what kept him up at night, he replied, "The biggest concern is always for an influenza pandemic . . . [It] really is the worst-case scenario."

So where are we now? What are the lessons?

Before addressing those questions, we need to understand the commonalities of the few pandemics we have information about: 1889, 1918, 1957, 1968, and 2009.

First, all five came in waves. (A few scientists argue that the difference in lethality between 1918's first and second waves mean that these were caused by different viruses, but evidence showing otherwise seems overwhelming. For one thing, exposure to the first wave provided as high as 94 percent protection against the second wave, far better protection than the best modern vaccine affords, and that's just one piece of the evidence that the same virus caused both waves.)

In fact, some investigators now speculate that the 1918 virus circulated in humans for several years before mutations allowed it to spread easily. If true, this would of course explode the hypothesis that Haskell was the origin. The 1889 pandemic virus did follow this pattern, generating two and a half years of sporadic outbreaks around the world, including in such large cities as London, Berlin, and Paris, before becoming fully pandemic, blanketing the world in the winter of 1891–92.

We also know that every wave of every pandemic has been at least a little different. In 1918, of course, that difference was dramatic, but 1968 may be more puzzling. In the United States, 70 percent of pandemic deaths occurred in the 1968–69 influenza season, with the rest in 1969–70. Europe and Asia were the opposite, with few deaths in 1968–69 and the overwhelming majority in 1969–70—even though a vaccine was available by then. Incidentally, the 1968 pandemic gave us the H3N2 virus, which has continued to cause the most severe disease of several circulating influenza viruses ever since.

Speculative explanations of that phenomenon

come down to the fact that the virus mutates rapidly, which explains why a mantra at the U.S. Centers for Disease Control is "When you've seen one influenza season, you've seen one influenza season."

In the end, for all we know about influenza—and we know a lot—at this point does not do us much good.

There is one answer to all this: a universal vaccine, i.e., a vaccine that works against all influenza viruses.

Current vaccines target the hemagglutinin, the antigen most exposed to the immune system (see 103–104), which looks something like the head on broccoli. Unfortunately, the vaccines target the head portion, which mutates rapidly and is a part of the virus that can change without interfering with the functioning of the virus. That's part of the reason influenza vaccines are not particularly good: between 2003 and 2017 their effectiveness ranged only from 10 percent to 61 percent. (Even at those levels, they prevent millions of cases and thousands of deaths and are well worth getting.) For the elderly, with their less robust immune systems, in some years the vaccine did not generate any protection at all.

But other parts of the virus, including the stalk on the hemagglutinin, akin to the stalk on broccoli, are "conserved," i.e., shared by most if not all influenza viruses, likely because if they mutate the virus will be unable to infect a cell and replicate (see 167–168). Current research focuses on developing a vaccine that incites the immune system to target the stalk. If successful, this vaccine will work against the influenza viruses that have a history of infecting humans—and it would likely also be far more effective than the best current vaccines; thus it would save hundreds of thousands of lives every year.

Of course, if developing a universal vaccine were easy it would have been done, but for decades few resources went to such research. Consider for a moment that prior to the emergence of H5N1, the U.S. government was spending more money on the West Nile virus than on influenza. While influenza was killing as many as 56,000 Americans a year, West Nile in its deadliest year killed 284. And West Nile will never be a major threat; it is not a disease that will ever explode through the human population. Yet it was receiving more research dollars than influenza.

That has changed, and significant progress toward a universal vaccine has been made, but more resources should still go to the effort. Developing this vaccine should be one of the very highest priorities for medical research.

The question of vaccines aside—where are we? How prepared are we for a new pandemic?

Here is what has gone right:

For one, the World Health Organization and governments have developed a good surveillance system. The problem is that it is incomplete—too many countries still do not participate—and dependent on governments to cooperate. In 2003, the system even picked up SARS, which was originally thought to be a new influenza virus, and contained it, but SARS was infinitely easier to control than influenza would be. As it was, the world was put at risk by China, which initially lied and hid the disease. China's candor has improved significantly, but China is still not fully transparent. And China is not the only reluctant partner.

Obviously, surveillance matters because it provides the earliest possible alert of potential pandemic viruses, which in turn accelerates the production of a vaccine—and with all its flaws, a vaccine remains the best defense against a pandemic.

Even a few weeks could make a difference. The vaccine against the 2009 pandemic virus was as effective as the best seasonal vaccines, but it arrived late in the second wave.

In addition to surveillance, investment has also gone into better and faster vaccine manufacturing technologies. For more than seventy years and continuing into the present, influenza viruses have been grown in eggs, harvested, killed (a small amount of attenuated, live-virus vaccine is made), and purified. But egg-based production is slow, and the virus adapts itself to eggs—another reason it is not more effective in humans. Finally, since 2009, production has begun shifting into two better and faster technologies. One grows the virus in mammalian cells. The second uses recombinant molecular biology techniques to insert the hemagglutinin antigen into an entirely unrelated virus, then grows that virus in insect cells and harvests the hemagglutinin.

Yet even under a best case scenario, even with the new technologies, it will still take months to deliver large quantities of vaccine. In addition, much of the U.S. vaccine supply is manufactured outside the country; in a lethal pandemic, there is a question whether another government would allow its export before its own population was protected.

Several anti-viral drugs, particularly oseltamivir and zanamivir, are of incremental use in lessening the severity of an attack, and taken prophylactically, they can also cut the risk of getting the disease, but only while they are being taken. However, they too have limited effectiveness and resistance may develop.

So current pharmaceuticals would fall far short of solving the problem of a pandemic.

What else can be done? In the past several years numerous governments have looked at NPIs—i.e., ways to mitigate a pandemic's impact using public health measures.

No easy answers exist. The virus is airborne, so it can be inhaled, which seems to be the primary manner of transmission, but it can also survive on a surface—a doorknob, say, or a can of beer—at least for hours or, depending on temperature and humidity, possibly for days. So it can also be transmitted if someone opens a door, then covers a yawn. The only way to avoid it is to completely isolate oneself from society for the six to ten weeks it takes an outbreak to burn through a community, including not accepting deliveries, not going out, and so forth.

That is infeasible, just as it is infeasible except in extraordinary circumstances for a community to successfully isolate itself completely from the rest of the world. (In 1918, a few islands and communities did do this, but even fewer could do so successfully today.)

So NPIs, whether imposed by governments or taken by individuals, will have limited usefulness. And even to the limited extent an intervention might be successful, it must be sustained. Based on studies of what U.S. cities did in 1918, modelers have concluded that "layering" several interventions—most of them different kinds of "social distancing"—would at least stretch out the length of an influenza outbreak in a local community, easing the strain on the health care system. The historical data used in some of these models was flawed, and in assessing such 1918 actions as closing schools, none of the models considered that the cities that experienced the spring wave likely had a population with some immunity, which may have affected the model's results.

Nonetheless, these NPIs are the only tools available. One tool of no use is widespread quarantine. For some diseases quarantine makes good sense, and in theory in some circumstances it could help even for influenza—but only in theory. An unpublished 1918 study of army camps demonstrates this. The army had data on 120 training camps—99 imposed quarantine and 21 did not. But there was no difference in mortality or morbidity between camps implementing quarantine and those that didn't; there was not even any difference in how long it took influenza to pass through the camp. The story, however, isn't quite that simple: the epidemiologist who performed the study looked not just at numbers but at actual practice, and found that out of the 99 camps that imposed quarantine, only a half dozen or so rigidly enforced it. Those few did benefit. But if the overwhelming majority of army bases in wartime could not enforce a quarantine rigidly enough to benefit, a civilian community in peacetime certainly could not.

Closing borders would be of no benefit either. It would be impossible to shut down trade, prevent citizens from returning to the country, etc. That would shut down the entire economy and enormously magnify supply chain problems by ending imports—including all health-related imports like drugs, syringes, gowns, everything. Even at that, models show that a 90 percent effective border closing would delay the disease by only a few days, at most a week, and a 99 percent effective shutting of borders would delay it at most a month.

That doesn't leave much for an individual to do

other than mundane tasks such as washing one's hands. Doing it in a disciplined way every time, every day, for weeks, is difficult. But discipline matters. The SARS outbreak is illustrative: most of the dead were health care workers, and it's strongly suspected most of them infected themselves by failing to strictly follow safety protocols they were familiar with. At the very first meeting to discuss NPIs, the chief of infection control of the Hong Kong hospital, with by far the best safety record, emphasized that he made certain that everyone followed those protocols rigorously. (The same can be said for virtually all hospital infections; the hospitals with the best infection control records have staffs who pay attention to detail and take no shortcuts. Success depends on rigor, emphasis, and discipline.)

Surgical masks are next to useless except in very limited circumstances, chiefly in the home. Putting a mask on someone sick is most effective because it will contain droplets otherwise expelled into the room—a fact that experiments in 1918 proved. Will a parent put a mask on a sick child and make that child more uncomfortable? Maybe, if he or she knows it will protect the rest of the family. And even a surgical mask when combined with rigorous hand washing may provide some protection for those in close contact with a sick person. N95 masks would be more appropriate in that situation and they do protect, but they need to be properly fitted and properly worn. This is harder than it sounds.

A study of professionals wearing N95s to protect themselves from toxic mold found that more than 60 percent did not wear them properly. In addition, they are extremely uncomfortable. For a few individuals and situations N95 masks may make sense, but for the general public over a period of weeks they do not.

Other recommendations are generally simple and obvious: for example, keeping sick children home from school—which is standard behavior—and having sick adults stay home from work—which is not standard behavior. Another is exercising "cough etiquette"—coughing and sneezing into one's elbow and not one's hand, since that hand will eventually reach for a doorknob. Telecommuting is another obvious action, although the so-called last mile cannot support a significant surge in Internet usage.

In a truly lethal pandemic, state and local authorities could take much more aggressive steps, such as closing theaters, bars, and even banning sports events—in 1919 even the Stanley Cup finals were canceled—and church services.

Possibly the most controversial NPI is closing schools—most controversial because such extreme steps as those listed above would occur only in a major emergency. Closing schools could occur in a much less serious situation, making it a much more difficult call.

The argument for school closing: Because adults have much more cross-protection from exposure to other influenza viruses than children do, children usually suffer higher attack rates. They are also less careful about, for example, disposing of tissue when they sneeze, washing their hands, and so forth, so they routinely spread influenza and other infectious diseases—not only to each other, but to adults. (Inoculating children with a pneumococcal vaccine caused from a 38 percent to 94 percent decline in pneumonia in the elderly—their grandparents.) Without a doubt schools played a significant role in spreading the 1957, 1968, and 2009 pandemics, and continually do so in spreading seasonal influenza.

But closing schools places an economic burden on working parents because it, like the other interventions, has to be sustained for weeks. Accepting this economic cost might well make sense in a lethal pandemic, but it does not in a mild one. In 2009, the CDC initially recommended—it has no enforcement authority and can only recommend—that if a school had a single case, it close for two weeks. Dr. D. A. Henderson, a public health expert who earned tremendous cachet for running the World Health Organization program that eliminated smallpox from the world, raised hell and the CDC reversed itself, saying closings were "not effective" against the virus. I supported the reversal. Now the CDC will recommend school closure only in a severe pandemic. That is the right decision.

There is also data from 1889, 1918, and a 1920 recrudescence that undermines the conclusion that

children are important "super-spreaders" of influenza. Four different studies by three different investigators in England, Boston, and Detroit found
that the first cases in 80 to 85 percent of households were adults, not schoolchildren. The Detroit
study also showed that as the disease progressed
over time, adults became a smaller percentage of the
cases and children an increasing percentage—this
would mean adults were spreading the disease to
children, not the other way around. Unfortunately,
when I told a CDC investigator about this, his response was "I don't believe the data." That was not
the right response. The data is almost certainly accurate; these studies could be outliers, statistical
anomalies, but good epidemiologists compiled it.
Their findings need to be explored and understood;
the policy implications are too significant. (One
possible explanation is that the 1889 and 1918 viruses were so different from previously circulating
viruses that adults had no cross-protection, so the
immune systems of children and adults were equal.
It was as if no one had been exposed to them. In
1920, by contrast, virtually everyone had been exposed, so again their immune systems were equal.)

Finally, if any NPIs are to have any effect, the
public has to comply with the recommendations
and sustain that compliance. That will be difficult.
In Mexico City in 2009, for example, the government recommended people use masks on public
transit (a near-useless intervention) and gave out

free ones. At the height of the fear, usage peaked at 65 percent—and four days later fell to 27 percent.

Meanwhile, continued monitoring of the virus is absolutely necessary. A shift in the behavior of the virus—as from the first wave in 1918 to the second—may call for a shift in the response to it. Surveillance is critical not only in advance of but during a pandemic.

So the problems presented by a pandemic are, obviously, immense. But the biggest problem lies in the relationship between governments and the truth.

Part of that relationship requires political leaders to understand the truth—and to be able to handle the truth. If there's a lesson from the 2009 pandemic, it's that too many governments were incapable of doing so. Every Western government and many non-Western ones had prepared plans for a pandemic, as did the World Health Organization. They were reasonable plans that included good recommendations. Many of the plans attempted to limit the role of personality by laying out explicit steps to take—or not take—based on certain triggers. But planning does not equal preparation, and too many political leaders ignored the plans.

Mexico's emergency health manager was initially excluded from many high level meetings about the pandemic. Brazil was slow to release information and its southern regions had the world's highest fatality rates. Chinese Minister of Health Chen Zhu said the pandemic was a foreign disease and he would keep it out of China, declaring, "We are confident and capable of preventing and containing an H1N1 influenza epidemic." The French wanted the European Union to cancel all flights to and from Mexico. Egypt slaughtered all the pigs in the country. India considered quarantining villages with influenza. All these actions would have accomplished absolutely nothing. Mexico spent $180 million to fight the disease, but suffered $9 billion in economic losses because of the irrational response from trading partners—not exactly positive reinforcement if the goal is to encourage candor the next time.

It's unclear whether actions evolved purely out of political calculation—in Egypt, for example, only politically isolated Coptic Christians eat pork, and slaughtering pigs allowed the government to appear to be doing something—or whether public officials were just reacting emotionally, not rationally, or both. Emotion is not the absence of reason; emotion corrupts reason.

Either way, whether a politician saw an advantage and knowingly did something at best unproductive or whether he or she acted out of incompetence or fear, the human factor, the political leadership factor, is the weakness in any plan, in every plan. The 2014 experience with Ebola is only another reminder of that.

■   ■   ■

There was terror afoot in 1918, real terror. The randomness of death brought that terror home. So did its speed. And so did the fact that the healthiest and strongest seemed the most vulnerable.

But as horrific as the disease itself was, public officials and the media helped create that terror—not by exaggerating the disease but by minimizing it, by trying to reassure. A specialty among public relations consultants has evolved in recent decades called "risk communication." I don't much care for the term. For if there is a single dominant lesson from 1918, it's that governments need to tell the truth in a crisis. Risk communication implies managing the truth. You don't manage the truth. You tell the truth.

Terror rises in the dark of the mind, in the unknown beast tracking us in the jungle. The fear of the dark is an almost physical manifestation of that. Horror movies build upon the fear of the unknown, the uncertain threat that we cannot see and do not know and can find no safe haven from. But in every horror movie, once the monster appears, terror condenses into the concrete and diminishes. Fear remains. But the edge of panic created by the unknown dissipates. The power of the imagination dissipates.

In 1918 the lies of officials and of the press never allowed the terror to condense into the concrete. The public could trust nothing and so they knew nothing. Society is, ultimately, based on trust; as trust broke down, people became alienated not only from those in authority, but from each other. So a terror seeped into the society that prevented one woman from caring for her sister, that prevented volunteers from bringing food to families too ill to feed themselves and who starved to death because of it, that prevented trained nurses from responding to the most urgent calls for their services. The fear, not the disease, threatened to break the society apart. As Victor Vaughan—a careful man, a measured man, a man who did not overstate to make a point—warned, civilization could have disappeared within a few more weeks.

So the final lesson of 1918, a simple one yet one most difficult to execute, is that those who occupy positions of authority must lessen the panic that can alienate all within a society. Society cannot function if it is every man for himself. By definition, civilization cannot survive that.

Those in authority must retain the public's trust. The way to do that is to distort nothing, to put the best face on nothing, to try to manipulate no one. Lincoln said that first, and best.

A leader must make whatever horror exists concrete. Only then will people be able to break it apart.

Acknowledgments

THIS BOOK was initially supposed to be a straightforward story of the deadliest epidemic in human history, told from the perspectives of both scientists who tried to fight it and political leaders who tried to respond to it. I thought it would take me two and a half years to write, three at the most.

That plan didn't work. Instead this book took seven years to write. It has evolved (and, I hope, grown) into something rather different than originally conceived.

It took so long partly because it didn't seem possible to write about the scientists without exploring the nature of American medicine at this time, for the scientists in this book did far more than laboratory research. They changed the very nature of medicine in the United States.

And, finding useful material on the epidemic proved remarkably difficult. It was easy enough to find stories of death, but my own interests have always focused on people who try to exercise some kind of control over events. Anyone doing so was far too busy, far too overwhelmed, to pay any attention to keeping records.

In the course of these seven years, many people helped me. Some shared with me their own research or helped me find material, others helped me understand the influenza virus and the disease it causes, and some offered advice on the manuscript. None of them, of course, is responsible for any errors of commission or omission, whether factual or of judgment, in the book. (Wouldn't it be entertaining to once read an acknowledgment in which the author blames others for any mistakes?)

Two friends, Steven Rosenberg and Nicholas Restifo at the National Cancer Institute, helped me understand how a scientist approaches a problem and also read parts of the manuscript and offered comments. So did Peter Palese at Mount Sinai Medical Center in New York, one of the world's leading experts on the influenza virus, who gave very generously of his time and expertise. Robert Webster, at St. Jude Medical Center, like Palese a world leader in influenza research, offered his insights and criticisms as well. Ronald French checked the manuscript for accuracy on the clinical course of the disease. Vincent Morelli introduced me to Warren Summers, who along with the entire pulmonary section of the Louisiana State University Health Sciences Center in New Orleans helped me understand much of what happens in the lung during an influenza attack; Warren was extremely patient and repeatedly helpful. Mitchell Friedman at the Tulane Medical School also explained events in the lung to me.

Jeffrey Taubenberger at the Armed Forces Institute of Pathology kept me abreast of his latest findings. John Yewdell at the National Institutes of Health also explained much about the virus. Robert Martensen at Tulane made valuable suggestions on the history of medicine. Alan Kraut at American University also read and commented on part of the manuscript.

I also particularly thank John MacLachlan of the Tulane-Xavier Center for Bioenvironmental Research, who very much helped make this book possible. William Steinmann, head of the Center for Clinical Effectiveness and Life Support at the Tulane Medical Center, gave generously of his office space, knowledge of disease, and friendship.

All of the above have M.D.s or Ph.D.s or both. Without their assistance I would have been lost trying to understand my own cytokine storm.

People who write books are always thanking librarians and archivists. They have good reason to.

Virtually everyone at the Rudolph Matas Medical Library at Tulane University was extraordinarily helpful to me, but Patsy Copeland deserves truly special mention. So do Kathleen Puglia, Sue Dorsey, and Cindy Goldstein.

I also want to thank Mark Samels of WGBH's **American Experience,** who made available all the material collected for its program on the pandemic; Janice Goldblum at the National Academy of Sciences, who did more than just her job; Gretchen Worden at the Mutter Museum in Philadelphia; Jeffrey Anderson, then a graduate student at Rutgers, and Gery Gernhart, then a graduate student at American University, both of whom generously offered me their own research; and Charles Hardy of West Chester University, who gave me oral histories he had collected; and Mitch Yockelson at the National Archives, who gave me the benefit of his knowledge. Eliot Kaplan, then the editor of **Philadelphia Magazine,** also supported the project. I also want to thank Pauline Miner and Catherine Hart in Kansas. For help with photos I want to especially thank Susan Robbins Watson at the American Red Cross, Lisa Pendergraff at the Dudley Township Library in Kansas, Andre Sobocinski and Jan Herman at the Bureau of Navy Medicine, Darwin Stapleton at the Rockefeller University archives, and Nancy McCall at the Alan Mason Chesney archives at Johns Hopkins. I also want to thank Pat Ward Friedman for her information about her grandfather.

Now we come to my editor, Wendy Wolf. Although this is only my fifth book, counting magazine articles I've worked with literally dozens of editors. Wendy Wolf very much stands out. She edits the old-fashioned way; she works at it. On this manuscript she worked particularly hard, and working with her has been a pleasure. It is a true statement to say that, for better or worse (and I hope better), this book wouldn't exist without her. I'd also like to thank Hilary Redmon for her diligence, reliability, and just general assistance.

Thanks also to my agent Raphael Sagalyn, as good a professional as there is. I've had many editors but only one agent, a fact that speaks for itself.

Finally I thank my brilliant wife, Margaret Anne Hudgins, who helped me in too many ways to enumerate, including both in concept and in the particular—but chiefly by being herself. And then there are the cousins.

Notes

Abbreviations

APS	American Philosophical Society, Philadelphia
HSP	Historical Society of Philadelphia
JHU	Alan Mason Chesney Medical Archives, the Johns Hopkins University
LC	Library of Congress
NA	National Archives
NAS	National Academy of Sciences Archives
NLM	National Library of Medicine
RG	Record group at National Archives
RUA	Rockefeller University Archives
SG	Surgeon General William Gorgas
SLY	Sterling Library, Yale University
UNC	University of North Carolina, Chapel Hill
WP	Welch papers at JHU

PROLOGUE

Page

2   **the smartest man:** Personal communication with Dr. David Aronson, Jan. 31, 2002, and Dr. Robert Shope, Sept. 9, 2002.

7   **fifty million deaths:** Niall Johnson and Juergen Mueller, "Updating the Accounts: Global Mortality of the 1918–1920 'Spanish' Influenza Pandemic," **Bulletin of the History of Medicine** (2002), 105–15.

7   **"doubly dead":** Sherwin Nuland, **How We Die** (1993), 202.

10 **college degree:** Kenneth M. Ludmerer, **Learning to Heal: The Development of American Medical Education** (1985), 113.

11 **"vibrate and shake":** William James, "Great Men, Great Thoughts, and Environment" (1880); quoted in Sylvia Nasar, **A Beautiful Mind** (1998), 55.

11 **" 'Tis writ, 'In the beginning' ":** Johann Wolfgang Goethe, **Faust, Part One** (1949), 71.

Part I: The Warriors

CHAPTER ONE

16 **"the hostile Sioux": Washington Star,** Sept. 12, 1876.

17 **"For God's sake": New York Times,** Sept. 12, 1876.

18 **"great change in human thought":** H. L. Mencken,

"Thomas Henry Huxley 1825–1925," **Baltimore Evening Sun** (1925).

19   **"voice was low, clear and distinct":** For accounts of this speech, see **New York Times, Washington Post, Baltimore Sun,** Sept. 13, 1876.

20   **endowed chairs of theology:** Simon Flexner and James Thomas Flexner, **William Henry Welch and the Heroic Age of American Medicine** (1941), 237.

24   **theories that attributed epilepsy:** Roy Porter, **The Greatest Benefit to Mankind** (1997), 56.

24   **"a theory is a composite memory":** Quoted in Charles-Edward Amory Winslow, **The Conquest of Epidemic Disease: A Chapter in the History of Ideas** (1943), 63.

25   **four kinds of bodily fluids:** For a discussion of the theory, see Porter, **The Greatest Benefit to Mankind,** 42–66, passim.

26   **"the true path of medicine":** Ibid., 77.

27   **"recognizable only by logic":** Vivian Nutton, "Humoralism," in **Companion Encyclopedia to the History of Medicine** (1993).

29   **"our own observation of nature":** Quoted in Winslow, **Conquest of Epidemic Disease,** 126.

29   **"unequalled . . . between Hippocrates and Pasteur":** Ibid., 142.

30   **"Don't think. Try.":** Ibid., 59.

31   **"I placed it upon a rock":** Quoted in Milton Rosenau's 1934 presidential address to the Society of American Bacteriologists, Rosenau papers, UNC.

32 **"more simple and consistent system":** For an excellent review of this, see Richard Shryock, **The Development of Modern Medicine,** 2nd ed. (1947), 30–31.

33 **"sagacity and judgment":** Ibid., 4.

35 **still seen as a manifestation:** Charles Rosenberg, "The Therapeutic Revolution," in **Explaining Epidemics and Other Studies in the History of Medicine** (1992), 13–14.

35 **natural healing process:** Ibid., 9–27, passim.

35 **"profuse perspiration":** Benjamin Coates practice book, quoted in ibid., 17.

37 **never had a peaceful bath again:** Steven Rosenberg in personal communication to the author.

39 **"withered arm of science":** Quoted in Richard Shryock, **American Medical Research** (1947), 7.

41 **Michel Foucault condemned:** John Harley Warner, **Against the Spirit of the System: The French Impulse in Nineteenth-Century American Medicine** (1998), 4.

42 **"The practice of medicine":** Ibid., 183–84.

44 **"Why think?":** See Richard Walter, **S. Weir Mitchell, M.D., Neurologist: A Medical Biography** (1970), 202–22.

44 **"Nature answers only":** Winslow, **Conquest of Epidemic Disease,** 296.

45 **"if all disease were left to itself":** Quoted in Paul Starr, **The Social Transformation of American Medicine** (1982), 55.

46 **In 1862 in Philadelphia:** Charles Rosenberg,

Explaining Epidemics and Other Studies in the History of Medicine (1992), 14.

46 **"popular crafts of every description":** **Thomsonian Recorder** (1832), 89; quoted in Charles Rosenberg, **The Cholera Years: The United States in 1832, 1849, and 1866** (1962), 70–71.

47 **"False theory and hypothesis":** John Harley Warner, "The Fall and Rise of Professional Mystery," in **The Laboratory Revolution in Medicine** (1992), 117.

47 **"priests' and Doctors' slavery":** Quoted in Rosenberg, **Cholera Years,** 70–71.

47 **"a greater humbug":** John King, "The Progress of Medical Reform," **Western Medical Reformer** (1846); quoted in Warner, "The Fall and Rise of Professional Mystery," 113.

48 **only thirty-four licensed physicians:** Burton J. Bledstein, **The Culture of Professionalism: The Middle Class and the Development of Higher Education in America** (1976), 33.

48 **"the Diminished Respectability":** Shryock, **Development of Modern Medicine,** 264.

49 **court-martialed and condemned:** Ludmerer, **Learning to Heal,** 10, 11, 23, 168.

49 **not to treat malaria:** Rosenberg, "The Therapeutic Revolution," 9–27, passim.

49 **"all the worse for the fishes":** Bledstein, **Culture of Professionalism,** 33.

50 **"a vast deal to be done":** Quoted in Donald Fleming, **William Welch and the Rise of American Medicine** (1954), 8.

50 **7,000 to 226,000:** Edwin Layton, **The Revolt of the Engineers: Social Responsibility and the American Engineering Profession** (1971), 3.

51 **fail four of nine courses:** Ludmerer, **Learning to Heal,** 37 (re: Harvard), 12 (re: Michigan).

51 **"truths that lie about me so thick":** Quoted in ibid., 25.

52 **not know how to use a microscope:** Ibid., 37.

52 **"something horrible to contemplate":** Ibid., 48.

52 **"can't pass written examinations":** Bledstein, **Culture of Professionalism,** 275–76.

52 **"No medical school has thought":** Ludmerer, **Learning to Heal,** 15.

53 **"simply horrible":** Ibid., 25.

53 **Against the advice:** James Thomas Flexner, **An American Saga: The Story of Helen Thomas and Simon Flexner** (1984), 125; see also ibid., 294.

54 **"strongest evidence of this demand":** Benjamin Gilman, quoted in Flexner, **American Saga,** 125.

CHAPTER TWO

57 **eightieth-birthday celebration:** Flexner and Flexner, **William Henry Welch,** 3–8, passim.

59 **fifteen hundred stores:** Ezra Brown, ed., **This Fabulous Century, The Roaring Twenties 1920–1930** (1985), 105, 244.

59 **"beyond the capacity of an individual**

parent": Quoted in Sue Halpern, "Evangelists for Kids," **New York Review of Books** (May 29, 2003), 20.

60 **work of Rudolf Virchow:** Flexner and Flexner, **William Henry Welch,** 33.

60 **"accurate observation of facts":** Ibid.

61 **filled him with repugnance:** Ibid., 29.

61 **begged his cousins:** Fleming, **William Welch,** 15.

63 **"every noble and good quality":** Flexner and Flexner, **William Henry Welch,** 50.

64 **"the light of his own mind":** Quoted in ibid., 49.

65 **"the labyrinths of Chemistry":** Ibid., 62–63.

66 **scientists had met in Berlin:** Shryock, **Development of Modern Medicine,** 206.

67 **"I can only admire":** Flexner and Flexner, **William Henry Welch,** 64, see also 71.

67 **"the easiest examination":** Ibid, 62.

68 **"a voyage of exploration":** Ibid., 76.

69 **fifteen thousand American doctors:** Thomas Bonner, **American Doctors and German Universities: A Chapter in International Intellectual Relations, 1870–1914** (1963), 23.

69 **"those who have studied abroad":** Welch to father, March 21, 1876, WP.

70 **"a source of pleasure and profit":** Welch to step-mother, March 26, 1877, WP.

70 **"Germany has outstripped":** Flexner and Flexner, **William Henry Welch,** 83.

70 **"certain important methods":** Welch to father, Oct. 18, 1876, WP.

71   **"carry on investigations hereafter":** Welch
      to father, Feb. 25, 1877, WP.
71   **"observe closely and carefully":** Welch to
      father, Oct. 18, 1876, WP.
71   **"He is almost the founder":** Welch to father,
      Sept. 23, 1877, WP.
72   **"The facts of science":** Quoted in Flexner and
      Flexner, **William Henry Welch,** 87.
73   **"constantly astonished at the wealth of
      experience":** Quoted in Shryock, **Development
      of Modern Medicine,** 181–82.
73   **"the greatest and most useful":** Quoted in
      ibid., 182.
74   **"the first men to be secured":** Quoted in Flexner
      and Flexner, **William Henry Welch,** 93.
75   **"a modest livelihood":** Ibid., 106.
76   **"cannot make much of a success":** Ibid., 112.
76   **"the drudgery of life":** Ibid.

CHAPTER THREE

77   **"leak knowledge":** Ibid., 70.
78   **"a larger circle of hearers":** Quoted in
      ibid., 117.
80   **"poisoning of half the population":** John
      Duffy, **A History of Public Health in New
      York City 1866–1966** (1974), 113.
81   **the zymote theory:** For more on zymotes see
      Phyllis Allen Richmond, "Some Variant Theories
      in Opposition to the Germ Theory of Disease,"
      **Journal of the History of Medicine and Allied
      Sciences** (1954), 295.

85   **laurel wreath "such are given to the brave":** Paul De Kruif, **Microbe Hunters** (1939), 130.

85   **"What was theory":** Charles Chapin, "The Present State of the Germ Theory of Disease," Fiske Fund Prize Essay (1885), unpaginated, Chapin papers, Rhode Island Historical Society.

86   **"powerless to create an epidemic":** Michael Osborne, "French Military Epidemiology and the Limits of the Laboratory: The Case of Louis-Felix-Achille Kelsch," in Andrew Cunningham and Perry Williams, eds., **The Laboratory Revolution in Medicine** (1992), 203.

88   **"however bright the prospect":** Flexner and Flexner, **William Henry Welch,** see 128–32.

89   **"not be so cheaply earned":** Welch to stepmother, April 3, 1884, WP.

89   **"in no way discuss with him":** Ibid.

90   **"on a high plane of loneliness":** Flexner and Flexner, **William Henry Welch,** 136, see also 153.

91   **"deliberately break off relationships":** According to Dr. Allen Freeman, quoted in ibid., 170.

92   **"already has a German reputation":** Welch to father, Jan. 25, 1885, WP.

92   **the greatest name in science:** Florence Sabin, **Franklin Paine Mall: The Story of a Mind** (1934), 70.

94   **"a small chemical lab":** Sabin, **Franklin Paine Mall,** 24.

94   **"What we shall consider success":** Flexner and Flexner, **William Henry Welch,** 225.

94 **"which will cost $200,000"**: Sabin, **Franklin Paine Mall,** 112.

95 **"You make the opportunities"**: Ibid.

95 **"the real pioneer of modern"**: Martha Sternberg, **George Sternberg: A Biography** (1925), see 5, 68, 279, 285.

99 **build a theory on the right ones:** An anecdote related by Dr. Steven Rosenberg, July 1991.

100 **"keystone of the arch"**: Flexner and Flexner, **William Henry Welch,** 165.

101 **"putting an opponent down"**: Ibid., 151.

102 **"the richness of the world"**: Ibid., 230.

102 **"atmosphere of achievement"**: Ibid., 165.

104 **"never anything quite like it"**: John Fulton, **Harvey Cushing** (1946), 118.

CHAPTER FOUR

107 **"no evidence of preliminary education"**: Flexner and Flexner, **William Henry Welch,** 222.

108 **"long and painful controversy"**: Ludmerer, **Learning to Heal,** 53.

108 **"The talk was of pathology"**: Fulton, **Harvey Cushing,** 121.

108 **"what was true of Harvard"**: Shryock, **Unique Influence of Johns Hopkins,** 8.

109 **"and want no others"**: Quoted in Ludmerer, **Learning to Heal,** 75.

109 **"to one man—Franklin P. Mall"**: Shryock, **Unique Influence,** 20.

109 **"whether they were saved"**: Michael Bliss, **William Osler: A Life in Medicine** (1999), 216.

110 **fifty-three became professors**: Bonner, **American Doctors and German Universities,** 99.

110 **"the whole still concert"**: William G. MacCallum, **William Stewart Halsted** (1930), 212.

111 **"violate all the best precedents"**: Flexner and Flexner, **William Henry Welch,** 263.

111 **"flick of a wrist"**: Ludmerer, **Learning to Heal,** 128.

112 **endowments totaled $500,000**: Shryock, **Unique Influence,** 37.

115 **marvelous curative agent**: Victor A. Vaughan, **A Doctor's Memories** (1926), 153.

116 **"an epoch in the history of medicine"**: Flexner and Flexner, **William Henry Welch,** 207.

117 **"a body of research"**: Wade Oliver, **The Man Who Lived for Tomorrow: A Biography of William Hallock Park, M.D.** (1941), 238.

118 **"little less than lunatic"**: Frederick T. Gates to Starr Murphy, Dec. 31, 1915, WP.

118 **"to become a pioneer"**: Ibid.

119 **accepting the Jew**: James Thomas Flexner, **American Saga,** 241–42.

120 **"every letter handwritten"**: Ibid., 278.

121 **"not to have anything to do with"**: Benison and Nevins, "Oral History, Abraham Flexner," Columbia University Oral History Research Office; Flexner, **American Saga,** see 30–40.

121 **"never heard a heart or lung"**: James Thomas Flexner, **American Saga,** 133.

122   **"great gaps":** Ibid., 421.

122   **"He read . . . as he ate":** Benison and Nevins, "Oral History, Abraham Flexner."

122   **"days of acute fear":** James Thomas Flexner, **American Saga,** 239.

122   **"a museum in print":** Peyton Rous comments, Simon Flexner Memorial Pamphlet, Rockefeller Institute of Medical Research, 1946.

123   **"His mind was like a searchlight":** Corner, **History of the Rockefeller Institute,** 155.

123   **"final as a knife":** Ibid.

123   **"or they can be bled further":** Flexner to Cole, Jan. 21, 1919, Flexner papers, APS.

123   **"Individuals were as nothing":** Peyton Rous comments, Simon Flexner Memorial Pamphlet.

125   **mortality rate fell to 31.4 percent:** Simon Flexner, "The Present Status of the Serum Therapy of Epidemic Cerebro-spinal Meningitis," **JAMA** (1909), 1443; see also Abstract of Discussion, 1445.

125   **"Remarkable results were obtained":** Ibid.

125   **a shouting match ensued:** Wade Oliver, **Man Who Lived for Tomorrow,** 300.

125   **"mortality rate of 25 percent":** M. L. Durand et al., "Acute Bacterial Meningitis in Adults—A Review of 493 Episodes," **New England Journal of Medicine** (Jan. 1993), 21–28.

126   **"I advise the publication":** Flexner to Wollstein, March 26, 1921, Flexner papers.

126   **"Before night your discovery":** Corner, **History of the Rockefeller Institute,** 159.

126   **"frequent ballyhoo of unimportant stuff"**: Ibid., 158.

127   **"he also was tender"**: Saul Benison, **Tom Rivers: Reflections on a Life in Medicine and Science, An Oral History Memoir** (1967), 127.

127   **"made to believe"**: Corner, **History of the Rockefeller Institute,** 155.

127   **"I won't expect anything"**: Ibid., 158.

128   **"a great inspiration"**: Heidelberger, oral history, 1968, NLM, 66.

128   **"an organism, not an establishment"**: Peyton Rous comments, Simon Flexner Memorial Pamphlet.

129   **"science isolated Dr. Koch"**: For an account of this meeting see Wade Oliver, **Man Who Lived for Tomorrow,** 272–76.

CHAPTER FIVE

131   **"wasn't afraid to fight"**: Benison, **Tom Rivers,** 30, 70, 204.

131   **"quite remarkable in that way"**: Heidelberger, oral history, 83.

132   **"Cole was adamant"**: Benison, **Tom Rivers,** 70.

132   **"urged to undertake experimental work"**: Benison, **Tom Rivers,** 68.

134   **"results were better than the system"**: Quoted in Flexner and Flexner, **William Henry Welch,** 61.

134   **Not until 1912 would Harvard:** Fleming, **William Welch,** 4.

135 a blistering . . . report: Vaughan, **A Doctor's Memories,** 440.

135 fifty-seven medical schools: Ludmerer, **Learning to Heal,** 116.

136 only eight thousand members: Paul Starr, **The Social Transformation of American Medicine** (1982), 109.

136 "my initial visit to Baltimore": Ludmerer, **Learning to Heal,** 172.

137 "make better farmers": Ibid., see 169–73.

138 6,843 locations: Meirion Harries and Susie Harries, **The Last Days of Innocence: America at War, 1917–1918** (1997), 15.

138 "to . . . legitimize . . ." capitalism: E. Richard Brown, **Rockefeller's Medicine Men** (1979), quoted in Starr, **Social Transformation,** 227.

139 thirty-one states denied licensing: Ludmerer, **Learning to Heal,** 238–43.

139 still 25 percent less: Shryock, **Development of Modern Medicine,** 350; Ludmerer, **Learning to Heal,** 247.

139 "The AMA deserved . . . the credit": Fulton, **Harvey Cushing,** 379.

140 $154 million into medicine: Ludmerer, **Learning to Heal,** 192–93.

142 "the sole argument for putting": Charles Eliot to Abraham Flexner, Feb. 1 and Feb. 16, 1916, WP.

Part II: The Swarm

CHAPTER SIX

146 **"A slow rain fell": Santa Fe Monitor,** Feb. 28, 1918.

147 **didn't suffer fools:** Material on L. V. Miner comes from an interview with his daughter-in-law Mrs. L. V. Miner Jr. on Aug. 27, 1999, and granddaughter Catherine Hart in July 2003, and from **Kansas and Kansans** (1919).

149 **hold the train for him:** For a description of a typical western practice, especially in Kansas, see Arthur E. Hertzler, **The Horse and Buggy Doctor** (1938) and Thomas Bonner, **The Kansas Doctor** (1959).

150 **"sick with pneumonia": Santa Fe Monitor,** Feb. 14, 1918.

151 **"influenza of severe type": Public Health Reports** 33, part 1 (April 5, 1918), 502.

152 **"Most everybody over the country": Santa Fe Monitor,** Feb. 21, 1918.

152 **"John will make an ideal soldier": Santa Fe Monitor,** Feb. 28, 1918.

153 **"animosity towards me":** Maj. John T. Donnelly, 341st Machine Gun Battalion, Camp Funston, RG 393, NA.

154 **"to exercise command":** Commanding General C. G. Ballou, Camp Funston, to Adjutant General, March 12, 1918, Camp Funston, RG 393.

154 **"overcrowded and inadequately heated":** Maj. General Merritt W. Ireland, ed., **Medical**

Department of the United States Army in the World War, v. 9, **Communicable Diseases** (1928), 415.

CHAPTER SEVEN

157 **"arrival of American troops in France":** F. M. Burnet and Ellen Clark, **Influenza: A Survey of the Last Fifty Years** (1942), 70.

163 **"a special instance" among infectious diseases:** Bernard Fields, **Fields' Virology,** (1996), 265.

168 **mutate much faster:** Ibid., 114.

168 **"mutant swarm":** J. J. Holland, "The Origin and Evolution of Viruses," in **Microbiology and Microbial Infections** (1998), 12.

169 **"certain randomness to the disease":** Ibid., 17.

CHAPTER EIGHT

170 **resist putrefaction:** Quoted in Milton Rosenau notebook, Dec. 12, 1907, Rosenau papers, UNC.

176 **influenza kills more people:** Harvey Simon and Martin Swartz, "Pulmonary Infections," and R. J. Douglas, "Prophylaxis and Treatment of Influenza," in section 7, Infectious Diseases, in Edward Rubenstein and Daniel Feldman, **Scientific American Medicine** (1995).

179 **"It's equally likely":** Peter Palese, personal communication with the author, Aug. 2, 2001.

180 **"attacked at once":** W. I. B. Beveridge,

Influenza: The Last Great Plague: An Unfinished Story of Discovery (1977), 26.

180 "entirely depopulated": Ibid.

181 "as in a plague": John Duffy, Epidemics in Colonial America (1953), 187–88, quoted in Dorothy Ann Pettit, "A Cruel Wind: America Experiences the Pandemic Influenza, 1918–1920, A Social History" (1976), 31.

181 "youngest as well as the oldest": Beveridge, Influenza, 26.

181 "all weer sick": Quoted in Pettit, "Cruel Wind," 32.

181 more people died from influenza: Beveridge, Influenza, 26–31.

Part III: The Tinderbox

CHAPTER NINE

188 "The rat serves one useful function": Major George Crile, "The Leading War Problems and a Plan of Organization to Meet Them," draft report, 1916, NAS.

189 "The war sentiment": Randolph Bourne, "The War and the Intellectuals," The Seven Arts (June 1917), 133–46.

190 "I am sure that my heart": Arthur Walworth, Woodrow Wilson, v. 2 (1965), 63.

190 "I will not cry 'peace'": Walworth, Woodrow Wilson, v. 1, 344.

191 "Once lead this people into war": Walworth, Woodrow Wilson, v. 2, 97.

191 **"It isn't an army we must shape":** Stephen Vaughn, **Holding Fast the Inner Lines: Democracy, Nationalism, and the Committee on Public Information** (1980), 3.

193 **"the poison of disloyalty":** David Kennedy, **Over Here: The First World War and American Society** (1980), 24.

193 **"Thank God for Abraham Lincoln":** Walworth, **Woodrow Wilson,** v. 2, 101.

193 **"an imperative necessity":** Walworth, **Woodrow Wilson,** v. 2, 97.

194 **"governed by public opinion":** Kennedy, **Over Here,** 47.

194 **"casual or impulsive disloyal utterances":** Vaughn, **Holding Fast the Inner Lines,** 226; Kennedy, **Over Here,** 81.

194 **"from good motives":** Richard W. Steele, **Free Speech in the Good War** (1999), 153.

195 **two hundred thousand APL members:** Joan Jensen, **The Price of Vigilance** (1968), 115.

196 **"seditious street oratory":** Ibid., 96.

196 **"ninety percent of all the men":** Kennedy, **Over Here,** 54.

196 **"What the nation demands":** Quoted in Jensen, **Price of Vigilance,** 79.

196 **"Every German or Austrian":** Ibid., 99.

197 **"What had been folly":** Kennedy, **Over Here,** 74.

197 **"spreads pessimistic stories":** Vaughn, **Holding Fast the Inner Lines,** 155.

197 **"sinister intrigue":** Jensen, **Price of Vigilance,** 51.

197 **Two Communist parties:** Robert Murray, **Red Scare: A Study in National Hysteria** (1955), 16, 51–53.

197 **"That community is already in the process":** Learned Hand speech, Jan. 27, 1952, quoted in www.conservativeforum.org/authquot.asp?ID915.

199 **"Truth and falsehood are arbitrary":** Vaughn, **Holding Fast the Inner Lines,** 3.

199 **most citizens were "mentally children":** Kennedy, **Over Here,** 91–92.

199 **climbed onto a chandelier:** Interview with Betty Carter, April 1997.

200 **"one white-hot mass":** Vaughn, **Holding Fast the Inner Lines,** 3.

200 **"intellectual cohesion—herd-instinct":** Bourne, "War and the Intellectuals," 133.

200 **"the noblest of all mottoes":** Vaughn, **Holding Fast the Inner Lines,** 141.

200 **"I am Public Opinion":** Ibid., 169.

201 **"every printed bullet":** Murray, **Red Scare,** 12.

201 **"To fight for an ideal":** Vaughn, **Holding Fast the Inner Lines,** 126.

202 **"questionable jokes": Philadelphia Inquirer,** Sept. 1, 1918.

202 **"Force to the utmost!":** Walworth, **Woodrow Wilson,** v. 2, 168.

203 **"exert itself in any way":** Red Cross news release, Aug. 23, 1917, entry 12, RG 52, NA.

203 **"delivered at any point":** Aug. 24, 1917 memo, entry 12, RG 52, NA.

206 **"Confectioners and restaurants":** See, for example, the **Arizona Gazette,** Sept. 26, 1918.

206 **"go down to roll bandages":** William
     Maxwell, unaired interview re Lincoln,
     Illinois, Feb. 26, 1997, for "Influenza 1918,"
     American Experience.

207 **"Military instruction under officers":**
     Committee on Education and Training: A
     Review of Its Work, by the advisory board,
     unpaginated, appendix. C. R. Mann, chairman,
     RG 393, NA.

207 **"mobilization of all physically fit registrants":**
     Memo to the Colleges of the U.S. from Committee
     on Education and Training, Aug. 28, 1918; copy
     found in Camp Grant files, RG 393, NA.

CHAPTER TEN

211 **"The Academy now considers":** Quoted in
     Simon Flexner and James Thomas Flexner,
     William Henry Welch and the Heroic Age of
     American Medicine (1941), 366.

214 **More soldiers had died of disease:** United
     States Civil War Center, www. cwc.lsu.edu/cwc/
     other/stats/warcost.htm.

215 **not a single microscope:** Victor Vaughan,
     A Doctor's Memories (1926), 410.

215 **"virgin" human population:** Interview with
     Dr. Peter Palese, March 20, 2001.

215 **killing 5 percent of all the men:** Memo on mea-
     sles, undated, RG 112, NA; see also Maj. General
     Merritt W. Ireland, ed., **Medical Department**
     of the United States Army in the World War,
     v. 9, **Communicable Diseases** (1928), 409.

217 **rotating his attention:** David McCullough, **The Path Between the Seas: The Creation of the Panama Canal, 1870–1914** (1977), 425–26.

220 **"extremes the sexual moralist can go":** William Allen Pusey, M.D., "Handling of the Venereal Problem in the U.S. Army in Present Crisis," **JAMA** (Sept. 28, 1918), 1017.

220 **"A Soldier who gets a dose":** Kennedy, **Over Here,** 186.

220 **"no longer a danger":** C. P. Knight, "The Activities of the USPHS in Extra-Cantonment Zones, with Special Reference to the Venereal Disease Problem," **Military Surgeon** (Jan. 1919), 41.

221 **test the antitoxin:** Flexner and Flexner, **William Henry Welch,** 371.

222 **"[U]nit will be arranged":** Colonel Frederick Russell to Flexner, June 11, 1917, Flexner papers, APS.

223 **no mere cosmetic change:** George A. Corner, **A History of the Rockefeller Institute: 1901–1953, Origins and Growth** (1964), 141.

224 **"best from these classes":** Notes on meeting of National Research Council executive committee, April 19, 1917, NAS.

224 **half of all those . . . fit for service:** Arthur Lamber, "Medicine: A Determining Factor in War," **JAMA** (June 14, 1919), 1713.

224 **army had fifty-eight dentists:** Franklin Martin, **Fifty Years of Medicine and Surgery** (1934), 379.

225 **replaced labels on drug bottles:** Lavinia Dock,

1909, quoted in Soledad Mujica Smith, "Nursing as Social Responsibility: Implications for Democracy from the Life Perspective of Lavinia Lloyd Dock (1858–1956)" (2002), 78.

226   **"at once sever my connection":** Lavinia Dock et al., **History of American Red Cross Nursing** (1922), 958.

226   **"carry out the plans":** Ibid., 954.

CHAPTER ELEVEN

229   **"Every single activity":** Editorial, **Military Surgeon** 43 (Aug. 1918), 208.

230   **"The consideration of human life":** John C. Wise, "The Medical Reserve Corps of the U.S. Navy," **Military Surgeon** (July 1918), 68.

230   **"they should be bayonetted":** "Review of **Offensive Fighting** by Major Donald McRae," **Military Surgeon** (Feb. 1919), 86.

230   **"I was very glad":** Flexner and Flexner, **William Henry Welch,** 371.

233   **lowered the death rate:** H. J. Parish, **A History of Immunization** (1965), 3.

234   **banned all sales:** Wade Oliver, **The Man Who Lived for Tomorrow: A Biography of William Hallock Park, M.D.** (1941), 378.

234   **enough typhoid vaccine for five million:** Vaughan to George Hale, March 21, 1917, Executive Committee on Medicine and Hygiene, general file, NAS.

234   **"sent to any one of the camps":** Flexner to Russell, Nov. 28, 1917, Flexner papers.

234 **"prevention of infectious disease":** Flexner to Vaughan, June 2, 1917, Flexner papers.

235 **"Although pneumonia occurs":** Rufus Cole et al., "Acute Lobar Pneumonia Prevention and Serum Treatment" (Oct. 1917), 4.

236 **"as if the men had pooled their diseases":** Flexner and Flexner, **William Henry Welch,** 372.

236 **"How many lives were sacrificed":** Vaughan, **A Doctor's Memories,** 428–29.

237 **"Not a troop train":** Ibid., 425.

237 **three thousand were sick enough:** Ireland, **Communicable Diseases,** 415.

238 **complications of measles:** Vaughan, **A Doctor's Memories,** 57.

238 **average death rate from pneumonia:** Dorothy Ann Pettit, "A Cruel Wind: America Experiences the Pandemic Influenza, 1918–1920, A Social History" (1976), 56.

239 **"never in their confidence":** Ibid., 3.

240 **"seem to have deserted me":** John M. Gibson, **Physician to the World: The Life of General William C. Gorgas** (1989), 242.

240 **"send directions for Avery's":** Welch diary, Jan. 2, 1918, WP.

CHAPTER TWELVE

243 **evidence that the influenza virus:** J. A. McCullers and K. C. Bartmess, "Role of Neuraminidase in Lethal Synergism Between Influenza Virus and Streptococcus Pneumoniae,"

William Osler, **Osler's Textbook Revisited** (1967), **Journal of Infectious Diseases** (2003), 1000–1009.

246 **"To bleed at the very onset":** 00.

246 **"Pneumonia is a self-limited disease":** Ibid.

250 **"true inwardness of research":** Quoted in McLeod, "Oswald Theodore Avery, 1877–1955," **Journal of General Microbiology** (1957), 540.

250 **"An acute need for privacy":** René Dubos, "Oswald Theodore Avery, 1877–1955," **Biographical Memoirs of Fellows of the Royal Society,** 35.

250 **"as if a mask dropped":** Ibid.

250 **"a natural born comedian":** Donald Van Slyke, oral history, NLM.

251 **about Landsteiner's personal life:** René Dubos, **The Professor, the Institute, and DNA** (1976), 47.

252 **notified he'd won the Nobel:** Saul Benison, **Tom Rivers: Reflections on Life in Medicine and Science, an Oral History Memoir** (1967), 91–93.

252 **"motives that lead persons to art or science":** Quoted in Dubos, **Professor,** 179.

253 **"a sweeping metabolic theory":** Ibid., 95.

CHAPTER THIRTEEN

258 **"Protection in man is inferior":** Rufus Cole et al., "Acute Lobar Pneumonia," 4.

259 **"lead all diseases":** Ibid.

259 **"diseases amongst the troops":** See, for example, Gorgas to Commanding Officer, Base Hospital, Camp Greene, Oct. 26, 1917, entry 29, file 710, RG 112, NA.

260 **All of them had negative reactions:** Scientific reports of the Corporation and Board of Scientific Directors of Rockefeller Institute, April 20, 1918.

260 **Camp Gordon outside Atlanta:** Ireland, **Communicable Diseases,** 442.

260 **"the matter of prophylactic vaccination":** Cole to Russell, Dec. 14, 1917, entry 29, RG 112, NA.

261 **controls suffered 101:** Memo from Flexner to Russell, Oct. 3, 1918, entry 29, RG 112, NA.

261 **Pasteur Institute was also testing:** Ireland, **Communicable Diseases,** 125.

262 **to meet Gorgas and Welch:** Welch to Flexner wire, April 15, 1918; Flexner to Cole, April 16, 1918, Flexner papers.

262 **"really a privilege":** Michael Heidelberger, oral history, NLM, 83.

263 **checking on everything:** Ibid.

263 **"chiefly in epidemic form":** Rufus Cole, "Prevention of Pneumonia," **JAMA** (Aug. 1918), 634.

265 **the Canadian army:** W. David Parsons, "The Spanish Lady and the Newfoundland Regiment" (1998).

265 **"detention camps for new recruits":** Welch diary, Dec. 28, 1917, WP.

Part IV: It Begins

CHAPTER FOURTEEN

270   **Thirty of the fifty largest cities:** Edwin O. Jordan, **Epidemic Influenza** (1927), 69.

270   **"convenient to follow":** F. M. Burnet and Ellen Clark, **Influenza: A Survey of the Last Fifty Years** (1942), 70.

271   **of 172 marines:** W. J. MacNeal, "The Influenza Epidemic of 1918 in the AEF in France and England," **Archives of Internal Medicine** (1919), 657.

271   **appearance in the French army:** Burnet and Clark, **Influenza,** 70.

271   **36,473 hospital admissions:** Quoted in Jordan, **Epidemic Influenza,** 78.

271   **"At the end of May":** Ibid.

272   **"broken clean through":** Harvey Cushing, **A Surgeon's Journal 1915–18** (1934), 311.

272   **"The expected third phase":** Ibid.

272   **"the epidemic of grippe":** Ibid.

273   **"a grievous business":** Ray Stannard Baker, **Woodrow Wilson: Life and Letters/ Armistice March 1–November 11, 1918** (1939), 233.

274   **"abuts on the harbor":** Jordan, **Epidemic Influenza,** 85.

274   **"swept over the whole country":** Ibid., 87.

275   **10,313 sailors fell ill:** David Thomson and Robert Thomson, **Annals of the Pickett-Thomson Research Laboratory,** v. 9, **Influenza** (1934), 178.

275   **"of a mild form":** Jordan, **Epidemic Influenza,** 93.

275 **doubt that it was influenza:** MacNeal, "Influenza Epidemic," **Archives of Internal Medicine** (1919), 657.

275 **"not influenza":** From **Policlinico** 25, no. 26 (June 30, 1918), quoted in **JAMA** 71, no. 9, 780.

275 **"very short duration":** T. R. Little, C. J. Garofalo, and P. A. Williams, "B Influenzae and Present Epidemic," **The Lancet** (July 13, 1918), quoted in **JAMA** 71, no. 8 (Aug. 24, 1918), 689.

276 **"fatal in from 24 to 48 hours":** Major General Merritt W. Ireland, ed., **Medical Department of the United States Army in the World War,** v. 9, **Communicable Disease** (1928), 132.

276 **"a new disease":** Jordan, **Epidemic Influenza,** 36.

276 **688 men were ill:** George Soper, M.D., "The Influenza Pandemic in the Camps," undated draft report, RG 112, NA.

277 **"any definite information":** Cole to Pearce, July 19, 1918, NAS.

277 **put more resources:** Cole to Pearce, July 24, 1918, NAS.

278 **declared the epidemic over:** "The Influenza Pandemic in American Camps, September 1918," memo to Col. Howard from Office of the Army Surgeon General, Oct. 9, 1918, Red Cross papers, War Council notes, RG 200, NA.

278 **"completely disappeared":** Letter from London of Aug. 20, 1918, quoted in **JAMA** 71, no. 12 (Sept. 21, 1918), 990.

278 **"mistaken for meningitis":** Late summer report quoted in **JAMA** 71, no. 14 (Oct. 5, 1918), 1136.

278 **"No letter from my beloved":** Dorothy Ann Pettit, "A Cruel Wind: America Experiences the Pandemic Influenza, 1918–1920, A Social History" (1976), 97, 98.

279 **"some interesting cases":** Ibid., 67.

CHAPTER FIFTEEN

281 **most influenza experts:** Interview with Robert Webster, June 13, 2002.

281 **At the fifteenth passage:** William Bulloch, **The History of Bacteriology** (1938, reprinted 1979), 143.

282 **Changing the environment:** Jordan, **Epidemic Influenza,** 511.

283 **As the bacteria adapted to rabbits:** Richard Shryock, **The Development of Modern Medicine,** 2nd edition (1947), 294–95.

283 **1 million pigs:** Bulloch, **History of Bacteriology,** 246.

284 **"primarily virus influenza":** Burnet and Clark, **Influenza,** 40.

284 **"We must suppose":** Ibid., 69, 70.

285 **a ward was sealed off:** Soper, "Influenza Pandemic in the Camps."

285 **"they had influenza":** Ibid.

286 **"not like the common broncho-pneumonia":** Adolph A. Hoehling, **The Great Epidemic** (1961), 21.

286 **"an outbreak of epidemic influenza": Public Health Reports,** 33, part 2 (July 26, 1918), 1259.

287 **"I am confidentially advised":** Entry 12, index card 126811, RG 52, NA.

288 **"a progressive increase in cases":** Ireland, **Communicable Diseases,** 83, 135.

289 **"indistinguishably blend with":** Ibid., 135.

289 **"the seamen were prostrate":** Jordan, **Epidemic Influenza,** 114.

289 **"a well-nourished people":** John Duffy, **A History of Public Health in New York City 1866–1966** (1974), 286.

289 **children were malnourished:** Ibid., 287.

289 **two steamships from Norway:** Soper, "The Influenza Pandemic in the Camps."

290 **outbreak with high mortality:** Ireland, **Communicable Diseases,** 137.

290 **overwhelmed the naval hospital:** Director of Labs, AEF, to SG, Dec. 10, 1918, entry 29, RG 112, NA.

290 **"number of American negroes":** Quoted in Pettit, "Cruel Wind," 94.

291 **two natives died:** Burnet and Clark, **Influenza,** 72.

291 **five hundred of the six hundred laborers:** A. W. Crosby, **America's Forgotten Pandemic: The Influenza of 1918** (1989), 37.

291 **7 percent of the entire crew died:** Burnet and Clark, **Influenza,** 72.

292 **struck down nine hundred:** Ibid.

292 **115 more deaths:** Director of Labs, AEF, to SG, Dec. 10, 1918, entry 29, RG 112, NA.

292 **"grossly overcrowded":** Crosby, **America's Forgotten Pandemic,** 38.

293   **"The Bible":** From Medical Officers Training Camp at Camp Greenleaf, Georgia, Nov. 18, 1918, Rosenau papers, UNC.

CHAPTER SIXTEEN

296   **"mess officer is well informed":** Major R. C. Hoskins, "Report of Inspection on Sept. 30, 1918," Oct. 9, 1918, RG 112, NA.

296   **inoculating a series of human volunteers:** Undated report by Major Andrew Sellards, entry 29, RG 112, NA.

296   **only eighty-four patients:** "Influenza Pandemic in American Camps, September 1918"; see also Paul Wooley to SG, Aug. 29, 1918, RG 112, NA.

297   **"very significant increase": Boston Health Department Monthly Bulletin,** Sept. 1918, 183, quoted in Jordan, **Epidemic Influenza,** 115.

297   **diagnosed as having meningitis:** Major Paul Wooley, "Epidemiological Report on Influenza and Pneumonia, Camp Devens, August 28 to October 1, 1918," entry 29, RG 112, NA.

298   **"which attacked so many":** Ibid.

298   **"occurred as an explosion":** Ibid.

299   **Eight of the twelve collapsed:** "Steps Taken to Check the Spread of the Epidemic," undated, unsigned, entry 29, RG 112, NA; see also Katherine Ross, "Battling the Flu," **American Red Cross Magazine** (Jan. 1919), 11.

299   **"These men start with what appears to be":** Dr. Roy N. Grist to "Burt," **British Medical Journal** (Dec. 22–29, 1979).

300   "only a matter of a few hours": Ibid.

301   "we are all well": Russell to Flexner, Sept. 18, 1918, Flexner papers, APS.

302   "You will proceed immediately": Victor Vaughan, **A Doctor's Memories** (1926), 431.

302   "hundreds of young stalwart men": Ibid., 383–84.

302   in excess of six thousand: Vaughan and Welch to Gorgas, Sept. 27, 1918, entry 29, RG 112, NA.

303   "dead bodies are stacked": Vaughan, **A Doctor's Memories,** 383–84.

303   "step amongst them": Cole to Flexner, May 26, 1936, file 26, box 163, WP.

304   "too much for Dr. Welch": Ibid.

305   "influenza be kept out of the camps": "Memo for Camp and Division Surgeons," Sept. 24, 1918, entry 710, RG 112, NA.

306   "New men will almost surely": Brigadier General Richard to adjutant general, Sept. 25, 1918, entry 710, RG 112, NA; see also Charles Richard to chief of staff, Sept. 26, 1918, entry 710, RG 112, NA.

308   "spread rapidly across": J. J. Keegan, "The Prevailing Epidemic of Influenza," **JAMA** (Sept. 28, 1918), 1051.

308   Around the world from Boston: I. D. Mills, "The 1918–1919 Influenza Pandemic—The Indian Experience," **The Indian Economic and Social History Review** (1986), 27, 35.

Part V: Explosion

CHAPTER SEVENTEEN

313 **three hundred sailors arrived:** "Sanitary Report for Fourth Naval District for the Month of September 1918," entry 12, file 584, RG 52, NA.

314 **tenements still had outhouses:** "Philadelphia— How the Social Agencies Organized to Serve the Sick and Dying," **The Survey** 76 (Oct. 19, 1918); oral history of Anna Lavin, July 14, 1982, courtesy of Charles Hardy, West Chester University.

314 **"death rate . . . has gone up":** Mrs. Wilmer Krusen reports, Feb. 4, 1918, entries 13B-D2, RG 62.

315 **no high school until 1934:** Allen Davis and Mark Haller, eds., **The Peoples of Philadelphia: A History of Ethnic Groups and Lower-Class Life, 1790–1940** (1973), 256.

315 **"worst-governed city":** Quoted in Russell Weigley, ed., **Philadelphia: A 300-Year History** (1982), 539.

318 **"took control of police":** Major William Snow and Major Wilbur Sawyer, "Venereal Disease Control in the Army," **JAMA** (Aug. 10, 1918), 462.

319 **left Philadelphia for Puget Sound: Annual Report of the Surgeon General of the U.S. Navy for Fiscal Year 1918,** Government Printing Office.

321 **put the body on a stretcher:** Robert St. John, **This Was My World** (1953), 49–50, quoted in Dorothy Ann Pettit, "A Cruel Wind: America

Experiences the Pandemic Influenza, 1918–1920" (1976), 103.

321 **"33 caskets to Naval":** "Journal of the Medical Department, Great Lakes," entry 22a, RG 52, NA.

322 **toe tags on the boys':** Carla Morrisey, transcript of unaired interview for "Influenza 1918," **American Experience,** Feb. 26, 1997.

322 **"what it would feel like":** Ibid.

322 **"this threat of influenza invasion":** Howard Anders to William Braisted, Sept. 12, 1918, RG 52, NA.

323 **refused to release six:** Board of Trustees minutes, Sept. 9 and Sept. 30, 1918, Jefferson Medical College, Philadelphia.

325 **"When obliged to cough or sneeze": Philadelphia Inquirer,** Sept. 19, 1918.

325 **"No concern whatever": The Evening Bulletin,** Sept. 18, 1918.

326 **"can successfully be prevented":** Department of Public Health and Charities minutes, Sept. 21 and Oct. 3, 1918.

327 **"ideas of whole populations":** Quoted in Victoria De Grazia, "The Selling of America, Bush Style," **New York Times** (Aug. 25, 2002).

327 **"world lives by phrases":** Quoted in Joan Hoff Wilson, **Herbert Hoover: Forgotten Progressive** (1974), 59.

328 **"'Every Scout to Save a Soldier'":** Quoted in ibid., 105 fn.

329 **"If you find a disloyal":** Gregg Wolper, "The Origins of Public Diplomacy: Woodrow Wilson,

George Creel, and the Committee on Public Information" (1991), 80.

329 "The IWW agitators": Kennedy, **Over Here,** 73.

330 "nobody can say we aren't loyal": Ellis Hawley, **The Great War and the Search for a Modern Order: A History of the American People and Their Institutions, 1917–1933** (1979), 24.

330 "In spite of excesses such as lynching": Ibid.

331 "most powerful of human motives": William McAdoo, **Crowded Years** (1931), 374–79, quoted in David Kennedy, **Over Here** (1980), 105.

331 "Every person who refuses": David Kennedy, **Over Here,** 106.

332 "a ready-made inflammable mass": Howard Anders, letter to **Public Ledger,** Oct. 9, 1918, in which he cites his earlier opposition to the rally; quoted in Jeffrey Anderson, "Influenza in Philadelphia 1918" (1998).

CHAPTER EIGHTEEN

336 "excellent chief of service": Frederick Russell and Rufus Cole, Camp Grant inspection diary, June 15–16, 1918, WP.

337 "keep our eye on him": Welch to Dr. Christian Herter, treasurer, Rockefeller Institute for Medical Research, Jan. 13, 1902, WP.

337 "different type of pneumonia": Ibid.

337 "an important contribution": Richard Pearce to Major Joseph Capps, July 10, 1918, Camp Grant, influenza file, NAS.

337 **"a very important matter"**: Rufus Cole to Richard Pearce, July 24, 1918, influenza file, NAS.

338 **"vital measures in checking contagion"**: Joseph Capps, "Measures for the Prevention and Control of Respiratory Disease," **JAMA** (Aug. 10, 1918), 448.

338 **"one of the most brilliant"**: Chicago Tribune, Oct. 9, 1918.

339 **had issued warnings**: George Soper, M.D., "The Influenza Pandemic in the Camps," undated draft report, entry 29, RG 112, NA.

340 **"None of these diseases"**: A. Kovinsky, Camp Grant epidemiologist, report to SG, Sept. 4, 1918, entry 31, RG 112, NA.

341 **"Until further notice"**: Quoted in Kovinsky, report to SG, Nov. 5, 1918, entry 29, RG 112, NA.

341 **"crowding of troops"**: Charles Hagadorn, Sept. 20, 1918, entry 29, box 383, RG 112, NA.

342 **"No visitors will be permitted"**: Kovinsky, report to SG, Nov. 5, 1918.

342 **the first soldier died**: "Bulletin of the Base Hospital," Camp Grant, Sept. 28, 1918, RG 112, NA.

344 **"except under extraordinary circumstances"**: "Bulletin of the Base Hospital," Oct. 3 and Oct. 4, 1918, RG 112, NA.

344 **"formalin should be added"**: Ibid.

345 **"Devoting special personal care"**: "Bulletin of the Base Hospital," Oct. 6, 1918, RG 112, NA.

345 **escorts of the dead . . . be prohibited**: Dr. H. M. Bracken, Executive Director,

Minnesota State Board of Health, Oct. 1, 1918, entry 31, RG 112, NA.

345 **"No power on earth":** Victor Vaughan, **A Doctor's Memories,** 425.

346 **"movements of officers and men":** See telegram from adjutant general, Oct. 3, 1918, RG 92.

347 **two thousand of the 3,108 troops:** "Analysis of the Course and Intensity of the Epidemic in Army Camps," unsigned, undated report, 4, entry 29, RG 112, NA.

347 **likely that the death toll:** Camp Hancock, Georgia, entry 29, RG 112, NA.

348 **twenty-eight hundred troops would report ill:** Soper, "The Influenza-Pneumonia Pandemic in the American Army Camps, September and October 1918," **Science** (Nov. 8, 1918), 451.

348 **"very carefully controlled":** Stone to Warren Longcope, July 30, 1918, entry 29, RG 112, NA.

348 **only 16.7 percent died:** Alfred Gray, "Anti-pneumonia Serum (Kyes') in the Treatment of Pneumonia," entry 29, RG 112, NA.

348 **Desperate efforts were being made:** Maj. General Merritt W. Ireland, ed., **Medical Department of the United States Army in the World War,** v. 9, **Communicable Diseases** (1928), 448.

349 **"the duty of the Ward Surgeon":** "Bulletin of the Base Hospital," Oct. 7 and 8, 1918, RG 112, NA.

349 **"friends of persons dying":** "Bulletin of the Base Hospital," Oct. 3 and 4, 1918, RG 112, NA.

349   **"winning their fight":** Chicago Tribune, Oct. 7, 1918.

350   **"verandas must be used":** "Bulletin of the Base Hospital," Oct. 5, 1918, RG 112, NA.

350   **"too early to foretell":** George Soper, "The Influenza-Pneumonia Pandemic in the American Army Camps, September and October 1918," **Science** (Nov. 8, 1918), 451.

CHAPTER NINETEEN

352   **$100 bribes:** Visiting Nurse Society minutes, Oct. and Nov., 1918, Center for the Study of the History of Nursing, University of Pennsylvania.

352   **"no doctors available":** Selma Epp, transcript of unaired interview for "Influenza 1918," **American Experience,** Feb. 28, 1997.

353   **average weekly death toll: Public Health Reports** 33, part 2, (July 26, 1918), 1252.

355   **"Don't get frightened": Public Ledger,** Oct. 8, 1918.

357   **"another crepe and another door":** Anna Milani, transcript of unaired interview for "Influenza 1918," **American Experience,** Feb. 28, 1997.

357   **"People were dying like flies":** Oral history of Clifford Adams, June 3, 1982, provided by Charles Hardy of West Chester University.

357   **"My uncle died there":** Anna Lavin oral history, June 3, 1982, Charles Hardy oral history tapes.

357   **"caskets stacked up outside":** Michael Donohue, transcript of unaired interview for "Influenza 1918," **American Experience** interview, Feb. 28, 1997.

358   "'Let me get a macaroni box'": Louise Apuchase, June 3, 1982, Charles Hardy oral history tapes. June 24, 1982.

358   "They couldn't bury them": Clifford Adams, Charles Hardy oral history tapes, June 3, 1982.

359   "may also die of the plague": North American, Oct. 7, 1918.

359   "cyanosis reached an intensity": Isaac Starr, "Influenza in 1918: Recollections of the Epidemic in Philadelphia," Annals of Internal Medicine (1976), 517.

360   "no truth in the black plague assertion": Unidentified newspaper clipping in epidemic scrapbook, Dec. 29, 1918, College of Physicians Library, Philadelphia.

360   ports and naval facilities: Public Health Reports, Sept. 13, 1918, 1554.

360   "an influenza-like disease": Ibid., Sept. 20, 1918, 1599.

363   did not come again: Charles Scott to William Walling, Oct. 1, 1918, RG 200, NA.

364   "After gasping for several hours": Starr, "Influenza in 1918," 517.

364   "the city had almost stopped": Ibid. 518.

Part VI: The Pestilence

CHAPTER TWENTY

369   "two groups of symptoms": Edwin O. Jordan, Epidemic Influenza (1927), 260, 263.

369   "In nonfatal cases": Maj. General Merritt W.

Ireland, ed., **Medical Department of the United States Army in the World War,** v. 9, **Communicable Diseases** (1928), 159.

370   **"didn't care if I died":** Clifford Adams, Charles Hardy oral history tapes, West Chester University, June 3, 1982.

370   **"sick as a dog":** Bill Sardo, transcript of unaired interview for "Influenza 1918," **American Experience,** Feb. 27, 1997.

370   **"time was a blur":** William Maxwell, transcript of unaired interview for "Influenza 1918," **American Experience,** Feb. 26, 1997.

370   **"ice would rattle":** Josey Brown, transcript of unaired interview for "Influenza 1918," **American Experience,** Feb. 26, 1997.

371   **"happened to my hind legs":** John Fulton, **Harvey Cushing** (1946), 435.

371   **"something like typhoid":** Dorothy Ann Pettit, "A Cruel Wind: America Experiences the Pandemic Influenza, 1918–1920, A Social History" (1976), 91.

372   **"on a narrow ledge over a pit":** Katherine Anne Porter, "Pale Horse, Pale Rider," **The Collected Stories of Katherine Anne Porter** (1965), 310–12.

373   **"pain above the diaphragm":** Richard Collier, **The Plague of the Spanish Lady: The Influenza Pandemic of 1918–1919** (1974), 35.

374   **"Many had vomiting":** Ireland, ed., **Medical Department of the United States Army in the World War,** v. 12, **Pathology of the Acute Respiratory Diseases, and of Gas Gangrene Following War Wounds** (1929), 13.

374 **In Paris, while some:** Diane A. V. Puklin, "Paris," in Fred Van Hartesfeldt, ed., **The 1918–1919 Pandemic of Influenza: The Urban Impact in the Western World** (1992), 71.

374 **"general throughout Spain": Public Health Reports** 33, part 2 (Sept. 27, 1918), 1667.

374 **"beginning in the neck":** W. S. Thayer, "Discussion of Influenza," **Proceedings of the Royal Society of Medicine** (Nov. 1918), 61.

374 **bowl of Rice Krispies:** Carla Morrisey, transcript of unaired interview for "Influenza 1918," **American Experience,** Feb. 26, 1997.

375 **"rupture of the drum membrane":** Ireland, ed., **Medical Department of the United States Army in the World War,** v. 9, **Communicable Diseases** (1928), 448.

375 **"bulging eardrums":** Ireland, **Pathology of Acute Respiratory Diseases,** 13.

375 **"destructive action on the drum":** Burt Wolbach to Welch, Oct. 22, 1918, entry 29, RG 112, NA.

375 **eye involvement with special frequency:** David Thomson and Robert Thomson, **Annals of the Pickett-Thomson Research Laboratory,** v. 10, **Influenza** (1934), 751.

375 **ability to smell:** Ibid., 773.

376 **"symptoms were of exceeding variety":** Ireland, **Pathology of Acute Respiratory Diseases,** 13.

376 **"Intense cyanosis":** Ibid., 56, 141–42.

377 **"even to an indigo blue":** Ireland, **Communicable Diseases,** 159.

377 **"suffered from epistaxis":** Ireland, **Pathology of Acute Respiratory Diseases,** 13, 35.

378 **"pint of bright red blood":** Jordan, **Epidemic Influenza,** 260.

378 **"died from loss of blood":** Ireland, **Pathology of Acute Respiratory Diseases,** 13.

378 **"hemorrhages ... interior of the eye":** Thomson and Thomson, **Influenza,** v. 9, 753.

378 **"subconjunctional hemorrhage":** Ireland, **Pathology of Acute Respiratory Diseases,** 13.

378 **"uterine mucosa":** Ibid., 76.

378 **Many mechanisms can cause bleeding:** Interview with Dr. Alvin Schmaier, University of Michigan, Oct. 2, 2002; J. L. Mayer and D. S. Beardsley, "Varicella-associated Thrombocytopenia: Autoantibodies Against Platelet Surface Glycoprotein V," **Pediatric Research** (1996), 615–19.

378 **chief diagnostician . . . diagnosed:** Jordan, **Epidemic Influenza,** 265.

379 **47 percent of all deaths:** Thomson and Thomson, **Influenza,** v. 9, 165.

379 **average life expectancy:** Jeffrey K. Taubenberger, "Seeking the 1918 Spanish Influenza Virus," **American Society of Microbiology News** 65, no. 3 (July 1999).

380 **South African cities:** J. M. Katzenellenbogen, "The 1918 Influenza Epidemic in Mamre," **South African Medical Journal** (Oct. 1988), 362–64.

380 **In Chicago the deaths:** Fred R. Van Hartesveldt, **The 1918–1919 Pandemic of Influenza:**

The Urban Impact in the Western World
(1992), 121.

380   A Swiss physician: E. Bircher, "Influenza
Epidemic," **Correspondenz-Blatt fur Schweizer
Aerzte, Basel** (1918), 1338, quoted in **JAMA** 71,
no. 23 (Dec. 7, 1918), 1946.

381   "doubly dead in that": Sherwin Nuland, **How
We Die** (1993), 202.

382   from 23 percent to 71 percent: Jordan,
Epidemic Influenza, 273.

382   26 percent lost the child: John Harris,
"Influenza Occurring in Pregnant Women: A
Statistical Study of 130 Cases," **JAMA** (April 5,
1919), 978.

382   "interesting pathological experience":
Wolbach to Welch, Oct. 22, 1918, entry 29,
RG 112, NA.

383   "convolutions of the brain": Douglas
Symmers, M.D., "Pathologic Similarity Between
Pneumonia of Bubonic Plague and of Pandemic
Influenza," **JAMA** (Nov. 2, 1918), 1482.

383   "relaxed and flabby": Ireland, **Pathology of
Acute Respiratory Diseases,** 79.

383   damage to the kidneys: Ireland, **Communicable
Diseases,** 160.

383   "necrotic areas, frank hemorrhage": Ireland,
Pathology of Acute Respiratory Diseases, 392.

384   "comparable findings . . . death from toxic
gas": Ireland, **Communicable Diseases,** 149.

384   "inhalation of poison gas": Edwin D.
Kilbourne, M.D., **Influenza** (1987), 202.

CHAPTER TWENTY-ONE

385 **"died within twelve hours"**: Transcript of influenza commission appointed by governor of New York, meeting at New York Academy of Medicine, Oct. 30, 1918, SLY.

385 **"One robust person"**: E. Bircher, "Influenza Epidemic," **JAMA** (Dec. 7, 1918), 1338.

386 **the conductor collapsed, dead:** Collier, **Plague of the Spanish Lady,** 38.

387 **"a new disease":** Jordan, **Epidemic Influenza,** 36.

390 **"Physical signs were confusing":** Ireland, **Communicable Diseases,** 160.

390 **"old classification . . . was inappropriate":** Ireland, **Pathology of Acute Respiratory Diseases,** 10.

390 **"little evidence of bacterial action":** F. M. Burnet and Ellen Clark, **Influenza: A Survey of the Last Fifty Years** (1942), 92.

391 **"lesion of characterization":** Ireland, **Communicable Diseases,** 150.

394 **inhibits the release of interferon:** Fields, **Fields' Virology,** 196.

395 **weakened immune responses:** Thomson and Thomson, **Influenza,** v. 9, 604.

398 **"acute inflammatory injection":** Ibid., 92.

399 **"not previously described":** P. K. S. Chan et al., "Pathology of Fatal Human Infection Associated with Avian Influenza A H5N1 Virus," **Journal of Medical Virology** (March 2001), 242–46.

399 **had seen the same thing:** Jordan, **Epidemic Influenza,** 266–68, passim.

400 **mortality rate for ARDS:** Lorraine Ware and Michael Matthay, "The Acute Respiratory Distress Syndrome," **New England Journal of Medicine** (May 4, 2000), 1338.

401 **Recent research also suggests:** J. A. McCullers and K. C. Bartmess, "Role of Neuraminidase in Lethal Synergism Between Influenza Virus and Streptococcus Pneumoniae," **Journal of Infectious Diseases** (March 15, 2003), 1000–1009.

402 **almost half the autopsies:** Ireland, **Communicable Diseases,** 151.

402 **the same conclusion:** Milton Charles Winternitz, **The Pathology of Influenza,** (1920).

402 **deaths came from complications:** Frederick G. Hayden and Peter Palese, "Influenza Virus" in Richman et al., **Clinical Virology** (1997), 926.

403 **still roughly 7 percent:** Murphy and Werbster, "Orthomyxoviruses," in Fields, **Fields' Virology,** 1407.

403 **35 percent of pneumococcal infections:** "Pneumococcal Resistance," Clinical Updates IV, issue 2, January 1998, National Foundation for Infectious Diseases, www.nfid.org/publications/clinicalupdates/id/pneumococcal.html.

Part VII: The Race

CHAPTER TWENTY-TWO

412 **Three Hopkins medical students:** Dorothy Ann Pettit, "A Cruel Wind: America Experiences the Pandemic Influenza, 1918–1920" (1976), 134.

412 **"could not have dreamed":** Comments at USPHS conference on influenza, Jan. 10, 1929, file 11, box 116, WP.

412 **went to bed immediately:** Welch to Walcott, Oct. 16, 1918, Frederic Collin Walcott papers, SLY.

413 **"the Flip-flap railroad":** Simon Flexner and James Thomas Flexner, **William Henry Welch and the Heroic Age of American Medicine** (1941), 251.

414 **"temperature has been normal":** Welch to Walcott, Oct. 16, 1918, Walcott papers.

417 **"astonishing numbers":** Quoted in David Thomson and Robert Thomson, **Annals of the Pickett-Thomson Research Laboratory,** v. 9, **Influenza** (1934), 265.

417 **the cause of influenza:** William Bulloch, **The History of Bacteriology** (1938), 407–8.

423 **"Surely there is a time":** Quoted in Wade Oliver, **The Man Who Lived for Tomorrow: A Biography of William Hallock Park, M.D.,** (1941), 218.

423 **"Everyone believed it":** Saul Benison, **Tom Rivers: Reflections on a Life in Medicine and Science, An Oral History Memoi**r (1967), 237–40, 298.

424 **"No influenza bacilli":** A. Montefusco, **Riforma Medica** 34, no. 28 (July 13, 1918), quoted in **JAMA** 71, no. 10, 934.

CHAPTER TWENTY-THREE

428 **"a new bronchopneumonia":** Pettit, "Cruel Wind," 98.

430 **Copeland was sworn in:** Ibid., 9: 555.

430 **his loyalty to Tammany:** Ernest Eaton, "A Tribute to Royal Copeland," **Journal of the Institute of Homeopathy** 9: 554.

431 **perform it within thirty minutes:** Charles Krumwiede Jr. and Eugenia Valentine, "Determination of the Type of Pneumococcus in the Sputum of Lobar Pneumonia, A Rapid Simple Method," **JAMA** (Feb. 23, 1918), 513–14; Oliver, **Man Who Lived for Tomorrow,** 381.

432 **"so-called Spanish influenza":** "New York City letter," **JAMA** 71, no. 12 (Sept. 21, 1918): 986; see also John Duffy, **A History of Public Health in New York City 1866–1966** (1974), 280–90, passim.

432 **"prepared to compel":** "New York City letter," **JAMA** 71, no. 13 (Sept. 28, 1918), 1076–77.

432 **"We mourn for him":** Letter of Jan. 5, 1890, quoted in Oliver, **Man Who Lived for Tomorrow,** 26.

435 **despite their animosity:** Benison, **Tom Rivers,** 183.

435 **"secret of course":** Oliver, **Man Who Lived for Tomorrow,** 149.

436 **"wanted to go places":** Anna Williams, diary, undated, chap. 26, pp. 1, 17, carton 1, Anna Wessel Williams papers, Schlesinger Library, Radcliffe College.

436 **"no one particular friend":** "Marriage" folder, undated, Williams papers.

436 **"degrees to everything, including friendship":** "Religion" folder, March 24, 1907, Williams papers.

436 **"if we were sure, oh!":** "Religion" folder, Aug. 20, 1915, Williams papers.

437 **"discontent rather than happiness":** "Affections, longing, desires, friends" folder, Feb. 23, 1908, Williams papers.

437 **"I have had thrills":** "Marriage" folder, undated, Williams papers.

437 **no advice to give:** Diary, Sept. 17, 1918, Williams papers.

438 **"Death occurring so quickly":** Diary, undated, chap. 22, p. 23, Williams papers.

440 **quadrupled the number of horses:** Oliver, **Man Who Lived for Tomorrow,** 378.

440 **"Will your lab undertake":** Pearce wire to Park, Sept. 18, 1918, influenza files, NAS.

440 **"Will undertake work":** Park wire to Pearce, Sept. 19, 1918, influenza files, NAS.

441 **dismissed most of it:** William Park et al., "Introduction" (entire issue devoted to his laboratory's findings, divided into several articles), **Journal of Immunology** 6, no. 2 (Jan. 1921).

441 **in fifteen minutes could fill three thousand**

tubes: **Annual Report of the Department of Health,** New York City, 1918, 86.

443   **arbitrarily stopped counting:** Mortality figures for the epidemic were no longer tabulated after March 31, 1919. By then the disease had died out in every major city in the country except New York City.

443   **Nurses were literally being kidnapped:** Permillia Doty, "A Retrospect on the Influenza Epidemic," **Public Health Nurse** (1919), 953.

443   **"we are justified in":** William Park and Anna Williams, **Pathogenic Microroganisms** (1939), 281.

444   **"our methods . . . did not take into account":** Park et al., "Introduction," 4.

444   **"We had plenty of material":** Diary, undated, chap. 22, p. 23, Williams papers.

445   **220,488 test tubes: Annual Report of the Department of Health,** New York City, 1918, 88.

445   **"only results so far":** Park to Pearce, Sept. 23, 1918, NAS.

447   **she would find it:** Edwin O. Jordan, **Epidemic Influenza** (1927), 391.

447   **"the most delicate test":** Park et al., "Introduction," 4.

447   **"the starting point of the disease":** Park to Pearce, Sept. 26, 1918, NAS.

CHAPTER TWENTY-FOUR

450   **"[h]is heart lies in research":** Smith to Flexner, April 5, 1908, Lewis papers, RUA.

450 **"one of the best":** Flexner to Eugene Opie, Feb. 13, 1919, Flexner papers, APS.

451 **the smartest man:** Interview with Dr. Robert Shope, Jan. 31, 2002; interview with Dr. David Lewis Aronson, May 16, 2002.

451 **"special service in connection":** Lewis to Flexner, June 19, 1917, Flexner papers.

451 **"no onerous routine duties":** Lewis to Flexner, Oct. 24, 1917, Flexner papers.

451 **"capacity to inhibit the growth":** See assorted correspondence between Flexner and Lewis, esp. Lewis to Flexner, Nov. 13, 1916, Flexner papers.

453 **only one had died:** W. R. Redden and L. W. McQuire, "The Use of Convalescent Human Serum in Influenza Pneumonia" **JAMA** (Oct. 19, 1918), 1311.

454 **suspected a virus:** On Dec. 9, 1918, Lewis received permission from the navy to publish "The Partially Specific Inhibition Action of Certain Aniline Dyes for the Pneumococcus," entry 62, RG 125, NA; see also polio clipping in epidemic scrapbook, College of Physicians Library, Philadelphia, which mistakenly referred to a vaccine used by the city as being produced according to methods used in New York for polio. The specificity of this error almost certainly came from a misunderstanding of Lewis's work.

455 **"badly decomposed" bodies:** Transcript of New York influenza commission, meeting, Nov. 22, 1918, Winslow papers, SLY.

455 **"armed the medical profession": Philadelphia Inquirer,** Sept. 22, 1918.

456 **only three people developed pneumonia:** Transcripts of New York influenza commission, first session, Oct. 30, 1918; second session, Nov. 22, 1918; and fourth session, Feb. 14, 1919, Winslow papers.

458 **failed to cure:** Thomson and Thomson, **Influenza,** v. 10, (1934), 822.

458 **"Technically, I am not well-trained":** James Thomas Flexner, **An American Saga: The Story of Helen Thomas and Simon Flexner** (1984), 421.

459 **"cleanliness of the glassware":** Steven Rosenberg was the student. See Rosenberg and John Barry, **The Transformed Cell: Unlocking the Secrets of Cancer** (1992).

CHAPTER TWENTY-FIVE

463 **"Every case showed":** Wolbach to Welch, Oct. 22, 1918, entry 29, RG 112, NA.

463 **"causative agent":** George Soper, M.D., "The Influenza-Pneumonia Pandemic in the American Army Camps, September and October 1918," **Science** (Nov. 8, 1918), 455.

463 **"It is established":** Vaughan and Welch to Gorgas, Sept. 27, 1918, entry 29, RG 112, NA.

466 **"utter concentration on a few chosen goals":** Dubos, **The Professor, the Institute, and DNA** (1976), 78.

467 **"explore theoretical implications":** McLeod, "Oswald Theodore Avery, 1877–1955," **Journal of General Microbiology** (1957), 541.

467 **"imaginative vision of reality":** Dubos, **Professor,** 177, 179.

467 **"not random products of chance":** Quoted in McLeod, "Oswald Theodore Avery," 544–46.

468 **"hunter in search of his prey":** Dubos, **Professor,** 173.

469 **"Disappointment is my daily bread":** Ibid., 91.

469 **"compelled to take care of the cases":** Cole to Russell, Oct. 23, 1918, entry 710, RG 112, NA.

470 **the highest rate of pneumonia:** "Annual Morbidity Rate per 1000 Sept. 29, 1917 to March 29, 1918," entry 710, RG 112, NA.

470 **"as you interpret them":** Callender to Opie, Oct. 16, 1918, entry 710, RG 112, NA.

470 **thirteen thousand . . . hospitalized simultaneously:** "Red Cross Report on Influenza, Southwestern Division," undated, RG 200, NA, 9.

470 **offered all headquarters:** Memo from Russell, Oct. 3, 1918, entry 29, RG 112, NA.

471 **"not to be depended upon":** Maj. General Merritt W. Ireland, ed., **Medical Department of the United States Army in the World War,** v. 12, **Pathology of the Acute Respiratory Diseases, and of Gas Gangrene Following War Wounds** (1929), 73, 75.

471 **six of 198 autopsies:** Unsigned Camp Grant report, 6–7, entry 31d, RG 112, NA.

471 **"inclined to take the stand":** Ibid., 8.

473 **"technical difficulties in the isolation":** Oswald Theodore Avery, "A Selective Medium

for B. influenzae, Oleate-hemoglobin Agar," **JAMA** (Dec. 21, 1918), 2050.

473 **"seems to me still doubtful":** Cole to Russell, Oct. 23, 1918, entry 710, RG 112, NA.

474 **had just cured twenty-eight:** Cole, "Scientific Reports of the Corporation and Board of Scientific Directors 1918," Jan. 18, 1918, NLM.

474 **took two months:** Heidelberger oral history in Sanitary Corps, 84, NLM.

474 **twenty-five liters a day:** "Scientific Reports of the Corporation and Board of Scientific Directors 1918," April 20, 1918, RUA.

Part VIII: The Tolling of the Bell

CHAPTER TWENTY-SIX

481 **"what the Prussian autocracy":** David Kennedy, **Over Here: The First World War and American Society** (1980), 166.

484 **"no more worries":** John Eisenhower and Joanne Eisenhower, **Yanks: The Epic Story of the American Army in World War I** (2001), 221.

485 **"not permitted to embark":** Richard to March, Sept. 19, 1918, entry 29, RG 112, NA.

485 **"that of a powder magazine":** Surgeon, Port of Embarkation, Newport News, to Surgeon General, Oct. 7, 1918, entry 29, RG 112, NA.

485 **quarantining . . . for one week:** See Richard to Adjutant General, various correspondences and cables, Sept. 25 through Oct. 10, 1918, entry 29, RG 112, NA.

486 **Franklin Roosevelt . . . on a stretcher:** Eleanor Roosevelt, **This Is My Story** (1937), 268.

488 **"a true inferno reigned supreme":** A. A. Hoehling, **The Great Epidemic** (1961), 63.

488 **tracked the blood through the ship:** John Cushing and Arthur Stone, eds., **Vermont and the World War, 1917–1919** (1928), 6, quoted in A. W. Crosby, **America's Forgotten Pandemic: The Influenza of 1918** (1989), 130.

489 **orderlies carried away bodies:** Crosby, **America's Forgotten Pandemic,** 130.

489 **"died on board":** Log of **Leviathan,** RG 45, NA.

489 **"death in one of its worst forms":** Quoted in Crosby, **America's Forgotten Pandemic,** 138.

490 **more Third Division:** Ibid., 163.

490 **"dying by the score":** George Crile, **George Crile, An Autobiography,** v. 2 (1947), 350–51, quoted in Crosby, **America's Forgotten Pandemic,** 166.

491 **to freeze the movement:** Undated **Washington Star** clipping in Tumulty papers, box 4, LC; see also Arthur Walworth, **Woodrow Wilson,** v. 2 (1965), 183–89, 462–63.

491 **"decline to stop these shipments":** Walworth, **Woodrow Wilson,** v. 2, 462–63.

492 **"Every such soldier who has died":** Ibid.

492 **continued the voyages:** Ibid.

493 **picked a PHS scientist:** Vaughan to George Hale, Aug. 23, 1917, Council of National Defense papers, NAS.

493 **when Tammany took over:** Haven Anderson

to Rosenau, Dec. 24, 1917, Rosenau papers, UNC.

494   **"interests in the State . . . harmonized":** Morris Fishbein, **A History of the American Medical Association, 1847 to 1947** (1947), 736.

495   **"health insurance will constitute":** Blue, presidential address, reprinted in **JAMA** 66, no. 25 (June 17, 1916), 1901.

496   **"not immediately necessary to the enforcement":** Blue's office to McCoy, July 28, 1918, entry 10, file 2119, RG 90, NA.

497   **"Owing to disordered conditions":** Cole to Pearce, July 19, 1918, NAS.

497   **"local health authorities": Public Health Reports,** Sept. 13, 1918, 1340.

497   **"manifestly unwarranted":** Blue, undated draft report, entry 10, file 1622, RG 90, NA.

497   **first influenza death: Washington Post,** Sept. 22, 1918.

498   **"Surgeon General's Advice to Avoid Influenza": Washington Evening Star,** Sept. 22, 1918.

499   **"arrange for suitable laboratory studies":** Blue to Pearce, Sept. 9, 1919, NAS.

500   **last yellow-fever epidemic:** John Kemp, ed., **Martin Behrman of New Orleans: Memoirs of a City Boss** (1970), 143.

501   **appealed to the War Council:** "Minutes of War Council," Oct. 1, 1918, 1573, RG 200, NA.

502   **"contingent fund for . . . influenza":** "Minutes of War Council," Sept. 27, 1918, RG 200.

502   **"appear with electric suddenness":** George Soper, M.D., "The Influenza-Pneumonia

Pandemic in the American Army Camps, September and October 1918," **Science** (Nov. 8, 1918), 454, 456.

CHAPTER TWENTY-SEVEN

505 **"depend upon its own resources":** Quoted in "Summary of Red Cross Activity in Influenza Epidemic" (undated), 6, box 688, RG 200; see also Evelyn Berry, "Summary of Epidemic 1918–1919," July 8, 1942, RG 200, NA.

506 **"forty nurses ill":** Jackson to W. Frank Persons, Oct. 4, 1918, box 688, RG 200, NA.

506 **"telegraphed to all my chapters":** Ibid.

507 **"unable to handle adequately":** Ibid.

511 **72,219 physicians:** Franklin Martin, **Fifty Years of Medicine and Surgery,** (1934), 384.

513 **stripped hospitals of their workforce:** Lavinia Dock et al., **History of American Red Cross Nursing** (1922), 969.

514 **"no nurses left in civil life":** Ibid.

CHAPTER TWENTY-EIGHT

517 **"not planned specifically for your time":** Flexner to Lewis, July 8, 1908, RUA.

520 **"sever my connection":** Mrs. J. Willis Martin to Mayor Thomas Smith, Oct. 8, 1918, Council of National Defense papers, HSP.

521 **use that same organization:** Undated memo, entries 13B–D2, RG 62, NA.

521 **"death toll for one day":** Ibid.

522 **ceded to the group control:** "Minutes of Visiting Nurse Society for October and November, 1918," Center for the Study of the History of Nursing, University of Pennsylvania.

523 **"death rate for the past week":** Krusen to Navy Surgeon General William Braisted, Oct. 6, 1918, entry 12, RG 52, NA.

523 **"heartily endorse":** Blue to Braisted, Oct. 7, 1918, entry 12, RG 52, NA.

523 **"filth allowed to collect": Philadelphia Public Ledger,** Oct. 10, 1918.

523 **"condition . . . spreads the epidemic":** Ibid.

525 **"undertakers found it impossible": Mayor's Annual Report for 1918,** 40, Philadelphia City Archives.

525 **"took her to the cemetery":** Anna Lavin, June 3, 1982, Charles Hardy oral history tapes, West Chester University.

525 **"brought a steam shovel":** Michael Donohue, transcript of unaired interview for "Influenza 1918," **American Experience,** Feb. 28, 1997.

526 **"corpse on the front porches":** Harriet Ferrell, transcript of unaired interview for "Influenza 1918," **American Experience,** Feb. 27, 1997.

527 **"drawn by horses":** Selma Epp, transcript of unaired interview for "Influenza 1918," **American Experience,** Feb. 28, 1997.

528 **"Everything was quiet":** Clifford Adams, Charles Hardy oral history tapes.

528 **"Nursing Halting Epidemic": Philadelphia Inquirer,** Oct. 16, 1918.

528 **"calls not filled, 2,758":** "Directory of

Nurses," College of Physicians of Philadelphia papers.

528 **Ten of the fifty-five:** Joseph Lehman, "Clinical Notes on the Recent Epidemic of Influenza," **Monthly Bulletin of the Department of Public Health and Charities** (March 1919), 38.

529 **"Calls for Amateur Nurses":** In at least three Philadelphia newspapers, including the **Philadelphia Inquirer** and two unidentified newspaper clippings in epidemic scrapbook, Oct. 6, 1918, College of Physicians Library, Philadelphia.

530 **"all persons with two hands":** Unidentified newspaper clipping in epidemic scrapbook, Oct. 9, 1918, College of Physicians Library, Philadelphia.

530 **"must have more volunteer helpers": Philadelphia Inquirer,** Oct. 14, 1918.

531 **"they will work all the harder":** "Minutes of Philadelphia General Hospital Woman's Advisory Council," Oct. 16, 1918, HSP.

531 **118 officers responded: Mayor's Annual Report for 1918,** 40, City Archives, Philadelphia.

532 **"[V]olunteers . . . are useless":** "Minutes of Philadelphia General Hospital Woman's Advisory Council," Oct. 16, 1918, HSP.

532 **"they still hold back":** Undated clipping in epidemic scrapbook, College of Physicians Library.

532 **"fear in the hearts":** Susanna Turner, transcript of unaired interview for "Influenza 1918," **American Experience,** Feb. 27, 1997.

533 **Day after day he carried:** Ibid.

CHAPTER TWENTY-NINE

536 **"not a soul to be seen":** Geoffrey Rice, **Black November: The 1918 Influenza Epidemic in New Zealand** (1988), 51–52.

536 **had died overnight:** See "Reminiscences Dana W. Atchley, M.D." (1964), 94–95, Columbia oral history, quoted in Dorothy Ann Pettit, "A Cruel Wind: America Experiences the Pandemic Influenza, 1918–1920," (1976), 109.

536 **"first casualty when war comes":** Many citations of this comment originally made in 1917, including **Newsday,** June 15, 2003.

536 **"plenty of gasoline":** See, for example, **Arizona Republican,** Sept. 1, 1918.

537 **possibility of plague:** E. Bircher, "Influenza Epidemic," **Correspondenz-Blatt fur Schweizer Aertze,** Basel (Nov. 5, 1918), 1338, quoted in **JAMA** 71, no. 24 (Dec. 7, 1918), 1946.

537 **"similarity of the two diseases":** Douglas Symmers, M.D., "Pathologic Similarity Between Pneumonia of Bubonic Plague and of Pandemic Influenza," **JAMA** (Nov. 2, 1918), 1482.

538 **"sorrow and sadness sat":** Wade Oliver, **The Man Who Lived for Tomorrow: A Biography of William Hallock Park, M.D.** (1941), 384.

538 **"may actually be reassuring": Providence Journal,** Sept. 9, 1918.

539 **"To dispel alarm":** Run in many newspapers, for example, **Arizona Republican,** Sept. 23, 1918.

539 **"epidemic is on the wane"**: **JAMA** 71, no. 13 (Sept. 28, 1918): 1075.

539 **"no cause for alarm"**: **Washington Evening Star,** Oct. 13, 1918.

540 **"ought to see this hospital tonight"**: Quoted in Pettit, "A Cruel Wind," 105.

540 **"Spanish influenza is plain la grippe"**: **Arkansas Gazette,** Sept. 20, 1918.

540 **"something constructive rather than destructive"**: Report from **Christian Science Monitor** reprinted in **Arizona Gazette,** Oct. 31, 1918.

541 **said nothing at all**: See **Review Press and Reporter,** Feb. 1972 clipping, RG 200, NA.

541 **"Fear kills more than the disease"**: Ibid.

541 **"If ordinary precautions"**: Quoted in Crosby, **America's Forgotten Pandemic,** 92.

542 **"Nothing was done"**: John Dill Robertson, **Report of an Epidemic of Influenza in Chicago Occurring During the Fall of 1918** (1919), City of Chicago, 45.

542 **"Worry kills more"**: **The Survey** 41 (Dec. 21, 1918), 268, quoted in Fred R. Van Hartesveldt, **The 1918–1919 Pandemic of Influenza: The Urban Impact in the Western World** (1992), 144.

542 **mortality rate at Cook County**: Riet Keeton and A. Beulah Cusman, "The Influenza Epidemic in Chicago," **JAMA** (Dec. 14, 1918), 2000–2001. Note the 39.8 percent corrects an earlier report in **JAMA** by Nuzum on Nov. 9, 1918, 1562.

542   **"Fear is our first enemy":** Literary **Digest** 59 (Oct. 12, 1918), 13–14, quoted in Van Hartesveldt, **1918–1919 Pandemic of Influenza,** 144.

542   **"Don't Get Scared":** Albuquerque **Morning Journal,** Oct. 1, 1918, quoted in Bradford Luckingham, **Epidemic in the Southwest, 1918–1919** (1984), 18.

542   **"epidemic under control":** Arizona **Republican,** Sept. 23, 1918.

543   **deaths in New Orleans:** Compare **Arizona Republican,** Sept. 19, 1918, to **New Orleans Item,** Sept. 21, 1918.

543   **utterly silent:** See **Arizona Republican** of Sept. 25, 26, 27, 28, 1918.

543   **"most fearful are . . . first to succumb":** **Arizona Gazette,** Jan. 9, 1919.

543   **"refrain from mentioning the influenza":** **Arizona Gazette,** Nov. 26, 1918.

543   **"Simply the Old-Fashioned Grip":** See Vicks VapoRub ad run repeatedly all over the country, for example, in **Seattle Post-Intelligencer,** Jan. 7, 1919.

544   **"come up through the grapevine":** Dan Tonkel, transcript of unaired interview for "Influenza 1918," **American Experience,** March 3, 1997.

544   **"not inclined to be as panicky":** Gene Hamaker, "Influenza 1918," **Buffalo County, Nebraska, Historical Society** 7, no. 4.

544   **"do much toward checking the spread":** See, for example, **Washington Evening Star,** Oct. 3, 1918.

544   **"Every person who spits":** Unidentified,

undated clipping in epidemic scrapbook, College of Physicians Library.

545 **"Remember the 3 Cs"**: For example, **Rocky Mountain News,** Sept. 28, 1918, quoted in Stephen Leonard, "The 1918 Influenza Epidemic in Denver and Colorado," **Essays and Monographs in Colorado History,** essay no. 9 (1989), 3.

545 **"The danger . . . is so grave"**: JAMA 71, no. 15 (Oct. 12, 1918), 1220.

548 **"None of the cases . . . serious"**: **Arizona Republican,** Sept. 23, 1918.

548 **"My first intimations"**: William Maxwell, "Influenza 1918," **American Experience.**

548 **"we were next"**: Lee Reay, "Influenza 1918," **American Experience.**

549 **"Spanish hysteria"**: Luckingham, **Epidemic in the Southwest,** 29.

549 **"What's true of all the evils"**: Quoted in Sherwin Nuland, **How We Die** (1993), 201.

551 **gone back to being a doctor:** interview with Pat Ward, Feb. 13, 2003.

551 **nothing but brief obituaries:** See, for example, JAMA 71, no. 21 (Nov. 16, 1918).

552 **"Germans have started epidemics"**: Doane made the statement in Chicago and was quoted by the **Chicago Tribune,** Sept. 19, 1918. The story appeared in many papers nationally, for example, the **Arizona Republican,** same date.

552 **"prepared the public mind"**: Parsons to Blue, Sept. 26, 1918, entry 10, file 1622, RG 90, NA.

553 **"well back of the lines":** Ibid.

553 **"we wonder which":** Ibid.

553 **Police ruled it suicide:** Associated Press, Oct. 18, 1918; see also **Mobile Daily Register,** Oct. 18, 1918.

554 **41 percent of the entire population:** U.S. Census Bureau, **Mortality Statistics 1919,** 30–31; see also W. H. Frost, "Statistics of Influenza Morbidity," Public Health Reports (March 1920), 584–97.

554 **"this help never materialized":** A. M. Lichtenstein, "The Influenza Epidemic in Cumberland, Md," **Johns Hopkins Nurses Alumni Magazine** (1918), 224.

555 **"everything possible would be done":** Parsons to Blue, Oct. 13, 1918, entry 10, file 1622, RG 90, NA.

555 **"Panic incipient":** Parsons to Blue, Oct. 13, 1918, entry 10, file 1622, RG 90, NA.

555 **"[W]hole city in a panic":** J. W. Tappan to Blue, Oct. 22 and Oct. 23, 1918, entry 10, file 1622, RG 90.

556 **125 died:** Leonard, "1918 Influenza Epidemic," 7.

556 **"shot gun quarantine": Durango Evening Herald,** Dec. 13, 1918, quoted in Leonard, "1918 Influenza Epidemic," 8.

557 **"which may be deemed appropriate":** Memo by E. L. Munson, Oct. 16, 1918, entry 710, RG 112.

557 **"a terrible calamity": Gunnison News-Chronicle,** Nov. 22, 1918, quoted in Leonard, "1918 Influenza Epidemic," 8.

557 **"right at our very doors":** Susanna Turner, transcript of unaired interview for "Influenza 1918," **American Experience,** Feb. 27, 1997.

557 **"almost afraid to breathe":** Dan Tonkel, transcript of unaired interview for "Influenza 1918," **American Experience,** March 3, 1997.

558 **"Farmers stopped farming":** Ibid.

558 **"It kept people apart":** William Sardo, transcript of unaired interview for "Influenza 1918," **American Experience,** Feb. 27, 1997.

559 **"Nobody was coming in":** Joe Delano, transcript of unaired interview for "Influenza 1918," **American Experience,** March 3, 1997.

559 **illegal to shake hands:** Jack Fincher, "America's Rendezvous with the Deadly Lady," **Smithsonian Magazine** (Jan. 1989), 131.

560 **"starving to death not from lack of food":** "An Account of the Influenza Epidemic in Perry County, Kentucky," unsigned, Aug. 14, 1919, box 689, RG 200, NA.

560 **arrived . . . Saturday and left Sunday:** Shelley Watts to Fieser, Nov. 11, 1918, box 689, RG 200, NA.

560 **mortality rate reached 30 percent:** Nancy Baird, "The 'Spanish Lady' in Kentucky," **Filson Club Quarterly,** 293.

560 **"he'd spray the money":** Patricia J. Fanning, "Disease and the Politics of Community: Norwood and the Great Flu Epidemic of 1918" (1995), 139–42.

561 **"send for the priest":** From Red Cross pamphlet: "The Mobilization of the American National

Red Cross During the Influenza Pandemic 1918–1919" (1920), 24.

561 **"shouted orders through doors"**: Leonard, "1918 Influenza Epidemic," 9.

562 **"taught that they were safer at work"**: C. E. Turner, "Report Upon Preventive Measures Adopted in New England Shipyards of the Emergency Fleet Corp," undated, entry 10, file 1622, RG 90, NA.

562 **absentee records were striking:** Ibid.

563 **"the first problem": Arizona Republican,** Nov. 8, 1918.

563 **"H. G. Saylor, yellow slacker": Arizona Gazette,** Oct. 11, 1918.

564 **"a city of masked faces": Arizona Republican,** Nov. 27, 1918.

564 **"Phoenix will soon be dogless": Arizona Gazette,** Dec. 6, 1918.

564 **"BONG! BONG! BONG!":** Mrs. Volz, transcript of unaired interview "Influenza 1918," **American Experience,** Feb. 26, 1997.

565 **"Ice is also great":** Robert Frost, "Fire and Ice," originally published in **Harper's,** 1920.

565 **"akin to the terror of the Middle Ages":** "Mobilization of the American National Red Cross," 24.

CHAPTER THIRTY

566 **"two colored physicians":** Converse to Blue, Oct. 8, 1918, entry 10, file 1622, RG 90, NA.

566 **"urgent need of four nurses":** Rush wire

to Blue, Oct. 14, 1918, entry 10, file 1622. RG 90, NA.

566 **"No colored physicians":** Blue to Converse, Oct. 10, 1918, entry 10, file 1622, RG 90.

566 **"impossible to send nurses":** Rush wire to Blue, Oct. 14, 1918, entry 10, file 1622, RG 90, NA.

567 **house to house searching:** Report, Oct. 22, 1918, box 688, RG 200, NA.

567 **go to the ticket booth:** Josey Brown, transcript of unaired interview for "Influenza 1918," **American Experience,** Feb. 26, 1997.

567 **"urgent call on physicians":** See, for example, **JAMA** 71, no. 17 (Oct. 26 1918): 1412, 1413.

568 **"Infection was prevented":** James Back, M.D., **JAMA** 71, no. 23 (Dec. 7, 1918), 1945.

569 **"saturated with alkalis":** Thomas C. Ely, M.D., letter to editor, **JAMA** 71, no. 17 (Oct. 26, 1918): 1430.

569 **injected people with typhoid vaccine:** D. M. Cowie and P. W. Beaven, "Nonspecific Protein Therapy in Influenzal Pneumonia," **JAMA** (April 19, 1919), 1170.

569 **"results were immediate and certain":** F. B. Bogardus, "Influenza Pneumonia Treated by Blood Transfusion," **New York Medical Journal** (May 3, 1919), 765.

570 **forty-seven patients; twenty died:** W. W. G. MacLachlan and W. J. Fetter, "Citrated Blood in Treatment of Pneumonia Following Influenza," **JAMA** (Dec. 21, 1918), 2053.

570 **hydrogen peroxide intravenously:** David Thomson and Robert Thomson, **Annals of the**

Pickett-Thomson Research Laboratory, v. 10, **Influenza** (1934), 1287.

570 **homeopaths claiming no deaths:** T. A. McCann, "Homeopathy and Influenza," **The Journal of the American Institute for Homeopathy** (May 1921).

571 **"effect was apparent":** T. Anastassiades, "Autoserotherapy in Influenza," **Grece Medicale,** reported in **JAMA** (June 1919), 1947.

571 **therapy in The Lancet:** Quoted in Thomson and Thomson, **Influenza,** v. 10, 1287.

572 **"prompt bleeding":** "Paris Letter," Oct. 3, 1918, in **JAMA** 71, no. 19 (Nov. 9, 1918).

573 **In disease as in war:** Quoted in Van Hartesveldt, **1918–1919 Pandemic of Influenza,** 82.

573 **"keep your feet dry":** Arizona Gazette, Nov. 26, 1918.

574 **"a powerful bulwark for the prevention":** All these and others reproduced under title "Propaganda for Reform" in **JAMA** 71, no. 21 (Nov. 23, 1918), 1763.

574 **"Use Vicks VapoRub":** Seattle Post-Intelligencer, Jan. 3, 1919.

574 **"vaccinated . . . immune to the disease":** Numerous papers both in and outside New York City, see, for example, Philadelphia **Public Ledger,** Oct. 18, 1918.

574 **thousands of dosages more:** John Kolmer, M.D., "Paper Given at the Philadelphia County Medical Society Meeting, Oct. 23, 1918," **Pennsylvania Medical Journal** (Dec. 1918), 181.

575 **"some prophylactic value":** George Whipple, "Current Comment, Vaccines in Influenza," **JAMA** (Oct. 19, 1918), 1317.

575 **death rate . . . 52 percent:** Egbert Fell, "Postinfluenzal Psychoses," **JAMA** (June 7, 1919), 1658.

576 **"now has available":** E. A. Fennel, "Prophylactic Inoculation against Pneumonia," **JAMA** (Dec. 28, 1918), 2119.

576 **"none is available for distribution":** Major G. R. Callender to Dr. W. B. Holden, Oct. 7, 1918, entry 29, RG 112, NA.

576 **"still in the experimental stage":** Acting surgeon general to camp and division surgeons, Oct. 25, 1918, entry 29, RG 112, NA.

577 **"health officers in their public relations":** Editorial, **JAMA** 71, no. 17, (Oct. 26, 1918), 1408.

577 **"may arouse unwarranted hope":** Editorial, **JAMA** 71, no. 19 (Nov. 9, 1918), 1583.

577 **eighteen different kinds:** Fincher, "America's Rendezvous," 134.

578 **"large doses hypodermically":** Friedlander et al., "The Epidemic of Influenza at Camp Sherman" **JAMA** (Nov. 16, 1918), 1652.

578 **"No benefits were gained":** Ibid.

580 **Sentries guarded all trails: Engineering News-Record** 82 (1919), 787, quoted in Jordan, **Epidemic Influenza,** 453.

580 **could become "extinct":** Kilpatrick to FC Monroe, Aug. 7, 1919; see also Mrs. Nichols, "Report of Expedition," July 21, 1919, RG 200.

580   **"people of Alaska consider":** U.S. Congress, Senate Committee on Appropriations, "Influenza in Alaska" (1919).

581   **176 of 300 Eskimos:** W. I. B. Beveridge, **Influenza: The Last Great Plague: An Unfinished Story of Discovery** (1977), 31.

581   **"frozen to death before help arrived":** U.S. Congress, Senate Committee on Appropriations, "Influenza in Alaska."

582   **"few adults living":** Mrs. Nichols, "Report of Expedition."

582   **"heaps of dead bodies":** Ibid.

583   **"starving dogs had dug their way":** Ibid.

584   **"Whole households lay inanimate":** Eileen Pettigrew, **The Silent Enemy: Canada and the Deadly Flu of 1918** (1983), 28.

584   **"left us to sink or swim":** Ibid., 31.

584   **killed over one hundred dogs:** Richard Collier, **The Plague of the Spanish Lady: The Influenza Pandemic of 1918–1919** (1974), 300.

585   **laid 114 bodies in the pit:** Pettigrew, **Silent Enemy,** 30.

585   **one-third of the total population died:** Ibid., 33.

585   **Metropolitan Life Insurance:** Jordan, **Epidemic Influenza,** 251.

585   **In Frankfurt the mortality:** Van Hartesveldt, **1918–1919 Pandemic of Influenza,** 25.

585   **"too exhausted to hate":** Fincher, "America's Rendezvous," 134.

586   **"remarkable for the severity":** Pierre Lereboullet, **La grippe, clinique, prophylaxie, traitement** (1926), 33, quoted in Diane A. V.

Puklin, "Paris," in Van Hartesveldt, **1918–1919 Pandemic of Influenza,** 77.

586   "obliterating whole settlements": Jordan, **Epidemic Influenza,** 227.

586   only a single sailor died: Crosby, **America's Forgotten Pandemic,** 234.

587   46 percent of the blacks would be attacked: Jordan, **Epidemic Influenza,** 204–5.

587   the state of Chiapas: Thomson and Thomson, **Influenza,** v. 9, 165.

587   attack rate of 33 percent: "Rio de Janeiro Letter," **JAMA** 72 no. 21, May 24, 1919, 1555.

587   In Buenos Aires: Thomson and Thomson, **Influenza,** v. 9, 124.

587   In Japan: Ibid., 124.

588   die in the sixteen days: Jordan, **Epidemic Influenza,** 224.

588   "filled with bodies": Ibid., 225.

588   <u>Talune</u> brought the disease: Rice, **Black November,** 140.

588   In Chungking one-half the population: **Public Health Reports,** Sept. 20, 1918, 1617.

589   doubled that of the: Jordan, **Epidemic Influenza,** 222.

589   case mortality rate: Mills, "The 1918–19 Influenza Pandemic—The Indian Experience," **The Indian Economic and Social History Review** (1986), 27.

589   arrived with the dead and dying: Richard Gordon, M.D., **Great Medical Disasters** (1983), 87; Beveridge, **Influenza: The Last Great Plague,** 31.

589 **For Indian troops:** Jordan, **Epidemic Influenza,** 246.

589 **7,044 of those patients died:** Memo to Dr. Warren from Dr. Armstrong, May 2, 1919, entry 10, file 1622, RG 90, NA.

589 **"littered with dead and dying":** "London Letter," **JAMA** 72, no. 21 (May 24, 1919), 1557.

589 **firewood was quickly exhausted:** Mills, "The 1918–19 Influenza Pandemic," 35.

589 **Close to twenty million:** Ibid., 4; Kingsley Davis, **The Population of India and Pakistan** (1951), 36.

590 **"civilization could easily . . . disappear":** Collier, **Plague of the Spanish Lady,** 266.

Part IX: Lingerer

CHAPTER THIRTY-ONE

593 **measles requires an unvaccinated:** Quoted in William McNeill, **Plagues and Peoples** (1976), 53.

594 **"no longer a master":** H. G. Wells, **War of the Worlds,** online edition, www.fourmilab.ch/etexts/www/warworlds/b2c6.html.

597 **worst numbers came from Camp Sherman:** George Soper, M.D., "The Influenza Pandemic in the Camps," undated, unpaginated, RG 112, NA.

597 **last five camps attacked:** Ibid.

598 **"failed when . . . carelessly applied":** Ibid.

599 **"when it first reached the state":** Wade Frost

quoted in David Thomson and Robert Thomson, **Annals of the Pickett-Thomson Research Laboratory,** v. 9, **Influenza** (1934), 215.

599 **"relatively rarely encountered":** Edwin O. Jordan, **Epidemic Influenza** (1927), 355–56.

601 **"influenza has not passed":** "Bulletin of the USPHS," Dec. 11, 1918, quoted in **JAMA** 71, no. 25 (Dec. 21, 1918), 2088.

602 **twenty-seven epidemic ordinances:** Dorothy Ann Pettit, "A Cruel Wind: America Experiences the Pandemic Influenza, 1918–1920, A Social History" (1976), 162.

602 **places closed—for a third time:** Ibid., 177.

603 **"99% proof against influenza":** June Osborn, ed., **Influenza in America, 1918–1976: History, Science, and Politics** (1977), 11.

603 **teachers volunteered as nurses:** See Alfred W. Crosby, **America's Forgotten Pandemic: The Influenza of 1918** (1989), 91–116, passim.

603 **"how gallantly the city":** Quoted in ibid., 106.

604 **worst on the West Coast:** Osborn, **Influenza in America,** 11.

604 **quarantine of incoming ships:** W. I. B. Beveridge, **Influenza: The Last Great Plague: An Unfinished Story of Discovery** (1977), 31.

604 **not even one-quarter that of Italy:** K. D. Patterson and G. F. Pyle, "The Geography and Mortality of the 1918 Influenza Pandemic," **Bulletin of the History of Medicine** (1991), 14.

605 **"the influenza plague":** Quoted in Lucy Taksa, "The Masked Disease: Oral History, Memory,

and the Influenza Pandemic," in **Memory and History in Twentieth Century Australia** (1994), 86.

605 **"I can recall the Bubonic Plague":** Ibid., 79.

605 **"inoculated against the Bubonic Plague":** Ibid., 83.

606 **"I can remember that":** Ibid., 79–85, passim.

CHAPTER THIRTY-TWO

608 **"not considered in this report":** Egbert Fell, "Postinfluenzal Psychoses," **JAMA** (June 1919), 1658.

609 **"profound mental inertia":** Thomson and Thomson, **Influenza,** v. 10, 772.

609 **"influenzal psychoses":** G. Draggoti, "Nervous Manifestations of Influenza," **Policlinico** (Feb. 8, 1919), 161, quoted in **JAMA** 72 (April 12, 1919), 1105.

609 **"serious mental disturbances":** Henri Claude, M.D., "Nervous and Mental Disturbances Following Influenza," **JAMA** (May 31, 1919), 1635.

609 **"an active delirium":** Martin Synnott, "Influenza Epidemic at Camp Dix" **JAMA** (Nov. 2, 1918), 1818.

610 **"mental depression":** Jordan, **Epidemic Influenza,** 35.

610 **"Nervous symptoms":** Maj. General Merritt W. Ireland, ed., **Medical Department of the United States Army in the World War,** v. 9, **Communicable Diseases** (1928), 159.

610 "melancholia, hysteria, and insanity":
Thomson and Thomson, **Influenza,** v. 10, 263.

610 "involvement of the nervous": Ireland,
Influenza, 160.

610 "muttering delirium which persisted": Ireland,
ed., **Medical Department of the United States
Army in the World War,** v. 12, **Pathology of
the Acute Respiratory Diseases, and of Gas
Gangrene Following War Wounds** (1929),
141–42.

610 "central nervous system": Ibid., 119.

610 "Infectious psychosis": Ibid., 13.

610 increase in Parkinson's: Frederick G. Hayden
and Peter Palese, "Influenza Virus," in **Clinical
Virology** (1997), 928.

611 "influenza may act on the brain": Jordan,
Epidemic Influenza, 278–80.

611 "profound influence on the nervous system":
Thomson and Thomson, **Influenza,** v. 10, 768.

611 "influence suicide": I. M. Wasserman, "The
Impact of Epidemic, War, Prohibition and Media
on Suicide: United States, 1910–1920," **Suicide
and Life Threatening Behavior** (1992), 240.

611 "wide spectrum of central nervous system":
Brian R. Murphy and Robert G. Webster,
"Orthomyxoviruses" (1996), 1408.

612 "membranes surrounding the brain":
P. K. S. Chan et al., "Pathology of Fatal Human
Infection Associated with Avian Influenza A
H5N1 Virus," **Journal of Medical Virology** 63,
no. 3 (March 2001), 242–46.

612 "meninges of the brain": Douglas Symmers,

M.D., "Pathologic Similarity Between Pneumonia of Bubonic Plague and of Pandemic Influenza," **JAMA** (Nov. 2, 1918), 1482.

612 **"hemorrhages into gray matter":** Claude, "Nervous and Mental Disturbances," 1635.

612 **"across to central nervous systems":** Interview with Robert Webster, June 13, 2002.

614 **"have been exceeding miserable":** Diaries, House collection, Nov. 30, 1918, quoted in Pettit, "Cruel Wind," 186.

614 **"all too generous": New York Telegram,** Jan. 14, 1919, quoted in Ibid.

614 **"lost the thread of affairs":** Quoted in Arthur Walworth, **Woodrow Wilson,** v. 2 (1965), 279.

615 **"a greased marble":** Tasker Bliss, quoted in Bernard Baruch, **Baruch: The Public Years** (1960), 119, quoted in Crosby, **America's Forgotten Pandemic,** 186.

616 **1,517 Parisians died:** From Great Britain Ministry of Health, "Report on the Pandemic of Influenza" (1920), 228, quoted in Crosby, **America's Forgotten Pandemic,** 181.

616 **"grave proportions . . . in Paris":** "Paris Letter," March 2, 1919, **JAMA** 72, no. 14 (April 5, 1919), 1015.

617 **"the principles laid down":** Walworth, **Woodrow Wilson,** v. 2, 294.

617 **"severe cold last night":** Grayson wire to Tumulty, 8:58 A.M., April 4, 1919, box 44, Tumulty papers, LC.

618 **"The President was taken violently sick":** Grayson to Tumulty, April 10, 1919, marked

PERSONAL AND CONFIDENTIAL, box 44,
Tumulty papers.

618 "taking every precaution": Grayson wire to
Tumulty, 11:00 A.M., April 8, 1919, box 44,
Tumulty papers.

618 "he manifested peculiarities": Walworth,
Woodrow Wilson, v. 2, 297.

619 "we will go home": Edith Wilson, **My Memoir**
(1939), 249, quoted in Crosby, **America's
Forgotten Pandemic,** 191.

619 "a cook who keeps her trunk": Quoted in
Walworth, **Woodrow Wilson,** v. 2, 398.

619 "began to drive himself": Cary Grayson,
Woodrow Wilson: An Intimate Memoir
(1960), 85.

620 "push against an unwilling mind": Herbert
Hoover, **America's First Crusade** (1942),
1, 40–41, 64, quoted in Crosby, **America's
Forgotten Epidemic,** 193.

620 "lacked his old quickness": Hugh L'Etang, **The
Pathology of Leadership** (1970), 49.

620 obsessed with such details: Elbert Smith,
**When the Cheering Stopped: The Last Years
of Woodrow Wilson** (1964), 49.

620 "never the same after": Irwin H. Hoover, **Forty-
two Years in the White House,** (1934) 98.

621 "so worn and tired": Grayson to Tumulty,
April 10, 1919, box 44, Tumulty papers.

621 "could not remember": Margaret Macmillan,
**Paris 1919: Six Months That Changed the
World** (2002), 276.

622 "nervous and spiritual breakdown": Lloyd

George, **Memoirs of the Peace Conference** (1939), quoted in Crosby, **America's Forgotten Epidemic,** 193.

622   "terrible days for the President": Grayson to Tumulty, April 30, 1919, box 44, Tumulty papers.

622   "What abominable manners": Walworth, **Woodrow Wilson,** v. 2, 319.

622   "I should never sign it": Ibid.

623   suffering from arteriosclerosis: Archibald Patterson, **Personal Recollections of Woodrow Wilson** (1929), 52.

623   "arteriosclerotic occlusion": Rudolph Marx, **The Health of the Presidents** (1961), 215–16.

623   "thrombosis": Elbert Smith, **When the Cheering Stopped: The Last Years of Woodrow Wilson** (1964), 105–6.

623   "a little stroke": Edward Weinstein, "Woodrow Wilson's Neurological Illness," **Journal of American History** (1970–71), 324.

623   "a minor stroke": Macmillan, **Paris 1919,** 276.

624   "final breakdown": Grayson, **Woodrow Wilson,** 82.

625   "the dead season of our fortunes": John Maynard Keynes, **Economic Consequences of the Peace** (1920), 297.

626   "you did not fight": "Papers Relating to the Foreign Relations of the United States, The Paris Peace Conference" (1942–1947), 570–74, quoted in Schlesinger, **The Age of Roosevelt,** v. 1, **Crisis of the Old Order 1919–1933,** (1957), 14.

CHAPTER THIRTY-THREE

628 **"felt very ill"**: Quoted in Michael Bliss, **William Osler: A Life in Medicine** (1999), 469. For more on Osler's illness, see Bliss 468–76, passim.

628 **"broncho-pneumonias so common after influenza"**: Ibid., 469.

628 **"with it the pain"**: Ibid., 470.

628 **"shall not see the post mortem"**: Ibid., 472.

628 **"how can I hope"**: Ibid., 470.

629 **"might have saved him"**: Ibid., 475.

629 **"Hold up my head"**: Ibid., 476

629 **"dealing with any recurrences"**: Pettit, "Cruel Wind," 234.

630 **"No publicity is to be given"**: Red Cross files, undated, RG 200, NA.

630 **"rapid spread of influenza"**: Memo to division managers from chairman of influenza committee, Feb. 7, 1920, RG 200, NA.

630 **more cases would be reported**: Pettit, "Cruel Wind," 248.

630 **victim's home was tagged**: Ibid., 241.

631 **"Enforce absolute quarantine"**: R. E. Arne to W. Frank Persons, Jan. 30, 1922, RG 200, NA.

631 **twenty-one thousand children . . . made orphans**: Associated Press wire, appearing in **Arizona Republican,** Nov. 9, 1918.

631 **"sixteen motherless children"**: Alice Latterall to Marjorie Perry, Oct. 17, 1918, RG 200, NA.

631 **one hundred children orphaned**: "Report of Lake Division," Aug. 12, 1919, RG 200, NA.

631   **orphaned two hundred children:** JAMA 71,
       no. 18 (Nov. 2, 1918), 1500.

632   **"havoc is wide spread":** General manager to di-
       vision managers, March 1, 1919, RG 200, NA.

632   **"What bones are they":** Quoted in Pettit, "A
       Cruel Wind," 173.

634   **"how sick the world is":** John Dewey, **New
       Republic** (Jan. 1923), quoted in Dewey,
       **Characters and Events: Popular Essays in
       Social and Political Philosophy,** v. 2 (1929),
       760–61.

634   **"all faiths in man shaken":** F. Scott Fitzgerald,
       This Side of Paradise (1920), 304.

635   **"a motivating force in four books":** William
       Maxwell, "A Time to Mourn," **Pen America**
       (2002), 122–23, 130.

636   **"almost nothing in literature":** Personal com-
       munication from Donald Schueler, July 5, 2003.

636   **"an epidemic of discreet, infectious fear":**
       Christopher Isherwood, **Berlin Stories** (New
       York: New Directions, 1951), 181.

637   **"foreign settlements of the city": Rocky
       Mountain News,** Oct. 31, 1918, quoted
       in Stephen Leonard, "The 1918 Influenza
       Epidemic in Denver and Colorado," **Essays and
       Monographs in Colorado History** (1989), 7–8.

637   **"negligence and disobedience": Durango
       Evening Herald,** Nov. 26, 1918, quoted in
       Leonard, "1918 Influenza Epidemic in Denver
       and Colorado," 7.

637   **"penalty for filth is death":** Shelley Watts to
       Fieser, Nov. 13, 1918, RG 200, NA.

641 **may have reached 20 million:** Kingsley Davis, **The Population of India and Pakistan** (1951), 36, cited in and see also I. D. Mills, "The 1918–19 Influenza Pandemic—The Indian Experience" (1986), 1–40, passim.

641 **"in the order of 50 million":** Niall Johnson and Juergen Mueller, "Updating the Accounts: Global Mortality of the 1918–1920 'Spanish' Influenza Pandemic," **Bulletin of the History of Medicine** (spring 2002), 105–15, passim.

641 **as many as 100 million:** Ibid.

642 **those aged twenty-one to thirty:** Virtually all studies showed similar results. See, for example, Thomson and Thomson, **Influenza,** v. 9, 21.

642 **most conservative estimate:** Ibid., 165.

Part X: Endgame

CHAPTER THIRTY-FOUR

648 **"The appointment of Dr. Opie":** Winslow to Wade Frost, Feb. 1, 1930, Winslow papers, SLY.

649 **"Jordan seems at first":** Winslow to Frost, Jan. 16, 1930, Winslow papers.

649 **"distinctly prefer Emerson":** Frost to Winslow, Jan. 20, 1930, Winslow papers.

650 **"the Black Death":** Quoted in Michael Levin, "An Historical Account of the Influenza," **Maryland State Medical Journal** (May 1978), 61.

651 **"we were so helpless":** Transcript of Influenza Commission minutes, Oct. 30, 1918, Winslow papers.

654 **precise epidemiological investigations:**
"Association Committee Notes on Statistical
Study of the 1918 Epidemic of So-called
Influenza," presented at American Public Health
Association meeting, Dec. 11, 1918, entry 10, file
1622, RG 90, NA.

655 **"an opportunity to show":** Ibid.

655 **"ultimately in the laboratory":** Transcript of
Influenza Commission minutes, Feb. 4, 1919,
Winslow papers.

656 **isolated for seven days:** George Soper, M.D.,
"Epidemic After Wars," **JAMA** (April 5, 1919), 988.

657 **"every effort to collect":** Russell to Flexner,
Nov. 25, 1918, Flexner papers, APS.

658 **"this business off our hands":** Quoted in
Dorothy Ann Pettit, "A Cruel Wind: America
Experiences the Pandemic of Influenza,
1918–1920, A Social History" (1976), 229.

659 **two units of seasoned troops:** Maj. General
Merritt W. Ireland, ed., **Medical Department
of the United States Army in the World War,**
v. 9, **Communicable Diseases** (1928), 127–29.

660 **"cyclic variation in air pressure":** David
Thomson and Robert Thomson, **Annals of the
Pickett-Thomson Research Laboratory,** v. 9,
Influenza (1934), 259.

660 **"the outstanding objective":** F. M. Burnet,
"Portraits of Viruses: Influenza Virus A,"
Intervirology (1979), 201.

661 **"humiliating but true":** Comments by Welch
on influenza bacillus paper, undated, file 17,
box 109, WP.

CHAPTER THIRTY-FIVE

664 **"the specific inciting agent":** Thomson and Thomson, **Influenza,** v. 9, 499.

664 **"blood agar plates":** Capt. Edwin Hirsch to SG, Oct. 7, 1919, entry 31D, RG 112.

664 **"investigation of the bacteriologic methods":** J. Wheeler Smith Jr. to Callender, Feb. 20, 1919, entry 31D, RG 112, NA.

665 **They found the bacteria everywhere:** Maj. General Merritt W. Ireland, ed., **Medical Department of the United States Army in the World War,** v. 12, **Pathology of the Acute Respiratory Diseases, and of Gas Gangrene Following War Wounds** (1929), 180–81.

665 **"in every case":** Ibid., 58.

666 **"absence of influenza bacilli":** Ibid., 140.

666 **"were not discovered":** Ibid., 144.

667 **"other respiratory diseases":** Ireland, **Communicable Diseases,** 62.

667 **only five of sixty-two cases:** Edwin O. Jordan, **Epidemic Influenza** (1927), 393.

668 **"the most slipshod manner":** Thomson and Thomson, **Influenza,** v. 9, 512.

668 **"found in nearly every case":** William H. Park, "Anti-influenza Vaccine as Prophylactic," **New York Medical Journal** (Oct. 12, 1918), 621.

670 **"ten different strains":** Park comments, transcript of Influenza Commission minutes, Dec. 20, 1918, Winslow papers.

670 **"important secondary invaders":** Thomson and Thomson, **Influenza,** v. 9, 498.

670 **"evidence points to a filterable virus":** Carton 1, chapter 22, p. 24, Anna Wessel Williams papers, Schlesinger Library, Radcliffe College.

671 **"not recognizable by our microscopic methods":** William MacCallum, "Pathological Anatomy of Pneumonia Following Influenza," **Johns Hopkins Hospital Reports** (1921), 149–51.

672 **failed to infect:** Thomson and Thomson, **Influenza,** v. 9, 603–8.

672 **claimed success for three:** Charles Nicolle and Charles LeBailly, "Recherches experimentales sur la grippe," **Annales de l'Institut Pasteur** (1919), 395–402, translated for the author by Eric Barry.

673 **"jumped to the conclusion":** Saul Benison, **Tom Rivers: Reflections on a Life in Medicine and Science, An Oral History Memoir** (1967), 59.

674 **Fleming found:** Thomson and Thomson, **Influenza,** v. 9, 287, 291, 497.

675 **"reducing the resistance":** Welch comments, USPHS Conference on Influenza, Jan. 10, 1929, box 116, file 11, WP. Conference itself reported in **Public Health Reports** 44, no. 122.

676 **"the best claim to serious consideration":** Thomson and Thomson, **Influenza,** v. 9, 512.

676 **"scientific problems were almost forced on him":** René Dubos, **The Professor, the Institute and DNA** (1976), 174.

677 **"not as broad":** Ibid., 74.

677 **"narrow range of techniques":** Dubos, "Oswald

Theodore Avery, 1877–1955," **Biographical Memoirs of Fellows of the Royal Society** (1956), 40.

679 "'the whole secret . . . in this little vial'": Michael Heidelberger, oral history, 70, NLM.

679 "extreme precision and elegance": Dubos, **Professor, Institute and DNA,** 173.

683 "never published a joint paper": Ibid., 82.

684 "digging a deep hole": Ibid., 175.

684 "fundamental to biology": Heidelberger, oral history, 129.

685 "what more do you want": Dubos, **Professor, Institute and DNA,** 143.

686 "likened to a gene": Oswald Avery, Colin McLeod, and Maclyn McCarty, "Studies on the Chemical Nature of the Substance Inducing Transformation of Pneumococcal Types," **Journal of Experimental Medicine** (Feb. 1, 1944, reprinted Feb. 1979), 297–326.

686 "little influence on thought": Gunther Stent, Introduction, **The Double Helix: A Norton Critical Edition** by James Watson (1980), xiv.

687 "obviously of fundamental importance": Nobelstiftelsen, **Nobel, the Man, and His Prizes** (1962), 281.

687 "Avery showed": James Watson, **The Double Helix: A Norton Critical Edition,** see 12, 13, 18.

688 "Avery gave us": Horace Judson, **Eighth Day of Creation: The Makers of the Revolution in Biology** (1979), 94.

688 "we were very attentive": Ibid., 59.

688   **"nonsense to say that we were not aware"**: Ibid., 62–63.

688   **"dark ages of DNA"**: Watson, **Double Helix,** 219.

689   **"opening . . . the field of molecular biology"**: Dubos, **Professor, Institute and DNA,** 156.

689   **"keeping his own counsel"**: Ibid., 164.

CHAPTER THIRTY-SIX

691   **solid evidence:** Transcript of Influenza Commission minutes, first session, Oct. 30, 1918; second session, Nov. 22, 1918; fourth session, Feb. 14, 1919, Winslow papers.

691   **"Lewis's mind working, the depth of it"**: Interview with Dr. David Aronson, Jan. 31, 2002, and April 8, 2003.

692   **"disinfectant power of light"**: Lewis to Flexner, Nov. 29, 1916, Flexner papers, APS.

692   **"interesting and important"**: Flexner to Lewis, Jan. 29, 1919, Flexner papers, APS.

693   **"I do not thrive on routine"**: Lewis to Flexner, April 21, 1921, Flexner papers, APS.

693   **"All I have heard"**: Flexner to Lewis, April 22, 1921, Flexner papers, APS.

694   **"your new honor"**: Flexner to Lewis, Jan. 21, 1921, Flexner papers, APS.

695   **"let me take a little trouble for you"**: Flexner to Lewis, Dec. 21, 1921, Flexner papers, APS.

695   **"'father' to me"**: Lewis to Flexner, Sept. 8, 1924, Flexner papers, APS.

696   **"you may well feel gratified":** Flexner to Lewis, Jan. 26, 1923, Flexner papers, APS.

696   **"rehabilitation of a . . . mind":** Lewis to Flexner, Jan. 20, 1923, Flexner papers, APS.

697   **"to go to work again":** Lewis to Flexner, Jan. 24, 1923, Lewis papers, RUA.

697   **"I shall be rejoiced":** Flexner to Lewis, undated response to Lewis's Jan. 20, 1923, letter, Flexner papers, APS.

698   **"to deserve your confidence":** Lewis to Flexner, Jan. 24, 1923, Lewis to Flexner, Jan. 30, 1923, Lewis papers, RUA.

699   **"free of any entanglement":** Lewis to Flexner, June 26, 1924, Lewis papers, RUA.

700   **"the first chance to make a second center":** Flexner to Lewis, summer 1924 (probably late June or July), Lewis papers, RUA.

700   **"I am secure":** Lewis to Flexner, Sept. 8, 1924, Lewis papers, RUA.

701   **"one of the finest investigators":** Benison, **Tom Rivers,** 341, 344.

702   **understanding of the immune system:** "Scientific Reports of the Corporation and Board of Scientific Directors" (1927–28), RUA, 345–47; see also George A. Corner, **A History of the Rockefeller Institute: 1901–1953 Origins and Growth** (1964), 296.

703   **"aiming higher than his training":** Smith to Flexner, Nov. 2, 1925, Lewis papers, RUA.

703   **diet of the guinea pigs:** Lewis and Shope, "Scientific Reports of the Corporation" (1925–26), 265, RUA.

704   **"no change in my line of work":** Ibid.

704   **"doubt expressed about your future":** Flexner to Lewis, draft letter, Dec. 1, 1925, Lewis papers, RUA.

704   **"unequivocally opposed":** Flexner to Lewis, Dec. 1, 1925, Lewis papers, RUA.

707   **"have not been very productive":** Lewis to Flexner, Aug. 4, 1927, Lewis papers, RUA.

707   **"rather barren subject":** Flexner to Lewis, Sept. 22, 1927, Lewis papers, RUA.

708   **"this diagnosis in pigs":** Richard Collier, **The Plague of the Spanish Lady: The Influenza Epidemic of 1918–1919** (1974), 55; W. I. B. Beveridge, **Influenza: The Last Great Plague: An Unfinished Story of Discovery** (1977), 4; J. S. Koen, "A Practical Method for Field Diagnosis of Swine Diseases," **Journal of Veterinary Medicine** (1919), 468–70.

708   **filtered the mucus:** M. Dorset, C. McBryde, and W. B. Niles, **Journal of the American Veterinary Medical Association** (1922–23), 62, 162.

709   **"our future Lewis problem":** Flexner to Smith, phone message, June 21, 1928, Lewis papers, RUA.

709   **he could still be master:** Flexner to Smith, June 20, 1928, Lewis papers, RUA.

710   **"in all kindness":** Flexner to Smith, June 22, 1928, Lewis papers, RUA.

710   **"not essentially . . . investigator type":** Flexner to Smith, June 29, 1928, Lewis papers, RUA.

710   **double the median income:** Paul Starr, **The**

Social Transformation of American Medicine
(1982), 142.

711 **"no doubt as to the risk":** Flexner to Smith,
June 29, 1928, Lewis papers, RUA.

712 **"I don't think Noguchi was honest":** Benison,
Tom Rivers, 95.

712 **"objections were very unreasonable":** Corner,
History of Rockefeller Institute, 191.

714 **"learn about Shope's Iowa work":** Flexner to
Lewis, Nov. 21, 1928, Lewis papers, RUA.

714 **in some herds:** Richard E. Shope, "Swine
Influenza I. Experimental Transmission and
Pathology," **Journal of Infectious Disease**
(1931), 349.

715 **"went right to work":** Lewis to Flexner, Feb. 1,
1929, Lewis papers, RUA.

715 **"Lewis well":** Russell to Smith, Jan. 28 through
May 23, 1929, "our weekly cable arrived containing the words 'Lewis well,'" each with notation "copy mailed to Mrs. Lewis," Lewis
papers, RUA.

716 **"'Lewis's illness began'":** Russell to Flexner,
June 29, 1929, Lewis papers, RUA.

716 **"Lewis condition critical":** George Soper to
Russell, June 29, 1929, Lewis papers, RUA.

716 **"Marked renal involvement":** Davis to Russell,
June 28, 1929, Lewis papers, RUA.

717 **"Probably laboratory infection":** unsigned
to Russell, July 1, 1929, Lewis papers, RUA.

717 **Shope walked down Maple:** Lewis to
David Aronson, Aug. 21, 1998, provided by
Robert Shope.

717　**"order some flowers":** Smith to Shope, July 16, 1929, Lewis papers, RUA.

718　**"Dear Sirs":** Janet Lewis to Board of Scientific Directors, July 30, 1929, Lewis papers, RUA.

718　**"study of light phenomena":** "Scientific Reports of the Corporation" (1929), 6, RUA.

718　**"recrudescence of poliomyelitis":** Ibid., 11.

718　**"unfinished work of Dr. Noguchi":** Ibid., 10.

719　**"white paint and some other improvements":** Flexner to Sawyer, March 17, 1930, Lewis papers, RUA.

719　**blamed cigarettes:** Interview with Robert Shope, Jan. 2002; interview with David Aronson, April 8, 2003.

720　**"in association with Sewall Wright":** Simon Flexner, "Paul Adin Lewis," **Science** (Aug. 9, 1929), 133–34.

721　**Shope did demonstrate:** Paul A. Lewis and Richard E. Shope, "Swine Influenza II. Hemophilic Bacillus from the Respiratory Tract of Infected Swine," **Journal of Infectious Disease** (1931), 361; Shope, "Swine Influenza I," 349; Shope, "Swine Influenza III. Filtration Experiments and Etiology," **Journal of Infectious Disease** (1931), 373.

721　**took him hunting and fishing:** C. H. Andrewes, **Biographical Memoirs, Richard E. Shope** (1979), 363.

Afterword

726　**Between 2003 and 2017:** See http://www.who.int/influenza/human_animal_interface/

Influenza_Summary_IRA_HA_interface_10_ 30_2017.pdf?ua=1. Accessed January 19, 2018.

727 **segments of the 1918 virus are of avian origin:** Michael Worobey, Guan-Zhu Han, and Andrew Rambaut, "Genesis and Pathogenesis of the 1918 Pandemic H1N1 Influenza A Virus," **Proceedings of the National Academy of Sciences of the United States of America** 111, no. 22 (June 3, 2014): 8107–12.

730 **all five came in waves:** W. T. Vaughan, **Influenza:** An **Epidemiologic Study,** American Journal of Hygiene, Baltimore, 1921, 45–46; Jordan, **Epidemic Influenza** (1927), passim; F. L. Dunn, "Pandemic Influenza in 1957. Review of International Spread of New Asian Strain," **JAMA** 166, no. 10 (1958): 1140–48.

731 **70 percent of pandemic deaths:** Cécile Viboud et al., "Multinational Impact of the 1968 Hong Kong Influenza Pandemic: Evidence for a Smoldering Pandemic," **Journal of Infectious Diseases** 192, no. 2 (July 15, 2005): 233–248.

732 **10 percent to 61 percent:** Presentation by Anthony Fauci, Nov. 13, 2017, at Smithsonian Conference on Influenza, https://www .smithsonianmag.com/science-nature/watch -livestream-next-pandemic-are-we-prepared -180967069/.

737 **99 imposed quarantine:** George Soper, M.D., "The Influenza Pandemic in the Camps," undated draft report, box 394, RG 112, NA.

742 **fell to 27 percent:** Bradly J. Condon and Tapen Sinha, "Who Is That Masked Person:

The Use of Face Masks on Mexico City Public Transportation During the Influenza A (H1N1) Outbreak (July 4, 2009)," **Health Policy** 95, no. 1 (Apr. 2010): 50–56. doi: 10.1016/j.healthpol .2009.11.009. Epub Dec. 4, 2009. https://www .ncbi.nlm.nih.gov/pubmed/19962777. Accessed Jan. 19, 2018.

743 **$9 billion in economic losses:** Presentation by Ciro Ugarte, Nov. 13, 2017, at Smithsonian Conference on Influenza, https://www .smithsonianmag.com/science-nature/watch -livestream-next-pandemic-are-we-prepared -180967069/.

Selected Bibliography

Primary Sources

ARCHIVES AND COLLECTIONS

Alan Mason Chesney Archives, Johns Hopkins University
Stanhope Bayne-Jones papers
Wade Hampton Frost papers
William Halsted papers
Christian Herter papers
Franklin Mall papers
Eugene Opie papers
William Welch papers

American Philosophical Society
Harold Amoss papers
Rufus Cole papers
Simon Flexner papers
Victor Heiser papers
Peter Olitsky papers
Eugene Opie papers
Raymond Pearl papers
Peyton Rous papers

City Archive, Philadelphia
Alms House, Philadelphia General Hospital Daily
    Census, 1905–1922 Census Book
Coroner's Office, Interments in Potters Field, 1914–1942
Department of Public Health and Charities Minutes
Journal of the Board of Public Education
Journal of the Common Council
Journal of Select Council
Letterbook of Chief of Electrical Bureau, Department
    of Public Safety

College of Physicians, Philadelphia
William N. Bradley papers
Arthur Caradoc Morgan papers
Influenza papers

Columbia University, Butler Library, Oral History Research Office
A. R. Dochez oral history
Abraham Flexner oral history

Historical Society of Philadelphia

The Advisory Committee on Nursing, Philadelphia Hospital for Contagious Disease, Report for Feb. 1919

Council of National Defense papers

Benjamin Hoffman collection

Dr. William Taylor collection

Herbert Welsh collection

Woman's Advisory Council, Philadelphia General Hospital collection

Jefferson Medical College

Annual Report, Jefferson Hospital, year ended May 31, 1919

Library of Congress

Newton Baker papers

Ray Stannard Baker papers

George Creel papers

Joseph Tumulty papers

Woodrow Wilson papers

National Academy of Sciences

Executive Committee of Medicine 1916–1917 files

Medicine and Related Sciences, 1918 Activities Summary

Committee on Medicine and Hygiene 1918 files

Committee on Psychology/Propaganda Projects files

Influenza files

Biographical files for Oswald Avery, Rufus Cole, Alphonse Dochez, Eugene Opie, Thomas Rivers, Hans Zinsser

National Archives
Red Cross records
U.S. Army Surgeon General records
U.S. Navy Surgeon General records
U.S. Public Health Service records

National Library of Medicine
Stanhope Bayne-Jones papers and oral history
Michael Heidelberger oral history
Frederick Russell papers
Donald Van Slyke oral history
Shields Warren oral history

New York City Municipal Archives
Annual Report of the Department of Health of the City of New York for 1918
Collected Studies of the Bureau of Laboratories of the Department of Health of the City of New York for the Years 1916–1919, v. 9
Collected Reprints of Dr. William H. Park, v. 3, 1910–1920

Rhode Island Historical Society
Charles Chapin papers

Rockefeller University Archives
Paul Lewis papers
Reports to the Board of Scientific Directors

Sterling Library, Yale University
Gordon Auchincloss papers
Arthur Bliss Lane papers

Vance C. McCormick papers
Frederic Collin Walcott papers
Charles-Edward Winslow papers

Temple University Special Collections
Thomas Whitehead papers

Temple University Urban Archives
Carson College for Orphan Girls
Children's Hospital, Bainbridge
Clinton Street Boarding Home
Housing Association of Delaware Valley papers
Rabbi Joseph Krauskopf papers
Pennsylvania Hospital
Pennsylvania Society to Protect Children from Cruelty
Philadelphia Association of Day Nurseries
Whosoever Gospel Mission of Germantown
Young Women's Boarding Home Association
of Philadelphia
Report of the Hospital of the Women's Medical College
of Pennsylvania, 1919

Tennessee Historical Society
Oswald Avery papers

University of North Carolina, Chapel Hill
Milton Rosenau papers

University of Pennsylvania Archives
George Wharton Pepper papers

Secondary Sources

NEWSPAPERS

Arizona Gazette
Arizona Republican
Boston Globe
Chicago Tribune
London Times
Los Angeles Times
New Orleans Item
New Orleans Times-Picayune
New York Times
Philadelphia Inquirer
Philadelphia North American
Philadelphia Public Ledger
Providence Journal
San Francisco Chronicle
Santa Fe Monitor (Kansas)
Seattle Post-Intelligencer
Seattle Times
Washington Post
Washington Star

ARTICLES

"Advertisements in the **Laryngoscope:** Spanish
    Influenza—1918." **Laryngoscope** 106, no. 9, part 1
    (Sept. 1996): 1058.
Anastassiades, T. "Autoserotherapy in Influenza." **Grece
    Medicale,** reported in **JAMA** 72, no. 26 (June 28,
    1919): 1947.
Andrewes, C. H. "The Growth of Virus Research

1928–1978." **Postgraduate Medical Journal** 55, no. 64 (Feb. 1979): 73–77.

Ashford, Bailey K. "Preparation of Medical Officers of the Combat Division in France at the Theatre of Operations." **Military Surgeon** 44 (Feb. 1919): 111–14.

Austrian, R. "The Education of a 'Climatologist.'" **Transactions of the American Clininical Climatolology Association** 96 (1984): 1–13.

Avery, Oswald Theodore. "A Selective Medium for B. Influenzae, Oleate-hemoglobin Agar." **JAMA** 71, no. 25 (Dec. 21, 1918): 2050–52.

Avery, Oswald Theodore, Colin MacLeod, and Maclyn McCarty. "Studies on the Chemical Nature of the Substance Inducing Transformation of Pneumococcal Types." **Journal of Experimental Medicine** (1979, originally published Feb. 1, 1944): 297–326.

Baer, E. D. "Letters to Miss Sanborn: St. Vincent's Hospital Nurses' Accounts of World War I." **Journal of Nursing History** 2, no. 2 (April 1987): 17–32.

Baird, Nancy. "The 'Spanish Lady' in Kentucky." **Filson Club Quarterly** 50, no. 3: 290–302.

Barnes, Frances M. "Psychoses Complicating Influenza." **Missouri State Medical Association** 16 (1919): 115–20.

Benison, Saul. "Poliomyelitis and the Rockefeller Institute: Social Effects and Institutional Response." **Journal of the History of Medicine and Allied Sciences** 29 (1974): 74–92.

Bernstein, B. J. "The Swine Flu Immunization Program." **Medical Heritage** 1, no. 4 (July–Aug. 1985): 236–66.

Bircher, E. "Influenza Epidemic." **Correspondenz-Blatt fur Schweizer Aerzte, Basel.** 48, no. 40, (Nov. 5, 1918): 1338, quoted in **JAMA** 71, no. 24 (Dec. 7, 1918): 1946.

Bloomfield, Arthur, and G. A. Harrop Jr. "Clinical Observations on Epidemic Influenza." **Johns Hopkins Hospital Bulletin** 30 (1919).

Bogardus, F. B. "Influenza Pneumonia Treated by Blood Transfusion." **New York Medical Journal** 109, no. 18 (May 3, 1919): 765–68.

Bourne, Randolph. "The War and the Intellectuals." **The Seven Arts** 2 (June 1917): 133–46.

Brown P., J. A. Morris, and D. C. Gajdusek. "Virus of the 1918 Influenza Pandemic Era: New Evidence About Its Antigenic Character." **Science** 166, no. 901 (Oct. 3, 1969): 117–19.

Burch, M. "'I Don't Know Only What We Hear': The Soldiers' View of the 1918 Influenza Epidemic." **Indiana Medical Quarterly** 9, no. 4 (1983): 23–27.

Burnet, F. M. "The Influence of a Great Pathologist: A Tribute to Ernest Goodpasture." **Perspectives on Biology and Medicine** 16, no. 3 (spring 1973): 333–47.

————. "Portraits of Viruses: Influenza Virus A." **Intervirology** 11, no. 4 (1979): 201–14.

Capps, Joe. "Measures for the Prevention and Control of Respiratory Disease." **JAMA** 71, no. 6 (Aug. 10, 1918): 571–73.

Centers for Disease Control. **AIDS Surveillance Report** 13, no. 2 (Sept. 24, 2002).

Chan, P. K. S. et al. "Pathology of Fatal Infection Associated with Avian Influenza A H5N1 Virus."

Journal of Medical Virology 63, no. 3 (March 2001), 242–46.

Charles, A. D. "The Influenza Pandemic of 1918–1919: Columbia and South Carolina's Response." **Journal of the South Carolina Medical Association** 73, no. 8 (Aug. 1977): 367–70.

Chesney, Alan. "Oswald Theodore Avery." **Journal of Pathology and Bacteriology** 76, no. 2 (1956): 451–60.

Christian, Henry. "Incorrectness of Diagnosis of Death from Influenza." **JAMA** 71 (1918).

Claude, Henri, M.D. "Nervous and Mental Disturbances Following Influenza." Quoted in **JAMA** 72, no. 22 (May 31, 1919): 1634.

Clough, Paul. "Phagocytosis and Agglutination in the Serum of Acute Lobar Pneumonia." **Johns Hopkins Hospital Bulletin** 30 (1919): 167–70.

Cole, Rufus. "Pneumonia as a Public Health Problem." **Kentucky Medical Journal** 16 (1918): 563–65.

———. "Prevention of Pneumonia." **JAMA** 71, no. 8 (August 24, 1918): 634–36.

Cole, Rufus, et al. "Acute Lobar Pneumonia Prevention and Serum Treatment." Monograph of the Rockefeller Institute for Medical Research 7 (Oct. 1917).

Condon, Bradly J., and Tapen Sinha. "Who Is That Masked Person: The Use of Face Masks on Mexico City Public Transportation During the Influenza A (H1N1) Outbreak (July 4, 2009)." **Health Policy** 95, no. 1 (Apr. 2010): 50–56. doi: 10.1016/j.healthpol.2009.11.009. Epub Dec. 4, 2009. https://www.ncbi.nlm.nih.gov/pubmed/19962777.

Cowie, D. M., and P. W. Beaven. "Nonspecific Protein

Therapy in Influenzal Pneumonia." **JAMA** 72, no. 16 (April 19, 1919).

Cumberland, W. H. "Epidemic! Iowa Battles the Spanish Influenza." **Palimpsest** 62, no. 1 (1981): 26–32.

Davenport, F. M. "The Search for the Ideal Influenza Vaccine." **Postgraduate Medical Journal** 55, no. 640 (Feb. 1979): 78–86.

Davenport, R. M., G. N. Meiklejohn, and E. H. Lennette. "Origins and Development of the Commission on Influenza." **Archives of Environmental Health** 21, no. 3 (Sept. 1970): 267–72.

De Grazia, Victoria. "The Selling of America, Bush Style." **New York Times,** Aug. 25, 2002.

Dingle, J. H., and A. D. Langmuir. "Epidemiology of Acute Respiratory Disease in Military Recruits." **American Review of Respiratory Disease** 97, no. 6 (June 1968): 1–65.

Doty, Permillia. "A Retrospect on the Influenza Epidemic." **Public Health Nurse,** 1919.

Douglas, R. J. "Prophylaxis and Treatment of Influenza." In **Scientific American's Medicine,** edited by E. Rubinstein and D. Federman. New York: Scientific American Inc., 1994.

Dowdle, W. R., and M. A. Hattwick. "Swine Influenza Virus Infections in Humans." **Journal of Infectious Disease** 136, supp. S (Dec. 1977): 386–89.

Draggoti, G. "Nervous Manifestations of Influenza." **Policlinico** 26, no. 6 (Feb. 8, 1919) 161, quoted in **JAMA** 72, no. 15 (April 12, 1919): 1105.

Dubos, René. "Oswald Theodore Avery, 1877–1955." **Biographical Memoirs of Fellows of the Royal Society** 2 (1956): 35–48.

Dunn, F. L. "Pandemic Influenza in 1957. Review of International Spread of New Asian Strain." **JAMA** 166, no. 10 (1958): 1140–48.

Durand, M. L. et al. "Acute Bacterial Meningitis in Adults: A Review of 493 Episodes." **New England Journal of Medicine** 328, no. 1 (Jan. 1993) 21–28.

Eaton, Ernest. "A Tribute to Royal Copeland." **Journal of the Institute of Homeopathy** 31, no. 9: 555–58.

Ebert, R. G. "Comments on the Army Venereal Problem." **Military Surgeon** 42 (July–Dec. 1918), 19–20.

Emerson, G. M. "The 'Spanish Lady' in Alabama." **Alabama Journal of Medical Science** 23, no. 2 (April 1986): 217–21.

English, F. "Princeton Plagues: The Epidemics of 1832, 1880 and 1918–19." **Princeton History** 5 (1986): 18–26.

Ensley, P. C. "Indiana and the Influenza Pandemic of 1918." **Indiana Medical History** 9, no. 4 (1983): 3–15.

"Epidemic Influenza and the United States Public Health Service." **Public Health Reports** 91, no. 4 (July–Aug. 1976): 378–80.

Feery, B. "1919 Influenza in Australia." **New England Journal of Medicine** 295, no. 9 (Aug. 26, 1976): 512.

Fell, Egbert. "Postinfluenzal Psychoses." **JAMA** 72, no. 23 (June 7, 1919): 1658–59.

Fennel, E. A. "Prophylactic Inoculation Against Pneumonia." **JAMA** 71, no. 26, (Dec. 28, 1918): 2115–18.

Fincher, Jack. "America's Rendezvous with the Deadly Lady." **Smithsonian Magazine,** Jan. 1989: 131.

Finland, M. "Excursions into Epidemiology: Selected Studies During the Past Four Decades at Boston City Hospital." **Journal of Infectious Disease** 128, no. 1 (July 1973): 76–124.

Flexner, Simon. "Paul Adin Lewis." **Science** 52 (Aug. 9, 1929): 133–34.

———. "The Present Status of the Serum Therapy of Epidemic Cerebro-spinal Meningitis." **JAMA** 53 (1909) 53: 1443–46.

Flexner, Simon, and Paul Lewis. "Transmission of Poliomyelitis to Monkeys: A Further Note." **JAMA** 53 (1909): 1913.

Friedlander et al. "The Epidemic of Influenza at Camp Sherman." **JAMA** 71, no. 20 (Nov. 16, 1918): 1650–71.

Frost, W. H. "Statistics of Influenza Morbidity." **Public Health Reports** 7 (March 12, 1920): 584–97.

Galishoff, S. "Newark and the Great Influenza Pandemic of 1918." **Bulletin of the History of Medicine** 43, no. 3 (May–June 1969): 246–58.

Gear, J. H. "The History of Virology in South Africa." **South African Medical Journal** (Oct. 11, 1986, suppl): 7–10.

Glezen, W. P. "Emerging Infections: Pandemic Influenza." **Epidemiology Review** 18, no. 1 (1996): 64–76.

Goodpasture, Ernest W. "Pathology of Pneumonia Following Influenza." **U.S. Naval Bulletin** 13, no. 3 (1919).

Grist, N. R. "Pandemic Influenza 1918." **British Medical Journal** 2, no. 6205 (Dec. 22–29, 1979): 1632–33.

Guerra, F. "The Earliest American Epidemic: The Influenza of 1493." **Social Science History** 12, no. 3 (1988): 305–25.

Halpern, Sue. "Evangelists for Kids." **New York Review of Books,** May 29, 2003.

Hamaker, Gene. "Influenza 1918." **Buffalo County, Nebraska, Historical Society** 7, no. 4.

Hamilton, D. "Unanswered Questions of the Spanish Flu Pandemic." **Bulletin of the American Association of the History of Nursing** 34 (spring 1992): 6–7.

Harris, John. "Influenza Occuring in Pregnant Women: A Statistical Study of 130 Cases." **JAMA** 72, no. 14 (April 5, 1919): 978–80.

Harrop, George A. "The Behavior of the Blood Toward Oxygen in Influenzal Infections." **Johns Hopkins Hospital Bulletin** 30 (1919): 335.

Hayden, Frederick G., and Peter Palese. "Influenza Virus." In **Clinical Virology,** edited by Douglas Richman, Richard Whitley, and Frederick Hayden, 911–30. New York: Churchill Livingstone, 1997.

Heagerty, J. J. "Influenza and Vaccination." **Canadian Medical Association Journal** 145, no. 5 (Sept. 1991, originally published 1919): 481–82.

Herda, P. S. "The 1918 Influenza Pandemic in Fiji, Tonga and the Samoas." In **New Countries and Old Medicine: Proceedings of an International Conference on the History of Medicine and Health,** edited by L. Bryder and D. A. Dow, 46–53. Auckland, New Zealand: Pyramid Press, 1995.

Hewer, C. L. "1918 Influenza Epidemic." **British Medical Journal** 1, no. 6157 (Jan. 1979): 199.

Hildreth, M. L. "The Influenza Epidemic of 1918–1919 in France: Contemporary Concepts of Aetiology, Therapy, and Prevention." **Social History of Medicine** 4, no. 2 (Aug. 1991): 277–94.

Holladay, A. J. "The Thucydides Syndrome: Another View." **New England Journal of Medicine** 315, no. 18 (Oct. 30, 1986): 1170–73.

Holland, J. J. "The Origin and Evolution of Chicago Viruses." In **Microbiology and Microbial Infections,** v. 1, **Virology,** edited by Brian W. J. Mahy and Leslie Collier, 10–20. New York: Oxford University Press, 1998.

Hope-Simpson, R. E. "Andrewes Versus Influenza: Discussion Paper." **Journal of the Royal Society of Medicine** 79, no. 7 (July 1986): 407–11.

———. "Recognition of Historic Influenza Epidemics from Parish Burial Records: A Test of Prediction from a New Hypothesis of Influenzal Epidemiology." **Journal of Hygiene** 91, no. 2 (Oct. 1983): 293–308.

"How to Fight Spanish Influenza." **Literary Digest** 59 (Oct. 12, 1918).

Hyslop, A. "Old Ways, New Means: Fighting Spanish Influenza in Australia, 1918–1919." In **New Countries and Old Medicine: Proceedings of an International Conference on the History of Medicine and Health,** edited by L. Bryder and D. A. Dow, 54–60. Auckland, New Zealand: Pyramid Press, 1995.

Irwin, R. T. "1918 Influenza in Morris County." **New Jersey Historical Community Newsletter** (March 1981): 3.

Jackson, G. G. "Nonbacterial Pneumonias:

Contributions of Maxwell Finland Revisited." **Journal of Infectious Disease** 125, supp. (March 1972): 47–57.

Johnson, Niall, and Juergen Mueller. "Updating the Accounts: Global Mortality of the 1918–1920 'Spanish' Influenza Pandemic." **Bulletin of the History of Medicine** 76 (spring 2002): 105–15.

Kass, A. M. "Infectious Diseases at the Boston City Hospital: The First 60 Years." **Clinical Infectious Disease** 17, no. 2 (Aug. 1993): 276–82.

Katz, R. S. "Influenza 1918–1919: A Further Study in Mortality." **Bulletin of the History of Medicine** 51, no. 4 (winter 1977): 617–19.

————. "Influenza 1918–1919: A Study in Mortality." **Bulletin of the History of Medicine** 48, no. 3 (fall 1974): 416–22.

Katzenellenbogen, J. M. "The 1918 Influenza Epidemic in Mamre." **South African Medical Journal** 74, no. 7 (Oct. 1, 1988), 362–64.

Keating, Peter. "Vaccine Therapy and the Problem of Opsonins." **Journal of the History of Medicine** 43 (1988), 275–96.

Keegan, J. J. "The Prevailing Epidemic of Influenza." **JAMA** 71 (Sept. 28, 1918), 1051–52.

Keeton, Riet, and A. Beulah Cusman. "The Influenza Epidemic in Chicago." **JAMA** 71, no. 24 (Dec. 14, 1918): 2000–2001.

Kerson, T. S. "Sixty Years Ago: Hospital Social Work in 1918." **Social Work Health Care** 4, no. 3 (spring 1979): 331–43.

Kilbourne, E. D., M.D. "A History of Influenza Virology." In **Microbe Hunters—Then and Now,** edited by H. Koprowski and M. B. Oldstone, 187–204. Bloomington, Ill.: Medi-Ed Press, 1996.

———. "In Pursuit of Influenza: Fort Monmouth to Valhalla (and Back)." **Bioessays** 19, no. 7 (July 1997): 641–50.

———. "Pandora's Box and the History of the Respiratory Viruses: A Case Study of Serendipity in Research." **History of the Philosophy of Life Sciences** 14, no. 2 (1992): 299–308.

King, John. "The Progress of Medical Reform." **Western Medical Reformer** 6, no. 1846: 79–82.

Kirkpatrick, G. W. "Influenza 1918: A Maine Perspective." **Maine Historical Society Quarterly** 25, no. 3 (1986): 162–77.

Knight, C. P. "The Activities of the USPHS in Extra-Cantonment Zones, With Special Reference to the Venereal Disease Problem." **Military Surgeon** 44 (Jan. 1919): 41–43.

Knoll, K. "When the Plague Hit Spokane." **Pacific Northwest Quarterly** 33, no. 1 (1989): 1–7.

Koen, J. S. "A Practical Method for Field Diagnosis of Swine Diseases." **Journal of Veterinary Medicine** 14 (1919): 468–70.

Kolmer, John, M.D., "Paper Given at the Philadelphia County Medical Society Meeting, Oct. 23, 1918." **Pennsylvania Medical Journal,** Dec. 1918.

Krumwiede, Charles, Jr., and Eugenia Valentine. "Determination of the Type of Pneumococcus in the Sputum of Lobar Pneumonia, A Rapid Simple Method." **JAMA** 70 (Feb. 23, 1918): 513–14.

Kyes, Preston. "The Treatment of Lobar Pneumonia

with an Anti-pneumococcus Serum." **Journal of Medical Research** 38 (1918): 495–98.

Lachman, E. The German Influenza of 1918–19: Personal Recollections and Review of the German Medical Literature of that Period." **Journal of the Oklahoma State Medical Association** 69, no. 12 (Dec. 1976): 517–20.

Lamber, Arthur. "Medicine: A Determining Factor in War." **JAMA** 21, no. 24 (June 14, 1919): 1713.

Langmuir, A. D. "The Territory of Epidemiology: Pentimento." **Journal of Infectious Disease** 155, no. 3 (March 1987): 349–58.

Langmuir, A. D., et al. "The Thucydides Syndrome: A New Hypothesis for the Cause of the Plague of Athens." **New England Journal of Medicine** 313, no. 16 (Oct. 17, 1985): 1027–30.

Lautaret, R. L. "Alaska's Greatest Disaster: The 1918 Spanish Influenza Epidemic." **Alaska Journal** 16 (1986): 238–43.

Lehman, Joseph. "Clinical Notes on the Recent Epidemic of Influenza." **Monthly Bulletin of the Department of Public Health and Charities** (Philadelphia), March 1919.

Leonard, Stephen, "The 1918 Influenza Epidemic in Denver and Colorado." **Essays and Monographs in Colorado History,** essays no. 9, 1989.

Levin, M. L. "An Historical Account of 'The Influence.'" **Maryland State Medical Journal** 27, no. 5 (May 1978): 58–62.

Lewis, Paul A., and Richard E. Shope. "Swine Influenza II. Hemophilic Bacillus from the

Respiratory Tract of Infected Swine." **Journal of Infectious Disease** 54, no. 3 (1931): 361–372.

Lichtenstein, A. M. "The Influenza Epidemic in Cumberland, Md." **Johns Hopkins Nurses Alumni Magazine** 17, no. 4 (Nov. 1918): 224–27.

Lyons, D., and G. Murphy. "Influenza Causing Sunspots?" **Nature** 344, no. 6261 (March 1, 1990): 10.

MacCallum, William G. "Pathological Anatomy of Pneumonia Following Influenza." **Johns Hopkins Hospital Reports** 20 fasciculus II (1921): 149–51.

————. "The Pathology of Pneumonia in the U.S. Army Camps During the Winter of 1917–18." **Monographs of the Rockefeller Institute for Medical Research** (10), 1919.

McCann, T. A. "Homeopathy and Influenza." **Journal of the American Institute for Homeopathy,** May 1921.

McCord, C. P. "The Purple Death: Some Things Remembered About the Influenza Epidemic of 1918 at One Army Camp." **Journal of Occupational Medicine** 8, no. 11 (Nov. 1966): 593–98.

McCullers, J. A., and K. C. Bartmess. "Role of Neuraminidase in Lethal Synergism Between Influenza Virus and Streptococcus Pneumoniae." **Journal of Infectious Diseases** 187, no. 6 (March 15, 2003): 1000–1009.

McCullum, C. "Diseases and Dirt: Social Dimensions of Influenza, Cholera, and Syphilis." **Pharos** 55, no. 1 (winter 1992): 22–29.

Macdiarmid, D. "Influenza 1918." **New Zealand Medical Journal** 97, no. 747 (Jan. 1984): 23.

McGinnis, J. D. "Carlill v. Carbolic Smoke Ball Company: Influenza, Quackery, and the Unilateral Contract." **Bulletin of Canadian History of Medicine** 5, no. 2 (winter 1988): 121–41.

MacLachlan, W. W. G., and W. J. Fetter. "Citrated Blood in Treatment of Pneumonia Following Influenza." **JAMA** 71, no. 25 (Dec. 21, 1918): 2053–54.

MacLeod, Colin. "Theodore Avery, 1877–1955." **Journal of General Microbiology** 17 (1957): 539–49.

McMichael, A. J. et al. "Declining T-cell Immunity to Influenza, 1977–82." **Lancet** 2, no. 8353 (Oct. 1, 1983): 762–64.

MacNeal, W. J. "The Influenza Epidemic of 1918 in the AEF in France and England." **Archives of Internal Medicine** 23 (1919).

McQueen, H. "Spanish 'Flu'—1919: Political, Medical and Social Aspects." **Medical Journal of Australia** 1, no. 18 (May 3, 1975): 565–70.

Maxwell, William. "A Time to Mourn." **Pen America** 2, no. 4 (2002).

Mayer, J. L., and D. S. Beardsley. "Varicella-associated Thrombocytopenia: Autoantibodies Against Platelet Surface Glycoprotein V." **Pediatric Research** 40 (1996): 615–19.

Meiklejohn, G. N. "History of the Commission on Influenza." **Social History of Medicine** 7, no. 1 (April 1994): 59–87.

Meltzer, Martin, Nancy Cox, and Keiji Fukuda. "Modeling the Economic Impact of Pandemic Influenza in the United States: Implications for

Setting Priorities for Intervention." In **Emerging Infectious Diseases,** CDC, 1999, www.cdc.gov/ncidod/ eid/vol5no5/melt back.htm.

Mencken, H. L. "Thomas Henry Huxley 1825–1925." **Baltimore Evening Sun,** May 4, 1925.

Mills, I. D. "The 1918–19 Influenza Pandemic—The Indian Experience." **Indian Economic and Social History Review** 23 (1986): 1–36.

Morens, D. M., and R. J. Littman. "'Thucydides Syndrome' Reconsidered: New Thoughts on the 'Plague of Athens.'" **American Journal of Epidemiology** 140, no. 7 (Oct. 1, 1994): 621–28, discussion 629–31.

Morton, G. "The Pandemic Influenza of 1918." **Canadian Nurse** 69, no. 12 (Dec. 1973): 25–27.

Mullen, P. C., and M. L. Nelson. "Montanans and 'The Most Peculiar Disease': The Influenza Epidemic and Public Health, 1918–1919." **Montana** 37, no. 2 (1987): 50–61.

Murphy, Brian R., and Robert G. Webster. "Orthomyxoviruses." In **Fields' Virology,** third edition, Bernard Fields, editor in chief. Philadelphia: Lippincott-Raven, 1996.

Nicolle, Charles, and Charles LeBailly. **"Recherches experimentales sur la grippe."** Annales de l'Institut Pasteur 33 (1919): 395–402.

Nutton, Vivian. "Humoralism." In **Companion Encyclopedia to the History of Medicine,** edited by Bynum and Porter. London: Routledge, 1993.

Nuzum, J. W. et al. "1918 Pandemic Influenza and Pneumonia in a Large Civil Hospital." **Illinois Medical Journal** 150, no. 6 (Dec. 1976): 612–16.

Osler, William. "The Inner History of Johns Hopkins Hospital." Edited by D. Bates and E. Bensley. **Johns Hopkins Medical Journal** 125 (1969): 184–94.

"Outbreak of Influenza, Madagascar, July–August 2002." **Weekly Epidemiological Report 77**, no. 46 (2002): 381–87.

Oxford, J. S. "The So-Called Great Spanish Influenza Pandemic of 1918 May Have Originated in France in 1916." In **The Origin and Control of Pandemic Influenza**, edited by W. Laver and R. Webster, Philosophical Transactions of the Royal Society 356, no. 1416 (Dec. 2001).

Palmer, E., and G. W. Rice. "A Japanese Physician's Response to Pandemic Influenza: Ijiro Gomibuchi and the 'Spanish Flu' in Yaita-Cho, 1918–1919." **Bulletin of the History of Medicine** 66, no. 4 (winter 1992): 560–77.

Pandit, C. G. "Communicable Diseases in Twentieth-Century India." **American Journal of Tropical Medicine and Hygiene** 19, no. 3 (May 1970): 375–82.

Pankhurst, R. "The Great Ethiopian Influenza (Ye Hedar Beshita) Epidemic of 1918." **Ethiopian Medical Journal** 27, no. 4 (Oct. 1989): 235–42.

————. "A Historical Note on Influenza in Ethiopia." **Medical History** 21, no. 2 (April 1977): 195–200.

Park, William H. "Anti-influenza Vaccine as Prophylactic." **New York Medical Journal** 108, no. 15 (Oct. 12, 1918).

Park, William H. et al. "Introduction." **Journal of Immunology** 6, Jan. 1921: 2–8.

Patterson, K. D., and G. F. Pyle. "The Diffusion

of Influenza in Sub-Saharan Africa During the 1918–1919 Pandemic." **Social Science and Medicine** 17, no. 17 (1983): 1299–1307.

———. "The Geography and Mortality of the 1918 Influenza Pandemic." **Bulletin of the History of Medicine** 65, no. 1 (spring 1991): 4–21.

Pennisi, E. "First Genes Isolated from the Deadly 1918 Flu Virus." **Science** 275, no. 5307 (March 21, 1997): 1739.

Persico, Joe. "The Great Spanish Flu Epidemic of 1918." **American Heritage** 27 (June 1976): 28–31, 80–85.

Polson, A. "Purification and Aggregation of Influenza Virus by Precipitation with Polyethylene Glycol." **Prep Biochemistry** 23, nos. 1–2 (Feb.–May 1993, originally published 1974): 207–25.

Porter, Katherine Anne. "Pale Horse, Pale Rider." **The Collected Stories of Katherine Anne Porter.** New York: Harcourt, 1965, 304–317.

Pusey, William Allen, M.D. "Handling of the Venereal Problem in the U.S. Army in Present Crisis." **JAMA** 71, no. 13 (Sept. 28, 1918): 1017–19.

Raff, M. J., P. A. Barnwell, and J. C. Melo. "Swine Influenza: History and Recommendations for Vaccination." **Journal of the Kentucky Medical Association** 74, no. 11 (Nov. 1976): 543–48.

Ranger, T. "The Influenza Pandemic in Southern Rhodesia: a Crisis of Comprehension." In **Imperial Medicine and Indigenous Societies,** edited by D. Arnold, 172–88. Manchester, England, and New York: Manchester University Press, 1988.

Ravenholt, R. T., and W. H. Foege. "1918 Influenza,

Encephalitis Lethargica, Parkinsonism." **Lancet** 2, no. 8303 (Oct. 16, 1982): 860–64.

Redden, W. R., and L. W. McQuire. "The Use of Convalescent Human Serum in Influenza Pneumonia." **JAMA** 71, no. 16 (Oct. 19, 1918): 1311–12.

"Review of **Offensive Fighting** by Major Donald McRae." **Military Surgeon** 43 (Feb. 1919).

Rice, G. "Christchurch in the 1918 Influenza Epidemic: A Preliminary Study." **New Zealand Journal of History** 13 (1979): 109–37.

Richmond, Phyllis Allen. "American Attitudes Toward the Germ Theory of Disease, 1860–1880." **Journal of the History of Medicine and Allied Sciences** 9 (1954): 428–54.

———. "Some Variant Theories in Opposition to the Germ Theory of Disease." **Journal of the History of Medicine and Allied Sciences** 9 (1954): 290–303.

Rivers, Thomas. "The Biological and the Serological Reactions of Influenza Bacilli Producing Meningitis." **Journal of Experimental Medicine** 34, no. 5 (Nov. 1, 1921): 477–94.

———. "Influenzal Meningitis." **American Journal of Diseases of Children** 24 (Aug. 1922): 102–24.

Rivers, Thomas, and Stanhope Bayne-Jones. "Influenza-like Bacilli Isolated from Cats." **Journal of Experimental Medicine** 37, no. 2 (Feb. 1, 1923): 131–38.

Roberts, R. S. "A Consideration of the Nature of the English Sweating Sickness." **Medical History** 9, no. 4 (Oct. 1965): 385–89.

Robinson, K. R. "The Role of Nursing in the Influenza

Epidemic of 1918–1919." **Nursing Forum** 25, no. 2 (1990): 19–26.

Rockafellar, N. "'In Gauze We Trust': Public Health and Spanish Influenza on the Home Front, Seattle, 1918–1919." **Pacific Northwest Quarterly** 77, no. 3 (1986): 104–13.

Rogers, F. B. "The Influenza Pandemic of 1918–1919 in the Perspective of a Half Century." **American Journal of Public Health and Nations Health** 58, no. 12 (Dec. 1968): 2192–94.

Rosenberg, Charles. "The Therapeutic Revolution." In **Explaining Epidemics and Other Studies in the History of Medicine.** Cambridge, England, and New York: Cambridge University Press, 1992.

———. "Toward an Ecology of Knowledge." In **The Organization of Knowledge in Modern America, 1860–1920.** Edited by A. Oleson and J. Voss. Baltimore: Johns Hopkins University Press, 1979.

Rosenberg, K. D. "Swine Flu: Play It Again, Uncle Sam." **Health/PAC Bulletin** 73 (Nov.–Dec. 1976): 1–6, 10–20.

Ross, Katherine. "Battling the Flu." **American Red Cross Magazine** (Jan. 1919): 11–15.

Sage, M. W. "Pittsburgh Plague—1918: An Oral History." **Home Health Nurse** 13, no. 1 (Jan.–Feb. 1995): 49–54.

Salk, J. "The Restless Spirit of Thomas Francis, Jr., Still Lives: The Unsolved Problems of Recurrent Influenza Epidemics." **Archives of Environmental Health** 21, no. 3 (Sept. 1970): 273–75.

Sartwell, P. E. "The Contributions of Wade Hampton

Frost." **American Journal of Epidemiology** 104, no. 4 (Oct. 1976): 386–91.

Sattenspiel, L., and D. A. Herring. "Structured Epidemic Models and the Spread of Influenza in the Central Canadian Subarctic." **Human Biology** 70, no. 1 (Feb. 1998): 91–115.

Scott, K. A. "Plague on the Homefront: Arkansas and the Great Influenza Epidemic of 1918." **Arkansas Historical Quarterly** 47, no.4 (1988): 311–44.

Shope, Richard E. "Influenza: History, Epidemiology, and Speculation." **Public Health Reports** 73, no. 165 (1958).

———. "Swine Influenza I. Experimental Transmission and Pathology." **Journal of Infectious Disease** 54, no. 3 (1931): 349–60.

———. "Swine Influenza III. Filtration Experiments and Etiology." **Journal of Infectious Disease** 54, no. 3 (1931): 373–390.

Shortt, S. E. D. "Physicians, Science, and Status: Issues in the Professionalization of Anglo-American Medicine in the 19th Century." **Medical History** 27 (1983): 53–68.

Shryock, Richard. "Women in American Medicine." **Journal of the American Medical Women's Association** 5 (Sept. 1950): 371.

Simon, Harvey, and Martin Swartz. "Pulmonary Infections." In **Scientific American's Medicine,** edited by Edward Rubinstein and Daniel Feldman, chapter 20. New York: Scientific American, 1994.

Smith, F. B. "The Russian Influenza in the United Kingdom, 1889–1894." **Social History of Medicine** 8, no. 1 (April 1995): 55–73.

Snape, W. J., and E. L. Wolfe. "Influenza Epidemic. Popular Reaction in Camden 1918–1919." **New Jersey Medicine** 84, no. 3 (March 1987): 173–76.

Soper, George, M.D. "Epidemic After Wars." **JAMA** 72, no. 14 (April 5, 1919): 988–90.

———. "The Influenza-Pneumonia Pandemic in the American Army Camps, September and October 1918." **Science,** Nov. 8, 1918.

Springer, J. K. "1918 Flu Epidemic in Hartford, Connecticut." **Connecticut Medicine** 55, no. 1 (Jan. 1991): 43–47.

Starr, Isaac. "Influenza in 1918: Recollections of the Epidemic in Philadelphia." **Annals of Internal Medicine** 85 (1976): 516–18.

Stephenson, J. "Flu on Ice." **JAMA** 279, no. 9 (March 4, 1998): 644.

Strauss, Ellen G., James H. Strauss, and Arnold J. Levine. "Viral Evolution." In **Fields' Virology,** Bernard Fields, editor in chief. Philadelphia: Lippincott-Raven, 1996.

Stuart-Harris, C. H. "Pandemic Influenza: An Unresolved Problem in Prevention." **Journal of Infectious Disease** 122, no. 1 (July–Aug. 1970): 108–15.

Sturdy, Steve. "War as Experiment: Physiology, Innovation and Administration in Britain, 1914–1918: The Case of Chemical Warfare." In **War, Medicine and Modernity,** edited by Roger Cooter, Mark Harrison, and Steve Sturdy. Stroud: Sutton, 1998.

"Sure Cures for Influenza." **Public Health Reports** 91, no. 4 (July–Aug. 1976): 378–80.

Symmers, Douglas, M.D. "Pathologic Similarity Between Pneumonia of Bubonic Plague and of Pandemic Influenza." **JAMA** 71, no. 18 (Nov. 2, 1918): 1482–83.

Taksa, Lucy. "The Masked Disease: Oral History, Memory, and the Influenza Pandemic." In **Memory and History in Twentieth Century Australia,** edited by Kate Darian-Smith and Paula Hamilton. Melbourne, Australia: Oxford Press, 1994.

Taubenberger, J. K. "Seeking the 1918 Spanish Influenza Virus." **ASM News** 65, no. 7, (July 1999).

Taubenberger, J. K. et al. "Initial Genetic Characterization of the 1918 'Spanish' Influenza Virus." **Science** 275, no. 5307 (March 21, 1997): 1793–96.

Terris, Milton. "Hermann Biggs' Contribution to the Modern Concept of the Health Center." **Bulletin of the History of Medicine** 20 (Oct. 1946): 387–412.

Thayer, W. S. "Discussion of Influenza," **Proceedings of the Royal Society of Medicine** 12, part 1 (Nov. 13, 1918).

Thomson, J. B. "The 1918 Influenza Epidemic in Nashville." **Journal of the Tennessee Medical Association** 71, no. 4 (April 1978): 261–70.

Tomes, Nancy. "American Attitudes Toward the Germ Theory of Disease: The Richmond Thesis Revisited." **Journal of the History of Medicine and Allied Sciences** 52, no. 1 (Jan. 1997): 17–50.

Tomes, Nancy, and Warner John Harley. "Introduction—Rethinking the Reception of the Germ Theory of Disease: Comparative Perspectives."

Journal of the History of Medicine and Allied Sciences 52, no. 1 (Jan. 1997): 7–16.

Tomkins, S. M. "The Failure of Expertise: Public Health Policy in Britain During the 1918–19 Influenza Epidemic." **Social History of Medicine** 5, no. 3 (Dec. 1992): 435–54.

Turner, R. Steven et al. "The Growth of Professorial Research in Prussia—1818–1848, Causes and Context." **Historical Studies in the Physical Sciences** 3 (1972): 137–182.

Van Helvoort, T. "A Bacteriological Paradigm in Influenza Research in the First Half of the Twentieth Century." **History and Philosophy of the Life Sciences** 15, no. 1 (1993): 3–21.

Viboud, Cécile, et al. "Multinational Impact of the 1968 Hong Kong Influenza Pandemic: Evidence for a Smoldering Pandemic." **Journal of Infectious Diseases** 192, no. 2 (July 15, 2005): 233–248.

Wallack, G. "The Waterbury Influenza Epidemic of 1918/1919." **Connecticut Medicine** 41, no. 6 (June 1977): 349–51.

Walters, J. H. "Influenza 1918: The Contemporary Perspective." **Bulletin of the New York Academy of Medicine** 54, no. 9 (Oct. 1978): 855–64.

Ware, Lorraine, and Michael Matthay. "The Acute Respiratory Distress Syndrome." **New England Journal of Medicine** 342, no. 18 (May 4, 2000): 1334–49.

Warner, John Harley. "The Fall and Rise of Professional Mystery." In **The Laboratory Revolution in Medicine,** edited by Andrew Cunningham and

Perry Williams. Cambridge, England: Cambridge University Press, 1992.

"War Reports from the Influenza Front." **Literary Digest** 60 (Feb. 22, 1919).

Wasserman, I. M. "The Impact of Epidemic, War, Prohibition and Media on Suicide: United States, 1910–1920." **Suicide and Life Threatening Behavior** 22, no. 2 (summer 1992): 240–54.

Waters, Charles, and Bloomfield, Al. "The Correlation of X-ray Findings and Physical Signs in the Chest in Uncomplicated Influenza." **Johns Hopkins Hospital Bulletin** 30 (1919): 268–70.

Webb, G. F. "A Silent Bomb: The Risk of Anthrax as Weapon of Mass Destruction." **Proceedings of the National Academy of Sciences** 100 (2003): 4355–61.

Wein, L. M., D. L. Craft, and E. H. Kaplan. "Emergency Response to an Anthrax Attack." **Proceedings of the National Academy of Sciences** 100 (2003): 4346–51.

Weinstein, Edward. "Woodrow Wilson's Neurological Illness." **Journal of American History** 57 (1970–71): 324–51.

Weinstein, L. "Influenza—1918, A Revisit?" **New England Journal of Medicine** 294, no. 19 (May 1976): 1058–60.

Wetmore, F. H. "Treatment of Influenza." **Canadian Medical Association Journal** 145, no. 5 (Sept. 1991, originally published 1919): 482–85.

Whipple, George. "Current Comment, Vaccines in Influenza." **JAMA** 71, no. 16 (Oct. 19, 1918).

White, K. A. "Pittsburgh in the Great Epidemic of 1918." **West Pennsylvania History Magazine** 68, no. 3 (1985): 221–42.

"WHO Influenza Surveillance." **Weekly Epidemiological Record** 71, no. 47 (Nov. 22, 1996): 353–57.

Wilkinson, L., and A. P. Waterson. "The Development of the Virus Concept as Reflected in Corpora of Studies on Individual Pathogens, 2: The Agent of Fowl Plague—A Model Virus." **Medical History** 19, no. 1 (Jan. 1975): 52–72.

"Will the Flu Return?" **Literary Digest** (Oct. 11, 1919).

Wilton, P. "Spanish Flu Outdid WWI in Number of Lives Claimed." **Canadian Medical Association Journal** 148, no. 11 (June 1, 1993): 2036–37.

Winslow, Charles-Edward. "The Untilled Fields of Public Health." **Science** 51, (Jan. 9, 1920): 30.

Wise, John C. "The Medical Reserve Corps of the U.S. Navy." **Military Surgeon** 43 (July 1918): 68.

Wooley, Paul. "Epidemic of Influenza at Camp Devens, Mass." **Journal of Laboratory and Clinical Medicine** 4 (1919).

Wright, P., et al. "Maternal Influenza, Obstetric Complications, and Schizophrenia." **American Journal of Psychiatry** 152, no. 12 (Dec. 1995): 1714–20.

Yankauer, A. "Influenza: Some Swinish Reflections." **American Journal of Public Health** 66, no. 9 (Sept. 1976): 839–41.

BOOKS AND PAMPHLETS

Ackerknecht, Erwin. **Medicine at the Paris Hospital, 1794–1848.** Baltimore: Johns Hopkins University Press, 1967.

American Red Cross. "A History of Helping Others." 1989.

Andrewes, C. H. **Biological Memoirs: Richard E. Shope.** Washington, D.C.: National Academy of Sciences Press, 1979.

Baruch, Bernard. **Baruch: The Public Years.** New York: Holt Rinehart, 1960.

Benison, Saul. **Tom Rivers: Reflections on a Life in Medicine and Science: An Oral History Memoir.** Cambridge, Mass.: MIT Press, 1967.

Berliner, Howard. **A System of Scientific Medicine: Philanthropic Foundations in the Flexner Era.** New York: Tavistock, 1985.

Beveridge, W. I. B. **influenza: The Last Great Plague: An Unfinished Story of Discovery.** New York: Prodist, 1977.

Bledstein, Burton J. **The Culture of Professionalism: The Middle Class and the Development of Higher Education in America.** New York: Norton, 1976.

Bliss, Michael. **William Osler: A Life in Medicine.** Oxford and New York: Oxford University Press, 1999.

Bonner, Thomas. **American Doctors and German Universities: A Chapter in International Intellectual Relations, 1870–1914.** Lincoln: University of Nebraska Press, 1963.

————. **The Kansas Doctor.** Lawrence: University of Kansas Press, 1959.

Brock, Thomas. **Robert Koch: A Life in Medicine.** Madison, Wisc.: Science Tech Publishers, 1988.

Brown, E. Richard. **Rockefeller's Medicine Men.** Berkeley: University of California, 1979.

Brown, Ezra, ed. **This Fabulous Century: The Roaring Twenties 1920–1930.** Alexandria, Va.: Time-Life Books, 1985.

Bulloch, W. **The History of Bacteriology.** London: Oxford University Press, 1938.

Burnet, F. M., and Ellen Clark. **Influenza: A Survey of the Last Fifty Years.** Melbourne: Macmillan, 1942.

Cannon, Walter. **The Way of an Investigator.** New York: Norton, 1945.

Cassedy, James. **Charles V. Chapin and the Public Health Movement.** Cambridge, Mass.: Harvard University Press, 1962.

————. **Medicine in America: A Short History.** Baltimore, Md.: Johns Hopkins University Press, 1991.

Chase, Marilyn. **The Barbary Plague.** New York: Random House, 2003.

Chesney, Alan. **The Johns Hopkins Hospital and the Johns Hopkins University School of Medicine.** Baltimore, Md.: Johns Hopkins University Press, 1943.

Clark, P. F. **Pioneer Microbiologists in America.** Madison: University of Wisconsin Press, 1961.

Cliff, A. D., J. K. Ord, and P. Haggett. **Spatial Aspects of Influenza Epidemics.** London: Pion Ltd., 1986.

Coleman, William, and Frederic Holmes, eds. **The Investigative Enterprise: Experimental Physiology in Nineteenth Century Medicine.** Berkeley: University of California Press, 1988.

Collier, R. **The Plague of the Spanish Lady: The Influenza Pandemic of 1918–1919.** New York: Atheneum, 1974.

Collins, Selwyn et al. **Mortality from Influenza and Pneumonia in 50 Largest Cities of the United States 1910–1929.** Washington, D.C.: U.S. Government Printing Office, 1930.

Corner, George A. **A History of the Rockefeller Institute: 1901–1953, Origins and Growth.** New York: Rockefeller Institute Press, 1964.

Creighton, Charles. **A History of Epidemics in Britain.** London: Cambridge University Press, 1894.

Crile, George. **George Crile, An Autobiography.** Philadelphia: Lippincott, 1947.

Crookshank, F. G. **Influenza: Essays by Several Authors.** London: Heinemann, 1922.

Crosby, Alfred W. **America's Forgotten Pandemic: The Influenza of 1918.** Cambridge, England, and New York: Cambridge University Press, 1989.

Cunningham, Andrew, and Perry Williams, eds. **The Laboratory Revolution in Medicine.** Cambridge, England: Cambridge University Press, 1992.

Cushing, Harvey. **A Surgeon's Journal 1915–18.** Boston: Little, Brown, 1934.

Cushing, John, and Arthur Stone, eds. **Vermont and the World War, 1917–1919.** Burlington, Vt.: published by act of legislature, 1928.

Davis, Allen, and Mark Haller, eds. **The Peoples of

Philadelphia: A History of Ethnic Groups and Lower-Class Life, 1790–1940. Philadelphia: Temple University Press, 1973.

Davis, Kingsley. **The Population of India and Pakistan.** Princeton, N.J.: Princeton University Press, 1951.

De Kruif, Paul. **Microbe Hunters.** New York: Harcourt, Brace and Company, 1939.

———. **The Sweeping Wind, A Memoir.** New York: Harcourt, Brace & World, 1962.

Dechmann, Louis. **Spanish Influenza (Pan-asthenia): Its Cause and Cure.** Seattle, Wash.: The Washington Printing Company, 1919.

Dewey, John. **Characters and Events: Popular Essays in Social and Political Philosophy.** New York: Henry Holt, 1929.

Dock, Lavinia et al. **History of American Red Cross Nursing.** New York: Macmillan, 1922.

Dorland's Illustrated Medical Dictionary, 28th ed. Philadelphia: W.B. Saunders and Company, 1994.

Dubos, René. **The Professor, the Institute, and DNA.** New York: Rockefeller University Press, 1976.

Duffy, John. **Epidemics in Colonial America.** Baton Rouge: Louisiana State University Press, 1953.

———. **A History of Public Health in New York City 1866–1966.** New York: Russell Sage Foundation, 1974.

Eisenhower, John, and Joanne Eisenhower. **Yanks: The Epic Story of the American Army in World War I.** New York: Free Press, 2001.

Fee, Elizabeth. **Disease and Discovery: A History of the Johns Hopkins School of Hygiene and**

Public Health, 1916–1939. Baltimore, Md.: Johns Hopkins University Press, 1987.

Fields, Bernard, editor in chief. **Fields' Virology,** third edition. Philadelphia: Lippincott-Raven, 1996.

Finkler, Dittmar. **Influenza in Twentieth Century Practice,** v. 15. London: Sampson Low, 1898.

Fishbein, Morris, M.D. **A History of the American Medical Association, 1847 to 1947.** Philadelphia: W.B. Saunders & Co., 1947.

Fitzgerald, F. Scott. **This Side of Paradise.** New York: Scribner's, 1920.

Fleming, Donald. **William Welch and the Rise of American Medicine.** Boston: Little, Brown, 1954.

Flexner, James Thomas. **An American Saga: The Story of Helen Thomas and Simon Flexner.** Boston: Little, Brown, 1984.

Flexner, Simon, and James Thomas Flexner. **William Henry Welch and the Heroic Age of American Medicine.** New York: Viking, 1941.

Foucault, Michel. **The Birth of the Clinic: An Archaeology of Medical Perception.** New York: Vintage Books, 1976.

Fox, R., and G. Weisz, eds. **The Organization of Science and Technology in France, 1808–1914.** Cambridge, England, and New York: Cambridge University Press, 1980.

Fulton, John. **Harvey Cushing.** Springfield, Ill.: Chas. Thomas, 1946.

Fye, W. Bruce. **The Development of American Physiology: Scientific Medicine in the Nineteenth Century.** Baltimore: Johns Hopkins University Press, 1987.

Garrison, F. H. **John Shaw Billings: A Memoir.** New York: Putnam, 1915.

Geison, Gerald, ed. **Physiology in the American Context. 1850–1940.** Bethesda, Md.: Williams and Wilkins, 1987.

George, Lloyd. **Memoirs of the Peace Conference.** New Haven: Yale University Press, 1939.

Gibson, John M. **Physician to the World: The Life of General William C. Gorgas.** Tuscaloosa: University of Alabama Press, 1989.

Goethe, Johann Wolfgang. **Faust, Part One.** New York: Penguin Classics, 1949.

Gordon, Richard, M.D. **Great Medical Disasters.** New York: Stein & Day, 1983.

Grayson, Cary. **Woodrow Wilson: An Intimate Memoir.** New York: Holt, Rinehart, & Winston, 1960.

Harries, Meirion, and Susie Harries. **The Last Days of Innocence: America at War, 1917–1918.** New York: Random House, 1997.

Hausler, William Jr., Max Sussman, and Leslie Collier. **Microbiology and Microbial Infections,** v. 3, **Bacterial Infections.** New York: Oxford University Press, 1998.

Hawley, Ellis. **The Great War and the Search for a Modern Order: A History of the American People and Their Institutions, 1917–1933.** New York: St. Martin's Press, 1979.

Hertzler, Arthur E. **The Horse and Buggy Doctor.** New York: Harper & Brothers, 1938.

Hirsch, August. **Handbook of Geographical Historical Pathology.** London: New Sydenham Society, 1883.

Hirst, L. Fabian. **The Conquest of Plague: A Study of the Evolution of Epidemiology.** London: Oxford University Press, 1953.

Hoehling, Adolph A. **The Great Epidemic.** Boston: Little, Brown, 1961.

Hoover, Herbert. **America's First Crusade.** New York: Scribner's, 1942.

Hoover, Irwin H. **Forty-two Years in the White House.** New York: Houghton Mifflin, 1934.

Hope-Simpson, R. E. **The Transmission of Epidemic Influenza.** New York: Plenum Press, 1992.

Ireland, Merritt W., ed. **Medical Department of the United States Army in the World War,** v. 9, **Communicable Diseases.** Washington, D.C.: U.S. Army, 1928.

————. **Medical Department of the United States Army in the World War,** v. 12, **Pathology of the Acute Respiratory Diseases, and of Gas Gangrene Following War Wounds.** Washington, D.C.: U.S. Army, 1929.

Jensen, Joan. **The Price of Vigilance.** New York: Rand McNally, 1968.

Johnson, Richard T., M.D. **Viral Infections of the Nervous System,** 2nd ed. Philadelphia: Lippincott-Raven, 1998.

Jordan, Edwin O. **Epidemic Influenza.** Chicago: American Medical Association, 1927.

Judson, Horace. **The Eighth Day of Creation: The Makers of the Revolution in Biology.** New York: Simon & Schuster, 1979.

Kansas and Kansans. Chicago: Lewis Publishing Co., 1919.

Kennedy, David. **Over Here: The First World War and American Society.** New York: Oxford University Press, 1980.

Keynes, John Maynard. **Economic Consequences of the Peace.** New York: Harcourt, Brace and Howe, 1920.

Kilbourne, E. D., M.D. **Influenza.** New York: Plenum Medical, 1987.

Layton, Edwin. **The Revolt of the Engineers: Social Responsibility and the American Engineering Profession.** Cleveland: Press of Case Western Reserve University, 1971.

Lereboullet, Pierre. **La grippe, clinique, prophylaxie, traitement.** Paris: 1926.

L'Etang, Hugh. **The Pathology of Leadership.** New York: Hawthorn Books, 1970.

Luckingham, B. **Epidemic in the Southwest, 1918–1919.** El Paso: Texas Western Press, 1984.

Ludmerer, Kenneth M. **Learning to Heal: The Development of American Medical Education.** New York: Basic Books, 1985.

McAdoo, William. **Crowded Years.** Boston and New York: Houghton Mifflin Company, 1931.

MacCallum, William G. **William Stewart Halsted.** Baltimore, Md.: Johns Hopkins University Press, 1930.

McCullough, David. **The Path Between the Seas: The Creation of the Panama Canal 1870–1914.** New York: Simon & Schuster, 1977.

Macmillan, Margaret. **Paris 1919, Six Months That Changed the World.** New York: Random House, 2002.

McNeill, William. **Plagues and Peoples.** New York: Anchor Press/Doubleday, 1976.

McRae, Major Donald. **Offensive Fighting.** Philadelphia: J.B. Lippincott, 1918.

Magner, Lois. **A History of Medicine.** New York: M. Dekker, 1992.

Mahy, Brian W. J., and Leslie Collier. **Microbiology and Microbial Infections,** v. 1, **Virology.** New York: Oxford University Press, 1998.

Martin, Franklin B. **Fifty Years of Medicine and Surgery.** Chicago: Surgical Publishing Company, 1934.

Marx, Rudolph. **The Health of the Presidents.** New York: Putnam, 1961.

Murray, Robert. **Red Scare: A Study in National Hysteria.** Minneapolis: University of Minnesota Press, 1955.

Nasar, Sylvia. **A Beautiful Mind.** New York: Simon & Schuster, 1998.

Nobelstifelsen. **Nobel, The Man, and His Prizes.** New York: Elsevier, 1962.

Noyes, William Raymond. **Influenza Epidemic 1918–1919: A Misplaced Chapter in United States Social and Institutional History.** Ann Arbor, Mich.: University Microfilms, 1971, c1969.

Nuland, Sherwin. **How We Die.** New York: Vintage, 1993.

Oliver, Wade. **The Man Who Lived for Tomorrow: A Biography of William Hallock Park, M.D.** New York: E. P. Dutton, 1941.

Osborn, June. E. **Influenza in America, 1918–1976:**

History, Science and Politics. New York: Prodist, 1977.

Osler, William. **Osler's Textbook Revisited,** edited by A. McGehee Harvey and Victor A. McKusick. New York: Appleton Century Crofts, 1967.

Packard, Francis, M.D. **History of Medicine in the United States.** New York: Hafner, 1963.

Papers Relating to the Foreign Relations of the United States: The Paris Peace Conference, v. 11. Washington, D.C.: Government Printing Office, 1942–1947.

Parish, H. J. **A History of Immunization.** Edinburgh: Livingstone, 1965.

Park, William H. **Collected Reprints of Dr. William H. Park,** v. 3, **1910–1920.** City of New York.

Park, William H., and Anna Williams. **Pathogenic Microorganisms.** Philadelphia: Lea & Febiger, 1939.

Patterson, Archibald. **Personal Recollections of Woodrow Wilson.** Richmond, Va.: Whittet & Shepperson, 1929.

Patterson, K. D. **Pandemic Influenza, 1700–1900: A Study in Historical Epidemiology.** Totowa, N.J.: Rowan & Littlefield, 1986.

Peabody, F. W., G. Draper, and A. R. Dochez. **A Clinical Study of Acute Poliomyelitis.** New York: The Rockefeller Institute for Medical Research, 1912.

Pettigrew, E. **The Silent Enemy: Canada and the Deadly Flu of 1918.** Saskatoon, Sask.: Western Producer Prairie Books, 1983.

Porter, Roy. **The Greatest Benefit to Mankind: A Medical History of Humanity.** New York: Norton, 1998.

Pyle, Gerald F. **The Diffusion of Influenza: Patterns and Paradigms.** Totowa, N.J.: Rowman & Littlefield, 1986.

Ravenel, Mayzyk, ed. **A Half Century of Public Health.** New York: American Public Health Association, 1921.

Rice, G. **Black November: The 1918 Influenza Epidemic in New Zealand.** Wellington, New Zealand: Allen & Unwin, 1988.

Richman, Douglas, Richard Whitley, and Frederick Hayden, eds. **Clinical Virology.** New York: Churchill Livingstone, 1997.

Robertson, John Dill. "Report of an Epidemic of Influenza in Chicago Occurring During the Fall of 1918." City of Chicago.

Roosevelt, Eleanor. **This Is My Story.** New York, London: Harper & Brothers, 1937.

Rosenberg, Charles. **The Cholera Years: The United States in 1832, 1849, and 1866.** Chicago: University of Chicago Press, 1962.

————. **Explaining Epidemics and Other Studies in the History of Medicine.** Cambridge and New York: Cambridge University Press, 1992.

Rosenberg, Steven, and John Barry. **The Transformed Cell: Unlocking the Secrets of Cancer.** New York: Putnam, 1992.

Rosenkrantz, Barbara Gutmann. **Public Health and the State: Changing Views in Massachusetts, 1842–1936.** Cambridge, Mass: Harvard University Press, 1972.

Rubenstein, Edward, and Daniel Feldman. **Scientific American Medicine.** New York: Scientific American, 1995.

Sabin, Florence. **Franklin Paine Mall: The Story of a Mind.** Baltimore: Johns Hopkins University Press, 1934.

St. John, Robert. **This Was My World.** Garden City, N.Y.: Doubleday, 1953.

Schlesinger, Arthur. **The Age of Roosevelt,** v. 1, **Crisis of the Old Order 1919–1933.** Boston: Houghton Mifflin, 1957.

Sentz, Lilli, ed. **Medical History in Buffalo, 1846–1996, Collected Essays.** Buffalo: State University of New York at Buffalo, 1996.

Shryock, Richard. **American Medical Research Past and Present.** New York: Commonwealth Fund, 1947.

————. **The Development of Modern Medicine,** 2nd ed. New York: Knopf, 1947.

————. **The Unique Influence of the Johns Hopkins University on American Medicine.** Copenhagen: Ejnar Munksgaard Ltd., 1953.

Silverstein, Arthur. **Pure Politics and Impure Science: The Swine Flu Affair.** Baltimore, Md.: Johns Hopkins University Press, 1981.

Simon Flexner Memorial Pamphlet. New York: Rockefeller Institute for Medical Research, 1946.

Smith, Elbert. **When the Cheering Stopped: The Last Years of Woodrow Wilson.** New York: Morrow, 1964.

Starr, Paul. **The Social Transformation of American Medicine.** New York: Basic Books, 1982.

Steele, Richard W. **Free Speech in the Good War.** New York: St. Martin's Press, 1999.

Stent, Gunther. Introduction to **The Double Helix: A Norton Critical Edition,** by James Watson, edited by Gunther Stent. New York: Norton, 1980.

Sternberg, Martha. **George Sternberg: A Biography.** Chicago: American Medical Association, 1925.

Thompson, E. Symes. **Influenza.** London: Percival & Co., 1890.

Thomson, David, and Robert Thomson. **Annals of the Pickett-Thomson Research Laboratory,** vols. 9 and 10, **Influenza.** Baltimore: Williams and Wilkens, 1934.

U. S. Census Bureau. **Mortality Statistics 1919.** Washington, D.C.: General Printing Office.

U.S. Congress, Senate Committee on Appropriations. "Influenza in Alaska." Washington, D.C.: Government Printing Office, 1919.

Van Hartesveldt, Fred R., ed. **The 1918–1919 Pandemic of Influenza: The Urban Impact in the Western World.** Lewiston, N.Y.: E. Mellen Press, 1992.

Vaughan, Victor A. **A Doctor's Memories.** Indianapolis: Bobbs-Merrill, 1926.

Vaughn, Stephen. **Holding Fast the Inner Lines: Democracy, Nationalism, and the Committee on Public Information.** Chapel Hill: University of North Carolina Press, 1980.

Vogel, Morris, and Charles Rosenberg, eds. **The Therapeutic Revolution: Essays on the Social History of American Medicine.** Philadelphia: University of Pennsylvania Press, 1979.

Wade, Wyn Craig. **The Fiery Cross: The Ku Klux Klan in America.** New York: Simon & Schuster, 1987.

Walter, Richard. **S. Weir Mitchell, M.D., Neurologist: A Medical Biography.** Springfield, Ill: Chas. Thomas, 1970.

Walworth, Arthur. **Woodrow Wilson.** Boston: Houghton Mifflin, 1965.

Warner, John Harley. **Against the Spirit of System: The French Impulse in Nineteenth-Century American Medicine.** Princeton, N.J.: Princeton University Press, 1998.

Watson, James. **The Double Helix: A Norton Critical Edition,** edited by Gunther Stent. New York: Norton, 1980.

Weigley, Russell, ed. **Philadelphia: A 300 Year History.** New York: Norton, 1982.

Wilson, Edith. **My Memoir.** Indianapolis and New York: Bobbs-Merrill, 1939.

Wilson, Joan Hoff. **Herbert Hoover: Forgotten Progressive.** Boston: Little Brown, 1974.

Winslow, Charles-Edward Amory, **The Conquest of Epidemic Disease: A Chapter in the History of Ideas.** Princeton: Princeton University Press, 1943.

————. **The Evolution and Significance of the Modern Public Health Campaign.** New Haven: Yale University Press, 1923.

————. **Life of Hermann M. Biggs,** Philadelphia: Lea & Febiger, 1929.

Winternitz, Milton Charles. **The Pathology of Influenza.** New Haven: Yale University Press, 1920.

Young, James Harvey. **The Medical Messiahs: A**

Social History of Health Quackery in Twentieth Century America. Princeton, N.J.: Princeton University Press, 1967.

————. The Toadstool Millionaires: A Social History of Patent Medicines in America before Federal Regulation. Princeton, N.J.: Princeton University Press, 1961.

Zinsser, Hans. As I Remember Him: The Biography of R. S. Gloucester, Mass.: Peter Smith, 1970.

————. Rats, Lice, and History. New York: Black Dog & Leventhal, 1963.

UNPUBLISHED MATERIALS

Allen, Phyllis. "Americans and the Germ Theory of Disease." Ph.D. diss., University of Pennsylvania, 1949.

Anderson, Jeffrey. "Influenza in Philadelphia, 1918." MA thesis, Rutgers University, Camden, 1998.

Fanning, Patricia J. "Disease and the Politics of Community: Norwood and the Great Flu Epidemic of 1918." Ph.D. diss., Boston College, 1995.

"Influenza 1918." The American Experience, Boston, Mass.: WGBH, 1998.

Ott, Katherine. "The Intellectual Origins and Cultural Form of Tuberculosis in the United States, 1870–1925." Ph.D. diss., Temple University, 1990.

Parsons, W. David, M.D. "The Spanish Lady and the Newfoundland Regiment." Paper presented at Newfoundland and the Great War Conference, Nov. 11, 1998.

Pettit, Dorothy Ann. "A Cruel Wind: America

Experiences the Pandemic Influenza, 1918–1920, A Social History." Ph.D. diss., University of New Hampshire, 1976.

Smith, Soledad Mujica. "Nursing as Social Responsibility: Implications for Democracy from the Life Perspective of Lavinia Lloyd Dock (1858–1956)." Ph.D. diss., Louisiana State University, 2002.

Wolper, Gregg. "The Origins of Public Diplomacy: Woodrow Wilson, George Creel, and the Committee on Public Information." Ph.D. diss., University of Chicago, 1991.

Index

Photographic Credits

Figures 1, 2, 3: The Alan Mason Chesney
 Medical Archives of The Johns Hopkins
 Medical Institutions
Figures 4, 5: American Review of Respiratory
 Disease; Reuben Ramphal, Werner Fischlschweiger,
 Joseph W. Shands Jr., and Parker A. Small Jr.;
 "Murine Influenzal Tracheitis: A Model for
 the Study of Influenza and Tracheal Epithelial
 Repair"; Vol. 120, 1979; official journal of the
 American Thoracic Society; copyright American
 Lung Association.
Figure 6: National Museum of Health and Medicine
 (#NCP-1603)
Figures 7, 8, 15, 17, 22: Courtesy of the National
 Library of Medicine

Figures 9, 23, 24, 25: Courtesy of the American Red
  Cross Museum. All rights reserved in all countries.
Figure 10: Library of the College of Physicians
  of Philadelphia
Figures 11, 12: Temple University Libraries, Urban
  Archives, Philadelphia, Pennsylvania
Figures 13, 14: National Archives
Figure 16: Courtesy of the Rockefeller Archive Center
Figure 18: The Schlesinger Library, Radcliffe
  Institute, Harvard University
Figure 19: Courtesy of The Bureau of Naval Medicine
Figure 20: Courtesy of The Naval Historical Center
Figure 21: California Historical Society, Photography
  Collection (FN-30852)
Figure 26: Courtesy of Professor Judith Aronson
Figure 27: Courtesy of Dr. Thomas Shope

THE GREAT INFLUENZA

John M. Barry is the author of four previous books: **Rising Tide: The Great Mississippi Flood of 1927 and How It Changed America; Power Plays: Politics, Football, and Other Blood Sports; The Transformed Cell: Unlocking the Mysteries of Cancer** (cowritten with Steven Rosenberg); and **The Ambition and the Power: A True Story of Washington.** He lives in New Orleans and Washington, D.C.